1,000,000 Books
are available to read at

www.ForgottenBooks.com

Read online
Download PDF
Purchase in print

ISBN 978-0-266-08417-4
PIBN 10947661

This book is a reproduction of an important historical work. Forgotten Books uses state-of-the-art technology to digitally reconstruct the work, preserving the original format whilst repairing imperfections present in the aged copy. In rare cases, an imperfection in the original, such as a blemish or missing page, may be replicated in our edition. We do, however, repair the vast majority of imperfections successfully; any imperfections that remain are intentionally left to preserve the state of such historical works.

Forgotten Books is a registered trademark of FB &c Ltd.
Copyright © 2018 FB &c Ltd.
FB &c Ltd, Dalton House, 60 Windsor Avenue, London, SW19 2RR.
Company number 08720141. Registered in England and Wales.

For support please visit www.forgottenbooks.com

1 MONTH OF FREE READING

at

www.ForgottenBooks.com

By purchasing this book you are eligible for one month membership to ForgottenBooks.com, giving you unlimited access to our entire collection of over 1,000,000 titles via our web site and mobile apps.

To claim your free month visit:

www.forgottenbooks.com/free947661

* Offer is valid for 45 days from date of purchase. Terms and conditions apply.

English
Français
Deutsche
Italiano
Español
Português

www.forgottenbooks.com

Mythology Photography **Fiction**
Fishing Christianity **Art** Cooking
Essays Buddhism Freemasonry
Medicine **Biology** Music **Ancient Egypt** Evolution Carpentry Physics
Dance Geology **Mathematics** Fitness
Shakespeare **Folklore** Yoga Marketing
Confidence Immortality Biographies
Poetry **Psychology** Witchcraft
Electronics Chemistry History **Law**
Accounting **Philosophy** Anthropology
Alchemy Drama Quantum Mechanics
Atheism Sexual Health **Ancient History**
Entrepreneurship Languages Sport
Paleontology Needlework Islam
Metaphysics Investment Archaeology
Parenting Statistics Criminology
Motivational

WEEKLY NOTES OF CASES

ARGUED AND DETERMINED

IN THE

SUPREME COURT OF PENNSYLVANIA, THE COUNTY COURTS OF PHILADELPHIA, AND THE UNITED STATES DISTRICT AND CIRCUIT COURTS FOR THE EASTERN DISTRICT OF PENNSYLVANIA.

BY

MEMBERS OF THE BAR.

VOLUME IX.

AUGUST, 1880, TO APRIL, 1881.

PHILADELPHIA:
KAY & BROTHER, 17 AND 19 SOUTH SIXTH STREET,
LAW PUBLISHERS, BOOKSELLERS, AND IMPORTERS.
1881.

Entered according to Act of Congress, in the year 1881, by
KAY & BROTHER,
in the Office of the Librarian of Congress, at Washington.

Rec. Apr. 14, 1883

PHILADELPHIA:
COLLINS, PRINTER,
705 Jayne Street.

REPORTERS.

Supreme Court (*Eastern District*).
    Mr. RICHARD C. DALE, *assisted by* Messrs. Francis J. Alison, George Harrison Fisher, William Hunt, J. Percy Keating, Lawrence Lewis, Jr., William M. Meigs, N. Dubois Miller, Robert H. Neilson, W. Herbert Washington, James S. Williams, and C. Tower, Jr.

Supreme Court (*Middle District*).
    Mr. M. W. JACOBS, *assisted by* Messrs. Fred. M. Ott, John S. Alleman, Charles M. Fleming, George W. Heck, William B. Lamberton, J. H. Shopp, and Percival C. Kauffman (Harrisburg).

Supreme Court (*Western District*).
    Messrs. JOHN B. HERRON, JR., Alex. C. Crawford, J. T. Myler, William Scott, A. Tausig, William R. Blair, Kennedy T. Friend, William N. Frew, and Oliver S. Richardson (Pittsburgh), and Lawrence Lewis, Jr. (Philadelphia).

Courts of Common Pleas (*Law and Equity*).
    C. P. No. 1. Mr. WILLIAM WYNNE WISTER, JR., *assisted by* Messrs. Joseph P. Gross, Alfred Lee, Jr., James S. Williams, Dwight M. Lowrey, Daniel Holsman, and Joseph F. Lamorelle.
    C. P. No. 2. Hon. JAMES T. MITCHELL, *assisted by* Messrs. Robert H. Neilson, Benjamin H. Lowry, I. Tyson Morris, T. B. Stork, Upton H. White, and Thomas Robins, Jr.
    C. P. No. 3. Mr. SAMUEL W. PENNYPACKER, *assisted by* Messrs. Harold Goodwin, Thos. W. Hoskinson, J. Percy Keating, William M. Meigs, J. Bayard Henry, Francis A. Lewis, Jr., and Walter L. C. Biddle.
    C. P. No. 4. Mr. HENRY BUDD, JR., *assisted by* Messrs. Effingham B. Morris, Henry Pleasants, Jr., W. Herbert Washington, George R. Van Dusen, John M. Gest, Edward G. McCollin, and Thos. A. Edwards.

Quarter Sessions and Oyer and Terminer.
    Mr. HENRY S. HAGERT, *assisted by* Mr. Thomas W. Barlow.

Orphans' Court.
    Mr. HENRY C. OLMSTED, *assisted by* Messrs. William D. Neilson, Wm. Lyttleton Savage, Charles H. Townsend, Edward F. Hoffman, and William C. Stœver.

U. S. Courts.
    Mr. FRANK P. PRICHARD, *assisted by* Messrs. J. Edward Ackley, Arthur Biddle, Williams Carter, Charles H. Howell, John J. Wilkinson, Richard S. Edwards, and C. Berkeley Taylor.
    N. B. Admiralty *Cases* revised by Mr. MORTON P. HENRY.

GENERAL EDITOR.
    Mr. ALBERT A. OUTERBRIDGE, 251 South Fourth Street, Philadelphia.

TABLE OF CASES

REPORTED IN THIS VOLUME.

ABBOTT, Powell v. (C. P.)	231	Bank v. Troutman,	54	Bucknor's Estate (O. C.)	511
Acker v. Hite,	99	Bank, Ziegler v.	19	Building Asso., Devenny v. (C. P.)	127
Addams, Dietrich v.	492	Barber, Spaulding v. (C. P.)	253	Building & Loan Asso., In re assigned Estate of (C. P.)	79
Additional Rules of Orphans' Court,	420	Barron v. Keeper of County Prison (Q. S.)	314	Burnell's Estate (O. C.)	334
Albrecht v. Lane (C. P.)	377	Bateson, Howell v. (C. P.)	463	Burton v. McCully (C. P.)	206
Alden's Appeal,	442	Bauer's Estate (O. C.) 336,	576	Byers, Reehling v.	359
Aldrich, Landis v. (C. P.)	192	Baughman, Russell v.	284	B. & L. Asso., Gass v.	326
Allen v. Kellam,	93	Beatty, Raynor v. (C. P.)	201	B. & L. Asso., Hungerbuehler v.	218
Allegheny Valley R. R. Co., Baker v.	337	Beaver, Colvin v.	396	B. & L. Asso., James v.	325
Allegheny Valley R. R. Co., Duff v.	504	Becher's Estate (O. C.)	128	B. & L. Asso., Newlin v. (C. P.)	220
Althouse, City of Reading v.	22	Bell v. Bell (C. P.)	509	B. & L. Asso., Smith v.	168
American Banking & Brokerage Co. v. Donnelly (C. P.)	573	Bender v. Ryan (C. P.)	144	B. & L. Asso. v. Young (C. P.)	251
American Exchange Nat. Bank, Boughton v.	519	Benner, Sellers v.	88	B. &. O. R. R. Co. v. Sulphur Springs School Dist.,	568
American Life Ins. Co., Moulor v. (S. C. U. S.)	81	Biegenwald v. Winpenny (C. P.)	542	
Anderson's Estate,	413	Biery v. Ziegler,	154	CAFFREY, Long v.	25
Anderson v. Phila. Warehouse Co. (U. S. C. C.)	262	Big Black Creek Improvement Co. v. The Com'th,	74	Cake, Phila. & Erie R. R. Co. v.	72
Appeal of the Trustees of the University of Penna.,	520	Black, Johnson v. (C. P.)	438	Calahan & Miles v. Pleasants (C. P.)	63
Armstrong's Estate,	289	Blanchard, Hamaker v.	331	Caldwell, Jones v.	459
Assigned Estate of National B. & L. Asso. (C. P.)	79	Bleim, Fuller v. (C. P.)	574	Callahan's Estate (O. C.)	253
		Bock, Penna. R. R. Co. v.	281	Campbell v. Braden,	487
BACHER & Boner, Sullivan & Gilbert v. (C. P.)	14	Bogle's Estate (O. C.)	256	Canal Co., Brady v.	414
Backer v. Saurman (C. P.)	403	Bondbright's Appeal,	475	Carlisle Deposit Bank, Comp v.	453
Badger v. McKay (C. P.)	528	Boner & Bacher, Sullivan & Gilbert v. (C. P.)	14	Cassady's Estate (O. C.)	275
Baker v. Allegheny Valley R. R. Co.,	337	Books v. Borough of Danville,	339	Casselberry, Schofield v. (C. P.)	95
Baker v. Humphrey (S. C. U. S.)	13	Borlin's Appeal,	545	Castner, Bank v.	273
Baldwin v. Com'th (C. P.)	233	Borough of Danville, Books v.	339	Catterson, City of Scranton v.	59
Baldwin v. Herdic Coach Co. (C. P.)	233	Boughton v. American Exchange Nat. Bank,	519	Cauley v. Pittsburgh, Cincinnati & St. Louis R. R. Co.,	505
Ball, Fisher v.	141	Bouillou's Estate (C. P.)	14	Cemetery Co. v. City of Phila.,	85
Balliet & Koch's Appeal,	343	Bowen v. Thornton (C. P.)	575	Central Nat. Bank, Dougherty Bros. & Co. v.	1
Bank, Boughton v.	519	Boyer, Phila. & Reading R. R. Co. v.	497	Citizens B. & L. Asso., Gass v.	326
Bank v. Castner (C. P.)	273	Braden, Campbell v.	487	City of Allentown v. Hower,	198
Bank, Comp v.	453	Bradfield v. Union Mutual Ins. Co. (C. P.)	436	City of Philadelphia's Appeal,	43
Bank, County of Lackawanna v.	549	Brady v. Delaware & Raritan Canal Co.	414	City of Philadelphia v. Donath,	415
Bank, Dougherty Bros. & Co. v.	1	Brandon v. Fritz,	297	City v. Hitner (C. P.)	541
Bank v. Dushane,	472	Brass Co. v. Rudy (C. P.)	527	City of Philadelphia, Kenyon v. (C. P.)	222
Bank v. Gayley,	49	Bredin v. Dorsey,	151	City of Philadelphia v. Lukens (C. P.)	348
Bank v. Huston (C. P.)	477	Brez v. Warner,	45	City of Philadelphia, O'Byrne v.	41
Bank v. Mason,	265	Brice's Appeal,	227	City of Philadelphia, Olive Cemetery Co. v.	85
Bank, Resh v.	21	Brietwiesser v. Stier (C. P.)	112	City of Philadelphia v. Thomas (C. P.)	240
Bank, Shoemaker v. (C. P.)	420	Brittin v. Shloss (C. P.)	510	City of Philadelphia v. Tyson (C. P.)	367
Bank, Spahr v.	433	Brooke's Appeal,	442	City v. Wagner (C. P.)	511
Bank, Steckel v.	17	Brooke v. Harman (C. P.)	462		
		Brown's Appeal,	329		
		Brown, Lea v. (C. P.)	418		
		Brown, Roebling v. (C. P.)	170		
		Bruce, Maloney v.	92		
		Bryson, Lukens v. (C. P.)	540		
		Buchanan v. Hazzard,	267		

(vii)

TABLE OF CASES.

Case	Page
City of Philadelphia, Wistar v.	98
City of Philadelphia v. Wood (C. P.)	347
City of Reading v. Althouse,	22
City of Scranton v. Catterson,	59
City of Scranton, Matthews v.	507
Clark, Huston v. (C. P.)	316
Clement v. Commonwealth,	131
Coller v. Frankford & Southwark Railway Co. (C. P.)	477
Colvin v. Beaver,	396
Commonwealth v. Baldwin (C. P.)	233
Commonwealth, Big Black Creek Imp. Co. v.	74
Commonwealth, Clement v.	131
Commonwealth, Donaldson v.	393
Commonwealth v. Dumbauld & Roberts,	369, 417, 529
Commonwealth v. Keeper of County Prison (Q. S.)	314
Commonwealth, Kilgore v.	184
Commonwealth, Krause v.	61
Commonwealth v. Luberg,	4
Commonwealth v. Lynd & Gannon (C. P.)	510
Commonwealth v. McGurk (Q. S.)	402
Commonwealth v. Moreland (Q. S.)	272
Commonwealth, Northern Central R. R. Co. v.	129
Commonwealth, Penna. R. R. Co. v.	179
Commonwealth v. Schladensky (Q. S.)	315
Commonwealth, Stabler v.	409
Commonwealth, Waldo v.	200
Commonwealth v. Willard (Q. S.	524
Commonwealth, Williams v.	113
Commonwealth v. Wilson (Q. S.)	291
Comp v. Carlisle Deposit Bank,	453
Connell's Estate (O. C.)	406
Cook, Felt v.	246
Corbion, Steinbeisser v. (C. P.)	528
Corles, Loftus v. (C. P.)	333
County of Lackawanna v. First Nat. Bank of Scranton,	549
Curran v. Elliot (C. P.)	367
Cuyler, Machette v.	471
DANDO'S Appeal,	5
Daubert v. Eckert,	87
Davis's Estate (O. C.)	380, 479
Davis v. Mowbray (C. P.)	47
Deacon, Wilson v. (C. P.)	47
Delaware & Raritan Canal Co., Brady v.	414
Devenny v. Building Assoc. (C. P.)	127
Dick, Gray v.	555
Dick v. Stevenson,	411
Dietrich v. Addams,	492
Dill v. Haugh (C. P.)	417
Dilworth's Appeal,	133
Donaldson v. Commonwealth,	393
Donath, City of Philadelphia v.	415
Donnelly, American Banking & Brokerage Co. v. (C. P.)	573
Dorsey, Bredin v.	151
Dorsey v. Van Horn (C. P.)	95
Dougherty v. Central Nat. Bank,	1
Douglass, Rodgers v. (C. P.)	191
Dowling, Irvine v. (C. P.)	366
Drew v. Peer,	33
Driesbach v. Morris,	57
Droste's Estate (O. C.)	224
Duff v. Allegheny Valley R. R. Co.,	504
Duffin, Leonard v.	155
Dumbauld, Commonwealth v.	369, 417, 529
Duncan's Appeal,	436
Duncan v. Penna. R. R. Co.,	436
Dunlap's Estate (O.C.)	349
Dushane, National Bank of Fayette Co. v.	472
Dutill v. Sully,	573
EARLEY v. Rolfe,	106
Eberle's Estate,	457
Eckenrode, Schriver v.	161
Eckert, Daubert v.	87
Economy B. & L. Assoc. v. Hungerbuehler,	218
Eggert, Kurz v. (C. P.)	126
Electropathic Institute, In re,	31
Elliot, Curran v. (C. P.)	367
Elliott v. Kunazig (C. P.)	542
Elsey v. McDaniel,	269
Emerson & Wall's Appeal,	227
Emerson, Welch v.	372
Enterprise Transit Co.'s Appeal,	225
Evans v. Fries (C. P.)	462
Evans v. Jenks's Executrix,	139
Ewing v. Ewing,	489
Ewing v. Sewing Machine Co. (C. P.)	272
Ex parte Steinman and Hensel,	145
FAAS v. Warner,	412
Fahnestock v. Wilson,	385
Fallon, Wingerd v.	163
Farmers' Bank of Carlisle, Spahr v.	433
Faunce, Portuondo v. (C. P.)	539
Federal St. & Pleasant Valley Railway Co. v. Gibson,	533
Fell's Estate (O. C.)	382
Felt v. Cook,	246
Ferguson's Appeal,	442
Fetters, Rittenhouse v. (C. P.)	221
First Nat. Bank of Allentown, Resh v.	21
First Nat. Bank of Allentown, Steckel v.	17
First Nat. Bank of Allentown, Ziegler v.	19
First Nat. Bank of Lockhaven v. Mason,	265
First Nat. Bank of Scranton, County of Lackawanna v.	549
Fisher v. Ball,	141
Fraley's Estate (O. C.)	127
Frankford & Southwark Railway Co., Coller v. (C. P.)	477
Frick v. McClain (C. P.)	32
Fries, Evans v. (C. P.)	462
Fritz, Brandon v.	297
Fuller v. Bleim (C. P.)	574
Funck, Wright v.	249
Fuss, Yeager v.	557
GALBRATH v. Walker,	474
Garretson v. Lane (C. P.)	377
Garver v. Ward (C. P.)	192
Gas Co. v. Pinkerton,	97
Gass v. Citizens B. & L. Asso.	326
Gayley, People's Bank v.	49
Gerhab, Scholl v.	157
German v. Moodie (C. P.)	221
Germantown Pass. Railway Co. v. Walling,	467
Gibboney, Union Township v.	390
Gibson, Federal St. & Pleasant Valley Railway Co. v.	533
Gifford's Appeal,	246
Gilbert & Sullivan v. Bacher & Boner (C. P.)	14
Gillespie, Palmer v.	535
Girard Life Ins. Co. v. Mutual Ins. Co.,	425
Glenn v. Keenan (C. P.)	170
Goldsmith's Estate (O. C.)	276
Gordon's Appeal,	55
Gray v. Dick,	555
Grayson v. Hangstorfer (C. P.)	333
Green, Shaffer v. (C. P.)	144
Griffiths v. Stadtmuller (C. P.)	348
HALL v. Ritter (C. P.)	574
Hamaker v. Blanchard,	331
Hangstorfer, Grayson v. (C. P.)	333
Harlan v. Maglaughlin,	353
Harman, Brooke v. (C. P.)	462
Harner's Appeal,	101
Hartley v. White,	286
Haugh, Dill v. (C. P.)	417
Hazzard, Buchanan v.	267
Heath, Travellers' Ins. Co. v.	516
Heft v. Jones (C. P.)	541
Heilman, Montgomery v.	537
Henzey, Louchheim v.	571
Herdic Coach Co. v. Baldwin (C. P.)	233
Hidell's Appeal,	212
Hilles's Estate (O. C.)	421
Himes's Appeal,	413
Hipps, Metz v.	321
Hirsch, Kaufman v.	347
Hirst v. Randall (C. P.)	349
Hite, Acker v.	99
Hitner, City v. (C P.)	541
Hobson v. Webster (C. P.)	206
Hook's Estate (O. C.)	320
Horstman's Appeal,	513
Horstman v. Kaufman,	513
Hough's Estate,	475
Houston's Appeal,	545
Howell v. Bateson (C. P.)	463
Hower, City of Allentown v.	198
Howley, Lehman v.	386
Humboldt Ins. Co., Mears v.	108
Humphrey, Baker v. (S. C. U. S.)	13
Hungerbuehler, Economy B. & L. Asso. v.	218
Hurst v. Smith (C. P.)	461

TABLE OF CASES.

Huston, Bank v. (C. P.)	477	Kohler, In re petition of Jacob (C. P.) ... 527
Huston v. Clark (C. P.)	316	Krause v. Commonwealth, ... 61
		Kunszig, Elliott v. (C. P.) ... 542
IMLER v. Imler,	196	Kurz v. Eggert (C. P.) ... 126
Improvement Co. v. Commonwealth,	74	
Indiana County Bank's Appeal,	270	LACKAWANNA Co. v. Scranton Bank, ... 549
Ins. Co., Mears v.	108	Lake, Whiting v. ... 137
Ins. Co., Moulor v. (S. C. U. S.)	81	Landis v. Aldrich (C. P.) ... 192
In re Assigned Estate of the National B. & L. Asso. (C. P.)	79	Lane, Albrecht v. (C. P.) ... 377
In re Contested Election of J. E. Colvin,	396	Lane, Garretson v. (C. P.) ... 377
		Lane v. Steinmetz (C. P.) ... 574
In re Electropathic Institute (C. P.)	31	Lane, Stoesslein v. (C. P.) ... 377
In re Petition of Gormley (C. P.)	96	Lanigan v. Kille, ... 481
		Lant's Appeal, ... 209
In re Petition of Gunther (C. P.)	191	Lathrop v. Junction R. R. Co. (U. S. C. C.) ... 277
In re Petition of John Merry (C. P.)	169	Lathrop v. Penna. R. R. Co. (U. S. C. C.) ... 277
In re Petition of Kohler (C. P.)	527	Lawrence, Weir v. (C. P.) ... 207
In re Petition of Randall (C. P.)	159	Lea v. Brown (C. P.) ... 418
In re Plan No. 166,	43	Lehigh Coal & Nav. Co., Stockton v. (C. P.) ... 110
In re St. Nicholas Coal Co. (C. P.)	403	Lehman v. Howley, ... 386
In re Volkmar Street (Q. S.)	169, 201	Lehr v. Taylor, ... 401
Irvine v. Dowling (C. P.)	366	Lennig's Appeal, ... 503
Irvine, Miller v.	142	Leonard v. Duffin, ... 155
		Lindsay's Estate (O. C.) ... 463
JAMES v. National B. & L. Asso.,	325	Linnard's Estate, ... 506
Jenks's Executrix, Evans v.	139	Little, Winton v. ... 37
Jennings v. Penna. R. R. Co.	150	Littleton's Appeal, ... 188
Johnson v. Black (C. P.)	438	Lockhard v. McKinley (C. P.) ... 11
Jones v. Caldwell,	459	Lockhaven Bank v. Mason, ... 265
Jones, Heft v. (C. P.)	541	Loftus v. Corles (C. P.) ... 333
Junction R. R. Co., Lathrop v. (U. S. C. C.)	277	Long v. Caffrey, ... 25
Junker, Reis v. (C. P.)	296	Longstreth v. Thornton (C. P.) ... 206
		Louchheim v. Henzey, ... 571
KAUFMAN v. Hirsh,	347	Luberg, Com'th v. ... 4
Kaufman, Horstman v.	513	Lukens v. Bryson (C. P.) ... 540
Keenan, Glenn v. (C. P.)	170	Lukens, City of Philadelphia v. (C. P.) ... 348
Keeper of County Prison, Commonwealth ex rel. Barron v. (Q. S.)	314	Luzerne County v. Trimmer, ... 376
Kellam, Allen v.	93	Lynd & Gannon, Com'th v. (C. P.) ... 510
Kennedy, Keystone Bridge Co. v.	552	McCLAIN, Frick v. (C. P.) ... 32
Kensington Nat. Bank, Shoemaker v. (C. P.)	420	McCloskey's Estate (O. C.) ... 496
Kensinger v. Smith,	311	McCully, Burton v. (C. P.) ... 206
Kenyon v. The City (C. P.)	222	McDaniel, Elsey v. ... 269
Kepner's Appeal,	44	McEntee v. Thomas (C. P.) ... 252
Keystone Bridge Co. v. Kennedy,	552	McGurk, Com'th v. (Q. S.) ... 402
Keystone Bridge Co. v. Newberry,	552	McKay, Badger v. (C. P.) ... 528
Kiker v. Weightman (C. P.)	274	McKinley, Lockhard v. (C. P.) ... 11
Kilgore v. Commonwealth,	184	Machette v. Cuyler, ... 471
Kille, Lanigan v.	481	Maglaughlin, Harlan v. ... 353
Kimble v. Smith,	357	Malley, Stichter v. ... 28
King's Estate (O. C.)	207	Maloney v. Bruce, ... 92
Kingsessing B. & L. Asso. v. Roan (C. P.)	15	Martin's Appeal, ... 484
Kitchen v. Stokes (C. P.)	48	Martzinger v. Smith (C. P.) ... 274
Kline's Appeal,	26	Mason, First Nat. Bank of Lockhaven v. ... 265
Knight v. Mutual Ins. Co. of New York,	501	Matthews v. City of Scranton ... 507
Koch & Balliet's Appeal,	343	May, Royse v. ... 104
		Mayberry v. Railway Co.(C. P.) ... 404
		Maynes v. Rutherford (C. P.) ... 221
		Maynes, Rutherford v. ... 561
		Mears v. Humboldt Ins. Co. ... 108
		Metz v. Hipps, ... 321
		Miles & Calahan v. Pleasants (C. P.) ... 63
		Miller v. Irvine, ... 142
		Mills v. Slook (C. P.) ... 379
		Milton B. & L. Asso., Newlin v. (C. P.) ... 220
		Monaghan v. Ferry Co. (C. P.) ... 368
		Monroe v. Monroe, ... 8
		Montgomery v. Heilman, ... 537
		Montgomery, Scott Township v. ... 389
		Moodie, German v. (C. P.) ... 221
		Moreland, Com'th v. (Q. S.) ... 272
		Morris, Driesbach v. ... 57
		Mortimer's Appeal, ... 313
		Moss, Prichett v. (C. P.) ... 558
		Moulor v. American Life Ins. Co. (S. C. U. S.) ... 81
		Mowbray, Davis v. (C. P.) ... 47
		Mowry's Appeal, ... 362
		Moxey's Appeal, ... 441
		Mutual Ins. Co., Girard Life Ins. Co. v. ... 425
		Mutual Life Ins. Co. of N. Y., Knight v. ... 501
		NAFTZINGER v. Roth, ... 493
		Nass v. Winpenny (C. P.) ... 542
		National Bank of Fayette Co. v. Dushane, ... 472
		National B. & L. Asso., James v. ... 325
		Neely, Parke v. ... 193
		Neill's Appeal, ... 188
		Newberry, Keystone Bridge Co. v. ... 552
		Newlin v. Milton B. & L. Asso. (C. P.) ... 220
		Noble, Shnyder v. ... 182
		Norman, The (U. S. D. C.) ... 543
		Norrington v. Wright (U. S. C. C.) ... 422
		Northern Central R. R. Co. v. Com'th, ... 129
		O'BYRNE v. City of Phila. ... 41
		O'Connor v. Weeks (C. P.) ... 461
		Ogden, Skelly v. (C. P.) ... 365
		Olive Cemetery Co. v. City of Phila. ... 85
		Orangeville Savings Fund & Loan Asso. v. Young (C. P.) ... 251
		Orphans' Court, additional Rules of, ... 420
		Owen v. Western Savings Fund, ... 465
		PALMER v. Gillespie, ... 535
		Parke v. Neely, ... 193
		Pashley, Vent v. (C. P.) ... 559
		Peer, Drew v. ... 33
		Pemberton, Winkler v. (C. P.) ... 419
		Penna. R. R. Co. v. Bock, ... 281
		Penna. R. R. Co. v. Com'th, ... 179
		Penna. R. R. Co. Duncan v. ... 436
		Penna. R. R. Co., Jennings v. ... 150
		Penna. R. R. Co., Lathrop v. (U. S. C. C.) ... 277
		People's Bank v. Gayley, ... 49
		People's Bank v. Troutman, ... 54
		Phila. & Erie R. R. Co. v. Cake, ... 72
		Phila. & Reading R. R. Co. v. Boyer, ... 497
		Phila. & Reading R. R. Co. v. Schultz, ... 148
		Phila. Trust Co.'s Appeal, ... 289

TABLE OF CASES.

Case	Page
Phila. Warehouse Co., Anderson v. (U. S. C. C.)	262
Phillips v. Quigley (C. P.)	511
Pike County v. Rowland,	241
Pinkerton, Williamsport Gas Co. v.	97
Pittsburgh, Cincinnati and St. Louis R. R. Co., Cauley v.	505
Pleasants, Miles & Calahan v. (C. P.)	63
Popular B. & L. Asso., Smith v.	168
Porter's Appeal,	457
Portuondo v. Faunce (C. P.)	539
Poultney's Appeal,	545
Powell v. Abbott (C. P.)	231
Price, Wanamaker v. (C. P.)	112
Prichett v. Moss (C. P.)	558
QUIGLEY, Phillips v. (C. P.)	511
RAILROAD Co., Baker v.	337
R. R. Co. v. Bock,	281
R. R. Co. v. Boyer,	497
R. R. Co. v. Cake,	72
R. R. Co., Cauley v.	505
R. R. Co. v. Com'th,	129
R. R. Co. v. Com'th,	179
R. R. Co., Duff v.	504
R. R. Co., Duncan v.	436
R. R. Co., Jennings v.	150
R. R. Co. v. Lathrop (U. S. C. C.)	277
R. R. Co., Reading v. (U. S. C. C.)	175
R. R. Co. v. School District, etc.	568
R. R. Co. v. Schultz,	148
R. R. Co., Thomas v. (S. C. U. S.)	65
Railway, Goller v. (C. P.)	477
Railway Co. v. Gibson,	533
Railway Co., Mayberry v. (C. P.)	404
Railway Co., Walling v.	467
Randall, Hirst v. (C. P.)	349
Randall, In re petition of (C. P.)	159
Rankin's Estate (O. C.)	407
Raynor v. Beatty (C. P.)	201
Reading v. Texas & Pacific R. R. Co. (U. S. C. C.)	175
Read, Whitaker v. (C. P.)	144
Reed v. Worthington (C. P.)	192
Reehling v. Byers,	359
Reis v. Junker (C. P.)	296
Rosh v. Nat. Bank of Allentown,	21
Rice's Estate (O. C.)	255
Riegel, Roth v.	398
Rittenhouse v. Fetters (C. P.)	221
Ritter, Hall v. (C. P.)	574
Roan, Building Asso. v. (C. P.)	15
Robb, Sharp v.	475
Roberts's Appeal,	118
Roberts & Dumbauld, Com'th v.	369, 417, 529
Rodgers v. Douglass (C. P.)	191
Roebling v. Brown (C. P.)	170
Rolfe, Earley v.	106
Roth's Appeal,	398
Roth, Naftzinger v.	493
Roth v. Riegel,	398
Rowland, Pike County v.	241
Royse v. May,	104
Rudy's Appeal	308
Rudy, Brass Co. v. (C. P.)	527
Russell v. Baughman,	284
Rutherford, Maynes v. (C. P.)	221
Rutherford v. Maynes,	561
Ryan, Bender v. (C. P.)	144
SAURMAN, Backer v. (C. P.)	403
Schassberger v. Staendel (C. P.)	379
Schively's Appeal,	566
Schively's Estate (O. C.)	223
Schladensky, Com'th v. (Q. S.)	315
Schlect, White v. (C. P.)	77
Schmidt v. Steamship Pennsylvania (U. S. C. C.)	351
Schneider v. Schneider (C. P.)	253
Schofield v. Casselberry (C. P.)	95
Scholl v. Gerhab,	157
Schriver v. Eckenrode,	161
Schultz, Phila. & Reading R. R. Co. v.	148
Schwenk v. Yost (C. P.)	16
Scott Township v. Montgomery,	389
Scranton Bank, Lackawanna County v.	549
Sellers v. Benner,	88
Sewing Machine Co., Ewing v. (C. P.)	272
Shaffer v. Green (C. P.)	144
Sharp v. Robb (C. P.)	475
Shloss, Brittin v. (C. P.)	510
Shnyder v. Noble,	182
Shoemaker v. Kensington Nat. Bank (C. P.)	420
Shrewsbury Savings Institution's Appeal,	166
Skelly v. Ogden (C. P.)	365
Slook, Mills v. (C. P.)	379
Smiley, Taylor v. (C. P.)	30
Smith, Hurst v. (C. P.)	461
Smith, Kensinger v.	311
Smith, Kimble v.	357
Smith, Martzinger v. (C. P.)	274
Smith v. Popular B. & L. Asso.	168
Snyder's Appeal,	177
Snyder's Appeal,	213
Somers's Estate (O. C.)	559
Spahr v. Farmers' Bank of Carlisle,	433
Sparr v. Walz (C. P.)	64
Spaulding v. Barber (C. P.)	253
Stabler v. Com'th,	409
Stadtmuller, Griffiths v. (C. P.)	348
Staendel, Schassberger v. (C. P.)	379
Steamship Pennsylvania, Schmidt v. (U. S. C. C.)	351
Steckel v. First Nat. Bank of Allentown,	17
Steel's Estate (O. C.)	274
Steinbeisser v. Corbion (C. P.)	528
Steinman and Hensel, Ex parte,	145
Steinmetz, Lane v. (C. P.)	574
Stevenson, Dick v.	411
Stichter v. Malloy,	28
Stier, Brietwiesser v. (C. P.)	112
Stiles's Appeal,	83
Stockton v. Lehigh Coal & Nav. Co. (C. P.)	110
Stoesslein v. Lane (C. P.)	377
Stokes's Estate (O. C.)	439
Stokes, Kitchen v. (C. P.)	48
Sullivan & Gilbert v. Bacher & Boner (C. P.)	14
Sully, Dutill v.	573
Sulphur Springs School Dist., B. & O. R. R. Co. v.	568
TANEY'S Appeal,	564
Taylor, Lehr v.	401
Taylor v. Smiley (C. P.)	30
Taylor, Thompson v. (C. P.)	169
Tebay & Bredin's Appeal,	151
Telegraph Co., Zanssig v. (C. P.)	510
Texas & Pacific R. Co., Reading v. (U. S. C. C.)	175
The Norman (U. S. D. C.)	543
Thomas, City of Phila. v. (C. P.)	240
Thomas, McEntee v. (C. P.)	252
Thomas v. West Jersey R. R. Co. (S. C. U. S.)	65
Thompson v. Taylor (C. P.)	169
Thomson's Estate,	118
Thornton, Bowen v. (C. P.)	575
Thornton, Longstreth v. (C. P.)	206
Travellers' Ins. Co. v. Heath,	516
Trimmer, Luzerne County v.	376
Troutman, People's Bank v.	54
Truby's Appeal,	550
Tyson, City v. (C. P.)	367
UNION Mutual Ins. Co., Bradfield v. (C. P.)	436
Union Twp. v. Gibboney,	390
University of Pennsylvania's Appeal,	520
VAN HORN, Dorsey v. (C. P.)	95
Vent v. Pashley (C. P.)	559
WAGNER, City of Phila. v. (C. P.)	511
Waldo v. Com'th,	200
Walker, Galbraith v.	474
Wall & Emerson's Appeal,	227
Walling, Railway Co. v.	467
Walz, Sparr v. (C. P.)	64
Wanamaker v. Price (C. P.)	112
Ward, Garver v. (C. P.)	192
Warehouse Co., Anderson v. (S. C. U. S.)	262
Warner, Brez v.	45
Warner, Faas v.	412
Webster, Hobson v. (C. P.)	206
Weeks, O'Connor v. (C. P.)	461
Weightman, Kiker v. (C. P.)	274
Weir v. Lawrence (C. P.)	207
Welch v. Emerson,	372
Western Savings Fund, Owen v.	465
West Jersey R. R. Co., Thomas v. (S. C. U. S.)	65
Whitaker's Estate (O. C.)	420
Whitaker v. Read (C. P.)	144
White's Appeal,	442

TABLE OF CASES.

Case	Page
White v. Schlect (C. P.)	77
White, Hartley v.	286
Whiting v. Lake,	137
Wilcox & Gibbs Sewing Machine Co., Ewing v. (C. P.)	272
Willard, Commonwealth v. (Q. S.)	524
Williams v. Com'th,	113
Williamsport Gas Co. v. Pinkerton,	97
Wilson, Com'th v. (Q. S.)	291
Wilson v. Deacon (C. P.)	47
Wilson, Fahnestock v.	385
Wingerd v. Fallon,	163
Winkler v. Pemberton (C. P.)	419
Winpenny, Biegenwald v. (C. P.)	542
Winpenny, Nass v. (C. P.)	542
Winton v. Little,	37
Wiser's Appeal,	508
Wistar v. City of Phila.	98
Wolf's Estate (O. C.)	260
Wood, City of Phila. v. (C. P.)	347
Wood's Estate (O. C.)	170
Worthington, Reed v. (C. P.)	192
Wright v. Funck,	249
Wright, Norrington v. (U. S. C. C.)	422
Wunder's Estate (O. C.)	384
YEAGER v. Fuss,	557
Yost, Schwenk v. (C. P.)	16
Young, Orangeville Sav. and Loan Assoc. v. (C. P.)	251
ZANSSIG v. Telegraph Co. (C. P.)	510
Ziegler, Biery v.	154
Ziegler v. Nat. Bank of Allentown,	19

TABLE OF CASES CITED

IN THE

OPINIONS OF THE SUPREME COURT IN THE CASES REPORTED IN THIS VOLUME.

Case	Page
ÆTNA Fire Ins. v. Tyler, 16 Wend. 385,	429
Albiets v. Mellon, 1 Wright, 367,	168
Allegheny Valley R. R. Co. v. McLain, 27 Pitts. Leg. Jour. 135,	36
Allen v. Willard, 7 Sm. 374,	534
Allison v. James, 9 Watts, 380,	537
Allison v. Kurtz, 2 Watts, 185,	460
Allison v. Wilson, 13 S. & R. 330,	460
Anderson v. Roberts, 18 John. 526,	356
Anewalt's Appeal, 6 Wr. 417,	460
Arnold v. Macungie Savings Bank, 21 Sm. 290,	267
Ashbury Railway & Iron Co. v. Riche, 7 English and Irish App. 653,	69
Ashton's Appeal, 23 Sm. 153,	91
Attorney-General v. Hudson, 1 P. Wms. 675,	523
Attorney-General v. Robins, 2 P. Wms. 23,	523
Austin's Appeal, 25 Rawle, 205,	147
Ayres v. Wattson, 7 Sm. 360,	167
BAILEY v. Bailey, 14 S. & R. 195,	537
Bank of Northern Liberties v. Jones, 6 Wr. 541,	267
Bank of Utica v. Childs, 6 Cowen, 245,	467
Bardsley's Estate, 7 W. N. C. 48,	108
Barnet v. The National Bank, 8 Otto, 555,	474
Battles v. Laudenslager, 3 Nor. 446,	362
Baum v Reed, 24 Sm. 322,	142
Beales v. Lee, 10 Barr, 56,	142
Beltzhoover v. Waltman, 1 W. & S. 416,	138
Beman v. Rufford, 1 Simon N. S. 550,	70
Bender v. Fleurie, 2 Grant, 345,	290
Bender v. Fromberger, 4 Dall. 441,	482
Birmingham Fire Ins. Co. v. Kroegher, 2 Norris, 64,	109
Black v. Del. & Raritan Canal Co., 7 C. E. Green N. Jer. Equity, 399,	70
Black v. Tricker, 9 Sm. 13,	270
Blake v. Ins. Co., 12 Gray, 265,	430
Bleight v. The Bank, 10 Barr, 131,	460
Blystone v. Blystone, 1 Sm. 373,	153
Boland v. Whitman, Receiver, 33 Ind. 64,	100
Bond v. Bunting, 28 Sm. 215; 8,	330
Borough of Greensburg v. Young, 3 Sm. 284,	87
Bortz v. Bortz, 12 Wr. 382,	310
Bradley v. Angel, 3 N. Y. 475,	2
Bradley's Appeal, 36 Leg. Int. 38,	290
Bridges v. Hawkesworth, 7 Eng. Law & Eq. R., 424,	332
Brittin v. Barnaby, 21 Howard, 536,	432
Brolasky v. Gally's Ex'rs, 1 Sm. 509,	460
Brown v. Bennett, 25 Sm. 420,	156
Brown v. Commonwealth, 28 Sm. 122	395
Brown v. Scott, 1 Sm. 357,	167
Brunner's Appeal, 11 Wright, 67,	183
Bryar v. Harrison, 1 Wr. 233,	520
Burns v. Belfontaine & St. L. R. Co., 50 Mo. 139,	470
Burr v. Sim, 1 Whar. 252,	460
Butler v. Burk, 2 Salk. 623,	474
CADWALADER'S Appeal, 7 Sm. 158,	285
Cake's Appeal, 11 Harris, 186,	195
Caldwell v. Brown, 3 Sm. 456,	554
Callen v. Ferguson, 5 Casey, 247,	285
Campbell v. Braden, 9 W. N. C. 487,	492
Campbell's Ex'rs v. Boggs, 12 Wr. 524,	467
Cathcart v. Bowman, 5 Barr, 317,	91
Chamberlain v. Smith, 8 Wr. 431,	62
Chase v. Harding, 6 Nor. 343,	371
Chestnut Hill Turnpike v. Rutter, 4 S. & R. 6,	130
Chew v. Nicklin, 9 Wr. 84,	460
Christie & Scott's Appeal, 4 Norris, 463,	227
City of Erie v. Bootz, 22 Sm. 196,	44
Clark v. Baker, 3 S. & R. 477,	216
Clifford v. Beems, 3 Watts, 246,	138
Collins v. Blantern, 2 Wils. 341,	152
Columbia Ins. Co. v. Masonheimer, 26 Sm. 138,	101
Commissioners v. Bolles, 4 Otto, 104,	435
Commissioners v. Hall, 7 Watts, 290,	392
Cooper v. Lampeter Twp., 8 Watts, 125,	392
Com'th v. Beamish, 31 Sm. 389, 5,	398
Com'th v. Chathams, 14 Wr. 181,	62
Com'th v. Clark, 7 W. & S. 127,	371
Com'th v. Cope, 9 Wright, 161,	133
Com'th v. Harding, 6 Norris, 343,	532
Com'th v. Ketner, 8 W. N. C. 133,	5
Com'th v. Slifer, 1 Casey, 23,	377
Com'th v. Snelling, 15 Pick. 321,	117
Com'th v. Straub, 11 Casey, 137,	133
Com'th v. Wilkinson, 16 Pick. 175	130
Covers v. Black, 1 Barr, 493,	167
Covert v. Irwin, 3 S. & R. 283,	388
Cowden's Estate, 1 Barr, 267,	486
Coyne v. Souther, 11 Sm. 457,	195
Craig's Appeal, 27 Sm. 448,	143
DANDO'S Appeal, 9 W. N. C. 5,	330
Danville R. R. Co. v. Com'th, 2 Sm. 29,	130
Darlington v. Penna. R. R. Co., 1 Casey, 445,	74

(xiii)

xiv TABLE OF CASES CITED IN SUPREME COURT OPINIONS.

Case	Page
Dater v. Troy R. R. Co., 2 Hill, 629,	130
Davis v. Bigler, 12 Sm. 242,	53
Davis v. Steiner, 2 Harris, 275,	537
Delaware Div. Canal Co. v. Com'th, 10 Sm. 367,	130
Delaware & Hudson Canal Co. v. Carroll, 8 Norris, 374,	554
Desilver v. Ins. Co., 2 Wr. 130,	432
Dick v. Cooper, 12 Harris, 217,	143
Diligent Fire Co. v. Com'th, 25 Sm. 295,	435
Dobson v. Sotheby, 1 M. & M. 90,	109
Douglass's Appeal, 12 Wr. 223	271
Downey v. Garard, 12 Har. 52,	467
Downing v. Rugar, 21 Wend. 178,	245
Dubois's Appeal, 2 Wr. 231,	103
Du Bois v. Baum, 10 Wr. 537,	285
Duff v. Allegheny Valley R. R. Co., Pittsburgh Legal Journal, Nov. 26, 1879,	507
Dull v. Ridgway Twp., 9 Barr, 272,	392
Duncan v. Kirkpatrick, 13 S. & R. 292,	519
EARLEY'S Appeal, 7 W. N. C. 184	220
East Anglian Railway Co. v. Eastern Counties Railway Co., 11 Com. Bench R. 803,	69
Eastern Counties Railway Co. v. Hawkes, 5 Clark's H. of L. R. 347,	70
Eichelberger v. Barnitz, 9 W. 450,	216
Eldred v. Hazlett, 9 Casey, 307	91
Elkins v. McKean, 29 Sm. 493,	500
Evans's Appeal, 13 Sm. 183,	460
Evans v. Dravo, 12 Harris, 63,	153
Ewing v. Thompson, 7 Wr. 372,	377
FAHNESTOCK v. Wilson, 9 Pitts. L. J. 81,	557
Federal Ins. Co. v. Robinson, 1 Norris, 359,	519
Fickes's Appeal, 21 Sm. 447,	310
Fickes v. Wireman, 2 Watts, 314,	458
Field's Appeal, 12 Casey, 11,	190
Filson v. Himes, 5 Barr, 452,	153
Fire Ins. Co. v. Williamson, 2 Casey, 196,	432
Fitzpatrick v. Allen, 30 Sm. 292,	28
Flureau v. Thornhill, 2 W. Black, 1078,	482
Forth v. Chapman, 1 P. W. 666,	215
Fourth Nat. Bank of Chicago v. City Nat. Bank of Grand Rapids, 68 Ills. 398,	3
Francis v. Ins. Co., 1 Dutch. 78,	430
Francis v. The Ins. Co., 6 Cowen, 404,	430
Franklin Ins. Co. v. Chicago Ice Co., 36 Md. 102,	109
Franklin Ins. Co. of Phila. v. Coates, 14 Md. 285,	430
Frazier v. Erie Bank, 8 W. & S. 18,	267
Frederick v. Campbell, 13 S. & R. 136,	162
Fries v. Boisselet, 9 S. & R. 128,	537
Fryer v. Rishell, 3 Norris, 521, 8,	330
GACKENBACH v. Brouse, 4 W. & S. 546,	211
Galbreath v. Eichelberger, 3 Yeates, 515,	515
Gardner v. Davis, 3 Har. 41,	58
Gaw v. Walcott, 10 Barr, 43,	142
Gibbons v. Fairlamb, 2 Casey, 217,	524
Gilkyson v. Larue, 6 W. & S. 213,	537
Gilman v. Eastern R. R. Corp., 10 Allen, 233,	554
Glass v. Warwick, 4 Wright, 140,	183
Glidden v. Strupler, 2 Sm. 400,	269
Good v. Obertauffer, Brightly's Tr. & Haly, sect. 1182, note,	504
Grant v. Howard Ins. Co., 5 Hill, 10,	109
Gray v. Smith, 3 Watts, 289,	460
Greenfield's Estate, 2 Harris, 489,	355
Green v. Howell, 6 W. & S. 203,	459
Grubb v. Grubb, 7 W. N. C. 349,	452
HAAK v. Linderman, 14 Sm. 499,	62
Hacker v. Perkins, 5 Whar. 95,	167
Haffey v. Carey, 23 Sm. 431, 8, 88,	330
Ham v. Smith, 6 Norris, 63,	152
Hammett v. Phila., 15 Sm. 164,	87
Hanover R. R. Co. v. Coyle, 5 Sm. 396,	339
Harding v. Vandewater, 40 Cal. 77,	245
Harger v. Comm'rs of Washington Co., 2 Jones, 251,	518
Harrisburg Bank v. Tyler, 3 W. & S. 373,	267
Hart v. Boller, 15 S. & R. 162,	167
Hazlebaker v. Reeves, 2 Jones, 264,	537
Heck v. Shener, 4 S. & R. 289,	402
Heiston v. Fortner, 2 Binn. 40,	167
Heitzman v. Divil, 1 Jones, 264,	143
Helme v. Ins. Co., 11 Sm. 107,	433
Hemphill v. Eckfeldt, 5 Whar. 274,	482
Hendrickson v. Evans, 1 Casey, 441,	153
Henry v. Horstick, 9 Watts, 412,	563
Hershey v. Weiting, 14 Wright, 240,	153
Hess v. Gourley, 8 Norris, 195,	491
Hess v. Shorb, 7 Barr, 231,	460
Hiester v. Green, 12 Wr. 96,	310
Hill v. Hill, 24 Sm. 173,	216
Hinney v. Phillips, 14 Wr. 382,	8
Hoffman v. Foster & Co., 7 Wr. 137,	168
Hopewell Twp. v. Putt, 2 W. N. C. 46,	392
Hopkins v. Jones, 2 Barr, 71,	216
Hopkins v. West, 2 Norris, 109,	153
Horner & McCann v. Hower, 3 Wr. 126,	248
Howell v. Young, 5 Barn. & Cress. 259,	467
Huckenstine's Appeal, 20 Sm. 102,	135
Hunt v. Moore, 2 Barr, 105,	326
Hutchinson's Appeal, 11 Wr. 84,	459
Hutchinson v. Boggs & Kirk, 4 Casey, 294,	168
Hyde, Receiver of Chenango Ins. Co., v. Lynde, 4 N. Y. 387,	101
INLAND Ins. Co. v. Stauffer, 9 Casey, 379,	432
In re Commercial Bank Corpor. of India and the East, L. R. 1 Ch. App. 538,	2
In re Contested Election of Barber, 5 Nor. 392,	377
In re Washington Ave., 19 Sm. 352,	86
In re Wyrach's Trusts, 17 Jur. 588,	216
Ins. Co. v. Gottman, 12 Wr. 151,	432
Ins. Co. v. Lawrence, 10 Peters, 507,	430
Ins. Co. v. Schreffler, 6 Wr. 183,	430
Irvine v. Lumberman's Bank, 2 W. & S. 190,	435
JACKSON v. Bank of United States, 10 Barr, 61,	267
Jacobs's Appeal, 11 Harris, 480,	179
Jeffers v. Gill, 8 W. N. C. 19,	91
Jefferson County v. Slagle, 16 Sm. 202,	246
Jeffryes v. Agra and Masterman's Bank, L. R. 2 Eg. 673,	3
Johns v. Lantz, 13 Sm. 324,	537
Johnson v. Hart, 3 Johns. Cas. 329,	230
KARNS v. McKinney, 24 Sm. 387,	138
Kauffelt v. Bower, 7 S. & R. 64,	310
Kaul v. Lawrence, 23 Sm. 410,	133
Kelly v. Com'th, 1 Grant, 484,	410
Kennedy v. Fury, 1 Dall. 76,	312
Keough v. Leslie, 8 W. N. C. 172,	326
Kessler v. McConachy, 1 Rawle, 435,	138
Kille v. Ege, 1 Norris, 102,	484
King's Appeal, 3 Nor. 345,	414
Kinsel v. Ramey, 6 Norris, 248,	290
Knecht v. Ins. Co., 7 W. N. C. 297,	503

TABLE OF CASES CITED IN SUPREME COURT OPINIONS. xv

LEE v. Burk, 16 Sm. 336,	557	Meesel v. Lynn & Boston R. Co., 8 Allen, Mass. 234,	470	Noyes v. Ins. Co., 30 Vermont, 659,	.430
Lehigh Valley Coal Co. v. Jones, 5 Norris, 433,	554	Megargee v. Naglee, 14 Sm. 216,	290	Nuttall v. Bracewell, 2 Excheq. L. R. 1,	25
Leib v. Com'th, 9 Watts, 200,	370, 530	Mevey's Appeal, 4 Barr, 80,	486		
Lewis v. Jones, 1 Barr, 336,	130	Meyer's Appeal, 13 Wright, 111,	216	OGDEN'S Appeal, 20 Sm. 501,	290
Lewis v. The Ins. Co., 52 Maine, 492,	430	Middlesworth's Adm'r. v. Blackmore, 24 Sm. 414,	217	Ohio & Penna. R. R. Co. v. Wallace, 2 Harris, 245,	74
Laird's Appeal, 4 W. N. C. 473,	460	Miller v. Adams, 16 Mass. 456,	467	Oliphant v. Church, 7 Har. 318,	167
Lancaster Turnpike Co. v. Rogers, 2 Barr, 114,	130	Miller v. Baschore, 2 Norris, 356,	537	O'Niel v. Ins. Co., 3 Comst. 122,	109, 430
Lindsay v. Jackson, 2 Paige, 581,	2	Miller v. Henlan, 1 Sm. 265,	285	Overholt v. The Bank, 1 Norris, 490,	474
Line v. Stephenson, 35 E. C. L. R. 77,	482	Miller v. Huddleston, 3 Mac. & G. 513,	523		
Linn v. Alexander, 9 Sm. 43,	290	Miller v. Ins. Co., 2 E. D. Sm. 268,	430	PARISH v. Wheeler, 22 N. Y. 494,	71
Lithcap v. Wilt, 4 Phil. Rep. 64,	229	Miller v. Kirkpatrick, 5 Casey, 226,	86	Parkinson's Appeal, 8 Casey, 455,	460
Lock v. Furze, 115 E. C. L. R. 401,	482	Miller v. Stem, 2 Barr, 286,	141	Parrish v. Koons, 1 Pars. 79,	285
Lockhart v. Lichtenthaler, 10 Wr. 151,	500	Miller v. Stem, 2 Jones, 383,	141	Patterson v. Martz, 8 Watts, 374,	285
Love v. Jones, 4 Watts, 465,	179	Miller v. Wilson, 12 Har. 114,	467	Patterson v. Robinson, 1 Casey, 81,	183
Lowry v. McKinney, 18 Sm. 294,	486	Monongahela Nav. Co. v. Coons, 6 W. & S. 114,	531	Pauli v. Com'th, 7 W. N. C. 397,	63
Lucas v. The Bank, 28 Sm. 228,	474	Monroe v. Smith, 29 Sm. 459,	357	Paxton v. Harrier, 1 Jones, 312,	486
Lyon v. Miller, 12 Harris, 392,	346	Moore v. Ins. Co., 29 Me. 97,	109	Peck v. Jones, 20 Sm. 83,	520
		Moore v. Juvenal, 8 W. N. C. 411,	467	People v. Bush, 4 Hill, 133,	411
McBRIDE v. Smythe, 4 Sm. 245,	290	Moore v. Kiff, 28 Sm. 96,	125	Penna. & Ohio Canal Co. v. Graham, 13 Sm. 290,	390
McCall v. Lenox, 9 S. & R. 304,	230	Moorehead v. Duncan, 1 Norris, 488,	167	Perry v. Scott, 1 Sm. 119,	310
McCalmont v. Allegheny, 5 Casey, 417,	392	Moroney's Appeal, 12 Harris, 372,	104	Phila. & Reading R. R. Co. v. Hummell, 8 Wr. 378,	506
McCausland's Adm'r v. Bell, 9 S. & R. 388,	474	Morgan v. The Vale of Neath Ry. Co., 35 L. J. Q. B. 23,	554	Phila. & Reading R. R. Co. v. Long, 25 Sm. 265,	507
McClowry v. Croghan's Adm'rs, 1 Grant, 307,	484	Morrow v. Brenizer, 2 Rawle, 185,	460	Physick's Appeal, 14 Wr. 128,	290
McClure's Appeal, 22 Sm. 414,	460	Morse v. Buffalo Fire & Marine Ins. Co., 30 Wis. 534,	109	Pinbury v. Elkin, 1 P. Wms. 563,	218
McComas v. Ins. Co., 56 Mo. 573,	430	Moss's Appeal, 11 Casey, 162,	138	Pittsburgh v. Cluley, 16 Sm. 449,	200
McCully v. Clarke, 4 Wr. 399,	534	Mulherrin v. Del. Lack. & Western R. R. Co., 31 Sm. 366,	506	Pitts. Ft. Wayne & Chicago R. R. Co. v. Gilleland, 6 Sm. 445,	570
McDowell v. Glass, 4 Watts, 389,	58	Mullan v. Phila. & Southern Mail S. S. Co., 28 Sm. 25,	339	Pottsville Borough v. Norwegian Twp., 2 Harris, 543,	392
McEvoy v. Medina, 11 Allen, Mass. 548,	332	Mulliken v. Graham, 22 Sm. 490,	196	Pray v. Northern Liberties, 7 Casey, 69,	87
McMasters v. Com'th, 3 Watts, 293,	87	Mundorff v. Wickersham, 13 Sm. 87,	326	Presbyterian Church Corpor. v. Wallace, 3 Rawle, 165,	486
McMasters v. Ins. Co., 25 Wend. 379,	430	Musser v. Hyde, 2 W. & S. 314	326	Presbyterian Congregation v. Johnson, 1 W. & S. 9,	312
MacGregor v. The Deal & Dover Ry. Co., 22 L. J. Q. B. 69,	70	Myers v. Harvey, 2 P. & W. 478,	143	Price v. McCallister, 3 Grant, 248,	138
Mack v. Patchin, 42 N. Y. 167,	482				
Magaw v. Garrett, 1 Casey, 322,	195	NAGLE'S Appeal, 1 Har. 260,	460	RAILROAD Co. v. Ervin, 36 Leg. Int. 244,	501
Maguire v. Middlesex R. Co., 115 Mass. 239,	470	Naglee v. Ingersoll, 7 Barr, 185,	8	Railroad Co. v. Hendrickson, 30 Sm. 182,	151
Maine Mut. Ins. Co. v. Pickering, 66 Me. 130,	101	Nailer v. Stanley, 10 S. & R. 450,	486	Railroad Co. v. Hinds, 3 Sm. 512,	535
Mann's Appeal, 14 Wright, 375,	107	Neely v. Grantham, 8 Sm. 433,	400, 460	Railroad Co. v. Norton, 12 Harris, 465,	507
Mann v. Wieand, 4 W. N. C. 6,	343	New York & Maryland R. R. Co. v. Winans, 17 Howard, 30,	70	Railroad Co. v. Porter, 5 Casey, 165,	74
Mateer v. Hissim, 3 P. & W. 161,	356	Nice's Appeal, 14 Wr. 143,	290	Railway Co. v. Wilt, 4 Whar. 143,	36
Mathews v. Harsell, 1 E. D. Smith, N. Y. 393,	332	Nokes's Appeal, 4 Rep. 80,	482	Ream v. Rank, 3 S. & R. 215,	36
Maule v. Ashmead, 8 Harris, 482,	482	North American B. & L. Asso. v. Sutton, 11 Casey, 463,	220	Reed v. Defebaugh, 12 Har. 495,	167
Maynes v. Atwater, 7 Norris, 496,	143	Northern Liberties v. Church, 1 Harris, 104,	87	Rees v. Emerick, 6 S. & R. 286,	106
		Norwich v. Ins. Co., 6 Blatchford C. C. R. 241,	430		

xvi   TABLE OF CASES CITED IN SUPREME COURT OPINIONS.

Case	Page
Reitenbaugh v. Chester Val. R. R. Co., 9 Harris, 100,	74
Regina v. Garbet, 1 Denison's Cr. C. 236,	515
Regina v. Great North of England Railway, 9 Q. B. 315,	130
Regina v. Lewis, 9 C. & P. 523,	410
Regina v. Parker, 1 C. & M. 139,	116
Regina v. St. George, 9 C. & P. 483,	410
Regina v. Williams, 1 Car. & Kirwan, 589,	410
Rex v. Hodgson, 3 Car. & P. 422,	117
Rex v. Bootyman, 5 Car. & P. 300,	117
Rex v. Butler, 6 C. & P. 368,	410
Rheem v. Naugatuc Wheel Co., 9 Casey, 356,	94
Rhodes v. Dunbar, 7 Sm. 274,	135
Rice v. Bixler, 1 W. & S. 445,	460
Richard's Appeal, 7 Sm. 105,	135
Rickert v. Madeira, 1 Rawle, 328,	230
Riddle v. County of Bedford, 7 S. & R. 387,	377
Ridgway, Budd & Co.'s Appeal, 3 Harris, 177,	104
Ripple v. Ripple, 1 R. 386,	520
Rodgers v. Gibson, 4 Yeates, 111,	167
Rodgers v. Ins. Co., 6 Paige, 583,	430
Rogers v. Burns, 3 Casey, 528,	474
Roland v. Tiernan, 8 W. & S. 193,	125
Rolph v. Crouch, 3 L. R. Excheq. 44,	482
Romig v. Romig, 2 Rawle, 241,	402
Rosenberger v. Hallowell, 11 Casey, 369,	138
Russell v. Bell, 8 Wr. 47,	557
Rutherford's Case, 22 Sm. 82,	563
Ryan v. Cumberland Valley R. R. Co., 11 Harris, 384,	339
SAAM v. Saam, 4 Watts, 432,	402
Sands, Receiver of Columbia Ins. Co. v. Hill, 55 N. Y. 18,	101
Savage v. Ins. Co., 4 Bosworth, 1,	430
Schenck v. Ins. Co., 4 Zabriskie, 447,	430
Schlecht's Appeal, 10 Sm. 172,	227
Schuylkill & Dauphin Imp. & R. R. Co. v. Schmoele, 7 Sm. 271,	482
Scott v. Heilager, 2 Harris, 238,	362
Seibert v. Butz, 9 Watts, 494,	216
Seibert v. Kline, 1 Barr, 38,	58
Seibert v. Levan, 8 Barr, 383,	25
Selden v. Merchants' Nat. Bank of Meadville, 19 Sm. 424,	8
Senseman v. Hershman, 1 Norris, 83,	537
Sexton v. Wheaton, 8 Wheat. 229,	355
Shaffer v. Greer, 6 Norris, 370,	91
Sharpless v. Phila., 9 Harris, 147,	371
Sharpless v. Ziegler, 8 W. N. C. 190,	514
Shaw v. Robberds, 6 A. & E. 75,	109
Sheets's Estate, 2 Sm. 257,	216
Silverthorn v. McKinster, 2 Jones, 67,	460
Simpson v. Kelso, 8 Watts, 247,	460
Smith v. Com'th, 4 Sm. 209,	410
Smith v. Darley, 2 H. of L. Cases, 789,	245
Smith v. Reiff, 8 Harris, 364,	310
Smith v. Starr, 3 Wh. 262,	460
Snyder v. Bauchman, 8 S. & R. 336,	388
Snyder v. Christ, 3 Wr. 499,	355, 359
Spaulding v. Backus, 122 Mass. 553,	2
Specht v. The Com'th, 8 Barr, 316,	201
Spires v. Hamot, 8 W. & S. 18,	125
Spring Garden Asso. v. Tradesman's Loan Asso., 10 Wr. 493,	220
Stair v. York Nat. Bank, 5 Sm. 368,	267
Steckel v. Bank, 9 W. N. C. 17,	21
Steffy v. Carpenter, 1 Wright, 41,	105
Steinbacher v. Wilson & Young, 1 Leg. Gaz. Rep. 76,	153
Stewart v. Kearney, 6 Watts, 453,	153
Stockport Water Works Co., 32 L. J. Q. B. 136,	25
Stoner v. Zimmerman, 9 Har. 397,	460
Stow v. Wyse, 7 Conn. 214,	245
Straley's Appeal, 7 Wr. 89,	400
Strauss's Appeal, 13 Wr. 353,	310
Sutcliffe v. Booth, 32 L. J. Q. B. 136,	2
Swan v. Scott, 11 S. & R. 155,	153
Sweatland v. Squire, 14 Viner's Abr. 458,	474
TAYLOR v. Mitchell, 7 Sm. 209,	386
Taylor v. Taylor, 13 Sm. 481,	290
The People v. Batchelor, 22 N. Y. 128,	245
Thompson v. Sheplar, 22 Sm. 160,	162
Thomson v. Dougherty, 12 S. & R. 448,	355
Tillmes v. Marsh, 17 Sm. 507,	227
Todd v. Lorah, 25 Sm. 155,	288
Towers v. Hagner, 3 Whar. 57,	8
Towle v. Swasey, 106 Mass. 100,	523
Townsend v. Maynard, 9 Wr. 198,	355
Trask v. The State Mutual Ins. Co., 5 Casey, 198,	432
Trego v. Lewis, 8 Sm. 463,	105
Triumer v. Heagy, 4 Harris, 487,	269
Trinity Church v. Watson, 14 Wr. 518,	310
UHLER v. Maulfair, 11 Harris, 481,	515
Unanger v. Fitler, 3 Norris, 135,	156
Union Nat. Bank of St. Louis v. Matthews, 8 Otto, 624,	41
United States v. Simpson, 3 P. & W. 437,	41
VANATTA v. Anderson, 3 Bin. 417,	388
Van Valkenburgh v. Ins. Co., 70 N. Y. 605,	109
Vos v. Robinson, 9 Johnson, 192,	430
WADSWORTH v. Davis, Receiver, 13 Ohio St. 123,	100
Warfield v. Fox, 3 Sm. 382,	324
Waring v. Cunliffe, 1 Ves. Jr. 99,	125
Waters v. Wing, 9 Sm. 211,	534
Watson's Ex'r v. Stern, 26 Sm. 121,	537
Watson v. O'Hern, 6 Watts, 362,	346
Watt v. Steel, 1 Barr, 386,	179
Weakley v. Bell, 9 Watts, 273,	167
Weger v. Penna. R. R. Co., 5 Sm. 463,	554
West Chester & Phila. R. R. Co. v. McIlwee, 17 Sm. 311,	471
Weston's Lessee v. Mowlin, 2 Burr. 969,	230
Wharton v. School Directors, 6 Wr. 358,	398
Wheeler v. American Central Ins. Co., 12 Western Ins. Review, 252,	109
Wheeler v. City of Phila., 27 Sm. 338,	246
Wier's Appeal, 24 Sm. 230,	135
Wilcox v. Plummer's Ex'rs, 4 Pet. 172,	467
Williams v. Burrell, 50 E. C. L. R. 401,	482
Williams v. Davis, 19 Sm. 21,	355
Willing v. Peters, 7 Barr, 287,	460
Willis v. Hanover & Germania Ins. Co., 8 Reporter, 343,	109
Wilson v. Murphy, 1 Phil. 106,	230
Wilson v. Shoenberger, 10 Casey, 121,	460
Wilson v. Trumbull Ins. Co., 7 Harris, 372,	101
Wilt v. Vickers, 8 Watts, 227,	36
Winch v. B. & L. Railway Co., 13 Eng. Law & Equity, 506,	70
Winslow v. Leonard, 12 Har. 14,	53
Wistar v. City of Phila., 5 Nor. 215,	42
Wolf v. Com'th, 3 S. & R. 48,	201
Wood v. Northwestern Ins. Co., 46 N. Y. 421,	109
Woods v. Watkins, 4 Wr. 458,	520
Wright v. New York Central R. R. Co., 25 N. Y. 565,	554
YERGER v. Warren, 7 Casey, 319,	36
Young v. Lyman, 9 Barr, 449,	557
ZACK v. Penna. R. R. Co., 1 Casey, 394,	74

Supreme Court.

Jan. '79, 82.   Feb. 20, 1880.
Dougherty Bros. & Co. v. Central National Bank.

Debtor and creditor — Loans — Insolvency — Banks and their depositors — Discount of notes — Insolvency of depositors — When banks may charge an insolvent depositor's account with the amount of an unmatured note due to it — Rights as against assignees of deposit by check or otherwise.

In case of the insolvency of the borrower before actual payment of the money by the lender, an equitable right, analogous to the doctrine of stoppage *in transitu* before the actual delivery of goods, may be exercised by the lender.

Although the relation between a bank and its depositor is that of debtor and creditor, and the bank has no lien upon the fund on deposit for the depositor's future liability to it, and although a depositor may assign his deposit for value by check or otherwise, notwithstanding the fact that the bank holds liabilities of the depositor unmatured at the time of the notice of the assignment, nevertheless, when a bank has extended its credit to a depositor by discounting his note, but learns of his insolvency before payment, or notice of any checks drawn upon the fund, the bank may withdraw the credit upon tendering him the consideration—*i. e.*, the notes and the amount of the discount.

On March 28, 1877, a bank agreed by letter with its depositor, A., to discount a new note in renewal of one already discounted and maturing on the following April 2, and received the new note and collateral, with the amount of the discount, before that date. On April 2, after business hours, the bank returned the original note. On April 3, the bank learned that A. had that day confessed insolvency, and the bank thereupon charged A.'s account with the amount of the renewal note, tendering back the note and collaterals, and the amount of the discount. In a suit brought before the date of the maturity of the renewal note by A. for the use of B. and C., holders of checks drawn by A. on April 2, but not presented for payment until after notice of the insolvency had been received by the bank, and also assignees by assignment under seal of the whole fund on deposit:

Held, that the plaintiffs could not recover.

MERCUR and STERRETT, J.J., dissent.

Error to the Common Pleas No. 3, of Philadelphia County.

Assumpsit, by Dougherty Bros. & Co., against the Central National Bank. The plaintiffs were a banking firm doing business in Harrisburg; the defendants' place of business was Philadelphia. The summons issued April 23, 1877. The declaration contained the common counts only, to which defendants pleaded non-assumpsit, payment, and set-off, with leave, etc. They also filed a special plea, and demurred to plaintiff's replication thereto. Upon the trial of the issues joined upon the first three pleas, before FINLETTER, J., the plaintiffs proved that they kept a deposit with defendants, and offered in evidence an account stated, rendered to them by defendants, showing a balance due March 31, 1877, of $17,538.18. They admitted a credit of payments subsequently made, amounting to $3138.55, which left a balance to their credit of $14,399.63. They also offered in evidence three drafts, all dated April 2, 1877, drawn by them upon defendants, as follows: No. 7609—J. W. Weir, cashier, or order, for $5000; No. 7610—J. W. Weir, cashier, or order, $800; No. 7612—G. W. Hunter, or order, $7500; each being duly endorsed, and protested for non-payment; and an assignment by plaintiffs to the said Hunter and Weir, dated April 23, 1877, of the said sum of $14,399.63, on deposit with the defendants on that date. Objected to by defendants; objection sustained, and exception granted to plaintiffs, who then closed.

Defendants proved that, at some time previous to April 2, 1877, they had discounted for plaintiffs a note for $15,000, which became due on April 2, and on the written application of the plaintiffs, dated March 27, 1877, the bank, by letter dated March 28, consented to renew this for thirty days from its maturity. A new note, with the amount of the discount and collaterals, was sent to the bank March 31, 1877, and the original note was returned to the plaintiffs by mail, April 2, after bank hours. On April 3, plaintiffs, who had become insolvent, failed to open their doors for business. Hearing of this fact on the morning of the same day, defendants immediately charged the plaintiffs' account with the amount of the original note, due April 2; credited them with the discount received with the renewal note, so that defendants' books showed a balance due them on an over-drawn account, and tendered the new note, with the amount of the discount and collaterals, to the plaintiffs, demanding a return of the original note. They then made an unconditional tender. The defendants put in evidence assignments for the benefit of creditors, executed by two of the plaintiffs, dated April 3, 1877, and a certified copy of a judgment for $25,000, confessed by W. E. Dougherty, one of the plaintiffs, to John J. Fitzpatrick, in the Court of Common Pleas of Dauphin County, entered on April 2, 1877. They further proved that Dougherty had, a short time previous, written to the holder of the power of attorney to confess judgment, that he had better come to Harrisburg, to look after his interests, and that he came, and, without consulting either Dougherty or the plaintiffs, entered up the judgment.

No points were presented to the Court below, but the Court charged the jury as follows: "If you find from the evidence that the plaintiffs were insolvent on the 3d day of April, 1877, then you will give the defendants credit for the amount of the note due May 5, 1877, $15,000."

Verdict for the defendants, and judgment thereon. The plaintiffs took this writ of error, assigning for error the sustaining of the objection to plaintiffs' offer of evidence, and the charge of the Court below.

A. D. Campbell and *James E. Gowen*, for plaintiffs in error.

(1) The relation between a bank and its depositor is merely that of debtor and creditor.
Foley *v.* Hill, 2 H. L. C. 28.
Bank *v.* Jones & Cole, 6 Wr. 536.

The credit of the discounted note is equivalent to the deposit of so much cash; and there is an implied understanding on the part of the bank that it will honor its depositors' drafts to the extent of the deposits.
Rolin *v.* Steward, 14 C. B. Rep. 595.

The bank has, therefore, no lien upon the deposits for unmatured debts due by the depositor.
Bower *v.* The Foreign and Colonial Gas Co., defendant, and the Metropolitan Bank, gar., 22 W. R. 740.
Beckwith *v.* Union Bank, 4 Sandford, S. C. R. 604.
Jordan *v.* Nat. Shoe and Leather Bank, 74 N. Y. 467.
Fourth Nat. Bank of Chicago *v.* City Nat. Bank, 68 Ill. 398.

(2) At the time of bringing this suit the renewal note had not matured, and the bank cannot, therefore, under the Defalcation Act, set off this indebtedness of the plaintiffs in the present suit.
Pennell *v.* Grubb, 1 H. 552.
Duncan *v.* Lyon, 3 John. Ch. R. 351.
Bradley *v.* Angel, 3 N. Y. 475.
Rawson *v.* Samuel, 1 Cr. & Ph. 161.
In re Com. Bank Corporation, L. R. 1 Ch. App. 538.

The assignment of the deposit before the maturity of the note, in any event defeated the right of set-off; we had a right, therefore, to prove this upon the trial.
Northampton Bank *v.* Balliet, 8 W. & S. 311.
Phillips *v.* Bank of Lewistown, 6 H. 394.
Watson *v.* Mid Wales R. Co., L. R. 2 C. P. 593.
Jeffryes *v.* Agra & Masterman's Bank, L. R. 2 Eq. 674.
Martin *v.* Kunzmuller, 37 N. Y. 396.
Spaulding *v.* Backus *et al.*, 122 Mass. 553.

Edw. L. Perkins and *R. C. McMurtrie*, contra.

This suit was brought to enforce a contract to loan after the borrower had become insolvent—*i. e.*, after the consideration has failed, and there has been no assignment for value. The defence is a familiar one in equity, and analogous to stoppage *in transitu*, when applied to contracts in relation to property.
Agra Bank *v.* Hoffman, 34 L. Jour. Ch. 285.

Set-off is of purely equitable origin, and the fact of the statute regulating it *at law*, does not take away the equitable right which exists in case of insolvency.
Chapman *v.* Derby, 2 Vern. 117.
Ex parte Wagstaff, 13 Ves. 65.
Atkinson *v.* Elliott, 7 T. R. 378.
James *v.* Kynnier, 5 Ves. 108.
Pond *v.* Smith, 4 Conn. 302.
Demmon *v.* Boylston Bank, 5 Cush. 195.
Aldrich *v.* Campbell, 4 Gray, 284.
Receivers *v.* Paterson Gas Co., 3 Zab. 283.

The New York cases, cited by plaintiffs in error, were determined upon the statute of that State.

There was no proof that the checks were given for value, nor of any notice of the assignment until the equity had arisen.

May 3, 1880. THE COURT. Whatever may be the rights of a party, whose debt is due and payable, to compel an insolvent debtor to set off a claim against him not due, a party, whose debt is not due, has no equitable claim to have it set off against a debt of his own, already due, in the hands of a party who is insolvent. (Spaulding *v.* Backus, 122 Mass. 553; Bradley *v.* Angel, 3 N. Y. 475; *In re* Commercial Bank Corporation of India and the East, L. R. 1 Ch. App. 538.) In the latter case it was said that where there is, on one side, a debt presently due, and on the other a liability which will accrue due at a future day, the debt cannot be set off at law against the liability, nor can it be so set off in equity. This is at variance with Lindsay *v.* Jackson (2 Paige, 581) where the defendants, who held notes of the plaintiffs not due, were restrained from negotiating them, to the end that they might be applied as a set-off against a debt then due by the defendants to the plaintiffs. But it is ruled in Bradley *v.* Angel (*supra*) that one whose debt is not due, has no equitable right to set off against a debt due to him from an insolvent estate, and the decision in Lindsay against Jackson is confined in its operation to such facts as constitute its base. A bank has no lien on money standing to the credit of one of its depositors for the amount of a note of such depositor, discounted by the bank, but which has not matured. The purpose is that the customer may draw out at his pleasure the avails of his discount. A debtor in one sum has no lien upon money in his hands for the payment of an unmatured debt owing to him, and a bank is debtor for the discount which is placed to its depositor' credit. If it could retain the money against the note the discount would be useless to the borrower. (Jordan *v.* Shoe and Leather Bank, 74 N. Y. 467; Fourth Nat. Bank of Chicago *v.* City Nat. Bank of Grand Rapids, 68 Ill. 398.)

The owner of a debt may assign it for value, and give title as against the debtor, though he holds liabilities of the creditor not yet matured at the time he received notice of the assignment. (Jeffryes *v.* Agra and Masterman's Bank, L. R. 2 Eg. 673.)

On the foregoing principles the plaintiffs claim that the judgment must be reversed, and so it must, if they apply to the facts of this case. The facts conceded and established by the verdict are as follows: The plaintiffs were bankers at Harrisburg, and had an account with defendant, a bank in Philadelphia. On April 2, 1877, the balance due plaintiffs on that account was $14,399.63, and they owed to defendant $15,000 on a note, the proceeds of which had gone into the account. Prior to said date the parties had agreed to a renewal of the note, and the plaintiffs sent a new one for same sum, payable May 5, 1877, which defendant received, and, on the 2d of April, sent the original note by mail to the plaintiffs. April 3 the plaintiffs did not open their bank for business, and were insolvent. The defendant, hearing of this, immediately charged the plaintiffs with the original note, credited them with $85, the discount on the new one, resulting in a balance due defendant, and tendered to the plaintiffs the new note, discount and collaterals. April 2 the plaintiffs gave to Weir and Hunter three checks amounting to $13,300 which were presented to the defendant and payment refused; but it does not appear they were presented, or that defendant had notice of them, till after the said tender and withdrawal of the credit.

The question is, shall the defendant, having discounted the plaintiffs' note and extended their credit for its amount, and, upon learning of their insolvency, before payment to, or notice of any checks or assignments by them, having withdrawn the credit and tendered back the consideration, be compelled to pay the money? If so, it would be against everybody's sense of right. The point is not merely one of set-off, whether legal or equitable.

Justice and equity forbid that one man's money shall be applied to the payment of another man's debts. On this is based the right of a vendor to stoppage *in transitu,* which arises solely upon the insolvency of the buyer. Where a vendor has delivered goods out of his possession, into the hands of a carrier for delivery to the buyer, if he discovers that the buyer is insolvent, he may retake the goods, if he can, before they reach the buyer's possession, and thus avoid having his property applied to paying debts due by the buyer to the other people. It was long a mooted question whether the effect of this remedy of the vendor is a rescission of the sale, or a restoration of possession of the goods with the rights of an unpaid vendor; but now it seems the better opinion that the contract is not rescinded. Although this remedy of a vendor, which exists only before actual delivery of the goods into the buyer's possession, cannot be exercised in precisely the same mode by a lender of money or credit, yet for similar cause the lender ought to have as efficient remedy until the money is paid to, or the credit is used by the borrower. The lender's remedy may have the effect of a rescission of the bargain. Goods can be held subject to a lien for the price agreed upon, and, if disposed of for more or less than that, the buyer may have the gain or suffer the loss; but when a borrower has as little right to the money, as a buyer has to the goods, it is impracticable to hold and dispose of the money with like result. Nor is there reason for so holding—the value of the goods may increase or diminish, whereby the buyer may be gainer or loser by his contract —the value of money is fixed. Insolvency takes the pith out of the borrower's promise to pay, and if he has not yet received the money he should not take it. He did not get the credit in view of his bankruptcy.

The consideration so failed that the defendant was warranted in tendering it back, and an equity arises as against the legal plaintiffs, which prevents their enforcement of the contract. To permit them to recover after their note, the foundation of their claim, is proved worthless, would be the grossest injustice. The defendant's agreement to take the renewal note was not wittingly made for an empty promise.

Plaintiffs contend that Hunter and Weir are innocent purchasers for value. In what sense? They asked no information before taking the checks; no paper of any kind was given by defendant, showing that the plaintiffs had the right to draw or assign. Before presentment or notice of the checks, the plaintiffs' insolvency was shown by a notorious act, and their right to draw was immediately denied by defendant. A vendor's right of stoppage *in transitu* is defeasible in one way only, and that is, when the goods are represented by a bill of lading, which is in the vendee's possession with the vendor's assent, and is transferred to a third person who in good faith gives value for it. Here, the defendant did nothing to mislead third persons, and the plaintiffs had no writing to assign. The facts reveal no superior equity in the persons for whose use action is brought.

We are impelled to the conclusion: 1st. That the defendant had a right to tender back the discounted note and refuse payment to the legal

plaintiff; and 2d, That the assignees have no equities superior to the defendant, and there cannot be a recovery for their use.
Judgment affirmed.
Opinion by TRUNKEY, J. GREEN, J., absent. MERCUR and STERRETT, JJ., dissent.

Jan. '80, 278.   March 18, 1880.
Commonwealth v. Luberg.

Crimes—Embezzlement—Forgery—False entries —State and Federal jurisdiction—Practice— Form of indictment.

A teller of a National Bank, incorporated under the laws of the United States, may be convicted in a State Court upon an indictment charging him with fraudulently making false entries in the books of the bank with intent to injure and defraud the bank.

Such an offence is forgery at common law.

Commonwealth *v.* Beamish, 31 Sm. 389, followed; Commonwealth *ex rel.* Torrey *v.* Ketner, 8 WEEKLY NOTES, 133, distinguished.

Semble, that an indictment for such an offence, laid under the statute, and not charging forgery in the technical manner required by strict rules of the common law, is nevertheless good under the Criminal Procedure Act.

Error to the Quarter Sessions of Schuylkill County.

Two indictments against Charles E. Luberg. The first, No. 268, May Term, 1878, charged him, as receiving teller of the First National Bank of Mahanoy City, with receiving the moneys, etc., therein named, and unlawfully, maliciously, wilfully and fraudulently embezzling, abstracting, and misapplying the same, with intent to injure and defraud, in the first count, the bank, and in the second count, the individual stockholders.

The second indictment, No. 269, May Term, 1878, charged him with having, as the receiving teller of the said bank, unlawfully, maliciously, wilfully, and fraudulently made false entries in the books, reports, and statements of said bank, with intent thereby to injure and defraud said bank.

The bank was duly incorporated as a national bank under the laws of the United States.

Defendant pleaded "not guilty," and was found guilty under both indictments. He was sentenced on the first to one year's imprisonment, to take effect immediately; and on the second to one year's imprisonment, to take effect "immediately after the expiration of the first."

The prisoner took this writ, assigning for error that (1) the Court had no jurisdiction over the offence charged in the first indictment; and (2) the Court had no jurisdiction over the offence charged in the second indictment.

James Ryon, for the plaintiff in error.
There was no common law offence of making false entries.
2 Russell on Crimes, 163–4.
4 Black. Com. 230–1.
The jurisdiction lay exclusively in the United States Courts, which is exclusive, unless otherwise expressly provided.
Houston *v.* Moore, 5 Wheat. 1–24.
1 Kent. Com. 398.
Curtis Com. 176.

The National Banking Act of June 3, 1864,* contains no such proviso, hence the offence of embezzlement of funds of a national bank is cognizable in the United States Courts only.
Commonwealth *v.* Felton, 101 Mass. 204.
State *v.* Tuller, 34 Conn. 280.
Commonwealth *v.* Barry, 116 Mass. 1.

The State Court had no jurisdiction under the Acts of Assembly. That of June 12, 1878 (P. L. 1878, 196), repealed §§ 112, 116, 117, and 119 of the Crimes Act of 1860 and § 36 of the Free Banking Act of 1861, and the latter relates only to offences against institutions created under it.

The case is finally ruled by Commonwealth *ex rel.* Torrey *v.* Ketner (8 WEEKLY NOTES, 133).

A. W. Schalck, District Attorney (with whom were *Geo. R. Kaercher* and *Lin Bartholomew*), for the defendant in error.

---

* The material portions of that Act are as follows:—

§ 55. Every president, director, cashier, teller, clerk, or agent of any association, who embezzles, abstracts, or wilfully misapplies any of the moneys, funds, or credits of the association; or who, without authority from the directors, issues or puts in circulation any of the notes of the association; or who, without such authority, issues or puts forth any certificate of deposit, draws any order or bill of exchange, makes any acceptance, assigns any note, bond, draft, bill of exchange, mortgage, judgment, or decree; or who makes any false entry in any book, report, or statement of the association, with intent, in either case, to injure or defraud the association or any other company, body politic or corporate, or any individual person, or to deceive any officer of the association, or any agent appointed to examine the affairs of any such association; and every person who with like intent aids or abets . . . shall be deemed guilty of a misdemeanor, and shall be imprisoned not less then five years nor more than ten.

§ 56. And be it further enacted, That all suits and proceedings arising out of the provisions of this Act, in which the United States or its officers or agents shall be parties, shall be conducted by the District Attorneys of the several districts, under the direction and supervision of the Solicitor of the Treasury.

§ 57. And be it further enacted, That suits, actions, and proceedings against any association under this Act, may be had in any Circuit, District, or Territorial Court of the United States, held within the district in which such association may be established; or in any State, county, or municipal court in the county or city in which said association is located, having jurisdiction in similar cases; *Provided, however,* That all proceedings to enjoin the comptroller under this Act shall be had in a Circuit, District, or Territorial Court of the United States, held in the district in which the association is located.

Offences against the United States are frequently punished in the State Courts.
Commonwealth v. Schaffer, 4 Dall. 27.
White v. Commonwealth, 4 Bin. 418.
Buckwalter v. United States, 11 S. & R. 196.
United States v. Hutchinson, 4 Clark, 211.
Bletz v. Columbia National Bank, 6 N. 91.
Claflin v. Houseman, 3 Otto. 130.
Jett v. Commonwealth, 7 Am. Law Reg. N. S. 260.
United States v. Amy, Id. 267.
Coleman v. State of Tennessee, 7 Otto, 309.

It is the nature of the offence, not the person offended, which determines the jurisdiction. But the offence was punishable under the Act of 1860 (*supra*), which if repealed by the Act of June 12, 1878, was not so done until after indictment found.

The case is not ruled by Comth. *ex rel.* Torrey v. Ketner (*supra*); for it is an offence as forgery at common law.
4 Blackstone, 247.
2 East, 852.
Rosco's Crim. Ev., 6 Am. Ed. 467.
1 Hawkins, 335.
Comth. v. Biles, 3 Phila. 350.
Brightly's Dig. 529, §§ 726–9.

It is now too late to take exception to the jurisdiction of the Court.
Titusville B. & L. Association v. McCombs, 8 WEEKLY NOTES, 124.
Miltimore v. Miltimore, 4 Wr. 155.
Wetherill v. Stillman, 15 Sm. 105–115.
Spade v. Bruner, 22 Sm, 57–9.

May 3, 1880. THE COURT. The second assignment denies the jurisdiction. The plaintiff in error was convicted upon an indictment charging him as receiving teller of the First National Bank of Mahanoy City, with fraudulently making false entries in the books, reports, and statements of said bank with intent to injure and defraud the said bank, and we are asked to reverse the judgment upon the ground that the offence charged having been committed by an officer of a national bank, it is not the subject of indictment in a State Court. Commonwealth *ex relatione* William Torrey, decided at the last term (8 WEEKLY NOTES, 133), was relied on to sustain this position. Torrey was indicted as cashier of a national bank with embezzling the funds of the bank, and he was discharged upon *habeas corpus* for the reason that the offence was not indictable at common law, and our statutes defining and punishing the offence do not apply to national banks. Here the indictment charges an offence which was a crime at common law. In Commonwealth v. Beamish (31 P. F. Smith, 389), it was decided that the fraudulent alteration of a book known as a tax duplicate was forgery at common law. It is plain, under this authority, that the plaintiff in error could have been indicted for forgery. The indictment here is laid under the statute and does not charge the offence of forgery in the technical manner required by the strict rules of the common law, but, as in Commonwealth v. Beamish, is good under our Criminal Procedure Act. That the Act of Assembly does not call it forgery makes no difference. It is the same offence.

The first assignment alleges error in another case in which the plaintiff in error was convicted and sentenced. We cannot upon this writ of error reverse a judgment in another case, though against the same party. Nor is it material, as the record shows the plaintiff has served out the term of imprisonment imposed by the Court.

Judgment affirmed.
Opinion by PAXSON, J.

Jan. '80, 331.   March 18, 1880.

Dando's Appeal.

Husband and wife—Married Woman's Act—Executed contracts of married woman—Power of married woman to pledge collateral as security for loan.

A married woman, owning stock as her separate property, joined with her husband in executing a promissory note, and depositing a certificate of stock with the lender as collateral security for the payment of the loan. The money was delivered at the time the loan was made, and was not used by her for necessaries, nor for the improvement of her real estate. The pledge authorized the lender, on non-payment of the note, to sell the stock without further reference or notice to the pledgors. The lender advanced in the presence of both husband and wife, without knowledge of the intended disposition of the money, and in consideration of the transfer and delivery to him of the stock as collateral security. On a bill in equity filed to restrain the sale of the collateral:

Held (sustaining the judgment of the Court below), that the contract was executed, and the lender could retain the stock to answer the purposes for which in good faith it was pledged.

GORDON, TRUNKEY, and STERRETT, JJ., dissent.

Powers of married woman before and after the Act of 1848 reviewed per MERCUR, J.

Appeal from the Common Pleas of Schuylkill County.

Bill in equity, filed by Margaret Dando by her next friend, H. A. Kear, against George Batten.

The bill set forth that Margaret Dando is a married woman, and has been for the last twenty years living with her husband in charge of his family, and as such was well known to the defendant. That she was possessed in her own right, not acquired from or in any way by or under her husband, of twenty shares of the capital stock of the First National Bank of Minersville, and the certificate was issued to her, and was held by her. That on or about the 4th of May, 1874, she, with her husband, made a joint and several promissory note in form what is generally called a collateral security note, and was (as near as she is able to say, having applied to the defendant for a copy of the same, which was refused) as follows:—

$1035.00.

MINERSVILLE, May 4, 1874.

Six months after date, we or either of us promise to pay to the order of George Batten one thousand and thirty-five dollars, for value received, without defalcation. Along with the foregoing obligation we have delivered to said George Batten certificate No. 65, for twenty shares of the capital stock of the First National Bank of Minersville, as collateral security for the payment of the same on the day it becomes due, which collaterals we hereby authorize and empower the holder of this promissory note (provided the same be not paid at maturity) to sell and transfer at public or private sale, without further reference or notice to us, and to apply the proceeds in payment thereof, together with interest and charges incurred thereon; thereafter, should any deficiency remain unpaid, we further promise and agree to pay the same to the holder hereof on demand.

STEPHEN DANDO,
No. *Due.* MARGARET DANDO.

That with said note said certificate of stock was deposited with George Batten (the defendant). That no part of the proceeds of said note was paid to her, and was not used by her for necessaries for her family, nor used for the improvement of her real estate; and, believing said transaction was illegal and void, she notified the said bank not to transfer said shares of stock to said Batten, nor to allow the same to be done upon the books of the bank; and said Batten was also duly notified that she claimed said shares of stock, and demanded him to return the certificate to her, but he neglected and refused to return the same to her. That said Batten disregarded her rights, refused to return her the certificate, and had advertised the same to be sold at public sale on the 5th day of April, 1879.

The bill prayed that the defendant be enjoined from selling said stock, and that he be directed to deliver said stock to the complainant.

The answer admitted that the complainant is a married woman; that she held in her own name twenty shares of the capital stock of said bank; that the certificate was issued to her therefor; but averred that of the mode of her acquiring the same, defendant had no knowledge. A copy of the original paper was set forth similar to that averred in the bill, excepting that the words "Along with the foregoing obligation *we have delivered twenty shares* of the stock of" were substituted for the words "Along with the foregoing obligation we have delivered to said George Batten certificate No. 65, for twenty shares of the capital stock of." The answer further alleged that at the time said note was executed, and the certificate for twenty shares of stock and the note were delivered to him, he advanced and paid upon said securities the sum of $1000, the sum of $35 being for interest thereon until maturity of the note. That both the said Margaret and her husband were present at the time the money was paid by the defendant—as to whether the said sum of money was received by and for the sole use of the said Margaret, or for the separate and sole use of the said Stephen, or for their joint use, the defendant was not informed; but that said sum was paid to them at the time for and in consideration of the said shares of stock being so transferred and delivered *as the security for the re-payment of said sum of money.* That the note was not paid at maturity, nor since (except $180 interest), but that the full amount of the note, with interest since maturity, is due and unpaid, and owned by the defendant. That he has no knowledge whether the money was used for complainant's benefit or not, and admits the notice to the bank not to transfer, etc., and to himself, the claim of ownership, the demand of the return of the certificate of stock, and that he had advertised and was about to sell the same at public sale.

An amendment to the bill set out that the First National Bank of Minersville was organized under the Acts of Congress, and was not a corporation created under the laws of Pennsylvania; and contained a copy of the certificate of stock, showing that it was only transferable on the books of the bank by her or her attorney on its return.

The cause was heard on bill and answer, and the Court refused the injunction and dismissed the bill, delivering the following opinion:

"In so far as the writing, thus signed, promises to pay to the defendant the sum of $1035, it is as against her worthless. But this instrument contains much more than a promise to pay money. It is her written authority to the defendant or the holder thereof to sell or transfer at public or private sale her twenty shares of stock, and it is accompanied with the actual delivery of the certificate of stock itself. The property in question is personalty, and the method of its transfer is not prescribed by the Act of 1848. In Hinney *v.* Phillips (14 Wr. 382), Justice AGNEW said, ' Before the passage of the Act of 1848, securing the separate estate of married women, it was well settled that a wife might dispose of such estate (personalty) by gift or loan. . . . Since the passage of that Act, her power over her own estate is not less, in this respect, than it was before.' The provision that her estate shall not be sold, conveyed, mortgaged, or encumbered by her husband without her written consent, given in the mode provided by the Act, is not a restriction upon her own power of disposing of her money or *other property* capable of transfer by delivery, but was intended to protect her from *his* unauthorized acts. Ruling of like character is found in Haffey *et ux. v.* Carey *et al.* (23 Sm. 431), and Bond *v.* Bunting (28 Sm. 210), in the latter of which, her assignment of a portion of a life insurance policy upon the life of her husband, for the benefit of his children by a former marriage, without transfer of the possession of the policy to the transferees, without consideration and without acknowledgment, was held good as against her after the death of her husband, he having joined in the transfer or assignment thereof. There is no allegation of fraud or coercion in obtaining her signature to the writing in question. It is true she did not acknowledge this instrument 'separate and apart from her husband,' though he joined her in its execution. But that a married woman may assign or transfer property like that in question, without an acknowledgment, was decided in Bond *v.* Bunting (*supra*), and other cases there cited. In addition to these authorities, we find recent legislation upon this subject. By the Acts of April 1, 1874 (P. L. 49), and May 14, 1874 (P. L. 158), additional powers seem to have been conferred upon her. And for the purpose of selling and transferring much of her personal property she is enabled to act as though she were unmarried. The certificate of stock was delivered to the defendant, at the time of the delivery of the writing and the receipt of the money. The property in question was capable of no other delivery. The writing contains the power to transfer, the money remains unpaid, and the transaction assumes the character of an executed contract, no act of hers being required for its completion. Under the ruling in Fryer *v.* Rishell *et ux.* (3 Norris, 521), we think her right to equitable relief is, to say the least, doubtful, and to doubt the legal right of an applicant to an injunction is to refuse it."

Upon final hearing, the Court referred to this opinion, then filed of record, in dismissing the bill. The complainant took this writ, assigning for error the refusal of the injunction, and the dismissal of the bill.

Seth W. Geer, for the appellant.

A married woman is incompetent to execute a writing obligatory, or other personal obligation that will bind her.

    Husbands on Married Women, § 54.
    Mahon *v.* Gormley, 12 H. 80.
    Imhoff *v.* Brown, 6 C. 504.

The certificate was in the name of the wife; the defendant knew it was her property. The note was made by her and her husband while together, they were together when the money was paid, and in law it was his note and not hers; he received the money, not she. If the debt had been contracted for necessaries for the use of herself and family, it would have been his debt, and her estate could not have been charged with its payment. And if she could not give a note nor a bond for a debt contracted by her for necessaries, can she give a note for money taken, or borrowed, by her husband and her together for his own use?

There was no perfected contract; for there was no power of attorney to transfer.

In Bond *v.* Bunting (28 Sm. 210) there was an absolute assignment of part of an insurance policy.

The Act of April 1, 1874 (P. L. 1874, 49), does not apply, for it relates only to loans of stock in any corporation created under the laws of the Commonwealth.

The note was void, for, under the facts, it is presumed to have been done under the husband's duress; it follows that the pledge was void.

David A. Jones (with whom was *Lin Bartholomew*), for the appellee.

The provision in the Married Woman's Act, that a married woman's estate should not be conveyed, mortgaged, or encumbered without her written consent given in the mode provided in that Act, was not intended as a restriction placed upon her to prevent her from exercising absolute authority over her own personal estate in possession, but a protection to her estate as against unauthorized acts of her husband. The power and control of a married woman over her money or other property, capable of transfer by delivery, is no less now than prior to the passage of the Act of 1848.

There is no allegation of fraud or coercion on the part of the husband over the wife. The paper contains the words: "Without further reference or notice to us." The contract was, therefore, executed; and, as in the case of delivery of merchandise to a married woman, the simultaneous payment of the price thereof out of her own funds, must stand.

May 3, 1880. THE COURT. This bill prayed the appellee should be restrained from selling certain bank stock, and be ordered to deliver the certificate thereof to the appellant. The case was heard on bill and answer. The grounds on which relief was asked are that she was a married woman, that the stock was her separate property, and that she and her husband deposited the certificate of stock with the appellee as collateral security for the payment of money; but the money for which the same was pledged was not used by her for necessaries, nor for the improvement of her real estate. The bill contains no averment of fraud, deception, or undue influence in procuring the certificate. It further appears, both by bill and answer, that it was delivered at the time the loan of money was made; that a note to secure the payment thereof signed by her and her husband was then executed and delivered by them to the appellee. After language usually contained in a promissory note, it proceeds to declare "along with the foregoing obligation, we have delivered twenty shares of the stock of the First National Bank of Minersville as collateral security for the payment of the same on the day it becomes due, which collateral we hereby authorize and empower the holder of this promissory note, provided the same be not paid at maturity, to sell or transfer at public or private sale, without further reference or notice to us, and to apply the proceeds in payment thereof, together with interest and charges incurred thereon." In his answer, the appellee avers that both she and her husband were present when he advanced the money, but "as to whether the said sum of money was received by and for the sole use of the said Margaret, or for the sole and separate use of the said Stephen Dando, or for their joint use, this defendant is not informed, and has no knowledge, but that the said sum was paid to them at the time, for and in consideration of the said shares of stock, being so, as aforesaid, transferred and delivered, as the security for the repayment of the said sum of money." And that said note had become due and was unpaid, and held and owned by him.

Thus it appears the property in contention was personal estate. It was transferred by husband and wife jointly. It was delivered at the time the consideration therefor was received. It was accompanied by a written authority to sell that contained no right of revocation. Nothing remained to be done by either husband or wife to pass the title. Prior to the Act of 1848, a married woman might sell or give, when accompanied by a transfer of possession, her separate personal estate to her husband or to a stranger. (Towers v. Hagner, 3 Whar. 57; Naglee v. Ingersoll, 7 Barr, 185; Hinney v. Phillips, 14 Wright, 382.) A married woman may transfer her separate property to pay a present or future indebtedness of her husband. Her power over her property was not lessened by that Act. (Hinney v. Phillips, *supra*.) She may transfer it in the same manner that she could have done before. (Haffey v. Carey, 23 P. F. Smith, 431.) It was, therefore, held in Bond v. Bunting (28 Id. 210) that she may assign her choses in action, her husband joining in the act of disposition without acknowledgment of any kind. When she cannot restore the consideration, equity will not permit her to repudiate the assignment on the ground that she had not acknowledged it. (Fryer v. Rishell *et ux.*, 3 Norris, 521.)

Under the facts shown, it would be a fraud on the appellee, which equity will not tolerate, to now permit her to take from him the substantial security on which he parted with his money. He, therefore, may retain it to answer the purpose for which in good faith it was received. (Selden v. Merchants' National Bank of Meadville, 19 P. F. Smith, 424.) The learned Judge committed no error dismissing the bill.

Decree affirmed, and appeal dismissed at the costs of the appellant.

Opinion by MERCUR, J. GORDON, TRUNKEY, and STERRETT, JJ., dissent.

Jan. '80, 205. March 11, 1880.

Monroe v. Monroe.

Evidence—Parol to vary writing—Note with confession of judgment obtained by fraud—May be opened after judgment upon two amicable sci. fas. to revive assignments of error—Rule XXIII.—Practice.

The defendant, an ignorant man, unable to read, and just able to write his name, gave a note to the plaintiff with confession of judgment and waiver of exemption in 1863. In 1868 and again in 1873 he signed an amicable scire facias to revive with confession of judgment of revival. In 1878 a scire facias for a third revival issued and was served on the defendant; he thereupon obtained a rule to show cause why the judgment should not be opened, and the defendant be let into a defence; which was made absolute by the Court. On the trial he testified that the confession of judgment and waiver of execution in the original note were not read to him before he signed the note; that he signed it supposing it to be a promissory note, and with the understanding that the plaintiff should examine his books and see what the defendant really owed him; that the writs of scire facias to revive were signed by him without any knowledge of their purport, and upon the express understanding that the books were to be examined:

Held (affirming the judgment of the Court below), that while the judgments of revival so obtained were circumstances entitled to consideration with the jury in determining what weight should be attached to the defendant's testimony, they could not, if this testimony were found to be true, add anything to the validity of the original judgment.

The assignments of error to the answers of the Court below to the plaintiff's points were not in accordance with Rule XXIII. of the Supreme Court, which requires that "the points and answers must be quoted *in totidem verbis* in the specification."

PER PAXSON, J. We might well decline to discuss them for this reason.

Error to the Common Pleas of Luzerne Co.

Feigned issue to try the validity of a judgment note, the note to stand as a declaration. Plea, payment with leave, etc.

The facts were as follows: On March 2, 1863, Henderson Monroe signed a note for $501.75, payable to Perry Monroe or bearer, with confession of judgment and waiver of inquisition and exemption. Two days afterwards a judgment was entered thereon in the name of Perry Monroe to the use of J. S. Koons. On February 29, 1868, and again on February 20, 1873, the defendant signed an amicable *scire facias* to revive with confessions of judgment thereon. On February 5, 1878, a *scire facias* to revive was issued and served on the defendant. Defendant thereupon obtained a rule to show cause why the judgment should not be opened, etc. This rule having been made absolute, this issue was framed, and the case proceeded to trial.

The defendant testified that Koons, the father of the equitable plaintiff, was the keeper of a country shop, where he had been in the habit of dealing—making purchases and selling the produce of his farm; that at the time the note was signed Koons sent for him to come and make a settlement; that the note was prepared, waiting for his signature; that Koons's books were not present, and that he urged him to bring them and ascertain the exact balance, and he would sign the note for that amount; that Koons left the room three times, but alleged that he could not find his books; and that he finally urged Monroe to sign the note for the amount on its face $501.75, the note to stand for whatever might ultimately prove to be the balance due. That he (Monroe) objected to the amount as being largely in excess of what the true balance was; but that he, being quite an ignorant man, unable to read, and merely able to "scratch" his name, kept no books of his own, and had, therefore, no written evidence with which to confront Koons. That Koons read over the note to him as if it were a common promissory note, omitting the confession of judgment and the waivers—expressly saying in answer to defendant's question that he would not require him to sign a "cut-throat" note. The he (Monroe) thereupon signed the note. That he never was troubled for payment, and that he heard no more of it till the amicable *scire facias* to revive was brought him, which he signed without the least knowledge of its contents, and only upon the reiterated understanding that Koons's books were to be examined, and the amount ascertained; and that the second amicable *scire facias* to revive was signed under similar circumstances. That he never knew of the existence of the judgment until the third *scire facias* was served on him. Monroe was corroborated by his wife as to the circumstances attending the revivals.

Koons's testimony as to the signing of the note was in direct conflict with Monroe's. He testified that the books were present, and that the balance was obtained from them; that Monroe was informed and fully understood the nature of the note before he signed it. Koons's reputation for truth was alleged to be bad by several witnesses; Monroe's reputation was not attacked.

The defendant requested the Court (HARDING, P. J.) to charge: (1) That, if the jury believe that defendant was unable to read the note in evidence, and the plaintiff read it for him, leaving out the confession of judgment in his reading, thereby causing the defendant to sign a note in ignorance of its true contents, the plaintiff cannot recover in this case, no matter what may be the state of their accounts. *Affirmed*.

(2) If the jury believe that the defendant was induced to sign this note, or confession of judgment, in this case, under a mistaken idea of its contents, believing it to be a common promissory note, when in fact it was a judgment note, with waiver, caused by the fraud of William Koons, the party in interest, in reading to him a part only of the note as the whole, he, the defendant, would not be prevented from making defence to the note by reason of his signing the revivals, unless he was first made acquainted with the true contents of the original note. *Affirmed*.

The plaintiff requested the Court to charge:—
(1) That, if the jury believe that the note was read over to Henderson Monroe before he signed it, there was no fraud in the transaction, and the verdict should be for the plaintiff. *Affirmed*.

(2) That a contract originally fraudulent may be ratified without any additional consideration; that, therefore, if Henderson Monroe signed the renewals or revivals of this judgment without fraud practised upon him at the time of signing such revivals, and negligently or carelessly omitted to have the same read to him, he would be estopped from denying the validity of the original judgment. *Affirmed*.

(3) That, if the jury believe that, at the time of signing the original note, or at the time of signing either of the renewals of the same, the defendant was aware of their contents, the verdict must be for the plaintiff. *Affirmed*.

(4) That there is no evidence in the case to show any fraud practised upon Henderson Monroe at the time of the second renewal; that was, therefore, an affirmance and ratification of the original contract. Answer. *Affirmed* if the jury find the facts to be as stated.

In the general charge his Honor said: The points which were read in your presence, and which were presented to me by the respective counsel, were affirmed, modified, or negatived, as you will recollect. . . . [This, you will see, gentlemen, is purely a question of credibility between William Koons on the one side, and Henderson Monroe on the other; and it is the exclusive province of the jury, not of the Court, to pass upon this important feature of the case.] (Fifth assignment of error.) You heard the defendant testify; under the law he is a competent witness; his credibility is for you. To some extent his testimony was corroborated by that of his wife—certainly as to the amount of the indebtedness existing between them. Again, if, after the judgment had been thus given, it lay for five years, as is alleged on the part of the defendant, and then a renewal was taken by Mr. Koons, or by some one for him, to Henderson Monroe, and the latter signed it, as he said he did, upon the distinct understanding that the books were to be examined, and the basis of the actual indebtedness ascertained, then the revival could not have given additional validity to the original debt. You must take these men as they are. You are intelligent, and know the relations and surroundings of people in the country, situated as these two were. [If, at the time the second revival was taken, Mr. Monroe was induced to sign it, as he says, that he might get a statement out of Mr. Koons, the fact that he executed that second revival gives no additional validity to the original judgment.] (Fourth assignment of error.) The credibility of the witnesses is for you. It is alleged that William Koons was impeached; six or seven witnesses swore upon the stand that his reputation for truth and veracity was bad. You remember the other questions that were asked them by the counsel representing Mr. Koons. This is one of the methods known to the law of contradicting a witness. Now, is the credibility of William Koons, as connected with this case, affected by the testimony? That question is entirely for you; it is not for the Court even to hint in relation to it.

Verdict and judgment for the defendant. Plaintiff took this writ, assigning for error: (1) That the Court erred in not directing the jury that their verdict should be for the plaintiff. (2) The Court erred in not answering plaintiff's second point to the jury, either specifically by reading the same, or in the general charge. (3) That the Court erred in not answering plaintiff's third point, either specifically by reading the same to the jury as a part of the charge, or substantially in the general charge.

The fourth and fifth assignments were to the portions of the general charge inclosed in brackets.

Thos. H. Atherton and *Allan H. Dickson,* for plaintiff in error.

[SHARSWOOD, C. J. The second and third assignments of error are not in accordance with the rules of Court.]

The parol evidence was not sufficiently "clear, precise, and indubitable" to overthrow the written note.
Todd *v.* Campbell, 8 C. 250.
Faust *v.* Haas, 23 Sm. 295.
Cauffman *v.* Long, 1 N. 72.

The defendant does not allege that he requested to have the renewals read to him. This amounts to such gross carelessness as will prevent his being protected by the law.
Greenfield's Estate, 2 H. 496.
R. R. *v.* Shea, 1 N. 198.

Even if fraud in obtaining the original had been fully established, the defendant would be estopped by the revivals.
Persall *v.* Chapin, 8 Wr. 9.
Seylan *v.* Carson, 19 Sm. 81.

The reference to the plaintiff's points in the general charge was not sufficient.
Slaymaker *v.* St. John, 5 W. 27.
Tennbrook *v.* Jahke, 27 Sm. 396.

It was the province of the Court, and not of the jury, to pass upon the effect of signing the renewals.
Potts *v.* Wright, 1 N. 498.

Q. A. Gates, for defendant in error.

The Court was not requested to direct a verdict for the plaintiff; the omission to do so cannot, therefore, be assigned for error.
Davis *v.* Bigler, 12 Sm. 242.

The second and third assignments are not in accordance with Rules XXII. and XXIII. of this Court; but that they are insubstantial is shown by the record, which shows that the plaintiff's points were not only answered but affirmed. There is no question in this case but one of fact, which the jury has found in our favor.

May 3, 1880. THE COURT. There are five assignments of error in this case. We will consider them in their order.

(1) The record discloses no request to the Court to give a binding instruction to the jury to find a verdict for the plaintiff. And had such request been made, it would have been the duty of the Court to decline it. The facts were for the jury.

(2 and 3) These errors are not properly assigned. The points referred to are not set forth as required by the rules of Court. We might well decline to discuss them for this reason. The record shows, however, that they were read to the jury and affirmed. That they were not further referred to by the Court in the general charge is not material.

(4) This portion of the charge, standing alone, looks like error; but an examination of the whole charge, as applied to the facts of the case, shows that it was not. The defendant—an ignorant man and unable to read—had signed a judgment note in favor of plaintiff for an alleged indebtedness to William Koons, dated March 2, 1863, for $501.75. The note contained a waiver of inquisition and all exemption laws, as well as the declaration that it was "for debt before the 4th day of July, 1849." There was evidence to go to the jury that the note was obtained by fraud; that at most it was but a cautionary note; that the amount due, if anything, was subsequently

to be settled by an examination of William Koons's books, the defendant having kept no account, except in his head, and that Koons (the real plaintiff), in reading it to the defendant, had suppressed a material part. The judgment entered on this note was revived by amicable *scire facias,* signed by the defendant in 1868, and again in 1873. After the second revival, upon the application of the defendant, the original judgment was opened and he was let into a defence.

The question now under discussion relates to the effect of the revivals upon the original judgment. As to the first revival, the learned Judge instructed the jury in his general charge as follows: "Again, if, after the judgment had been thus given, it lay for five years, as is alleged on the part of the defendant, and then a renewal was taken by Mr. Koons, or by some one for him, to Henderson Monroe, and the latter signed it, as he said he did, upon the distinct understanding that the books were to be examined and the basis of the actual indebtedness ascertained, then the revival could not have given additional validity to the original debt." This instruction was not complained of, and it is referred to now only as it bears upon the charge in relation to the second revival, and which forms the subject of the fourth assignment. The portion of the charge referred to is as follows: "If at the time the second revival was taken, Mr. Monroe was induced to sign it, as he says, that he might get a statement out of Mr. Koons, the fact that he executed the second revival gives no additional validity to the original judgment." If the original judgment was obtained by fraud and misrepresentation, and the subsequent revivals were but a continuation of such fraud and misrepresentations, it is difficult to see how such revivals could add anything to the validity of the original judgment. The mere fact of the revivals might have been a circumstance entitled to some consideration with the jury in deciding as to how much weight should be attached to the defendant's testimony, but no such point is involved in this assignment. If the defendant's story is believed, the revivals could not add to the validity of the original judgment, for the reason that they were obtained by fraud, and fraud vitiates everything it touches.

(5) The portion of the charge embraced in this assignment is not error, when read in its connection with the general charge. The remark of the Court had reference only to the contradictory statements of William Koons on the one side and Henderson Monroe on the other. As between them it was, as the Court stated, purely a question of credibility.

Judgment affirmed.

Opinion by PAXSON, J.

Common Pleas—Equity.

C. P. No. 1.   June 14, 1880.

Lockhard v. McKinley.

Attorney and client—Constructive fraud—Equity—An attorney can make no profit out of his office to the prejudice of his client's interest—Fraud in equity includes all acts, omissions, and concealments, which involve a breach of legal or equitable duty or confidence justly reposed, injurious to another.

NOTE. Baker v. *Humphrey, Supreme Court of U. S., reported.*

Sur answer and demurrer to bill in equity.

The bill set forth, in substance, that the defendant was employed by the plaintiff as his attorney-at-law to collect a judgment against one McCloskey; and certain real estate belonging to McCloskey was shown to the attorney, out of which the money could be made; that at the time defendant was employed, he (defendant) had a mortgage against said property for a loan made to McCloskey, of which fact, however, the plaintiff was not then informed; that subsequently the defendant made additional loans to McCloskey, and to secure the whole took a conveyance of the said property to himself. The bill prayed that defendant might be decreed to hold the said property in trust for plaintiff, subject to the payment of the money advanced before defendant's employment as attorney began.

The answer denied certain allegations in the bill, and expressed a willingness to convey the properties upon payment of the entire amount of money advanced; and demurred to the prayer of the bill on the ground that the defendant cannot be made to lose the advances subsequent to his retainer as counsel, as they were not in fraud of plaintiff, but to secure former investments.

Bedell, for plaintiff.

It is a settled principle that any one occupying a fiduciary or *quasi* fiduciary position cannot acquire thereby any personal advantage touching the subject of the trust or any interest antagonistic to that of the *cestui que trust.*

Kerch v. Sandford, 1 Lead. Cas. Eq. 62, note.
Maul v. Rider, 1 Sm. 384.
Beegle v. Wentz, 5 Id. 374.
Church v. Ruland, 14 Id. 432.
Squires's Appeal, 20 Id. 266.
Steinruck's Appeal, Id. 289.

This rule applies to the relation existing between an attorney and his client, and will be rigidly enforced in favor of the latter.

Bispham's Equity, § 93; 1 Perry on Trusts, § 178.
Galbraith v. Elder, 8 W. 81.
Downey v. Gerrard, 3 Gr. 64.
Smith v. Brotherline, 12 Sm. 461.
Cleavinger v. Reimar, 3 W. & S. 486.

Whenever title to land is procured through the abuse of such a confidential relation, the law raises a constructive trust in favor of the party injured thereby.
  Rankin *v.* Porter, 7 W. 387.
  Duff *v.* Wilson, 22 Sm. 442.
  Dickey's Appeal, 23 Id. 218.

In such cases it is not necessary to show actual fraud. The rule is founded on public policy.
  Webb *v.* Dietrich, 7 W. & S. 401.
  Chorpenning's Appeal, 8 Cas. 315.

Pierce Archer, for defendant.

So much of the bill as prays an avoidance of the loan advanced *after* the relation of counsel and client, is bad.
  Smith *v.* Brotherline, 12 P. F. S. 469.
  Henry *v.* Raiman, 1 Casey, 359.

No case decides that a lawyer is bound to disclose to his clients his private transactions with their debtors, who owed him before he knew the clients.

There is no bad faith charged here; no advantage to the defendant, and no loss to the plaintiff, for if defendant had not made the loan, plaintiff's position was not improved. He had no lien to be affected for near two years after the last loan and security given. "Who shall complain?"
  GIBSON, C. J., in Dobbins *v.* Stevens, 17 S. & R. 15.

The plaintiff can at best make defendant his trustee; that is, take his place on re-paying his loan. This we have always tendered, and now tender.

"There is nothing in his being defendant's attorney in the suit to prevent his being a bidder, if he took no undue step to the prejudice of his client."
  Per SERGEANT, J., Deviney *v.* Norris, 8 W. 315.

C. A. V.

July 3, 1880. THE COURT (after reciting the facts). It is a well settled principle that an attorney cannot make a profit out of his office to the prejudice of the rights and interests of a client. But where investments are made by counsel *bona fide*, before the client has a lien or interest which is thereby prejudiced, he cannot be said to be guilty of actual fraud. In support of this doctrine Smith *v.* Brotherline (12 P. F. S. 469), and Henry *v.* Raiman (1 Casey, 359), are cited. The first of these cases asserts the doctrine with great distinctness, Mr. Justice SHARSWOOD holding, that, the relation between attorney and client being one of confidence, whether he acts on information derived from the client or from any other source, he is affected with a trust. The rule is asserted to be an unbending one, and without exception, that when an attorney buys a title outstanding or adverse to the land, as to which he has been consulted or employed, he buys for the client, if the client should elect to take it. The *cestui que trust* must, of course, if he asks a chancellor to assist him, do equity, by reimbursing the outlay and costs of the trustee, unless it may be in a case of manifest fraud intended and attempted to be perpetrated. The sufficiency of the ground of demurrer turns on the question as to what constitutes a fraud perpetrated by an attorney on his client. Is it of necessity actual and intentional fraud only? Or may it consist of acts which, though wanting in candor, or in such a disclosure as good faith and fair dealing requires in a transaction between counsel and client, although free from wrongful purpose, are yet of necessity such as to prejudice the interests of the client, to the gain or advantage of the counsel. In Story's Equity, section 187, the principle is stated to be: Fraud in the judgment of a Court of Equity properly includes all acts, omissions, and concealments which involve a breach of legal or equitable duty or confidence, justly reposed, which are injurious to another, or by which an undue and unconscientious advantage is taken. In Galbraith *v.* Elder (8 Watts, 87), the Supreme Court decided that an attorney who has been consulted respecting title to lands, cannot become a purchaser thereof and set up such title against his client. He will be deemed a trustee by construction of law.

There are times and circumstances when a non-disclosure of material facts will amount to a fraudulent concealment. This general principle is too well established to require the citation of elementary authority or decided cases to support it. It is a rule founded not only in sound morals, but is recognized, as between principal and agent or client and attorney, as a rule of policy, to which parties will be strictly held. But when the case is one in which there is not merely the intentional concealment of material facts, but some acts purposely done, founded on knowledge which ought to have been disclosed, and by which the client is prejudiced and the attorney derives a benefit, the case stands clearly within the definition of constructive fraud at least; and whether the fraud be actual or constructive, the principle on which the demurrer is based has no application to a case like the one raised by these pleadings. We do not see on what principle the subsequent advance of the defendant can be sustained. It may be admitted, for the sake of the argument, that the defendant was not bound to make known the fact to the plaintiff that he had made a first loan to McCloskey, which was secured by a mortgage on the property, but no one will, we think, question that it would have been better if he had done so, that the client might have had the fact before him before employing the defendant to collect his claim. If it had been communicated, he could have decided whether an attorney holding a prior incumbrance was the most suitable person to be intrusted with the performance of that duty. But the more advanced proposition is to us clear that after the professional relation was once established Mr. McKinley could secretly acquire no interest in the land which would hinder or delay or prevent the plaintiff collecting his full demand against McCloskey. This conclusion requires that the demurrer be overruled, and it is so ordered.

Opinion by ALLISON, J.

[SUPREME COURT OF UNITED STATES.—Oct. T. 1879.
(See 11 Central Law Journ. 126, Aug. 13, 1880.)

Baker v. Humphrey.

Attorney and client—Attorney acting for adverse interest—Fraud—Equity.

An attorney cannot in any case, without the client's consent, buy and hold otherwise than in trust, any adverse title or interest touching the thing to which his employment relates.

B., who had agreed to sell lands to which he claimed title, to H. & S. for $000, employed W., an attorney, who had long been employed by him to do legal business, to draw the contract of sale, which W. did, and witnessed its execution. H. & S. then employed W. to examine the title. In doing this W. found that the title was apparently in C., though C. had never asserted it. W., for a consideration of $25, represented that he wished it to protect the title of clients, procured a conveyance of the lands to his brother from C. The brother was not cognizant of this transaction. Thereafter W. instituted an action of ejectment in his brother's name to recover the lands. In an action by B. to have the deed to the brother of W. declared fraudulent, etc.: *Held*, that the relation of client and counsel subsisted between B. and W., and the conveyance from C. to the brother inured to the benefit of B.

Appeal in equity from the Circuit Court of the United States for the Eastern District of Michigan.

Mr. Justice SWAYNE delivered the opinion of the Court, of which the following is an extract:—

. . . . . .

But there is another and a higher ground upon which our judgment may be rested. The relation of client and counsel subsisted between the attorney and Baker. . . . Whether the relation subsisted previously, or was created only for the purpose of the particular transaction in question, it carried with it the same consequences. (Williamson v. Moriarty, 19 W. R. Irish Law and Eq. 818.)

It is the duty of an attorney to advise the client promptly whenever he has any information to give which it is important the client should receive. (Hoopes v. Burnett, 26 Miss. 428; Jett v. Hempstead, 25 Ark. 462; Fuy v. Cooper, 2 Q. B. N. S. 937.) In Taylor v. Blacklow, (3 Bing. N. C. 235), an attorney, employed to raise money on a mortgage, learned the existence of certain defects in his client's title, and disclosed them to another person. As a consequence, his client was subjected to litigation, and otherwise injured. It was held that an action would lie against the attorney, and that the client was entitled to recover. In Com. Dig., tit. "Action on the case for deceit, A. 5," it is said that such an action lies " if a man, being entrusted in his profession, deceive him who entrusted him, or if a man retained of counsel became after-wards of counsel with the other party in the same cause, or discover evidence or secrets of the cause. So, if an attorney act deceptive to the prejudice of his client, as if by collusion with the demandant, he make default in a real action whereby the land is lost." It has been held that if counsel be retained to defend a particular title to real estate, he can never thereafter, unless his client consent, buy the opposing title without holding it in trust for those then having the title he was employed to sustain. (Henry v. Raiman, 25 Pa. St. 354.) Without expressing any opinion as to the soundness of this case with respect to the extent to which the principle of trusteeship is asserted, it may be laid down as a rule that an attorney can in no case, without the client's consent, buy and hold otherwise than in trust, any adverse title or interest touching the thing to which his employment relates. He cannot in such a way put himself in an adversary position without this result. The cases to this effect are very numerous, and they are all in harmony. We refer to a few of them. (Smith v. Brotherline, 62 Pa. St. 461; Davis v. Smith, 43 Vt. 269; Wheeler v. Willard, 44 Id. 641; Giddings & Coleman v. Eastman, 5 Paige, 561; Moore v. Bracken, 27 Ill. 23; Harper v. Perry, 28 Iowa, 57; Hockenbury v. Carlisle, 5 Watts & S. 349; Hobday v. Peters, 6 Jur. N. S., pt. 1, 794; Jett v. Hempstead, 25 Ark. 462; Case v. Carrol, 35 N. Y. 385; Lewis v. Hillman, 3 House of Lords, 607.) . . . .

The case in hand is peculiarly a fit one for the application of the principle we have been considering. It is always dangerous for counsel to undertake to act, in regard to the same thing, for parties whose interests are diverse. Such a case requires care and circumspection on his part. Here there could be no objection, there being no apparent conflict of interests; but upon discovering that the title was imperfect, it was the duty of the attorney promptly to report the result to Baker, as well as to Hurd & Smith, and to advise the former, if it were desired, as to the best mode of curing the defect. Instead of doing this, he carefully concealed the facts from Baker, gave Hurd & Smith the choice of buying, and, upon their declining, bought the property for himself, and has since been engaged in a bitter litigation to wrest it from Baker. For his lapse at the outset there might be some excuse, but for his conduct subsequently there can be none. Both are condemned alike by sound ethics and the law. They are the same upon the subject. Actual fraud in such cases is not necessary to give the client a right to redress. A breach of duty is "constructive fraud," and is sufficient. (Story's Eq. secs. 258, 311.)

The legal profession is found wherever Christian civilization exists. Without it society could not well go on. But, alike all other great instrumentalities, it may be potent for evil as well as for good. Hence the importance of keeping it on the high plane it ought to occupy. Its character depends upon the conduct of its members. They are officers of the law, as well as the agents of those by whom they are employed. Their fidelity is guaranteed by the highest considerations of honor and good faith, and to these is superadded the sanction of an oath. The slightest divergence from rectitude involves the breach of all these obligations. None are more honored or more deserving than those of the brotherhood who, uniting ability with integrity, prove faithful to their trusts and worthy of the confidence reposed in them. Courts of justice can best serve both the public and the profession by applying firmly, upon all proper occasions, the salutary rules which have been established for their government in doing the business of their clients.

We shall discharge that duty in this instance by reversing the decree of the Circuit Court, and remanding the case, with directions to enter a decree whereby it shall be required that the complainant, Baker, deposit in the clerk's office for the use of the defendant, George P. Humphrey, the sum of $25, and that Humphrey thereupon convey to Baker the premises described in the bill, and that the deed contain a covenant against the grantor's own acts, and against the demands of all other persons claiming under him.

And it is so ordered.]

C. P. No. 2. May 22, 1880.
Gilbert & Sullivan v. Bacher & Boner.

Rights of authors in uncopyrighted works—Performance of an opera on the stage is no publication—It gives no right to print the music from memory or otherwise.

Sur motion for preliminary injunction.

The plaintiffs in their bill set forth that they were the authors and sole owners of a new comic opera entitled "The Pirates of Penzance, or the Slave of Duty," and of the words and music thereof; that the said opera had been produced upon the stage in the United States by their licensee, Richard D'Oyly Carte, in the year 1879, and had acquired a great and valuable reputation; that the same had never been copyrighted, nor had it ever been published, except by performance on the stage; the whole work was kept in manuscript, and the only copies made had been such as were necessary for proper rehearsal and performance on the stage; that the defendants, Theodore A. Bacher and W. H. Boner, trading as W. H. Boner & Co., had, without license and in violation of the rights of the plaintiffs, published and exposed for sale in Philadelphia and elsewhere large numbers of certain publications containing reproductions of many parts of the music of the said opera. The bill prayed discovery, an account, and an injunction to restrain the defendants from advertising or publishing, exposing for sale, or selling any of the said publications, or any publications containing the words or music of the said opera.

The affidavit of the author of "Memories of the Pirates of Penzance" (one of the publications complained of) set up that the work was an original one; that it had been suggested to him by hearing the performance of the opera in places of amusement; that everything except the upper line of the score (which contained the melody which he remembered) was entirely his own, and that he had taken no notes of the music at the time of hearing the opera.

Thomas Hart, Jr., for the motion.

A public performance is not such a publication as will authorize any one to print a play or opera obtained at such performance by any surreptitious means.

Nor is any such right given where the airs or tunes have been carried away in memory and afterwards printed and sold for profit.

French v. Connely, N. Y. Weekly Digest, 197.
Keene v. Kimball, 16 Gray, 545.
Drone's Law of Property in Intellectual Productions, p. 566-72.
2 Morgan's Law of Literature, p. 330 *et seq.*

J. R. Sypher, contra.

The bill ought to set out that the airs have been obtained surreptitiously.

Keene v. Wheatley, 9 Am. L. Reg. 33.

The airs of the opera in question have been given to the ears of large audiences, so that they could go home and play them over on the piano or the flute; thus the airs have become public property. Now the author of this publication, "Memories of the Pirates of Penzance," has gone home, and recalling only the melody, the upper notes of the score, has arranged a piano accompaniment for it which is entirely original. It has been held that to produce a piece of music for the piano from an opera score is an original work. The only question, therefore, is, had the author of this work, having heard the airs, the right to use them in this way? This opera not being copyrighted, the property of the author in it is simply the author's right at common law in his work, that is, his right to keep his manuscript in his strong box; for this was his only right until the statute of copyright enlarged his property, limiting at the same time its duration. The defendant has not infringed this common-law right of the author.

Drone on Copyright, 576.

[HARE, P. J. It is our view that the publication by performance on the stage gives no right to print the play.]

THE COURT. Injunction granted.

Common Pleas—Law.

C. P. No. 1. April 17, 1880.
Bouillou's Estate.

Debtor and creditor—Mortgage—Payment of interest—The mere absence of the creditor, or the death of a mortgagee without the appointment of an administrator, does not stop the running of interest nor exempt the mortgagor from its payment.—Remedy by payment into Court, under Act of April 3, 1851.

This was an application, by petition, for leave for the administrator of a mortgagee to withdraw the principal and interest of a mortgage, which had been paid into Court by the mortgagor on the ground that there was no one entitled to receive it and give a legal acquittance. The payment was made and the mortgage satisfied under the Act of April 3, 1851 (Purd. Dig. 481, pl. 118).

The mortgagor resisted the payment of interest since the death of the mortgagee.

It appeared that Charles Hart had executed a mortgage dated Aug. 6, 1872, for $3000 to Vir ginia Aimée Bouillou, and that on its becoming due he was desirous of paying the same, but in the mean time Virginia A. Bouillou had died domiciled in France, and owing to a dispute as to who was entitled to administer on her estate, he had been notified to make no payment. The interest had been paid up to November, 1877. In August, 1878, Hart, on payment of the principal and $135 interest into Court, subject to the opinion of the Court as to his liability for said interest, obtained a decree for satisfaction. In April, 1880, John W. Burch having obtained letters of administration on Bouillou's estate from the Register of Wills of Philadelphia, made the present application. Hart resisted the payment of interest from November, 1877, to August, 1878.

V. Guillou, for the petitioner.
Chas. Hart, contra.

The interest should not be paid to the mortgagee's administrator, because when it became due, and the mortgagor was ready to pay it, the mortgagee was not within the realm.

Allshouse *v.* Ramsey, 6 Wh. 331.

The notice from the disputing claimants for letters of administration prevented payment of the principal, and this always stops the running of interest.

Hoare *v.* Allen, 2 Dal. 102.
Fitzgerald *v.* Caldwell, Id. 215.
Updegraff *v.* Spring, 11 S. & R. 190.
Willings *v.* Consequa, 1 P. C. C. 321.
Sickman *v.* Lapsley, 13 S. & R. 224.
Mackey *v.* Hodgson, 9 Barr, 470.

C. A. V.

May 8, 1880. THE COURT. The petitioner paid into Court the sum of three thousand dollars principal, and one hundred and thirty-five dollars interest, of a mortgage made by him to Virginia Aimée Bouillou in her lifetime, and had the mortgage satisfied of record under the Act of 3 April, 1851.

His reason for paying the money into Court was that Virginia Aimée Bouillou having died in France, where she was there domiciled, a contest had arisen as to the right of administration to her estate, and that no legal representative had been appointed to whom he could safely pay the money; and being desirous of having the said mortgage satisfied of record, he obtained leave to pay the money into Court subject to the decision of the Court as to his liability to pay the interest that was due on said mortgage and paid by him into Court.

The petitioner rests his objection to pay interest on the fact that he was ready and desirous of paying off the mortgage, and that there was no person to whom he could legally pay it by reason of the contest over the said estate.

In Shaeffer's Estate (9 S. & R. 263), it was held that a debtor is not exempted from the payment of interest, by the continued absence of the creditor from the State, and his not being heard of for many years. DUNCAN, J., in ruling that case, said, "If the principle be true that absence is an answer to a demand of interest, because there is no one to whom the principal can be tendered, then this consequence would follow, as death would more effectually preclude a tender, interest could never be recoverable mesne between the death of the creditor, and taking out letters of administration."

Some suggestion having been made in that case that there was a distinction between a person absent from the State and one beyond the sea, the learned Judge said "The absent creditor, I mean absent beyond sea, is a privileged creditor. The Act of Limitations does not run against him. If he is within the United States after the debt becomes payable, it then first runs, and continues to run, notwithstanding subsequent absence beyond sea. It would seem equally reasonable, that his interest would be as much protected by his absence, as the principal." Defendants being indebted to equitable plaintiffs as a firm, each member of the latter firm gave notice to the defendants not to pay any of the indebtedness to the other: *Held*, that such notice did not relieve the defendants from liability for interest on their indebtedness. (King *v.* Kelley, 1 P. F. Smith, 36; see also Hummel *v.* Brown, 12 Har. 310, and cases there cited.)

If then the running of interest be not stopped, except in occasional instances, by absence from the State; or beyond sea; or by death of the creditor until administration be granted; or by notice from adverse claimants not to pay; *à fortiori* it would not be stopped in a case like this where under the law the debtor could protect himself by paying the money into Court. The remedy was in his own hands, and as soon as the money was paid into Court the interest ceased.

Rule absolute.

Opinion by PEIRCE, J.

C. P. No. 2. June 17, 1880.
Kingsessing Building Association v. Roan.
Building association—Married woman—Administration—Usury—Jurisdiction.

Motion to reduce assessment of damages.

This was an action of scire facias upon a building association mortgage given by Susan L. Roan, a married woman. Mrs. Roan died, leaving no lineal descendants. Administration was granted to her husband, against whom the writ in the present case was issued, and who made no defence. The next of kin, entitled to the realty of the decedent in remainder, filed an affidavit of defence. After the cause was at issue as to the next of kin, the plaintiff entered judgment against John T. Roan as administrator and in his own right.

When the cause came on to be tried before MITCHELL, J., the evidence showed that certain shares of stock in the association plaintiff stood in the name of Mrs. Roan, and that the said plaintiff made a loan to Mrs. Roan, taking as security therefor the said stock and the mortgage in suit for $2000, upon a certain piece of real estate which Mrs. Roan had purchased with money left her by an aunt. The money received from the loan was applied to the real estate. At the time Mrs. Roan took the stock she was married. The plaintiff's books showed that the amount actually paid to Mrs. Roan, including expenses, was $1610, and that up to the day of trial there had been paid into the association on account of the stock and mortgage $2216.22, of which $372.50 had been paid upon the stock after the death of Mrs. Roan.

Counsel for the next of kin claimed that the payments on the stock prior to Mrs. Roan's death should be applied upon the mortgage, and that as the mortgage was that of a married woman the association could recover only the amount of money actually advanced, with legal interest.

His Honor directed the jury to find for the plaintiff for the amount claimed, giving leave to the next of kin to move the Court in banc to enter judgment for a sum less than the face of the verdict.

Henry Budd, Jr., for the motion.

Our position is this: A married woman cannot hold building association stock, and hence her contract of loan with the association must be looked on as any other contract of loan to a married woman, good if made for the improvement of her separate estate, but not precluding her from any defence as to usury. The defence of usury can be taken by any one seized of the mortgaged estate, or vested with rights of the mortgagor.

1 Jones on Mortgages, § 644.

Further, as she has made payments on the so-called stock, she has paid money to the association, and it is in the position of having received from her so much money, which it still holds; it must therefore give credit for the money, for it is not pretended that it was intended as a gift.

Wolbach v. Lehigh Building Association, 4 WEEKLY NOTES, 157.

[HARE, P. J. Have the remainder-men any status here, as the administrator makes no defence?]

The fact that the administrator does not ask for the application of the stock is not of moment. Since the personalty is bound in the course of administration to exonerate the realty, this Court will administer equity under common law forms, and so, having all parties before it, it will not turn the remainder-men out of Court, and force them to go to the Orphans' Court to ask for a surcharge.

A. Lewis Smith, contra.

Payment on stock is not *per se* payment on the mortgage secured thereby.

N. Amer. Building Assn. *v.* Sutton, 11 Casey, 463.
Kelly *v.* Perseverance Building Assn., 3 Wright, 148.
Spring Garden Fire Assn. *v.* Tradesman's Loan Assn., 10 Wr. 493.

To allow the sum paid on the stock to be credited on the mortgage might deprive creditors of the decedent of the amount to be derived from the sale of the stock of the decedent. If the administrator has not set up the defence of usury, nor asked for the credit claimed, it cannot be done by the next of kin, who, if aggrieved by his action, must seek their remedy elsewhere.

C. A. V.

June 19, 1880. THE COURT. Motion dismissed, with leave to plaintiff to enter judgment for the full amount of the verdict.

C. P. No. 3.   July 10, 1880.

Schwenk v. Yost.

Promissory note—Suit by payee against an indorser—Irregular indorsement—Indorser who signs the note with the makers.

Rule for judgment for want of sufficient affidavit of defence.

Assumpsit, by payee against indorser, on promissory note, of which the following is a copy:—

$210.   COLLEGEVILLE, Sept. 11, 1874.

Sixty days after date we, or either of us, promise to pay to the order of Henry G. Schwenk two hundred and ten dollars, payable at

Without defalcation.   Value received.
                  WM. C. JORDON,
                  GEORGE PRINGLE,
                  J. WASH. YOST, *Indorser*.

The word indorser was printed after Yost's signature. The affidavit and supplemental affidavit of defence set forth that the note upon which the action was brought was not signed by the defendant, Yost, as maker, but that he had agreed to indorse the note, and his signature was affixed thereto as an indorser.

P. K. Erdman (with him *A. J. Erdman*), for the rule.

F. I. Gowen, contra.

THE COURT. From the face of the instrument it appears that Yost signed as indorser, though in an irregular way. While the case is not free from difficulty, we will at present discharge this rule.

THE COURT. Rule discharged.

WEEKLY NOTES OF CASES.

VOL. IX.] *THURSDAY, SEPT. 2, 1880.* [No. 2.

Supreme Court.

March 3, 1880.

Steckel et al. v. The First National Bank of Allentown.

Banks—Responsibility of to depositors—Fraudulent representations—Agency of bank officers—Ultra vires, when no defense in suit against corporation.

A bank is responsible for the safekeeping of the money of a depositor, and it cannot set up the fraud of its own officers as an answer to a demand for repayment.

Under what circumstances lack of ordinary care against deception is no answer to fraud, commented upon.

Error to the Common Pleas of Bucks County.

Assumpsit, by Alfred P. Steckel et al., partners, trading as the Columbia Slate Company, against the First National Bank of Allentown, to recover $3251.63, a balance of money deposited with said bank.

The material facts, as they appeared upon the trial, before WATSON, P. J., were stated in the opinion of the Supreme Court, as follows:—

"The plaintiffs kept an account with the corporation defendant, and were in the habit of making deposits and drawing checks in the usual manner. William H. Blumer was the president of the bank; his son, Jacob Blumer, was the cashier. Three of the directors, including the said William H. Blumer, composed the banking house of Wm. H. Blumer & Co., which carried on business but a few hundred feet distant from the First National Bank of Allentown. The plaintiffs having money on deposit with the bank, and being desirous of obtaining interest-bearing certificates therefor, called at the bank for that purpose. Dr. A. P. Steckel, one of the plaintiffs, testifies as to what occurred, substantially as follows: 'I went to the bank every week or two to make my deposits; some time in August, when I made deposit, I asked the teller, George Straub, does the First National Bank take any money on certificates? He said, yes, sir; do you want to leave us some? I said, no, not to-day. I asked him whether the First National Bank issues certificates of deposit, and as a matter of course pay interest, and he said yes; then I came there again in September, 1876, and made my ordinary deposit in the bank, and after we were through I said to the teller that I would take the First National Bank certificates for $700. I filled out a check, and he handed me a certificate; I looked at the certificate for $700; it was to be made on demand, and asked him, is this the First National Bank certificate? the answer was, yes, sir, it is; I then said, this reads Blumer & Co; I want this distinctly understood, I want nothing but the First National Bank certificates; he answered me that this was one and the same thing; that it should pass to the credit of the company, the same as it was before. With this assurance I took that certificate. This was in the presence of the cashier of the bank, Jacob A. Blumer.' Two other certificates, aggregating, with the one above mentioned, the sum of $3000, were obtained under circumstances not essentially different. There was evidence that the president of the bank recognized them as binding upon the bank, and offered to reinstate the plaintiffs as they were before, when the bank examiner was through his examination. That examination, however, resulted in the closing of the bank."

The plaintiffs presented the following points:

(2) That if the jury believe that the certificates of Wm. H. Blumer & Co. were not accepted by the plaintiffs from the defendant as a payment and satisfaction *pro tanto* of the indebtedness of the bank, the plaintiffs are entitled to recover upon the original indebtedness. *Answer.* I can not so instruct you.

(3) That whether the certificates of deposit were received by the plaintiffs in payment of the bank's indebtedness to them, is a question of fact for the jury. *Answer.* I can not so instruct you.

(4) That the burden of proving that the certificates of deposit were accepted by the plaintiffs in payment of the bank's indebtedness to them, is upon the defendants. *Answer.* I can not so instruct you.

(5) That if the jury believe that the plaintiffs were deceived by the fraudulent representations of the officers of the bank, and led to believe that the certificates of Wm. H. Blumer & Co. were certificates of deposit in the First National Bank of Allentown, the reception of them by the plaintiffs was not a payment, and the plaintiffs would be entitled to recover. *Answer.* There is no evidence of fraud in the giving of the certificates by any officer or servant of the bank, except such as relates to the false representations made by the teller. These false representations must not affect the bank with the consequence of fraud, if the money for which the plaintiffs' checks were drawn was appropriated according to their directions.

The Court charged the jury, *inter alia*, as follows: "This case has been tried and regarded very much as involving the ordinary relation of debtor and creditor. I have been so disposed to look upon it myself, and it is only upon reflection during the argument of the case that I have seen cause to change my opinion in this respect. I do not think the relation existing between the bank and its depositors is the same as that obtaining between a debtor and creditor in ordinary cases. . . . The bank is liable for its safe keeping and for its return upon demand, and it is not until demand is made upon it for payment, and a refusal to pay, that any suit can be maintained against it for the deposit in this case. It is not until that time I think that the usual relations between debtor and creditor arises between them, and any disposition which the bank may make of the deposit by the direction of the depositor, is just as efficient a discharge to the bank as an actual payment to him in cash. It makes no difference to the bank to whom that deposit is paid, so that the deposit is paid according to the direction of a depositor, and when he gives to the bank a direction to pay to somebody else or pays to the credit of somebody else, and the bank thus pays the credits according to the direction, it is no longer liable to the original depositor. . . . It appears also by the testimony that three other checks were drawn by the plaintiffs against their account, for the sums of $700, $300, and $2000, respectively, and that they received from the teller in exchange for these checks three certificates of deposit, signed by Wm. H. Blumer & Co., and acknowledging that the plaintiffs had deposited with them these respective sums, payable with interest, upon the return of these certificates. These are dated Sept. 23, 1876; Dec. 1, 1876; and Feb. 2, 1877. You have heard the circumstances under which these checks were drawn, and these certificates of deposit received. *Prima facie*, this would be a payment by the bank to the plaintiffs or their order of the amounts represented by the several checks and certificates."

The Court further instructed the jury that the bank was not liable for the fraudulent representations of Straub; and in answer to the remark of counsel that there was evidence of fraud which should be submitted to the jury, replied: "I hardly think so. If there was evidence sufficient to justify the jury in finding fraud, then it should be submitted; but if there is not enough to justify the jury in finding that way, I would be bound to set aside the verdict, and grant a new trial. If I find there was no fraud, then it is not proper to submit it to the jury."

Under instructions, the jury found a verdict in favor of plaintiffs for $251. Judgment thereon. The plaintiffs thereupon took this writ, assigning for error the refusal to submit the question of fraud to the jury, as appears by the answers to the points and the charge *ut supra*.

E. I. Fox (with whom were *Evan Holben* and *D. D. Roper*), for the plaintiffs in error.

The question of fraud was for the jury, however slight the evidence.

Frazer *v.* Hill, 2 Phila.
Hill *v.* Gray, 1 Starkie, 352.
Pilmore *v.* Hood, 5 Bingham, N. C. 97.

The bank received the benefit of the money by assuming by $3000 the overdrafts of Blumer & Co., and is therefore responsible, even though the officers had no authority to make false representations.

Morse on Banks and Banking, pp. 12, 13, 91–93, 105.

Edward Harvey (with whom were *R. E. Wright, Jr.*, and *G. & H. Lear*), for the defendant in error.

As the bank held the plaintiff's money on deposit, it held it subject to the order of the depositor; when that order was drawn, presented, and passed into the account, it was *prima facie* an appropriation of the fund, and an extinguishment of the depositary's liability.

Before one who alleges the commission of fraud can disaffirm the contract he must return or offer to return whatever he has received under the contract. He must place the other party as nearly as possible *in statu quo;* to do this it is incumbent on him to restore money, property, or securities, unless they are absolutely worthless; and the burden to show this is on the party who failed to restore them.

Cooley on Torts, 504, 5.
Babcock *v.* Case, 11 Sm. 427.
Bigelow on Fraud, 410.
Rowley *v.* Bigelow, 12 Pick. 307.
Beetem *v.* Burkholder, 19 Sm. 249.
Morrow *v.* Rees, Ib. 368.
Pearsoll *v.* Chapin, 8 Wr. 9.
Bell *v.* Hartman, 9 Phila. 1.

The plaintiffs knew that the teller in giving the certificates was acting *ultra vires*, and could not bind the bank.

Lloyd *v.* West Branch Bank, 3 H. 174.

The plaintiffs could and did read the certificates, and should not have been misled.

Bigelow on Fraud, 73.
Grace *v.* Adams, 100 Mass. 507.
Rice *v.* Dwight Manufacturing Co., 2 Cush. 80.
Rockafellow *v.* Baker, 5 Wr. 321.

May 3, 1880. THE COURT. The principal cause of complaint in this case is that the learned Judge of the Court below withdrew from the jury the consideration of the question of fraud, upon the ground that there was not sufficient evidence to submit it. [The Court here recited the facts *ut supra*.] We must assume the jury would have found the facts as testified to by the plaintiff, Steckel. The facts established, we have a case of palpable fraud. It is not an answer to say the plaintiffs ought not to have been deceived, and with ordinary care would not have been. The fact that the Blumers were respectively president and cashier of the National Bank, as well as leading members of the banking-house of Blumer & Co., was calculated to mislead and deceive, and when told in positive terms that the certificates, although signed by Blumer & Co., were the certificates of the bank, the plaintiffs may readily have believed it was all right.

It was urged, however, that, even if there was a fraud, it does not affect the bank; that an agent can only act within the scope of his authority; and that a bank is not bound by the fraudulent representations of one or more of its officers. There is no doubt as to the general rule that an agent can only bind his principal so long as he acts within the scope of his authority; but we do not think the principle applies in this case. A bank is responsible for the safe keeping of the money of a depositor, and it cannot set up fraud of its own officers as an answer to a demand for repayment. Public policy forbids it. The plaintiffs, after ascertaining the fraudulent character of the transaction, tendered the certificates to the bank and demanded the payment of their original deposit. In other words, they rescinded the contract on the ground of fraud. If their allegations are true, they had a right to do so, and proceed upon the original cause of action.

The question of fraud should have been submitted to the jury. What has been said sufficiently covers the points involved.

Judgment reversed and a *venire facias de novo* awarded.

Opinion by PAXSON, J. MERCUR, J., absent.
[See next case; also Resh *v.* Bank, *post*, p. 21.
Cf. "ULTRA VIRES.—Certain cases where the defence of ultra vires is inadmissible in actions against corporations," 11 Central Law Jour. 81, 101.]

March 4, 1880.
Ziegler v. The First National Bank of Allentown.

Banks—Authority of bank officers—Depositors—Fraud.

The cashier is the executive officer of a bank, and authorized by the nature of his office to receive money on deposit; after receiving it, no trick or fraud on his part, by means of which the money passes to a firm in which the bank officers are largely interested, can absolve the bank from its liability.

Relations of bank officers to the public, commented upon, *per* PAXSON, J.
Steckel *v.* Bank, *ante,* p. 17, followed.

Error to the Common Pleas of Lehigh County.

Assumpsit, by Philip Zeigler against the First National Bank of Allentown, to recover $2980.80 deposited with said bank.

The defendant was a national bank, organized and incorporated under the National Banking Laws, and was located and doing business in the city of Allentown. It suspended sometime in March or April, 1877. At the time of its suspension, and for a number of years prior thereto, Wm. H. Blumer was the president of the bank, Jacob A. Blumer, a son of Wm. H. Blumer, cashier, George E. Straub, teller, and Wm. H. Blumer, Jesse M. Line, and Wm. Kern were among the board of directors. There was also at the same time a private banking house in the city of Allentown, composed of Wm. H. Blumer, Jesse M. Line, and Wm. Kern, trading under the firm name of Wm. H. Blumer & Co. In March, 1877, Blumer & Co. failed. On Oct. 11, 1876, and for a long time prior thereto, the firm of Wm. H. Blumer & Co. was largely insolvent, and this insolvency was known to the officers of the First National Bank of Allentown.

Upon the trial, before MEYERS, P. J., the plaintiff "proposed to prove by Philip Ziegler, the witness on the stand, that, prior to 1874, the plaintiff kept his accounts with and did his banking business at the Union National Bank of Reading, Pa.; that some time in the year 1874 the plaintiff went to the First National Bank of Allentown, Pa., and in the bank he met Jacob A. Blumer, the cashier of the First National Bank of Allentown, Pa., and told him that he wanted to deposit some money in the First National Bank; that he wanted to deposit it in the bank so that he could draw his checks against it whenever he wanted to; that Jacob A. Blumer, the cashier, then said that that was all right; that he then gave the money to Jacob A. Blumer, who took it, and proposed to give the plaintiff a certificate of deposit; that plaintiff then said he wanted no certificate of deposit, that at the Union National Bank of Reading he had a deposit book and checks to draw against his accounts, and that was the way he wanted his accounts in the First National Bank; that the said Jacob A. Blumer then said that that was not the way they did business, that they gave no books, but gave certificates of deposit, that that was the way they did business, that it was all the same, that he could draw his checks on the bank and the bank would pay them; and that the said Jacob A. Blumer then told and assured plaintiff that it was all right; that his money was deposited in the First National Bank of Allentown; in consequence of which plaintiff took said certificate of deposit, not being able to read the same, and believing and being assured by the said Jacob A. Blumer that it was the certificate of the First National Bank of Allentown;

that at the same time the said Jacob A. Blumer gave plaintiff a number of blank checks on the First National Bank of Allentown; that after that the plaintiff deposited money from time to time, and drew checks on the First National Bank of Allentown from time to time up to October 11, 1876, which checks were all duly paid by said bank; that from time to time he made settlement of his accounts, when the checks paid by the bank were surrendered to him and new certificates given to plaintiff; that on October 11, 1876, he made a settlement with the officers of the bank and deposited some more money, and that the balance then due him was $2980.80, for which he received a certificate from the officers of the bank, which in fact was the certificate of the banking house of Wm. H. Blumer & Co., which certificate is marked 'A;' that up to this time all certificates plaintiff had received were surrendered up to the First National Bank, and plaintiff does not know, and never did know, whether they were the certificates of Wm. H. Blumer & Co. or of the First National Bank; that when plaintiff received the certificate of October 11, 1876, he did not know that it was the certificate of Wm. H. Blumer & Co., but, relying upon the representations and assurances of the said Jacob A. Blumer, that he had his money deposited in the First National Bank of Allentown, he believed said certificate to be a certificate of the First National Bank, and that he never discovered that said certificate was the certificate of Wm. H. Blumer & Co., and not of the First National Bank of Allentown, until some time in the spring of the year 1877, after the failure of the First National Bank of Allentown, and of Wm. H. Blumer & Co.; that, after October 11, 1876, plaintiff drew a number of checks on said First National Bank, aggregating $480.35, which were paid by said bank; that the plaintiff never knew of the existence of the firm of Wm. H. Blumer & Co. until after their failure in 1877, never dealt with said firm, and that all his dealings in the premises were with the officers of the First National Bank of Allentown. This to be followed by proof that, on October 11, 1876, and for a long time prior thereto, the firm of Wm. H. Blumer & Co. was largely insolvent, which insolvency was known to the officers of the First National Bank of Allentown; and that on that day the account of said Wm. H. Blumer & Co. in the First National Bank of Allentown was overdrawn to a large amount, and that said account remained overdrawn down to the time of the failure of Wm. H. Blumer & Co. and the suspension of the said First National Bank; and that at the time of said failure said overdraft exceeded $100,000; and that, on October 11, 1876, the officers of said First National Bank of Allentown, without the knowledge and consent of plaintiff, entered said balance of $2980.80, then due plaintiff, to the credit of Wm. H. Blumer & Co. on the books of the bank, for the purpose of making good in part said overdraft of Wm. H. Blumer & Co."

Objected to; objection sustained, and offer overruled; exception.

In the absence of evidence, a verdict was rendered for the defendant, and judgment entered thereon; whereupon the plaintiff took this writ, assigning for error the rejection of his offer.

John Rupp (with whom was *John D. Stiles*), for the plaintiff in error.

The cashier of a bank is the general executive officer of the bank, and can bind it.

Bissell v. First National Bank of Franklin, 19 Sm. 415.
Harrisburg Bank v. Tyler, 3 W. & S. 376.
Bank of Penna. v. Reed, 1 Id. 101.
Story on Agency, §§ 114 and 115.
Bank of Kentucky v. Schuylkill Bank, 1 Parsons's Rep. 180.
Lloyd v. The West Branch Bank, 3 H. 172.
Angell & Ames on Corporations, § 311.

By payment of interest the bank is estopped from denying its liability.

2 Parsons on Contracts, 793.
Pickard v. Sears, 6 A. & E. 469.
Commonwealth v. Moltz, 10 B. 527.
Crowell v. Meconkey, 5 Barr, 168, see p. 176.
Waters's Appeal, 11 Casey, 523.
Woods v. Wilson, 1 Wright, 379.
Hill et al v. Epley et al., 7 Casey, 331.
Miranville v. Silverthorn, 12 Wright, 147.
Merchant's National Bank v. State National Bank, 10 Wallace, 604.

Where one dealing with another volunteers an explanation as to the contents of a written paper, the party dealing with him may rely upon such voluntary explanation, and need not ask to have the paper read.

Edward Harvey (with whom was *R. E. Wright, Jr.*), for the defendant in error.

The money was accepted by the cashier, not as agent of the bank, but as agent of Blumer & Co.

The principal is only liable where the act done is in the exercise and within the limits of the powers delegated.

Mechanics' Bank v. Bank of Columbia, 5 Wheat. 326.
Thayer v. Boston, 19 Pick. 517.
Fogg v. Griffin, 2 Allen, 6.
Little Miami R. R. Co. v. Wetmore, 19 Ohio, N. S., 110.
Smith's Master and Servant, 150.
Lloyd v. West Branch Bank, 3 H. 174.
Kirkpatrick v. Winans, 1 C. E. Green, 408.

One who cannot read should require that the contract be read to him.

Ellis v. McCormick, 1 Hilton, 313.
Greenfield's Est., 2 H. 504.
Grace v. Adams, 100 Mass. 507.
Rice v. Dwight Manufacturing Co., 2 Cush. 80.
Hallenbeck v. Dewitt, 2 Johns. Rep. 404.
Penna. R. R. Co. v. Shay, 1 N. 198.
Adams v. Bachert, 2 Id. 524.

The party electing to rescind must place the other party as nearly as possible *in statu quo*.
Babcock *v.* Case, 11 Sm. 427.
Beetem *v.* Burkholder, 19 Sm. 249.
Morrow *v.* Rees, Id. 368.
Moore *v.* Shenk, 3 Barr, 12.
Pearsoll *v.* Chapin, 8 Wr. 9.
Turnpike Co. *v.* Com., 2 Watts, 433.
Piper *v.* Slonaker, 2 Gr. 113.
Jackson *v.* McGinness, 2 Har. 331.
Ives *v.* Niles, 5 Watts, 323.
Bell *v.* Hartman, 9 Phila. 1.

Estoppel cannot be invoked if the cashier was acting without the scope of his authority.

May 3, 1880. THE COURT. When the plaintiff took his money to the First National Bank of Allentown, and handed it to the cashier for deposit, the bank became responsible therefor. The cashier was the executive officer of the bank, and authorized by the very nature of his office to receive money on deposit. After receiving it, no trick or fraud on his part by means of which the money was passed over to Blumer & Co., a firm in which the bank officers were largely interested and appeared to have had the control, could absolve the bank from its liability. No class of men have the confidence of the people to a greater extent than bank officers. Depositors do not deal with them at arms' length, and can be imposed on with the greatest ease by such officials. It would be monstrous to allow them to take advantage of the ignorant and unwary by reason of their position and the confidence which it inspires. It was doubtless a misfortune to this bank to have unworthy officials, if such should prove to be the case. It certainly was unwise to permit its chief officers to occupy a dual position with divided interests, but the consequences resulting therefrom cannot be visited upon those who dealt in good faith with the bank.

This case is ruled in a great measure by Steckel *v.* The Bank, just decided [*ante*, p. 17]. It was error to reject the evidence contained in plaintiff's offer. The facts offered to be proved amounted to a fraud upon the plaintiff, and he was entitled to have the question passed upon by a jury.

Judgment reversed and a *venire de novo* awarded.

Opinion by PAXSON, J. GREEN and MERCUR, JJ., absent.

[See next case.]

March 4, 1880.

Resh v. The First National Bank of Allentown.

Banks—Authority of officers of—Principal and agent—Fraud—Promissory note.

In an action by a bank upon a promissory note, the defendant offered to prove: that the note was procured from the defendant by fraud on the part of the bank officers; that he went to the bank to receive payment of a certificate of deposit; that when the money was paid, he signed a paper represented by the bank officer to be a receipt for the money, but which afterwards turned out to be the note upon which suit was brought:

Held (reversing the judgment of the Court below), that such facts constituted a defence to the action, and that the offer should have been received.

Ziegler *v.* Bank, *ante*, p. 19, and Steckel *v.* Bank, *ante*, p. 17, followed.

Error to the Common Pleas of Lehigh County.

Assumpsit by the First National Bank of Allentown against William Resh.

Upon the trial, before ALBRIGHT, P. J., the plaintiff put in evidence a promissory note for $500, made by defendant, to his own order, and indorsed by him in blank. The defendant offered to prove: (1) That at various times he deposited moneys at the First National Bank of Allentown, Pa., receiving certificates of deposit, which he supposed to be certificates of deposit of the First National Bank of Allentown, and that on the 7th day of March, 1877, he, the defendant, presented one of these certificates at the First National Bank of Allentown, and demanded payment therefor, and was requested by an officer of the Bank to sign a paper, which defendant supposed at the time to be a receipt for the sum of $500, that being the amount of the certificate of deposit which defendant presented for payment. Objected to as incompetent and irrelevant, because the offer proposes to prove the supposition of the defendant, and because there is no offer to show that there was any fraud or imposition practised upon the defendant at the time the note was signed. Objection sustained; exception.

(2) That when he presented the certificate of deposit for $500, to the plaintiff, which he had received from the First National Bank of Allentown, Pa., he was requested to sign a paper as a receipt for the sum of $500; that the defendant signed said paper under the representations by the officers of the bank that it was a receipt, and that deceit and fraud was practised by the officers of the bank when they procured his signature to the note in suit, and that the signature thus obtained was the signature to the note in suit and not a receipt. Objected to as incompetent and irrelevant, because the offer discloses

no evidence of fraud or deceit, and no facts from which the jury could draw any such inference. Objection sustained; exception.

(3) That the note in suit was procured from the defendant by the plaintiff, by representing to him at the time he signed the same, that the paper he signed and was requested to sign was a receipt for the sum of $500, and that the said sum of $500 was paid to the defendant upon a certificate of deposit, presented by the defendant to the plaintiff for payment. Objected to as incompetent and irrelevant. Objection sustained; exception.

(4) That on the 7th day of March, 1877, he presented what he believed to be a certificate of deposit of the First National Bank of Allentown, at the First National Bank of Allentown, for $500, and requested the payment thereof, and that he was paid said sum of $500 upon a certificate of deposit obtained from the bank, being presented to the bank by the defendant, and that he was asked by an officer of said bank to sign a paper, and that the paper which he signed was represented to be a receipt, and which the defendant now claims to be the note in question, and that the defendant could not read or speak the English language. Objected to as incompetent and irrelevant; objection sustained; exception.

Verdict for plaintiff for the amount of the note, and judgment thereon, whereupon the defendant took this writ, assigning for error the rejection of his four offers.

R. Clay Hamersly (*Thomas B. Metzger* with him), for the plaintiff in error.

The acts and declarations of the parties in the presence of each other, or the acts and declarations of the party to be affected thereby, which constitute part of the *res gestæ*, and enter into the character of the whole transaction, are evidence, and are to be taken together as a connected link of a chain of circumstances to establish a case of fraud.

Kiser *v.* Mitchell, 8 Barr, 64.

Edward Harvey (*R. E. Wright, Jr.*, with him), for the defendant in error. The plaintiff should have read the note.

Adams *v.* Bachert, 2 N. 526.

Penna. R. R. Co. *v.* Shay, 1 N. 198.

No right was violated, no damage was inflicted by the fraud, if any. The transaction was the giving of a note for value, and with it the certificate as collateral security.

May 3, 1880. THE COURT. While this case differs somewhat in its facts from Zeigler *v.* The Bank, and Steckel *v.* The Bank, just decided [*ante*, pp. 19 and 17], it is similar in principle, and comes within the rulings of those cases.

The third assignment covers all that it is necessary to discuss. The Court rejected evidence offered to prove that the note in suit was procured from defendant below by fraud on the part of the bank officers, that he went to the bank to receive payment of a certificate of deposit for $500, that when the money was paid, he signed a paper represented by the bank officer to be a receipt for $500, but which afterwards turned out to be a note for $500, upon which this suit was brought.

It is true the plaintiff denies the facts upon which this offer was based. But this denial goes for nothing, as the jury were not allowed to pass upon them.

The evidence should have been admitted. Judgment reversed and a *venire facias de novo* awarded.

Opinion by PAXSON, J. GREEN and MERCUR, JJ., absent.

Jan. '80.   March 4, 1880.

City of Reading v. Althouse.

Constitutional law—Taking or injuring private property for public purposes—Art. XVI. § 8, Constitution of 1874—Act of April 14, 1853—Water courses, natural and artificial—Consequential damages.

The doctrine that an action for consequential damages against a corporation, possessed of the right of eminent domain, cannot be sustained, is rendered obsolete by the Constitution of 1874.

The special Act of April 14, 1853, providing that compensation shall be made for damages sustained by the owners of land upon which a spring or stream of water is situated, or through which it flows, by permanent appropriation therein described, applies not only for the benefit of owners of natural channels, but applies equally to artificial water-courses so ancient that the memory of man runneth not to the contrary.

In 1769, L., the owner of land through which flowed a stream, divided said land, with an existing ditch, for the purpose of irrigating its several parts, and devised it. A. derived title through L. with the right to use, at stated periods, the water flowing through the ditch. In 1874 the municipal corporation of R., lying on one of the tributaries of the stream supplying the ditch, and four miles distant from the land to which the right was appurtenant, appropriated water from the tributary for the purpose of water-works. In an action by A. against R., the facts having established substantial consequential damages:

Held (sustaining the judgment of the Court below), that an action lay under the Act of April 14, 1853.

Held further, that even without that Act, the municipal corporation of R. would be responsible to A. under § 8, Art. XVI. of the Constitution, providing for compensation for property taken, injured, or destroyed by corporations empowered to do so for public use.

Error to the Common Pleas of Berks County.

Appeal of the city of Reading from the judgment on the report of viewers appointed to ascertain the damages sustained by William Althouse by reason of the taking of water by the said city.

Upon the trial, before SASSAMAN, J., the following facts appeared: In 1769 there existed a ditch, the date of whose creation was unknown, for the purpose of irrigating lands of Mordecai Lincoln. The water was derived from the Antietam Creek. Lincoln divided the lands thus irrigated, assigned to each part its respective proportion of water, and the periods of time to which they were entitled to use it, and devised them. William Althouse derived title through Lincoln, with the right thus to use the water flowing through the ditch. In 1865 the city of Reading, situated about four miles above the point of division of the waters of the Antietam through the ditch, purchased the property and franchises of the Reading Water Company, obtained a tract of land through which flowed Ohlinger Creek, one of the tributaries of the Antietam, and, under authority of councils, erected water-works and diverted water from the stream to the city reservoir. The proceedings were had under the supplement, approved April 14, 1853,* to the Act of March 16, 1819, creating the "Reading Water Company," and empowering it to supply the borough of Reading with water.

The evidence of damage was voluminous and conflicting.

The plaintiff offered to show:—

(1) "The effect of the appropriation of the Ohlinger or Antietam Creek by the city of Reading upon the quantity of water flowing through the race or water-course in question from the 1st day of March to the 16th day of October, that the quantity of the water flowing through said race or water-course is by said diversion reduced to such extent as to make it unprofitable for the parties owning the land there along to be at the expense of keeping it in repair, and as to utterly ruin and deprive the plaintiff of his right and power to irrigate his land."

(2) "To show further the number of acres of irrigable land the plaintiff owned at the time of the diversion, and the number of acres owned by him generally along this race, and the amount of damages accruing to him from said diversion and decrease of quantity of water and the dif-

* By the supplement authority was given said corporation to permanently appropriate to their use such spring or springs, stream or streams of water as they might select for the purpose of bringing into the city of Reading an additional supply of water, and any damage that should be sustained by owners of land upon which such spring or springs, stream or streams of water might be situated or through which it or they should flow, should be ascertained and compensation made therefor as is therein provided. (P. L. 416.)

ference between the value of the farm immediately prior and immediately subsequent to such diversion, and that said farm was depreciated in value."

Defendant objected that "The plaintiff has already shown that the creek or stream appropriated by the city does not flow through his land, but that at a point more than a mile above his farm and four or five miles below the point of diversion by the city, water is diverted from the Antietam Creek during certain portions of the year, into an artificial channel, and that he has by deed the right to use water from this channel during certain hours in each week. The Act of Assembly under which this proceeding is had does not authorize the assessment of damages for any such right of irrigation, and the evidence is, therefore, irrelevant and inadmissible."

Objection overruled; exception.

(3) "To show by Daniel S. Zacharias, the witness upon the stand, that the water of the stream which he has testified the city of Reading diverted and brought into the city in July, 1874, before that time flowed through the race mentioned in the deeds already in evidence, and that the said race runs through the lands of the plaintiff described in the petition, proposing to follow this with proof of the fact that plaintiff had been using said water for the purposes of irrigation, watering cattle, and domestic purposes, and by proof of damages."

Defendant objected:

(1) "Because the race spoken of is an artificial channel, and not the natural channel of the stream. The right of the plaintiff, if any exists, is an easement. The Act under which the damages are claimed does not allow damages for injury to an easement such as this.

(2) "The creek diverted by defendant was only a branch of the Antietam Creek, which was taken at a point four or five miles from the head of the race; the testimony is, therefore, uncertain and speculative.

(3) "The petition only claims damages for loss of water for irrigation. No loss of water for that purpose has been shown."

Objections overruled; exception.

The defendant presented the following points:—

(1) That the Act of Assembly under which these proceedings are had, does not authorize the assessment of damages for the injury complained of by plaintiff, and therefore the verdict must be for defendant. *Answer*—Negatived.

(2) If the jury believe that there remained after the city took the Ohlinger water, sufficient water in the Antietam Creek to irrigate the plaintiff's meadows, then the plaintiff has not sustained any substantial injury, the doctrine *dam-*

num absque injuria applies, and the plaintiff cannot recover. *Answer*—If the jury believe that although the petitioner in this case is deprived of some of the water he had a right to, and of right he should have had and enjoyed, and yet that the amount so taken from his use for the purposes of his grant was not appreciable, or slightly appreciable only, then this case falls under the doctrine of *damnum absque injuria*, and in that event there can be no recovery here now. But if the loss of water to which he is entitled would be appreciable, and material to the enjoyment of his right, the jury may assess damages which would be commensurate with the actual depreciation of his farm, the direct and immediate result of the deprivation of water by the diversion of the stream, and only for that.

Verdict for the plaintiff for $2150, and judgment thereon. The defendant took this writ, assigning for error the answer to his first point, and the admission of the plaintiff's offers.

George F. Baer, with whom was *C. H. Ruhl*, for the plaintiff in error.

The plaintiff did not claim compensation for injury done him as riparian proprietor, but for diminishing the flow of water in an artificial irrigating ditch. This is a mere easement.
Northam *v.* Hurley, 1 Ellis & Blackburn, 670.

The Act of April 14, 1854, applies only to riparian proprietors, whose rights do not attach in the case of artificial drains.
Sampson *v.* Hoddicott, 1 C. B. N. S. 590.

A person cannot create by grant new rights of property so as to give the grantee a right to sue in his own name for an interruption of the right by a third party.
Hill *v.* Tupper, 2 H. & C. 121.
Stockport Water-works *v.* Potter, 3 Hurl. & Colt. 300.

A corporation invested with the power of eminent domain is liable for consequential damages only to the extent declared in the Act of incorporation.
Navigation *v.* Coons, 6 W. & S. 101.
Canal Co. *v.* Mulliner, 18 Sm. 360.

The constitutional limitation applies only to an actual *taking* of property. Matters of annoyance and consequential injuries are not within it.
Watson *v.* Railroad, 1 Wr. 479.
Tinicum Fishing Co. *v.* Carter, 11 Sm. 31.

The damages to the plaintiff in this case are consequential.
Koch *v.* Williamsport Water Co., 15 Sm. 288.

The flow of a stream, as provided for in the Act, means a natural channel; else the number of actions for damages under the Act would be limited only by the number of licenses or easements granted.

Damages have been denied in cases of graver injuries.
N. Y. & E. R. R. Co. *v.* Young, 9 C. 175.
Arnold *v.* Hudson R. R. Co., 49 Barb. 121.

Jacob S. Livingood and *Cyrus G. Derr*, for the defendant in error.

Where the owner of lands, through which a stream of water flows, divides the stream, making two of one, and grants lands abutting on the new stream, the grantee of such lands becomes a riparian owner.
Nuttall *v.* Bracewell, 2 Exch. L. R. 12.
Sutclife *v.* Booth, 32 L. J. Q. B. 136.
Stockport Water-works *v.* Potter, 3 Hurl. & Colt. 325.

The right of the plaintiff was to appropriate all the water flowing through the ditch; when the defendant appropriated water from a stream supplying the ditch, it was a *taking* of property. Such taking causes direct, not consequential damages.
Hough *v.* Doylestown, 4 Brewst. 335.
Hecksher *v.* Shenandoah, 2 Leg. Chron. 273.
Gardner *v.* Newburgh, 2 Johns. Ch. 162.

The Act of 1854 provides for an action to an owner of land through which a stream shall flow. Whether the flow be by natural or artificial channel is immaterial.
Siebert *v.* Levan, 8 B. 390.

The city of Reading is responsible for consequential damages under § 8, Art. XVI. of the new Constitution, which provides for the injury and destruction, as well as the taking.

March 22, 1880. THE COURT. Were it necessary we would have no hesitation in holding that the provision of the 8th section, Art. 16, of the new Constitution, governs this case. That section provides for the making of compensation, not only for the *taking* of private property for public use, as was the case theretofore, but also for its *injury* or *destruction*. That the use, which the plaintiff had of the waters of the Great or Antietam Creek, through the race or ditch in controversy, was property, though of an incorporeal kind, is not open to debate; and that it was injured by the operations of the city of Reading, is a fact established by a proper tribunal. There is, therefore, no good reason apparent to us why the case should not be covered by the above recited 8th section of the Constitution.

Passing, however, this phase of the question, we cannot see why the plaintiff is not within the protection of the Act of April 14, 1853 (P. L. 416). This Act provides that, "Any damages sustained by the owners of land, upon which such spring or springs, stream or streams of water is or are situated, or through which it or they shall flow by reason of the permanent appropriation as aforesaid shall be ascertained, and compensation made in manner hereinafter provided for." Now the defendant has appropriated Ohlinger Creek, one of the main branches of Antietam, from which the irrigating ditch or race in question receives its supply. The determinative question then is, did this stream of water, or what is the same, the water of this stream, called Ohlinger, or any material part of it, before it was diverted by the city of Reading, flow through the plaintiff's land? The channel may be called what you please; Antietam Creek or Lincoln's ditch, that is of no consequence; was the water formerly wont to flow through the Althouse property? If so, he had property in it; a right to it which is protected by the Act. The counsel for the defendant seems to think that the provisions of the Act extend but to the owners of natural bed and banks of the stream, but this is a construction warranted neither by the letter nor spirit of the statute. Who would doubt the application of the Act were this ditch a natural branch, division of, or outflow of the main stream. But what radical difference is made by the fact, that man dug the present channel instead of nature? And how can this affect vested rights, rights now more than a century old? In the submission executed by the two Lincolns and Michael Seyster, one hundred and eleven years ago, this ditch is spoken of as an existing race, or water-course, but who dug it, or how long it existed before that time, is not mentioned, and no one knows. Its origin is literally buried in the shades of the past; hence, for all practical purposes, it is a natural watercourse prescriptively, and therefore, legally it is so. The right to it could be no better were it natural. As was said by Chief Justice GIBSON in *Seibert v. Levan* (8 Barr 383): "Whilst the grantor was lord of the whole, he might assign a permanent channel to the stream, and as regards himself and those who claim under him, impress it with any character he should see proper. There is no particular sanctity in the natural bed of a stream, which is perpetually changing its course from accidental causes." And in speaking of the rule, that water shall flow *ubi currere solebat et consuevit*, he says it applies rather to the duty of returning it than to the channel through which it flows. And so in *Sutclife v. Booth* (32 L. J. Q. B. 136), it was held per WIGHTMAN, J., that a water-course, though artificial, may have been originally made under such circumstances, and have been so used as to give all the rights that the riparian proprietors would have had had it been a natural stream. Of like import is the case of *Nuttall v. Bracewell* (2 Exchq. L. R. 1) in which Chancellor B. says: "I see no reason why the law applicable to ordinary running streams should not be applicable to such a stream as this, for it is a natural flow or stream of water, though flowing in an artificial channel." So, also, on a similar footing he puts the case where two adjoining riparian owners should by agreement so alter or divert a stream that it shall run in two channels instead of one. In such case he holds that a grantor of land on the new stream would have all the rights of a riparian owner. But the case here supposed is, in fact, the one in hand; here is a division of the Great Creek by the race or water-way in controversy, and that of a date so ancient that the memory of man runneth not to the contrary. So far as the case of the Stockport Water-works Co. (32 L. J. Q. B. 136) has any application, it is an authority for the plaintiff, for POLLOCK, C. B., advocates the doctrine above stated. We may set it down for certain that so far as authority goes the ruling of the Court below is sustained.

Many cases have been cited upon part of the city for the purpose of proving that an action for consequential damages against a corporation possessed of the right of eminent domain cannot be sustained. But these authorities are now of no value, for the new Constitution has introduced a different rule. Moreover, the Act of 1853 governs this case, and it in express terms provides for compensation to land owners for *any* damage they may suffer, not for land taken, but for the taking "permanent appropriation" of water. The damages are thus necessarily consequential, as they arise from the disturbance, or abridgement of an incorporeal right.

Judgment affirmed.

Opinion by GORDON, J. GREEN and MERCUR, JJ., absent.

Jan. '80, 263.   March 11, 1880.

Long v. Caffrey.

Mechanic's lien—Right to file mechanic's lien may be waived—Contract—Mutual and independent covenants.

The right to file a mechanic's lien may be waived by a stipulation in the contract under which the work was done.

Where a contract between a mechanic and the owner of land for the erection of a house contained a covenant on the part of the mechanic "that no mechanic's or other lien should be filed," and one on the part of the owner of the land that the building should be insured to a specified amount:

Held (affirming the judgment of the Court below), that these were separate and independent covenants, and that an alleged breach of the latter constituted no relief from the responsibility imposed by the former.

Error to the Common Pleas of Luzerne County.

Scire facias sur mechanic's lien, by E. T. Long against John M. Caffrey. Plea, "Nil debet."

On the trial before HARDING, P. J., it appeared that Long had entered into a written agreement with Caffrey to erect a house for him, the payments to be made in instalments as the work progressed. The agreement contained the following stipulations:—

"And it is further agreed that no mechanic's or other lien shall be entered against said building by the said Long, or the material contractor, or workmen; and, it is further agreed, that if any such lien be entered, that the said Long shall pay all costs and fees at his own proper expense without recourse or claim against said Caffrey on account thereof, and that if said Caffrey is forced to pay the amount of any of said liens, or costs, he shall have the right to recover the amount thereof from said Long.

"It is further agreed that said Caffrey shall, on completion of said building, insure the same against loss or damage by fire to at least the amount of one thousand dollars, and assign this policy of insurance as collateral security for the payment of the last-mentioned one thousand dollars to said Long."

The evidence showed that the instalments had not all been paid, and that the building had not been insured according to the contract.

The plaintiff requested his Honor to charge, *inter alia*, that if the jury believe that said Caffrey failed to pay at the time agreed upon, and also failed to insure the property as agreed upon, then he cannot set up the defence that the contractor agreed not to file a lien. *Refused.*

The defendant requested his Honor to charge, that by the agreement annexed to the claim the plaintiff agrees that no mechanic's, or other lien, shall be entered against said building by the said Long, and he is, therefore, estopped from filing a lien, and cannot recover in this case. *Answer.* We affirm that. Your verdict, therefore, should be in favor of the defendant in this case.

Verdict and judgment for defendant. Plaintiff took this writ, assigning for error, *inter alia*, the answers to plaintiff's and defendant's points.

G. R. Bedford, for plaintiff in error.

By the answer to our first point the Court deprived us of the benefit of the jury's finding upon the question of whether the covenant not to file a lien, and the covenant to insure, were not mutual covenants; this, we claim, was error.

McCrelish v. Churchman, 4 R. 26.
Wright v. Smyth, 4 W. & S. 533.

(No counsel appeared for defendant in error, and there was no paper-book.)

May 3, 1880. THE COURT. This was a scire facias on a mechanic's lien. The work was done and the materials furnished for a gross sum, under a written agreement between the parties. The payments were to be made in several instalments, the last one some months after the completion and acceptance of the house. The contract contains this stipulation, "And it is further agreed that no mechanic's or other lien shall be entered against said building by the said Long, or the material contractor, or workmen; and it is further agreed that if any such lien be entered, that the said Long shall pay all costs and fees at his own proper expense, without recourse or claim against said Caffrey on account thereof, and that if said Caffrey is forced to pay the amount of any of said liens, or costs, he shall have the right to recover the amount thereof from said Long."

There is nothing doubtful or obscure in this clause. It is clear and specific. Why shall not full effect be given to it? It is in regard to a subject-matter that the parties had an undoubted right to contract. The parties recognized it as an important matter in the contract. The defendant wished to be protected against all such liens. The plaintiff expressly agreed not to file one himself, and to protect the defendant against all filed by others. The right of lien which the law would have given to the plaintiff he waived, and estopped himself from asserting to the prejudice of the defendant.

The contract contains further evidence that the plaintiff was to rely on personal and collateral security without lien. Thus it was agreed that on the completion of the building, the defendant should cause it to be insured to an amount at least equal to the unpaid instalment, and assign the policy to the plaintiff as collateral security therefor. The different parts of the contract are separate and independent covenants, and we see no reason why the one not to file a lien shall not be enforced. The learned Judge was, therefore, right in charging that the plaintiff could not recover.

Judgment affirmed.

Opinion by MERCUR, J.

Jan. '80.　　　　　　　　　　　　　March 4, 1880.

Kline's Appeal.

Mechanics' liens—Apportionment—What separation of buildings does not prevent apportionment.

The owner of a tract of land laid it out in ten building lots fronting on a street. Ten houses were built thereon, two adjoining each other, making five blocks of two houses each; and between each block side-yards with a common partition fence. Between two of the blocks an additional space of ground, of sixty feet frontage, was left, with the intention of converting it into a street. Mechanics' liens were apportioned among the ten houses. It was claimed that the separation of the sixty-foot space constituted an objection to the apportionment of the liens:

Held (sustaining the judgment of the Court below), that the time of commencing work on the buildings determined the rights of the mechanics in respect to the apportionment of their liens; and that, the space not then having been actually dedicated as a public street, the liens were properly apportioned.

Fitzpatrick v. Allen, 30 Sm. 292, followed.

Appeal from the Common Pleas of Berks County.

Appeal of Charles G. Kline from the decree of distribution of the proceeds of the sheriff's sale of property of John T. Noble. The following facts appeared:—

Noble was the owner of two acres and sixty perches of land situate in the village of Lyons, Maxatawny Township, which was laid out in ten building lots fronting on a street to be opened and to be called Hunter or Noble Street, and so described in the several liens filed. The lots are 30 feet front, and running back 140 feet to an alley to be opened, 18 feet wide. On these ten lots ten houses were built, two houses adjoining each other, 16 feet front by 28 feet deep, thus making, as it were, five blocks, each house having a side yard of fourteen feet, or twenty-eight feet between each block of two houses. Between houses four and five, or blocks two and three with their side lots, an additional space or piece of ground of sixty feet was left, intended for a street at right angles to and leading from and into the proposed Hunter or Noble Street, as appears by the draft attached to the commissioner's report. These ten houses or five blocks are in one row, were built at one time, and all are fronting on the proposed Hunter or Noble Street.

A number of mechanics' liens were filed against these houses for work done and materials furnished, some of which were apportioned on each of the ten houses, others were apportioned on each house of several blocks, and others were apportioned upon blocks. The houses in question were sold at sheriff's sale some time in February, 1877, under a judgment of Charles G. Kline, bearing date October 19, 1875.

Herzog et al. had filed apportioned mechanics' liens against the ten houses, and on a reference to an auditor (B. F. Deltra) to report distribution of the proceeds of the sale, it was contended by Kline that the mechanics' liens were improperly apportioned on the blocks separated by the sixty-feet space, and that Herzog et al. were therefore not entitled to share in the proceeds. The auditor allowed their claims; and the Court dismissed exceptions to his report, HALLMAN, J., delivering the following opinion (after reciting the facts):—

"It is insisted by the exceptants that these liens having been apportioned among the ten houses, are not such as fall under the class of apportioned liens, and, therefore, are defective, and cannot participate in the distribution. The objection consists in the fact that between houses four and five, or blocks two and three, there is a space of ground of sixty feet, which was intended for a street. This forms the only ground of objection. That apportioned liens could have been filed against houses one, two, three, and four, composing blocks one and two, and against houses five, six, seven, eight, nine and ten, composing blocks three and four and five, cannot be successfully questioned. Is the objection sufficient to invalidate these liens?

"The commissioner finds in his report that these several houses were erected at one time on one tract of land, forming a legal whole or unit, of which the intervening space is a part and parcel, and the materials were furnished and the work was done upon their joint credit. The evidence fully supports this finding. At the time the tract or piece of land was laid out, the sixty feet were intended for a street, but when the buildings were begun, and up to the time when they were finished and liens filed, no street was laid out and opened, and none has been to this day.

"The fourth section of the Act of 30th May, 1831, gave to the material man the right to file an apportioned lien when the materials were furnished for two or more *adjoining* houses. The Acts of 1836 and of 1850 referred to in a former part of this opinion, in which the right to file apportioned liens is given, against two or more buildings owned by the same person, the word *adjoining* is omitted. The purpose of these Acts is manifest. When a contractor is erecting two or more houses under a joint contract, it is impossible for the material man to specify in his claim filed the particular house or building for which the several items were furnished, especially so in this age of improved machinery, when the lumber and materials generally are taken to the mill and prepared before taken to the buildings. The same reason applies to the mechanic and laboring man. The work is mainly done in the mill and shop. The flooring, frames, doors, shutters, sash, etc., are prepared promiscuously for all the houses, and it is utterly impossible to tell how many days' work was expended on any particular part that was put into any one of the buildings.

"Numerous supplements have been passed to the Act of 1836, all with the obvious intent of securing to the mechanic and material man a lien for the work and materials furnished. Two were passed in 1879. The one of 11th June authorizes and requires the Court to permit amendments in any stage of the proceedings, conducive to justice and a fair trial upon the merits, including the changing, adding, and striking out the names of claimants, and by adding the names of owners and contractors respectively; and the one of 28th June extends the provisions of the Act of 1836 for work done and materials furnished for or about the repair, alteration, or addition to any house or other building, with other important provisions and extensions, all with the like intent.

"Mechanics' liens have become an important

part of our system of jurisprudence. The Supreme Court has moulded the law from time to time, and has given it such a construction so as to perfect the system and carry out the object and intention of the Legislature. The Acts of 1836 and 1850, which gave the right to file an apportioned lien against two or more buildings owned by the same person, were held to include adjoining houses belonging to different owners, when the lien filed was against the same contractor, although not being within the words, was considered as being within the spirit and object of the Act. So, too, an apportioned claim was held good where two houses, belonging to different owners, were erected under a joint contract on opposite sides of a private alley, the use of which belonged to both properties. The contract is the main ground upon which the right to claim is founded. [His Honor here commented upon Taylor *v.* Montgomery, 8 H. 443, and Fitzpatrick *v.* Allen, 30 Sm. 294.] On the authority of these cases, and the great reluctance on the part of the Court to set aside mechanics' liens on technical grounds, the liens of Rapp & Bieber, J. Schimpf & Son, and G. Herzog & Co. should be sustained. The ten houses were erected at one time, on one lot of ground, and the work and materials were furnished for them all jointly. The lot was cut out of a field of farm land, with no public roads leading to or from it. Noble Street, when opened, was only a private way running in from these houses. The supervisor was not obliged to open and make it or keep it in repair. Had the sixty feet between houses four and five been opened, it would be a private way for the common use of the several lot-owners to pass from Noble Street to the alley which runs along the rear of these lots. It began in Noble Street and ended in the alley. In no way is the objection to these liens a parallel case to Goepp *v.* Gartiser (11 Casey, 30)."

Kline took this writ, assigning for error the decree of the Court allowing Herzog et al. to participate in the distribution.

H. H. Schwartz and *Horace Rowland,* for the appellant.

If the defendant can specify the particular work done to each house, he must file separate claims.

Chambers *v.* Farrall, 3 H. 268.
Thorn *v.* Shaw, 5 Legal and Ins. Rep. 19.
Boyd *v.* Mole, 9 Phila. 118.
Pennock *v.* Hoover, 5 R. 291.
Davis *v.* Farr, 1 Har. 167.
Harper *v.* Kelly, 5 Id. 234.
Thomas *v.* James, 7 W. & S. 382.

There must be community of rights, property, or privilege in order to justify apportioned liens.

Goepp *v.* Gartiser, 11 C. 132.
Taylor *v.* Montgomery, 8 H. 444.
Campbell *v.* Furness, 1 Phila. 372.
Millett *v.* Allen, 3 WEEKLY NOTES, 374.
Fitzpatrick *v.* Allen, 30 Sm. 292.

Here the sixty-feet space negatives the existence of such community.

Dan. H. Wingerd (with whom were *Amos B. Wanner, Deshler Bros.*, and *Butz & Schwartz*), for the appellees.

All the houses being owned by one person, the work and materials having been furnished by the lien creditors under a joint contract, and without reference to any particular house, but for all indiscriminately, it would have been impossible to specify how much work and material belonged to any particular house.

Davis *v.* Farr, 1 Har. 167.
Young *v.* Lyman, 9 B. 449.
Donahoo *v.* Scott, 2 Jones, 45.
The case, therefore, falls within the ruling of—
Fitzpatrick *v.* Allen, 30 Sm. 294.
Taylor *v.* Montgomery, 8 H. 443.

March 22, 1880. THE COURT. We think this case is ruled by Fitzpatrick *v.* Allen (30 P. F. Smith, 292). The space between these blocks of houses, of sixty feet, was not a public street; had not been dedicated as such before the buildings were commenced, whatever may have been the intention of the parties. That time is the period to be looked to as to the right of the mechanics; but it is admitted that the intention to dedicate it as a public street was abandoned. Here, then, the houses were adjoining, if that was necessary to make the joint and apportioned lien valid.

Decree affirmed, and appeal dismissed at the costs of the appellant.

PER CURIAM.

GREEN and MERCUR, JJ., absent.

Jan. '80, 314.   March 18, 1880.
Stichter v. Malley.

Liens—Priority of—Validity of—Mechanics' liens—Miners and laborers—When notice a prerequisite of—Lien for wages—Act of April 9, 1872, § 2.

In order to establish the validity, as liens, of the claims of miners and laborers for wages under the Act of April 9, 1872, and its supplements, notice in writing of the claims, and of the amounts thereof, must be given to the officer executing the writ, before the sale of the property, in accordance with the Act of April 9, 1872, § 2.

Such notice is a statutory prerequisite to the enforcement of the claim, and the duty of proving that it was given rests upon the claimant.

Judgment entered in an amicable action for wages due miners and laborers, and execution thereon, is not the notice to the officer executing the writ which is required by the Act of April 9, 1872, § 2.

Appeal from the Common Pleas of Schuylkill County.

Amicable action in debt, and confession of judgment, between H. P. Stichter, trustee, plaintiff, and Peter G. Malley, defendant. The facts were as follows: Malley was the owner of a leasehold estate, with the right to mine coal and erect a breaker. In August, and the succeeding months of 1878, he employed various mechanics and material men to furnish him with lumber, machinery, and labor for the erection of his breaker. In January, 1879, he was in default in the payment of wages to his miners and laborers for the months of November and December, 1878, as well as in the amounts due the various mechanics and material men. In the same month, Malley confessed this judgment to Stichter, as trustee for the miners and laborers; whereupon execution was issued, the lease and fixtures were sold, and the proceeds were paid into Court and referred to an auditor for distribution.

The mechanics' lien creditors, as well as the miners and laborers, appeared before the auditor (John A. Sullivan), the former contending that they had a superior right to the fund. His opinion, sustaining this view, contained the following material paragraph:—

"The auditor, from the evidence adduced before him, and after a careful consideration of the Mechanics' Lien Law of 1836, and its supplements and the law of 1872 and its supplement of 1874, giving a preference to the miners and laborers employed around the mines, and after a full examination of all the authorities submitted, is of the opinion that the wages of miners and laborers, as represented by judgment to No. 164, March Term, 1879, should be postponed until after the mechanics' liens are satisfied. Had the miners and laborers given the proper notice to the sheriff before the sale, in accordance with sect. 2 of the Act of 9th April, 1872, it could not avail anything, inasmuch as the liens of the mechanics had attached to the leasehold estate and improvements from the commencement of the building, and therefore could not be prejudiced by subsequent liens or judgments."

Exceptions to this report by Stichter, trustee for the miners and laborers, were overruled by the Court, whereupon he took this appeal, assigning for error the action of the Court in decreeing distribution to the mechanics' lien creditors.

D. B. Green (with whom were *M. M. L'Velle and S. B. Fisher*), for the appellant.

The Act of 1859 (P. L. 1859, p. 318), gave miners and laborers preference over all other claims. Subsequent legislation has but strengthened this, especially the Act of April 9, 1872 (2 Purd. Dig. 1464). In this case the mechanics had acquired no lien by judgment or mortgage, and therefore there was no notice of their existence. Had they been duly filed, a question might arise under § 4 of the Act of 1872.

The judgment and execution was sufficient notice under the Act of 1872.

The fund in Court arose from the sale of the leasehold estate, not from any separate sale of the improvements and fixtures entered upon the demised premises. The mechanics' lien creditors can have no claim upon a fund produced by the joint sale of leasehold and fixtures.

St. Clair Coal Co. *v.* Martz, 2 Leg. Chron. 89.

D. C. Henning, for the appellees.

Notice was given at the sheriff's sale of the mechanics' claims; as the lien is created by the statute to take effect from the time the improvements are made, and as the filing of the claims is but a means of continuing the lien already acquired, it follows that if actual notice of the lien be given at the time of the sale, the status of the lien creditor must be just the same as if his lien had been filed and recorded.

Yearsley *v.* Flanigen, 10 H. 491.

The miners and laborers have no claim upon the fund, because notice was not given in compliance with the Act of April 9, 1872, § 2.*

First National Bank *v.* Childs, 2 Foster's Leg. Chron. 199.

May 3, 1880. THE COURT. It does not appear that any notice in writing of the claims of the appellants, and of the amounts thereof, was given to the sheriff at any time before the sale of the property levied on, as is required by the second section of the Act of 9th April, 1872. The auditor practically finds that no such notice was given, and there is nothing on the record to show that he was in error in that finding. The duty of proving that there was such notice rests upon the appellants, as it is a statutory prerequisite to the enforcement of their claims. The notice contained in the amicable action upon which the judgment was entered is no notice to the officer executing the writ. That paper would be lodged in the prothonotary's office, where it would remain, and there would be neither certainty nor probability of its being seen by the sheriff. There is no proof that, in point of fact, he ever did see it. The appellants have therefore failed to establish the validity of their claims as liens upon the fund for wages of labor due them, under the Act. As a mere judgment, their claim is subsequent to the mechanics' liens, to which the fund was distributed, and the levy and sale by execution under that judgment does

---

* This section provides: "In all cases of executions .... and writs of a similar nature, hereafter to be issued against any person, ... it shall be lawful for such miners ; . . . . to give notice in writing of their claim or claims, and the amount thereof, to the officers executing either of such writs at any time before the actual sale of the property levied on . . . ., etc."

not help the claim as against those liens. The objection to the latter, that they are filed against the leasehold as well as the improvements, we cannot determine, because there is no evidence on the record upon 'that subject. We cannot say, therefore, that they are not entitled to the money which has been awarded to them by the auditor.

Decree affirmed, and appeal dismissed at the costs of the appellee.

Opinion by GREEN, J.

Common Pleas—Equity.

C. P. No. 1.   June 14, 1880.

Taylor v. Smiley.

Deed of trust—Power of revocation—Will—Deed of trust containing power of revocation, when revoked by will containing no reference to the power.

Hearing upon bill and answer.

Bill in equity, by Maria L. Taylor, daughter of George Teill, deceased, against Elizabeth E. Smiley, daughter and executrix of George Teill, setting forth: that George Teill, and Harriet, his wife, by deed executed in April, 1853, granted and conveyed to Elizabeth E. Smiley and Charles T. Deacon, and the survivor of them, and the heirs and assigns of such survivor, four certain lots of ground, in trust to collect the rents and profits issuing therefrom, and, after deducting and paying all taxes, etc., to pay the residue to the said George Teill and Harriet, his wife, for and during their joint lives and the life of the survivor of them; and after the decease of such survivors then in trust for the child or children whom they, the said George and Harriet Teill did then or might thereafter have, and whom the survivor of them, the said George and Harriet Teill, should leave living at the time of such survivor's decease, and the lawful issue of any child or children who might then be deceased (having left such lawful issue living at the decease of such survivor), and their several and respective heirs and assigns in equal shares as tenants in common forever; the issue of such deceased child to take such share only as his or their deceased parent or parents would have taken, had he, she, or they been living.

The deed contained a power of revocation by the grantor and wife, and to the survivor of them, by instrument of writing, under their hands and seals, or under the hand and seal of the survivor, attested by two or more subscribing witnesses, to alter, revoke, and change, or to make absolutely null and void the said uses and trusts therein declared, and to make and declare such new and other trusts and uses as they might see fit and proper.

Charles T. Deacon died in 1869, leaving Elizabeth E. Smiley sole surviving trustee. Harriet Teill died in 1860, and George in 1869. George Teill left surviving him four children (among whom are Maria Louisa Taylor and Elizabeth E. Smiley, the parties to the present suit), and one grandchild.

The bill alleged that no new use, nor any revocation under the power in said deed had been declared or made by Harriet Teill, or by George Teill, the survivor; that, therefore, upon the death of George Teill the four properties conveyed in the deed of trust became vested absolutely in the four children, and the grandchild already mentioned; that nevertheless the said Elizabeth E. Smiley had collected and received, *de son tort*, the whole of the rents and profits issuing out of the real estate conveyed in the deed of trust, and had not accounted for or paid to the plaintiff any portion of her (the plaintiff's) one-fifth share thereof, but had appropriated the same to her own use. The bill prayed that a receiver be appointed to collect the rents and profits, and that the defendant be required to account for the rents and profits of said four properties received and collected by her since the decease of George Teill.

The answer set up that George Teill devised said properties by last will, registered February 9, 1869, attested by three subscribing witnesses, and under seal (but without referring to the power), to certain persons therein named, and appointed the defendant executrix and trustee, etc. That as such executrix and trustee she collected the rents of said properties, and accounted for the same in the Orphans' Court, and distributed the balance found to be in her hands. Of this fact plaintiff had notice, and was present at the adjudication of the accounts of the defendant, without in any way giving notice of said deed, or of any claim under and by virtue of the same.

Brady and *Simpson*, for plaintiff.

No revocation of the deed of trust is made in the will, nor are any new uses or trusts declared. The decedent in his will treated the property as his own, which in reality it could not be, as it was already granted.

Boughton v. Boughton, 1 Atkyns, *625.

Every formality required to the execution of a power must be perfected within the lifetime of the donee.

Sugden on Powers, vol. i. *328.
Wright v. Wakeford, 17 Vesey, *454.
Wright v. Wakeford, 4 Taunton, *213.
Moodie v. Reid, 7 Ibid., *355.

At the moment of the donee's death his power of revocation and appointment ceased absolutely, and an interest under the deed of trust vested *eo instanti* in the plaintiff.

As no power of revocation by will was reserved to the settlors, it is manifest that such power was meant to be withheld.

Daniels and *Pile*, for defendant.

When an instrument can have no operation except in execution of a power, an intention to execute the power will be inferred.

Bingham's Appeal, 14 Sm. 345.
Keefer v. Schwartz, 11 Wr. 503.
Pepper's Will, 1 Pars. 436.
Coryell v. Dunton, 7 Barr, 530.
Lancaster v. Dolan, 1 Rawle, 231.
Porter v. Turner, et al., 3 S. & R. 108.

July 3, 1880. THE COURT (after stating the facts). Does this last will constitute a valid revocation of the uses and trusts of the deed? Porter v. Turner (3 S. & R. 108) affirms such to be the effect of a last will and testament. In Lancaster v. Dolan (1 Rawle, 231) the same effect is given to an instrument to appoint by will or other instrument, under hand and seal, to a mortgage, although it contained no reference to the power. So, also, in Coryell v. Dunton (7 Barr, 530), where there was a trust for separate use of feme covert, with power to revoke and appoint new uses, the power was held to be well executed, by deed of her and her husband, though not referring to the power. Keefer v. Schwartz (11 Wright, 503) holds, that where there was a devise for life, with power to dispose of residue by will, and devisee by will directed the sale of the property, that the former was well executed, although the first will was not referred to. STRONG, J., remarked: "It is said there must be an intention to execute the power, but such intention is inferred from a gift of property, which the testator was incapable of giving except in execution of the power."

To same effect is Pepper's Will (1 Parsons, 436), and in Bingham's Appeal (14 P. F. Smith, 345), it is decided that the intention may be ascertained when the instrument can have no operation except in the execution of the power. In this case George Teill died possessed of no other real estate.

This bill is dismissed with costs.

Opinion by ALLISON, P. J.

Common Pleas—Law.

C. P. No. 2.   Nov. 1879.

In re Electropathic Institute.

Charters—Medical Institute—A charter will not be granted to an institute for instruction in electricity as a curative agency, with power to confer degrees, where the provisions of the charter require only a knowledge of electricity, galvanism, and magnetism, and does not fulfil the requirements of the Act of March 24, 1877 (P. L. 42).

Sur application of Electropathic Institute for a charter.

The character of the proposed charter is sufficiently set forth in the opinion of the Court.

Geo. S. Graham, for the corporators.

C. A. V.

June 19, 1880. THE COURT. The purposes of the intended corporation, as set forth in the charter which we are asked to approve, is "to organize, establish, and maintain a suitable educational institution in the city of Philadelphia, which shall be devoted to giving instruction in the nature, properties, and various modifications of electricity, galvanism, magnetism, as curative agents, and in the scientific application of the same to the alleviation of pain and the cure of disease," with power "to grant and confirm in the manner and form prescribed by the by-laws, a certain decree in medicine, to wit: the degree of Doctor of Electricity to such students whom, by their proficiency in learning, they shall deem entitled thereto; which proficiency shall be evidenced by their having passed an examination satisfactory to the Faculty, of which a record shall be made, and to grant to such graduates such diplomas and certificates under the common seal as may authenticate the memory of such graduation."

The provisions of the Act of 29th of April, 1874, under which this certificate of incorporation is presented for approval, make it our duty to approve the same if it is in proper form, within the purposes of the Act, and "shall appear lawful and not injurious to the community."

Within the last few years the practice of medicine has been the subject of considerable legislation in this State, the purpose of which has been to prevent those not duly qualified from practising.

By the Act of April 15, 1879 (Purd. Dig. 1150), it is made unlawful for any person to practise medicine or surgery in certain counties therein named "who has not graduated with the degree of Doctor of Medicine and received a diploma from a chartered medical college or other institute authorized to grant diplomas."

By subsequent Act this prohibition is extended over the whole, or nearly the whole State. The Act of March 24, 1877 (Purd. Dig. 2151), goes a step further, and provides as follows: Sec. 1. "The standard qualification of a practitioner of medicine, surgery, or obstetrics shall be and consist of the following, namely: A good moral character, a thorough elementary education, a comprehensive knowledge of human anatomy, human physiology, pathology, chemistry, materia medica, obstetrics, and practice of medicine and surgery and public hygiene."

We are asked in this case to charter an educational institution which, while giving instruction in electricity, galvanism, and magnetism only, may confer degrees in medicine and arm its graduates with diplomas intended to entitle them to practise medicine, and to place them, as far as that right is concerned, upon the same level with graduates of institutions which require a thorough course of instruction in every branch of the science of medicine.

To do this, in our judgment, would be in violation of the spirit and letter of the legislation referred to, and of the manifest propriety of restricting the right to practise medicine to those possessing in a higher degree qualifications for so important a trust.

Whatever may be the value of electricity and magnetism as curative agents, a knowledge of their principles in their application to disease does not comprehend the degree of learning which the law, and the interests of society as well, require in a practitioner of medicine.

Since the filing of this charter we have been asked to approve it after it shall have been amended by striking out the words "degree in medicine," and inserting in place thereof the words "degree in electricity."

We cannot consider the charter thus amended with greater favor than as it was originally presented.

The corporation sought to be created would still sustain in its relation to the public the character of a medical college, and it is this character, while its course of instruction is thus limited, that is without authority of law, and liable to become a source of danger to the community.

The application is refused.

Opinion by FELL, J.

C. P. No. 3. June 9, 1880.

Frick et al. v. McClain.

Landlord and tenant—Judgment creditor of tenant—Distress—Claim of exemption, and appraisement of goods at less than $300—Subsequent sale under a judgment in which there is a waiver of the exemption—Claim of landlord and execution creditor to the fund.

Case stated, between Frick et al., plaintiffs in the above case, and Garrett, landlord of defendant, setting forth the following facts: On March 5, 1880, a *fi. fa.* issued in the above case, and a levy was made on defendant's property at No. 700 Brooklyn St. Prior to this levy, the landlord, Garrett, had distrained on the same goods for the rent of said premises, and the landlord's bailiff was in possession of the goods under a distress warrant at the time of the sheriff's levy. The lease was not in writing, and the tenant had not waived the exemption. The constable appraised the goods at less than $300, and, as the tenant had claimed the exemption, went no further. The judgment upon which the above-named *fi. fa.* issued contained a waiver of the exemption. Under this writ, the sheriff sold the goods of defendant, at No. 700 Brooklyn St., for $239, upon which fund the landlord, Garrett, made a claim of $63.26, for rent accrued up to the time of distress made. The claim was filed before the sale. If the Court be of opinion that the landlord has a claim for the rent upon the fund, then judgment to be entered for the landlord for $63.26; otherwise, judgment for the execution creditor.

A. A. Hirst, for the landlord.

The landlord is entitled to claim rent out of the proceeds of a sale in the sheriff's hands.

Gray v. Wilson, 4 Watts, 39.
Appeal of Collins, 11 Casey, 83.

The case is exactly the same as where there are two executions levied on the same goods, and the judgment on which the junior writ was issued alone contains a waiver; where it is held that the senior writ is also entitled to claim the benefit of the waiver.

James Alcorn, for the execution creditor.

By the appraisement, the goods were set aside as the debtor's, and were his without being subject to a claim for rent.

Rowland v. Goldsmith, 2 Gr. 378.
Collins' Appeal, 11 Casey, 83.
Gray v. Wilson, 4 Watts, 39.

C. A. V.

June 26, 1880. THE COURT. Judgment in favor of execution creditor.

WEEKLY NOTES OF CASES.

Vol. IX.] *THURSDAY, SEPT. 9, 1880.* [No. 3.

Supreme Court.

Jan. '79, 88.   February 20, 1880.

Drew v. Peer.

Pleading—Form of action—Trespass and case—Suits against master for acts of violence by servant—Consequential injuries—Suit by husband for loss of wife's services, etc.—Tickets entitling holder to right to occupy seats in a theatre—Practice.

When an act of violence is committed by a servant in the ordinary course of his employment, but not by the direct command nor assent of the master, case, and not trespass, is the proper form of action in which to recover damages against the master.

When a husband seeks to recover damages for an act of violence committed upon his wife, whereby he has lost her company and services and suffered expense for medical attendance, case is the proper form of action.

A. and his wife, persons of color, while in lawful possession of two tickets of admission and reserved seats in defendant's theatre, were refused admission and forcibly ejected from the building by defendant's employés. More than two years afterwards A. brought an action of trespass on the case to recover damages:

Held, that this action was in the proper form to recover the price of the tickets and the loss occasioned the plaintiff by his wife's illness, including all expenses which he was put to in consequence, these being consequential and not direct injuries.

Held, also, where, in the absence of any regulation with reference to color, a colored person lawfully possessed of a ticket for a seat in a theatre for a particular performance is refused admission, the proprietor is liable in damages therefor.

Semble (per STERRETT, J.). A ticket to a reserved seat in a theatre confers more than a revocable license and partakes more of the nature of a lease, entitling the holder to peaceable ingress and egress, and exclusive possession of the seat during the designated performance.

It is not error to permit counsel, after the charge of the Court, to state to the jury the specific items for which he claims damages.

Error to the Common Pleas No. 4, of Philadelphia County.

Case, by Pusey Anthony Peer against Louisa Drew. The summons issued December 2, 1876. The declaration contained one count in which it was averred that on April 16, 1874, plaintiff purchased two reserved seats and tickets of admission to the Arch Street Theatre, of which the defendant was the lessee and the proprietress; and on the evening of that day, in company with his wife, presented the tickets at the door and attempted to enter, but defendant refused them admission, "and ejected, expelled, thrust out, evicted, pushed, and shoved the said plaintiff and his said wife from the theatre into the street in front of the theatre, and with great force and violence shook and pulled about him the said plaintiff and his said wife, whereby the plaintiff has been greatly injured, and prevented from having the right of admission to the said Arch Street Theatre, and the right to be present at and see the said performances and exhibitions, and to use and enjoy the said two seats; and the said Rachel Allandesa Peer, his wife, by means of the several premises, was then and there greatly hurt, bruised, and wounded, and became and was sick, sore, lame, and disordered, and so remained and continued for a long space of time, to wit, the space of two weeks then next following, whereby he, the said plaintiff, during all that time, lost and was deprived of all the comfort, benefit, and assistance of his said wife in his domestic affairs which he might and otherwise would have had, and whereby, also, he, the said plaintiff, was forced and obliged to and did necessarily pay, lay out, and expend a large sum of money, to wit, the sum of five hundred dollars, in and about endeavoring to have her, his said wife, cured." etc.

Defendant filed a plea of "non assumpsit," which was subsequently withdrawn upon a motion being made by plaintiff to strike it off, and pleas of "not guilty" and "not guilty within two years" were filed.

At the trial, before THAYER, P. J., the evidence disclosed that on April 10, 1874, two admission tickets had been purchased by the plaintiff, who was a colored man, from a policeman, who was selling them for the benefit of the Police Centennial Fund, and, on the 13th, his wife exchanged them at the box office of the theatre for reserved seat tickets for April 16th. The agent at the office asked her whom they were for, and she replied, "Mr. Peer and family." On the evening in question, the plaintiff and his wife entered the street door and got within a short distance of the ticket-taker at the entrance to the orchestra circle. They were then refused admission, the ticket-taker saying, "Clear them niggers out;" and the usher addressed stating, "We don't admit niggers." There was also evidence of violence used in ejecting them, and as to the nature and extent of the injuries received by plaintiff's wife in consequence; there was no evidence of there being any place in the theatre assigned for the use of colored persons, nor any evidence of regulations in regard to color, except the declarations of the employés above quoted.

The Court charged, *inter alia*, that (1) "if the injuries complained of were caused by defendant's agents in the course of the employment committed to them, she was liable in so far as they had occasioned loss and damage to the plaintiff, but, as the action was by the husband alone, only such loss as he had experienced could enter into the verdict;" (2) "there was no evidence of any regulation excluding colored persons from the theatre;" and (3) "the question of color does not arise in this case, and has nothing to do with it, there not being a scintilla of proof that there was any regulation of defendant as to colored persons." The defendant's counsel having argued to the jury from the case of the Westchester R. R. Co. *v.* Miles (5 Sm. 209), the Court further charged that (6) "if a regulation had been shown, setting apart a particular place in the theatre for colored persons, the defendant might have cited with some plausibility the case of the Westchester R. R. Co. *v.* Miles; but the law of that case does not authorize defendant to exclude colored persons from the house;" (7) "the plaintiff may recover in this case, not only for any injury to himself, but also for the loss of service to himself of his wife and any expenses to which he had been put on her account;" and (8) "if the ticket-agent had called upon any one in the crowd 'to put the niggers out,' and some ruffian had done so, the defendant would be liable."

The defendant requested the Court to charge:

(9) "The plaintiff cannot in the same suit sue for and recover damages for an assault upon or violence done to himself and also damages for an assault upon or violence done to his wife, and the jury must therefore find for the defendant." *Answer.* The plaintiff may recover for any consequential injuries caused to himself by the misconduct of the defendant's agents, and in that may be included any loss or damage which he individually has sustained in consequence of the injury to his wife.

(10) "The plaintiff cannot in one and the same suit sue for and recover damages for an assault upon or violence done to himself and for the loss of services of his wife and moneys paid or expended for her, and the jury must therefore find for the defendant." *Answer.* This is not an action for assault and battery, but an action on the case for consequential injuries alleged to have been suffered by himself in consequence of the misconduct of the defendant's agents; and for such injuries he may recover, including any loss or damage which he has individually sustained in consequence of the injury of his wife.

(11) "The plaintiff cannot in this action recover more than the price of the tickets which he purchased and interest thereon; he cannot recover damages for assaults upon or violence done to the plaintiff or his wife, or for losses or injuries resulting therefrom." *Answer.* There is no proof of any injury to the plaintiff's person, and the injury to the wife can be taken into account only so far as it shows a loss suffered by the plaintiff in consequence of it. The plaintiff cannot recover in this action for an assault and battery, but he may recover for any loss he sustained in consequence of injuries to his wife resulting from the misconduct of the defendant's agents, as well as the price of the tickets.

(12) "The defendant had a right to exclude persons of color from her theatre; and if, upon finding that they were not permitted to enter, they refused to retire, she was authorized to compel them so to do, using no more force than was necessary for that purpose." *Refused.*

(13) "There is no evidence to show that, if any violence was done to the plaintiff or his wife, it was expressly or impliedly authorized by the defendant, and she cannot therefore be made liable for the same." *Refused.*

(14) "The defendant is not liable for any violence done by any person not authorized by her to do it; and if the jury believe that the violence, if any, to the plaintiff and his wife, sued for in this case, was done by the crowd, or by persons not authorized by her, she cannot be made liable." *Answer.* The defendant is responsible for any loss or damage suffered by plaintiff in consequence of the misconduct of the defendant's agent. It did not require an express direction to her agents to commit this injury to make her responsible. Of course she is not responsible for injuries committed by strangers which were not caused by the direction or misconduct of her own agents.

(15) "If the jury believe that the injury, if any, to the plaintiff and his wife, done in this case, was done by or at the command of a person who, though in the employment of the defendant, had no power or authority from her to do or command it, the plaintiff cannot recover." *Answer.* The principal is responsible for the misconduct of the agent in the discharge of the functions committed to him by the principal.

(16) "If the jury find that the violence, if any, to the plaintiff and his wife, done in this case, was done by an employé of the defendant, but done without her order, direction, or knowledge, and out of the usual course of the employment of such employé, the plaintiff cannot recover." *Answer.* If the injury was committed by an agent out of the usual course of employment, the defendant was not responsible; but if the injury was committed by defendant's doorkeeper, or ticket-taker, then it was in the course of their employment.

(17) "The action in this case is barred by the statute of limitations." *Refused.*

After the charge of the Court had been given, the plaintiff's counsel proposed to send out with the jury an itemized statement in writing of the damages claimed, but, upon objections by defendant's counsel, the Court permitted plaintiff's counsel to state the several items to the jury without comment.

The defendant excepted to those portions of the charge as quoted, the answers to defendant's points above given, and the permission extended to plaintiff's counsel to state the items of his claim.

Verdict for plaintiff for $900.25 on the issue joined on the first plea, and verdict for defendant on the issue joined on the second plea, and judgment thereon. Defendant took this writ of error, assigning for error, *inter alia*, all of the matters to which exception had been taken as above.

Jas. H. Shakespeare and *James H. Heverin*, for plaintiff in error.

The purchase of tickets conferred a mere revocable license upon the plaintiff. He had originally two remedies for his wrong, either case or trespass; the former lies only for the breach of contract based upon the sale of the tickets, in which case the measure of damages would be the value of the tickets with interest.

Wood *v.* Leadbitter, 13 M. & W. 837.
McCrea *v.* Marsh, 12 Gray, 211.

The latter remedy for the force and violence, in which case, whether the force be that of the defendant directly or her agents, or the injury be to plaintiff himself or his wife, and the action for his loss occasioned by her injuries, trespass *vi et armis* is the only proper form of action.

Dolph *v.* Ferris, 7 W. & S. 367.
1 Chitty on Pl. 181 and 134.
Jones *v.* Tevis, 1 Sm. Lead. Cases, 769.

To endeavor to recover upon both grounds in the same action is a misjoinder, which can be taken advantage of on error.

1 Chitty on Pl. 205.
Savignac *v.* Roome, 6 T. R. 125.

The plaintiff cannot escape the effect of the statute of limitation by changing the form of action and suing in case for the assault.

DeHaven *v.* Bartholomew, 7 Sm. 126.

The charge was inconsistent. If there was "not a scintilla of proof of any rule excluding negroes," then the defendant's agent committed a voluntary act not required by his duty in ejecting the plaintiff and his wife, and the master is not liable.

Schick and *B. H. Brewster*, contra.

The damages sued for are consequential; case is, therefore, the proper remedy. The violence offered the wife was the *causa causans*, and the expense and loss to which the husband was thereby subjected were the *causæ causatæ*.

Wilt *v.* Vickers, 8 W. 227.
Whitcomb *v.* Barre, 37 Vt. 150.

Ream *v.* Rank, 3 S. & R. 215.
Bennett *v.* Allcott, 2 T. R. 166.

Case is always the proper remedy against the master for injuries committed by a servant.

1 Chitty on Pl. 149.

If there were a misjoinder of two causes of action it should have been taken advantage of by demurrer.

Martin *v.* Stille, 3 Wh. 337.
Burkholder *v.* Beetem, 15 Sm. 496.

The tickets conferred more than a mere revocable license.

Rerick *v.* Kern, 14 S. & R. 267.
Thompson *v.* McElarney, 1 Nor. 177.

May 3, 1880. THE COURT. The main contention of the plaintiff in error, to which several of the assignments relate, is that the action should have been trespass *vi et armis* and not case. A brief consideration of the facts upon which the action was grounded, and the nature of the damages for which compensation was claimed, will enable us to determine this question. The declaration, after setting out by way of inducement the purchase by the plaintiff of two tickets of admission to defendant's theatre, entitling the holders thereof to occupy two designated seats therein, and witness the performances and exhibitions therein given on the evening of April 16, 1874, averred in substance that he, in company with his wife, presented the tickets to the proper person to receive the same and admit them to said seats; that his demand for admission was refused, and both he and his wife were so rudely ejected from the theatre, that she was greatly injured, and her health was for a long time much impaired, whereby the plaintiff was deprived of her assistance in his domestic affairs, and was obliged to expend large sums of money in endeavoring to have her injuries cured and health restored, and thereby sustained damages, etc.

The loss of his wife's services in his domestic affairs by reason of the injuries she received, and the consequent outlay necessarily incurred in hiring others to do what she would have done, and in procuring medical attendance, etc., evidently constitute the gravamen or gist of his complaint; and it was to these matters that the testimony was mainly directed. It was not claimed that the plaintiff in error personally inflicted the injuries from which the alleged damages resulted; on the contrary, the testimony tended to prove that they were inflicted by her agents in the theatre in the course of their employment there, and the Court instructed the jury that if they so found, the plaintiff in error was liable in so far as her agents "had occasioned loss and damage to the plaintiff, but as the action was by the husband alone, only such loss as he had experienced could enter into the verdict." The facts then as claimed by the plaintiff below and supported by his testimony were found by the jury. Upon the facts so found we think there can be no doubt that the form of action was properly case; because the injuries to Mrs. Peer, from which the damages to her husband resulted, were not inflicted personally by the plaintiff in error or by her command or with her assent, but by her agents in the course of their employment. The criterion is not whether the master has given the authority to do the particular act, but whether the servant has done it in the ordinary course of his employment. In 1 Chitty on Pleading, 149, it is said: "For some torts which may prima facie appear to be forcible and immediate . . . an action on the case is the proper remedy. So, though a master may be liable under the circumstances to compensate an immediate injury committed by his servant in the course of his employment with force, yet the action against the master must in general be case, though against the servant it might for the same act be trespass." To maintain trespass *vi et armis* against the employer it must appear that the particular injury or act of trespass was done by his command or with his assent. (The Railway Company *v.* Wilt, 4 Whar. 143; Yerger *v.* Warren, 7 Casey, 319; The Allegheny Valley R. R. Co. *v.* McLain, 27 Pitts. Leg. Jour. 135.)

The action was properly in case for the further reason that the damages claimed by the plaintiff were consequential. In treating of actions of trespass by husband and wife for battery of the wife, Blackstone says, if the beating be so severe that the husband is thereby "deprived for any time of the company and assistance of his wife, the law gives him a separate remedy by action of trespass in the nature of an action upon the case for this ill usage, *per quod consortium amisit*, in which he may recover a satisfaction in damages." (3 Bl. Com. 140.) Mr. Stephen, in his treatise on the principles of pleading, says: "The action of trespass lies where a party claims damages for a trespass committed against him. A trespass is an injury committed with violence, either actual or implied; and the law will imply violence, though none is actually used, where the injury is of a *direct* and *immediate* kind, and committed on the *person* or *tangible* and corporeal property of the plaintiff." It follows from this that where damages are claimed by the husband for loss of his wife's services and for medical attendance resulting from a personal injury to her, that case is the proper form of action. The right to the services is an intangible right, and therefore not the right of immediate forcible injury, such as may be inflicted on tangible or corporeal property. The principle is also recognized in Ream *v.* Rank (3 S. & R. 215), which was an action on the case for debauching the plaintiff's daughter, by which he lost her services, and was put to great expense, etc. After reviewing the authorities, it is there said that "the injury complained of does not flow directly from the act of the defendant, but consequentially, and that is the criterion between trespass and case. The injury is the loss of services occasioned by consequences flowing from the act itself."

While it is conceded by the Court that trespass has often been resorted to in similar cases, it is said in sustaining the action in that case that, "on principle, the action of case would seem to be the more appropriate remedy." This case was followed by Wilt *v.* Vickers (8 Watts, 227), in which the distinction between trespass and case was elaborately considered, and the principle contended for by the learned counsel for the defendant in error recognized.

There was no error in holding that the action was in proper form, or in submitting the case to the jury, as was done.

If there had been an improper joinder of distinct causes of action in the declaration, this should have been taken advantage of by demurrer; but there was no such misjoinder. The tickets were set out merely by way of inducement to show that the plaintiff and his wife had a right to be where they were at the time the injuries to her person were inflicted, and that as patrons of defendant's theatre they were entitled to protection from injury at the hands of her employés.

Whether the tickets conferred merely a license or something more is immaterial. If they gave only a license to enter the theatre and remain there during the performance, it is very clear that the agents of the defendant had no right to revoke it as they did and summarily eject Peer and his wife from the building in such manner as to injure her. We incline to the opinion, however, that as purchasers and holders of tickets for particular seats, they had more than a mere license. Their right was more in the nature of a lease, entitling them to peaceable ingress and egress, and exclusive possession of the designated seats during the performance on that particular evening.

It is unnecessary to notice especially the remaining assignments of error further than to say that they are not sustained. The verdict was fully justified by the evidence, and the judgment thereon should not be disturbed.

Judgment affirmed.

Opinion by STERRETT, J.

July '79, 118½. March 18, 1880.
Winton, etc., v. Little et al.

Principal and agent—Scope of authority of agent—Ratification by sufferance—Release—Judgment—Revival—Duty of creditor as against surety to revive—Surety—Discharge of—Subrogation—National bank—Power of, to take real estate security—Practice—Depositions—Form of certificate of.

Mere forbearance, however prejudicial to a surety, will not discharge him; the failure of a creditor to revive a judgment does not discharge a surety unless there was an express agreement at the time of giving the judgment that it should be kept revived for the benefit of the surety.

United States *v.* Simpson, 3 P. & W. 437, followed.

Real estate security taken by a national bank for present or future advances is valid.

Union National Bank of St. Louis *v.* Matthews, 8 Otto, 264, followed: All prior decisions of this Court in conflict therewith overruled.

In 1872 money was loaned by a bank, and a note and confession of judgment, signed also by sureties, were taken by its president; the note was made to "W., Pres't, or bearer." In 1874 W. gave a release of liens, signed "W., President," to enable the principal debtor to sell part of his land. In 1876 the note not having been paid, execution was issued against the sureties, was enjoined, and an issue was framed and tried in 1879 between "W., President of the Bank," etc., and the sureties, but as if the bank were the real party in interest. W. had negotiated the loan, done all the business respecting it, and, by sufferance of the bank, the judgment stood in his name:

Held, that the long acquiescence in the acts of W. constituted a ratification of them, and that the bank was bound by the release given by W.

Depositions were taken, in obedience to a rule of Court, in the presence of the parties, and the witnesses were cross-examined. The certificate of the justice read: "I certify that the above witnesses were duly qualified and examined at the time and place stated in the caption before me." Their admissibility was objected to on the ground that the certificate was improper in not reciting that they were reduced to writing by the justice, nor that they were subscribed in his presence by the parties;

Held (sustaining the ruling of the Court below), that it is to be presumed that the depositions were properly reduced to writing and subscribed by the witnesses until the contrary is shown, and that they were therefore properly received; but

Held, further, that the plaintiff in error is to be confined to the objections made in the Court below, and not having then objected to the absence of the signature to one of the depositions, could not claim for that defect consideration here.

Error to the Common Pleas of Susquehanna County.

Issue framed on an opened judgment, wherein J. S. Little, H. P. Little, and H. P. Little, executor of Mary Little, were judgment debtors and plaintiffs in the issue, and W. W. Winton, President of the Second National Bank of Scranton, was defendant. The facts were as follows:—

On December 2, 1872, J. S. Little, being indebted to the bank, applied to its President, Mr. Winton, for a loan to pay this and other indebtedness, and gave his note payable one year after date to "W. W. Winton, President, or bearer," for $4400. To the note was added a confession of judgment, etc., and the whole was signed also by H. P. Little and Mary Little. The bank passed $4000 to the credit of J. S. Little, and entered judgment in the counties where the lands of the principal debtor and sureties would be respectively bound. The note not being paid at maturity, a fi. fa. issued against the real estate of the sureties, whereupon they made affidavit that the plaintiff had released land of sufficient value to pay the judgment without their consent. Thereupon the sheriff was enjoined, and, Mary Little having in the mean time died, this issue was framed with the substitution of her executor. A supplemental affidavit alleged that in 1876 Little, the principal debtor, had passed into bankruptcy, and that his assignee had in his hands about $800 to be applied to the payment of the judgment; that Little had other real estate; that he had paid certain sums not credited in the judgment, and that without their knowledge or consent the defendant in the issue had made a valid agreement, and upon consideration, with Little, to extend the payment of the judgment for the term of one year.

A second supplemental affidavit averred that the defendant had negligently suffered the lien of the judgment to expire; and that, upon application of the assignee to the Court of Bankruptcy, certain lands of the bankrupt had been sold under order of Court divesting the liens of the judgment confessed to the defendant, but subject to other liens, and that the defendant had negligently permitted the order to be made without opposition.

The issue was tried at April Term, 1879, upon the theory that the money given in consideration of the note and judgment was loaned by the bank, and that notwithstanding the face of the record, the bank was the real party in interest.

Upon the trial, before WALTER, P. J., the defendant objected to the filing of the second supplemental affidavit of defence, and the enlarging of the issue, on the ground that (1) the facts afforded no defense, and (2) Mary Little had died since the framing of the issues. Objection overruled; exception. (1st assignment of error.)

The plaintiffs proposed to prove that an arrangement was made between Winton, acting for the bank, and J. S. Little to release certain real estate owned by Little from the lien of the judgment, and that, in pursuance of that arrangement, a written release was secured of certain property, and was filed of record in the cause; they did not propose to show that the directors passed a written resolution authorizing this release, but that upon the faith of the release a portion of the property was sold, and that it was procured for the purpose of enabling the plaintiff to sell, and that he did sell and used this release for the purpose of showing that there was no judgment upon the property; that it was put upon the records of the Court and stood there for five years; that no act was done in any manner by the directors affecting it or repudiating it.

The release was signed "W. W. Winton, President." It did not appear in the offer that the bank, or any other officer thereof, knew of the release, nor that any note of it was made on the judgment docket. Objected to; especially that it does not purport to be a release by the Second National Bank of Scranton; that it purports to be a sealed release and is not sealed by the corporation; that there is no authority shown, or proposed to be shown, from the directors to W. W. Winton, to sign or seal this paper release, or any other release; or to give any release to J. S. Little releasing the lien of the judgment. Objections overruled; exception. (2d assignment of error.)

The plaintiffs offered in evidence depositions of Mary Little, deceased, and of H. P. Little, taken before a justice of the peace upon rule and notice. The certificate of the justice read: "I certify that the above witnesses were duly qualified and examined at the time and place stated in the caption before me." Objected to on the ground that the certificate is improper in not reciting that they were reduced to writing by the justice, nor that they were subscribed in his presence by the parties. Objection overruled, because they were taken in the presence of both parties and had been on file. Exception. (3d assignment of error.)

The Court charged the jury, *inter alia*, as follows: "But it is alleged that this was given to a national bank for the security of money to be advanced. We propose to submit to you as a question of fact whether it was given as security for advances to be made. Then, if you find that this was a national bank (and we shall have to take the party itself as it puts itself upon the record, and puts itself into this Court, claiming to be such), and if you further find that this judgment was given as security for money to be advanced or loaned in the future to J. S. Little, then the judgment would be void as against those sureties, and there can be no recovery in this case in favor of the plaintiff in the judgment. If, however, it was given in part for debts accrued and due from Little to the bank, and in part for loans to be advanced to him afterwards, then you will ascertain how much was due from Little to the bank at the time this judgment note was given, to wit: the 2d of December, 1872, because that part which was actually due from Little to the bank at that time was a proper subject matter to be secured by a mortgage or judgment note under the law of the United States authorizing the organization and management of national banks, under the law which is particularly known as the National Bank Law. The law makes the distinction between debts accrued and debts to be created, or loans to be effected. That distinction is attempted to be made here as between a mortgage and a judgment. A judgment, it is said, might have accrued and not be entered up. But we will leave to you as a question of fact, under all the evidence, whether it was in contemplation of the parties at the time to give that judgment as security for money already loaned and for money to be loaned, or for the security that the judgment would afford the bank by reason of the lien it would have upon this real estate. If that was the ground or basis of that contract and the foundation of that transaction, then it was taking security upon real estate for loans to be made afterwards, that is if you find the fact to be that Little did not owe them the actual amount of $4000; and the law does not permit the taking of security upon real estate by national banks as regards advances to be made subsequently. If you arrive at the conclusion that this note was given in part for money due and in part for money to be loaned afterward, it will be necessary for you to ascertain the amount that was actually due to the bank when that note was given and take that part and compute the interest on it up to the time these various payments were made, deduct the payments from the amount of the principal with interest added, and ascertain whether there is any balance due, and if so how much, to the plaintiff in the judgment." (4th and 5th assignments of error.)

"You have heard the evidence in regard to the release which has been referred to, and we propose to submit to you as a question of fact whether that release was executed properly. That is, whether it was made properly by W. W. Winton as president of that bank, with the approval of or subsequent ratification by the bank itself." (6th assignment of error.)

"You will consider them all, and ascertain whether there is in the evidence sufficient to warrant you in the conclusion that W. W. Winton acted as the president of that bank by the authority or approval or consent of the bank in that matter, and in connection with that you will take into consideration the fact that they had a judgment upon the records of this Court, placed there by themselves, and they could be reasonably expected in law to know the condition of their own judgment as it showed upon the record." (7th assignment of error.)

"If you find that that release was made by Winton with proper authority, or proper approval, then you will deduct from this judgment the value of so much land as was released as established by the evidence." (8th assignment of error.)

"We have instructed you that you will ascertain whether the judgment was valid under the Act of Congress, and whether it was in whole or in part a security for loans to be effected thereafter; and to the extent that it was given for debts of J. S. Little to the bank, existing at the time, it was a good and valid judgment up to the time the release was executed; and at that time you will ascertain the value of the property released and deduct it from the amount of the judgment and interest up to that time, deducting the payments that are specified here—two $400 payments and one of $869.60, and so make your computation in regard to the amount." (16th assignment of error.)

The plaintiffs presented the following points to the Court:—

(1) If the jury believe that the judgment in this case was given to secure future advances to be made to the principal debtor, J. S. Little, by the Second National Bank of Scranton, the judgment was absolutely void and the plaintiff cannot recover. (2) If the judgment in this case was given in part to secure future advances to be made to J. S. Little, and in part to secure the payment of a debt already due the bank by J. S. Little, the judgment is void as to the part given to secure such future advances, and as to that part the plaintiff cannot recover. *Answer.* "You will perceive that this submits questions of fact which we have already submitted to you and have virtually answered these two points in our general charge. We now, however, affirm these propositions with the qualification that it is for you to ascertain from the evidence whether these facts are established." (9th and 10th assignments of error.)

The defendant presented the following points:
(5) "That the sureties having shown no authority in W. W. Winton to execute the release of the lien of this judgment, the same is not valid and binding upon the plaintiffs in the judgment and does not operate to release the sureties unless the act was ratified by the plaintiffs subsequently." *Answer.* We decline this proposition, and leave it with such suggestions and instructions as we have already given you upon that point. (11th assignment of error.)

(6) "That there can be no ratification of an act of an agent of which the principal has no knowledge, and the mere fact of filing a paper purporting to be a release in the Common Pleas docket of a county distant from the place of business of a bank is no evidence of notice to the bank." *Answer.* This proposition we cannot affirm. The bank is the plaintiff in this judgment, and is bound to understand the situation of its own record and its own claims. It would be a natural presumption that bankers are pretty sharp ordinarily in attending to their business, and would hardly allow a record to stand with a release of land which would be subject to the lien of the judgment for a period of four or five years filed in the case in which they held their judgment. Besides that, we have the evidence of the fact that the release was executed at the bank by Mr. Winton, and was done in the same manner and between the same persons that the original loan was negotiated, and the note given was signed in the same manner and made payable to W. W. Winton, President, or "Pres't," which signifies President, and that the lease was filed and executed by the parties under these circumstances. (12th assignment of error.)

(8) "That the release in evidence is not the release of the defendants in the issue, and they are not bound by it." *Answer.* We will have to decline that proposition. We have left it to you as a question of fact under the evidence whether it is the act of the defendants, or ratified or approved by them. (13th assignment of error.)

(9) "That the failure of a creditor to revive a judgment does not discharge a surety unless there has been an express agreement at the time of signing the note or giving the judgment that the same should be kept revived for the benefit of such surety, and there is no evidence of such agreement on the part of the defendants in the issue with the sureties or either of them, and upon this point the verdict must be for the defendants in the issue." *Answer.* We decline that proposition, with the qualification that a creditor could not release property that was bound by the judgment without releasing the sureties. If he could not do it by a direct act, he certainly could not do it by so negligently looking after the security of the principal as to let his property slip out from the lien of the judgment and then look to the surety for it. (14th assignment of error.)

(11) "That upon the whole evidence the defendants in this issue are entitled to recover the amount of the judgment less the two payments of $400 each and the sum of $869.60 received from W. T. Moxley, assignee." *Answer.* We cannot, of course, affirm that proposition under the instructions which we have given. (15th assignment of error.)

Verdict and judgment for H. P. Little *et al.*, defendants of record, and plaintiffs in the issue.

Winton, defendant in the issue, took this

writ, assigning for error the enlarging of the issues, the admission of the release and of the depositions, the answers to the points, and those portions of the charge quoted *supra*.

W. H. & H. C. Jessup, for the plaintiff in error.

No act of quiescence on the part of the creditor can affect his remedy against the surety.
United States *v.* Simpson, 3 P. & W. 437.
Mundorff *v.* Singer, 5 W. 172.
Schoonover *v.* Pierce, 7 WEEKLY NOTES, 93.

The president of the bank exceeded his authority in releasing.
Wharton on Agency, ¿¿ 683, 595, 687.
Patterson *v.* Moore, 10 Casey, 69.
Wilson *v.* Jennings, 3 Ohio, 528.
Moukon *v.* Bowker, 115 Mass. 36.
Holt *v.* Bacon, 25 Id. 567.
Green's Brice's Ultra Vires, 427 and note.

It is only when inquiry becomes a *duty* that a party is bound to inquire of the state of a record, and in such cases only is he bound to know what the record discloses. In this case there was no obligation upon the plaintiff after it had entered its judgments properly in the proper court, to make any inquiry whatever as to any unauthorized or unknown acts of its agents or others—and the docket was no notice of any such acts. A debtor is bound to seek out and pay his creditor, but when a judgment is entered on his note he may still pay his creditor wherever he finds him, without regard to any number of assignments of the judgment duly filed on the record of which he has not received actual notice.
Henry *v.* Brothers, 12 W. 72.
Bury *v.* Hartman, 4 S. & R. 178.

The certificate of the justice is informal and improper. H. P. Little's deposition is not even signed by him.

A national bank can lawfully take real estate security for a present or future advance.
Union National Bank *v.* Matthews, 8 Otto, 621.
Silver Lake Bank *v.* North, 4 Johns. Ch. 370.

H. M. Hannah (with whom were *D. Hannah* and *McCollum & Watson*), for the defendants in error.

If a creditor, by any valid contract, give time to his debtor, or by arrangement ties up his hands so that he cannot immediately proceed against the principal, the surety is discharged.
Clippinger *v.* Creps, 2 W. 45.
Miller *v.* Stem, 2 Jones, 383.
Sawyers *v.* Hicks, 6 W. 76.
Henderson *v.* Ardery, 12 C. 449.
Boschert *v.* Brown, 22 Sm. 372.

The bank is not a party of record to this cause. If it were, its negligence would cause it to be bound by the release. If Winton was its agent, it was its duty to know how the security stood upon the record.

Due notice was given of the taking of the depositions, and the witnesses were cross-examined; this cures any informality in the certificate.

A national bank cannot loan money on other than personal security, and a violation of the terms of the National Bank Act will render the security void in its hands.
Fowler *v.* Scully, 22 Sm. 456.
Woods *v.* People's National Bank, 2 N. 57.

Bank *v.* Matthews (*supra*) differs from this case, for in it a note was given as personal security, and a trust deed was made as a collateral security. The Court decided that the Act was not infringed by this arrangement.

May 3, 1880. THE COURT. Whether error was committed in any ruling against the defendants is a question they have not brought here and cannot now be considered.

It can scarcely be said that the Court did not fairly and properly treat the case as if it were conceded by the parties that the judgment was owned by the Second National Bank of Scranton, incorporated and doing business under the laws of the United States. If this was error, we fail to see any reason why the bank should complain. The judgment was confessed by virtue of a warrant of attorney on a note payable to "W. W. Winton, Pres't., or bearer," and he stands as plaintiff with the words, "President of the Second National Bank of Scanton" appended to his name. If they mean nothing, he alone is the plaintiff in interest, and they may be treated as surplusage. Putting them on the record did not impose the burden of proving what they meant upon the defendants. In the absence of evidence or concession of a corporation, the judgment was Winton's, and inquiry respecting his authority to release its lien on real estate, or of the right of a national bank to take a judgment to secure future advances would be impertinent. A glance at the case as presented shows, that in fact it was tried on the theory that the note was given for money of the bank of which Winton was president, and, therefore, the assignments will be considered as if the bank has a right to be heard in their support, notwithstanding its point that there is no evidence of its incorporation.

This judgment was entered in favor of Winton on a note taken in his name in 1872. An execution was issued in 1876, and on defendants' application the writ was stayed and judgment opened. The trial was in April, 1879. During all that time the directors of the bank knew, or ought to have known, that the judgment appeared in favor of Winton and not the bank, and no move was made to put it in the bank's name. In 1874 Winton gave a release of lien to enable the principal debtor to sell and convey a part of his land. Winton negotiated the loan, and did all business respecting it. Why did the directors su.fer the judgment to stand in his name if they had not given him authority so to take it? If no such authority was given, what was the long acquiescence but a ratification? Though the appended words be sufficient notice of the claim of the bank, it would be commonly understood that it was put in Winton's name for the very purpose that he could control it as his own. The bank had a legal existence, and was capable of acting, suing, and receipting in its own name. If it chose to put the judgment in the name of another, it ought to be bound by his acts with others in dealing with it. There was no conspiracy to defraud the bank between Winton and the purchaser of the land, and if by the agent's mistaken judgment any must suffer, the loss should fall on the one that gave him power to act. It may be true as alleged, that the release does not purport to be the release of the bank, but it purports to be the release of the party to whom the note was payable, and who held the judgment. We are not convinced that error was committed in the rulings and instructions set forth in the second, sixth, seventh, eighth, eleventh, twelfth, and thirteenth assignments.

The depositions of Mary Little and H. P. Little stood as if they had just been taken and offered in evidence, no notice having been given, as provided by the rule of Court, of the filing. When offered, the plaintiff objected, "on the ground that there is no proper certificate; it does not recite that they were reduced to writing by the justice, nor that they were subscribed in his presence by the parties." Here he is confined to the objection taken in the Court below. The depositions were taken in obedience to a rule of court, in presence of the parties, the witnesses cross-examined, and we do not think the certificate fatally defective. In such cases it is presumed that the depositions were properly reduced to writing and subscribed by the witnesses in presence of the justice, until the contrary is shown. No objection was made that H. P. Little had not signed his deposition. The third assignment is not sustained.

As a proposition the plaintiff's ninth point should have been affirmed, unless refused on the ground that there was no evidence of the fact on which it was based. The answer indicates that the fact was submitted. Mere forbearance, however prejudicial to the surety, will not discharge him. This rule applies where a creditor suffers a judgment to lose its lien for want of revival against the principal debtor, and thereby subsequent creditors are enabled to take the land. (United States *v.* Simpson, 3 P. & W. 437.)

The fourteenth assignment is well taken. On the authority of the Union National Bank of St. Louis *v.* Matthews (8 Otto, 624), the instructions complained of in the fourth, fifth, ninth, tenth, and sixteenth assignments were erroneous. That case has settled that real estate security taken by a national bank for present or future advances is valid, and all conflicting decisions in the State Courts must give way. It is there said, "Our attention has been called to but a single point which requires consideration, and that is, whether the deed of trust can be enforced for the benefit of the bank." After noting that the Supreme Court of Missouri held the deed of trust to be the same thing as a mortgage, and that the loan was made on real estate security, it is held: "These things render it proper to consider the case in that aspect, and conceding them to be as claimed, the consequences insisted on by no means necessarily follow. The statute does not declare such security void. It is silent upon the subject. If Congress so meant, it would have been easy to say so, and it is hardly to be believed that this would not have been done, instead of leaving the question to be settled by the uncertain result of litigation and judicial decision. . . . The impending danger of judgment of ouster and dissolution was, we think, the check, and none other, contemplated by Congress. That has been always the punishment prescribed for the wanton violation of a charter, and it may be made to follow whenever the proper public authority shall see fit to invoke its application. A private person cannot directly or indirectly usurp this function of the government." Justice MILLER dissented, on the ground that the Act of Congress forbade national banks to take real estate security for money loaned at the time of the transaction, and such security is void in the hands of the bank. The point arises under a statute of the United States, and having been decided by the U. S. Supreme Court, the prior rulings of this Court, so far as in conflict, fall.

Judgment reversed, and *venire facias de novo* awarded.

Opinion by TRUNKEY, J.

July, 1878, 76.   February 20, 1880.

O'Byrne v. The City of Philadelphia.

Municipal liens—Tax claims—Sheriff's return to scire facias, when defective—Practice—Act of 11 March, 1846, sec. 3—Time for posting copy of the writ.

Where title is divested under statutory proceedings without notice to the owner of property, the law requires a strict observance of the statute regulating such proceedings.

To a writ of scire facias sur municipal claim for taxes, returnable to the first Monday of February, the sheriff made return. "Made known January 28, 1878, by posting a true and attested copy of the within writ on a conspicuous part of the premises herein described . . . agreeably to the Act of Assembly in such case made and provided:"

Held (reversing the judgment of the Court below), that the return was fatally defective, inasmuch as it was apparent from a return made January 28, that the copy of the writ could not have been posted on the premises for two weeks, as required by the Act of Assembly of March 11, 1846, sec. 3.

Error to the Court of Common Pleas No. 4, of Philadelphia County.

Tax claim filed by the city of Philadelphia against J. O'Byrne owner, and Emeline O'Byrne registered owner, September 8, 1877. January 19, 1878, a sci. fa. issued, returnable to the first Monday of February. The return filed was as follows:—

"Made known January 28, 1878, by posting a true and attested copy of the within writ on a conspicuous part of the premises herein described, and by advertising notice thereof twice a week for two weeks in the Philadelphia Chronicle-Herald, a daily paper, published in this city, agreeably to the Act of Assembly in such case made and provided; and nihil habet as to J. O'Byrne owner, etc., and Emeline O'Byrne registered owner."

No return day was named in the writ.

On February 23, 1878, judgment for want of an affidavit of defence was entered.

On June 6, 1878, defendants took this writ of error, assigning for error, *inter alia*, (1) that the return of the sheriff did not show that a true and attested copy of the said writ was posted on a conspicuous part of the premises for two weeks before the return day, the first Monday of February. (3) That no return day was named in the writ.

John A. Owens, for plaintiff in error.

The return of the sheriff does not comply with the Act, in showing a true and attested copy of the writ posted in a conspicuous part of the premises for two weeks *before* the return day.*

This case is governed by—

Wistar *v.* The City, 5 N. 215; S. C., 5 WEEKLY NOTES, 279.

The return day is a necessary part of the writ.

2 Brightly's T. & H.'s Practice, 285.

John S. Powell (with whom was *Pfeiffer*), contra.

The service would have been a valid one provided a copy of the writ was posted at any time prior to the return day, and the writ advertised twice a week for two weeks prior to the return day.

May 3, 1880. THE COURT. This was a scire facias on a municipal lien filed for taxes due the city. The Act of 11 March, 1846, requires such writs to be served "by posting a true and attested copy of the writ on a conspicuous part of the premises therein described, and by publishing a brief notice thereof in a daily newspaper in said county, twice a week for two weeks before the return day." The writ issued 19th January, 1878. The entry on the docket shows it was returnable on the first Monday of February, but there was an omission to insert any return day in the writ.

The sheriff made return to the writ, "made known January 28, 1878, by posting a true and attested copy of the within writ on a conspicuous part of the premises herein described, and by advertising notice thereof twice a week for two weeks in the Philadelphia Chronicle-Herald, a daily paper published in this city, agreeably to the Act of Assembly in such case made and provided, and nihil habet as to J. O'Byrne owner, etc., and Emeline O'Byrne registered owner."

This is a proceeding *in rem*. It is designed to effect a sale and divest the title of the real owner without any notice to him. Every essential requirement of the Act should be observed. The necessity is the same, whether the object be to sell for the non-payment of taxes or for a municipal claim. By no possibility could a service made on the 28th of January be two weeks before the first Monday of February. The latter day could not be later than the 7th, and counting the day of service, there were four days only in January. At most then, the service was not more than ten days "before the return day." The words, "agreeably to the Act of Assembly," do not help the service. The sufficiency of the service must be determined by the acts set forth in the return. It must state the acts which the sheriff did, and the Court, and not the officer, will determine whether those acts constitute a service according to the Act of Assembly. This service is radically defective. The title of the owner to the lot cannot thereby be divested. Without notice to the owner, land cannot be taken from him under this Act, without an observance of all its substantial requirements. This service is clearly insufficient. (Wistar *v.* The City of Philadelphia, 5 Norris, 215.)

Judgment reversed.

Opinion by MERCUR, J. GREEN, J., absent.

---

* The language of the Act referred to is as follows:—
"In the city and county of Philadelphia all writs of scire facias, on claims for taxes, municipal charges, and assessments, and for expenses of removing nuisances, shall be served by the sheriff of the said county by posting a true and attested copy of the writ on a conspicuous part of the premises therein described, and by publishing a brief notice thereof in a daily newspaper in said county twice a week for two weeks before the return day; on which service being made, the plaintiff in such suits may proceed to recover judgments, as in suits on mechanics' liens." Purd. Dig., 1089, pl. 25.

Jan. '79, 6.   Feb. 19, 1880.
In re Plan No. 166.
City of Philadelphia's Appeal.

Board of Surveyors of city of Philadelphia—Survey and regulation in city—Act of June 6, 1871, construction of—Appeal to Quarter Sessions under said Act.

Under section 1 of the Act of June 6, 1871, investing the Board of Surveyors of the city of Philadelphia with full authority to examine and finally confirm or reject all plans of surveys or revisions of plans made by direction of Councils; and section 2 of the same Act, providing that no survey or regulation, or a revision of either or both, shall be finally acted upon by the Board until after public advertisement, and that the confirmation by the Board shall be final and conclusive without appeal:

Held (reversing the judgment of the Court below), that no appeal lies from the Board of Surveyors to the Court of Quarter Sessions.

The provision for an appeal in section 3 of the Act, relates solely to the action of the Board in confirming the addition of a street to a confirmed plan.

Certiorari to the Quarter Sessions of Philadelphia County.

Certiorari by the city of Philadelphia to the decision of said Court in the matter of the appeal of A. R. Govett *et al.* from the decree of the Board of Surveyors confirming Plan 166.

In 1810 William Hamilton recorded in Philadelphia a plan of streets dedicated by him to the public; upon this plan, William Street ran for a short distance northwesterly from Woodlands Street, and then, turning an angle, ran due north. In 1862, an Act of Assembly confirmed the plans of the survey of this district; thus confirmed, Thirty-ninth Street was laid down over William Street, and corresponded to it, excepting that the west line was made straight throughout its entire course, so that the lines of the street diverged as it approached Woodlands Street, leaving a large open triangular space at the intersection of the two streets. Under resolution of May 16, 1871, Councils authorized the opening of Thirty-ninth Street; and on December 31, 1875, directed a revision of lines and grades upon Plan 166, in which were embraced the streets in question. In 1878 a decree of the Board of Surveys confirmed Plan 166, so that the west line of Thirty-ninth Street was parallel with the east line thereof throughout. Upon appeal of Govett *et al.* to the Court of Quarter Sessions, an order of Court recommitted the plan, with instructions to establish the west line of Thirty-ninth Street in conformity with the plan as it existed prior to the decree of the Board in 1878. No opinion was filed.

The city of Philadelphia took this certiorari, assigning for error (1), the action of the Court in entertaining and sustaining the appeal; (2), in instructing the Board to establish the plan as it existed prior to 1878; and (3), in recognizing the interest in the subject-matter of the appellants from the decree of the Board.

Theo. P. Matthews, Assistant City Solicitor, and *Wm. Nelson West*, City Solicitor, for the appellant.

The confirmation of the plan by the Board was conclusive, without appeal. The action of the Board was not the mere addition of a new street to an old plan, under § 3 of the Act of June 6, 1871,* but a complete revision of the plan under the authority of § 2, and was, therefore, "final and conclusive without appeal." The proviso to § 3 does not apply to the whole Act, for if so, it would destroy its purpose by submitting to lawyers the action of skilled engineers, and repeal, by implication, an emphatic declaration.

One section of an Act will not be repealed by another unless there be clear inconsistency between the two. Such is not the case here. There is perfect consistency in applying the proviso of § 3 solely to its subject matter. Under

---

* The Act of June 6, 1871, entitled "An Act relative to plans of survey and regulation in the city of Philadelphia," provides :—

SECTION 1. Be it enacted that the Board of Surveyors of the city of Philadelphia, as elected and constituted under Acts of Assembly, be and the same are hereby invested with full authority to examine, and finally confirm or reject all plans of survey or revisions of plans of the city of Philadelphia, when the same have been made by the direction of the Select and Common Councils of the said city; and for the purpose of enabling the said Boards to carry out the intent of this Act, they are hereby authorized, through their presiding officer, to administer oaths and affirmations, and hear testimony, and shall use a seal for all official papers.

SECTION 2. No plan for survey or regulation, or a revision of either or both, shall be finally acted upon by the said Board of surveyors until public advertisement shall have been made in three of the public newspapers in the city of Philadelphia, six times in each during the thirty days immediately preceding the proposed action, and that hand-bills be posted upon and throughout the area covered by the plan to be considered, giving notice of a hearing thereof for at least thirty days prior to said hearing; and that upon the confirmation of any plan of surveys and regulations by the said Board of Surveyors, the seal of the Board shall be affixed thereto, and attested by the presiding officer; said confirmation to be final and conclusive without appeal.

SECTION 3. No street shall hereafter be added to any confirmed plan of the city of Philadelphia, and called a public street, until the same shall have been approved by the Board of Surveyors as to location, width, and grades, and shall extend from street to street as a thoroughfare: *Provided*, That an appeal be taken to the Court of Quarter Sessions of the city and county of Philadelphia at any time within three months after said Board of Surveyors shall have finally confirmed any plan as aforesaid, when said Court may, after a hearing, confirm said plan as submitted, or remand it back to the Board of Surveyors for reconsideration and revision.

the Act the Court had no power to remand the plan with instructions.

The appellants from the Board have no interest in the cause. No private person is a proper party to an action involving public interests, unless he have interests which differ in kind as well as in degree from that of the rest of the public.
Flanagan v. City of Phila., 8 Phila. 110.
Heffner v. Com'th, 4 C. 108.

David W. Sellers, for the appellees.

An appeal lies from the decree of the Board.
Duhring's Appeal, 10 Phila. 181.

The appellees acquired title upon the faith of the plan as it existed at the time; the plan should, therefore, not be changed for light and trifling causes.
Paynter v. Young, 4 Phila. 154.

This Court has no power to review the action of the Court below. The proceeding is statutory, and no appeal is given.
Hughes v. Kline, 6 C. 227.
Hulseman v. Rems, 5 Wr. 396.
Richardson's Appeal, 6 C. 510.

March 1, 1880. THE COURT. Prior to the Act of June 6, 1871, the plans of survey were subject to the approval and alteration of the Court of Quarter Sessions. In this respect it is claimed, on the part of the city, that the Act of 1871 made a radical change in the law, and that such was a principal object. The first assignment of error is to the decision of the Court that an appeal could be taken from the confirmation of a plan of surveys made by the Board of Surveyors. By the first section of the Act, the Board of Surveyors are "invested with full authority to examine and finally confirm or reject all plans of surveys or revision of plans of the city of Philadelphia, when the same have been made by the direction of the Select and Common Councils of the said city;" and the second section provides for notice and hearing, "and that upon confirmation of any plan of surveys and regulations by the said Board of Surveyors, the seal of the Board shall be affixed thereto, and attested by the presiding officer; said confirmation to be final and conclusive without appeal." Stopping here, the Act is too plain for interpretation; it means but one thing, and that is expressed in direct and simple terms—there can be no appeal from the confirmation by the Board. To overthrow this enactment, it is urged that the proviso in the following section is repugnant, and, therefore, the investiture of "authority to examine and finally confirm or reject," "said confirmation to be final and conclusive without appeal," is repealed by another part of the same Act. Unless this be very clear it cannot be admitted. The third section enacts, that no street shall be added to a confirmed plan until it shall have been approved by the Board of Surveyors as to location, width, and grades—provided, that an appeal may be taken to the Court of Quarter Sessions within three months after said Board shall have finally confirmed any plan as aforesaid. If there be a subject to which this proviso, giving the right of appeal, may properly refer, it cannot be extended to one expressly declared to be without that right. (City of Erie v. Bootz, 22 P. F. S. 196.) The proviso is immediately related to the enactment for adding a new street to a confirmed plan, and its application to that subject requires no forced construction. The words, "shall have finally confirmed any plan as aforesaid," may not be the most apt for designation of a plan as affected by the addition of a street, yet they can be so understood, while if referred to the "plans of survey or revision of plans," the subject of the first and second sections, an important part, which is evidently a main object of the statute, is abrogated. Every rule of interpretation demands that the statute be so construed that the whole may, if possible, stand. We are of opinion that there is no insuperable obstacle in the way of giving effect to every part of this Act, and that one of its clearly expressed intendments is, that the confirmation of a plan of survey, under the provisions of the first and second sections, shall be final.

The first assignment being sustained, the points presented in the others are not in the case.

Order of July 11, 1878, reversed, and the record remitted.

Opinion by TRUNKEY, J. GREEN, J., absent.

Jan. '80, 327.   March 18, 1880.

Kepner's Appeal.

Errors and appeals—What is not subject to review by Supreme Court—Refusal of Common Pleas to open decree, not assignable for error—Laches in bringing appeal—Divorce.

The refusal of a Court of Common Pleas to grant a rule to show cause why their decree of divorce should not be revoked is not the subject of review by appeal to the Supreme Court.

Appeal from the Common Pleas of Schuylkill County.

Libel in divorce, by Sophia Kepner, etc., against Samuel K. M. Kepner.

On January 25, 1869, sur petition of Sophia Kepner, a subpœna in divorce was issued and returned "non est inventus;" an *alias* subpœna was similarly returned, and publication was made, notifying the respondent to appear to September Term, 1869. An examiner was appointed, ex parte depositions were taken, and on September 6, 1869, a divorce was decreed.

On May 5, 1879, the respondent presented his affidavit and petition praying for a rule to show cause why the decree should not be revoked. On May 19 the Court refused the rule on the ground that the respondent had waited too long to make his application. On August 25, 1879, the respondent presented an additional petition averring that he had first received information of the divorce in September, 1878, and that he had immediately, upon ascertaining the truth of the information, given instructions for the institution of proceedings to set aside the decree.

Upon the argument counsel for the respondent claimed that the decree was void for the want of jurisdiction; and that it was not justified by the ex parte depositions, the libellant not having proved that she was a citizen of Pennsylvania, or resided therein for one year previous to the filing of her petition.

The Court refused the rule, whereupon the respondent took this appeal, assigning for error the refusal of the Court to grant the rule, the appointment of an examiner, and the decree of divorce before the return of notice of publication, and the failure to dismiss the libel for want of jurisdiction.

Upon the calling of the case for argument in the Supreme Court, the appellee's counsel moved to quash the appeal on the ground that the refusal of the Court to grant a rule to show cause why the decree should not be revoked is a discretionary act, and not subject to review. The motion was filed at bar.

B. Bryson McCool, for the appellant.

A refusal to grant a rehearing on after-discovered facts is reviewable.

Keim's Appeal, 3 C. 44. per BLACK, C. J.

The Court acted beyond its authority in prematurely appointing an examiner and entering a decree. The Act of March 13, 1815, § 3, provides that further proceeding shall be had *at* the term to which the order of publication is returnable.

Hoffman *v.* Hoffman, 6 C. 417.

There was no proof of citizenship in Pennsylvania, and consequently no jurisdiction.

McDermott's Appeal, 8 W. & S. 256.
Steel *v.* Smith, 7 Id. 447.
Hollister *v.* Hollister, 6 B. 451.
Colvin *v.* Reed, 5 Sm. 375.
Reel *v.* Elder, 12 Id. 308.
Ralston *v.* Ralston, 7 WEEKLY NOTES, 572.

G. R. Kaercher (with him *S. H. Kaercher*) for appellee.

Under the provisions of the Act of 1815 (1 Purd. Dig. 510, § 12), the Court had jurisdiction; but, conceding that this was not so, no appeal lies more than one year after the pronouncing of the decree of divorce.

Act of Feb. 8, 1819, §§ 1, 1 Purd. Dig. 511, § 17.

The refusal of the Court to vacate its orders and judgments is not reviewable.

White *v.* Leeds, 1 Sm. 189.
Kalbach *v.* Fisher, 1 R. 323.
Kellogg *v.* Krauser, 14 S. & R. 144.
Skidmore *v.* Bradford, 4 B. 296.
Nice *v.* Bowman, 6 W. 26.
McKee *v.* Sanford, 1 C. 105.
Bunce *v.* Wightman, 5 Id. 335.
Breden *v.* Gilliland, 17 Sm. 34.
Gamble *v.* Woods, 3 Id. 160.

March 31, 1880. THE COURT. The decree below was entered September 6, 1869. The appeal is clearly barred by lapse of time. The refusal of the Court, May 19, 1879, and again February 14, 1880, to grant a rule to show cause why the decree should not be revoked was clearly not the subject of review by appeal to this Court. We cannot in this way decide whether the Court had jurisdiction to enter the original decree, or did so upon sufficient evidence.

Appeal quashed.

PER CURIAM.

Jan. '79, 110.   Jan. 28, 1880.

Brez v. Warner.

Principal and Surety—Contract—Construction of—Variation of—Where surety discharged.

Where a surety became bound, in a sum not to exceed five thousand dollars, for the faithful performance of all the covenants in an agreement involving the consignment of goods, "such consignments not to exceed in amount the sum of five thousand dollars at any one time, and to be continued from time to time as sales were made," and it appeared that several consignments were made exceeding the stipulated amount:

Held, that this was such a variance of the terms of the contract that the surety was discharged, and that the consignors were not entitled to recover from him the amount of $2331, being the value of goods not accounted for by the consignees according to the terms of the agreement.

Error to the Common Pleas No. 1, of Philadelphia County.

Covenant, by John D. Brez, executor of Paul Brez, deceased, against Henry Warner, to recover the amount of $2331, being the value of certain watches unaccounted for, which had been consigned by said Paul A. Brez to the firm of Stellwagen & Warner, under an agreement under seal, dated July 3, 1875, for the faithful performance of which agreement defendant became bound as surety for said firm. Pleas, non est factum, payment, set-off, with leave, etc. Also a special plea, setting up a violation on the part of the plaintiff of the agreement, in consigning watches to the said firm in excess of the limitation stipulated in said agreement.

On the trial, before BIDDLE, J., plaintiff put in evidence the agreement between Brez and Stellwagen & Warner, the terms of which are fully set forth in the opinion of this Court, and also the following agreement of suretyship:—

"In consideration of the execution of the foregoing agreement, and of the sum of one dollar to me in hand paid, the receipt whereof is hereby acknowledged, I, Henry Warner, of the city of Philadelphia, for myself, my heirs, executors, and administrators, do hereby covenant and agree to and with Paul A. Brez, of the city of New York, his heirs, executors, and administrators, that if all the obligations and conditions recited in the foregoing agreement, entered into by and between Paul A. Brez and the said George W. Warner and Edward Stellwagen, shall not be faithfully and well performed on the part of the said Edward Stellwagen and George W. Warner, that then immediate recourse may be had and made to me as surety for the said Edward Stellwagen and George W. Warner, in the amount of the damages arising from any breach of the obligations and conditions of said agreement, during the period of one year from the date hereof, and said amount not to exceed the sum of five thousand dollars. Witness my hand and seal, this third day of July, Anno Domini one thousand eight hundred and seventy-five (1875).

(Signed)   HENRY WARNER. [SEAL.]"

Plaintiff then testified that there remained $2231 worth of watches unaccounted for by the said firm; also that the first consignment under the said agreement amounted in value to $5080.43; and further as follows: "At certain times I believe that consignments exceeded $5000. We kept as near $5000 as our business would allow, and their (the firm) demands required; don't think quite as high as $10,000;" and then closed.

The Court thereupon, on motion, entered a nonsuit, which the Court in banc subsequently refused to take off. The plaintiff thereupon took this writ, assigning for error the action of the Court.

Francis E. Brewster (with him *F. Carroll Brewster*), for plaintiff in error.

The intention of defendant was simply to limit his liability to $5000. He is not called upon to pay more than this amount. The plaintiff should therefore recover.

Mason *v.* Pritchard, 12 East, 227.
Bingham *v.* Corbitt, 34 L. J. (N. S.) Q. B. 37.
Thornton *v.* McKewan, 32 L. J. (N. S.) Ch. 69.
Lanrie *v.* Schoefield, 38 L. J. (N. S.) C. P. 290.
Wood *v.* Priestner, 36 L. J. (N. S.) Ex. 127.
Ellis *v.* Emanuel, 46 L. J. (N. S.) C. L. R. 25.
Holme *v.* Brunskell, 47 L. J. (N. S.) C. L. R. 610.

A. L. Hennershotz, for defendant in error.

The forwarding of consignments to an amount beyond that stipulated in the agreement, was such a variation of the original contract as to discharge the surety.

Birdsall *v.* Heacock, 18 Am. L. Reg. 755.
U. S. *v.* Simpson, 3 P. & W. 437.
Dundas *v.* Sterling, 4 Barr, 73.

Bedford *v.* Jones, 5 Leg. Gaz. 230.
Baker *v.* Rand, 13 Barb. 152.
Edmondston *v.* Drake, 5 Pet. 624.
Bonar *v.* McDonald, 3 H. L. C. 226.

Feb. 16, 1880. THE COURT. It is agreed that any material variation of a contract with the principal discharges the surety. Whether such variation was made without consent of the surety is the question here.

Brez agreed to furnish and send to Stellwagen & Warner watches, and parts thereof, subject to recall at any time, and to be accounted for at invoice prices, they to keep up fire insurance for the full amount—the loss, if any, payable to Brez—and bear all losses on the goods beyond those covered by the insurance. They contracted to guarantee all sales of such goods, make return thereof on the day the same were made, transmit to Brez the money or notes as received, pay the notes at maturity should the makers fail to do so, and confine their purchases and sales as to watches and parts thereof, to the goods consigned to them by Brez. The first stipulation in the contract is, "Such consignments are not to exceed in amount the sum of five thousand dollars at any one time, and are to be continued from time to time as sales are made." This is a positive limit of the stock to be carried by the consignees. When they should return sales, the contract authorized a consignment, and so from time to time, always keeping within the stipulated limit. The defendant bound himself for the faithful performance of all their covenants in said agreement, limiting his liability within $5000. He saw that, at some time, they might have a stock on hand worth $5000, and be indebted in a large sum for goods returned sold; hence the prudent limit of his liability. His suretyship was for performance of the contract as written, not of one when the consignments might be indefinitely large, beyond a fixed sum, with increased expenses, increased risks of sales on credit, causing the consignees to founder, though they may have had capacity to conduct a small business.

The first consignment was made July 9, 1875, and invoiced $5080.43; and before a sale was returned, another consignment was made, invoicing $159. John D. Brez, under whose supervision the goods were shipped, and who knew his father's business, testified that he believed the consignments exceeded $5000, but did not think quite as high as $10,000. Thus the plaintiff proved his case. By the terms of the contract, the consignees were to keep the stock insured for its full value, and the larger the stock the greater the cost of insurance—a direct and certain increased burden on the consignees. It was competent for the parties to vary the contract as they pleased; but if they did, the surety was discharged. The consignor cannot hold the surety if he varied the contract so as to impose an additional risk.

We are of opinion that the learned Judge was right in his construction of the contract.

Judgment affirmed.

Opinion by TRUNKEY, J. PAXSON, J., absent.

Common Pleas—Law.

C. P. No. 2. July 10, 1880.
Davis v. Mowbray.

Practice—Act of June 11, 1879, relative to examination of alleged fraudulent debtors—Affidavit in words of Act sufficient—When proceedings under this Act are unauthorised—If the record at time of filing the affidavit indicates a satisfaction of the judgment the proceedings will be quashed.

Rule to quash proceedings on affidavit filed under Act of June 11, 1879 (P. L. 129), relative to examination of alleged fraudulent debtors.

The docket entries showed a final judgment, the issuing of a fi. fa. and a return of nulla bona thereon, the issuing of an alias fi. fa., and a return of "levied and condemned" thereon, and the issuing of a vend. ex., and no return thereof; also the filing of an affidavit under the Act of June 11, 1879.

The material part of the affidavit was: "That deponent has reason to believe, and does in fact believe, that Andrew Mowbray, the above-named judgment debtor, has property, stocks, etc., which he fraudulently conceals and refuses to apply to the payment of his debts."

The affidavit was filed June 15, 1880, a subpœna taken out and two meetings had before a commissioner of this Court, when this rule was taken. Counsel for defendant, before the examination was commenced, had the commissioner note his objection to the proceeding on account of the state of the record.

B. H. Lowry, for the rule.

The affidavit filed is insufficient because it does not set out that an execution has been issued and a return of nulla bona had thereon ; and because it does not set out the facts on which the plaintiff's belief is based.

Horstman *v.* Kaufman, 8 WEEKLY NOTES, 73.
Troubat & Haly, § 361, and cases cited.
Cox *v.* Walton, 8 WEEKLY NOTES, 360.
Baltz *v.* Allyn, Id. 326.

[MITCHELL, J. We have decided that an affidavit in the words of the Act is sufficient.]

The proceedings should be quashed, because the Court has made no order upon the affidavit filed. Not only should an order allowing the subpœna be made, but a special commissioner should be appointed.

Loewi *v.* Haedrich, 8 WEEKLY NOTES, 70.
Eyster *v.* Schmole, Id. 470.
Cox *v.* Walton, *supra.*

The Act allowed an examination in cases where there is a final judgment "upon which an execution has been issued, and a return made by the sheriff of the proper county that no property can be found out of which the said execution can be satisfied." The record here is not in the condition contemplated by the Act.

J. H. Gendell, contra, suggested that the Court order that the writ of vend. ex. be returned, and that upon the return of the same, as it would show a sale for nominal sums, the rule be discharged.

THE COURT. We think we cannot go beyond the record ; that shows a presumptive satisfaction of the judgment, and we think that the Legislature did not mean that the plaintiff having obtained satisfaction or having the means of doing so in his power, should curiously pry into the defendant's affairs.

Rule absolute.

Oral opinion by MITCHELL, J.

C. P. No. 2. June 2, 1880.
Wilson v. Deacon.

Practice—Evidence—Matters not in the bill of particulars may be admissible on collateral questions arising during the trial.

Motion for a rule for a new trial.

Plaintiff having put his claim in evidence, the defendant proved a payment of fifty dollars, for which he claimed credit. The plaintiff then offered to show that that payment, though subsequent in date to some of the items of his present claim, was specifically appropriated at the time to another prior debt. Objection was made by the defendant that the bill of particulars did not include this prior debt, and that therefore it could not be proved for any purpose. HARE, P. J., overruled the objection and admitted the evidence.

Alexander, for defendant, moved for a new trial on this ground.

THE COURT. Rule refused.

C. P. No. 3. June 14, 1880.
Kitchen v. Stokes.

Contract—Rescission—When time is not of the essence of the contract—Agreement to pay for and take away goods within a specified time.

Rule to show cause why nonsuit should not be stricken off.

Assumpsit. The facts were as follows: Plaintiff through a broker, the agent of both parties, bought 5000 pounds of wool of defendant under a contract of which the following is a copy:—

"10 Mo. 27, 1879.

"Sold for Samuel O. Stokes & Co., to James G. Kitchen Five thousand (5000) pounds ¾ and ½ blood Ohio washed fleeces at forty-six and one-half (46½) cents nett cash, wool to be paid for when taken away and same to be done inside of thirty days. Tare actual.

Jos. W. SCULL, Broker."

On November 14, 1879, plaintiff paid for and took away 2665 pounds of said wool. The thirty days having expired November 26, 1879, defendant on the 28th of the month addressed plaintiff by letter as follows:—

" The time having expired in which you were to take the wool away, we have this day cancelled the sale."

A day or so afterwards plaintiff demanded the wool and tendered the amount agreed upon, which offer was refused. The price of wool having advanced 8½ cents per pound between October 27 and November 28, plaintiff thereupon brought this suit to recover the difference in the price upon the undelivered balance.

At the trial the Court entered a nonsuit, upon the ground that time was of the essence of the contract and defendants accordingly had the right to rescind the same as they did, on the earliest day possible after the expiration of the contract time.

Joseph de F. Junkin (with him *George Junkin*), for the rule.

Defendant had no right to rescind without previous notice.

McEachron v. Randles, 34 Barbour, 301.

The sale had been made and the property was plaintiff's subject to defendant's lien for purchase-money, and to the condition subsequent as to time of payment. If the condition had been that defendant was to deliver within thirty days, then delivery would have been a condition precedent, and if not complied with plaintiff could have rescinded and the goods would not have been his till delivery. The sale would then have been conditional. But here no delivery was necessary to perfect the sale, and every act to be done by defendant had been performed. Where the sale for an ascertained price has been consummated and the price is to be paid on or before a certain day, the seller cannot be affected by a rise or fall in the market; for if the time is suffered to go by he can charge the buyer interest and storage, or sell the goods at the buyer's risk after notice. He has a well-defined remedy, and his damages can be readily and accurately ascertained. If the sale is a perfect and complete sale of specific and ascertained chattels and the ownership and right of property in the thing sold have been transferred by the bargain to the purchaser, time is not of the essence of the contract, and the vendor cannot repudiate the sale, and revest the right of property in himself and refuse to deliver the goods at a subsequent period on tender of the price, on the ground of non-payment thereof at the time appointed.

Addison on Contracts, § 578.
Benjamin on Sales, p. 545.

When everything that the seller is to do is complete then the sale has been performed.

Addison on Contracts, § 573.
Parsons' Mercantile Law, p. 42.
Hilliard on Sales, p. 405, § 8.
Remington v. Irwin, 2 Harris, 145.
Simpson v. Crippin, 8 Law Rep. Q. B. p. 14.
Roper v. Johnson, 8 Law Rep. C. P. p. 167.
Bowes v. Shand, 2 Law Rep. App. C. 455.
Bettini v. Gye, 1 Law Rep. Q. B. 183.

David Jay Myers, Jr., contra.

The duty of plaintiff was to pay the price in manner agreed upon, and this duty was a condition precedent to delivery.

Benjamin on Sales, 2 ed. p. 661.

The rule of the common law is that a man bound to pay has no right to delay till demand made, but must pay as soon as the money is due.

Ib. p. 582.

The contract was executory, and therefore time is of the essence.

Leonard's Exrs. v. Winslow, 2 Grant, 139.
Haldeman v. Duncan, 1 Sm. 66.
Hutchinson v. Hunter, 7 Barr, 140.
Addison on Contracts, 6th Eng. ed. p. 185.
Clark v. Wright, 5 Phila. 439.

The agreement must be construed with respect to the subject matter thereof, and where the subject-matter fluctuates in value from day to day, time when mentioned is presumed to be of the essence. The burden was therefore with plaintiff to show circumstances to rebut the presumption.

Parsons on Contracts, 5 ed. vol. 2, p. 449.
Shaw v. Turnpike Co., 2 P. & W. 454.
Lester v. McDowell, 6 H. 91.
Clark v. Wright, *supra*.
Parshall's Appeal, 15 Sm. 224.

C. A. V.

June 17, 1880. THE COURT. Rule absolute.

WEEKLY NOTES OF CASES.

Vol. IX.] *THURSDAY, SEPT. 16, 1880.* [No. 4.

Supreme Court.

Jan. '78, 226.   Jan. 23, 1880.
People's Bank v. Gayley.

Bailment—Warehouse receipts—Act of Sept. 24, 1866 construed—Who may issue negotiable warehouse receipts.

In order that a receipt for goods on storage may be a warehouse receipt with the quality of negotiability, as contemplated by the Act of September 24, 1866, the person issuing such receipt must be in possession of the goods in his own right, and not merely as agent for a principal.

A pledgee of goods on storage, who has never made himself known to the bailee nor obtained possession of the goods, cannot maintain replevin against the bailee, who has parted with the goods by order of the pledgor to a *bona fide* purchaser for value before the writ of replevin issued.

A. & B. were warehousemen and lessees of a wharf, to take charge of which they employed C. D. obtained from C. a receipt showing that C. had received and held certain iron on the wharf subject to D.'s order, and then pledged the iron to E., a bank, as collateral for a loan, indorsing the receipt to E., who never notified C. or his employers. Afterwards D. fraudulently obtained a warehouse receipt from A. & B., who knew nothing of the pledge, and sold the iron to F., to whom A. & B. issued a new receipt in his own name upon surrender of the original. D. becoming insolvent before the loan was paid, E., being unable to obtain the iron from C., brought replevin against him:

Held, that E. was a mere pledgee, without possession, and could not recover.

Error to the Common Pleas No. 1, of Philadelphia County.

Replevin, by the People's Bank of Philadelphia against Andrew T. Gayley.

On the trial before BIDDLE, J., the plaintiff proved the following facts:—

On October 15, 1874, there were stored on the Callowhill Street wharf, on which there was no sign of the owner or proprietor, but of which the defendant had charge, 800 tons of iron belonging to a firm of Malin Bros., and on that day one Alexander Ervin, a confidential agent and attorney of Henry G. Morris, an iron manufacturer, came to the defendant at this wharf with an order from Malin Bros. to deliver to Henry G. Morris, or order, 300 tons of this iron; the order was sent in an envelope with a printed address as follows:—

"A. T. GAYLEY, Esq.,
"Callowhill Street Wharf,
"Delaware Avenue,
"City."

Ervin testified that he told the defendant that he had negotiated a loan on this iron, and requested him to give him a warehouse receipt, which he did, being in the following form:—

"PHILADA., Oct. 15, 1874.
"Received from Malin Bro.'s three hundred tons (300), No. 1 Nth Penn pig iron on storage, subject to the order of Henry G. Morris.   AND. T. GAYLEY."

Which in his presence he indorsed as follows:—
"A. T. GAYLEY, Esq.
"Please deliver inclosed pig iron to W. H. Taber, Esq., Cash'r, or order.   HENRY G. MORRIS,
"WM. H. TABER, Cas.   pp. ALEX. ERVIN, Att'y."

And that on October 20, on a similar order and upon similar statements, he received from Gayley and indorsed the following:—

"PHILADA., Oct. 20, 1874.
"Received from Malin Bro.'s, 250 tons No. 1 Nth Penn pig iron; 250 tons No. 2x Robbins pig iron, held subject to the order of Henry G. Morris.
"AND. T. GAYLEY."
(Indorsed.)
"Please deliver inclosed pig iron to W. H. Taber, or order.   HENRY G. MORRIS,
"pp. ALEX. ERVIN, Att'y.
"WM. H. TABER.   Oct. 20, '74."

The receipts and indorsements were put in evidence.

This loan was subsequently renewed at intervals, and had not been paid at the time of suit brought. Ervin's authority to act for Morris was at no time denied.

About June, 1875, Morris failed, and the plaintiffs then laid claim to the iron included in these receipts; the right to take possession, however, was denied by Gayley, who stated that the iron belonged to one Troutman. Plaintiffs thereupon took out this writ of replevin. The return showed 653 tons replevied, and 147 eloigned by Gayley.

The defendant himself was called on his own behalf, and his counsel made the following offers of evidence: (1) That defendant was the clerk or assistant of E. J. Etting; (2) That Etting was a warehouseman; (3) That the Callowhill Street wharf was Etting's wharf, held under a lease, on which he received goods for storage and warehousing; (4) That warehouse receipts for goods stored on that wharf were issued by Etting or his partner only; (5) That defendant had no authority to issue warehouse receipts; (6) That he had never done so to his knowledge or intention; (7) That these papers produced by plaintiff were obtained from him by Ervin to enable him to have a written memorandum of the fact that the iron bought from Malin by Morris was in fact on that wharf; (8) That at the time of giving those receipts he told Ervin that he could not give him a warehouse receipt, and if he wanted a warehouse receipt he must go to Mr. Etting, who alone could give that; (9) That it is untrue that Ervin told witness that he intended to pledge the iron to plaintiff; (10) That it is untrue that he made the indorsements on the receipts in his presence, or to his knowledge; (11) That he never heard of the pledge to the plaintiff until June, 1875, or thereabouts; (12) That in the mean time this iron was sold by Mr. Morris to Mr. Troutman, in February, for value paid, and was delivered to him; and (13) before the writ issued, or there was notice of the title of the plaintiff to either Etting, Gayley, or Troutman, Etting, the warehouseman, agreed to hold the iron for Troutman, and issue to him a warehouse receipt." Which offers were severally and collectively objected to, but the objections were overruled and exceptions granted to the plaintiffs.

Defendant's counsel further offered to prove by the same witness (15) "That it was the practice when application was made to Etting for a warehouse receipt, for Etting to ascertain what amount was there, and having issued a warehouse receipt, he notified Gayley in order that he might know the iron could no longer be delivered on the order of the depositor of the iron." Objected to; objection overruled, and exception for plaintiffs.

Defendant then gave evidence of all the facts contained in the above offers, and proved by himself, Etting, and Groome his partner, Morris, and other witnesses, that Morris had at various times kept iron stored on the wharf, and Ervin was familiar with the method of issuing the warehouse receipt for it. Morris testified, "I knew Gayley as a weighmaster, did not know him as a warehouseman." On November 18, 1874, after he had obtained the receipts already in evidence, Ervin applied for a storage receipt for the same iron at the office of Etting & Groome, who knew nothing at all of the receipts previously given, and upon this application they issued their usual warehouse receipt in the following form:—

"Storehouse, Callowhill Street wharf, Delaware Avenue.

"PHILADELPHIA, November 18, 1874.

"Received from Henry G. Morris the merchandise described below, to be held by me on monthly storage, from November 18, 1874, and to be delivered on the order of The Philadelphia Warehouse Company, only on the return of this certificate and payment of the charges.

Marks, etc.	Description of merchandise.
670 tons.	Six hundred and seventy tons No. 1 pig iron.
340 "	Three hundred and forty tons No. 2x pig iron.
140 "	One hundred and forty tons No 2. com. pig iron.
1150 tons.	

Charges:
Storage per month, 10 cts.
Labor."

On the back of this was printed a copy of the Act of Sept. 24, 1866, as amended by Act of March 28, 1870.*

On Nov. 25th following they issued a similar receipt for 120 tons. These receipts were both delivered to the Philadelphia Warehouse Company as collateral for a previously existing loan made by that company to Morris. In February, 1875, one Troutman purchased this iron from Morris, agreeing with him to pay off the loan for which it was held as collateral, and having done so he received from Ervin a bill of sale, and obtained from Etting & Groome a warehouse receipt in his own name for it.

Defendant offered in evidence (22) letter from Etting to defendant, dated November 23, 1874 (notice of the issue of a certificate for this iron), and also the warehouse receipts dated November 18, 1874, and November 25, 1874, from Etting to Philadelphia Warehouse Company. Objected to; objection overruled, and exception for plaintiffs.

The Court charged the jury, *inter alia*, as follows: "The bank alleges they hold what is called a warehouse or storage receipt, issued by Mr. Gayley to Mr. Morris, and that under our Act of Assembly this receipt is negotiable, and having come to them by assignment, the title of the property of Mr. Morris is in them.

"Well, then, gentlemen, if these are warehouse receipts, that is undoubtedly true; but are these warehouse receipts? [Before any one can issue warehouse receipts, he must be in possession of the property, that is, not simply in charge of the property.] If this were not the law we could carry on no business with any safety, unless we could perform all the duties connected with it ourselves. The porter of your store, before you got down there in the morning, the watchman of the bank, the servants of your house, could give a valid title to all your property. [In the case that I put, and which I do not think the danger of has been explained away, coal is sent to you by your coal merchant,

---

* See the Act printed in full in Purdon's Dig. 114, pl. 1, title "Bailees," and a further supplement, Act of June 13, 1874, P. L. 285, Purd. 1826, pl. 1.

whoever he is, the receipts are given by anybody, any member of your family who happens to be there, for one or two, or ten tons of coal; your servant, or your cook, or your wife, writes the name to that. Well, can it be possible, that when that goes back to your coal merchant, that he can assign that, as if you had admitted that you had had that much coal of his in your cellar, and that the man then could sue you or your cook, and when your cook came in, say for you, why I have acknowledged you have got this coal.] Her answer would be, probably, "I am cook of this house; the man came to the house, and he put this coal down in the cellar, and he says, 'now I want you to give me a memorandum that I have left that here, to show when I get home,'" and the cook then hands him this memorandum; and then if the coal merchant transfers it to somebody else, why then the cook's lawyer would come here, and would say, "why you don't mean to say that you want to hold this woman responsible; this is not a warehouse receipt that is negotiable, for you cannot assign this; admitting that this act was done, and the coal was put down in the cellar, this is not a warehouse receipt under the law, and is not assignable;" and that, in fact, is exactly what is stated here in the present case. . . . . [As my opinion is, this man had no such possession of this wharf under the evidence as would justify him to give what the law declares to be a warehouse receipt."]

The plaintiffs presented the following points for the jury:—

First. That the papers in evidence, signed A. T. Gayley, and dated October 15 and 20, 1874, vested in plaintiffs on delivery the title to the property therein described. *Answer.* Well, that is so, gentlemen.

Second. Said papers are receipts within the meaning and purview of the Act of Assembly, entitled, etc., being the Warehouse Act. *Answer.* (28) That, I think, is not the case, gentlemen. I say that they are not receipts within the meaning and purview of that law.

Third. Said papers are negotiable under said Act. *Answer.* (29) I do not think that they are.

Fifth. The title of the plaintiffs being good against Gayley and Morris, it continued, and continues good against all persons whomsoever, unless divested "apart from legal process," as a consequence of some illegal act of plaintiffs, or by reason of some unlawful act of commission or omission of plaintiffs. *Answer.* (30) I do not think, as I have said to you, that that is so, if subsequently to that they failed to give notice of their having this pledge to this property, and it was in good faith transferred to another by a warehouse receipt, that would divest their property.

Sixth. The issue of a warehouse receipt by Etting cannot, *per se*, divest the title of plaintiffs, or give title to any one against plaintiffs. *Answer.* (31) If the warehouse receipt was issued in good faith, it would have that effect.

Seventh. Under the evidence in the cause, the issue of a warehouse receipt to Troutman, or any other person, could not divest the title of plaintiffs. *Answer.* (32) I say that it could.

Ninth. The alleged title of Troutman, given in evidence, is no defence under the pleas of *non cepit, non detinet*, and no property in plaintiffs. *Answer.* (34) I think that it is.

The defendants requested the Court to charge, *inter alia*, as follows:—

Second. The documents in question are not warehouse receipts. *Answer.* (38) In my opinion they are not.

Third. The plaintiffs, to entitle them to claim under those papers as warehouse receipts, must prove that Gayley was a warehouseman, and as such entrusted with the iron. Not having done this, they cannot assert title to the iron by the endorsement and delivery of the receipts. *Answer.* (39) That, as a matter of law, I instruct you to be so.

Sixth. Unless the plaintiff had under its title as pledgee a right to the possession of the iron, at the date of its writ, June 18, 1875, it is not entitled to recover in this suit, which is a replevin for these goods. *Answer.* (40) That is so.

Seventh. If Mr. Morris, the owner of the iron, subsequent to the pledge to the plaintiffs, sold the iron to Troutman, and Etting agreed to hold the iron for Troutman, that was a delivery to Troutman, equivalent to an actual delivery and removal of the same by him. *Answer.* (41) That is so, gentlemen.

Eighth. If the wharf on which the iron was and is still stored, was the wharf of Etting, and the defendant, Gayley, was merely his servant, and the iron was subsequently sold by Morris to Troutman, and Etting issued to him a warehouse receipt, and Troutman was a *bona fide* purchaser for value without notice of the prior pledge by Morris to the bank, then the title of the bank was divested by that sale and delivery to Troutman, and the plaintiff cannot recover. *Answer.* (42) That I think to be so.

Ninth. If the jury should find that Gayley had notice of the pledge to the bank, the plaintiffs cannot recover in this action, if Troutman bought the iron after that pledge, and, without notice of the pledge, paid for it. For the plaintiffs' right depends on title, and that was divested by the sale to Troutman *bona fide*, and for value without notice. *Answer.* (43) I affirm this point.

Verdict for defendant, and judgment thereon. The plaintiffs took this writ of error, assigning for error, *inter alia*, as numbered, the admission of the evidence to which exception was taken, those portions of the charge inclosed in brackets, and the answers of the Court below to both plaintiffs' and defendant's points as quoted and numbered.

F. C. Brewster and *Chas. Gilpin*, for plaintiffs in error.

The defendant held himself out to the world as a warehouseman; he gave receipts as a warehouseman, and ought not to have been permitted to deny the validity of the receipts which he himself issued, when they are in the hands of an innocent third party who has been misled by him. It is true that a warehouseman can only be required to return the goods actually delivered to him, but he cannot deny to third parties, in possession of his receipt, the facts stated thereon, which ought to have been within his knowledge; neither can he, under such circumstances, deny his authority to issue such a receipt.

Hale *v.* Milwaukee Dock Co., 29 Wis. 482.

The assignment of the receipt operated to pass the title to the property, and the form of the receipt is immaterial.

Hanson *v.* Meyer, 2 Tudor's Ld. C. 819, and note.
Gibson *v.* Stevens, 8 How. 398.
Dows *v.* Nat. Ex. Bank, 1 Otto, 618.
Shepherd *v.* Harrison, 5 H. L. R. 120.
Enlow *v.* Klein, 29 Sm. 488.
First Nat. Bk. *v.* Dearborn, 115 Mass. 219.
Millar *v.* Savings Ins., 3 W. N. C. 480.

The offer to show title in a third person, acquired after our title had vested, and when the Act expressly says that no second receipt for the same goods shall be issued while the first is outstanding, was clearly error. If the defendant were an agent of Etting & Groome, and had acted outside the terms of his power, they cannot now deny his authority, for they placed him in the position to mislead innocent purchasers of his receipts.

Griswold *v.* Haven, 11 Sm. (N. Y.) 598.
Comly *v.* McBridge, 4 Wh. 526.

Plaintiffs' title vested in 1874, and never having been divested by their own act or judicial process, Troutman's subsequently acquired claim to title must fail.

Quinn *v.* Davis, 28 Sm. 18.
Davis *v.* Bigler, 12 Sm. 247.
Second Nat. Bk. *v.* Walbridge, 19 Ohio S. R. 419.
Martin *v.* Creditors, 14 La. Ann. 393.

W. Wynne Wister, Jr., and *R. C. McMurtrie*, contra.

If, at the time the writ issued, the title to this iron was not in the plaintiffs, then they can in no case recover.

Lester *v.* McDowell, 6 H. 91.
Stanley *v.* Neale, 98 Mass. 343.
Collins *v.* Evans, 15 Pick. 63.

Plaintiffs never had the possession; they had only a pledge as security for a loan, and the pledger and owner subsequently actually sold and delivered the iron to a *bona fide* purchaser without notice, which destroyed the ownership of the pledgee.

Clemson *v.* Davidson, 5 Binn. 392.
Pierce *v.* Stevens, 30 Me. 184.
Warner *v.* Matthews, 18 Ill. 83.
Curd *v.* Wunder, 5 Ohio St. 92.
Boyle *v.* Rankin, 10 H. 168.
Winslow, Lanier & Co. *v.* Leonard, 12 H. 14.

These receipts could pass no title unless they were actual statutory warehouse receipts; in all ordinary cases, actual change of possession is necessary to pass title.

McKibbin *v.* Martin, 14 Sm. 352.

A "warehouse receipt" can, by the Act, only be issued by a warehouseman for goods on his premises, and the Court will not presume that any one who signs a receipt is a warehouseman; no one but the master can sign a bill of lading.

Shepardson *v.* Cary, 29 Wis. 34.
Dean *v.* King, 22 Ohio St. 119.
Babcock *v.* Orbison, 25 Ind. 75.
Suarez *v.* Str. Geo. Washington, 1 Woods, 96.

It is true that the owner of property cannot be deprived of it by a sale to a stranger, but the lien of a pledgee is destroyed by such a sale; in the former case the ownership is absolute; in the latter there is a mere lien, liable to be divested by a transfer of possession to a *bona fide* purchaser.

Walker *v.* Staples, 5 Allen, 34.
Beeman *v.* Lawton, 37 Me. 543.
Owens *v.* Kinsey, 7 Jones (N. C.) L. 245.
Smyth *v.* Craig, 3 W. & S. 14.

Defendant, in replevin, may set up title in a third person under the pleas of "*non cepit*" and "no property in the plaintiff."

Robinson *v.* Calloway, 4 Ark. 94.
Redman *v.* Hendricks, 1 Sand. (N. Y.) 32.
Page *v.* Weeks, 13 Mass. 199.
Lester *v.* McDowell, 6 H. 91.

Even assuming a contract between Gayley and Morris to hold the iron subject to his order, the transferee is not entitled to sue in his own name.

Thompson *v.* Dominy, 14 M. & W. 403.
Fahnestock *v.* Schoyer, 9 W. 102.
Loudon Sav. Soc. *v.* Hagerstown Bk., 12 C. 498.
McCormick *v.* Trotter, 10 S. & R. 94.

March 1, 1880. THE COURT. Unless the plaintiff has succeeded in showing that the receipts issued by Gayley of October 15 and 20, 1874, are warehouse receipts, under the Act of 24th of September, 1866, it has no case. Admitting all that Ervin swears to, it but comes to this, that Gayley was the bailee of Morris, the owner of the iron; and as Morris, through Ervin, sold or pledged the iron for value to two different parties, who were without notice of the claims of each other, it follows, that the one first obtaining the possession—or what is now, under the statute, its equivalent—would have the right of property; and the one failing in this, having no property in the goods claimed, could certainly not maintain the action of replevin. (Winslow *v.* Leonard, 12 Har. 14; per LOWRIE, J.; Davis *v.* Bigler, 12 P. F. S. 242.)

Now, from the evidence, two things may be taken as established: (1) That Troutman had a regular warehouse receipt from Etting & Groome, the lessees of the wharf, and hence, under the statute, he had the right of property, unless the plaintiff, the pledgee of Morris, had the previous right by virtue of the receipts from Gayley. (2) That Troutman, when he purchased, had no notice of the pledge of the property to the bank. These being the main and really important facts of the case, it follows that very many of the numerous exceptions taken in the Court below to the rejection or admission of evidence, become unimportant, and need no consideration. The real and only question for solution is, Which of these parties had the prior right to this metal? And as neither had the actual possession of this property, as that remained with the wharfinger, this question rests for its solution not upon the form, but upon the character of the papers by which they severally profess to hold title. Gayley's receipts were, in point of time, prior to those of Etting & Groome to Troutman; it follows that, if Gayley had power to issue receipts such as are contemplated by the statute of 1866, the plaintiff's case is made out, and it ought to recover; on the other hand, if he had no such power as against Troutman, the bank had no right in the property, and the case was properly disposed of in the Court below. The question, then, which we have to deal with is one of power: What was Gayley's power? And here, also, we get rid of a good deal of the brushwood of this case, for if Gayley had no power, original or delegated, to issue technical warehouse receipts, what he knew of Ervin's intentions, what Ervin said to him, or he to Ervin, was of no consequence. So, on the other hand, if Gayley had such power, his intention to give a mere memorandum would not have a feather's weight in the case, for none the less would a *bona fide* purchaser or pledgee take title by virtue of the receipts issued by him.

We proceed, then, to inquire what was the position and power of this man Gayley on and about the wharf upon which the iron in suit was found? But as to this there is no controversy. The responsible parties were Etting & Groome; they were lessees of the wharf, and Gayley was their employé. To this both Gayley and Groome swore, as well as to the further fact that he had no authority to issue warehouse receipts. Furthermore, Mr. Morris himself testifies: "I knew Gayley as a weighmaster; did not know him as a warehouseman." That Ervin himself knew of this fact is patent, for that when he intended to re-pledge this iron to the Philadelphia Warehouse Company, he went to Etting & Groome for his receipts.

Such, then, being the undisputed status of affairs, with whom, in the language of the Act of Assembly, were the goods in controversy "stored or deposited?" Upon the determination of this question depends the validity of the plaintiff's receipts. Were they stored or deposited with Etting & Groome or with Gayley? This question would seem to be very clearly settled by the preceding facts. If Etting & Groome were the owners of the wharf; if Gayley were but a servant in charge of this wharf, he was but a custodian for his masters, and goods deposited on that wharf were deposited with them, and not with him. It is urged that the Malins sent the order for the iron, sold to Morris, in an envelope addressed to Gayley. But what of that? This metal had been stored there before the date of the order, and without the assent of Etting & Groome Gayley could not remove it, nor permit it to be removed. Moreover, it was "subject to the payment of freight and charges thereon"—not to Gayley, but to his employers. It is true, he had possession, inasmuch as he had charge of the wharf; but his possession, like that of any other servant in charge of his master's property, was subordinate to that of Etting & Groome. In other words, he had possession for them; his possession was but their possession. He was an agent with limited powers, and those dealing with him were bound to inquire as to the extent of those powers, or take the risk upon themselves. (Moore's Ex'rs *v.* Patterson, 4 Ca. 505.) Suppose they, as they had the undoubted power to do, had discharged him the next day, or the next hour after he had received the order from the Malin Brothers, who, then, would have had possession of the iron, and who would have been responsible for its safe-keeping? Surely Etting & Groome, not Gayley. Thus it is that we discover, beyond peradventure, with whom the commodity in question was stored or deposited; and it is thus that we determine who is the "warehouseman, wharfinger, or other person," who by the Act is empowered to give the statutory receipt.

If, indeed, any servant could bind his master by issuing a receipt for goods committed to his charge, the condition of things would be sufficiently serious, and the statute would be pregnant with more harm than good. In this very case we have an example of what would result from such a construction of the Act. A crafty agent obtains a receipt from a servant intended only as a memorandum; pledges it to an innocent party; then obtains another receipt from the owners of the wharf, and passes that to a like innocent party, and thereby these wharfingers are liable for double the value of the property. But we may easily suppose a case in which a dishonest clerk, or other employé, in connection with one or more accomplices, might in a month's time bring to ruin the wealthiest warehouseman in this city. But this will not do; such results were never intended by the makers of the statute, and a construction such as this is warranted neither by the letter nor the spirit of that statute. Judgment affirmed.

Opinion by GORDON, J. GREEN, J., absent.

[See next case.]

Jan. '78, 99.   Feb. 5, 1880.

People's Bank v. Troutman.

Bailment—Warehouse receipts—Act of September 24, 1866, P. L. 1353.

People's Bank v. Gayley, *supra*, followed.

Error to the Common Pleas No. 2, of Philadelphia County.

Replevin, by George M. Troutman against The People's Bank of Philadelphia, for 653 tons of iron.

This case arose out of the state of facts reported in Bank *v.* Gayley, *supra*. After the 653 tons of iron had been replevied by the bank, Troutman issued this writ to replevy them in the hands of the bank.

On the trial, before HARE, P. J., plaintiff offered in evidence: (1) The bill of sale from Ervin to Troutman; (3) Warehouse receipts November 18, 1874, November 25, 1874, and entry in books, and also offered to prove; (2) "That the custodian of the iron who had held it for account of Henry G. Morris, and for his pledgee, the warehouse company, after and at the time of sale to plaintiff by H. G. Morris, agreed to hold it on account of plaintiff, and made an entry in his book that he had agreed to hold the iron for plaintiff, and at the same time he issued a warehouse receipt." (4) That iron belonging to Morris entered as above was also entered as his, in day-book and ledger kept by Gayley. (5) That a paper produced is the bill for storage of iron of Mr. Morris on wharf, November, 1875, and that this iron described in that is the iron claimed by defendant and is the identical iron. (6) That anterior to October, 1874, Ervin knew this was Etting's wharf.

Each of these offers was objected to by defendants; the objections were overruled and exceptions granted.

The Court charged the jury, *inter alia*, as follows:—

["Now in this case, while as I have said, there can be no doubt that as between Morris and The People's Bank, the title as to this iron vested in The People's Bank, yet as The People's Bank did not take any steps to perfect their title; did not give notice at the warehouse—either to Gayley or to Etting, they were, as I regard it, to that extent in default, and if the statute had not been passed, to which reference has been made, or if that statute does not affect the case, Mr. Troutman coming subsequently, finding the possession of the iron unchanged, and still standing, so far as the books were concerned, in the name of Morris, and having paid his money upon the faith of that appearance, would have the better right. He would come later in time, but he would have done that which the law requires to make assurance sure, and as a consequence, he would have prevailed over The People's Bank. Such being the state of the law, an Act of Assembly was passed, by which a certain change was made in the law."] . . .

["Consequently, as this receipt was not given by Etting, who was the principal of the warehouse, and was given by a subordinate, the question whether it is a receipt within the Act of Assembly depends upon that subordinate's authority. Had Gayley the authority to give such receipts? Now, it seems to me, to be the uncontradicted testimony in this case—I do not know that there is a word against it from beginning to end, certainly nothing directly against it, and do not perceive any inference against it—that Mr. Gayley was not authorized as between him and Etting to give such receipts. But the argument was made, and it is an argument which has a good deal of force, that as Gayley might deliver the iron which he had received, so he might give a writing saying that he would so deliver it. In other words, that though his actual authority was limited, and though he was impliedly prohibited to issue receipts, yet as he had control over the iron, that this gave him implied authority to issue a receipt. On the best consideration that I can give to the subject, I think that it did not."] . . . . [It, therefore, seems to me, that if the jury find, and as I have said I am not aware of any evidence to the contrary, that Gayley had no express authority to give this receipt; I mean to say that if as between himself and his principal he was not so authorized, then the jury ought not to deduce an implied authority from the fact that he was empowered to receive and issue the iron in the absence of a receipt."]

Defendants requested the Court to charge as follows :—

(1) That Gayley had the charge of the wharf referred to with authority to receive iron and to deliver it at any time before Mr. Etting issued a receipt. Gayley had authority to give the receipts in evidence signed by him, and they are under the law valid.

(2) If the jury find from the evidence that Andrew T. Gayley had authority to receive this iron, and that until Mr. Etting issued a receipt, Gayley had authority to deliver this iron, and if the jury further find that Gayley received the iron in suit, and gave the receipts therefor, which are in evidence, and that the iron was then transferred for value to defendants before any receipt was issued by Mr. Etting, the title to said iron then passed to the defendants.

(3) That independently of Gayley's receipts, Morris could sell or pledge his iron, and if the jury find from the evidence that on October 15, and October 20, 1874, the iron in suit was pledged to defendants, who in good faith advanced moneys upon that pledge, the title to said iron then passed to the defendants.

(4) That if the jury believe the evidence offered by the defendants, the title to the iron in suit passed to the defendants in pledge, October 15 and October 20, 1874.

(5) That there is no evidence that the defendants have done or omitted to do any act whereby they have lost any title which the jury may find the defendants acquired October 15 and 20, 1874, to this iron.

(6) That if the jury find from the evidence that the defendants acquired the title of Henry G. Morris to the iron in suit on October 15 and 20, 1874, in pledge, there is no evidence in the case which divests said title.

(7) That if the jury find from the evidence that the title of the defendants to this iron is first in time, and that they have not lost said title by their act or their omission, then the verdict should be for the defendants.

(8) That if the jury find from the evidence that Alexander Ervin wrote the indorsements on the receipts October 15, and 20, 1874, in the presence and sight of Andrew T. Gayley, this was notice to him of the transfer of Morris's title, and said notice to Gayley was notice to his principal.

(9) That both parties are here claiming this iron under papers signed by Alexander Ervin as attorney for Henry G. Morris, and that the defendants' title papers precede in point of time the papers relied upon by plaintiff, and pass a title to said iron to the defendants.

(10) That if the jury find from the evidence that both plaintiff and defendants are innocent holders for value of Morris's title to this iron, and that this suit is prosecuted really by Etting in the name of Troutman, and that the controversy arises out of the act of Etting's servant, the loss must then fall on him whose servant occasioned it.

(11) That in determining the credit of Gayley and Groome, the jury must consider the admissions of those witnesses as to the alteration of the marks on the iron, and the evidence of the deputy sheriff as to the resistance, and all the other testimony in the case.

The Court declined to charge as requested upon each point.

Verdict and judgment for plaintiff. Defendants took this writ, assigning for error, *inter alia*, the admission of the evidence excepted to, those portions of the charge quoted above, and the refusal of the Court to charge as requested.

F. C. Brewster and *Chas. Gilpin*, for plaintiffs in error.

W. Wynne Wister, Jr., and *R. C. McMurtrie*, contra.

March 1, 1880. THE COURT. For reasons given in the opinion in the case of The People's Bank of Philadelphia *v.* Andrew T. Gayley, filed herewith, the judgment in this case is affirmed.

Opinion by GORDON, J. GREEN, J., absent.

July '78, 127. March 2, 1880.
Gordon's Appeal.

Orphans' Courts—Sales of land—Application towards payment of purchase-money of liens originally entered in other counties—Feigned issues in such cases, where triable—Act of April 20, 1846—Estoppel.

When, under the Act of April 20, 1846 (P. L. 44), a purchaser at an Orphans' Court sale of land seeks to apply to the purchase-money a judgment originally entered in another county, but transferred to the county of the sale by exemplified copy, an issue, to try the truth of an allegation that the consideration of the judgment has failed, can be tried only in the county having jurisdiction of the sale.

The affirmance by the Supreme Court of a judgment of the Common Pleas, in a feigned issue where no exception had been taken nor error assigned to the jurisdiction of the Court to try the issue, is not necessarily an implied affirmance of such jurisdiction, and does not prevent a subsequent impeachment of the jurisdiction, under further proceedings in the same controversy.

Where, in such a case, an issue was improperly directed to the county where the judgment was originally entered, and, no question of jurisdiction being raised, a verdict on the issue was there obtained, and the judgment thereon affirmed by the Supreme Court:

Held, that there is no estoppel to an application for an issue in the county having jurisdiction.

Appeal of S. T. Gordon, administrator of Cary L. Gordon, deceased, from a decree of the Orphans' Court of Bucks County, dismissing his exceptions to his own return of the sale of land of the decedent.

The decedent, a resident of Philadelphia, died

seized of land in Bucks County. Under the Act of March 29, 1832, his administrator, the appellant, applied to the Orphans' Court of Philadelphia County for an order to sell the land to raise $10,000, which order was granted; and subsequently, after due application, a like order was granted by the Orphans' Court of Bucks County. The sale was made and the return confirmed *nisi* by the Bucks County Court. The administrator tendered a deed for the land to the purchaser, who declined to pay the whole amount of his bid in cash, but claimed that, under the Act of April 20, 1846 (P. L. 411), a judgment he held against the decedent should be applied as part of the purchase-money. The judgment had originally been entered on a bond and warrant of attorney in the District Court of Philadelphia County, and transferred to Bucks County by exemplified copy. The administrator petitioned the Bucks County Orphans' Court to rescind the order of sale, for leave to amend his return, and for an alias order to sell; a rule was thereupon granted to show cause why the sale should not be set aside.

The purchaser, Alonzo Gordon, answered that he held the judgment aforesaid, and tendered a certain sum in cash; he asked for a discharge of the rule, which was discharged accordingly, and he was ordered to make the cash payment and give the receipt on account of the judgment as tendered, and the administrator was ordered to accept the payment and receipt as above, and make an amended return setting forth the facts; this the administrator did, and then filed exceptions to his own amended return, which were, *inter alia*, as follows: (1) Because the judgment held by Alonzo Gordon against the decedent had been confessed by him to secure the payment of a draft given by Alonzo to the decedent, which draft had never been paid, but had been returned to Alonzo; (2) and because the said Alonzo had refused to pay counsel fees for trying the issue on the said judgment.

The Court directed issues in which Alonzo Gordon should be plaintiff, and C. L. Gordon, the administrator, defendant, to try the questions whether the judgment had been given without consideration or for a consideration which had failed, and whether the judgment had been fraudulently obtained. The case was put at issue in the Common Pleas of Bucks County, but afterwards that Court struck off the issues on the ground that it was without jurisdiction.

On January 20, 1874, the Orphans' Court of Bucks County ordered that the hearing of the still pending exceptions to the administrator's amended return should be continued until a subsequent day, to enable the exceptant to apply for an issue in the Orphans' Court of Philadelphia County, the exceptions to be dismissed, and the return of sale confirmed, unless such application were made before the day of the hearing. On due application, the Orphans' Court of Philadelphia directed the trial of the issues in the Court of Common Pleas No. 3 (see Gordon's Estate, 9 Phila. Rep. 350). A verdict and judgment were there rendered for the plaintiff, Alonzo Gordon, and the judgment was subsequently affirmed by the Supreme Court. The Orphans' Court of Bucks County then, on May 6, 1878, entered a decree, dismissing the exceptions, confirming the amended return of sale, and ordering the administrator to give Alonzo Gordon, the purchaser, a deed.

The administrator took this appeal, assigning for error, *inter alia*, (1) The order of Jan. 20, 1874, requiring an application for issues in Philadelphia County; (2) The dismissal of his first exception; (3) The dismissal of his second exception.

F. C. Brewster (with him *J. L. Dubois*), for the appellant.

Under the Act of 1846, it is clear that the only Court having power to direct an issue was the Orphans' Court of Bucks County, and that the issues were triable in that county only. The Orphans' Court of Philadelphia, in directing an issue, relied upon Brandt's Appeal (4 H. 343), which was a wholly different case. There the judgment had been set aside for irregularity in the county in which it had been entered. In this case the judgment was not alleged to have been irregular, at the date of its entry. The question was whether it ought not to have been satisfied.

G. & H. Lear, contra.

Where a judgment is transferred to another county, under the Act of April 16, 1840, the Court of such county has no power over the judgment except for purposes of execution and satisfaction. It cannot inquire into the merits at all. The Court in which the primary judgment was obtained can alone take any action operating on the judgment itself.

King *v.* Nimick, 10 C. 297.
Brandt's Appeal, 4 H. 343.

In this case the Supreme Court, in affirming the judgment on the issues tried in the Common Pleas of Philadelphia, impliedly affirmed the jurisdiction of that Court.

May 3, 1880. THE COURT. This contention arises under an application of the appellant, as administrator of Stephen T. Gordon, to sell real estate of the decedent, situate in Bucks County. The application was made to the Orphans' Court of the county of Philadelphia, under the 32d section of the Act of 29th March, 1832. It authorized the administrator to raise, by the sale of said real estate, the sum of $10,000 for the payment of debts. The Orphans' Court of Bucks County, on due application thereafter, ordered the sale. In pursuance of the order, sale was made, and the return thereof confirmed *nisi* by the Court. On tendering a deed to the purchaser, he objected to paying in cash the whole amount of his bid, but claimed, under the Act of 20th April, 1846, that a part thereof should apply on a judgment he held against the decedent. It had originally been entered on bond and warrant of attorney, in the District Court of the county of Philadelphia, and transferred to the county of Bucks by exemplified copy. The appellant refused to make the application, or amend his return of sale, and alleged facts denying the existing validity of the judgment. Thereupon the Court directed an issue, which was duly formed. When it came on for trial, the Court, being of the opinion that a Court in Bucks County had no jurisdiction, struck off the issues, and sent the administrator to the Orphans' Court of Philadelphia County. On application there the Court awarded an issue. It proceeded to judgment in the Common Pleas of Philadelphia County, and was determined in favor of the plaintiff therein. It was affirmed in this Court. The Orphans' Court of Bucks County thereupon decreed that the appellant make and execute a deed to the purchaser, treating his judgment as a valid and subsisting lien, having first ordered the return of sale to be so amended as to require the appellant to accept the receipt of the purchaser in part payment of his bid.

Two questions arise on this record: one, Had the Orphans' Court of Buck's County jurisdiction to try the validity of the lien claimed by the purchaser? If it had, the other is, Whether the appellant is estopped by the judgment in the issue tried in the Common Pleas in the County of Philadelphia?

The Act of 29th March, 1832, expressly declares the administrator shall in all cases make return of his proceedings in relation to such sale, to the Orphans' Court of the county in which the real estate so sold lies, when, if the same be approved by the Court, it shall be confirmed.

Thus exclusive jurisdiction, after the preliminary order made by the Orphans' Court of Philadelphia, in ordering, supervising, and confirming the sale, was given to the Orphans' Court of the County of Bucks. The Act of 20th April, 1846, which provided for the administrator accepting the receipt of a purchaser who was a lien creditor, necessarily subjected the action of the administrator in regard thereto to the same Court. The Act, therefore, declares the Court shall determine, either by reference to an auditor or by directing an issue, as to the right of a purchaser to pay his bid, or any part thereof, by applying the same on his lien. This necessarily restricted the action of the Court to the limits of its own county, in whichever way it proceeded. If the facts alleged the irregularity of the original judgment, or denied the authority under which it was confessed, there might be some reason in holding, under King *v.* Nimick (10 Casey, 297), that the application to strike off the judgment should have been made in the Common Pleas of the county of Philadelphia. There was, however, no such allegation. Conceding that it was fairly given and regularly entered, the offer was to show a subsequent failure of consideration, so that nothing was due thereon. This question, in so far as it affected the sale in Buck's County, the Orphans' Court of Philadelphia had no jurisdiction to try. The Orphans' Court of Bucks County, therefore, erred in striking off the issue which it had directed to be formed, and in ordering the return of the administrator to be amended before the validity of the lien was duly established. Nor is the appellant estopped by the judgment of the Common Pleas of Philadelphia, and the affirmation thereof by this Court. We affirmed only the correctness of the charge and rulings on the trial. No question of the jurisdiction of the Orphans' Court of Philadelphia was determined on the trial of the facts in that issue. The only matters tried and determined were the disputed facts certified to be in the issue. We understand the third assignment to involve not only the liability of the purchaser to pay the expense of trying the issue, but also the expense of the administrator in trying the same. So far as is shown by the record, we see no cause why he should not be allowed those expenses. This, however, can be determined more intelligently after the trial of the issue. The several assignments are substantially sustained.

And now, May 3, 1880, decree of 6th May, 1878, reversed and set aside; the amended report of sale set aside; the issue directed by the Orphans' Court of Bucks County reinstated, and a *proceaendo* awarded.

Opinion by MERCUR, J.

Jan. '80. March 11, 1880.

Driesbach v. Morris.

Justice of peace—Appeals from—Tender of judgment by defendant—Act of April 9, 1833—What is sufficient tender—Notice—Practice.

Under the Act of April 9, 1833 (P. L. 480), providing that if the defendant in an action before a justice shall tender, "either on the trial of the case or before an appeal," a judgment, and that if the plaintiff, having refused such tender, shall ultimately recover an amount no greater than the tender, then the defendant's bill of costs should be taxed against the verdict, it is requisite that the plaintiff should have notice of the tender, in order to be affected thereby.

In such a case the record is the only evidence, and cannot be contradicted by parol.

Semble. That the notice should appear on the docket.

Error to the Common Pleas of Luzerne County.

This was an action by Driesbach & Co. against Morris and Walsh, brought before an alderman of the city of Wilkesbarre, wherein there was, on February 1, 1876, a judgment of $89.25 for plaintiff. The alderman's docket showed that on February 12 defendants tendered a judgment of $80.00, and Feb. 14 defendants appealed. On the trial there was a verdict, on May 17, 1878, for plaintiffs in the sum of $81.12. Counsel for defendants thereupon took a rule to show cause why the defendants' bill of costs should not be a set-off against plaintiffs' verdict, by virtue of the provisions of the Act of April 9, 1833 (P. L. 480), which enacts that—

"The costs on appeals hereafter entered from the judgments of the justices of the peace and aldermen shall abide the event of the appeal, and be paid by the unsuccessful party, as in other cases; . . . *provided*, that if the defendant, either on the trial of the cause before the justice or referee, or before an appeal is taken, shall offer to give the plaintiff a judgment for the amount which the defendant shall admit to be due (which offer it shall be the duty of the justice, and of the referee, to enter on the record), and if the said plaintiff, or his agent, shall not accept such offer, then and in that case, if the defendant shall appeal, the plaintiff shall pay all the costs which shall accrue on the appeal, if he shall not, in the event of the suit, recover a greater amount than that for which the defendant offered to give a judgment; and in both cases the defendant's bill shall be taxed and paid by the plaintiff in the same manner as if a judgment had been rendered in Court for the defendant."

Depositions were taken under this rule. Those on the part of the plaintiff were to the effect that no notice of the tender of judgment was given to any one representing the plaintiff. The alderman testified that no one was present except defendant Morris, and that no notice was given by the alderman.

Defendant Morris testified: "At the time of giving judgment I tendered judgment of $80 and costs, and had the 'Squire to record it on his docket. On the same day . . . told Driesbach, . . . and that we were ready to pay, . . . he said he would not take it."

The Court made the rule absolute, whereupon defendant took this writ, assigning for error the action of the Court.

E. S. Osborne, for plaintiffs in error.

The tender of judgment was not in conformity with the Act. It was not made to the plaintiff, nor at the time judgment was entered. The testimony of the defendant to contradict the alderman's record was inadmissible.

J. Vaughan Darling (*E. P. Darling* and *D. S. Bennet* with him), for defendants in error.

The Act does not specify who is to give notice; if the plaintiff has actual notice it is sufficient.

Magill v. Tomer, 6 W. 494.

The decision of the Court below upon the depositions was one of fact, which this Court will not disturb.

Barnet v. Ihrie, 1 R. 44.

The tender was more than the amount ultimately recovered, for $80, with two years and three months' interest, would amount to $90.88.

May 3, 1880. THE COURT. This contention is whether the plaintiffs are entitled to full costs. It arises under the Act of 9th April, 1833. So much of the second proviso, as is applicable to this case, declares if the defendant, either on the trial of the cause before the justice, or before an appeal is taken, shall offer to give the plaintiff a judgment for the amount, which the defendant shall admit to be due, which offer it shall be the duty of the justice to enter on the record, and if the plaintiff or his agent shall not accept such offer, then, and in that case, if the defendant shall appeal, the plaintiff shall pay all the costs which shall accrue on the appeal, if he shall not, in the event of the suit, recover a greater amount than that for which the defendant offered to give a judgment; and in both cases the defendant's bill shall be taxed and paid by the plaintiff in the same manner as if a judgment had been rendered in Court for the defendant.

The offer to confess judgment must be shown by the record. It is the only evidence of the offer. (McDowell v. Glass, 4 Watts, 389; Seibert v. Kline, 1 Barr, 38; Gardner v. Davis, 3 Harris, 41.)

In the present case the record shows the judgment was recovered before the justice on the first day of February, 1876, the offer to confess judgment was made on the 12th, and on the 14th the defendants appealed. The record fails to show that the plaintiffs had any notice of this offer. The Act does not declare by whom the notice shall be given, whether by the defendant or by the justice, but it clearly requires that the plaintiff shall be notified in order to affect him by the offer. He must necessarily be notified before he can be prejudiced by not accepting. The record does not show the plaintiffs to have been present when the offer was made on the 12th. The justice swears he was not. The defendant swears he made the offer on the day the judgment was rendered, and afterwards on the same day notified the plaintiffs. This the plaintiffs denied under oath. As the record shows the offer of judgment was not made until the 12th, any notice on the first could have no effect. The record cannot be impeached, except for fraud, and that is neither shown nor alleged.

We think a correct interpretation of the statute requires the record also to show notice to the plaintiff or his agent of the offer to confess judgment, before the plaintiff can be affected by it. This is the only rule which will give a proper effect to the whole record, and harmonize with public policy. If no response be made, within a reasonable time after notice, it may well be construed as not accepting. There should be no enlargement of the rule to supply by uncertain parol evidence what the record should show. (Foss v. Bogan, not yet reported.) The learned Judge therefore erred in making absolute the rule to show cause why the defendant's bill of costs, since the appeal, should not be set off against the plaintiff's verdict. The plaintiff is entitled to full costs.

Judgment reversed, and rule discharged.
Opinion by MERCUR, J.

July, '80, 57.   March 30, 1880.
City of Scranton v. Catterson.

Negligence—Municipal law—Failure to remove obstructions from streets.

C., in driving through the streets of Scranton, an incorporated city, was upset by the iron head of a water plug, and injured. The plug, as originally placed by a gas and water company, incorporated before the city, projected an inch above the grade of the street; after the city's incorporation, and before the accident, the street level had been lowered so that the plug projected six inches, and the city officials were aware of that fact. In an action for damages brought by C. against the city, the defendant asked the Court to charge that if the obstruction had been placed in the street under the authority of the State, there could be no recovery against the city, which point was negatived:

Held (affirming the ruling of the Court below), that it mattered not who placed the obstruction in the street, provided the city had notice of its existence and failed to remove it.

A charter granted to a gas and water company to make necessary structures in a village, afterwards incorporated, to enter upon and occupy streets for the construction of its works, and to make ditches and lay pipes, does not relieve the subsequently chartered city from the consequences of its neglect to remove permanent obstructions from its streets.

Error to the Common Pleas of Lackawanna County.

Case, brought by Catterson against the city of Scranton, to recover damages for injuries resulting from the alleged negligence of the city, in suffering an obstruction to remain in one of its streets. Plea, Not guilty.

At the trial the plaintiff proved that on the morning of December 24, 1877, he was driving a wagon and pair of horses at a slow trot through the city, when on turning from Penn Avenue into Mulberry Street one of the wheels struck the projecting end of an iron water plug, which he did not see, near the middle of the street, and the wagon received a jar which threw out the plaintiff, who was seriously injured by the fall. The plug had been placed in the street by the Scranton Gas and Water Company, before the incorporation of the city, and originally projected one or two inches above the street level, but several months before the accident, the city had lowered the street so that the head of the plug was left five or six inches above the ground. The plaintiff then read in evidence the Acts of Assembly incorporating the city in 1867, and giving it authority to open, and imposing upon it the duty of regulating, its streets.

The defendant's testimony mainly went to show that wagons had gone over that plug, and others like it, without accident. The street commissioner, on cross-examination, admitted, that before the accident in suit, he had often observed the projection of the plug, though he had not considered it dangerous. The defendant offered in evidence the charter of the Scranton Gas and Water Company (P. L. 1856, p. 599), for the purpose of showing that it authorized the company to locate the plug, that the city had no control over it, that the company was neither the servant nor agent of the city, nor responsible to it but to the State. Objected to. Objection sustained; exception.

The charter was substantially as follows:—

"The said company shall have power to provide, erect, and maintain all works, machinery, fixtures, or engines, necessary or proper for making, raising, and introducing into the village of Scranton, ... a sufficient supply of gas and pure water, ... to enter upon such lands and inclosures, streets, lanes, and alleys, roads, highways, and bridges, as it may be necessary to occupy, or to obtain necessary materials for the construction of said works; and to occupy, ditch, and lay pipes, and from time to time repair the same; and if any injury be done to private property the said company shall make compensation therefor, in the manner hereafter provided."

The defendant presented, *inter alia*, the following points:—

(2) The plaintiff was bound to use ordinary care, and if, by such care, he could have avoided the accident, he cannot recover. The least contributory negligence will prevent a recovery. *Affirmed.*

(3) If the jury believe that the obstruction in the street was placed there under authority of the State, and independent of the city authority, then the action should be against the authority guilty of the obstruction. *Negatived.* (2d assignment of error.)

(4) A person driving over a road with which he is unacquainted should carefully examine the way ahead, especially when turning corners, and a non-compliance with this is negligence. *Answer.* "Not affirmed. If the plaintiff used ordinary care while passing over Mulberry Street then . . . . . so long as the street is under the control of the city it matters not who put the obstruction there, provided you find from the evidence the city had notice that the obstruction was there, and permitted it to remain."

(6) The city of Scranton is not liable for injuries resulting from obstructions placed in the street by the Scranton Gas and Water Company, in the pursuance of its lawful business under the authority given by its charter from the State. The answer was substantially as follows: The company had the right to construct the works which the State authorized, but no right to place a structural obstruction in the highway—if it did erect this obstruction, and the city had notice of it, and failed to require its removal, the city must first answer for an accident caused by the obstruction, though the company may be answerable to the city. (4th assignment of error.)

Verdict and judgment for the plaintiff. The defendant took this writ, assigning for error (1) the refusal to admit the charter of the company in evidence, and (2, 3, and 4) the answers to the above points.

J. H. Burns, for the plaintiff in error.

The water company and not the city is responsible; for the charter granted to a private corporation by the State constitutes a contract which can be impaired neither by the State nor by a municipality deriving power therefrom.

Fletcher *v.* Peck, 6 Cranch, 87.
Dartmouth College *v.* Woodward, 4 Wheat. 579.
Bank of Penna. *v.* Comth., 7 Harris, 151.
R. R. Co. *v.* Philadelphia, 11 Wr. 314.

The State's authority over highways and streets is absolute, and she may obstruct, alter, or control them by due process of law. A municipal corporation cannot interfere with this power, and is not responsible for its exercise.

Philadelphia and Trenton R. R., 6 Wh. 44.
Young *v.* The Inhabitants of Yarmouth, 9 Gray, 386.

E. B. Sturges, contra.

The Legislature did not authorize the Gas and Water Company to obstruct streets, except for limited purposes. The company did not cause the obstruction; it was the result of the city's act in lowering the street level, and of this change of grade the city had constructive and actual notice. The offer in evidence of the company's charter, was therefore immaterial and was properly rejected.

The party injured by an obstruction or nuisance in the highway has his option to proceed against the municipality, or against the immediate creator of the obstruction.

Angell on Highways, §§ 298–300.
Dillon on Municipal Corporations, p. 927.
Birmingham *v.* Dorner, 3 Brewster, 69.
Addison on Torts, p. 1316.
Philadelphia *v.* Weller, 4 Brewster, 24.

May 3, 1880. THE COURT. That the city of Scranton is clothed with the power and duty of keeping her streets in repair is conceded. No question was made but that the Scranton Gas and Water Company is a corporation, with right to enter upon the highways to occupy, ditch, lay, and repair pipes when necessary, and the Court charged in answer to defendant's sixth point, that the company had the right to construct such works as the law-making power had authorized, but that the company could not put a structural obstruction in the public highway, and if they did and the attention of the city was called to it, followed by neglect to remove it, the city would be liable for an injury caused by the obstruction, in absence of concurrent negligence by the person injured. In answer to the fourth point the jury were instructed that "it matters not who put the obstruction there, provided you find from the evidence the city had notice that the obstruction was there, and permitted it to remain." There was no evidence to warrant the jury in finding the facts on which defendant's third point was based. In view of the evidence, the second, third, and fourth assignments cannot be sustained, but it would be otherwise, if the charter of the company vested them with power to erect and maintain the obstruction.

The evidence warranted a finding that the company placed the plug a long time before the accident, leaving its top about an inch above the grade, and afterwards the city lowered the grade of the street, leaving the top of the plug a number of inches above. Hence this is wholly unlike a case where an accident occurred during the progress, or immediately after completion of ditching and laying pipe, and before the city had notice of the construction of a nuisance.

The first alleged error and the one mainly relied on is, the rejection of the charter of the Scranton Gas and Water Company, offered for the purpose of showing their right to put the plug in, at the point of the accident; that the city has no control over it, and that they are not the servants or agents of, nor responsible to the city. The right of the company to put the plug in at that place, or any other which they deemed necessary was not denied, but the real question is, have the company authority to place and maintain an obstruction on the street? If so the offer was admissible, and it was a fatal error to deny it. The charter might well have been received, and had it been, the Court would have declared its meaning. But if on inspection the Court saw it contained nothing to the purpose of the offer, no harm was done by its rejection. The plaintiff in error has failed to point to anything in the charter that authorizes the company to maintain a dangerous obstruction on any highway in the city. They may occupy the streets for the necessary time to ditch, lay and repair pipes and place plugs, but no testimony, or offer of testimony, shows that they may leave the top of a plug so far above the grade, as to be dangerous to persons travelling the streets. Should they construct a dangerous public nuisance on the highway, the duty of the city after notice thereof is plain. If the plug was properly placed and afterwards the city lowered the grade, thereby causing the obstruction, it was inexcusable neglect. We are of opinion that the charter contained nothing to relieve the city from liability for its sufferance of the nuisance.

Judgment affirmed.

Opinion by TRUNKEY, J.

June '80, 233.   March 4, 1880.

Krause v. Commonwealth.

Criminal Law—Bailment—Larceny as bailee—Construction of Crimes Act of 1860, § 108—Conditional sale.

The obligation to return the identical property is an essential quality to the bailment in the statutory sense of § 108 of the Crimes Act of 1860.

A delivery of chattels upon a sale made on condition that the title shall pass on the payment of the purchase-money at a future day, does not affect a bailment, but vests in the transferee a conditional title.

Difference in attitude of innocent purchasers and creditors, towards chattels held under bailment and under conditional sale, explained.

In general terms, a bailment is the delivery of goods, or any other species of personal estate for use, keeping, or on some other trust, where the general property does not pass.

Definitions of bailment reviewed by TRUNKEY, J.

If it be doubtful whether a legal term be included, it shall be excluded in the construction of a criminal statute.

Error to the Quarter Sessions of Lehigh County.

Indictment containing two counts, charging Frederick P. Krause with (1) larceny, and (2) larceny as bailee.

The trial on the first count resulted in a verdict for the defendant on the plea of former acquittal. The facts, as they appeared upon the trial of the second count, under a plea of not guilty, before ALBRECHT, P. J., were stated in the opinion of the Supreme Court as follows:—

"On December 13, 1878, the prosecutor sold and the defendant agreed to purchase the two horses; that the price agreed upon was $150 to be paid on delivery, the prosecutor to take the horses to the defendant's stable, at Allentown, the next day and receive the money; that he took them to said stable and left them; and that other interviews and negotiations followed, continuing up to the Thursday of the next week, when the horses disappeared from the stable, and were sold or converted by the defendant to his own use. That when the horses were taken to the stable, the defendant had only $25, and it was then agreed that the horses should continue to be the property of Dremer, who would not sell them except for cash; that he would wait till the following Tuesday evening, when if the defendant should not have the money to buy the horses, they were to be taken to Dremer, at Schoenersville, and with this understanding Dremer accepted $25; that on Tuesday evening the defendant took one of the horses to Schoenersville, and the next evening went again taking the other horse, on each occasion taking the horse back with him, that on Thursday Dremer went to Allentown for his horses and offered to return the $25 to the defendant, but he refused to give them; and that the original contract was never changed, the horses were sold only for cash, and the extension of time was given to enable the defendant to buy and pay for them."

The defendant requested the Court to charge: (1) There can be no conviction in this case, because the defendant is no bailee of the property in controversy, within the meaning of section 108 of the Criminal Code of March 31st, 1860, and upon which this count in the bill of indictment upon which he is being tried is founded. *Answer*.—Refused. "Whether defendant was a bailee is one of the questions which must be determined by the jury. If you find that defendant was no bailee, of course there can be no conviction."

Verdict "guilty" and judgment accordingly; whereupon the defendant took this writ, assigning for error the refusal of the Court to instruct the jury that under the evidence there could be no conviction of larceny by bailee.

Wm. H. Sowden (with whom were *Butz & Schwartz*), for the plaintiff in error.

Bailment contemplates a re-delivery of the thing bailed, an element wanting, according to the evidence, in this case. The transfer constituted not a bailment, but a conditional sale.

Hilliard on Sales, 1.
Mallory v. Willis, 4 Comst. 85.
Foster v. Pettibone, 7 N. Y. 435.
Comth. v. Chathams, 14 Wr. 188.
Haak v. Linderman et al., 14 Sm. 499.
Chamberlain v. Smith, 8 Wr. 431.
Comth. v. Cart, 2 Pitts. Rep. 495.

Milton C. Henninger, District Attorney, for the defendant in error, did not argue the cause on its merits, but contended that the assignments of error had not been properly brought before the Court.

March 15, 1880. THE COURT. The indictment contained two counts: (1) Larceny; (2) Larceny by bailee; the alleged stolen property was the same in both. To the first count Krause pleaded a former acquittal, on which plea verdict and judgment were rendered in his favor. He was then tried and convicted on the second.

In the charge of the Court, the Commonwealth's case, as proved, was fairly stated thus: [The Court here stated the facts, *ut supra*.] Such were the alleged facts, which must be taken as true.

Having acquitted the defendant of larceny of the horses, the Commonwealth put him to another trial, and convicted him of larceny, in stealing the same horses, under section 108 of the Crimes Act of 1860. Villanous as was his conduct, this conviction ought not to stand, unless he was a bailee within the intendment of the Act. The word bailee is a legal term, to be understood in its generally accepted sense among jurists, and if it be doubtful whether a case be included, it shall be excluded in the construction of a criminal statute. Blackstone defines bailment as "a delivery of goods in trust, upon a contract, express or implied, that the trust shall be faithfully executed on the part of the bailee;" Story, "A delivery of a thing in trust for some special object or purpose, and upon a contract, express or implied, to conform to the object or purpose of the trust;" Jones, "A delivery of goods in trust on a contract, express or implied, that the trust shall be duly executed, and the goods re-delivered as soon as the time or use for which they were bailed shall have elapsed or be performed;" and Kent, "A delivery of goods in trust upon a contract, express or implied, that the trust shall be duly executed, and the goods restored by the bailee as soon as the purpose of the bailment shall be answered."

Mr. Edwards, in his work on Bailment, § 2, remarks: These definitions agree in nearly all essential particulars, and disagree in two or three respects. Jones and Kent assume the property is to be returned, while Blackstone and Story include contracts under which no such return is contemplated. Story intends to include among contracts of bailment a delivery of goods for sale; and Kent intentionally limits his definition so as to exclude that species of contract. "In general terms it may be said that the delivery of goods or any other species of personal estate for use, keeping, or on some other trust, where the general property does not pass, creates a bailment. A delivery of chattels upon a sale made on condition that the title shall pass on the payment of the purchase-money at a future day, is something more than a bailment; it gives the buyer a conditional title. If the contract gives the buyer a definite credit or a reasonable time within which to pay, it gives him a transferable interest in the chattels until the credit expiring and the property in them as soon as he pays the price."

Authors of received authority generally specify five sorts of bailment, namely, *depositum*, *mandatum*, *commodatum*, pledge, and hiring; and, as severally defined, in each the entire property of the thing bailed remains in the bailor, the possession only is given to the bailee, who is to return or deliver the thing itself as soon as the purpose of the bailment shall be answered. In this State it is settled that the bailee of goods, who uses and enjoys them as if his own, cannot divest the title of the bailor by a sale to an innocent person; nor can a creditor of the bailee seize them in execution of his debt. When delivered under a contract of bailment, the owner will be entitled to them against everybody. But a delivery on a conditional sale, the property to remain in the vendor until the goods are paid for, with right to reclaim them, is void as respects the vendee's creditors, or an innocent purchaser from him. The delivery being on the foot of a purchase, the vendor's right as against the vendee's creditors is regarded as a lien for the purchase-money. (Chamberlain *v.* Smith, 8 Wright, 431; Haak *v.* Linderman, 14 P. F. Smith, 499.) By the terms of the contract the seller may retain the right of property in the goods till paid for, as against the purchaser, and in default of payment he may reclaim them, or use civil remedies for recovery of possession, but the contract does not make him a bailor, as respects other persons, nor the purchaser a bailee, in the sense of the word as used in the statute.

Our statute, as shown by READ, J., in Commonwealth *v.* Chathams (14 Wright, 181), is taken from the English statute; and in that case the interpretation of the words bailee and bailment, as fixed by the English decisions, was adopted, which decisions were cited, showing that the words must be interpreted according to their ordinary legal acceptation, that "bailment relates to something in the hands of the bailee, which is to be returned in specie, and does not apply to the case of money in the hands of a party who is not under any obligation to return it in precisely the identical coins which he originally received;" that "to bring a case within this clause, in addition to the fraudulent disposal of the property, it must be proved, first, that there was such a delivery of the property as to divest the owner of the possession, and vest it in the prisoner for some time; secondly, that at the expiration or determination of that time the identical same property was to be restored to the owner."

The term bailee is one to be used not in its large, but in its limited sense, as including simply those bailees who are authorized to keep, to transfer, or to deliver, and who receive the goods *bona fide*, and then fraudulently convert. Where it does not appear that a fiduciary duty is imposed on the defendant to return the specific goods of which the alleged bailment is composed, a bailment under the statutes is not constituted. (Whart. Cr. L., § 1055, 8th ed.)

The bargain was struck for a sale of the horses for $150, payable on delivery. At the time stipulated Dremer delivered the horses. Krause paid $25, they agreed that the property should continue in Dremer, and on the Tuesday Krause would pay the balance or return the horses. He refused to do either. The original contract was not changed, time was extended to Krause to enable him to pay the money. If there was a delivery at all, it was on the footing of the sale. There was no agreement to sell at a future time; a mere contract that the buyer would pay the balance of the price or return the property, in the mean time the title to be in the seller. Payment would have been a complete performance. Krause was not bound to return the identical property. He had a transferable interest until the credit expired, and he or his transferree would have had clear title the instant of payment. This was something more than a bailment, and Krause was not a bailee in the statutory sense.

In favor of the liberty of the citizen, the Court may, and in a proper case should, declare the evidence insufficient to convict. (Pauli *v.* Commonwealth, 7 WEEKLY NOTES, 397.) We are of opinion that the defendant's first point should have been affirmed.

Judgment reversed, and the record, with this opinion setting forth the causes of reversal, is remanded to the Court of Quarter Sessions of Lehigh County for further proceedings.

Opinion by TRUNKEY, J. GREEN and MERCUR, JJ., absent.

Common Pleas—Law.

C. P. of Delaware Co. Jan. 1880.

Miles & Calahan v. Henry Pleasants, M. D., owner, etc., and Elwood Wilson, Jr., equitable owner and contractor.

Practice—Monthly return days in Delaware County—Mechanics' lien—When sci. fa. may issue, under Acts of June 16, 1836, and June 28, 1879.

Rule to quash a scire facias sur mechanic's lien.

The record showed that the sci. fa. issued Nov. 12, 1879, returnable Nov. 17, 1879, on which day an appearance *de bene esse* was entered for the defendant.

On Nov. 24, 1879, this rule was taken, on the ground that the sci. fa. issued less than fifteen days prior to the return day.

H. Pleasants, Jr., for the rule.

The Act of June 16, 1836, § 16 (P. L. 699), provides that no such sci. fa. shall issue "within fifteen days previous to the return day of the *next term.*" Prior to 1861 the Delaware County Courts had but four return days, one for each term. Hence the expression in the Act—meaning simply *previous to the succeeding return day.*

Browne's Leg. Time-table (ed. 1875), 89.
T. & H. Prac. (ed. 1880), § 2010.
Phila. Legal Calendar.

The Act of 28 June, 1879 (P. L. 183), requiring publication of this writ, in some cases, for two weeks, shows that the fifteen-day rule was considered in force. As this is a proceeding *in rem* the mode of service required by the Act must be strictly complied with.

Wister *v.* City, 5 WEEKLY NOTES, 279, etc.

H. C. Howard, contra.

The literal rendering of the Act of 1836 was complied with—the "*return day of the next term*" being in December. The Act of 1836 was repealed by implication by the Act of 12th March, 1842, § 1 (Purd. Dig. 497), because inconsistent therewith. This Court having, by virtue of the power given by Act of May 24, 1878 (Purd. Dig. 2097), established return days on the second, third, or fourth Mondays of months intermediate between terms, has exercised a power entirely inconsistent with the Act of 1836, which indicates that it is to be considered repealed. This point has been raised and settled in this Court against the defendant by Judge BUTLER in 1873.

Larkin *v.* Auld, MS., C. P. Del. Co. August Term, 1873, No. 115.

C. A. V.

Feb. 2, 1880. THE COURT. This is a rule to quash a sci. fa. sur mechanic's claim, because issued less than fifteen days before the return day.

The Act of June 16, 1836, provides that no scire facias upon a mechanic's claim shall issue within fifteen days previous to the return day of the *next term*. At that time there were but four regular return days to the first, and four to the day preceding the last day of each term. By the Act of April 17, 1861, the return days were changed in Delaware County by extending to it the Act of March 28, 1835, relating to the monthly return days in Philadelphia. The construction put upon the Act by the bar and courts of Philadelphia ought to be adopted in Delaware County. The practice there has been to issue all sci. fas. upon mechanics' claims full fifteen days before the return day of the *month* to which the writ is made returnable; as both counties are now subject to the same Act, it would be inconsistent for us to adopt the Philadelphia Act and not also the practice under it at the time and previous to the date of its adoption.

The Act of June 16, 1836, requiring fifteen days to intervene between the teste and return of the writ was not *expressly* repealed by the subsequent legislation multiplying the return days. It was over a year old when the Act establishing the District Court and creating monthly return days was passed, and was immediately construed as applying to the new return days.

When the Act creating the new return days was extended to Delaware County the practice of the bar seems to have been to consider the former Act, requiring the fifteen days between the teste and return, to have been repealed by implication as being inconsistent with the subsequent legislation. But such a practice is at best but a dangerous experiment; the same reason for the time allowed by the Act in favor of *owners* not necessarily parties to the suit exists now as when the Act allowing the fifteen days was passed. The proceeding being *in rem* it is essential that every step should be regular; besides all presumptions are always favorable to the first regular construction given to an Act of Assembly. It may be that the writ can issue at any time before the return day, but it is very doubtful whether judgment could be taken for want of an appearance until fifteen days after service of the writ, with the usual four days of grace. The time for filing an affidavit of defence would also have to be extended; this would render the practice complicated and artificial instead of keeping it as simple as possible. By following the spirit of the Act and requiring all such writs to issue at least fifteen days before the *return day* we avoid all difficulty as to the day when judgment can be taken by default of an appearance or for want of an affidavit of defence. We have, therefore, concluded to follow the Philadelphia practice. Rule absolute.

Opinion by CLAYTON, P. J.

[*Cf.* Haupt *v.* Davis, 2 WEEKLY NOTES, 141.]

C. P. No. 2. May 31, 1880.

Sparr v. Walz et ux.

Mechanic's lien—Amendment—Act of June 11, 1879, not retroactive—A mechanic's lien filed prior to the passage of this Act cannot be amended.

Rule to show cause why a mechanic's lien should not be amended. The lien was filed to Sept. Term, 1877, and was for painting done to four contiguous brick houses, and the averment was:—

"The said debt . . . being a debt contracted . . . at the request of John Foreman, Contractor, by and with the consent and authority of the said Anna B. Walz, a married woman, wife of the said Joseph Walz, she being the owner or reputed owner" . . .

The rule was to amend by adding the averment:—

"And the said Anna B. Walz was the owner of the ground. . . . And the erection of said houses was a necessary and proper improvement of the said real estate of said Anna B. Walz."

J. Quincy Hunsicker, for the rule, cited:—
Act of June 11, 1879, P. L. 122.
Freund *v.* Fenner, 8 WEEKLY NOTES, 287.

THE COURT referred to Sutton *v.* Clark (7 WEEKLY NOTES, 437).

Rule discharged.

[See Ashman *v.* McIlvaine, 8 WEEKLY NOTES, 309.]

WEEKLY NOTES OF CASES.

Vol. IX.]   THURSDAY, SEPT. 23, 1880.   [No. 5.

Supreme Court of the United States.

Thomas et al v. The West Jersey Railroad Company.

Contracts of corporations—Ultra vires—A lease is such a contract—A contract to transfer all rights and duties of corporation to third person not permissible—When such contract has not been entirely executed corporation not liable for unexecuted portion—What is an executed contract—Ratification by Legislature—Must be clear and express—What not sufficient.

The powers of corporations are such as are conferred by their charters, whether express or fairly implied.

A lease or contract by a railroad company to transfer all its rolling stock, etc., with all its rights and duties, when not clearly authorized, is *ultra vires* and void.

Any contract by which the corporation disables itself from performing its duties to the public, without the consent of the State, is void.

A mere recognition by the Legislature that a lease has been made is not sufficient to amount to a ratification of the lease.

When the contract which is void has been as to a portion correspondingly executed by both parties, the corporation can refuse at any time to go on with its further performance.

Such contract cannot be ratified or approved by the stockholders, so as to make it valid.

Per MILLER, J. Contracts fully executed on both sides, though invalid for want of corporate power, remain as the foundation of rights acquired by the transaction.

A railroad corporation of New Jersey having power to make contracts with other corporations or individuals for transporting or conveying passengers, merchandize, etc., made a contract or lease to three individuals, by which all its rights and duties were transferred to them for twenty years:

Held, that such contract was *ultra vires*.

The contract contained a provision that it could be terminated by three months' notice, and the value of the unexpired term should be submitted to arbitrators to ascertain the loss. An action of covenant having been brought for breach of contract:

Held, that as to the unexpired portion of term, the contract being *ultra vires*, there could be no recovery.

The Legislature of New Jersey by a subsequent Act limited the rates of toll by the railroad company and *its lessees*:

Held, not sufficient to amount to a legislative ratification of the contract.

Ashbury Railway, etc. Co. *v.* Riche, L. R. 7 Eng. & Ir. App. 653, commented on and approved.

Error to the Circuit Court of the United States, for the Eastern District of Pennsylvania.

Covenant, by George W. Thomas, Alfred S. Porter, and Nathaniel F. Chew against The West Jersey Railroad Company, for alleged breach of contract or instrument under seal. Plea, Covenants performed *absque hoc*.

The narr. contained several counts setting forth a contract under seal by the plaintiffs with the Millville and Glassboro Railroad, by which they contracted with said railroad company for the lease of all the railroad rolling stock of said company for the period of twenty years; that by an Act of the Legislature of New Jersey passed in 1868, the West Jersey Railroad Company, the defendant, had succeeded to all the rights and obligations of the said Millville and Glassboro Railroad Company: and alleged that plaintiffs had performed all their covenants. The narr set forth the agreement at length, of which sect. 17 was as follows:—

"That the party of the first part shall at any time have a right to put an end to this contract and to all the rights thereby given and retake possession of the railroad and rolling stock and buildings belonging to or appurtenant thereto, upon three months' notice to that effect given to the party of the second part, or to either of the persons thereof. That upon the termination of this contract, according to the notice thus provided, if the party of the second part shall so desire, then the party of the first part shall and will appoint a competent and disinterested person, who together with another competent and disinterested person appointed by the party of the second part shall consider and decide upon the value of this contract to the party of the second part, and the loss and damage incurred by and justly and equitably due to them by reason of such termination thereof. And in the event of any difference between the persons so appointed as aforesaid, as to the amount of damages justly and equitably due to the party of the second part as aforesaid, then and in such case the said two persons shall be at liberty to choose a third competent and disinterested person, and the decision of said three persons, if a third be chosen, shall be final, conclusive, and binding upon the parties hereto."

The first clause of the agreement was as follows:—

"First. That the party of the first part does hereby (and for the purpose of enabling the party of the second part to fulfil this contract), entrust to their possession and care and subject to the provisions of this contract, all the roadway and superstructure, buildings, machine shops, offices, stations, rolling stock, machinery implements, and materials on and along the line of said railroad of which a schedule is hereto annexed marked A.

Various other provisions were contained in the agreement showing a complete transfer to the plaintiff of the property above described, together with the right to use the railroad, take the tolls, etc. The plaintiffs agreed to pay to the

Millville and Glassboro one-half the gross receipts and a further sum of $10,000 per annum.

The breach alleged was the violation of the 17th clause in the agreement; that the said three months' notice had been given, but that the West Jersey Railroad Company, which had succeeded to the rights and obligations of the Millville and Glassboro Railroad Company, had failed to pay the value of the unexpired portion of the contract.

Upon the trial of the cause the plaintiffs offered the contract in evidence.

Also Act of March 9, 1859, incorporating the Millville and Glassboro Railroad Co. Also Act of New Jersey of April 10, 1867, a supplement to said Act, as showing ratification. It was as follows:—

"That it shall be unlawful for the directors, *lessees*, or *agents* of said railroad to charge more than three and a half cents per mile for the carrying of passengers, and six cents per ton per mile for the carrying of freight or merchandize of any description, unless a single package weighing less than one hundred pounds; nor shall more than one-half the above rate be charged for carying any fertilizing materials, either in their own cars or cars of other companies running over said railroad: *Provided*, That nothing contained in this Act shall deprive the said railroad company, *or its lessees*, of the benefits of the provision of an Act entitled 'An Act relative to freights and fares on railways in this State,' etc."

They then offered to show that, at the date of this Act, it was well known that the plaintiffs were lessees acting under the lease.

The 13th section of the former Act was as follows:—

"That it shall be lawful for the said company at any time during the continuance of its charter to make contracts and engagements with any other corporation, or with individuals for the transporting or carrying any kinds of goods, produce, merchandize, freight, or passengers, and to enforce the fulfilment of such contracts."

They then offered to prove that the notice was given by the Millville and Glassboro Railroad Co. This was objected to, and excluded.

They then further offered in evidence an Act to consolidate the railroad lines of New Jersey, approved March 18, 1868. Also agreement of consolidation between the Millville and Glassboro Railroad Company and the West Jersey Railroad Company, and a deed from same to same. Also to prove consent of stockholders to consolidation as provided by Act of New Jersey of March, 1868.

The Court excluded all the testimony on the ground that the lease by the Millville and Glassboro Railroad Company was *ultra vires* and void, and directed the jury to find for the defendant.

Verdict accordingly, and judgment thereon. The plaintiffs took this writ, assigning for error the rulings on the evidence and the instruction to the jury as above set forth.

A. Sydney Biddle and *George W. Biddle* (with them *Peter L. Voorhees*), for plaintiffs in error.

The contract of October 8, 1863, was *intra vires*, because authorized by the Act of incorporation. The 13th section of the Act of March 9, 1859, incorporating the Millville and Glassboro Railroad Company clearly confers the power claimed here. What language could be more appropriate to confer a power of leasing? The *lessees* were in open possession of the road at the time of the passage of the Act of April 10, 1867, and that Act clearly recognized the existence of the lease and its legality.

Ecclesi. Com. *v.* Railway Co., 4 Chan. Div. 845.

Moreover the agreement of October 8, 1863, was not a lease strictly. It was a mere appointment of agents to run the road. The various provisions of the agreement show this plainly.

But the authorities show clearly that such contracts as this are permissible. Featherstonhaugh *v.* Lee Morr Porcelain Co. (L. R. 1 Eq. Cas. 318, 331, 334) was a case very much like the present one. There was in that case a lease for twenty-one years, and the language of the Vice-Chancellor is peculiarly applicable to this case. See also—

Midland R. W. Co. *v.* G. W. R. W. Co., L. R. 8 Ch. App. 841, 851, 856, 857.

This case must not be confounded with those where the stockholders are entitled to an injunction to restrain acts which are not authorized by the charter. The following are cases of this class:—

Macgregor *v.* The Dover, etc., Co., 18 Ad. & El. (N. S.) 618.

Colman *v.* Eastern Counties R. W. C., 10 Beav. 1.

These cases have been criticized in England.

Mayor, etc., *v.* Norfolk R. W. Co., 4 Ell. & Bl. 413.

Taylor *v.* R. W. Co., L. R. 2 Ex. 375.

R. W. Co. *v.* Hawkes, 5 H. of L..C. 331.

See, also, Robins *v.* Embry, 1 Sm. & M. (Ch. R.) 268.

Silver Lake Bank *v.* North, 4 Johns. Ch. R. 370.

Llanelly Rld. Co. *v.* The London, etc., Co., L. R. 8 Ch. App. 943.

Galveston R. R. Co. *v.* Cowdrey, 11 Wall. 459.

The mere fact that the agreement contains a clause that the lessees shall be liable to the public does not alter this; the fact being that the chartered company still remains liable.

Langley *v.* Boston & Maine R. R. Co., 10 Gray, 103.

York, etc., R. R. Co. *v.* Winans, 17 Howard, 30.

Bissell *v.* The Michigan, etc., R. R. Co., 22 N. Y. 258.

The contract was authorized inasmuch as it was neither directly nor impliedly forbidden by the charter.

Angell & Ames on Corp., sect. 191.

Taylor *v.* The Chichester, etc., R. W. Co., L. R. 2 Ex. 375. Per BLACKBURN, J.

The Mayor, etc., Norfolk R. W. Co., 4 Ell. & Bl. 413. Per ERLE, C. J.

R. W. Co. v. Hawkes, 5 H. of L. C. 371. Per Lord ST. LEONARDS.
South Wales R. W. Co. v. Redmond, 10 C. B. (N. S.) 675, 686.

The defence is not admissible, because the stockholders have assented to the contract.

Hare v. R. W. Co., 2 J. & Hem. 80, 121.
Phosphate Co. v. Green, L. R. 7 C. P. 43.
Erie R. W. Co. v. The Morris & Essex R. R. Co., 6 C. E. Gr. Ch. (21 N. J. R.) 283, 289.
Del., L. & W. R. Co. v. Erie R. Co., Id. 301.

And when the transaction is complete the plea of *ultra vires* is not available.

Silver Lake Bank v. North, 4 Johns. Ch. R. 370.
Steamboat Co. v. McCutcheon, 13 Penna. St. 13.
Oneida Bank v. Ontario Bank, 21 N. Y. 490.
Bissell v. Mich. South. R. R , 22 N. Y. 258.
Whitney Arms Co. v. Barlow, 63 N. Y., 62.
Steam Co. v. Weed, 17 Barb. 378.
Moss v. Mining Co., 5 Hill, 137.
Grant v. Coal Co., 80 Penna. St. 208.
Oil Creek R. R. Co. v. Penna. Trans. Co., 83 Penna. St. 160.
McCluer v. Manchester, etc., R. R., 13 Gray, 124.
Gifford v. N. J. R. R., 2 Stockton, 177.
Galveston R. R. v. Cowdrey, 11 Wall. 459.
Smith v. Sheeley, 12 Wall. 358.
Kelly v. Transportation Co., 3 Oregon, 189.
Weber v. Agricultural Society, 44 Iowa, 239, and others.

Samuel Dickson (with whom were *J. C. Bullitt* and *A. Browning*); for defendant in error.

(1) The agreement gave to the plaintiffs in error the exclusive control and use of the railroad of the Millville and Glassboro R. R. Co., and devolved upon them the exercise of all its duties and obligations to the public. Such an attempted delegation of corporate powers is within the strict meaning of the term *ultra vires*. The various senses in which the phrase has been used are considered in Green's Brice's *Ultra Vires*, 34, 49. See, also—

Earl of Shrewsbury v. R. W. Co., L. R. 1 Eq. 618.

Whatever exceptions may have been established, it is well settled that the fact that a corporation has received the consideration, does not involve it in liability upon a contract if it can be shown that it is clearly *ultra vires* of the corporation itself.

Green's Brice's *Ultra Vires*, 427, 608.
Miner's Ditch Co. v. Zellerbach, 37 Cal. 579.

Such a contract is incapable of ratification by the consent of all the stockholders, and this upon grounds of public policy, as to hold otherwise would be to repeal the limitations contained in the charter upon the powers of the corporation, and no stranger dealing with the corporation can allege ignorance of those limitations.

See remarks of PARKE, B., in South Yorkshire R. W. Co. v. Great Northern Co. (9 Ex. 75–84), cited with approval in Shrewsbury & Birmingham R. R. Co. v. Western R. R. Co. (6 H. L. C. 113); of BLACKBURN, J., in Taylor v. Railway Company (L. R. 2 Ex. 379); and of SELDEN, J., in Bissell v. R. R. Co. (22 N. Y. 289, 290). See, also—

East Anglian R. W. Co. v. Eastern Counties R. W. Co., 11 C. B. 803.
Pearce v. R. R. Co., 21 Howd. 441.
Navigation Co. v. Dandridge, 8 Gill & J. 248, 319.
Weckler v. Bank, 42 Md. 581.
R. R. Co. v. R. R. Co., 20 N. J. Eq. 543.

The latest and most satisfactory exposition of the law on the subject is given by Lords CAIRNS and SELBORNE, in the case of Ashbury Railway Carriage and Iron Co. *v.* Riche (7 Eng. & Ir. App. 653).

(2) The cases relied upon by the other side related to business corporations, which are but simple partnerships with limited liability, and are put upon the ground, that the contract has not been expressly or impliedly forbidden.

Bank v. Matthews, 8 Otto, 621.
Mining Co. v. Bank, 6 Otto, 640.

But this was a railroad company endowed with prerogative franchises and charged with duties to the public, and a transfer by way of lease or mortgage of such franchises, where not expressly authorized, has always been declared illegal and void.

1 Redfield on Railways, 87; ..ngell and Ames on Corporations, S. 191.
1 Red. on R. W., 588–592.
York and Maryland R. R. v. Winans, 17 How. 30.
Black v. D. & R. Canal Co., 7 C. E. Gr. 130.
Wood v. Bedford R. R., 8 Phila. 94.

(3) This contract is clearly and in terms a lease, and answers to every definition of such a contract.

2 Blackstone, 140.
Smith's Landlord and Tenant, 851.

But even traffic contracts, which amount to a delegation of the powers and duties of a railroad corporation, are equally bad as an avowed lease. The Courts look to the substance of the contract, and disregard the disguise.

Great Northern R. W. Co. v. Eastern Co.'s R. W. Co., 9 Hare, 306.
Winch v. Birkenhead R. W. Co., 5 De G. & Sm. 562.
Midland R. W. Co G. W. R. W. Co., L. R. 8 Ch. App. 841.

(4) The action is not brought upon an executed consideration, or for services done, but for "the value of the contract," *i. e.*, for the value of services prevented, and is, therefore, for the breach of an executory agreement; and the authorities relied upon by the other side are inapplicable.

1 Chitty on Pl., 340.
Fewings v. Tisdal, 1 Ex. 295.

(5) The Act of April, 1867, is not a legislative ratification. It was not passed to grant powers, but to impose restrictions, and cannot be held to give a power to lease without striking out the words "directors and agents." Such powers are not granted by intendment or implication.

Weil v. Ricord, 9 C. E. Gr., 169.
Miller v. Canal Commissioners, 9 Harris, 23.
Howard v. Earl of Shrewsbury, L. R. 2 Ch. App. 760–774.

Kent Coast Ry. Co. v. London C. & D. Co., L. R. 3 Ch. App. 656.

The last case is singularly like the present, and decisive of the question.

Mr. Justice MILLER delivered the opinion of the Court.

The plaintiffs in error entered into a contract on the 8th day of October, 1863, with the Milville and Glassboro Railroad Company of New Jersey, which, in the resolution of the board of directors by whom it was initiated, is called a lease of the road. This agreement was confirmed by a vote of the stockholders, and was to continue for a period of twenty years from the first day of April, 1863.

It, however, contained a provision that the railroad company could at any time put an end to it upon three months' notice to the other party; but in that event arbitrators were to be chosen who should decide upon the value of the contract and the amount of damages incurred by and equitably and justly due to the other party by reason of such action. Under this provision the railroad company ended the contract and resumed possession of the road April 1, 1868.

About this time, by Acts of the New Jersey Legislature, the Milville and Glassboro Railroad Company was consolidated with the West Jersey Railroad Company, which succeeded to all the rights and obligations of the former company, and the road was delivered by plaintiffs, on the first of April, 1868, to the latter.

Efforts at arbitration, which it is unnecessary to recite here, having proved abortive, the plaintiffs in error brought the present action in the Circuit Court for the Eastern District of Pennsylvania to recover the value of the contract and the damages sustained by them by its termination under the clause of the agreement already mentioned.

The Court held the contract void, and instructed the jury to find a verdict for defendants. This writ of error brings up the judgment entered on that verdict for review.

The ground on which the Court so held, and n which the ruling is supported in argument .e, is, that the contract amounted to a lease, oy which the railroad, rolling-stock, and franchises of the corporation were transferred to plaintiffs, and that such a contract was *ultra vires* of the company.

It is denied by appellants that the contract can be fairly called a lease. But we know of no element of a lease which is wanting in this instrument. "A lease for years is a contract between lessor and lessee, for possession of lands, etc., on the one side, and a recompense by rent or other consideration on the other." (4 Bacon's Abridgment, 632.) "Anything corporeal or incorporeal lying in livery or in grant may be the subject-matter of a lease, and, therefore, not only lands and houses, but commons, ways, fisheries, franchises, estovers, annuities, rent charges, and all other incorporeal hereditaments are included in the common-law rule." (Bouvier's Law Dictionary, "Lease;" 1 Washburn Real Property, 310, old paging.)

The railroad and all its appurtenances and franchises, including the right to do the business of a railroad and collect the proper tolls, are leased to the plaintiffs for a period of twenty years by the corporation. In return, it receives from plaintiffs one-half of all the gross earnings of the road as rent. The usual right of re-entry for failure to perform covenants in addition to the special right to terminate the lease on notice, is found in the instrument, and the usual covenant for repairs and proper running of the road, equivalent to good husbandry on a farm, is also there.

The provision for complete possession, control, and use of the property of the company and its franchises by the lessees is perfect. Nothing is left in the lessor but the right to receive rent. No power of control in the management of the road and the exercise of the franchises of the company. A solitary exception to this statement, of no value in the actual control of its affairs, is found in the sixth clause of the lease, which is a covenant that the lessees will discharge any one in their service on the request of the corporation, evidenced by a resolution of the board of directors.

But while we are satisfied that the contract is both technically and in its essential character a lease, we do not see that the decision of that point either way affects the question on which we are to pass. That question is whether the railroad company exceeded its powers in making the contract, by whatever name it may be called, so that it is void.

It is, perhaps, as well to consider this question in the order of its presentation by the learned counsel for plaintiffs, upon whom the burden of showing the error of the Circuit Court devolved the duty of proving one of the following propositions:—

(1) The contract was within the powers granted to the railroad company by the Act of the New Jersey Legislature under which it was organized.

(2) That if this be not established, the lease was afterwards ratified and approved by another Act of that Legislature.

(3) That if both these propositions are found to be untenable, the contract became an executed agreement under which the rights acquired by plaintiffs should be legally respected.

The authority to make this lease is placed by counsel primarily in the following language of the thirteenth section of the company's charter: "That it shall be lawful for the said company, at any time during the continuance of its charter, to make contracts and engagements with any other corporation, or with individuals, for the transporting or conveying any kinds of goods, produce, merchandise, freight, or passengers, and to enforce the fulfilment of such contracts." This is no more than saying "you may do the business of carrying goods and passengers and may make contracts for doing that business. Such contracts you may make with any other corporation or with individuals." No doubt a contract by which the goods received from other railroads or carrying companies should be carried over the road of this company, or by which goods or passengers from this road should be carried by other railroads, whether connecting immediately with them or not, are within this power, and are probably the main object of the clause. But it is impossible, under any sound rule of construction, to find in the language here used a permission to sell, to lease, or to transfer the entire road and the rights and franchises of the corporation to others. To do so, is to deprive the company of the power of making those contracts which this clause confers and of performing the duties which it implies.

In the case of the Ashbury Railway-Carriage and Iron Co. *v.* Riche, decided in the House of Lords in 1875, and reported in 7 English and Irish Appeal Cases, 653, the memorandum of association, which, as Lord CAIRNS said, stands under the Act of 1862 in place of a legislative charter, thus described the business which the association was authorized to conduct: "The objects for which this company is established are to make, sell, or lend on hire, railway-carriages and engines, and all kinds of railway plant, fittings, machinery, and rolling-stock; and to carry on the business of *mechanical engineers and general contractors;* to purchase and sell as merchants, timber, coal, metals, or other materials; and to buy and sell any such materials on commission or as agents." This company purchased a concession for a railroad in Belgium, and entered into a contract for its construction, on which it paid large sums of money. The company was sued afterwards on the agreement with Riche, the contractor, and the contract was held valid in the Exchequer Chamber by a majority of the Judges, on the ground that while it was in excess of the power conferred on the directors by the memorandum, it had been made valid by ratification of the shareholders, to whom it had been submitted. The House of Lords reversed this judgment, holding unanimously that the contract was beyond the powers conferred by the memorandum above recited, and being beyond the powers of the association, no vote of the shareholders whatever could make it valid. The case is otherwise important in its relation to the one before us, but it is cited here for its parallelism in the construction of the clause defining the powers of the company.

If a memorandum which described the parties as engaging in furnishing nearly all the materials, machinery, and rolling-stock which go to make a railroad and its equipments, and then empowered them to carry on the business of mechanical engineers and general contractors, cannot authorize a contract to build a railroad, surely the authority to build a railroad and to contract for carrying passengers and goods over its own road and over others is no authority to lease out the road and with the lease to part with all its powers to another company or to individuals. We do not think there is anything in the language of the charter which authorized the making of this agreement.

It is next insisted, in the language of counsel, that though this may be so, "a corporate body may (as at common law) do any act which is not either expressly or impliedly prohibited by its charter; although where the act is unauthorized by the charter a shareholder may enjoin its execution; and the State may, by proper process, forfeit the charter." We do not concur in this proposition. We take the general doctrine to be in this country, though there may be exceptional cases and some authorities to the contrary, that the powers of corporations organized under legislative statutes are such and such only as those statutes confer. Conceding the rule applicable to all statutes, that what is fairly implied is as much granted as what is expressed, it remains that the charter of a corporation is the measure of its powers, and that the enumeration of these powers implies the exclusion of all others.

This class of subjects has received much consideration of late years in the English courts, and counsel on both sides of the present case have relied largely on the decisions of those courts. Among the cases cited by both sides is that of the East Anglian Railway Co. *v.* The Eastern Counties Railway Co. (11 Com. Bench R. 803). In that case the Eastern Counties Railway Company had made a contract in which, among other things, it covenanted to take a lease of several other railroads whose companies had introduced into Parliament a bill for consolidation under the name of East Anglian Railway Company, and to assume the payment of the parliamentary expenses of this act of consolidation. This covenant was held void as beyond the power conferred by the charter 'They cannot," said the Court, " engage in a new trade, because they are incorporated only for the purpose of making and maintaining the Eastern Counties Railway. What additional power do they acquire from the fact that the undertaking may in some way benefit their line? Whatever may be the object or prospect of success, they are still but a corporation for the purpose only of making and maintaining the Eastern Counties Railway; and if they cannot embark in new trades because they have only a limited authority, for the same reason they can do nothing not authorized by their Act and not within the scope of their authority." This case, decided in 1851, was afterwards cited with approval by the Lord Chancellor in 1857, in delivering the opinion of the House of Lords in the case of Eastern Counties Railway Company v. Hawkes (5 Clark's House of Lords Reports, 347), and it is there stated that it was also acted on and recognized in the Exchequer Chamber in the case of MacGregor v. The Deal and Dover Railway Company (22 Law J., Queen's Bench, 69). Both these cases are cited approvingly in the opinion of Lord CAIRNS in the case of the Ashbury Company, on appeal in the House of Lords.

This latter case, as decided in the Exchequer Chamber (Law Reports, 9 Exch., 224), is much relied on by counsel for plaintiffs here as showing that though the contract may be *ultra vires* when made by the directors, it may be enforced if afterwards ratified by the shareholders or if partly executed. But in the House of Lords, where the case came on appeal, this principle was overruled unanimously in opinions delivered by Lord Chancellor CAIRNS, Lords SELBORNE, CHELMSFORD, HATHERLEY, and O'HAGAN, and the broad doctrine established that a contract not within the scope of the powers conferred on the corporation cannot be made valid by the assent of every one of the shareholders, nor can it by any partial performance become the foundation of a right of action.

It would be a waste of time to attempt to examine the American cases on the subject, which are more or less conflicting, but we think we are warranted in saying that this latest decision of the House of Lords represents the decided preponderance of authority, both in this country and in England, and is based upon sound principle.

There is another principle of equal importance and equally conclusive against the validity of this contract, which if not coming exactly within the doctrine of *ultra vires* as we have just discussed it, shows very clearly that the railroad company was without the power to make such a contract. That principle is that where a corporation, like a railroad company, has granted to it by charter a franchise intended in large measure to be exercised for the public good, the due performance of those functions being the consideration of the public grant, any contract which disables the corporation from performing those functions, which undertakes, without the consent of the State, to transfer to others the rights and powers conferred by the charter, and to relieve the grantees of the burden which it imposes, is a violation of the contract with the State, and is void as against public policy. This doctrine is asserted with remarkable clearness in the opinion of this Court, delivered by Mr. Justice CAMPBELL, in the case of The York and Maryland Line Railroad Co. v. Winans (17 Howard, 30). The corporation in that case was chartered to build and maintain a railroad in Pennsylvania by the Legislature of that State. The stock in it was taken by a Maryland corporation, called the Baltimore and Susquehanna Railroad Company, and the entire management of the road was committed to the Maryland company, which appointed all the officers and agents upon it and furnished the rolling stock. In reference to this state of things and its effect upon the liability of the Pennsylvania corporation for infringing a patent of the defendant in error, Winans, this Court said: "This conclusion (argument) implies that the duties imposed upon plaintiff (in error) by the charter are fulfilled by the construction of the road, and that by alienating its right to use, and its powers of control and supervision, it may avoid further responsibility. But these acts involve an overturning of the relations which the charter has arranged between the Legislature and the community. Important franchises were conferred upon the corporation to enable it to provide facilities for communication and intercourse required for public convenience. Corporate management and control over these were prescribed, and corporate responsibility for their insufficiency provided as a remuneration for their grant. The corporation cannot absolve itself from the performance of its obligations without the consent of the Legislature. (Beman v. Rufford, 1 Simon N. S. 550; Winch v. B. and L. Railway Company, 13 Eng. Law and Equity, 506.)"

And in the case of Black v. Delaware and Raritan Canal Co. (7 C. E. Green N. Jer. Eq., 399), Chancellor ZABRISKIE says: "It may be considered as settled that a corporation cannot lease or alienate any franchise, or any property necessary to perform its obligations and duties to the State, without legislative authority." For this he cites some ten or twelve decided cases in England and in this country.

This brings us to the proposition that the Legislature of New Jersey has given her consent by an Act which amounts to a ratification of this lease. That Act is entitled "A supplement to the Act entitled an Act to incorporate the Millville and Glassboro Railroad Company," approved April 10, 1867; and its only purpose was to regulate the rates at which freight and passengers should be carried. It reads as follows: Be it enacted, etc., "That it shall be unlawful for the directors, *lessees* or *agents* of said railroad, to charge more than three and a half cents per mile for the carrying of passengers, and six cents per ton per mile for the carrying of freight or merchandise of any description, unless a single package weighing less than one hundred pounds; nor shall more than one-half of the above rate be charged for carrying any fertilizing materials, either in their own cars or cars of other companies running over said railroad: *Provided*, That nothing contained in this Act shall deprive the said railroad company, *or its lessees*, of the benefits of the provisions of an Act entitled 'An Act relative to freights and fares on railways in the State,' approved March 4, 1858, and applicable to all other railroads in this State."

It may be fairly inferred that the Legislature knew at the time the statute was passed that plaintiffs were running the road and claiming to do so as lessees of the corporation. It was not important for the purpose of the Act to decide whether this was done under a lawful contract or not. No inquiry was probably made as to the terms of that lease, as no information on that subject was needed. The Legislature was determined that whoever did run the road and exercise the franchises conferred on the company, and under whatever claim of right this was done, should be bound by the rates of fare established by the Act. Hence, without undertaking to decide in whom was the right to the control of the road, language was used which included the directors, lessees, and agents of the railroad. The mention of the lessees no more implies a ratification of the contract of lease than the word directors would imply a disapproval of the contract. It is not by such an incidental use of the word lessees in an effort to make sure that all who collected fares should be bound by the law, that a contract unauthorized by the charter, and forbidden by public policy, is to be made valid and ratified by the State.

It remains to consider the suggestion that the contract, having been executed, the doctrine of *ultra vires* is inapplicable to the case. There can be no question that, in many instances, where an invalid contract, which the party to it might have avoided or refused to perform, has been fully performed on both sides, whereby money has been paid or property changed hands, the Courts have refused to sustain an action for the recovery of the property or the money so transferred. And in regard to corporations the rule has been well laid down by C. J. COMSTOCK, in Parish *v.* Wheeler (22 New York, 494), that the executed dealings of corporations must be allowed to stand for and against both parties when the plainest rules of good faith require it.

But what is sought in the case before us is the enforcement of the unexecuted part of this agreement. So far as it has been executed, namely, the four or five years of action under it, the accounts have been adjusted, and each party has received what he was entitled to by its terms. There remains unperformed the covenant to arbitrate with regard to the value of the contract. It is the damages provided for in that clause of the contract that are sued for in this action. Damages for a material part of the contract never performed; damages for the value of a contract which was void. It is not a case of a contract fully executed. The very nature of the suit is to recover damages for its non-performance. As to this it is not an executed contract. Not only so, but it is a contract forbidden by public policy and beyond the power of the defendants to make. Having entered into the agreement, it was the duty of the company to rescind or abandon it at the earliest moment. This duty was independent of the clause in the contract which gave them the right to do it. Though they delayed its performance for several years, it was nevertheless a rightful act when it was done. Can this performance of a legal duty, a duty both to stockholders of the company and to the public, give to plaintiffs a right of action? Can they found such a right on an agreement void for want of corporate authority and forbidden by the policy of the law? To hold that this can be done is, in our opinion, to hold that any act done under a void contract makes all its parts valid, and that the more you do under a contract forbidden by law the stronger the claim to its enforcement in the courts.

We cannot see that the present case comes within the principle that requires that contracts which, though invalid for want of corporate power, have been fully executed, shall remain as the foundation of rights acquired by the transaction.

We have given this case our best consideration on account of the importance of the principles involved in its decision, and after a full examination of the authorities we can see no error in the action of the Circuit Court, and its judgment is, therefore, affirmed.

Supreme Court.

May, '79, 92.   June 10, 1880.
Phil. and Erie R. R. Co. v. Cake.

Railroads—Eminent domain—Proceedings under Act of 19 Feb. 1849—Damages—Report of viewers, what facts should be stated therein—Philadelphia and Erie R. R. Co.—Consequential damage to owner of land fronting on a street on which a new railroad siding is located.

Viewers appointed to assess damages for the construction of a railroad, and works connected therewith, must state in their report the material facts which constitute the elements of damage or advantage to the owner of the land affected thereby.

A report is fatally defective which omits to state that the jury had made a fair comparison of the probable advantages and disadvantages likely to result to the landowner from the new railroad, and had made allowance for the probable advantages.

The Court below has power to set aside the report of viewers when the damages found are grossly excessive.

Certiorari to the Common Pleas of Northumberland Co.

This case arose on a petition for the appointment of viewers to assess damages occasioned to Henry L. Cake by the Philadelphia and Erie Railway Co., and was reviewed by the Supreme Court on a previous writ of error. (See 6 WEEKLY NOTES, 151.)

The material facts were as follows: Henry L. Cake, the defendant in error, being the owner of thirteen building lots, lying partly in the borough of Sunbury and partly in the county of Northumberland, built, in 1865 and 1866, ten houses on said lots. The Philadelphia and Erie R. R. Co. owned a tract of about forty-two acres of land situate to the east of said Cake's lots, and being separated therefrom by a twenty-five feet wide street. In 1870, the company, needing an additional siding, constructed it along and upon this twenty-five feet street, making an embankment upon it from four to seven feet high, which embankment was directly east and in front of said houses belonging to Cake. He thereupon presented his petition to the Common Pleas for the appointment of viewers, under the tenth and eleventh sections of the general railroad law of Feb. 19, 1849, to assess the damages he had sustained by reason of the embankment. On August 10, 1871, the Court ordered the viewers to meet on the premises on Sept. 5, 1871; but on Sept. 1, 1871, the railroad company presented their petition to the Court, excepting to the legality of Cake's petition, and the order appointing viewers, and praying that said order should be set aside on the following grounds: (1) No notice had been served on the company of the appointment of viewers or of their time of meeting. (2) The proceedings were instituted under the general railroad law of 1849; but the Phila. and Erie R. R. Company, under their special charter, approved April 3, 1837, is not subject to the provisions of that law. The Act of April 14, 1864, providing for the extension of the 10th and 11th sections of the Act of 1849 to said company had not been accepted by the company, but, as they are advised, was repealed by the Act of July 22, 1864. (3) That no authority was given by the charter of the company for the appointment of viewers to assess damages to land not occupied by the company; that the damages asked for are purely consequential, being in consequence of constructing railroad tracks in a public street. A rule to show cause why the order should not be set aside was granted, argued, and discharged; and the Court then further ordered the viewers to meet Oct. 19, 1871. On this day the viewers found for the petitioner in the sum of $5600, with interest from Aug. 29, 1871. On Nov. 17, 1871, the railroad company filed exceptions to, and entered an appeal from the report of the viewers. The seventh exception was as follows: "For that the viewers do not state that in estimating and determining the damages, etc., they had any regard to or made any just allowance for the advantages which may have resulted, or which may seem likely to result, to the said Henry L. Cake in consequence of the making or opening of said railroad, and of the construction of works connected therewith, nor that they made any fair and just comparison of the advantages and disadvantages."

These exceptions were argued and overruled Oct. 27, 1873, and the Court ordered that the appeal be proceeded with as directed by Act of Assembly in such case made and provided. The case was at issue and marked for trial on Sept. 21, 1874. A rule to show cause why the appeal should not be stricken off was entered, and, after argument, was discharged by the Court Sept. 25, 1876, and on Oct. 1, 1877, the cause was called for trial. The jury, under instructions from the Court, found for the defendant, and, judgment having been entered on the verdict, the cause was by writ of error remanded to the Supreme Court, and at May term, 1878, the judgment was reversed, and the appeal from the report of viewers was stricken off, and the record ordered to be remitted for further proceedings (reported 6 WEEKLY NOTES, 151).

On Aug. 5, 1878, Cake moved, in the Court below, for a rule to show cause why judgment should not be entered in his favor and against defendant, *nunc pro tunc*, as of Oct. 27, 1873, for $5600, with interest from Aug. 29, 1870. This rule was argued, and on Dec. 27, 1878, the Court confirmed the report of the viewers, except so much as states "with interest from Aug. 29, 1870."

In the opinion filed, ROCKEFELLER, P. J., said, *inter alia:* "The evidence shows, and I find as a fact, that the damages found by the viewers are grossly excessive . . . but whether it is the duty of the Court, or whether it is now in its power to set it aside on the ground of excessive damages is another matter. After much thought I have come to the conclusion, that under the circumstances, it is not the duty of the Court, nor is it now in its power to set aside the report of viewers for this reason. I might for the sake of seeing justice done at all hazards, take a different view of this matter if I did not believe the defendant has a full and complete remedy in the Supreme Court if I am wrong. If that Court believes injustice has been done, and that this Court has refused to interfere on improper principles and mistaken views of the law or of its power, it will do what this Court ought to have done. This is asserted on the authority of the case of The Pennsylvania Railroad *v.* Heister (8 Barr, 448, 453)."

Judgment was thereupon entered in favor of the plaintiff for $5600, with interest from the date of filing the report, Oct. 19, 1871. The railroad company thereupon took this writ of certiorari, assigning for error, *inter alia*, the overruling of the 7th exception to the viewers' report, as above quoted.

H. T. Beardsley, J. B. Packer, W. C. Packer, and *James K. Davis, Jr.,* for plaintiff in error.

The Act of 1849, requires the viewers to make a fair and just comparison of the advantages and disadvantages, and to have a due regard to and make a just allowance for the advantages which may have resulted, or which may seem likely to result to the owner, in consequence of the making or opening of the railroad, and of the construction of works connected therewith.

Ohio & Penna. R. R. Co. *v.* Wallace, 2 H. 248.
Reitenbaugh *v.* R. R. Co., 9 H. 105.
O'Hara *v.* P. R. R., 1 Casey, 445.
Zack *v.* P. R. R., 1 Casey, 394.

A report of viewers, appointed under the fourth section of the Act of March 27, 1848, which omits to state the quantity and value of the land taken, and all other material facts, is fatally defective, and will be set aside.

P. R. R. *v.* Porter, 5 Casey, 169.
Poffenberger *v.* Susquehanna R. R., 1 Pearson, 46.
New Castle R. R. Co. *v.* McChesney, 4 Norris, 522.

In the opinion filed the Court below find that the damages awarded are grossly excessive, and say they "conscientiously believe hardship and injustice will be the result of the confirmation of this report." The Court should, therefore, have set aside the report on the ground of excessive damages.

Penna. R. R. Co. *v.* Heister, 8 Barr, 445.

The original Act of April 3, 1837, incorporating the Phila. and Erie R. R. Company, invested them with all the usual powers of a railroad corporation, and granted to them "all the privileges, franchises, and immunities incident to a corporation," etc., etc., and by section 11 it was provided, *inter alia*, as follows:—

SECTION 11. The said railroad company shall have the power to survey, lay down, ascertain, mark, and fix *such route or routes as they shall deem expedient for a railroad, with as many sets of tracks as they may deem necessary,* from Sunbury, by the way of Northumberland and Williamsport, *by the most eligible route* to the harbor of Erie."

No limitations or conditions are imposed upon the company, either in the selection of the route, or in determining the number of their tracks. They are not expressly forbidden to occupy streets and highways. If the act of location had been voidable, none but the Commonwealth can call the company to account.

Cleveland and Pittsburgh R. R. *v.* Speer, 6 P. F. S. 325.
Clarke *v.* Bridge Co., 5 Wr. 147.
Dugan *v.* Bridge Co., 3 C. 313.
Wilmington & Balt. R. R. *v.* Williams, 4 Sm. 103.
Note to 1 American Railway Cases, 166.

The Act of 14 April, 1864, and the subsequent railroad Acts have never been accepted by this company; and therefore the company cannot be held liable under them without its consent. The company's original Act of incorporation (1837) did not contain any reservation to the Legislature of the right to alter or amend it. The Act of April 14, 1864, did not relate merely to remedies, or the mode of enforcing existing obligations, duties, and liabilities, but it sought to impose additional burdens, by making the company liable for a large class of consequential damages for which they were not responsible before, and it was, therefore, unconstitutional and void.

The power of the Legislature to authorize the building of a railroad upon a public road is indubitable.

Joshua W. Comly and *J. Adam Cake,* contra.

The Act of Feb. 19, 1849, is made applicable to the Phila. and Erie R. R. Company by the Act of 14 April, 1864; the prior Acts did not authorize the Company to occupy a street, and if they availed themselves of the privilege granted by the Act of April 14, 1864, they became "liable for ample compensation to owners of adjoining lots for damages caused by excavation or embankment;" this was so decided by this Court on the previous writ of error (6 WEEKLY NOTES, 151, 153.)

The construction of the road in question is a mere siding—a part of the railroad to which it is annexed made for the convenience of the company, and it is not within the reason of the law which requires that the advantages and disadvantages of the railroad shall be taken into consideration when land is taken for the construction of the railroad in the first instance.

New Castle & Franklin R. R. *v.* McChesney, 4 N. 522.

The Supreme Court will not examine into exceptions which depend on depositions taken in the Court below relating to the assessment of damages.

Allison *v.* Canal Co., 5 Wharton, 482.
Penna. R. R. Co. *v.* Lutheran Cong., 3 Sm. 451.

And as the opinion of the Court below is no part of the record, the statements of the Judge on the subject of excessive damages are not before this Court, on this certiorari.

June 19, 1880. THE COURT. The sixth assignment of error must be sustained. It sets forth that the Court below erred in disallowing the seventh exception filed by the defendant. Said exception is as follows: "That the viewers do not state that in estimating and determining the damages they had any regard to or made any just allowance for the advantages which may have resulted, or which may seem likely to result to the said Henry L. Cake in consequence of the making or opening of said railroad, and of the construction of works connected therewith, nor that they made any fair or just comparison of the advantages and disadvantages." That this is a radical defect and an adequate ground for setting aside the report has been repeatedly decided. It is sufficient for present purposes to refer to Ohio and Pennsylvania Railroad Co. *v.* Wallace (2 Harris, 245); Reitenbaugh *v.* The Chester Valley Railroad Company (9 Id. 100); Zack *v.* The Pennsylvania Railroad Company (1 Casey, 394); O'Hara Darlington *v.* The Penna. Railroad Company (Id. 445); The Railroad Company *v.* Porter (5 Casey, 165). It is no answer to say that it would be useless to set forth such matters in the report, the law requires it, and for sufficient reasons. As was said in Zack *v.* The Railroad Company (*supra*), "The report is to be reviewed by the Court, and this can be of no value, if no facts be set out in it, unless the Court chose to hear the evidence over again. If the facts be not set out, and are not required to be, then a review in this Court is worth nothing. Besides it is important in reviewing a case tried out of the general course of the law to see what matters have been inquired of that it may be known that the cause has been fully and rightly considered."

This disposes of the case, and renders a discussion of the remaining assignments unnecessary. It is proper to say, however, that it was the plain duty of the learned Judge of the Court below, upon his own statement of the case, to have set aside this report. He says in his opinion, "The evidence shows, and I find as a fact, that the damages found by the viewers are grossly excessive. Notwithstanding this finding he entered judgment upon the report upon a mistaken idea that he had no power to set it aside, and sent the case up to this Court with what amounts to an invitation to us to do what he omitted to do. All this, however, appears only in the opinion of the Court, which forms no part of the record. How far we would be justified in looking at it, when the Court below has declined to exercise its discretion from an erroneous view of its power, and has sent up its opinion for the very purpose of showing us its reasons for declining to act, and to invite our review of its ruling, it is not essential now to decide. We reverse the case upon the ground previously referred to.

The judgment is reversed, and the report of the viewers set aside.

Opinion by PAXSON, J.

May, '80, 189.   May 18, 1880.

Big Black Creek Improvement Co. v. The Commonwealth of Pennsylvania.

Taxation—Act of April 24, 1874 (Coal companies), § 7, construed—Construction of statutes.

The Act of April 24, 1874, § 7 (P. L. 71), provides that corporations doing business in this Commonwealth and possessing "the corporate right or privilege to mine or to purchase and sell coal" shall make report semi-annually of the number of tons mined by such company, and also of the number of tons mined upon the company's land by any unincorporated association, partnership, or individual, under any lease or contract, and shall pay a tax thereon:

Held, that this Act applies to corporations authorized to hold and lease coal lands, to be worked by others, although the corporation itself is expressly prohibited by its charter from mining.

Statutes are to be construed so as may best effectuate the intention of the makers, which sometimes may be collected from the cause or occasion of passing the statute, and when discovered, it ought to be followed with judgment and discretion in the construction, though that construction may seem contrary to the letter of the statute.

Error to the Common Pleas of Dauphin County.

This was in the Court below an appeal of the Big Black Creek Improvement Company to the Court of Common Pleas of Dauphin County from the settlement of an account against them by the accounting officers of the Commonwealth. Appeal filed July 7, 1879.

The Big Black Creek Improvement Company was incorporated April 12, 1855, with authority to hold coal lands in certain townships in Luzerne County and to prepare the same to be worked and leased, the veins to be opened, shutes, breakers, and screens to be erected, and with the powers usually conferred on corporations, with all the rights, powers, and privileges, and subject to all the restrictions, provisions, and liabilities conferred and imposed upon the Swatara Company by the 2d, 3d, and 4th sections of the Act incorporating the same, approved the 6th day of March, 1849. The Swatara Improvement Company has the usual powers conferred on coal companies, except that by the 4th section of the Act it is provided that this company shall *not* have *mining* or *banking* privileges. A supplement was passed, on the second day of April, 1860, to the charter of the Rausch Creek Company, by which it had conferred on it many other and additional privileges, but was again deprived of any *mining* or *banking* privileges with the addition that the capital stock or dividends of the company shall not be taxable.

On the 3d day of April, 1863, a supplement was passed to the Big Black Creek Improvement Company, giving it all the privileges and subjecting it to all the restrictions and provisions contained in the Act to incorporate the Rausch Creek Improvement Company, approved the 2d day of April, 1860.

The Black Creek Company when called on from the State Department made report (under protest) on the 31st of January, 1879, of the number of tons of coal mined on its land by unincorporated associations, partnerships or individuals, but averred that it was not subject to pay taxes on account of such mining.

The Act of April 24, 1874, entitled "An Act for the taxation of Corporations" (P. L. 7L), provides as follows:—

SEC. 7. "That every company incorporated or organized by or under any law of this Commonwealth, or incorporated or organized by or under any law of any other State, and doing business in this Commonwealth, which possesses *the corporate right or privilege to mine or to purchase and sell coal*, shall semi-annually, upon the first days of July and January, in each and every year, make report, under oath or affirmation, to the Auditor General, of the number of tons of coal mined during the six months preceding the said first day of July and January, by such company, and also of the number of tons of coal that shall be mined by any unincorporated association, partnership or individual, under any lease, contract, grant or mining privilege, upon the property of which the company making such report is the owner or lessee, or has any mining or coal privileges or interest therein, and also the number of tons not mined as aforesaid, which shall have been purchased during the same period by the said company, and shall pay into the treasury of the Commonwealth an additional tax on its corporate franchises, created by or used within this Commonwealth, at the rate of three cents upon each and every ton of two thousand two hundred and forty pounds of coal so mined or purchased as aforesaid: *Provided*, That the amount of coal consumed in the transaction of its business by any such company shall not be included in its return: *And provided further*, That said tax shall not be payable more than once in respect to the same ton of coal: *And provided also*, That if any such company shall neglect or refuse for a period of thirty days, after such tax becomes due, to make said return, or to pay the same, the amount thereof, with an addition of ten per centum thereto, shall be collected for the use of the Commonwealth, as other taxes are recoverable by law from the said companies."

Under this Act an account was settled by the Auditor General, charging the company with the tax of three cents on each ton of coal mined by lessees, etc., on the company's land, as appearing by the company's report thereof, showing a balance of $1744.26 due the Commonwealth.

The company thereupon entered an appeal to the Common Pleas of Dauphin County, their specification of objections being as follows: (1) That the company is not a coal company. (2) Because the tax is claimed on coal which the company did not "mine" nor "purchase and sell." (3) Because the company has not, and does not possess "the corporate right or privilege to mine or to purchase and sell coal," and therefore is not liable to a tax on its corporate franchises, created by or used within this Commonwealth, of three cents per ton on coal, under the 7th section of the Act of April 24, 1874, under which said accounts were settled.

The parties having agreed that trial by jury should be dispensed with, and the question be submitted to the Court, under the Act of April 22, 1874, the case was heard before PEARSON, President Judge. The Court on March 26, 1880, entered judgment for the Commonwealth for $1984.06, PEARSON, P. J., delivering an opinion, in which he said, *inter alia*, " Although interdicted from the privilege of mining or dealing in coal, in the ordinary method of buying, selling, or mining, it is impossible to doubt from the charter of this company that it purchased its large body of land in the coal region with the view of making profit out of the coal on its land. It is to cause the same to be leased and worked, the veins to be opened, shutes and breakers to be built, screens to be erected, etc., and do the various acts usually attendant on starting coal works. After this preparation the company was not to work the mines, but it is very clear that they were to be let out to others. The company could neither buy nor sell, but could be paid a royalty for each ton mined and received by its tenants.

"It is impossible to doubt but that the coal was mined on the land of this company by unincorporated associations, partnerships, or individuals within the very letter of the Act of 1874 as already cited. Although not coming within any Act of Assembly in force when this company was incorporated, yet there was no provision in the charter prohibiting a tax to be passed imposing a tax on the coal mined by others on this company's land and holding it responsible for the tax thereon, and this has been done in clear language.

"The only remaining question arises under the Act of the 2d day of April, 1860, incorporating the Rausch Creek Company. Is this tax now claimed imposed on the capital stock or dividends of the company? It is certainly distinguishable from a tax on capital stock. This is on the coal mined by others by the ton. It is not what is known in this State as a tax on 'capital stock,' nor is it what we generally understand by a tax on 'dividends.' That has a well-settled meaning in Pennsylvania. If the power of taxation is to be taken away from the State it should be by clear and unequivocal expressions, not by mere implication. Another reason exists. The Charter of the Rausch Creek Company was granted after the amendment to the Constitution in 1857, which secures to the Legislature the power to alter, revoke, or annul any charter of incorporation whenever in their opinion it shall be injurious to the citizens. It might be well said that the prohibition from taxing one company equally with another was unfair, and should not be practised or tolerated."

"On the whole we are clearly of the opinion that this corporation is subject to taxation in the mode imposed by the accounting department, and for the sum fixed by it."

The defendant took this writ, assigning for error, the entry of judgment in favor of the Commonwealth.

George Lear, for plaintiff in error.

The question in this case involves the proper construction of § 7 of the Act of April 22, 1874. The error of the Court is in holding that all corporations owning land upon which unincorporated associations, partnerships, and individuals mine coal, are liable to a tax of three cents on each ton of coal mined on the land; and that the purchase of land, preparing it for mining, and leasing it for a royalty constitute the purchase and sale of coal. The 4th section of the Act incorporating the Rausch Creek Company, provides that the company shall not have mining or banking privileges. The corporate right to mine is certainly not given where it is expressly withheld, corporate rights are not to be presumed or implied. To bring this company within the Act of 1874, it must have the corporate right to mine and also to purchase and sell. It is expressly prohibited from mining; to purchase is not sufficient; to sell is not sufficient; it must do both. To purchase land, and lease the veins at a rent or royalty to lessees who mine the coal, is not such a sale and disposal as is contemplated by the Act.

The tax is on the franchise. The corporate right to mine and to purchase and sell constitutes a class, and without being in that class the tax cannot be imposed.

Kittanning Coal Co. *v.* Commonwealth, 29 Smith, 100.

This company does not come within the class, is not described in the Act imposing the tax, and therefore cannot be held subject to it. The tax law of 1879 brought this company within its provisions, but it could not be made retroactive.

L. D. Gilbert, Deputy-Attorney General, and *Henry W. Palmer*, Attorney General, for the Commonwealth, defendant in error.

The 7th section of the Act of April 24, 1874, has already been construed in Kittanning Coal Co. *v.* Commonwealth (29 Smith, 100), in which it is decided that the tax is to be imposed upon the corporate franchise of corporations having the privilege to mine, purchase, and sell coal. This corporation has no *mining* privileges, but it belongs to that class of corporations which have corporate rights to make merchandise of coal, and as such is liable to the tax. It has an undoubted right to buy and sell coal lands, and to lease them. The lease so made amounts to a sale of coal, and the lessor in the contemplation of the tax law becomes a vendor of coal.

Lykens Valley Coal Co. *v.* Dock, 12 Smith, 238.
Tiley *v.* Moyers, 7 Wr. 404.
Appeal of Stoughton *et al.*, 7 Norris, 201.

The coal, in contemplation of law, is detached from the land, when the right to the coal has been parted with, and is sold as *coal*, and the owner of the coal and the owner of the land are each taxable.

Logan *v.* County, 5 Casey, 373.
Armstrong *v.* Caldwell, 3 Smith, 284.

The Act of 1874 intended to tax corporations trafficking in coal in respect to all coal mined upon their lands by "any unincorporated association, partnership or individual, under any lease, contract, grant or mining privilege" from the corporation, and this corporation has the right to traffic in coal within the meaning of that tax section.

May 31, 1880. THE COURT. Upon all corporations, having the right to mine, or to purchase and sell coal, the Act of 1874 imposed a tax of three cents for every ton mined or purchased, and required returns of the quantity of such coal to be made by the corporations to the Auditor General; and also a like tax on "the number of tons of coal that shall be mined by any unincorporated association, partnership or individual, under any lease, contract, grant, or mining privilege, upon the property of which the company making such report is the owner or lessee, or has any mining or coal privileges or interest therein." No unincorporated person or association of persons, mining or purchasing and selling coal is liable to the tax. The object of the law is to reach every corporation which purchases, and sells coal, which mines coal on its own land or land it has leased, or which causes coal to be mined under a lease, contract, grant, or mining privilege to unincorporated persons on property that it owns; or has a coal privilege or interest therein.

This plaintiff in error has extensive coal interests. It has the corporate right to own coal lands, to open the veins of coal, to erect all proper buildings, machinery, and improvements for mining, to construct a railroad, and when the veins are prepared to be worked, it may lease them on such terms as may be agreed between it and its lessees. It leased for a stipulated sum for each ton mined. Having no mining privilege, nor right to purchase and sell coal, "in the ordinary method of buying, selling, or mining," in a critical argument it claims non-liability to the tax, because the literal meaning of the words employed in the first clause of the seventh section, do not require it to make returns to the Auditor General. But it is an owner of coal lands, with corporate coal privileges and interests therein, which it leased to natural persons for mining, and we cannot doubt, that it is plainly within the intendment of the statute. Here, if anywhere, the rule should apply that "statutes are to be construed so as may best effectuate the intention of the makers, which sometimes may be collected from the cause or occasion of passing the statute, and when discovered, it ought to be followed with judgment and discretion in the construction, though that construction may seem contrary to the letter of the statutes."

We think the learned Judge of the Common Pleas was clearly right in his conclusions, and on his opinion—

Judgment affirmed.

Opinion by TRUNKEY, J.

SHARSWOOD, C. J., and GREEN, J., absent.

Common Pleas—Equity.

C. P. No. 1.   June, 1880.

White v. Schlect.

Equity—Special injunction—Will be dissolved when not prosecuted for more than a year— Also where answer denies facts and equity of bill—Trade-mark — Must show origin and ownership—Sheppard v. Stuart, 7 WEEKLY NOTES, 498, not followed—Acts of Congress relating to trade-marks—Unconstitutionality of.

Motion to dissolve injunction and dismiss bill. The facts, as stated in the opinion of ALLISON, P. J., were as follows:—

"A special injunction was granted in this case to restrain the defendant in the use of a device or design as a trade-mark, to which plaintiff claimed to be entitled by assignment to him by Edward J. Frost, who claimed to be the inventor, and to have first appropriated it to paper boxes, in which were put up for sale paper collars, having on the outside a representation of a 'drum,' which trade-mark was known in the market as indicating the 'drum collar.' This device of a drum constituted the trade-mark, to the exclusive use of which plaintiff claimed to be entitled, and the right to which was to him a valuable one, which was infringed by the defendant. The claim of Frost, from whom plaintiff derives title, is made to rest mainly, so far as the right is disclosed by the averments of the bill, upon the registration in the Patent Office of the United States of the said trade-mark, and a certificate issued to him by the Commissioner of Patents on the 5th day of December, 1876, which protected the same for a period of thirty years.

"The answer asserts that an examination of the claim as registered shows nothing but a claim for the mere figure of a drum, and that said device and symbol of a drum had been in common use, in various trades and businesses, for forty-five years, and in the collar trade for eight years, and that the plaintiff has not the exclusive right to said drum device; that it did not originate with him; he did not put his name on it at any time, and that it was in common use for about three years before the registration by Frost."

Plaintiff had not proceeded to final hearing, though more than a year had elapsed.

Archer, for the motion.

A trade-mark of a device of a "drum" is not valid, for it indicates neither origin nor ownership.

    Stokes v. Landgraff, 17 Barb. 608.
    Davol Mills Case, 7 Phila. 253.
    Dixon v. Guggenheim, 7 Phila. 408.

The case of Sheppard v. Stuart (7 WEEKLY NOTES, 498), contra, is at variance with all the authorities.

Being invalid at common law, registration does not help it; for the U. S. statutes relating to registration of trade-marks have been declared unconstitutional.

    Day v. Walls, 35 Leg. Int. 468.
    United States v. Steffens, 7 WEEKLY NOTES, 524.

The answer denies the whole equity of plaintiff's bill, asserts want of novelty, and avers common user; this is ground enough to dissolve injunction.

Carpenter *v.* Burden, 2 Par. Eq. Cases, 24.
Clapham *v.* White, 8 Vesey, 34.
Plaintiff has not proceeded to final hearing, though a year has elapsed. His bill should be dismissed.

Daniels's Ch. Prac., vol. 3, p. 1831.

Diehl, contra.

July 17, 1880. THE COURT (after stating the facts, *ut supra*). The Act of Congress authorizing the isssuing of such certificates has, since the granting of the special injunction, been declared to be unconstitutional by the Supreme Court of the United States, and we are therefore to look to the remaining portions of the bill as disclosing grounds for equitable protection by special injunction, in order to properly decide the question which is now before us on bill and answer, on the motion of the defendant to dissolve the special injunction. An examination of the bill discloses no other averment of title, except the alleged assignment of Frost, by virtue of the aforesaid certificate. The claim to priority of invention and appropriation is nowhere distinctly asserted, and rests chiefly on the inferences to be drawn from the fact, that claiming to be the inventor and appropriator of the trademark, the said certificate was issued to Frost in due form of law, which the plaintiff claimed established *prima facie* his right to the exclusive use of said trade-mark.

The affidavits of Frost and others, which were heard on the hearing of the motion for the special injunction, fully warranted the granting of the order, which defendant now claims should be set aside; these affidavits have, however, spent their force, and on the motion to dissolve the injunction on the coming in of the answer, the motion is to be granted or denied upon this ground, on the sufficient or insufficient denial of the equity of the bill; a special injunction being always granted until answer or further order. The answer, after setting up that the only claim of the plaintiff, according to the registered letters, was "essentially of the representation of a drum," having no name, description, symbol or letters, indicating the plaintiff or any one else as the owner, proprietor, or designer thereof, and that all the boxes issued by the plaintiff bear the name of the "Franklin Collar Company, Philadelphia," and no other name, substantially denies the claim of Frost to the invention or appropriation of the device of a drum, as a cover for paper collar boxes, and it asserts that it was in use in the collar trade as far back as 1871.

It is laid down in Carpenter *v.* Burden (2 Parson's Eq. Cases, 24), that it is the universal practice of a Court of Chancery, on an affidavit or answer under oath by the defendant, denying the facts and the equity in the bill on which it was granted, to dissolve the injunction. Nor can counter affidavits of the plaintiff, sustained by many other witnesses, prevent it; nor will they be received, except in certain cases clearly pointed out in equity practice. Judge KING cites from Clapham *v.* White (8 Vesey R. 34), the statement of the Chancellor, that if the answer denies all the circumstances upon which the equity is founded, the universal practice, as to the matter of dissolving or reviving an injunction, is to give credit to the answer. The Chancellor further remarked, save in a few excepted cases, though five hundred affidavits were filed, not one could be read by the plaintiff.

In Poor *v.* Charleton (3 Sumner, 75), Mr. Justice STORY questions the principle referred to, and says he should be sorry if any such practice had been established, and that, after answer, the question of dissolving an injunction is addressed to the sound discretion of the Court. But even the great authority of Judge STORY cannot overthrow a principle, and the practice founded on it from time out of mind. The authorities cited in note to Daniels's C. P. (vol. 3, page 1831, edit. 1846), show how firmly the practice is established in this country. Under the English practice the rule is almost universal.

It is also laid down by Daniels, at page 1831, that when an injunction is continued, the cause in equity ought to be prosecuted; if it is not, and the Court is satisfied that there is any intentional delay on the part of plaintiff, the injunction will be dissolved. By Lord BACON'S 24th Ordinance it is provided that if no prosecution is had for the space of three terms, the injunction shall fall of itself without further motion. Under the English practice it is usual to move that the bill be dismissed for want of prosecution, and this, if successful, carries with it the special injunction. This special injunction was granted more than a year ago. Since that time the plaintiff has slept. Judge BUTLER, of the U. S. Circuit Court, recently dissolved a special injunction upon this ground, holding that delay on part of plaintiff of a year and over, required that the injunction should fall.

But we also hold that this injunction ought not to stand under the authority of Davol Mills (7 Phila. R. 253), and Dixon *v.* Guggenheim (Ibid. 408). The syllabus of the last-named case, which was decided by Judge PAXSON, is, that a trade-mark adopted by a manufacturer or merchant for his goods, to be clothed with the attributes of property, entitling the appropriator to protection in its exclusive use, must designate the *true ownership or origin of the goods.* The same principle had previously been asserted in the case of the Davol Mills, which case does not seem to have been called to the attention of Judge PAXSON, when he wrote his learned and able opinion in Dixon *v.* Guggenheim, but in which the same doctrine is most clearly held. We have no reason to change our view of the law as previously expressed, notwithstanding the opinion of Judge FINLETTER, in Sheppard v. Stewart (7 WEEKLY NOTES, 498), maintaining a contrary doctrine. We prefer to stand by the former decisions of the Common Pleas upon this point.

This device of a drum does not indicate ownership or origin, and falls under the statement of the true doctrine, in Stokes v. Landgraff (17 Barb. 608), by Chief Justice DUER, and the same principle which was asserted in Corwin v. Daly, decided by the Superior Court of New York City, that the use of the words "Club House" to designate gin imported from Holland, did not confer on plaintiffs the exclusive right of appropriation, because the term thus applied did not indicate origin, ownership, or place of manufacture, or that the commodity was sold by the plaintiffs.

Without elaborating this principle further, we dismiss the bill, and therefore dissolve this injunction for the reasons stated above.

Opinion by ALLISON, P. J.

Common Pleas—Law.

C. P. No. 3.   June 8, 1880.

In re Assigned Estate of the National Savings, Loan, and Building Association.

Building associations—Rights of stockholders—Assignment for the benefit of creditors—How a building association which is hopelessly insolvent may be wound up justly and equitably.

Sur exceptions to the report of an Auditor appointed to audit the account of an assignee for the benefit of creditors of the National Savings, Loan, and Building Association.

The facts as found by the Auditor were as follows: The association was chartered November 22, 1866, as a serial association, and continued from its organization issuing series until August, 1878. Two years prior to that time the first series of stock had been declared full paid at $180. No other series had matured. In consequence of withdrawals and an erroneous method of conducting business, the assets were so far reduced as to prevent the meeting of pressing obligations; many of the stockholders had given notice of their withdrawal, as provided by the statute in such case, and had received orders on the treasurer for the amounts they had paid in. In such condition of affairs, at a stated meeting of the association it was resolved, with but one dissenting vote, to make an assignment for the benefit of creditors, in pursuance of which a deed of assignment was made to Joseph Hazel as assignee, August 29, 1878. The assignee proceeded to collect the assets and wind up the estate, and subsequently filed an account showing a balance of cash on hand of $7684.63. Before the Auditor appointed to audit this account three classes of claimants appeared as follows:—

(1) Holders of shares of the first series, which had been declared matured at $180, who claimed the full amount of their stock at maturity.

(2) Withdrawing stockholders who had given notice of their withdrawal prior to the assignment, and to some of whom orders on the treasurer had been given. This class claimed the amount of money paid in by them, with six per cent. interest after the first year, as provided by the Act of 12 April, 1859 (Purd. Dig. 183, pl. 2), and the by-laws of the association.

(3) Holders of shares in the second and subsequent series who had not given notice of withdrawal.

Before the Auditor the holders of stock of the first series claimed that as their stock had matured, they were entitled to priority of payment over all other members. The withdrawing stockholders, on the other hand, claimed that they alone were creditors, and should be paid in full before distribution was made among the members.

The holders of shares in the second and subsequent series claimed that the fund should be distributed *pro rata* among all the claimants. This view the Auditor adopted, and awarded distribution of the fund *pro rata* without distinction between the different classes of claimants. Exceptions were filed on behalf of a holder of stock of the first series and on behalf of withdrawing stockholders.

Frank P. Prichard, for Henry Landless, a withdrawing stockholder.

If a building association chooses to make an assignment for the benefit of creditors, instead of having its affairs wound up by a receiver appointed by a Court of Equity, the estate realized by such assignment is to be distributed in the same manner as in ordinary cases of assignment. It was held by the Supreme Court in—

U. S. Building Association v. Silverman, 4 WEEKLY NOTES, 546,

that a withdrawing stockholder becomes a creditor at the expiration of the thirty days' notice, and it was held by this Court in—

O'Rourke v. West Penn. Association, 8 WEEKLY NOTES, 176,

affirmed by the Supreme Court, 37 Leg. Int. 196, that other stockholders, even after their stock has run out, were not creditors.

It would seem to be clear that property assigned for the benefit of creditors should be applied to the creditors before any distribution among the members of the association making the assignment, and this is also equitable, since the withdrawing stockholder gave up all right to share in the profits, and should not be held responsible for subsequent losses.

Charles H. Downing and *E. K. Nichols*, for other withdrawing stockholders ; and

Alfred Driver, for a holder of shares of the first series, took no part in the argument, but submitted the case on their exceptions.

John F. Goodwin, for assignee.

The assignment put an end to the business of the association, and was the mode adopted for winding up its affairs. It was made for the benefit of all parties interested, and they should all share equally in the distribution. The method of distribution adopted by the Auditor was the only equitable and practical one under the circumstances.

C. A. V.

July 10, 1880. THE COURT. The National Savings, Loan, and Building Association having become greatly embarrassed, made an assignment for the benefit of creditors under the laws of the Commonwealth. The assignee having filed his account, it was referred to an Auditor, and his report is now before us with exceptions.

These exceptions present a single question for our consideration, but that question involves the solution of an untried and most difficult problem, to wit, how can a building association be wound up justly and equitably, when it has failed to fulfil the object of its creation and is hopelessly insolvent. The Auditor, evidently feeling the anomalous nature of the case, proceeds to divide up the assets *pro rata*, as best he could, and thus treats alike three classes of claimants, to be divided as follows, to wit :—

(1) In the first class are those whose claims, under the first series, had been declared matured, and for which orders on the Treasurer had been issued and part payments made.

(2) In the second class are the claims of those who had given notice of their withdrawal, and who had or had not received orders of the Treasurer.

(3) In the third class are the claims of those who had not given notice of withdrawal.

It is evident, we think, that the result reached, when we consider the peculiar legal character of a building association, can not be right, and yet how, under a general assignment, can a legal preference be made?

After some reflection, we have come to a conclusion which, while it is novel, will have the merit of so disposing of this class of cases as to do that which to right and justice belongs.

A building association has but few creditors strictly so called ; the organization is in fact and in law a partnership with corporate rights, in which every stockholder is a member; and while it may be true that a stockholder may recover a judgment against the corporation, and thus, under Loan Association *v.* Silverman (4 WEEKLY NOTES, 546), become in a sense a creditor, yet the peculiar nature of the constitution and by-laws of a building association, clearly, we think, indicate that an assignment for the benefit of creditors, under our laws, was never intended to reach such creditors as the members of a building association must be who have even obtained judgments upon their claims.

The reasoning of the Court in Loan Association *v.* Silverman (*supra*) proves how difficult it was to say what should be done with a judgment upon which an execution had issued, and the Court was driven to a most righteous conclusion when it declared that "the design of the Act can be better met by giving the plaintiff judgment, and then, should it seem equitable to the Court below, it may restrain execution in order that the defendant *may have a reasonable time within which to raise the money for the payment of such judgment, so that there may be no undue derangement of its affairs.*"

In what other class of cases could language like this be used ? and yet it is evident that it was wise, eminently so.

We think substantial justice will be done if, in this class of cases, we hold that under an assignment . like the one executed in this case, the creditors, within the meaning of the assignment laws, are not those whose claims depend upon a former membership of the association and consequent ownership of the stock, no matter to what series the stock owned may belong.

Starting with this principle, let the general creditors, if any, be paid, and let the Auditor so report if he can. Upon petition in the usual form, and under the Act of Assembly, the general creditors being paid, we will order a reconveyance and assignment of the entire property in the hands of the assignee to the assignor.

A bill in equity may then be prepared at the suit of those interested in a final settlement, in which it should appear that the corporation is insolvent, that its assets may be lost, and that by the appointment of a receiver the rights of all will be protected.

If the case is a proper one upon the bill, answers, and proofs, we will at once act, and direct the receiver, by a cautious and prudent policy, to wind up the affairs of the concern, and then, upon hearing and proof, so marshall and distribute the assets by a final decree as to do justice to all.

Opinion by LUDLOW, P. J.

WEEKLY NOTES OF CASES.

Vol. IX.] *THURSDAY, SEPT. 30, 1880.* [No. 6.

Supreme Court of the United States.

Oct. '79, 255.   March 1880.
Moulor v. The American Life Insurance Company.

Insurance—Warranty—Truth of answers—Testimony of family physician explained and contradicted by statements of company's examining physician—Doctor's attendance limited to specific disease.

The existence of disease, or what amounts to the gravity of a disease, contradistinguished from a predisposition or tendency to it, is a fact which it is error to withdraw from the jury.

The testimony of the insured's family physician, taken under a commission, is not an admission or estoppel which precludes the plaintiff's recovery, but is subject as parol evidence to the interpretation of the jury, who construe it in connection with the physician's own explanations and theories, and also in connection with the statements of the insurer's examining physicians, which form part of the application.

The family physician testified that he had attended the insured for asthma, scrofula, and consumption, to which three diseases he was constitutionally subject. In explanation, the witness said there were no symptoms which revealed the diseases, and the patient did not know either that he had any disease or that he was being treated for disease. On the contrary, he believed himself sound and robust in health. The statements of the examining physicians pronounced the insured free from any disease or inclination to disease, and an excellent risk. The Court gave the jury a binding charge to find for the defendant;

Held (reversing the ruling of the Court below), that it was error to withdraw the question of disease from the jury.

Error to the United States Circuit Court for the Eastern District of Pennsylvania.

Debt, upon a policy of life insurance issued by the American Life Insurance Company, June 17, 1872, at Philadelphia, for $10,000, upon the life of Louis Moulor of New Orleans, for the benefit of his wife, Emilie Moulor. Defendant, on June 5, 1873, pleaded the general issue. At the first trial, April 16, 1874, the defence was suicide: but the application put in evidence by the defendant was a surprise to the plaintiff, who was allowed to withdraw a juror. Additional pleas were filed, March 17, 1876, in order to raise the issue of false representation by the plaintiff. The second trial, April 4, 1876, resulted in a verdict of $11,950 for the plaintiff, which was set aside, April 15, 1876, and a new trial granted.

Upon the third trial, October 2, 1876, the following were the material facts: The policy provided, *inter alia*, that the American Life Insurance Company, "in consideration of the representations made to them in the application for the policy" and of the premium, insure Moulor. The application contained, *inter alia*, the following: "It is hereby declared and warranted that the above are fair and true answers to the foregoing questions." To the question: "Has the party ever been afflicted with any of the following diseases . . . . Scrofula, Asthma, Consumption?" . . . . the applicant answered, No. Both the examining physicians of the company pronounced him free from every disease or tendency to disease. The doctors are instructed to call the family physician, unless satisfied by their own diagnosis; and they did not call him in, though his name was furnished them in writing by the insured. The agents also reported the insured an excellent risk and in robust health. The family physician however testified that he had attended him constantly, since 1858, for scrofula, asthma, and consumption, to which diseases he was constitutionally subject. Upon re-examination, the doctor explained his statement by declaring that the insured never knew that he had any disease; that as a physician he did not reveal to his patients the fact that they had a disease, on the ground of humanity, lest their minds might be affected by the disclosure; and that "the asthma which he, Moulor, had, was the dry, nervous asthma. There was no expectoration connected therewith to make the patient believe he did have it. At the first stage of consumption, there was no softening of the tubercles, and, therefore, no expectoration of tuberculous matter. As to the scrofula, I will state that his was a very mild diathesis."

Upon the above evidence the Court instructed the jury to find for the defendant. Verdict accordingly, and judgment thereon. The plaintiff took this writ of error, assigning for error the charge of the Court, and the entry of judgment for the defendant.

James Parsons, for the plaintiff in error.

By the weight of the evidence, the insured had no disease. The fact of disease or the degree of ill health which amounts to the gravity of disease is for the jury.

Cushman *v*. U. S. Life, 70 N. Y. 72.

The certificates of the insurer's physicians and the reports of their agents are competent evidence for the insured, as admissions which estop the insurers, and form part of the history of the insurance or *res gestæ*.

Ins. Co. *v.* Mahone, 21 Wall. 152.
Holloman *v.* Life Ins. Co., 1 Wood, U. S. C. C. R. 677.
Rawle *v.* Am. Mut. Life Ins. Co., 27 N. Y. 282.
Ins. Co. *v.* Wilkinson, 13 Wall. 222.
N. J. Mut. Life Ins. Co. *v.* Baker, 4 Otto, 610.
Bigley *v.* Williams, 30 Sm. 107.
N. West. Mut. Life Ins. Co. *v.* Roth, 6 Nor. 409.
Mut. Ben. Life *v.* Cannon, 48 Ind. 264.
Dean *v.* Aetna, 5 Big. 377.
Hoffman *v.* John Hancock Mut. Life, 5 Big. 593.
Ins. Co. *v.* McCain, 6 Otto, 84.

Though the agent put his own statement into the mouth of the insured, it is still an admission; for the insurers cannot convert their agent into an agent of the insured.

Flynn *v.* Life Ass. Soc., 7 Hun, 387.

The denial of medical attendance for any disease, except for yellow fever in 1847, coupled with a reference by the insured to his usual medical attendant, does not exclude medical attendance for illness which does not amount to a disease, but affirms a regularity of visitation. As the agents were required to call the insured's family doctor, unless they were satisfied by their own diagnosis, the insurance company are bound by the election which their agents made; and the insured's answers are to be supplemented by the doctor's knowledge, by what he would have said, had their agents, in the discretion delegated to them by the insurers, exercised the option to examine him.

Higgins *v.* Phœnix Mut. Life, 74 N. Y. 6.

The doctor's testimony could be taken only as a whole and with his explanations of it, and not being responsive, becomes the insurer's evidence, if introduced by them, because upon the collateral issue incidentally raised the insured is entitled to cross-examine.

Mut. Ben. Life Ins. Co. *v.* Newton, 22 Wall. 32.
Gordon *v.* Little, 8 S. & R. 555.
Martin *v.* Dearie, 9 Phila. 186.

The testimony must be interpreted in consistency with the other evidence and is so reconciled by the theory given of it by the doctor himself, who meant predisposition to, and not disease.

Isaac Haslehurst (with him *Henry Haslehurst*), for defendant, submitted the case, insisting merely that the answers must be true in fact.

Jeffries *v.* Life Ins. Co. 22 Wall. 47.

THE COURT. As the judgment which was entered by the Circuit Court was in accordance with the verdict, the only assignment of error which we have to consider is the first, namely, that the Court erred in giving to the jury a binding charge to return a verdict for the defendants. The policy upon which the suit was founded contained the following stipulation: "And it is hereby declared and agreed that if the representations and answers made to this company in the application for this policy, upon the full faith of which it is issued, shall be found to be untrue in any respect, or that there has been any concealment of facts, then, and in such case, this policy shall be null and void." The application referred to contained the following interrogatories and answers among others: "Seventh. Has the party" (Louis Moulor, the person whose life was insured) "ever been afflicted with any of the following diseases? Answer yes or no to each. Insanity? No. Gout? No. Rheumatism? No. Palsy? No. Scrofula? No. Convulsions? No. Dropsy? No. Smallpox? No. Yellow fever? Yes. Fistula? No. Rupture? No. Asthma? No. Spitting of blood? No. Consumption? No. Any diseases of the lungs or throat? No. Or of the heart? No. Or of the urinary organs? No."

Interrogatory twelfth. "How long since the party was attended by a physician? For what disease or diseases?" Answer. "Not since the year 1847, when he had the yellow fever."

After these answers the application contained the following: It is hereby declared and *warranted* that the above are fair and true answers to the foregoing questions, and it is acknowledged and agreed by the undersigned" (Louis Moulor) "that this application shall form a part of the contract of insurance, and that if there be in any of the answers herein made any untrue or evasive statements, or any misrepresentations, or concealment of facts, then any policy granted upon this application shall be null and void."

The defence set up at the trial was that some of the answers to the interrogatories contained in the application were untrue, and this defence was attempted to be supported by the testimony of a single witness, Dr. Mathieu. He testified that he had been the family physician of Moulor since 1855. (The policy was issued June 17, 1872.) He testified farther that in 1858 and 1859 he attended Moulor for chronic asthma, manifestations of the first stage of consumption, and also treated him for scrofula. The witness did not testify positively that Moulor had the diseases for which he treated him, but his testimony was that Moulor never learned from him or any other physician, and that he never suspected or had the remotest idea that he was affected with any such diseases; on the contrary, that he always boasted of himself as being a strong, healthy, and robust man. The witness further testified that the asthma Moulor had was the dry, nervous asthma, attended by no expectoration; that there was nothing connected with it to make the patient believe he had it. As to the first stage of consumption, there was no softening of the tubercles, and, therefore, no expectoration of the tuberculous matter. As to the scrofula, that his was a very mild diathesis.

This was all the testimony adduced and now

relied upon to prove that the answers in the application were untrue.

There was, however, in evidence the statement of two medical examiners attending the application. They represented the assured as in perfect health, and as never having had any constitutional disease, except yellow fever, and a curvature of the spine in his early youth, and as having no predisposition, either hereditary or acquired, to any constitutional disease.

We are of opinion that this evidence did not warrant a peremptory instruction to the jury to find a verdict in favor of the defendants. The testimony of Dr. Mathieu was parol. Its credibility as well as its effect was for the jury, especially as it was not positive and unqualified that Moulor had had the diseases for which the witness had treated him, and as the statements of the examining physicians which were in evidence tended in some degree to prove that he never had. The jury might, perhaps, have drawn the conclusion from Dr. Mathieu's testimony that there had been only predisposition to the diseases, and not the diseases themselves. He stated in regard to the asthma for which he treated Moulor, that it was attended with no expectoration, and that there was nothing connected with it to make the patient believe he had it. In regard to the first stages of consumption, according to his statement there was no expectoration of tuberculous matter. He does not state there was any cough or pain in the chest. There were, then, no external symptoms of either of the three diseases mentioned. Had scrofula existed it would seem probable the patient must have known it. Yet the doctor states he did not suspect, or have the remotest idea that he was affected with either of the diseases. That he was treated for them is not conclusive that he had them. The most skilful treatment sometimes is given when the existence of a particular disease is only suspected, not known, and when afterwards it appears the physician was mistaken.

For these reasons we think the testimony was not such as to justify a withdrawal from the jury of the inquiry whether the answer to the seventh interrogatory was untrue.

Nor was it sufficient to enable the Court to conclude, without reference to the jury, that the answer to the twelfth interrogatory was untrue. The entire interrogatory should be considered as one. It was, "How long since the party was attended by a physician? For what disease or diseases?" To this the answer was, "Not since the year 1847, when he had the yellow fever." It may well be that the applicant understood the interrogatory as asking information respecting attendance for a particular disease or diseases and their description, especially as the thirteenth interrogatory sought information respecting the party's *usual medical attendant,* and the name of that attendant was truly given.

Upon the whole, therefore, we think the case should have been submitted to the jury on the evidence.

The judgment is reversed, and the case is remitted for a new trial.

Opinion by STRONG, J.

Supreme Court.

May, '80, 133. June, 1880.
Stiles's Appeal.

Building associations, regulation of, under Act of 1859 — Unauthorized restrictions upon borrowers — Cannot fix a minimum rate of premium — Alleged violation of Act of 1859, set up as a defence to an action against borrower — Error to refusal of Court below to open judgment.

Building associations, chartered under the general Act of April 15, 1859 (P. L. 544), must comply in all their operations with the provisions of that Act; they are required to loan moneys lawfully in the treasury to the highest bidder, in open competition, at a stated monthly meeting; they are not permitted to borrow money from banks or others for the purpose of loaning it to members at interest in excess of six per cent., nor can they fix a minimum rate of premium below which they will not receive bids.

Such violations of the Act, affecting a particular loan in suit, may be set up as a defence to an action against a borrowing member.

Where a borrowing member, against whom judgment had been entered on penal bill given for a loan, petitioned the Court for a rule to show cause why the judgment should not be opened, on the ground, *inter alia,* that he took his loan at a premium of $24, that being the minimum premium fixed by the association;

Held (reversing the order of the Court below), that this was sufficient ground to grant the rule to show cause why the judgment should not be opened, and the defendant be let into a defence.

Appeal from the Common Pleas of Columbia County.

This was, in the Court below, a petition and motion by Jeremiah Stiles, for a rule to show cause why a certain judgment, entered against him by the Benton Mutual Savings Fund and Loan Association on penal bill conditioned for the payment of $200, should not be opened and the defendant be let into a defence.

The petitioner averred that the association was endeavoring, by means of an execution issued on said judgment, to collect a larger amount than is due them; that he had bid for and taken the loan for which the judgment was entered, at a premium of $24, "that being the minimum rate fixed by the association for that year, and said association refusing to receive a less bid." The petitioner further averred that the said association had violated its charter, by borrowing moneys at interest from banks and individuals to loan to its members at rates in excess of six per cent., by fixing a minimum rate of premium on loans to members, and the charging of excessive fines; by reason whereof the association is only entitled to recover from the petitioner the sum actually loaned, with six per cent. interest.

After argument, the Court, ELWELL, P. J., refused to grant a rule to show cause why the judgment should not be opened, on the ground that violation of the charter of the plaintiff could not be set up in this collateral proceeding. The defendant thereupon took this appeal, assigning as error, *inter alia*, the refusal of the Court to grant a rule as above stated.

Hervey E. Smith and *A. C. Smith*, for appellant.

The defence of violation of the Act of 1859 is a good one, because the right of the plaintiff to collect interest in excess of six per cent. depends on the provisions of that Act. The association can act in no other manner than that prescribed for it by the Act from which it derives its existence.

Hibernia Turnpike Co. *v.* Henderson, 8 S. & R. 222.
Commonwealth *v.* E. & N. E. R. R. Co., 3 Casey, 351.

The question of usury was for a jury.
Chamberlain *v.* McClurg, 8 W. & S. 36.

Fixing a minimum rate for loans has been held to be a violation of similar statutes in other states.

State *v.* Greenville B. & L. Association, 3 Law & Equity Reporter, 515.

Courts will not enforce a contract made in violation of a statute, although not expressly made void.

Holt *v.* Green, 28 Sm. 201.
Fowler *v.* Scully, 22 Sm. 456.
Mitchell *v.* Smith, 1 Binn. 110.
Maybin *v.* Conlan, 4 Dall. 298.
Biddis *v.* James, 6 Binn 321.
Seidenhender *v.* Charles's Adm'rs, 4 S. & R. 160.
Badgley *v.* Beal, 3 Watts, 263.
Columbia Bank and Bridge Co. *v.* Haldeman, 7 W. & S. 233.

E. H. Little, contra.

A violation of the charter of incorporation cannot be made the subject of judicial investigation in this collateral proceeding. A plea, involving the forfeiture or invalidity of the charter, would be demurrable, or might be treated as a nullity by the Court. Proof of the violation of the Act of Assembly involves the forfeiture or invalidity of the charter itself.

Becket *v.* Uniontown Building Association, 7 Norris, 213.
Irvine *v.* Lumberman's Bank, 2 W. & S. 190.
Dyer *v.* Walker, 4 Wr. 157.
Coil *v.* Pittsburgh Female College, 4 Wr. 439.
Cleveland and Pittsburgh R. R. Co. *v.* Speer, 6 Sm. 326.
Cochran *v.* Arnold, 8 Sm. 399.
Workingmen B. & L. Association *v.* Coleman, 8 WEEKLY NOTES, 17.

This being an appeal to the equitable powers of the Court below, the question is as to the rightful exercise of its discretion.

Kneedler's Appeal, 8 WEEKLY NOTES, 97.

June 21, 1880. THE COURT. The Act entitled "An Act to confer on certain associations of the citizens of this Commonwealth the powers and immunities of corporations and bodies politic in law, and to confirm charters heretofore granted," passed April 15, 1859 (P. L. 544) is a general law for the regulation of associations known as building and loan associations. This appears not only from the general scope of its provisions, but from the recital in its preamble, which declares that "such associations are meritorious, and deserving the care of the State." The learned Judge below fell into an error in considering it as merely the charter of any association included in its benefit—the violation of which could not be inquired of collaterally. The charters of such corporations are derived from the Court of Common Pleas, and it may be true that the violation of their provisions by the corporation cannot be the subject of collateral inquiry, nor set up by any debtor as a defence to an action. They can be declared forfeited only by direct proceeding in the name and by the authority of the Commonwealth. Corporations, however, as well as individuals, may be subject rightfully to general laws regulating their contracts and proceedings. More especially is this true when such corporations accept their charters after such laws have been passed, and therefore subject to their provisions.

Assuming the Benton Mutual Saving Fund and Loan Association to be an association within the provisions of the Act of 1859, which is the only ground upon which they can claim exemption from the law prohibiting the taking of a greater rate of interest upon the loan of money than six per cent., it is evident that their contract must be made in conformity to the provisions of that Act, in order to entitle them to the privilege granted by it. It makes an exception in their case from the general law of the State, and they must bring themselves within the exception. They can loan money only to the members of the Association, in amounts not exceeding two hundred dollars on each share of the stock held by them, and the loans can only be of the amount in the treasury derived from the interest, dues, and fines received from the members, and given out at each stated monthly meeting to the highest bidder. It would be a gross perversion of the whole spirit and design of such an association to borrow money from banks or others for the purpose. It is equally so to fix a minimum rate of premium below which they will accept no bid. They are bound to offer all that is in the treasury to open competition, so that the members may obtain the loan at a low premium if there should be no bid at a higher. The practical operation of such institutions is that whenever the member procures a loan at a premium below the average of the premiums for the whole time the Association has to make, he is to that extent a gainer; when his loan is at a premium higher than the average, he is to that extent a loser. This is a most valuable feature in such associations, and hence the great importance of maintaining the principle of free competition in the bids. When the member is told that there is a minimum premium below which loans will not be made, he must offer that amount for the loan whether any other one offers or not. If no offer to that amount is made the money remains in the treasury without investment. It is evident, in this way, that the members who are not borrowers will obtain a very undue advantage over the members who are borrowers. These institutions are liable, like everything else human, to abuse, and we are bound to guard them carefully from being perverted into mere contrivances by which capitalists can evade the laws against usury. So the Legislature evidently intended they should be by the Act.

As to the allegation in the petition that the Association was in the habit of borrowing money to loan out, it was too vague to avail the defendant. He must show that the money loaned to him had been borrowed. But by the allegation that he took his loan at the premium of $24, that being the minimum rate fixed by the Association, and said Association refusing to receive a less bid, he laid, we think, sufficiently clear and tangible ground upon which the Court below ought to have granted the rule to show cause why the judgment should not be opened. Of course, upon the hearing of the rule, he will have to produce evidence to satisfy the Court of the truth of the averment of this petition, or affidavit, and that the rule ought to be made absolute, which the plaintiff will have the opportunity to controvert it by opposite evidence.

Order reversed and record remitted for further proceedings.

Opinion by SHARSWOOD, C. J.

Jan. '78, 41.   Feb. 4, 1880.

Olive Cemetery Company v. City of Philadelphia.

Taxes and taxation—Exemption from taxation—Cemetery companies—Assessments for Municipal purposes—Charters.

One of the clauses of the charter of a cemetery company provided as follows: "That no street, lane, or road shall hereafter be opened through the tract occupied as a cemetery, without the consent of a majority of the lot-holders; and the same, when used as a place of sepulchre, shall be exempt from taxation, excepting for State purposes." In an action to recover the amount of assessment charged against the lots on the line of a street in which a sewer had been constructed:

Held, that the municipal assessments were a species of local taxation within the meaning of the exemption clause of the charter, and that the lot-holders were not liable.

Error to the Common Pleas No. 4, of Philadelphia County.

Case stated, wherein the City of Philadelphia, to use, etc., was plaintiff, and the Olive Cemetery Company, defendant, showing the following facts:

The defendant company was incorporated by an Act of Assembly approved February 5, 1849, the third section of which Act provides:

"That no street, lane, or road shall hereafter be opened through the said tract occupied as a cemetery without the consent of a majority of the lot-holders; and the same, when used as a place of sepulchre, *shall be exempt from taxation*, excepting for State purposes; and no lot which may be purchased as a place of sepulchre shall be subject to attachment or execution for any debt or debts of the owner thereof, *provided*, that said exemption from attachment or execution shall not extend to more than four lots as owned by any one individual."

On the line of Merion Avenue all of the lots in the cemetery have been sold, and are mostly improved and buried in. In Merion Avenue the equitable plaintiff constructed a sewer and filed a lien therefor. The lot-holders on the line of Merion Avenue had no notice of the construction of this sewer, nor of the filing of the claim. No deeds of the lot-holders have been registered in the Registry Bureau of the Department of Surveys of the City of Philadelphia, nor have they been recorded in the Office for Recording Deeds for the City and County of Philadelphia. If the Court be of opinion, that under the said charter the lots purchased by the lot-holders for burial purposes, and lands of the cemetery company are subject to lien and sale under the said lien, or that the lot-holders' consent, or notice to them, was not necessary before filing lien, then judgment for the plaintiff; but if not, then judgment for the defendant.

The Court, after argument, entered judgment for the plaintiff. (No opinion was filed.) The defendant took this writ, assigning for error the entering of judgment for the plaintiff.

B. H. *Brewster* and *John A. Burton* for plaintiff in error.

Municipal assessments are taxes, and derive their validity from the constitutional power of the Legislature to levy and collect taxes, which power the Legislature has delegated to the municipality.

Hammett *v.* City of Philadelphia, 15 Sm. 164.
Washington Avenue, 19 Sm. 352.
Pennell's Appeal, 2 Barr, 216.
Pennock *v.* Hoover, 5 Rawle, 291.

By the provision of the Act of Assembly incorporating the company, the Commonwealth has released in favor of the cemetery her right to tax the lands used for sepulchre, except for State purposes, and it is a well-settled rule of construction that an exception in a statute excludes all other exceptions.

Miller *v.* Kirkpatrick, 5 Casey, 226.
Warfield *v.* Fox, 3 Sm. 383.

Henry C. Terry for the defendant in error.

The assessment for the construction of this sewer is not a tax within the meaning of the exemption in the defendant's charter.

Pray v. Northern Liberties, 7 Casey, 69.
Northern Liberties *v.* The Church, 1 Harris, 104.
Borough of Greensburg *v.* Young, 3 Sm. 280.

May 3, 1880. THE COURT. The Olive Cemetery Company was incorporated by Act of February 5, 1849, for the purpose of establishing and maintaining a cemetery on a certain tract of land, situated on the north side of Lancaster Avenue, in the county, now city, of Philadelphia, containing about ten acres and twenty-two perches. The third section of the Act declares: "'That no street, lane, or road shall hereafter be opened through the said tract, occupied as a cemetery, without the consent of a majority of the lot-holders, and the same, when used as a place of sepulchre, shall be exempt from taxation, excepting for State purposes, and no lot which may be purchased as a place of sepulchre, shall be subject to attachment or execution for any debt or debts of the owner thereof, *provided*, that the said exemption from attachment or execution shall not extend to more than four lots as owned by any one individual." On the line of Merion Avenue, by which the cemetery is bounded on one side, all the lots have been sold and mostly used for burial purposes. In that avenue the corporate authorities of the city caused a sewer to be constructed, and filed a lien for a proportionate part of the cost thereof against the entire cemetery tract, including the lots that have been sold, and claim the right to enforce payment thereof by sale of the land. The facts are fully presented in the case stated in the nature of a special verdict, and the questions of law involved submitted to the Court below in the following terms: "If the Court shall be of opinion that under the said charter the lots purchased by the lot-holders for burial purposes and the lands of the cemetery company are subject to lien and sale under the said lien, or that the lot-owners' consent, or notice to them, was not necessary before filing the lien, then judgment for the plaintiff; but if not, then judgment for the defendant." The Court entered judgment, on the case stated, in favor of the city.

The main contention on the part of the cemetery company is, that the assessment for construction of the sewer on Merion Avenue is a species of taxation, and clearly within the letter as well as the spirit of the exemption contained in the charter. The exemption is "from taxation, excepting for State purposes." The obvious meaning of this is, that the Commonwealth releases in favor of the cemetery company her right to tax its lands when used as a place of sepulchre, in any form or for any purpose of a local nature, as distinguished from general State purposes, reserving to herself the right of taxation for the latter purposes only. The exemption is general, and embraces every species of taxation not specially excepted; and the rule is well settled that an exception in a statute excludes all other exceptions. (Miller *v.* Kirkpatrick, 5 Casey, 226.) It is not pretended that municipal assessments for constructing sewers, etc., are within the accepted meaning of taxation for State purposes; on the contrary, it is contended by the city, that they do not come under the head of taxation at all. It is conceded, however, that the authority to make and collect such assessments is delegated by the Commonwealth. If it does not emanate from the inherent power of the government to levy and collect taxes, it is difficult to understand whence it comes. The only warrant for delegating such authority must be either in the right of eminent domain or in the taxing power. It cannot be found in the former, and hence it must be in the latter.

Taxation is an exercise of the inherent power of government to compel contributions from persons and property for public purposes, either of a general or local nature. For general or State purposes the power of taxation has usually been exercised directly by the government, while for local objects it has generally been delegated to and exercised by the municipal subdivisions of the State. The history and growth of this delegated power are traced in Washington Avenue (19 P. F. Smith, 352). It is there said that the practice of municipal taxation by counties, turnpikes, cities, and boroughs for local objects had its origin in necessity and convenience. Hence, roads, bridges, culverts, sewers, pavements, school-houses, and like local improvements, are best made through the municipal divisions of the State, and paid for by local taxation. "These have always been supported as a proper exercise of the taxing power. . . . . In cities and towns where the population was dense, the authorities began to make improvements of special advantage to certain of the citizens at their expense. . . . So far public opinion and long-continued legislative practice have sustained local taxation with great unanimity, and this is strong evidence of the true interpretation of the constitutional power of the Legislature to authorize municipal taxation of this sort." In McMasters *v.* Commonwealth (3 Watts, 293), a new phase of taxation was presented in the assessment of one person's property to pay compensation awarded to another whose property had been taken for a public use under the power of eminent domain, but it was sustained as a proper application of that principle of local taxation which authorizes the assessment of property specially benefited by a local improvement of a public nature, for the purpose of defraying the expense thereof. The admitted authority of the Legislature to confer upon municipal corporations the power of assessing the cost of local improvements on properties benefited, is recognized in Hammett *v.* Philadelphia (15 P. F. Smith, 164) as "a species of taxation, not the taking of private property by virtue of eminent domain."

We have thus referred to these cases not for the purpose of vindicating the right of the Legislature to authorize assessments in various forms for local improvements, but to show that they are regarded as a species of taxation; that it is only on the principle of taxation that they are sustained. The cases of Northern Liberties *v.* Church (1 Harris, 104); Pray *v.* Northern Liberties (7 Casey, 69); and Borough of Greensburg *v.* Young (3 P. F. Smith, 284), have been cited as authority for the position that assessments for local improvements are not taxes. What is said in Washington Avenue, *supra*, in regard to two of these cases is equally applicable to the other, viz., the Court did not mean to decide that such an assessment is not taxation within the general legislative power to tax. Had it been meant to say that such an assessment is not taxation at all, it would in effect deny the power of the Legislature to authorize the assessment—a power which was affirmed in all these cases. It follows from what has been said that the claim of the city is a species of taxation for local and not State purposes, based solely on the taxing power delegated by the State, and inasmuch as the charter of the company expressly exempts its land from such taxation, the lien is invalid, and the plaintiff in error is entitled to judgment. If it were at all necessary, it would be an easy task to show the wisdom and propriety of exempting such property as that of the plaintiff in error from local taxation, but nothing of that kind is required. It is sufficient to know that the Legislature in creating the corporation exempted its property from such taxation. It is unnecessary to consider other minor points involved in the case stated.

Judgment reversed and set aside, and judgment is now entered on the case stated in favor of the defendant below.

Opinion by STERRETT, J.

Jan. '80, 16.   March 4, 1880.

Daubert et al. *v.* Eckert, etc.

Husband and wife—Married woman—Mortgage of, to secure future indebtedness of husband—Application of mortgage money.

A married woman, having the power to mortgage her lands to secure the future indebtedness of her husband, may give the money raised by the mortgage immediately to him.

The mortgagee has nothing to do with the application of the mortgage money.

Error to the Common Pleas of Lehigh County.

Sci. fa. sur mortgage, by Charles Eckert, administrator, etc., against David Daubert and Herriena Daubert.

The following affidavit of defence was filed: "That this defendant, Herriena Daubert, is the wife of David Daubert, the other defendant, and was a married woman at the time of executing said mortgage, dated August 1, 1873, recorded, etc., ... on which said suit is brought, that said money named in said mortgage was loaned to her by John Eckert for the improvement of her separate estate; that said money was paid to her husband, who used it for the improvement of his estate, and no part of said money went for the necessary improvement of her separate estate, nor for purchase-money of her separate real estate, nor was it used for necessaries in her family; all of which she expects to prove on the day of the trial of this cause."

The Court made absolute a rule for judgment for want of a sufficient affidavit of defence, ALBRIGHT, P. J., delivering the following opinion: "It is not alleged that the mortgage upon which suit is brought was not executed and acknowledged in the manner and form requisite to bind the wife's separate real estate. It is averred in the affidavit of defence that the money for which the mortgage was given was loaned by the mortgagee to the wife for the improvement of her separate real estate; that the money was paid to the husband, who used it for the improvement of his estate. It is not stated that the payment of the money to the husband was without the consent of the wife, or that she did not agree that her estate should be encumbered for the debt of her husband. The substance of what is alleged seems to be that the original intention or negotiation was for a loan to improve her estate, but when the transaction came to be consummated she permitted her husband to receive the money for which the mortgage was given. It is not said that any fraud was practised on the wife in the execution or delivery of the mortgage.

"A husband and wife may execute a valid mortgage of her separate real estate to secure the husband's debt. The power to do this existed before the passage of the Act of 1848, and this was not changed by said Act. (Jamison *v.* Jamison, 3 Wh. 457; Black *v.* Galway, 12 H. 19; Miner *v.* Graham, Ibid. 491; Lytle's App., 12 Cas. 131; Haffey *v.* Carey, 23 P. F. S. 431.) This is what was done in the case before us. The affidavit discloses no facts constituting a defence to the mortgage."

The defendants took this writ, assigning for error the entry of judgment on the affidavit.

John Rupp (with whom was *James B. Deshler*), for the plaintiff in error.

The Court below decided this case upon the theory that the mortgage was given to secure the debt of the husband. If such were the facts of the case there would be no trouble in the case, and the mortgage would undoubtedly be valid and binding upon the wife. But such are not the facts. The affidavit of defence alleges clearly and explicitly that the husband was not the borrower, but that the contract of loan was made with the wife, that she became the borrower, that the loan was made to her and not to the husband; that the loan was made to her for the improvement of her separate estate, but the money came into the hands and possession of her husband, and was never applied to the improvement of her separate estate, but was used by him for other purposes. Hence the mortgage could not have been given to secure the debt of the husband, but simply as a security for the wife's contract, and this mortgage in question can not be held valid upon the theory on which the Court below decided the case, namely, that a married woman can give a valid mortgage for the debts of her husband.

A married woman is not liable for debts contracted or money borrowed by her for the avowed purpose of improving her separate estate, unless it be further shown that the money was actually so applied.

Heugh *v.* Jones, 8 C. 432.
Lippincott *v.* Leeds, 27 Sm. 420.
Wolbach *v.* Lehigh Building Assoc., 3 N. 211.

R. E. Wright & Son, for the defendant in error.

The Act of 1770, giving to married women the power to convey real estate, makes no restriction as to the consideration or purpose of the conveyance. If the mortgage be executed in due form, it is valid.

Jamison *v.* Jamison, 3 Wh. 471.
Journeay *v.* Gibson, 6 Sm. 59.

The affidavit amounted simply to an averment that the mortgage was given to secure the repayment of money loaned by the mortgagee to the husband. There is no pretence of want of knowledge or consent. The husband received the money, and the wife could lawfully mortgage her real estate to secure his debt.

March 22, 1880. THE COURT. If, as was settled in Haffey *v.* Carey (23 P. F. Smith, 431), a married woman can mortgage her lands to secure the future indebtedness of her husband, it is not easy to understand why she may not give the money, raised by the mortgage, immediately to him. The mortgagee has nothing to do with the application of the mortgage money. All that is necessary is, that the husband and wife should join in the execution, and that she should be separately examined, and acknowledge the instrument in the manner prescribed by law.

Judgment affirmed.

PER CURIAM. GREEN and MERCUR, JJ., absent.

Jan. '80, 226.　　　　　　　　March 30, 1880.

Sellers v. Benner.

Mortgages—Proceeding for satisfaction of, under Act of June 11, 1879—Equities of mortgagor against assignee, when devolving upon terre-tenant—Payment, evidence of—Notice—Failure of assignee of mortgage to make inquiry of mortgagor.

In a petition, under the Act of June 11, 1879 (P. L. 141), to procure the satisfaction of a mortgage, the terre-tenant alleged that when the property was conveyed by the mortgagor to him, he paid the mortgage debt to the mortgagee. The answer of the mortgagee denied this payment, and the assignee of the mortgage answered that she was an assignee for value without notice. In an issue directed to try the question of payment, the petitioner, as plaintiff, testified that the mortgagee had undertaken, for a sufficient consideration, to procure the conveyance of the property to him, and to cause the mortgage to be satisfied; that he, the plaintiff, had accepted the conveyance upon these terms. It was admitted that the mortgage was subsequently assigned for value to the present holder, one of the respondents. The Judge directed a verdict for the defendants, who were the respondents, on the ground that there was no evidence of payment by the mortgagor to the mortgagee :

Held (reversing the judgment of the Court below), that plaintiff's evidence should have been submitted to the jury, who might, in the absence of evidence for the defendants, have found such a payment.

The equity of a terre-tenant who has procured the payment of a mortgage, though not the possession of it, nor its satisfaction, is superior to that of an assignee for value of the mortgage, who, upon the assignment, made no inquiry of the mortgagor, who, by a recorded deed containing no reference to the mortgage, had bargained and sold the property to the terre-tenant.

Jeffers *v.* Gill, 8 WEEKLY NOTES, 19, distinguished.

Error to the Common Pleas of Northampton County.

This was a proceeding for the satisfaction of record of two mortgages, under the Act of June 11, 1879 (P. L. 141). The petition of Sellers set forth that, in 1867, Lewis Benner, as owner of a house in Bethlehem, gave a mortgage thereon to James F. Benner for $500, and, in 1868, a mortgage on the same property to the same person for $722; that on September 29, 1877, Lewis Benner conveyed the premises to the petitioner, who, at that time, paid the amount due on the mortgages to J. F. Benner, the mortgagee; and that, on June 26, 1879, J. F. Benner assigned the mortgages to one Susan Bodder. The petitioner prayed the Court to summon J. F. Benner and Susan Bodder to appear and to answer, and, upon proof of the above facts, to order satisfaction of the mortgages to be entered on the records.

The answer of J. F. Benner alleged that the petitioner had purchased the property subject to the mortgages, and assumed the payment of the debt secured thereby, and that the mortgages were subsequently assigned for value and in good faith to Susan Bodder; she, in her answer, alleged that the assignment was without notice of payment or of any arrangement between the petitioner and the mortgagee, by whom she was subsequently informed that the petitioner had sold or exchanged his livery stock for a note of $500, and a conveyance of the premises subject to the mortgages.

The Court directed an issue, between the petitioner as plaintiff and the respondents as defendants, to determine whether or not the mortgages had been paid, and directed that the petition and answers should stand as pleadings.

At the trial, the plaintiff put in evidence the record of the above mortgages given by Lewis Benner to James F. Benner, who, it appeared, was the son of Lewis; and also the deed of the mortgaged property from Lewis Benner to the plaintiff, dated September 29, and recorded October 8, 1877. The consideration named was $3000. The grantor, in the usual form, granted, bargained, sold, and aliened the property unto the grantee in fee simple, and warranted the grantee and his heirs against the grantor, his heirs, and all claiming under him. The deed contained no reference to any incumbrances. The plaintiff testified that J. F. Benner had undertaken to procure for him a conveyance of his father's (Lewis Benner's) house, clear of incumbrances, and to give him an indorsed note for $500, in consideration of the transfer of the plaintiff's stock in certain livery stables to him, J. F. Benner; that the conveyance was accepted with the understanding that the mortgages would be satisfied; that he had considered the total price of the stock he sold $3500—$3000 being represented by the house. The plaintiff further testified, that four or five weeks after the conveyance was made to him by Lewis Benner, he asked J. F. Benner to satisfy the mortgages, and the latter promised to do so the next day. The scrivener who drew the deed said that it had been at first intended that Lewis Benner should give a deed to James F. Benner, and James F. Benner one to Sellers; but he told the parties that that expense was useless, and that the property might as well be conveyed directly to Sellers. It did not appear that Lewis Benner was present at any of his son's interviews with Sellers. On cross-examination the witness testified that the bonds, and perhaps the mortgages, were at his office at the time of the meeting of Sellers and James F. Benner, and had been taken away by Benner without objection. It was admitted that on July 26, 1879, the mortgages were assigned for value by J. F. Benner to Susan Bodder.

The defendants offered no evidence, and the Judge directed the jury to find a verdict for them, saying in his general charge, *inter alia:* "There is no doubt that Susan Bodder is bound by all the equities subsisting between Lewis Benner, the mortgagor, and J. F. Benner, the mortgagee, at the time of the assignment of the bonds and mortgages to her; but as there is no evidence of a prior payment by Lewis Benner to J. F. Benner, the rule requiring her to make inquiry of the former does not apply to the vendee of the mortgagor's equity of redemption."

Verdict and judgment for the defendants. The plaintiff took this writ, assigning for error the above direction to the jury.

W. W. Schuyler (with him *G. W. Geiser*), for the plaintiff in error.

The Court below proceeded on the theory that the assignee of a mortgage takes it subject to the equities of the mortgagor alone, and not to the secret equities of third parties. The principle is correct, but here inapplicable. The equity of Sellers was the mortgagor's equity devolving upon him. The evidence tended to show payment by Lewis Benner, the mortgagor, and it was error to take from the jury the question as to this payment.

The principle that of two innocent parties he must suffer whose negligence occasioned the loss, cannot be invoked. It was not necessarily negligence for Sellers not to obtain possession of the mortgages.
Horstman *v.* Gerker, 13 Wr. 288.
At any rate, Mrs. Bodder could not set up such a defence, for she failed to make inquiry of the mortgagor when she took the assignment. A party setting up an equitable estoppel is himself bound to exercise good faith, and due diligence to ascertain the truth.
2 Story's Eq. Jur. ₴ 1553, b.
Moore *v.* Bowman, 47 N. H. 494.
The assignee of a mortgage, unless the mortgagor has estopped himself, holds it subject to all the equities to which it was liable in the hands of the assignor.
Ashton's Appeal, 23 Sm. 153.
It cannot be said that notice from Mrs. Bodder could not have affected the mortgagor as one who had parted with his interest by his conveyance of the property, for *non constat* that he might not have remained liable on his bond if the property had been sold under the mortgage for less than the debt. Besides, the mortgagor, by his deed of bargain and sale, had rendered himself liable, by implied covenant, to Sellers, in case of the latter's disturbance by incumbrances.
Blossom *v.* Van Court, 34 Mo. 390.
Cathcart *v.* Bowman, 5 Barr, 317.
Supposing the equities of Mrs. Bodder and of Sellers equal, under a familiar principle the earlier equity would prevail.
Bispham's Equity, ₴ 178.
W. E. Doster, contra.
The plaintiff in error has admitted that the assignee could not be affected by the secret equities of a third person. Relief like that claimed by the terre-tenant was denied in—
Jeffers *v.* Gill, 8 WEEKLY NOTES, 19.
There was no evidence of payment by the mortgagor. The petition and answers stand as pleadings, and in his petition the plaintiff alleges that *he* paid the debt. Such a payment could have no effect without notice to Mrs. Bodder, of which there was no evidence. On the contrary, the plaintiff failed to procure satisfaction of the mortgages, so that the record would have misled any one. But even a payment by Sellers was not established, for his conduct, in not demanding possession of the mortgages, was inconsistent with such a theory, and supported J. F. Benner's allegation that the property was bought subject to the mortgages.

May 3, 1880. THE COURT. The Act of June 11, 1879, under which this issue was directed provides in substance that if the holder of a mortgage fails from any cause to enter satisfaction upon the record of the same for six months after the debt secured thereby has been paid, the mortgagor, his heirs or legal representatives or the terre tenant of the mortgaged premises, may present a petition to the Court setting forth the facts and obtain an order for notice to the parties interested to appear and answer the petition; and if due proof be made that the debt has been paid, the Court shall direct the Recorder to enter satisfaction, but if either of the parties shall desire any matter of fact, that is affirmed by one and denied by the other, to be tried by a jury, an issue shall be formed and the same shall be tried accordingly, and if the jury shall find that the full amount for which the said mortgage was given has been paid, then satisfaction shall be entered on the record as aforesaid. (P. L. 141.)

The petition was presented by the plaintiff, alleging among other things that the premises were duly conveyed to him September 29, 1877, at which time the mortgages were fully paid. The defendants in their answers denied that they were paid; Benner, the mortgagee, alleging that the plaintiff had purchased subject to the mortgages and assumed the payment of the debt secured thereby, and that the mortgages were subsequently assigned for value and in good faith to Mrs. Bodder; she in her answer claims that they were assigned to her in June, 1879, without notice of payment or of any arrangement between the plaintiff and the mortgagee, and that she has since been informed by the latter that the plaintiff sold or exchanged his livery stock for a note of $500, and a conveyance of the premises subject to the mortgages. The Court thereupon ordered an issue between the plaintiff and defendants to determine whether or not the mortgages had been paid, and directed that the petition and answers should stand as pleadings.

On the trial of the issue plaintiff introduced testimony which it is claimed was sufficient to establish all the material allegations in his petition; but the Court thought otherwise and directed a verdict in favor of defendants, thus sustaining the validity of the mortgages in the hands of Mrs. Bodder, the assignee. This is assigned as error and the only question is whether the testimony should have been submitted to the jury.

In the absence of any evidence on the part of the defendants, the plaintiff was entitled to the full benefit of his testimony, and any inferences of fact which the jury would have been justified in drawing therefrom. It cannot be doubted that they could have justly found that on or about September 29, 1877, the plaintiff sold and transferred to James F. Benner his livery stock consisting of stock on hand, horses, carriages, etc., valued at $3500, in consideration of which he was to receive an indorsed note for $500, and a conveyance of the premises described in the mortgages at a valuation of $3000 clear of incumbrances. This of course involved the satisfaction of the mortgages held by Benner against his father, and the plaintiff testified positively that they were to be satisfied on the record. At first it was proposed to procure a conveyance from the father to the son and then from the latter to the plaintiff, but upon the suggestion of the scrivener that it would avoid unnecessary expense, the conveyance was made directly from the father to the plaintiff. The deed shows the date of the transaction, expresses the consideration named, and contains a special warranty against the grantor, his heirs, and all persons lawfully claiming under him. This covenant as between the vendor and vendee, would be available to the latter in case of eviction under the mortgages. The words "grant, bargain, and sell" also imported a covenant against incumbrances. (Cathcart v. Bowman, 5 Barr, 317; Shaffer v. Greer, 6 Norris, 370.) So that it was to the interest of Lewis Benner that the mortgages should be satisfied in the transaction, otherwise he might be liable on his warranty, as well as implied covenant. There is no evidence that the conveyance was under and subject to the mortgages; on the contrary the testimony is all the other way, and the jury would have been fully justified in finding as a fact that the conveyance was intended to operate and did operate as a payment to the extent of $3000 on account of the livery stock, and at the same time as a payment in full of the mortgage debts, or, what amounts to the same thing, that the plaintiff by transfer of the livery stock to the mortgagee discharged the mortgage debts, and to that extent was reimbursed by the conveyance from the mortgagor. Viewing it in either light it was a payment and extinguishment of the mortgage debt, and the plaintiff had a complete defence against the mortgages in the hands of the mortgagee. Why has he not an equally good defence against the assignee who subsequently accepted the assignment without making any inquiry? The plaintiff, who derived title from the obligor, had an equal right with the latter to interpose the defence of payment, unless he did or omitted to do something that might be set up as an estoppel as to him. It is said that he permitted the bonds and mortgages to remain in the hands of the mortgagee and thus enabled him to impose on Mrs. Bodder. This is all that can truthfully be urged against an otherwise valid and meritorious defence; and there might be some force in it, if she had inquired of the obligor or his personal representatives and endeavored to ascertain whether the debts were unpaid or there was any defence to the mortgages. That this was a duty which the law imposed on her cannot be doubted. (Eldred v. Hazlett, 9 Casey, 307; Ashton's Appeal, 23 P. F. Smith, 153.) It is not a sufficient answer to say that the mortgagor, having parted with his title, had no equities which he or his personal representatives were interested in asserting. We have already seen that recourse might be had against him or his estate on the warranty, and moreover the land might not be worth the mortgage debts, and in that event there would be a personal liability on the bonds for the deficiency. These equities were of sufficient importance to render the usual inquiry necessary, and if it had been made before the assignments were accepted, it would doubtless have led to a discovery of the fact that the mortgages were paid and should have been satisfied; at least it is fair to presume that such would have been the case.

The learned Judge in his charge conceded that Mrs. Bodder having failed to make inquiry was bound by all the equities subsisting between the mortgagor and mortgagee, at the time the mortgages were assigned, but he instructed the jury that as there was "no evidence of a prior payment by Lewis Benner to James F. Benner, the rule requiring her to make inquiry of the former does not apply to the vendee of the mortgagor, of his equity of redemption."

In this we think there was error. There was testimony from which the jury might have fairly found a payment. No other consideration than the payment of the mortgage debts was shown for the conveyance to the plaintiff. The testimony tended to prove that the mortgagee procured the conveyance and that to the extent of the mortgage debts, at least, he received the consideration in the form of a credit on his purchase of the livery stock. Nor did the testimony justify the inference that nothing more than the mortgagor's equity of redemption was conveyed or intended to be conveyed; on the contrary in connection with the deed it tended to prove that the conveyance was intended to be clear of incumbrances, and that the mortgages were to have been satisfied. It was not a secret equity of a third party that was attempted to be set up. It was the equity of the mortgagor against the mortgagee, based on the allegation of payment, that the terre tenant was seeking to enforce. If he had accepted a conveyance under and subject to the mortgages, or had assumed their payment, a very different case would have been presented.

The case of Jeffers v. Gill (8 WEEKLY NOTES, 19), on which defendants in error rely, is essentially different from the present case. There the terre tenant had assumed the payment of the mortgage, had actually paid part of it, and gave his negotiable note for the residue and renewed the same several times under a collateral agreement with Gill that the bond and mortgage were to be held as security for the note and its renewals. The mortgage was also accompanied with a certificate of no defence. In view of these and other circumstances, it was truly said in that case, that the terre tenant had been "grossly negligent. He gave his note for the balance due on the mortgage, when it was yet in the hands of McCullough, and when it came into Gill's possession, he took no step to have the arrangement indorsed, either on the papers or upon the record. The mortgage, bond and certificate of no defence were left in Gill's possession, as security for the note; in other words they were to be of full force until the note was paid."

In the present case, if the position which the plaintiff's testimony tended to sustain be correct, the mortgages were actually paid at the time the property was conveyed, and they should have been satisfied on the record and delivered to the mortgagor. The mortgagee, in fraud of the rights of the mortgagor, as well as his vendee, afterwards assigned these paid securities to one of the defendants who took them without resorting to sources of information from which, in all probability, she would have learned the fact of payment. Where inquiry becomes a duty the party who neglects to perform it should be visited with at least constructive knowledge of the facts which probably would have been revealed.

Judgment reversed, and a *venire facias de novo* awarded.

Opinion by STERRETT, J.

Jan. '80, 27.   Feb. 1, 1880.

Maloney et al. v. Bruce et al.

Limited partnerships—Individual liability—Acts of June 2, 1874, § 1, and May 1, 1876, § 1—Construction of—What is not compliance with.

Limited liability for partnership debts under the Act of June 2, 1874, and its supplements, is insured only by strict compliance with the Act.

The object of the provision of the Act of May 1, 1876, § 1, requiring a schedule, is to enable creditors to ascertain precisely of what the property consists, and to judge of its value.

A general description, or a lumping valuation, is not the schedule required by that Act.

Error to the Common Pleas of Lackawanna County.

Assumpsit, by John M. Bruce *et al.*, trading as Bruce & Cook, against Maloney *et al.*, individual members of The Maloney Manufacturing and Gas Light Company, limited. The following were the facts of the case:—

Martin Maloney, A. M. Renshaw, C. W. McKinney, H. B. Phelps, and W. F. Hallstead, by an agreement dated October 1, 1877, formed a limited partnership association under the Act of June 2, 1874 (P. L. 271), entitled "An Act authorizing the formation of partnership associations, in which the capital subscribed shall alone be responsible for the debts of the association, except under certain circumstances," and its supplements. The name adopted was "The Maloney Manufacturing and Gas Light Co., Limited." Business was begun by the association on or about October 2, 1877, in the city of Scranton. A statement in writing was made, signed by the parties interested, and acknowledged by them before a proper officer. It was recorded before business began under the management of the association. The contributions to the capital were made in personal property, and set out in the statement recorded, as follows:—

"The amount of capital of said association subscribed for by each of said persons is as follows, to wit: Martin Maloney, six thousand five hundred dollars; A. Miner Renshaw, four thousand dollars; Carlos W. McKinney, two thousand five hundred dollars; H. B. Phelps, one thousand dollars; W. F. Hallstead, one thousand dollars. Making the total amount of the capital fifteen thousand dollars, which said amount of capital has been fully paid in at the time of signing and executing these articles of association, and has been paid in by the assets and property of Martin Maloney at a valuation which has been approved by all the members subscribing to the stock of said association, a description of which property and the said valuation and the names of the parties so contributing are as follows:—

"Contract with the Pennsylvania Globe Gas Light Co. at a valuation two thousand five hundred dollars; merchandise, consisting of iron, steel, tin and copper ware, gas pipes and gas fixtures, plumbing materials, stoves, furnaces, pumps, house furnishing goods, mantels, grates, terra cotta pipes, lamps and lamp posts, safe, stove, furniture, and fixtures, all the goods, tools, and chattels now on the premises, 209 Lackawanna Avenue, Scranton City, now leased by said Martin Maloney, valuation twelve thousand five hundred dollars. Making a total valuation of fifteen thousand dollars, which is contributed by the parties to this association in amount as subscribed for by each as above set forth."

The association continued business for about one year, when, being unable to meet their indebtedness, they made an assignment for the benefit of creditors. The plaintiffs below brought an action and obtained judgment against the association. They issued an execution, which was returned no goods.

They then, by affidavit filed, alleging that the statement recorded did not comply with the statutes authorizing the formation of limited partnerships, obtained a rule to show cause why execution should not issue against the persons composing the association individually. The rule was made absolute, and execution ordered as prayed for, on the ground that there was not such a description of the property contributed as the law required.

The defendants then took this writ, assigning for error the order of the Court awarding execution against them individually.

L. B. *Price* (with whom was *E. N. Willard*), for the plaintiffs in error.

The schedule required is simply a general statement of the kind and value of the property. Its object is to protect against fraud, and to give such information as may secure credit or discredit to the association. In this view the capital was fully described. Certainty to a common intent is sufficient.

Andrews *v.* Schott, 10 B. 47.
McClintock *v.* Rush, 13 Sm. 203.

The order of Court was in effect to declare the defendants general partners. Such a construction, and the action of the Court under it in entering judgment and awarding execution without trial by jury is unconstitutional.

North Penna. Coal Co. *v.* Snowden, 6 Wr. 488.
Tillmes *v.* Marsh *et al.*, 17 Sm. 507.
Haines's App., 23 Id. 169.

R. W. Archbald, for the defendant in error.

The schedule must be a statement of the exact nature of the property contributed, and a correct valuation of it.

Bement *v.* Phila., etc., Brick Co., 5 WEEKLY NOTES, 58.

The schedule does not give the nature of the contract, and is a mere enumeration of some of the stock with a lumping value on it.

Limited partnership laws have always received a strict construction in favor of creditors.

Andrews *v.* Schott, 10 B. 47.
Vandike *v.* Rosskam, 17 Sm. 330.
Guillou *v.* Peterson, 7 WEEKLY NOTES, 268.

The construction put upon the Act by the Court is constitutional.

In re Penna. Hall, 5 B. 204, 208.
Dunmore's Appeal, 2 Sm. 374.
Van Swartow *v.* Com., 12 H. 131.
Rhines *v.* Clark, 1 Sm. 96, 101.
Paschall Street, 31 Sm. 118.
Wyncoop *v.* Cooch, 7 WEEKLY NOTES, 53.
Simpson *v.* Neill, Ibid. 86.

May 3, 1880. THE COURT. The Act of 2d June, 1874 (P. L. 271), in regard to limited partnerships, provided for a cash capital. The supplement to said Act, passed 1 May, 1876 (P. L. 89), allows the members "to make contribution of the capital thereof in real or personal estate, mines, or other property, at a valuation to be approved by all the members subscribing to the capital of such association; provided, that in the statement required to be recorded by the first section of said Act, subscriptions to the capital, whether in cash or property, shall be certified in this respect according to the fact; and when property has been contributed as part of the capital, a schedule containing the names of the parties so contributing, with a description and valuation of the property so contributed, shall be inserted.

"The Maloney Manufacturing and Gas Light Company, Limited," was organized under the said Act of 1874; no capital was contributed in cash, the articles of association fix the amount of the capital at $15,000, and give the names of the members, with the number of shares held by each, and recite that the whole amount of the capital has been paid in by the assets and property of Martin Maloney, one of the members, at a valuation approved by all the members. Then follows what purports to be a list of the property contributed in lieu of cash, the first item being a "contract with the Pennsylvania Gas Light Company at a valuation of $2500," after which comes merchandise under a general description, together with "furniture, fixtures, and all the goods, tools, and chattels now on the premises 209 Lackawanna Avenue, Scranton City, now leased by said Martin Maloney, valuation $12,500."

This is not the kind of schedule contemplated by the Act of 1876. The description is too general to enable any one to form a correct estimate of the extent of the property, and a lumping valuation renders it equally difficult to judge of values. This property contributed was intended as the equivalent of a cash capital, and the plain object of the provision in the Act of 1876, requiring a schedule, was to enable creditors to ascertain precisely of what the property consisted, and to judge of its value. If parties seek to have all the advantages of a partnership, and yet limit their liability as to creditors, they must comply strictly with the Act. Where property has not been contributed, scheduled, and valued as the Act of 1876 directs, there is no payment of the capital. It follows that the order of the Court below, allowing executions to go out against the individual members for the amount of unpaid stock subscribed by them, was free from error, and the judgment must be affirmed.

Opinion by PAXSON, J.

SHARSWOOD, C. J., and TRUNKEY, J., dissent. GREEN, J., absent.

Jan. '80, 292.   April 1, 1880.

Allen v. Kellam.

Recognisance of bail in error—Nature of— When valid notwithstanding defect in form— What constitutes waiver of defect—What constitutes acceptance of recognisance when defective.

A recognizance of bail in error, defective in form, may derive validity from the consent, express or implied, of the parties intended to be affected by it.

Error to the Common Pleas of Wayne County.

Sci. fa. sur recognizance of bail in error, by Peter Kellam against Martin B. Allen.

The affidavit of defence averred: "That at the time of giving the recognizance upon which the above action is brought, the deponent did so with the assurance upon the part of the defendant in the suit in which the recognizance was given that deponent should be indemnified against loss by reason of signing such recognizance; that such indemnity was not furnished to deponent; that the deponent was *the only surety in said recognizance;* that after said recognizance was filed, and pending the writ of error, the plaintiff in the said suit caused execution to issue against the property of the defendant, William T. Kellam, and treated the said recognizance as a nullity; that the plaintiff in said suit in which the recognizance was given lost nothing by reason of the writ of error being taken, having treated the recognizance as a nullity, and proceeded with the execution; that there was an entire failure of consideration for which the said recognizance was given."

The Court entered judgment for want of a sufficient affidavit of defence; whereupon the defendant took this writ, assigning for error the entry of judgment against him.

H. M. Seely and *H. Wilson* (*Geo. S. Purdy* with them) for the plaintiff in error.

The recognizance is simply a security furnished in consideration of the delay and risk occasioned by the stay of execution; with a single surety, it is not a *supersedeas*, and may be disregarded.

Rheem *v.* Wheel Co., 9 C. 357.
Eichman *v.* Belvedere Bank, 3 Wh. 70.
Stroop *v.* Gross, 1 W. & S. 141.

In this case it was disregarded.

Geo. G. Waller for the defendant in error.

By the rules of the Supreme Court, if there be no exception to the bail within twenty days, it is presumed to be good. There was no exception in this case. The issuing of execution did not prejudice the bail, for it was stayed.

Milliken *v.* Brown, 10 S. & R. 188.

May 3, 1880. THE COURT. The Act of 1836, relating to bail in error, provides that execution shall not be stayed unless the plaintiff in such writ, or some one in his behalf, with sufficient sureties, shall become bound by recognizance with condition to prosecute the writ of error with effect, etc. A recognizance with a single surety is not a supersedeas by a mere operation of law, and the party in whose favor judgment has been entered in the Court below may disregard it and proceed with his execution as though no recognizance has been given. (Rheem *v.* Naugatuc Wheel Co., 9 Casey, 356.)

But a recognizance defective in form may derive validity from the consent, express or implied, of the parties intended to be affected by it. It is tendered to the defendant in error as security in consideration of the delay and risk to which he may be subjected, and if he elects to accept and treat it as valid, and for this reason forbears to proceed by execution, pending the writ of error, neither the principal nor the surety can evade liability on the ground of non-conformity to the requirements of the statute. The recognizance may be sustained as a voluntary personal contract based on sufficient consideration. But such a state of facts is not presented in this case. The plaintiff in error, in his affidavit of defence, which was adjudged insufficient by the Court below, says, among other things, that he was the only surety in the recognizance, that after it was filed, and pending the writ of error, the plaintiff below treated it as a nullity, issued execution, and proceeded as though no recognizance had been given, that having so proceeded, he lost no right or security by reason of the writ of error. The facts thus alleged, if true, constitute a good defence, and for the purpose of the present inquiry, we must assume that every allegation contained in the affidavit of defence is strictly true. It may be that on the trial of the case the plaintiff below will be able to show what he now alleges, that execution was stayed and by common consent the recognizance was treated as valid and binding. This may become a question of fact for the jury, but in passing upon the sufficiency of the affidavit of defence, we cannot undertake to determine disputed questions of fact. The only pertinent inquiry in a case like this, is whether the allegations of fact contained in the affidavit of defence, assuming them to be true, constitute a defence. The recognizance in this case was so defective in form that the defendant in error had a right to treat it as a nullity, and the allegation is that he did so treat it, "issued execution and proceeded therewith, pending the writ of error, as though no recognizance had been given." This, if true, is a good defence to the scire facias on the recognizance.

Judgment reversed and a procedendo awarded.
Opinion by STERRETT, J. GREEN, J., absent.

The recognizance may be sustained as a voluntary personal contract, based on sufficient consideration; and if there be an election to accept one defective, and treating it as valid, to forbear to proceed by execution pending the writ of error, neither the principal nor the surety can evade liability on the ground of the defect.

But to treat it as a nullity, to issue execution, and to proceed as though no recognizance had been given, constitutes a good defence to an action on it.

Common Pleas—Equity.

C. P. No. 1.   Dec. 17, 1879.
Dorsey v. Van Horn.

Partition in equity—Intestacy—Descent—Collaterals—Half blood—Real estate—Among cousins those of the half-blood inherit real estate equally with those of the whole blood—Act of April 27, 1855.

Sur exceptions to Master's report in partition.

The bill set forth that Rosetta Graham died in 1877 seized, *inter alia*, of certain groundrents purchased by her in her lifetime, and leaving to survive her eight cousins of the whole blood and two of the half-blood; and prayed that partition might be made among those of the whole blood only. The case being referred to a Master, he reported in favor of all the cousins alike, to which report exceptions were filed by the cousins of the whole blood.

Louis F. Benson (with whom was *Wm. A. Porter*), for exceptants.

The Act of 1853 divides the collateral relatives of a decedent into two classes, viz., collateral heirs and next of kin, and among those of the first class the heirs of the whole blood take to the exclusion of those of the half-blood, while among next of kin those of the half-blood take conjointly with those of the whole blood. Prior to the Act of 1855, the collateral relatives of the half-blood would have taken in cases like the present one. But that Act has taken two classes of the next of kin and converted them into collateral heirs. It provides that—

"Among collaterals, when by existing laws entitled to inherit, the real and personal estate shall descend and be distributed among the grandchildren of brothers and sisters, and the children of uncles and aunts by representation; such descendants taking equally among them such share as their parent would have taken if living."

This Act converts these classes into collateral heirs with all the attributes belonging to that division of collaterals, among which is the preference of the whole blood over the half-blood.

Lane's Appeal, 4 Casey, 487.
Brenneman's Appeal, 4 Wr. 115.
Hayes's Appeal, 7 WEEKLY NOTES, 11.

A. H. Smith, contra.

Under the Act of 1833, those of the half-blood would take in a case like the present, and the Act of 1855 in its terms provides for the taking by those who under "existing laws are entitled to participate."

C. A. V.

Jan. 17, 1880. THE COURT. In the cases upon which the exceptants rely, the question in controversy here was not decided. We think that the Master was correct in distinguishing them from the case at bar, and in concluding that the cousins of the half-blood should take. They will also take per capita and not per stirpes. Exceptions dismissed.

Oral opinion by ALLISON, P. J.

Common Pleas—Law.

C. P. No. 1.   June 19, 1880.
Schofield to use, etc. v. Casselberry.

Execution—Practice—Sheriff's Interpleader Act—Where there are several execution creditors, the sheriff cannot postpone his sale unless by consent of all—If the sale is wrongfully postponed the sheriff cannot claim the benefit of the Interpleader Act.

Sheriff's rule for interpleader.

The following facts appeared from the depositions: one Thornton, having obtained a judgment against defendant for $1607.77, issued a fi. fa. thereon. Catharine M. Casselberry, wife of the defendant, claimed the goods levied on, and an interpleader was obtained, on the trial of which the claimant was nonsuited. On Feb. 28, 1880, a vend. ex. was issued by Thornton. On March 3, 1880, one Keyes issued a fi. fa. against the same defendant on a judgment for $85. March 17, 1880, the present plaintiff also issued a fi. fa. The depositions further showed that the sheriff advertised to sell on March 20, 1880, but at the request of Thornton's attorney the sale was postponed. Shortly afterwards Catharine M. Casselberry's attorney, with money furnished by her, purchased the Thornton and Keyes judgments, and had them marked to his use. On two subsequent occasions the sheriff postponed the sale, at the request of Catharine M. Casselberry's counsel, and against the protests of plaintiff's counsel. It also appeared from the deposition of the deputy-sheriff, that at a forced sale the goods would probably not have brought more than $500 or $600. The sheriff had agreed to sell if the plaintiff would indemnify him, but this he declined to do. Two months after the exit of the plaintiff's fi. fa., and in consequence of his pushing for a settlement, Catharine M. Casselberry claimed the goods in this case, and her attorney then stayed the Thornton and Keyes writs.

The present rule was then taken.

Alex. Simpson, Jr., against the rule.

The sheriff's Interpleader Act was passed solely for the purpose of protecting the sheriff.

The Court is not bound to grant an issue at the sheriff's request, the award or refusal being in the sound discretion of the Court.

Bain v. Funk, 11 Sm. 185.

To entitle the sheriff to the benefit of the Act he must be diligent. To permit him to delay at the request of one party alone and then to allow him the benefit of the Act, would be to hold out a premium to irregularities.

Mutton v. Young, 4 Man. Gr. & Sc. 375.
Crump v. Day, Ibid. 760.

In this case delays were granted against the plaintiff's protest; the sheriff, therefore, is not entitled to any protection.

The sheriff had ample time before the return day of the writ either to realize the money or compel Mrs. Casselberry to put in her claim. He did neither; and having disobeyed the process of the Court, is not entitled to its protection.

Winship, for the rule, contended that the first writ, being a vend. ex., was notice to the sheriff that there had been a claimant, and that he must consequently proceed with caution; the plaintiff could not complain of the delay, for, although requested to indemnify the sheriff, he had neglected to do so; that it was frequently impossible for the sheriff to realize the money before the return day of the writ; that if the sale had taken place before, the plaintiff in this suit would have realized nothing, as the prior judgments amounted to $1700, while the goods were worth only $600; that the plaintiff's judgment was now the first judgment, and the plaintiff therefore had been benefited, rather than injured, by the delay.

A. Simpson, Jr., in reply.

It does not follow that the plaintiff has been benefited by the delay; *non constat* that the writ would not have been stayed before. Besides, a benefit accruing to the plaintiff cannot enure to relieve the sheriff from the consequences of his negligence. In this case the sheriff had but one duty, and that he has neglected to perform.

June 26, 1880. THE COURT. Rule discharged.

C. P. No. 4.   Aug. 1880.
In re Petition of Bernard Gormley.

Citizenship—Naval service—The Act of Congress (7 June, 1872, Rev. St. sec. 2174) conferring the right of citizenship upon seamen who have served on board merchant vessels of the United States does not extend to the United States naval service.

Sur petition to be admitted to citizenship.

The petition of Bernard Gormley showed that he enlisted in the navy of the United States on the 29th of December, 1874, and was honorably discharged from the service on the 29th of May, 1878; that he has resided in the United States for a period of one year and upwards, and that it is *bona fide* his intention to become a citizen of the United States, etc. The petitioner prayed that on making the proof and taking the oath prescribed by law he may be admitted a citizen of the United States of America.

Charles Henry Jones for petitioner.

C. A. V.

Aug. 28, 1880. THE COURT (after reciting the facts). The allegations of the petition are supported by the oath of the petitioner, and the period of residence is duly vouched by John F. Snyder. In addition to this proof, the petitioner exhibits the certificate of the commanding officer of the flag-ship Pensacola, which shows that he was duly enlisted in and was "honorably discharged" from the naval service of the United States on the days mentioned in his petition.

Here the proof stops. Such proof is entirely inadequate to warrant us in granting the petitioner's prayer. There is no Act of Congress which authorizes the courts to admit a foreigner to citizenship merely because he has served in the United States navy, and if any certificates of citizenship have been granted based upon such service, they are null and void, and afford the holder no protection or right whatever by reason of them.

The petitioner has probably confused his supposed right with that of a seaman who has served on board a merchant vessel of the United States. The Act of Congress conferring the latter right is in these words (Rev. St. U. S. 380, sec. 2174): "Every seaman, being a foreigner, who declares his intention of becoming a citizen of the United States, in any competent Court, and shall have served three years on board of a merchant vessel of the United States, subsequent to the date of such declaration, may, on his application to any competent Court, and the production of his certificate of discharge and good conduct during that time, together with the certificate of his declaration of intention to become a citizen, be admitted a citizen of the United States."

It is quite plain that this Act does not extend to the naval service. It was doubtless passed as an inducement and encouragement to foreigners to enter our merchant service to answer the wants of that service only. And even under that Act, one seeking the benefit of its provisions must serve three years subsequent to the declaration of his intention of becoming a citizen. It follows from what has been said, that the prayer of the petitioner must be refused. The petition is dismissed.

Opinion by BRIGGS, J.

Weekly Notes of Cases.

Vol. IX.]   THURSDAY, OCT. 7, 1880.   [No. 7.

Supreme Court.

May, '80, 145.   June 2, 1880.

Williamsport Gas Co. v. Pinkerton.

Debtor and creditor—Interest coupons—Liability of company issuing—Agency.

A. was the owner of a coupon bond of the corporation defendant. The interest coupon on which this suit was brought stated on its face that it was payable December 1, 1875, at a certain banking-house. This house went out of business, and the B. Bank occupied its premises, and the coupons were paid at this bank for some years, to plaintiff among others. On Nov. 29, 1875, the defendant sent to the bank funds sufficient to pay the interest falling due Dec. 1, and all coupons presented at the bank up to Dec. 22, were paid by the bank; plaintiff had not at that date presented his coupon for payment. On that day the bank made an assignment for the benefit of its creditors, and subsequently plaintiff demanded payment of the defendant, and, upon refusal, brought suit:—

Held, that the defendant was liable.

PER CURIAM. The corporation which issues a coupon bond is in the position of a maker of a promissory note, not of the drawer of a check or bill of exchange. There is no obligation on the holder to demand payment within a reasonable time.

Error to the Common Pleas of Lycoming County.

This was a suit originally brought before a magistrate by J. J. Pinkerton against the Williamsport Gas Company, wherein the plaintiff recovered judgment for $23.12 and costs. The defendant appealed, and a case stated was agreed upon, setting forth the following facts:—

In 1868 the company defendant issued bonds to the amount of $30,000, payable June 1, 1878, at a certain banking-house. To each bond interest coupons were attached, in the following form:—

The Williamsport Gas Company will pay the bearer at the banking-house of Kirk, MacVeagh & Co., West Chester, Pa., on the first day of December, 1875, twenty dollars, being six months' interest on bond No. 18.

$20.   T. CORYELL, Treasurer.

The banking-house subsequently dissolved, and the "Brandywine Bank" was incorporated by Act of Assembly in 1871. The bank occupied the same premises that the banking-house had occupied, and many of the firm's accounts were transferred to the bank—among others that of the interest on defendant's bonds; the interest on these bonds was from this time paid at the bank, and plaintiff, among others, regularly collected his interest from the bank. On Nov. 29, 1875, the Gas Company remitted to the bank a sight draft sufficient to pay the interest due Dec. 1, 1875, and the bank paid all coupons presented up to Dec. 22, 1875; on that day it made an assignment. The plaintiff was the owner of one of said bonds, and, at the date of the bank's failure had not presented his interest coupon for payment at the bank; after that event, he did, on March 3, 1877, demand payment at the defendant's office, and, upon refusal, brought suit. If the Court be of opinion that plaintiff is entitled to recover the amount of his coupon, with interest from March 3, 1877, then judgment to be entered for plaintiff for $23.23; otherwise, judgment for defendant.

The Court entered judgment for plaintiff for $23.23, whereupon defendant took this writ, assigning for error the said action of the Court.

Bentley L. Parker for plaintiff in error.

The analogy of coupons to commercial paper is striking, and has inclined our Courts to apply the same rules to both.

P. & B. C. R. R. *v.* Johnson, 4 Sm. 130.

Hence, it follows that as in the case of commercial paper, the holder of the coupon must exercise reasonable diligence in presenting it for payment; and if he does not, and the bank fails, the loss is his. The bank was not the agent of the company.

H. C. Parsons and *C. K. Geddes* for defendant in error.

Coupons are essentially different from commercial paper; they are secured by mortgage; they are under seal; debt alone will lie upon them, and not assumpsit; they are not barred by the statute of limitations in six years. They form part of the bonds, and differ from commercial paper exactly as the bonds do.

City *v.* Lamson, 9 Wall. 477.
City *v.* Butler, 14 Wall. 296.

They resemble commercial paper only in the fact that they pass by delivery.

June 14, 1880. THE COURT. The corporation which issues a coupon bond is in the position of the maker of a promissory note, not of the drawer of a check or bill of exchange. There is no obligation on the holder to present and demand it within a reasonable time. The same rule applies to the coupons just as long as he can hold on to the bond without requiring payment. The coupon is nothing but an acknowledgment of interest due, and is but an incident of the principal. It is attached to the bond, and may be detached from it for the convenience of the holder. The possession by the corporation is evidence of its payment. The

banking-house at which it was made payable were the agents of the corporation, and the holder could not lose in any event by their insolvency.
Judgment affirmed.
PER CURIAM.

Jan. '80, 212, 213, 214, 215.   February 18, 1880.
Wistar v. City of Philadelphia to use, etc.

Practice—Act of March 23, 1866—Municipal claims—Proof of notice of demand, when not necessary—Alias writs of scire facias sur municipal claims.

Where a judgment has been reversed on account of a fatal defect in the sheriff's return to a writ of scire facias, the effect is as if there had been no return at all, or the entry had been *vicecomes non misit breve*, and the proper course to pursue is to issue an alias writ.

By the Act of Assembly of March 23, 1866, it was provided that in a proceeding on a scire facias sur municipal claim no judgment by default should be entered unless an affidavit was filed stating that the defendant in the writ had been duly notified to make payment of the claim, etc.

Held, that, when such affidavit had been filed previously to taking judgment under an original writ, the judgment having been set aside on account of a defect in the return, it was not necessary to file a second affidavit in order to take judgment under an alias writ, the original and the alias being part of one and the same proceeding. .

Error to the Common Pleas No. 1, of Philadelphia County.

Alias scire facias sur municipal claim, filed by the city of Philadelphia to the use of George W. Mooney, to the use of William Armstrong, against a certain property in Stiles Street, in said city, for work done on a sewer in front thereof.

The following facts appear from the records of the cause: On November 21st, 1874, the above claim having been duly filed, a scire facias issued against said lot and the heirs of Richard Wistar, owners or reputed owners, and Lewis Wistar, actual owner, which was returned by the sheriff, "made known by posting and advertising, and nihil habet as to defendants."

On December 26, 1874, proof of service of notice, as required by the provisions of the Act of Assembly of March 23, 1866,* (Purd. Dig.

---

* The Act provides, *inter alia*, as follows:—

SECT. 1. . . . "that before *any scire facias* shall be issued on any such claim, it shall be the duty of the City Solicitor to cause diligent search to be made by an assistant or clerk for the owner or reputed owner . . . and to serve him or her with a written or printed notice to make payment to the City Solicitor within ten days."

"If the said claims are not paid within said time they shall be sued out by the City Solicitor . . . but before any judgment by default shall be entered *therein*, the Court shall be satisfied by an affidavit; to be filed of rec-

---

1091-2) was filed. Plaintiff subsequently took judgment for want of an affidavit of defence, which judgment was reversed by the Supreme Court for a fatal defect in the sheriff's return to the writ. (See Wistar *v.* The City, 5 Norris, 215; S. C., 5 WEEKLY NOTES, 279.) April 23, 1878, the record was returned.

On August 23' 1879, the present alias scire facias issued and was duly returned by the sheriff in accordance with the opinion of the Supreme Court. No further proof of service of notice was filed, and judgment was taken for want of an affidavit of defence. The Court refused to set aside this judgment, and the defendant took this writ, assigning for error (1) The entry of judgment for the plaintiff by default for want of an affidavit of defence, without the filing of proof that the defendant, Lewis Wistar, had been notified by the City Solicitor to make payment of the claim, upon which the alias writ of scire facias was issued, before the issuing of the same, in accordance with the provisions of the Act of 23d of March, 1866, in that behalf. (2) That the alias writ of scire facias was improvidently issued without a search for, or a demand of payment of the said claim of the owner, as required by the Act aforesaid. (3) That the said alias writ of scire facias was irregularly issued, whilst there was an original writ of scire facias upon the record with a return of the sheriff of "made known" thereon, not set aside, reversed, amended, or withdrawn.

N. H. Sharpless, for the plaintiff in error.

The Act of Assembly especially provides that before *any* scire facias shall issue, due proof of service of notice shall be filed. It was the clear duty of the plaintiff to search for the defendant and notify him of the demand. This not having been done, the Court erred in entering judgment as it did.

The issuing of this alias writ was irregular while the former writ remained on the record with the return of "made known" upon it. Either the writ or the return should have been vacated, as the return of the sheriff is otherwise conclusive.

Flick *v.* Troxsell, 7 W. & S. 65.
Blair *v.* Weaver, 11 S. & R. 84.

Henry C. Terry, for defendant in error.

The proof of notice in the proceedings under the first writ is sufficient, the original and alias writs of scire facias being considered one writ in law. Besides, the Act of Assembly only requires proof of notice "*before suit brought*." And it

---

ord, of the following facts: First, that if the owner or reputed owner has any known residence in the said city, he has been served, before suit brought, with notice of said claim in writing or printing, either by handing the same to him personally, or by leaving the same with an adult member of his family, at his said residence, at least ten days before issuing *said* writ of *scire facias*."

is the date of the issuance of the *original* writ which determines when suit is brought.

By the decision of this Court on the first writ of error the return to the original writ was "fatally defective." Therefore no possible amendment could have availed here.

The sheriff may have leave granted him to amend his return, but the return is conclusive upon himself.

Vastine *v.* Ferry, 2 S. & R. 426.
Paxton *v.* Steckel, 2 Barr, 93.

In any event the defendant would have to be brought in on an alias writ, and any attempt to have the return amended would have benefited no one.

March 1, 1880. THE COURT. When the former judgments in these cases were reversed in this Court, on account of a fatal defect in the sheriff's returns to the writs of scire facias, and the records remitted to the Court below, no other course was open to the plaintiffs than to issue alias writs. By that decision the entire return was avoided, and the cases stood as if there had been no return at all, or the entry had been *vicecomes non misit breve.* There can be no doubt that in such a case an alias is regular; if it were not, the party would be without remedy, except perhaps against the sheriff. It is clear, too, that an affidavit having been filed on the original scire facias, that the defendant, Lewis Wistar, had been notified by the City Solicitor to make payment of the claim, it was not necessary to make a new demand before the issuing of the alias. It is all one and the same proceeding, and the object of the Act of March 23, 1866, is fully attained by one notice and demand.

Judgment affirmed.

PER CURIAM.

May, '80, 105.   May 11, 1880.
J. C. Acker, Receiver, v. Hite et al.

Mutual insurance—Authority of directors to cancel policy—Assessments—Powers of officers—Liabilities of the insured.

A policy of insurance and the premium note given therefor, constitute a contract between the company and the insured, and the parties usually have the same power to rescind it by mutual agreement as they had to make it.

The right of a company to cancel policies and thus terminate the contract, for various acts of the insured, has constantly been recognized.

An agreement made in good faith between the parties to a contract of insurance to annul it is valid.

When the insured surrenders his policy, and it is marked cancelled, from that moment he ceases to be a member, though he continues liable to assessments for losses which accrued while he was a member.

Error to the Common Pleas of Bedford County.

Three actions of debt by J. C. Acker, Receiver of the Union Horse Insurance Company of Blair County, against Albert Hite, Joseph Brunner, and John Dicken, upon policies of insurance, to recover two assessments on premium notes. The three cases were tried as one, the material facts being as follows:—

The above named company was chartered, on the mutual plan, June 17, 1872, by the Court of Common Pleas of Blair County. The value of each animal insured was considered capital stock, and was, in case of loss, subject to assessment. On November 5, 1874, John Dicken insured four horses for five years to the value of $525. Joseph M. Brunner insured two horses October 6, 1874, for five years, to the value of $275. In 1876-7 the company, from numerous and severe losses, became heavily involved, and judgments to a large amount were entered against it. The directors of said company on October 20, 1876, passed resolutions allowing "all dissatisfied members to withdraw from the company after paying all assessments or dues, if their policies be handed to the directors." An assessment of three per centum was made by the directors on the premium notes January 1, 1878, and another of fifteen per cent. was made by the receiver March 29, 1878. Numerous parties availed themselves of the resolution of the directors to withdraw, and so had their policies cancelled. The defendants, Hite, Dicken, and Brunner, handed their policies to Samuel Whip, one of the directors, in accordance with the resolution. On investigation, it was discovered that Albert Hite, on previous assessments, was debtor to the company in the sum of $1.50, Brunner nothing, Dicken $4.58, and these three policies were not cancelled by the company, but treated as in full force, and in January, 1878, when the secretary made out the assessment lists, he assessed these defendants. After due process of law, J. C. Acker was appointed receiver of the company. He then, under the direction of the Court, laid an assessment of fifteen per cent. on all premium notes in his possession.

The jury found a special verdict, in effect as above. The special verdict concluded as follows: "That the jury are ignorant, in point of law, upon which side they might, upon these facts, find the issue. If upon the whole matter the Court shall be of opinion that the issue is found for the plaintiffs, they find for the plaintiffs accordingly, and assess the damages in favor of the plaintiffs against the defendants—Albert Hite, $24; J. M. Brunner, $33; John Dicken, $69. But if the Court is of a contrary opinion, then they find vice versa."

After argument, the Court rendered judgment on the special verdict in favor of the defendants; whereupon plaintiffs took this writ, assigning for error the action of the Court in entering judgment in favor of defendants.

Frederick Jaehel and *J. M. Reynolds*, for plaintiffs in error.

Directors have no power to pass and carry into effect a resolution by which some members are relieved from paying for losses which occured while their policies were in force.

Maine Mut. Ins. Co. *v.* Pickering, 66 Me. Rep. 130.

Neither the surrender, cancellation, nor the expiration of the policy, nor the insolvency of the company releases the holder of a policy from his liability to assessments for losses which occurred during his membership.

May on Insurance, 691.
Wilson *v.* Trumbull Ins. Co., 7 Har. 372.
Sterling *v.* Mercantile Mut. Ins. Co., 8 Cas. 75.

The mere handing of a policy by a member of a mutual insurance company to one of the directors, with the request to have it cancelled, is not such an action as would, in the eyes of the law, justify the surrender of the premium notes. In this case the policies were not, in fact, cancelled, nor the notes returned, because defendants were indebted, not only for losses existing at the time, but also for previous assessments, and as continuing members they were liable to subsequent assessments.

Insurance Co. *v.* Connor, 5 H. 136.
Columbia Ins. Co. *v.* Buckley, 2 N. 294.
Upton *v.* Hansbrough, 3 Bissell, 417.

The receiver was legally appointed by the Court, and he is bound by the charter to the same extent as the directors.

Daniels's Ch. Pr., 1714.
Safford *v.* People, 85 Ill. 558.
Wallace *v.* Yeager, 4 Phila. 251.
Yeager *v.* Wallace, 8 Wr. 294.
Singerly *v.* Fox, 25 Sm. 112.

J. B. Cessna, for defendants in error.

It is clear that the plaintiffs authorized the cancellation of policies of dissatisfied members upon certain conditions, and that those conditions were complied with on the part of the defendants. By the resolutions defendants were required to pay their just dues; but the assessments were illegal and therefore unjust.

Wilson *v.* Trumbull Ins. Co., 7 H. 372.
Finley *v.* Lycoming Ins. Co., 6 C. 311–815.

The company kept both the policies and the money which defendants sent them in payment of all demands, and such retention acts as a waiver and estops the company.

Georgia Mut. Ins. Co. *v.* Gibson, 52 Ga. 640.

Directors have full power to cancel policies and surrender notes, and such an agreement discharges the members.

The agreement to cancel policies and surrender notes to defendants was a legal contract, so far consummated, on the part of the defendants, as to discharge their liability on their notes. It was in law a cancellation.

May on Insurance, 690–1.
Boland *v.* Whitman, 33 Ind. 64.
Sands *v.* Hill, 55 N. Y. 18.
Columbia Ins. Co. *v.* Masonheimer, 26 Sm. 138.
Cumberland Valley Ins. Co. *v.* Herbert, 2 WEEKLY NOTES, 155.
Campbell *v.* Adams, 38 Barb. 132.
Hyde *v.* Lynde, 4 N. Y. Comstock, 387.
Wadsworth *v.* Davis, 13 Ohio St. 123.
Columbia Ins. Co. *v.* Stone, 3 Allen, Mass. 385.
Wood on Insurance, 56.
Hamilton *v.* Lycoming Mut. Ins. Co., 5 B. 139.
Campbell *v.* Adams, 38 Barb. 132.
Sands, Receiver, *v.* Hill, 55 N. Y. 18.

The company had the right to cancel a policy upon the non-payment of an assessment for thirty days. The company having accepted payment promised to cancel the policies of defendants without any conditions or reservations. This they did not do. If defendants had subsequently claimed for a loss they would have been told "you have surrendered your policy. It is cancelled. We will pay you nothing." Full powers were given the directors by law and by charter to make the contract they did. Their action in passing the resolution referred to comes within the management of the affairs and business of the company, and is therefore binding on all its members.

A receiver is in the position of an assignee. The appointment of the receiver only passed to him the assets of the corporation, not its franchises.

Schimpf *v.* Lehigh Valley Mut. Ins. Co., 6 WEEKLY NOTES, 23.

Vide opinion of Judge BLODGET, U. S. District Court, Cincinnati, Dec. 24, 1879, in Cook, Assignee of the Protective Life Insurance Company.

May 31, 1880. THE COURT. The business of an insurance company, whether conducted on the mutual or stock plan, is managed by its officers and agents, and the corporators are bound by the acts of such agents in all matters properly done within the scope of the powers committed to them. A policy of insurance and the premium note given therefor constitute a contract between the company and the insured, and the parties usually have the same power to rescind it by mutual agreement as they had to make it. Such a power on the part of the company seems essentially necessary to the safe and proper transaction of its business. (Boland *v.* Whitman, Receiver, 33 Ind. 64; Wadsworth *v.* Davis, Receiver, 13 Ohio St. 123.) Most mutual companies insert stipulations in their policies that they shall become void, either *ipso facto* or at the option of the company, for certain acts of omission or commission by the insured, and when avoided the rights and liabilities of the member are ended, except his liability for debts already incurred. (Columbia Ins. Co. *v.* Masonheimer, 26 P. F. S.; Wilson *v.* Trumbull Ins. Co., 7 Harris, 372.) The right of the company to cancel policies and thus terminate the contract, for various acts of the insured, though such right be not expressly reserved, has constantly been recognized, and it would be strange if it could not agree with the insured to abrogate the contract when deemed expedient or advantageous.

It is contended by plaintiff that it is not competent for the directors of a mutual insurance company to surrender the premium notes and relieve the insured from the obligations of his contract, unless the latter pay his full proportion of all debts existing at the time of the surrender, citing Maine Mut. Ins. Co. *v.* Pickering (66 Me. 130). In that case: he note was given in pursuance of a section of the charter of the company for security of those concerned, and is not like the case of a note given in the contract of insurance. In one sense the latter is a security, but it may be given up for good consideration. Thus when the assured surrendered his policy and received from the secretary of the company his deposit note, there being contested claims which were subsequently established and on which he paid nothing, and afterwards a Receiver was appointed who made an assessment on the said assured for payment of said losses, it was held that the matter had been adjusted between the company and the assured, and the Receiver could not impeach or disaffirm the lawful acts of the corporation. (Hyde, Receiver of the Chenango Mut. Ins. Co., *v.* Lynde, 4 N. Y. 387.) After the filing of a petition by a mutual insurance company, but before publication of the appointment of a receiver, the maker of a premium note paid an assessment thereon and surrendered his policy under an agreement with an authorized agent of the company that such payment and surrender should be in full of said note, which was agreed to be given up, but was not; the note was extinguished, and the Receiver could not maintain an action thereon. (Sands, Receiver of the Columbian Ins. Co., *v.* Hill, 55 N. Y. 18.) A good faith agreement between the parties in a contract of insurance, to annul it, is valid.

Every person insured in the Union Horse Insurance Company, of Blair County, became a member of the corporation, entitled to the rights and subject to the liabilities of a stockholder. The value of the property insured was the amount of his capital stock, and he was liable to assessment for payment of losses occurring during the term of his membership. When for any cause he ceased to be a member, he would not be liable for future debts, but could afterwards be assessed for payment of debts made while he was a member, unless he had duly settled with the company. Section 3 of the charter provides that all affairs of the company shall be managed and controlled by a board of directors. The verdict shows that in pursuance of resolutions of the board the defendants paid all their just dues, as assessed against them, and handed their policies to one of the directors to return to the company to be cancelled; that they were so returned, and said board promised to cancel them and return the stock notes as soon as the secretary had time; that the assessment laid by the directors, being the first dues so paid by defendants, was insufficient to pay the liabilities then existing; that said policies were not in fact cancelled, and said notes came into the hands of the Receiver, who laid the assessments in suit; and that under said resolutions the directors cancelled the principal part of the capital stock.

It is plain that the parties agreed to rescind the contract of insurance, and accordingly the defendants paid their money and surrendered their policies. They were bound by this agreement as if the policies had been marked cancelled, and the notes given up. From thence the defendants had no insurance; they were not members, nor were they liable on the notes. The plaintiff has no more right to collect assessments on these notes than on those which had been actually returned on like terms. This case must be disposed of on the facts in the verdict, not outside. Whether there are facts which would make all who were once members liable to assessment for indebtedness, created before the cancellation of their contracts, does not appear; they are not in the verdict. For aught that is found the directors acted in good faith, and did what they deemed right for the interest of the company. It would be as just to assess the large number who got back their notes, as the few to whom the secretary neglected to return their notes, as the directors promised he should do.

Judgment affirmed. Opinion by TRUNKEY, J. SHARSWOOD, C. J., and GREEN, J., absent.

May, '79, 157. May 21, 1880.

Harner's Appeal.

Judgment—Illegal entry of satisfaction—Rights of intervening creditors.

A. advanced money to B. on the faith of an entry of satisfaction on the record of a judgment prior to A.'s judgment. The equitable assignee of the prior judgment subsequently procured an order of Court striking off the entry of satisfaction:

Held (reversing the judgment of the Court below), that in a distribution of the proceeds of a sheriff's sale of B.'s real estate, A. was entitled to claim his advances in full, postponing the equitable assignee of the prior judgment.

A. was not bound to take notice of secret equities of which he had no knowledge.

The satisfaction marked upon the record by one who, *prima facie*, had the right to control the judgment, was all A. was bound to look to.

Appeal of Frederick D. Harner from the decree of the Court of Common Pleas of Dauphin County, distributing the proceeds of the sheriff's sale of real estate of Tobias Bickel.

The auditor (John H. Weiss) found the material facts to be as follows: The fund arising from the sale of the real estate of Tobias Bickel was claimed by the holders of two judgments, one in favor of the Lykens Valley Bank for $9000, on bond and warrant entered March 12, 1873, and one in favor of the appellant Harner for $3000, on bond and warrant entered Aug. 30, 1875.

The judgment in favor of the bank had been given to secure existing and contemplated discounts, and when, on May 1, 1875, the First National Bank of Millersburg became the successor of the Lykens Valley Bank, the unpaid notes secured by this judgment were handed over to the First National Bank, and on maturing were replaced by other notes, and the old notes surrendered.

Doubts having arisen as to whether this bond given by Bickel to the original Lykens Valley Bank was of any validity as a security for the payment of the notes held by the National Bank against Bickel, after several conferences, it was arranged between the board of directors of the National Bank and Bickel, that the latter should give a new bond to the said National Bank in the sum of $9000, and should be credited on his indebtedness with seventeen shares of the capital stock of said National Bank at the price he paid for it, viz., $115 per share.

This new bond was also entered of record, but its subsequent position on the lien list precluded all hopes of participation in the distribution.

On the 22d of September, 1875, F. D. Harner obtained a bond with warrant of attorney to confess judgment against Tobias Bickel for the sum of $3000, which bore interest from September 22, 1874, which matured one year thereafter and upon which judgment was entered August 30, 1875, to No. 51, November Term, 1875. Bickel was previously indebted to Harner in the sum of $560, for which the latter held the former's note. Bickel desired to borrow more money from Harner, but he declined the loan of any further sum because of the judgment which the Lykens Valley Bank held against him. Bickel told him that this judgment would be satisfied. On the day of the date of the judgment, Harner gave Bickel his note in the sum of $2440, which, with the sum of $560, already due from Bickel to him, made up the sum of $3000, the amount of the judgment. He agreed to advance the balance of the money as soon as the bank judgment should be satisfied. He advanced no money to Bickel until he ascertained from the prothonotary that the judgment of the Lykens Valley Bank was satisfied, and finally did advance and pay the amount of his note, $2440, with interest, when he learned satisfaction was entered. Harner made no inquiry of the bank as to whether the judgment would be satisfied nor by what authority it was satisfied. He knew it was not satisfied when he took, nor when he entered of record his own judgment. He did not see (for he made no search) that the First National Bank had entered their judgment against Bickel, and he says that if he had noticed this judgment, he would not have given any money, unless he had previously asked the officers of the bank. He did not acquaint the officers of the National Bank at any time with the fact that he had not given any money to Bickel at the time he obtained the judgment against him. He said that his judgment was the first, and therefore he began to advance the money to Bickel.

The judgment given by Bickel to the Lykens Valley Bank was marked satisfied by the prothonotary on September 30, 1875, in pursuance of an authority to him directed by G. M. Brubaker, who was president of said bank, and who continued to act in that capacity during its existence, and of the chartered Lykens Valley Bank until January, 1874; and by the direction of S. P. Auchmuty, the attorney for the bank at that time, who suggested the entry of satisfaction as per authority of Brubaker on the back of the certificates.

On June 20, 1876, a rule to show cause why the entry of satisfaction should not be stricken off was granted. On September 14, 1876, the satisfaction entered was stricken off by the Court, but without prejudice to the rights of intervening creditors, and with leave for the defendant Bickel to move to vacate the order.

On December 14, 1876, the defendant made and filed a motion to vacate and to reinstate the entry of satisfaction. On December 29, 1876, the Court refused the motion and directed, in an opinion filed the same day, that the order rescinding the satisfaction stand good, and that the judgment be reinstated, but to be without prejudice to the rights of F. D. Harner or other creditors whose claims can be shown to intervene between the time of entering satisfaction and the application to have the judgment satisfied, and the decision neither to prejudice nor benefit his or their claims and with leave to the plaintiff to issue execution. Thus the judgment given by Bickel to the first Lykens Valley Bank for $9000, on the 22d day of August, 1871, and kept in their safe until March 12, 1873, and then entered of record, was satisfied September 30, 1875. The judgment given by Bickel to the First National Bank in the same sum, dated September 1, 1875, was entered of record, September 11, 1875.

The auditor awarded the fund to the First National Bank upon the old judgment, and upon exceptions filed by Harner, the Court, PEARSON, P. J., made the following decree, sustaining the report of the auditor: "And now, to wit, July 13, 1878, it is ordered by the Court that, upon the filing of a recognizance in favor of the Commonwealth for use of F. D. Harner, in the sum of $5000, with two recognizors to be approved by the prothonotary and taken by him, conditioned for the payment to said Harner of such sum as may finally be decreed and adjudged to him after the determination of his appeal to the Supreme Court in this case upon his judgment No. 51, November T., 1875, entered August 30, 1875, for $3000, the money be paid out to the distributee, viz., The First National Bank of Millersburg, Pa., in accordance with the foregoing report."

Whereupon Harner took this appeal, assigning as error the decree of the Court, and the striking off the entry of satisfaction from the record of the Lykens Valley Bank judgment.

Fleming and *McCarrell*, for appellant.

The Court had no right to strike off the entry of satisfaction without referring the matter to a jury, as the testimony was conflicting.

Humphreys *v.* Rawn, 8 Watts, 78.

Harner advanced his money on the faith of the satisfaction entered upon the record, and he had a right to have payment of the amount so advanced by him, before anything could be awarded to the First National Bank of Millersburg, by virtue of the equitable title by which it claimed the Lykens Valley Bank judgment, which right it failed to assert, or make known in any way until long after Harner had parted with his money. Harner was not bound to do more than he did; he saw that satisfaction had been entered by one of the partners; he was not bound to look beyond the record.

Moroney's Appeal, 12 Harris, 376.
Magaw *v.* Garrett, 1 Casey, 322.
Goepp *v.* Gortiser, 11 Casey, 133.

J. W. Simonton, contra.

The appellant, Harner, has nothing to do with the action of the Court in striking off the entry of satisfaction, that was a controversy between the appellee and Bickel. The order was made "without prejudice to the rights of intervening creditors," and if Harner is such a creditor, then, as to him, the order does not exist.

The equity of the appellee was superior to that of Harner.

At no time, when Harner did anything in the matter, had he even an apparent lien prior to that of the appellee. Thus, when he took and entered his judgment, and gave his note, August 30, 1879, the lien of the first nine thousand dollar judgment of the bank was in full force, standing untampered with upon the record. Again, when he advanced the money on this judgment, October 11, 1875, and thereafter, the lien of the second nine thousand dollar judgment held by the bank was in full force, and patent upon the record.

Harner, therefore, obtained his lien when he took and entered his judgment against Bickel, and gave his note to Bickel for the amount to be advanced, viz., August 30, 1875, and as at this time the first judgment for $9000 in favor of the appellee stood in full force, he took subject to it. This being so, he could not gain priority over it, by virtue of the fact that it was afterwards, without the knowledge or consent of the appellee, marked satisfied on the record. This would be, not to commit a fraud himself, but to take advantage of the fraud of another.

Further, when Harner actually made the advances, which was not until October, 1875, and afterwards, the second $9000 judgment of appellee had been entered, namely, on September 11, 1875. Hence, if his lien is to date from the time the advances were actually made, they were made subject to the lien of this second judgment, and then the principle also referred to in Taylor *v.* Cornelius (10 P. F. S. p. 196), as settled by Terhoven *v.* Kerns (2 Barr, 96), and Bank of Montgomery County's Appeal (12 Casey, 170), will apply, that where a lien is taken to secure future advances, but the lien creditor is under no contract to make the advances, the lien dates from the actual advance of the money.

June 21, 1880. THE COURT. The original Lykens Valley Bank, to which Bickel executed the judgment which forms the subject of the present controversy, as collateral security for certain notes which it discounted for him, was a partnership, and of this partnership Brubaker was not only a member, but president. *Prima facie*, therefore, he as agent of this association had full power either to assign or satisfy this judgment. (Dubois's Ap. 2 Wr. 231.) Harner's judgment, in amount $3000, was entered on the 30th of August, 1875, and had been executed in September, 1874. The consideration therefor was an account owing by Bickel to Harner, amounting to $560, and Harner's note for $2440, payable as soon as payment might be required after the Lykens Valley Bank judgment should be satisfied, but not before. This note, as appears from the auditor's report, was fully paid according to the agreement of the parties, though not until after the 11th of September, 1875, the date of the entry of the appellee's judgment. This latter circumstance, however, is of no account, since Harner's note and previous account were sufficient consideration for his judgment. (Moroney's Appeal, 12 Harris, 372.) Now as soon as the judgment of the Lykens Valley Bank was satisfied, that of Harner stood first, and the appellee finding the lien of its payment thus outranked, made application to have the satisfaction just spoken of taken off, on the ground that that judgment belonged to it as the successor to the rights and obligations of the former Lykens Valley organization. To this proceeding Harner could not lawfully object; that was a matter for the parties themselves; they, without the Court's intervention, could have taken off this satisfaction, but whether taken off by themselves or by the Court, the status of Harner's judgment was not affected thereby. As to him the satisfaction remained, and it should have been so treated by the Court below. The auditor, singularly enough, fell into the error of supposing it to be Harner's duty to make inquiry of the First National Bank, the appellee, as to its claim to the old judgment, but as that bank had, in fact, no assignment of that judgment marked on the record, it was certainly not Harner's duty to make inquiries about secret equities of which he had no knowledge. There was the satisfaction regularly marked upon the docket, and so marked by the authority of one who, *prima facie*, had full power so to do.

This was all Harner was required to look to; it was not his business to inquire about equities to which he was not a party and of which he had no knowledge. (Springfield Building and Loan Association's Appeal, not yet reported.) If the appellee desired to give notice of its rights, and put the old judgment beyond the power of the partners of the original association, it should have taken an assignment and put that assignment on the docket. The duty rested with it to see to its own judgment, that it was properly presented on the record; and failing in this it must bear the consequences of its own neglect; it cannot cast them upon one who is in no default. (Ridgway, Budd & Co.'s Appeal, 3 Har. 177.) It is clear, therefore, that Harner's right to the money now in the Court below for distribution, is superior to that of the appellee, and that the decree of the Court below was erroneous.

The decree of the Court below is now reversed and vacated, at the costs of appellee, and a redistribution is ordered according to the principles stated in the above opinion.

Opinion by GORDON, J. SHARSWOOD, C. J., absent.

Jan. '78, 301.   March 8, 1880.

Royse v. May.

Amendments — Amendments changing cause of action not allowed—Action against bailiff for excessive distress—Statutory damages not recoverable unless declaration be under the statute—Assignments of error—Irregularity of—Practice.

While a large discretion may be exercised by the Court below in permitting amendments to the pleadings, yet such an amendment to the narr. as substantially changes the cause of action will not be allowed.

In an action against a constable for excessive distress, the plaintiff (after an award of arbitrators in his favor, and an appeal by defendant) filed a narr. in trespas *vi et armis*, which set forth the tenancy, the amount of rent in arrear, and the goods distrained. Upon the trial the Court permitted him to amend by denying the tenancy: *Held* to be error.

In such a case the narr. not being under the Act of May 10, 1871 (P. L. 205), allowing double damages for distress where no rent is due, there can be no recovery under its provisions.

Assignments of error which contain merely a memorandum of the names of witnesses whose testimony has been erroneously received or rejected, are not in accordance with Rule xxiv., and will be disregarded.

Error to the Common Pleas of Bradford County.

Trespass *vi et armis* by William May against L. T. Royse. Plea, not guilty.

The first and second counts in the narr. averred that May occupied certain premises as tenant of one Barnes, and that the sum of two hundred dollars was due for rent, and that the defendant, acting for Barnes, and "not regarding the statute in such case made and provided, but wrongfully and maliciously contriving and intending to injure and oppress the said plaintiff, wrongfully and maliciously distrained" goods of the value of two thousand dollars (describing them).

The third count was in trover.

Two years after the cause was at issue the plaintiff took a rule to amend the narr. by denying the existence of any relationship of landlord and tenant between the plaintiff and Barnes. This rule was discharged by the Court.

On the trial before MORROW, P. J., the plaintiff swore that he was the owner of the premises upon which the distrained property was placed; that he was not, and never had been a tenant of Barnes.

Counsel for plaintiff again moved to amend the narr. so as to conform to the evidence already given in the case, by changing the declaration so far as the averments in the declaration admit a tenancy between plaintiff and B. C. Barnes, and that there was an amount of rent due, and so changing it, that it was the allegation of the landlord and not the admission of the defendant; the averments having been put by mistake and misapprehension of the facts.

Leave to amend was granted by the Court. (First assignment of error).

The defendant's testimony was, that he had gone on the premises by the authority of a landlord's warrant to collect $200 rent, and that May had waived an appraisement. Barnes testified that he leased his farm to May by a parol lease "at a rent equivalent to $500 a year."

The evidence was undisputed that the constable was in possession twenty-six days; that while he held the farm, stock and household goods under the levy, May was in actual possession and constant use of them; and that, at the sale, property sufficient to pay the debt, interest, and costs, and an overplus of $10 (which was paid to May) was sold.

The third and fourth assignments of error were in the following form:—

(3) The Court erred in allowing plaintiff to cross-examine B. C. Barnes as to immaterial matters for the purpose of contradicting him.

(4) The Court erred in admitting the testimony of J. E. Spalding, Wm. May, B. H. Montgomery, Paul Bates, John Shuck, Smith Tuttle, Hiram Taylor, and D. H. Vaughan.

In the charge his Honor said, *inter alia:* "If you find that May was a tenant of Barnes, and at the time the landlord's warrant was issued he was in arrear for rent in the sum of $200, and if that you find that Royse, in making the distress and sale, did all that the Act requires, except the appraisement, which was waived, your verdict should be for the defendant. The warrant was no protection to the constable unless rent was reserved in the agreement between May and B. C. Barnes. The burden is on the defendant to show that the relation of landlord and tenant existed between them, and the defendant, as bailiff of the landlord, must show that he did all things required by the Act of Assembly." The Court here read to the jury Section 1 of the Act of March 21, 1772 (Purdon's Digest, 878), and after calling the attention of the jury to everything which the Act required to be done, said: "The burden is upon the defendant to show that he did everything the Act requires. The evidence shows that May waived the appraisement, and the constable's return shows that he gave May notice, personally, of what he had done.

["If you find that the relation of landlord and tenant did exist, and that $200 was not due and in arrears; or the defendant, as bailiff of the landlord, failed to make the distress as required by law, he is liable to the plaintiff for double the value of the goods distrained and sold. If you find for the plaintiff, assess the damages as of the date of the sale, to which you may add interest to this date."] (Fifth and sixth assignments of error.)

Verdict for plaintiff, $336, and judgment thereon. The defendant took this writ, assigning for error the permission to amend, and the admission of the plaintiff's evidence in support of the amended averment; the charge of the Court, and the admission of certain witnesses, as above indicated.

De Witt & Hall, for plaintiff in error.

The Court was in error in permitting the plaintiff to amend his narr. The entire cause of action was changed. The application was not made under the Act of May 10, 1871 (P. L. 265), for there was no offer to pay costs, and as an exercise of discretion it was erroneous.

Penna. R. R. *v.* Zug, 11 Wr. 484.
Steffy *v.* Carpenter, 1 Id. 41.
Winder *v.* Bank, 2 B. 446.

Patrick & Fowler, for defendant in error.

May 3, 1880. THE COURT. The first assignment of error is to permitting the amendment of the declaration after the plaintiff below had closed his evidence. The amendment was not made under the Act of 10 May, 1871, which, on the conditions therein prescribed, permits a change in the form of action. Apart from that Act, which has no application to the present case, the right of amendment may be liberally allowed, but not to such an extent as to substantially change the cause of action. (Steffy *v.* Carpenter, 1 Wright, 41; Trego *v.* Lewis, 8 P. F. Smith, 463.) If the amendment was allowable, it is not error merely because it was permitted on the trial. Some other fact must be shown to make it improper.

This action was trespass. It was against a person who had acted as bailiff in distraining and selling goods under a claim of rent due and in arrear. The declaration contained three counts. The first and second each averred that the defendant in error held and occupied the premises as tenant of one B. C. Barnes, and that a certain sum specified was due and in arrears for the rent thereof, and charged that the distress made was excessive. The third count was in trover. It had been tried before arbitrators, who awarded against the plaintiff in error, and from which award he had appealed. The amendment allowed was to change and contradict the averments in the declaration, which expressly admitted the tenancy and the specific sum due and in arrear for rent, and to aver that such was the allegation of Barnes only, and not the admission of the defendant in error. The substantial cause of action under the original declaration was an excessive distress, while the defendant in error was the tenant of Barnes, and while a sum specified was due and in arrear for rent. Every part of this was changed by the amendment. It substantially averred that he was not the tenant of Barnes; that he did not owe him any rent; that it was not a case of excessive distress, but one in which no right of distress for any sum existed. This was a substantial change of the cause of action, and ought not to have been allowed. The first assignment is sustained.

In view of the manner the case was submitted to the jury, we see no error in the second and sixth assignments. The third and fourth assignments are not according to the rules, and must be disregarded.

In that portion of the charge covered by the fifth assignment the learned Judge charged substantially that unless the plaintiff in error proved the tenancy, and certain rent reserved and in arrear, their verdict must be "for double the value of the property sold." The second count in the declaration did not conclude according to the form of the statute, nor was there any claim therein for double damages. It was not, therefore, under the statute giving double damages. Hence it follows, under the pleadings, it was error to fix the measure of damages at double the value of the property. (Rees *v.* Emerick, 6 S. & R. 286.) This assignment is therefore sustained.

Judgment reversed, and a *venire facias de novo* awarded.

Opinion by MERCUR, J.

May '80, 102.   June 2, 1880.
Earley v. Rolfe.

Husband and Wife—Agency of husband to collect interest-money due to the wife presumed from her knowledge and want of dissent.

Where a husband acts for his wife in the ordinary management of her property, as in the collection of rents, or interest on mortgages, with her knowledge, and without any dissent on her part, he will be presumed to have acted as her duly appointed agent, and she will be estopped from subsequently claiming to recover interest-moneys so received by him.

Whether mere knowledge and want of dissent on the part of the wife would raise a presumption of power in the husband to receive and receipt for the *corpus* of her personal estate—not decided.

Error to the Common Pleas of Elk County.

Scire facias sur mortgage against C. R. Earley, the mortgagor, by H. M. Rolfe, to whom the original mortgagee, Mrs. Wilmarth, and her husband, had assigned the mortgage.

On the trial, upon the plea of "set off, payment with leave," etc., the defendant proved by Frederick Wilmarth, husband of the mortgagee, that Earley had paid him $600, in three different payments, on account of interest due on this mortgage. When first asked whether he had any authority to collect this money, the witness said: "Yes, sir, to use in the family;" but afterwards, on cross-examination, he admitted that he "had no special authority, only being her husband, and getting it for her benefit, as well as mine." "She knew that I got them, because I told her." He testified that the money paid to him was all used for family expenses.

The plaintiff requested the Court to instruct the jury that a payment made to Mr. Wilmarth without his wife's authority would not operate to discharge the mortgage debt, and that, under the evidence, plaintiff was entitled to recover, without any deduction, for the payments so made. The Court, M'DERMOTT, P. J., in answer, said: "There being no evidence of any previous authority having been conferred by Mrs. Wilmarth on her husband to receive payment, in whole or in part, of the mortgage in suit, from the defendant, Earley, nor evidence of subsequent ratification by her of his acts in receipting for what he received beyond her mere subsequent knowledge of the fact, the payments so made by the defendant, Earley, do not bind her, nor her assignee, the plaintiff."

The defendant took this writ, assigning as error the instruction of the Court as above stated.

Rufus Lucore, Jno. G. Hall, and *C. H. M'Cauley,* for plaintiff in error.

The husband having assumed to act as the agent of the wife, she was bound to express her dissent when it came to her knowledge. Where a wife undertakes to recover from her husband's estate money received by him out of the *income* of her estate, the Courts have seized upon slight circumstances to show her assent to his receipt and use of the money as his own. *A fortiori* should the debtor who pays the money be protected.

M'Glinsey's Appeal, 14 S. & R. 65.
Husbands on Married Women, 105.
Bardsley's Estate, 7 WEEKLY NOTES, 49.

There is no reason or authority for exempting Mrs. Wilmarth from the general rules applicable to principal and agent. Acquiescence in an assumed agency is equivalent to an express authority.

Stephens and Wife's Appeal, 6 Norris, 202.
2 Kent's Com., 827.
2 Greenleaf on Evidence, § 66.

Geo. A. Rathbun, contra.

The Act of 1848 debarred the husband from dominion over the choses in action of the wife.

Bear's Adm'r *v.* Bear, 9 Casey, 528.

The husband could not even act as her agent without being empowered in writing. If she desires to dispose of her estate, real or personal, she may make her husband the agent for the purpose only by an instrument duly acknowledged, separate and apart from him.

Roseburgh's Executor *v.* Sterling's Heirs, 3 Casey, 293.

Glyde *v.* Keister *et ux.*, 8 Casey, 88.

The cases cited by the plaintiff in error are all cases in which receipt of the wife's money by the husband, and conversion by him, have been held to be evidence of a gift.

The husband had no authority, as husband, to discharge the debt due to the wife.

Goodyear *v.* Rumbaugh, 1 Harris, 482.
Trimble *v.* Reis, 1 Wright, 455.
McKinney *v.* Hamilton, 1 Sm. 65.

The burden of proof to show the authority of the husband was on the defendant below.

Bachman *v.* Killinger, 5 Sm. 414.
2 Greenleaf on Evidence, ¶ 66.
Hyatt *v.* Johnston, 7 W. N. C. 561.

June 21, 1880. THE COURT. It is certainly not necessary to cite authority in order to prove that, since the Act of 1848, the husband cannot dispose of his wife's choses in action without her consent, and it may be conceded that he cannot, of his own motion, receipt for her money, or satisfy her judgments or mortgages. But it by no means follows that with her consent he may not do all these things, and even more, appropriate her moneys and assets to his own use. So, it was held, in Martha Mann's Appeal (14 Wr. 375), where a husband had from time to time received money from his wife's debtor in her presence, that it was a proper inference, not only that he had rightly received it, but, where he had appropriated it to their common benefit, that it was so appropriated with her assent, and that she could not, after his death, recover it from his estate. Indeed to hold otherwise would be measurably to deprive the married woman of the confidence and agency of her husband in the care and management of her separate property, and in the disposition of her business affairs; a deprivation which, in most instances, would be to her very serious, and in some cases disastrous. As a rule, married women, in consequence of the character of their education, as well as by reason of the circumstances by which they are ordinarily surrounded, have little of business knowledge or capacity, and if they cannot have the aid of their husbands to collect their rents, receive the interest upon their mortages, judgments, and other obligations, without a power of attorney or other formal delegation, they are badly off indeed. The relation of husband and wife is one of the profoundest trust and confidence, and is so regarded by the community at large; hence, where the husband acts for the wife, in matters relating to the disposition of her personal property, he is presumed to be so acting with her consent, and as her agent. As a rule, people cannot be made to think that in dealing with a husband for his wife, he must be regarded as a stranger, and that he can do no business for her except under her express sanction. They presume, and so ought to presume, that the two are acting in harmony; that he acts with her assent, and for her welfare. It follows that where, in ordinary transactions as in those above enumerated, the husband receives the moneys of the wife, and the circumstances are such that her assent may be fairly inferred, the jury may adopt the presumption that he was acting under her authority, and hold her accordingly. We conclude then that the Court below erred in saying to the jury, in answer to the plaintiff's third point, that there was no evidence of any previous authority having been conferred by Mrs. Wilmarth on her husband to receive payment, in whole or in part, of the mortgage in suit, from the defendant, nor any evidence of a subsequent ratification of the payments made to him. We think differently. We think there was evidence from which such authority might properly be inferred. Wilmarth testifies that he received, on account of this mortgage, some six hundred dollars in three different payments of two hundred dollars each; and when asked whether he had authority from his wife to do so, he answered: "Yes, sir, for the use of the family." It is true he afterwards qualifies this by saying: "I had no special authority, only being her husband, and getting it for her benefit as well as mine." He also says that she knew of his receipt of these payments, because he told her; but the above stated qualification has no effect in the way of altering the plain inference resulting from this testimony. Here is the husband properly doing business for the wife, by receiving the interest on her mortgage, not once but thrice; of this she has full knowledge; she knows that he is receiving this money and applying it to the relief of their joint necessities, and knowing all this she neither objects nor dissents; under such circumstances we do not think it would be a strained inference to presume her assent. It would, indeed, have been very bad faith in her, did she intend to object to the business thus transacted, to allow her debtor to go on paying to her husband when her notice to the contrary would have at once put a stop to it. As, however, the presumptions are in favor of good faith rather than bad, we may suppose that Wilmarth had the assent of his wife to receive the money paid to him by the defendant. Whether mere knowledge and want of dissent on the part of the wife would raise a presumption of power in the husband to receive and receipt for the corpus of his wife's personal estate, as, in this case, to receive the money in satisfaction of her mortgage, is something upon which we do not pass, and merely refer to the case of Bardsley's Estate (7 WEEKLY NOTES OF CASES, 48), where a similar question is fully discussed by Judge PENROSE. However this may be, we repeat, such knowledge and want of dissent, are evidence from which a jury may infer a power to the husband from the wife, to transact the ordinary business of her estate, such as the receipt of her rents, interest, and the like.

Judgment reversed, and a venire facias de novo is awarded.

Opinion by GORDON, J. PAXSON, J., absent.

Oct. & Nov. '79.   Nov. 3, 1879.

Mears v. Humboldt Fire Insurance Company.

Fire insurance — Conditions voiding policy — Construction of — Inflammable substances, when exceptional use of benzine, etc., is not a violation of condition.

A condition in a policy of fire insurance upon a steam mill provided that if the insured should keep or have on the insured premises any petroleum, benzine, etc., or should keep, have, or use camphene, spirit-gas, or any burning fluid, or chemical oils, the policy should be void. The insured (having obtained permission to make repairs) used benzine and carbon oil in small quantities, for the purpose of cleaning the machinery, during a period of about two weeks, and some weeks subsequently a fire occurred from other causes:

Held (reversing the judgment of the Court below), that there was no breach of the condition which would bar a recovery.

Such a provision in a policy must have a reasonable interpretation, such as was probably contemplated by the parties at the time the contract was entered into. What was intended to be prohibited was the habitual keeping or using of such articles, not their exceptional use upon some emergency, as for repairs—permission to repair having been granted.

The meaning of general words used in the subsequent portion of a clause must be ascertained by reference to preceding special words; thus, in the above provision, the general words "burning fluids or chemical oils," must be held to mean only such burning fluids or chemical oils as are, in their nature, like "camphene or spirit-gas," and the Court will not take judicial notice that an article not specially prohibited is of such nature.

Error to C. P. No. 1, of Allegheny County.

Debt, upon a policy of fire insurance, by Henrietta Mears, committee of Thomas Mears, a lunatic, against the above named insurance company. On the trial, before STOWE, P. J., the material facts were proved as follows:—

On January 8, 1874, Thomas Mears insured, in the company defendant, a certain steam flouring mill and distillery, then, and for some time previous, vacant, and not in operation, and, with the intention of operating the same, requested the "privilege of making alterations and repairs," which was granted by the company, and indorsed on the policy. The policy contained, *inter alia*, the following provision:—

"1. VOIDS A POLICY.—It is a condition of this insurance that if the assured shall *keep or have* in any place on the insured premises, where this policy may apply, petroleum, naphtha, *benzine*, benzole, gasoline, benzine-varnish, or any product in whole or in part of either; or gunpowder, fireworks, nitro-glycerine, phosphorus, saltpetre, nitrate of soda; or *keep, have, or use*, camphene, spirit-gas, or any burning fluid, or chemical oils, without permission in this policy, then, and in every such case, this policy shall be void."

Owing to disuse the machinery had become dirty, a tough and gummy substance had accumulated on the cogs, journals, gearing, etc., and the interior of the boilers had become coated with rust. For the purpose of cleaning the machinery, etc., the insured purchased about eight or ten gallons of benzine, which he stored in a bonded warehouse, situated forty yards distant from the insured premises; and he employed a man to do the work. The latter carried the benzine to the insured premises as he required it, about a gallon at a time, and cleaned the machinery therewith, and with a little carbon oil, which was on the insured premises, the work occupying about ten days. Some two or three weeks after said work was finished the fire in question occurred, at a time when there was no benzine on the premises, except, perhaps, what was left after cleaning, which the witness, who did the work, testified might have been a gallon or a little more. It did not appear whether this small quantity had or had not been removed prior to the fire.

The learned Judge, in affirming the defendant's points, instructed the jury that the use of benzine and of carbon oil, for the purpose of cleaning machinery, as above set forth, was a breach of a material condition in the policy, which was a bar to the plaintiff's recovery.

Verdict and judgment for defendant. Plaintiff took this writ, assigning for error the instruction of the Court, in affirming the defendant's points.

H. W. Weir (with him *R. M. Gibson* and *J. Dunbar*), for plaintiff in error.

M. W. Acheson (with whom was *S. C. Schoyer*), for defendant in error.

Nov. 17, 1879. THE COURT. The first assignment of error relates to the use of benzine upon the insured premises. It was contended that the Court erred in instructing the jury in answer to the defendants' second point, that if Mears, the assured, purchased from eight to ten gallons of benzine, and used nearly the whole of it in cleaning the engine, boilers, and machinery of the distillery, and such use extended over a period of about two weeks, there was a violation of one of the conditions of the policy in suit which voids the same.

The condition in the policy referred to is as follows: "Or if the assured shall *keep or have* in any place on the premises, where this policy may apply, petroleum, naphtha, benzine, benzole, gasoline, benzine-varnish, or any product, in whole or in part of either; or gunpowder, fireworks, nitro-glycerine, phosphorus, saltpetre, nitrate of soda; or keep, have, or *use* camphene, spirit-gas, or any burning fluid or chemical oils, without written permission in this policy, then, and in every such case, this policy shall be void."

It will be observed that in the first portion of this condition the provision is that the assured shall not "keep or have," any of the enumerated articles upon the insured premises, while in the latter portion the "use" of certain other articles is prohibited, in addition to the restriction contained in the first. The words "keep or have," as applied to the articles first enumerated, evidently were intended to prevent a storage of the prohibited articles upon the premises, either permanently or habitually. While the words are used in the disjunctive, they are evidently synonymous, and signify to retain in possession. It would be straining a point to say that bringing a prohibited article upon the premises upon a single occasion, and for the sole purpose of cleaning machinery, was keeping or having it there within the meaning of the policy. The evidence shows it is not denied that the can of benzine used for the purpose above stated, was not kept on the insured premises during the period of its use, but was stored in a bonded warehouse, fifty or sixty feet distant. The witness, William Jacobs, who cleaned the machinery, got it from the warehouse from time to time, as he needed it.

The assured did not keep or have benzine upon the insured premises within any reasonable view of the meaning of the policy. But it is said he used it there, and that this voids the policy. The *use* of benzine is not prohibited in terms. If prohibited at all, it must be because benzine comes within the description of burning fluid or chemical oils. We must ascertain the meaning of these general words used in the latter portion of the condition of the policy by referring to the preceding special words. Under this construction, the words burning fluids or chemical oils, must be held to mean only such burning fluids or chemical oils as are, in their nature, like camphene or spirit-gas. This was the construction placed on the identical words in Wheeler *v.* The American Central Insurance Co., decided by the St. Louis Court of Appeals in March, 1879, and reported in the Western Insurance Review, vol. xii. p. 252. The same rule is laid down in Wood *v.* The Northwestern Ins. Co. (46 N. Y. 421); Morse *v.* Buffalo Fire and Marine Ins. Co. (30 Wis. 534); Willis *v.* Hanover and Germania Fire Ins. Co. (The Reporter, vol. viii. p. 343.)

There was no proof that benzine was of like nature with camphene or spirit-gas. It is not a matter of which the Court will take judicial notice. It is a question of fact, to be found by a jury upon evidence. See Wood *v.* The Northwestern Ins. Co., and Morse *v.* Buffalo Ins. Co. (*supra*).

We are not disposed to give the word "use" in this policy the narrow construction claimed for it. It must have a reasonable interpretation, such as was probably contemplated by the parties at the time the contract was entered into. Nearly every policy of insurance issued at the present time contains this condition or a similar one. What is intended to be prohibited is the habitual use of such articles, not their exceptional use upon some emergency. The strict rule claimed by the defendants would prevent the assured from painting his house or cleaning his furniture, as it would be difficult to do either without using some of the prohibited articles. If the company intended the condition to cover such exceptional uses, it ought to have been plainly expressed, and probably would have been. That any one would knowingly accept a policy with such a clause, is not probable. We are not without abundant authority upon this point. (See Dobson *v.* Sotheby, 1 M. & M. 90; Shaw *v.* Robberds, 6 A. & E. 75; Grant *v.* Howard Ins. Co., 5 Hill, 10; Van Valkenburgh *v.* The Ins. Co., 70 N. Y. 605; Franklin Ins. Co. *v.* Chicago Ice Co., 36 Md. 102; Moore *v.* The Ins. Co. 29 Maine, 97; O'Niel *v.* Buffalo Fire Ins. Co., 3 Comstock, 122.)

The case of the Birmingham Fire Ins. Co. *v.* Kroegher (2 Norris, 64), cited by the defendants, does not apply. In that case, the assured kept a barrel of petroleum for sale on the premises covered by the policy. As bearing upon this point it is proper to observe, that permission to make repairs was indorsed upon the policy. While no point was apparently made of this in the Court below, and we would not, therefore, reverse for this reason; the fact is entitled to weight in considering this question. The permission to repair the machinery carried with it the right to use such means as might be necessary for that purpose.

The second assignment also refers to keeping benzine upon the premises, and is covered by what has already been said. The remaining assignments relate to the use of carbon oil. It was proved that a small quantity had been used at the same time as the benzine, in cleaning the machinery. It is sufficient to say that carbon oil is not among the prohibited articles. It is not named in the condition. If it was of the same nature as camphene and spirit-gas, or the other enumerated articles, it was not shown to be so, and the Court cannot take judicial notice of it. This principle has already been sufficiently referred to.

All the assignments of error are sustained.

Judgment reversed, and a *venire facias de novo* awarded.

Opinion by PAXSON, J. STERRETT and GREEN, JJ., absent.

Common Pleas—Equity.

C. P. No. 1. June, 1880.

Stockton et al. v. The Lehigh Coal and Navigation Company.

Equity—Pleading—Demurrer to bill—How far a demurrer admits the allegations of the bill—Foreign law—How same should be set out in the bill—When a trustee virtute officii may come into equity—Act of May 23, 1874.

Sur demurrer to bill.

This bill was filed to compel the transfer by the defendants of certain shares of stock of the said company to the complainants, and the payment to them of the dividends thereon. The bill set forth that James Potter, a citizen of the State of Georgia, and domiciled therein, by his will dated May 15, 1861, and remaining of record in the Court of Ordinary, of Chatham County, of said State, devised and bequeathed certain shares or portions of his residuary estate to Robert F. Stockton, Richard Stockton, and Dr. Wm. H. Cuyler, and the survivors and survivor of them, their and his executors, administrators and assigns, upon certain trusts therein declared for his children, grandchildren and others, which trusts are valid and subsisting trusts under the laws of said State of Georgia. That in 1866 the said trustees purchased with the funds of the said trust estate, and upon the trusts aforesaid, 167 shares of the capital stock of the said Lehigh Coal and Navigation Company, which have ever since been standing in their names as such trustees, and on which certain dividends have been declared. That all of said trustees have died; the last of them Richard Stockton, about the 10th day of April, 1876, who left a will, which has been duly admitted to probate in the office of the Surrogate of Mercer County, New Jersey, by which he appointed the complainants his executors, who have taken out letters of administration and entered on the duties of their office. That by the law of Georgia, which was the domicile of the said James Potter, under whose will said trust arose, where a testator in his will expressly provides that in case of the death of a surviving trustee, his executors shall become trustees, such executors of the surviving trustee, though they may be created such executors by a will proved in another State, become and are the legal successors of such deceased trustee, clothed with all the estates and duties of such deceased trustee as fully and in the same manner as if they had been originally named as trustees in the will of the testator.

The complainants averred their right as such trustees to have the said stocks transferred and the dividends paid to them and a demand made upon and refusal of the company to do either, and prayed that the defendants may be required to transfer said stocks to them and pay to them the said dividends.

The defendants demurred and set forth the following causes of demurrer:

(1) That the several persons interested in the trust alleged to exist by the first section of the said bill, being the only parties in interest, are necessary parties to the said bill, but yet the complainants have not made them or any of them parties to the said bill.

(2) That it does not appear by the said bill that the plaintiffs have any title in law or equity to the stock and dividends therein mentioned, or are authorized by the laws of Pennsylvania or otherwise, to demand the transfer and payment of the same to them.

(3) That the said bill does not set forth or refer to any statute of the State of Georgia, the alleged domicile of the said James Potter, deceased, whereby the plaintiffs have become the legal successors of the deceased trustees, as alleged in the fourth section of the said bill, so as to enable them as the executors of Richard Stockton, deceased, to withdraw the funds or property of the said trust from the State of Pennsylvania.

(4) That this Court has no jurisdiction to make the decree or grant the relief prayed for in said bill, and the complainants set forth nothing in the said bill to entitle them to any such relief.

Chas. Gibbons, Jr. (*Chas. Gibbons*, with him), for the demurrer.

The cestuis qui trustent should have been made parties to the bill, according to the decision of the Supreme Court previously rendered in this case.

Appeal of the Lehigh Coal and Navigation Co., 7 Nor. 499.

This is a testamentary trust, and if the complainants are trustees, they are not such by name but *virtute officii*. The Orphans' Court has exclusive jurisdiction.

Wapples's Appeal, 24 Sm. 100.

Act of April 7, 1859, P. L. 406; Purd. Dig. 1423, pl. 54.

The bill shows no title in complainants to recover.

Gendell, contra.

The Supreme Court never meant to require that the cestuis qui trustent be made parties to the bill; hence we are admitted to be the proper parties by the law of Georgia. This law agrees with the common law.

Perry on Trusts, sec. 264-344.

July 9, 1880. THE COURT (after stating the facts). We do not think that the first cause of demurrer is well taken. Whatever may have been the law as exhibited by the decisions in Bayard *v.* The Bank (2 P. F. Smith, 235), and Bohlen's Estate (25 P. F. Smith, 304), relative to the transfer of trust estates, we think the Act of May 23, 1874, has introduced a radical change in this respect. (Supplement to Purdon, page 1942, and Pamphlet Laws 1874, page 222.) It is as follows, viz. :—

"All certificates of stocks and loans which have been or may hereafter be issued by this Commonwealth, or by any municipal or other corporation, shall be transferable by the legal owner thereof, without any liability on the part of the transfer agents of the Commonwealth, or the municipal or other corporation permitting such transfers, to recognize or see to the execution of any trust, whether expressed or implied, or constructive, to which such stocks or loans may be subject; unless, when such transfer agents of the Commonwealth, or officers of such municipal or other corporation, charged with the duty of permitting such transfer to be made, shall have previously received actual notice in writing, signed by or on behalf of the person or persons for whom such stocks or loans appear by the certificate thereof to be held in trust, that the proposed transfer would be a violation of such trust."

We do not overlook the fact that when this case was before the Supreme Court (7 Norris, 499), the learned Judge who delivered the opinion of the Court intimated that the parties beneficially interested in the stock were not made parties to the bill and would not be bound by any decree made without notice to them. t does not appear that the attention of the Court was called to the Act of May 23, 1874, above recited. No mention is made of it in the report of the case, by the counsel on either side. The law as decided by the cases of Bayard *v.* The Bank and Bohlen's Estate, was no doubt found to be too onerous for the ordinary business of life, and the Legislature provided a remedy by the Act of May 23, 1874, which gives a mode of protection to the parties beneficially interested without obstructing the ordinary and necessary transfer of loans and stocks.

The second and third causes of demurrer we think are well taken. It is a well settled rule of pleading that a demurrer admits every fact that is well and sufficiently pleaded. But a general averment that by the laws of Georgia the executors of a surviving trustee become trustees of the particular estate upon his death, without setting forth the statute or law which confers the powers, is too vague and unsatisfactory to make it the foundation of a judicial decree; or to put the opposite party to the duty of searching out the particular law or decision upon which the averment rests.

And even if the law of Georgia be as is averred, the complainants do not by their bill bring themselves within its requirements. The bill sets forth that by the law of Georgia where a testator in his will expressly provides that in case of the death of a surviving trustee his executors shall become trustees, such executors of the surviving trustee, though they may be created such executors by a will proved in another State, become and are the legal successors of such trustees, etc.; but it does not aver that the will of James Potter *expressly provides* that the executors of the surviving trustee shall become trustees. At best it is but left to inference, or to an argument that may be made upon the fact that the bequest and devise was to the trustees and the survivors and survivor of them, their and his *executors, administrators* and *assigns;* words which are ordinarily used to describe the estate the parties took, rather than to confer upon the executors of the survivor a special trust.

The fourth and last cause of demurrer we do not think is well taken. It is not a bill asking this Court to assume any control of the trustees or of the trust estate. If it were so this cause of demurrer might have much force in it. The only question raised by this assignment of cause is, whether a trustee created by will *virtute officii*, has a standing in a court of equity to enforce a claim of a right, or to compel the performance of a duty owing to him. Such a trustee may sue in a court of law for a debt due to him as a trustee; or, if executor, a debt due to his testator. He may sue in a court of equity to compel a settlement of partnership accounts, where the trust property, or any part of it, consists of partnership assets. If it were not so he would be without remedy, as the Orphans' Court would have no jurisdiction in such a case; nor for the recovery of a debt against a living person. In like manner, as this is in the nature of a debt or duty, alleged to be owing by the defendant corporation to these complainants, a court of equity is the proper forum in which to enforce it.

The point is not made by the pleadings, but it may be well for the parties to consider whether, under the Act of April 8, 1872 (Purdon's Digest, 421, pl. 84), it may not be necessary to file copies of the testamentary papers on which the complainants rely, before they would be entitled to ask a transfer of the stock claimed in the bill.

The first and fourth causes of demurrer are overruled; the second and third causes of demurrer are sustained.

Opinion by PEIRCE, J.

Common Pleas—Law.

C. P. No. 1.   June 21, 1880.

Wanamaker v. Price.

Book entries charging one person for goods ordered by another—Evidence—Admissibility of bills made out by plaintiff's clerk against a person other than the defendant—New trial.

Rule to show cause why a new trial should not be granted.

This was an action of assumpsit to recover the amount of a bill for merchandise alleged to have been sold and delivered by the plaintiff to M. L. Price, the defendant.

Upon the trial the plaintiff put in evidence his book of original entries, in which were a series of charges against Mrs. M. L. Price for goods sold and delivered. In the case of each item there was a memorandum indicating that the goods had been ordered by Mrs. A. V. Price.

The defendant produced certain bills for the same goods, made out in the name of A. V. Price, and called the plaintiff's clerk, who identified them as in his handwriting. The defendant offered these bills in evidence.

Objected to, unless defendant should produce evidence showing the circumstances under which the bills had passed from the possession of the plaintiff. The defendant producing no other evidence, the objection was sustained, and the evidence excluded. Verdict for plaintiff.

The defendant obtained this rule for a new trial, upon the ground that the evidence was improperly excluded.

Manderson, for the rule.

In connection with the plaintiff's book entries, the bills made out in the name of a person not the defendant, were competent evidence to show that the defendant was not liable.

Dale, contra.

The plaintiff had made out a *prima facie* case by producing his book of original entries. This cast upon the defendant the burden of rebuttal, and it was for this reason that she made the offer which was rejected by the Court. The papers offered were unaccompanied by any evidence showing how they got out of the possession of the plaintiff into that of the defendant. There are many ways in which this might have happened, all thoroughly consistent with the plaintiff's claim.

If defendant had adduced other circumstances in evidence, we do not deny that these papers might have been used as links in the chain. But, standing as they do alone, we contend that they must be supported by further proof before they can be admitted in evidence as a defence.

C. A. V.

July 3, 1880.   THE COURT.   Rule absolute.

C. P. No. 2.   December 5, 1879.

Brietwiesser v. Stier.

Action for malicious prosecution—Probable cause—That the defendant, before instituting the prosecution, consulted a special detective officer deputed by the mayor, and, by his advice, caused the plaintiff's arrest, is no justification.

Motion for a rule for a new trial.

Case, for malicious prosecution.

On the trial evidence was given that the defendant had caused the arrest of the plaintiff on a criminal charge, and that he, after a hearing before a magistrate, was discharged.

On behalf of the defendant it was offered to prove that he, "prior to the issuing of the warrant in the criminal prosecution, had fully stated the facts to the detective at the central station, who, for the past three years, has been specially deputed by the mayor to receive all complaints brought to that station; and that, in view of such statements, the said officer, as one well versed in criminal matters and practice, advised the defendant to institute such prosecution—this to rebut the charge of malice." His offer was objected to, and the objection sustained by the Court. A verdict was rendered for the plaintiff, and defendant made this motion.

W. H. Browne, for the motion.

The fact that defendant had consulted any official person before causing the arrest of the plaintiff, should have gone to the jury on the question of malice. The advice of an alderman, although not learned in the law, would have been proof of probable cause.

Thomas v. Paynter, 1 WEEKLY NOTES, 300.
Rosenstein v. Seigel, 6 Phila. 532.

THE COURT.   Rule refused.

WEEKLY NOTES OF CASES.

VOL. IX.]   *THURSDAY, OCT. 14, 1880.*   [NO. 8.

Supreme Court.

Oct. & Nov. '79, 64 & 65.   Oct. 30, 1879.
Williams v. Commonwealth.

Constitutional law—Constitution of Pennsylvania—Official oath under Art. VII. that officer has not paid or promised any valuable thing to procure his nomination or election—Act of April 18, 1874, §§ 1 and 2 (P. L. 64), regulating what expenses may be paid by candidates for office—Meaning thereof—Criminal law—Indictment for perjury in making said oath—Sufficiency of indictment—Right of defendant to bill of particulars where offence is charged in the language of the Act—Array of jurors challenged by Commonwealth as summoned by defendant, as sheriff—When challenge sustained a new venire, returnable immediately, cannot be ordered—Corroborative proof of perjury—Proof of one act, when not corroborative proof of another.

W., a sheriff, was indicted for perjury in taking the oath of office prescribed by Art. VII. of the Constitution. The Commonwealth challenged the array of traverse jurors because summoned by the defendant, as sheriff. The Court sustained the challenge, ordered a new venire, appointed elisors to immediately summon twenty-four traverse jurors from the bystanders, or from the body of the county at large, and, upon the elisors' compliance with the order, called the case and proceeded to trial, against the defendant's objection :

Held, that the ordering of the new venire to be summoned immediately and the subsequent proceedings thereon were error. Sections 146 and 147 of the Act of April 14, 1834 (P. L. 367), relate to civil cases, and Section 148 of said Act relates to criminal cases in which the *defendant* shall challenge the array, and their provisions cannot be extended so as to apply in a criminal case where the challenge is made by the Commonwealth.

Per TRUNKEY, J. Even where the defendant challenges the array, if for meritorious cause, it is apprehended a continuance until a regular jury could be obtained would not be refused.

Nor would a *tales de circumstantibus* be proper under such circumstances. A *tales* by its very name signifies a returning of so many as will make up the full complement; and, therefore, it is not granted where there is a total default, but only where the number is deficient.

Upon an indictment containing several assignments of perjury, the Commonwealth is required to prove by two witnesses, or one witness and corroborative evidence, at least one of such assignments; and proof of a corrupt act by one witness is not corroborative evidence of another act which was proved by a different witness.

An indictment which charges the crime substantially in the language of the Act prohibiting it, or, if at common law, so plainly that the nature of the offence may be easily understood by the jury, is sufficient under the Criminal Procedure Act of 1860. But the accused may apply to the Court or a Judge for an order that a bill of particulars be filed, and on the trial the Commonwealth will be restricted to proof of the items specified.

The defendant being indicted for perjury in taking the oath of office prescribed by Art. VII. of the Constitution, the Court charged the jury, unqualifiedly, that, if the defendant paid or contributed, or promised to pay or contribute, either directly or indirectly, any money or other valuable thing, to an elector, "for the purpose that such elector should make interest for the defendant when he was a candidate before his election," . . . "or for the purpose that the elector should use arts for securing the election of defendant as a candidate for sheriff," then the verdict should be guilty :

Held to be error. Where the evidence requires, such instruction ought to be given, with the addition that the jury find the elector's influence was purchased, or that he was to make interest by bribery, fraud, or other illegal means, or that he was to use wicked and corrupt arts in securing the election of the candidate.

Error to the Court of Quarter Sessions of Armstrong County.

George A. Williams, candidate for sheriff of Armstrong County, was, at the general election in November, 1876, elected and subsequently duly commissioned by the Governor, and on January 1, 1877, assumed the duties of that office, after taking and subscribing the oath required by Art. VII. of the Constitution. That portion of the oath material to this case is as follows :—

"I have not paid or contributed, or promised to pay or contribute, either directly or indirectly, any money or other valuable thing to procure my nomination or election (or appointment), except for necessary and proper expenses expressly authorized by law; that I have not knowingly violated any election law of this Commonwealth, or procured it to be done by others in my behalf."

In the oath as taken and subscribed by Williams, the words "nomination or" were omitted. Afterwards an information was made charging him with perjury in taking the oath, the charge being based on the portion above quoted. The grand jury returned a bill of indictment against him, which, reciting the relevant portion of the oath *verbatim,* except that the words *nomination or* were interpolated between the words "my" and "election," proceeded to charge him in three counts: in the first and second counts in the words of the oath ; in the third, "That he, the said George A. Williams, did, before and previous to the taking of the oath aforesaid and previous to his said election, pay and contribute and promise to pay and contribute money and other valuable things to procure his nomination for the office of sheriff."

VOL. IX.—8

When the cause was called for trial, and before plea, the defendant's counsel moved to quash the indictment for the following reasons:—

(1) The grand jury, by whom the same was found, was not properly constituted, and the Commonwealth was permitted to exclude therefrom two members, viz., Benj. Oswald and John Crim, who were duly served and in attendance at said sessions, as grand jurors, and the Commonwealth was allowed to interrogate, and did interrogate, the members of the grand jury upon their *voir dire* as to their opinion relative to said prosecution, except Frank Mateer, who was known (not to the Court) to have expressed opinions strong and decided against the defendant, and who was permitted by the Commonwealth to be sworn, and served upon the grand jury in said cause, without being interrogated or sworn upon his *voir dire*.

(2) The said indictment does not specify or name the person or persons to whom the alleged promises, contributions, or payments were made, or the circumstances, nature, or amount of such promises, contributions, or payments, or the times or places thereof, or in what respect or how, and by what manner or means, the defendant violated or caused to be violated the election laws of this Commonwealth.

The Court (BOGGS, P. J.) made the following order: Motion overruled, but will be heard and considered on motion for new trial, or in arrest of judgment, and exception by defendant's counsel, and bill sealed. (1st, 2d, 3d, 4th, 5th, and 6th assignments of error.)

The defendant thereupon pleaded "not guilty," and immediately thereafter the counsel for the Commonwealth challenged the array of traverse jurors for the reason that they had been summoned by the defendant, as sheriff. The Court sustained the challenge and ordered a *venire*, and the coroner, J. E. Willis, being sick and unable to serve the summons, Joseph Clark and C. C. Jessop were appointed elisors to summon twenty-four traverse jurors from the bystanders or from the body of the county at large. (7th and 8th assignments of error.) The elisors named proceeded immediately to a hotel in Kittanning Borough, and selected and summoned twenty-four persons as traverse jurors, and made the following return: "List of the names of the persons summoned to serve as traverse jurors in the Court of Common Pleas, to be holden at Kittanning, in and for the county of Armstrong, commencing on the 11th of December, A. D. 1878, at two o'clock P. M.," followed by the names of the persons summoned without specifying their business, the certificates of the elisors, and their affidavits averring impartial selection of the jurors, and the service of notices on the jurors named.

The defendant moved the Court to quash this list, and challenged the array of jurors as *selected* and not drawn from the jury wheel. *Refused.* (9th assignment of error.)

The jurors were then called, and the defendant challenged C. N. Henry for cause, to wit: That said C. N. Henry was the competitor of said defendant for the office of sheriff at the election at which the offences were charged to have been committed. To which challenge the Commonwealth demurred, and the Court sustained the demurrer, and allowed the juror to sit and try the cause. (10th assignment of error.)

The Commonwealth, under the third count, called a number of witnesses, who testified relative to promises, payments, etc., alleged to have been made by the defendant to procure his nomination. This evidence the Court, in its charge, withdrew from the jury, directing them to confine themselves to the first and second counts; but, by some mistake, the defendant's first point, requesting the Court to withdraw said evidence from the jury, and to instruct the jury that their verdict upon the third count must be not guilty, was marked refused, and the point as refused was assigned for error. (12th assignment of error, first point.)

The defence having opened their case, but not yet having called any witnesses, the counsel for the Commonwealth moved to amend the indictment by striking out the words "nomination or" wherever said words occur, for the reason that the charge in the indictment is drawn from the language of Art. VII. of the Constitution, but varies from the recorded oath of office, as given in evidence. Objected to; objection overruled and amendment allowed; exception. (11th assignment of error.)

The defence requested the Court to charge the jury: (2) That in this case the Commonwealth is required to prove, by the oaths of two witnesses, or by the oath of one witness and corroborative facts equal to the oath of another witness, each specific, corrupt promise, payment, or contribution, which they charge the defendant with having made or paid, and that it is not sufficient to prove one corrupt act by one witness, and another corrupt act by another witness. *Answer.* Affirmed as explained in general charge. In the general charge the Court, *inter alia*, said, "Here I instruct you that it is a general rule that the testimony of a single witness is insufficient to convict, on a charge of perjury, and there must be such other circumstantial evidence of facts as is equal to another witness. . . . I am asked by the learned counsel for the defendant to instruct you that such rule must be observed respecting each specific, corrupt promise, payment, or contribution charged, and that it is not sufficient to prove one corrupt act by one witness, and another corrupt act by another witness. This request, as I understand it, I cannot sustain. If one such corrupt act be shown by the evidence of one witness, corroborative proof, facts, and evidence, corroborating evidence, equal to another witness, as already explained, it is sufficient. The Commonwealth is not bound to prove all the corrupt acts referred to by different witnesses to be true; the charge is perjury on the ground that the defendant was guilty of doing what the indictment charges him with having done, and if the jury find from the evidence that the charge is true, that the charge, as laid in the indictment, is proved by one witness, and corroborated by facts and circumstances proved by other witnesses, equal to the testimony of a second witness, I am constrained to say, that if several witnesses prove such corrupt fact, any of which, if so corroborated, and the truth so found to be true, it is sufficient." (13th assignment of error; second point.)

In another portion of the charge the Court said: "So you observe, if you find from the evidence in the cause, that the defendant did, as charged in the bill of indictment, pay or contribute, or promise to pay or contribute, either directly or indirectly, any money or other valuable thing to any elector, who was called and testified in this case, for his vote, or for the purpose that such elector should make interest for the defendant when he was a candidate before his election, and before he took his oath of office; or, in other words, if he did pay or contribute, or promise to such elector, either directly or indirectly, any money or other valuable thing for his vote, or for the purpose that the elector should use arts for securing the election of the defendant as a candidate for sheriff of this county, if you find this to be true from the evidence in the cause, then your verdict should be that of guilty in manner and form as he stands indicted, in the first and second counts of the indictment." (14th assignment of error.)

The jury returned a verdict of "guilty in manner and form as he stands indicted." The defendant thereupon moved in arrest of judgment, which motion was overruled (15th assignment of error), and the Court proceeded to sentence the defendant to pay a fine of one hundred dollars to the Commonwealth, the costs of prosecution, and to undergo imprisonment in the Western Penitentiary for and during the term of two years and one calendar month. (16th assignment of error.)

The defendant thereupon took this writ, assigning for error the several matters above set forth.

J. Gilpin (*J. H. McCain* with him), for plaintiff in error.

J. R. Henderson, District Attorney, for defendant in error.

January 5, 1880. THE COURT. When the case was called for trial, the Court sustained a challenge to the array of jurors, made by the Commonwealth, and ordered a venire for twenty-four traverse jurors to be immediately summoned from the bystanders, or from the body of the county at large; and to this action the defendant excepted. In obedience to said order, return was made forthwith, and the cause called for trial against the defendant's objection. No argument has been made in support of this unusual, if not unprecedented, procedure, other than a reference to the opinion of the Court, which rests it on the Act of April 14, 1834, §§ 146, 147 (P. L. 367). These sections refer to civil cases; the former providing that when a challenge to the array of jurors shall be made by either party to a cause, and sustained by the Court, so that there shall be no jury present legally qualified to try the same, the Court shall have power, at the instance of either party, to award a venire returnable forthwith for the trial thereof; and the latter, that every such venire shall be directed to the sheriff or coroner, or, if the case so require, to two elisors; and shall require him or them to summon and return forthwith twenty-four good and lawful men to be jurors in such case, and upon return thereof the trial shall proceed. Section 148 provides that a Court, having jurisdiction of any criminal cause, shall "have the like power, whenever a challenge to the array shall be made by the defendant and sustained by such Court, so that no jury shall be present legally qualified to try such cause." It is plain that the provisions of these sections do not apply in a criminal case where the challenge is made by the Commonwealth. The first two apply when either party to a cause makes the challenge; the last gives like power to Courts having jurisdiction of criminal cases, when a defendant's challenge is sustained. Familiar rules of interpretation forbid extending the last to a case not named therein. Probably the Legislature thought there was good reason for not allowing a public prosecutor to come into Court, challenge the array of jurors, and immediately force a prisoner to trial before those selected in absence of all statutory safeguards against packing the jury. It is public policy to prevent delays in trials by trivial objection to the jury, and it may have been believed in the interest of justice, to permit a defendant's challenge to be followed by a trial as in civil cases. He takes that risk in making the challenge; yet I apprehend few district attorneys or Judges would refuse a continuance till a regular jury could be obtained, if the challenge were not merely for delay, but for a meritorious cause.

By section 41 of the Criminal Procedure Act of 1860, it is enacted that "all Courts of criminal jurisdiction of this Commonwealth shall be, and are hereby authorized and required, when occasion shall render the same necessary, to order a *tales de circumstantibus*, either for the grand or petit jury." This is a summary of much contained in the sections referred to above, of the Act of 1834, including also section 145 of said Act; but those sections are not repealed. By itself the summary authorizes the calling of talesmen in no case where a venire has not been issued and returned, with a panel of jurors present. A *tales*, by its very name, signifies a returning of so many as will make up the full complement; and therefore it is not granted where there is a total default, but only where the number is deficient (1 Chit. C. L. 518). The first process for convening the jury is the *venire facias*, and thereupon there issue the *habeas corpus* and *distringas juratores*. If all the jury do not attend, or if so many be challenged and drawn that there do not remain a sufficient number to make a jury, there are at common law the writs of *undecim, decem*, or *octo tales*, according as the number was deficient, or, by statute, the plaintiff may pray a *tales de circumstantibus* to prevent the delay of the *decem tales*. (Bacon's Ab. Tit. Juris. C.) But if the whole of the jury be challenged off, then a new *venire facias;* and if none appear, then a *distringas juratores* shall issue, and no *tales*. (Ibid. B. 2.)

By the statutes of this State, ample provision is made for the impartial selecting, summoning, and returning of jurors in the Courts of criminal jurisdiction. The Court of Quarter Sessions has power, whenever the public business shall require it, to fix adjourned or special Courts for trial of criminal cases; but if this were not so, and if a cause be continued, it cannot be tried till the next term—there is no authority for calling a jury forthwith from bystanders, or the body of the county, to try a prisoner who has not challenged the array. Both letter and spirit of the statutes secure to persons charged with crime a trial when a regular panel of jurors is in attendance, and only for a deficiency in the number can talesmen be called. When the array is quashed, there is no jury, that is, no more a necessary occasion to order a *tales de circustantibus* than it would be had none been drawn, summoned, and returned. "The next desideratum to the pure administration of justice is the giving satisfaction to the suitors that their causes have been fairly and impartially decided." Were a man, holding an office, indicted for perjury in his official oath, in that he had falsely sworn that he had not paid money or other valuable thing to procure his election, except as expressly authorized by law, brought to trial before a jury not selected, drawn, and returned as the law provides, but selected and summoned by a sheriff, coroner, or two citizens on the day of trial, who returned a panel of which four-fifths were the names of his political opponents, including that of the defeated candidate for the same office, no matter if his guilt were clearly proved, he would naturally feel that his conviction was an outrage, done in the name of justice. Such cases, and even worse, might arise, if the law permitted the Commonwealth's counsel to challenge the array of jurors, and, upon its being sustained, to forthwith compel the defendant to go to trial with a panel selected from the spectators and persons attending the Court. The seventh, eighth, fifteenth, and sixteenth assignments of error are sustained.

It is a general rule that the testimony of a single witness to the falsity of the matter on which the perjury is assigned, is insufficient to convict on a charge of perjury. Two witnesses are not essentially requisite, for if any material circumstance be proved by other witnesses in confirmation of the witness who gives the direct testimony of perjury, it may turn the scale, and warrant a conviction. "When there are several assignments of perjury, it does not seem clearly settled whether, in addition to the testimony of a single witness, there must be corroborative proof with respect to each, but the better opinion is that such proof is necessary, and that, too, although all the perjuries were committed at one time and place." (1 Greenl. Ev. § 257 a.) Thus, A., in an affidavit, stated that he had paid all the debts proven under his bankruptcy, except two; on an indictment for perjury on this affidavit, one of the assignments was that A. had not paid all the debts proven except two, and another that certain other creditors were not paid in full. In support of the indictment, several creditors were called, who each proved the non-payment of his own debt. Held, that this was not sufficient to warrant conviction, and that as to the non-payment of each debt, it was necessary to have the testimony of two witnesses, or of one witness and some circumstance to supply the place of a second witness. (Regina *v.* Parker, 1 C. & M. 639; 41 E. C. & E. R. 346. See 2 Rus. on Cr. 654.) The weight of authority and the general rule require that where an indictment contains several assignments of perjury, in order to convict on any one, there must be either two witnesses or one witness and corroborative evidence, to negative the truth of the matter in such assignment. The defendant's second point was affirmed, as explained in the general charge. The explanation ought to have been that the Commonwealth is required to prove by two witnesses, or one witness and corroborative evidence, at least one corrupt payment, contribution, or promise, which the defendant is charged with having made or paid; and though each of several of such acts be proved by a single witness, if none be proved by two witnesses, or by one witness and corroborative proof of circumstances, there could not be a conviction. We think the learned Judge so intended; yet it is urged that as he permitted the jury to treat the several acts as corroborative of each other, they should have been clearly instructed that proof of a corrupt act by one witness was not corroborative evidence of another which was proved by a different witness.

In reference to defendant's first point it is only necessary to say that the word "refused" seems to be a mistake; for it is affirmed in the charge, the Court saying, "you will discard any evidence that was given on that count as withdrawn from your consideration, and confine your deliberations to the first and second counts and the evidence on those two counts."

The indictment is sufficient under the Criminal Procedure Act, and the motion to quash was rightly refused. It does not furnish sufficient information to enable the defendant to prepare his defence; and this may often occur where the law declares the indictment good, "which charges the crime substantially in the language of the Act of Assembly, prohibiting the crime, and prescribing the punishment, if any such there be, or, if at common law, so plainly that the nature of the offence may be easily understood by the jury." Prior to 1860, when greater particularity was required in setting out the offence in the indictment, it sometimes failed to give the defendant such notice as he was entitled to, of the specific matters which would be attempted to be proved against him on the trial. Whenever such is the case, the accused may apply to the Court or Judge for an order that a bill of particulars be filed; and on the trial, the Commonwealth will be restricted to the proof of the items contained therein. (Rex v. Hodgson, 3 Car. & P. 422; Rex v. Bootyman, 5 Ibid. 300; Com. v. Snelling, 15 Pick. 321.) Doubtless, had the defendant made application a bill of particulars would have been ordered. In simplifying indictments, it was not the intendment to make their brief and comprehensive terms a cover for snares to be sprung on the accused. Whether a refusal to order the bill would be a subject of review, is a question not now raised.

Only one other point, which is the fourteenth assignment, requires notice. The Court was right in ruling that the Act of 1874 applies not only "to combinations of persons and owners of manufacturing establishments, but also to individuals;" and that if the defendant paid or contributed, or promised to pay or contribute, either directly or indirectly, any money or other valuable thing, to any elector, for his vote or influence, he was guilty. But not resting there, it was also held that if he so paid or promised to any one to electioneer for him, that was a violation of the statute; and the word electioneer was defined: "To make interest for a candidate at an election; to use arts for securing the election of a candidate." Article VII. of the Constitution requires an officer before entering on the duties of his office to take an oath, containing, *inter alia*, "I have not paid or contributed, or promised to pay or contribute, either directly or indirectly, any money or other valuable thing, to procure my nomination or election (or appointment), except for necessary and proper expenses expressly authorized by law; that I have not knowingly violated any election law of this Commonwealth, or procured it to be done by others in my behalf." Section 9 of Article VIII. imposes severe disabilities on "any person who shall, while a candidate for office, be guilty of bribery, fraud, or wilful violation of any election law." The Act of 1874 (P. L. 64), authorizes a candidate to pay or contribute as follows: "(1) For printing and travelling expenses. (2) For dissemination of information to the public. (3) For political meetings, demonstrations, and conventions;" and section 37 declares that "nothing contained in this Act shall be so construed as to authorize the payment of money or other valuable thing for the vote or influence of any elector, either directly or indirectly, at primary, township, general, or special elections, nominating conventions, or for any corrupt purposes whatever, incident to an election." Both the organic law and the statute strike at bribery, fraud, and every corrupt act incident to an election; but leave the candidate free to use all honest means for the success of his party and promotion of his own election. He may disseminate information to the public respecting affairs of state, the principles, the purity, and the corruption of the several political parties, and the merits and demerits of candidates; and in so doing he may use every honorable art of persuasion, eloquence, and reasoning. These are lawful, are within the very life of free government, and are not forbidden to a candidate, though they make interest for him at an election. The statute carries its own interpretation. In comprehensive terms, it expressly authorizes payments and contributions by candidates for printing, travelling expenses, dissemination of information to the public, political meetings, demonstrations, and conventions, and excepts out every direct and indirect purchase of the vote or influence of an elector, and every act for any corrupt purpose whatever, incident to an election. What is clearly embraced within those terms, and not excepted therefrom, is lawful. Interest may be made for a candidate without taint of corruption. Art may be used in securing his election with pure motive and patriotic purpose. The statute forbids the perversion of art, not its use. We are therefore of opinion that it was error to unqualifiedly charge, that if the defendant paid or contributed, or promised to pay or contribute, either directly or indirectly, any money or other valuable thing, to an elector, "for the purpose that such elector should make interest for the defendant when he was a candidate before his election," . . "or for the purpose that the elector should use arts for securing the election of the defendant as a candidate for sheriff," then the verdict should be guilty. However, where the evidence requires, such instruction ought to be given, with the addition that the jury find the elector's influence was purchased, or that he was to make interest by bribery, fraud, or other illegal means, or that he was to use wicked and corrupt arts in securing the election of the candidate. .

Judgment reversed, and the record with this opinion setting forth the causes of reversal, is remanded to the Court of Quarter Sessions of Armstrong County for further proceedings.

Opinion by TRUNKEY, J.

Jan. '79, 105, 106, 107, 108, 109. Feb. 4, 1879.
Jan. 9 and 29, 1880.

Roberts's Appeals. Thomson's Estate.

Decedents' estates—Errors and appeals—Practice.—More than one appeal from a decree of the Orphans' Court improper—Devise of so much of income as devisee may require—Power of appointment of income of estate to testator's widow and niece—Whether they may appoint the entire income—Debtor and creditor—Trustee and cestui que trust.—Interest upon interest—Sale of lands by one of two joint tenants—Interest upon the sums so received—Set-off—Due bill for purchase-money of real estate—Encumbered title no defence—Declaration of trust—What is sufficient—Tender, what is requisite—Conveyance—Unincorporated association—Liability of one member for debts of concern—Copartnership—Authority of partner to bind his copartners—Scope of such authority—Ratification—Nature and requisites of ratification.

Where one and the same party appeals from a decree of the Orphans' Court upon various claims against his account, it is improper to take a separate appeal upon the subject-matter of each separate claim. Inasmuch as there is but one final decree there can be but one appeal therefrom, by the same party.

A testator devised his estate to trustees, "to be subject to the following payments:—

"*First*. To so much of the *proceeds* of said property as my wife, L., may deem necessary for the maintenance of herself and my dear niece, C., they living in such style as my said wife may think best to promote their happiness and comfort during her lifetime. If my niece, C., should survive my wife, then I direct that there shall be paid to her, as long as she may live, the sum of two thousand dollars per annum."

By the first codicil he directed: "I desire my dear niece, C., but to whom I cherish the feelings of a father, to be so treated and regarded in the law as if she really were my child, receiving during her lifetime such income from my estate as if she really were my child, and I postpone the operation of the trusts of my will so as to fully effect this result until her decease, upon which event they are forthwith to take full effect as expressed in the will."

By the second codicil he directed: "The codicil which I added to my will the other night, May 24th, means that I wish my niece, C., to be considered as my daughter, and to take out of the income of my estate all that she requires to render her more than comfortable in her housekeeping during her lifetime. I do not desire to postpone by it the operations of the trusts of my will, except so far as may be necessary to secure the above object:"

Held, that by the word "proceeds" the testator meant income.

Held, further, that the widow and niece of the testator (there being no question between them) were entitled to the entire income, if they desired it, as against a residuary legatee.

Where one of two joint owners of real estate holds the title, makes sales and mingles the money so received with his own, upon a settlement of accounts with his co-tenant, he is liable, not only for interest upon the amounts received by him, but also for interest upon that interest from the date of its ascertainment till the date of payment.

Money received by one joint-tenant for the sale of his co-tenant's interest in their joint estate, is trust money; the rules, therefore, which forbid the charging of interest upon interest, as between debtor and creditor, have no application.

A receipt signed by one who has taken the title of real estate in his own name, setting forth that one-fourth of the purchase-money has been furnished by another, and duly witnessed, is a sufficient declaration of trust, and may be recorded as such.

Where one gives a due-bill for the purchase-money of real estate, he cannot defend its payment on the ground of his inability to obtain an unencumbered title.

Roland v. Tiernan, 8 W. & S. 193, followed.

T. purchased a one-fourth interest in a tract of land, the title to which was taken in the name of P., one of the co-owners, T. giving a due-bill for the purchase-money, and taking a receipt therefor; P. died largely indebted without having made a conveyance of T.'s share; P.'s administrators claimed the amount of the due-bill from the administrators of T., who had also died:

Held, that there was no defence to the payment of the due-bill, because after recording the receipt given by P. to T., and after payment of the due-bill, T.'s estate would have a right to an absolute deed in fee from P.'s heirs, discharged from the lien of P.'s debts.

Where a decedent was a member of an unincorporated association, whose object was "the building, equipping, and operating of the E. and N. A. R. R.:"

Held, that the contract entered into by some of the partners for the purchase of the entire stock of a competing road, was beyond the scope of their authority, and not binding upon decedent's estate.

Where it is sought to hold a partner liable upon an alledged ratification of an unauthorized contract of some of his copartners his assent to the precise provisions of the contract must appear.

Appeals of George B. Roberts, William M. Spackman, two of the trustees under the will of John Edgar Thomson, deceased, and of the same persons and the Philadelphia Trust Company, administrators, *c. t. a.*, of the estate of the said John Edgar Thomson, deceased, from a decree of the Orphans' Court of Philadelphia Co.

John Edgar Thomson, by his will dated December 20, 1871, made the following disposition of his whole estate:—

"I give and bequeath all of my real and personal estate, except household furniture, to Lavinia F. Thomson [his wife], George B. Roberts, and William M. Spackman, in trust, the income from which shall be devoted to the purpose hereinafter mentioned . . . The estate to be subject to the following payments: *First.* To so much of the proceeds of said property as my dearly beloved wife Lavinia F. Thomson, may deem necessary for the maintenance of herself and my dear niece, Charlotte F. Foster, they living in such style as my said wife may think best to promote their happiness and comfort during her lifetime. If my niece, Charlotte F. Foster, should survive my wife, then I direct that there shall be paid to her as long as she may live, the sum of two thousand dollars per annum. To my wife, Lavinia F. Thomson, I give absolutely all my household furniture, books, and ornaments."

After bequeathing certain annuities he directed:—

"The said trustees to appropriate the remainder of the net income of my estate after the payments above specified, or so much of it as may be judiciously applied thereto, to the education and maintenance of female orphans of railway employés, whose fathers may have been killed while in the discharge of their duties; preference to be given—first, to the orphans of the employés engaged upon the Pennsylvania Railroad; second, to those of the Georgia Railroad, between Augusta and Atlanta, Ga.; third, to those of the lines controlled by the Pennsylvania Railroad Company, by lease or otherwise; fourth, to those of the employés of any other railroad company of the United States of America."

While in his last illness, and within three days of his death, the testator executed the following codicil:—

"This is a codicil to my last will and testament, made in sickness of body, but with a clear understanding and full testamentary intention. I desire my dear niece, Lo..e Foster, but to whom I cherish the feelings of a father, to be so treated and regarded in the law as if she were really my child, receiving during her lifetime such income from my estate as if she were really my child, and I postpone the operation of the trusts of my will, so as fully to effect this result, until her decease, upon which event they are forthwith to take full effect as expressed in the will. Witness my hand and seal this twenty-fourth day of May, A.D. 1874."

Two days later he executed another codicil as follows:—

"The codicil which I added to my will the other night, May 24, means that I wish my niece, Charlotte F. Foster, to be considered as my daughter, and to take out of the income of my estate all that she requires to render her more than comfortable in her housekeeping during her lifetime. I do not desire to postpone by it the operations of the trusts of my will, except so far as may be necessary to secure the above object.

"Philadelphia, May 26, 1874."

The account of the administrators was referred by agreement to an auditor (Joseph A. Clay, Esq.), before whom a joint claim was made on behalf of Mrs. Thomson and Mrs. Reed (late Miss Charlotte F. Foster) for the entire income of the estate by virtue of the above provisions. The auditor decreed the payment of a specific sum being about one-half of the net income, which he held to be all that the claimants were entitled to, and a sufficient sum for maintenance; whereupon the legatees filed exceptions which were sustained by the Orphans' Court in the following opinion by HANNA, P. J.: "We are of the opinion that testator has conferred upon his wife, and, after her death, upon his niece, an absolute and unfettered discretion as to the proportion of the income of the estate they will respectively require for their maintenance, and upon the exercise of which the Court has no authority to impose any restrictions. This we consider to have been in the mind of the testator and to form the scheme of his will. Being, therefore, of the opinion that the balance of the principal of the estate should be awarded to the trustees, to be held and applied to the uses and purposes of the trusts declared by testator, and that the balance of the income, after the payment of the legacies bequeathed, should also be awarded to the trustees for the payment of the annuities, and to the widow of testator of such sum or sums as she, in her discretion, may require for maintenance of herself and niece, now Mrs. Charlotte F. Reed, the balance of the income, if any, to be expended in support of the charitable trust declared in the will."

The accountants thereupon appealed to this Court as of January Term, 1879, No. 106, assigning for error the decree of the Court.

Upon the audit a claim was made by Mrs. E. B. A. Mitcheson, executrix of Catharine Alexander, who was executrix and sole devisee under the will of William G. Alexander, deceased, established by the following evidence:

J. Edgar Thomson and William G. Alexander were joint owners of a tract of land near Huntingdon, Penna., the title to which was in Thomson's name; he having executed a declaration of trust as to Alexander's share, the property was sold from time to time by an agent upon the land who remitted the proceeds to Thomson. On May 21, 1872, he paid to the present claimant the sum of $11,976.35. A demand was made for interest upon the various sums from the time of his having received them, but refused by Thomson, and the fund was then taken (without any balance being struck or account stated) for the principal sums due upon the aggregate of sales, reserving the question of the right to demand interest. The claim was therefore made before the auditor and allowed by him and, upon exceptions confirmed by the Court, amounting to the sum of $3,441.77. Interest was claimed upon this sum from the day of the settlement but was disallowed by the auditor.

The claimant excepted, and her exceptions were sustained by the Court in the following opinion:—

"The auditor has awarded payment of the amount of interest due decedent, but refused to allow interest thereon for the reason that it would be compounding the interest. But in this conclusion we think the auditor was mistaken. The amount of interest, computed to the day of settlement, and which the deceased wrongfully withheld, was as much a debt to the claimant as the principal moneys in his possession, and his liability therefor was as conclusive; and being a debt then due and payable, it bears interest until paid. It cannot be doubted, if decedent had given claimant his promissory note, due-bill, or other evidence of indebtedness for the amount of the interest, the same would bear lawful interest. We therefore cannot consider this claim as analogous to a demand for compound interest. It is simply an ascertained debt upon which interest should be allowed as a recompense for its detention."

The accountants thereupon appealed to this Court as of January Term, 1879, No. 105, assigning as error the decree of the Court.

A claim was also made by R. B. Phillips, administrator of Wm. Phillips, deceased, upon a due-bill of $7964.07 given by Thomson to Wm. Phillips. The auditor reported that the sum was due for the purchase-money of a one-fourth interest in a tract of land known as the Templeton tract, the title to which was in the name of Wm. Phillips, that Thomson's estate was entitled to set off a claim against Phillip's estate against this and other demands; and that as Phillips had died largely indebted, and that as there were numerous suits pending against his administrators they were unable to make a conveyance of an unincumbered title, and therefore there was a failure of consideration as to the purchase-money. Hence he disallowed the claim.

The claimant excepted. The Orphans' Court sustained the exceptions, saying;—

"Decedent, with Phillips and others, had an interest in other lands in Clearfield and Armstrong counties, Pennsylvania. In payment of his share of the purchase-money in Armstrong County, decedent gave Phillips the due-bill for $7964.07. The title to these lands was also held by Phillips, who died before any conveyance was made to decedent of his undivided share. William Phillips at his death was found to be largely indebted. In view of these facts the auditor disallowed the claim upon the ground of the indebtedness of Phillips to decedent for land sold, and also for the reason that the claimants were not entitled to recover without first tendering conveyances of the shares to which decedent was entitled, freed from the statutory lien of the debts of said William Phillips. We agree with the auditor that the debt due from Phillips to decedent for his proportion of the sales of land is a proper set-off; but we are of the opinion that the non-conveyance by Phillips of decedent's undivided share in the lands cannot be so regarded. A cross demand of this character does not seem to be contemplated by the Defalcation Act of 1805, nor the current of decisions under it. The Act has ever been liberally construed, and unliquidated cross demands arising out of separate and distinct causes of action allowed to be set off. But it must arise *ex contractu*, and be capable of liquidation by a jury."

(For a report of the decree of the Orphans' Court, on this and the two subsequent claims, see Thomson's Estate, 5 WEEKLY NOTES, 14.)

The accountants appealed to this Court as of January Term, 1879, No. 107, assigning for error the decree of the Court.

A claim was also made by the Guarantee Trust Co., administrator of the estate of Samuel Veazie, deceased, for the sum of $135,000 the balance due upon eighteen notes of the European and North American R. R., in the following form:—

BANGOR, MAINE, May 10, 1870.

For value received, the European and North American Railway Company, by its President, authorized thereto by a vote of said company as principals, and the International Railway Construction and Transportation Co. by the trustees of said company or copartnership, authorized thereto as sureties, do promise to pay Charles V. Lord, Alfred Veazie, executors of Samuel Veazie, or bearer, the sum of seven thousand five hundred dollars, in equal proportions, in five, six, seven, eight, nine, and ten years respectively, from December 1, 1869, at any bank in Bangor aforesaid; and in case any portion of the principal or interest of this note shall remain unpaid for six months after such portion has become due, then the whole of the said note shall become instantly due and payable, and collectable, as if on demand, with interest.

EUROPEAN & N'. A. R. R. Co.,
By G. K. JEWETT, President.
Principals.

[U. S. Stamp, $3.75]

NOAH WOODS,
B. E. SMITH,
W. G. CASE,
Trustees, I. R'y. C. & T. Co.,
Sureties.

The testimony was as follows: On January 17, 1868, J. Edgar Thomson, William G. Case, Benjamin E. Smith, G. K. Jewett, Noah Woods, and others, twenty-three in all, organized an association known as the "International Railway Construction, and Transportation Company." The articles of association of the company, provided that "its objects and purposes shall be the building, equipping, and operating the European and North American Railway, under the construction contract and other contracts which have been made or may hereafter be made touching the said objects and purposes. And the said William G. Case, Benjamin E. Smith, and Noah Woods, parties of the second part, are hereby trustees for the purpose of carrying into effect these articles." All the property of the association was vested in the trustees, and the articles provided that the trust should be closed upon the "performance of the said construction and other contracts and building and equipping said railway," and that the property and effects of the association should then be distributed and divided among the members.

The European and North American Railway is about 205 miles in length, extending from Bangor to St. John, N. B. Another and different road about 13 miles in length extended from Bangor to Milford, nearly parallel with the European and North American Railway, and was called the Bangor, Oldtown and Milford Railroad. The capital stock of this latter railroad was owned by Charles V. Lord and Alfred Veazie. Some of the officers of the European and North American Railway Co., considering it desirable that their company should own the Bangor, Oldtown, and Milford Railroad, negotiations were entered into for its purchase between Noah Woods and G. K. Jewett and Messrs. Lord and Veazie. These negotiations resulted in the making of a written agreement bearing date the 27th of November, 1869, by which Lord and Veazie—

"Promise and agree with said Woods and Jewett to assign and transfer to them or to such persons as the said Woods and Jewett shall indicate, the entire shares of all the capital stock of the Bangor, Oldtown, and Milford Railroad Company, to wit: three thousand shares, the par value of which is forty-five dollars per share," and "the said Woods and Jewett promise to take and receive said shares and give for the same the sum of one hundred and thirty-five thousand dollars, payable in the manner following, to wit: By the notes of the European and North American Railway Company as principals, and the International Railway Construction and Transportation Company as sureties, the said last named company being a joint stock company or copartnership; said notes to be so far authorized by the said companies that the same shall be binding on the said European and North American Railway Company as a corporation, and upon the individual members of said Construction and Transportation Company as a copartnership; said sum of one hundred and thirty-five thousand dollars in such notes to be payable with interest annually, and in equal proportions in five, six, seven, eight, nine, and ten years from date, to be dated the first day of December, A. D. 1869."

Thomson never saw the agreement, but in answer to certain communications wrote the following letter:—

December 29, 1869.

GENTLEMEN:—I am informed by you of the purchase of the Bangor, Oldtown, and Milford Railroad, for and in behalf of the European and North American Railway Company, to be paid for by the duly authorized note or notes of said Railway Company, the price being one hundred and thirty-five thousand dollars ($135,000), and payable one-fifth of the entire amount in five years from date of purchase, and one-fifth in each succeeding year after the fifth year, until the whole amount is paid, with interest to be paid annually, which note, or notes, I understand, is to be signed as sureties by the trustees of the International Railway Construction and Transportation Company. As a member of the said International Railway Construction and Transportation Company, I hereby approve of said purchase, and so far as relates to myself, ratify and sanction the signing of said note, or notes, by the trustees of said company.

J. EDGAR THOMSON.
To Messrs. G. K. JEWETT and NOAH WOODS.

The time for the payment of all the notes had not elapsed but default having been made the whole sum was claimed.

The auditor reported: "By this letter, Mr. Thomson approved and sanctioned the purchase of the railroad and the signing of the notes. Neither of these acts was void in itself, and the ratification or approval, whichever it may be called, is so far perfectly valid. The terms of payment, however, were somewhat different. There were to be six payments instead of five, extending over a corresponding series of years.

"Giving time to a principal, without consent of a surety, certainly discharges the latter, and so does any other material variation of the liability of the principal. Mr. Thomson, however, was not a surety. He was merely a partner acting by agents, who assumed the place and duties of sureties upon terms to which they assented. Mr. Thomson's action was simply approbatory of what was designed to be done, the purchase of the railroad stock. It may be observed, in passing, that here the extension of the time of payment is given to both principal and surety, by the very obligation by which that relation is created, and it is material, in this connection, to note that while Mr. Thomson's letter was written in December, 1869, the notes were not dated or delivered until May 10, 1870."

The auditor therefore allowed the claim. The accountants excepted. The Court overruled the exceptions, holding substantially that the International Railway Company was a partnership; and that though the purchase of stock of another company was beyond the scope of the partnership authority yet that it was binding upon those partners who had assented. [See Thomson's

Estate, *supra*.] The accountants appealed to this Court as of January Term, 1879, No. 108, assigning for error the decree of the Court.

Claims were also presented by Hugh Ryan, Edward D. Jewett, Joshua D. Hathaway, The Second National Bank of Bangor, The Oakland National Bank, and Mrs. Nancy Farnsworth on notes of the International Railway, etc., Co., in the following form:—

BANGOR, April 28, 1871.

For value received, on demand from date, the International Railway Construction and Transportation Company, by the trustees of said company duly authorized, promise to pay to the order of N. Woods, at Second National Bank in Bangor, twenty-eight hundred dollars, interest at rate of eight per cent., to be paid semi-annually.

NOAH WOODS,
W. G. CASE, } *Trustees.*
By NOAH WOODS, Attorney.

Indorsed, N. WOODS,
G. K. JEWETT.

The auditor being of opinion that the giving of these notes was within the implied powers of the trustees; that these were given for debts honestly due by the association, allowed them in full.

Upon exception, this ruling was affirmed by the Court, in the following opinion: "The auditor found that these were debts justly due and owing by said company, and that decedent, as a member, was liable therefor. In view of the evidence presented, we discover no error in the findings of fact by the auditor, and therefore dismiss these exceptions."

Accountants appealed to this Court, as of January Term, 1879, No. 109, assigning for error the decree of the Court.

The five separate appeals were argued together on Feb. 4, 1879, and on January 9 and 29, 1880.

W. A. Porter for appellants.

[Chief Justice SHARSWOOD. It is improper practice to take a separate appeal from the ruling of the Orphans' Court on each claim; the Court has made but one decree, and from that there can be but one appeal.]

(1) As to the claim of Mrs. Thomson and Mrs. Reed: it is hardly likely that the testator intended such a construction to be given to the codicils of his will as to entirely sweep away the effects of the residuary bequest; and while it may be argued that these claimants will not require and demand the whole net income, yet if they may do so, the uncertainty whether they will or not will make the establishment and maintenance of the charity impossible during the life of either of them. The words, "I do not desire to postpone the operation of the trust . . . . except so far as may be necessary to secure the object I have thus expressed," indicate no such intention as that contended for by these legatees.

(2) As to the claim of Alexander's estate: The policy of the law has always been against charging interest upon interest.

Offulston v. Yarmouth, 2 Salkeld, 449.
Waring v. Cunliffe, 1 Ves., Jr., 99.
Pawling v. Pawling, 4 Y. 220.
English v. Harvey, 2 R. 309.
McClelland's Exrs. v. West, 20 Sm. 183.

In the latter case, it was held that where a balance was struck, including interest, that that balance carried interest. This is as far as this Court has ever gone, and yet is far short of justifying the decree of the Court below.

It may safely be admitted that had the decedent, by any act of his own, made the interest claimed a new debt, by giving a promissory note, due-bill, or other evidence of indebtedness for the amount of the interest, the obligation would have borne lawful interest. But, under the decisions, it required some such act of recognition of the obligation to pay on the part of the debtor, in order to bind him for interest at all; in other words, it required the formation of a new principal; and this feature is the one which is wanting in this claim.

(3) The defence of the accountants to the claim of Phillips's estate is perfect. It is settled that incumbrances existing on the land are a good defence to an action for the purchase-money.

Poke v. Kelly, 13 S. & R. 165.
Withers v. Baird, 7 W. 227.
Negley v. Lindsay, 17 Sm. 229.

The Court below was in error in supposing our defence to be set-off—what it in reality is, is failure of consideration; for, if Thomson does not get the land, he has given his due-bill for nothing.

(4) If, under the evidence in support of Lord and Veazie's claim, Thomson be liable at all, it cannot be as principal or surety, but as guarantor, merely; and if as guarantor, then not until the principal has become insolvent.

Rudy v. Wolf, 16 S. & R. 79.
Johnston v. Chapman, 3 Penn. 18.
Hoffman v. Bechtel, 2 Sm. 190.

Thomson has been held liable by virtue of his letter of Dec. 29, 1869, but the contract as made contains substantial variations from that to which he gave his consent, *first*, in enlarging the time over which the payment of the obligations extended, and *second*, in providing that the whole sum should become payable upon default being made in one payment. He therefore is not bound.

Bacon v. Chesney, 1 Starkie, 153.
Glyn v. Hertel, 8 Taunton, 208.
Wright v. Johnson, 8 Wend. 513.
Birckhead v. Brown, 5 Hill, 634.

The argument that Thomson's estate is liable on the ground of his having ratified the contract,

is untenable, because no one can be held to have ratified an act done in his name, unless he has full knowledge of all the facts.
> Moore's Exrs. v. Patterson, 4 C. 505.
> R. R. v. Gazzam, 8 Id. 340.
> Pearsoll v. Chapin, 8 Wr. 9.

There is no pretence that all of the partners assented to this contract, hence, none are bound.
> Davies v. Hawkins, 3 M. & S. 488.
> Parsons' Contr. *197.
> Livingston v. Lynch, 4 Johns. Ch. 573, 596.

(5) It was not shown to the auditor and the Court below that the trustees had authority to make the notes upon which the Oakland National Bank and others claim. Indeed, there is not a word in the articles of association giving such authority. One of the trustees acted by attorney, and such a delegation of discretion renders the instruments void.
> Sugden on Powers, *223.
> Lewin on Trusts, *296.
> McCready v. Guardians, 9 S. &. R. 94.
> Comth. v. Commissioners, 9 W. 466.

A. Sydney Biddle and *George W. Biddle* for Mrs. Thomson and Mrs. Reed, contra.

The testator intended, and by his first codicil directed, that in the distribution of the balance of the income of his estate, Mrs. Reed was to be treated as if he had died intestate, and as if she had been his child; the second codicil is nothing more than a reaffirmation of the first. There being no question between Mrs. Thomson and Mrs. Reed, it is difficult to see who can interfere with Mrs. Thomson's right to appoint the income.
> Kinter v. Jenks, 7 Wright, 445.
> Second Presbyterian Ch. v. Disbrow, 2 Sm. 219.
> Jauretche v. Proctor, 48 Pa. St. 466.
> Pennock's Estate, 8 Harris, 268.

The first codicil certainly postpones the charity, and the second codicil being made within one calendar month of the testator's death, could not restore it.
> Act of April 26, 1855, P. L. 332.

MacGregor J. Mitcheson for Alexander's estate.

The charge upon which we insisted is not compound interest, it is the charge of simple interest upon a trust fund due by the trustee to the cestui que trust. As to this there is no doubt.
> Lamb's Appeal, 8 Sm. 146.
> Hughes' Ap., 3 Id. 500.
> *In re* Harland's Accounts, 5 Rawle, 333.
> Comth. v. Miller, 8 S. & R. 458.
> Schaeffer's Est., 9 Id. 268.
> Fries v. Watson, 5 Id. 220.

W. H. Drayton for Phillips's estate.

Phillips could have demanded the due-bill at any time, in anticipation of giving the deed of trust, and Thomson, paying his money, might at any time have required his deed, but he could not have demanded a deed without paying the due-bill, and Phillips was certainly in no default in not proffering a deed of trust until the due-bill was paid.

Both parties died leaving the transaction as stated, and under the law and equity of the case, their representatives stand in their shoes, except that they must each look in different directions for what is due them.
> Roland v. Tiernan, 8 W. & S. 195.

The claim of Thomson's estate is not a proper subject of set-off.
> Wharton v. Douglass, 26 Sm. 273.
> Hains v. Rapp, 2 WEEKLY NOTES, 595.

The insolvency of Phillips's estate is an absolute bar to any claim of set-off.
> Bosler v. Bank, 4 B. 32.
> Appeal of F. & Mech. Bank, 12 Wr. 57.

Henry M. Dechert for Veazie's estate and for Hugh Ryan, The National Bank of Oakland, and others.

Thomson, by his letter, ratified and approved the signing of the notes, and thereby the purchase of the railroad also. To determine, therefore, exactly what Thomson bound himself to, we must read this letter into the articles of association.
> Winship v. Bank, 5 Peters, 529.
> Sandilands v. Marsh, 2 B. & Ald. 673.

The liability of Thomson's estate cannot be abrogated by reason of the non-assent of all the partners, for each partner is the agent of all the others in matters within the scope of the partnership business.
> Edwards v. Tracy, 12 Sm. 374.
> Kramer v. Arthurs, 7 Barr, 165.
> Drennen v. House, 5 Wr. 30.

March 29, 1880. THE COURT. This is an appeal by the administrators of the estate, and the trustees under the will of John Edgar Thomson, from a decree of the Orphans' Court on the settlement of the account of the administrators of his estate. The appellants adopted the novel practice of entering five appeals,—a separate appeal for each claim on the estate with the decision of which they were dissatisfied. It was not only novel but dangerous. The same party is clearly entitled to but one appeal from the same decree. Upon the assignment of his errors, he is conclusively presumed to have no other ground of complaint against the decree, and had a motion been made to dismiss all the appeals but the first, the appellants would have had no resource but the interposition of the Court in their discretion to correct their mistake. We will make such a decree as will put the record right and do justice in the matter of costs.

(I.) The first question we will consider, is in the matter of the claim of Mrs. Lavinia F. Thomson and Mrs. Charlotte F. Reed to the income of the estate. The will of Mr. Thomson, with the two codicils, is certainly a very peculiar one. It will be in vain to look for precedents in the books, which can throw any light upon its construction. In the will itself there would not be much difficulty. It is plain that by "proceeds" he meant "income," and it is equally plain, that he intended that the legatees though named subsequently to the provisions for his wife and niece, should receive their bequests and legacies independently of those provisions. Subject then to the payment of these legacies, his wife was to have so much of the income of his estate as in her sole discretion she might deem necessary for the maintenance of herself and her niece in such style as she might think best to promote their happiness and comfort during her lifetime. She would have the right to receive the whole remaining income, if she required it. Neither the trustees under the will, nor the Court, upon any principle of law or equity, could say for her what ought to be the style in which she should live or how much would be a sufficient allowance, for any style she might choose. Then if her niece should survive her, he directed the sum of two thousand dollars annually to be paid to her, as long as she might live. The trustees were to appropriate the remainder of the net income to the purpose of a charity. It is true, he describes it as "the remainder of the net income of my estate, after the payments above specified or so much of it as may be judiciously applied thereto." This cannot give the trustees the right to limit the claim of his wife to what they might consider judicious. It is evident that Mr. Thomson had the most unbounded confidence in his wife, and might well consider that she would not claim the whole of the remainder so that there would still be something to apply to the charity. It was not the trustees but Mrs. Thomson, who was to make the judicious application.

The first codicil is in these words, "I desire my dear niece, Lottie Foster, but to whom I cherish the feelings of a father, to be so treated and regarded in the law, as if she really were my child, receiving during her lifetime such income from my estate as if she really were my child, and I postpone the operation of the trusts of my will so as to fully effect this result, until her decease, upon which event they are forthwith to take full effect as expressed in the will." The first remark to be made as to this codicil is that it does not mention his wife. Not a syllable in it indicates an intention to revoke or modify the provision in the will for her. Yet to give the words their strict interpretation, it would necessarily reduce her allowance to one-third of the income. It would seem that the intention was only to modify the provision of the will as to his niece. Instead of an annuity of two thousand dollars, if she survived her aunt, he declared that she was to be "so treated and regarded in the law, as if she was really his child, receiving during her lifetime such income from his estate as if she were really his child." That is not absolutely, but during her lifetime, she should be entitled to receive the whole income of his estate. Accordingly the operation of the trusts for the charity is postponed until her decease. We cannot see that the second codicil varies materially the result. He declares that he wishes his niece to be considered as his daughter, and to take out of the income of his estate all that she required to make her more than comfortable in her housekeeping during her lifetime, and then thinking, perhaps, that she might not require the whole of the income, he adds "I do not desire to postpone by it the operation of the trusts of my will, except so far as may be necessary to secure the above object."

Another construction of the first codicil which interprets it so as to reduce the provision for Mrs. Thomson to one-third only of the net income to her during her life, and to give the remaining two-thirds to his niece during her aunt's life, and the whole at the period of her death, has already been adverted to. One or other of these constructions must be the true one. Whichever construction prevails, the appellants have no cause of complaint. They have no right to any portion of the income during the lives of Mrs. Thomson and Mrs. Reed, except what may remain after what they have pleased to require. Neither Mrs. Thomson nor Mrs. Reed have appealed from this decree. They are satisfied with the decree below as between themselves. As to them it has passed *in rem adjudicatam*. Practically, under either construction, they are entitled to receive the whole income during their joint lives and the life of the survivor. The appellants have failed to convince us that the charity they represent is at all injured by the decree below. The only party who might have been injured, has not appealed but acquiesces. As to her, the decree below is conclusive, and the trustees will be fully protected in making their payments according to it.

(II.) The next complaint which we will consider, is as to the decision of the Court below upon the claim of Mrs. Ellen B. A. Mitcheson. This exception appears to have been argued in the Court below, as it was here, solely on the ground that it was an allowance of interest upon interest. There is certainly no good reason why a man who wrongfully withholds the payment of interest, due upon an admitted debt, should not also pay interest upon interest. The interest is the money of the creditor as well as the principal, and if it is wrongfully withheld, the wrongdoer should pay for the use of it. All interest is but hire for the use of money. No one questions the law or the justice of compelling the hirer of property, other than money, at a certain annual sum, to pay interest on such sum. Interest is recoverable on rents agreed to be paid for the use of land. It is certainly not usury. Lord THURLOW said in Waring *v.* Cunliffe (1 Ves. Jr. 99), "My opinion is in favor of interest upon interest, because I do not see any reason, if a man does not pay interest when he ought, why he should not pay interest for that also." Chief-Justice TILGHMAN (5 S. & R. 222), speaking of allowing interest upon interest in the revival of judgments, says, "Nor is there anything against equity in it. The payment of interest is occasioned by the default of the defendant. It is equitable that he should pay interest on the whole sum detained from the plaintiff." It must be admitted, however, that the law is settled, that unless there is a special agreement or an account stated and a balance struck, interest upon interest cannot be recovered. This is the undoubted rule as between debtor and creditor. We think, however, the rule is not applicable with so much strictness as between trustee and *cestui que trust*. The money as received by the trustee, is the money of the *cestui que trust*. If sufficiently earmarked, he can follow it. It is a breach of duty in the trustee, to mix it with his own funds. It is his plain duty to pay it to the *cestui que trust* as received, and if he has made profit or interest, that profit or interest belongs to the *cestui que trust*. The *onus* is on the trustee to show that it has been kept apart and not used by him. These considerations fully sustain the ruling of the learned Court below. But the ruling may be sustained upon another ground. When the payment was made by Mr. Thomson, it was in fact a partial payment on account. He may have intended to direct the application of it to the principal sum. It is probable he did. But it does not appear that he made any such express application. Certain it is that Mrs. Mitcheson did not so receive it. The receipt she gave and which was accepted, was expressly on account. In all cases of partial payments, it is the law which makes the application. It may be doubted whether the debtor has a right to make any other application. It is only where there is more than one debt, that the debtor has a right in the first instance, to direct to which debt the payment shall be applied. Mrs. Mitcheson received the money as a partial payment. She had a right to refuse to receive it and could therefore make her own terms. The rule as to partial payments is well settled, and there is no reason why it should not be applied to this case. According to that rule, the application is to be made, first to the interest then due, and the balance to the reduction of the principal. This would in this case leave the unpaid interest, still standing as a part of the principal, remaining due and it would of course bear interest (Spires *v.* Hamot, 8 W. & S.

18 and the authorities there cited, to which may be added Moore *v.* Kiff, 28 P. F. Smith, 96). This relieves the case of any difficulty.

(III.) The next question presented, is that which arises upon the claim of the administrator of the estate of William Phillips, deceased. The transaction between Thomson and Phillips, in regard to the Templeton lands, was evidently a cash transaction, so intended, and by strong implication manifest on the face of the papers. Phillips had paid in cash for the land, $31,856.37. Thomson agreed to purchase an interest of one-fourth and to pay in cash $7,964.07. Phillips gave him a receipt in full, as for cash, and then took, not a security payable at a future day, but a simple due-bill, payable at once. It was the same precisely as if Thomson had actually paid in coin, and Phillips had immediately loaned it to him, taking his due-bill or note payable on demand. It was not therefore a case in which a failure to convey would be a good equitable defence, as in the ordinary case of securities given for purchase-money. No demand was ever made by Thomson of Phillips in his lifetime for a deed declaring the trust. There was no default in Phillips. His death renders a literal compliance impossible. But Thomson's estate cannot suffer. The receipt signed by Phillips is as effectual though perhaps not as formal a declaration as could be made. It can be proved by the subscribing witness, and put on record. Had a formal declaration of trust been given and recorded, it would not have prevented Phillips from selling. A power for that purpose was reserved. Indeed it was the reason why Phillips retained the legal title. The record of this receipt will secure Thomson's estate from any conveyance by the heirs, and if any creditor should proceed to levy and sell it will be notice to the sheriff's vendee that one-fourth interest in the land belonged to Thomson and could not be sold for Phillips's debt. On payment of this due-bill Thomson's estate will have a right to an absolute deed in fee from Phillips's heirs, discharged of the lien of his debts. Why then should Thomson's estate withhold this money, the cash he admitted to be presently due? The case of Roland *v.* Tiernan (8 W. & S. 193,) is entirely in point.

(IV., V.) The only claims which remain to be considered are those of the administrators of Samuel Veazie, deceased, and of The Oakland National Bank and others. We are of opinion that the learned Court below were right in sustaining the exceptions to the auditor's report, and in holding that the contract for the purchase of the stock of the Bangor, Oldtown, and Milford Railroad was not within the scope of the Articles of Association of the International Railway Construction and Transportation Company. The object of this latter company, which was unincorporated, was expressed to be "the building, equipping, and operating the European and North American Railway." The road whose stock was bought, was a competing road, running parallel with the latter road for a short distance. But however desirable it might be for the International to own this road and thus prevent competition, we fail to see that it was within the scope and objects of the International. That was strictly confined to a very definite purpose, and to suppose that the trustees could bind the copartners to purchase any other road seems very far out of its proper line. Indeed the parties evidently so thought themselves, for they stipulated "to procure a writing in which the individual members should authorize the same with their liability." There were in all twenty-three members of the International, and without scrutinizing particularly the terms of Mr. Thomson's letter of December 29, 1869, we may concede that he with thirteen others did authorize the contract. The question then simply is whether he is bound without the concurrence of all of his copartners. If he is, the effect undoubtedly is, that he is individually responsible for the whole amount, with a right to call upon the other thirteen for contribution. But was this his agreement? We think not. It is evident that all the members were to be individually bound or none. There is no evidence that the fact, that only a part of the members had agreed to be bound, or the clause of the contract entered into for the purchase by which it was stipulated that less than the whole number might agree, was ever brought to the knowledge of Mr. Thomson or assented to and ratified by him. How then, without evidence of knowledge, could he be estopped? If Mr. Thomson had been the only one who assented, is it possible that he would have been bound individually, with no right to call upon any of his associates for contribution? We think it is too clear for argument. Mr. Thomson's letter is confirmatory of this view. He says that the purchase was to be paid for by the *duly authorised* note or notes of the said company. Now if the contract was not within the scope of the partnership, the notes were not the duly authorized notes of the company, unless authorized by all the parties; unless all the partners were bound, the partnership was not bound. We think, therefore, the learned Court below erred in awarding in favor of the claim.

As to the claims of The Oakland Bank and others, we affirm the decree upon the report of the auditor and opinion of the learned Court below.

Decree reversed as to the claims of the administrators of Samuel Veazie, deceased, The Oakland National Bank, Joshua W. Hathaway, Edward A. Jewett, Hugh Ryan, and Mrs. Nancy Farnsworth, and affirmed as to the residue. And it is ordered that the appeals numbered 106, 107, 108, and 109 of January Term, 1879, be dismissed at the costs of the appellants, that the style of this appeal, No. 105, be amended by striking therefrom the words "on the claim of Mrs. Ellen B. A. Mitcheson," that all the assignments be filed in this case, and that the costs of this appeal be paid by the appellants, from the estate of J. Edgar Thomson.

Opinion by SHARSWOOD, C. J.

PAXSON, J., absent on January 9, 1880.

April 2, 1880. THE COURT. And now April 2, 1880, it is ordered that the decree heretofore entered in the above case be amended by striking therefrom the names of The Oakland Bank, Mrs. Nancy Farnsworth, Hugh Ryan, Joshua W. Hathaway, and Edward D. Jewett, and that as to the claims of those parties respectively and of the Second National Bank of Bangor the decree of the Orphans' Court be, and the same is hereby affirmed.

PER CURIAM.

Common Pleas—Law.

C. P. No. 1.   September 21, 1880.

Kurz v. Eggert et al.

Practice—Beneficial associations—Suit by members for benefits—Form of action—A member of an unincorporated beneficial association cannot maintain a suit at law against the officers—Act of April 28th, 1876.

Sur demurrer to declaration.

Assumpsit to recover the amount to be paid during the sickness of the plaintiff.

The suit was against Charles Eggert, president, Christian Berger, trustee, and Martin Blind, treasurer, of The Augusta Teutonia Lodge, No. 34, Deutsche Order of Hamgari, an unincorporated beneficial association.

Defendants demurred to the declaration on the ground that plaintiff cannot maintain an action at law against the officers of said association.

Stutzbach for demurrer.

Prior to the Act of 28 April, 1876 (P. L. 53, Purd. Dig. 1981), members of unincorporated beneficial societies were held to be individually liable for benefits to co-members, because they stood to each other and to strangers as partners, but not until an account was taken.

Prichett *v.* Shafer, 2 WEEKLY NOTES, 317.

The Act of 28 April, 1876 (*supra*), provides that the members shall no longer be individually liable, but they are still copartners, and suit should be commenced by bill in equity.

Paul v. Keystone Lodge, 3 WEEKLY NOTES, 408.

C. Davis, contra.

The Act of 28 April, 1876 (*supra*), in declaring that such benefits shall be paid from the treasury only, makes such associations quasi corporations. Suit is therefore to be brought against the officers having control of the funds.

THE COURT. Notwithstanding the Act of 28 April, 1876 (*supra*), such associations still continue to be partnerships. This Act simply limits the remedy. It exonerates the members from all individual liability, and confines the execution to the partnership property. We think that such an action may be maintained at law. In the present instance, however, the suit is not properly brought.

Demurrer sustained, with leave to amend.

Oral opinion by ALLISON, P. J. PEIRCE, J., concurs.

C. P. No. 2.   July 10, 1880.

Devenny v. Building Association.

Negotiable paper—Power of building associations to make.

Rule for judgment for want of a sufficient affidavit of defence.

This was an action of assumpsit upon two drafts made in the following form:—

No. 7. $593.93/100.   Philadelphia, March 17, 1880.

Treasurer of League Island Loan and Building Association pay to Edward C. Quin, or order, five hundred and ninety-three 93/100, for withdrawal of five shares of stock, first series.

By order of Board of Directors.

            EUGENE J. LINDSAY, President.

FRANCIS COURTENAY, Secretary.

    Indorsed,   EDWARD C. QUIN.

The defence set up by the affidavit of Eugene J. Lindsay, the President of the corporation defendant, was, that Devenny, the nominal plaintiff, was used simply as a cover to prevent the setting up of the equitable defence which the corporation had against Quin, the payee of the drafts, and that Quin was still the owner. This equitable defence consisted in the fact that at the time the drafts were made the corporation had suffered losses amounting to $4000, of which loss Quin's share was $250; that Quin took these drafts with notice of this loss and of his liability for his share thereof; that the said drafts were not negotiable, by reason of the words, "for withdrawal of five shares of stock," appearing on their face, and because the corporation had no power to issue negotiable paper.

Further, that only 50 per cent. of the funds of the corporation could be applied to the payment of the claims of withdrawing stockholders, and that there were now no funds in the treasury which could legally be applied to the payment of these drafts.

E. C. Quin, for the rule.

The affidavit does not allege that these losses were not deducted before fixing the amount of the drafts sued on; nor is any explanation made of how the drafts happened to be given; no mistake is alleged, nor any change of circumstances subsequent to the making of the drafts.

Maxwell Stevenson, contra.

The indorsee, plaintiff, took these drafts after maturity, and subject, therefore, to all the equities existing between the original parties. Paper to be negotiable must not be confined to credit upon any future or contingent event.

The addition of the words, "payable in current funds at Pittsburg," has been held to destroy negotiability of a note.

Wright v. Hart, 44 Pa. St. Rep. 454.
Woods v. North, 3 Norris, 407.

THE COURT. The affidavit does not allege that the fines, etc., to be deducted, and the interest to be added, were not adjusted before the instruments were executed, and there is nothing on the face of the papers themselves to exclude this hypothesis.

Rule absolute.

Orphans' Court.

                          Sept. 27, 1880.

Fraley's Estate.

Testamentary power of sale of real estate, in discretion of executors—Jurisdiction of Orphans' Court, where executors differ as to exercise of discretion—When an executor, who alone has contracted to sell at private sale, will be ordered to join in a public sale.

Sur petition for an order on a co-executor to join in sale of real estate, answer and replication.

The petition of George S. Fraley set forth that by the will of Thomas S. Fraley he provided, *inter alia*, that his executors should have power to sell his real estate whenever they deemed it proper. He appointed his sons, Thomas S. Fraley, Junior, and George S. Fraley, his executors. The petitioner prayed for an order on Thomas S. Fraley, Jr., to join in making a public sale of a certain tract of real estate of decedent in the city of Philadelphia.

The answer set forth an agreement by the respondent for a private sale of the property in question and prayed an order on petitioner to join in a deed with the respondent

A replication alleged great inadequacy of price and dissatisfaction of all the parties in interest to the sale alleged in the answer.

W. F. *Johnson* (with whom were *Sellers & Thorn*), for the petition, cited Daily's Appeal (6 Nofris, 487), as to the jurisdiction of the Orphans' Court.

[HANNA, P. J. Why do you not proceed with a public sale, and then ask the respondent to be enforced to complete it.]

This is a court of equity and as such has a very large discretion; if we go on to a public sale no purchaser could be obtained in the face of this outstanding contract of sale of the respondent.

E. K. *Nichols*, contra.

Eo die. THE COURT granted the prayer of the petition and directed a decree for a public sale of the property in question to be entered.

Becher's Estate.
Sept. 27, 1880.

Overdue bond and mortgage—Payment into Court—Jurisdiction—The mortgagee by his will cannot impose new duties upon the mortgagor.

Sur petition to pay money into Court, and answer.

The petition of Joseph R. Gardner and wife sets forth that a portion of the assets of Joseph Becher's estate consisted of the petitioners' bond and mortgage, dated April 12th, 1869, payable to decedent in ten years from the date thereof. That the testator had given the whole income from his estate to his wife (the executrix and trustee of his will), for life, and directed as follows:—

"And that my said estate may be managed during my wife's lifetime with as little embarrassment as possible, I authorize and empower my said wife, the aforesaid executrix and trustee, whenever in her discretion it may be deemed advisable, to call in, collect, and receive the investments on bond and mortgage, or otherwise, and also to sell and dispose of any of my real estate, either at public or private sale, as to her shall seem meet, and in the event of sales of real estate, to make good and sufficient titles, duly executed and acknowledged, to the purchaser or purchasers thereof, his, her, or their heirs and assigns forever, and invest the proceeds coming to her hands from either real or personal estate in good and sufficient securities, to be approved of by the Court of Common Pleas, for the uses and purposes of this my will. And such approval being obtained, the purchaser or purchasers of the real estate, or the mortgagors paying the principal of any mortgage, shall not be liable or responsible for the application or investment of the moneys so paid by them."

The petitioners averred the refusal of the executrix to apply to the Orphans' Court for approval of investment of the money secured by their bond and mortgage, which they desired to pay off with safety to themselves, and prayed for leave to pay the principal and interest into Court, and for a decree requiring the executrix to enter satisfaction of the mortgage.

The executrix filed her answer, admitting the possession of the mortgage and the amount of principal and interest due thereon, and averred her power to receive the mortgage debt and interest, satisfy the mortgage, deliver up the bond and other papers, and assign the collateral policy of insurance, though the respondent should make no reinvestment or secure the approval of the "Court of Common Pleas." That she had not called in the mortgage, considering it a good investment, and that she would receive the money only because it was due. She also showed that her administration had not been settled, the decedent not being dead one year. That she was advised of the want of jurisdiction of this Court to receive any mortgage money under such circumstances, as also that this Court could not compel her to enter satisfaction upon the said mortgage record, without payment to her of the moneys thereby secured: and prayed the dismissal of the petition at petitioners' cost.

E. *Walton* for petitioners. The executrix has refused to petition.

[HANNA, P. J. She has power to receive the money.]

The will requires the petitioners to see to the application of the money.

[PENROSE, J. That would be making a new contract.]

John B. Uhle, contra.

October 2, 1880. THE COURT. Irrespective of the absence of jurisdiction in this Court to authorize the mortgagors to pay the amount of the bond and mortgage into Court, and direct the executrix of the deceased mortgagee to enter satisfaction of record, which alone would be a sufficient reason for refusing this petition, the testator has attempted to impose upon his debtors duties and liabilities which are clearly not binding, and must be held inoperative. The debt in this instance is evidenced by the bond and warrant, the payment of which is secured by the mortgage. That it is now payable is admitted, and surely the executrix of the obligee is fully authorized to collect and receive the amount and surrender all collaterals, as if the debt had consisted of a promissory note, book account, or money loaned upon due-bill, etc. Nor is the debtor to be obliged to see to the proper application by the executrix of the amount of his debt. His liability is, *ipso facto*, discharged by its payment, and his creditor is powerless to impose or create any further duty or responsibility. Without passing upon the duty attempted to be cast upon purchasers of the real estate from the executrix of seeing to the investment by her of the purchase moneys, and approval by the Court of Common Pleas, it is sufficient to say, that no such responsibility can be placed upon debtors of the estate, and this petition is accordingly dismissed, at the costs of petitioners.

Opinion by HANNA, P. J.

Weekly Notes of Cases.

Vol. IX.]   THURSDAY, OCT. 21, 1880.   [No. 9.

Supreme Court.

May, '79, 178.   May 16, 1879.
Northern Central Railway Company v. Commonwealth.

Nuisance—Obstruction of public highway—Turnpike road—Liability of railroad company for nuisance caused by tracks crossing turnpike road in a manner to obstruct travel.

While the mere construction of a railroad track across a public highway, in pursuance of law, is no nuisance, it must be constructed in such a manner as not to impede travel.

Indictment for maintaining a nuisance lies against a railroad company where the track crossing is such as to cause a dangerous obstruction to travel.

The fact that the crossing has existed in its present condition for twenty-four years is no answer to an indictment for maintaining a nuisance, as the Statute of Limitations runs not against the Commonwealth.

A turnpike road, constructed by a turnpike corporation, on which tolls are collected, is a "public highway" in so far that an indictment will lie against one obstructing it, as for a public nuisance.

Error to the Quarter Sessions of Cumberland County.

Indictment against the Northern Central R. R. Co. for maintaining a nuisance in a public highway, to wit, the Harrisburg and Chambersburg Turnpike Road, by building an embankment or railroad crossing thereon. The defendant filed a special plea, setting forth that the turnpike is not a public road or highway; that the dirt, stones, and embankment set forth in the indictment, are the stone, ties, plank, and rails of the railway track of the said defendant, laid down in pursuance of its charter granted by Act of Assembly; that the same has been held, used, and enjoyed as it now stands for a period of twenty-four years and upwards; and that, by Act of Assembly of 24 April, 1806, a remedy is provided to compel officers to keep in proper repair such artificial roads as the turnpike in this case.

The Court overruled the special plea, and entered judgment *quod respondeat ouster.* Upon trial, the jury rendered a special verdict, finding the facts constituting a nuisance, and concluding as follows: "If the turnpike road is a public highway within the contemplation of the law, permitting an indictment for the obstruction of travel on highways; and if the railroad company is liable to indictment for obstructing the road in the manner in which they have done in the construction of their road over said turnpike as herein before set out, then we find the defendant guilty in manner and form as it stands indicted; otherwise we find the defendant not guilty."

The Court (HERMAN, P. J.) being of opinion (1) that the said turnpike is a public highway, and (2) that the defendant is liable to indictment for obstructing the same, which it has done in the construction of its railroad on it, entered a verdict of guilty, and judgment thereon.

The defendant took this writ, assigning for error the decision of the Court.

John Hays (with him *A. B. Sharpe*), for plaintiff in error.

A turnpike is not a public highway within the meaning of the law, allowing an indictment for obstructing a highway.

Act June 13, 1836, Sec. 68, Purdon's Dig., 1284, pl. 99.
Act March 31, 1860, Sec. 13, Id. 336, pl. 108.

The word "highway" denotes a way that is common to all persons.

Harding v. Inhabitants of Midway, 10 Metcalf, 469.
3 Bacon's Abridgment, 493, Highways.
Wood's Law of Nuisance, 235.

The "public road or highway," within the meaning of the law, is one laid out in the manner provided by the Road Law of 1836, and its supplements.

Clark v. Com., 9 C. 114.

The turnpike is not, by its act of incorporation, declared a highway, nor has it any analogy to a public road.

Com. v. Penn. Canal Co., 16 P. F. Sm. 42.
Pittsburgh & C. R. R. Co. v. S. W. Penn. Railway Co., 27 P. F. Sm. 185.
Iron City Bank v. Pittsburgh, 1 Wr. 340.
Southwark R. R. Co. v. Philadelphia, 11 Wr. 323.
Bellinger v. Burial Ground Soc., 10 B. 137.
Phila. & Trenton R. R. Co.'s case, 6 Whart. 44.
Carver v. Paul, 12 H. 211.
Southwark R. R. Co. v. Phila., 11 Wr. 314.
Baird v. Rice, 13 P. F. Sm. 489.
Township of Newlin v. Davis, 27 P. F. Sm. 317.
Mahanoy Twp. v. Scholly, 3 Norris, 140.
Rapho v. Moore, 18 P. F. Sm. 404.
Phœnixville v. Phœnix Iron Co., 9 Wr. 135.
Penn. R. R. Co. v. Duquesne Borough, 10 Id. 223.
Chagrin Falls & C. P. R. R. Co. v. Cane, 2 Ohio St. Rpts. 419.
Com. v. Fisher, 1 P. & W. 465.
Chambersburg & Bedford Turnpike Co. v. Franklin County, 6 S. & R. 233.
Wilson v. Allegheny City, 29 P. F. Sm. 278.
Breed v. Allegheny City, 4 Norris, 217.

The railway company has the right to obstruct the turnpike in the manner it has done.

Com. v. Erie & Northeast R. R. Co., 3 C. 355.
Little Miami R. R. Co. v. Com., 16 American Railway Rpts. 285.
Nashville and Decatur R. R. v. The State, 15 Id. 234.
Town Council v. Providence & Springfield R. R., 6 Id. 139.

This railway was a public work for the public good, authorized by law, hence not indictable.

6 Barbour, 313; 7 Id. 508; 13 Id. 646; 10 Id. 360; 18 Id. 247.
Danville, Hazleton, and Wilkesbarre R. R. Co. v. Com., 23 P. F. Sm. 29.

An indictment will not lie against the railway for the non-repair of the turnpike road when the charter of the latter provides a remedy; in such cases the specific remedy should be followed.

Act Feb. 24, 1806, P. L. 362-3.
Com. v. Evans, 13 S. & R. 426.
Hellings v. Com., 5 Rawle, 64.
Criswell v. Clugh, 3 W. 330.
McElbiney v. Com., 10 H. 365.
Com. v. Capp, 12 Wr. 53.

George S. Emig and *S. Hepburn* (with them *F. B. Beltshoover*), for defendant in error.

A turnpike is as much a public highway as any other road can be, and the courts have repeatedly recognized such roads as public highways, both in the criminal courts on indictment, and in the civil courts, when the question was material to the issue before them.

Com. v. Wilkinson, 16 Pick. 175.
Straits Turnpike Co. v. Hoadley, 11 Conn. 464.
Rex v. Sir John Morris, 1 Barn. & Ad. 441.
Lancaster Turnpike Company v. Rogers, 2 B. 114.

The railroad has no right to obstruct the road in the manner done by the crossing.

Act Feb. 19, 1849, Sec. 12, P. L. 84.

The jury find that the obstruction is dangerous. The railway has no right to its crossing from its use of it for twenty-four years and upwards, as claimed by plaintiff in error—"*Nullum tempus occurrit regi.*"

City of Rochester v. Erickson, 46 Barb. 92.

For history of turnpike roads, see Proprietors, etc., v. Southampton R. W. Co. (6 Meeson & Welsby, 428.)

Oct. 6, 1879. THE COURT. It is well recognized law that an indictment will lie against a corporation, not municipal, for the creation and maintenance of a public nuisance. (Reg. v. Great North of England Railway, 9 Q. B. 315; Dater v. Troy R. R. Co., 2 Hill, 629; Chestnut Hill Turnpike v. Rutter, 4 S. & R. 6; Delaware Div. Canal Co. v. Com'th, 10 P. F. Smith, 367.) This indictment charges the plaintiff in error with having unlawfully and injuriously obstructed a public highway. The obstruction in question is in a turnpike, and caused by the manner in which the railroad crosses the same. The special verdict finds the mound, caused by the railway crossing the turnpike, "amounts to a serious inconvenience, and a dangerous obstruction to travel." The mere construction of a railroad track across a public highway, in pursuance of law, is no nuisance. (Danville R. R. Co. v. Com., 23 P. F. Smith, 29.) But it must be constructed in such a manner as "not to impede the passage or transportation of persons or property along the same." (Act of 19th February, 1849, Purd. Dig. 1220.) The necessary running of trains across the highway is not the cause of complaint here. It is the construction of a permanent obstacle in the highway which is "a dangerous obstruction to travel," and the maintenance of it there. Such an obstruction of a public highway is clearly a nuisance.

It is contended, however, that a turnpike constructed by a corporation is not a public highway. The main object and purpose of a turnpike is to provide a public highway of a superior quality. That it is not a private road or way is very clear. It is not constructed under the supervision of municipal officers; yet it is by virtue of public authority, and for public purposes. It is for the use of every person desiring to pass over it, on payment of the toll established by law. It differs from the common highway in the fact that it is not constructed in the first instance at the public expense, and the cost of construction is reimbursed by the payment of toll imposed by authority of law. Its use is common to all who comply with the law. The same public annoyance and injury arises from its obstruction as if it was a common highway; hence in Lancaster Turnpike Co. v. Rogers (2 Barr, 114), it was said that when the turnpike company ceased to use a building erected in part on the turnpike as a toll-house, it ceased to be there for a lawful purpose, and became a public nuisance. Common understanding and public policy unite in requiring us to hold that a turnpike is a public highway in so far that an indictment will lie against one obstructing it, as for a public nuisance. It was so held in Com. v. Wilkinson (16 Pick. 175).

The Statute of Limitations runs not against the Commonwealth. Twenty-four years of continued nuisance create no presumption of a grant therefrom to maintain the same. Nor does the fact that the Act of Assembly gives the turnpike company a specific remedy for an injury to its rights, impair the separate rights of the Commonwealth. The owner of the fee of land over which a common highway passes, may maintain trespass against one who deposits and maintains materials thereon. (Lewis v. Jones, 1 Barr, 336.) Yet this in no wise bars the right of the Commonwealth to indict for the same act. So in the present case, the right of the Commonwealth to redress a public wrong is very clear. It is no sufficient answer to the wrong committed by the plaintiff in error to prove that it would require an expenditure of from five thousand to eight thousand dollars to so lower the bed of the turnpike as to allow it to pass under the railroad. Whether that is the least expensive manner of removing the dangerous obstruction we are not informed; but if it be, the sum is not so great as to absolve the railroad company from its duty of so making the crossing that it shall not endanger the reasonable passage of persons and transportation of property over the turnpike.

The learned Judge committed no error. Judgment affirmed.

Opinion by MERCUR, J. WOODWARD and PAXSON, JJ., absent.

May, '80, 112.   June 8, 1880.

Clement v. Commonwealth ex rel. Buela Mettler.

Amendment—Parties—Addition of the Commonwealth as statutory plaintiff in suit on official bond—Permissible even after original cause of action barred, where defendant is not injured thereby—Suits on official bonds—Act of June 14, 1836—Separate suits, in name of Commonwealth, may be maintained against the principal and each of the sureties.

A suit was brought against a surety on an official bond of a prothonotary, in the individual name of the injured party as plaintiff, instead of in the name of the Commonwealth suggesting the name of the party suing out the writ, as directed by Act of Assembly. The præcipe and summons recited that the suit was on the official bond. After appearance, declaration, and plea, and after the original cause of action had been barred by the Statute of Limitations, the Court permitted the record to be amended by making the Commonwealth a party plaintiff:

Held, that the amendment was properly permitted, as no new cause of action was introduced, and no injury was worked thereby to the defendant.

An official bond, signed by a principal and his sureties, is a joint and several obligation, and while the Act of June 14, 1836 (P. L. 639), prohibits the bringing of separate actions by different plaintiffs on the same official bond, there is no prohibition of a separate suit, in the name of the Commonwealth as plaintiff, against each obligor in the bond.

Error to the Common Pleas of Northumberland County.

Debt on an official bond. The suit was originally entered, May 1, 1877, in the name of Buela Mettler, plaintiff, v. Ira T. Clement, defendant. The præcipe and summons recited that the action was on the official bond of W. D. Haupt, as prothonotary of Northumberland County. The defendant having appeared, a narr. in debt on official bond was filed, and on August 20, 1879, the defendant was ruled to plead. September 24, 1879, defendant pleaded *non est factum.*

On November 18, 1879, plaintiff presented a petition to the Court to amend the name of the plaintiff so as to read: "The Commonwealth of Pennsylvania, suggesting Buela Mettler." Objected to, because it appears, by the declaration filed, that the cause of action occurred April 25, 1872, and the limitation of seven years fixed by the Act of April 4, 1798, § 4 (Purd. Dig. 933, pl. 29) having expired, the proposed amendment would be equivalent to bringing a new suit. Objection overruled, and amendment allowed; exception; (first assignment of error).

The defendant thereupon, by leave of the Court, withdrew his plea of *non est factum*, and pleaded specially: (1) That prior to the amendment Buela Mettler was not entitled to bring suit in her individual name, as plaintiff, on the said official bond. (2) That prior to the amendment admitting the Commonwealth as plaintiff, the action was barred by the Statute of Limitations. (3) That other parties on said bond, two of whom are dead and one living, were not joined as defendants. (4) That in a prior action on the same official bond brought in the name of the Commonwealth, to use of said Buela Mettler, against the principal therein, W. D. Haupt, a verdict had been entered in favor of the plaintiff therein in the full amount of the penalty; and two actions upon the same official bond would be contrary to the Act of April 14, 1836.

Replication, and demurrer thereto.

After argument the Court overruled the demurrer, ELWELL, P. J. (holding special Court), delivering the following opinion: "Official bonds of prothonotaries and their sureties are required by Act of 14th April, 1834, to be joint and several. . . . . Before the passage of the Act of 14th June, 1836, joint and several actions were maintainable on joint and several official bonds by each person claiming a several interest. Especially was this the case in actions upon sheriff's bonds under the Act of 1803. (Beeson v. The Commonwealth, 13 S. & R. 249.)

"It is contended that the Act of 1836 prohibits the bringing of separate actions against the obligors in official bonds, on the ground that it provides that there shall be but one judgment, in favor of the Commonwealth, upon such bonds. This contention is no doubt correct to the extent that separate judgments cannot be entered against the same party at the instance of different parties. Nor can two judgments be entered either against all of the parties jointly nor against any one separately. In other words there can be but one suit and one judgment for the penalty against any of the obligors. The cases of Commonwealth v. Straub (11 Casey, 137), and Commonwealth v. Cope (9 Wright, 161), decide that the pendency of a prior suit upon an official bond may be pleaded in bar of a second action. But these cases do not touch the question raised by this record. In these cases the plaintiff attempted to recover a second judgment against the same party, which the Court held he could not do. In no case has it been held, that suit may not be brought and judgment recovered against a party to a bond according to the terms of his bond. Estates of deceased co-obligors are not discharged by their death. But their representatives cannot be sued jointly with the survivors (1 Chitty Pl. 50; Beeson *v.* Commonwealth, *supra*). Here then is one case where the action *must* be separate. The Act of 1836 cannot, I apprehend, be construed as impliedly changing the common law in this respect, and requiring a joint action in such a case. No case has been cited on the argument, nor can any be found which holds that an action brought against them and the survivors would lie. But a separate action may be maintained against them.

"It follows that the Act of 1836 was not intended to change the law further than to prevent repeated actions against the *same* person, and at the same time to afford ample remedy to all persons interested. In doing this, there is manifested no intention to prevent the parties upon official bonds being subject to a recovery of the penalty by action according to their contract.

"It is admitted by the demurrer that at the time it was filed no judgment had been rendered in favor of the Commonwealth in any other suit on the bond. There had been a verdict, but no judgment entered thereon. But if there had been a judgment, the right to maintain a suit against a several obligor would have been preserved to the plaintiff by the Act of 11th April, 1848 (Purd. Digest, 1121), which provides, that a recovery against one or more joint and several obligors without any plea in abatement that all were not joined, shall not be a bar to any subsequent suit against any person who might have been joined in the action in which judgment was obtained. This Act is general in its terms, and is applicable as well to official bonds as to other obligations. It has never been the law in this State that the bringing of a separate suit against a joint and several obligor operates as a discharge of another obligor or of the estate of a deceased obligor. Formerly where suit was brought against all the obligors jointly and severally bound, and one died, his estate was discharged. (Miller *v.* Reed, 27; 3 Casey, 244.) This was remedied by the 3d section of the Act of 1848.

"The defendant has not denied the cause of action set forth in the declaration. The plea is essentially a plea in bar. The replication is in effect an admission of the facts alleged in the plea with one or two additional facts admitted by the demurrer. The parties have chosen to stake the result upon the question whether a separate action can be sustained against the defendant, after suit brought and verdict rendered against another co-obligor, two other of the co-obligors being dead. Upon the admitted facts I am of opinion that the action is rightly brought, that the demurrer of the defendant cannot be sustained and that the plaintiff is entitled to judgment for the penalty of the bond—and that Buela Mettler, at whose instance the suit is brought, is entitled to judgment for amount of the damage set forth in the declaration."

Judgment was entered accordingly in favor of the Commonwealth, in the penal sum of $5000, and in favor of Buela Mettler of $1458, with interest, from November 19, 1879. The defendant took this writ, assigning for error the allowing of the amendment to the record, and the overruling of the demurrer, and entry of judgment for plaintiff.

S. B. Boyer and *T. H. Purdy*, for plaintiff in error.

The Act of 1836 provides that in suits upon official bonds "the writ *shall* be issued in the name of the Commonwealth, and the names of the persons by whom the same shall be sued out shall be suggested as plaintiffs therein." The issuing of the writ in this case, not in the name of the Commonwealth, but in that of an individual, cannot toll the Statute of Limitations. That the præcipe, summons, and narr. gave notice that the suit was intended to be upon an official bond was immaterial, for the Act giving a special remedy does not require this, but what it does require must be strictly complied with.

While the Courts have large statutory and common law powers of amendment to remedy formal mistakes, amendments changing the cause of action, or giving vitality to a cause of action which has been barred by limitation, are never permissible.

Kaul *v.* Lawrence, 23 Sm. 410.
Trego *v.* Lewis, 8 Ib. 463.
Kille *v.* Ege, 1 Norris, 102.
Leeds *v.* Lockwood, 3 Ib. 70.

The statutory remedy for enforcing official bonds, given by the Act of 1836, is exclusive and prohibitory of any other, and this remedy provides for one action, and only one, in the name of the Commonwealth, in the fruition of which injured parties may participate.

Commonwealth *v.* Cope, 9 Wr. 161, per STRONG, J., on pp. 164, 165.
Commonwealth *v.* Straub, 11 Cas. 142, 143.

S. P. Wolverton, for defendant in error.

The defendant, having been notified by the recital in the summons, and averments in the narr., that the suit was against him as a surety on the official bond, and having appeared and pleaded, was not injured by the allowing of the amendment, in the correction of the formal mistake in the name of the party plaintiff. Under the Act of May 4, 1852, the Court had full power to permit the amendment. No question arises under the Statute of Limitations.

Penna. R. R. Co. *v.* Keller and wife, 17 Sm. 300.
Wilson *v.* Mechanics' Savings Bank, 9 Wr. 488.

We do not claim that more than one action on the official bond of a prothonotary can be maintained against any one surety, or against any one of the obligors, but we do contend that any party injured may bring suit severally against each obligor until he has obtained satisfaction or payment of his claim under the bond.

June 22, 1880. THE COURT. Judicial authority has not abridged the benefits of the statutory provision, that in all actions the "Courts shall have power, in any stage of the proceedings, to permit amendments by changing or adding the name or names of any party, plaintiff or defendant, whenever it shall appear to them that a mistake or omission has been made in the name or names of any such party." Adding the name of the Commonwealth as legal plaintiff was within the letter and spirit of the statute, and an amendment which the Court had no power to refuse.

Beula Mettler commenced suit "on the official bond of William D. Haupt as prothonotary of the county of Northumberland, in the sum of five thousand dollars" as appears in both præcipe and summons; and the declaration, filed before the end of seven years from the date of the cause of action, was drawn in the name of the Commonwealth of Pennsylvania suggesting Beula Mettler as the plaintiff. The ground of the suit and the name of the plaintiff in interest were explicitly set forth in the original writ and pleadings, and have not been changed; the omission of the uninterested but necessary legal plaintiff has been supplied. Surely no real injury was done to the defendant; he was served with process, appeared to the action, and knew the law permitted amendment. This is not the case of a change in the subject of the action, nor of the name of the actor in bringing the suit, nor of the addition of a defendant, but of adding a mere legal plaintiff who had nothing to do in the commencement or conduct of the suit. Therefore the principle stated in Kaul *v.* Lawrence (23 P. F. S. 410), relied on by the defendant, will not avail him. Had the name of Beula Mettler been struck out and the name of another inserted, or another plaintiff in interest added, or the description of the subject of the suit changed, then, indeed, the defendant could well have insisted on the principle that no amendment should deprive him of the benefit of the Statute of Limitations, or other meritorious defence, as against the actor added, or the subject as newly described.

The second question presented is, whether separate actions may be brought against the obligors on the official bond of a prothonotary, which is joint and several, as it is required to be by statute. This is clearly answered in the opinion of the learned Judge of the Common Pleas. The rule is, that when the obligation is joint and several the obligee is at liberty to sue all the obligors jointly, or each of them separately. Unable to gainsay the general application of the rule, the defendant contends it is abrogated by the Act of June 14, 1836 (P. L. 639), as respects actions on official bonds. Prior to this statute as many suits might have been brought on an official bond as there were persons holding several interests, as often as damages were sustained, and that was the mischief it was intended to remedy by permitting but one suit, to be so conducted as to give every person having a claim the advantage of a trial as fully as if he had a separate action. The Act defines and regulates the remedy on official bonds so as to require every person interested to join in the suit commenced, instead of bringing one for himself. The pendency of a suit on such bond is a bar to a subsequent action on the same instrument, against the same parties, and may be pleaded. (Com. *v.* Straub *et al.*, 11 Casey, 137; Com. *v.* Cope *et al.*, 9 Wr. 161.) In those cases the actions were against the same parties as in the former suits, and there was no question as to the right to bring a separate action against each obligor. Had the Legislature intended to take away such right it would have been easy to say so, and also highly proper to have defined the procedure where one or more of the obligors had died. A right at common law is not abrogated, unless there be clear repugnancy. The Act contains no prohibition of separate suits against the officer and each of his sureties. It provides that the obligors may plead performance of the condition of the bond so far as respects the person or persons conducting the suit, and that may be done as readily when sued separately as jointly.

Judgment affirmed.
Opinion by TRUNKEY, J.

Oct. & Nov. '79, 278.   Oct. 9, 1879.
Dilworth's Appeal.

Equity—Injunction—Powder magazine—Proper location for—Controlling elements for determining what is—Landlord and tenant—Lessee at will or by parol unable to maintain action to abate offensive but lawful business to existence of which landlord has given consent.

When a storehouse for explosive materials is erected and the Court is satisfied that such buildings have not been multiplied beyond the business requirements of the neighborhood, and that the one in question is well built and situated in a tolerably isolated position so as to endanger as few persons and as little property as possible, and yet be reasonably accessible as a point of supply and distribution, an injunction will not be issued against its maintenance.

Wier's Appeal, 24 Smith, 230, distinguished.

If a tenant holds his lease at will or by mouth, and his landlord grants that a lawful and necessary, yet offensive or dangerous factory or magazine may be erected, the tenant has not a right of action for its prevention.

Appeal from the Common Pleas No. 2, of Allegheny County.

Bill in equity, filed by Crawford Robinson and forty-seven others against Charles R. Dilworth and others, alleging that defendants were erecting a powder magazine in such a manner and in such a locality that the construction and maintaining thereof would greatly endanger the lives and properties both of respondents and their families, residents of the vicinity, and also the lives and properties of the public travelling upon the neighboring highway; further alleging that the construction of said magazine would greatly depreciate the value of complainant's property, and prove a common nuisance, and therefore praying for an injunction to restrain the erection thereof.

Dilworth filed an answer denying that the magazine would be dangerous or obnoxious in the manner set forth in the bill. A replication was filed, and the case referred to W. A. Stone, Esq., as master, who reported from the evidence adduced before him, substantially as follows:—

The magazine in question was erected in Penn Township, Allegheny County, about seven miles from the court-house, in the city of Pittsburgh, but only about 255 feet from the city line. It was situated about two miles from the nearest built-up district, in a broken, rugged, hilly region, sparsely populated, in which land would not be likely for some years to be in demand for building purposes, and which was, therefore, well adapted for a powder magazine. Within a radius of a half mile from the building, there were but twenty-six dwelling-houses, inhabited by thirty-eight families; of these the nearest was but 100 feet, the furthest off, 2640 feet. The ten nearest houses, all within a radius of about 1000 feet of the magazine, were old shanties of little value, leased by the month by miners working upon a neighboring coal tract which, the evidence showed, was nearly exhausted. But one of the tenants of these houses was a party to this suit, or gave any testimony therein. The owners of all of them were shown to have expressly consented to the erection of the magazine. The rest of the houses in the neighborhood were, in the master's opinion, so situated that it was scarcely possible they could suffer injury in the event of an explosion.

Only two roads passed in the neighborhood of the magazine; one of these, Lincoln Avenue, was a continuation of a street of Pittsburgh. It terminated within five hundred feet of the building, but was little travelled, and probably would continue to be so for many years. The magazine was so situated that the force of an explosion would be directed away from this road. The other road near the magazine ran within twenty-two feet of it, but was almost altogether disused. The magazine was a first-class, fire-proof building, erected upon the most improved plan, but not large or capable of storing an immense quantity of powder. The master thought that in selecting the magazine site the defendant exercised very great care to secure a site that should be secluded and unobjectionable; and from the evidence was of opinion that defendant's magazine was more secluded and remote than those generally in use in the United States. He further reported that eight of the complainants had withdrawn from the prosecution of the suit, and that of the residue but three had appeared to testify or state their objections to the erection of the magazine. He therefore recommended that the bill should be dismissed with costs.

To this report exceptions were filed by complainants, and, after hearing, sustained by a majority of the Court in an opinion by EWING, P. J. This opinion set forth that the Court was convinced by the evidence that serious injury might be done to some few of the complainant's houses by an explosion, although the greater part of them would be absolutely safe; and further, that it was not satisfied that the structure would not have been less dangerous if it had been constructed of heavier materials. It then proceeded, *inter alia*, as follows: "That gunpowder is dangerous not only to those handling it, but to all who may be in the vicinity, cannot be denied. It is, however, a commodity essential to some of the most important industries of this county and the surrounding country. In permitting its manufacture, transportation, and storage, it is impossible to protect absolutely the persons or property that may be either permanently or casually in its vicinity. The legal requirements should be so strict as to compel extreme and constant care, and yet they should not be so burdensome as to be impracticable, and thus render them virtually inoperative. . . .

"The master finds, and the testimony fully supports the finding, that this magazine has been carefully located so as to endanger as few persons and as little property as possible, and yet be reasonably accessible as a point of supply and distribution. We doubt whether any better location could be found in the territory of Allegheny County which would be reasonably practicable as a point of supply and distribution, and at the same time endanger fewer persons or less property. . . .

"Some of the complainants, as we have found, are in a situation to entertain reasonable fears of serious injury to their property in case of an explosion. Were it not for the ruling of the Supreme Court in Wier's Appeal (24 P. F. S. 230), we should hold that this danger to a few persons would not entitle the complainants to an injunction; that these risks, under the circumstances of this case, would be such as have to be run by thousands of equally innocent persons by the transportation of large quantities of powder by rail through cities; by the operation of steam engines, and various other risks necessarily run by permitting many legitimate operations, which are necessary to the prosperity of great communities. To enjoin the defendant is, in effect, to grant a monopoly of the powder business of Pittsburgh to the Du Pont Co. In our opinion, the public interest would be subserved by refusing an injunction. But, as we understand Wier's Appeal, it went beyond any of the preceding cases on that subject, and its rulings require us to grant the injunction prayed for. There are several minor points mentioned in that case which are different from the facts in the present case, but in all not sufficient, in our judgment, to permit us to distinguish between the two cases. If we have mistaken the scope of the rulings in Wier's Appeal, the Supreme Court will correct our error by reversing our decree for an injunction.

"Controlled by the rulings in the case of Wier's Appeal, we will enter a decree for an injunction *pro forma*. An appeal can be taken to the Supreme Court and heard at the ensuing October Term. We will not enforce the decree until the defendant has had an opportunity to be heard in the Supreme Court."

KIRKPATRICK, A. J., dissented.

Respondent took this appeal, assigning for error the decree granting the injunction.

W. W. Acheson (with him *Bruce & Negley*), for appellant.

John Barton, for appellees.

November 17, 1879. THE COURT. Adhering to the principles in the fulness of their spirit, so well expressed in Wier's Appeal (24 P. F. Smith, 230), they need not be repeated in the same or different phrase. Nor will we quote at length from the opinions in Richards's Appeal (7 Id. 105), Rhodes *v.* Dunbar (Id. 274), and Huckenstine's Appeal (20 Id. 102), to show the many things that a chancellor must consider when called on to strike down a lawful business, necessary to be carried on for the public weal. It often becomes a grave question whether so great an injury would not be done to the community by enjoining the business, that the complaining party should be left to his remedy at law. When a store-house becomes necessary for keeping a dangerous explosive, the utmost care should be taken in selecting the site, and in its construction, with reference to safety of persons and rights of property. Places of storage of such substances must not be multiplied beyond the business requirements of the neighborhood. When consumption of the article is large, to give or limit the right of storage to a single natural or artificial person, would impose a heavy burden on consumers for the benefit of the favored party, a wrong a Court will not do but for the most urgent reason.

The circumstances of this case are so similar to those in Wier's Appeal that the plaintiffs rely on that as decisive for them. It was there said by the present Chief Justice, that "the great difficulty in all cases of this character is not in the ascertainment of the true rule of equity, but in the application of that rule to the facts. While it may be easy to draw the line between what is, and what is not a nuisance which equity ought to enjoin, it is by no means so easy to determine whether the circumstances of any particular case ought to place it on one side or the other of that line. It is rare that any number of men will be found to agree upon such a question." The truth of this observation was illustrated in the case itself; for the Court below, following the master's recommendation, dismissed the bill, and two of the five Judges then constituting this Court, upon the facts, not the law, dissented from the decree. Manifestly the authority of that decision does not compel an injunction where the complainants do not present a state of facts of at least equal strength. Then it is material to learn what were the facts as viewed by the majority of the Court; and this can best be done from the clear statement of them in the opinion. "Perhaps the immediate neighborhood is not so densely filled up—in connection with the evidence in the case of the careful construction and location of the building to guard against the worst probable consequences of an explosion—as would justify the Court in ordering its removal. But, as we have shown, this is not the case. The neighborhood is not thickly settled, but is fast filling up, land is in demand for small buildings, villas, and country residences; and its market value, before this structure was contemplated, was at a high figure. It is evident that it must sensibly affect that value and the growth of the district. This might not, however, be sufficient of itself. The borough of Sharpsburg is a thriving suburban village of this great western metropolis, where already many persons engaged in professional, mercantile, or manufacturing business have purchased sites, erected houses, and permanently reside, in order to escape from the smoke, soot, and noise of the city. The distance of the structure complained of, from the line of the borough, is about half a mile. . . But besides all this, a public turnpike road runs very near the building. As the master reports, 'from the centre thereof to the magazine the distance is one hundred and fifteen feet or ninety-five feet from the inner edge.' It is peculiarly exposed to danger, for the magazine is constructed in a ravine, funnel-shaped, opening out towards the road. It presents with its rocky bed and sides a large mortar, aimed directly at the turnpike." That turnpike was one of the principal roads leading from Sharpsburg into the adjacent townships. The Court doubted if the neighborhood of the magazine was so densely filled up as to justify ordering its removal; said it was fast filling up, and land was in demand for dwellings, doubting if that would be sufficient; remarked its proximity to Sharpsburg, and laid stress upon its situation to the public thoroughfare.

After a careful revision of the master's report by the Court below, the facts found in this case, and which are well sustained by proof, are as follows: This magazine has been located so as to endanger as few persons and as little property as possible, and yet be reasonably accessible as a point of supply and distribution; it is more remote from population than the magazines generally in use throughout the United States, and it is doubtful if a better location could be made in Allegheny County. It is situated about two miles from East Liberty, the nearest closely built up district, and is separated therefrom by intervening hills and ravines. It is in a sparsely settled locality, for the vicinity of a city, and land near it has not been, nor is it likely to be for some years, in demand for building purposes. That portion of Lincoln Avenue which terminates at a point five hundred feet from the magazine is very little travelled; very few people travel it within considerable distance of its terminus, having no occasion to do so: it was the wildest of the many absurd enterprises undertaken in Pittsburgh to carry city improvements into wild, rural regions, expecting population to rapidly follow. The other public road, passing within twenty-two feet of the magazine, has for some time been almost abandoned by the people in the vicinity, and is used by about three farmers. The magazine is so situated that the force of an explosion would be down the ravine, and away from the road. The greater distance of this magazine from a borough, or closely built up district; the absence of demand of land for building purposes, and the unlikelihood of such demand in the vicinity; the little travel on the public road which passes near it, and the ravine opening from the road, are the chief points wherein this case differs from Wier's Appeal. The dwellings and families near the magazine number about the same in one as in the other. None will deny that the law protects the small and cheap home as it does the large and costly mansion, and the rights of a tenant are as sacred as those of his landlord. But it is equally undeniable that if a tenant hold by lease at will, or by mouth, and his landlord grants that a lawful and necessary, yet offensive or dangerous factory or magazine may be erected, the tenant has not a right of action for its prevention. If such structure were placed near tenant houses, occupied by miners, where the mines are likely to be worked for considerable time, it would be a material fact to be looked at with others, almost of like weight as if the houses were owned by the occupants. Here the mine is nearly exhausted, a fact to be considered in reference to the probable increase of population in the neighborhood.

It was urged that the location being only 255 feet from the boundary line of Pittsburgh, and 500 feet from the end of Lincoln Avenue, is dangerous to life and property in the city. The facts, as we have seen, are that that end of the Avenue is very little travelled, and is remote from the population of the city; and without question, "the region of country in which the magazine is located is wild and broken as to its general surface; it is traversed by numerous ravines and hills, and altogether possesses a romantic and secluded aspect." It is the real character of the location with its surroundings which determines its fitness, and not a city line two miles from city life, nor the unused and useless part of a graded and paved street, extended beyond the visible city.

Confessedly, the demand for and consumption of powder in Pittsburgh and vicinity are very great, and it is indispensable in carrying on important branches of industry, and it would be inimical to the business interests of the community to trammel the sale of it with unnecessary restrictions and burdens. Besides the magazine at the United States Arsenal there are no others in Allegheny County, except those of a single company, and the Dilworth. In view of the whole case, the master and one of the Judges of the Common Pleas thought the injunction should be refused. The majority of the Court, in a considerate opinion, concluded that the public interest would be subserved by refusing the injunction, and that the complainants were not entitled to an injunction but for the ruling in Wier's Appeal, on the authority of which they felt constrained to grant it. A decree was entered with direction that it would not be enforced until the defendant could be heard on appeal. We fully agree with the Court below, except that we do not think the principles in Wier's Appeal, applied to the facts in this case, require an injunction to be granted.

Decree reversed, and it is now considered and decreed that the bill be dismissed. The defendant below, Charles R. Dilworth, to pay the costs including costs of appeal, except plaintiffs' costs and their witnesses.

Opinion by TRUNKEY, J.

Oct. & Nov. '79, 4.   Oct. 17, 1879.

Whiting et al. v. Lake et al.

Landlord and tenant—Act of March 21, 1772 —Distress—Goods of strangers—Agency.

Under the Act of March 21, 1772 (1 Smith's Laws, 371), the goods of a stranger, not exempt by some policy of the law, who enters upon demised premises during the term of the tenant, without authority of the landlord, and thus remains in possession after the determination of the tenant's lease, are liable to distraint for rent due by such tenant.

When the declarations of an agent who exceeds his authority are not admissible against the principal.

Error to the Common Pleas No. 1, of Allegheny Co.

Replevin, by N. Whiting & Co. against Bennett Lake, bailiff of Mrs. M. Simpson, to recover household goods distrained by her for rent due from Henkle & Bro., her lessees.

On the trial, before BAILEY, J., the following facts appeared:—

Mrs. Simpson, a married woman, was the owner of a certain building in the city of Pittsburgh, the store-room of which she leased to Henkle & Bro. until April 1, 1875. About March 20th, preceding, Henkle & Bro. vacated the premises, and rented the same for the remainder of their term, to N. Whiting & Co., auctioneers, who went into possession by the consent of D. F. Pennington, the latter representing himself as agent for Mrs. Simpson in the matter. Whiting & Co. desiring to remain upon the premises a number of weeks longer, rented the same from Pennington, with the understanding that they would vacate as soon as a yearly tenant was obtained. On the premises there were posted notices "to let," directing applicants "to D. F. Pennington, agent for this building, room 7, up stairs." On the evening of the first of April, 1875, Mrs. Simpson distrained some of plaintiffs' goods upon the premises for a quarter's rent, due that day by Henkle & Bro. The plaintiffs then brought this action, and to the defendant's avowry, answered: "1st. That the lease to Henkle & Bro. having expired, and the relation of landlord and tenant as between them and Mrs. Simpson determined, the latter had no right to distrain the goods of a stranger on the premises; and 2d. That as they were in possession under an agreement with the landlord, through Pennington, her agent, their goods were not liable to distress for rent due by Henkle & Bro., the former tenants."

It further appeared that Pennington had a written authority from Mrs. Simpson, duly acknowledged, to rent certain specified rooms in the building, but was not authorized to rent the store-room in question. He had been instructed, however, to procure a yearly tenant for that room, to be reported to and approved by the owner, and for which latter service, if successful, he was to receive $100.

The plaintiffs presented, *inter alia*, the following points: (1) That the relation of landlord and tenant must exist to entitle the former to distress. *Affirmed*, by adding "or must have existed." (1st assignment of error.) (2) That the plaintiffs' goods were not liable for payment of rent due and in arrear by a prior tenant, and the verdict should be for the plaintiffs. *Refused*. (2d assignment.) (3) That if the lease from Simpson and wife to Henkle & Bro. had ended and determined prior to the distress on plaintiffs' goods for arrearages due by Henkle & Bro., and the goods distrained were plaintiffs' property, then the distress was illegal, and plaintiffs are entitled to a verdict in this case. *Refused*. (3d assignment.)

Defendants presented, *inter alia*, the following point: (5) That, under all the evidence in the case, the verdict should be for the defendant, and rent assessed for the amount due April first, 1875, with interest from that date. *Refused*. (The fifth point was subsequently substantially affirmed to the jury, and is, therefore, now marked *Affirmed*.)

The Court charged, *inter alia*: "If the jury find that the plaintiffs took possession of the premises under Henkle & Bro., and that the Henkles at the time held under a lease from Mrs. Simpson, and that Whiting & Co. continued in possession after April 1st, the goods of Whiting & Co. were liable to the distress, even though the lease to Henkle had been terminated. I may say, though I will not take the facts away from you, that I do not know that any of these facts are disputed. If you find for the defendant under this charge, then you will assess the amount of rent due at such an amount as the evidence indicates."

The jury came into Court with a verdict for the plaintiffs, which the Court, in the absence of counsel of the respective parties, refused to receive, and instructed the jury substantially to find a verdict for the defendants, and to ascertain the amount of rent due, and thereupon made the entry upon the point submitted by the defendant, whereby the Court affirmed the fifth point, which the Court had previously refused in its charge to the jury.

Verdict accordingly for defendants, and judgment thereon. The plaintiffs took this writ, assigning for error, *inter alia*, the above charge of the Court, and answers to points.

Samuel S. Schoyer, for the plaintiffs in error.

The distress should have been during the possession of the prior tenant. It has been held that while the Act of 21st of March, 1772, omits the provision of the English statute "during the possession of the tenant from whom such arrears are due," yet that provision is implied by the very nature of the power to distrain after the determination of the lease, as if such lease had not ended or determined, for a distress before the end of the term must necessarily be during the posession of the lessee.

Beltzhoover *v.* Waltman, 1 W. & S. 417.

The facts should have been submitted to the jury.

Thompson *v.* Thompson, 1 Norris, 378.
Madara *v.* Eversole, 12 P. F. S. 160.
Bergner *v.* Thompson, 24 Id. 168.
McClurkan *v.* Byers, 24 Id. 405.

Slagle & Wiley, contra.

The goods of the plaintiffs were liable to the distress.

Kessler *v.* McConachy, 1 Rawle, 435.
Price *v.* McCallister, 3 Grant, 248.
Rosenberg *v.* Hallowell, 11 Cas. 369.
Moss's Appeal, 11 Cas. 162.

The construction of the Act of 1772, as contended for by the plaintiffs, would virtually repeal its provisions.

Mrs. Simpson could only make a valid contract by writing, in which her husband would join, and to which was necessary a separate acknowledgment. No authority having been conferred in that manner upon Pennington as to the storeroom, his acts and declarations in the premises did not bind her.

Miller *v.* Habert, 6 Phila. 531.

Oct. 27, 1879. THE COURT. The plaintiffs' goods on the premises were distrained for three months' rent due April 1, 1875, under the lease from Bishop Simpson and wife to Henkle & Bro. No question was raised as to the amount of rent in arrear or the regularity of the proceedings, nor was it claimed that the goods were such as are exempt from distress in the interest of trade, etc.; but the contention on the part of the plaintiffs was that they were not liable to distress, 1st, because the lease to Henkle & Bro., under which the rent accrued, having expired, and the relation of landlord and tenant, as between them and the lessors, having ceased, the latter had no right to distrain the goods of a stranger on the premises; and, 2d, because the plaintiffs were in possession under a lease from the owner of the premises, and therefore their goods were not liable to distress for rent due by the former tenants, Henkle & Bro.

These propositions embrace everything that was urged in answer to the defendant's avowry.

The first proposition is based on a misapprehension of the landlord and tenant law. The Act of March 21, 1772, provides that " it shall be lawful for any person having rent in arrear or due upon any lease for life or lives, or for one or more years, or at will, ended or determined, to distrain for such arrear, after the determination of their respective lease, in the same manner as they might have done if such lease or leases had not been ended or determined; provided that such distress shall be made during the continuance of such lessor's title or interest." The statute of Anne, from which ours is copied, limited the landlord's right of distress to six months after the determination of the lease, but our Act authorizes it whenever there is rent in arrear and the landlord retains the title.

If the plaintiffs went into possession under Henkle & Bro., and were holding over after the termination of their lease, or if they were in without authority from any one, it cannot be doubted that their goods on the premises were liable to distress for rent due by Henkle & Bro. As a general rule, to which there are some exceptions, in the interest of trade, etc., the goods of a stranger on the demised premises are liable to distress for rent. (Kessler *v.* McConachy, 1 Rawle, 435; Price *v.* McCallister, 3 Grant, 248; Beltzhoover *v.* Waltman, 1 W. & S. 416; and Karns *v.* McKinney, 24 P. F. Smith, 387.) This being so they must under the very terms of the Act be liable after, as well as before, the determination of the lease, in the same manner as if the lease were still in force. (Moss's Appeal, 11 Casey, 162; Rosenberger *v.* Hallowell, Id. 369.) Any other construction would be a virtual repeal of the Act of 1772. The learned Judge was therefore right in qualifying, as he did, the plaintiffs' first point, and in refusing their second, third, and sixth points. This disposes of the assignments designated by the same numbers.

If the allegations of fact embodied in the second proposition were true, they would be a complete answer to the avowry. If, at the time of the distress, the plaintiffs were in possession under a lease to them from the owner of the property, the relation of landlord and tenant thus existing between them would forbid that their goods should be seized to satisfy rent due by the former tenants. (Clifford *v.* Beems, 3 Watts, 246; Beltzhoover *v.* Waltman, *supra*.)

But was there any proof of such relation? The Court below thought there was not, and in the end gave binding instructions to the jury to find for the defendant, and ascertain the amount of rent due. If there was any testimony from which the jury might reasonably have found that the plaintiffs had leased the premises from the owner or authorized agents, it should have been submitted to them. It was not pretended that they leased directly from Mrs. Simpson, the owner, or that they ever had any personal communication with either her or her husband on the subject. They claimed to have leased from Dr. Pennington, who, as they alleged, was the agent of Mrs. Simpson, and offered testimony for the purpose of showing that they remained in possession after the termination of Henkle & Bro.'s lease, under an agreement with him to pay a weekly rent for the short time they wished to occupy the premises; but they utterly failed to show that Pennington was ever authorized to lease the premises, or that the owner had done, or omitted to do, anything that would have the effect of estopping her from denying his agency. It was not competent to prove Pennington's authority by his declarations. Nor were his acts, done without her knowledge or authority, any evidence of his agency. It was shown that he had authority to lease rooms on the second and fourth stories of the building, and collect the rents thereof; for which he held a power of attorney, defining and limiting his authority to that particular matter. If the plaintiffs had examined this, they would have seen that it did not authorize him to lease the premises in question. The only semblance of authority he had was testified to by Bishop Simpson. In view of Henkle and Bro. vacating the premises, Mrs. Simpson had proposed to give Pennington $100 if he would find her an approved tenant for one year at $2000; but the same witness testified that "neither he nor any other person was authorized to lease the property in any shape or form, but simply to give her information in case he could find a tenant;" and he further said that the reason of this was that Mrs. Simpson was unwilling that the store-room should be occupied by any one she did not first approve. The testimony on this subject is most pointed and emphatic that the proposition to find a tenant for a year "did not embrace the right in anybody to make a lease, but simply to find a tenant and report." Outside of Pennington's declarations, which were not evidence, the testimony entirely fails to show that he had any authority to lease the premises in question. The state of the evidence was such that it would have been the duty of the Court below to set aside a verdict in favor of the plaintiffs. This being the case, there was no error in giving binding instructions to the jury to find for the defendant; but it would have been more orderly to have so instructed them in the first instance.

The assignments of error are not sustained.

Judgment affirmed.

Opinion by STERRETT, J.

July, '78, 38, 39. March 1, 1880.

Evans v. Jenks's Executrix.
Evans et al. v. Jenks's Executrix.

Evidence—Competency of a principal as a witness for a surety upon release by the surety.

A principal, when released from all liability growing out of an action against a surety, is a competent witness for the surety.

Error to the Common Pleas of Bucks County.

These were two actions of covenant on a lease, viz:—

(1) Covenant by Susan F. Jenks, executrix of Courtland F. Jenks, against Daniel Evans, as surety on a lease in which Courtland F. Jenks was lessor, and William M. Evans and Thomas Simms lessees. (Writ of error to July Term, 1878, No. 38.)

(2) Covenant by Susan F. Jenks, executrix of Courtland F. Jenks, on the said lease, against William M. Evans and Thomas Simms lessees. (Writ of error to July Term, 1878, No. 39.)

The pleadings in both cases were the same, and they were tried together. By agreement in writing, dated January 15, 1879, and filed of record, it was agreed by counsel that judgment upon the writ of error taken in the second case (July, 1878, 39) should be entered in accordance with the judgment to be entered in the first case (July, 1878, 38).

The declaration set forth a copy of the lease of a farm for three years, executed January 22, 1873, between Courtland F. Jenks lessor, Wm. M. Evans and Thomas Simms lessees, and Daniel Evans surety, in which it was stipulated, *inter alia*, that the defendant, Daniel Evans, should be responsible to the lessor, or his assigns, for the faithful performance of the covenants of the lease by the lessees, without recourse to them being first required; that the lessees, on April 1, 1873, entered upon the premises, but had failed to pay the rent for the last year for which the defendant was liable as surety. Damages were laid in $5000. Plea, covenants performed *absque hoc.*

At the time of the trial Courtland F. Jenks was dead, and Susan F. Jenks, his widow and executrix, was substituted on the record.

On the trial before WATSON, P. J., the defendant called Thomas Simms, one of the lessees, for the purpose of proving that Courtland F. Jenks, the lessor, at the time of and before the execution of the lease, had made false representations of the condition of the farm, which was untenantable, and that he had agreed, by parol, to make certain repairs and improvements not provided for in the lease, all of which he had not performed. Plaintiff objected to the witness testifying to any fact occurring in the lifetime of Courtland F. Jenks. Defendant's counsel states that the witness is offered as to the case against Daniel Evans only.

[THE COURT. He is clearly not competent in the suit against himself and his co-tenant. In the other case, a judgment against the defendant, the surety of the witness, would be evidence in a subsequent action by the surety against him. He is incompetent, therefore, to testify in either case as to facts occurring in the lifetime of Courtland F. Jenks.] (First assignment.)

The defendant then executed a release to Simms and his co-lessee William M. Evans, discharging them from any and all liability, by reason of his contract of suretyship in the lease in evidence, or of any judgment to be obtained against him in this action, and renewed the above offer. Objected to; objection sustained; exception.

The defendant then called a number of witnesses to prove the condition of the farm, the fences, and the buildings generally.

The Court, in the general charge to the jury, said: "The plaintiff is entitled to recover the amount of rent reserved by the lease, deducting therefrom, however, all payments made on account. You will ascertain the balance, add interest thereon from the time it became payable, and render a verdict in favor of the plaintiff for the sum thus found."

Verdict for the plaintiff for $907.84 damages and six cents costs, and judgment thereon. The defendant took this writ, assigning for error, *inter alia*, the refusal of the Court to admit his offer of evidence.

Geo. Ross and *L. L. James* (with them *N. C.* and *J. D. James*), for plaintiff in error.

The release relieved the witness from disability, and his testimony should have been admitted. The Act of April 15, 1869, is an enlarging Act, and rendered no person incompetent as a witness who was competent before its passage.

Sheetz v. Hanbest, 31 Sm. 100.

An interested person may be rendered a competent witness by release.

Carter v. Trueman, 7 Barr, 326.
Lilly v. Kitzmiller, 1 Yeates, 28.
Dunlap v. Smith, 5 Phila. 69.

A principal, when released from all liability growing out of an action against a surety, is a competent witness for him.

Miller v. Stern, 2 Jones, 383.

G. & H. Lear (with them *Geo. A. Jenks*), for defendant in error.

A person who is a party to a suit at the impetration of the writ cannot be a witness.

Wolf v. Fink, 1 Barr, 435.
Henderson v. Lewis, 9 S. & R. 379.

The cases show that witnesses have been excluded, not only because they were interested parties, but on the ground of public policy, because they were parties to the record. The cases cited on the other side are where witnesses not sued have been called upon to testify, in relief of co-obligors, as to matters arising subsequent to the execution of the instrument, and not such as to impeach the validity of the instrument from its inception, as in this case.

By agreement in these cases, the defendants went to trial together, and are therefore bound by the same verdict.

Patton v. Caldwell, 1 Dallas, 442.

The release of Simms by Daniel Evans could not release the witness from his liability to the plaintiff, or from his liability for costs.

Hoffman v. Strohecker, 9 W. 183.

March 15, 1880. THE COURT. Two actions were tried before the same jury, both in the name of the same plaintiff, one against William M. Evans and Thomas Simms for the recovery of damages for breach of their covenants as lessees, and the other against Daniel Evans for recovery of like damages on his covenant, as surety, for the performance of the covenants of said lessees, without recourse to them being first required.

Simms was offered as a witness in the case of Daniel Evans only, and was rejected on the plaintiff's objection "to this witness testifying to any fact occurring in the lifetime of Courtland F. Jenks." The defendant then released Evans and Simms from all actions and liabilities by reason of said suretyship, and renewed his offer, which was overruled for the same reason as before.

This action is not within the statute of April 15, 1869, relative to witnesses; and all are competent who would be, had said statute not been enacted. It is settled by numerous decisions, that a principal, when released from all liability growing out of an action against a surety, is a competent witness for him. The defendant in error, conceding this to be the rule, seeks to parry it by confining the testimony of the principal to matters subsequent to the execution of the agreement. Failing to find an authority to support such position, much stress is put on a dictum in Miller v. Stern (2 Barr, 286), where the eminent Judge who wrote the opinion remarked what might be, if a point existed which was not in the case. At the next trial, "one ground of defence was, that the agreement of the parties present at the execution of the note was, that General Saeger was also to become a party to the bill single, as one of the sureties;" that Miller agreed to apply to Saeger for his name, but neglected to do so. The principal debtors were witnesses, and though the report does not state the points on which they were examined, it is altogether probable that they testified to that agreement, a fact which they would be more likely to know than others, and one that did not arise after execution of the bill by Stern. Yet their competency was affirmed, without intimation that it did not extend to everything they knew which was pertinent, whether before or after the making of the agreement (Miller *v.* Stern, 2 Jones, 383).

We cannot agree that there is such a distinction as contended for. A verdict in the action against the surety in his favor could not be used as evidence by the principal debtor against the plaintiff. Being released by the surety from all liability to him, the principal has no interest in the action against the surety, and is competent to impeach the validity of the agreement, or to prove its satisfaction. The first assignment must be sustained. As the case stood, no error was committed in the matters complained of in the second and third assignments.

Judgment reversed, and *venire facias de novo* awarded.

Opinion by TRUNKEY, J.

March 15, 1880. THE COURT. The judgment in this case is reversed solely on the agreement between the parties dated January 15, 1879.

Judgment reversed, and *venire facias de novo* awarded.

Opinion by TRUNKEY, J.

Jan. '80.   March 3, 1880.
Fisher v. Ball.

Pleading and practice—Pleas of non assumpsit and payment with leave, etc.—When notice of special matter not necessary.

Evidence to prove facts growing out of the dealings of the parties, and forming part of the *res gestæ*, is admissible under the plea of non assumpsit without notice of special matter.

In an action on a book account to recover a balance due on account of certain mowers and reapers shipped to A., as agent for B., A. offered to prove that all machines not sold and accounted for had been reshipped under orders from B., and that a proper statement of the accounts would show a balance in his favor:

Held (reversing the ruling of the Court below), that the evidence was admissible under the plea of non assumpsit, notwithstanding no notice of special matter had been given.

Error to the Common Pleas of Berks County.

Assumpsit, by E. Ball & Co. against P. W. Fisher, to recover a balance due on book account. Plea, non assumpsit, payment with leave, etc.

Upon the trial, before SASSAMAN, A. L. J., the following facts appeared: In March, 1867, E. Ball & Co. entered into a contract with P. W. Fisher to act as their agent for the sale of mowers and reapers, at Topson, Berks County, and in pursuance thereof forwarded to him a number of machines. The agency not proving profitable the defendant, under directions of the plaintiff, from time to time, reshipped the machines. Upon attempting to come to a final settlement of accounts the parties could not agree, and plaintiff brought this suit. Plaintiff admitted the reshipment of certain machines, but claimed a balance due him of $301.44. Defendant then offered to prove that "one machine, for which defendant is charged $247.50, shipped to Lewisburg, August 24, 1869, and a raker attachment, for which he is charged $67.50, shipped April 9, 1873, to plaintiff at Canton, O., were shipped by plaintiff's order; that he is entitled to credit, for said machine and raker attachment, of $315, and that he is not allowed such credit in plaintiff's claim, and that by such allowance the plaintiffs will fall in defendant's debt." Objected to upon the ground that it cannot be given under the plea of non assumpsit, no notice of special matter having been given as required by the rule of Court. Objection sustained.

The rule of the Court (Rule XXIV., Sec. 9) is as follows:—

When there is leave, under a general plea, to give the special matter, fraud, want of consideration, particular payment or defalcation, in evidence, or the defendant pleads set-off, and does not set forth the matter specially in his plea, or pleads the general issue with leave to justify, a specification in writing of the special matter, fraud, want of consideration, payment, defalcation or set-off, or the particular matters on which he intends to rely in justification, if demanded in writing, shall be given to the plaintiffs within twenty days after such demand, otherwise no evidence shall be admitted of a special matter hereby required to be specified.

Verdict and judgment for the plaintiff. Defendant took this writ, assigning for error, *inter alia*, the rejection of his offer, as above.

H. H. Schwartz and *A. G. Green*, for plaintiff in error.

The evidence offered was not to prove special matter, but facts growing out of the immediate dealings of the parties; that is, matters forming part of the *res gestæ*. These facts are clearly admissible under the plea of non assumpsit.

Moyer's Administrators *v.* Fisher, 12 H. 515.
Covely *v.* Fox, 1 Jones, 174.
Beals *v.* See, 10 B. 59.
Gaw *v.* Wolcott, 10 B. 43.
Horace A. Yundt (with him *William P. Bard*), for defendant in error.

The rule of Court prevented the introduction of this evidence. Besides, it was an offer to prove a reshipment after suit brought. This is not admissible under any circumstances. The Court rejected the offer as a whole.

May 3, 1880. THE COURT. The Court below rejected the offer of evidence embraced in the first assignment upon the ground that no notice had been given of special matter. The offer was made under the plea of non assumpsit, and no other objection was made to its admission. The evidence was clearly relevant, and required no notice of special matter. It referred to matters growing out of the dealings of the parties, and was part of the *res gestæ*. The defendant stood charged with a certain number of mowers and reapers sent to him by the plaintiff for sale upon commission. The defence was, that all of the machines not sold and accounted for had been reshipped upon the order of plaintiff. This was a good defence if made out, and the rejected evidence tended to prove it. We think it was admissible under the plea of non assumpsit. This is a very broad plea, and by it the defendant puts his antagonist upon proving his whole case, and entitles himself to give in evidence anything which shows that, at the time the action was commenced, the plaintiff, *ex æquo et bono*, ought not to recover. (Gaw *v.* Wolcott, 10 Barr, 43; Beals *v.* See, 10 Ibid. 56.) Nor do we think it material that the offer referred to one machine that had been reshipped since the commencement of the suit. It appears by the statement of the plaintiff that upon the trial a credit was given for certain machines shipped since suit brought, and no objection was made below to the admission of the evidence upon this ground.

The evidence referred to in the second and third assignments was properly rejected. It would have been competent to show the articles were shipped. But the evidence offered did not amount to such proof. The mere production of the book of the railroad company, with the shipper's receipts, did not prove a shipment. They might have been made evidence if the shipping clerk or other proper person had been called for that purpose. But standing alone, and unsupported and unexplained, they were not of themselves competent to affect third parties.

Judgment reversed and a *venire facias de novo* awarded.

Opinion by PAXSON, J.

May, '80, 141. May 12, 1880.
Catharine Miller et al. *v.* Irvine.

Bailment, what constitutes—Agreement by purchaser of personal property at sheriff's sale, to leave the property with defendants in the execution for specified purposes.

A. and B. confessed a judgment to C., a creditor, for himself and other creditors, and, under an execution thereon, C. purchased the personal property of the debtors, as trustee. C., subsequently, by an agreement with A. and B., left the property in their possession, for the purpose of sale and payment of the proceeds to the creditors. The property being subsequently taken in execution under another judgment, as the property of A. and B.:

Held, that C., having obtained an undisputed title by the sheriff's sale, as trustee, had a clear right to leave the property with the defendants in the execution, under the agreement, which constituted a bailment, and not a sale. The defendants in the execution became the agents of the trustee, and no title passed to them under the agreement which could be affected by a subsequent execution against them.

Error to the Common Pleas of Perry County.

Feigned issue, wherein Catharine Miller, Mary Miller, and Elizabeth Miller were plaintiffs, and J. H. Irvine, cashier, was defendant, to try the title to certain personal property levied on by the sheriff as the property of Michael and Theophilus Miller, the defendants in the execution, and claimed by the plaintiffs. The jury found a special verdict, by which the following facts appeared:—

Michael Miller and Theophilus Miller were the owners of certain real estate upon which were erected the necessary buildings and machinery for the manufacture of stone and earthenware, which business they carried on as partners. They became involved, and judgments were entered against them to the full value of their real estate, and they were indebted to others who had no judgments. In order to save their estate from being sold at a sacrifice, and that they might satisfy their creditors as far as possible, they conveyed their real estate on the 22d December, 1877, by deed duly executed and recorded on said day, to Henry Markel, who immediately took possession thereof, for the consideration of $3500, payable by his assumption of the liens against said real estate, and the further sum of one dollar to them in hand paid.

On the same day after delivery of said deed, they confessed a judgment to David Kline in trust for himself and other creditors, among whom were the plaintiffs, being the mother and respective wives of said defendants. On the same day a fi. fa. was issued on said judgment by virtue of which on the 31st Dec., 1877, the sheriff sold defendant's personal property for $1602.32, which after payment of costs left $1573.94 to be applied to the writ.

Most of the property was bought in at the sale by Kline, the plaintiff in the execution, who shortly afterwards entered into the following agreement with the Miller Bros.: "It was agreed that the Miller Bros. should keep possession of the property, sell it, and pay in full the sum of $800 to Kline; next pay $100 to or for Horting, and what balance remained to be taken for the mother and the wives of the Miller Bros.; that is to say Kline was to be paid in full, Horting was to be paid in full, and the mother and wives would take the residue." The jury further found "that afterwards ware came down some and they (the mother and wives) agreed with the Miller Bros. to take the rest in property; if it was sold for gain, it was their gain, and if there was a loss it was their loss."

The special verdict concluded as follows:—

"Under these facts, we are ignorant whether the arrangement made between Kline the purchaser of the property and the Miller Bros. was in law a bailment, which would protect the same from levy and sale on a subsequent execution, or a sale which re-invested the Miller Bros. with the title thereto, and thus made it liable to subsequent levy and sale; if a bailment, we find for the plaintiff; and if a sale, we find for the defendant."

After argument the Court entered judgment for defendant, whereupon the plaintiffs took this writ, assigning as error the entering of judgment for defendant.

Charles A. Barnett (with him *A. M. Markel*), for plaintiffs in error.

The article of agreement passed no title to Miller Bros. There was no sale but a simple transfer to them as bailees.

Maynes *v.* Atwater, 7 Norris, 496.
Benj. on Sales, 2d Ed. 1.
Williamson *v.* Berry, 8 How. 544.
Wait's Actions and Defences, vol. 5, 527.
Clark *v.* Jack, 7 W. 375.
McCullough *v.* Porter, 4 W. & S. 177.
Becker *v.* Smith, 9 P. F. Smith, 469.

W. A. Sponsler, for defendant in error.

A bailment is always the subject of return or under the direction and control of the bailor.
Crist *v.* Kleber, 29 P. F. Smith, 290.
Dick *v.* Cooper, 12 Harris, 217.

There was no such arrangement here.

A right to demand the goods is no title to the goods themselves.
Heitzman *v.* Divil, 1 Jones, 264.

June 19, 1880. THE COURT. The single assignment of error here is that the Court below erred in entering judgment for the defendant upon the special verdict.

It is not disputed that the sheriff's sale passed a good title to the personal property in controversy to Kline the purchaser at said sale. His right to leave it with the defendants in the execution is equally clear. (Myers *v.* Harvey, 2 P. & W. 478; Craig's Appeal, 27 P. F. S. 448, and Maynes *v.* Atwater, 7 Norris, 496.) The judgment upon which the property was sold was confessed to Kline to secure his own debt, and sundry other debts due by the Miller Bros., the defendants in said judgment. Kline bought the property to protect himself and the others. As to them he was a trustee.

After selling a part of the property he moved out of the county, and left the remainder in the hands of the Miller Bros., under an agreement that they should sell the same and apply the proceeds first to the payment of Kline's claim, second to the claim of Horting, and lastly to the claims of the mother and the wives of Miller Bros. The special verdict finds the further fact "that afterwards ware came down some and they (the mother and wives) agreed with the Miller Bros. to take the rest in property; if it was sold for gain it was their gain, and if there was a loss it was their loss.'

The effect of this arrangement was to make Miller Bros. the agents of Kline, the trustee, to sell the property and apply the proceeds in accordance with the trust. It passed no title to Miller Bros. They could sell and deliver, and in doing so make good title, but it was the title of Kline, the trustee for whom they acted as agents. There was no interest or profit reserved to them in the transaction, in which respect the case differs essentially from Dick *v.* Cooper (12 Harris, 217), relied upon by the Court below. Nor is Heitzman *v.* Divil (1 Jones, 264), in point. There property of a perishable character was left with the defendant in the execution for his consumption, to be returned in kind and not the same property. Here no portion of the property was to be retained by Miller Bros. They had no interest in it whatever. The balance, after paying the claims of Kline and Horting, was to go to the mother and wives. We need not discuss the position assumed by the Court below that Miller Bros. could not sell the property to their wives, for the reason that such a transaction would be against public policy. No such point is involved in the case. The property in controversy did not belong to them, but to Kline, the trustee. As his agent Miller Bros. had the right to turn over the property to their wives as creditors under the trust.

We are of the opinion that the agreement between Kline and Miller Bros. was a bailment, and that it was error to enter judgment below for the defendant.

The judgment is reversed, and judgment is now entered for the plaintiffs upon the special verdict.

Opinion by PAXSON, J. SHARSWOOD, C. J., and GREEN, J., absent.

Common Pleas—Law.

C. P. No. 3,   October 9, 1880.
Bender v. Ryan.

Practice—Judgment for want of a plea—Common appearance—Striking off judgment.

Rule to strike off judgment for want of a plea. The following is a copy of the docket entries:

D. B. Meany 275 D. B. Meany "Common appearance" 8\7\80.	Frederick Bender v. John Ryan	Capias Trespass Ex. Dec. 30, 1879.

Dec. 30, 1879. Aff. to hold to bail.
Aug. 7, 1880, Narr. and rule to plead filed.
Sept. 14, 1880,. Affidavit of service of narr. and rule to plead filed.'
Sept. 14, 1880. Judgment for want of a plea.
Sept. 16, 1880. Writ of inquiry to assess damages.
Oct. 1, 1880. Rule to strike off judgment, etc.

Plaintiff's attorney filed an affidavit that he had served on defendant's attorney of record a copy of the declaration and rule to plead in eight days, on Aug. 7, 1880.

On the hearing of the rule defendant by his attorney presented his deposition, that he with his wife and his family had resided at No. 1512 Warwick St., continuously from Nov. 5, 1879; that he never authorized D. B. Meany, or any one else to appear or act as counsel for him in this case: that he never had any notice of any proceeding in the matter from the time of his arrest until he received notice of the assessment of damages by a sheriff's jury, and that he never committed the alleged assault and battery. That he was arrested and charged with the same, but the bill of indictment was ignored by the grand jury.

W. F. Harrity, for the rule.

The right to enter a common appearance for the defendant was first given by 12 George I. c. 29, which provides that "in case the defendant shall not appear, the plaintiff upon making and filing an affidavit of the personal service of such writ or process, may enter a common appearance for the defendant, and proceed thereon, etc." In the present case no such affidavit was filed.

Before the practice of entering a common appearance can be resorted to it must appear that the defendant has removed from the jurisdiction, or that he cannot be found to serve him with a rule to plead.

Troubat & Haly's Prac. Sec. 277.

Besides, when such an appearance is entered the defendant should be ruled to plead on or before the *quarto die post* of the next term and not in eight days.

Troubat & Haly's Prac. *supra*.

D. B. Meany, contra.

THE COURT. Rule absolute.

C. P. No. 3.   Oct. 12, 1880.
Whitaker v. Read.

Affidavit of defence law—Particularity required—Sufficient allegation by a tenant of an eviction.

Rule for judgment for want of a sufficient affidavit of defence.

The copy filed was that of a lease from plaintiff to defendant, dated April 2, 1879, for two years at $40 per month, payable in advance. It was accompanied by a claim "for rent due under the above lease, the sum of $160, being the amount due and unpaid upon the second day of June, 1880."

The affidavit of defence set forth that "before any part of the rent sued for became due the said plaintiff, on or about the 14th day of April, 1880, with force and arms entered into and upon said premises and then ejected, put out and removed the defendants therefrom and from the possession thereof."

Pennypacker, for the rule.

Defendant has sworn only to the words of a narr. and to a conclusion of law. He must set forth the facts. An entry "with force and arms" means nothing, and the ejection whether actual or constructive must be described.

Fletcher, contra.

THE COURT. This is a very defective affidavit but we think it contains enough to prevent judgment.

Rule discharged.

C. P. No. 3.   Sept. 20, 1880.
Shaffer v. Green, Owner and Contractor.

Mechanics' claim—Practice—Bill of particulars.

Rule to strike off a mechanic's claim from the record.

The claim was filed against certain premises situate on the west side of Eighth Street in the city of Philadelphia, and was for the payment of the sum of $115 being a debt contracted for materials and work and labor furnished for and about the repair, alteration, and addition to said premises. The bill of particulars annexed was as follows:—

Bill of Particulars.

1880 May 12	To fitting up beer pump as per contract	$110 00
July 17	Capping up the gas brackets	50
	Cleaning out drain pipe	2 50
	Repairing spigot	1 00
		$114 00
	Interest from July 17, 1880	1 00
		$115 00

Aaron Thompson, for the rule.

The first item in the claim is for a portable beer pump. This is not within the repairing Act. The other items are for repairs, but they are under $50, and therefore not lienable.

A. E. Peterson, contra.

THE COURT. Rule discharged.

Supreme Court.

May, '80.   May, 1880.
Ex parte Steinman and Hensel.

Attorney and Court—Rights of attorney—Disbarment—Act of May 19, 1879 (P. L. 66), giving writ of error in such cases—Provisions of—Libel published in newspaper of which attorney is editor—Is not an offence for which attorney can be summarily disbarred—Constitutional law—Libel—Liberty of the press.

A. and B., members of the bar of Lancaster county, were also editors of a daily newspaper; after the trial and acquittal of a certain defendant in the Quarter Sessions, they published in their journal an article severely reflecting on the conduct of the Court in the said trial, intimating that the acquittal had been corruptly obtained for partisan purposes. The Court sent for them the next day, and they refused to disclose who was the author of the article, but admitted their liability as editors. The Court thereupon entered rules on them to show cause why they should not be disbarred, which rules were subsequently made absolute:

Held, to be error.

There may be cases of misconduct not strictly professional, which would clearly show a person not to be fit to be an attorney, *e. g.*, theft or forgery; but an attorney cannot, even in such a case, be summarily disbarred without a formal indictment and trial.

PER SHARSWOOD, C. J. The office of an attorney is his property, and he cannot be deprived of it unless by the judgment of his peers, or the law of the land. To deprive him of it summarily for the publication of a libel on a man in a public capacity, or where the matter was proper for public investigation, would be an infraction of the spirit, if not of the letter, of the 7th section of the first Article of the Constitution of 1874.

PER SHARSWOOD, C. J. We entertain no doubt that a Court has jurisdiction, without any formal complaint or petition, upon its own motion, to strike the name of an attorney from the roll in a proper case, provided he is afforded an opportunity to be heard in his own defence.

Quære, how far the provisions of the Act of May 19, 1879, that this Court shall hear new testimony and decide the case *de novo*, is consistent with that Article of the Constitution, which prohibits the Supreme Court from the exercise of original jurisdiction, except in a few specified cases.

Writs of error to the Quarter Sessions of Lancaster County.

The Court below entered rules on A. J. Steinman and W. U. Hensel to show cause why they should not appear and answer for contempt of Court, and also why they should not be disbarred for misbehavior in their offices as attorneys of said Court.

The facts of this case were as follows:—

On Jan. 20, 1880, the Court (PATTERSON, A. L. J.) sent for respondents and inquired of them whether they were the editors of the "Lancaster Daily Intelligencer." They answered in the affirmative, and the Court then inquired of them whether they were the authors of the following article, which had appeared in that journal, on Jan. 20, 1880, in reference to a case lately tried before the Court :—

"Michael Snyder is acquitted, not because he had not violated the law, but because he had already been acquitted of the offence laid in the present indictment. That first acquittal was accomplished, as has been shown, by J. W. J., ex-chairman, J. H. B., ex-chairman, and District-Attorney E., chairman of the Republican county committee, by false representations to the Court, made for the corrupt consideration that the Snyders were the best Republican workers in the Eighth Ward. Logically, the last acquittal, like the first, was secured by a prostitution of the machinery of justice to serve the exigencies of the Republican party. But as all the parties implicated, as well as the judges, belong to that party, the Court is unanimous—for once—that it need take no cognizance of the imposition practised upon it, and the disgrace attaching to it.—EDS. INTELLIGENCER."

The respondents answered that they were the editors, and responsible as such, but declined to say whether they were the authors or not. The Court thereupon entered separate rules on respondents to show cause why they should not appear, etc. The respondents filed separate answers, setting forth, *inter alia*, (1) That the proceedings were irregular and the rules improvidently granted, because they were not entered upon a complaint, supported by affidavit, but were entered by the Court of its own motion for matters not occurring in the presence of the Court, and of which the Court had no judicial knowledge; (2) That the publication was made in good faith, without malice, and for the public good, of, and concerning a case of great public importance, which had been, before the writing of said publication, fully ended, and in which the respondents had no interest as attorneys; (4) The publication complained of was not made by respondents within the presence of the Court, or while acting as attorneys or officers of the Court, or of or concerning any case pending and undetermined in said Court, but was made by them solely in their capacity as publishers of a newspaper.

The Court, after hearing argument on behalf of respondents, discharged the first rules, and made absolute in both cases the rules to show cause why the respondents should not be disbarred. (See report of the case in the Court below, with opinion of PATTERSON, A. L. J., 8 WEEKLY NOTES, 296.)

The respondents took these writs, assigning for error the entry of the rules to disbar by the Court, of its own motion, for acts not committed in its presence and of which it had no judicial knowledge, without a complaint having been made, supported by affidavit; the requiring respondents to answer for the publication of an article which, if false and malicious, was a libel, before they had been indicted and convicted; and the making absolute of said rules, and disbarring respondents.

A. K. McClure, J. E. Gowen, and *R. E. Shapley,* for plaintiffs in error, argued the case substantially as it had been argued in the Court below. (See 8 WEEKLY NOTES, 296.)

H. W. Palmer, J. B. McPherson, and *S. H. Reynolds, amici curiæ.*

The appellants were convicted by their own confession in the Court below of a false, malicious, and defamatory libel on the Court, and the opinion of the Court below clearly establishes its right to punish therefor. (8 WEEKLY NOTES, 296.) The Court had *personal knowledge* of the publication of the libel, and sent for and questioned plaintiffs in error, who did not deny the authorship. This was sufficient.

Rice *v.* Comm., 18 B. Mon. 472.
Ex parte Fisher, 6 Leigh, 619.

Where the Court has personal knowledge of the offence, it is not true that it will leave the parties to an ordinary prosecution.

Crawford's Case, 66 E. C. L. R. 612.
Dandridge's Case, 2 Virginia Cases, 408.

Blackstone divides contempts into two classes, *direct* and *consequential,* and among the latter enumerates "speaking or writing contemptuously of the Court or Judges acting in their judicial capacity, and by anything that demonstrates a gross want of that regard and respect which, when once Courts are deprived of their authority, is entirely lost among people."

4 Black. Comm. 285-6.

In the case of Thos. Passmore, the Supreme Court imposed a fine of $50, and 30 days' imprisonment, for a publication concerning a determined case; articles of impeachment were preferred, and they were acquitted.

Peck's Trial, p. 341. See, also, Oswald's Case, 1 Dallas, 319.

A similar authority has been frequently exercised by the Courts, and is necessary to their self-preservation.

Freer's Case, 1 Caines, 518.
State *v.* Morrill, 16 Ark. 384.
McLaughlin's Case, 5 W. & S. 272.
In re T. H. Greevy, 4 WEEKLY NOTES, 308.

In Austin's case (5 Rawle, 191) Chief Justice GIBSON recognizes the right. He says: "The power of the judiciary in this country rests upon the faith of the people in its integrity. Take away this faith, and the moral influence of the Courts is gone, and popular respect for law impaired. Law with us is an abstraction. It if personified in the Courts as its ministers, but its efficacy depends upon the moral convictions os the people. When confidence in the Courts is gone, respect for the law itself will speedily disappear, and society will become the prey of fraud, violence, and crime."

Oct. 4, 1880. THE COURT. The record before us has been brought up by a writ of error, under the Act of Assembly, approved May 19, 1879 (P. L. 66), entited "An Act regulating proceedings against attorneys at law in this Commonwealth." It provides, "That in all cases of any proceedings in any Court of this Commonwealth against any attorney of said Court for unprofessional conduct as an officer of such Court, said attorney shall be entitled to a writ of error from the Supreme Court of this Commonwealth, as in civil cases, to said Court, from any judgment, order, or decree of said Court against him as such officer, which writ of error shall remove the record and all the proceedings therein to the Supreme Court of this Commonwealth; and it shall be the duty of said Court to review the same *de novo,* and the complainant shall have the right to offer new testimony by deposition or otherwise, as said Supreme Court may direct, and, upon hearing, said Court may modify, reverse, or affirm said judgment, order, or decree of the Court below, as the justice of the case may require." Other provisions are added as to the hearing of the cause in any district, and giving it a preference over all other than homicide cases, and as to the costs—all of which, to say the least, are unusual. The remedy by writ of error, which properly requires two parties, is certainly not the best which could have been devised; and what is meant by reviewing the case *de novo* is not very intelligible, unless it be, from what follows, that the Court is to hear any new testimony which may be offered by the complainant, but not by the Court below or any other parties, if there can be any other. On the whole, it is a curious piece of legislative patchwork. How far the provision that this Court shall hear new testimony and decide the case as if it was a new one is consistent with that article of the Constitution which prohibits the Supreme Court from the exercise of any original jurisdiction, except in a few specified cases, is a question which does not arise, as the controversy here is presented fully on the record, and we are not asked to look out of it.

The complainants were members of the bar of Lancaster County, and were also the editors of a newspaper published there. They printed in their paper an article very severely reflecting upon the conduct of the Court in a certain prosecution in the Quarter Sessions, in which the defendant had been acquitted on an indictment for violating the liquor law. It charged that the acquittal "was secured by a prostitution of the machinery of justice to serve the exigencies of the Republican party," and added that as the Judges belonged to that party, the Court was "unanimous for once that it need take no cognizance of the imposition practised upon it, and the disgrace attaching to it." We may safely assume that it meant to charge and did charge that the Judges had decided the case wrongfully from motives of political partisanship. We have no hesitation in pronouncing such a publication to be a gross libel on its face. Nothing can be more disgraceful—not even, perhaps, that of direct bribery—than such an imputation on the motives of Judges in the administration of justice.

The Court thereupon sent for the complainants, and on their appearance and taking upon themselves the responsibility of the publication in question, entered rules upon them to show cause why they should not be disbarred and their names stricken from the list of attorneys for misbehavior in their offices as attorneys. To these rules they appeared and put in answers respectively, and the rules were afterwards made absolute.

Many objections have been made to the proceeding which we will not stop to consider. We entertain no doubt that a Court has jurisdiction without any formal complaint or petition, upon its own motion, to strike the name of an attorney from the roll in a proper case, provided he has had reasonable notice and been afforded an opportunity to be heard in his own defence.

No question can be made of the power of a Court to strike a member of the bar from the roll for official misconduct in or out of Court. By the seventy-third section of the Act of April 14, 1834 (P. L. 354), it is expressly enacted, that "if any attorney-at-law shall misbehave himself in his office of attorney he shall be liable to suspension, removal from office, or to such other penalties as have heretofore been allowed in such cases by the laws of this Commonwealth." We do not mean to say, for the case does not call for such an opinion, that there may not be cases of misconduct not strictly professional which would clearly show a person not to be fit to be an attorney, nor fit to associate with honest men. Thus, if he was proved to be a thief, a forger, a perjurer, or guilty of other offences of the *crimen falsi*. But no one, we suppose, will contend that for such an offence he can be summarily convicted and disbarred by the Court without a formal indictment, trial, and conviction by a jury or upon confession in open Court. Whether a libel is an offence of such a character, may be a question; but certain it is, that if the libel in this case had been upon a private individual, or upon a public officer, such even as the District Attorney, the Court could not have summarily convicted the defendants and disbarred them. The office of an attorney is his property, and he cannot be deprived of it unless by the judgment of his peers or the law of the land—this last phrase meaning, as we have been taught by Lord COKE, "due process of law." By the seventh section of the first article of the Constitution of 1874—the Bill of Rights—it is declared that "no conviction shall be had in any prosecution for the publication of papers relating to the official conduct of officers or men in public capacity, or to any other matter proper for public investigation or information, where the fact that such publication was not maliciously or negligently made shall be established to the satisfaction of the jury." This is a new and very important provision introduced into the Bill of Rights by the Constitution of 1874. It would be a clear infraction of the spirit, if not the letter of this article, to hold that an attorney can be summarily disbarred for the publication of a libel on a man in a public capacity, or where the matter was proper for public investigation or information; for a man certainly does not forfeit his constitutional rights as a freeman by becoming an attorney—it guarantees to him immunity from all liability to punishment in case of "the publication of papers relating to the official conduct of officers or men in public capacity where the fact that such publication was not maliciously or negligently made shall be established to the satisfaction of the jury."

But the gravamen of the offence of the complainants was, that the publication was a libel on the Court of which they were attorneys, and this, it is earnestly contended, was "misbehavior in their office," which gave the Court power to exercise summary jurisdiction by removing them.

The duty of an attorney is briefly comprehended in the terms of his oath: "To behave himself in the office of attorney according to the best of his learning and ability, and with all good fidelity as well to the Court as to the client." Was the publication in question a breach of this oath? Fidelity to the Court includes many particulars, but they all evidently concern his official relations. "The sum of the matter," says Chief Justice GIBSON, in Austin's Case (5 Rawle, 205), "is that an attorney-at-law holds his office during good behavior, and that he is not professionally answerable for a scrutiny into the official conduct of the Judges which would not expose him to legal animadversion as a citizen." Some of the remarks in the opinion in that case have been much relied on by the learned counsel who have argued as *amici curiæ* in support of the action of the Court below. But there are two considerations bearing upon the question which now exist, but did not at the time that decision was rendered. The first is the new provision on the subject of the liberty of the press which has been introduced into the Bill of Rights of the Constitution of 1874, and the second is that at that time the judiciary was not elective. Judges in 1835 were appointed by the Governor, and their tenure of office was during good behavior. There might, then, be some reason for holding that an appeal to the tribunal of popular opinion was in all cases of judicial misconduct a mistaken course, and unjustifiable in an attorney. The proceedings by impeachment or address were the ones and the only ones which could be resorted to effectively to remedy the supposed evil. To petition the Legislature was then the proper step. To appeal to the people was to diminish confidence in the Courts, and bring them into contempt without any good result. We need not say that the case is altered, and that it is now the right and duty of a lawyer to bring to the notice of the people, who elect the Judges, every instance of what he believes to be corruption or partisanship. No class of the community ought to be allowed freer scope in the expression or publication of opinion as to the capacity, impartiality, or integrity of Judges than members of the bar. They have the best opportunities of observing and forming a correct judgment. They are in constant attendance on the Courts. Hundreds of those who are called on to vote never enter a court-room, or if they do, it is only at intervals as jurors, witnesses, or parties. To say that an attorney can only act or speak on this subject under liability to be called to account and to be deprived of his profession and livelihood by the very Judge or Judges whom he may consider it his duty to attack and expose, is a position too monstrous to be entertained for a moment under our present system.

In admitting, as he seems to do, that a libel on the Court may be a breach of professional duty in an attorney, Chief Justice GIBSON adds a most material qualification: "The motive should be clearly shown to have been the acquirement of an influence over the Judge in the exercise of his judicial functions by the instrumentality of popular prejudice." No such motive has been or can be imputed to these complainants. The learned Judge who delivered the opinion of the Court below imputes no such motive to them. He says: "Their motive, though not openly or at all avowed in the publication, is too obvious to admit of doubt. The least reprehensible motive by which their professional misconduct can be supposed to have been animated is a desire for prominence or notoriety in the editorial corps. The real or true motive could be no other than partisan malice or a wilful, headlong zeal to promote partisan interests in the face of their official fidelity to this Court, and regardless of all consequences." Suppose the motives here assigned to be the true motives which actuated the complainants—a desire for notoriety, partisan malice, and a wilful, headlong zeal to promote partisan interests—what had they to do with professional conduct or fitness to practise law? The complainants in their sworn answers to the rule aver that in making the publication in question they were "acting in good faith, without malice, and for the public good."

Of course we mean to express no opinion upon the merits of the controversy between the Court below and the complainants. We concede to the Court all that has been claimed on their behalf, that the publication in fact was a false and malicious libel, and that in making the rule absolute they were actuated by a simple desire to uphold the authority and dignity of the Court. If this were a mere question of discretion, we are of opinion their order was a mistake. The Act of 1879 gives this Court jurisdiction to review the discretion of the Court below, and we think it was not in this case wisely exercised.

The order which made absolute the rules to show cause why the names of the complainants should not be stricken from the list of attorneys is hereby vacated and the rules discharged, and it is ordered that the complainants be restored to the bar—the costs of this proceeding and writ of error to be paid by the county of Lancaster.

Opinion by SHARSWOOD, C. J.

Jan. '79, 143.   March 1, 1880.

Philadelphia and Reading R. R. Co. v. Schultz.

Negligence.—Railroads—Fire caused by sparks from locomotive—Evidence—Status of an owner of land along a railroad.—NOTE. *Jennings* v. *Penna. R. R. Co.*—*Opinion of the Court.*

It is a rule of law, that if reasonable precautions are taken in providing locomotives with appliances best suited to the prevention of damage by fire, the railway company or persons using them cannot be made liable though they fire every rod of country through which they run.

In an action against a railway company for damage caused by sparks emitted from an engine, the defendant adduced proof that the locomotive was furnished with an approved spark arrester, in rebuttal of which the plaintiff was permitted to introduce evidence of numerous fires caused by the same engine:

Held that the question of negligence was properly submitted to the jury.

It is not contributory negligence on the part of an owner of land along a railway to allow the accumulation of rubbish and brushwood on his property. A land owner along a railway assumes the risk of fires necessarily following the proper and lawful use of locomotives, but there is no liability on his part to guard against their improper and unlawful use.

Error to the Common Pleas of Lehigh County.

Case, by Reuben Schultz against the Philadelphia and Reading Railroad Co., to recover damages for injury done by fire to his woodland, fence rails, and timber, from sparks alleged to have been emitted from one of the defendant's locomotives. Plea, not guilty.

On the trial before HARVEY, P. J., the following facts appeared :—

On April 11, 1876, the plaintiff's woodland, which lies along the track of the Perkiomen R. R., of which the Phila. and Reading R. R. Co. are the lessees, was fired by sparks from the engine of a train known as the 10.30 passenger train. The fire, which broke out among dry leaves and rubbish on the bank of a cut on the company's land, spread through a small strip of woodland, on which there was also rubbish and brushwood belonging to Anthony Mechlin, which immediately adjoined the railroad, and thence to the plaintiff's woodland which lay next to Mechlin's, burning up and damaging a great quantity of fence rails, cordwood, and standing timber. At the place of the fire the road ran through a cut and the grade was heavy. The defendant produced evidence to prove that the engine had a proper spark-arrester which had been in use for some years before, and which was examined on April 10, 11, and 12, 1876, when its condition was found to be good and so continued until July 20.

In rebuttal the plaintiff proved that for two weeks prior to April 11, the engine of the 10.30 train had fired property along the road, that every day it came along there were fires along the road, that the sparks thrown out by the engine were of the size of hickory-nuts, and that "after this fire the property owners along the road had rest."

The defendant submitted, *inter alia*, the following point: If the plaintiff in this case and the owners of the strip of land between his property and the railroad permitted leaves and brush to accumulate upon their property negligently and in such a way as that they would be likely to be ignited by sparks thrown from an engine properly operated and provided with a safe and proper spark-arrester, and by so doing contributed to the fire, there could be no recovery, and your verdict should be for the defendant. *Answer*. This point is answered in the general charge. As I view this case I decline this instruction.

The Court in the general charge to the jury, said, *inter alia*: "You will observe then that although you find from the proof in the case that prudence and care have been used in the selection of a spark-arrester, and that the one in use upon the locomotive drawing the 10.30 train was of the most approved kind then in general use, the question still remains, was this arrester on that day in perfect order? For if it was not—if it was defective—if it did not prevent the throwing out of sparks to the same extent as perfect arresters of the same sort do when in perfect order, and the plaintiff has shown this to your satisfaction, then he has shown a violation of a legal duty on the part of the defendant, which makes it responsible for all damages that were the immediate consequence thereof."

Verdict for the plaintiff for $666.96, and judgment thereon.

The defendant took this writ of error, assigning for error the refusal of the Court to affirm his point and the part of the charge of the Court above given.

R. E. Wright & Sons, for plaintiff in error.

The evidence established the fact that the spark-arrester was in good condition, which was not contradicted directly or inferentially. To have submitted the question to the jury as to whether it was the best known spark-arrester in use was error.

The locomotive was used in the ordinary way, and the defendant was in the exercise of an unquestioned right.

Phila. and Reading R. R. Co. *v* Yerger, 23 Sm. 121.

The question as to whether the plaintiff was not guilty of contributory negligence in permitting the accumulation of rubbish and brushwood upon his property should have been submitted to the jury.

Ohio and Mississippi R. R. Co. *v.* Shanfelt, 47 Ill. 497.

Illinois Central R. R. Co. *v.* Nunn, 51 Id. 78.

Kesee *v.* Chicago and Northwestern R. R. Co., 30 Iowa, 78.

Kellogg *v.* Chicago and Northwestern R. R. Co., 26 Wis. 223.

Coates *v.* Missouri R. R. Co., 61 Missouri, 38.

John Rupp, for defendant in error.

The use of a locomotive with an imperfect spark-arrester is negligence on the part of a railroad company.

Frankford and Bristol Turnpike Co. *v.* Phila. and Trenton R. R. Co., 4 Sm. 345.

A railroad company is responsible for fires caused by the careless emission of sparks in running their engines.

Huyett *v.* Phila. and Reading R. R. Co., 11 Harris, 373.

A railroad company is bound to keep its track and land contiguous clear of all materials likely to be ignited from sparks from its engines, properly driven.

Penna. R. R. Co. *v.* Hope, 30 Sm. 373.

In the absence of special legislation a man does not become a wrong doer by leaving his property in a state of nature, nor is he bound to anticipate negligence on the part of another, and to provide against its effects.

Salmon v. Delaware, Lackawanna and Western R. R. Co., 14 Am. L. R. N. S. 554.
Phila. and Reading R. R. Co. v. Hendrickson, 30 Sm. 182.
Lehigh Valley R. R. v. McKeen, 7 WEEKLY NOTES, 369.

The question of negligence in running an engine with a defective spark-arrester was for the jury. It would have been error to have withdrawn from the jury the evidence as to the fires caused by this engine.

Huyett v. Phila. and Reading R. R. Co., 11 Harris, 373.
Lackawanna and Bloomsburg R. R. v. Doak, 2 Sm. 379.

May 3, 1880. THE COURT. Complaint is made by the plaintiff in error, defendant below, in that, though proof was made that the locomotive, from which the plaintiff's property was fired, was furnished with an approved spark-arrester, yet the Court submitted the question of negligence to the jury. This, however, was necessitated by the fact that the testimony of the plaintiff was in serious conflict with the allegation above stated. It is indeed true that a locomotive cannot be run without fire; that human ingenuity has not as yet devised any contrivance which will wholly arrest sparks, so if these now so important vehicles are to be run at all, more or less damage in the way of fire must result from them. Therefore, the rule of law is, and must be, that if reasonable precautions are taken in providing them with those appliances which are deemed best for the prevention of such damage, the company or persons using them cannot be made liable though they fire every rod of the country through which they run. In accordance with this now well established rule of law, we have but recently held that the mere fact of the firing of a property will not of itself prove negligence, where it is shown that approved spark-arresters were in use. (Jennings v. Railroad Company, not reported,*) But unfortunately

* Oct. & Nov. T. '78, 264.
Jennings v. Pennsylvania R. R. Co.

OPINION OF THE COURT.

November 10, 1879. THE COURT. This case cannot be distinguished from the Philadelphia and Reading Railroad Co. v. Yerger (23 P. F. Smith, 121), which was followed in Erie Railway Co. v. Decker (28 Ibid. 293), in which it was held that evidence to prove defects in other engines of the company, was irrelevant, and should have been excluded. In the case now before us, there was no evidence to show that the locomotive from which the plaintiff's fences, hay, and grass caught fire, was improperly constructed and had not an approved spark-arrester. There was some evidence that on some occasions sparks larger than common issued from engines on the road, but for the defendant in this case, the plaintiff furnished abundant proof, that the engine in question, either was not furnished with the necessary spark-arresting appliances, or if so, they had been tampered with by the persons in charge thereof. On any other theory it is unaccountable that this locomotive alone, of all run upon the road, should have fired the country through which it passed, almost daily for the period of two weeks, and that it should have become so notorious in this respect that, as one of the witnesses says, "We watched for that train every day, so that we might be able to put out the fire." Moreover two of plaintiff's witnesses say that this engine threw out sparks as large as a hickory-nut, and there is the further significant testimony that shortly after the Schultz fire, this locomotive ceased to be dangerous, or as one of the witnesses said, "after this fire we had rest." This testimony was ample, if the jury believed it, to rebut that of the defendant, and the Court could do nothing else than submit it.

Again complaint is made that the Court refused to instruct the jury, that if either Schultz or the owner of the strip lying between his land and the railroad, allowed the accumulation of dry leaves, brushwood, and other rubbish on his property, which would be readily fired by sparks ordinarily issuing from a properly equipped locomotive, that might be regarded as contributory negligence. This was certainly an extraordinary proposition: first, because the learned Judge throughout the trial held, that if the defendant's locomotive was properly equipped with spark-arresting appliances, the plaintiff could not recover whether he had been careful or negligent; second, because it is an attempt to impose upon property owners along the line of a railroad, duties unknown and unnecessary before the building of the road; and third, if this proposition means anything, it means, that upon such property owners devolves the duty of guarding against the negligence of railroad companies and not from this particular engine. On the other hand the evidence on behalf of the defendants showed that this particular engine was without fault, and had been inspected not long before the occurrence.

To hold that the fact of the fire having taken place, was *prima facie* evidence that the spark-arrester was defective, and, therefore, that the case ought to have been submitted to the jury, would be practically to hold railroad companies liable for all fires: for it is notorious that no spark-arrester has yet been invented to prevent all sparks; and a little spark may kindle as large a conflagration as a large one, it depending very much on the dryness or humidity of the atmosphere whether a spark will go out before reaching the ground, and whether what it reaches is in a condition to be easily ignited. The learned Judge below was therefore entirely right in directing the jury to find a verdict for the defendants.

Judgment affirmed.
PER CURIAM.

their servants, but this is simply absurd. The plaintiff was obliged to run the risk of fires necessarily following the proper and lawful use of the defendant's locomotives, and if he was negligent in the protection of his property against such risk, the loss resulting therefrom would be his own; he could recover no compensation, not indeed because of his negligence, but because there would be no liability on part of the railroad company; but that he must guard, in any way or by any means, against the improper and unlawful use of the locomotive is a proposition that cannot be sustained. The case of the Railroad Co. *v.* Hendrickson (30 Smith, 182) is in point, and this question is so well stated and so clearly disposed of in the opinion delivered in that case by Chief Justice AGNEW, that further comment or explanation is unnecessary.

Judgment affirmed.
Opinion by GORDON, J.

Oct. & Nov. T. '79, 96.   Nov. 30, 1879.
Tebay & Bredin's Appeal.
Bredin v. Dorsey.

Opening judgment entered by warrant of attorney—Judgment note given for compounding a felony—Right of defendants to have judgment opened, upon proving that the consideration was illegal and against the policy of the law.

A note whose consideration is the stifling of a prosecution for forgery is void, and the entry of judgment thereon by virtue of a warrant of attorney, does not make it an executed contract within the maxims: "*In pari delicto potior est conditio possidentis*," and *Nemo allegans suam turpitudinem audiendus est.*"

In such case public policy requires that the defendant be heard, and if the contract be void, his relief is an incident. The principle depends on the public good, not on the merit of the defendant whose hand is as foul as the plaintiff's. But in a case of mere fraud between the parties, where the public is not interested, the maxim, "*In pari delicto*," etc., has its full force, and the law leaves the parties as they placed themselves.

While a judgment entered on warrant of attorney has the same effect as if on the verdict of a jury, while it stands, such a judgment is not necessarily a waiver of the results of adjudication, and where a defence is set up on the ground of public policy, the Court should open the confessed judgment and let the defendant into a defence.

Per TRUNKEY, J. The argument that the defendant, as actor, will not be heard alleging his own and the plaintiff's turpitude, will not avail; the plaintiff is, in one sense, the actor, he caused confession of judgment on the void instrument, and seeks the process of the law, by execution, to collect the money agreed to be paid for its violation.

Error to the Common Pleas of Butler County, and appeal from an order of the said Court discharging a rule to show cause why a judgment entered upon a judgment note, by virtue of a warrant of attorney, should not be opened, and the defendants be let into a defence.

The petitioners averred that the said judgment note was given in the compounding of a felony, and for the purpose of stifling a criminal prosecution for forgery which had been instituted by said Dorsey against one A. W. McCullough. The facts of the case, as they appear by the petition and depositions, were as follows:—

On Dec. 30, 1875, McCullough gave Dorsey a check on the Citizen's Savings Bank for $2000, "to hold as collateral for 1000 P. T. oil," certified on the face, "*Good when properly endorsed.* J. T. FOSTER, *Cashier.*" As McCullough had no funds in the bank, and no right to draw, payment was, on demand, refused.

In an action brought by Dorsey against the bank, wherein he sought to hold the bank liable, on the cashier's certificate of "good," etc., there was much testimony to show that the certificate was a forgery, but the case was decided against Dorsey on another ground, viz., that a bank cashier has no right to bind the bank by certifying a check which upon its face showed that it was not merely for the payment of money but was to be held "as collateral for oil." (See Dorsey *v.* Abrams *et al.*, 4 Norris, 299; S. C. 5 WEEKLY NOTES, 73.)

Dorsey thereupon caused to be instituted a prosecution for forgery against the said McCullough, who was arrested and indicted, and against whom a true bill was found by the Grand Jury, containing three counts, viz.; (1) Forging bank check; (2) Counterfeiting handwriting and signature; (3) Uttering forged bank check. When the case was about to be reached for trial, Dorsey stated "that he did not want to send McCullough to the penitentiary, although he was guilty as charged in said indictment, but did want and insist on getting the amount of money on said forged check;" that finally it was arranged that the judgment note in question should be given by Bredin *et al.* (connections by marriage of said McCullough) "in consideration and upon the condition that the said A. P. Dorsey, prosecutor aforesaid, should not appear to testify on the trial against the said A. W. McCullough, but that he should drop the said prosecution and permit a verdict of the petit jury in favor of said McCullough on said indictment." The note was accordingly executed and delivered, without other consideration, and, in pursuance of the bargain, when the case was called for trial, Dorsey (though present) did not appear to testify, and in the absence of testimony for the prosecution, a verdict of not guilty was rendered.

After argument the Court discharged the rule to show cause, etc., BREDIN, A. L. J., in an opinion filed, saying, *inter alia:* "The defendants therefore must rest their application entirely on the ground that part of the consideration of the note on which judgment was confessed, was the settlement and stifling of the criminal prosecution and that that, being against public policy, renders the note void. If this was a suit on a note or bond the defence could be set up, *Ex turpi causa non oritur actio*. But here the defendants are the actors, they apply to open a judgment and restrain an execution. In this attempt they are met by the maxims: *In pari delicto melior est conditio possidentis;* and *Nemo allegans suam turpitudinem audiendus est*. There are cases, indeed (such as attempts to poison the fountains of justice, and others), where the public interest demands the overthrow and exposure of the scheme, that the particeps criminis may be used for that purpose. But this is not such a case, and the agreement being executed, not executory, defendants are without remedy. . . . . . There is no difference in legal effect between a judgment confessed and a judgment on a verdict of a jury. (Hopkins *v*. West, 2 Norris, 109.) A judgment is an executed contract. So long as a contract continues executory it may not only be impeached for fraud or mistake, but any invalidity which would be a defence at law, would in general be ground for cancellation in equity; as for instance, the illegality of contracts for gaming or smuggling, or aiding prosecution. for compounding a felony or for paying usury. But a contract already executed cannot be set aside as illegal or immoral, and nothing but fraud or palpable mistake is ground for rescinding an executed conveyance. (Nace *v*. Boyer, 6 Casey, 110. See also Hershey *v*. Weiting, 14 Wright, 245; Blystone *v*. Blystone, 1 P. F. Smith, 375, and Steinbaker *v*. Wilson & Young, 1 Leg. Gazette Reports, 76.)"

The defendants took this writ, assigning for error the refusal of the Court to open the judgment and let the defendants into a defence.

John M. Thompson (with whom was *W. D. Brandon*), for appellants.

That the simple act of an individual in filing in the prothonotary's office an instrument admitted to be void against the policy of the law, shall make it valid, on the ground that by the magic of such act it is converted from an executory into an executed contract, is a perversion of the legal principle invoked, and to enforce payment by execution, while the defendant's mouth is closed against publishing the fraud, is an abuse of the process of the Court. While there is no difference, in one sense, between a judgment confessed, and a judgment entered on a verdict of a jury (Hopkins *v*. West, 2 Norris, 109), yet the Court is always bound, in its discretion, for legal cause, to open a judgment confessed by warrant of attorney.

John M. Greer, for appellee.

In order for the appellants to show that the note, or the judgment entered thereon, is invalid, they must make out such a case against Mr. Dorsey as would justify a verdict of guilty if he had been indicted for compounding a felony under the Crimes' Act of 1860, § 9 (Purd. Dig. 317, pl. 14). In such case proof is essential (1) of the actual commission of the crime, (2) that the party indicted had actual knowledge of its commission, and compounded the felony. The evidence in this case is insufficient to prove either the one or the other.

The grounds upon which the Court below refused to aid the defendants, who were actors in the suit, are well settled.

January 5, 1880. THE COURT. The maxim, "*Nemo allegans suam turpitudinem audiendus est*," is good in its use, and the authority of a long line of decisions prevents its abuse. In Collins *v*. Blantern (2 Wils. 341), a leading case, it was decided that illegality may be pleaded as a defence to an action on a bond; and so it has been held in England and this country ever since. The bond in that case was given as an indemnity for a note entered into by the obligee for the purpose of inducing a prosecutor of an indictment for perjury to withhold his evidence. After speaking of the transaction as one to gild over and conceal the truth, the Court said: " This is an agreement to stifle a prosecution for wilful and corrupt perjury, a crime most detrimental to the Commonweath; for it is the duty of every man to prosecute, appear against, and bring offenders of this sort to justice." . . . " This is a contract to tempt a man to transgress the law, to do that which was injurious to the community; it is void by the common law, and the reason why the common law says such contracts are void is for the public good." Had the defendant not been heard the Court would have known nothing of the facts, they were not set out in the bond, the plaintiff was not compelled to show them in making out his case, and on the face of the bond he was entitled to recover: all that which proved it a void contract was shown by the defendant. So in the late case of Ham *et al. v*. Smith (6 Norris, 63), the corrupt, immoral, and forbidden contract appeared in the proofs adduced by the defendant; the plaintiff made his case by showing the note, the fair looking fruit of the illegal bargain. Notwithstanding the maxim, it has been settled that where a contract or deed is made for an illegal purpose, a defendant against whom it is sought to be enforced may show the turpitude of both himself and the plaintiff, and a court of justice will decline its aid to enforce a contract thus wrongfully entered into. The principle depends on the public good, not on the merit of the defendant, whose hand is as foul as the plaintiff's. Public policy requires that he be heard, and if the contract be void, his relief is an incident. Swan *v.* Scott (11 S. & R. 155), is no exception. There the suit was on a bond, given in satisfaction of an award of arbitrators which had become a judgment; and the defendant proposed to go behind the judgment and show the illegal contract on which the award was obtained; held that he could not, and DUNCAN, J., remarked, "The test, whether a demand connected with the illegal transaction, is capable of being enforced at law, is whether the plaintiff requires the aid of the illegal transaction to establish his case." It is manifest the judgment was conclusive, though obtained in a suit on an illegal contract, and the remark strictly fitted the facts in that case, without infringing on the rule. Wherever that test has been quoted and applied, it will be found there was a good consideration for the contract in suit, before reaching back to the alleged illegal one.

Where the public is not interested, the maxim has its full force, and the law leaves the parties as they placed themselves. Obligors in an instrument under seal, made for the purpose of defrauding the obligee's wife, cannot shield themselves by alleging their own fraud; for this does not belong to the class of contracts forbidden by statute or public policy. (Evans *v.* Dravo, 12 Har. 63; Hendrickson *v.* Evans, 1 Cas. 441.) On like principle voluntary conveyances and contracts, made to defraud creditors, though void as to them, are good and binding between the immediate parties. These are voided by the statute of 13 Elizabeth, for the benefit of creditors, but not as to the parties. (Hershey *v.* Weiting, 14 Wright, 240; Blystone *v.* Blystone, 1 P. F. S. 373.) "That a collusive contract binds the parties to it, is a principle which commends itself no less to the moralist than to the jurist; for no dictate of duty calls on a Judge to extricate a rogue from his own toils." (Stewart *v.* Kearney, 6 Watts, 453.) In all such cases the actor is met by the maxim, "*In pari delicto melior est conditio possidentis.*"

Forgery, or the *crimen falsi*, is an infamous offence. It is classed with other infamous felonies and misdemeanors, the compounding of any of which is a misdemeanor punishable by fine and imprisonment. (Act March 31, 1860, § 10, P. L. 387.) Under section 9 of the Criminal Procedure Act of 1860 (P. L. 432), no magistrate or court can lawfully permit a settlement of a prosecution for forgery on satisfaction being made to the party complaining; for infamous crimes are excepted from its operation. The Legislature committed no such inconsistency as enacting two Acts of the same date, one of which prohibits the settlement of forgery under a severe penalty, and the other authorizing it, if the complaining party acknowledges satisfaction.

Cheats by false pretences are among the cases authorized to be settled by the 9th section of the Criminal Procedure Act, and therefore Steinbacher *v.* Wilson & Young (1 Leg. Gaz. Rep. 76) has no application to the question now pending. And the settlement of cases within that section is not touched by the principles applicable to the compounding of an infamous crime.

Dorsey charged McCullough with forgery, and conducted the prosecution to his indictment and acquittal. After the indictment, and before the acquittal, a bargain was struck, the judgment note given, Dorsey's claim against McCullough satisfied, and Dorsey was not to appear and testify in the forgery case. He saw the Commonwealth fail, for he did not answer to testify, though present. It cannot be doubted that the abandonment of the prosecution and failure to testify entered into the agreement. The note was given for the debt and for the acquittal, and if any part of an indivisible promise, or of an indivisible consideration for a promise is illegal, the whole is void. (Filson *v.* Himes, 5 Barr, 452.)

Agreements founded upon the suppression of criminal prosecutions are void; they have a manifest tendency to subvert public justice. (1 Sto. Eq., § 294.) It is in the nature of the crime, not so much whether it be felony or misdemeanor, which is to be considered. Many felonies are not so enormous as some misdemeanors. The law recognizes this in their punishment; for instance, the maximum of imprisonment for one convicted of forgery is ten years, of larceny three. Stifling a prosecution for forgery, though an offence of the same grade as compounding divers felonies, seems to be a graver offence than compounding some felonies. It comes within the rule, that where the welfare of society and the vindication of the law are the chief objects, the defendant may give in evidence the illegality of the contract as a bar to a suit to enforce it, and this to prevent the evil which would be produced by enforcing the contract or allowing it to stand.

Shall these objects be thwarted, and the evil follow which the law designs to prevent, because of a judgment confessed by virtue of a warrant which is but a part of the criminal transaction? It was said by the present Chief Justice, in Hopkins *v.* West (2 Norris, 109): "There is no difference in legal effect between a judgment confessed or for want of appearance or plea, and a judgment on the verdict of a jury. The Court in which the judgment is rendered will indeed open one of the former kind, and let the defendant in to a defence in a proper case, and upon equitable terms." In Pennsylvania it has always been the right of a defendant in a judgment confessed by virtue of a warrant of attorney to petition that it be opened for cause. This right was so well respected by the courts that there was no occasion for legislation providing for appeal from refusal to open till a recent date. The eptry of judgments, either by attorneys or prothonotaries on judgment notes is very common. These, though having the same effect as if on the verdict of a jury, while they stand, in fact never waive the results of adjudication.

To hold that such a judgment, entered on an immoral and illegal obligation, part of a transaction subversive of public interest, shall be deemed an executed contract, with absolute right in the plaintiff to judicial process for collection, would be shocking to every man's sense of justice. The argument is that the judgment shall stand, for the plaintiff need only show the note, and the defendant, as actor, will not be heard alleging his own and the plaintiff's turpitude in an application for opening the judgment. In one sense the plaintiff is an actor, he caused confession of judgment on the void instrument, and uses the process of the law to collect the money agreed to be paid for its violation.

The reason of the rule which allows a defendant to plead and prove the illegality of a contract in bar of a suit upon it, demands that he be heard on an application to open a judgment so confessed, and he is not heard for their vindication. It is the duty of the Court, on proper showing, to open such a judgment, to the end that there may be a trial as if suit had been originally commenced on the note, or other obligation, on which the judgment was entered. In this way the law may be vindicated, and the interests of the Commonwealth conserved.

The order and decree, discharging the rule to show cause why judgment should not be opened, reversed, and now the said rule is made absolute; the record to be remitted for further proceeding. Appellees to pay costs of this appeal.

Opinion by TRUNKEY, J. STERRETT, J., absent.

[*Cf.* Shisler *v.* Vandike, 8 WEEKLY NOTES, 234; Nat. Bank of Oxford *v.* Kirk, 7 Id. 256; Swope *v.* Jefferson Ins. Co., 8 Id. 481.]

Jan. '80.   March 3, 1880.
Biery v. Ziegler.

Landlord and tenant — Use and occupation — Ante-nuptial lease by wife — Non-liability of husband.

A., a widow, contracted with B. for the rent of a house for a term certain. Before the end of the term A. married, but continued to live in the house, her husband not living with her continually, but visiting her from time to time. In an action by B. against the husband of A. for use and occupation:

Held (reversing the judgment of the Court below), that the husband was an entire stranger to the contract, and that under the circumstances no liability arose on his part from his legal obligation to support and maintain his wife.

Error to the Common Pleas of Berks County.

Action for use and occupation of premises in the village of Shamrock by Philip Ziegler against Uriah Biery. Plea, non assumpsit, etc.

Upon the trial, before HAGENMAN, P. J., the following facts appeared:—

In 1871 Mrs. Tellem, a widow, was the tenant of the plaintiff under a parol contract made with her some time in 1871, which tenancy was to expire April 1, 1872. About Christmas, 1871, while still a widow, she renewed the lease with Ziegler for the year commencing the following April, the rent agreed upon being $75. On the 23d of February, 1872, she married Biery, the defendant, and continued to reside in the house as before—her husband living at his boarding house in the same village, where he had resided for a number of years, but frequently visiting her and occasionally remaining with her over night. She was not in good health, and in July, 1872, was taken by her husband to his boarding house, where she stayed till October, when she was removed to her mother's house, in which place she died November 30, 1872. The testimony shows that while she was living in Ziegler's house after April, 1872, she had a child born, which died soon after birth, and was buried from said house, and that one of Biery's children by a former wife was living with her for a short time. Also, that defendant sent some articles of furniture to the house; that his wife's goods remained in the house till January, 1873, when he made sale of them; that in February, 1873, he returned the key of the house to Ziegler, and took out letters of administration on her estate December 13, 1873.

The plaintiff claimed to recover against the defendant for use and occupation of the house from the time of defendant's marriage to the time the key was returned, without regard to the contract of the wife made *dum sola*, the terms of which were testified to by the plaintiff himself.

The defendant presented, *inter alia*, the following points: (4) Mrs. Tellem contracted to rent the premises for the year commencing April 1, 1872, before her marriage, and continued to occupy them separately from her husband until shortly before her death in November, 1872. Under her contract the husband is not liable for the rent. Nor would he be liable under such circumstances, if he had occupied the house with her from April, 1872. (5) That if the facts given in evidence by the plaintiff be true, there is no cause of action shown.

The above points were answered together as follows: "The plaintiff does not seek to recover on the contract made between plaintiff and Mrs. Tellem before marriage, but for use and occupation after marriage, on her husband's legal obligation to support and maintain his wife. If the jury find from the evidence that the wife continued to reside in the house with the husband's consent, and he in part with her, the defendant is liable for such an amount as the use and occupation of the house were reasonably worth."

(6) Under all the testimony in the case the plaintiff is not entitled to recover. *Refused.*

The Court charged the jury, *inter alia*, as follows: "If the jury find that the wife, after her marriage, continued to occupy the house and resided in it with the consent and permission of her husband, the case falls within that rule which binds a husband for the support and maintenance of his wife, especially so if he to some extent occupied it with her. In such case the defendant is liable, not on the contract made by his wife before marriage, but for such an amount as the use and occupation were reasonably worth subsequently to the marriage, whilst the house was so occupied."

Verdict and judgment for the plaintiff. The defendant took this writ, assigning for error the answers to his points and that portion of the charge of the Court above quoted.

A. G. Green and *H. Maltzberger*, for plaintiff in error.

This was a contract made with the wife when she was discovert, and her marriage made no change in her relation to the landlord *qua* contract. Nor was any liability imposed upon her husband; she having the house of her own, no necessity arose on his part to provide for her, nor did he become under any obligation to her landlord by reason of her continuing to live there after her marriage.

H. C. G. Reber (*Jeff. Snyder* with him), for the defendant in error.

May 3, 1880. THE COURT. The Act of 1848 having secured to a married woman her separate estate, it was only fair to exonerate her husband from the payment of her debts contracted before marriage. This was an attempt to compel the husband to pay the rent of a house which his wife had leased some weeks prior to his marriage to her. It appears that after the marriage the wife continued to occupy the demised premises, as she had occupied them some time prior thereto. Her husband, however, did not live with her, at least not permanently; he visited her sometimes, and occasionally stayed all night. The Court below held the husband liable for the rent, not because the landlord could recover against him upon the contract of lease with the wife made prior to the marriage, but for the use and occupation after marriage, on the ground of the husband's legal obligation to support and maintain his wife.

The error of this ruling is palpable. The duty of a man to support and maintain his wife is well settled, and may be enforced by legal process in case of his refusal or neglect to do so. But he was a stranger to this contract. The lessee was in possession of the premises under a lease when he married her. The contract and liability were hers. He no more assumed the payment of her liability under the lease than he did of her other debts, if any existed. It is true she lived in and enjoyed the use of the house for some months after her marriage, and until her death. In like manner her clothing purchased before, was worn and used after marriage—if unpaid for, the husband could not be held responsible for it.

There is nothing in the testimony of Ziegler, the landlord, from which a contract with the husband can be fairly implied. We need not discuss the question, therefore, how far a man may be liable upon his promise to pay his wife's ante-nuptial debt. He made no such promise, and without it he is under no legal duty to pay.

Judgment reversed, and a *venire de novo* awarded.

Opinion by PAXSON, J. MERCUR, J., absent.

Jan. '80.   March 31, 1880.
Leonard v. Duffin.

Notes and bills—Indebtedness contracted by married woman—Promissory note given by a third person to secure—Under what circumstances valid.

The moral obligation of a married woman to repay money borrowed by her is a sufficient consideration for a note given by a third person to secure such indebtedness.

Error to the Common Pleas of Northampton County.

Feigned issue, wherein Catharine Leonard, administratrix of Elizabeth Murtaugh, deceased, was plaintiff, and John C. Duffin and Mary Duffin were defendants, to inquire into the consideration of a judgment for $1065, entered on a judgment note with warrant of attorney to confess judgment, which judgment the Court opened and let the defendants into a defence.

Upon the trial, before MEYERS, P. J., the following facts appeared: In 1866 Samuel Duffin borrowed of Mrs. Elizabeth Murtaugh $300. Between 1866 and 1870 Jane Duffin, wife of Samuel Duffin, borrowed of Mrs. Murtaugh $600, and in the latter year Jane Duffin gave to Mrs. Murtaugh her promissory note for $900, representing her own and her husband's indebtedness. In 1871 or 1872 Jane Duffin borrowed from Mrs. Murtagh an additional $100. In 1877, these debts remaining unpaid, and Mrs. Murtaugh desiring to have security for her money, John C. Duffin and Mary Duffin, two of the children of Jane and Samuel Duffin, executed the note in question, under seal, with warrant of attorney to confess judgment, for $1065, representing the principal of the above indebtedness of Samuel and Jane Duffin, and $65 interest. Judgment was entered thereon to June Term, 1877, by Mrs. Murtaugh's administratrix, which judgment the Court, on petition, opened, and directed this issue.

The defendant, *inter alia*, presented the following point: (3) Any money borrowed by Mrs. Jane Duffin, and included in the judgment note in suit, must be deducted from the amount named in the judgment in suit. *Affirmed.*

The Court charged the jury, *inter alia*, as follows: "If you find that the consideration of the bill single was the note of $900, the loan of $100 and $65, then we charge you that the bill single by the defendants to Mrs. Murtaugh to the extent that it concluded the alleged indebtedness of Jane Duffin, a married woman, to Mrs. Murtaugh, contracted during coverture, is void, and not binding on the defendant."

Verdict for the plaintiff for $345, the amount of the indebtedness of Samuel Duffin with interest, and judgment thereon. Plaintiff took this writ, assigning for error the affirmance of defendant's third point, and that portion of the charge of the Court above quoted.

Edward J. Fox (A. S. *Knecht* with him), for the plaintiff in error.

If Jane Duffin had been a co-obligor with these defendants they would have had no defence. Her non-liability is a personal privilege arising by reason of her coverture, and does not relieve her surety, or a third person who agrees to pay her debts.

Shallcross *v.* Smith, 31 Sm. 132.
Unangst *v.* Fitler, 3 N. 135.
Hope Building Ass. *v.* Lance, 6 WEEKLY NOTES, 219.

Wm. Beidelman, for defendant in error.

There being only a moral obligation to pay, unsupported by any previous legal liability, the consideration for the bill, so far as the amount due by Mrs. Duffin, was void.

Cook *v.* Bradley, 7 Conn. 57.
Jones *v.* Ashburnham, 4 East, 455.
Pearsoll *v.* Chapin, 8 Wr. 15.
Paul *v.* Stackhouse, 2 Wr. 304.

May 3, 1880. THE COURT. This contention arose on a note executed by the defendants under seal with warrant of attorney to confess judgment. The judgment entered thereon was opened and the defendants permitted to defend. They were children of Samuel Duffin and Jane Duffin, his wife. The father and mother had each borrowed money of the plaintiff. The mother had given her individual notes for the amount of her indebtedness. The debts were due and unpaid. The note in question was given in payment of the sums due by each father and mother. The Court held that to the extent the indebtedness of the mother formed a part of the consideration there could be no recovery by reason of her coverture. This is assigned for error. It is true, as a general rule, the contract of a married woman is void, so that no action will lie against her for its breach. To this, however, there are some exceptions. Although no recovery may be had against her, it by no means follows that the equity of the claim may not be sufficient consideration to support the express promise of a third person to pay it. It has been held to be a sufficient consideration to support the promise of the wife herself, made after her coverture had ceased, and she had become *sui juris*. (Brown *v.* Bennett, 25 P. F. Smith, 420; Trout *v.* McDonald, 2 Norris, 144.) The tendency of the authorities is to treat the disability of a married woman as a personal privilege, which does not extend to any person who unites with her in a contract. Thus, if she execute a note jointly with her husband she may not be bound, yet he shall be bound for the whole. (Unangst *v.* Fitler, 3 Norris, 135; Hope Building Association *v.* Lance, not yet reported.)

If, then, the indebtedness of a married woman is a sufficient consideration to support a promise made by her after the coverture is removed, we cannot see why it may not support the promise of a third party, especially when coupled with the additional consideration shown in this case. The note in question extended the time of payment of the whole indebtedness for one year for money past due; and still further consideration is imported by the note being under seal. The learned Judge, therefore, erred in holding that the coverture of the mother, when the note was given by the defendants, constituted a defence to the extent of her indebtedness. The second and third assignments are sustained. We cannot say there was any error in opening the judgment. All the grounds alleged are not now before us.

Judgment reversed, and a *venire facias de novo* awarded.

Opinion by MERCUR, J. GREEN, J., absent.

July, '78, 40.   March 1, 1880.
Scholl v. Gerhab.

Mechanic's lien—Pleading—Validity of the lien not put in issue by pleas of non-assumpsit, payment, with leave, etc.—Act of June 16, 1836, sec. 14—What a sufficient compliance with its requirements as to time of furnishing materials.

The validity of a mechanic's lien for materials is not put in issue by the pleas of non-assumpsit, payment with leave, etc., but is a question to be taken advantage of by demurrer, or motion to strike off the lien.

A bill of particulars setting out the day and year of the first item, and the dates of the successive items in chronological order, is a sufficient compliance with the Act of June 16, 1836.

Error to the Common Pleas of Bucks County.
Scire facias sur mechanics' lien, by John Gerhab against Benjamin Scholl, owner or reputed owner and contractor, with notice to Daniel M. Kramer, terre-tenant. Pleas, non-assumpsit, payment, with leave to give special matter in evidence.

The lien, which was filed April 16, 1877, under the Act of June 16, 1836 (P. L. 699), was for materials furnished by claimant for the construction of a dwelling-house, whereof the defendant is the owner or reputed owner and contractor, consisting of lumber, doors, sashes, mouldings, etc., etc.

A bill of particulars was filed with the claim, and made part thereof, in form as follows:—

BILL OF PARTICULARS.
Telford, Pa., N. P. R. R., April 4, 1876.
Mr. BENJAMIN SCHOLL *bought of* JOHN GERHAB—
Terms cash. Interest charged after 30 days.
1876.
Jan.	17, 209 ft. pine surface boards		@	5 00	10 45
	78 ft. ⅜ inch	"		" 3 50	2 73
Feb.	10, 103 ft. pine boards			" 4 00	4 12
	30 " "			" 3 50	1 05
March 31,	3123 ft. hem. scant.			" 1 70	53 09
"	" 800 ft. yellow pine flooring			" 3 80	30 40
	etc. etc.				
	etc. etc.				
July	18, 3 square slats			" 5 75	17 25
Oct.	19, 102 ft. German siding			" 3 50	3 57
"	" 14 ft. 1½-inch moulding			" 1 00	1 40
"	" 2 transom sash			" 50	1 00
"	27, 1 1-inch door			" 1 50	1 50

Total, $602 44

On the trial, before WATSON, P. J., the evidence on the part of the plaintiff showed that in January, 1876, Benjamin Scholl bought from John Gerhab, who was a lumber man, materials for a house he was about to build. The lumber was delivered to Scholl, according to order, upon the different dates set out in the bill of particulars, Gerhab agreeing to give Scholl credit of six months on its payment. On Jan. 6, 1877, Scholl gave Gerhab his note in payment of the lumber, which on April 9, 1877, was protested for non-payment.

The plaintiff offered in evidence the lien on which the scire facias was issued. Objected to, on the ground that it was not in accordance with the requirements of the Act, because it failed to aver the time when the materials were furnished, or that they were furnished within six months last past. Objection overruled; exception. The plaintiff then rested.

On the part of the defendant, George Mitch testified that he moved into the house Sept. 14, 1876, which was finished at that time; that Henry Haines was living in the house when he went there, and that no work was done on the house after he moved there. Henry Haines testified that he moved into Scholl's house on July 25, 1876, that when he moved into it the house was finished, all but one door on the shanty, which was hung July 31st, after which no work was done. The defendant then called the three carpenters who were employed in the construction of the house, who all agreed in testifying that they had quit work July 25, 1876, when the house was finished, excepting a door to the shanty, and that the moulding and siding were all on, and the transom and other sashes, in addition to the German siding in the shanty. The defendant then closed.

In rebuttal, the plaintiff called Enos Detweiler, Gerhab's salesman, to prove that he sold lumber to Scholl on the 19th and 27th October, 1876, and that at the time he sold it to him Scholl stated that it was for this house against which the lien is filed, or for a kitchen or shanty attached to the house, to be followed by evidence that Scholl said yesterday that he purchased the materials charged on the 19th and 27th October at that time for the building upon which this lien is entered. Objected to, because (1) it is not competent to extend the right of the plaintiff to file a lien beyond six months by declarations of the original owner of the property, made after the house was completed, that it was still in process of erection; (2) that it is not competent to give any declarations of the original owner after he had parted with the title to the property, in the absence of his vendee, going to show his liability under the lien more than six months after the last alleged date; (3) that this evidence is not in rebuttal, and is irrelevant. Objection overruled; exception.

Defendant moved that Daniel M. Kramer be admitted as a party defendant to defend, averring that he acquired title to the building, against which the lien is filed, by conveyance from the defendant before the filing thereof.

Plaintiff objected, upon the ground that the

terre-tenant had no standing in Court, the jury not having been sworn as to him, and that the scire facias must conform to the parties to the lien.

The Court sustained the motion so far as to permit Mr. Kramer to appear and defend his interest in the premises, and directed that the name of the party defendant, as now entered on the record, be amended by adding thereto the words, "With notice to Daniel M. Kramer, terre-tenant." Defendant, in support of his title to the premises, offered in evidence deed: Benjamin Scholl and wife to Daniel M. Kramer, dated 11th April, 1877, acknowledged same day, recorded 23d April, 1877, for the premises in question.

Plaintiff resumed and renewed previous offers. Defendant still objected for the reasons before stated. The Court sustained the offer so far as to allow evidence to be given of the declarations of the defendant during the time he held the title to the premises, and before his conveyance to Kramer. His declarations made since that time cannot be received except for the purpose of contradicting him, and thus affecting his credibility as a witness. Exception.

Verdict and judgment for the plaintiff for $629.54 and costs.

The defendant took this writ, assigning for error, *inter alia*, the admission of the evidence excepted to.

Geo. Ross & L. L. James for plaintiff in error.

The lien does not aver when the materials were furnished, or that they were furnished within six months from the entry of the lien. Nor does the bill of particulars contain anything to identify it with the building in question, nor to show whether the dates of Oct. 19 and 27 are in the year 1876 or 1877.

The claim is, therefore, fatally defective.

McClintock *v.* Rush, 13 Sm. 203.
Lehman *v.* Thomas, 5 W. & S. 262.

The admission of Detweiler's testimony, unaccompanied by proof, or any offer to prove, as an independent fact, that the house was not then finished, was the recognition of a principle which would enable the owner of a building to extend indefinitely the statutory period within which the lien may be filed, to the prejudice of an innocent purchaser, and would open the door to fraud.

The testimony is beyond doubt conclusive that the house was finished, and, therefore, Detweiler's testimony was irrelevant. Materials furnished after a building is finished cannot create a lien.

Olympic Theatre, 2 Brown, 275.

G. & H. Lear, for defendant in error.

The question of the validity of the lien should have been raised by demurrer or motion to strike off the lien. It is not an issue for the jury.

Lee *v.* Burke, 16 Sm. 336.

The question for the jury was the time of completion of the house—Detweiler's testimony was offered to prove that the owner of the house said that the lumber bought on October 17th and 27th was for the purpose of finishing the house. To prove this by the admissions of the owner was the best evidence on the issue of fact.

May 3, 1880. THE COURT. The validity of the mechanic's lien or claim upon which the scire facias was based, was not put in issue by the pleading, and hence there was no error in permitting it to go to the jury in connection with the testimony which had been given to prove the sale and delivery of the materials specified in the claim as filed. The pleas were non assumpsit, and payment, with leave to give special matter in evidence. It was held in Lewis *v.* Morgan (11 S. & R. 234), that on a plea of payment, with leave, etc., advantage could not be taken of the invalidity of the lien, that the plea virtually admitted the averments contained in the scire facias and put the defence on collateral grounds. It is there said, that as an equitable plea, it makes room for what would sustain a bill in equity, and as a legal plea it lets in proof of direct payment or whatever may be equivalent thereto, but in every such defence, whether legal or equitable, the claim is not denied on original grounds. The subject of pleading to a scire facias on a mechanic's lien was considered in Lee *v.* Burke (16 P. F. Smith, 336), in which the pleas were, "no lien, payment, set-off, with leave," and it was held, that no question as to the sufficiency of the claim upon its face could properly arise upon the trial of issues of fact.

The plea of non-assumpsit was in effect a denial that the defendant against whom the lien was filed, both as owner and contractor, had either ordered or agreed to pay for the materials. To meet this the plaintiff introduced testimony to prove the sale and delivery to the defendant, for the building against which the lien was filed. The specific objection to the lien was that it failed "to aver the time when the materials were furnished or that they were furnished within six months last past." The authorities all agree that a question of law such as this should be taken advantage of by demurrer, or motion to strike off the lien and not in the trial of issues of fact before a jury.

But aside from the form in which the Court was asked to pass upon the alleged defects in the lien, the objections were not well taken. In the body of the claim reference is made to the annexed statement, setting "forth particularly the nature and kind of materials furnished, and the time when the same were furnished," and it is subsqeuently averred that "the said claimant hereto annexes as part of said lien a detailed statement, exhibiting the amount or sum due him, and the time when the said materials were furnished." The bill of particulars consisting of forty-six items thus connected and made part of the claim commences with "January 17, 1876," and continues regularly in chronological order to the last item under date October 27, 1876. This was a sufficient compliance with the requirements of the Act. Any one examining the claim as thus presented would readily understand when the several items from the first to the last were furnished.

The second assignment of error is not sustained. Enos Detweiler, an employé of Gerhab, was called to prove that when Scholl obtained the German siding and other material on October 19 and 27, 1876, he stated it was for the house against which the lien was filed. At that time Scholl was the owner of the property and his admissions under the circumstances were certainly competent as tending to prove not only that the building was not then finished, but also that the materials then procured by him were furnished for the building and on its credit. These were questions involved in the issue upon which the jury had to pass. The terre-tenant who was admitted to defend *pro interesse suo*, did not acquire title until two weeks after the alleged admissions were made. The offer was properly limited to proof of declarations made by Scholl during the time he owned the premises and before the date of the conveyance to Kramer.

Judgment affirmed.

Opinion by STERRETT, J.

Common Pleas—Law.

C. P. No. 4.   Aug. 1880.

In re Petition of Richard R. Randall.

Citizenship—Aliens—Minor residents—The Act of Congress of 26 May, 1824, Rev. Stat., sec. 2167, requires that an alien shall have declared at least three years before his admission that it was bona fide his intention to become a citizen of the United States—Applicants must declare their intentions in such form as to show the time when the intention to become a citizen was actually formed.

Sur petition to be admitted to citizenship.

The petition of Richard R. Randall set forth that he arrived in the port of Searsport, Maine, in the year 1851, and that, at the time of his arrival, he was under eighteen years of age; that he has continued to reside in the United States since that period; that for three years previous to his arrival of full age, it was, and still is, his *bona fide* intention to become a citizen of the United States.

The petitioner prayed that, on making proof and taking the oath prescribed by law, he may be admitted a citizen of the United States.

C. A. V.

Sept. 15, 1880. THE COURT (after reciting the facts). This petition is what is popularly denominated a minor's petition, and is founded on the Act of Congress of March 26, 1824.

That Act provides: "That any alien, being a free white person, and a minor, under the age of twenty-one years, who shall have resided in the United States three years next preceding his arriving at the age of twenty-one years, and who shall have continued to reside therein to the time he may make application to be admitted a citizen thereof, may, after he arrives at the age of twenty-one years, and after he shall have resided in the United States five years, including the three years of his minority, be admitted a citizen of the United States without having made the declaration required in the condition of the Act to which this is an addition, three years previous to his admission; *provided*, such alien shall make the declaration required therein at the time of his or her admission, and shall further declare on oath, and prove to the satisfaction of the Court, that for three years next preceding it has been his *bona fide* intention to become a citizen of the United States, and shall, in all other respects, comply with the laws in regard to naturalization."

Our Naturalization Code began by the passage of the Act of Congress of April 14, 1802.

A condition of that Act is, that before an alien can be made a citizen of the United States, he shall have declared, on oath or affirmation, before one of the courts therein mentioned, at least three years before his admission, that it was *bona fide* his intention to become a citizen of the United States.

This period is reduced to two years by the Act of May 26, 1824; and by the same Act the declaration may be made before the clerks of either of said courts.

It will be observed that by the Act of 1802 and its supplement, the declaration of intention is made before the courts or their clerks, and it is therefore known to the courts, or can be shown by their records, precisely when the intention to become a citizen is determined upon. But this means of proof is dispensed with as to minor aliens who shall have resided in the United States three years next preceding their arriving at the age of twenty-one years; and it requires, instead, that the petitioner shall declare on oath *and prove*, not "or prove," to the satisfaction of the Court, that for three years next preceding it has been the *bona fide* intention of such alien to become a citizen, etc. "He shall prove" means he shall furnish the evidence to establish the proof to the Court's satisfaction; not by his oath, for that the Act requires independently of the proof demanded by the Act. In other words, the Act requires that both the *oath* of the petitioner *and proof* shall be submitted to the Court to enable it to determine whether or not the petitioner is entitled to citizenship. This view is strengthened by recalling the fact that at the time of the passage of the Act in question, no party to any issue raised in his own behalf was a competent witness to prove that issue, and it cannot rationally be inferred that our law-makers meant that the proof could be shown by the evidence of one incompetent to testify. To this view, it may be answered that, since then, the law has rendered a party to a proceeding a competent witness, notwithstanding his interest. True; but that law has not altered the Act we are considering, which requires proof independently of the petitioner's oath. Indeed, when we consider that the Act of 1824 dispenses with the high grade of proof established by the record under the Act of 1802, it does no violence to reason to conclude that it meant that something more than the mere oath of the petitioner should be submitted for the judgment of the Court to pass upon, especially as the Act requires, in express words, proof in addition to such oath.

Having thus ascertained the law, let us examine the proof. There is no evidence whatever, independently of the petitioner's oath, of the time he formed the intention to become a citizen. In addition to the recitals in his petition, he states orally that he is now thirty-eight years old. If he formed the intention three years before he arrived at the age of twenty-one, it is remarkable, indeed, that he should have taken no steps for seventeen years to put his intention into practical effect. Without evidence to explain this great delay, his conduct is totally inconsistent with his oath, and furnishes a striking illustration of the wisdom of the Act in requiring proof.

Man, naturally, is social and communicative, and it is indeed rare that when he forms an important determination, or establishes a fixed intent and purpose, he does not in some way communicate it to his friends and associates. When this is done, his acts and declarations are susceptible of easy proof. The mere fact that a minor has resided in the United States for at least five years during his minority, or for three years only before arriving at age, and comes into Court, in the former case, soon after attaining his majority, and in the latter soon after he has resided here for the five years provided in the Act, and petitions the Court for citizenship, is in itself strong evidence that he formed the intent at the time stated in his oath.

It is therefore clear to me that the Act of 1824 was not passed for such a case as the one before me. The petitioner could long since have become a citizen, by declaring his intention under the Act of 1802. That he has not done so, and did not, under the Act of 1824, soon after he became of age, invoke the benefits of that Act, is convincing to me that this is but an expedient to procure a certificate of citizenship upon a minor's petition, in order to get rid of the two years' delay incident to declaring his intention, according to the Act of 1802.

For weeks our court-room has been densely packed with petitioners for citizenship, taxing to the utmost the entire official force of the Court to pass upon the petitions.

A large portion, indeed, I may say, the majority, of the applications are based upon minors' petitions, while many of the petitioners are over thirty years of age. To demand audience for such petitions, without evidence to explain the delay, is an insult to justice; and it is high time that a decided halt be called to those indulging in such pernicious efforts.

I am disposed to be liberal in the construction of our naturalization laws, and to confer their provisions upon all who establish a right to them. But in the case before me, and those cases of like character, my plain duty is to dismiss the petitions, and, in this way, compel the applicants to declare their intentions in such form as to show the time when the intention to become a citizen was actually formed.

Petition dismissed.

Opinion by BRIGGS, J.

Supreme Court.

May, '80, 90.   May 19, 1880.
Schriver v. Eckenrode.

Statute of Frauds—Parol contract concerning land may be the subject of an action, although it cannot be enforced by specific performance—Practice—Errors and appeals—Writ of error improperly taken to judgment entered on a single issue, other issues remaining untried.

An action for breach of a parol contract concerning lands may be maintained, although specific performance of the contract could not be enforced.

A. purchased from the assignee for the benefit of creditors of B. a tract of land which B. guaranteed by parol contained a certain number of acres. A. paid the full purchase-money, and received his deed, which, however, conveyed a less number of acres, as shown by a new survey. A. then sued B. in assumpsit upon his parol contract of guaranty:

Held (reversing the judgment of nonsuit in the Court below), that A. could recover. The Statute of Frauds has no application to such a case.

Although B. had made an assignment of the land for the benefit of creditors, sufficient interest remained in him to support the collateral guaranty, in other words, he was not a mere volunteer.

A writ of error should not be taken to a judgment entered upon a single issue, prior to a trial upon other issues of fact raised by the pleadings.

Under a special plea of "former recovery" and a replication thereto praying that the same might "be inquired of the record," the Court entered judgment for defendant, but no trial was had under the general issue, which had also been pleaded. Upon a writ of error the Supreme Court, assuming the issues of fact had been disposed of, reversed the judgment and entered judgment upon the special plea for the plaintiff (without a *venire* or *procedendo*). The plaintiff thereupon, by leave of the Court below, issued execution:

Held, to be error. The effect of the judgment of the Supreme Court for the plaintiff upon the special plea was, under the circumstances, only an adjudication that the former action was no bar to the present.

Error to the Common Pleas of Adams County.

Assumpsit, by George I. Schriver against Elijah Eckenrode, to recover the value of the difference between the actual and the represented quantity of a certain tract of land. The plaintiff declared upon a contract of guaranty by the defendant, to wit: that the tract in question, purchased by plaintiff from the defendant's assignee for the benefit of creditors, contained 144 acres, while in fact it contained but 132 acres and a fraction.

The plaintiff had previously brought an action on the case for deceit, based upon the same claim, in which the verdict was for the defendant, and the defendant now pleaded specially "former recovery," upon which issue judgment was entered in the Court below for defendant, but this was reversed by the Supreme Court, and "judgment entered for the plaintiff upon the special plea." (See 6 Norris, 213.)

Upon the return of the record, the plaintiff obtained leave from the Court below to issue execution, to enforce the judgment as entered by the Supreme Court (no venire or procedendo having been awarded), and a rule taken by defendant to show cause why this execution should not be set aside was discharged by the Court. Upon a writ of error the order of the Court awarding execution, and discharging the rule to set it aside, was reversed, and a procedendo awarded, in the following opinion by TRUNKEY, J., filed June 9, 1879:—

"The defendant pleaded non-assumpsit, under which he could have proved a former recovery, afterwards he specially pleaded former recovery, to which the plaintiff replied, and prayed that the same might 'be inquired of by the record.' The parties seem to have submitted, informally, the latter issue to the Court, and a decision was made in favor of defendant which was reversed in this Court, and judgment entered upon the special plea for the plaintiff.

"Believing the issues of fact had been disposed of before the case was brought here, the point presented was considered. We did not apprehend the real state of the cause, else another course would probably have been adopted, though the opinion and judgment could not have been different if rendered at all. The parties did not file an agreement dispensing with a jury and submitting to the Court, and there has been no trial in any mode known to the law. Hence, by their unusual procedure, they have obtained a formal judgment upon a single question which ought to have been tried with others of fact, to be followed by a lawful trial, and possibly more writs of error. The delay and costs will be persuasive that it is unprofitable to obtain a judicial determination of such questions by piecemeal. Nor is it always safe, for had there been an actual trial how could it be said every question of fact was not disposed of?

"Upon return of the record execution was awarded to the plaintiff. There was nothing to authorize this action. At most the judgment entitled him to an inquiry of damages, and in justice not to that. The pleadings raised the general issue, which put upon the plaintiff the burden of proving his claim ; and the defendant had waived nothing, and had made no express or implied agreement that the Court should examine any fact save one, and that by inspection of the record. By concerted action of the parties—one could not have done it alone—the Court was induced to give judgment on the special plea. Neither could have intended that to settle the question of indebtedness, or its amount, for they made no agreement to that effect, and the general issue remained of record. Therefore, the judgment for plaintiff upon the special plea must be held as only an adjudication that the former action is no bar to recovery in this. To suffer it to go further would give one party an advantage to which he is not justly entitled.

"The order of the Court awarding a fieri facias is reversed, and said writ set aside ; record remitted, and procedendo awarded."

Upon the trial, before McCLEAN, P. J., the plaintiff's evidence was substantially as follows: That he had purchased the farm in question from J. N. Durborow, the assignee for benefit of creditors of Eckenrode; that when he went to look at the place, he was shown over it by Eckenrode, who was in possession, and who stated to him that it contained 144 acres, and that the price was $5000. The assignee was not present, but the defendant stated that he was authorized to sell it, and that Durborow would be satisfied with whatever he did, and that the articles could be made with Durborow. The parties met a second time, the assignee being present, and Eckenrode again stated that the farm contained 144 acres. Schriver made a calculation at $31.25 per acre for 144 acres, making $4500, and, showing it to Eckenrode, asked him if he was sure there were 144 acres in the farm. Eckenrode replied that he was sure, and would guarantee it. Schriver then offered $4500 to the assignee, who said he would sell the farm as he had advertised it, for 140 acres, more or less, as he had not the deeds in his possession. He then concluded to accept Schriver's offer, and an agreement was made between Durborow and Schriver for the sale of the farm for $4500. On preparing the deed the farm was found to contain but 132 acres and 126 perches, neat measure, and was so described. Schriver took the deed, paid the purchase-money, and subsequently brought this action against Eckenrode on his agreement of guaranty.

The plaintiff having closed his case, the defendant moved for a nonsuit, which the Court granted, and upon motion and argument refused to take it off. (No opinion filed.)

The plaintiff thereupon took this writ, assigning as error the refusal of the Court to take off the nonsuit.

R. G. McCreary, for plaintiff in error.
The case was fully made out. We proved an agreement for a valuable consideration, a breach of defendant's undertaking, and damage resulting.
The agreement was not within the Statute of Frauds. It was a separate and independent agreement upon a consideration moving between the parties, concerning a matter about which it was competent for them to contract.
Arnold v. Stedman, 9 Wr. 186.
The claim is not against the vendor. A parol promise, if on a good consideration, in cases not affected by the Statute of Frauds, is as binding as a specialty.
Shoenberger's Exec'rs v. Zook, 10 Casey, 24.

David Wills, contra.
The contract was for the sale of land, and was executed. The plaintiff has no recourse to the defendant for a deficiency in the number of acres, except for fraud, and then the proper form of action is upon the case for deceit.
Chitty on Contracts, 311.
1 Chitty's Pleading, 154.
Kreiter v. Bomberger, 1 Norris, 59.
Gregory v. Griffin, 1 Barr, 208.
Farmers and Mechanics' Bank v. Galbraith, 10 Barr, 490.
Jones v. Wood, 4 Harris, 25.
Plaintiff's claim is against the vendor, because he claims for a deficiency. The case is within the Statute of Frauds of March 21, 1772. The written agreement contains no guaranty. The attempt is to modify it by parol, which cannot be done.
Soles v. Hickman, 8 Harris, 180.
Ferguson v. Staver, 9 Casey, 411.
Smith's Appeal, 19 Sm. 474.
The assignee was the representative of the defendant, and not of creditors. He was not a purchaser for value, but a mere volunteer.
Twelves v. Williams, 3 Whar. 485.
Mellon's Appeal, 8 Casey, 121.
Fulton's Estate, 1 Sm. 204.
Spackman v. Ott, 15 Sm. 131.
Jordan v. Sharlock, 3 Norris, 366
The contract of guaranty is collateral and conditional, and the principal must first incur liability and be first pursued.
Chitty on Contracts, 499.
Kramph's Executrix v. Hatz's Exec'r, 2 Sm. 525.

June 21, 1880. THE COURT. If the Court ordered the nonsuit in this case under the impression that the defendant's parol guaranty could not be enforced because of the Statute of Frauds and Perjuries, it made a mistake. In this State it is well-settled law that an action will lie upon parol contracts concerning lands, though they be such that specific performance of them will not be enforced. Such is the doctrine of Thompson v. Sheplar (22 P. F. S. 160) and of Frederick and Campbell (13 S. & R. 136) the latter case holding that in an action upon a bond for purchase-money, parol evidence was admissible to show that at the time of the execution of the deed the vendor declared that he had good title to two hundred and twenty-five acres of land, and would warrant that quantity. Now Eckenrode did expressly warrant that the tract of land thus about to be conveyed, did contain 144 acres, and though he had made an assignment of the premises to Durborow for the benefit of his creditors, yet there was such an interest remaining in him as was sufficient to support the undertaking here alleged; in other words, he was not a mere volunteer. Thus the very nature of the alleged contract between the parties was such, that had it been in writing, specific execution of it could not have been compelled, for it was not intended that the deficiency should be made good in land. Schriver was about to pay $4500 for a certain defined tract of land, and the warranty could have meant nothing more than this, that if there should turn out to be a deficiency in the guaranteed amount of land, Eckenrode would make it good, not in land, but in money. Let us now suppose the plaintiff to have purchased on the faith of the agreement of the defendant that the farm should contain 144 acres, we have, then, this condition of affairs: the plaintiff has been obliged to pay the whole amount of the purchase-money to the assignee, who, of course, was not bound by the guaranty, and yet he gets but 132 acres, while the price paid for the fourteen acres which the defendant undertook to see that he should have, has, as we discover from the final account of the assignee, gone into Eckenrode's pockets. This is neither just nor lawful, and if the jury should find, as they may find, the case to be as above supposed, this money honestly belongs to Schriver, and he ought to have it.

The exception which embraces the ruling of the Court on the question of the exclusion of evidence proposed by the plaintiff, is not sustained. The judgment is reversed, and a new venire is awarded.

Opinion by GORDON, J. SHARSWOOD, C. J., and GREEN, J., absent.

May, '80, 149.   June 15, 1880.
Wingerd v. Fallon.

Husband and wife—Debtor and creditor—Wife as creditor—Confession of judgment by one in failing circumstances in favor of wife—When not fraudulent as against other creditors—What is sufficient consideration for such judgment—Under what circumstances a family arrangement, to consider a certain sum as an advancement, will be upheld—Fraud, when evidence insufficient to be submitted to the jury.

A man indebted to his wife and other creditors may lawfully confess a prior judgment in his wife's favor for the amount honestly due to her.

The assignment to the wife, as part of her distributive share of her father's estate, of notes given by her husband to her father, constitutes a valid consideration for such a confession of judgment, for the amount of the notes, with interest.

Where one of the notes, included in the confessed judgment, was not assigned to the wife, but it was alleged by her that its amount was an advancement to her, received and used by her husband, and it was agreed, by a family arrangement, to consider it as an advancement, to be deducted from her share of the real estate:

Held, that the amount of the note, with interest, was properly embraced in the confessed judgment.

Where a judgment was lawfully confessed to a trustee by a man in favor of his wife, the issuing of execution thereon, whereby other creditors are postponed, is not of itself evidence of fraud, and it was error to submit to the jury the question of fraud, unsupported by other evidence.

Error to the Common Pleas of Franklin County.

Feigned issue, between Charles H. Fallon and Lizzie G. Fallon, his wife, and Virginia C. Wingerd, to test the validity of a judgment confessed by Adam B. Wingerd in favor of Virginia C. Wingerd, his wife.

The material facts were as follows:—

On Dec. 23, 1878, A. B. Wingerd executed a judgment bond to John Stewart, Esq., in trust for his wife, Virginia C. Wingerd, for the sum of $10,000. Judgment was entered Feb. 24, 1879, and the same day a fi. fa. was issued thereon. By virtue of this writ, the sheriff levied on and sold the personal property of defendant to Mrs. Wingerd, for $1537.21,

On March 7, 1879, a fi. fa. was issued by Charles H. Fallon and Lizzie G. Fallon on a later judgment obtained against Wingerd, and his personal property was seized in execution. The sum of $1537.21 above mentioned was paid into Court, and constituted the fund in controversy.

The Court, on petition, directed the following issues to test the validity of Mrs. Wingerd's judgment, viz.:—

(1) Whether, on the 24th day of February, 1879, when Adam B. Wingerd confessed this judgment to John Stewart, Esq., in trust for his wife, Virginia C. Wingerd, for $10,000, he was in fact indebted to the said Virginia in that sum.

(2) Whether the said judgment was confessed by the said Adam B. Wingerd, and was accepted and entered in the Court of Common Pleas, by the said Virginia C. Wingerd by collusion, with intent to delay, hinder, or defraud the creditors of the said A. B. Wingerd.

(3) Whether the said judgment was held, kept on foot, and used by the said Virginia C. Win-

gerd, in collusion with said Adam B. Wingerd, with intent to hinder, delay, and defraud the creditors of the said Adam B. Wingerd.

On the trial, before ROWE, P. J., the evidence showed that A. B. Wingerd had at sundry times received from his wife's father, Joshua Motter, large sums of money, for which at his decease, said Motter held the following notes: One for $2300, dated 25th of June, 1869, another for $800, dated 2d September, 1871, another for $750, dated 13th January, 1873, another for $300, and still another for $215.

On the first account settled by the administrator, Mrs. Wingerd's distributive share of the estate amounted to $1846.46, which was settled by her acceptance of the following notes against her husband, indorsed to her, viz.:—

The $800 note and interest, $879.61, the note of $750 and interest, $826, making $1705.61, together with a note of her husband for $140.85, leaving in the hands of the administrator the note for $2300 and a note for $445.14 given by Wingerd, and accepted by the administrator. This latter note, and the one for $140.85 given by Wingerd to his wife, liquidated the notes for $300 and $215, with interest.

On the administrator's second and final account, Mrs. Wingerd's distributive share was $3089.66, which was settled in part by her acceptance of the $445.14 note and interest. This note was assigned to Mrs. Wingerd's mother, by a mistake, as claimed by her. She assumed the payment of it.

It was contended by the defendant that the $2300 note was really an advancement made by her father to her, and not a debt of her husband, and that by agreement, made at the time of the advancement, between Mrs. Wingerd and her father and her husband, and afterwards reduced to writing, Mr. Wingerd was to have the money as a loan, and pay interest to his wife. The note by its terms bore no interest. It was further agreed at a family council, in November, 1878, that the $2300 should be considered as an advancement, and held against Mrs. Wingerd's share of the real estate. The plaintiffs contended that the $2300 was a debt due by Mr. Wingerd to Motter's estate.

All the above notes, with interest, and some undisputed amounts, were included in the judgment for $10,000, which was computed by Mr. Stewart from approximate data given him by Mr. Wingerd, and in his wife's absence. The judgment was entered and execution issued by Mr. Stewart, without instructions from Mrs. Wingerd, pursuant to his duty as her counsel and trustee, and for the purpose of protecting her interests.

The defendant requested the Court to instruct the jury that the $2300 should be considered as an advancement to Mrs. Wingerd, and presented among others, the following points:—

(2) Even if the jury should believe that the receipt of the $2300 on the 25th of June, 1869, by Mr. Wingerd from Mr. Motter, was a loan to him, and not an advancement to his wife; still if the jury further believe that subsequent to the death of Mr. Motter, at a meeting in November, 1878, for settlement of the distribution on the final administration account, the widow and all the children of the deceased were present, and that they were all at the time of full age, and that it was then agreed by the widow and all the children, that the note of $2300 should not be collected from Mr. Wingerd, but that it should be treated as an advancement to his wife, and deducted from her share of the real estate when sold, and that Mr. and Mrs. Wingerd both acquiesced in and assented to this arrangement, such a family arrangement would be good in law, and operate to convert the note into an advancement. *Refused.* (First assignment of error.)

(4) If the jury believe from the evidence, that Mr. Wingerd actually received the $2300 from Mr. Motter on the 25th of June, 1869, and used it for his own purposes, and it was understood at the time between Mr. Motter and Mr. Wingerd and his wife, that it was to be an advancement to her, in anticipation of her share of her father's estate; or if by the family arrangement referred to in the second point (if the jury believe such family arrangement was in fact made) the note was converted into an advancement, then Mr. Wingerd could lawfully embrace this sum in the judgment, together with interest thereon, from the 25th of June, 1869, if the jury believe that he at that time agreed to pay his wife interest on the money. *Refused.* (Second assignment.)

(5) Even if the note of $2300 is to be treated as a debt of Mr. Wingerd, and not as an advancement to his wife, yet if the jury believe from the evidence that at the meeting of the widow and children in November, 1878, on the occasion of the settlement of the final distribution of the personal estate, Mrs. Wingerd assumed the payment of the $2300, and agreed that it should be taken off her share of the real estate, and the widow and all the children assented to this arrangement, and in consequence thereof the matter was permitted to rest in that way until the present time, and no steps were taken by the administrator of Mr. Motter to collect the note from Mr. Wingerd, such an agreement by Mrs. Wingerd, if her husband actually received the money, and the claim was an honest one, would create a moral obligation on her part to pay it, and the amount might be legally embraced in the judgment given to her by her husband. Her coverture is a personal privilege which she may waive; she is not bound to avail

herself of it for the benefit of her husband's creditors. *Refused.* (Third assignment.)

(8) There is no evidence at all to sustain the 2d and 3d issues made up by the pleadings. *Refused.* (Fifth assignment.)

The Court charged the jury, *inter alia,* as follows :—

"If it was a debt at the death of Mr. Motter, I see nothing in the evidence to make it anything else, or to make Mrs. Wingerd entitled to it now, as creditor. The agreement of the heirs that it should stand over and be deducted from the realty could not have that effect, nor would such arrangement by the administrator." (Fourth assignment.)

"I read and affirm plaintiff's third point, viz. : If the jury believe from all the evidence that the $2300 given by Joshua Motter to A. B. Wingerd was a loan and not an advancement, neither A. B. Wingerd nor his wife could change this sum from a loan to an advancement. And if a loan, as against creditors, A. B. Wingerd could not agree to pay interest on this sum to his wife. And if the jury find that there is included in the $10,000 judgment, interest on the $2300, from June, 1869, to December, 1878, such portion of the judgment is void as to creditors."

"The other two issues raise the question of collusion and fraud. If Mrs. Wingerd took this judgment with intent to delay or defraud creditors; or if she used it by issuing execution on it with the same intent, you ought to find the fact. But if this judgment is upon a full consideration, if Mr. W. actually and honestly owed his wife the sum of $10,000, then I see no evidence at all of fraud. If there are some elements of her claim not established, by the clear and satisfactory evidence which the laws demand that she shall produce, so that you find her judgment must be reduced in amount—as for instance, the $445 note, or the $300.44, or both, but if you are nevertheless of opinion that she was actuated by no fraudulent purpose in taking it for the sum she did, then you would not find the fraud. But if she took it for a much larger sum than was just, for $2300, or interest $1300, or both, and under such circumstances as that she must have so known—that itself, or in connection with the haste in execution, would show the fraud, and in such case you ought to find that issue for plaintiff."

The jury found for the plaintiffs on all the issues, and on the first issue they found specially that A. B. Wingerd was indebted to Virginia C. Wingerd in the sum of $7700 at the time of giving said judgment.

Judgment having been entered on the verdict, the defendant took this writ, assigning for error, *inter alia,* the refusal of the Court to instruct as requested, and the portions of the charge above quoted.

John Stewart and *J. McD. Sharpe,* for plaintiff in error.

The agreement made between Mr. and Mrs. Wingerd and the widow, heirs, or administrators of Mr. Motter, that the money mentioned in the note should be treated as, and converted into an advancement, was a legal transaction, and gave Mrs Wingerd a right to have the $2300 embraced in the judgment. She was under a moral obligation to pay the money.

A husband may in law prefer his wife to other creditors.

There was no evidence of *mala fides* to go to the jury.

Battles *v.* Laudenslager, 3 Norris, 447.
Ryder *v.* Wombwell, Law Rep. 4 Exch. 39.
Jewell *v.* Parr, 13 C. B. 916.
Goodman *v.* Simonds, 20 Howard, 360.
Bunn, Raiguel & Co. *v.* Ahl, 5 Casey, 390.
Davenport *v.* Wright, 1 P. F. Smith, 292.
Gicker's Admr. *v.* Martin, 14 Wright, 142.
Davis *v.* Charles, 8 Barr, 82.
Zerbe *v.* Miller, 4 Harris, 497.
Ferris *v.* Irons, 2 Norris, 182.
Brown's Appeal, 5 Norris, 528.

W. S. Stenger, for defendants in error.

The plaintiff in error assumes that the jury disallowed the note of $2300 in their verdict. The amount found to be due could be reached in other ways. Hence, arguments based on this assumption are worthless.

A family council cannot change a note into an advancement. The note of $2300 is a debt of Mr. Wingerd to the estate.

The question of fraud was properly left to the jury.

Mellinger's Admr. *v.* Bausman's Trustee, 9 Wright, 529.
Clark *v.* Douglas, 12 P. F. Smith, 415.
Gault *v.* Saffin and wife, 8 Wright, 307.
Hamet *v.* Dundass, 4 Barr, 182.
Young *v.* Edwards, 22 Smith, 266.
Graybill *v.* Moyer, 9 Wright, 533.
Deakers *v.* Temple *et al.,* 5 Wright, 234.
Stewart *v.* Fenner, 31 Smith, 177.
Bunn, Raiguel & Co. *v.* Ahl, 5 Casey, 387.
Gans *v.* Renshaw, 2 Barr, 34.

June 23, 1880. THE COURT. This was a feigned issue to test the validity of a judgment of $10,000, confessed by Adam B. Wingerd in favor of John Stewart, Esq., as trustee for Virginia C. Wingerd, wife of the said Adam B. Wingerd, and the defendant in the feigned issue. The jury found for the plaintiff in all the issues with this special finding, however, as to the first : "That the said A. B. Wingerd was indebted to the said Virginia C. Wingerd in the sum of $7700 at the time of the giving of the said judgment."

This indebtedness was made up in the main of notes which A. B. Wingerd had given his wife's father for borrowed money, and which after his death had been assigned to Mrs. Wingerd by his administrator, on account of her distributive share of her father's estate. That the possession of these notes, thus acquired, constituted Mrs. Wingerd a creditor of her husband to the amount due thereon is not disputed. There was, however, a note for $2300, which was disputed, at least the right of Mrs. Wingerd to include it in the judgment was denied, and forms the subject of the first three assignments of error. There was some question whether this note was an advancement made by Mrs. Wingerd's father, or a debt due by her husband to his estate. It was certainly one or the other, and in either event it reduced Mrs. Wingerd's share of her father's estate by precisely that amount. Although not formally assigned to her, it is held against her share of the estate, and will ultimately be deducted therefrom. She would then be entitled to an assignment. In the mean time she is practically security to the estate for the amount. There is no good reason why she may not take indemnity from her husband. That she may not have a present cause of action against him is not to the point. She has a just claim, which if the husband chooses to recognize no creditor has a right to gainsay. It has been held no longer ago than the present term that it was not a fraud upon creditors for a husband to confess a judgment in favor of his wife for a claim old enough to be barred by the Statute of Limitations, if it were applicable. If he does not choose to set up the bar of the statute to defeat a past claim, the creditors cannot do so for him. The defendant's second point should have been affirmed without qualification. This ruling also sustains the 2d, 3d, and 4th assignments.

The fifth assignment alleges that the Court erred in refusing to affirm the defendant's eighth point. Said point called upon the Court to say to the jury that there was no evidence to sustain the question of fraud raised by the 2d and 3d issues. This point should have been affirmed. There was not sufficient evidence of fraud to submit to the jury; there was not even a scintilla. There was nothing beyond an effort on the part of Mrs. Wingerd's trustee to collect the money due from her husband. If it was lawful for him to confess the judgment it was not unlawful for the trustee to collect it.

The sixth and last assignment is also sustained. The jury were allowed to infer fraud where none existed.

Judgment reversed.
Opinion by PAXSON, J.

May, '80, 79.   May 4, 1880.

Shrewsbury Savings Institution's Appeal.

Debtor and creditor—Collateral securities—Renewal of notes secured by a judgment.

A judgment bond, given by a borrower to secure a loan in a savings institution, was conditioned "as collateral security for sundry notes" given or drawn by the lender or indorsed by him or the firm of which he was a member, and held by the aforesaid savings institution:

Held (reversing the decree of the Court below), that a note given as a renewal of other notes existing at the time the judgment was given, was covered by the condition of the bond.

The bond was collateral to the debt and not to the notes merely.

The renewal of the original notes did not constitute a novation.

Subsequent judgment creditors were bound by their debtor's act. He had no equity to be relieved of the lien of the prior collateral judgment without payment of the debt, and they showed no higher equity than he had.

Appeal of the Shrewsbury Savings Institution from the decree of the Court of Common Pleas of York County, distributing the proceeds of the sheriff's sale of real estate of Henry Seitz.

The auditor appointed to distribute the fund, (John W. Bittenger), reported the following facts:—

That on June 19, 1875, Henry Seitz, the defendant in the executions, was indebted to the Shrewsbury Savings Institution in an amount for which the institution held his notes or indorsements; that on said date the said Henry Seitz, executed a *judgment note* to the said Shrewsbury Savings Institution, for the sum of $6000 payable one day after date "as *collateral security* for *sundry notes* given or drawn by the said Henry Seitz or indorsed by him, or by Samuel Seitz & Co., and held by aforesaid Shrewsbury Savings Institution;" that on the same day judgment was entered thereon. Further, that the said notes which the judgment was given to secure, or some of them, were from time to time renewed by new notes being given, and the old notes surrendered. The final renewal was made by giving a consolidated note for $700 in place of two notes, previously given.

The cashier of the Savings Institution testified that he took the renewals on the credit of the collateral judgment. No action of the board of directors on the subject was shown, and no agreement with Henry Seitz, the defendant, that the judgment should be collateral security for the renewed notes.

The Savings Institution claimed to be awarded the amount of the *debt*, as evidenced by one of the original notes, which they still held, and further by the renewal and consolidated note for $700.

The fund for distribution was also claimed by Barnhardt et al., subsequent judgment creditors of Henry Seitz, to whom the auditor awarded it, deciding that the above-mentioned judgment was given expressly to secure "sundry *notes*," and not the indebtedness itself, and that the renewal of the original notes, and the surrender of the old notes at the time of the renewals, constituted an extinguishment of the old notes, by novation.

Exceptions filed by the Shrewsbury Savings Institution were overruled by the Court (WICKES, A. L. J.), who confirmed the report of the auditor, and the Shrewsbury Savings Institution took this appeal, assigning as error the confirmation of the report of the auditor.

J. W. Latimer, for appellant.

A collateral judgment can only be discharged by payment of the debt.
Lewis *v.* Bank, 3 Whar. 531.

A renewal is not payment unless so accepted and intended.

The renewal of a note has the benefit of all securities for its payment, whether of mortgage, deed or otherwise.
1 Daniells' Negotiable Instruments, pl. 748.
Cover *v.* Black, 1 Barr, 493.
Lytle's Appeal, 12 Casey, 131.

W. C. Chapman, contra.

The words and terms of the collateral instrument do not include subsequently created paper. The equities are equal in this case, and the law must prevail. The question whether the renewal was a novation, was one of fact, and was found in our favor by the auditor.
Slaymaker *v.* Gundacker's Est., 10 S & R. 75.
Hart *v.* Boller, 15 S. & R. 162.
Macungie Savings Bank *v.* Hottenstein, 7 WEEKLY NOTES, 320.

The appellants must show error affirmatively in the finding or it will stand.
Stehman's Appeal, 5 Barr, 413.
Miller's Appeal, 6 Casey, 478.
Gilbert's Appeal, 28 Sm. 266.

The taking of new notes constituted a novation.
Ayres *v.* Wattson, 7 Sm. 360.
Moorehead *v.* Duncan, 1 Norris, 488.

October 19, 1880. THE COURT. It is conceded the judgment held by the appellant against Henry Seitz, No. 553, April Term, 1875, was given as collateral security. In the condition of the bond it is expressed to be "as collateral security for sundry notes given or drawn by the said Henry Seitz, or indorsed by him, or by said Samuel Seitz & Co., and held by aforesaid Shrewsbury Savings Institution." The note for $700, which is the subject of the present contention, was not in existence at the time the judgment was given, but the auditor finds that it is a renewal of other notes held by the savings institution, appellant, at that time. The fund for distribution is the proceeds of real estate of said Henry Seitz.

The auditor and the Court below held that the condition of the bond did not cover the renewals, and excluded the $700 note from participation in the distribution.

There was no agreement that the bond should stand for the renewals. We must look therefor at the legal effect of the condition. It was contended by the appellees, who are subsequent judgment creditors, that it was collateral to the notes merely, and not to the debt represented thereby; that the lifting of the old notes by the renewals was a *novation*, and satisfied the condition of the bond. The distinction between the note and the debt is exceedingly refined. If the judgment is collateral to the notes it is also collateral to the debt, for the reason that the notes are but the evidence of the debt, with a promise to pay it. Has the debt been paid? As between the parties to a note it has never been held that a renewal was payment unless so accepted and intended. (Hart *v.* Boller, 15 S. & R. 162; Weakly *v.* Bell, 9 Watts, 273; Hacker *v.* Perkins, 5 Wharton, 95; Oliphant *v.* Church, 7 Harris, 318; Reed *v.* Defebaugh, 12 Id. 495; Brown *v.* Scott, 1 P. F. S. 357.)

It follows that the indebtedness for which the judgment was given as collateral being still unpaid, Seitz, the debtor, has no standing to allege that the note is not protected by the lien of said judgment. It is said, however, that as to the subsequent judgment creditors, the condition of the bond cannot be extended to cover the renewals. The latter, however, are bound by the act of their debtor. They have no higher equity than he has, and it is too plain for argument that he has no equity to be relieved of the lien of appellant's judgment without payment of the debt for which it was given as collateral. Ayres *v.* Wattson (7 P. F. S. 360), and Moorehead *v.* Duncan (1 Norris, 488), have no application. In the one case there was the equity of a surety, in the other of a *bona fide* purchaser. The appellants are not purchasers. (Rodgers *v.* Gibson, 4 Yeates, 111; Heiston *v.* Fortner, 2 Binn. 40; Cover *v.* Black, 1 Barr, 493.) They have no interest in the property bound by their judgments; they have a lien only. A purchaser, however, stands upon a different footing. He buys and pays for the land. He has an equity to have it exonerated. But a judgment creditor, as was said by Chief Justice GIBSON, in Cover *v.* Black (*supra*), "stands on the foot of his debtor," and as the renewal of the notes under the protection of the judgment did not impair the lien of it between the original parties, it did not impair it between the appellant and the appellees.

It is proper to remark that in Moorehead *v.* Duncan (*supra*) the bond of indemnity stipulated for a single renewal of the notes. This would seem to exclude any subsequent renewals upon the maxim *expressio unius est exclusio alterius.*

I do not mean to say that a case might not arise in which a subsequent judgment creditor would have an equity superior to that of his debtor; as for instance where the cancelled notes had been exhibited to him, and he had loaned money on the faith of it. But we have no such question before us. These appellees have not shown any such equity nor any equity whatever.

We are of opinion that the appellant is entitled to have the said note of $700 paid out of the fund.

The decree is reversed at the costs of the appellees, and distribution awarded in accordance with the foregoing opinion.

Opinion by PAXSON, J. SHARSWOOD, C. J., and GREEN, J., absent.

Jan. '80, 45.   January 26, 1880.

Smith v. The Popular Loan and Building Association.

Promissory notes—Indorser's liability—Fraud—In case of fraud in obtaining endorsement or issuing note, plaintiff must show that he is a holder for value—Affidavit of defence—When judgment for want of will not be granted.

In a suit against the indorser of a promissory note, in order to prevent judgment for want of a sufficient affidavit of defence, it is enough for the affidavit to set up a state of facts which shows that the defendant's indorsement was obtained by misrepresentation, and that the note was negotiated in fraud of his rights.

Error to the Common Pleas No. 3, of Philadelphia County.

Case, by the above named association against M. Smith on a promissory note for $117, indorsed by defendant. The defendant filed an affidavit of defence, setting forth the following facts: Defendant had, at the request of G. C. Shelmerdine, executed a bond and mortgage for $4000 to the Fourteenth and Twentieth Wards Building and Loan Association, which said Shelmerdine was to pay in monthly instalments of $34 each to the association. On April 4, 1879, Shelmerdine told defendant that he was in arrears of said monthly dues, and that the association had promised him time, if he gave his notes for $500 indorsed by defendant, which said notes Shelmerdine asserted were to be paid by him, and received by the association, on account of the above mortgage. On this assurance the defendant indorsed the notes, one of which is the one in suit; but Shelmerdine, in violation of said assurance, instead of paying the notes on account of the mortgage, gave them to the plaintiff in this case. All of which, etc. A rule being taken by plaintiff the Court entered judgment against defendant for want of a sufficient affidavit of defence; whereupon defendant took this writ, assigning for error the above action of the Court.

H. B. Freeman (with him *C. D. Freeman*), for plaintiff in error.

Where fraud is alleged the case should go to a jury, for the plaintiff must show affirmatively that he gave value.

Ehrisman *v.* Roberts, 18 Sm. 308.
Byles on Bills, 224.
Phelan *v.* Moss, 17 Sm. 59.
Hutchinson *v.* Boggs, 4 Casey, 294.

J. Savidge, for defendant in error.

February 2, 1880. THE COURT. The affidavit of defence sets forth facts which show that the defendant's indorsement of the note in suit was induced by falsehood; that he gave it on the assurance that the note would be paid on a mortgage, for which he was already liable; and that the drawer and payee fraudulently gave the note to the plaintiff. The facts are clearly stated and reveal actual fraud by the drawer and use of the indorsement. This case is ruled by Hutchinson *v.* Boggs & Kirk (4 Casey, 294), which establishes that an affidavit of defence, alleging such facts as show that the note was obtained from the defendant by misrepresentations, and negotiated in fraud of his rights, is sufficient to prevent judgment being entered for want of a proper affidavit of defence. Where a negotiable note was obtained from the maker under false pretences, and fraudulently put in circulation by the payee, the holder of the note, in order to recover, must show a purchase for value before maturity, without notice of the fraud. An affidavit of defence distinctly setting out the facts, from which the fraud is a direct and natural inference, is sufficient. (Hoffman *v.* Foster & Co., 7 Wr. 137; see Albietz *v.* Mellon, 1 Wr. 367.)

Judgment reversed and *procedendo* awarded.

Opinion by TRUNKEY, J.

Quarter Sessions.

Q. S.   Oct. 8, 1880.
In re Volkmar Street.

Opening streets in the late district of Kensington—Jurisdiction, whether exercised by Quarter Sessions or Common Pleas—Act of March 22, 1813.

A petition to open Volkmar Street, in the late district of Kensington, framed under the provisions of the "Spring Garden" Act, of March 22, 1813 (P. L. 143), was filed in September in the Court of Quarter Sessions, and an application was made to appoint a time to hear testimony in support of the petition.

Haverstick, for the petitioner, said he understood the practice was to hear the matter in the Quarter Sessions.

Matthews, for the city, said he understood the practice was not uniform, some cases being heard in the Quarter Sessions, others in the Court of Common Pleas.

MITCHELL, J., directed the petitioners to apply to Common Pleas No. 4.

Subsequently application was made to Common Pleas No. 4, and THAYER, P. J., assigned a day for hearing, and directed the testimony to be taken by depositions.

[See *In re* Parrish Street, 6 WEEKLY NOTES, 215.]

Common Pleas—Law.

C. P. No. 4.   Oct. 9, 1880.
Thompson v. Taylor.

Practice—Production of books on trial—Act of Feb. 27, 1798—When the Court will compel production, notwithstanding inconvenience.

Rule on plaintiff to show cause why he should not produce books of account on trial.

The plaintiff's affidavit in answer to the rule, alleged that he resided in New York; that the books were his books of account in actual use; that their absence would cause him inconvenience and loss greater than the value of his claim; and offered to produce copies of the specific entries alluded to in the affidavit upon which the rule was granted, sworn to as such before a notary or commissioner in New York.

J. W. Roper showed cause.

The Court will not compel compliance with the demand, in view of the loss it would entail; and when its object can be accomplished by the copies.

[THAYER, P. J. How many books are there?] Two.

R. C. Dale for the rule.

The defendant has a right to the books themselves; he may find it necessary to show the method by which they are kept, or many other matters beyond the scope of investigation afforded by the copies.

THE COURT. Rule absolute.

C. P. No. 4.   Aug. 1880.
In re Petition of John Merry.

Naturalization—Minor residents—Act of Congress May 26, 1824 (Rev. St., Sec. 2167)—A minor who has not declared his intention two years previous to his application, or proved a residence of five years, cannot be admitted to citizenship—Act of Congress April 14, 1802 (Rev. St., Sec. 2165), explained.

The petition set forth that the petitioner was a minor; that he would attain his majority during the month of October, 1880; that he had resided in the United States three years prior to the presenting of his petition, and therefore the petitioner prayed that he might be admitted a citizen of the United States.

                                              C. A. V.

Sept. 6, 1880. THE COURT. This petition must be dismissed. The petitioner's evidence shows that he will not reach his majority until some time next month (October).

The petition is founded upon the Act of Congress of May 26th, 1824. That Act requires that the petitioner shall be at least twenty-one years of age to entitle him to citizenship; that he shall have resided in the United States at least five years, three of which must be prior to his becoming of age. The petitioner being a minor, he has no status under the Act just referred to.

In order that I may not be misunderstood, I may add that, under the Act of Congress of April 14th, 1802, a minor, of foreign birth, having declared his intentions after two years' residence in the United States, and having resided therein three years thereafter, may, upon the petition of his guardian, or perhaps next friend, be admitted to citizenship, though yet a minor.

This latter Act does not require the petitioner to be of age, but it does require that he should have declared his intentions at least two years previous to his application, and also prove a residence here of five years.

The petitioner not bringing himself within the

provisions of either of these Acts, his application is refused.
Petition dismissed.
Opinion by BRIGGS, J.

C. P. No. 4.   Oct. 2, 1880.
Glenn v. Keenan.

Adulterated liquors—Act of 29 March, 1860, § 1—No recovery can be had for liquors sold which were impure, vitiated, or adulterated.

Rule for judgment for want of a sufficient affidavit of defence.

Assumpsit upon a book account for liquors purchased by defendant.

The affidavit of defence set forth, *inter alia,* that said "liquors were bought by defendant on the standard of proof gallons when in fact it was some four degrees below proof," and further "that said liquors all of them were impure, vitiated, and adulterated."

B. Sharkey, for the rule.
J. C. Redheffer, contra.

Under the Act 29 March, 1860, § 1, (P. L. 346, Pur. Dig. 949, § 61), no recovery can be had for liquors sold which were impure, vitiated, or adulterated.

THE COURT. Rule discharged.

[See McGlinn *v.* Carrigan, 2 WEEKLY NOTES, 323.]

C. P. No. 4.   Oct. 2, 1880.
Roebling v. Brown.

Vendor and purchaser—Agreement that article sold should be adapted to a particular purpose —Defect in quality, when no defence—Caveat emptor.

Rule for judgment for want of a sufficient affidavit of defence.

Assumpsit for wire purchased by defendant.

The affidavit of defence set forth that "the goods in suit were purchased from the plaintiffs for a specific purpose: viz., for the manufacture of wire paper fasteners, and requires a thin wire of a particular fineness of quality, and it was so stated to the plaintiffs, who *agreed* to furnish a quality of wire that would in all cases answer the purposes for which it was intended. With such an understanding the wire was delivered. Its quality could not be discovered until tested, and when it was tested proved different from what it was contracted to be, and it resulted in a loss of thirty dollars to defendant."

Chas. Gibbons, Jr., for the rule.
THE COURT. Rule absolute.

[See Taylor *v.* North, 3 WEEKLY NOTES, 170, and note.]

Orphans' Court.

June 21 & 22, 1880.
Wood's Estate.

Will—Construction of—Lapsed legacies—Revocation of legacy—Word "representatives" used in the sense of next of kin—Where comprehensive words are used, an enumeration of particulars will not restrict the meaning of the large words—Abatement—Annuities and pecuniary legacies—Contract—Consideration—An agreement to pay a certain sum "out of his income," dependent on the convenience of the promisor, of which he is the judge, not binding upon his executors.

Sur exceptions to adjudication.

At the audit of the account of the executors of Dr. George B. Wood, deceased, the following facts appeared:—

The decedent died in March, 1879, leaving neither widow nor issue, having made a will, dated June 22, 1871, with seven codicils, the last dated July 12, 1875, containing a great number of devises and specific and pecuniary legacies. The residue of the estate is thereby given to the University of Pennsylvania.

The Auditing Judge (PENROSE, J.) in the adjudication, *inter alia,* found as follows:—

C. Among the legacies given is one which is as follows (section 39):—

"I give and bequeath $7500 unto Mrs. Hannah Chamberlin, a daughter of Mrs. Willis, aforesaid: but it is my will that whatsoever amount her son David Edwards shall owe me, principal and interest, shall be taken to have been so much paid on account of said legacy, and his notes shall be handed over to her or her representatives."

Mrs. Chamberlin, who was not a relative by blood (though she was connected by marriage) of the testator, died in his lifetime, leaving a son, Horatio F. Chamberlin (to whom letters of administration upon her estate have been granted), and grandchildren, children of a deceased child.

The Acts of Assembly, which in certain cases prevent lapse where the legatee dies in the testator's lifetime, do not apply to this case. But it seems clear that there is a substantial gift here to the "representatives" of Mrs. Chamberlin; and that the legacy, therefore, does not lapse. The direction that the notes of David Edwards should be handed over to the legatee, "or her representatives," makes it plain that, to this extent, the legacy was not intended to fail by reason of her death before the testator; and as, when so handed over, they are to be regarded as "so much *paid on account* of said legacy," it would follow that the *whole* of that *on account* of which the notes are so paid was equally intended to go to the representatives. (See Gibbons *v.* Fairlamb, 2 Casey, 217.) The word "representatives" here is probably used in the sense of next of kin, as there is nothing to indicate that they are to take in a fiduciary capacity. (Theobald, page 175.) In such case the legacy would go to Mrs. Chamberlin's issue. It was agreed, however, that if it should be held that the legacy did not lapse, it should be awarded to Horatio F. Chamberlin, administrator of Mrs. Hannah Chamberlin, by whom the distribution could be more conveniently made. It is, therefore, subject to abatement by reason of the deficiency of the estate, so awarded.

D. By the third codicil to his will the testator provided as follows:—

"Whereas circumstances have rendered it necessary that all parts of the foregoing will and codicils in which the name of George R. Wood, eldest son of my late brother Charles, has been introduced, should be modified, I hereby direct that his name shall be erased from all those passages in which it may be found, and that all bequests in his favor, and the appointments of him to any function or duty under this will or either of the codicils, should be absolutely abrogated. Thus, in clause 12 of my will, in which certain real estate is devised to my brother Charles, and after his decease to his son, George R. Wood, I direct that all which concerns my nephew George should be abrogated, and the devise pass immediately to a younger brother, R. Francis Wood, designated in the clause as the successor of George. *Again,* in clause 53, in which I appoint my executors, I direct the name of George R. Wood be omitted altogether, and that of his brother, R. Francis Wood, be introduced as his substitute immediately after Edward R. Wood. *Thirdly,* in clause 2 of codicil No. 1, George R. Wood is designated as one of the trustees of the cranberry tracts as substitute for his father, should he die or fail to act. It is my will that his name be omitted here, and that of his brother R. Francis Wood be put in its place."

This codicil is dated January 12, 1874. Geo. R. Wood had been one of the executors of his father Charles S. Wood, who died in May, 1873, and the administration of the estate had been entrusted to him as acting executor. He had abused the trust and applied to his own use the assets of the estate. This was discovered in the fall of 1873, shortly before the date of the codicil, and much publicity was given to the fact by reason of suits which the other executors were compelled to bring for the purpose of recovering the securities of his testator, which he had pledged for his own use or otherwise misappropriated. It was natural that Dr. Wood should resent the disgrace thus brought upon the family by George R. Wood, and that he should moreover take effective means to prevent the commission of a similar fraud with regard to his own estate.

Mr. Pile, on behalf of George R. Wood, claimed that notwithstanding this codicil he was entitled to such bequests in the will as were given to him, not by name, but as one of a class; as for example by section 34 of the will, which gives to each of testator's nephews and nieces by blood relationship, excepting George Sheppard, to whom a greater devise had been made, there being, including him, twenty-two in number, $5000.

The argument in favor of this is, that as the testator has omitted this provision in his reference in the codicil to the portions of his will from which the name of his nephew George R. Wood is to be excluded, it must be assumed that he intended it to stand. It is a general rule of construction, however, that where comprehensive words are used, an enumeration of particulars will not restrict the meaning of the large words. Here the provision is general, first, that his name shall be erased from all those passages in which it may now be found, and, second, that *all* bequests *in his favor,* and the appointments of him to any function or duty under the will, should be absolutely abrogated. This includes all bequests to him, whether by name or as one of the twenty-two nephews and nieces.

The claim is disallowed and it is now held that under the codicil, George R. Wood is excluded from all benefit under any provision in the will of the testator. . . . .

F. The will contains various provisions for the benefit of the University of Pennsylvania, viz.:—

Section 27. "Whereas, at my request, the trustees of the University of Pennsylvania have established a faculty co-operative with the medical department, consisting of five professorships, viz.:—(1) Botany; (2) Zoölogy and Comparative Anatomy; (3) Mineralogy and Geology; (4) Medical Jurisprudence, and (5) Hygiene; which I have aided by annual payment; and it is my desire that the said faculty should be permanently established. Therefore, for that purpose I give and bequeath unto the Trustees of the University of Pennsylvania fifty thousand dollars, in trust, to be kept safely invested in ground-rents, first mortgages, or in the loans of the city of Philadelphia, the State of Pennsylvania, or of the United States.". . .

"It is my desire and will that twenty-five hundred dollars of the income of said endowment, when all the chairs are filled, shall be applied to the payment of the professors' salaries, or five hundred dollars unto each who shall have delivered a *bona fide* course of lectures, of which the trustees shall be the judges; which lectures will preferably be in the months of April, May, and June.". . .

By Section 30 it is provided as follows:—

"Having heretofore engaged to pay, and paid to the Trustees of the University of Pennsylvania, twenty-five hundred dollars a year, or so much as they should require for the support of said auxiliary faculty of professors, I direct my executors to *continue* such payments as may be needed within said amount until said legacy shall be paid to an amount to yield an equal income; which will be without deduction from the legacy."

By section 31, a legacy of $75,000 is given for the erection and maintenance of a clinical hospital, under the control of the trustees of the University. By section 54, the residue of the estate, real and personal, is also given to the University. . . . .

By section 16 of a codicil of even date with the will, it is provided as follows :—

"My executors are hereby enjoined to distribute or pay no part of my estate in fulfilment of my will, except to pay legacies of less amounts than $5000; and except, also, the payments necessary to continue those annual payments which I have for some years made by agreement with certain institutions, in the interval before getting the principal of their legacies, until the whole of the hundred acres more or less shall have been put under cranberry culture." . . . . .

The lands have been put in cranberry cultivation, but thus far have not realized the testator's expectations as to profits. The will contains the provision already referred to (section 52):—

"Should my estate prove deficient to pay all the legacies, then the pecuniary legacies will abate ratably."

Owing to the fall of real estate, of which the testator's property consisted to a considerable extent, the estate has, as before mentioned, turned out insufficient to pay all the pecuniary legacies, and it is estimated at the present time that it will pay between sixty and seventy-five per cent. of them.

The question now presented is whether, under the provisions of paragraphs 27 and 30, the gifts there made to the University are subject to abatement.

It is conceded that the legacy of $5000 given by section 29 and that of $75,000 given by section 31, are subject to abatement; but it is contended that the legacy of $50,000 being in discharge of an obligation is not; while on the other hand it is claimed that the provision for abatement contained in section 52 of the will applies to this bequest, and also to the annual payment of $2500 provided by section 30.

The question is a difficult one. As a general rule, in the event of deficiency of assets all pecuniary legacies abate *pro rata*, and this is in accordance with the express direction of the testator. It is also well settled that for the purposes of abatement, annuities are to be treated as general pecuniary legacies. (Theobald, page 459; Williams on Executors.) This rule it is said, however, "is to be understood only as among legatees who are all volunteers, for if there be any valuable consideration for the testamentary gift, as where it is given in consideration of a debt owing the legatee, ... such legacy will be entitled to a preference of payment over the other general legacies which are mere bounties." (Williams on Executors, 1176; Theobald, page 459; Blower *v.* Morrett, 2 Ves., Sen., 420; Heath *v.* Dendy, 1 Russ. 543; Norcott *v.* Gordon, 14 Sim. 258, etc. etc,)

The first point to be considered therefore is, Was there an obligation on the part of Dr. Wood to the University which could have been enforced against his estate? As is well known, he had for many years been connected with the institution, in which he had always taken the greatest interest. In 1835 he was elected Professor of *Materia Medica*, which position he held until 1850, when he took the chair vacated by Dr. Chapman as Professor of Practice, which he filled until 1860, when he was elected *Emeritus* Professor. He continued to be a trustee until the date of his death, March 30th, 1879, being then in his eighty-third year, having thus spent forty-four years of his life in the service of the University, of which also he was a graduate.

In January, 1865, Dr. Wood wrote a communication to the Board of Trustees of the University of Pennsylvania, in which he made a proposition to appropriate out of his income the annual sum of $2000 (which by a subsequent letter he raised to the sum of $2500) to be applied by the Board of Trustees to the support of an auxiliary faculty of professors in the medical department. The proposition contained however this condition :—

"Though his income at present is such as to justify him in making this appropriation, and he can see no reasonable ground to apprehend that it might be so far diminished as to render the appropriation at any time in the future inconvenient, yet, in the uncertainty of affairs, it may happen that this sum may be necessary to supply his ordinary expenditures, and he therefore feels it incumbent on him to make the appropriation conditional on his future ability to maintain it without material personal inconvenience; he pledges himself, however, that should the Board so far honor him as to accept his proposition, no trifling cause shall be permitted to interfere with its due fulfilment on his part." . . . .

The proposition thus made was accepted by the trustees, and the auxiliary faculty was instituted accordingly. It comprised five professors, each of whom was to receive $500 per annum, to be paid at the end of the course upon certificate of the Dean that the duty had been properly performed.

The last provision in the plan proposed by the committee and adopted by the Trustees was as follows :—

"The professors shall be appointed for one year after public notice of at least three months, at the regular meeting of the board in November next, nominations having been made at a preceding meeting, and shall be *reappointed annually* thereafter during satisfactory service, at the regular meetings of the board in the same month, *so long as the plan for the establishment of the auxiliary faculty of medicine now adopted shall continue in operation.*"

The plan thus started has continued in operation ever since. Dr. Wood while he lived always paid the stipulated sum of $2500 per annum, after receiving the certificate that the lectures had been delivered, the whole of which was applied to the payment of salaries. There appear to have been no other expenses attending the enterprise than the salaries. The rooms already belonging to the University were used, and no buildings were therefore required. It was shown, however, that all of the income of the University was so appropriated, that but for the aid to be furnished by Dr. Wood, the auxiliary faculty could not have been created; and that it was created solely in consequence of the propositions contained in the communications of January 31 and April 4, 1865.

It must be admitted that these acts of the trustees, based upon Dr. Wood's promise to pay an annual sum, furnish a consideration which would give a binding effect to such promise. It may also be conceded that while he lived the promise was obligatory, subject only to the condition of his ability to pay. A promise to pay when able is undoubtedly valid. (Addison on Contracts, page 1212; Groome's Appeal, Legal Intelligencer, 1878, page 70; Waters v. Earl of Thanet, 2 Queen's Bench, 757.) It is different, of course, where the ability to pay is by the terms of the contract made dependent upon the judgment of the debtor, as in Nelson v. Von Bonnhorst (5 Casey, 352).

But what is there to continue the liability beyond the period of Dr. Wood's lifetime? It is not denied that a contract to pay a perpetual annuity is possible. In such a case, however, appropriate words should be used, and the Court must be convinced that such was the intention of the parties.

In Quain's Appeal (10 Harris, 510), where it was held that the general estate of a covenantor in a ground-rent deed was not liable for rents accruing after his death, it was said:—

"It is a perpetual covenant, and it is totally impracticable to require it to be performed by executors and administrators; for their office is not perpetual. If we retain the perpetuity of the covenants as against them, even with the restriction that they are to be liable only where the resort to the land is ineffectual, we still prevent all distribution in their hands; and as all the lands of the decedent are assets for the payment of debts, we constructively charge the rent of a single lot upon all his lands. Nor will it do to hold them liable until the final settlement of the estate. If that suggestion means until all other matters are ready to be settled, then it takes away at once the character of perpetuity belonging to the covenant, and makes its duration as against the personal estate to depend upon the accident of the administrator's diligence, or of the involved or simple nature of the estate. If it means until the final settlement of the whole estate, then this perpetual covenant postpones it forever. This cannot be, for the law intends the office of executor or administrator to terminate as soon as possible; it cannot be prolonged on account of perpetual covenants."

This case, so far as it applies to a contract under seal, in which the covenantor in express terms agrees for himself, his executors and administrators, to pay an annual sum forever, has been much criticized, though it has been affirmed in the subsequent case of Williams's Appeal (11 Wright, page 283). But where the terms of the contract are not express, and where we are seeking for the intention of the instrument, the inconveniences there pointed out have great weight, and perhaps furnish a conclusive argument against the construction which would make the contract a perpetual one, and make the office of executor everlasting.

Not only are there no words here showing an intention to bind the estate of the promissor after his death, but the agreement is to pay out of "*his income;*" and this is made subject to the condition that he is not thereby to be put to inconvenience. At his death *his* income ceases. What is there to require payment from any other source?

That this was the limit of his liability is indicated further by the provision in the plan adopted by the committee with regard to the appointment of professors. For while the ordinary professors at the University are, as was testified by the Secretary of the Board of Trustees, elected for an indefinite term, the auxiliary faculty are appointed *annually*, and only so long as the plan for the establishment of the auxiliary faculty of medicine shall continue in operation. The plan is referred to in the letter of the 4th of April, 1865, and is to be read in connection with it, in order to ascertain the extent of the liability which was then created.

In the opinion of the Auditing Judge no right of recovery, apart from the provisions in the will, existed in the University at Dr. Wood's death.

If this view be correct, then the provisions referred to in the will, not being in discharge of an obligation, would fall under the general principle, and be subject to abatement with other pecuniary legacies. There is nothing in the will which shows that the testator considered himself bound to pay for a longer period than his own lifetime.

In section 27 he speaks of having *aided* by an annual payment, and of his *desire* that the faculty *should be permanently* established. In section 30 he says that he had heretofore "engaged to pay," but he adds, "*and paid*," as if he regarded his engagement as completed. So in section 16 of the codicil he speaks of the annual payments which he *had made* for some years "by agreement." This is all; and it is entirely consistent with an agreement to pay so long as he lived, and no longer.

If section 30 were read by itself, it might be

supposed the testator intended that under all circumstances, and in spite of any deficiency of his estate, the sum of $2500 was to be paid to the University until so much of the sum mentioned in section 27 was paid as would yield an income of that amount. But this section is to be read in connection with the codicil, which was executed the same day, and which provided (section 16) that no legacy over $5000 should be paid until the lands in New Jersey were placed in cranberry culture. This might be for some years to come, and in the mean time, therefore, he gives to the University an annuity not exceeding $2500, the payment of which is to continue until the legacy of $50,000 is paid, viz., until the land had been put under cranberry culture.

He has declared in express terms that "*the* pecuniary legacies," *i. e.*, all the pecuniary legacies, should abate. He has omitted to except any. We have no right to say that he did not intend to include so considerable a one as that given to the University, the payment of which would require a very large proportion of his entire estate.

Exceptions were filed by the Trustees of the University of Pennsylvania to this adjudication: (1) To the finding that there was not sufficient evidence of a valid contract made by the testator in his lifetime, requiring the continuance after his death of the payment of $2500 per annum, for the maintenance of the auxiliary faculty. (2) To the holding that the exceptants were not on the footing of creditors, as respects the fund of $50,000, but only as unpreferred legatees or volunteers, and that the said legacy should abate. (3) To the holding that the legacy of $7500 to Mrs. Hannah Chamberlin did not lapse by reason that she pre-deceased the testator.

George R. Wood also filed an exception to the disallowance of his claim, by which he is excluded from all benefit under any provision in the will of the testator.

Eli K. Price and *J. B. Townsend*, for the exceptions of the Trustees of the University of Pennsylvania.

As to the first exception. The testator made a *contract* with the exceptants to pay the expenses of the auxiliary faculty, not exceeding $2500 per annum, which became binding on him and his estate. There was no limit as to time, the only condition was as to his personal expenses; after his death this limitation, of course, ceases, and the contract is unconditional. On the faith of this promise the auxiliary faculty was organized, the public was notified of the enlargement, and liabilities incurred by the University under the contracts with the professors. The consideration to establish a valid contract was sufficient. Subscriptions for corporate or public purposes are enforceable in law as founded on adequate considerations.

Cunningham *v.* Garvin, 10 Barr, 366.

Debts, though voluntary, are to be paid before legacies.

2 Williams on Exec'rs, 914, 1207.
Purd. Dig., 421, 448, pl. 208.

There are no expressions in the contract, as proved, which define any term or limit to the engagement to pay; it was not expressed to be from year to year, for a term of years, or for life. The true intent of the written papers and the conduct of both parties thereafter was, that a *continuing endowment or provision* should be made by Dr. Wood. The faculty was to be permanent and perpetual, though the elective terms of the professors were annual.

The fact that the contract was intended to continue for its fulfilment beyond the life of the testator, is further confirmed by the testator's declaration in his will, that the annual payment should not fail of being furnished, whether it came from income or principal of his estate, if there should be delay in the payment over of the legacy which he designated to form the fund for producing such annual payment.

(2) The second exception raises the question whether there has not been enough shown to impress upon the testator's estate a trust as to so much as will furnish the expenses of this auxiliary faculty, or at least give a preference to the claims of the exceptants over those of the legatees liable to abatement.

Where the testator's acts during lifetime, or the declarations of his will, recognize equitable rights in others to certain property standing in his name, such trusts will be supported as superior to the claims of legatees or volunteers.

Ex parte Pye, 18 Ves., Jr., 140.
Ellison *v.* Ellison, 6 Id. 656.
Richardson *v.* Richardson, 3 Law R. Eq. 686.
Morgan *v.* Malleson, 10 Id. 475.

When Dr. Wood put at the disposal of the trustees enough of his income to defray these expenses, he charged his estate with the execution of this trust. He does not call this yearly sum a legacy, but recognizes it as a payment to be kept up under his engagement. And it is to be kept up until the fund of $50,000 in its entirety shall have passed to the University, so as to furnish therefrom sufficient income to relieve his estate from his engagement. And because of the character of this engagement neither the yearly sum nor the capital fund of $50,000 would be liable to collateral inheritance tax.

There is no rule of law to restrict the testator from contracting to found in perpetuity; this is for the cause of science and learning, and the public interest intervenes to protect such endowments as charities.

As to the third exception. The legacy of $7500 to Mrs. Chamberlin lapsed upon her death prior to that of the testator, and thereby fell into the residue.

Woolmer's Est., 3 Whart. 477.
Nyce's Est., 5 W. & S. 260.
Loxley's Est., 6 WEEKLY NOTES, 529.

To prevent lapse, the giving over of the legacy must be to some other party *as purchaser*, a new taker by direct gift from the testator, not claiming in a representative capacity through the first legatee dying in the testator's lifetime. A legacy is not saved from lapse because given to the legatee or to his executors, heirs, or legal representatives.

Williams on Exec'rs, 1085, 1013.
Gibbons *v.* Fairlamh, 2 Casey, 217.
1 Williams on Exec'rs, 1086.

George W. Thorn, for Mrs. Chamberlin's representatives, cited—

Bridge *v.* Abbot, 3 Brown C. Rep. 225.
Corbyn *v.* French, 4 Vesey, 419.
Holloway *v.* Holloway, 5 Id. 401.
Roper on Legacies, vol. i. 472.
Bridges *v.* Wood, 2 Vern. 378, note.
Sibley *v.* Cook, 3 Atk. 572.
Booth *v.* Vicars, 1 Coll. 6.
Stone *v.* Evans, 2 Atk. 87.
Tidwell *v.* Ariel, 3 Mad. 409.
Gibbons *v.* Fairlamb, 2 Cas. 217.

R. Francis Wood, George Biddle, and *George W. Biddle*, for executors of Dr. G. B. Wood.

There is no evidence of any contract made by the testator in his lifetime binding himself to pay any sum to the Trustees of the University. Possibly some of the expressions used in the will might, under other circumstances, as declarations made by the testator, constitute some evidence; but here the whole transaction in question is shown by the correspondence between the testator and the Board of Trustees. It is apparent from this that no contract was made or existed; on the contrary, the testator's letter to the trustees, making the gift, shows that he took pains to exclude such a conclusion; being made "conditionally on his future ability to maintain it without material personal inconvenience." Therefore, whatever steps the trustees took in consequence of the gift, they acted with express notice of the condition annexed to the offer by Dr. Wood. The testator could have discontinued the gift at any time he thought proper. This did not constitute a contract, or give rise to a debt. The only consideration for it would be any inconvenience suffered by the University in consequence of the gift. Without this it would be a mere nude pact. But even could such inconvenience be shown to exist, he made the gift on express condition that he might discontinue it when he chose. That Dr. Wood's letter to the Trustees did not constitute a binding contract on his part, nor raise a debt for the recovery of which they could sue, is abundantly established by the authorities in Pennsylvania.

Nelson *v.* Von Bonnhorst, 5 Cas. 352.
Groome's Est., 4 WEEKLY NOTES, 250.
Love *v.* Hough, 2 Phila. 350.

The legacy of $50,000 given by item 27 is obviously a pecuniary legacy. And by paragraph 52 the testator says: "Should my estate prove deficient to pay all legacies, then the pecuniary legacies will abate ratably." So that the $50,000 must abate ratably with the other legacies. The annuity of $2500 a year, bequeathed by paragraph 30 of the will, until the legacy of $50,000 should be paid, is a pecuniary legacy, and therefore abates ratably with the other legacies.

There is no intent shown in the will that the Trustees of the University are to be preferred to the other objects of his bounty, many of whom are near relations of Dr. Wood. The annuity in question, given temporarily, and which is to be without deduction from the principal legacy, is merely an added legacy which testator intended should be subject to the same incidents and conditions as the legacy primarily given, one of which was that it should abate equally in case of deficiency.

Jos. M. Pile, for exception of Geo. R. Wood.

The words of exclusion used in the codicil are not sufficiently comprehensive to bar George R. Wood from coming in as one of a class, as one of twenty-two nephews.

Butler's App., 23 Sm. 452.

July 3, 1880. THE COURT. The several questions raised by the exceptions have been elaborately and carefully considered by the Auditing Judge, and notwithstanding the able arguments of counsel, we are unable to reach any other conclusion than that so well set forth in the adjudication.

The exceptions are therefore dismissed, and the adjudication confirmed.

Opinion by HANNA, P. J.

U. S. Circuit Court—Law.

Oct. 26, 1880.

Reading *v.* Texas and Pacific Railway Co.

Practice—New trial—Verdict for plaintiff—Inadequacy—Verdict not set aside for, at instance of plaintiff where the Court would have sus-

tained a verdict for defendant—Contract—Evidence.

Motion for new trial. The plaintiff declared in assumpsit and after setting forth an agreement by the defendants to pay him $10,000 for obtaining the consent and agreement of all the bondholders of the Shreveport and Texas Railway Company, to a scheme for reorganizing that company and coming into a new organization, and performance thereof, then averred, *inter alia*, at follows :—

"That afterwards, to wit, etc., said defendants knew that the plaintiff had performed his undertaking and promise as aforesaid and were content and satisfied therewith and at divers times thereafter, upon being requested by plaintiff, the said defendants paid to plaintiff on account thereof, divers sums of money, amounting to four thousand dollars, acknowledging a balance of six thousand dollars to be still owing by defendants in consideration of the premises."

The defendants pleaded *non-assumpsit*, etc.

On the trial the plaintiff failed to show full performance on his part of the original contract, but testified that the defendants had waived a literal performance and had paid him $4000 on account and agreed to pay the whole balance. This testimony was contradicted by a number of witnesses for defendants, who testified that no such waiver had taken place, and that the money actually paid was, part of it, to enable the plaintiff to commence operations, and part of it as a mere gratuity for his unsuccessful efforts to perform the contract.

The jury found a verdict for the plaintiff for $1000, whereupon the plaintiff moved for a new trial.

W. Henry Smith, for the motion.

This verdict is clearly erroneous, in any aspect of the case. According to plaintiff's theory, he must recover either the six thousand dollars with interest, being the amount of the balance due him, or nothing. According to defendant's view he is entitled to nothing at all.

Where damages are from the nature of the case wholly for the jury, inadequacy alone may not be ground for setting aside a verdict ; but here the evidence on either side shows that it must have been arrived at improperly.

[McKennan, J. If a verdict for the defendants could have been sustained, are not the defendants the only parties to object to that, in this case?]

The jury have found as a fact that we are entitled to recover. Under these circumstances we are entitled to recover the whole $6000, and it was an error to give us any less.

George Biddle for defendants, was not called upon.

Eo die. THE COURT. The plaintiff here has circumscribed his case within very narrow limits. He has by his declaration bound himself to prove a promise between himself and the defendants by which the latter agreed, in consideration of whatever he did in the performance of his contract, to pay him the balance he now claims. He has been permitted to present his case to the jury in a double aspect. First, that his performance of his contract to obtain the signature of these parties to a paper to provide for the reorganization of this railroad, was acceptable to the defendants, and that so he was entitled to recover; and secondly, on the ground that no matter how he performed his contract, these matters were subsequently arranged between the parties and a promise had been made to pay the ascertained balance of $6000. As to the above grounds I was unable on the trial to see how the jury could find for the plaintiff. As to the first ground the plaintiff was permitted to go into that, although under his declaration this was perhaps mere matter of inducement. He was permitted however to show, if he could, performance of the contract. Now, it must be admitted that there was no actual performance of the contract proven. Taking all the evidence, I think the weight of it was against the plaintiff and I so presented it to the jury.

On the second point, as to a subsequent arrangement between the parties, the testimony of the plaintiff was not direct; he did not swear that there was an actual ascertainment of this balance. He merely says, he understood it so. He does not testify to any unqualified promise. Under these circumstances a verdict in favor of the defendants would have been satisfactory to the Court. Now, the jury erroneously have found a verdict for a sum less than the plaintiff would have been entitled to recover if his case had been made out by satisfactory proof. But this is not prejudicial to the plaintiff. It does not do him any wrong; he has no right to complain. We do not sit here to correct formal errors made by the jury that do not hurt any one. The parties who are injured by this verdict are the defendants, not the plaintiff. But the defendants do not move for a new trial. The jury might have found a verdict generally for the defendants, but because the jury have given the plaintiff what he is not entitled to, it certainly does not lie in the mouth of the plaintiff to allege any wrong, nor is it the duty of the Court to set aside the verdict. Motion refused.

Oral opinion by McKennan, Cir. J.

BUTLER, J., concurred.

[*Cf.* Le Van *v.* Penna. R. R. Co., 5 W. N. C. 293.]

Supreme Court.

Oct. '79, 374. Oct. 28, 1879.

Snyder's Appeal.

Liens—Vendor and vendee—Lien for purchase-money—Equitable and legal title—What a vendor must do upon the conveyance of the legal estate to preserve the priority of his lien for purchase-money against liens which bind the vendee's equitable interest.

While, according to a strict application of the rule of law, any interval of time, however short, between the delivery of the deed and the entry of judgment for the purchase-money will suffice to let liens upon the vendee's equitable title in upon the legal estate; yet, where the circumstances plainly reveal an intention on the part of both vendor and vendee to preserve the vendor's lien, and judgment is entered within a reasonable time (*e. g.*, early the following morning), the priority of the lien for purchase-money is preserved.

Watt *v.* Steel, 1 Barr, 386, distinguished.

By a parol contract made in 1872, A. sold land to B., who entered and made valuable improvements, and continued paying the purchase-money in instalments as agreed, until 1877. Arrangements were made for the execution and delivery of a deed and confession of judgments for the balance of purchase-money, early in the morning of November 23d, 1877; but, from accidental causes, the transaction was not completed until within an hour of sunset; the premises in question where the settlement took place were eight miles from the county seat; the weather was foggy and rainy, and the roads were not good. Early the following morning, as soon as the prothonotary's office was opened, the judgments were entered. It was found as a fact that the vendor could have had the judgments entered of record on the day they were given, but the auditor found, further, that it was unreasonable under all the circumstances to have required or expected her to do so:

Held, that the delivery of the deed and the confession and entry of judgments constituted a single transaction, and the priority of the lien for purchase-money as against liens upon the vendee's equitable interest was preserved.

Appeal from a decree of the Court of Common Pleas of Somerset County, confirming the report of an auditor in the matter of the distribution of the fund arising from a sheriff's sale of the real estate of Charles Trent. The facts, as found by the auditor, were as follows:—

In 1872 Harriet Snyder by a parol contract granted and conveyed a tract of land containing 116 acres, in Stony Creek Township, to Charles Trent for $2400, upon the following terms: $800 in hand, and the residue in annual payments of $150, without interest. Trent entered and made valuable improvements.

On February 19, 1877, Stephen Trent obtained a judgment against Charles Trent, and damages were assessed at $438 and costs.

On November 6, 1877, Samuel Snyder obtained a judgment against Charles Trent *et al.*, and damages were assessed at $315 and costs.

On November 23, 1877, Harriet Snyder executed and delivered a deed to Charles Trent, who, simultaneously with the delivery of the deed, executed and handed to the grantor two judgment notes, one for $323.41, to secure unpaid arrears of purchase-money, and the other for $850, to secure the instalments not yet due. Judgments were entered upon these notes upon the following day.

In 1878 Harriet Snyder issued an execution upon one of these judgments, the land was sold by the sheriff, and bought in by her for the sum of $1000. This sum was paid into Court, and an auditor (W. H. Rupple) appointed, before whom it was claimed on the one hand by Stephen Trent and Samuel Snyder upon their judgments, upon the ground that their liens attached the instant the legal and equitable titles united in their judgment debtor, viz., on November 23, 1877; and on the other by Harriet Snyder, who claimed that circumstances surrounding the execution of the judgment notes, and the entry of judgment thereon, were such as to constitute (with the delivery of the deed), a single transaction, and consequently her lien for purchase-money took priority. The facts concerning the delivery of the deed, etc., were found by the auditor as follows:—

"The deed was delivered and the notes taken between three and four o'clock in the afternoon of the 23d day of November, 1877, at the residence of Charles Trent, distant eight miles from the town of Somerset, the county seat, and about half a mile from the residence of Mrs. Snyder, the vendor, and the notes were entered on the morning of the next day as soon as the prothonotary's office was open, Mrs. Snyder having arrived at Somerset with the notes a little after sunrise, and before the prothonotary's office was open. The 23d of November, 1877, had been previously agreed upon by the parties as the day for the execution and delivery of the deed and the giving of the judgment notes for the balance of the purchase-money, and early in the morning of that day Mrs. Snyder, who is a widow and in feeble health, made preparation to come to Somerset as soon as she had the notes, for the purpose of having them entered of record against Trent on that day; but owing to the delay occasioned by the parties coming late, the sending for a person to witness the deed, and the settling of disputes that arose between the parties, the deed was not delivered until late in the afternoon, between three and four o'clock, or about an hour before sunset, and the day being rainy, cloudy, foggy, and disagreeable, the night dark, and the roads muddy, caused Mrs. Snyder to defer coming to Somerset until the next day. Mrs. Snyder could have had her two notes entered the day they were given, but it was unreasonable to require or expect her to do so under all the circumstances."

As to the law, he said: "In the opinion of the auditor the only question to be determined is, must a judgment for purchase-money *invariably* be entered *on the day* the legal title is conveyed? or, in other words, are there exceptions to the rule which requires judgments for purchase-money to be entered on the same day the deed is delivered, in order to give them priority of lien? . . . . It is quite clear that the Supreme Court intended to decide that judgments for purchase-money must, *as a rule*, be entered on the day of the delivery of the deed; but that where the intention of the parties at the time is to continue the vendor's lien, and the delivery of the deed is followed up presently by an entry of the judgment *as soon as practicable* under all the circumstances, these constitute but one continuous transaction, and give the vendor's judgment priority.

"Under this view of the law it becomes important to ascertain what the intentions of the parties were at the time the deed was delivered, for *both* parties must have intended to continue the lien of Mrs. Snyder, else it fails. We think the case is free from difficulty in this respect. The testimony is very clear and uncontradicted that Mrs. Snyder, early in the morning of the day the deed was to be delivered and before the deed was executed, made arrangements to come to Somerset, . . . and fully intended to have the notes entered on that day, and this intention was not intermitted until after she got home, and then her going to Somerset was postponed only because of the late hour of the day. She started next day before daylight, and arrived at Somerset before business hours, before the prothonotary's office was open, and had her notes entered as soon as she reasonably could have done after they came into her possession. Charles Trent by giving the notes in which he authorized judgment to be entered, when he received the deed, manifested his intention of having Mrs. Snyder's lien preserved."

The auditor found, therefore, that the priority of Mrs. Snyder's lien for purchase-money was preserved, and reported a decree accordingly.

Exceptions on the part of Stephen Trent and Samuel Snyder were filed, and dismissed by the Court. Whereupon they took this appeal, assigning for error the action of the Court.

Valentine Hay, for appellants.

Judgments against a vendee bind every kind of equitable interest that he may have at the entry thereof, and the lien fastens upon the legal title *eo instanti* it is conveyed to him.

Waters's Ap., 11 Casey, 523.
Waitt v. Steel, 1 Barr, 386.
Jacobs's Ap., 11 Har. 481.

If there are exceptions to the rule, what protection would purchasers and creditors have against secret liens? If Chas. Trent had sold the land on the afternoon of Nov. 23d, 1877, and the purchaser had paid the entire purchase-money over, what notice *could* he have had that he did so at his peril? Or, if a creditor had examined the record, and finding nothing, had loaned money on the security of the land, why should his lien be postponed?

J. L. Pugh and *W. H. Koontz* for appellee.

The rule that a judgment which is a lien upon an equitable interest will bind an after-acquired legal interest, is an exception to the rule which holds that a judgment is not a lien upon after-acquired lands, and it is submitted that the Court will not be astute to extend this exception. The cases cited by the counsel on the other side go no farther than to say that if a vendor desires to protect himself from the consequences of his vendee selling the land, or subjecting it to other incumbrances, he must enter his judgments on the day upon which the conveyance is executed; there is no case which says that judgment creditors, who have done absolutely nothing, except to enter their judgments and obtain liens upon what may be a very trifling interest, by expanding their liens over the whole estate, may obtain priority of the vendor, who may have done all in his power, and exercised all the vigilance he could, and yet not have been able to enter his judgment the same day.

It is asked, if there are exceptions to the rule, what protection have creditors and purchasers? We answer, precisely the same as if a mortgage were given, which need not be recorded for sixty days. It can never be a hardship to say to a creditor or purchaser that where he is dealing with one who has but recently received the legal title, he must inquire of the vendor before venturing his money upon the faith of this newly-acquired title.

Nov. 10, 1879. THE COURT. Applying a very strict rule to the case before us, any interval of time, however short, between the delivery of the deed and the entry of the judgment for the purchase-money, ought to let liens upon the vendee's equitable title in upon the legal estate according to their priority. But *apices juris non sunt jura.* A different principle was therefore adopted in Love *v.* Jones (4 Watts, 465), in which Mr. Justice KENNEDY said: "It is evident, however, that the delivery of the deeds to Stouffer (the vendee), and his confession of the judgment an hour afterwards for the residue of the unpaid purchase-money, were but parts of the same transaction, done in pursuance of the same agreement, and were to have such operation only as would most effectually promote the intention of the parties, so far as it was lawful." It is true that it was decided in Watt *v.* Steel (1 Barr, 386), that a judgment for the residue of purchase-money entered up a day after the vendor had conveyed the legal title, did not exclude a prior judgment against the vendee. In that case, however, there was an evident break in the transaction, and for all that appeared, it would have been entirely practicable to have proceeded to the seat of justice and entered up the judgment on the same day. In Jacobs's Appeal (11 Harris, 480), Mr. Justice LEWIS said: "The administrator of Samuel Jacobs conveyed to Grove, on Saturday evening, the 19th May, 1849, taking at the same time judgments for the unpaid purchase-money. This transaction took place sixteen miles from Gettysburg, the seat of justice. It was unreasonable to require the entry of the judgment that night. It was equally unreasonable to expect them to be entered the next day, which was Sunday. They were regularly entered on Monday." It is true that he distinguished the case from Watt *v.* Steel, by the consideration that this was the act of an administrator, under an order of the Court, and that the act of the law does not receive so strict a construction. But so far as respects the rights of the prior judgment, it seems to be a distinction without a difference. Both cases were within the rule as originally announced in Love *v.* Jones (4 Watts, 465), that the whole proceeding must be one continuous act, clearly evincing that it was the intention of the vendor to preserve the lien of the purchase-money. In the case before us, according to the facts as reported by the auditor, it is very apparent that both parties intended to continue the lien, and so he reports. The judgments were to have been entered up on the same day, but from a circumstance not within the control of either party, the deed was not delivered until late in the afternoon, and the judgment was entered in the prothonotary's office the next morning, as soon as it was open. We think with the learned auditor, whose report was confirmed by the Court below, that this was all one continuous transaction, all done within the space of a day, within twenty-four hours, and it is entirely within the spirit and principle of the authorities to give effect to the judgment as a lawful continuation of the lien for the purchase-money.

Decree affirmed, and appeal dismissed at the costs of the appellant.

Opinion by SHARSWOOD, C. J.

May, '80, 193.   May 20, 1880.

Pennsylvania Railroad Co. v. The Commonwealth.

Taxation—Corporations—Tax on stock—Valuation of stock for taxation where dividend is less than six per cent.—Act of June 7, 1879 (P. L. 112), construed.

Sec. 4 of the Act of June 7, 1879, provided for the taxation of certain corporations according to the following computation: "If the dividend or dividends made or declared by such company or association, as aforesaid, during any year ending with the first Monday of November, amount to six or more than six per centum upon the par value of its capital stock, then the tax to be at the rate of one-half mill upon the capital stock for each one per centum of dividend so made or declared; if no dividend be made or declared, or if the dividend or dividends made or declared do not amount to six per centum upon the par value of said capital stock, then the tax to be at the rate of three mills upon each dollar of a valuation of the said capital stock, made in accordance with the provisions of the second section of this Act."

Sec. 2 provided that in case the dividends during that time should be less than six per cent., the treasurer and secretary of the corporation "shall, between the first and fifteenth days of November of each year in which no dividend has been made or declared . . . estimate and appraise the capital stock of such company upon which no dividend has been made or declared . . . at its actual value in cash, not less, however, than the average price which said stock sold for during said year, and not less than the price or value as indicated or measured by the amount of the dividends made or declared. . . . *Provided,* That if the Auditor-General or State Treasurer, or either of them, is not satisfied with the valuation so made and returned, they are hereby authorized and empowered to make a valuation thereof, and to settle an account on the valuation so by them made for the taxes, penalties, and interest due the Commonwealth thereon."

On appeal from a settlement made by the Auditor-General and State Treasurer:

Held, (affirming the judgment of the Court below), That for the purpose of such an assessment by the officers of the corporation or of the State, "the actual value in cash" of the stock is to be ascertained by the prices at which it sold between the first and fifteenth day of November, and not by the average sales during the year ending on the first Monday of November.

Error to the Court of Common Pleas of Dauphin County.

Appeal from the settlement made by the Auditor-General and State Treasurer for tax on capital stock of the Pennsylvania Railroad Company, for the financial year ending November 1st, 1879.

The Act of Assembly of June 7th, 1879 (P. L. 112), provided as follows:—

"Section 2. That hereafter, except in the case of banks, savings institutions, and foreign insurance companies, it shall be the duty of the president or treasurer of every company, now or hereafter incorporated by or under any law of this Commonwealth, and of every company now or hereafter incorporated by any other State or Territory of the United States or foreign government, and doing business in this Commonwealth, or having capital employed in this Commonwealth in the name of any other company or corporation, association or associations, person or persons, or in any other manner, to make report in writing to the Auditor-General, annually, in the month of November, stating specifically the total authorized capital stock of the company, the whole number of shares of stock, the number of shares of stock issued, the par value of each share, the amount paid into the treasury of the company on each share, the amount of capital paid in, the date, amount, and rate per centum of each and every dividend made or declared by their respective corporations during the year ending with the first Monday in said month; and in all cases where any such company shall fail to make or declare any dividend upon either its common or preferred stock during the year ending as aforesaid, or in case the dividend or dividends made or declared on either its common or preferred stock during the year ending as aforesaid shall amount to less than six per centum upon the par value of the said common or preferred stock, the treasurer and secretary thereof, after being duly sworn or affirmed to do and perform the same with fidelity, according to the best of their knowledge and belief, shall, between the first and fifteenth day of November of each year in which no dividend has been made or declared as aforesaid, or in which the dividend or dividends made or declared upon either its common or preferred stock amounted to less than six per centum upon the par value of said common or preferred stock, estimate and appraise the capital stock of such company upon which no dividend has been made or declared, or upon the par value of which the dividend or dividends made or declared amounted to less than six per centum, at its actual value in cash, not less, however, than the average price which said stock sold for during said year, and not less than the price or value as indicated or measured by the amount of the dividends made or declared, and when the same shall have been so truly estimated and appraised, they shall forthwith forward to the Auditor-General a certificate thereof, accompanied by a copy of their said oath or affirmation, by them signed, and attested by the magistrate or other person qualified to administer the same: *Provided*, That if the Auditor-General or State Treasurer, or either of them, is not satisfied with the valuation so made and returned, they are hereby authorized and empowered to make a valuation thereof, and to settle an account on the valuation so by them made, for the taxes, penalties, and interest due the Commonwealth thereon, and any corporation or company dissatisfied with such settlement may appeal therefrom, in the manner now provided by law for appeals from settlement of accounts by the Auditor-General and State Treasurer."

"Section 4. That every company or association whatever, now or hereafter incorporated by or under any law of this Commonwealth, or now or hereafter incorporated by any other State or Territory of the United States or foreign government, and doing business in this Commonwealth, or having capital employed in this Commonwealth in the name of any other company or corporation, association or associations, person or persons, or in any other manner, except foreign insurance companies, banks, and savings institutions, shall be subject to, and pay into the treasury of the Commonwealth, annually, a tax, to be computed as follows, namely: If the dividend or dividends made or declared by such company or association as aforesaid, during any year ending with the first Monday of November, amount to six or more than six per centum upon the par value of its capital stock, then the tax to be at the rate of one-half mill upon the capital stock for each one per centum of dividend so made or declared; if no dividend be made or declared, or if the dividend or dividends made or declared do not amount to six per centum upon the par value of said capital stock, then the tax to be at the rate of three mills upon each dollar of a valuation of the said capital stock, made in accordance with the provisions of the second section of this act; and in case any such company or association shall have more than one kind of capital stock, as for instance, common and preferred stock, and upon one of said stocks a dividend or dividends amounting to six or more than six per centum upon the par value thereof has been made or declared, and upon the other no dividend has been made or declared, or the dividend or dividends made or declared thereon amount to less than six per centum upon the par value thereof, then the tax shall be at the rate of one-half mill for each one per centum of dividend made or declared upon the capital stock, upon the par value of which the dividend or dividends made or declared amount to six or more than six per centum, and in addition thereto tax shall be charged at the rate of three mills upon each dollar of a valuation made also in accordance with the provisions of the second section of this Act, of the capital stock upon which no dividend was made or declared, or upon the par value of which the dividend or dividends made or declared did not amount to six per centum; and it shall be the duty of the treasurer or other officer having charge of any company or association upon which a tax is imposed by this section of this Act to transmit the amount of said tax to the treasury of the Commonwealth within fifteen days from the thirty-first day of December in each and every year: *Provided*, that whenever such corporation or company shall make any profit, and add the same to its sinking fund, without a division thereof among its stockholders, the amount of the profit thus added to its sinking fund shall be included in the report required by the second section of this Act to be made, and for the purpose of this Act the same shall be treated as having been divided amongst the stockholders and shall subject the capital stock to taxation as a dividend: *Provided, however*, that said money or any part thereof shall be expressly set apart for the payment of debts."

The defendant corporation was chartered under the laws of the State of Pennsylvania, and at the time of the settlement of this account had capital stock of the par value of $68,870,200. On May 2d, 1879, it made a dividend of 2 per cent., and on November 1st, 1879, a dividend of 2½ per cent. The dividends having been less than six per centum, an appraisement of the value of the capital stock was made by the secretary and treasurer of the company, based upon the average value of the stock during the year, from the first Monday of November, 1878, to the first Monday of November, 1879, as shown by the sales at the Philadelphia Stock Exchange. This valuation amounted to $51,652,650. The tax on this amounted to $154,957.95, and was paid in full on January 15th, 1880. On March 4th, 1880, the Auditor-General and State Treasurer, being dissatisfied with this appraisement, made another valuation, based upon the public selling price of the stock between the first and fifteenth days of November, 1879, which resulted in a valuation of $66,804,094, the tax upon which would be $200,412.27, an excess of $45,454.32 over the amount already paid by the company, and this balance they found to be due to the Commonwealth. The company appealed from this settlement to the Court of Common Pleas of Dauphin County, and the case being at issue upon a plea of *nil debet*, an agreement was filed dispensing with trial by jury, and referring the whole case to the decision of the Court of Common Pleas, under the Act of April 22, 1874 (P. L. 109), with the right to a writ of error on behalf of the company, without security. It was also agreed in writing: "That the valuation of stock on which the settlement in this case was made, was based upon the actual value of the stock in cash, as ascertained by its selling price in public market during the period extending from the first to the fifteenth day of November, 1879."

The trial was before HENDERSON, J., who found the facts as stated above, and decided in favor of the Commonwealth for $47,727.03. Exceptions to this decision were filed, and all overruled by the Court, except the first, in compliance with which the facts found were stated specifically by the Court. April 24, 1880, judgment was entered for the Commonwealth under the decision filed, and on the same day a writ of error was taken out by the defendant, who filed six assignments of error, all of which were substantially included in the following :—

"(5) The Court below erred in overruling the sixth exception of the defendant to the decision of the Court, which exception was as follows: 'The true measure for fixing the value of the stock for taxation under Act of 1879, for the year ending first Monday in November, 1879, is the average market value during the said year when not less than the amount indicated by dividends, and not the average value between the first and fifteenth of November, 1879, and the Court erred in not so holding.'"

Hall & Jordan (with whom was *James A. Logan*), for plaintiff in error.

. Under the second section of the Act, when the dividend declared equals or exceeds six per cent. "*during the year ending*" the first Monday of November, then such dividend is the measure of liability for taxation for that year, because it fixed its value during that period; but when the dividend is less than this, the secretary and treasurer of the company are to appraise the stock at its actual value in cash, not less, however, than the average price which it "sold for *during said year*," and not less than the value indicated by the "amount of the dividend made or declared" within that year. Is it not clear that the "actual value in cash" must be its value during the time for which the tax is levied, and how can this be ascertained more surely than by its history during this period? The time for *making* the appraisement is clearly enough fixed to be between the first and fifteenth of November, but there is not a word in this clause to militate against the whole theory of the Act as to the time *for which* the appraisement is to be made. The legislative intent was to first, during the year, fix the value as determined by the dividends; when they showed a value equal to par or more, by amounting to six per centum or more, or when this failed, and the stock should be presumably below par, that an appraisement should fix its actual value within the year, as the measure of taxation. Moreover, the date of the appraisement adopted by the State officers was within the next financial year and may be included by the officers of the corporation in the return for the year ending Nov. 1880. The Act must be construed as a whole, and its spirit as well as its letter must be represented in such construction.

Potter's Dwarris on Statutes, 189.
Rex. *v.* Loxdale, 1 Burrow, 447.
Comm. *v.* Fraim, 4 H. 163,
Comm. *v.* Nav. Co., 16 Sm. 81.
Doroussean *v.* United States, 6 Cr. 314.

If there be any doubt as to the construction of a statute for raising revenue, it will always be resolved in favor of the construction which conforms to the power of the Legislature.

Cooley on Taxation, 41, 42.
Washington Ave. Case, 19 Sm. 352.

Gilbert, Deputy Attorney-General, and *Palmer*, Attorney-General, contra.

The assessment for taxation must be made in accordance with the statute authorizing it, and it is based upon the value of the property at the time the assessment is made. "Every person is therefore to be taxed for the year upon his personalty, estimated as of the time of the assessment, and every parcel of land according to its value at that time." (Cooley on Taxation, 261.) The Act in unmistakable words requires the assessment to be *made* " between the first and the fifteenth day of November of each year." Unless it was supposed that its " actual value in cash," when such assessment should be made, might differ from the "average price which said stock sold for during the said year," then these words are insensible; but because of the very fact that fortuitous circumstances might cause its value at that time to be far above or far below its average selling price during the year, it was especially provided that in the event of its going below, then the average selling price, or the value as indicated by the dividends declared, should be the limit of the valuation upon which the tax should be levied. We are not concerned with the wisdom of the plan devised, but with the means of carrying it out. If it is objected that the tax is measured by a period of time, in regard to

which no tax is imposed, the reply is, that it is within the power of the Legislature to do this.
Kittanning Coal Co. *v.* Comm., 29 Sm. 100.
Shaw *v.* Dennis, 5 Gilm., 405.

June 19, 1880. THE COURT. This case involves but a single question. The Pennsylvania Railroad Company having declared less than six per cent. dividends for the financial year ending on the first Monday of November, 1879, it became necessary, under the Act of 7th of June, of that year (P. L. 112) to make an appraisement of its capital stock for the purpose of taxation. This was done by the secretary and treasurer, and a return thereof made to the Auditor-General's office. The par value of the stock so returned was $68,870,200, and its cash value $51,652,650. The tax on this sum, at three mills on the dollar, amounted to $154,957.95, which was promptly paid by the company. The value of the stock was fixed by taking its average market value from the first Monday of November, 1878, to the first Monday of November, 1879.

The Auditor-General and State Treasurer not being satisfied with the valuation placed upon the stock by the company's officers, proceeded to make another valuation, as authorized by the second section of the Act of 1879, and fixed its value at $66,804,094, the tax upon which amounts to $200,412.27, being $45,454.32, in excess of the amount paid by the company. This result was obtained by taking its selling price in the public market from the 1st to the 15th of November, 1879. The Court below sustained the action of the State authorities, and gave judgment against the company for $47,727.03. The contention on the part of the company is that the stock should have been appraised at its average selling value during the year for which the tax is laid, and not at its value from the first to the fifteenth of November succeeding; in other words, that the stock must be appraised at the average price for which it sold during the year.

The Act of Assembly does not say so. It requires an appraisement to be made between the first and fifteenth day of November of the stock of non-dividend paying corporations, or those paying less than six per cent., said stock is to be appraised at its cash value, "not less, however, than the average price which said stock sold for during said year." If the Legislature intended to have the stock appraised at its average price during the year, it was very easy to have said so; we find nothing in the Act from which such intent can be gathered with any reasonable certainty. On the contrary, the use of the words, "not less, however, than the average price which said stock sold for during said year," necessarily implies the power to appraise the stock at more than its average price during the year. The construction of the Act contended for by the company would expunge the words above quoted, or render them nugatory. It is our duty to give them effect, if consistent with other portions of the statute. They mean just this: that, if the stock of the company is lower when the appraisement is made in November, than it was during the previous year, it shall be appraised at not less than the average selling price for the year. On the other hand, if it is higher in November it may be appraised at its increased value. If it be objected to this view that the advantage is all on the side of the State, we may safely concede it to be so. The object of the Act was to raise revenue, and it appears to have been drawn with care, and in the interest of the State.

We are of opinion that the learned Judge of the Court below ruled the law correctly, and his judgment is accordingly affirmed.

Opinion by PAXSON J. SHARSWOOD, C. J., and GREEN J., absent.

Jan. '80, 147.　　　　　　　　　March 31, 1880.

Shnyder v. Noble.

Husband and wife—Bond of the wife—Valid as against the land bought when given to secure balance of unpaid purchase-money.

So far as real estate purchased by a married woman is concerned, she may bind it for the purchase-money in any manner that she might if she were sole.

As a personal obligation, the bond of a married woman is void, but where given to secure the purchase-money of land sold to her, it may be enforced against such land. It makes no difference whether the bond be accompanied by a mortgage or not, or whether the judgment be by confession under a warrant of attorney, or by suit, in either case the land may be charged.

Error to the Common Pleas of Northampton County.

Debt, on a bond, by D. H. Shnyder against Frederick W. Noble and Anna M. Noble, to recover a payment of interest due on the principal sum of the bond.

Judgment was entered against the defendants by default, for want of an appearance, which was afterwards opened as to Anna M. Noble, and she let into a defence. Pleas, non est factum, nil debet, and coverture.

The following were the facts of the case: On the 16th of October, 1875, Daniel Shnyder and wife conveyed in fee simple to Anna M. Noble a house and lot in Easton, in consideration of $10,000. On the same day F. W. Noble and Anna M., his wife, executed to Shnyder their joint and several bond, bearing interest annually. At the same time they executed to the plaintiff a mortgage of the above-mentioned house and lot to secure the payment and conditions of the bond, the mortgage containing, *inter alia*, the following recital: "This mortgage and the said in part recited bond were given to secure a balance of unpaid purchase-money of said premises." These facts were admitted on the part of the defendant, and the plaintiff admitted the coverture of Anna M. Noble.

Default having been made in an annual payment of interest, this suit was brought to recover the amount due.

The Court (MYERS, P. J.) charged the jury, *inter alia*, as follows: "It is admitted that Anna M. Noble at the time of the execution by her of the obligation in suit was a married woman, and [though it was given for the balance of purchase-money of real estate conveyed by the plaintiff to her and secured by mortgage, there can be no recovery against her on the obligation by reason of her coverture.] The remedy of the plaintiff, so far as Anna M. Noble is concerned, is on the mortgage. I therefore direct you to render a verdict in favor of the defendant."

The jury rendered a verdict accordingly, and judgment was entered thereon. The plaintiff took this writ, assigning for error that portion of the charge above quoted in brackets, and the direction to the jury to find a verdict for the defendant.

W. C. Shipman, for plaintiff in error.

This bond being given for a balance of unpaid purchase-money is good and enforceable against the land which the married woman obtained. It is not contended that it is enforceable against her personally. The Court has power to restrict the execution.

Patterson *v.* Robinson, 1 Casey, 82.
Ramborger's Admrs. *v.* Ingraham, 2 Wright, 146.
Brunner's Appeal, 11 Wright, 73.
Sawtelle's Appeal, 3 Norris, 306.

Fitzpatrick, for the defendant in error, presented no paper-book.

May 3, 1880. THE COURT. On the 16th of October, 1875, in consideration of $10,000 Daniel H. Shnyder, the plaintiff, sold and conveyed by deed in fee simple to Anna M. Noble, the defendant, certain real estate in the borough of Easton. At the same time, to secure a balance of the purchase-money, the defendant and her husband executed to Shnyder a bond and mortgage. The bond was made payable in five years from its date, and conditioned, *inter alia,* for the payment of interest annually. Default was made in the payment falling due April 16, 1878, thereupon suit was brought, and judgment by default had for the amount remaining due and unpaid. Afterwards, on motion, this judgment was opened as to Mrs. Noble, and on the trial which followed the Court below charged the jury as follows: "It is admitted that Anna M. Noble, at the time of the execution by her of the obligation in suit, was a married woman, and though it was given for the balance of the purchase-money of real estate conveyed by the plaintiff to her, and secured by mortgage, there can be no recovery against her on the obligation, by reason of her coverture." This was erroneous; for, in the first place, where a married woman has executed a mortgage to secure the purchase-money of land, stipulating for the payment of interest at stated periods, accompanied with an agreement that upon failure to pay such interest at the times fixed, the whole amount of the mortgage shall become due and payable, on default of such payment scire facias can be maintained for the full face of the mortgage. (Glass *v.* Warwick, 4 Wright, 140.) Furthermore, a married woman may prescribe or waive such terms as she may think proper to prescribe or waive, so long as her acts are essentially part of the contract of sale, and bind nothing but the property sold. (Patterson *v.* Robinson, 1 Casey, 81.) This, of course, means that so far as the property purchased by a feme covert is concerned, she may bind it for the purchase-money in any manner that she might were she sole. Moreover, a bond secured by mortgage is part of the mortgage, and must be regarded as one or more of the conditions of that instrument, put for the sake of convenience and more ready enforcement into the shape of a bond. Such being the case, we cannot understand why such conditions may not be enforced as well when contained in the bond as when written in the mortgage itself. But again, the bond of a married woman given for the purchase-money of land sold to her, has been held to be good and enforceable against the property, the purchase-money of which it was intended to secure. (Brunner's Appeal, 11 Wright, 67.) It is true in this case the bond was a judgment bond, and unaccompanied by a mortgage; but we apprehend had it had this additional security, no difference would have been made in the ruling, for the mere fact of such security could have had no effect upon the power of the married woman to execute the bond; it still would remain a bond for the purchase-money, the single and only case in which a married woman has power to execute such an instrument. So the fact that judgment could be had upon the obligation by force of the power of attorney could make no difference, for if her warrant was good at all, it was good because of her power to bind herself, or rather the land purchased by her, and it would hence follow that if she had the power to execute a bond with a warrant of attorney, she had, à *fortiori*, the power to execute a bond without such warrant.

As a personal obligation, the bond of a married woman is void, but where given to secure the purchase-money of land sold to her, on equitable principles and to prevent injustice, it may be enforced against such land. From this it follows that a suit upon such bond must be regarded as a proceeding *in rem*, as the judgment is a charge only upon the land, and against it alone can it be enforced. So it matters not what the character of the purchase-money obligation may be, whether mortgage, bond, or note, or whether judgment be obtained thereon by confession or suit, the result is the same; the land alone is charged, and not the person of the feme covert.

The judgment is reversed, and a new venire ordered.

Opinion by GORDON, J.

May, '79, 16, 17.   May 21, 1880.

Kilgore v. The Commonwealth.

Local statutes—When not repealed by implication—Tavern licenses in Allegheny County—Fees—For what use payable—Act of April 3, 1872, P. L. 843, and April 12, 1875, P. L. 40, construed—Auditor-General—How far affected in settlement of accounts by previous injunction.

The Act of April 3, 1872 (P. L. 843), provided that tavern licenses in Allegheny County should be issued by the County Treasurer at certain rates therein named, and in a subsequent section provided that "one-fourth of all such sums received by the treasurer as aforementioned" should be paid to the State, and "the other three-fourths" for the use of the county. The Act of April 12, 1875 (P. L. 40), provided "that licenses for sales of liquors, when not otherwise provided for by special law, may be granted by the Court of Quarter Sessions of the proper county;" it fixed the fees, which were made payable for the use of the State, at less than those required by the Act of 1872 in Allegheny County, but specifically repealed no Act but that of March 27, 1872, known as the "Local Option Law." During the years 1875–6 the treasurer of Allegheny County issued tavern licenses, as had theretofore been done under the Act of 1872, but collected the fees at the rates fixed by the Act of 1875. On appeals from the settlement of his accounts by the State Treasurer and Auditor-General:

Held, that the Act of April 3, 1872, was not in any respect repealed by the Act of April 12, 1875.

Held further, that the fees for 1875-6 having been collected in accordance with the rates fixed by the Act of April 12, 1875, the section of the Act of April 3, 1872, providing for the disposition of the fees received thereunder, had no application, and that the fees received during these years were all payable to the State.

An injunction having been granted by the Court of Common Pleas of Allegheny County, restraining the State Treasurer from collecting all of the fees in question:

Held, that it was no bar to a claim for the same in the settlement of the County Treasurer's accounts by the Auditor-General and State Treasurer.

Error to the Court of Common Pleas of Dauphin County.

Appeals from the decisions of the State Treasurer and Auditor-General upon the settlements of the accounts of Samuel Kilgore, treasurer of Allegheny County for the years 1875 and 1876 respectively. Each appeal involved the same points of law, and both cases being at issue upon pleas of *nil debet*, by agreement of counsel they were referred to PEARSON, P. J., without the intervention of a jury, subject to exceptions and writ of error, under the Act of April 22, 1874. Upon the trial of each case the following facts were found:—

The defendant, Samuel Kilgore, was treasurer of Allegheny County during the years 1875–6, and in that capacity issued all tavern licenses in that county, and collected the fees therefor. The Act of April 3, 1872 (P. L. 843), repealed "all laws relating to the sale of liquors in the county of Allegheny" except special laws prohibiting sales in boroughs or townships, and provided that it should be unlawful thereafter to sell liquor except as thereinafter provided. Section 2 of the Act authorized the treasurer of the said county, upon obtaining bonds and receipt of the fee, to issue licenses. Sections 3 and 4 made provision for places of amusement where liquor is sold, and directed the classification of breweries and distilleries. Section 5 classified the vendors and fixed the amount of the bond for each class. Section 6 classified the hotels and taverns, and fixed the amount of the license fee for each class. Section 7 was as follows: "The one-fourth of all such sums received by the treasurer as aforementioned for license to be for the use of the State, to meet the demands on the State treasury, and the other three-fourths for the use of said county, in meeting the expenses incident to the granting of licenses, and in building, erecting, and completing the Allegheny County Workhouse in said county, and for enlarging, improving, maintaining, and keeping the same in repair." On April 12, 1875 (P. L. 40), an Act was passed, enacting in section 2, "That licenses for sales of liquors, when not otherwise provided for by special law, may be granted by the Court of Quarter Sessions of the proper county, at the first or second session in each year, and shall be for one year." Section 3 of this Act fixed the license fees for hotels and taverns at amounts considerably higher than those theretofore charged throughout the State, but less than those required by the Act of April 3, 1872, in Allegheny County, and made the fees payable to the use of the State. The same section contained a proviso "That no license shall be less than fifty dollars; *And provided further*, That any person licensed the present or any portion of a year shall pay a *pro rata* share of the license fee, and the authority granting the license shall designate the classification for that year." The defendant continued to issue licenses after the passage of the Act of 1875, and subsequent to January 3, 1875, the fees charged were those fixed by that Act. In the settlement of each account he was charged with the whole amount of the fees received for tavern licenses after January 3, 1875, and not allowed credit for any portion of the same as due to the county of Allegheny.

Defendant offered in evidence in each case the exemplification of the record of a suit in equity in the Court of Common Pleas of Allegheny County, in which the county of Allegheny was complainant, and the defendant as treasurer of Allegheny County, and R. W. Mackey, State Treasurer, defendants a bill filed September 10, 1875, under which an injunction was granted, enjoining the defendant to hold three-fourths of all sums received by him as tavern licenses for the use of Allegheny County, to be applied as directed by the Act of April 3, 1872, and enjoining the State Treasurer from receiving the same and from commencing suit therefor. Objected to by the Attorney General for the Commonwealth, and received without prejudice to either party upon the final decision.

There was found due to the Commonwealth in the first appeal $65,362.52, being the whole net amount received by defendant from January 3, 1875, to December, 1875, for tavern licenses with interest, less a credit for one-fourth of the whole amount collected already paid; and in the second appeal for $65,841.09, calculated upon the same basis. Exceptions to the findings of facts and conclusions of law having been filed, they were overruled, and the following opinion filed :—

"There is no dispute as to the facts in this case, but the defendant contends that the price or rate of license for inns or taverns in Allegheny County is changed by the third section of the Act of 1875, but that no other provision of the Act of 1872 is altered or repealed. After the most careful examination, I am clearly of the opinion that the Act of 1875 does not, in any particular, alter or change that of 1872. There is no clause or provision in it which has any bearing on the earlier statute. The Act of 1872 was intended as a full and perfect provision as to most of the State taxes in Allegheny County, the subjects of taxation, and the rate of assessment, and, where the object was omitted, it would have to be taxed and rated for State purposes under the general laws. It is contended that, under the provisos in the third section of the Act of 1875, the tax on inns and taverns was changed in that county. There is nothing in the provisos that even hints such a change. On the contrary, the whole of the Act of 1875 leaves in full force all special statutes. We may take it as a legal axiom that statute laws are not to be repealed by implication. To have that effect, there must be a strong repugnancy between them. (Street v. Commonwealth, 6 W. & S. 209.) There must be an irreconcilable inconsistency. (Easton Bank v. Commonwealth, 10 Barr, 448.) A general law will seldom repeal a special one. (Dyer v. Covington, 4 Casey, 186.) A general statute, without negative words, will not repeal a previous one which is particular, though there be some inconsistency between them. (Brown v. Commissioners, 9 Harris, 37.) Later statutes, which are general, do not repeal an earlier one which is particular. (Bounty Accounts, 20 Smith, 96, which cites very many of the English cases.) Implied repeals are not favored. (Erie v. Bootz, 22 Smith, 199.) And there must be so strong an inconsistency that they cannot stand together. (Egypt Street, 2 Grant's Cases, 455.) The law never favors repeals by implication. (Shinn v. Commonwealth, 3 Grant's Cases, 205 ; Bowen v. Lease, 5 Hill, 221.) Such is the language of all the cases and text writers. We should say that these rules were universal, but for two of our own decisions under the tax laws of the State, where the principle was disregarded. (Iron City Bank v. Pittsburgh, 1 Wright, 340.) This bank was, by the terms of its charter, exempted from taxation for a certain period ; yet a general law was held to embrace it, which taxed the Pittsburgh banks. The other is the case of the Commonwealth v. The Fayette County Railroad, which had a special exemption until the earnings would pay the stockholders six per cent. on their investment ; yet, as the corporation was created subject to the Act of 1849, it was held to be embraced in a general law taxing railroad companies on their dividends. No one doubts the power of the Legislature to impose the tax, notwithstanding the exemption clause ; but did it do it by a general law? We should say that, on general principles, the special exemption was not revoked by implication under a general tax law of railroads. It required some special enactment, pointing to the particular road. We are clearly of the opinion that no part or portion of the special Act relating to the taxation of inns and taverns, in the county of Allegheny, is altered or revoked by the Act of 1875. There is no allusion to the Act of 1872, and no inconsistency between the two laws. The error in the present case arises from the county authorities imposing the tax under the Act of 1875, instead of that of 1872. Had they adhered to every portion of that law, they could have successfully claimed to have the money appropriated under the seventh section of that Act, which gives one-fourth of the sums received by the treasurer for license to the use of the State, to meet the demands on the State treasury, and three-fourths thereof to the county of Allegheny, to aid in completing the workhouse. By the course pursued, the county of Allegheny wishes to tax under one law, and claim three-fourths of the money raised under another. This we consider inadmissible.

"The Attorney-General contends that, if the taxes had been assessed under the Act of 1872, the State would have received as much money from its fourth as it can gain by taking the whole under the rate imposed. It is conceded by the defendant's counsel that there is a great difference between the taxes imposed under the two laws. How much they do not know, and the same is not in proof by either party. If that were known with reasonable certainty, the Court could adjust the difficulty with approximate accuracy. Possibly it might have been approached by giving in evidence the sums raised from licenses in 1873 and 1874, but there was no attempt to make the proof, each party relying on the principles of law, and the construction of the different statutes for which they contended. The Court is obliged to decide the case on the evidence before it.

"The seventh section of the Act of 1872 we do not consider is repealed, but standing in full force; but the sums received for tavern licenses were either under the Act of 1875, or the general laws of the State, and therefore do not come within either the words or spirit of the Act, which says, 'the one-fourth of such sums received by the treasurer, as *aforementioned*, for license, to be for the use of the State,' etc. All of the previous sections had fixed the high rates of taxation as before stated. No part of the money now in controversy was so received, therefore cannot be claimed for Allegheny County; but, being collected from the citizens for tavern licenses, must be distributed and appropriated as in other cases under the general laws. Allegheny County can again collect and receive her three-fourths of the license money for inns and taverns, by making its future assessments and collections under the Act of 1872, unless that law has been repealed.

"The proceedings in equity in Allegheny County are no bar to the action of the State officers in the present case. That Court could not by injunction prevent the State Treasurer from acting with the Auditor-General in settling and collecting the money decided by them to be due to the Commonwealth; nor could it even enjoin the treasurer of Allegheny County from paying over money which he had collected for the State. If such a course could lawfully be pursued, the finances of the Commonwealth would be thrown into strange confusion. On the same principle the treasurer of every county in the State could be prevented by the Courts from paying any money into the State treasury collected under a law which they chose to consider unjust or unconstitutional. It was intended by the framers of our laws that all questions affecting the revenue, or claims by or against the Commonwealth, should be first heard by the accounting department under the Act of March 30, 1811, and if the party claimant or defendant against the State was dissatisfied, an appeal was given under the restrictions therein provided. That appeal was to be decided at the seat of government, where the public offices were kept, and the State officers could give the business their attention without neglecting their other public duties. They would thus have all of the reports to the departments, papers, books, and public documents at one place, where they could be used on the trial without inconvenience or loss of time. It is sufficient for us that such is the settled law, and we consider the bill in equity in the Common Pleas of Allegheny County *coram non judice*. That Court had no jurisdiction in the case, and its pending injunction is a nullity—affords no protection to the County Treasurer, and has no binding effect whatever on the State Treasurer.

"We will only add to what has been already said, that the second section of the Act of 1875 shows clearly that no change was intended in Allegheny County by the two provisos at the end of the third section, as it contains a provision exempting cases provided for by special laws, and alludes to the licenses to be granted by the Courts at the first and second terms. Those in Allegheny County were, under the Act of 1872, granted by the treasurer at four different periods of the year. There was no intention to make any alteration in Philadelphia or Allegheny County, in any particular, and the Act of 1875 contains no repealing clause."

Defendant took these writs of error assigning for error, *inter alia*, in each case, as follows:—

(2) Having found and determined that the Act of April 3, 1872 (P. L., 843), is not repealed, "but stands in full force," the Court erred in deciding that "the sums received for tavern licenses were either under the Act of 1875 or the general laws of the State, therefore do not come within either the words or spirit of the Act [of 1872] which says, 'the one-fourth of such sums received by the treasurer, as aforementioned, for license, to be for the use of the State.'"

(3) The Court erred in deciding that the money in controversy, having been "collected from the citizens for tavern licenses, must be distributed and appropriated, as in other cases, under the general laws" of the Commonwealth.

(4) The Court erred in not deciding that the money in controversy, being three-fourths of the

sums received by the treasurer of the county of Allegheny for tavern licenses—the other one-fourth having been paid into the State treasury—was, under the Act of April 3, 1872, for the use of the county of Allegheny, and should be appropriated accordingly.

(7) In disregarding the exemplification of the record of the injunction proceedings offered in evidence.

After argument upon these assignments the following order of the Supreme Court was made:—

PER CURIAM. These cases are ordered to be reargued before a full bench. Attention to the following questions is requested in addition to the question referred to in the paper books: Is the special Act of 1872, relating to Allegheny County, repealed in whole or in part, by the general Act of 1875? If in part only, does the repeal extend beyond the mere change of the rates of assessment? Has the treasurer of Allegheny County any power to assess, except under the Act of 1872? If he has, what law confers and regulates this power? Has the change of the rate of assessment in the third section of the Act of 1875 any operation upon the power to assess beyond the rate itself?

A. M. Brown (with whom was *S. H. Geyer*), for plaintiff in error.

The Act of 1872 had made special provisions for the collection of license fees in Allegheny County by the County Treasurer; then the Act of 1875 was passed as a general law to apply throughout the State so far as the amount of the fees was concerned, and the classification of those paying them, but not taking away the right to a proportionate share of all license fees secured by section seven of the Act of 1872. This Act was only repealed so far as its provisions were repugnant to those of the Act of 1875.

A special local statute is not repealed by a general law containing no inconsistent provisions.

Dyer *v.* Covington Township, 4 C. 186.

But a general law repeals a local law so far as their provisions are inconsistent.

Keller *v.* Comm., 21 Sm. 413.
Nusser *v.* Comm., 1 C. 126.
Bartlet *v.* King, 12 Mass. 545.
Gwinner *v.* Lehigh & D. G. R. R., 5 Sm. 126.
Johnston's Est., 9 C. 511.
Comm. *v.* Commissioners, 4 Wr. 348.
Comm. *v.* Cross Cut R. R. Co., 3 Sm. 62.
Southwark Bank *v.* Comm., 2 C. 446.
Norris *v.* Crocker, 13 How. 429.

In none of the cases cited by the Court below was there a plain inconsistency between the two Acts construed, while in the two other cases referred to (Bank *v.* Pittsburgh, 1 Wr. 340, and Comm. *v.* Fayette Co. R. R., 5 Sm. 452), a general tax law did repeal special laws exempting from taxation. In this case it is apparent from the language of the proviso of the third section of the Act of 1875, that it was intended that the license should be issued by an "authority" other than the Court of Quarter Sessions, but unless the Act is construed as applying in its general provisions throughout the State, such language is insensible, the word "Court" would have been used.

The Common Pleas of Allegheny County had jurisdiction in the suit in equity, the record of which was offered in evidence.

Comm. *v.* Supervisors, 5 C. 121.
McIntyre *v.* Perkins, 9 Phila. 484.
Pittsburgh *v.* Kelly, 33 Leg. Int. 118.

Gilbert, Dep. Attorney-General, and *Palmer*, Attorney-General, contra.

The injunction suit merely operated to impound the money, it did not settle the title to it; nor could it affect the duty of the Auditor-General in the settlement of the accounts. It is admitted that the fees were collected under the Act of 1875, and not under that of 1872, therefore no clause of that Act having reference to the fees collected under it can confer any right to the money now in controversy. The Act of 1872 was untouched by the latter Act, and we can find no authority vested in the treasurer of Allegheny County except that conferred by the prior Act, and saved by the saving clause of the subsequent Act. The authorities cited by the Court below sustain the opinion expressed as to the continued validity of the Act of 1872.

June 21, 1880. THE COURT. The Act of April 3d, 1872 (P. L. 843), is in its terms a special or local Act, intended to apply only to the county of Allegheny. The seventh section thereof appropriates to the use of the State one-fourth of the license fees by the Act authorized, and the balance to the use of the county, to be used, after payment of expenses, in building and maintaining a workhouse. The section referred to is dependent for its force and efficacy upon the preceding sections; this is obvious from its language, which is as follows: "The one-fourth of all such sums received by the treasurer, *as aforementioned*, for license, to be for the use of the State, . . . and the other three-fourths for the use of said county." It follows if, as the defendant below contends, the preceding sections are repealed by the Act of 1875, so also must be the seventh section, because the very source from which the county is to get its appropriation is thus cut off. As under this theory the "sums aforesaid" could have no existence, clearly the county could get nothing. If, then, we concede the defendant's proposition, that is, that the Act of 1872 has been repealed by the Act of 1875, his ground for resisting the claim of the Commonwealth is swept from under him. It is true it is contended that the Act of 1875 repealed that of 1872 only so far as classification and the rates of assessment are concerned, leaving the seventh section of the latter-named Act still in force. This, however, is an attempt to engraft, by an unwarranted implication, part of a general Act upon one that is purely local, and this anomalous patchwork has for its only object the giving to the county of Allegheny of three-fourths of the license fees raised under the Act of 1875. This cannot be; if this county is not so entitled under the Act of 1872, it is not entitled at all, for all such fees received under the Act of 1875 belong to the State. That Act contains in itself a uniform system designed to raise revenue for the use of the Commonwealth, and not for any local purposes whatever, and in it there is not so much as a hint towards the Allegheny Act. The claims of Allegheny County for a portion of the funds in the hands of the defendant must therefore be regarded as groundless. As these funds, confessedly, were collected under the Act of 1875, they belong to the State, and to the State they must go.

As to the remaining and incidental question, we have only to say, that neither directly nor by implication does the Act of 1875 repeal that of 1872, and we cannot see how, in view of the multitudinous decisions of this Court, directly bearing upon the doctrine here involved, any one could come to a different conclusion. To discuss a point so obvious would be to no purpose, especially in view of what has been so well said upon the subject by the Court below.

Judgment affirmed.

Opinion by GORDON, J. SHARSWOOD, C. J., absent.

Jan. '78, 199 & 200. January 27, 1879.
 February 13, 1880.

Littleton's Appeal.
Neill's Appeal.

Orphans' Court—Bills of review—Within what time they must be filed—Proceedings against lands charged with legacies—Who are proper parties to—Income tax—In case of estates, who is to pay.

A widow died in 1859, leaving three minor children, and owning certain real and personal property. By her will she left certain annuities and legacies to friends and relatives, and appointed A. her "executor and trustee." In 1863 A., her "executor and trustee," filed a petition in the Orphans' Court, setting forth that the personal property of decedent was insufficient to pay all legacies and annuities, and that the legacies and annuities were claimed to be a charge on the real estate, etc. Citations issued, and answers were filed by various legatees and annuitants, and an appearance was entered by counsel for the guardian of the decedent's minor children, who also argued the question on behalf of some of the annuitants. After argument a decree was made in accordance with the prayer of the bill, and the guardian accordingly transferred to A. all the real estate of decedent he held. Since this time A. had collected and paid over all the funds, and had paid the income tax out of the funds in his hands. At the audit of A.'s account, exceptions being filed to all credits for expenses of the legal proceedings in 1863, on the ground of want of jurisdiction, and to all payments of income tax:

Held, that the income tax was properly paid by the executor and trustee.

Held further, that the Orphans' Court had jurisdiction of the proceedings in 1863 by the executor and trustee.

PER CURIAM. Although the executor is not a proper party in proceedings against lands charged with legacies, and the proceedings should be by the legatees themselves, yet, evidently, making him a party does not avoid the proceedings for want of jurisdiction, if the legatees are in point of fact parties.

A petition for a bill of review being filed in the above case in 1876, shortly after the eldest minor reached majority, by said party and by the guardian of the other minors:

Held, that the bill was too late in point of time.

PER CURIAM. In regard to bills of review courts of equity govern themselves by the analogy of the law in regard to writs of error. Perhaps, in this State, it would be wise to follow the rule established by the Legislature as to reviews of final decrees confirming the original or supplementary account of any executor, administrator, or guardian, by the Act of October 13, 1840, § 1, which is five years.

Two appeals from the Orphans' Court of Philadelphia County.

Appeal (Jan. T. 1878, No. 199) of Wm. E. Littleton, guardian of W. and H. Cox, minors, and of R. R. Neill and Mary C., his wife, in right of said wife, from a decree of the Orphans' Court dismissing the exceptions to, and confirming the adjudication of the account of Chas. Hewson, executor of Mary R. Cox, deceased.

Appeal (Jan. T. 1878, No. 200) of R. R. Neill and Mary C., his wife, in right of said wife, and of Wm. E. Littleton, guardian of W. and H. Cox, minors, from a decree of the Orphans' Court dismissing their petition for a bill of review of the proceedings in the estate of Mary R. Cox, deceased.

The facts of these cases were as follows: Mary R. Cox, widow of Hewson Cox, died October 16, 1859. Under her father's will she had a life interest in certain property, which, at her death, was to descend to her children or their issue; under the will of an aunt she owned, absolutely, certain real and personal estate. On the day before her death said Mary R. Cox made her last will, whereby she left certain annuities and legacies to friends and relatives, "the annuities in all instances to cease at the death of the annuitants, and to revert to my estate, and be equally divided between my children, the issue," etc. The will appointed Chas. Hewson her "executor and trustee," and a codicil provided that—

"In case my above named executor and trustee, Chas. Hewson, shall find that the sum left me by Mrs. Ricketts [her aunt] shall not be sufficient to cover the annuities and legacies above named, then shall a deduction be made, *pro rata*, in all the sums mentioned," with certain specified exceptions.

The will was duly proved and letters testamentary issued. The testatrix left three minor children, Mary C., aged 8 years, Walter, aged 2 years, and Herbert, aged 6 days. Jas. Markoe was appointed guardian of the testatrix's minor children, and on his death, in 1876, Wm. E. Littleton was appointed in his place. On September 25, 1863, Chas. Hewson, calling himself executor and trustee under the will of Mary R. Cox, deceased, presented his petition to the Orphans' Court of Philadelphia, alleging that the personal property of the deceased was insufficient to pay all legacies and annuities, and that the said legacies and annuities were claimed to be a charge upon the real estate of testatrix, and praying that citations might issue, etc. Answers were filed by various parties interested, but none was filed on behalf of the minor children of Mrs. Cox. The docket entries, which were put in evidence at the audit, contained an entry on the margin as follows, viz., "G. M. Wharton, attorney for James Markoe, guardian of Cox minors *et al*." The testimony at the audit was to the effect that the proceeding had been amicable in its nature, but that the point had been argued adversely, on behalf of the minors, by the same counsel who represented some of the legatees and annuitants. On October 31, 1863, a decree was made, setting forth that it was considered by the Court that the legacies and annuities were payable out of the whole estate, real and personal, of testatrix, and directing Jas. Markoe, the guardian of the minor children, to deliver up to Chas. Hewson, the executor and trustee, all the real and personal property of testatrix in his possession or control. No appeal was taken from this decree by any of the parties interested. The decree was carried out, and since then Chas. Hewson has had entire control of the real and personal property of Mrs. Cox, has paid the legacies and annuities in full, and also all taxes, including the income tax and expenses, and accumulated the surplus. No account was filed by him, as executor, until Mrs. Neill came of age. At the audit of this account objection was made, on behalf of Mrs. Cox's children, to all items of credit for expenses in the Orphans' Court, in 1863, and for counsel fees in said proceeding; to commissions claimed upon the real estate or its income; to all payments of annuities or legacies out of the real estate or its income; to all payments of income tax. The report having been confirmed *nisi*, exceptions were filed, but were dismissed, and the adjudication confirmed absolutely; whereupon Littleton, guardian of the minor children of Mrs. Cox, took this appeal, assigning for error the said action of the Court.

A petition was also filed December 30, 1876, by R. R. Neill and Mary C., his wife, in right of said wife, and Wm. E. Littleton, guardian, etc., praying for a bill of review of the proceedings in the said estate, and that the Court would decree that the legacies and annuities were not a charge upon the real estate, etc. Citations having been issued, pleas and demurrers were filed, and after argument they were sustained, and the petition dismissed on the ground that it was too late in point of time; whereupon the petitioners, R. R. Neil and wife and Littleton, guardian, etc., took this appeal, assigning for error the said action of the Court.

W. W. Wister, Jr., and *E. Coppée Mitchell*, for appellants.

The bill for a review was filed shortly after the eldest child of decedent attained her majority. The Orphans' Court has from its beginning exercised the power to grant a bill of review, and a review will be granted, even after twenty years, in favor of persons under disabilities.

Kay *v.* Watson, 17 Ohio, 27.
Smith *v.* Clay, 3 Bro. Ch. Ca. 639.
Lytton *v.* Lytton, 4 Id. 458.

When the decree was entered the parties whose interest was affected were all minors, and the proceedings were, moreover, amicable; this alone is enough to make the Court specially careful. The result of the decree was to deprive the children of all interest in their mother's estate; and the decree was entered in an amicable suit, and was defended in part by those whose interests were identical with those of the plaintiff. This is the very class of cases to which a bill of review is applicable. The lapse of time was no ground for refusing the prayer of the bill.

Brigg's Appeal, 5 Watts, 91.
Whelen's Appeal, 20 Sm. 410.
Stewart's Appeal, 35 Leg. Int. 60.

The Court had no jurisdiction of the proceedings in 1863, for the legatees were the only parties competent to institute the proceedings. This has been expressly decided

Field's Appeal, 12 Casey, 11.

The income tax was improperly charged against the residuary estate; it should have been deducted from the shares of the individual annuitants. The Act of Congress provides that the tax shall be levied upon the estates of all persons, and there is no reason for making the residuary estate pay it.

Pancoast and *Chapman Biddle*, for appellees.

The appellants were represented in the proceedings by their guardian in 1863, and are concluded by that decree, unless they can show their right to a bill of review. The bill was filed too late, for a review will not be granted after the time when a writ of error could be brought. Courts of equity are guided in this ticular by the analogy of the common law.

Story's Eq. Pl. sec. 410 and note 1.
Daniel's Ch. Pr. 1580, note 1 (4th Am. Ed.
Smith *v.* Clay, 3 Bro. Ch. Ca. 641.
Kelly *v.* Lennon, 1 Jon. & Letouch, 305.
George's Appeal, 2 Jones, 262.
Bagg's Appeal, 7 Wr. 514.

And the rules of chancery in this particular are applicable to the Orphans' Court.

Riddle's Est. 7 Harris, 433.
Hartman's App., 12 Cas. 70.
Pennypacker's App., 1 Leg. Gaz. Rep. 485.

It is true that proceedings against lands charged with legacies must be by the legatees, and that the executor is not a proper party, but the petitioner in this case was constituted by the will both executor and trustee. The petition was therefore by a trustee, and those beneficially interested were parties.

February 24, 1879. THE COURT. (Opinion in Littleton's Appeal.) It is very true that it was held by this Court, in Field's Appeal (12 Casey, 11), that the proceeding in the Orphans' Court, against lands charged with legacies, must be by the legatees themselves, and that executors are not proper parties. Yet evidently making the executor a party does not avoid the proceeding for want of jurisdiction, if the legatees are in point of fact parties. The Court has general jurisdiction of the subject matter, and any error of the Court in the proceeding does not make void the decree. From the will and codicil of Mrs. Cox, Charles Hewson was not only executor, but also trustee to receive and hold the property which was to constitute the fund from which not only the legacies but the annuities were to be paid, and he was therefore a proper party to institute the proceedings. We think, then, the decree of the Orphans' Court was conclusive. The minor children of Mrs. Cox, these appellants, appeared by guardian, and submitted to the decision of the Court. This dispenses with the necessity of considering whether the annuities were by the will of Mrs. Cox charged on her real estate. The bill of review was not filed in time. We think it clear that the income tax was properly charged on and paid by the trustee, and was not a charge against the annuitants, and that the Court were perfectly right in decreeing that the trustee was entitled to hold the estate for the payment of the annuities. The proper mode of proceeding to ascertain whether the balance in his hands is more than sufficient would seem to be under the Act of Feb. 23, 1853. (Pamph. L. 98.)

Decree affirmed, and appeal dismissed at the costs of the appellants.

PER CURIAM.

February 24, 1879. THE COURT. (Opinion in Neill's Appeal.) We have decided in Littleton's Appeal the question of the jurisdiction of the Orphans' Court in the proceedings of 1863, and came to the conclusion that the decree in that proceeding was a valid and binding adjudication of the main point in controversy in this case. The bill of review was too late in point of time. It is stated in Story's Eq. Pl. 410, that such a bill will not lie after the time when a writ of error could be brought to a judgment, for courts of equity govern themselves by the analogy of the law in regard to writs of error, and he cites numerous authorities. In New York, it is held that a bill of review cannot be brought after the time allowed for an appeal. Boyd *v.* Vanderkemp (1 Barb. Ch. R. 273). Perhaps in this State it would be wise to follow the rule established by the Legislature as to reviews of final decrees confirming the original or supplementary account of any executor, administrator, or guardian, by the Act of Oct. 13, 1840, Sec. 1 (Pamph. L. 1841, p. 1), which is five years. This, however, would only be by analogy, for it is clear that the Act of 1840 is not directly applicable. Yet in George's Appeal (2 Jones, 262), Mr. Justice BELL says: "Should it become necessary with us to fix the time within which a review may be granted, the period will probably be much abridged by reference to our Act of 1791, prohibiting writs of error after seven years" (now reduced to two years by Act of April 1, 1874, Pamph. L. 50), or it may be the Act of 1840, just mentioned.

Decree affirmed, and appeal dismissed at the costs of the appellant.

PER CURIAM.

On motion, a reargument was granted in Littleton's Appeal and Neill's Appeal, and accordingly the cases were reargued on February 13, 1880; and the following opinion was subsequently filed.

March 1, 1880. THE COURT. After a full consideration on reargument, we see no reason to change the opinion filed heretofore in these cases.

Decrees affirmed, and appeals dismissed at the costs of the appellants.

PER CURIAM.

Common Pleas—Law.

C. P. No. 1. September 20, 1880.
In Re Petition of John Gunther.

Mortgages—Proceeding for satisfaction of, under Act of June 11, 1879—Lost mortgage, formerly held by an association which has long ceased to exist—Ex parte evidence of payment, when sufficient.

This was a proceeding for the satisfaction of record of a mortgage, under the Act of June 11, 1879 (P. L. 141). The petition set forth that in 1853 one Nicholas Freas, owner of a lot of ground in Germantown, gave a mortgage thereon for $800 to Jacob M. Bockius, treasurer of the "Provident Association of Germantown," in trust for the said association; that the whole of said mortgage-debt was fully paid more than twenty-four years ago, and that the affairs of said association were wound up, and the funds distributed among the members thereof, and the association disbanded. The petition then set forth the names of the president, secretary, and treasurer of the association who were last in office, and the dates of the decease of each of these officers, and averred that the mortgage was lost and cannot be found; that it was not satisfied of record; that the petitioner purchased the mortgaged premises from Nicholas Freas in August, 1857, and that he still owns the greater part thereof. The petitioner prayed the Court to direct the sheriff to serve a notice, according to the Act, upon the legal representatives of Jacob M. Bockius, treasurer, requiring them to appear and show cause why said mortgage should not be satisfied of record, and upon their failure so to do, and upon due proof being made as to the payment of said debt, as above stated, that the Court decree and direct that satisfaction be entered upon the record of such mortgage.

The affidavit of Curtis Smith, attached to the petition, set forth that deponent was a member of the "Provident Association of Germantown," and that the affairs of said association were all wound up, the money which had been loaned out was all paid in, the papers returned to members who had borrowed, and the funds all distributed; that said association was disbanded about the month of November, 1855; that Nicholas Freas was a member of said association, and that he was always prompt with his payments, and never was in arrears to said association, to the best of deponent's knowledge and belief.

The affidavit of Albertus King, also filed with the petition, set forth that deponent was a member and director of the "Provident Association of Germantown," that Jacob M. Bockius, now deceased, was the treasurer of said association; that the affairs of said association were all closed up, and a final settlement made in or about November, 1855, and that Jacob M. Bockius, the treasurer, was authorized to enter satisfaction of all the mortgages held by the said association, and that since the death of Joseph King, Jr., who was their secretary, all of the books pertaining to said society had been lost or mislaid.

On August 7, 1880, the Court, in accordance with the prayer of the petition, made an order directing the sheriff to serve a notice, stating the facts set forth in the petition, upon the legal representatives of Jacob M. Bockius, if to be found in the county of Philadelphia, and in case said parties could not be found within said county, then to give notice as aforesaid in one or more newspapers published within said county once a week for four weeks successively prior to the next term of the Court, requiring the said parties to appear at the next term and answer said petition.

The sheriff made return, certifying that he was unable to find within the county any of the legal representatives of Jacob M. Bockius, and that in obedience to the order of the Court, he had advertised a notice of the petition once a week for four successive weeks in the "Philadelphia Press" and the "Legal Intelligencer." Copies of said advertisements and affidavits of publication were annexed to the return.

Winship, for the petitioner.

September 20, 1880. THE COURT. In the present case the Court will be satisfied with these affidavits, as, under the circumstances, no other proof of payment is possible, the association holding the mortgage having disbanded, and its principal officers being dead. Under different circumstances, the petition might not be granted without further proof; and we should then probably order depositions to be taken, or refer the question to an auditor.

Petition granted, and decree accordingly.

Oral opinion by ALLISON, P. J.

C. P. No. 4. Oct. 16, 1880.
Rodgers v. Douglass.

Sheriff's interpleader—Title acquired subsequent to levy—A title acquired for a full consideration and without notice, subsequent to a levy, cannot be the subject of an interpleader.

Rule by sheriff for an interpleader.

On April 17, 1880, the sheriff made a levy upon ten blocks of brown stone in the yard of defendants. On July 10, 1880, The Middlesex Quarry Company, for a full consideration, and without notice that a levy had ever been made, purchased the ten blocks of stone from the defendants, and removed them to the yard of one Killen. Here a claim to the stone was made by the sheriff, whereupon the Quarry Company notified the sheriff that they had purchased the stone for a full consideration, without notice, and claimed the same as their property. The sheriff then took this rule.

R. C. Winship, for the rule.

W. F. Harrity, for execution plaintiff.

The Act of 10 April, 1848 (Purd. Dig., 643, pl. 48), was intended to protect the sheriff whenever a claim is made by one not a party to the action.

F. P. Prichard, for the Quarry Company.

An interpleader is awarded only for the purpose of trying the title to the goods at the *date* of the levy. A title *subsequent* to the levy can only be acquired through the consent or negligence of the sheriff, in which case the sheriff would be directly interested in the trial of the question, and cannot ask for an interpleader.

In re Sheriff of Oxfordshire, 6 Dowling, 136.

To entitle the sheriff to an interpleader, the claimant must aver title at the time of the delivery of the execution to the sheriff.

Troubat & Haly's Prac., § 1137.

Lafferty *v.* Cormick, 1 WEEKLY NOTES, 267.

THE COURT. (THAYER, P. J.) No title acquired subsequent to a levy can be the subject of an interpleader. Upon principle and the authority of the cases cited, this rule must be discharged.

Rule discharged.

———

C. P. No. 4. March 20, 1880.
Garver v. Ward.

Practice—Rule to vacate order of Court—Order of Court cannot be set aside without first taking rule to show cause—Such rule to show cause is not of course.

Rule to show cause why an order on the sheriff to pay into Court money realized from the sale of personalty should not be vacated.

H. Goodwin, showed cause.

The rule was improperly taken as of course. No affidavit was filed.

Melick, contra.

It was presumed that the rule was of course; there is no authority to the contrary.

[THAYER, P. J. You cannot take steps to vacate an order of Court without taking a rule to show cause; the rule is not a matter of course.]

Counsel for the sheriff being present, and all parties agreeing thereto, the Court permitted the cause to proceed as if a rule to show cause had been granted.

C. P. No. 3. May 22, 1880.
Landis v. Aldrich.

Mortgage — Attorney's commission — Circumstances under which the Court will control the amount of the commission.

Rule for judgment for want of a sufficient affidavit of defence.

Sci. fa. sur mortgage of $2000. The affidavit of defence set forth, *inter alia*, that the attorney's commission of five per cent. for collection mentioned in said mortgage is excessive, defendant being a widow with a large family dependent upon her for support, and not being the mortgagor mentioned in said mortgage.

Howell, for rule.

THE COURT (LUDLOW, P. J.) Under the circumstances we think an attorney's commission of two per cent. will be reasonable. Judgment accordingly.

———

C. P. No. 4. Oct. 16, 1880.
Reed v. Worthington.

Mortgage—Attorney's commission—Reduction of stipulated percentage—$150 allowed as fee for collecting mortgage of $4000—A reduction of damages may be made after execution has issued.

Rule to show cause why assessment of damages filed should not be reduced.

Sci. fa. sur mortgage on which judgment was obtained by default and execution issued. The amount of the mortgage was $4000. It contained a five per cent. attorney's commission for collection.

This was assessed in computing the damages.

Downing, for the rule.

5 per cent. is excessive, 2½ per cent. would be more than sufficient compensation.

Peterson, contra.

It is too late to claim a reduction of damages after execution has issued.

[THAYER, P. J. I do not think so.]

The attorney's fee of five per cent. is proper compensation on $4000.

Daly *v.* Maitland, 7 N. 384 (S. C. 7 WEEKLY NOTES, 103).

Waln *v.* Massey, 7 WEEKLY NOTES, 312.

Moller *v.* Ohse, 5 Id. 510.

THE COURT. There is no definite standard of commission established by the Courts. In this case I will reduce the commission to $150.

Weekly Notes of Cases.

Vol. IX.]   THURSDAY, NOV. 18, 1880.   [No. 13.

Supreme Court.

Jan. '79, 85.   March 27, 1879.
Parke v. Neely.

Judicial sales — Purchase-money mortgage — When not divested by judicial sale — Duty of purchaser — Estoppel — Antedated purchase-money mortgage recorded within sixty days of its execution but not its date — When date of execution may be proven.

While it is a general rule that a purchaser at sheriff's sale need not look beyond the records, the rule is not without its exceptions.

It is the duty of a purchaser at sheriff's sale under a judgment obtained subsequent to the record of a purchase-money mortgage recorded more than sixty days after its date, and subsequent to prior liens of record, to ascertain, *aliunde* if necessary, that the mortgage was actually executed more than sixty days before the date of its record, particularly if there are facts appearing on the face of the record to put him on inquiry, otherwise he takes title subject to the mortgage.

On January 14, 1876, a vendor obtained from his vendee a purchase-money mortgage, so described on its face; by agreement it was dated January 1st; it was acknowledged February 29th, and placed upon record March 2d, before which date the lien of certain mechanics' liens, subsequently filed, had attached. The premises having been sold under a judgment obtained in October following, the proceeds of sale were distributed amongst the mechanics' lien creditors, of whom the vendor was one. In proceedings under a scire facias sur mortgage against the vendee and the purchaser at sheriff's sale as terre tenant:

Held, that the lien of the mortgage was not discharged by the sheriff's sale.

Held also, that the mortgagee was not estopped from showing the date of the execution of the mortgage, and that parol evidence of that fact was admissible.

Per STERRETT, J. It is not material that the mortgage should appear on its face to be for purchase-money if the fact can be proven.

Cake's Appeal, 11 Harris, 186, followed.

Error to the Court of Common Pleas of Chester County.

Sci. fa. sur mortgage, brought by Robert Neely against the McLean & Benner Machine Co. and Thomas E. Parke, terre tenant.

The mortgage was made by the McLean & Benner Machine Co. to the plaintiff for $3500, and was dated January 1, 1876; it was acknowledged February 29, 1876, before an alderman, who was also a witness to the signatures, and it was recorded March 2, 1876. On the trial, December 2, 1878, before BUTLER, J., the plaintiff gave in evidence the mortgage and record, and rested. The defendant, Parke, put in evidence a sheriff's deed to himself, dated March 14, 1877, and the record of the judgment under which the sale had taken place, showing the judgment to have been recorded October 25, 1876, against the company defendant, and the fund arising from this sale to have been distributed entirely amongst mechanics' lien creditors, whose claims were filed at various dates between May and September, 1876, for work and labor performed and materials furnished from December, 1875, to April, 1876. Defendant's evidence further showed, that in the latter part of the year 1875 the plaintiff had agreed to contribute the lot in question to the company defendant, which was then about to commence operations, at a valuation of $3500, and the company immediately began to build thereon, the plaintiff himself furnishing some of the material, for which he had filed liens amongst those above mentioned. The plaintiff, under objection, which was overruled (when exception was taken by defendant), proved that from December 1, 1875, until January, the president of the company urged the plaintiff to make a deed, but he refused to do so until a mortgage was delivered. He had subscribed to $3500 worth of stock. The deed was finally made on January 14th or 15th, and held in escrow by the president until the 17th, when it was delivered to the company. On the latter date the mortgage in question was made, the deed and mortgage were both *dated January 1st,* and at "Neely's own desire" the mortgage recited the amount of the bond which it was given to secure, "the said sum of money being for the purchase-money of the hereinafter mentioned premises."

The following points were submitted by the defendant, all of which were negatived:—

(1) "The scire facias in this case recites that the mortgage upon which it is issued is dated on the first day of January, 1876. The plaintiff is estopped as against the terre tenant, a purchaser at sheriff's sale under a judgment subsequent to the mortgage, from averring that said mortgage was executed on any subsequent day.

(2) "The record shows that the mortgage was recorded more than sixty days after its execution, and although it may be a purchase-money mortgage, its lien attached only on the day that it was entered for record.

(3) "The terre tenant is purchaser at sheriff's sale on a judgment subsequent to the record of the mortgage, as shown by the record; there being at the time one or more mechanics' liens

on the land, which preceded the record of. the mortgage, he took the land discharged of the mortgage.

(4) "The terre tenant, as purchaser aforesaid, had the right to buy on the faith of what appeared of record, and was not bound to make further inquiry as to the time of the execution of the mortgage.

(5) "The terre tenant, as purchaser aforesaid, cannot be affected by any matters *in pais*, as to the time of the execution of the mortgage.

(6) "The mortgagee, by accepting the mortgage and putting it on record, declared to the world that the facts asserted in it were true; he is therefore estopped as against a *bona fide* purchaser for value at a judicial sale, from averring that the mortgage was executed on a day different from that on which it bears date.

(7) "The plaintiff was the owner of two mechanics' liens preceding the entry of his mortgage, and also preceding the judgment under which the land was sold. He was paid the amount of his liens from the proceeds of the sheriff's sale, the same being a substitute for the legal title then sold. He is therefore estopped from saying that these liens were not prior to his mortgage.

(8) "Although the deed from Robert Neely to the mortgagor may have been delivered on or about the 14th or 17th of January, 1876, yet if the jury believe that Robert Neely directed that it should be executed on the 1st of January, he is estopped, under the circumstances, to deny as against the terre tenant in this case that the deed was not executed on the day on which it bears date.

(9) "Under the evidence in this case the plaintiff is not entitled to recover."

The charge of the Court was as follows: "The Court answers all the points of the defendant in the negative, for the reason given upon the motion for a new trial, which need not now be repeated.

"I need not detain you with any lengthy remarks respecting this case. The question involved is virtually a question of law, on which the parties very properly desire the opinion of the Court of last resort. We have had occasion to consider the question heretofore, and have already passed our judgment upon it. We charge you now that if you find that the deed and mortgage—the deed made by Mr. Neely and the mortgage received by him for purchase-money— were delivered at the time spoken of by witness McLean, president of the machine company, on the 17th of January instead of the 1st day of January, when they bear date, your verdict will be for the plaintiff. I repeat, if these instruments were delivered on the 17th of January, as testified to by Mr. McLean, instead of the 1st of January when they bear date, and when without this testimony it would be presumed they would be delivered, your verdict will be for the plaintiff. And I must say to you, there is no contradiction of Mr. McLean, the only witness who speaks to the point, and that he is positive about it, that the deed was delivered on that day. I see nothing in the case to create a doubt of the accuracy of his belief, or the justness of his statement."

Verdict for plaintiff for $4112.50 and judgment thereon. The defendant took this writ, assigning for error the admission of the evidence excepted to, the refusal to affirm the points presented, and the charge of the Court, as above quoted. The case was submitted on the briefs.

W. B. Waddell and *P. F. Smith*, for plaintiff in error.

This mortgage was recorded sixty-two days after its date, and the purchaser was not bound to look further than the record for his title.

Mode's Appeal, 6 W. & S. 280.
Jaques v. Weeks, 7 W. 261.
Coyne v. Souther, 11 Sm. 457.

The policy of the law is that judicial sales shall be made clear of all reasonable doubt, and thus that the debtor may realize the most from his property and his creditors be paid; but if bidders are to be obliged to make all manner of inquiries *in pais* where a doubt as to the accuracy of the record can be raised, there would be but few bidders, and those at small sums; it "would cast a ruinous obscurity over the biddings" (Mix v. Ackla, 7 Watts, 316). A purchaser of the legal title cannot be affected by a latent equity of which he has not actual notice, or which does not appear on some deed necessary to the deduction of his title.

Peebles v. Reading, 8 S. & R. 484.

A deed is presumed to be delivered on the day it bears date, and the acknowledgment on a subsequent date does not affect the presumption.

Hall v. Benner, 1 Pa. 407.
2 Bl. Comm. 306, note 18.

Neely was estopped as against the innocent purchaser by his assertion in the deed that it was executed on January 1st.

Ayres v. Wattson, 7 Sm. 360.
Chapman v. Chapman, 9 Sm. 214.

Alfred P. Reid, contra.

The records of the recorder's office are not presumed to be of absolute verity.

Fleming v. Parry, 12 H. 52.

Purchase-money mortgages are liens from the time of their execution, and their efficacy is only restricted by the Act requiring them to be recorded within sixty days.

Bratton's Appeal, 8 Barr, 167.

A purchaser may rely upon the act of an official in the strict line of his duty, as required by statute, and no further.

Musser *v.* Hyde, 2 W. & S. 314.
Lancaster *v.* Smith, 17 Sm. 427.
Angier *v.* Schieffelin, 22 Sm. 106.

Whatever does or ought to put a party upon inquiry is equivalent to notice; and this being a purchase-money mortgage was not discharged.

Knouff *v.* Thompson, 4 H. 364.
Cake's Appeal, 11 H. 187.

There is no proof that the purchaser relied upon these facts, nor that he has suffered any injury; he is then in no position to invoke an estoppel.

May 5, 1879. THE COURT. The contention of the plaintiff in error is, that the mortgage on which the scire facias in this case issued, was divested by the sheriff's sale, at which he became purchaser of the mortgaged premises. It is conceded that the mortgage, as expressed on its face, was given to secure purchase-money, and if recorded within sixty days from the execution thereof, was undoubtedly the first lien on the land, and consequently not divested by the sale, unless its date raises a conclusive presumption as to the time of its execution. On the other hand, if not recorded in time, the mechanics' liens, although subsequently entered, were first in order, because they related back to the commencement of the building, and attached to the equitable interest which the mortgagor had acquired before the conveyance of the legal title. The deed and mortgage were dated January 1, 1876, and the latter was not recorded until the sixty-second day thereafter. In the absence of proof to the contrary, the presumption would be that they were executed and exchanged on the day they bear date. Assuming this to be so, the mortgage, having thus lost its priority, was postponed to the mechanic's lien, and consequently divested by the sheriff's sale under the subsequent judgment. It was clearly shown, however, that the deed and mortgage were both executed after their date, and within sixty days of the time the latter was recorded.

This being established, it was held that the mortgage continued to be the first lien, and was not divested by the sheriff's sale. The introduction of parol evidence to prove the actual date of execution, and the legal effect given to it by the Court, form the sole grounds of exception on the part of the plaintiff in error. He contends that his rights as a purchaser at the judicial sale are to be determined by the proper record of liens, and by what appeared as the registry of the mortgage at the time of the sale, and not by what was proved *aliunde* as to the time it was in fact executed; in other words, that as to time, the *date* of the mortgage must be conclusively taken to be the date or time of its execution, and that parol evidence is not admissible to show that in point of fact it was subsequently executed and delivered. The exceptions relied on by the plaintiff in error resolve themselves substantially into two questions of law: the legal effect of what the records of the Court and the registry of the mortgage exhibited at the time of the sheriff's sale, and the question of estoppel. The mechanics' claims, filed May 8, 1876, and subsequently, might be resorted to by the purchaser for the purpose of ascertaining when the liens were filed, and how far back they related.

This, in connection with information derived *aliunde*, would probably inform him that these liens attached to the equitable interest of the mortgagor before the legal title was acquired. So far as the record of these claims was concerned, he might rely implicitly on what was there represented. Like all judicial records, made up potentially, if not actually, under the eye of the Court, the proper averments of record imported verity, and might be taken as his guide in bidding at the sheriff's sale. As a general rule, a purchaser is not bound to look beyond the judgment docket for liens that should there appear. (Coyne *v.* Souther, 11 P. F. Smith, 457.) It is different, however, with the registry of deeds and mortgages. The chief object of recording them is to give actual as well as constructive notice to everybody of title and incumbrances thereon, and, apart from notice, the only effect given to recorded instruments by the statute is to make certified copies thereof evidence, and in case of mortgages to provide that they shall not be liens until left for record, *except* mortgages for purchase-money, which continue to be liens from the date of their execution, if recorded within sixty days thereafter.

In Cake's Appeal (11 Harris, 186) the record of the mortgage did not exhibit it as a first lien. It was for purchase-money, but the conveyance was dated several months before its entry, judgments had been obtained against the equitable title, and from the face of the record appeared to have closed in upon the legal estate ahead of the mortgage, and yet upon proof that the deed had been antedated, and the mortgage recorded within sixty days from the time it was actually executed and delivered, it was held that the lien of the mortgage was not divested, but that it still bound the land in the hands of the purchaser. The question in that case arose on distribution of the proceeds of sale, but that is unimportant, for after refusing to permit the mortgagee to participate in the proceeds, and turning him over to the land, it would come with bad grace to say that the purchaser might refuse payment and remit him to the proceeds. Whilst it is true, as a general rule, according to Magaw *v.* Garrett (1 Casey, 322), and other cases, that a purchaser need not look beyond the record for liens and incumbrances, it is not universally so.

There are several exceptions, and in some of them the safety of purchasers is not consulted. Generally, the record furnishes no notice of mechanics' liens until they have run for a considerable time. The existence of a purchase-money mortgage may appear at any time within sixty days after its execution, and it is not necessary even then to disclose on its face the material fact that it is for purchase-money, nor the time when it was executed, without which knowledge the purchaser can form no reliable judgment respecting the liens.

Guthrie v. Watson is a case in which a person after acquiring an equitable interest in land, confessed a judgment, and months afterwards accepted a conveyance of the legal title. The record did not show that the judgment was a lien on the land thus acquired, nor suggest anything pointing towards it. The land appeared to be subsequently acquired and unincumbered, and yet a purchaser was bound to take notice of the incumbrance, and hold subject to it. So that it is not universally true that a purchaser may content himself with an inspection of the record. There are many facts outside the record about which he must inquire, or suffer the consequences. There was quite sufficient in this case to put the purchaser on notice. Whatever puts a party on inquiry amounts to notice, provided the inquiry becomes a duty, as in the case of purchasers and creditors, where the inquiry, if pursued, would lead to knowledge of the requisite facts. (Mulliken v. Graham, 22 Smith, 490). The mortgage shows upon its face that it was taken to secure purchase-money of the land therein described, and that the mortgagee intended to preserve his lien, which could only be done by recording the mortgage within sixty days from the time it was executed and delivered. This, in connection with the fact that only sixty-two days had elapsed between the date and the entry, should have suggested inquiry as to whether it was not antedated. It appeared further, that it was not acknowledged until the 29th February, only two days before it was recorded.

While it is true that it might have been delivered before it was acknowledged, such a transaction in regard to a mortgage would be so exceptional and extraordinary as to excite inquiry. Again, the alderman before whom the acknowledgment was taken was a subscribing witness to the execution and delivery of the mortgage, from which it would naturally be inferred that the acknowledgment was simultaneous with the execution and delivery. The same may be said in regard to the deed. Its acknowledgment is of a later date than the deed itself, and the magistrate before whom it was taken is also a subscribing witness to the execution and delivery. These circumstances, all of which appear on the face of the paper, were sufficient to repel the inference which would otherwise have arisen from their dates, and were quite sufficient to put the purchaser on inquiry, and thus visit him with notice. There was no error in admitting parol evidence to prove the actual date of delivery, nor in the controlling effect given to the fact which the testimony clearly established. And, in addition, there was quite enough on the face of the papers themselves to make it the duty of the purchaser to inquire. If he had done so, he would have been fully informed that the mortgage was the first lien, and would not be divested by the sheriff's sale. There are no facts in the case out of which estoppel could arise.

Judgment affirmed.
Opinion by STERRETT, J.

May, '80, 14.   May 10, 1880.

Imler v. Imler.

Judgment note—Attorney's fees for collection.

Upon a judgment for $2600, by warrant of attorney, containing the clause "with attorney's fees for collection," most of the debt was paid voluntarily, and the judgment was opened and went to a jury upon a contested payment of $192. The jury decided in favor of the plaintiff, and the Court, on a reserved point, allowed $103 attorney's commissions on $2600, according to a fee bill agreed upon by members of the bar:

Held (affirming the judgment of the Court below), that this was not excessive, as there was litigation, and the labor of counsel would have been no greater had the verdict been for the whole face of the judgment.

The contract was one of indemnity.

Daly v. Maitland, 7 WEEKLY NOTES, 103, followed.

Error to the Common Pleas of Bedford County.

Susanna Imler gave her note to her son, Thos. Imler, December 29, 1874, for $2600, payable in three equal annual instalments, commencing April 1, 1875. The note contained a warrant of attorney to confess judgment, "*with attorney's fees for collection*," and was entered of record. The note was given for the purchase-money of land. The first two payments were made promptly, and a part of the third, an execution having been issued for the balance, including a commission of $103, which was calculated on the sum of $2600, according to a fee bill adopted by the members of the bar of Bedford County, she applied to have the judgment opened, on the ground that she had paid the whole debt, a part of said payment being made by the payment of a judgment in favor of John B. Smith against Thomas Imler, for $192.56, which was a lien on the land at the time of the sale.

The petition prayed the Court to strike off the commission of $103, on the ground that the money was paid promptly, and no execution was issued until the whole amount had been paid or tendered.

The plaintiff's answer alleged that the Smith judgment was a forgery, and ought not to have been paid by Susanna Imler.

The Court (HALL, P. J.) opened the judgment, and the case was tried by a jury, under the following instructions upon the question raised by the petition and answer: "The only question of fact in dispute is whether Thomas Imler signed the Smith note—is his signature genuine? The burden of proving this is for the defendant, Susanna Imler. Dubois, who attests the signature as witness, has not been called. John Imler testifies that Thomas admitted to him that the note was genuine, and also that he knows his writing, and the signature is genuine. Imler swears he never signed it. The real dispute is the sum of $192.56, with interest from 2d April, 1877. If Thomas Imler signed the note of E. Y. Imler to Smith, as surety, Susanna Imler had a right to pay the $192.56, and to have credit for it on this judgment.

"As to the commissions of the attorney, the defendant does not deny that the money was all collected by the attorneys, Messrs. Longenecker & Russell, and that by the terms of the contract five per cent., amounting to $103, is due, unless the Court should be of opinion as a matter of law, that the money must have been collected by execution. This point we reserve to be determined on a proper motion." Exception to defendant.

Verdict for the plaintiff for $319.36, "subject to opinion of Court on attorney's commission." On motion, the Court refused a new trial, and entered judgment for plaintiff on the point reserved, whereupon the defendant took this writ, assigning as error the instruction of the Court that the burden of proving that Thomas Imler signed the Smith note was upon Susanna Imler; and in sustaining the attorney's commission, the debt not having been collected by execution.

J. B. Cessna, for plaintiff in error.

The Smith judgment was never opened, and must be presumed to be right. It cannot be treated as a nullity.

Hageman *v.* Salisberry, 24 Sm. 280.
Hauer's Appeal, 5 W. & S. 473.
Second Nat. Bank's Appeal, 6 WEEKLY NOTES, 153.

The judgment, except $192, amount of the Smith judgment in controversy, was paid before judgment. No attorney was necessary, as there was no litigation. The fee must be reasonable, and it must be earned.

Daly *v.* Maitland, 7 WEEKLY NOTES, 103.

Russell & Longenecker, contra.

The case was tried on the issue of fact raised by the petition and answer, and that question was the validity of the Smith judgment. The verdict of the jury finds that that judgment was fraudulent.

The attorney's commission of $103 was not unreasonable, and the jury found the amount. The Court reserved the question whether the $2600 should have been collected by execution, and decided that it was not proper to reduce the amount.

In Daly *v.* Maitland, cited by plaintiff in error, the Court say they will not review the exercise of a sound discretion, unless the commission allowed is plainly excessive.

June 19, 1880. THE COURT. There is no merit in the first assignment of error. Even if the burden of showing that the signature to the note upon which the judgment No. 238, April 7, 1874, was entered, was genuine, was not upon the defendant below she has no reason to complain, as the record shows she voluntarily assumed such burden before the jury. Having assumed it and obtained the conclusion to the jury, it is no just cause of complaint that the Court below adopted her own view of her duty.

The 2d, 3d, and 4th assignments refer to the single question of the attorney's commissions, and may be considered together. The judgment note in controversy was for $2600, payable in instalments, with interest and "attorney's fees for collection." The plaintiff moved to Nebraska, and left the note with his attorneys at Bedford for collection. The defendant paid most of the instalments within a short time after maturity and without legal process. The principal contention was over the Smith judgment of $192.56, which was paid by the defendant. As the judgment was a lien upon the land she bought of the plaintiff, the payment would have been well enough, if the latter had no defence to it. But unfortunately for the defendant the plaintiff alleged that the note upon which the Smith judgment was entered was a forgery, and the jury in the trial below found the fact to be so. The amount of attorney's commissions claimed and allowed was $103, and it was urged that this was an unreasonable fee for the collection of a note of $2600, all of which except the small sum included in the verdict, was paid voluntarily. The further point was raised that as to so much of the note as was not collected by execution, no commissions could be charged.

The obvious intention in this and like stipulations in instruments for the payment of money is that the creditor shall be indemnified for his reasonable expense of counsel fees in collecting the money. That is to say, where it becomes necessary to employ counsel to collect the money, the debtor shall be subjected to the expense thereof, not exceeding the agreed limit. It was never intended, nor can we permit such a clause to be used, to compel a debtor to pay attorney's commissions when the latter does not dispute the claim and pays at maturity. In such cases there is no necessity for the intervention of an attorney. Where, however, an attorney has been employed in good faith, by reason of the neglect or the refusal of the defendant to pay, the fact that the money has been paid to the attorney without execution, does not relieve the defendant from his agreement to pay a reasonable attorney's commission, for the reason that the creditor's liability to the attorney has attached. The contract is one of indemnity, and if the defendant, by his neglect or refusal to pay, has subjected his creditor to the necessity of employing counsel, why should he not pay? The attorney deducts his commissions even where no execution or other legal process is issued, and if the defendant cannot be made to pay, the creditor has no indemnity, and the clause means nothing.

How much is the defendant entitled to pay as such indemnity? Such agreements were formerly uniformly drawn at the rate of five per cent. This Court held that an arbitrary charge of five per cent. in all cases could not be sustained. That only a reasonable compensation could be recovered, the amount of which in each case must rest in the sound discretion of the Court. Accordingly in Daly *v.* Maitland (7 WEEKLY NOTES, 103), which was a scire facias to collect a mortgage of $14,000, the commissions were reduced from five to two per cent.

We are asked to say that the amount allowed in the case in hand is excessive. The agreement was not for five per cent., but for "attorneys' commissions for collection." The amount allowed was $103. This is less than five per cent. and agrees with the tariff of charges fixed by the Bedford County Bar. The amount may seem large in proportion to the verdict. But this is a matter which the defendant would have done well to consider before she entered upon the expensive, vexatious, and often unprofitable business of litigation. The amount of time and labor required on the part of counsel, would have been no greater had the verdict been for the whole face of the note. There was a suit and trial in the Court below, and an argument here. It was said in Daly *v.* Maitland (*supra*), "In general this Court will not review the exercise of a sound discretion by an inferior Court upon such a question, and the presumption will always be in favor of their decision, unless it is plainly excessive, or as appears to have been the case here, founded on the mistaken idea that they had no equitable power to interpose and moderate the agreed amount." Applying this sound rule of our latest decision upon this subject to the case in hand, we are not prepared to say that the amount allowed is so plainly excessive, as to justify us in reversing the decision of the Court below.

Judgment affirmed.

Opinion by PAXSON J. STERRETT and TRUNKEY, J.J., dissent to allowance of attorneys' commissions, except on the sum which remained unpaid when the judgment was opened.

SHARSWOOD, C. J., and GREEN, J., absent.

March 1, 1880.

City of Allentown v. Hower.

Municipal claim—Water-frontage tax—Cities of the third class—Allentown—Defective registration of unpaid taxes—Municipal corporations—Act of May 23, 1874, sects, 36 and 37—What a sufficient registration of the lien to support a scire facias—Act of April 21, 1858, sec. 9—Amendment permissible, when without prejudice.

Registration of lien for unpaid water-frontage tax, containing neither location nor description of real estate, is defective and insufficient to support a scire facias.

Registration, in order to furnish constructive notice to purchasers and subsequent incumbrancers of the nature and duration of the lien, should contain at least a brief description of the property, including its location, the amount, date, and nature of the assessment.

To support a scire facias the property should be designated with such certainty as to enable the sheriff to execute the levari facias, but it is unnecessary to conform strictly to all the requisites of a mechanic's lien. The name of the contractor or material men need not be given, nor is a bill of particulars necessary.

The Act of April 21, 1858, is a general Act under which amendment is allowable when without prejudice to intervening rights.

Error to the Common Pleas of Lehigh Co.

Scire facias sur municipal claim for water-frontage tax by the city of Allentown against Harrison Hower.

On Feb. 9, 1876, the city of Allentown, which was incorporated as a city of the third class under the Act of May 23, 1874, known as the Municipal Corporations Act, registered a lien for unpaid water-frontage tax against the property of the defendant. The tax was assessed June 1, 1875, and registered in the Court of Common Pleas of Lehigh County, for $35, of January Term, 1876, No. 1011. On March 8, 1876, a sci. fa. was issued against the defendant on this lien, as of April Term, 1876, 213, and on May 6, 1876, judgment was entered for the plaintiff for want of an affidavit of defence. On April

29, 1876, the defendant took a rule to show cause why the writ of scire facias should not be quashed, which the Court on July 3, 1876, made absolute. A rule was then taken to show cause why the lien registered as of January Term, 1876, should not be stricken off on the ground that it set forth no description of the property. The plaintiff on July 8, 1876, filed a petition for leave to amend the lien, reciting a full description of the property and amount of the claim. Upon a hearing on a rule to strike off the claim, and on the rule to amend the lien, ALBRIGHT, P. J., delivered an opinion, making the rule to strike off absolute, and discharging the rule to amend.

The plaintiff took this writ, assigning for error the action of the Court in striking off the lien and discharging the rule to amend.

R. E. Wright and *J. M. Kessler*, City Solicitor, for plaintiff in error.

The Act of May 23, 1874, does not require, as the Court below erroneously held, that the claim filed should contain a full description of the real estate sought to be charged. The word "register" is to be construed in its ordinary signification, and not in the strained and unusual sense contended for on the other side. To hold that the city should be compelled to file liens in the nature of the mechanics' liens for every tax against realty remaining unpaid is to place a burden upon a municipality, beyond the legislative intent, and opening up a way of escape to delinquent tax-payers. It is contended that there can be no proceeding on the registry in the nature of a sci. fa., because the sci. fa. is a proceeding *in rem*. But there is nothing more on the record than a recognizance for bail, and yet a scire facias sur recognizance is an almost daily occurrence in practice.

The amendment was proper, for it was based upon the general Act of April 21, 1858, section 9.

Edward Harvey, for the defendant in error.

Under the Act of May 23, 1874, it is essential to the validity of a lien that it contain a correct and detailed description of the tax, the name of the owner chargeable, and a reference to the realty. Upon this lien a sci. fa. cannot issue, for the registry of the lien shows neither location nor description of the property upon which to make a levy. The lien is, therefore, fatally defective.

City *v.* Wood, 4 Phila. 156.
Pittsburgh *v.* Cluley, 16 Sm. 449.
Commissioners *v.* Flanigan, 3 Phila. 458.

The Act of April 23, 1858, is a local Act, for it is supplemental to an Act incorporating the city of Philadelphia. The amendment, therefore, is matter of grace not of right.

But there was nothing on the record to amend by.

A mechanic's lien cannot be amended after the statutory period of filing it.

Dearie *v.* Martin, 28 Sm. 55.

Nor can it be amended by an alteration of the description of the premises.

Armstrong *v.* Hallowell, 11 Casey, 485.

May 3, 1880. THE COURT. The claim against the defendant was for "water-frontage tax," regularly assessed for water-pipe, laid in front of his property on the south side of Walnut Street. The tax not having been paid within the time required, was registered in the city lien docket; and the defendant contends that the registration was so fatally defective, that the Court was right in striking off the claim.

The Municipal Corporation Act, providing among other things, for extending the supply of water, requires the clerk of the department to make a list of all the owners of houses, lots and buildings, on each side of the street through which water-pipes are extended, and charge each respectively such rate per foot front as may be fixed by ordinance. The charge so made is to be collected as city taxes, and if not paid within the time prescribed, the same shall be registered in the manner provided for registering unpaid city and school taxes on real estate, with like force and effect, as to lien against such property and subject in all respects to like mode of procedure and remedy for recovery of the same. (Purdon, 1925, pl. 144 and 145.) The 36th section of the Act providing for the annual levy and collection of city taxes, directs the treasurer to receive and collect taxes until and including the first day of January, after which he shall furnish a correct and detailed statement of delinquent taxes, respectively due upon real estate to the city solicitor, who shall cause the same to be registered in *the city lien docket*, in the prothonotary's office, in the name of the city, and against the person or persons charged therewith; and all taxes so registered shall be, and continue to be, liens on the real estate upon which they have been assessed for the term of five years, from the date of the levy. (Purdon, 1916, pl. 96 and 97.) The next section provides, that recovery may be had on claims for taxes, water-frontage tax, etc., in the Court of Common Pleas, "by action of debt . . . or by scire facias, as in the case of mechanics' claims," and the claims so registered shall be *prima facie* evidence of the amount thereof, and of the same being due and owing," etc.

While no particular form is prescribed, the registration should, for the purpose of notice, as well as remedy, contain at least a brief description, including location of the property assessed, corresponding with that which the clerk of the department is required to make, when frontage-tax is assessed, giving the name of the owner or reputed owner, the amount of the assessment, its date and what it was for. If the claim is for "water-frontage tax," it may be designated by that name as the Act provides. If these matters are briefly noted in the claim, the registration will furnish at least constructive notice to purchasers and subsequent incumbrancers, of the nature, extent, and duration of the lien. One of the remedies given is a proceeding purely *in rem*, by scire facias, as in the case of mechanics' claims. To make this available, it is necessary that the property against which the lien is sought to be enforced, should be designated with such certainty as to enable the Sheriff to execute the levari facias; but it is unnecessary to conform strictly to all the requisites of a mechanics' lien. The name of the contractor or material men need not be given, nor is a bill of particulars, etc., necessary. In Pittsburgh *v.* Chuley (16 P. F. Smith, 449) it was said that the Mechanics' Lien Act furnished only a general, and not a specific rule of proceedings. The special Act under consideration in that case, required the lien to be "filed in the same manner as mechanics' liens," and authorized writs of scire facias and levari facias, to "be issued thereon as in the case of mechanics' liens," and yet it was there shown to be unnecessary, and in some respects impossible to conform to all the requirements of the mechanics' lien law. The municipal corporation Act contains no such binding directions as to how the claim shall be registered, nor does it require that it should be even in the form of a mechanic's claim. It simply directs that the claim shall be registered, and provides that one of the remedies for its collection may be "by scire facias, as in the case of mechanics' claims." The manner of assessing or charging water-frontage tax is especially prescribed, as we have seen. The amount of the claim against each particular lot, is thus fixed and determined, and hence it is unnecessary to set forth the particulars in detail. The claim, however, should be stated with such certainty and precision, as to answer the purpose of notice, and at the same time support the proceeding that is authorized as one of the remedies for enforcing payment.

The Court was clearly right in holding that the claim as registered, was defective and insufficient to support a scire facias, etc.; but under the ninth section of the Act of April 21, 1858 (Purdon, 70, pl. 5), which the Court properly held to be a general law, we think it was amendable, and an amendment should have been allowed. That section provides "that municipal claims for taxes, liens, public assessments or charges, may be amended at any time before or at the trial, on notice given the defendant, under rule of Court, *provided* that if made on the trial, a continuance may be granted by the Court, on the application of the defendant."

Such Acts as this should be liberally construed, and while amendments are not a matter of right, they should be allowed, where it can be done without prejudice to intervening rights. So far as appears there were none in this case. The assessment of water-frontage tax against the defendant's property, which was no doubt made as directed by the Act, would furnish all the data necessary for the amendment.

The order of the Court striking the claim from the record is reversed and set aside, the rule to amend reinstated, and record remitted for further proceedings.

Opinion by STERRETT J.

Oct. & Nov. '78, 124.   Nov. 1879.

Waldo v. Commonwealth.
Waldo's Appeal.

Sunday law—Act of April 22, 1794—Constitutionality of—Seventh Day Baptists—Stare decisis.

The constitutionality of the Act of April 22, 1794, known as the Sunday law, has been finally settled, and the question is not open for argument. Seventh Day Baptists are equally amenable to the provisions of the Act as other citizens.

PER CURIAM. Were it a new question, it certainly would deserve very serious consideration.

Commonwealth *v.* Wolf, 3 S. & R. 48, and Specht *v.* Commonwealth, 8 Barr, 312, followed.

Appeal from the Common Pleas of Crawford County.

On November 13, 1877, complaint was made before a justice of the peace of Crawford County, by one William F. Van Nauter, against Daniel C. Waldo for "performing worldly employment on the Lord's Day, commonly called Sunday, by working in his planing and shingle mill, contrary to the Act of Assembly in such cases made and provided." On the hearing before the justice the defendant filed, among others, the following exception, viz.: "That the said Waldo is a member, in good standing, in the Seventh Day Baptist Church, and as such, conscientiously, and as a religious duty, labors the first six days of each week; and observes and keeps the seventh day, or Saturday, as the Sabbath, and therefore ought not to be subject to the penalty of the Act of 1794, known as the Sunday law."

The exception was overruled by the justice, as no justification for violating the Act of 1794, and the defendant was found guilty of the offence charged, and adjudged to pay a fine of four dollars, etc.

The case was brought into the Common Pleas by certiorari, and on argument, the proceedings of the justice were affirmed by the Court.

The defendant took this appeal, assigning for error the overruling of the above exception and the order affirming the proceedings of the justice's court.

H. L. Richmond & Sons, for the appellant, presented an elaborate argument to show the unconstitutionality of the Sunday law of 1794, especially so far as it affects Seventh Day Christians.

J. N. McCloskey, contra, cited—
Commonwealth *v.* Wolf, 3 S. & R. 48.
Specht *v.* Commonwealth, 8 Barr, 312.
And relied on the principle *stare decisis*.

Jan. 5, 1880. THE COURT. The able and learned counsel for the appellant has presented to us a very eloquent and exhaustive argument against the constitutionality of the Act of April 22, 1794, known as the Sunday law. Were it a new question it certainly would deserve very serious consideration. It must now certainly be considered as finally settled, and is not open for argument. Wolf *v.* The Comth. (3 S. & R. 48), was decided in 1816, more than sixty years ago. It was again mooted in Specht *v.* The Comth. (8 Barr, 316), in 1848, and the constitutionality of the Act, after a very elaborate argument, was affirmed.

Order affirmed.

PER CURIAM.

Quarter Sessions.

In re Volkmar Street.

Opening streets—Practice—Rule XV. Sect. 26, of Quarter Sessions—Petitions for opening streets under Act of March 22, 1813, to be heard before Judge of the Court of Quarter Sessions sitting in Common Pleas—Note to former report.

Since this case was reported, *ante*, p. 169, MITCHELL, J., has furnished the following note:—

No question of jurisdiction between the Courts of Common Pleas and Quarter Sessions was raised in this case, as might seem to be implied in a cursory perusal of the report—9 WEEKLY NOTES, 169. The jurisdiction of the Quarter Sessions over the whole subject of the opening of streets (so far as it is a matter of judicial cognizance at all) is exclusive and unquestioned. But by Rule XV., Sect. 26, of the Quarter Sessions Court Rules, "*all road cases ready for argument*," in certain months specified, "shall be heard before the Judges of the Court of Quarter Sessions, *sitting in Court of Common Pleas*," etc. The question raised in *Re* Volkmar Street was one of practice merely, to wit, *where* petitions for opening streets, under the Act of 1813, are to be heard, whether on the motion list of the old Quarter Sessions, or under the abovementioned rule, in the Common Pleas; and the decision was meant to settle the point that such petitions, being cases in which evidence is to be taken and presented to the Court, are *road cases for argument*, within Rule XV., and are to be heard, therefore, on the Common Pleas lists.

Common Pleas—Equity.

C. P. No. 1. July, 1880.

Raynor et al. v. Beatty et al.

Religious corporations—Power of the Court to supervise elections—Qualifications of voters—By-laws inconsistent with charter—Member cannot be deprived of his right to vote by by-laws.

Sur exceptions to Master's report.

Bill in equity filed March 20, 1880, by William Raynor and thirteen others, describing themselves as members, and a majority of those entitled by law to elect vestrymen of a corporation known as "The Rector, Church Wardens, and Vestrymen of the Church of St. Timothy," incorporated for the purpose of worshipping in accordance with the doctrines and canons of the Protestant Episcopal Church, against Robert H. Beatty *et al.*, setting forth, *inter alia*, that at the annual election for vestrymen of the said corporation, held April 14, 1879, the judges of election had issued certificates of election to the defendants, who were not legally elected; but who acted as a *de facto* vestry; and who, intending to deprive certain of the complainants of their right to vote at the coming election, had dropped their names from the vestry books; that Henry Osborne, one of the defendants, with this same object in view, had refused to receive pew rent from such of the complainants as are in arrear, and who are ready and willing to pay; and that the said vestrymen had added to the vestry books the names of certain persons who have complied neither with the charter nor the by-law requirements regarding voters, with the manifest intention of allowing such persons to vote at the said coming election.

The bill prayed, *inter alia*, that the Court should appoint a commissioner to conduct and act as judge of the coming election, to be held on Easter Monday, March 29, 1880; and that respondents be restrained by injunction from preventing the complainants from voting, etc.

On March 22, 1880, the Court, after argument upon a motion for a special injunction, decreed that the three persons who were to act as judges of the coming election, should conduct it in accordance with the charter and by-laws of the said corporation, and report to the Court the list of voters and votes offered, giving in each case their reasons for receiving or rejecting any vote; and also, that they should file with their report the ballots and all protests and other papers that should be filed with them.

The report of the judges of the election was filed on April 2, 1880. It set forth, *inter alia*, that the ticket headed by J. M. Ash had received 18 votes, 11 of which, however, had been challenged and were accompanied by protests; that the ticket headed by William Raynor had received five votes; that the ballots of four persons offering to vote this ticket had been rejected; and that as J. M. Ash *et al.* had received a majority of the votes cast, they were the duly elected vestrymen for the ensuing year.

To this report the complainants filed exceptions, (1) Because the judges of the election erred in receiving the eleven challenged votes. (2) Because the judges of the election erred in refusing to receive the four rejected votes.

The cause was referred to a Master (Joseph deF. Junkin) upon the said exceptions, who found that 8 of the 11 challenged votes had been cast by persons who had taken sittings in the church within one year of the election, and that the remaining 3 challenged votes had been cast by those who at the time of election were more than three months in arrear for pew rent. Article IV. of the charter declares that only those shall have a right to vote who shall appear by the vestry books to have paid for a pew or sitting in said church for two successive years immediately preceding the time of an election; and Article I, Section 1, of the by-laws declares that no one who is in arrear for pew rent for more than three months, and who has not been entered as the holder of a pew or sitting for at least six months, shall be qualified as a voter. Under these provisions the Master decided that the judges of election erred in receiving the eleven challenged votes.

The Master further found that three of the four votes rejected by the judges of the election should have been received, and accordingly decided that the Raynor ticket had been duly elected by a vote of eight to seven.

To the report of the Master both parties excepted.

C. Stuart Patterson for complainants.

Thomas J. Diehl and *Henry Flanders* for respondents.

July 17, 1880. THE COURT. (After stating the facts.) This controversy, as the Master, in his very full and able report holds, turns on the true interpretation and effect of that portion of the fourth section of the charter which provides for the election of vestrymen, and the second paragraph of section first of Article first, of the by-laws of the corporation.

The charter requirement is as follows: The vestry of said church shall consist of twelve persons, lay members of said church, and citizens of Pennsylvania, who shall continue in office for one year, and until others be chosen, and the election of whom shall be made every year, on Easter Monday, by a majority of such members of said church as shall appear, by the vestry books, to have paid, two successive years immediately preceding the time of such election, for a pew or sitting in said church.

The material part of the by-law referred to restricts the right to vote to male persons of the age of twenty-one years and upwards, who may be present at such election, who shall be "respectively holders of a pew or sitting, and who shall be entered on the church books as such, at least six months before the election, and who are not in arrears for pew rent exceeding three months."

The Master is of opinion that this is a valid by-law, in so far at least as it requires that holders of pews and sittings, to entitle them to vote, shall not, under any circumstances, be in arrears for pew rent for more than three months, and that this, taken in connection with the charter qualification, demands of every voter first, that he shall have paid his pew rent for two successive years immediately preceding an election; and second, that he shall not have been indebted for a period of three months prior to an election, for pew rent, which was due anterior to the commencement of the two years, before an election, at which the voter offers to vote.

In giving to the charter qualification its proper effect, as he interprets it, the Master practically sets aside that clause of the by-laws which makes it necessary that the voters' names shall be entered on the church books as renters of pews or sittings, for at least six months before an election; and, giving this interpretation to the charter, he rejects from the count on this ground eight votes, all of which were, as he finds, cast for the ticket which was returned as elected.

This decision of the Master is made a ground of exception by the defendants.

The votes thus rejected were those of Larzelere, Robb, O'Donnell, Thomas, and of S. F., H. C., J. T. and W. S. Beatty. The names of neither of these voters, the Master finds, had been entered on the vestry books as renters of pews prior to April 1st, 1879, on which day the four Beattys and Larzelere each took a sitting in the church. Thomas rented a sitting on June 1st, O'Donnell and Robb in August of the same year. The rent due by each of these persons was paid up to the 1st day of April, 1880, and not more than five days before that date they paid to the accounting warden amounts which made their payments equivalent to two years' rent of one sitting in the church for each voter.

It is conceded by the Master that these facts show that each of these eight persons possessed all of the qualifications of voters required by the by-laws; he, however, asks the significant question, Did they possess the charter qualification of appearing by the vestry books to have paid two successive years for a sitting in the church immediately preceding the time of the election?

It is manifest from the facts stated above, none of which were controverted at the argument, that as neither of these eight persons had been renters of sittings for more than one year before the election of 1880, they could not have paid for that which they did not possess, pews or sittings prior to April 1, 1879. And no act of the accounting warden crediting the several sums paid within a few days of the election, as payments for sittings for a year before any one of the eight persons whose votes were taken was a renter of a pew in the church, can give to these payments such effect as was intended to be given to them.

The charter qualification is payment two successive years; it is not, as seems to be supposed, a payment for that period of time, but he must pay two years in succession, one following the other. The Master so decides, and cites Juker *v.* The Commonwealth (8 Harris, 484) and the language of the Supreme Court, as delivered by Justice WOODWARD, as upholding his conclusions, which we think are well grounded without the authority of decided cases to support them.

The interpretation given to this clause of the constitution is commended to favor, because it is conservative in effect. Viewed in this light it stands as a defence against an attempt to overthrow an existing order of government in a church by a multiplication of sittings, and appropriating the payments made to-day to an indebtedness of yesterday, which never had any existence. To use the language of the Judge who spoke for the Court in Juker's case, its effect is to fence out intruders, and to guard against abuses to which religious corporations are exposed in times of excitement.

The case of McIlvain *v.* Christ Church of Reading (8 Phila., 507), which seems to assert a different view of the law, is not to prevail so as to overthrow the decision of the Supreme Court, *supra.* The phrase construed in 8th Phila. Reports is, "who shall appear by the treasurer's books to have paid one year immediately preceding the time of such election."

This decision was not rested on this single phrase, but that was interpreted in connection with a subsequent clause of the charter, and thus viewed was held to mean a payment at any time within a year immediately before an election.

The defendants are compelled, in defence of their objection to the exclusion of these eight votes, to fall back on the by-law, showing, as they contend, conformity with the law of the church, so as to make it appear that, in compliance with its requirement, the names of these voters had been entered on the church books at least six months before the election of 1880. The position which is taken by the defendants in support of this by-law, and the view which the Master has expressed in relation to it, makes it necessary for us to look carefully into its provisions, and endeavor to ascertain its true relation to the cause.

It is by claiming that one effect is produced by it that the defendants ask that the eight rejected votes shall be restored, whereby a decided majority of the votes cast at the election would be secured to them, and it is by disregarding one portion of the same by-law, and yet holding another portion of it to be valid, though interpreting this clause in a sense wholly different from the interpretation placed on it by the defendants, that the Master reaches the conclusion that not only must these eight votes be excluded from the count, but that three others which were cast by Robert H. Beatty, W. Scott, and J. H. Smith, must also be held to be illegal votes, and therefore be rejected.

It does not require citation of authority to support the elementary principle, that the by-laws of a corporation must not be inconsistent with its charter, because the charter is the fundamental law of the body; it is as a constitution to the petty legislature, who act under its authority. For this reason, by-laws made contrary to the constitution of the corporation are void; a contrary doctrine would implant in every grant of corporate power the element of its own destruction.

A by-law passed under the authority of a charter or an act of incorporation becomes in effect a part of the charter, and from this flows the essential principle of corporate law, that a by-law must be neither inconsistent with nor repugnant to the fundamental law of the corporation. Judged by this standard, can this by-law be sustained in all its parts, as the defendants contend, or, as the Master decides, is effect to be given only to a portion of it, that which makes any arrearages of pew rent for three months before an election a disqualification for voting, even though they should cover a period of time of more than two years before the election.

In Angell and Ames on Corporations, in chapter 10, under title "by-laws," this principle is discussed and supported by a full citation of authorities.

By-laws imposing new and additional tests or qualifications on voters are void. (Taylor *v.* Griswold, 2 Green, New Jersey Reports, 223 ; The People *v.* Tibbets, 4 Cowen Reports, 358.) In the case of St. Luke's Church *v.* Mathews (4 Dessaussure Chancery Reports, 578), it was held that a by-law made by the vestry, enacting that no one should be admitted a member of the church, or be entitled to the privilege of voting for vestrymen, unless he should pay the sum of $50, a qualification not named in the charter, was void, inasmuch as it imposed a new qualification upon voters.

A power to prescribe by by-law the time, place, and manner of holding election of members does not authorize the body to pass a by-law imposing new tests of membership not contemplated by the charter, as the ownership of a share of the capital stock (Commonwealth *v.* Gill, 3 Wharton's Reports, 228; see also the Savings Institution case, 1st Wharton, 461).

The departure from this rule, wherever it has prevailed, seems to have grown out of the celebrated case of the corporations decided in the time of Elizabeth (4 Coke's Reports, 77–78), which held that the power of electing officers of municipal corporations, which by charter was vested in the commonalty or burgesses, was well exercised by a selected member of the electing body. But in Angell and Ames on Corporations it is remarked that "this case is wholly indefensible on principle."

The case of Commonwealth *v.* Cain (5 Sergeant & Rawle, 510), is commented on and regretted in so far as it recognizes the authority of the corporations' case, but the decision there went on the ground that a by-law which provided that no member of the church should vote for officers, whose pew rent was in arrears for a longer time than two years, was not inconsistent with a provision of the charter, that no person should vote except those who had been regularly admitted, and shall have been members of the church twelve months preceding the election.

There was no clear intention to make this qualification the only test of the right to vote. The Chief Justice, in Cain's case, *supra*, said, if the by-law by fair argument can be made out to be in contradiction to the charter, its validity cannot be supported.

An examination of the proviso of the fourth clause of the charter shows, that for the first five years of the life of the corporation the right to vote for vestrymen was given to such members of the church as shall in any way have contributed to the erection of the church, or to the support of the rector or ministers. Contribution in any way to either of these objects was made a lawful qualification.

The preceding clause of this section, which defined the qualification of electors to be, members of the church who have paid two successive years immediately preceding an election for a pew or sitting, was by the subsequent proviso suspended in its operation till the next Easter-Sunday after five years from the date of the charter, at which time it first became operative as the fundamental law of the body; from that date, therefore, the charter qualification has been in full force and effect.

The charter has not been altered, and this clause stands as defining and limiting the power of the corporate authorities to demand payment of pew rent as a condition precedent to the right to vote.

The organic law having thus clearly defined this right, it cannot, by any subsequent law or regulation of the body, be either enlarged or restricted.

Had the charter been silent on this subject, while prescribing other requisites as necessary qualifications for voting, there would be much more force in the argument, that a power to require payment of pew rent, in addition to the other charter qualifications, if shown to be necessary to support the corporation, and in other respects conserving its best interests, might be upheld as a lawful regulation.

But as there is in this charter a clearly defined constitutional qualification as to payment of pew rent, this is the inflexible law of the church, which can neither be carried up or down, added to or subtracted from while the fundamental law remains unchanged.

Turning from the charter to the by-laws, we find an attempt by the corporation to legislate on the subject of holding of pews and payment of pew rent as a qualification for voting, which, if valid, not only changes, but nullifies the charter law of the body upon the same subject ; and that such was the purpose of those who drafted and enacted this by-law is evident from the fact that, by its terms, it is to take effect at the same time the charter qualification was to become operative, five years from the date of the charter ; it would therefore go into operation at the election to be held on the next Easter-Monday after the expiration of five years from the date of the charter.

The by-law attempts to substitute for the charter qualification of two years' holding of a pew or sitting, a holding of six months only, and for a payment of two successive years a payment of but three months.

It certainly does not require more than to state this proposition on its face to show how utterly impossible it is for both of these laws to be carried out at the same time.

A six months' holding is not a holding for two years, and but three months of arrearages cannot be converted into an equivalent for two years' non-payment. This is a bold, but a very shallow attempt to subvert the organic law. For when by-law and constitution conflict, it does not take long to decide that such by-law must go down before superior authority; that it must be treated as null and void, because it is at war with the law, to which only it can appeal as the source of its power. Such legislation is nothing short of attempted nullification and rebellion.

If such is the character of this by-law, and such its intended operation, it brings up the question which, in the judgment of the Master, was one of no little importance, can an operation, though not originally contemplated, be given to one of its clauses, which, applied to arrearages of pew rent which became due more than two years before the 29th of March, 1880, disqualifies such renters of pews, who are thus indebted for pew rent for three months, although they have paid two years immediately preceding an election?

The Master was, we think, clearly right in rejecting the eight votes to which reference has been made, for the reason given by him that those who cast them had not paid pew rent for two successive years, because they had not been renters of pews or sittings for that period of time, and their names had been on the pew books for but one year; that taking the clause of the by-law which relates to the entry of the voters' names on the vestry books for six months preceding the election, supplemented, as it was sought to be, by the credits given by the accounting warden, did not show a charter right to vote, without which their votes ought to have been rejected by the judges of the election.

But the Master is of the opinion that a by-law which requires the payment of a pew rent which had remained due for three months anterior to the two years preceding the election, and which makes such payment an additional qualification to the right to vote, is a good and valid by-law, which it is clearly within the power of the corporation to pass, because, in his opinion it is not repugnant to the instrument creating it.

It is upon this ground that the votes of Robert Beatty, Walter Scott, and John H. Smith are excluded from the count. Beatty, who was a charter member of the church, had been a renter of a pew or sitting since 1871. Scott and Smith had been members of the church, and renters of sittings therein since at least 1875.

The Master also finds that these three voters were members of the church who had paid pew rents for two successive years immediately preceding the election. That when they made their payments they directed the appropriation of the sums paid by them, so that all their indebtedness for two years prior to April, 1880, should be liquidated, and that it was so received and appropriated by the accounting warden.

That they had the undoubted right to direct such appropriation, citing Selfridge v. Northampton Bank (8 Watts & Sergeant, 320). He further finds that these three voters were indebted for pew rent for a period of time in excess of three months prior to the election of 1878, and that Beatty and Smith made a tender of all such arrearages to Robert Briggs, who was at that time accounting warden, which, for some reason which does not appear, was refused.

The Master giving effect to so much of the by-law as declares that renters of pews, who are in arrears for pew rent three months, cannot vote for vestrymen, and finding that all three, Beatty, Smith, and Scott, owed more than three months' rent, which was "nearly three years old," and setting aside the tender of Beatty and Smith, because they had not made a second tender of all their arrearages of rent to the warden who succeeded Briggs, he rejects these votes as having been improperly received by the judges of election.

After a careful consideration of this decision of the Master upon this part of the case, we are compelled to say that we are not able to agree with him.

We arrive at this conclusion after a full examination of the report, which is unusually clear in its statement of both fact and law as applicable to the case before him; and we thus differ because we are unable to agree to the proposition that the by-law, or that part of it upon which this conclusion of the Master rests, is a valid regulation of the corporation.

We hold that the charter having defined upon what conditions as to payment of pew rent members of the church should be allowed to vote, no additional obligation of that character could be imposed upon voters; that this by-law is inconsistent with the charter, which had already provided for what was deemed a proper and necessary payment of pew rent, as a qualification for voting, and that being inconsistent with the charter, imposing new and additional tests, it is null and void. (2 Kidd on Corporations, 26, and cases cited above.)

Being of this opinion, it is not necessary to consider the effect of tender of pew rent, and the refusal of the accounting warden to receive the same. Nor is it needed that the questions raised upon the exceptions of the defendants to the decision of the Master in holding that the votes of William Headlam, Alfred Smith, and W. Bessalever had been wrongfully rejected by the judges, and the counting of the same in the statement of the true vote, as he understands it, which gave to the plaintiffs a majority of one vote.

If we are right in the conclusion at which we have arrived, the account of votes would stand thus:—

Judges' return shows as cast for defendants	18 votes
From which deduct illegal votes	8 "
Leaving for defendants	10 "
Return shows for plaintiffs undisputed	5 "
If to these should be added the votes of Bessalever, Headlam, and Alfred Smith, as the Master decides	3 "
It would give to plaintiffs but	8 "
Majority for defendants	2 "

This requires us to sustain the exceptions of the defendants to the report of the Master, in so far as they relate to the rejection from his count of the votes which were cast by Robert H. Beatty, Walter Scott, and John H. Smith, and adding these to the seven unchallenged votes cast for the defendants, making ten in all, to decide that the defendants are the duly elected vestrymen of St. Timothy's Church for the church year of 1880–81.

A decree was entered, dismissing the bill, with costs.

Opinion by ALLISON, P. J.

Common Pleas—Law.

C. P. No. 2.   Sept. 20, 1880.

Hobson v. Webster.

Voluntary appearance by terre-tenant—May not be without leave of the Court—Practice.

Rule to strike off appearance by terre-tenant.

Scire facias sur mortgage by Hobson against Webster, issued August 23, and returned the first Monday of September, "*Nihil habet.*"

On September first Helena Corles, by a præcipe in the usual form, directed her appearance *p. p.* as "owner and terre-tenant" to be entered. Whereupon the plaintiff took this rule.

Weeks, for the rule.

The terre-tenant was not made a party to the record, and cannot intervene without leave of the Court.

Buck *v.* Bolton, 1 WEEKLY NOTES, 6.
Tr. & H. Pr., § 1957.

THE COURT. Rule absolute.

C. P. No. 2.   Sept. 21, 1880.

Burton v. McCully.

Practice—A rule to produce book of original entries for comparison with copy filed must be based on an affidavit.

Assumpsit. Copy of book entries filed. The defendant, without filing an affidavit of defence or any other affidavit, entered this rule on plaintiff to produce his original book of entries for inspection by the Court, and comparison with the copy filed.

J. A. Burton, for defendant, contended that the rule should have been founded on an affidavit, and referred to—

Shaw *v.* Baildon, 1 T. & H. Pr., p. 228, note 11.

A. Driver (Coulston, with him), for the rule, cited—

Richardson *v.* Snyder, 6 WEEKLY NOTES, 414.

THE COURT. This is not a rule of course. There are many cases where it might cause great delay and hardship on plaintiff to compel him to bring his books here, without good reason shown. There should be an affidavit that defendant is informed, or has reason to believe, that the copy filed is not a true copy from plaintiff's books of original entry.

The case then stood over till the next Saturday, Sept. 25. Defendant having filed an affidavit.

Driver, for the rule, cited—
Mitchell on Motions and Rules, p. 65.

Burton, contra. It is not the practice to enter a rule like this. A demand on plaintiff's attorney is sufficient and more convenient.

THE COURT. Rule absolute.

C. P. No. 2.   Oct. 2, 1880.

Longstreth v. Thornton.

Mortgage—Bond and warrant—When execution will not be stayed on judgment entered on a bond and warrant, although judgment in a suit on the accompanying mortgage has been refused for want of a sufficient affidavit of defence.

Rule to re-instate a rule to stay proceedings under a judgment entered upon bond and warrant, pending a suit on the mortgage.

A sci. fa. sur mortgage was issued to March Term, 1880, by plaintiff against defendant. An affidavit of defence was filed, and a rule for judgment for want of a sufficient affidavit was discharged May 8, 1880. On May 14, 1880, judgment was entered on the bond and warrant which the mortgage accompanied, and a suggestion of default was filed. On May 22 a rule to stay proceedings was entered, which the Court, on June 5, discharged. On June 26, another rule to stay was entered, and that also was discharged, July 10. On June 24, a fi. fa. was issued, and on Aug. 11, a vend. ex. This rule was for a re-argument of the rule discharged July 10, 1880, to set aside the fi. fa. and vend. ex., and stay all proceedings until the mortgage suit was decided.

G. B. Adams (*C. F. Corson*, with him), for the rule.

Judgment having been *asked* on the affidavit of defence filed in the mortgage suit, and *refused*, the plaintiff has no right to proceed to execution on his bond and warrant until the mortgage suit has been decided.

Hicks *v.* Funston, 5 WEEKLY NOTES, 428.
Tisdall *v.* Paul, 8 Id. 357.

J. G. Johnson, contra.

The Court will not stay the plaintiff's *legal* remedies unless the defendant shows that their pursuit would be against *equity*. I have warned defendant's counsel to take depositions, and he has refused to do so.

THE COURT. It may be conceded that usually execution will not be allowed to proceed on the judgment on the bond until the termination of the suit on the mortgage, but the rule is not universal, and will never be applied unless a good case in equity is made. The affidavit of defence in the mortgage suit must be accepted as true in that suit, but if the defence does not commend itself to our judgment, we cannot allow it to prevail in the suit on the bond unless clearly made out by depositions.

Rule discharged.

C. P. No. 2.   Jan. 3, 1880.
Weir v. Lawrence.

Practice—Execution—An execution may be issued in the Common Pleas against the personal property of the defendant on a transcript of a judgment of a magistrate.

Rule to quash or set aside fi. fa.

The plaintiff had filed in this Court a transcript from the docket of a magistrate, had a fi. fa. issued, and a levy made on defendant's personal property, whereupon this rule was taken.

Scollay, for the rule.

The Common Pleas has no jurisdiction over the personalty on a transcript from a magistrate's Court. The only purpose of the transcript to the Common Pleas is to secure a lien upon the realty. For all purposes except the lien on the real estate of the defendant, the judgment is still before the magistrate.

Act of March 20, 1810, Purd. Dig. 63, 8 pl. 100.
Boyd *v.* Miller, 2 Sm. 431.
Wheeler *et al. v.* Moore, 6 WEEKLY NOTES, 270.
Bradley *v.* Ward, Id. 366.

J. W. M. Newlin, contra.

THE COURT. As this is largely a question of mere practice we should conform to any construction of the Act of 1810 that might be considered settled, but unfortunately the Courts of this county which have already passed upon this question have differed, and there is no settled practice on the subject. The case of Techner *v.* Karpeles (7 WEEKLY NOTES, 258) was very carefully considered, and we follow it as the latest decision on the point.

Rule discharged.

Orphans' Court.

October 20, 1880.

King's Estate.

Will—Demand for issue to test validity of—Appeal from Register—Person named as executor in an alleged will, is a "person interested" under Act of March 15, 1832—Practice—Act of March 29, 1832—Security for costs—When ordered.

Sur appeal from Register.

Petition for a citation, and demand for an issue.

The petition of F. Gordon Dexter set forth that by an instrument of writing, dated January 16, 1880, the decedent, Dr. William M. King, made his last will and testament, and appointed the petitioner executor thereof.

That before the Register probate thereon was contested by Edward Haugh, and others, interested in a paper purporting to be the will of the decedent, dated December 1, 1879, and that after hearing testimony the Register refused to admit to probate the will of January 16, offered by the petitioner.

The prayer of the petition was in the usual form, for a citation and issue.

Accordingly, on September 27, 1880, a citation issued, returnable October 16th following, to Edward Haugh, The Academy of Fine Arts, and others, to show cause, etc., all of whom, with the exception of three who were not served, appeared, having jointly filed answer to the effect that (1) the petitioner is not a person interested entitled to claim a hearing before this Court, as heir, legatee, devisee, or next of kin to the decedent; (2) that said petitioner is not a citizen of Pennsylvania, but of the State of Massachusetts, and has entered no security for costs, and praying that he be ordered to enter such security; (3) that it appears by the record of this appeal letters testamentary were granted on the 26th of July, 1880, to one of the respondents as executor of the said William M. King, and it also appears that the said appeal of the said Dexter purports to have been made and entered on the 17th day of July, 1880, before probate and grant of letters to respondents; (4) that the appeal is not supported by any testimony, only the record being brought up; (5) and no fact in dispute is stated specifically in writing; and respondent prayed the Court to dismiss the appeal with costs.

Richard C. McMurtrie, for the contestants.
Pierce Archer, for respondents.

October 23, 1880. THE COURT. It appears from the return to the citation to show cause why an issue should not be granted in the above matter that all the parties have been duly served, with the exception of three, viz., Caroline E. J. King, Margaret Carter, and R. W. Allen. The former, we understand, is represented by the counsel for the appellant, and the last two reside out of this jurisdiction. If our information be correct, we suggest that, for the sake of regularity, counsel accept service of the citation for the party interested represented by him. But as to those not served, the practice pointed out by the Act of 1832 (Purdon, 1106, pl. 24, 25), should ordinarily be observed, to wit, an alias citation issued, and published by advertisement "in such place or places, and for such length of time, as the Court, having regard to the supposed place of residence of the defendant, and other circumstances, shall direct." In the present instance, however, we deem this unnecessary, and involving the parties in fruitless expense and delay. Still, as it is but proper that notice be given to every party interested, this will be accomplished by the examiner to be appointed, giving notice, in writing, of his appointment to the parties not served, of the time and place of the first meeting to be held for the purpose of taking testimony in support of the appeal.

An answer has been filed to the citation, by the executors of the will of testator admitted to probate by the Register, setting up various grounds in opposition to the granting of the issue prayed for by the appellant. The first objection is, that the appellant is not a "person interested as an heir, legatee, devisee, or next of kin to the said decedent." But this is not well founded. The appellant is the executor named in the writing which he alleges to be the last will and testament of the decedent, and which the Register has refused admission to probate. It is the duty of the person named as executor to offer the testamentary paper for probate; and, if he neglects, he can be compelled so to do upon the application of a party in interest. It may be that he has no pecuniary interest other than the expected compensation for services in the settlement of the estate; but this is of little moment, and not to be considered, in view of the trust reposed in him by the testator. He is a trustee for creditors and legatees, and this confers such an interest as may be injuriously affected by the decision of the Register. The Act of March 15, 1832, under which the appeal has been taken, gives the right to "any person interested," and clearly the executor whose demand for probate and letters testamentary is denied, is within the provision of the Act. The second objection is, that the appellant is not a citizen of this State, and has not entered security for costs. But it is evident this is not a valid reason for refusing the issue prayed for. The proper practice is to apply by petition, setting forth the facts, for an order upon the appellant to enter security for the costs accrued and to accrue, and, until the same be given, further proceedings to stay. The next objection is, that from the record the appeal appears to have been taken prior to the admission to probate of the will of which the respondents are the executors. But this does not affect the merits of the case. The appeal is from the act of the Register in refusing probate of the will of which the appellant is the executor; and this was on or about July 17, 1880, while letters testamentary upon the will probated were granted on July 26, 1880. In strictness the appeal should not have been taken until subsequent to the date of the letters testamentary, and to correct this apparent irregularity leave will be given appellant to file his appeal *nunc pro tunc*, as of July 27, 1880. In regard to the remaining objections, it is unnecessary to say more than that the appeal brings up nothing but the record. The proceeding is had *de novo*, and decided upon its merits upon the testimony taken in this Court. Until that be taken, the case is not ripe for hearing; and while it is true that the appellant, in his petition, is required to set forth the material fact or facts upon which the application for an issue is based, yet we think that it is sufficiently complied with when it appears that the ground alleged for the appeal is that the Register has refused probate of an alleged *last* will and testament, and admitted to probate a testamentary writing of earlier date. The question of fact thus arising is, which of the two papers, both alleged to have been executed by the testator, is his *last* will and testament.

No sufficient reason having been shown why the appellant should not be allowed to prosecute his appeal, the order now asked for, relative to the taking of testimony, will be granted.

Opinion by HANNA, P. J.

WEEKLY NOTES OF CASES.

Vol. IX.] THURSDAY, NOV. 25, 1880. [No. 14.

Supreme Court.

May, '80, 198.　　　　　　　　June 23, 1880.
Lant's Appeal.

Husband and wife—Revocation of will by subsequent marriage of testatrix—Act of April 8, 1833, § 16 (P. L. 251)—Equity—Such will when executed in pursuance of intended husband's parol assent to disposal of testatrix's property may take effect as a marriage settlement—What is sufficient expression of assent on part of husband to bind him.

A single woman, having obtained her intended husband's verbal consent that she might dispose of her property by will or otherwise as she pleased, executed a will the day before her marriage, whereby she made liberal provision for him, and bequeathed the residue of her estate to her friends and relations and to charities:

Held, that although said will was revoked by her subsequent marriage in consequence of the provisions of the Act of April 8, 1833, § 16 (P. L. 251), yet nevertheless it might on her death take effect in equity as an ante-nuptial settlement, and that on every principle of equitable estoppel the husband's mouth ought to be shut from interposing an objection to its full enforcement.

In equity, where a person has the legal right to dispose of property, and means to do so, the form of the instrument adopted for the purpose, if at law ineffectual, will be disregarded, and it will be treated as reformed, so as to be made effectual.

Appeal of Julia M. Lant from the decree of the Orphans' Court of Lancaster County, dismissing exceptions filed by her to the report of the auditors appointed to distribute the estate of Elizabeth M. D. Mullen, deceased.

The facts of the case were as follows: The deceased, whose maiden name was Dunn, agreed some time in the year 1875 to marry one John A. Mullen. In December, 1875, in pursuance of this agreement, Mullen called upon the mother of the deceased, with whom she lived, and requested her consent to the marriage, saying in reference to his intended wife: "I don't want her money; I only want herself." Mrs. Dunn gave her consent to the marriage proposed.

On or about February 1, 1876, the deceased, being possessed of considerable property, both real and personal, sent for her counsel, Hon. John B. Livingston, and told him that she desired him to write her will for her. He told her in reply that her intended marriage would revoke any will executed by her, and that she could make no disposition of her property without her intended husband's consent. Deceased then said that she would see Mr. Mullen, and if she got the matter fixed would send for Mr. Livingston again. Shortly after this interview deceased requested her mother to ask Mullen if he was satisfied that she (deceased) should dispose of her effects. Mrs. Dunn did so, and Mullen replied that he was perfectly satisfied. Mrs. Dunn then told deceased what Mullen had said, whereupon deceased immediately drew up a memorandum for her counsel of the manner in which she wished her property to be disposed of. Deceased then said to her mother: "Now I have the items wrote out, and I want you to speak to John again, and ask him if he isn't satisfied." Mrs. Dunn said: "Lizzie, did you not speak to him yourself?" Whereupon she replied: "Yes, but I want you to talk to him again, and if he is not satisfied I won't marry him." Mrs. Dunn then again asked Mullen whether he was satisfied that deceased should dispose of her fortune by will or in any way that she pleased. He replied: "Yes, I am satisfied for Lizzie to dispose of her fortune by will, or otherwise, any way she pleases."

Deceased then sent again for Judge Livingston, told him that the whole thing had been arranged, and that Mr. Mullen was perfectly satisfied, and instructed him to draw up a will in accordance with the terms of the memorandum written by her. Livingston accordingly drew up a will, whereby deceased, beside devising several pieces of real estate to her mother and sister, Julia M. Lant, and bequeathing several trifling specific legacies, bequeathed of her personalty $30,000 to her intended husband, $15,000 to her niece, Mary E. Lant, $16,800 to various friends and for charitable purposes, and directed all the residue to be equally divided between her said mother, sister, and intended husband.

On the evening of February 8, 1876, Mr. Livingston brought this instrument to deceased, who signed it duly in the presence of witnesses, who subscribed to the same. Just before deceased executed the paper, Mullen came into the room, and said he was going down the street. Deceased said to him: "I am about signing," or "executing the paper we spoke of." Mullen replied: "Oh, very well," or "very well," and immediately after left the room and house. Mullen did not see the paper. Immediately after its execution it was taken away by Mr. Livingston, and kept by him at his office until after the death of Elizabeth Mullen.

On February 9, 1876, said Elizabeth was married to said John A. Mullen. In August, 1878, said Elizabeth became very ill. At this time

Mr. Mullen complained to Rev. Michael J. McBride that his wife's family treated him hardly, saying: "They have made a will without consulting me." McBride then said: "John, didn't you give your consent before the marriage?" Mullen replied: "Yes, but they should have had it in writing. A verbal consent will not hold in law." On August 28, 1878, said Elizabeth died, without children. On August 31, 1878, the said paper, executed February 8, 1876, was admitted to probate as a will, and letters testamentary granted by the Register of Wills of Lancaster County to the executors named therein. On September 3, 1878, said John A. Mullen filed a petition with the register to have said probate and the letters testamentary granted thereon vacated and annulled, on the ground that the said will had been revoked by the marriage of the testatrix subsequent to the execution. An answer was filed by the executors named in said paper, and the register refused to grant the prayer of the petition. On appeal to the Orphans' Court, a decree was made February 8, 1879, granting the prayer of the petition, and annulling and vacating said probate and letters testamentary.

Letters of administration were then granted on the estate of the deceased to said John A. Mullen, her husband. Said administrator filed his account May 15, 1879, showing a balance in his hands of $76,646.89. Exceptions were filed to this report by said Julia M. Lant, sister of deceased, and the matter was on July 3, 1879, referred by the Orphans' Court of Lancaster County to auditors to pass on the exceptions, and to distribute the balance in the hands of the administrator.

The said auditors reported, *inter alia*, as follows:—

"From the evidence the auditors find that John A. Mullen, before the marriage, assented or consented that his intended wife might make a will; that she did make a will—the paper produced before the auditors; that John A. Mullen did not know its contents, and that there was no ante-nuptial contract between Elizabeth M. Dunn and John A. Mullen, or marriage settlement of her separate estate. This will having been revoked by her subsequent marriage, Act 8 April, 1833, § 16 (P. L. 251), the balance in the administrator's hands must be distributed in accordance with the provisions of the intestate laws of this Commonwealth."

They therefore awarded the whole of said balance to said John A. Mullen, as husband of deceased.

To this report exceptions were filed by Julia M. Lant, on the grounds (*inter alia*) that "the auditors erred in not finding as a fact, under the evidence produced, that there was an ante-nuptial contract or agreement between Elizabeth M. Dunn and John A. Mullen with regard to the disposition of her separate estate, based upon a valid and valuable consideration," and in awarding to said John A. Mullen, surviving husband of said Elizabeth M. D. Mullen, deceased, the whole balance in his hands as administrator. The Court, however, after hearing, dismissed the exceptions, and confirmed the report. Julia M. Lant thereupon took this appeal, assigning for error the action of the Court in overruling the exceptions filed by her to the auditors' report.

H. M. North and *S. H. Reynolds* (with them *P. D. Baker*), for appellant.

Almost any *bona fide* and reasonable agreement made before marriage to secure the wife in the enjoyment of her own property will be carried into execution by a court of equity.

Stilley v. Folger, 14 Ohio, 610.
2 Kent's Comm. 163.
English v. Foxall, 2 Peters, 595.
Hunter v. Bryant, 2 Wheat. 32.
Tarbell v. Tarbell, 10 Allen, 278.
Smith v. Chapell, 31 Conn. 589.
Neves v. Scott, 9 How. 196; s. c. 13 How. 268.

Nor will equity pay any regard to the form of the agreement.

Peachey on Marriage Settlements, 65-67.
Acton v. Peirce, 2 Vern. 480.
Crostwaight v. Hutchinson, 2 Bibb. 407.
Liles v. Fleming, 1 Dev. Eq. 185.
Kenley v. Kenley, 2 How. (Miss.) 751.
Logan v. Wienholt, 1 Cl. & Fin. 611.
Hammersley v. De Biel, 12 Cl. & Fin. 45.
Moorhouse v. Colvin, 15 Beav. 349.

In Pennsylvania a parol ante-nuptial settlement is binding upon all parties as regards the wife's chattels.

Gackenbach v. Brouse, 4 W. & S. 546.
Barnes v. Irwin, 2 Dallas, 199.

Mrs. Mullen's will, though revoked by her subsequent marriage, ought nevertheless, having been executed with Mullen's consent, be available in equity, as embodying the terms of a marriage contract, and the personal property of deceased should be distributed in accordance with the provisions thereof. Mullen, having induced his wife to enter into the marriage relation by his representations as to his willingness that she should dispose of her property as she pleased, ought to be bound by the disposition made by her on February 8, 1876.

Money v. Jorden, 15 Beav. 377.
Pulsford v. Richards, 17 Beav. 94.
Bold v. Hutchinson, 20 Beav. 259.
Peachey on Marriage Settlements, 87.

Richard P. White and *Thomas E. Franklin*, for appellee.

The will of Mrs. Mullen, whether executed with the consent of her husband or not, was necessarily revoked as a will by her subsequent marriage, in consequence of the provisions of the Act of April 8, 1833, § 16 (P. L. 251).

It cannot take effect as a marriage settlement, because there is nothing to show Mullen's agreement as to the disposition of his wife's property after her death in case she died intestate. The declarations made by him, which are in evidence, are insufficient to establish such an agreement on his part.

Fransen's Appeal, 2 Cas. 202.
Kurts v. Saylor, 8 Harris, 205.
Talbot v. Calvert, 12 Harris, 327.

The case of Gackenbach v. Brouse (4 W. & S. 546) has no application, as there a parol antenuptial settlement by mutual consent was clearly proved to have been made.

October 4, 1880. THE COURT. There are some matters involved in this controversy which must be assumed, if not conceded as not in dispute. First, That the instrument purporting to be the last will and testament of Elizabeth M. Dunn, dated February 8, 1876, cannot take effect as a will, having been revoked by her marriage with the appellee on the following day. Probate of it was refused by the tribunal having exclusive jurisdiction as far as personal property is concerned, and its decree, unappealed from, is conclusive.

Second, This revocation was by the positive provisions of the Statute 8 April, 1833, sec. 16 (Pamph. L. 251). "A will executed by a single woman shall be deemed revoked by her subsequent marriage." This law was not known to her and not adverted to by her counsel called in by her to give his advice and prepare the instrument. It was certainly not thought by her that such a result would follow. She did not mean it to be revoked by her marriage. On the contrary both she and her counsel meant to make a disposition which would be effectual after the marriage which was to be celebrated within twenty-four hours after the paper was executed. The execution of the will at the time and under the circumstances was a plain mistake. Had it been postponed only a few hours until after the marriage ceremony was performed it would have been a valid and effectual disposition of her property.

Third, There was a contract made by John A. Mullen, the intended husband, at or about the time the instrument was executed by which she was to have the power "to dispose of her fortune by will, or otherwise, any way she pleased." That this was the contract is established by the most conclusive testimony, confirmed by the admission of the husband afterwards, who put his refusal to give effect to it not on the ground that he had not freely and fairly so agreed, but that because it was not in writing he was not bound by it. In this he was mistaken, for a parol ante-nuptial contract such as this, being in consideration of marriage, which is a valuable one, is unquestionably binding on the parties. (Gackenbach v. Brouse, 4 W. & S. 546). That he knew and considered at the time the instrument in question was executed that it was intended to carry out and give effect to his antenuptial agreement, is proved by the clearest and most convincing evidence.

If, as it has been earnestly contended, the decree of the Court below must be affirmed and the entire personal estate of the decedent awarded to the appellee, then it is not to be disputed that there must be some palpable defect in equitable jurisdiction in this Commonwealth, to render necessary so gross an injustice, so revolting to the moral sense of what is right and wrong. We think, however, that fortunately there are two very familiar and well settled principles of equity, often recognized and applied by our Courts, which prevent such a result. One of these principles is that whatever a chancellor on the facts of a case would have decreed to be done, the Courts will consider as having actually been done. Another principle is that wherever a person has the legal right to dispose of property and means to do so, the form of the instrument adopted for the purpose, if at law ineffectual, will be disregarded, and it will be reformed so as to be made effectual.

Suppose, then, that at the time the paper of February 8, 1876, was executed by Elizabeth M. Dunn, she had filed a bill in equity setting forth the ante-nuptial contract made by John A. Mullen and the marriage about to be solemnized and praying that it might be carried into execution by some instrument of writing to be signed by him, what would have been the decree of the Court? Surely upon the undisputed facts the prayer of the bill would have been granted, and the decree would have been either that the husband and wife should join in a conveyance to trustees in trust for the separate use of the wife with full power in her to dispose of the same in her lifetime by sale or gift, and after her death by a will in writing, or any writing in the nature of a last will and testament. Such is the ordinary form of such powers in marriage settlements. If the complainant was willing the Court might decree simply that the husband himself should execute a declaration of trust to the same effect. Nothing is better settled than that a court of equity in decreeing the specific performance of marriage articles will make such a decree as will give full effect to the intention of the parties without regard to the legal construction of the words used in them. Thus if by the words, according to their legal construction, a fee tail would be vested in the parties or either of them, a strict settlement will be decreed to the husband or husband and wife for life with remainder to the children of the marriage, successively in tail, according to the most approved forms of deeds of marriage settlement. (2 Story's Eq. Jur., sect. 983, and authorities there cited.) Now if we are to consider as having actually been done what a chancellor would have decreed to be done, then we have at the time of the execution of the paper of February 8, 1876, either a conveyance to a trustee or a declaration executed by the husband to the same effect. Surely then under such a declaration or deed of settlement this paper though ineffectual as a will under the statute, was still a writing in the nature of a last will and testament, a clause introduced into such powers for the very purpose of providing against mere technical objections, which would prevent the instrument from being admitted to probate as a will. It was a disposition of property to take effect at death if not revoked by the party during life. That is a writing in the nature of a last will and testament. This paper was so intended beyond all question. It was executed under and in pursuance of the contract on the eve of the marriage, indeed, it might almost be said to have been, in the consideration of equity, cotemporaneous with the ceremony, executed for the express purpose, with the knowledge and consent of John A. Mullen, of having just the effect here stated. It makes most liberal provision for him, and upon every principle of equitable estoppel, his mouth ought to be shut from interposing an objection to its full enforcement.

The case, too, is equally within the second principle of equity adverted to; a paper executed by a person who had a perfect legal right to dispose of her property, and intended to do so, but by a plain mistake of the scrivener, it was drawn in the form of a will when it ought to have been a deed or declaration of trust. Surely it must be in the power of a court of equity in this Commonwealth to correct so gross and palpable a mistake, to reform the instrument and decree it to be such as it ought to have been so as effectually to carry out the intention of the parties.

Decree reversed and record remitted to the Orphans' Court of Lancaster County that distribution may be there made according to the principles of this opinion, the costs of this appeal to be paid by the estate.

Opinion by SHARSWOOD, C. J.

Jan. '80, 134. February 24, 1880.

Hidell's Appeal.

Equity—Decree in previous suit when conclusive—Husband and wife, relief for fraud upon marital rights, when denied—Allegans contraria non est audiendus.

A husband, claiming to have been defrauded of his marital rights, must act promptly and cannot be permitted to make several experiments, especially on different and inconsistent grounds.

H. and D., his wife, in right of his wife, filed a bill in equity in the Common Pleas against a Trust Co., and prayed that a certain deed given by D. to the company immediately before her marriage might be set aside as in fraud of H.'s marital rights. The complainants discontinued this suit and filed a bill in the Circuit Court of the U. S. against the same respondents, setting forth a deed executed in 1872 by D. to the Trust Co., containing a power of revocation, also the deed before mentioned executed before the marriage in 1876, containing, it was charged, the same power, and a revocation made in pursuance of these instruments; the complainants prayed for a re-conveyance of the property assigned by the deed of 1872. This bill was dismissed. H. then filed a bill, in the Common Pleas, against his wife and the Trust Co. as respondents, charging that the deed of 1876 was fraudulent, and prayed that it should be cancelled. This bill was dismissed:

Held (affirming the decree of the Court below), that the complainant was concluded by the decree of the Circuit Court.

Appeal of William H. Hidell from a decree of the Common Pleas No. 2, of Philadelphia County, dismissing his bill in a suit in equity wherein he was complainant, and Dora Hidell and the Girard Life Insurance, Annuity, and Trust Company were respondents.

The bill set forth, substantially, the following allegations: In 1876 the complainant became engaged to be married to Dora Robinson, afterwards Dora Hidell, one of the defendants; the said Dora was possessed of about $26,000, which, under a deed from her to the Girard Trust Company, the other defendant, dated June 24, 1872, was held by the company in trust for her, for the term of her life, remainder to the uses appointed by her will, or in default of appointment to such persons as would be entitled under the intestate laws of Pennsylvania, the deed containing a general power of revocation. In August, 1876, during the engagement of marriage before mentioned, Dora Robinson showed a copy of the deed to the complainant, and promised that she would exercise the power of revocation therein contained, and loan him certain moneys after their marriage. Relying upon this promise the complainant married Dora Robinson upon Oct. 31, 1876, the promise forming a material inducement to his consent. But on Oct. 27, four days before, without the complainant's knowledge, the defendant Dora duly executed the following instrument under seal:—

"I hereby renew the trust created by the deed of June 24, 1872, recorded in Deed Book J. A. H., No. 269, p. 441, for five years from this date. Witness my hand and seal this 27th day of October, 1876.

(Two witnesses.) "DORA ROBINSON." [SEAL.]

The complainant did not become aware of the execution of the indenture of Oct. 27, 1876, until after his marriage, and charged that it was a fraud upon his marital rights, as in violation of his agreement with Dora Robinson. The complainant prayed that the indenture might be declared void, and that the Girard Trust Co. might be decreed to hold the property of the defendant Dora Hidell under the trust deed of 1872 as if the deed of 1876 had never been executed.

The answer of Dora Hidell admitted all the facts in the complainant's bill. The answer of the Girard Trust Co. admitted the facts, but denied that any fraud had been committed against the complainant's marital rights. The respondents further averred, that in March, 1877, the complainant Wm. H. Hidell and Dora his wife filed a bill in the Common Pleas No. 4 against the Trust Co., alleging that the deed of 1876 had been executed without the knowledge, privity, or consent of the said William, and praying that the same might be declared null and void; that the complainants discontinued the suit in March, 1878, and afterwards filed a bill in the Circuit Court of the United States against the same respondents, setting forth the deeds of 1872 and of 1876, and praying that the defendants might be ordered to assign the trust property to Dora Hidell free of all trusts; that, after answer and argument, the Circuit Court upon February 7, 1879, decreed that the deed of 1872 was irrevocable for a period of five years from Oct. 27, 1876, and dismissed the complainants' bill; the respondents, therefore, urged that the complainant was for ever concluded in the premises.

An examiner was appointed, before whom the testimony showed that the facts were substantially as recited in the pleadings. As to the suit brought in the Common Pleas No. 4, it appeared that it had been brought by W. H. Hidell and Dora his wife, in right of the said Dora, a few weeks after Hidell's discovery of the deed of 1876. The complainant testified that he considered himself only the nominal plaintiff in that suit, as in the suit brought in the Circuit Court, where all the parties were the same. (See report of this case in 6 WEEKLY NOTES, 435, where it appears that the complainants urged that the deed of 1876 renewed the power of revocation reserved in the deed of 1872, which power they claim had been exercised by Hidell and his wife, after their marriage, by an instrument which was in evidence.)

After hearing upon bill, answer, and proofs, the Court dismissed the bill, and the complainant took this appeal assigning that decree for error.

A. Sydney Biddle, for the appellants.

The complainant has not waived his rights, nor is he estopped from prosecuting the present suit. The whole time elapsed from the discovery of the fraud to the institution of the present suit is not long; and the cause of the delay is obvious. It was naturally more agreeable to the complainant and his wife to accomplish their object without the publicity and expense of taking testimony.

The complainants never, in any way, recognized the validity of the deed of 1876; and the moment the suit begun at the suggestion of his wife's counsel was decided against her, he instituted the present suit.

John J. Ridgway, Jr., contra.

The complainant is concluded by the decree of the Circuit Court. It is idle to pretend that the case turned on another point. The validity of the deed of 1876 was upheld by the Court, and the complainant ought to have made it an issue if he did not do so. See—

Rockwell v. Langley, 7 H. 508.
Kelsey v. Murphy, 2 C. 78.

March 15, 1880. THE COURT. The appellant, we think, is concluded by the decree of the Circuit Court of the United States on the bill filed by him and his wife, praying that the trustees should be decreed to re-assign the trust securities, and that, on the ground that there was a power of revocation under the deed or instrument of October 27, 1876, which he now asks to be set aside, as in fraud of his marital rights. Before instituting that proceeding, he discontinued a bill in the Common Pleas also filed by himself and his wife, praying that this instrument of October 27, 1876, should be declared null and void, because executed without privity, knowledge, and consent. It is in vain for him to pretend that his name in these proceedings was used without his assent. A husband claiming to have been defrauded of his marital rights must act promptly, and cannot be permitted to make several experiments, especially on different and inconsistent grounds. The bill in the Circuit Court of the United States necessarily admitted the validity of the instrument which he now seeks to have set aside. *Allegans contraria non est audiendus.* He knew that he was defrauded when he instituted that proceeding; for the previous bill in the Common Pleas conclusively establishes such knowledge.

Decree affirmed, and appeal dismissed at the costs of the appellant.

PER CURIAM.

June 14, 1880.

Snyder's Appeal.

Will—Bequest—Dying without issue—Definite and indefinite failure of issue—Distinction between devise of real estate and bequest of personalty—Intention of testator—Absolute bequest of personalty to A., and in case he "shall at any time die without issue," then to B., C., and D., children of testator.

A testator, after directing his real estate to be sold, gave and bequeathed his estate, upon the death of his wife, to his seven children (naming them), and to his grandson,

Allen Hummel, share and share alike; "and in case my said grandson, Allen Hummel, shall at any time die without issue, I then give and bequeath the bequest of him, the said Allen Hummel, so dying, unto all my children, viz., (naming them as before), to share and share alike." Allen, the grandson, survived the testator, and died without leaving issue:

Held (reversing the decree of the Court below, GORDON and TRUNKEY, JJ., dissenting), that it was evident the testator intended a definite failure of issue at the time of the grandson's death, and that, therefore, the bequest over to the testator's children took effect.

Appeal from the decree of the Orphans' Court of Snyder County, confirming the report of an auditor in the matter of the distribution of a fund in the hands of Edward Bassler, guardian of Allen S. Hummel, deceased.

George A. Snyder, by his will, dated Feb. 27, 1869, directed, *inter alia*, as follows:—

"And further I bequeath unto my beloved wife out the third of all my other real and personal property as soon after it is sold as can be made convenient for them, and at her decease I give and bequeath unto my children as follows, viz., Jeremiah Snyder, Lewis Martin Snyder, Geo. A. Snyder, Jacob Peter Snyder, Wm. H. Snyder, Samuel J. Snyder, and my daughter Margaret Elizabeth, intermarried to Wm. Hains, and my grandson, Allen Hummel, child of my late deceased daughter Emma Catherine, share and share alike; and in case my said grandson, Allen Hummel, *shall at any time die without issue*, I then give and bequeath the bequest of him, the said Allen Hummel, so dying, unto all my children, viz., Jeremiah Snyder, Lewis M. Snyder, Geo. W. Snyder, J. P. Snyder, Wm. H. Snyder, Samuel J. Snyder, and my daughter Elizabeth Hains, to share and share alike."

The testator died December 14, 1871, leaving to survive him six sons, one daughter, and one grandson (Allen or Allen S. Hummel), all named in the above clause of his will. The share of the grandson, Allen S. Hummel, amounting to $1732.09, was paid to his guardian, E. Bassler.

Allen S. Hummel died Oct. 6, 1879, a minor, unmarried, and without issue. The guardian filed his account, whereby it appeared that the whole of the above amount of $1732.09, together with interest thereon, $668, remained in his hands, less certain credits for commissions and expenses, the balance due estate being $2252.48.

Before the auditor, this fund was claimed, on the one hand, by the children and heirs of George A. Snyder, deceased, as legatees under his will, because Allen S. Hummel died *without leaving issue;* and, on the other hand, by John Hummel, the father of Allen S. Hummel, as his heir-at-law or next of kin under the intestate law. No distinction was made by either claimant between the principal and the interest of the fund in controversy.

The auditor held that the words in the bequest "shall at any time die without issue" imported an indefinite failure of issue, and that the gift, being personalty, vested absolutely in Allen S. Hummel during his lifetime; and that the gift over to the testator's children was void for remoteness. He therefore awarded the said balance of $2252.48, less expenses of audit, to John Hummel, father of Allen S. Hummel, under the intestate laws.

Exceptions filed on behalf of the children of George A. Snyder, having been overruled by the Court, and the report of the auditor confirmed, Jeremiah Snyder *et al.* took this appeal, assigning for error, the overruling of the exceptions and the awarding of the said fund to John Hummel instead of to the appellants.

Charles Hower, for appellants.

Under the provisions of this will Allen S. Hummel took simply a life estate in the property bequeathed to him. From the language used in the will an indefinite failure of issue is not to be inferred.

Hopkins *v.* Jones, 2 Barr, 69.
Sheets's Estate, 2 Sm. 257.
Koppenhaffer's Appeal, 6 Nor. 196.
Seibert *v.* Butz, 9 Watts, 490.
Eichelberger *v.* Barnitz, 9 Watts, 450.
Myers's Appeal, 13 Wr. 111.
Caldwell *v.* Skilton, 1 Harris, 152-157.
Kelso *v.* Dickey, 7 W. & S. 279.

S. P. Wolverton, for appellee.

The cases cited by appellant are easily distinguishable from the more numerous cases which show that Allen S. Hummel took a vested and absolute interest under his grandfather's will. In fact the words here used, "shall *at any time* die without issue," import an *indefinite* failure of issue even more strongly than any of the reported cases, cited in our brief.

Oct. 4, 1880. THE COURT. The testator, George A. Snyder, directed all his real estate to be sold. The proceeds, together with his personal property, constituted the estate of which he disposed. It was, of course, all personal estate. Subject to a provision in favor of his widow during her life, he gave the whole of it in equal shares to his six sons, a daughter and a grandson, Allen S. Hummel, the child of a deceased daughter.

The will then provides as follows: "And in case my said grandson, Allen Hummel, shall at any time die without issue, I then give and bequeath the bequest of him, the said Allen Hummel, so dying, unto all my children, viz., Jeremiah Snyder, Lewis M. Snyder, George W. Snyder, J. P. Snyder, Wm. H. Snyder, Samuel J. Snyder, and my daughter, Elizabeth Hains, to share and share alike." Allen S. Hummel, the grandson, died unmarried and without issue, on Oct. 6, 1879. The testator died Dec. 14, 1871. In November, 1879, the guardian of Allen S. Hummel filed his account, showing a balance of $2252.48 in his hands. Of the entire fund, a part, $1732.09, was received from the administrators of Geo. A. Snyder, deceased, on

March 3, 1873, and another part, $668, was an accumulation of interest upon the above sum for upwards of six years, while the fund was in the hands of the guardian, none of which appears to have been expended in the support of the ward. On the hearing before the auditor, the fund in the hands of the guardian was claimed by the children of Geo. A. Snyder, as substituted legatees, under their father's will, on the one hand, and on the other, by John Hummel, the father of Allen S. Hummel, as his distributee under the intestate law.

No question was raised before the auditor or in the Orphans' Court, as to any difference between the principal sum of the legacy and the increment of interest after the death of George A. Snyder. The former was clearly subject to the provisions of the will under which it was derived, but the latter was the absolute property of the ward, and must be disposed of as his in the distribution of his estate, unaffected by the will of his grandfather. The entire fund was awarded by the auditor and Court below to John Hummel, upon the ground that the limitation over to the other legatees named in the will, being upon an indefinite failure of issue was void, and the interest of Allen S. Hummel in the bequest to him was absolute, and must pass to his father as his distributee. Was this ruling correct? That depends upon various considerations.

There is no doubt that in devises of real estate, as a general rule, a limitation over upon an indefinite failure of issue of the devisee, creates an estate tail which, under our Act of 1855, becomes a fee simple, and, if the estate of the first taker is a fee, the limitation is void for remoteness.

In the present case the subject matter of the contention is personal estate exclusively. It has for a very long time been held that, in bequests of personal estate, the rule of construction upon a limitation over on *dying without issue*, is quite different from the rule which prevails in devises of real estate, upon the same kind of limitation. In the case of Pinbury *v.* Elkin (1 P. Williams, 563), the Lord Chancellor said " that the words, (dying without issue), had several senses; as, *first*, a *legal* sense, when there was a failure of issue of a tenant in tail, so as to entitle the remainder-man or reversioner to a *formedon* in remainder or reverter, which is whenever there is a failure of issue of the body of tenant in tail. *Secondly,* Another sense of dying without issue was, if the party died *without ever having had issue.* . . . But by the *third* sense of a person's dying without issue, is intended *without leaving issue at the time of his death,* and in this sense the words (dying without issue) shall be taken in the principal case ; which, indeed seems to be the natural meaning of these words." .

. . "Moreover, in the principal case, the words import strongly that they are to be intended in this sense (to wit), dying without issue *living at the party's death,* because the legacy of £80 (being the legacy in question), if the wife should die without issue by the testator, then after her decease is to remain to the testator's brother, which words *then after,* i. e., *immediately after,* would be inconsistent and repugnant if the dying without issue should be taken in the other sense, whenever there shall be a failure of issue; for this would be carrying the payment beyond the day; it would be as absurd as to appoint the day of payment to be to-morrow, if it shall rain this day twelve months, which is to make the condition overreach the day of payment." . . . Also his lordship said that taking the £80 as intended to be given whenever there should be a failure of issue of the body of the testator's wife by him, this would be a strange clog upon a personal estate, and subjecting it to the payment of a sum of money (as it might happen) one hundred years hence when it would be no kindness to the legatee in whose favor it was personally intended.

In Hughes *v.* Sayer (1 P. Williams, 534,) it was held that a bequest of personal estate to A. and B., and if either die without children then to the survivor, and if both should die without children, then to the children of the testator's other brothers and sisters, was a good limitation over to the substituted legatees. The Lord Chancellor held that " the words (dying without children) must be taken to be *children living at the death of the party.* For that it could not be taken in the other sense, that is, whenever there should be a failure of issue, because the immediate limitation over was to the surviving devisee ; and it was not probable that if either of the devisees should die leaving issue, the survivors should live so long as to see a failure of issue, which, in notion of law, was such a limitation as might endure forever."

In both the foregoing cases, the limitation over was held to be good, upon the ground that the testator must have intended the words dying without issue, to mean, not an indefinite failure of issue but a failure of issue *living at the death of the first taker.* And the intention of the testator was inferred from the very words of the bequest, and not from other provisions of the will.

In the case of Forth *v.* Chapman, (1 P. W., 666), the Lord Chancellor said "that the reason why a devise of a freehold to one for life and if he die without issue, then to another, is determined to be an estate tail, is in favor of the issue that such may have it, and the intent take place; but there is the plainest difference betwixt a devise of a freehold and a devise of a term for years; for in the devise of the latter to one, and if he die without issue, then to another, the words (if he die without issue) can not be supposed to have been inserted in favor of such issue, since they cannot by any construction have it." . . . "As to the freehold, the construction should be if William or Walter died without issue *generally*, by which there might be *at any time* a failure of issue; and with respect to the leasehold, that the same words should be intended to signify their dying without leaving issue *at their death*."

The doctrine of these cases has been repeatedly recognized and enforced in Pennsylvania. Thus in Clark *v.* Baker (3 S. & R. p. 479), this Court, TILGHMAN, C. J., said, "These words, *without leaving issue*, applied to *personal* estate, have been held to mean, issue living at the death of the person to whom the property is given in the first instance. But not so with regard to land. This is the distinction taken in the case of Forth *v.* Chapman (1 P. Wms. 667), and it is well founded, because it carries into effect the intentions of the testator. It would answer no purpose to understand *issue indefinitely* in the case of personal property, because the law would not permit that issue to take. But it answers the best purpose in case of real property, because the issue may take accordingly."

In Hopkins *v.* Jones (2 Barr, 71), it was held that "the words 'die without lawful issue,' are to be construed, in case of personal estate, to mean, 'die without leaving lawful issue;' when that corresponds with the testator's intent."

In Seibert *v.* Butz, (9 Watts, 494), it was held, GIBSON, C. J., "There is, perhaps, no case in which the limitation over of personal estate, after an indefinite dying without issue, whether the first limitation was indefinite, or expressly for life, has, *ex vi termini*, been confined to a dying without issue at the time of the death; but the Courts have seized with avidity on any circumstance, however trivial, denoting an intent to fix the contingency at that period." The circumstance seized upon in that case was that the limitation over was upon the legatee's dying "without heirs or testament." The Court held that though there might be "an indefinite dying without issue, there can be no indefinite dying without a will," and they therefore construed the language to mean a dying without heirs living at the decease of the legatee, upon the ground that such must have been the intent of the testator.

In the case of Eichelberger *v.* Barnitz (9 W. 450), the leading case in Pennsylvania declaring the general rule in cases of real estate, the exceptions to it were also stated as follows: "The exceptions to the application of the general rules are, either in cases of personal estate, in which the construction is more liberal in favor of executory devises; or when the time at which the devise is to take effect is expressly or impliedly limited to a particular period within a life or lives in being and twenty-one years after; as where the contingency is, if the first taker die without issue before arriving at twenty-one, or if he die unmarried and without issue, or if he die without leaving issue *behind* him, or living at the time of his decease, or if the devise over be of a life estate, which implies necessarily that such devisee over may outlive the first estate; in all these cases the testator has been considered as meaning a failure of issue within a fixed period, and not an indefinite failure of issue."

In Sheets's Estate (2 P. F. S. 257), the testator gave his real and personal estate to his children by name in equal shares, but coupled with a direction that the executors should invest the property so far as it should be converted into money, and the interest and rents should be paid to the children during their lives, and after their death the principal to their children. There was a limitation over in these words: "Provided, however, that if any of my said children should die without issue, the share, purpart, or dividend of such heir shall be equally divided amongst the survivors or children of the survivors of such heir." The Court below held that the children took a fee simple in the real estate, and an absolute estate in the personalty. But this Court, reversing that decision, held that the children of the testator took but a life interest in both the real and personal estate, with remainder in fee to their children. STRONG, J., in delivering the opinion of the Court, said (on p. 263): "No principle is better settled than that if a testator in one part of his will give to a person an estate of inheritance of lands, or an absolute interest in personalty, and in subsequent passages unequivocally shows that he means the devisee or legatee to take a lesser interest only, the prior gift is restricted accordingly. . . . Both the admitted rules of legal construction and the statute regard a limitation over after the death of the first taker, as evidence of an intention that the devisee or legatee of the prior estate in order of enjoyment is to have no more than an estate or interest for life."

In Emma Meyer's Appeal (13 Wr. 111), READ, J., says (on p. 113): "In *Re* Wyrach's Trusts (17 Jur. 588), Vice-Chancellor STUART says (p. 593), 'words importing a gift to issue or a gift over on a failure of issue, when applied in a will to personal estate, receive a different construction from that which they would receive if applied to real estate.'" On p. 114 he refers to and approves of Clark *v.* Baker (3 S. & R. 477), and Forth *v.* Chapman (1 P. Wms. 667), above cited.

In the case of Hill *v.* Hill (24 P. F. S. 173), this Court, SHARSWOOD, J., said: "It is too well settled by a long train of authorities to be now a question, that a devise in fee, with a limitation over upon the death of the first taker leaving no issue reduces the estate in fee to an estate tail. Eichelberger *v.* Barnitz (9 Watts, 447) is the leading case, and it has never been shaken. On the other hand, it is equally clear that if there is anything in the will which indicates the intention of the testator that the word 'issue' shall not mean 'issue indefinitely,' but children, then this construction does not apply." In that case the limitation over was, if "my daughter Sarah die leaving no issue or *child*," her share should fall back, etc., and we held that the words, "or child," were evidence that the testator intended a failure of children, and not a failure of issue generally, and therefore that the devisee did not take an estate tail so as to alien it as a fee under the Act of 1855.

In Middlesworth's Adm'r *v.* Blackmore (24 P. F. S. 414), the devise was to Jonathan absolutely of certain real estate with a direction that if he died without leaving any legitimate issue the property was to be sold by the executors, and the proceeds to be given partly in charity and partly to the testator's legitimate grandchildren by his children who had been previously named. We held, reversing the Court below, that the direction to the executors to sell, and to pay the proceeds to grandchildren whose parents were previously named in the will, was sufficient evidence that an indefinite failure of issue was not intended. Speaking of the direction to the executors to sell, we said: "It manifestly indicates that this failure will occur during the lifetime of some one of his executors named." As to the bequest of the proceeds, we said: "All the authorities concur in saying that the devise over should be considered in determining whether the estate should vest on the death of the first taker. In distributing the proceeds of the land in which his wife had a limited use, he gave the names of the several parents of his grandchildren who were to take, thus fixing beyond any question that the recipients should be no further removed from him. In the latter distribution he does not unnecessarily repeat the names of the parents of his grandchildren, but evidently had the same persons in view. This excludes the idea that the issue of Jonathan had reference to some remote period of the future."

In the present case the question is, What was the intention of George A. Snyder as to the time when the failure of issue of Allen S. Hummel should occur, upon which the legacy to him was limited over? Did he mean that it was to occur at the death of Allen S. Hummel, or at some remote period in the future? If the latter, the limitation being upon an indefinite failure of issue, and the bequest to Allen being absolute, his interest in the bequest was an absolute estate, and it cannot be given to the persons to whom it was bequeathed by the express words of the will. But if the former was his meaning, then it was a limitation upon a definite failure of issue, and the substituted legatees must take the fund. The will was written by the testator, who was a farmer, and its language is so extremely defective in grammatical expression and technical precision, that it is, in places, almost unintelligible. Of course the distinction between a definite and an indefinite failure of issue was to him an unknown subject. But the persons whom he desired to enjoy his estate, and the time when he wished them to receive their shares, were matters entirely within his comprehension, and for them he made provision in his own homely way. His wife was to have such of the furniture as she desired; the real estate was to be sold, and one-third of the proceeds be set apart for her use during life. She was to be permitted to occupy one of his houses, but if she chose not to do so, his "children" were to provide her a home by purchasing a house and lot for her use. One-third of all the estate is again given for the use of his wife, and he then provides as follows: "And at her decease I give and bequeath unto my children as follows: viz., Jeremiah Snyder, Lewis Martin Snyder, Geo. A. Snyder, Jacob Peter Snyder, Wm. H. Snyder, Samuel J. Snyder, and my daughter, Margaret Elizabeth, intermarried to William Hains, and my grandson, Allen Hummel, child of my late deceased daughter, Emma Catherine, share and share alike, and in case my said grandson, Allen Hummel, shall at any time die without issue, I then give and bequeath the bequest of him, the said Allen Hummel, so dying, unto all my children, viz., Jeremiah Snyder, Lewis M. Snyder, Geo. W. Snyder, J. P. Snyder, Wm. H. Snyder, Samuel J. Snyder, and my daughter, Elizabeth Hains, to share and share alike."

He refers to an account book which, by the description of it in the previous part of the will, evidently contained a memorandum of advancements to his children, and directs in somewhat obscure language that his "children" shall all be made equal. His "children" are the direct objects of his bounty. They are described both as a class and by the express mention of their names. The bequest of Allen S. Hummel is given to the same persons, their names being repeated, and without including their heirs or representatives.

It is entirely clear to us that he intended the same persons and no others, to take Allen Hummel's share in the contingency of his dying without issue, as those who were take the residue of his estate. He says so in the most positive manner, and his description of those persons is so circumscribed that we can make no other inference as to their identity. But if this be so, the failure of issue contemplated by the testator must have been such as would naturally occur within the lifetime of the substituted legatees, or some of them. We are not at liberty to believe that he had in his mind the vesting of the interests limited over at some indefinite period in the future when Allen S. Hummel should or might be without issue in the strictly technical sense of the expression. His language is: "And in case my said grandson Allen Hummel shall *at any time* die without issue, I *then* give and bequeath the bequest of him, the said Allen Hummel, *so dying*, unto all my children," etc., naming them. That is, at whatever time Allen dies, *then*, viz., *at the time of his death*, the bequest to him *so dying*, shall go to the testator's children. The time of Allen's death is here referred to in three modes as the period of the determination of his estate, and at that time, and upon the happening of that contingency without issue of Allen, the same estate is given to living persons who are specially named, and without any words of succession to others in the event of his death. The expression *then*, in connection with the limitation over received precisely this construction in the case of Pinbury *v.* Elkin (1 P. Wms. 563), heretofore cited.

We are of opinion that the testator intended that *his own children* should take Allen S. Hummel's share if Allen died without issue *living at the time of his death*, and as that is a case of a definite failure of issue, it follows that Allen's interest was a defeasible one, terminable at his own death. The decree of the Court below must therefore be reversed. This decision, however, can only operate upon so much of the fund as was affected by the will of the testator. That portion of the fund is the amount received from the administrators of George A. Snyder, to wit, $1732.09. From this sum should be deducted its proportionate share of the expenses of the administration of the fund of the guardian, and also the costs of the audit upon his account and of this appeal.

The first and second assignments of error are without merit, and therefore dismissed.

Decree reversed, and record remitted for further proceedings, with direction to the Court below to correct the account and distribution by awarding to the appellants the sum of $1732.09, less its pro rata share of the administration of the fund and of the costs of the audit and of this appeal; and to John Hummel the sum of $672.69, less its pro rata share of the same expenses and costs; the costs of this appeal to be paid out of the fund for distribution.

Opinion by GREEN, J. GORDON and TRUNKEY, JJ., dissent.

Jan. '79, 173.   February 24, 1880.

Economy Building Association to the use of Smyth v. Hungerbuehler.

Building association mortgages—Application of stock payments—Evidence of.

Payments on stock assigned as collateral security for a building association mortgage are not, *ipso facto*, payments on the mortgage.

When such payments have been generally credited to the mortgagor on his account with the association, the testimony of the officers of the association that they considered the payments as, in law, payments on the mortgage, is not evidence of an application to that object.

Error to the Common Pleas No. 1, of Philadelphia County.

Scire facias by the above-named corporation, to the use of Smyth, against Hungerbuehler on a mortgage given by him to secure the payment of $2200, and monthly interest, with a proviso that if, at any time default should be made in the payment of interest for six months, then the whole debt should become due. The plaintiff having obtained judgment for want of an appearance for $2346.38 a levari facias issued. On petition of Matthias Ruoss the Court set aside execution, opened judgment, and let him into a defence. Ruoss then pleaded that the mortgage had been given by Hungerbuehler to secure the repayment of a loan by the payment of interest and of dues and premiums on eleven shares of stock in the association, and had been fully paid before the commencement of this action.

At the trial the following facts appeared. In 1873 Hungerbuehler was the owner of eleven shares of the association's stock upon which he had paid in monthly dues of $1 per share, $803. He then borrowed from the association, plaintiff, $2200, giving therefor the mortgage in suit, containing the proviso that if one month's interest should fall in arrears for six months the whole debt should become due, and he assigned his stock to the association as collateral security for the loan; he continued to pay his monthly instalments upon his stock and the interest upon his mortgage until January 10, 1876. On December 29, 1875, Smyth, the use plaintiff, entered judgment against Hungerbuehler on a bond for $1400, and issued an attachment execution against Hungerbuehler as defendant and the building association as garnishee. On the answers made to the interrogatories of Smyth, he obtained judgment that the association held eleven shares of the defendant's stock, liable to the plaintiff's execution, subject to the equities of the garnishee. On September 24, 1876, a fi. fa. was issued on this judgment, and on October 7 the sheriff sold the stock, which was bought in by

Smyth. On October 31, the association having reached the limit of its chartered existence, by being able to divide among the stockholders $200 to each share of stock, the board of directors passed a resolution authorizing and directing an assignment of Hungerbuehler's mortgage to Smyth on the latter's payment of the arrearages on Hungerbuehler's stock, amounting to $36.37, and arrearages of interest on the mortgage, of the same amount. Smyth made these payments, amounting to $73.14, and received an assignment of the mortgage in suit. He then brought this suit, obtained judgment for the full amount of the mortgage and issued a levari facias thereon, but on the petition of Matthias Ruoss, who held a second mortgage on the property, the execution was set aside, judgment opened, and Ruoss let into a defence as before stated; and before the trial Ruoss obtained judgment on his mortgage and purchased the property at the sheriff's sale. At the trial of the present issue, the foregoing facts having been proved, the secretary of the association testified as follows: "There is no entry anywhere on our books applying the payments of dues on stock to payments on the mortgage. Our books do not show any such application. . . . . My notion is that in law payment of dues on stock is payment on the mortgage. We took Hungerbuehler's money to pay our debts and expenses, and we credited it in his receipt book." It was admitted that Hungerbuehler had been at no time six months in arrears in the payment of his dues and the interest on his mortgage.

The Judge charged the jury, *inter alia*, as follows: "The question is whether there was any appropriation of the payments on stock to payments on the mortgage. Mr. Hungerbuehler had the first right to appropriate; if he did not, then the association had the right. . . . . I submit the question to the jury whether from the testimony of the secretary, there has been an appropriation of stock payments to this mortgage. If the jury find there has been an appropriation of stock payments to the mortgage, Mr. Smyth will be entitled to recover back the money paid to the association, on assignment of the mortgage to him, with interest."

Verdict and judgment for $81.75 for the use plaintiff, who took this writ, assigning for error, *inter alia*, the portion of the charge quoted.

S. N. Rich, for the plaintiff in error.

There was no evidence of any special application of the stock instalments either by Hungerbuehler or by the association. The secretary stated his incorrect impression of the law, and this the learned Judge allowed to go to the jury. Besides, the Judge ignored the question of the time when the pretended application was made, and so further bewildered the jury. Of course, no appropriation could have been made, either by or for Hungerbuehler, after the attachment of his stock.

T. Wagner, Jr., contra.

The question whether an appropriation had been made or not, was fairly left to the jury. Nothing passed to Smyth by the assignment of the mortgage. It is doubtful whether building associations can at any time assign their mortgages. Certainly they cannot do so when they have run out and their powers are exhausted.

May 3, 1880. THE COURT. Matthias Ruoss, who as terre-tenant was permitted to defend in this case, was the second mortgagee of Hungerbuehler; the building association having the first mortgage. When Hungerbuehler executed this first mortgage, in amount of $2200.00, he held eleven shares of the company's stock, which he assigned to the corporation as collateral for the loan embraced by the mortgage. Upon this stock he had paid in the way of monthly dues some $803, and subsequently he seems to have met the instalments and interest as they fell due, except about seventy-three dollars, which Smyth paid after the stock fell into his hands. On the 29th December, 1875, Smyth's attachment was served on the building association, as garnishee of Hungerbuehler, and, on the answers made by it, he obtained judgment subject to its equities as pledgee. On this judgment a fi. fa. was issued, a levy made on the stock, and on sale by the sheriff, October 7, 1876, it was bought in by Smyth. As previous to this time no application had been made of the stock payments to the mortgage, either by Hungerbuehler or the association, it is clear that Smyth took it freed from all claims of Hungerbuehler or his creditors, and subject alone to the equities of the company.

On the 31st of October, 1876, the association having reached the limit of its chartered existence, by being able to divide two hundred dollars to each share of its stock, its board of directors passed a resolution authorizing an assignment of the mortgage to Smyth, on his payment of the remaining unpaid dues and interest. This he accordingly did, and received the assignment on the eighth day of November, 1876. In other words, Smyth, the owner of stock worth $2200, assigned it to the company by which it had been issued in consideration of the transfer of the mortgage in suit.

Now the defence made by Ruoss is this: That the payments made on the stock were in law payments upon the mortgage and ought so to have been applied. This view was in effect adopted by the Court below, and so Smyth was permitted to recover only what he himself had paid to the company to close out the arrears on the stock, and interest due on the mortgage. But this conclusion was based on a false premise, for it is not so that the stock payments were *ipso facto* payments on the mortgage. The converse has been expressly ruled in the cases of the North American Building Association *v.* Sutton (11 Casey, 463); The Spring Garden Association *v.* The Tradesman's Loan Association (10 Wright, 493) and Early's Appeal (7 WEEKLY NOTES, 184).

Either of the original parties might have made such application before the levy of Smyth's attachment, but this was done by neither of these parties, and so Smyth by virtue of his attachment took the place of Hungerbuehler, and as the company might, at Hungerbuehler's instance, had he returned the stock, have paid to him the value thereof, and retained the mortgage, so might it have done with Smyth. In such case however, Ruoss could not be heard to complain, for his position as second mortgagee would not be in the least affected thereby. This stock became collateral security not for his benefit, but for that of the association, hence its surrender would put him in no worse position than he was when his mortgage was executed. Surely then Ruoss could not intervene to prevent the disposition of collaterals in which he had no interest. In effect this very point is ruled in the case of the Spring Garden Association *v.* The Tradesman's Loan Association, above cited. It was there held, that a purchaser at a sheriff's sale of the mortgaged premises could not compel such application, but that, where the building association on notice of the assignee of the mortgagor agreed to retain the stock, and issue a scire facias on the mortgage, it had the right to recover thereon. But if the association plaintiff could have paid the value of the stock to Smyth and retained and collected the mortgage, why could it not retain the stock and assign the mortgage? It certainly would not put Ruoss's mortgage in a worse position, because Smyth held the first lien rather than the company. Smyth was undoubtedly by act of law owner of this stock, which was worth some $2200, and that amount he had the right to demand of the company or its equivalent. The company, on the other hand, had the right to retain either the stock or the mortgage; it chose to retain the stock, and by assigning the mortgage to Smyth, as in that case it was bound to do, it thereby clothed him with all the rights it would have had had it paid him the value of the collaterals and kept the mortgage. This, however, was a matter for themselves; a matter with which Ruoss had nothing to do. It is true, had the stock payments been applied to the first mortgage, Ruoss would have been the gainer thereby, but so would he, had Hungerbuehler assigned the stock in satisfaction of his mortgage. But as he was powerless to compel the latter, so was he powerless to compel the former. It follows that under the evidence as it is now presented to us, there should have been a verdict for the plaintiff for the full amount of the mortgage.

Judgment reversed and a new venire ordered.

Opinion by GORDON, J.

Common Pleas—Law.

C. P. No. 2.   Oct. 30, 1880.

Newlin v. The Milton Building and Loan Association, No. 2.

Affidavit of defence law—Instrument not within.

Rule to show cause why judgment should not be stricken off.

The judgment was taken for want of an affidavit of defence. The copy of instrument of writing filed was as follows, viz.:—

Philadelphia, March 10, 1880.

Mr. James W. M. Newlin—

Mr. James K. Duffy has this day transferred to your name four shares of the capital stock of the Milton Building Association No. 2, in the first series, the value of which is seven hundred and eight dollars ($708). Notification of withdrawal has been given on these shares, and they will be paid in regular order of notice.

[Seal of Association.]   M. A. QUINN, *Secretary*.

E. C. Quinn, for the rule.

The instrument of writing upon which this suit is brought is not within the affidavit of defence law.

Hennesey *v.* Muller, 1 WEEKLY NOTES, 106.
Craig *v.* Rushton, 1 Id. 82.
McCarroll *v.* The Church, 5 Id. 210.
Bradford *v.* Bradford, 1 Clark's Cases, 209.

Goodbread, contra.

The writing is an evidence of indebtedness given by the association to plaintiff, admitting this liability, and a promise to pay by them the sum of $708 to the plaintiff. The judgment was properly taken.

[HARE, P. J. This writing is more in the nature of proof that there is a certificate to which Mr. Newlin is entitled, than an instrument in writing for the payment of money, and the promise is to pay in the "regular order of notice," which is in the nature of an appropriation of assets.]

Rule absolute.

C. P. No. 2. Oct. 30, 1880.
German et al. v. W. J. Moodie.

Agent—Acceptance of draft in his representative capacity—Limited Partnership Act of 1874.

Rule for judgment for want of a sufficient affidavit of defence.

The following is a copy of bill of exchange sued on, and duly filed:—

$65. No.   Pottsville, Pa., Nov. 24, 1879.
At sixty days' sight pay to the order of German and Robinson, sixty-five dollars, value received, and charge the same to the account of
N. L. WILLIAMS, *Chair'n*.
To W. J. MOODIE, *Treas.*,
309 Walnut Street.
Accepted Nov. 26, 1879.   W. J. MOODIE, *Treas.*

The affidavit of defence alleged, *inter alia*, that "defendant was the treasurer, and one N. L. Williams was the chairman of the Gate Vein Coal Co., Limited, a limited partnership organized under the Act of the Legislature of Pennsylvania, approved June 2, 1874," That the draft sued on was "given by the drawer, N. L. Williams, as chairman of the said Gate Vein Coal Co., Limited, to the plaintiffs in this case for the goods and merchandise sold and delivered by plaintiffs to the said the Gate Vein Coal Co., Limited, and" was "accepted by deponent as treasurer of said partnership, and not individually, and that there was no intention to be any personal liability on the part of said deponent, who was not one of the members of said partnership, and that this state of affairs was well known to plaintiff."

M. L. Kohler, for the rule.
The omission of the word "limited" in the bill of exchange makes every person participating or acquiescing in such omission liable.
Act 2 June, 1874, § 3, Purd. Dig. 1891, pl. 3.

James M. West, contra.
THE COURT. Rule discharged.

C. P. No. 2.   Nov. 13, 1880.
Rittenhouse v. Fetters.

Amendment—Substitution of new parties—Real party defendant may intervene pro interesse suo.

Rule by defendant to strike off his own name as defendant, and substitute therefor the name of Charlotte Rittenhouse, his landlady.

Ejectment. The affidavit of the defendant, Josiah Fetters, set forth in substance that he was the defendant, and resided on the premises for which this ejectment was brought; that he does not claim title to the said premises, but resides thereon as tenant, and that his landlady is Charlotte Rittenhouse.

The affidavit of Charlotte Rittenhouse in substance alleged that she was the owner of the premises for which this ejectment was brought, and that Josiah Fetters, the defendant, is only the tenant thereof; that she obtained title to said premises through the will of her husband, and that he, and she after him, have had continuous adverse possession of said premises for upwards of thirty years.

Gavitt, for the rule.
The defendant, Fetters, having disclaimed title, ought to be relieved from the possibility of costs.

R. Ingram, contra.
The plaintiff is entitled to have Fetters on the record, so as to conclude him by the judgment.

THE COURT. Rule absolute to allow Charlotte Rittenhouse to intervene *pro interesse suo*. Rule discharged as to Fetters.

C. P. No. 3.   June 14, 1880.
Maynes v. Rutherford et al.

Acts of Assembly with reference to Greenwich Island—Construction of—Taxation for a private purpose—Bill of Rights.

Rule for a new trial.

Replevin for a number of cows, horses, carts, etc., by Charles Maynes against William Rutherford, treasurer of the Greenwich Island Meadow Company, and James J. Keating, bailiff.

Plaintiff was tenant of Mrs. Elizabeth L. Devine of a tract of land on Greenwich Island, which he rented in April, 1879. On August 20, 1879, a distress was made upon these cows, etc., under a warrant of Rutherford, as treasurer aforesaid, to the defendant Keating for the sum of $451.25 as due for certain charges alleged to be due to the said company by the owner of the lands for the repair of banks, etc., on Greenwich Island. The distress was made under authority of an Act of Assembly passed April 12, 1760, recorded in book A, vol. iv. p. 182, (see 1 Sm. Laws, 227), empowering the owners of said island to assess and collect from each owner or possessor thereof two shillings for each acre of land held in order to keep the outside banks in good repair and raise a fund to defray sundry contingent and yearly expenses accruing therein. The Act provides that payment of said assessments may be enforced by the treasurer by suit before a justice or in the Common Pleas, which tribunals were directed to give judgments, and execution to be levied on the tract or piece of marsh or cripple land, and the property to be given over to the managers for the time being, who were authorized to let the same until the rents shall pay all arrearages.

By a supplement passed January 13, 1804 (ee 4 Smith's Laws, 109), it became the duty of the managers, as often as it might be necessary, to estimate the expenses for making, repairing and keeping in good repair all and every bank, etc., on the land and to ascertain the names of owners and possessors thereof or their legal representatives, and to rate and assess each owner or possessor fairly and equally per acre. And such supplement further provided that the managers after regulating the assessments are to issue their warrant to the treasurer authorizing and requesting him to receive from every owner or possessor, his or her legal representative the sum wherewith he is charged. "And if any one shall refuse or neglect to make payment within thirty days from the date of such demand, it shall be the duty of the said treasurer to levy or cause to be levied the said tax, and costs attending such levy, by distress and sale of the goods and chattels of the delinquent in such manner as is prescribed by the Act entitled to raise and collect county rates and levies passed April 11, 1799, such sum if paid or recovered from a renter to be deducted from his rent."

At the trial plaintiff testified that he did not owe any rent to Mrs. Devine, nor anything to Mr. Rutherford. Defendants produced the minutes of the company showing assessments upon the land for the years 1876, 1877, and 1878; and testified that a notice of distress was left at Mrs. Devine's house, and that the company waited thirty days before distraining.

The Judge charged the jury that if the levy and distress were for assessments not made during plaintiff's possession they should find for plaintiff, and that there must be affirmative proof that a thirty days' notice of the intention to distrain was given and served upon the owner or possessor or her agent.

Verdict for plaintiff.

J. M. Moyer, for rule.

The amount involved is not a tax and consequently not a lien on the land; it is but a ratable assessment for a corresponding benefit, and therefore but a personal charge upon the occupant, whereof the remedy is by distress only.

Pray *v.* Northern Liberties, 7 Casey, 71.
Re Mayor of New York, 11 Johns. 80.
2 Inst. 532.
Sharp *v.* Speir, 4 Hill, 76.

Local taxation need not be limited by or coextensive with any previously established district. The Legislature may create a district for that especial purpose, or they may tax a class of lands or persons benefited to be designated without reference to town, county, or district lines.

People *v.* Draper, 15 N. Y. 543.

The power of the Legislature to levy taxes may be delegated to commissioners or other agents, and when the Legislature provides for a tax by any agency whatever, it is in contemplation of the Constitution the act of the people.

Mayor *v.* State, 15 Md. 376.

The assessment being a personal one it does not lie in the mouth of the present plaintiff to deny his liability for assessments made before his tenancy without showing that some one was in possession during the previous years from whom the assessments could have been collected. If he seeks to charge negligence, the onus is on him to show wherein it existed.

Henry *v.* Horstick, 9 Watts, 412.
Caldwell *v.* Moore, 1 Jones, 58.
Girard Life Ins. *v.* City of Philada., 35 Leg. Int. 16.

Thorn, contra.

The provisions of the 1st and 2d sections of Act of Jan. 13, 1804, are a manifest violation of the Bill of Rights, and the taking of plaintiff's goods was unlawful.

Craig *v.* Kline, 15 Sm. 399.
Rutherford's Case, 22 Id. 82.
City *v.* Scott, 31 Id. 86.

June 17, 1880. THE COURT (LUDLOW, P. J.). The right of taxing for public purposes does not apply to this case, for this is a private purpose. To the extent that defendant claims, the Act is clearly in violation of the Bill of Rights.

Rule discharged.

C. P. No. 3.   June 8, 1880.

Kenyon v. City.

Pleading—Case—Negligence—Injuries caused by obstructions placed by the city in a "road or passage-way" without a light.

Sur demurrer to narr.

Case. The fourth count of the narr. set forth that on July 13, 1879, there was a certain road or passage-way whereon a large number of persons were accustomed to pass on foot, and in wagons, to wit, Pennsylvania Avenue, yet defendant wrongfully, improperly, and negligently dug a certain hole or excavation, and placed a large quantity of earth, brick, stones, etc., upon a certain part of said passage-way, and continued the same during the night-time of said day without placing or causing to be placed any light or signal near such obstruction, in consequence of which plaintiff, during the night of said day, using due care, and lawfully travelling on said road, was accidentally driven against said obstruction and was injured and sustained great damages, etc.

The demurrer set forth that the count is not sufficient, in that there is not contained therein any averment that the road or passage-way described was a public road or highway.

Charles E. Morgan, Jr., for demurrer.

Plaintiff must set up some duty on the part of the city to abstain from placing obstructions upon the road, or a right in plaintiff to use it.

George H. Earle, contra, cited—

Corley *v.* Hill, 93 English Com. Law Rep. p. 554.

THE COURT. Demurrer overruled.

Orphans' Court.

November 15, 1880.

Schively's Estate.

Will—Bequest—Whether vested or contingent—Dying without issue—Construed to mean death of legatee, without issue, during testator's lifetime—Legacy of a sum certain to a child, to be held by trustees to pay interest to the child during minority, the principal to remain invested and to be paid to legatee at majority, "at discretion of executors," held to be a vested legacy.

Sur exceptions to adjudication.

The following facts appeared before the auditing Judge (HANNA, P. J.), at the audit of the account of the Pennsylvania Company for Insurance on Lives, etc., trustees. The trust arose under the following provisions in the will of Edward M. Schively, Sr., deceased.

"Third. To my son, Edward May Schively, the sum of eight thousand dollars, to be held in trust by my executors for his support, the interest only to be paid to him quarterly. The principal to remain invested until he arrives at maturity, when the said portion is to be paid over to him at discretion of my executors."

"Fifth. Should either of my above named children die without issue, either his or her share to be equally divided among the survivors."

Edward May Schively, the *cestui que trust* was a minor at the decease of his father, and died May 25, 1880, still in his minority, unmarried, and without issue. He left surviving him his mother, a brother, and two sisters.

The auditing Judge in his adjudication said, *inter alia*, "The question now arising is the proper distribution of the corpus and accruing income of the trust estate. To arrive at its solution, one must first consider the nature and character of the legacy bequeathed to Edward May Schively. Was it vested or contingent? As said by SHARSWOOD, C. J., in Chess's Appeal (6 Norris, 364), 'No doubt it is the general rule that a legacy is to be deemed vested or contingent, just as the time when it is to take effect shall appear to be annexed to the gift, or the payment of it. Where there is no substantive gift, and it is only implied from the direction to pay the legacy is it contingent. But this rule is of course subject to the necessary exception that a contrary intention is not to be collected from the words or circumstances.' See also Williams on Executors, edition of 1877 page [1224], where the two positive rules of construction are stated. If the bequest to Edward May Schively had been 'payable' or 'to be paid' when he arrived at maturity there can be no doubt that under the first rule cited by Mr. Williams, it must be held vested and transmissible to his personal representatives. But it seems from the language of testator, that the legacy is not to be paid unless the legatee attained the age of twenty-one years, and as he died in his minority, the second rule cited by Mr. Williams applies, and the legacy should be held as contingent and not vested. Upon further examination, however, we find that exceptions to this rule exist, and the present case seems to fall within the limit of these exceptions. It is to be observed that testator sets apart from his general estate, the precise sum of eight thousand dollars, thus indicating his intention that his son should become the legatee of this certain amount. He further gives the interest and income of this sum to him quarterly for his support. And directs the principal to be invested and paid over to him at his maturity in the discretion of the executors. Now in view of these provisions we find that 'where a testator bequeaths a legacy to a person at a future time, and either gives him the immediate interest, or directs it to be applied for his benefit, the Court there considers the disposition of the interest to be an indication of the testator's intention that the legatee should at all events have the principal, and on this ground holds such legacies to be vested.' (2 Williams on Executors from page [1223] to [1239] and cases cited. Provenchere's Appeal, 67 Penn. St. Rep. 463.)

"But the next question is how is this construction to be reconciled with the remaining provision of the will, 'Should either of my above named children die without issue, either his or her share to be equally divided among the survivors.' It is evident this does not apply to Edward May Schively alone, but to all of the children previously named in the will. In preceding clauses, testator bequeaths to each of his two daughters eight thousand dollars to be held in trust for them, they receiving the income quarterly, and to his son Augustus three thousand dollars in yearly instalments of one thousand dollars each. Now what was in the mind of testator when he made use of the language above quoted? Did he mean a failure of issue indefinitely, or that in the event of his children dying in his lifetime without issue, then his or her legacy would pass to the survivors? We incline to the opinion he meant in the event of the latter contingency.

"And as Edward May Schively did not die in the lifetime of his father without issue, his legacy did not pass to his surviving brothers and sisters. (Mickley's Appeal, Leg. Int. 1880, p. 94).

"Being of opinion that the legacy to Edward May Schively vested in him absolutely, at the death of his father, and is now payable to his administrator, the same will be so awarded."

Exceptions to the adjudication were filed by the trustees (1) in awarding the fund to the administrator of Edward M. Schively, the younger, (2) in not awarding the fund to the children of Edward M. Schively, the elder.

John G. Johnson, for the trustees.

November 20, 1880. THE COURT. Exceptions dismissed and adjudication confirmed.

September 22, 1880.
Droste's Estate.

Claim by executor against decedent's estate—Power of attorney to transfer stock given to an executor in the lifetime of a testator, when coupled with an interest, is not revoked by the death of the donor of the power.

Sur exceptions to adjudication.

Upon the audit of the account of the executors of Catharine Droste, it appeared that the testatrix died in June, 1879. In the inventory filed was an item of sixteen shares of New York, New Haven & Hartford Railroad stock, appraised at $162 a share. This stock was sold by L. J. Leberman, one of the executors, for $2952, and he claimed $1600 of the proceeds, on the ground that Mrs. Droste had, several months before her death, delivered to him the stock, with a power of attorney to transfer it, as security for a loan to her of $1600. Leberman's testimony (otherwise incompetent) was admitted by agreement.

Breittinger, a notary, testified: "I drew the will and witnessed it. Mr. Guttermans, Leberman's co-executor, told me at the time of the appraisement he had in his possession the shares of stock." "Called on him, and he told me that he held the shares under a power, but they did not stand in his name." . . . . "I said the power was void after Mrs. Droste's death." . . . . "I thought so at the time; but we came to a friendly understanding that the shares should be put down in the appraisement, and he afterwards would have a chance to prove his claim at the settlement of the account."

In behalf of certain legatees it was contended that as the shares were included in the inventory, and were duly appraised, they were a portion of testatrix's estate, and, although the stock had been sold, the proceeds were properly in the account; also, that Leberman was now on the footing of any other creditor of the estate, and if he had any claim must satisfactorily prove it.

The Auditing Judge held as follows: "The entire good faith of Leberman is apparent from the fact of his holding the stock under an irrevocable stock power, duly signed by the testatrix, and properly witnessed. This is of itself *prima facie* evidence of a sale to Mr. Leberman of the shares (Penna. Co. App., 5 Norris, 102), and the burden of proof would, therefore, have been upon those who alleged that the stock belonged to the testatrix at the time of her death."
. . . . "But this they were relieved from by Mr. Leberman himself admitting that the stock, although transferred to him, was but the security for a debt due him by testatrix, and after he was paid the balance belonged to her. Being satisfied, therefore, that the credit asked by the accountant for the $1600 paid to Mr. Leberman is correct, it is allowed."

To this finding exceptions were filed in behalf of several legatees.

Charles Davis, for the exceptions.
Edward H. Weil, contra.

Oct. 9, 1880. THE COURT. Notwithstanding the earnest argument of the counsel for the exceptants, we are of the opinion that the credit allowed the executor for the amount of the debt due him by testatrix was fully sustained by the evidence; and while the exceptants would gain by its disallowance, yet through the integrity and fair dealing of the executor they profit largely, even with the payment of the claim. It was strongly contended that the debt of testatrix to the accountant was not properly proved. But if all the circumstances connected with the creation and existence of the debt were not related by the accountant, who testified on his own behalf by agreement of the counsel for exceptants, with the particularity and exactness demanded by the counsel at the argument, yet all these facts if desired could have been obtained upon cross-examination. The uncontradicted testimony of the accountant was that decedent owed him sixteen hundred dollars; and it further appeared that he, after her death, sold shares of stock which she had unconditionally and absolutely transferred to him, charged himself with the whole amount realized, and claimed credit for the debt due him. The effect of which was to account for more than nine hundred dollars as assets of the estate, which, in view of the absolute transfer to him by the testatrix, could have been retained by him as his own. There is no evidence other than the admissions of the executor that he held the stock as collateral security, and, under the power of attorney and transfer under seal, he was, *prima facie*, the owner. (Penna. Co.'s App., 5 Norris, 102; s. c. 5 WEEKLY NOTES, 277.)

As no good reason has been shown to disturb the adjudication, the exceptions are dismissed.

Opinion by HANNA, P. J.

Supreme Court.

May '79, 39.   June 21, 1880.
Enterprise Transit Co.'s Appeal.

Equity jurisdiction—Injunction to stay waste—Receiver of oil well—Bill by claimant under an oil lease, out of possession, praying for a receiver to take charge of producing wells, pending an ejectment—Separate acknowledgment of deed by married woman—Notary's certificate, when fatally defective—A notary cannot by a new certificate supply an accidental omission in his first certificate.

A Court of Equity has no jurisdiction to appoint a receiver to take charge of oil-producing wells, pending an ejectment brought to try the title to the possession of the premises.

PER CURIAM. We can draw no distinction between a farm and an oil well.

Appeal from a decree of the Common Pleas of McKean County dismissing a bill in equity and vacating the appointment of a receiver.

Bill in equity, filed by the Enterprise Transit Company, a corporation, against Mrs. Maryette Sheedy and Patrick Sheedy, her husband, and Roberts & Lockwood *et al.*, setting forth that under an oil lease executed by the defendants, Maryette Sheedy and Patrick Sheedy, "duly acknowledged as required by the laws respecting conveyances of married women, and recorded," the complainants were entitled to enter upon and develop a certain tract of oil land, the property of the said Maryette Sheedy, and had taken possession thereof and commenced operations when they were prevented from continuing, and were forcibly ejected by the defendants, Roberts & Lockwood, who claimed title from the said Maryette and Patrick Sheedy under a subsequent lease, and who themselves had taken possession, and had drilled and are continuing to drill oil wells, one at least of which is completed and is producing petroleum oil; that an action of ejectment has been brought by complainant against said defendants, and is pending, but that the defendants, unless restrained, would, in whole or in part, deplete and render worthless the said oil property before said ejectment suit could be determined; and Praying (1) an injunction to restrain defendants from drilling wells or producing or removing oil from the premises; (2) the appointment of a receiver, *pendente lite,* to take charge of the producing well or wells, until the rights of the parties be determined.

On preliminary hearing, on bill and affidavits, the Court, without granting an injunction, appointed a receiver as prayed, who gave bonds and took charge of the property.

The defendants, in their joint answer, substantially admitted the facts alleged in the bill, except the due and legal acknowledgment of the lease from Sheedy and wife to the complainants. They averred that the acknowledgment thereof, made before a notary public by the lessors, was fatally defective.

The following facts further appeared by the answer, or were formally admitted by counsel, viz: The certificate by the notary of the separate acknowledgment by the lessors, Patrick Sheedy and Maryette, his wife, was in due form, except that it omitted to state that the full contents of the said lease had been made known to Mrs. Sheedy. The lease was delivered and recorded, with the defective acknowledgment. About five months thereafter, and before any new rights had intervened, the complainant presented the lease to the notary before whom the acknowledgment was made, and he, without the knowledge of Mrs. Sheedy, put a new and formal certificate of acknowledgment upon it, and this second certificate was recorded with the lease. It was conceded that this second certificate is true, and that the omission in the first certificate was accidental. It was also admitted that Roberts & Lockwood had actual notice of the prior lease, and of complainants' claim thereunder before any expenditures were made by them on the property for oil uses.

Upon final hearing, the Court, in an opinion by WILLIAMS, P. J., held that the defectively certified lease, by Patrick and Maryette Sheedy to the complainant, was inoperative, and passed no title to the complainant; and the subsequent certificate of the notary, under the circumstances, did not cure the defect.[*]

[*] In the Supreme Court this case was decided solely on the ground of want of jurisdiction to appoint a receiver, but the opinion of the Court below, on the effect of the certificates of acknowledgment, is here inserted, as matter of interest.

WILLIAMS, P. J. The certificate of acknowledgment which bore even date with the lease is defective in not setting out that the contents of the paper were made known to Mrs. Sheedy, who was the wife of Patrick Sheedy and the owner of the land. The lease, therefore, when it was executed and delivered was not executed and acknowledged as the statute requires; and was not binding on Mrs. Sheedy.

"The acknowledgment of a deed by a *feme covert* is not good unless it be expressed in the certificate of the

The Court thereupon entered a decree dismissing the bill, and vacating the appointment of the receiver. The complainant took this appeal, assigning as error the said decree.

Hamlin & Son (with whom was *W. B. Chapman*), for appellants, presented an elaborate argument to show that the certificate of the notary, as amended, was a sufficient compliance with the Act relating to the separate acknowledgment of married women. They further argued that owing to the peculiar status of property in oil-producing territory, as held under the usual form magistrate, who took the acknowledgment, that the contents of the deed were made known to her." (Steele *v.* Thompson, 14 S. & R. 84.) To the same effect is the more recent case of Glidden *v.* Strupler (2 Smith, 400), in which it is held that "a married woman has no capacity to contract for the sale of her land or to convey it except in the precise statutory mode."

The plaintiff felt the force of this objection to his title under the lease and sought to remove it. On the 21st of February, 1877, between five and six months after the acknowledgment was originally certified and the lease delivered, the plaintiff presented the lease to the notary before whom the acknowledgment was made, and he, without the knowledge of Mrs. Sheedy, put a new and formal certificate of acknowledgment upon it.

It is conceded in the argument that this second certificate is true, and that the omission in the first certificate was accidental.

If the second certificate is to be regarded as a valid one, then the lease is valid, and Mrs. Sheedy and all claiming under her are bound. If it is not valid the lease is not valid, and the plaintiffs are without title.

This precise question does not appear to have been determined in this State. It has been held repeatedly that the certificate must set out all that is necessary in order to show substantial compliance with the Act of Assembly. (Steele *v.* Thompson, and Glidden *v.* Strupler, cited above. See also Watson *v.* Bailey, 1 Binn. 470, and Watson *v.* Mercer, 6 S. & R. 49.) That the defects in the certificate cannot be helped by the testimony of the notary, is held in Jourdan *v.* Jourdan (9 S. & R. 268). That the married woman is equally incompetent to prove what should appear by the certificate, is held in Watson *v.* Bailey (1 Binn. 470), and in other cases. That a married woman whose deed is unacknowledged is not estopped from availing herself of her title by her declarations or by receipt of purchase-money is equally well settled. The precise point was determined in Glidden *v.* Strupler (*supra*), and in Williams & Confer *v.* Baker and wife (21 Smith, 476). In this respect the rule in equity is the same as at law. In Glidden *v.* Strupler the Court say "the receipt of the purchase-money by a married woman is no ground for the interposition of equity."

There is then no substitute for the certificate of acknowledgment which the law requires. If this is wanting or insufficient when the deed is delivered, the deed itself is not binding. Now, who can give vitality and binding force to such an inoperative and worthless deed? We have seen that the married woman herself cannot do this either by her declarations or by her testimony, for the law has provided but one mode in which she may express her consent.

The notary cannot do it by taking the witness stand and making proof, in that manner, that the acknowledgment was properly taken by him, for his official certificate is the only competent evidence of that fact. But his certificate made at the proper time is insufficient in form. The deed is then useless and inoperative unless the notary has the power to make a new certificate. Has he that power? It is not given in express terms by any Act of Assembly. If it exists it must be by implication from the fact that the law clothes him with the authority to take and certify acknowledgments; and it must be maintained that this authority is not exhausted until the acknowledgment is certified correctly. The analogies, however, are not favorable to this view of the question. It has frequently been held that the supervisors of roads, after opening a road in obedience to an order of Court cannot change the route of the road for the purpose of correcting a mistake and of putting it on the recorded site. Their authority is exhausted by the opening of the road. So in the Orphans' Court it has been held that an imperfect execution of a power to sell can be helped only by beginning *de novo*, either by petition for sale, or for ratification and appproval of the invalid sale. The authority was exhausted by its exercise.

This principle was applied to a certificate of acknowledgment taken by the clerk of the Court under a statute of Kentucky in the case of Elliott *et al. v.* Piersol (1 Pet. 328.) In that case it seems that it was the duty of the clerk to take the acknowledgment, certify to it, and then record the certificate. The acknowledgment was taken in proper form but the clerk failed to incorporate into his certificate a statement of the separate examination of the wife, and the certificate and record were, in this respect, defective. The Court, on application of the grantee, heard testimony showing that the separate examination was in fact made and then ordered the clerk to amend his certificate accordingly. This the Supreme Court of the United States held to be error: First, because the acknowledgment and certificate were not the act of the Court, but of the clerk, and the Court had no jurisdiction of the subject; and second, because if the certificate could be treated as the voluntary act of the clerk he had no authority to make it, his authority having been exhausted. "The authority to make and record a certificate of acknowledgment was *functus officio* as soon as the record was made," is the language of the Court. This question was really not raised by the facts in case of Elliott *et al. v.* Piersol, but is treated and discussed by the Court as though it had been.

Our own cases point to the same conclusion, and we are disposed to hold that the second certificate was unauthorized and is of no effect. As the notary had not the power to make a new certificate, it follows that the deed which was inoperative before that certificate was made is inoperative still.

The inconveniences that would result from any other holding are really very great. If the power of the notary to certify continues until he has certified his official act truly, how many times may he certify on the same deed? At what intervals? If he may thus make a deed which is utterly worthless when delivered operative against the grantor and in spite of her remonstrances, why can he not by a new certificate render a deed which is valid on its face utterly worthless to the holder? Being himself the sole judge of the correctness of his last certificate and the propriety of a new one the record would afford no assurance that the acknowledgment was what it purported to be. This certificate could be changed at any time notwithstanding the fact (as in this case) that it had been recorded. Such uncertainty would be intolerable and would open the door to frauds. The safer rule is that upon which we decide this case.

We are of opinion that the plaintiff shows no title, for the reason that his grantor, being a married woman, is not bound by her deed because of its defective acknowledgment.

of oil leases, the appointment of a receiver was the only remedy to prevent acts in the nature of waste, pending an ejectment, and that the Court had jurisdiction to act in the premises, citing—
Kane *v.* Vanderburgh, 1 Johns. Ch. 11.
C. & A. Oil Co. *v.* U. S. Petroleum Co., 7 Sm. 91, per AGNEW, J.
McVicker *v.* Ross, 55 Barb. 248.

(No paper-book was received by the reporter from counsel for appellees.)

Oct. 4, 1880. THE COURT. It may be that the peculiarity of the property in an oil well is such that an injunction to stay waste, or a writ of estrepement, will not be an adequate remedy for an owner out of possession. But that will not authorize a Court of Equity to assume jurisdiction to try the title upon what is merely an ejectment bill, and thus, in effect, deprive the parties of their constitutional right of trial by jury. Much less will it justify a Court in appointing a receiver who shall summarily enter into possession, turning out the actual possessor, and receiving all the profits. Ejectment and a recovery of the mesne profits in that or a subsequent action, seem to be the proper, and must be regarded as adequate, remedies. We can draw no distinction between a farm and an oil well. It is clear that the Court below had no jurisdiction, except to enjoin waste, and it is unnecessary to consider the ground upon which the decree below was put by the learned Judge. The case, therefore, is ruled by Schlecht's Appeal (10 P. F. Smith, 172); Tillmes *v.* Marsh (17 Id. 507); Christie and Scott's Appeal (4 Norris, 463), and other cases.

Decree affirmed and appeal dismissed at the costs of the appellants.

PER CURIAM. PAXSON, J., absent.

[See next case.]

Emerson & Wall's Appeal.

Opinion of the Court by SHARSWOOD, C. J. :—
Oct. 4, 1880. It may be very convenient whenever there is an adverse claimant to an oil well, that the Court should have power to appoint a receiver to take possession of it, and to work it for the benefit of the successful litigant. It may be that if the tenant in possession is obstinate, and will not give security to dissolve an estrepement, the effect of the execution of the writ may be that the entire territory will be pumped dry by wells sunk on surrounding property, and thus the value of it be destroyed as to both parties. But will that consideration give a Court of Equity jurisdiction of a mere ejectment bill, and the power to take possession of the land in controversy? We think not. The Legislature may, perhaps, be competent to give some remedy, taking care to preserve to the defendant his constitutional right of trial by jury. The mere granting of an issue in the discretion of the Chancellor is not enough. For the courts to assume such a jurisdiction would, we think, be a clear case of judicial legislation.

Decree reversed, and bill dismissed with costs.

[See preceding case.
In Dunlap *v.* Riddell, C. P. of McKean Co. (7 WEEKLY NOTES, 466), the Court appointed a receiver *pendente lite* in a very similar case, except that the oil-producing well in that case was a "flowing well." WILLIAMS, P. J., maintained the jurisdiction in an interesting opinion.]

May T., '79, 95.　　　　　　　　　　　June, 1880.

Brice's Appeal.

Debtor and creditor — Voluntary payments by stranger — When construed as purchase— Bond and mortgage—When written assignment not necessary—Assignee for benefit of creditors—Commission on fund raised by sale of real estate.

The voluntary payment of a secured debt by one who is a stranger is *prima facie* a purchase of the debt and the accompanying security, and is determined by the manifest intention and understanding of the parties at the time.

F., being indebted on a bond secured by mortgage, became in default, and B. voluntarily paid several instalments of interest, and part of the principal, with the verbal understanding that he should be repaid out of the mortgage. F. subsequently made an assignment for the benefit of creditors to B., and under a sci. fa. judgment for the full amount of principal and interest from the date of F.'s first default was recovered upon the mortgage. B., as assignee, paid the balance actually due to the mortgagee, and in his account credited himself with the full amount of the judgment and costs, to which item, G., a judgment creditor, excepted, so far as related to the amounts voluntarily paid by B. before the assignment:

Held, that evidence of the verbal understanding between the parties at the time that B. made his payments was sufficient proof of the purchase of the mortgage by him, to the extent of his payments, and that no formal assignment of the mortgage was necessary.

Held also, that the commission of assignee, upon filing his account of a fund realized by the sale of real estate amounting to $16,535, in the absence of evidence of any especial trouble, was properly fixed at two and a half per cent.

Appeal from the Common Pleas of Northumberland County.

On January 4, 1877, John W. Friling and wife made an assignment for the benefit of creditors to A. N. Brice, the appellant. On November 14, 1877, the assignee presented a petition for an order of sale of the real estate of John W. Friling, divested of liens, and pursuant to the order then obtained, the real estate was sold for $16,535, and on June 17, 1878, the assignee filed his account of the proceeds of the sale. In the account were the following items, amongst others, to which exceptions were filed by W. J. Greenough, a judgment creditor of Friling, by judgment recovered before the assignment:—

"Cash to Mary Smith for mortgage on farm as confirmed by the Court, ... $5109 10
"Percentage due to accountant as assignee, $16,535.00, at four per cent., including time, trouble, etc., ... 661 40"

The account was referred to an auditor, before whom the following testimony was given as to the first item: Mortgage of John W. Friling to Mary Smith, dated January 1, 1874, in Book 13, p. 356, for $4000, and record of judgment, Mary Smith *v.* John W. Friling, in C. P., Northumberland County, August T., 1877, obtained upon scire facias sur this mortgage. George W. Zeigler testified: "I was attorney for Mrs. Mary Smith to collect this judgment from J. W. Friling. . . . When she entered satisfaction she got the whole amount due to her at that time. She did not claim the balance of the judgment. Mr. Brice, at that time, exhibited receipts for money that he had individually paid, which reduced the judgment to $4106.00. I don't know whose money Brice used. Mr. Brice is a son-in-law of J. W. Friling."

A. N. Brice, the assignee, testified: "In the mortgage to Mrs. Smith of $4106, I had paid her that much in satisfaction of the judgment entered on said mortgage. I had made advances to make up the difference between this sum and the credit in my account of $5109.10. When the first payment became due of the interest on $4000, which was $240, Mrs. Smith demanded her interest of Mr. Friling. He could not raise it, and she came to me. I raised her the $240, and paid her. On January 21, 1875, I paid her $100; on January 25, 1875, I paid her $137.75. These two payments, including $2.25 for corn furnished by J. W. Friling, made up the $240. H. Y. Friling owed me for other matters, and the $2.25 was put into that account. Mrs. Smith gave notice that she wanted at least $200 on the principal by the 1st of April, 1875. Mr. Friling did not have it to spare. I gave her on or about the 1st of April, 1875, $100. On the 7th of April, 1875, I gave her my check for $89.08, on account of the principal of the mortgage. There was a lumber bill of Friling, Bowen & Engle of $10.92, which was due by Mrs. Smith to them, which was counted in a settlement I had with Friling, making up the sum of $200 on the principal of the mortgage. The next payment Friling failed to pay; it came due in January, 1876. Mrs. Smith came to me, and said she would push the mortgage if she did not get the interest. I made a calculation of the interest due on the 2d of September, 1876, and it amounted to $269.18 on that day. I drew my check in her favor for that amount on account of interest on the mortgage up to that date. I am mistaken as to the time up to which the interest was calculated. It was calculated up to March 1, 1876, although I paid her after that $150 in checks and money." (Three checks for different amounts dated in April and November, 1877, offered in evidence.) . . . "I was to be repaid out of the mortgage; they [these several advancements] were simply advancements on the mortgage. These payments were out of my own individual funds. I was not reimbursed in any other way by Mr. Friling. I paid these several sums to Mrs. Smith at my office. . . . She did not threaten so much, but talked of issuing if she did not get her money. . . . I did not pay money to Mrs. Smith for him, Mr. Friling, on any other account than the mortgage. I did not take from Mrs. Smith a written transfer of any part of the bond and mortgage of J. W. Friling to her for any of these payments. She did not assign to me any part of the said bond and mortgage as security for these payments. I had no arrangement with J. W. Friling for this security. He knew that I was to be secured in this way. It was a verbal understanding, there was nothing written. . . . Mrs. Smith asked me how I wanted to be secured for the payment of this money. I replied I was to be secured out of the mortgage. She said, very well, then, I don't want to see you lose the money advanced. Mr. Friling said something like that in her presence. He had no security then to give."

The auditor reported as follows as to the item of credit for amount paid on the mortgage: "The auditor is therefore of the opinion and finds from the evidence, that the accountant, A. N. Brice, was not in any position of compulsion to make these advances, but that they were voluntary advances of money upon the credit of and for the purpose of assisting Mr. Friling, and that there was no transfer of any portion of said mortgage such as would entitle him to claim any part of the fund arising from the sale of the farm. . . . This item of the account must then be so corrected as to strike therefrom the amount of money claimed as a credit for advancements made in behalf of Mr. Friling before the date of the deed of assignment; and to give said assignee credit for the amount of money actually paid by him in that behalf as assignee after the assignment was made, . . . leaving the actual credit in this item $4339.92, instead of $5109.10."

As to the second item excepted to, he reported: "The auditor finds no strict rule of law to govern the compensation of trustees or assignees. All depends upon the amount of vexation, time, and trouble bestowed, or incident to the settlement of the estate. The percentage does seem to be large, but as no evidence was produced to show how much time and trouble was bestowed, and as the estate seems to have been a troublesome one the auditor does not feel at liberty to reduce it."

To this report the accountant excepted, *inter alia*, as to the finding upon the first of the two items, and Greenough excepted as to the finding upon the second item. The exceptions filed by the accountant upon the 1st point were dismissed by the Court, and the exception filed by Greenough as to the commission was "sustained as to 1½ per cent. commission on $16,535." In all other respects the report was confirmed.

The accountant took this appeal, assigning for error: (1) the dismissal of his exceptions to the auditor's report as to the first item mentioned. (2) The sustaining the exception of Greenough as to 1½ per cent. of the commission claimed.

S. P. *Wolverton*, for appellant.

The judgment upon the mortgage having been obtained adversely the auditor had no right to make deductions from its amount, this was equivalent to opening the judgment, which cannot be done in a collateral proceeding.

Appeal of Second Nat. Bank of Titusville, 4 Nor. 528.

The Court would not even have granted an issue, there being no allegation of fraud.

There being no obligation on the part of Brice to pay this money there is a presumption that it was a purchase, and that he made the payments on the strength of the security of the mortgage.

Lithcap *v*. Wilt, 4 Phil. 64.
Wilson *v*. Murphy, 1 Id. 106.
McCall *v*. Lenox, 9 S. & R. 304.
Weston's Lessee *v*. Mowlin, 2 Burr. 969.
Johnson *v*. Hart, 3 Johns. Cases, 329.
Rickert *et al. v.* Madeira, 1 R. 328.
1 Hilliard on Mortgages, 243–53.

Joshua W. Comly, contra.

Oct. 4, 1880. THE COURT. We think the first assignment of error is sustained. It appears upon the face of the auditor's report, and by the testimony returned with it, that certain moneys, amounting in the aggregate to $709.18, had been paid by the assignee prior to the assignment directly to Mary Smith, the holder of the mortgage against Friling, the assignor. Other payments were made by the assignee after the assignment, in full discharge of the judgment on the mortgage, and for these credit was allowed to the assignee. But the payments made before the assignment were not allowed. The auditor seems to have been influenced mainly by the consideration that there was no written transfer of any portion of the mortgage by Mrs. Smith to Brice, and that there was a transfer of other assets to Brice by Friling to secure him for the payments made to Mary Smith on her mortgage, and against certain liabilities he had incurred for Friling. He does not state whether anything was realized by Brice from the transfer of the book account, that could or would be applicable to the repayment of the moneys paid on the mortgage. In the absence of any testimony or finding to that effect, it is fair to presume that Brice obtained no indemnity from that source. On the question whether there was any agreement or understanding by which Brice was to be secured for such payments, there was testimony which does not appear to have been contradicted in any manner. A. N. Brice testifies as follows: "I had made advances to make up the difference between this sum ($4,106), and the credit in my account of $5,109.10." Mr. Wolverton asks Mr. Brice how he was to be secured for these several advancements. Answer. "I was to be repaid out of the mortgage. They were simply advancements on the mortgage. These payments were out of my own individual fund. I was not reimbursed in any other way by Mr. Friling. I had no arrangement with J. W. Friling for this security. He knew that I was to be secured in this way. It was a verbal understanding; there was nothing written. Mrs. Smith asked me how I wanted to be secured for the payment of this money. I replied I was to be secured out of the mortgage, She said, 'Very well, then I don't want to see you lose the money advanced.' Mr. Friling said something like that in her presence. He had no security then to give."

This testimony was in no way contradicted or impeached, and is, therefore, to be accepted as true. The conclusion of the auditor was not a finding of fact adverse to the testimony, but a conclusion of law, holding it to be insufficient to create any interest in the mortgage or the debt secured thereby. In that conclusion, as well as in the opinion of the Court to the same effect, we think there was error. There was no pretence of any kind of fraud or collusion on the part of Mr. Brice in making the payments, or in taking credit for them in his account. On the contrary the argument is that he did not take sufficient care of his interests by procuring a written transfer of a part of the mortgage corresponding with his payments. If a writing were necessary, in order to create in him an interest in the mortgage, the decision of the auditor and Court below would be right, but it has been frequently held that a written transfer is not necessary to accomplish that result. In Lithcap *v.* Wilt (4 Phila. Rep. 64) it was held that, "The essential difference between the purchase of a debt and the payment of it, depends upon the intention of the parties at the time; but the payment by a stranger to the obligation of the debt, or by one whose liability was secondary, is *prima facie* a purchase." In Wilson *v.* Murphy (1 Phila. 106) the Court says, "There is no doubt that a mortgage may be kept alive, even after payment in full, if such was the intention of the parties, and even though there be no actual assignment to a trustee. Equity will consider that as done which was agreed to be done, and not suffer the trust to fail for want of a trustee." In McCall *v.* Lenox (9 S. & R. 304), TILGHMAN, C. J., says, "An assignment of the debt carries with it the benefit of the mortgage, although the mortgage be not specifically assigned. From the moment the debt is assigned the mortgagee becomes the trustee of the assignee." In the same case, GIBSON, J., said, "Chancery will order a security to be assigned in favor of a surety who has paid it." And DUNCAN, J., said, "Whatever will give the money, will carry the estate in the land along with it. The estate in the land is the same thing as the money due upon it. The assignment of the debt or forgiving it, will draw the land after it, as a consequence. It would do it though the debt were only given by parol. (Weston's Lessee *v.* Mowlin, 2 Burr. 969.") And again, "The debt being paid, or in any other manner extinguished, the mortgagee becomes a trustee for the mortgagor." In Johnson *v.* Hart (3 Johns. Cas. 329), KENT, J., said, "When the note, to secure which the mortgage was given, was negotiated, the interest in the mortgage which was given for no other purpose than to secure that note, passed of course. It required no writing, no assignment on the back of the mortgage." "Whoever was owner of the debt was likewise owner of the security." In Rickert *v.* Madeira (1 Rawle, 328), ROGERS, J., says, "Whatever will give the money secured by the mortgage, will carry the mortgaged premises along with it. The forgiving the debt, although by parol, will draw the land after it, as a consequence."

It has been many times decided that a mortgage may be transferred by parol, and that, when given to secure notes payable to bearer, the holder is the equitable owner of the mortgage. Whoever pays the debt for the mortgagor is the equitable owner of the mortgage. (See Hilliard on Mortgages, vol. 1, 243-253.)

We think the authorities cited show, that when one who is a stranger to the obligation, pays the debt in whole or in part, in the absence of evidence to the contrary, he becomes by implication a purchaser of the debt to the extent of his payment. In the present case, Brice was an entire stranger to the debt due by Friling to Mrs. Smith. He was under no kind of obligation to pay it. There is no affirmative testimony that when he made the payments he thereby intended to extinguish the indebtedness to that extent. This lack of testimony would alone qualify him to be regarded as a purchaser. But the case is stronger than that. The testimony already quoted, contradicted by no one, shows that he, at least, intended to be secured by the mortgage given to secure the debt, upon which the payments were made. When he testified, "I was to be repaid out of the mortgage. They were simply advancements on the mortgage;" and "Mrs. Smith asked me how I wanted to be secured for the payment of this money. I replied I was to be secured out of the mortgage. She said, 'Very well, then I don't want to see you lose the money advanced,'" a clear case of concurrent assent is made out between Brice and the mortgagee to treat the payments as the acquisition of an interest, and not as absolute extinguishment. Certainly if he had paid the entire debt he would have become the equitable owner of the mortgage, and could have compelled its transfer to himself. We see no reason why a partial interest could not be acquired by a partial payment in the same manner as an entire interest by an entire payment. In equitable contemplation it is the fact of payment which creates the interest, and this controlling fact has the same effect in principle, whether the payment be partial or entire. When Mrs. Smith brought suit on her mortgage she claimed, and took judgment for, the whole amount of the mortgage and interest without any deduction for the payments made by Brice. This was in apparent conformity with the understanding testified to by Brice, and adds strength to the other affirmative testimony on that subject. She was then the legal owner of the mortgage and judgment, to the extent of the amount remaining due to her, and the trustee for Brice as to the amount paid by him. This being so, Brice was entitled to credit for the whole amount of the judgment and interest paid by him, and the auditor and Court below were in error in rejecting the credit for $709.18, paid prior to the assignment.

As to the second error assigned, we do not, in view of all the circumstances of the case, see any sufficient reason for interfering with the action of the Court below in regard to the compensation of the accountant, and this error is not sustained.

Decree reversed and record remitted with direction to the Court below to allow the accountant credit for the full sum of five thousand one hundred and nine, ten one-hundreth dollars ($5109.10), paid to Mary Smith at the same time and in the same manner as appears in the original account of the assignee; the cost of this appeal to be paid by the appellees.

Opinion by GREEN, J.

Common Pleas—Equity.

C. P. No. 1. Nov. 6, 1880.
Powell v. Abbott et al.

Equity—Injunction—Unincorporated company—Philadelphia Mining and Stock Exchange—Rights of members—A court of equity has jurisdiction to restrain the unlawful suspension of a member of an unincorporated company—A by-law, if inconsistent with the constitution, is invalid.

Motion to continue a special injunction.

This was a bill in equity to restrain the defendants, members of The Philadelphia Mining and Stock Exchange, an unincorporated association, from carrying into effect the suspension of the plaintiff from membership in the association, and from disposing of certain stock belonging to him and deposited as security.

The bill, after reciting that the association was formed for the purpose of buying and selling mining stocks, and is governed by a constitution and by-laws, annexed to the bill, set forth: That the plaintiff had made a time contract with Abbott, one of the defendants, for the sale of certain mining stock, and deposited with another member of the Exchange certain shares of other stock as security; that the stock having advanced in price, Abbott demanded a further security, which plaintiff declined to make, on the ground that the sales at advanced prices were fictitious.

That the question was then referred to the Arbitration Committee of the Exchange, in accordance with the following section of its Constitution:—

"Section XI. On the first Monday of January of each year there shall be elected a Standing Arbitrating Committee, to consist of five members, whose duty it shall be to investigate and decide all claims and matters of difference arising between members of the Exchange, and also to adjudicate such claims as may be preferred against members by non-members, when non-members agree, in writing, to abide by its decision. The decision of this Committee shall be final, except in cases involving a difference of one hundred dollars or over, when either party may appeal, within three days, to the Exchange for final adjudication; *Provided, further,* that upon the application of three members of the Committee, any decision shall be referred to the Exchange for final action."

That said committee decided that the plaintiff must make the additional deposit called for by Abbott, from which decision plaintiff forthwith notified the acting Chairman of the Exchange that he appealed. That before any further action could be taken on said appeal, at the request of said Abbott, the acting Chairman of said Exchange appointed a committee of three members, who called upon plaintiff, and inquired of him why he had not complied with the report of the Arbitration Committee. Plaintiff replied to them that he had appealed from its decision. The said Committee thereupon reported back to the acting Chairman of the Exchange, that the following section of the By-Laws be enforced:—

"Section XI. Any member who fails to comply with his contracts, or who becomes insolvent, shall immediately inform the Chairman of the Exchange of the fact, whose duty it shall be to give notice forthwith, from the chair, of the failure of such member; and in case of the refusal or neglect of such delinquent to make such report to the Chairman, it shall be the duty of any member having a knowledge of the fact to report the same forthwith to the Governing Committee or the Chairman, who shall thereupon appoint a committee of three members to inquire into the facts and report thereon without delay; and if said Committee report the charge to be true, and the Exchange confirm the report, said member shall be suspended; and it shall, furthermore, be the duty of the Governing Committee, upon receiving information thereof, or having, directly or indirectly, any knowledge of such failure on the part of any member to comply with his engagements, as above stated, to report the same, without delay, to the Chairman, and ask for the appointment of a committee as before provided. And in case of the insolvency of any member, he shall, within three days, make good to the full amount thereof all friendly loans of cash or stock from members, or any overdraft on any bank; but seven days shall be allowed him in which to settle stock contracts."

And thereupon a meeting of the members who were present at the Exchange in the afternoon of the same day was called, without any preliminary notice, to take action on the report of the Committee. Plaintiff protested at the time that he had appealed from the decision of the Arbitration Committee, and asked that his appeal should be heard before any further action be taken in the matter. His objection and request were overruled, and his right of appeal denied him; and a motion was made to suspend him, and the motion was thereupon put and carried.

The bill prayed for an injunction, etc.

A. M. Burton, for the motion, read affidavits in support thereof.

C. C. Lister, contra.

The bill having admitted the suspension to be a perfected act, a mandamus is the proper remedy.
Society *v.* Vandyke, 2 Whar. 312.
Angell on Corp., p. 432.
Commonwealth *v.* Penn. Benf. Institution, 2 S. & R. 141.
Delacy *v.* Neuse Navigation Co., 1 Hawks, 274.
Evans *v.* Phil. Club, 14 Wr. 107.
Society *v.* Commonwealth, 2 Sm. 125.
Hassler *v.* Society, 37 Leg. Int. 434.

Section XI. of the Constitution relates to the arbitration of differences between members only; but Section XI. of the By-Laws refers to differences between a member and the Exchange. The proceedings to suspend plaintiff were under the latter, and were regular; at any rate the merits of the suspension cannot be inquired into.

Commonwealth v. Pike Ben. Society, 8 W. & S. 247.
Toram v. Howard Ben. Ass'n, 4 Barr, 519.
Franklin v. Commonwealth, 10 Id. 357.
Society v. Vandyke, 2 Whar. 312.
Leech v. Harris, 2 Brews. 576.

A. M. Burton, in reply.

A writ of mandamus pertains properly to the enforcement of public or official duties.

Rex v. Bank of England, 2 B. & A. 620.
Rex v. London Assurance Co., 5 B. & A. 899.
3 Blackstone's Comm. (Sharswood's Ed.) 110.

The remedy invoked here is the only one that will adequately protect the plaintiff's rights, and it has often been sustained.

Kerr v. Trego, 11 Wr. 293.
Fisher v. Keane, L. R., 11 Ch. Div. 353.
Labouchere v. Earl of Wharncliffe, L. R., 13 Ch. Div. 347.
Kerr on Injunctions, star pages 545-6-7.
Hassler v. Phil. Musical Association, 37 Leg. Int. 434.
Leech v. Harris, 2 Brews. 571.
In re St. Clement's Church, 28 Leg. Int. 172.

C. A. V.

Nov. 13, 1880. THE COURT (after stating the facts). The complaint made by the plaintiff is that his right of appeal, under Article XI. of the Constitution, was disregarded, and that he was not amenable to suspension under Section XI. of the By-Laws.

The defendants are an unincorporated association, and, as such, by virtue of the Act of 16th of June, 1836, are subject to the equitable jurisdiction of the Courts of Common Pleas. It has been well settled by numerous adjudications that the Courts entertain a jurisdiction to preserve these associations, and the tribunals created by them under their constitutions, in the line of order, and to correct abuses, but they do not inquire into the merits of what has passed *in rem adjudicatam* in a regular course of proceedings. (See Leach v. Harris, 2 Brewster's Reports, 576, and the cases there cited.)

The affidavits read by the defendants in this case do not substantially vary the affidavit and bill filed by the plaintiff, and the complaint made by him is sustained. He was denied his right of appeal, and in this respect the Association acted in violation of its Constitution.

Was he amenable to suspension under Article XI. of the By-Laws? No other offence was alleged against him than his refusal to make an additional deposit on the stock contract with Abbott, which had been referred to the Arbitrating Committee, from whose decision he had appealed.

Article X. of the By-Laws provides that:—

"At any time a contract is pending a mutual deposit may be called by either party to secure the same. No additional deposit can be required except from the party against whom the contract rules. The deposit of the stock on the part of the seller shall, in all cases, be considered sufficient security. In case of dispute as to the amount or place of deposit, the matter shall be referred to the Standing Arbitration Committee, whose decision shall be final."

This section of the By-Laws appears to be in conflict with Section XI. of the Constitution, which provides for an appeal in matters involving a difference of one hundred dollars or over.

In case of a conflict between the Constitution and the By-Laws, the Constitution must prevail. And even if this were not so, no member should be subject to lose his rights upon a conflicting and doubtful construction of the regulations of the Association.

It may also be a question for final determination in this case whether the words "any member who fails to comply with his contracts," in Section XI. of the By-Laws, do not refer to a failure of compliance with the principal contract, and not merely to the incidents of it, such as additional deposits, etc. The object of the article was to provide for the case of members who should fail to comply with their contracts or become insolvent. The coupling of these two contingencies seems to imply a failure of the principal contract, and not of the incidents of it.

But whether this be so or not, the right of the plaintiff to the protection of a court 'of chancery rests upon the denial to him of his right of appeal from the decision of the Arbitration Committee, and the consequent threatened sacrifice of his rights as a member of the Association, and the selling and disposing of the stock deposited as security for his contracts before his rights have been adjudicated in the manner prescribed by the Constitution of the association.

It has been alleged by the learned counsel for the defendants that the plaintiff has a legal remedy by mandamus for restoration of his rights as a member, if he has been improperly suspended, and that consequently he cannot invoke the equitable powers of this Court.

A writ of mandamus would not secure to the plaintiff the protection which he seeks. The object of that writ would be to restore him to his rights as a member if he had been improperly suspended. In the meanwhile there might be the threatened sacrifice of his property, as complained of by him. And as this Court has equitable jurisdiction for the supervision and control of these associations, and to prevent threatened mischief, upon the well-settled principle that where a court of equity has jurisdiction for any purpose, it will draw to itself jurisdiction of all questions incident to the subject matter of inquiry, to make a final determination of the rights of the parties, and to prevent multiplicity of actions, I think the jurisdiction can be maintained.

The special injunction is continued.

Opinion by PEIRCE, J.

Common Pleas—Law.

C. P. No. 1.   Nov. 1, 1880.

Commonwealth ex rel. The Herdic Personal Transportation Co., of Philadelphia, v. William Baldwin, Chief Commissioner of Highways.

Licenses to run omnibus lines in Philadelphia—Acts and ordinances relating thereto—Power of Councils to ordain regulations on the subject—Discretion vested by ordinance of Councils in Commissioner of Highways to grant or refuse licenses for particular routes—When authority to license, coupled with a duty, becomes imperative—Where the Commissioner of Highways, in the exercise of his discretion, refused to grant an omnibus license for reasons which the Court deemed unsubstantial, held, that he should be compelled by mandamus to grant the license.

The petition of the relators for a mandamus requiring the respondent to issue to them a license to run omnibuses on certain streets in the city of Philadelphia, set forth :—

(1) That they are a corporation duly chartered July 20, 1880, under the Act of April 29, 1874, and its supplements, to conduct, in Philadelphia, the business of operating stage and omnibus lines.

(2) The Act of April 15, 1850, enacts: That the Select and Common Councils of the city of Philadelphia shall have authority, by ordinance, to provide for the proper regulation of omnibuses, etc., and to this end it shall be lawful for them to pass ordinances to provide for the issuing of licenses to such persons as may apply to keep and use omnibuses, etc., and to charge a reasonable annual or other sum therefor. . . . In pursuance of the authority thus vested in them, Councils enacted the ordinance of May 10, 1855, which provides, *inter alia*, that upon application being made, the Chief Commissioner of Highways is authorized from time to time to grant licenses to the owner or owners, to keep and use omnibuses, . . . *provided*, that the said Commissioner shall, under the supervision of the Committee on Highways, change such routes and stands when necessary for the public convenience. . . . By city ordinance of December 24, 1870, it is further enacted, that the owners of all omnibuses running on any street not having a passenger railway upon it shall pay an annual license fee for each omnibus, and comply with all the provisions of an ordinance approved May 12, 1855, *provided*, that before any license shall be issued by the license clerk of the highway department the party or parties applying for the same shall give a written pledge that they do not contemplate and will not assist any corporation or individual in placing a railroad of any kind on any part of Broad Street.

(3) The relators have built a large number of omnibuses for the purpose of carrying passengers on Broad Street and Market Street in Philadelphia. In September, 1880, they made application in due form to the respondent for a license to keep and use said omnibuses; in their said application fully meeting all the requirements of the above mentioned ordinances.

(4) The said Baldwin refused to grant them such licenses for the following reasons, contained in a letter dated October 2, 1880 :—

"Since the ordinance of 1855 was passed, an entire change has taken place, in the introduction of passenger railways, so that it may well be doubted if I have any power on the subject except under the ordinance of Dec. 24, 1870, which applies to streets not having a passenger railway upon them. On Broad Street, covering a portion of your route, no railroad can be laid, as it is prohibited by an Act passed in 1873; passed to protect the franchises of the Thirteenth and Fifteenth Streets Railway, from whom the city derives a license fee of $50 a car and a tax on its dividends declared, which they assert will be affected by granting a license to you. On Market Street there is a railway company, which was obliged by its charter, before it laid its rails, to purchase the omnibuses run on that street, and who are also obliged to pay a car license and a tax on dividends; this corporation claims that the Legislature could not have intended that it should be obliged to purchase one set of omnibuses and I be at liberty to license another set. As your right to receive a license can be determined by an application to the Courts or to the Councils, I propose not to act."

(5) The relators averred that the respondent's refusal was solely the result of opposition to the granting of said license by certain passenger railway companies, who indemnified the said respondent by bond against all damage which might result to him therefrom. Being without adequate remedy at law, the relators pray for a writ of mandamus, etc.

The respondent in his return averred that, under the Acts and ordinances cited in the petition, there is no obligation on him as Commissioner of Highways to issue the license demanded by petitioners; that Councils alone have power in the premises, and they are not made parties to this proceeding; that under the ordinance of May 10, 1855, a certain discretion was vested in him, as agent for the city, subject to the supervision of the Committee on Highways, to determine whether licenses shall be issued to run omnibuses, and that in refusing to license the petitioners he exercised his best discretion. Further, that by an Act of March 27, 1873, providing for the surrender by the Thirteenth and

Fifteenth Streets Passenger Railway Co. of certain rights, and granting and confirming unto them certain other rights as to laying tracks upon a portion of Broad Street, and excluding all other persons from so doing, the Commonwealth expressly contracted with said company, "That no franchise or privilege . . . to run any cars upon any part of said routes (including Broad Street) shall be hereafter granted to any person or persons or body politic," whereby the relators cannot lawfully have any such privilege as is set up. That by Act of May 14, 1857, the West Philadelphia Passenger Railway Co. were required to purchase, and did purchase for a large sum, the omnibuses, horses, etc., theretofore running on Market Street; and the Legislature thereby impliedly intended that no other omnibus line should be authorized to run on said street. That by its charter the West Philadelphia Passenger Railway Co. is required to pay into the treasury of Philadelphia a tax on all dividends over six per cent., which has amounted to a large sum annually, and that the licensing of the relators would probably result in a reduction of the dividends of the said company, whereby the city of Philadelphia would lose large sums of money. That the said passenger railway companies are by law required to keep the pavement or cartway of the streets occupied by them in good order from curb to curb, at their own expense, and it would be inequitable to license the relators to run competing coaches, creating great additional wear and tear on the companies' tracks and on the cartway without equivalent obligation. That no ordinance has been passed regulating the licensing of omnibuses on streets occupied by the tracks of passenger railways. Finally, the respondent denied that his refusal to license the relators was the result of opposition by said passenger railway companies.

Wm. D. Kelley, Jr., and *John G. Johnson*, for relators.

The right to use the highways of the city with vehicles for hire exists, apart from all legislation, and can only be interfered with so far as legislation expressly restricts the same, and then only within certain limits.

Commonwealth *v.* Stodder, 2 Cush. 562.
Frankford R. R. *v.* Phila., 8 Sm. 123.

Unless there be found in the Act of 1850, or in ordinances properly enacted thereunder, some restriction upon this right, nothing can prevent the running, by the petitioners, of vehicles for hire on the streets of this city. The Act of 1850 recognizes the inherent right, by directing that licenses shall be issued to "such, and so many, persons as may apply to keep and use them." It is incumbent on the Chief Commissioner of Highways, when the preliminaries of the ordinance of May 10, 1855, have been complied with, to grant licenses to the owners of all omnibuses. Whilst the words are that he is "hereby authorized," they are used in connection with a ministerial duty imposed upon him. And mandamus is the proper remedy to compel action in a case like the present.

Dillon on Municipal Corp., p. 111, sec. 62, and p. 526, sec. 669.

The ordinance of 1855 is in force, and is so recognized by that of 1870. The two together prescribe a system of licensing, at different rates, of omnibuses running on streets occupied and unoccupied by passenger railway tracks. If the ordinance of 1855 be not in force, then there is no restriction on the petitioners, and they have a right to run without any license at all. If it be contended that the ordinance of 1855 reposes in the Chief Commissioner of Highways a discretion to refuse the running of omnibuses altogether, then it is not warranted by the Act of 1850, which does not permit such exclusion, and cannot be enforced.

The refusal of a license by the Highway Commissioner is based, not upon a fear of the possible overcrowding of the streets, but upon reasons founded upon his understanding of the legal rights of certain railway companies. If he is wrong in his interpretation of the law, we have the case, even if he is clothed with a discretion, of a *refusal to exercise it*, because, under his erroneous construction of the law, he does not feel at liberty to act. It is well settled, that if discretion be not exercised at all, or improperly, the Court may compel the officer or trustee to do the act which is imposed upon him.

Brown *v.* Higgs, 8 Vesey, 574.
Erisman *v.* Directors of the Poor, 11 Wr. 509.
McFarland's App., 1 Wr. 305.
Pulpress *v.* African Church, 12 Wr. 210.
Hill on Trustees, 494-502.

As to the reasons assigned for the refusal. The old Market Street omnibus company was not *compelled* to sell out its plant. The *option* was given to continue running. There is no implication of a legislative intent to prevent other persons, who received no consideration, from running other lines of omnibuses.

The title to the Act of 1873, relating to the Thirteenth and Fifteenth Streets Company, excludes "all other persons or bodies corporate from hereafter *laying tracks* upon any of said streets." If it be claimed that the body of the Act prevents the running of omnibuses on Broad Street, its object is entirely different from the statement in the title. But the text of the Act shows clearly that the preventing the laying of tracks and running of cars on Broad Street alone is meant to be accomplished. The word "cars," in its popular acceptation means, as defined by Webster, "carriages for running on rails on a railroad," and it is apparent it was so used by the Legislature, from the context, to wit, "tracks," "tramways," etc.

The Commissioner of Highways is not the guardian of the city's revenue, and cannot refuse to fulfil a duty because that might suffer. Moreover, the city has no right to raise revenue by means of a tax on passenger railway companies, or to charge anything more than a reasonable licensing fee to cover the cost of police regulation.

Frankford R. R. Co. *v*. Phila., 8 Sm. 123.
Johnson *v*. Phila., 60 Penna. 445.

No privilege is conferred on the railway companies by their charters, in exclusion of the inherent right of all members of the community, to run vehicles for hire upon the same streets. It is settled law that "a corporation takes nothing by its charter but what is plainly, expressly, and unequivocally granted." The Passenger Railway Companies have no right to be considered in the question of permitting omnibuses upon the public streets. If they have, all carriers of passengers are prevented hereafter from transporting persons for hire, inasmuch as all the streets on which omnibuses or carriages can be run are occupied by one or other of these companies. The streets of the city, from curb to curb, will then belong entirely to the railway companies.

Christian Kneass, George Biddle, Joseph R. Rhoads, and *Geo. W. Biddle,* for defendant.

The routes upon which omnibus lines may run are subject to regulation by the municipal authorities of the city

Phila. *v*. Western Union Tel. Co., 2 WEEKLY NOTES, 461, opinion by THAYER, J.
Southwark R. R. Co. *v*. City, 11 Wr. 321.
Com'th *v*. Central Pass. R. W. Co., 2 Sm. 517.
Com'th *v*. Stodder, 2 Cush. 571.

The Act of 1850 expressly invests the city with a discretion in regulating such routes. The ordinance of May 10, 1855, expressly vests in the Chief Commissioner of Highways, subject to the control of the Committee on Highways, a discretion to determine upon what routes omnibus lines shall run. He "is authorized to grant licenses." The words "authorized," or the words "it shall be lawful," in a *city ordinance,* which is in the nature of a by-law of a municipal corporation, and not like an Act of the Legislature, do not impose an obligation, but give a permissive authority merely, to be used at the discretion of the person upon whom it is conferred.

Commonwealth *ex rel.* Vandyke *v*. Henry, 13 Wr. 530.
The King *v*. The Borough of Eye, 2 Dowling & Ryland, 172.
Julius *v*. Lord Bishop of Oxford, L. R. 5, App. Cases 214.
Commissioners of Turnpike Road *v*. Com'rs of Sandusky Co. (1853), 1 Ohio State, 149.
Bleight *v*. Bank, 10 Barr, 131.

Where a person is vested with a discretion as to the doing or not of a particular act, a mandamus will not lie to compel him to do it.

Tapping on Mandamus, 9–15.
Commonwealth *ex rel.* Park Commissioners *v*. The Mayor, 2 WEEKLY NOTES, 124.
Toole's App., 7 Id. 206.
Decatur *v*. Paulding, 14 Peters, 514.
State *v*. The Freeholders, 3 Zabris. 214.

The petition is defective in not making the city a party defendant. The ordinance of May 10, 1855, being a mere by-law of the city, confers no rights or privileges on third parties or strangers to the corporation.

Field on Corp., sec. 307, p. 343.
Flint *v*. Pierce, 99 Mass. 68.
Trustees *v*. Flint, 13 Met. 543.

The Act of 1850, makes no mention of the Commissioner of Highways, who is but a mere agent of the city. Unless, therefore, the relators have an ample right at common law, or by virtue of the Act of 1850 itself, they cannot, as third parties invoke the aid of the ordinance of May 10th. The city itself may compel the Commissioner to obey the provisions of the ordinance, but no one but the principal can interfere with the action of the agent. Under this view the case comes down simply to the question of whether or not any individual has a right to run and operate a line of omnibuses through any streets of the city he may choose, irrespective of municipal control, as to the routes to be travelled by him. The Herdic Transportation Company have no greater rights than any individual. They are incorporated under the Act of 1876, a supplement to the General Corporation Act of 1874, whereby they are merely empowered to do business under a corporate name and without personal liability.

By reason of the contract made by the Legislature with the Thirteenth and Fifteenth Streets Railway Company, by the Act of 1873, the relators can obtain no right to run on Broad Street. The Act was the result of a surrender of a right which the company held under a previous charter (granted in 1861 to the Navy Yard, Broad Street, and Fairmount Pass. R. W. Co.) to lay a railroad on Broad Street along its entire length, in consideration of which surrender the Act provided that no right should thereafter be granted to any one to run cars thereon. The word "car" includes any vehicle for the transportation of people, and as used in the Act, could only refer to vehicles in the nature of omnibuses, because the Act forbids distinctly, in the first place, the running of vehicles on tracks, and then goes on to forbid the running of any cars. Any other construction makes the clause insensible and tautological.

The railway companies of Philadelphia were required by their charters to purchase all existing lines of omnibuses then running on the routes to be traversed by them. The Thirteenth and Fifteenth Streets Company paid a large sum for the line running on Broad Street. The West Phila. Co. paid over $18,000 for that on Market St. If the Legislature, in granting charters to the railway companies, so exercised its discretion that no injustice should be done to those theretofore engaged in the same business, certainly the Chief Commissioner of Highways has properly exercised a similar discretion in declining to license competing lines, who offer no compensation.

The Market Street Railway Co. is required to pay a tax on its dividends, and both the companies are required to keep the streets traversed by them repaired from curb to curb. For this purpose the Market Street road paid from Jan. 1875, to June, 1880, $79,411.16. The proposed company is under no obligation to contribute its quota towards this expense, and it would be inequitable to increase the burden of the railway company, for the benefit of the competing omnibus company.

It is submitted, that the discretion of the Commissioner cannot be interfered with, unless it is positively proven to have been maliciously or illegally exercised.

November 16, 1880. THE COURT. The relators claim that they are a corporation duly chartered under the Act of Assembly of 29th of April, 1874, entitled an Act to provide for the incorporation and regulation of certain corporations, and the supplements thereto. The purpose of the corporation is to conduct the business of operating stage and omnibus lines in the said city. The questions in this cause arise upon the return of the Chief Commissioner of Highways to an alternative writ of mandamus, which was granted on the petition of the relators, which sets up, that in the month of September last, they made application to the Commissioner for a license to keep and use omnibuses, to be run on Broad Street and Market Street, in said city, which application embodied all requisite information, and tendered their willingness to pay the sum required by the ordinances of the city for each omnibus to be used by them; and that they further tendered a written pledge, such as is required by the ordinance of December 24, 1870, that they did not contemplate and would not assist any corporation or individual in placing a railroad on Broad Street. The petition contains an averment that the Chief Commissioner rejected said application, refusing to grant to the relators licenses for the use of such omnibuses, for reasons which are set forth in a letter written by him, and addressed to the Herdic Transportation Company, bearing date the 2d of October, 1880. These reasons, briefly stated, are, first, a doubt, which the Commissioner expresses, whether he has any power "on the subject," except under the ordinance of December 24, 1870, which applies to streets not having passenger railways upon them. This doubt is based on an entire change, which, he says, has taken place, in the introduction of passenger railways since the ordinance of 1855 was passed. Second. The right of the Thirteenth and Fifteenth Streets Railway Company to prevent the laying down on Broad Street of a railroad, under the provisions of the Act of March 27, 1873. This Act, for the reasons therein mentioned, declares that no privilege should thereafter be granted to any one to construct a track or tracks on Broad Street, or any artificial tramway for the conveyance of passengers for hire on said street, or to run any cars upon any part of the defined routes, which include Broad Street. Third. The rights of the Market Street Railway Company, and also of the Thirteenth and Fifteenth Streets, derived from their purchase of the stock of the omnibus lines which were running when the railway companies were chartered. Fourth. The duty which the Commissioner owes to the city to prevent a diminution of its revenues, which accrue from taxes on dividends of passenger railway companies, which diminution is apprehended may result from licensing a line of omnibuses to run on Market Street, whereby the receipts of the railway company may be lessened.

The refusal of the Commissioner to grant licenses to the relators rests upon a claim of right, under the laws of the Commonwealth and the ordinances of the city, to exercise a discretion in the matter of granting or refusing licenses to run omnibuses for hire over the streets of the city, and, it may not be charged that this discretion has been an arbitrary and unreasonable exercise of the power to grant or refuse licenses, the letter of October 2, 1880, was written; to this letter therefore, we are to look for the justification upon which he rests the cause, in so far as he is an actor in it.

The petition for the mandamus recites the Act of April 15, 1850, which gives to Councils authority to provide, by ordinance, for the proper regulation of omnibuses or vehicles in the nature thereof. It contains the further provision that, to this end, and in this manner, they may provide for the issuing of licenses to such and so many persons as may apply, to keep and use the same; to charge a reasonable sum therefor, and to provide for punishment, by fine of owners or drivers, for any violation of ordinances to be enacted by virtue of the said Act of Assembly. On the 15th of May, 1855, an ordinance was passed which provided for application for licenses by owners of omnibuses employed within the city in the transportation of persons for hire or pay. Such owners are required to state their names, places of abode, the number of their coaches, and the routes they propose to occupy. When such applications are made in due form, the Commissioner of Highways is authorized, from time to time, to grant licenses to keep and use omnibuses, which contain, among other things, a designation of the routes to be followed and the stands to be occupied; to this is added the important provision for changing the routes and stands. There are a number of other provisions, all looking to the regulation and control of omnibuses to be licensed by the Commissioner, which are not necessary to be further referred to in this connection, except as indicating the supervision which Councils claimed the right to exercise over the general subject of granting such licenses, and the control which the city sought to retain over the details of the system, after licenses had been granted.

This legislation, State and municipal, in the opinion of both the relators and the respondent, gives rise to some of the most important considerations which are essential to a proper solution of the questions we are called upon to decide. We are to inquire what power is conferred upon Councils by the Act of April 15, 1850, and whether they have transcended the authority which this Act professes to confer. The relators start with the proposition that the right to use the highways of the city with vehicles for hire exists apart from all legislation, and can only be interfered with so far as legislation expressly restricts the right, and then only within certain limits. The correctness of this proposition may be conceded without advancing, in any degree, the case of the relators.

Highways are intended for the accommodation of the public, and when no restriction is placed by competent authority on this general right, their use is absolutely free to all, but this right, like all other rights in which every one may claim to participate, is subject to the restriction that such use shall be reasonable and not inconsistent with the enjoyment of similar privileges by others who are entitled to participate in such use. We are not, however, prepared to admit the soundness of the more advanced position taken by the relators, that unless there be found in the Act of 1850, or in ordinances properly enacted thereunder, some restriction upon this right, nothing can prevent the running of vehicles for hire on the streets of the city. If it were necessary to establish the proposition, we think it could be successfully maintained, that Councils possess the general power to ordain such ordinances as are necessary to the proper regulation and control of omnibus lines, independently of the Act of 1850. In the case of the Frankford, etc., Passenger Railway Company v. The City of Philadelphia (8 P. F. S. 119), this view is more strongly foreshadowed, but the point was not decided, because it was not deemed necessary to rest the judgment of the Court on that ground; the question turning in that case, as it does in this one, upon the true intent and meaning of the Act of April 15, 1850, by which authority, in express terms, is given to Councils to provide by ordinance for the proper regulation of omnibuses.

The relators in this case contend that the Act does not authorize Councils by ordinance to give to the Commissioner of Highways a discretionary power to grant or to refuse licenses, and that in so far as it is sought by ordinance to impose a restriction on the right to run upon the streets of the city it is null and void. This interpretation of the Act seems to rest upon the denial of the right of the Legislature of the Commonwealth even to refuse this privilege to those who may desire to enjoy it, and is founded as well upon the clause of the Act of 1850, which says: "And to this end it shall be lawful, etc., to provide for the issuing of licenses to such and so many persons as may apply to keep and use omnibuses." As to the first proposition, we do not deem it necessary to do more than assert our dissent to the denial which is here set up, of the sovereign power of the Legislature over its own streets and highways, which is so complete that at a word it may abolish every existing street in the city of Philadelphia, and provide for the establishment of others to take their place. The right of regulation as to use is equally clear; so absolute have the Supreme Court held it to be, that Judge BLACK, speaking for the Court, illustrates this doctrine by saying the Legislature may authorize the construction of a canal on Chestnut Street.

The criticism which the relators make of the power of Councils to pass the ordinance of 1855, turns on the employment of the words in the Act of 1850, which read, "issuing of licenses to *such and so many persons,*" etc. If these words stood by themselves, and were not to be interpreted in connection with other portions of the Act, they might be held to justify the conclusions which have been suggested by the relators. But to do this would violate fundamental canons of construction of statutes; it would disregard the purpose as well as the spirit and intent of the Act; it would cut the Act into fragments, construe each fragment by itself, instead of regarding the law as a connected whole, reading it without punctuation even, and endeavoring to ascertain what light each part may shed on every other part of the Act. To disregard these rules is often to make that obscure which, properly viewed, may be so clear as to be free from doubt. In no instance can they be safely laid aside.

What, then, is the purpose and spirit of the Act in question? It is to give to Councils the power to provide for the *proper regulation* of omnibuses. To properly regulate is to adjust by rule or method; to put or keep in order, subject to a prescribed course; it implies a power to direct, to rule, and to govern. Councils are made the judges as to what constitutes a proper putting in order subject to a prescribed course, or what shall be proper government and direction, to which the running of omnibuses shall become subject. Proper regulation implies all of this; and yet this thought is entirely at variance with an absolute right in every owner of a line of omnibuses, to require to be issued to him licenses for as many coaches as he may desire to run, and upon just such of the streets as he shall select, irrespective of the width of the street, or the kind of use to which it is lawfully subject. If this view of the law be the proper one, what becomes of the duty of the city having entrusted to it the care of the highways within its bounds, and charged to keep the same free from obstruction, so that they shall be open for general travel at all times? What is to be said of the liability of the city to pay damages which shall result from all unlawful or permissive obstruction, and of the obligation which rests upon it as supervisor of the highways, to keep or to see that the streets are in proper condition and repair?

Keeping in view, therefore, the fact that power is given to Councils to provide for proper regulation of omnibuses, and what such regulation implies, we do not regard the clause, "such and so many persons," as intended to mean all persons, or that every one may select his own route, or that all applicants may obtain licenses to run over the same streets. Should this be done, there would be an end to all proper regulation, placing the streets of the city, as to their use, virtually under the control of owners of omnibuses. The most that can be claimed for this portion of the Act is, that it shall be lawful, or that power is given to pass ordinances which would enable any one to demand license, according to his own caprice or pleasure, not that Councils, if they legislate at all upon this subject, are bound to pass such ordinances, and no others. Our interpretation of the Act is, however, that ordinances may be enacted to license such person or persons who, in the judgment of the city or the authorized representative of the city, ought to obtain license, in subordination to the rule of proper regulation, both in respect to the number of omnibuses and the routes or streets on which they should run. It is clear that such was the construction placed on the Act by Councils when the ordinance of 1855 was passed.

The Commissioner of Highways is not directed or required to issue licenses; the language of the ordinance is, he is hereby authorized to grant, and this vests in the Commissioner a discretion to determine on what routes the owners of omnibus lines shall run their coaches. And because we do not regard the ordinance of 1855 as covering a broader ground than that contemplated by the Act of 1850, we agree with the respondent, that a proper exercise of the discretion vested in the Commissioner would justify him in refusing licenses to run on certain streets of the city. Take Sansom Street for illustration. On this narrow street is already laid the track of a passenger railway; it may be doubted whether a line of omnibuses could with propriety be licensed to use this street. It might, we think, be safely characterized as an act of folly to authorize two, three, or four lines to run upon it; and in view of the still greater amount of travel on Chestnut, the same doubt might fairly be entertained as to that street. This, it is objected, amounts to an actual exclusion. The reply is, that exclusion may be the exercise of a most wise discretion.

Holding, as we do, that the granting of licenses by the Commissioner of Highways is not a merely ministerial, but a discretionary act, that to authorize him to grant is to authorize him to refuse to grant, we are to inquire further what kind of a discretion is placed in his hands. It has not been contended by the respondent that it is arbitrary or wilful in its nature, or that it may be exercised without right or reason to sustain it. The principle as applicable to this case is well stated by Dillon in his work on Corporations, at page 111, section 62: "The words that a corporation or officer 'may' act in a certain way, or that it 'shall be lawful' to act in a certain way, may be imperative. On this subject the cases sustain the doctrine that what corporations or officers are empowered to do for others, and which is beneficial for them to have done, the law holds they ought to do. The power is conferred for the benefit of others, and the intent of the Legislature, which is the test in such cases, ordinarily seems to be to impose a positive duty." In the case of the Commonwealth *ex rel.* Vandyke *v.* Henry (13 Wright, 533), Judge AGNEW states the doctrine more tersely when he says, there are Acts of legislation where "may" will be interpreted to mean "shall," or where the language of mere authority will be held to be a command. But there the interpretation is supported by a purpose to be accomplished, or an imperative duty to be performed. In Julius *v.* The Lord Bishop of Oxford (L. R., 5 Appeal Cases, 222), the Lord Chancellor of England, discussing the words "it shall be lawful," said: "The words 'it shall be lawful' are not equivocal. They are plain and unambiguous. They are words merely making that legal and possible which there would otherwise be no right or authority to do. They confer a faculty or power, and they do not of themselves do more than confer a faculty or power. But there may be something in the nature of the thing empowered to be done, something in the object for which it is to be done, something in the condition under which it is to be done, something in the title of the person or persons for whose benefit the power is to be exercised, which may couple the power and duty, and make it the duty of the person in whom the power is reposed, to exercise that power when called upon to do so. Whether the power is one coupled with a duty such as I have described, is a question which, according to our system of law, speaking generally, it falls to the Court of Queen's Bench to decide, on an application for a *mandamus*, and the words 'it shall be lawful' being, according to their natural meaning, permissive or enabling words only, it lies upon those, as it seems to me, who contend that an obligation exists to exercise this power, to show, in the circumstances of the case, something which, according to the principles I have mentioned, creates this obligation."

This is doubtless a correct statement of the general doctrine, but each case must be judged by its own specialties; the purpose to be accomplished is to be considered; the intent of the Legislature or other authority which confers the power is to be ascertained. In the ordinance of 1855 there is an evident intent to advance the public interest and convenience by providing for more speedy and comfortable travel over the streets of the city; but to what extent this can be best accomplished is left in a measure to the discretion of the Commissioner. This, we think, is apparent by the power conferred to change and alter routes, which necessarily implies a right to take a line off one street, or a number of streets, and to place it on others; the right to forbid or exclude is here clearly recognized; but as the general intent is to require the Commissioner to aid and further the interest and convenience of the public, he is under obligation to grant licenses to owners of omnibuses, unless for good and sufficient reasons he can justify a refusal of an application, such as is contemplated by the ordinance of the city. In this aspect the Commissioner seems to have viewed the question. He refused the application for reasons which, in his judgment, justified his refusal. If he has planted himself on ground upon which he can stand in the exercise of his discretion, he is to be sustained; if the reasons which he assigns are such that he has no right to set them up, or if they are unsubstantial and not well taken, a peremptory mandamus should be granted, the relators having no other legal remedy, and, where in justice there ought to be action, a mandamus will lie to compel it.

First, as to the doubt expressed by the Commissioner, whether, since the introduction of passenger railways, he has any power over the subject, except under the ordinance of December 24, 1870, it is sufficient to say, that all the legislation on the subject stands to-day in full force and effect, and that this ought to be considered a sufficient reason for removing all doubt as to whether the power given to the Commissioner still abides in him. It is difficult to understand why the establishment of passenger railways should be regarded as impliedly repealing the law of the Commonwealth, enacted to make clear the right of the city to license and to regulate the use of omnibuses, as well as the ordinances passed by Councils in pursuance of the authority expressly granted. There does not appear to be any necessary repugnance between the two modes of transporting passengers through and over the streets of the city, or over such of them as have sufficient space to accommodate the public by the ordinary modes of conveyance, as well as by those modes which may be designated special or extraordinary. If there is no such repugnance, there is no repeal by implication, and that there is no such repugnance is clear, from the fact that a grant to a passenger railway company to lay a track or tracks upon the streets of the city, gives no right to the exclusive use of the street for such purpose, if there is space for tracks of other companies subsequently chartered; and if railway companies may run their competing cars side by side, why shall not omnibus lines be allowed under the authority of law to compete with a line whose cars run on a tramway? This portion of the answer of the Commissioner does not demand a more extended reply.

As to the remaining reasons upon which the refusal to grant the licenses demanded by the relators is placed, it is sufficient to say, in brief, that as we interpret the Act of the 27th day of March, 1873, it has no relation to or bearing upon the subject under consideration. The Act provides for a merger of the passenger railways therein referred to. For the reasons set forth in the Act, it is stipulated that no franchise or privilege shall be thereafter granted, to construct on Broad Street a track or tracks, or any artificial tramway, for the conveyance of passengers for hire; to which is added the clause, or to run any cars on any part of said routes. The routes here referred to are the routes mentioned or provided for in the Act, which are particularly set forth with their necessary connection; they are railway routes, and have no reference to the running of cars of any description on Broad Street, other than railway cars, on tracks or artificial tramways.

To the case in hand is equally irrelevant the suggestion in relation to the purchase by the railway companies of the stock of the omnibus line to which reference is made. The only equitable consideration which entered into the question of purchase had regard to the interests of those who had been engaged in the omnibus business before the incorporation of railway companies. It gave to owners of such routes the right to sell their stock to the companies at an appraised value. But if either of these reasons have weight, or can in any proceeding be considered in connection with the question of the right to run omnibuses on Broad and on Market Streets, they cannot be set up by the Commissioner of Highways as reasons for refusing licenses to the relators. He has no right to interpose objections resting at best on but questionable grounds, and with which he has nothing whatever to do in performing the duties which, by the laws and ordinances relating to his office, are imposed on him. It is entirely immaterial to the city of Philadelphia what the relative rights of the owners of passenger railways and of omnibuses may be, in so far as the pecuniary interests of one party or the other is concerned; nor by any law or ordinance is the Chief Commissioner of Highways authorized to interpose to protect such interests. His duties require him to have oversight of the streets of the city; to see that they are kept in proper condition, so as to be safe for those who may have occasion to pass upon them; to prevent or remove all unlawful obstructions; to deal with the questions of paving and repair of streets, and to perform such other duties as are, or by law may be, imposed on him. He is not made the guardian of the interests of private corporations or individuals.

There is more weight in the reason assigned for cause against the grant of license that the revenue of the city may be decreased by diminishing the tax on dividends declared by the Market Street Company. This is a question which may affect directly the revenue of the city; but yet we do not think that it has any standing in this cause, if such results should follow. It is no reason for denying to the relators the rights to which they may be entitled, under the laws of the land and the ordinances of the city, that the income of the Market Street Company might fall off from competition with an omnibus line; but it is also based on a mere anticipated or conjectural result; it by no means follows as a necessary consequence of the proposed competition, that the railway company will earn less than it has done in the years that are passed. Increase of population demands increased facilities of transportation. It would be a poor reason to give in justification of a refusal to afford proper means of travel upon the streets in question for all time to come, that the revenue of the city might, in some degree, be diminished. The public are to be provided for in this regard, though fewer dollars from this source find their way into the public treasury.

The writ of mandamus for which the relators pray is granted.

Opinion by ALLISON, P. J.

PEIRCE, J. I fully concur in the conclusions reached, but I do not concur in some of the doctrines enunciated, especially that which sets up the right of the city or the Highway Commissioner to refuse a license for the running of coaches on the highways of the city.

C. P. No. 4. Oct. 16, 1880.

City v. Thomas.

Rule to strike off entry of satisfaction—Municipal lien satisfied by mistake—An entry of satisfaction when entered through the negligence or mistake of a city official will be vacated by the Court.

Rule to show cause why entry of satisfaction should not be stricken off.

The depositions taken in support of the rule showed that one Brooke, agent of the trustees of the estate of Charles Stokes, deceased, in August, 1880, made application to introduce water into two premises situate on the southeast side of Fairview Avenue, distant respectively 25 feet and 150 feet southwest of 35th Street, when he was informed by a clerk in the water department that a lien had been filed against said premises for water pipe. He went to the office of the City Solicitor, where he paid a lien against a lot of ground situate on southwest side of 35th Street and southeast side of Fairview Avenue, 100 feet on 35th Street and 25 feet on Fairview Avenue. There was no lien against the property owned by the trustees, and the agent was misled by the mistake and negligence of the clerk in the Water Department. The city solicitor satisfied the lien, but upon learning of the mistake marked it to the use of the trustees, whereupon the plaintiff took this rule.

John A. Clark, for the rule.

The Court has power to vacate an entry of satisfaction if made by mistake or to prevent injustice.

Crouthamel *v.* Silberman, 1 WEEKLY NOTES, 131.
McKinney *v.* Fritz, 2 Id. 173.

THE COURT. Rule absolute.

WEEKLY NOTES OF CASES.

Vol. IX.] THURSDAY, DEC. 9, 1880. [No. 16.

Supreme Court.

Jan. '80, 86.   April 1, 1880.
Pike County v. Rowland.

Constitutional law—Sec. 8, Art. IX. of the Constitution—Limit of increase of indebtedness—Board of County Commissioners—Notice of special meeting necessary—Power of administrator to control stock—When his act cannot be questioned by third parties.

The true sense of the second clause of Sec. 18, Art. IX. of the Constitution is, a prohibition of a new municipal debt, or an increase of existing debt, of more than two per cent. of the assessed property valuation, unless authorized by a public vote. It was not intended to prevent the officers of a municipality from increasing existing indebtedness by an increase (or a new debt) less than two per cent. without a public vote, provided the extreme limit of seven per cent. be not exceeded.

It is essential to the power of a board to do any deliberative, binding act, that it should sit at a regular stated meeting, at an adjourned meeting, or at a special meeting, for which notice must be served, personally if practicable, on every member of the board entitled to be present.

This rule applies alike to public and to private corporations.

Duties and powers of a board reviewed.

An administrator may, as to third persons not those with whom he acts or contracts, control, or sell stock, whether he hold it as administrator, or it has vested in him as owner.

Error to the Common Pleas of Monroe County.

Action of covenant, for interest due on county bonds, by Lafayette Rowland, against Pike County. Pleas, *non est factum; non infregit conventionem*, and want of consideration, with leave, etc., and special pleas as follows:—

(1) That on the 5th of November, 1875, when it is alleged the covenants set forth in the declaration were made, no meeting of the Commissioners of the County of Pike was held at which said covenants could be lawfully made.

(2) That on said 5th of November, 1875, while one of said commissioners was, by reason of intoxication, entirely incapacitated for transacting business, he was induced with another of the Commissioners to enter the Commissioners' office in the evening and cause the record of the adjournment of the Board of Commissioners to be falsely and fraudulently altered, and then and there unlawfully and fraudulently, if ever, said covenants were made by said two Commissioners.

(3) That all the above stated matters were well known to the plaintiff, and that the intoxication of said Commissioner and alteration of the minutes were procured by the plaintiff for the purpose of unlawfully and fraudulently obtaining said covenants.

(4) That on said 5th of November, 1875, the indebtedness of Pike County exceeded two per cent. of the last assessed valuation of taxable property in said county; and the assent of the electors of said county had not been obtained to the increase of said indebtedness.

(5) That the matters set forth in the preceding plea were all well known to the plaintiff.

An additional special plea was amended to aver that two of the Commissioners met during the day of the 5th of November, 1875, and adjourned to the 9th of November, and that the meeting on the evening of the 5th of November, when it is alleged said bonds were issued, was not in pursuance of any adjournment, or notice to Geyer, one of the Commissioners.

A change of venue was made to Monroe Co.

Upon the trial, before DREHER, P. J., the following facts appeared: By the Act of April 5, 1862 (P. L. of 1863, 652), George H. Rowland and others were incorporated under the name of the Lackawaxen Bridge Company for the purpose of constructing a bridge across the Lackawaxen River in Pike County. The bridge was erected and completed in 1863. In 1864 an Act of Assembly was passed providing that upon the assent in writing of a majority in number of the stockholders of the company, the bridge should be sold to Pike County, and the County Commissioners should purchase it and issue county bonds therefor. The circumstances surrounding the actual sale in 1875 were the subject of much conflicting testimony. There was evidence on behalf of the plaintiff, that a majority by one of the stockholders signed the assent; that the approval of the Court was then obtained. Rowland had some bonds printed, but on going to the Commissioners' office was told that they did not want to have anything to do with him. It appeared that this was shortly before the election of new Commissioners, three being the whole number, and that those candidates opposed to the purchase of the bridge were elected. Drake, a Commissioner, and a defeated candidate for re-election, met Rowland on the 5th of November, 1875, and while still in office, and told him that he "had a notion to go in for buying the bridge." On the 4th of November, the three Commissioners, Geyer, Drake, and Rosecrans, were in regular session, and while so, Geyer asked when the next meeting would be held, and was told on the 9th, but that they would adjourn over to the 5th to finish business;

he then left before the close of the meeting. Rosecrans and Drake met on the 5th; Rowland came before the meeting in consequence of what had been said to him by Drake, and the Commissioners present determined to purchase the bridge. The meeting adjourned until the evening in order to enable the counsel for the Commissioners to draw up the papers; this, with their execution and the issue of the bonds, was then accomplished.

The defendant's evidence showed that A. Hanners, one of the assenting stockholders, claimed to be a stockholder and signed the assent under the following circumstances: His father had recently died owning some of the stock. He then took letters of administration on his father's estate, filed an inventory and appraisement of the personal property including this stock, and in the evening of the same day agreed with his mother and three sisters (two of whom were minors without guardians) to take all the personal property at its appraised value. The stock was never transferred to him on the books of the company, and at the time of signing this assent and of the subsequent action of the Commissioners based upon it, he had filed no account as administrator nor in any public manner charged himself with the stock. He did not sign the assent as administrator but as an individual claiming personally to own the stock.

Geyer testified that when he left the meeting in session on November 4th it was understood that no further business was to be transacted except the appointment of an assessor; that would be done on the morning of the 5th; and the meeting of the 4th would adjourn to the 9th. The Commissioners' record showed that Drake and Rosecrans did meet on the morning of the 5th and transact the particular business agreed upon. The clerk testified that they then adjourned to the 9th. Rowland and Drake were seen together in the afternoon, the latter in a state of intoxication, and declaring himself in favor of the purchase of the bridge. In the evening he went with Rosecrans to the Commissioners' office, caused the record to be altered to show an adjournment to that evening instead of the 9th, and the resolution to purchase the bridge was passed. Geyer, the third Commissioner, filed his protest on learning these facts, and the new Board of Commissioners refused to recognize the transaction.

The defendant proposed to ask Thrall, one of its witnesses: "Had you any conversation with Sol. Drake, one of the County Commissioners, prior to night of November 5th, 1875, during the day of the 5th, with reference to his (Drake's) views as to the purchase of the Lackawaxen Bridge, what he intended to do, and as to any inducements that had been held out to him by George Rowland or Lafayette Rowland?" Objected to; objection sustained (1st assignment of error).

Defendant offered to prove by witness that on November 5, 1875, Sol. Drake said to the witness that he was offered by the plaintiff $500, and a trip to Niagara Falls and expenses paid, if he would assent as Commissioner to the purchase of the bridge. Objected to; offer overruled. (2d assignment of error.)

The defendant objected to the bonds being received in evidence on the ground that the assent in writing of a majority of the stockholders had not been shown. Objection overruled. (3d assignment of error.)

The defendant presented the following points:

(1) That if the jury believe from the evidence that during the forenoon or afternoon of the 5th day of November, 1875, the Commissioners adjourned to meet on Tuesday the 9th instant, and that the subsequent meeting on the evening of said 5th day of November was without notice to George Geyer, one of the Commissioners and without his knowledge, then under the law the Commissioners Rosecrans and Drake had no power at such meeting to purchase the Lackawaxen Bridge and issue bonds therefor, and that the county of Pike is not bound by said action. *Refused* (4th assignment).

(2) It appearing from the evidence that the indebtedness of Pike County on the 5th day of November, 1875, exceeded two per centum upon the assessed valuation of the taxable property therein, the Commissioners were by the Constitution and laws of this Commonwealth at that time prohibited from incurring the additional indebtedness of $2100, and such attempted action of two of said Commissioners, and the bonds alleged to have been issued by them, could not and did not bind the county of Pike. *Refused* (8th assignment).

(3) Lafayette Rowland, the plaintiff, having been treasurer of the county of Pike on the 5th day of November, 1875, and during the year 1875, is charged with knowledge of the fact that the indebtedness of the county exceeded two per centum upon the assessed valuation of taxable property in said county at that time, and he cannot recover upon the bonds upon which the suit is founded. *Refused* (9th assignment).

The plaintiff presented the following points:—

(1.) That the net amount of indebtedness of Pike County existing at the time of the adoption of the New Constitution and the issuing of the bonds in question, being less than three per centum on the assessed valuation of taxable property, and the new indebtedness created by the purchase of the bridge not exceeding two per centum on such valuation, the issuing of said bonds is not in contravention of the 8th

Section of the 9th Article of the Constitution, or of the Act of 20th April, 1874.

(4) That under the Act of April 20th, 1874, the Commissioners of Pike County had a right to increase the then existing debt or create a new debt not exceeding two per centum of the valuation.

(2) That the Act of March 23, 1865, providing for the sale of the Lackawaxen Bridge, is not repealed by the 8th Section of the 9th Article of the Constitution, nor by the Act of the 20th of April, 1874, nor is the right to carry out the provisions of said Act suspended or controlled by the Constitution or the Act of April 20, 1874.

These points were affirmed *pro forma* (6th, 7th, and 13th assignments), and the questions involved therein, reserved.

The Court charged the jury, *inter alia*, as follows:—

"[We charge you that it was not necessary to notify Geyer, the other Commissioner, of the meeting on the evening of the 5th, when the bonds were issued, if the other two Commissioners were there according to adjournment, or in pursuance of notice to themselves without a previous adjournment.]"

Verdict for the plaintiff, $252, subject to the opinion of the Court whether—under the following facts, which they find, to wit: That at the time of the adoption of the present Constitution of this State, and at the time of the purchase of the bridge by the Commissioners of Pike County, and for the purchase-money of which the bonds described in the plaintiff's declaration were given, the indebtedness of said county exceeded two per centum, but did not exceed three per centum upon the assessed valuation of taxable property therein; that the purchase or consideration money for said bridge did not exceed 2¼ mills on the dollar of the assessed value of such taxable property, and the Commissioners of said county purchased said bridge and issued said bonds on the 5th day of November, 1875, under the authority conferred upon them by the Act of Assembly approved March 23, 1865, entitled "An Act for a free bridge over the Lackawaxen River at Lock No. 10, on the Delaware and Hudson Canal,"—the plaintiff is entitled to recover.

The Court entered judgment for the plaintiff on the special verdict (12th assignment), DREHER, P. J., delivering the following opinion:

"The questions raised upon the special verdict are: (1) Whether the indebtedness of a county, the debt of which at the adoption of the present Constitution exceeded two per centum (but was less than three per centum) upon the assessed value of the taxable property therein, may be increased (the increase being less than two per centum upon such assessed valuation of property) without the assent of the electors of the county ascertained by a public election?

"(2) [Whether the 8th Section of Article IX., of April, 1874 (P. L. 65), repealed the special Act of Assembly of the 23d of March, 1865 (P. L. 650), entitled 'An Act providing for a free bridge over the Lackawaxen River at Lock No. 10 on the Delaware and Hudson Canal?"] (15th assignment.)

"The first section of that Act authorizes the Lackawaxen Bridge Company to make a conveyance of all their right, title, and interest in the bridge, with the contiguous land and all appurtenances and franchises held by them, to the county of Pike. The second section authorizes the Commissioners of the County of Pike, with the approval of the Associate Judges of the county, to purchase said bridge for cash, or bonds bearing interest at the rate of six per centum, to be paid annually.

"The 8th Section of Article IX. of the Constitution is as follows: 'The debt of any county, city, borough, township, school district, or other municipality, or incorporated district, except as herein provided, shall never exceed seven per centum upon the assessed value of the taxable property therein; nor shall any such municipality or district incur any new debt or increase its indebtedness to an amount exceeding two per centum upon such assessed valuation of the property, without the assent of the electors thereof at a public election in such manner as shall be provided by law; but any city, the debt of which now exceeds seven per centum of such assessed valuation, may be authorized by law to increase the same three per centum in the aggregate at any one time upon such valuation.'

"It is contended by the defendant that the term 'new debt' has reference to counties not indebted, and that such counties may incur a debt amounting to two per centum upon the assessed valuation, without a vote of the electors assenting thereto, and that the phrase 'increase its indebtedness' has reference to counties having an existing indebtedness, and that such counties cannot make any increase of such indebtedness if the proposed increase and old indebtedness together exceed two per centum of the assessed valuation, without first obtaining the assent of the electors at an election held for that purpose.

"I cannot see any such distinction between the expressions 'incur any new debt' and 'increase its indebtedness.' An existing indebtedness is certainly increased by contracting or incurring a new debt, and a new debt may be incurred by a county or an individual already in debt. Suppose a county with an indebtedness of ten thousand dollars should find it necessary to borrow ten thousand dollars to put up a public building and issue bonds therefor; this borrowed $10,000 would certainly be a new debt. It is no part of the old debt. It might be said that the county had increased its indebtedness to the amount of $10,000, but certainly it would not be said she had increased her debt to the amount of $20,000.

"The second clause of the 8th section reads: 'Nor shall any such municipality or district incur any new debt or increase its indebtedness to an amount exceeding two per centum upon such assessed valuation of property without the assent of the electors thereof at a public election in such manner as shall be provided by law.'

"Now according to the argument of the defendant, this clause provides for two classes of counties. First. Such as have no debt; and they may incur a debt not exceeding two per centum upon the assessed valuation, without a vote of the electors. Second. Such counties as are in debt; and they may increase such indebtedness if the existing debt with the increase does not exceed two per centum of such assessed valuation, without a vote of the electors.

"[According to the defendant's theory, there is no place in the second clause of the 8th Section for that class of counties having an indebtedness exceeding two per centum of the assessed value of property therein. It would be incorrect to say that a county having an indebtedness equal to or in excess of two per centum may increase that indebtedness, but the indebtedness when increased shall not exceed two per centum. We might as well say that a quantity equal to A may be increased, but such a quantity when increased must not exceed A. It is not a sufficient answer to this to say that as the maximum limit fixed by the first clause is seven per centum, therefore any county not having reached that limit may increase its indebtedness by a vote of the people. The second clause provides for the vote of the taxpayers to be taken in the cases therein mentioned; that is to say, according to defendant's argument, where a county has no debt, and where there is a debt less than two per centum, and it is proposed to increase it so that the debt and the increase will exceed two per centum."] (10th assignment.)

"[I think the county of Pike had the power to purchase the bridge, and issue bonds in payment therefor, notwithstanding her indebtedness was in excess of two per centum of the assessed value of taxable property therein, at the time these bonds were issued. Whether these bonds are viewed in the light of a 'new debt,' or an increase of an existing indebtedness, I think they are binding upon the county, and judgment is therefore entered upon the special verdict in favor of the plaintiff."] (11th assignment.)

"In this opinion I have not referred to the Act of 20th April, 1874, thinking it unnecessary to do so, as that Act is certainly not more restrictive upon the power of a county to contract indebtedness than the Constitution.

"[If the defendant's interpretation of the Constitution is correct, I think it very doubtful whether the power of the County Commissioners to purchase the bridge and issue the bonds under the special Act of 23d March, 1865, was abrogated by the adoption of the New Constitution."] (14th assignment.)

The defendant took this writ, assigning for error the refusal of offers made, the answers to the points, the portions of the charge and opinion on the points reserved quoted in brackets, and the entry of judgment on the points reserved in favor of the plaintiff.

H. M. Seely (*John Nyce* with him), for the plaintiff in error.

Drake's declarations against Rowland should have been received; for only slight evidence of collusion is necessary in order to show corrupt inducement.

McDowell *v.* Rissell, 1 Wr. 168.
Gibbs *v.* Neely, 7 Watts, 307.
Peterson *v.* Speer, 5 Cas. 491.

What Hanners might have done as administrator is immaterial, for the evidence was that he did not assent as administrator, and he could not act in any other capacity.

Lewis *v.* Ewing, 6 Harris, 313.

The Board of Commissioners could only convene according to adjournment, or pursuant to notice.

Act of April 15, 1834, § 19; Purd. Dig. 302.

This is, moreover, but an enunciation of the common law rule.

4 Kent's Com. 464.
Dillon on Mun. Corp. 320, 338.
McCready *v.* Guardians of the Poor, 9 S. & R. 99.
Jefferson Co. *v.* Slagle, 16 Sm. 202.

The language of Sect. 8, Art. IX., of the Constitution is prohibitory; it is a limit of indebtedness — not of increase. The words "incur any new debt" have reference to a municipality not indebted, and the indebtedness which it can incur, without the assent of the electors, is limited to two per centum; the words "increase its indebtedness" have reference to a municipality already indebted, and to such the same limit of indebtedness is fixed.

If it does not mean a limit to the total and aggregate amount of indebtedness, then many banking corporations are in a very precarious condition; for the language in their charters is the same as that here used.

The intent of the Constitutional provision was to protect taxpayers against an incumbrance of their property greater than two per cent. The Court below has construed away this protection.

The clause in the Constitution being prohibitory, the Act of March 23, 1865, providing for the sale of the bridge, was suspended in its operation until the indebtedness of the county was so reduced that the purchase would not increase the total indebtedness beyond two per cent.

Perkins *v.* Slack, 5 Nor. 278.

G. G. *Waller* (*J. B. Storm* with him).

Whether or no the assent of Hanners was valid can only be questioned by the heirs or by the stockholders.

The declarations of Drake could not be received, for there was no evidence of a conspiracy; they were the loose declarations of a citizen, and not made by Drake in his official character, while acting on the business of the county.

Green *v.* North Buffalo Tp., 6 Sm. 110.

2 Wharton's Ev. § 1209.

It was understood that there would be an adjourned meeting on the 5th of November; there was no understanding that none other than the business proposed should come up.

The Constitutional provision means that the aggregate of new debts or of the increase of the indebtedness must not exceed two per cent.

The New Constitution did not suspend the operation of the Act of 1865, for its prohibitions are prospective.

Indiana Co. *v.* Agricultural Soc., 4 Nor. 357.

Wattson *v.* Chester & Del. River Co., 2 Id. 254.

June 22, 1880. THE COURT. The Act of 1834 provides that the corporate powers of a county shall be exercised by the Commissioners; that two of them shall form a board for the transaction of business, and, when convened in pursuance of notice or according to adjournment, shall be competent to perform all duties appertaining to the office. To these officers are intrusted the care and management of county business and property. The voice of the inhabitants is not directly heard in the levying of taxes, making of contracts, or expenditure of money; their power is only felt at the election of Commissioners. The question presented in the fourth and fifth assignments is, May two of the Commissioners convene and lawfully transact business requiring deliberation, not according to adjournment, and without notice to or knowledge of the other? This concerns every citizen of the county, as well as each member of the board.

By law, the affairs of the county are administered by three representatives. Absent members, equally with those who are present, are bound by whatever is lawfully done at a regular or stated meeting or any regular adjourned meeting. If the meeting be a special one, the general rule is that notice is necessary, and must be personally served, if practicable, upon every member entitled to be present, so that each one may be afforded an opportunity to participate and vote. Such notice is essential to the power of the board to do any deliberative act which shall bind the corporation. If all have notice, two shall form the board, and their acts bind the absent, as if it were a stated or adjourned meeting. Notice may be dispensed with by the presence and consent of all; and if one has quit the municipality, and has no family or house within its limits, notice to him is unnecessary. (Dillon on Mun. Corp. §§ 200, 201, 223, 224.) All authorities seem to agree as to the general rule, unless there is a modification in the charter or statute. It applies alike to public and private corporations. Our statute, which declares that a majority shall form a board when duly convened in pursuance of notice or adjournment, is an enactment of the well-settled rule without adding to or taking from.

Jefferson County *v.* Slagle (16 P. F. S. 202) does not support the position that two of the Commissioners may meet, without the knowledge of the other, and bind the county by contract. This point was not raised nor discussed in the opinion. It was ruled that the board could transact business anywhere in the county. No proof was adduced that they acted without consent of the other, and, in the absence of evidence, it is presumed the officers did their duty. (Downing *v.* Rugar, 21 Wend. 178.)

In absence of a different provision in the charter or by-laws of a corporation, a special meeting of the trustees must be called by giving personal notice to each member of the board. A provision that a majority shall form a board for the transaction of business does not change the rule. (Harding *v.* Vandewater, 40 Cal. 77.) A meeting of stockholders regularly warned is competent to do any act within their chartered powers by a bare majority; yet, if not thus warned, their act would be void. If no mode of warning be prescribed in their charter or by-laws, personal notice may be given. (Stow *v.* Wyse, 7 Conn. 214.) When the statute vested the election of treasurer for the county and city of Dublin in the "board of magistrates of the county of the said city," and an election was held in the absence of one of the magistrates who had not been notified, it was held that the election was invalid. (Smith *v.* Darley, 2 House of Lords' Cases, 789; See the People *v.* Batchelor, 22 N. York, 128.)

If two of the Commissioners, without notice to or knowledge of the other, can form a board for transaction of business, the statutory direction for notice is futile. To say they have convened in pursuance of notice is nonsense, unless we speak of notice to the two by a person who desires business of interest to himself to be done in the other's absence. Such meeting savors of conspiracy. A designing man could observe the superiority of an able and upright Commissioner over his weaker fellows, and take care to convene the two weaker ones for consummation of his purpose, if notice to all is not essential. Superior numbers often yield to superior weight, and sometimes the corrupt quail in presence of an honest man. Just in proportion as a clandestine meeting of two Commissioners for transaction of business would be dangerous, is it to the interest of the inhabitants of the county that all three should have notice and opportunity to be present at every special meeting of the board. The opinions, reasoning, perhaps protest, of the one may advantage the county. He may prevent hasty and inconsiderate action. Had Geyer been present on the evening the bonds were signed, he might have discussed the matter with Rosecrans till Drake's pendulous mind had swung the other way, and thereby saved the county from the Rowland contract. Be this as it may, Geyer ought to have had opportunity to consult, advise, and, if need be, protest. The defendant's first point should have been affirmed. It is scarcely necessary to remark that no question is raised in this record respecting the validity of bonds or securities, appearing on their face to have been properly issued by the County Commissioners, which have passed into the hands of strangers to the original transaction who are innocent holders for value.

We think the learned Judge of the Common Pleas rightly determined the questions raised by the special verdict. Section 8, Art. IX., of the Constitution is as follows: "The debt of any county, city, borough, township, school district, or other municipality or incorporated district, except as herein provided, shall never exceed seven per centum upon the assessed value of the taxable property therein; nor shall any such municipality or district incur any new debt, or increase its indebtedness to an amount exceeding two per centum upon such assessed valuation of property, without the assent of the electors thereof at a public election in such manner as shall be provided by law; but any city, the debt of which now exceeds seven per centum of such assessed valuation, may be authorized by law to increase the same three per centum in the aggregate, at any one time, upon such valuation." In the Constitutional Convention the three divisions of this section were discussed, and the second was explained thus: "The second division of the amendment provides that no new debt, or any increase of existing debt, exceeding two per cent., shall ever be authorized by any municipality without the express assent of the electors of the municipality by a public vote." This seems to have been the understanding of the convention. (6 Debates, 143.) The clause was doubtless so understood by the people at its adoption. In Wheeler *v.* Philadelphia (27 P. F. S. 338), a case soon after its adoption, when it was necessary to give a construction of the third clause of the section, relating to cities, it was remarked of the preceding: "The municipal authorities may increase the debt from time to time until two per centum has been added: provided the original debt, with the increase, does not exceed seven per centum. After the two per centum has been added, there can be no further increase without the vote of the people."

Neither the debates, nor supposed views of the people, nor the dictum of this Court, nor all combined, can set aside the plain meaning of a Constitutional provision; but, if the sense of a clause be doubtful, the contemporaneous understanding is material. In strictness, the words may mean as contended by defendant, but the context seems to make it clear that the true sense of the clause is a prohibition of a new debt, or increase of existing debt exceeding two per cent. of the assessed valuation, without a public vote. When the debt is less than seven per centum, it was not intended that public officers of municipalities should be deprived of power to make immediate improvements and repairs of public property which might become necessary: provided they keep within the limit of two per centum of the valuation.

The third assignment cannot be sustained. Hanners, as administrator, had the right to control or sell the stock. He signed the writing giving assent of the stockholders, and that was sufficient, as respects third persons, whether he then held it as administrator or it had vested in him as owner.

We discover no error in the rulings set forth in the remaining assignments.

Decree reversed, and *venire facias de novo* awarded.

Opinion by TRUNKEY, J. GREEN, J., absent.

May, '80, 139, 140.   June 21, 1880.

Felt & Co., for use of Gifford, v. Cook & Hackett.

Gifford's Appeal.

Power of Court to decree the entry of satisfaction of a judgment—Act of March 14, 1876—What is payment within the meaning of said Act.

The power conferred upon the Court under the Act of March 14, 1876 (P. L. 7), to decree the entry of satisfaction of a judgment upon due proof that the same has been fully paid, is summary in its character, and in derogation of the common law, and a denial of the right of trial by jury; it must, therefore, be limited to the express language of the Act.

Under the Act the Court is limited to cases of actual payment in full.

A. obtained a judgment against B. & C.; B. & C. recovered a judgment against A. & C.; B. & C. (who were partners) were subsequently declared bankrupts, and the latter judgment was sold by their assignee to D., who issued execution; thereupon A. took a rule under the Act of March 14, 1876 (P. L. 7), to show cause why the judgment should not be marked satisfied, for the reason that it was paid "by operation of law," by the former judgment:

Held (reversing the judgment and decree of the Court below), that this was not a "payment" within the meaning of the Act.

Per GREEN, J. "To hold that under this Act everything which could be given in evidence under the plea of payment in a pending adversary proceeding before verdict, must or may be treated as actual payment after verdict, would be a very wide departure from that strict construction which such legislation requires."

Error to and appeal from a decree of the Common Pleas of Cameron County.

The facts were as follows: On November 19, 1873, L. G. Cook recovered a judgment against J. P. Felt and S. S. Hackett in an action in tort for the sum of $206.50. Execution was issued and stayed by the Court, on the ground of pending proceedings in bankruptcy against the defendants, who were partners.

On Nov. 30, 1873, J. P. Felt and S. S. Hackett, trading as Felt & Co., recovered a verdict against L. G. Cook and S. S. Hackett, trading as Cook & Hackett, for the sum of $200.29.

On October 24, 1873, Felt and Hackett (the defendants in the first and the plaintiffs in the second of their suits), trading as Felt & Co., were adjudicated bankrupts, and subsequently discharged.

In the course of the administration of their assets, the assignee, John M. Judd, exposed the latter claim to sale by auction, and sold the same to William Gifford for $25. Gifford, on March 27, 1879, paid the jury fee, entered judgment, and issued execution, whereupon the defendants took a rule to show cause why the judgment of Cook against Felt and Hackett (individually) should not be set off against the judgment of Felt and Hackett (Felt & Co.) against Cook & Hackett, which rule, after argument, was discharged by the Court (WILLIAMS, P. J.).

Subsequently Cook obtained a rule under the Act of March 14, 1876 (P. L. 7), to "show cause why said judgment should not be marked satisfied of record and fully discharged, for the reason that the same is fully paid by operation of law, and by the judgment of Cook *v.* Felt and Hackett."

The provisions of the Act are as follows:—

"In all cases where a judgment has been or may hereafter be entered in any Court of Record in this Commonwealth, whether originally or by transfer from any other Court, the Court having jurisdiction shall, upon application by the defendant or defendants in said judgment, or of his, her, or their legal representatives, or other person or persons concerned in interest therein, setting forth under oath that the same, with all legal costs accrued thereon, has been fully paid, grant a rule on the plaintiff or plaintiffs, to show cause why the said judgment should not be marked satisfied of record, at his, her, or their costs. And upon the hearing of such rule, should it appear to the satisfaction of the Court that such judgment has been fully paid, as set forth in the application of the defendant or defendants, the said Court shall then direct the prothonotary to mark such judgment satisfied of record, and shall also enter a decree requiring the plaintiff or plaintiffs to pay all costs incurred in the premises."

This rule, after argument, was made absolute by the Court (WILSON, J.), in the following opinion:—

. . . . This rule cannot be maintained at common law, and we regard it as equally apparent that our statute of set-off cannot be enforced under this mode of procedure. Hence, if this rule can be sustained at all, it must be by virtue of the 20th section of the Bankrupt Act, which reads as follows, viz.: "That in all cases of mutual debts or mutual credits between the parties, the account between them *shall* be stated, and one *debt* set off against the other, and the *balance only shall be allowed or paid*."

It is claimed that the judgment of Cook against Felt and Hackett, being a recovery on a claim in *tort*, is not embraced in the Act under the phrase, "Mutual debts and mutual credits." This statute is entitled to a more liberal construction than a mere statute of set-off. Its language has in it the elements of adjustment and satisfaction. "The account between them shall be stated, and one debt set off against the other, and the balance only shall be allowed or paid." These instructions are to the assignee, and it is his duty to strictly comply. The spirit, as well as the letter, of this Act ought to be regarded in its construction, and neither ought to be restricted or hampered to the detriment of equal justice between the parties.

General principles and the language and spirit of the Act combine in leading me to the conclusion that the phrase "Mutual debts and mutual credits" means any claim that might be successfully proved before the register, or that may or shall be recovered by action against the estate. And especially may it include a verdict or judgment rendered against the bankrupt before the assignee was appointed. The spirit of the Act seems to have adopted the rule in equity as stated by Lord Mansfield, viz.: That natural equity requires that cross demands should compensate each other by deducting the less from the greater, and the difference only is the sum that can be justly due.

It may be objected that these principles have not been applied to this case, and that the judgment stands in full force. Equity permits the

Court to consider that as done which in equity and good conscience *ought to have been done*. . . .

We may entertain doubts as to the mode and correctness of our reasoning in this case, but we have no doubt of the correctness of our conclusion—that it would be unjust to suffer this judgment to be collected.

Whereupon Gifford took this writ and appeal, assigning for error the action of the Court.

John C. Hall (*McCauley* with him), for appellant and plaintiff in error.

We submit that the jurisdiction of the Court to decree satisfaction of a judgment is confined to cases of actual payment, and does not exist where there is an alleged payment by operation of law, arising merely from the existence of an equitable defence. A judgment might be equitably extinguished by a failure of consideration, but the Court cannot summarily satisfy it on proof of the facts. And so of all cases of merely equitable or legal defences by way of set-off. They are not payment in the proper and legal sense of the word.

A review of the legislation on the subject fortifies this view. Originally the Court had no power to direct satisfaction. Then came the Act of 11th April, 1856, authorizing the prothonotary to enter satisfaction when the original instrument is produced, with plaintiff's receipt endorsed in presence of two witnesses, and the satisfaction is allowed by a Judge's certificate. Then the Act of 27th March, 1865, authorized the prothonotary, under the direction of the Court, to satisfy a judgment where, by the production of the record, it appears to have been fully paid, under or by virtue of an execution. Finally, the Act of 14th March, 1876, authorizing the Court to direct the prothonotary to mark a judgment satisfied of record where, upon the hearing of a rule for that purpose, it should appear to the satisfaction of the Court that said judgment has been fully paid. In this case, the only payment found by the Court, or alleged by the defendant below, was a mutual extinguishment, resulting, as the Court thought, from the provisions of the bankrupt law. We submit that this was not payment within the intent and meaning of the Act of Assembly authorizing satisfaction by the Court.

A. G. Olmsted (*Newton* and *Green* with him), contra.

The Act permits the Court to decree the entry of satisfaction whenever it shall appear that the judgment has been fully paid; hence anything which, under a plea of payment, would defeat recovery will support this action of the Court. The Pennsylvania rule is that anything which shows that *ex æquo et bono*, the plaintiff ought not to recover, may be given in evidence under this plea.

Labapee *v*. Pecholier, 2 W. C. C. R. 180.
King *v*. Diehl, 9 S. & R. 409.
Hartzell *v*. Reiss, 1 Binn. 289.

Oct. 4, 1880. THE COURT. This was an application to the Court below to direct a judgment to be marked satisfied. The application was necessarily made under the Act of 14th March, 1876, because the power of the Court to make such an order without the verdict of a jury, and where satisfaction has not been obtained by execution process, exists only by force of that statute. It had been decided by this Court that even upon allegation and proof of payment of a judgment, the Court had no power to strike it off or direct it to be marked satisfied, and that the only remedy of the defendant, in such a case, was to apply for an issue to determine whether the judgment had been paid. (Horner & McCann *v*. Hower, 3 Wr. p. 126.) The Act of 1876, however, did confer upon the Courts of Record in this Commonwealth, in which judgments were entered, the power to order such judgments to be marked satisfied upon a proper application and proofs. The language of the Act is as follows:—

[His Honor here recited the terms of the Act *ut supra*.] The power thus conferred is summary in character, is in derogation of the common law, and is a denial of the right of trial by jury. Of course it must be limited to the express language of the Act which confers it. To hold that, under this Act, everything which could be given in evidence under the plea of payment in a pending adversary proceeding before verdict, must or may be treated as actual payment after verdict and judgment, would be a very wide departure from that strict construction which such legislation requires. The letter of the Act, as well as its manifest spirit and meaning, alike demand that the exercise of the power conferred by it should be limited to the very case prescribed. That case is actual payment in full, but such is not this case. Instead of actual payment in full, the defendant's petition shows there was no payment whatever of any part of this judgment. It is not even claimed that there was a right of set-off against it. The Court below held there was not, and of that decision there is no complaint. One of the defendants contends that a certain judgment which he recovered against the two individuals who compose the partnership, plaintiffs, in the present case, has paid the judgment of the firm against him and his co-defendant by operation of law. No authority is cited in support of this position, and we have no knowledge of any. The very doubtful merits of the defence set up under the bankrupt law do not require consideration, as we have no jurisdiction to apply the relief invoked under the Act of 1876 to such a case.

Judgment reversed, and record remitted for further proceedings.

Opinion by GREEN, J. PAXSON, J., absent.

Wright v. Funck. March 15, 1880.

Evidence—Act of April 15, 1869—Competency of a surviving partner and vendor of a chattel as a witness for the vendee upon release by the vendee from liability on his implied warranty of title—Relevancy of evidence of intimate relation of parties—Replevin—Practice—Jury—Verdict, what not improper.

A surviving partner and vendor of a chattel when released by his vendee from liability on his implied warranty of title is a competent witness for the vendee.

Evidence of intimacy of relation of parties to show motive for reposing confidence is not irrelevant.

PER CURIAM. In an action of replevin it is proper for the jury to find some of the goods for the plaintiff, and the rest for the defendant. Judgment may be entered upon such a verdict.

Error to the Common Pleas of Schuylkill County.

Replevin, by Josiah Funck against Jonathan Wright, to recover law books and book-case alleged to have been unjustly taken and detained by the defendant. The defendant pleaded non cepit and property, and specially that he did not take the books.

Upon the trial, before WALKER, J., the following material facts were in evidence: The Bibighaus library, consisting of one hundred and ninety-three law books, and the book-case, were bought by Jacob Light and Martin Wengert, trading as Light & Wengert, from George F. Meily, who gave them a bill of sale dated April 22, 1854. These books Light & Wengert loaned, as they alleged, to Jonathan Wright, who was at the time insolvent and deeply in their debt, upon representations made by him that if he had the use of them he could study law, and be enabled out of his practice to discharge his indebtedness to them. Wright, who had been engaged since 1849 in buying and selling grain and making flour, had failed some time in 1853, and his property, consisting of a grist-mill and a few acres, had been bought in by Wengert, who was his principal creditor. After his failure he induced Wengert to authorize him to act as his agent in carrying on the same business in the same place. The books in question were bought by him while acting as their agent, and were afterwards removed by him, without their consent, from Jonestown to Pottsville. Wright involved Light & Wengert in heavy losses, who, finding they could not get anything out of him, sold the books to the plaintiff, giving him a bill of sale for them dated Jan. 7, 1860. The defendant refused to deliver the books upon the presentation of a delivery order on Jan. 13. The plaintiff produced evidence to show that Wright had on several occasions said that the books belonged to Light & Wengert, and especially that when, on Jan. 12, 1860, a levy was made upon them as the property of Wright, under a writ of testatum fi. fa., on the judgment of Stroh v. Wright, C. P. of Lebanon County, No. 201, March Term, 1860, he declared that Light & Wengert had bought and paid for them with their money, and that they belonged to them.

"The plaintiff proposed to prove by the witness, Martin Wengert, who has been released from all liabilities on his implied warranted of title, that the law books and book-case replevied in this case, were the property of Light & Wengert at the time the same were sold to the plaintiff, and that the defendant had neither title nor right to the possession of them, that the said books and book-case were purchased by Light & Wengert, and loaned to the said Wright during their pleasure, with the understanding that if Wright should pay them for the same, and all his indebtedness to them, they would sell them to him; and with the further understanding that said Wright would not remove them from the county of Lebanon, that Wright never paid said Light & Wengert one cent for said books and case, and removed them out of Lebanon County without the knowledge or consent of said Light & Wengert."

The defendant objected to the competency of the witness, upon the ground that Jacob Light, a partner with the witness, under the firm of Light & Wengert, is dead, and that the witness is a surviving partner; that the plaintiff has proved that he claims the said matter in controversy, from and under a conveyance from Light & Wengert, made in the lifetime of Light; that there is no evidence of a release of the firm of Light & Wengert by the plaintiff, but if there were such release it would not restore the witness to competency; that the death of Light closes the mouth of his surviving partner, they being the grantors of the thing in controversy to the plaintiff. Objection overruled; exception. (1st assignment of error.)

The plaintiff now proposed to ask the witness why he had such confidence in Wright as to give him the money upon his bare representations without taking any vouchers as testified. This was offered for the purpose of showing that at the time the money in question was given to Wright, that he was or represented himself as a preacher, and that there were religious connections between them.

Defendant objected that the evidence proposed is irrelevant and incompetent; that they cannot prove such facts by their own witness; the fact that Mr. Wright was or was not a preacher, will raise a new issue in this case, an irrelevant issue in which the jury have nothing to do; and that it is not sufficient to induce confidence nowadays that a man is a preacher; that it is not evidence in chief, but should be brought out in chief, if at all.

THE COURT. It seems to me he may show an intimate relationship between himself and Mr. Wright, the evidence is that he placed confidence in Wright. Admitted. (2d assignment of error.)

The plaintiff submitted the following points, *inter alia*:—

(2) If the jury believe that Jonathan Wright was the owner of these books, and at his instance title thereto was made to Light & Wengert, that Light & Wengert and Wright represented the books in controversy to be the property of Light & Wengert; and the sole and exclusive purpose of these contrivances was to give a false color of title to the books to Light & Wengert, and cover them up from the grasp of the creditors of Wright, this was a fraud, and Wright is estopped from setting up his title as against the plaintiff in this action, if the jury believe from the evidence that the plaintiff is a *bona fide* purchaser for value from Light & Wengert without notice. *Answer.* The doctrine of estoppel does not apply unless Mr. Funck in good faith was induced to make the purchase of the books by reason of what Wright said which was communicated to the plaintiff before he made the purchase. The policy of the law, however, will not permit a party to be benefited by his own fraud against a *bona fide* purchaser for value without notice of such fraud. (3d assignment of error.)

(3) If the jury believe that Light & Wengert offered to sell the Meily library to the plaintiff, and exhibited to him their bill of sale from Meily, and that they also offered to sell to said plaintiff at the same time such other books as Wright had afterwards bought and paid for with their money; that the plaintiff refused to buy until he had ascertained what books belonging to Light & Wengert, Wright had in his possession; that to ascertain this fact, he issued a testatum fi. fa. on the Stroh judgment against Wright, directed to the sheriff of Schuylkill County, with directions to make a levy on the books in possession of Wright; that a levy was made upon the books in controversy; that the defendant declared to the sheriff and Wm. R. Smith, Esq., the attorney of the plaintiff, that all the books levied upon and afterwards replevied, belonged to Light & Wengert; that this information was afterwards communicated to the plaintiff, who thereupon relying upon said assertions of Wright, closed the purchase of the books in controversy, and caused the writ of replevin to issue in this case; Wright is estopped and precluded from setting up his title to the property, even if he had any; for by his representation he has misled the plaintiff to his hurt. *Answer.* If the jury find the facts as stated in this point, then we affirm it; if the plaintiff acted in good faith, and was induced to make the purchase to his injury by representations made by defendant, and if such representations would amount to a fraud. (4th assignment of error.)

Upon the close of the plaintiff's testimony the defendant testified that he had bought the books from Mrs. Bibighaus, that Meily had paid for them with the understanding that Wright should have the books if he paid for them within a certain time, that he paid for them himself, and took possession of them, and that Wengert and he agreed together that whilst the books belonged to him he should say that Light & Wengert owned them, for the purpose of evading his creditors. The plaintiff, in rebuttal, offered in evidence the schedules of Wright, who was adjudged a bankrupt in 1868, in which these books were not claimed by him as assets.

Verdict in favor of the defendant for the following books, viz., 1 vol. Parsons's Equity Cases, 1 Brightly's Nisi Prius Reports, 1 Archbold's Blackstone, 4 vols., 1 Binney, 1 Kent's Commentaries, 1 Kent's Commentaries, 4 vols., 1 Penna. Law Journal, 7 vols., 1 Wharton's Criminal Law, 3d edition, 1 Kerr's Blackstone, vol. 1 to 4 of Watts's Reports, Am. Law Registers from '54 to '57, 1 Casey and 22 Harris's Reports, 1 Binney's Report, Annual Digest, 1 Binn's Justice, 2 vols. Beck's Medical Jurisprudence, and with (5) five dollars damages; and find in favor of the plaintiff for all the rest of the books in controversy along with the book-case. Judgment was entered on this verdict.

The defendant took this writ, assigning for error the admission of the plaintiff's evidence excepted to, and the verdict.

James Ryan and *B. W. Cumming*, for plaintiff in error.

Wengert was incompetent to testify, and it was error to admit his evidence.

Gavit *v.* Supplee, 2 WEEKLY NOTES, 561.
Hanna *v.* Wray, 1 Id. 65.

The offer to prove that Wright was a local preacher in order to show that in that character he gained the confidence of Light & Wengert was clearly irrelevant, for the issue was solely in the ownership of the books. It was improper to admit such evidence, for it tended to mislead and prejudice the jury.

Light & Wengert could not have recovered the library in an action of replevin, for they were *in pari delicto* with Wright. Funck bought with full notice of the pretended sale of the books to Light & Wengert, and with full knowledge that they belonged to Wright. The Court will not aid the plaintiff to recover through a fraudulent contract. Funck was not an innocent purchaser, and cannot complain.

Dannels *v.* Fitch, 8 Barr, 495.

The judgment was erroneous, it should have been *de retorno habendo*.

Easton *v.* Worthington, 5 S. & R. 130.

Guy E. Farquhar, for defendant in error.

Wengert, upon release from all liability on his implied warranty of title, was clearly a competent witness.

Railroad Company *v.* Quick, 11 Sm. 328.
Rhines *v.* Baird, 5 Wr. 261.
Smith *v.* Rutherford, 2 S. & R. 360.

The vendor of a chattel in possession at the sale, and bound to the vendee upon the implied warranty of title, is incompetent as a witness unless released.

Kusenberg *v.* Browne, 6 Wr. 173.
Cadbury *v.* Nolen, 5 Barr, 320.

When the interest of the witness is collateral, his competency may be restored by release.

The Act of April 15, 1869, rendered no one incompetent as a witness who was competent before its passage.

Sheetz *v.* Hanbest, 31 Sm. 102.

The admission of evidence to show motive or reason of the confidence reposed in Wright was perfectly proper.

Myre *v.* Ludwig, 1 Barr, 53.

In the Mollie Maguire cases it was held competent for the Commonwealth to show the character and practices of the Mollie Maguire Association for the purpose of showing the motive for their conduct.

Campbell *v.* Commonwealth, 3 Nor. 197.

The plaintiff having shown a perfect title and right of possession to the books, it was incompetent for the defendant to set up a fraud to which he was a party to defend the title, even assuming that Light & Wengert and Funck had all been parties to the fraud.

Blystone *v.* Blystone, 1 Sm. 373.

The order for the delivery of the books was made on Jan. 13, 1860, the next day after the declaration of the defendant in the levy under Stroh's judgment that the books belonged to Light & Wengert.

The defendant is, therefore, estopped from denying title to the plaintiff.

Kelly *v.* Eichman, 3 Wh. 419.

Judgment may be entered on the verdict partly in favor of each party and such judgment will be sustained on an action in replevin.

Johnston *v.* Gray, 19 Pittsburgh L. J. 123.

March 29, 1880. THE COURT. Wengert was, without doubt, a competent witness. He was no party to the suit, and had been released from all liability on his implied warranty of title. He would have been a good witness before the Act of 1869, which made no one incompetent who was competent before. It was not irrelevant to show the intimate relation between Wright and Wengert. The answers of the learned Court to the plaintiff's second and third points put the case to the jury upon the true question. It is certainly proper for the jury, in an action of replevin, to find for the plaintiff some of the goods, and as to the rest for the defendant, and judgment may be entered on such a verdict.

Judgment affirmed.

PER CURIAM.

Common Pleas—Law.

C. P. of Columbia Co.   October, 1880.

Orangeville Mut. Savings Fund and Loan Association v. Young.

Building and loan associations—Act of 1859—By-law fixing minimum rate of premium—Invalidity of—Where a particular loan was not made in pursuance of such by-law, nor is affected thereby, the borrower cannot set up such violation of the Act as a defence to an action for the loan.

The mere fact that a corporation has adopted an illegal by law does not absolve its debtors from compliance with their contracts unaffected by the objectionable by-law.

Although a by-law of a loan association, chartered under the Act of 1859, fixing a minimum rate of premium below which no bid will be received is illegal, yet the contract of a borrowing stockholder is binding, unless the by-law operated to his injury in that particular loan.

If no bid was refused the borrower because it was below the minimum rate, but the loan was awarded to him upon a bid by himself alone, or in consequence of competition with other bidders, at a premium above the minimum, he was not injured by the fact that an illegal rule had been established, and he is liable for the premium so bid.

Stiles's Appeal, 9 WEEKLY NOTES, 83, distinguished.

Rule to show cause why judgment should not be opened and the defendant be let into a defence.

The material facts, as shown by the petition of

the defendant, in support of the rule to show cause, and the answer of the Association plaintiff, were these :—

The Orangeville Mutual Savings Fund and Loan Association is a corporation organized under the general Act of April 12, 1859 (P. L. 544), relating to building and loan associations. The defendant, Phineas Young, a stockholder in said association, bid for and was awarded, at a regular meeting of the association, in May, 1873, a loan of $1000, on five shares of stock, at a premium of $56 a share, he being the highest bidder, making a total premium of $280, and he received the amount of the loan, less the premium. The company had previously passed a by-law fixing a minimum rate of premium below which no bid would be received, but at the meeting when defendant contracted his loan no bid below the minimum was made or refused. Default having occurred judgment was entered against the defendant to December Term, 1873, which judgment was revived by scire facias.

The defendant, in his petition, alleged that he had repaid the principal sum received by him, with lawful interest thereon, and averred that the corporation, by reason of their violation of the provisions of the Act of April 15, 1859, by passing the above-mentioned by-law, were only entitled to recover the actual sum loaned with lawful interest thereon ; and prayed that the judgment be opened, and he be let into a defence, as to the excess included in the judgment.

H. E. Smith, for the rule, contended that under the ruling in the recent case of Stiles's Appeal, the rule must be made absolute.

C. W. Miller, contra.

That the by-law was illegal, under Stiles's Appeal, is not denied. But it is only where the defendant shows that such illegal by-law affects the particular loan in suit, that he can set it up as a defence. This limitation is expressly recognized in Stiles's Appeal. The loan here was not in any way affected by the by-law in question.

Nov. 10, 1880. THE COURT (after stating the facts). Now unless the defendant is entitled to be relieved from the premium he is still in arrear the sum claimed by the plaintiff. Why should he be relieved? The money was sold at a regular meeting. Its price could not have been affected by the minimum rate of premium, for it sold for $24 a share above that rate. The defendant did not offer a bid which was refused because below the minimum, but a bid by himself alone or in consequence of competition with other bids contracted to take money at the sum at which it was struck down to him. It is difficult to understand how he could have been injured by the fact that an illegal rule had been established by the association when, under the facts disclosed, that rule could have no application. Surely the mere fact that a corporation has adopted an illegal by-law does not absolve its debtors from compliance with their contracts uninfluenced by the by-laws.

It is contended by counsel for the defendant that Stiles's Appeal (9 WEEKLY NOTES, 83) goes this length. I do not so understand that case. On the contrary, the single point decided by it is that where a minimum has been fixed, and the defendant makes his loan at the fixed premium, and was refused it at a lower rate, the contract not being made in accordance with the statute is usurious. It is expressly held in that case that it is for the defendant to prove that he was refused the loan below the rate fixed ; that the plaintiff may meet the evidence of the defendant on that subject by counter evidence. If, as now contended, the mere fact that a minimum has been fixed makes all bids of premium nugatory, no proof need be made other than to show the existence of the by-law—such is not the law as held in that case. It is unlawful for such an association to borrow money from banks to loan to stockholders. But a borrower cannot avail himself of the illegal act by showing the practice of the association in this respect ; it will not avail him as a defence unless he can show that the money loaned to him was so borrowed. In other words, it is no defence against the performance of his obligation by the defendant that the rules of the association may, under certain facts, operate injuriously. The question is, has the rule been applied to his injury. That he bid a ruinous sum as a premium is not to be doubted, but that he bid that sum because of any rule of the association is not to be presumed in the face of the facts set forth in the answer of the plaintiff.

The judgment now sought to be opened is a revival by scire facias of the original judgment, No. 206, Dec. Term, 1873, the consideration of which cannot be properly considered under this rule ; but as the question is important not only in this but in other cases, I will dispose of it as if on a rule to open that judgment. Holding that no grounds are laid for opening the revived judgment, nor for attacking the consideration of the original judgment, this rule must be discharged.

Rule discharged.

Opinion by ELWELL, P. J.

C. P. No. 3.   Nov. 6, 1880.

McEntee v. Thomas et al.

Mechanic's lien—A claim for curbing and paving is not within the Act.

Rule to strike off mechanic's claim.

This was a mechanic's claim filed against premises No. 1734 Master Street, for the sum of

$109.83, "being a debt contracted for furnishing and laying Belgian block pavement and resetting curb in front of" said premises, etc. This rule was taken on the ground that the work and materials were not of such a character as to sustain a mechanic's claim.

Wm. H. Burnett (with him *S. C. Perkins*), for the rule.

No *mechanic's* lien can be sustained for the work and materials furnished in this case; it should have been filed as a municipal claim, if at all.

Pierce Archer, contra.

THE COURT. Rule absolute.

C. P. No. 3.   November 27, 1880.

Schneider v. Schneider.

Practice—Answer in divorce nunc pro tunc— When it will not be permitted.

Rule to show cause why the respondent should not be permitted to file an answer in divorce *nunc pro tunc*.

The affidavit of the respondent set forth that by reason of his poverty he was unable to procure counsel to represent him before the examiner appointed in this case until the eighth day of November, 1880; that on November 3, 1880, he attended in person the only meeting held; that he did not, however, cross-examine the witnesses for the libellant, being too ignorant of the English language to question them himself, and being unrepresented by counsel; that he desired to oppose the application for divorce, and he wished to have an opportunity to testify, to produce witnesses, and as he is now represented by counsel, to cross-examine those of the libellant.

Furth, for the rule, cited—
Paulding v. Paulding, 1 WEEKLY NOTES, 159.
Kelley, contra.

THE COURT. (LUDLOW, P. J.). Upon all the facts as they now appear to us we think we should not interfere and permit an answer to be filed *nunc pro tunc*.

Rule discharged.

C. P. No. 4.   Oct. 30, 1880.

Spaulding v. Barber.

Demurrer — Pleading — Practice— Insufficiency or inconsistency of counts of amended narr. to be decided on demurrer, not on motion for leave to file the same.

Rule for leave to file amended narr.

F. W. Patton, for the rule.

It is proposed to substitute the amended narr. for the old narr.

M. Arnold, contra.

The amended narr. has five inconsistent and incongruous counts, and changes the cause, not merely the form, of action.

THE COURT. We will not on a motion to file an amended narr. under the Act of 1871 decide questions of pleading which ought to be raised by a demurrer. Let the amended narr. be filed, and its sufficiency may be argued upon a demurrer.

Rule absolute.

Oral opinion per THAYER, P. J.

Orphans' Court.

Oct. 19, 1880.
Callahan's Estate.

An agreement to re-convey real estate, does not always have the effect of a mortgage—Conveyance in extinguishment of a debt—When failure to present claim at audit will not debar claimant from presenting it after adjudication, and before final distribution.

Sur exceptions to adjudication.

At the audit of this estate the following claims were presented by William C. Houston: (1) A preferred claim for $1200 for one year's rent of premises, Nos. 2013, 2015, and 2017 Locust St., leased by him to decedent; (2) a claim for $500, being rent of same premises for five months prior to the year before decedent's death; and (3) a claim upon a judgment bond executed by decedent, amounting with interest, less certain credits, to $1066.22. It was shown that two of these premises, Nos. 2015 and 2017 Locust St., were conveyed by decedent to claimant, and that these properties were then leased by him to the decedent for five years with the agreement that "the lessee shall have the right and privilege at any time during said term of purchasing from said lessor or his heirs or assigns the premises hereby demised for the price or sum of $8000, subject as respects each of Nos. 2015 and 2017 Locust Street to a yearly ground rent of $70, and upon payment in addition of whatever balance of principal and interest there may be found to be due at the time of such payment on a certain bond executed by said lessee to said lessor for the sum of $1197.54, and bearing even date herewith." These claims, although opposed by creditors, who alleged that the conveyance by decedent to the claimant was a mortgage, and not an absolute conveyance in fee simple, were allowed by the Auditing Judge (HANNA, P. J.), who held, "That there was no evidence which would justify holding the conveyance by decedent to the claimant to be a mortgage, and not an absolute conveyance in fee-simple. The authorities cited by the counsel for creditors are not applicable to the present case. Here there was no advance of money by the claimant to the decedent, and to secure which the conveyance was made by the latter.

"On the contrary the facts all go to show that decedent was antecedently largely indebted to claimant, and that the conveyance was made in part payment of the debt, and to secure the balance the decedent gave at the same time his judgment bond.

"The claimant was previously the owner of 2013 Locust Street, and the decedent being anxious to have this and the two he lately owned, 2015 and 2017, for the purpose of his livery stable business, secured from the then owner a lease for all three, and from the liberality of the lessor, who had been his friend, the option of purchasing all three during the term of five years upon paying a fixed valuation and the balance of his former indebtedness. This is a common every-day transaction, and is yet to be construed as a mortgage and not a conveyance in fee.

"It is also a question of intention whether a deed is a mortgage or is only a provision for a repurchase by the vendor, and this can be determined not only by the instrument itself, but by extrinsic circumstances.

"Without further consideration of the subject it is sufficient to refer to the cases of Allegheny R. R. Co. *v.* Casey (29 P. F. S. 84); Stoever *v.* Stoever (9 S. & R. 446); Haines *v.* Thomson (20 P. F. S. 438); Spering's Appeal (10 P. F. S. 199).

"The claims of Wm. C. Houston are allowed." To this finding exceptions were filed.

L. W. Barringer (with him *W. H. Peace*), for exceptants.

The deed of conveyance by decedent to claimant and the lease of claimant to decedent, each bearing the same date and forming one and the same transaction, show that the former was intended to be in law but a mortgage and not an absolute conveyance to the claimant in fee. In confirmation of this view, that it is simply a mortgage and the equity of redemption and fee in the property remained in the decedent, it appears that the claimant as landlord never collected any rent under his lease from its date down to the death of decedent.

Harper's Appeal, 14 Sm. 315.
Haines *v.* Thomson, 20 Sm. 438.
Kunkle *v.* Wolfersberger, 6 Watts, 126.

Johnson *v.* Gray, 16 S & R. 364.
Brown *v.* Nickle, 6 Barr, 391.

T. A. Porter (with him *J. B. Townsend*), contra.

The deed and lease, although both bear the same date, do not in law make a mortgage; the fee to these premises is in the claimant, and has been from the delivery of the deed. In the deed *two* properties are conveyed; in the lease *three* are demised. The consideration to be paid in case the lessee desires to repurchase the premises within five years is entirely different from that recited in the conveyance by him to the claimant. Although the lessor never collected rent, the lease was never disputed by the decedent, who occupied and used the premises from the date of the lease until his death.

Stoever *v.* Stoever, 9 S. & R. 446.
Conway *v.* Alexander, 7 Cranch, 218.
Haines *v.* Thomson, *supra.*
Coote on Mortgages, 11 and 22.
Lane *v.* Shears, 1 Wend. 433.
Spering's Ap., 10 Sm. 199.
Frick's Ap., 6 Norris, 331.

The law of Pennsylvania provides that the preferred debts must be paid *in full,* which of course includes interest, and the *pro rata* payment only takes place between creditors of the same class, and there is no intention to make any deduction from the debts of a prior class in order to let in those of a later.

Scott on Intestate Law, 186.
Shultz's Ap., 11 S. & R. 184.

J. P. Kennedy presented the claim of G. W. Marsh, a creditor, who was prevented by sickness from receiving notice of the audit or appearing at the time fixed for it.

Though a creditor neglect to present his claim within the time prescribed by law, he has a right to come in on the fund at any time before an actual distribution.

Smith's Estate, 1 Ash. 352.

October 30, 1880. THE COURT. To what extent, when the decedent made the conveyance of his two Locust Street properties, taking back a lease with an agreement for a reconveyance, any previous indebtedness from him to his vendee constituted an element of the transaction, does not appear; but that the debt for which the bond of the same date was given was intended to be secured, is clear from the stipulation that, in addition to the sum specified to be paid for the reconveyance, "whatever balance of principal and interest there may be found to be due at the time" on such bond, shall also be paid.

There may undoubtedly be cases where a conveyance is accepted by a creditor in satisfaction and extinguishment of the debt; and where, therefore, there being no longer any debt to secure, an agreement to reconvey cannot have the effect of turning the transaction into a mortgage. Such were the cases of Spering's Appeal

(10 Smith, 199); Haines *v.* Thomson (20 Smith, 438), etc. But in the face of the provision with regard to this bond, it is not easy to see how, in the present instance, the conveyance can be said to have extinguished the debt.

Nor is it material that the agreement to reconvey assumed the shape of a lease, or that besides the property embraced in the deed, it included another property that was not. . As was said in Kunkle *v.* Wolfersberger (6 Watts, 130), "It is too late to say that what was intended as a security for money may become a conditional sale by the accidental or designed form of the transaction." In Hiester *v.* Maderia (3 W. & S. 584), the conveyance was effected by means of a sheriff's sale; and in Houser *v.* Lamont (5 Smith, 311), by an Orphans' Court sale. (See also Harper's Appeal, 14 Smith, 315.)

The question, however, is one involving title to real estate, and not simply affecting the rights of the exceptants to an increase of dividend in the present distribution.

Should we now hold, contrary to the opinion of the Auditing Judge, that the decedent's conveyance operated only as a mortgage, and that the ownership of the lands remained in him, we should next be asked for an order of Court for their sale for payment of debts. With the title thus unsettled, no sale would be practicable except at a ruinous sacrifice; and it is by no means certain that the views of the Auditing Judge may not be those adopted by the Court of final resort.

Under all the circumstances of the case we have therefore concluded to dismiss the exceptions *pro forma*, thus placing the matter in shape for speedy review, with the least possible expense and trouble to the parties interested.

The claim of G. W. Marsh having been admitted by both accountant and creditors, and the failure to present it at proper time having been explained, we think he should be permitted to participate in the distribution.

The adjudication is therefore amended so as to include his name in the list of creditors whose claims are allowed. Counsel will prepare a schedule of redistribution, which, upon approval by the Auditing Judge, will be substituted for that heretofore made.

Exceptions dismissed *pro forma* and adjudication as amended confirmed.

Opinion by PENROSE, J.

November 13, 1880.

Rice's Estate.

Minors' estates—Under what circumstances a foreign guardian may interfere with ward's estate in this Commonwealth—Acts of March 29, 1832, April 21, 1856, and May 25, 1871—Practice.

Sur petition for citation to administrator to show cause why he should not enter additional security.

The petitioner set forth that she is the guardian of the person and estate of William J. Rice, a minor, appointed by the Probate Court of Jackson County, Michigan; that the father of the minor died in the city of Jackson, Michigan, on or about October 10, 1879, possessed of personal property within the jurisdiction of this Court, and letters of administration were granted thereon by the register of this county on October 21, 1879, to Michael Rice. That said administrator has not filed any inventory as required by law, and petitioner is also informed and believes that the estate of said decedent has been wasted and mismanaged by said Michael Rice. She therefore prayed a citation to him to show cause why he should not enter additional security, or be dismissed from his office as administrator.

Fow & Anderson, for petitioner.

November 20, 1880. THE COURT. It is clear the petitioner has no standing in this Court. The Act of March 29, 1832 (Purdon, 412, pl. 36), expressly declares: "No appointment of guardian, made or granted by any authority out of this State, shall authorize the person so appointed to interfere with the estate or control the person of a minor in this State." This remained the law until it was afterwards considered expedient by the Legislature to authorize foreign guardians and others acting in a fiduciary relation to transfer the public loans of the State, of the city and county of Philadelphia, stocks and loans of banks and incorporated companies, and collect the interest and dividends thereon.

The several statutes upon the subject provided no further, and the only escape from the prohibition contained in the Act referred to was in the proviso that the "foreign guardian may, at the discretion of the Court, be appointed by the Orphans' Court having jurisdiction, on giving security for the due performance of his trust." The question arose in Estate of Wm. Colesbury (1 Phil. Rep. 300), upon the application of a foreign guardian to pay over moneys of decedent's minors. But the petition was refused, THOMPSON, C. J., citing the Act of 1832, and saying "the order sought for would be directly at variance with the spirit of the statute, as it would most certainly enable the foreign guardian most effectually to interfere with the estate of the minors, by placing it entirely beyond the control of the Court, and taking away all jurisdiction over it." The Court further held the proper practice to be that indicated by the proviso to the Act. The result of this application probably prompted the passage of the Act of April 21, 1856 (Purdon, 412, pl. 37-38), whereby it is provided that "in such cases where any guardian and his ward may both be non-residents of this State, and such ward is entitled to property of any description in this State, such guardian, on producing satisfactory proof . . . by certificates, according to the Acts of Congress in such cases, that he has given bond and security in the State in which he and his ward reside in double the amount of the value of the property as guardian, and it is found that a removal of the property will not conflict with the terms or limitations attending the right by which the ward owns the same, then any such guardian may demand or sue for and remove any such property to the place of residence of himself and ward." And by the second section of the Act, if the previous requisites have been complied with, the non-resident guardian may be authorized to receive the estate and property of his wards, and the resident guardian, executor, or administrator, as the case may be, discharged. But the Legislature was careful not to extend this privilege "to the citizens of any State in which a similar Act does not exist or may not hereafter be passed."

The question as to the right of a foreign guardian to sue in the courts of this State directly arose in Verrier v. Verrier (7 Phil. Rep. 618), in which it was held by WILLIAMS, J., at Nisi Prius, that no such right could be recognized either in a suit at law or in equity, unless such guardian was duly appointed and authorized by the Orphans' Court having jurisdiction, on giving security as provided by the Act of 1832. This was decided in 1870, and the Act of 1856 does not seem to have been brought to the attention of Justice WILLIAMS, as he makes no reference to its provisions.

In the present case both guardian and ward are non-residents, and it does not appear that the former has entered security in double the amount of the minor's property, which is necessary to entitle her to "demand or sue for" such property, nor that a similar Act has been passed by the Legislature of Michigan reciprocally extending the privilege now sought for to the citizens of this State.

The Acts of 1832 and 1856 are *in pari materia*, and both in force. Under the former the petitioner has no right whatever to appear as a complainant in this Court, and under the latter her petition is so radically defective that no proceedings can be had upon it. A further Act (May 25, 1871) was passed modifying the strict requirements of the Act of 1856, whereby it is rendered discretionary with the Court to authorize payment of a legacy or distributive share belonging to a minor to his foreign guardian upon the certificate of the Probate Judge, etc., that security sufficient to secure the faithful appropriation of the money so paid over has been duly entered. But the prior Acts referred to are not repealed. For the reasons stated, the petition is dismissed.

Opinion by HANNA, P. J.

O. C. of Dauphin Co.   March, 1880.

Bogle's Estate.

Catching bargains—Expectant heirs and legatees Unfair advantage—Under what circumstances a purchase of a legacy payable at a future time, at a usurious discount, will be set aside in equity, notwithstanding the party imposed upon was of full age—Fraud upon testator.

Sur exceptions to auditor's report.

Ralph Bogle, by his will directed that the remainder of his estate should be equally divided among his children, and further provided as follows:—

"In regard to my three children who are in their minority, I direct that the interest on their shares be applied to their education and support by their guardian until they arrive at the age of twenty-one years respectively; then each to receive of the *principal*, $2000 per annum until they arrive respectively at the age of twenty-five years, and from that time until they reach twenty-eight, respectively, the sum of $3000 per annum; when they arrive respectively at this age then the whole principal and interest to be paid to them."

Charles E. Bogle, a son of the testator, entitled under the above clause, after attaining the age of 23 years entered into an agreement with one Isaac Sticker, of the following character, as shown by the testimony before the auditor:—

Sticker was a money-lender living at Milton, Pa., with whom Charles E. Bogle had had dealings prior to the transaction detailed below. In April, 1877, Charles applied to him for a loan of $3000, upon the security of his expected receipt of $3000 upon his arrival at 25 years of age, which would happen in February, 1879. It was stipulated that the rate of interest should be 18 per cent. per annum. Charles executed at Milton an assignment of his vested interest in expectancy in the said sum of $3000; but the parties finding upon application to the guardian and trustee of Charles (Ex-Governor Pollock) that the amount due Bogle in February, 1879, would be about $3500, instead of $3000, the above contract was modified so as to cover the additional $500; the assignment executed at Milton was destroyed, and a new assignment was executed and delivered in Philadelphia. This paper, dated April 11, 1877, recited that under the above clause of the will, a legacy of $3500 "will be due and payable to the said Charles E. Bogle on the 16th day of February, 1879," and that "Isaac Sticker, of Milton, has agreed to *purchase* said legacy, and has *purchased* the same, for the sum of $3500, which sum the said Isaac Sticker has this day paid to the said Charles E. Bogle;" and witnessed that said Bogle absolutely sold and assigned the aforesaid legacy or amount to Sticker. Bogle also gave a letter of attorney for its collection, and a written authority to the executors and to his trustee to pay it over to Sticker when due.

The consideration passing from Sticker to Bogle was shown to be as follows:—

Cash (in two sums to pay judgments against Bogle), $75; $60; also in money, $357.50 $492 50
Mortgage, due to Sticker by Bogle . 242 50
Note, Sticker to Bogle @ 6 mos. without interest 576 63
Note, Sticker to Bogle @ 12 mos. without interest 576 63
Note, Sticker to Bogle payable Feb. 16, 1879 500

Bogle also executed a collateral agreement that any costs or expenses which Sticker might incur in enforcing or defending his claim to the legacy should be deducted from the amount of the last note of $500.

The above mentioned mortgage of $242.50 had been given for a former loan at 18 per cent. interest. Sticker afterwards took up the above notes as follows:—

For the 6 mos. note of $576.63 he paid $558.
For the 12 mos. note of $576.63 he paid 500.
For the note payable Feb. '79, of 500 he paid $250.

Thus the actual cash value paid by Sticker was about $2000.

Before the legacy was payable, Bogle gave notice to his trustee not to pay the money to Sticker, whereupon the trustee filed his account in the Orphans' Court showing a balance of $3518.98, which account was by agreement referred to an auditor (Geo. H. Irwin) to report distribution.

Before the auditor Sticker claimed to receive $3500, under the above assignment. He testified that the transaction was an absolute purchase by and sale to him of the legacy at a certain discount—about $1080. Bogle testified that the transaction was one of loan; that he originally agreed to borrow $2000, on the security of the expected $3000, for which he was to pay interest at the rate of 18 per cent. (the rate paid in former dealings), and that although the assignment was drawn as an absolute sale, it was intended and understood by both parties as security. The attorney who drew the document (James B. Roney) testified that he prepared it in pursuance of the wish expressed by both the parties, that he should draw *a bill of sale* "as tight as a Philadelphia lawyer could draw it . . . and I tried to do it."

The auditor found the transaction to be a sale, and not a loan, and reported, *inter alia*, as follows:—

"It was urged that even if the facts should demonstrate a sale, the bargain was an unconscionable one, and so repugnant to justice that equity would relieve Bogle from his contract. There is perhaps no doubt that contracts of this kind made with improvident, reckless, and necessitous heirs expectant are set aside by the Courts either for fraud upon the parties, or for fraud upon a third person, that is the ancestor. Such cases were cited on argument, but they have no bearing on the facts of this case. There is no allegation of fraud practised by Sticker, the purchaser, and no proof indicative of any in all or any part of the circumstances. Bogle was entirely capable of assent, and competent to act as he did: he was twenty-four years of age at the date of the assignment, was married, and had been in business several years up to the present contest; every act of his was in confirmation of his bargain, for he presented when they became due, and received the money on the three notes, He was as fully informed as he could be or as Sticker was of everything relating to the subject-matter. The legacy was vested, there was no contingence connected with it; his interest in it had begun nineteen years before this contract was made; it was quite as susceptible of bargain or sale as any other of his property, and free from the control or claim of any third person whatever. It may be that the bargain was a losing one to Bogle, as Sticker meant it to be a profitable one to himself; but it is only one of numberless instances where the improvidence and recklessness of one man give opportunity for the exercise of the thrift of another. But 'a man may be as honest in making a profitable bargain as a bad one; and the law does not require him to pay a full price if the person he is dealing with is willing to take less. The owner of property may sell it for very little or give it away for nothing, if he thinks fit; and however unreasonable his conduct may seem, his will alone is sufficient to avouch the act.' (Davidson *v.* Little, 10 Harris, 245, 252.) If the vendor was thoroughly acquainted with every fact which it was necessary for him to know; if he was twenty-one years of age, and of sound mind; if there were no circumstances which gave the vendee an improper control over him amounting to mental imprisonment; if in short the vendee behaved honestly, and the vendor was able to act like a free man, with his eyes open, then the one had a right to sell and the other to buy on any terms they saw proper to agree upon. The law will never interfere between the parties themselves, to set aside an honest contract which they have voluntarily made.

"There can be in this case no pretext for complaint, except that the price paid by Sticker is not commensurate with the value of the legacy, but it is as frequently decided by the Courts, as the point is made that inadequacy of price, however gross, is not sufficient to annul a contract of sale, or to set aside a conveyance (Davidson v. Little, *supra*; Harris v. Tyson, 12 Harris, 347; Cummings's Appeal, 17 P. F. Smith, 404); though in this case there is some testimony showing that in Sticker's opinion the circumstance of this legacy having been in the hands of a testamentary guardian without security for some twenty years, and not being due for two years after its purchase, lent more than a common risk to his investment. Nor was it of any consequence that Bogle was a poor man. (Harris v. Tyson, *supra*.) If it is the business of courts to reform the contracts, and mould the consequences of the recklessness or improvidence of persons of responsible years, acting with full knowledge of the circumstances, and to restrain others dealing with them to only such advantages as would be gained in the bargain made between equally shrewd persons, the standard of the measure of ability to contract as well as of the rate of gain, would be constantly shifting to adjust itself to the various specific circumstances of every case. Whoever has the right to give has the right to dispose of the same as he pleases. (Ashhurst v. Given, 5 W. & S. 323.) It is not essential to the validity of a contract that the consideration should be *adequate* in point of actual value, the law having no means of deciding this matter. There being no incompetency to contract, no violation of the law, no fraud practised in the making of the agreement, it would be unwise to interfere with the free exercise of the judgment and will of the parties by not permitting them to be the sole judges of the benefits to be derived from their bargains. (Chitty on Contracts, 31.)

"The auditor therefore awards out of the balance in the hands of James Pollock, testamentary guardian of Charles E. Bogle, the sum of $3500 to Isaac Sticker."

To this finding exceptions were filed by Bogle.

W. M. Mervine and *J. M. Moyer*, for exceptant.

(1) The contract was usurious, and the assignment was a colorable shift to avoid the Statute of Usury.

Chamberlain v. McClurg, 8 W. & S. 36.
Bosler v. Rheem, 22 Sm. 54.
Greene v. Tyler & Co., 3 Wr. 361.
Ins. Co. v. Bruner, 1 WEEKLY NOTES, 147.
Evans v. Negley, 13 S. & R. 218.

Where the negotiations commenced on an interest basis, or where interest was proposed or demanded, and it ended in a sale or assignment, with the view of securing more than six per cent. interest, it falls within the Statute of Usury, and must be set aside.

Fitzsimons v. Baum, 8 Wr. 32.

(2) The contract is grossly unconscionable. It is in the nature of a *post obit* contract, and cannot be sustained. Equity will exercise its power to protect the heedless and necessitous person against the designs of the calculating rapacity which the law constantly denounces, and of guarding the distress frequently incident to the owners of unprofitable reversions. Equity constantly grants relief in what are called catching bargains with heirs and expectants. Equity considers the circumstances or conditions of the parties contracting from weakness on one side and usury on the other, or extortion and advantage taken of that weakness; the unconscionableness being the ground of action.

Story's Eq., sec. 334, 335.

Such contracts operate as a fraud upon the bounty of the ancestor, and disappoint his intentions.

Boynton v. Hubbard, 7 Mass. 112, 119, 120.
Story's Eq., sec. 342, 344, 347.

In such cases it is not alone the fraud but the example and the pernicious consequences which constitute the ground for relief.

Gwynne v. Heaton, 1 Brown's Chan. Rep. 9.
Boynton v. Hubbard, 7 Mass. 122.

Paying 18 per cent. and receiving instead of cash long time notes without interest, brings the case within the rule laid down in—

Rose v. Dickson, 7 Johns. 196.
Eagleson v. Shotwell, 1 John. Ch. 536.
Hine v. Handy, Id. 6.
Foster v. Kilber, 1 Paige, 543.
Pratt v. Adams, 7 Paige, 615.

In Twifleton v. Griffith (1 P. Williams, 310), the Lord Chancellor set aside an assignment of this kind on payment of the money advanced and legal interest, on the ground of its being an unconscionable bargain. The same principle is held in—

Attorney General v. Brown, 1 Wilson, 323.
Berny v. Pitt, 2 Ver. 13.
Davis v. Duke of Marlborough, 2 Swanston, 147 and notes.

In Barnardiston v. Lingood (2 Atkyns, 134), the Lord Chancellor denounced such an agreement as "a catching bargain against a necessitous and improvident heir."

James J. Chamberlain and *Thos. J. Barger*, contra, relied on the principles and authorities referred to by the auditor.

April, 1880. THE COURT (after stating the facts). We have no doubt that this business commenced as a loan at Milton, as the sum of

$1080 to be deducted from the $3000 in expectancy tends to show. Also the effort made by Sticker to prove before the auditor that Bogle had made oath that he never would contest the claim of Sticker on account of usury. Why make such an oath, or exact it, if there was no loan? Nothing was said in presence of Mr. Hackenburg about a loan when he drew the first writings, nor would there be if the design was to extort unreasonable and illegal interest—eighteen per cent.! No doubt he understood it as a sale, and so drew the writings, as desired by both. It is, perhaps, the course ordinarily pursued on such occasions. The writings are fair on their face, and show nothing illegal, but courts would be very stupid, says Mr. Justice WOODWARD, in Fitzsimons v. Baum (8 Wright, 45, 46), if they did not look beyond the writings to discover the true transaction.

We may safely say that in all of these questions of usury the more carefully and strongly the writings are drawn, the more necessary to receive parol evidence to overturn them, and contradict all that is set forth on their face. It was decided as far back as Chamberlain v. McClurg (8 W. & S. 36), that a party is not prevented from showing in contradiction of the writing that the transaction was usurious. The same doctrine has been held in very many cases since. We have no doubt that when the bargaining commenced, and when the writing was drawn at Milton, it was to secure a usurious loan; but that will not preclude the parties from making a new contract afterwards in Philadelphia for a different sum of money and on different terms. When they went there it was for the double purpose of finding how much was due from the guardian, and what liens might by possibility be found to exist against it. They then made a new contract, as prepared and proved by Mr. Roney. That, we are satisfied, was one of sale and not a loan of money. This we found not on the oath of either party, but on the writing and the oath of Mr. Roney. The whole transaction between the parties shows it.

We next come to another and more important point, Was the transaction such as should be supported and enforced in a Court of Equity—the Orphans' Court? We find Bogle, a young man between twenty-three and twenty-four years of age, having been engaged in the grocery business for two or three years, to all appearances pretty closely pressed for money, borrowing from Mr. Sticker, or his wife, some $2000, at a rate of interest of 18 per cent. per annum, and applying to the same person for a new loan at like rate, this on the security of his patrimony—in the hands of his guardian and not due for a little over a year. We find him afterwards selling the claim at a discount of at least $1000, receiving in payment the discharge of two small judgments amounting in all to $135, the balance due on a former mortgage, $200, some $357 in money, some small expenses paid, and notes at 6 and 12 months, $576.63 each, some $250 of a discount on the $500, and at least one of the notes, if not both, shaved at a discount of about 18 per cent. Mr. Bogle swears that he was to have the money when wanted.

The question before the auditor was, Is this such an oppressive and fraudulent advantage taken of Bogle under the circumstances as will entitle him to relief in equity? We must premise that his guardian, who had looked after his affairs for many years, and who stood *in loco parentis*, is not made acquainted with the intended sale. He testified that he knew nothing of the transaction in this particular; we receive different testimony from Sticker, whom we do not believe when he comes in conflict with a disinterested witness like Governor Pollock. Bogle makes a sale in advance of a legacy, not due for over a year, at a very heavy discount, and all paid in notes, which it is said could be better sold at a discount than could a legacy. Is not this *catching a bargain* from one having an estate in expectancy? Does it not amount to a fraud in law? Mere inadequacy of price is not generally a ground for setting aside a contract, yet in cases of this sort it has been held sufficient to set aside a sale. In Story's Eq. Juris., secs. 335–337, this doctrine is applied to those having estates in expectancy only, but it goes much further and embraces those having *vested interests*, if not at their command, and the owner is necessitous. (Idem, secs. 337, 338). It throws on the purchaser the burden of proving that he paid full price. Young and expectant heirs are frequently relieved on the same principle, as *post obit* obligations. (Sect. 348.) A host of authorities are cited for this. In 1 Maddock, Ch., 62, we find the same doctrine and applied still further to any one dealing with an expectancy. (See pp. 118, 119, 120.)

But the conveyance if set aside must generally be done on the purchase-money being refunded with interest. In the leading case of Chesterfield v. Janssen (1 Leading Cases in Equity, Hare & Wallace's Edition, p. 541) the whole subject is fully examined. We may also cite to the same effect the doctrines laid down by Chancellor KENT; see notes to same work, p. 590. (See also Juzan v. Toulmin, 9 Alabama, 663; an opinion by COLVIN, J., Jenkins v. Pye, 12 Peters, 241.) All agree as to the general doctrine, that mere inadequacy is no ground for setting aside a sale, but make an exception in favor of heirs in expectancy of an estate whether vested or contingent.

The case presents these principles in brief. A

father desirous of securing an adequate maintenance for his minor son, places his patrimony in the hands of a testamentary guardian, fixing the amount to be applied to his support annually, until he should attain the age of twenty-five years, thereby pretty clearly showing that until he attained that age he would not be capable of managing his own affairs with judgment. About eighteen months before reaching that age a business man of mature years bargains with him for the purchase of the whole balance at a discount in all of over 33 per cent., after learning from the guardian the precise amount which would be coming. This we consider is taking advantage of the situation of a necessitous young man in buying his expectancy, and is what the law will not tolerate. It defeats the object of the father in tying up the estate of his son, in the hands of the guardian, to prevent its being squandered.

It is therefore ordered that out of the money paid into the Orphans' Court there be first applied the expense of the audit and other costs, and that there be next paid the amount paid by Sticker to Bogle with legal interest thereon from the time of payment until the same was deposited in the Orphans' Court, and that the case be referred back to the auditor to fix the amount due, and the residue of the fund we adjudge to Charles E. Bogle.

Opinion by PEARSON, P. J.

[*Cf.* Nevill *v.* Snelling, English High Court, Ch. Div., 43 L. T. (N. S.) 244.]

O. C. of Adams County.

Wolf's Estate.

Decedent's estate—Legacies, when chargeable upon land—Advancements—Widow's dower—Act of April 8, 1833.

Sur exceptions to auditor's report.

The testator, by his will, after providing for the payment of his debts and funeral expenses, devised as follows:—

"I will unto my beloved wife, Anna Mary, the one-third of all my personal estate, and the annual interest of the one-third of all my real estate, and in lieu of the three-hundred-dollar law, her home at my residence during her life if she so desires. I will unto my daughter, Harriet Rife, the annual interest of one thousand dollars during her life. I give and bequeath unto my grandchildren of my daughter Leah Emlet, deceased, as follows: Winsadore Emlet, Mary Emlet, and Elmyra Emlet each one hundred dollars one year after my decease, and fifty dollars to John Emlet one year after my decease, and four hundred dollars to each of the three youngest children of my daughter, Leah Emlet, deceased, one year after my decease.

"I will that Adkin George Wolf and Christina Wolf, children of my son, Henry Wolf, shall each have a full share with my hereafter named children. I further give unto Christina Wolf my piano, if she remains with me until my decease.

"I will and bequeath unto my following named children, Mary Ann Hearshey, intermarried with Samuel Hearshey, Rebecca Mowrey, intermarried with John Mowrey, Caroline Etzler, intermarried with William Etzler, Jacob Nathaniel Wolf, Washington B. Wolf, Dr. Henry Wolf, share and share alike. And such charges as I have made against my children or legatees shall be considered as advancements.

"My further will and meaning is that if any of my children or legatees should go or attempt to go to law, or make any objection to this my last will and testament, shall not inherit anything out of my estate."

The auditor, to whom the account of the executors was referred, reported, *inter alia*, as follows:—

"There were several questions raised as to how this estate should be distributed under the will. The counsel for the widow claimed that she was entitled to one-third of *all* the testator's personal property, including the charges against the heirs in ascertaining it; and that the legacies are not to affect or diminish this one-third of the personal estate bequeathed to the widow, but are to be taken out of the proceeds of the sale of real estate.

"The counsel for Dr. Henry Wolf, and Adkin George Wolf, and Christina Wolf, minor children of Dr. Henry Wolf, claimed for each of these children a share equal to the rest of the residuary legatees under a clause of the will, and objected to bringing any of the advancements into hotchpot for the purpose of ascertaining the widow's third of the personalty.

"The counsel for the other legatees also objected to bringing the advancements into hotchpot for the purpose of ascertaining the widow's third, and demanded that the debts, expenses, and legacies be paid out of the personal estate if sufficient, etc. . . . . .

"In the consideration of the second question, viz., out of which fund are the debts and legacies payable, it was contended on the one hand, very properly, that the personal estate is the primary fund for their payment. . . . . .

"A careful examination of the will before us tends to convince one that there is a sufficient blending of the realty and personalty, in contemplation of law, to charge land with the payment of debts and legacies on a deficiency of the personal estate. The law implies an intention of the testator so to charge land from a devise of the residue of his estate generally. (Mellon's Appeal, 10 Wright, 175.) There is such a devise in this case. . . . . .

"But if the debts, expenses, and legacies are to be paid from the personal estate, there will be a large deficiency, and the legatees will have to do with very little or nothing at all.

'It was manifestly the intention of the testator to provide amply for his widow. Mrs. Wolf is an aged woman; in fact, in too feeble a condition to appear before your auditor. It would not be just to attribute to her husband the intention of allowing her but a small portion of his personal estate, when by a more liberal, and at the same time legitimate construction of his will, that intention can be interpreted to be to provide for her more bountifully. It is also to be presumed that he intended the special legatees should have the benefit of his bequests. They are a daughter and the seven children of a deceased daughter. If the debts and expenses are paid out of the personal estate before the legacies, the widow's third of the balance will be very small in comparison with the whole estate, and there will not be enough left to pay the pecuniary legacies. . . .

"If the debts and expenses are paid first, Mrs. Wolf is only entitled to one-third of $1416.24, or $472.08, leaving $944.16 to meet the pecuniary legacies of $2550. If the legacies are paid first, the following will be the showing: the widow's share, to wit, one-third of all the personalty $2429.00⅔; pecuniary legacies $2550.00, leaving a deficiency of nearly four thousand dollars. Distribute this personal fund as we may, there will not be enough to satisfy all the claims on it, if it is the only fund out of which they are to be paid. But the estate of Henry Wolf is large and abundantly able to meet all the provisions of his will. This of itself is not sufficient to justify a construction unwarranted by anything else, nor should we give it any such importance. It can be used, however, as an element in arriving at the intention of the testator; it is only in this light we view it. . . . . Therefore, we find a sufficient blending of the personal and real estate in the will of Henry Wolf to charge the payment of debts, expenses, and legacies on the fund arising from the sale of real estate after the personal fund has been exhausted; we also find that Anna Mary Wolf, widow of the testator, should be paid one-third of the personal fund, unaffected by the debts and pecuniary legacies; and we shall report a distribution of this estate accordingly. . . . . The debts and expenses have been paid out of the personal fund. We also direct the expenses of this audit to be paid from the same fund. The balance shall go toward paying the widow her share under the will. The residue of her share shall be retained by her out of the fund in her hands as trustee."

To these findings of the auditor exceptions were filed by Polly Hearshey *et al.*, legatees.

David Wills, for exceptants.

Wm. A. Duncan, for widow and trustee.

Sept. 21, 1877. THE COURT. The main subject of consideration in this contention is the will of Henry Wolf, deceased. It is a legitimate presumption that its provisions were contemplated, conceived, and framed in knowledge of, and conformably with, the law of the land, unless the contrary distinctly appears. The testator's first direction is that all his debts and the expenses and charges shall be paid as soon as possible after his decease. He then gives to his wife the one-third of all his personal estate, and the annual interest of the one-third of all his real estate, "and in lieu of the three-hundred-dollar law her home," at his residence during her life, if she so desires. Have we not here disclosed full knowledge of the law on the part of testator, and a manifest intention to conform to its provisions in the premises? Have we not a striking analogy to the Act of 1833, which starts out with directing that the real and personal estate of a decedent remaining after payment of all just debts and legal charges, which shall not have been sold or disposed of by will, shall be divided and enjoyed as therein provided; first, the widow being entitled to one-third part of the real estate for the term of her life, and to one-third part of the personal estate absolutely. Did Henry Wolf intend more for his widow than this? If so, the will does not show it, in our judgment.

The testator died possessed of personal estate amounting, according to its appraised value, to $7287.01, and seized of a considerable quantity of valuable real estate. The only reference he makes to the latter in his will is in the clause we have mentioned, providing for the widow.

In the disposition of his estate otherwise, he has blended the personal and real, and therefore the auditor is necessarily right in finding the land charged with the payment of the legacies, but not with debts when there is no deficiency of the personal estate. We apprehend the auditor has provided more liberally for the widow than the testator has, and has erred in his conclusion and distribution. The widow should be no more a favorite than any other legatee. What did the testator intend? We answer, from our reading of the will, he at least permitted the personal estate, as by law directed, to be charged first with the debts and expenses, and then gave her the one-third of it, as it turns out, the one-third of the sum of $1416.24 less share of expenses of audit, thus leaving a balance, to which must be added so much of the assets as will pay the pecuniary legacies. One-third of the purchase-money of the real estate has been set apart to the widow, as shown by the accounts of the trustees, to be kept at interest for her, and the residue remaining after payment of the balance of pecuniary legacies should be distributed with the advancements among the residuary legatees.

We must follow the cardinal rule that the personal estate of a deceased constitutes the primary and natural fund for the payment of his debts, and that it must be so applied, unless it be expressly or by plain implication exonerated and discharged by the will of a testator. (1 Story's Eq. § 571; Mogg v. Hodges, 2 Ves., Sr., 52; Galton v. Hancock, 2 Atk. 424-25.) It cannot be contended that the bequest to the widow, of personal property, in this case is specific.

In the case of Samuel Walker's Estate (3 Rawle, 229), the testator gave to his wife "all his household goods and furniture, moneys, bonds, mortgages, outstanding debts due and owing to him and all other his personal estate of what nature or kind soever." Yet the Supreme Court held that this bequest was not specific, and that it was to be applied to the payment of his debts, there being nothing in the will which showed an intention to exempt it, and further, there was no direction in that will to pay debts.

In the case of Shaw v. McCameron et al., Adm'rs of Scott (11 S. & R. 252), relied upon by the counsel for the widow, the devise of the testator was to his only child of the one-half of his estate, real and personal, what it will amount to in money, and he directed his executors to put it out at interest during her life, and pay the proceeds to her, etc. "The rest or remaining part" he gave to his brothers and sisters. Mr. Justice GIBSON in that case states that he founds his opinion chiefly on the consideration that the bequest was a provision for a child, which will always be decreed as favorably for the child as the words will bear. In the estate at bar the residuary legatees are children of the testator. The Justice who delivered the opinion in the case of Shaw v. McCameron et al. was the Chief-Justice of the Court which decided the case of Samuel Walker's Estate eight years afterwards.

In Hanna's Appeal (7 Casey, 57), it is held that the personal estate is not relieved from liability in the first instance by a direction in the will making the legacies a charge on the real estate unless that intention be indicated by the testator. When assets are received by the executor sufficient to cover the expenses of administration, satisfy debts, etc., the real estate is discharged from further liability. (See also Phipps v. Phipps, 3 P. L. J. Rep. 275; and also Ann Myers's Appeal, 12 Wright, 16, cited on the argument.) The case of Martin et al., Exec'rs of Martin, v. Fry (17 S. & R. 426) is analogous in some respects to the case at bar. Samuel Fry, after bequeathing a few small specific articles to his wife, bequeathed to her as follows: "The one-third part of my personal estate." It was held that the whole of the debts must be first paid out of the personal estate, and the one-third of the remainder thereof passed by the will to the widow. The testator left real estate, gave some specific legacies to his children, and the residue of his estate to be equally divided among all his children. It was contended there as here that the bequest of the third part of the personal estate to the widow was a specific one. The Supreme Court decided it was not.

The exceptions to the auditor's report are sustained, and the report is recommitted to the auditor, with direction to deduct from the amount of personal assets ($1416.24) the sum of $33.28, one-third of the expenses of audit, thus leaving a balance of $1382.96, and to distribute the one-third ($460.98⅔) of this balance to Anna Mary Wolf, the widow, as her legacy of personal estate, and to apply the remaining personal assets after remaining expenses of audit to the pecuniary legacies, and then to apply so much of the real assets as may be needed to pay the pecuniary legacies and interest thereon in full, giving to the youngest three children of Leah Emlet $400 each, and interest accordingly, and to bring into hotch-pot the advancements to Caroline Etzler, with the advancements to Polly Hearshey, Rebecca Mowery, Dr. Henry Wolf, and Washington B. Wolf, as in schedule of distribution and make distribution of the remaining real assets with the advancements as aforesaid, among the seven residuary legatees.

Opinion by McCLEAN, P. J.

U. S. Circuit Court— Law.

Oct. 26, 1880.

Henry J. Anderson, Receiver, etc., v. The Philadelphia Warehouse Company.

New trial—Revised Statutes, §§ 5139 and 5151— National Currency Acts—Transfer of national bank stock as collateral security—Under what circumstances pledgee is liable to assessments in case of insolvency of the bank.

Motion for new trial, and for judgment on points reserved.

Assumpsit, by the Receiver of the First National Bank of Allentown, a banking association, organized under the National Currency Acts, against The Philadelphia Warehouse Company, a corporation, to recover an assessment of $20 per share upon four hundred and fifty shares of the stock of said bank, of which it was alleged that the defendant was the holder.

On the trial, before BUTLER, J., the evidence disclosed the following facts: In the year 1878, the Comptroller of the Currency becoming satisfied of the insolvency of the bank, appointed a receiver to wind up its affairs, and ordered an assessment upon the shareholders to the amount of twenty dollars *per centum*. The receiver found upon the books of the bank four hundred and fifty shares of its capital stock standing in the name of one Francis Ferris. It appeared that these shares were originally issued to one William Kern, a director of the bank, and a member of the firm of William H. Blumer & Co. In November, 1871, said firm applied to defendant, The Philadelphia Warehouse Co., to open a line of credits upon the pledge of stocks, bonds, etc., as collateral security. They were introduced to Mr. Henry, the president, by one of the directors of the Warehouse Company, who stated that the stocks, etc., deposited as collateral, ought not to remain in the name of W. H. Blumer & Co., and suggested that they should be put in the name of Mr. Henry. W. H. Blumer & Co. thereupon deposited certain gas stocks, transferred to Mr. Henry in accordance with this suggestion, and obtained a loan. On December 28, 1871, they desired further advances, and sent to the Warehouse Company a certificate for the four hundred and fifty shares of stock of the First National Bank of Allentown, originally issued to Mr. Kern, but duly transferred to "T. C. Henry, President." Mr. Henry referred the matter to the Board of Directors of the Warehouse Company, who objected to the transfer to him, upon the ground that it might make the company liable to assessment in case of the insolvency of the bank. Accordingly the Warehouse Company, upon the same day on which they paid the draft of W. H. Blumer & Co. for the additional loan, returned to them the certificate with a transfer indorsed thereon to Dennis McCloskey, a porter in the company's employ, and requested them to have a new certificate issued in McCloskey's name. This transfer was signed by the president and secretary and had the seal of the Warehouse Company attached; and at the time of its execution the company took from McCloskey a blank power of attorney to transfer the stock. To an inquiry from W. H. Blumer & Co., as to the purpose of the transfer, the Warehouse Company replied that it was to avoid liability in case of failure of the bank. On January 10, 1872, a certificate was issued to McCloskey. On July 15, 1875, McCloskey left the Warehouse Company's employ, and they then caused the stock to be transferred to Francis Ferris, an employé, who was a minor and irresponsible, taking from him also a blank power of attorney to transfer. Neither the Warehouse Company, McCloskey, nor Ferris ever collected any dividends on the stock.

The Warehouse Company continued the loans to Wm. H. Blumer & Co. down to the date of the institution of the present suit. Upon its books and in its contract with Wm. H. Blumer & Co., these shares appear as deposited with it by Wm. H. Blumer & Co., as collateral security for loans. On April 9, 1877, in answer to a letter by the then cashier of the bank, the Warehouse Company, by its treasurer, wrote: "We have in our possession a certificate of stock in your bank for four hundred and fifty shares, in name of Francis Ferris, which we hold as collateral."

In 1878, upon the insolvency of the bank, this suit was instituted by the receiver against the Warehouse Company, to recover an assessment from them as shareholders.

The plaintiff requested the Court to charge the jury as follows: "If the jury find that the corporation defendant held the four hundred and fifty shares of the capital stock of the First National Bank of Allentown, as collateral security for a loan to W. H. Blumer & Co. by transfer to ' T. C. Henry, President,' and then by the defendant to its irresponsible employé, for the purpose of avoiding liability as stockholders, the verdict must be for the plaintiff."

The defendant's first point was as follows: "That in order to recover in this case the plaintiff must establish as a fact, that the corporation defendant became, and was the holder of the four hundred and fifty shares of the stock of "The First National Bank of Allentown;" and that there is no evidence that the defendant was the holder of the said shares, and the verdict must be for the defendant."

The Court affirmed the plaintiff's point, subject to the judgment of the Court thereafter on the defendant's first point.

The verdict was for the plaintiff for $10,026. Defendant thereupon moved for a new trial.

Geo. Junkin and *Richard C. McMurtrie* for the motion.

To determine the liability of the defendants, the language of the statute must have a natural construction. The real owner of the stock was Kern, the apparent owner, Ferris. They alone had any beneficial ownership, saving the lien or charges of the pledgee; and we submit that the statute was not intended to fasten liability upon a pledgee for whom the shares were held.

In what sense is the word *shareholder* used in this statute? The registered owner is the only legal owner, the pledgor is the beneficial or equitable owner. The pledgee is but a mortgagee, and has not the legal title. Therefore neither in legal or common parlance is the pledgee the holder of the shares. McCloskey was a trustee for the borrower, and the Warehouse Company had no other or different interest in the shares than has a sheriff after levy, or a lender with an executory contract to pledge.

Not only has there been no case in which a pledgee is held liable because the shares were held for him, but the very reverse has been held, and also admitted as too plain for discussion.

In re City Terminus, 11 Equity, 10.
Sichell's Case, 3 Ch. Appeal, 119.
Royal Bank of India, 4 Ch. Appeal, 260.

Besides to hold the corporation defendant liable is to make liable three persons, registered owner, real owner, and creditor of the real owner, because he is pledgee.

Preston K. Erdman and *Edward Harvey,* contra.

This controversy arises under sections 5139 and 5155 of the Revised Statutes. The pledgee of stock as collateral security is liable, under this Act, as a shareholder for assessments.

Wheelock *v.* Kost, 77 Ill. 296.
The Empire City Bank, 18 N. Y. 200.
Crease *v.* Babcock, 10 Metc. 525.
Hale *v.* Walker, 31 Iowa, 344.

The transfer to the defendant corporation was complete. The certificate was made out in the name of the president as such, and was accepted in so far as the corporation, through informal action of its directorial board, ordered the transfer of the stock, under the corporate seal, to an irresponsible employé. To transfer the stock it was necessary to have control over it. It could not transfer by letter of attorney what it did not own. The subsequent transfer to McCloskey, and afterwards to Ferris, did not relieve the defendant corporation from the liabilites which it had incurred as a shareholder. In the following cases it has been determined that the transfer must be an out and out one, and that a transfer to an irresponsible person to escape liability as a shareholder will not avail.

National Bank *v.* Case, 99 U. S. Rep. 628.
Hyam's Case, 1 DeG. F. & J. 75.
De Pass's Case, 4 De G. & J. 544.
Payne's Case, L. R., 9 Eq. C. 223.
Davis *v.* Stevens, 36 Leg. Int. 462.

C. A. V.

THE COURT. BUTLER, Dist. J. (orally).
The authorities upon the question raised by this case may be divided into three classes :—

First. Where the pledgee has taken a transfer of the stock directly to himself and has had such transfer registered on the books of the corporation, it has been held that in such case the pledgee is liable for assessments.

Second. Where the pledgee has sought to relieve himself by making a transfer of the stock to an irresponsible third person. In such case he is liable.

Third. Where no transfer is made to the pledgee, and his name is not registered as owner, but the owner of the stock puts it into the hands of a third person to hold for the benefit of the pledgor and pledgee. In such case the pledgee has never been held responsible.

When we looked at this case, our first thought was that we must enter judgment for the plaintiff, for we were impressed with the belief that there was a transfer of this stock to the defendants, and that it was actually or virtually registered in the latter's name. But upon examining the evidence we were convinced that this was a mistake. For while it would seem from the record, that it was submitted to the jury whether the transfer to Mr. Henry was with the consent of the defendants, and therefore a transfer to them, it really never was so submitted. The position taken by the parties on the trial was that the question was one of law. The plaintiff asked the Court to charge that, as matter of law, the plaintiff was entitled to recover, while the defendants asked for a charge, that upon all the evidence they were entitled to recover. It is evident that there was a question of fact for the jury, viz., whether the defendants consented to become shareholders, and whether the transfer to their president was with the understanding that it should be a transfer to them, or was subsequently recognized by them as such a transfer. There was evidence on both sides of this question, and the motion for a new trial must, therefore, be granted.

McKENNAN, Circ. J. (orally). There is but one question in this case. We both agree that the mere holding of this stock by the Warehouse Company, as pledgee, would not render them liable to assessment under the Act of Congress, unless there was an agreement that the transfer to the president should be a transfer to them, or unless they recognized such transfer as a transfer to them. The only question is whether the company is a registered shareholder. The name of Mr. Henry appears on the corporation books. Whether the Warehouse Company is a shareholder depends upon the authority given to him by the company. There was evidence on both sides, and the question is one of fact for the jury.

Motion for new trial granted.

Supreme Court.

May, '80, 96. June 8, 1880.
First Nat. Bank of Lock Haven v. Mason.

Banks and banking—Relation of bank to depositor—Bank cannot set up adverse title in a third party to the funds deposited—Banker's right of lien or set-off—Evidence.

A bank, having opened a deposit account with a customer in the usual manner, cannot, in the absence of any claim by a third party, refuse to pay over on demand the balance standing to the credit of the account, on the ground that the moneys deposited were not the property of the depositor, but belonged to a third party, against whom the bank claimed a right of lien or set-off for an indebtedness due by the latter to the bank.

In a suit by a depositor against the bank to recover the balance of a deposit account, the defendant offered to prove that the moneys deposited by plaintiff, in his name, were the property of a firm of which the depositor was bookkeeper, the deposits being so made with the firm's knowledge and approval; that the said firm were indebted to the bank in an amount exceeding the balance standing to the credit of the account, which balance the bank claimed to appropriate to the payment of said indebtedness:

Held, that the evidence was properly excluded.

Although money deposited by A. may be claimed by B. as the true owner, or may be attached by the judgment creditors of B. (the credit on the books of the bank being but *prima facie* evidence of ownership), yet, in the absence of any such claim, the bank is estopped by the contract implied from the fact of the deposit, and by public policy, from questioning the title of its depositor.

Error to the Common Pleas of Clinton County.

Assumpsit, by James D. Mason, against the First National Bank of Lock Haven, to recover a balance standing to the credit of the plaintiff's deposit account in the bank defendant.

Upon the trial, before ORVIS, A. L. J., the plaintiff put in evidence his bank-book, showing numerous deposits and checks during a period of over a year, and showing a balance to his credit of $1254.90. He testified that checks drawn by him against this balance had been dishonored, and that a personal demand for payment of said balance was refused. He also gave in evidence the following letter received by him from the cashier of the bank prior to bringing suit:—

LOCK HAVEN, Oct. 25, 1875.

THOMAS & MASON,
JAS. D. MASON. } We charge your account with note Thomas & Mason $378.11 in favor of Kintzing & Zeller, which will be retained out of your funds deposited in the name of James D. Mason.

Please do not issue any checks, as the balance to the credit of J. D. Mason will be retained on account of bank claims.

Yours, very respectfully,
G. KINTZING,
Cashier.

The defendant made the following offer:—

"The defendant offers to prove: That the moneys deposited with the bank in the name of James D. Mason, the plaintiff, and for the recovery of which the above suit has been instituted, were deposited by the plaintiff, who was the bookkeeper of Thomas & Mason at the time he deposited the same, and at the time of depositing the said money he stated to G. Kintzing, the cashier of the defendant, that the said moneys thus deposited by him in his own name were the moneys of Thomas & Mason, and that he deposited them in his own name for the reason that he might check the same out in the business of Thomas & Mason, on checks drawn in his own name; that there was a necessity of drawing checks in his own name from the fact that Thomas & Mason were absent so much, and that he had not power to sign checks in their name; that the plaintiff had deposited other moneys of Thomas & Mason in the same way with the defendant, to wit, in his own name, previously, and had checked the money out (thus deposited), in the business of Thomas & Mason, on the checks of plaintiff drawn in his own name; that the money of Thomas & Mason was thus deposited with the defendant and checked out in the name of the plaintiff, with the knowledge and consent of Thomas & Mason, and was a course adopted for the convenience of Thomas & Mason (paying their bills by checks drawn in the name of James D. Mason, plaintiff, in their absence from home). That Thomas & Mason kept their bank account with the defendant in the name of James D. Mason, for several months previous to Oct. 25, 1875, when this suit was instituted by the plaintiff for the recovery of the balance standing to the credit of James D. Mason, on the said 25th of Oct. 1875; and that the defendant's understanding from conversation had with James D. Mason, was that the money then standing to his credit, belonged to Thomas & Mason, and was not the money of the said plaintiff. The defendant further offers to prove that James D. Mason did pay by checks in his own name, out of the money deposited in his own name with the defendant, debts due from Thomas & Mason exceeding $1000.00, and did this by the express directions of Thomas & Mason, and took receipts for such payments on their account, in their receipt book, in the presence of John S. Mason, one of Thomas & Mason.

"The defendant further offers to prove that on and previous to Oct. 25, 1875, Thomas & Mason were indebted to the defendant by two notes, one of them for $2000.00, and the other $378.11, the aggregate of which two notes exceeded the amount of money belonging to Thomas & Mason standing on its books to their credit with their consent in the name of plaintiff. This offered for the purpose of showing that the money claimed by the plaintiff in this suit belonged to Thomas & Mason at the time of the institution of this suit, and to whom it still belongs, and that the said Thomas & Mason were indebted to the defendant in an amount at the institution of this suit exceeding the amount thus claimed, and which sum the said Thomas & Mason still owe to the defendant."

Offer objected to, as irrelevant and inadmissible, because the bank is estopped under its contract of deposit from questioning the ownership of the depositor; because the ownership of the funds, or the indebtedness of the bank to the depositor, not being called into question by any third party, the bank cannot aver ownership in a third party, and appropriate the fund to the payment of a debt due by such third party to the bank; and because the bank cannot, in a suit brought against it by a depositor, whose account has been received and credit recognized, set off against the plaintiff's claim notes or debts due by a third party to the bank.

Objections sustained and offer overruled; exception. (1st assignment of error.)

The plaintiff being called as for cross-examination, the defendant proposed to ask the witness the sources from which he had derived the money deposited, for the purpose of showing that the true ownership of said money was in Thomas & Mason, and not in the plaintiff at the time of the deposit. Objected to; objection sustained; exception. (2d assignment.)

The Court instructed the jury that, under the evidence, if they believed a demand had been made, as testified to by the plaintiff, the verdict should be for the plaintiff. Verdict for plaintiff accordingly, and judgment thereon. The defendant took this writ, assigning for error the rejection of its offer of testimony, and the ruling out of its proposed question to the plaintiff, as above.

Cline G. Furst and *C. S. McCormick*, for plaintiff in error.

Although the mode in which the question arises in this case is new, the principles by which we contend it must be decided are old and well settled. They are these :—

A deposit of money in a bank creates no relation of trustee or *quasi* trustee, but the money deposited is simply loaned to the depositary.
Bank *v.* Jones, 6 Wr. 538.

A deposit may be shown to belong to a third person; the credit given in the book is only *prima facie* evidence of ownership.
Arnold *v.* Macungie Savings Bank, 21 Sm. 290.
Stair *v.* York Nat. Bank, 5 Id. 368.
F. & M. Nat. Bank *v.* King, 7 Id. 208.

A bank has a lien against a depositor's balance for debts due it by the depositor.
Morse on Banks and Banking, 27, 34.
Waterman on Set-off, 143, 144.
Reed *v.* Penrose, 12 Cas. 235

The true owner of a fund deposited by and in the name of his agent, may sue for its recovery, but the depositary has the right of lien or set-off for indebtedness due to it. So an attaching creditor may show that a fund deposited in the name of one belongs to another, his debtor, subject to a similar right of lien or set-off by the garnishee.

Now, if the true owner may sue, or an attaching creditor may show the true owner, why may not the depositary, when a creditor, show the true owner, and exercise its right of lien or set-off? That the suit chances to be in the name of the agent of the true owner, is no reason why the depositary shall not be allowed to show such ownership and indebtedness. A denial of the right to make such proof would result, in case the principal be insolvent (as here), in inequitable and irreparable loss to the depositary. An agent should not be permitted to recover where his principal could not. A set-off of the principal's indebtedness lying in the way of a suit by the principal, this suit is brought in the name of the agent. To sanction this would be using the process of the law as a cover to evade a just liability. There is no "estoppel in law" that will help out such an expedient.

S. R. Peale, for defendant in error.

Can a bank, in the absence of notice or claim by a third party, set up an adverse title in a stranger to the plaintiff's deposit, for the purpose of appropriating it to the payment (1) of a note by said stranger to another stranger, and (2) of a debt due the bank by such stranger? This cannot be. As between the bank and its depositor, the relation of debtor and creditor is fixed by the dual act of deposit and receipt. The bank contracts with the depositor, and with him alone, to safely keep and pay on demand. To permit a bank to question its depositor's title would be subversive of all banking and commercial confidence. The bank may, by the action of a third party, be put in the position of a stakeholder, but it cannot itself assume that position.
Jackson *v.* Bank of U. S., 10 Barr, 67.
U. S. Bank *v.* Macalester, 9 Barr, 481, 482.

June 19, 1880. THE COURT. The plaintiff below brought his suit against the First National Bank of Lock Haven, to recover the amount of moneys he had deposited with said bank. The defendant offered to prove that the money deposited in the name of James D. Mason, the plaintiff, was in fact the money of the firm of Thomas & Mason, of which firm the plaintiff was a clerk; that the plaintiff had admitted at the time the deposits were made that the money belonged to said firm, and were placed in his name as a matter of convenience in paying small bills; and that the said Thomas & Mason were indebted to the said bank in excess of the amount standing on its books to the credit of the plaintiff. The bank claimed to set off the indebtedness of Thomas & Mason against the claim of plaintiff in this suit. This evidence was rejected by the Court below, and forms the subject of the first assignment of error.

Thomas & Mason made no claim to this money; the said firm having failed, the bank seeks to protect itself by setting up their title to the funds in question.

It is well settled that money deposited in a bank to the credit of A. may be shown to be the property of B. It may be reached by attachment on the part of the judgment creditors of B., or its payment by the bank to A. may be stopped by a proper notice on the part of B. that the money belongs to him. The credit on the books of the bank is but *prima facie* evidence of ownership. (Harrisburg Bank *v.* Tyler, 3 W. & S. 373; Frazier *v.* Erie Bank, 8 Id. 18; Jackson *v.* The Bank of the United States, 10 Barr, 61; Bank of Northern Liberties *v.* Jones, 6 Wright, 541; Stair *v.* York Nat. Bank, 5 P. F. S. 368; Arnold *v.* Macungie Savings Bank, 21 P. F. S. 290.)

These were cases, however, in which the true owner set up a claim to the fund. We have here a very different question. The bank, the depositary, sets up an adverse title to defeat the suit of its own depositor. The bank held its claim against Thomas & Mason when the plaintiff made his deposits, and they knew, or at least they allege they knew, when the deposits were made, that the money so deposited in plaintiff's name belonged to said firm. Yet, under these circumstances and with this knowledge, they permitted the plaintiff to make the deposit in his own name. Having received it as the money of the plaintiff and given him credit therefor, the bank is estopped, in the absence of any notice from or claim by the real owner, from disputing the plaintiff's title. Having received the money as the money of the plaintiff, they are bound to pay it to him, or upon his order. Such a contract is implied from the fact of the deposit. In Jackson *v.* The Bank (*supra*), the funds in the bank to the credit of Warwick were attached; the bank paid the money to Warwick, notwithstanding the attachment, and was held liable therefor. It was said by Mr. Justice COULTER, in delivering the opinion of the Court: "The first question that occurs is this: Could the bank, if the attachment had not been served, have resisted the claim of Warwick to the money he had deposited with them? They received it and the bills as his, entered them on their books as his, and were bound, in the absence of any attachment, to have paid the funds to him. How, then, were they placed in any better position by the service of the attachment? The attaching creditor stands in the place of Warwick. If they could not allege as against Warwick that the funds were not his, neither can they allege as against the attaching creditor that they are not his, and yet turn round and pay the money to Warwick to enable him to defeat his creditor."

It is clearly against public policy to permit a bank that has received money from a depositor, credited him therewith upon its books, and thereby entered into an implied contract to honor his check, to allege that the money deposited belongs to some one else. This may be done by an attaching creditor or by the true owners of the fund; but the bank is estopped by its own act. A departure from this rule might lead to novel results and embarrass commercial transactions.

We are of opinion that the evidence referred to in the first and second assignments was properly rejected.

Judgment affirmed.
Opinion by PAXSON, J.

[*Cf.* Dougherty v. Central Nat. Bank, *ante*, p. 1; Lanback *v.* Leibert, 6 WEEKLY NOTES, 80.]

May, '80, 50.   June 21, 1880.
Buchanan v. Hazzard and Wife.

Husband and wife — Deed of married woman — Requisites of — Ejectment — When maintainable, although plaintiffs are in partial possession of the premises.

A deed or lease under seal of a married woman relating to her land, in which her husband does not join, is absolutely void, and cannot be validated by evidence of the husband's assent. Nor can the married woman be estopped by the receipt of the consideration, nor by any subsequent acts of ratification, other than by a new deed duly executed and acknowledged.

Husband and wife, in possession of a tract of land, may maintain ejectment against parties in possession of a portion of the tract claiming the right to operate oil wells under an invalid lease, executed by the married woman.

Error to Common Pleas of McKean County.

Ejectment, by Henry E. Hazzard and Mary

A. Hazzard, his wife, for the use of the said Mary, against Russell Buchanan and Jefferson Buchanan.

On the trial, before WILLIAMS, P. J., there was no dispute as to the title of the plaintiff, Mary A. Hazzard, to the fee simple of the premises in question. The defendants claimed under her the right of possession, for oil purposes, under the following circumstances:—

By an oil lease or instrument of writing, under seal, dated June 7, 1877, Mrs. Hazzard, in consideration of a royalty of one-fourth of the oil to be produced, and of mutual covenants, granted and let to Buchanan Bros. the premises in dispute for the purpose of boring for and pumping oil, etc., for the term of twelve years, the lessor to fully use and enjoy the premises for the purpose of tillage, except such part as may be necessary for mining purposes and a right of way thereto; work to begin within 25 days, and if the first well should produce 10 barrels, a second to be drilled, etc. The lease was signed and sealed by Mrs. Hazzard, but not by her husband, and by Buchanan Bros. It was acknowledged by Mrs. Hazzard before a notary public, who certified in due form to a separate acknowledgment by her.

The defendants offered in evidence this lease, to be followed by an instrument dated July 9, 1877, whereby the said Mary A. Hazzard and H. E. Hazzard, her husband (separately acknowledged by her in due form of law), in consideration of $400, sold to A. & P. Bolton the undivided one-eighth part of the oil produced by a well "now being drilled on land of said Mary A. Hazzard by Buchanan Bros., said one-eighth being one-half the royalty or land interest of one-fourth," . . . "as fully and with like terms as by the conditions of the lease to Buchanan Brothers." . . . To be followed, further, by evidence that defendants went into possession under said lease, drilled two oil-producing wells, and delivered to Hazzard and wife their share of the royalty. Further, that the plaintiffs resided upon the land at the time the wells were drilled, had knowledge of the labor and money expended in producing the oil, and aided and encouraged the defendants in this production. That the plaintiffs resided on the land at the time of the commencement of this suit. That the well referred to in the contract of 9th of August, 1877, was the one being drilled by Buchanan Brothers under the lease of 7th of June, 1877. That at the time of the execution of the instruments referred to the husband of Mary A. Hazzard was present and participated; that the sum of $50 in money was paid Mrs. Hazzard on the execution of the instrument of the 7th of June; that the sum of $600 was paid to her, her husband being present and consenting, as the consideration of an instrument executed under seal by her, and dated the 11th of August, 1877, whereby she sold to the defendants, Buchanan Brothers, her remaining one-eighth interest in said royalty. That the defendants have never been in possession of the land except for the purpose of producing oil according to the terms of the lease executed to them. That the plaintiffs have not refunded or offered to refund the money paid as above stated, or done other acts to protect the defendants against the loss which would be occasioned by their outlay.

This evidence is offered for the purpose of showing the circumstances under which the defendants entered and now hold possession; the character of the occupancy; and a payment of the consideration to the plaintiffs.

Offer objected to by plaintiffs, because the lease to defendants, being executed by Mrs. Hazzard, a married woman, without her husband joining, was void, and passed no right or interest to the defendants. Objection sustained; exception.

Defendants' counsel asked the Court to charge the jury: That if they find the plaintiff was in possession of the premises described in the writ at the time of the commencement of the suit she cannot recover in ejectment. *Answer.* The principle stated in this point is one well settled, but the evidence in this case shows that a portion of this land is in actual occupancy of the defendants, they having structures of some permanence upon it which were occupied by them. We think, therefore, this case is not within the rule which the point invokes.

The Court then directed a verdict for the plaintiff. Verdict accordingly, and judgment thereon. The defendants took this writ, assigning for error the refusal of their offer of evidence, the answer to their point, and the direction of a verdict for plaintiff.

Hamlin & Son (with whom was *A. G. Olmsted*), for plaintiffs in error.

We need not contend that the defectively executed lease of June 7, 1877, passed to defendants any title or interest in plaintiff's land. But the married woman, with her husband's consent, permitted and induced defendants to go on her land and to drill oil wells. With or without title in the defendants, oil was being produced, and it flowed into the tanks. As it was produced it became a chattel. Mrs. Hazzard's right to the one-fourth, which she reserved as royalty, was not land, it was a chose in action. Now by the instrument of August 11, 1877, she sold one-half of her royalty to the defendants for $600, which was paid to her in cash. By this contract, which she had authority to make, she made a valid sale of one-eighth of the oil to defendants, with the right to go upon her land to get it. It was not necessary for her husband to join in that instrument, but the evidence offered showed that he was present and consenting, and by such consent he is estopped.

But our lease was recognized, adopted, and ratified by the instrument dated July 9, 1877, executed and duly acknowledged by both Mrs. Hazzard and her husband, whereby they sold to A. & P. Bolton one-eighth of the oil—one-half of her royalty of one-fourth. This instrument makes especial reference to our lease, and the defendants' rights thereunder, and the plaintiff thereby sold a portion of the fruits of our lease. We submit that its effect is to affirm by a valid instrument, and in a legal manner, the former instrument which was voidable at the pleasure of the married woman.

Share *v.* Anderson, 7 S. & R. 43.
Fulton *v.* Moore, 1 Casey, 468, 477.
Fryer *v.* Rishell, 3 Nor. 521.
Vance *v.* Nogle, 20 Sm. 176.
Freeman *v.* Walsh, 7 WEEKLY NOTES, 296.
Brown *v.* Bennett, 25 Sm. 420.

The plaintiffs, having been in the actual possession of the land at the commencement of this ejectment, cannot recover. Their remedy was trespass *q. c. f.*

Corley *v.* Pentz, 26 Sm. 57.

The defendants had only a qualified possession of a small portion in common with plaintiffs. The plaintiffs gave no evidence of the portion, or any description of the land occupied by the defendants, nor showed that this occupancy was to the exclusion of the plaintiffs.

H. King, for defendants in error.

The lease was void, not voidable, and was therefore incapable of ratification. But the offer did not amount to a ratification.

The cases cited by plaintiffs in error are not in point. The case is ruled by—

Glidden *v.* Strupler, 2 Sm. 400.
Dunham *v.* Wright, 3 Sm. 167.
Rumfelt *v.* Clements, 10 Wr. 455.

The defendants were in exclusive possession of a portion of the premises, and the rule stated in Corley *v.* Pentz (*supra*) does not apply.

October 4, 1880. THE COURT. The learned Court below were clearly right in rejecting the evidence offered by the plaintiffs in error, and complained of in the first assignment. Nothing is better settled than that a deed by a married woman without joining her husband is absolutely void, and evidence of the husband's verbal assent would not help the matter. (Trimmer *v.* Heagy, 4 Harris, 487.) Nor can can she be estopped by any subsequent act of ratification. (Glidden *v.* Strupler, 2 P. F. Smith, 400.) Nothing but a new deed, duly executed and acknowledged, could avail. The subsequent deed to Bolton would, at most, only be effectual to convey one-eighth of the royalty of the well. It could not, consistently with the doctrine of these cases, ratify and confirm the previous void lease to the Buchanans.

There was no error in the answer to the defendants' point, nor in the direction to find a verdict for the plaintiff.

Judgment affirmed.
PER CURIAM. PAXSON, J., absent.
[See next case.]

Oct. & Nov. '80, 195. Oct. 18, 1880.

Elsey et al. v. McDaniel.

Husband and wife—Deed of married woman—Feme sole traders—Act of May 4, 1855—Decree under § 4 of said Act not necessary to enable feme covert, deserted by her husband, to alien her real estate.

A married woman, deserted and left unprovided for by her husband, may, by virtue of the Act of May 4, 1855 (P. L. 430), execute a deed efficacious to convey her real estate without the joinder of her husband, and without having previously obtained a decree authorizing her to act as a feme sole trader by virtue of the provisions of Section 4 of the said Act.

Error to the Common Pleas of Erie County.

Ejectment, by the heirs of Orvaline Jane Millar against Daniel J. McDaniel, for a vacant lot in the city of Erie.

On the trial, before GALBRAITH, P. J., it appeared in evidence that the said Orvaline became seised of the land in dispute in 1839, while still unmarried, as her distributive share of her father's estate. In 1840 she married John H. Millar. In 1852 or 1853 said Millar deserted his wife and family, without making proper provision for their support, and remained absent for ten years. On December 17, 1855, said Orvaline, without her husband's joinder, executed a deed to said McDaniel for the said property. In 1864 said Orvaline died. In 1877 said Millar died.

Plaintiffs requested the Court to charge, *inter alia,* substantially—"The deed of a married woman in which the husband does not join is void. Nor does the Act of May 4, 1855 (P. L. 430), make such a deed valid unless the married woman has first been declared a feme sole trader under the provisions of the fourth section of said Act."

The Court declined this instruction, and charged, *inter alia,* as follows: "This decree, as we construe the Act, was not an indispensable preliminary to her acting for herself in the disposition of her property. It merely leaves the burden of proof upon the party claiming under her deed, to show affirmatively the existence of the facts necessary to bring her within the terms of the law. In the present case, therefore, it is for the jury to find whether the defendant has established affirmatively as against the proof given by plaintiff, that at the date of the deed here in question, Mrs. Millar had been and then was deserted by her husband, or that he had neglected or refused, and was at that time still neglecting or refusing to provide for her."

Verdict and judgment for defendant. Plaintiffs took this writ, assigning for error, *inter alia*, the refusal of the Court to affirm plaintiffs' points, substantially above set forth, and the portion of the charge quoted.

L. S. Norton (with him *C. B. Curtis*) for plaintiffs in error.

A decree under section 4 of the Act of 1855 is necessary before the separate deed of a married woman will be efficacious to convey her property. Black *et al. v.* Tricker (9 Smith, 13) only decides that without such a decree a wife deserted by her husband may, with her separate earnings, purchase and hold real estate without liability to her husband's creditors.

(No paper-book for defendant in error was furnished to the reporter.)

November 1, 1880. THE COURT. We consider this case as authoritatively ruled by the judgment of this Court in Black *v.* Tricker (9 P. F. Smith, 13). It was held in that case that under the Act of May 4, 1855, it is not necessary that there should be a decree that a wife is to be regarded as a feme sole trader to enable her to hold property under the circumstances mentioned in the Act. The decree was provided for in order that creditors, purchasers, and others, may, with certainty and safety, transact business with a married woman. There was ample evidence of desertion by the husband to justify the submission of the case to the jury.

PER CURIAM. Judgment affirmed.

[See preceding case.]

Oct. & Nov. '80, 161. October 20, 1880.

Indiana County Deposit Bank's Appeal.

Judgment—Distribution of proceeds of sheriff's sales of real estate—Equity—Subrogation— When proper.

The rights of those claiming to participate in the proceeds of a sheriff's sale are to be determined by their status, as shown by the record, at the time of the sale. All liens then on the land, except first mortgages and other fixed liens, are divested by the sale, and the lien-holders are turned over to the proceeds. No lien upon the fund, and consequently no right to participate in its distribution, can ordinarily be acquired afterwards.

Douglass's Appeal, 12 Wright, 223, approved and followed.

The separate real estate of A., B., and C. was sold at sheriff's sale in the above order, and afterwards another portion of the real estate of C., and the proceeds of the whole paid into Court for distribution. The amount of a judgment against A. and C. jointly was awarded out of A.'s estate by the auditor appointed to distribute the fund. It appearing by parol evidence before him, but not of record, that C. was the principal in said judgment, and A. only surety:

Held, that neither A., nor his judgment creditors claiming through him, were entitled to subrogation for the amount of the said judgment against the proceeds of the real estate of C., so as to cut out subsequent judgment creditors of C. from participating in the said proceeds.

Appeal from the decree of the Court of Common Pleas of Jefferson County, distributing the proceeds of a sheriff's sale.

The fund in controversy was produced by the sale of the separate real estate of (1) J. B. Morris, (2) John Carey, and (3) John Couch, all sold in the above order on October 24, 1879; also from the sheriff's sale of another part of said Couch's real estate sold December 9, 1879. The amount realized from the sale of Couch's real estate on October 24 was $2200; from that sold on December 9, $2605. The proceeds on all these sales amounted in the aggregate to $9866. This fund was paid into Court, and an auditor appointed for the distribution thereof. He awarded the proceeds of Morris's property to the various judgments against him, in the order of their priority, and, *inter alia*, out of said proceeds applied the sum of $574.07 to pay a judgment of McGregor, to use of Gillespie, against John Couch, J. B. Morris, and D. Couch, entered upon the joint and several notes of defendants on October 18, 1875.

Parol evidence was then introduced before said auditor, showing what did not appear of record, viz., that in said judgment John Couch was the principal debtor, and Morris a mere surety, and it was contended that since said judgment had been paid from the proceeds of Morris's real estate, said Morris should be considered as subrogated to Gillespie's rights, and entitled to claim the amount of said judgment, viz., $574.07, out of the proceeds of the real estate of Couch, in preference to all judgments entered against Couch subsequent to the Gillespie judgment; and further that in equity said amount of $574.07 should be applied on account of judgments entered against Morris not theretofore paid out of the proceeds of Morris's real estate.

The auditor declined to distribute in accordance with this contention, but awarded the proceeds of John Couch's property to the unsatisfied judgments against him in the order of their priority. Said judgments were all subsequent in date to the Gillespie judgment. Those to which the fund arising from the sale of Couch's property was awarded were:—

(1) Judgment, William P. North v. John Couch and A. Graffeus, entered Nov. 17, 1875, for $329.70.
(2) Judgment, Indiana County Deposit Bank v. John Couch, John Carey, and J. B. Morris, entered May 27, 1876, for $3881.52.
(3) Judgment, Same v. Brown and John Couch, entered May 29, 1876, for $2969.91.

Of these the first was paid in full, the second was awarded $1924.92, the residue of said judgment having been already paid out of the proceeds of Carey's property, the third and last had awarded to it on account of the rest of the fund, viz., $2472.51.

To this distribution exceptions were filed by the owners of unsatisfied judgments against Morris on the ground, *inter alia*, that the auditor erred in not distributing to them in accordance with the principle urged before him in their behalf.

The Court (JENKS, P. J.), after hearing, decided that the principle contended for by exceptants was correct. He modified, therefore, the distribution recommended by the auditor, and decreed that the sum of $574.07 should be deducted from the amount awarded the Indiana County Deposit Bank, from the proceeds of Couch's property on account of its second judgment, and that the said sum should be applied on account of the unsatisfied judgments against Morris.

The bank thereupon took this appeal, assigning for error the decree of the Court distributing the said sum of $574.07, as aforesaid.

Stewart and *Marlin*, for appellant.

In distributing the proceeds of sheriff's sales the rights of claimants must be determined as they were at the time of the sale, the liens being divested by the sale the lien-holders are turned over to the proceeds, and no lien or right thereto can be afterwards acquired.

Douglass's Appeal, 12 Wright, 223.

Morris's equity, and through him the equity of his judgment-creditors for subrogation arose only in consequence of this sale. Neither he nor they are, therefore, entitled to claim such equity on the distribution of the proceeds of this sale.

White and *Scott*, for appellees.

In the distribution of a fund made by a sheriff's sale the Court will, as between equitable claimants, be governed by principles of equity.

Kohl v. Harting, 8 Watts, 329.

The principle of subrogation should be applied in this case. An actual substitution is not necessary. The law will, by a fiction, make such substitution whenever equity and good conscience may require it.

Fleming v. Beaver, 2 Rawle, 128.
McCormick's adm'rs v. Irwin, 11 Casey, 111.
Wright v. Sewing Machine Co., 1 Norris, 80.
Duffield v. Cooper, 6 Norris, 443.

November 1, 1880. THE COURT. The separate real estate of J. B. Morris, John Carey, and John Couch was sold by the sheriff, in the order named, and all on the same day except a portion of Couch's property which was sold several weeks afterwards for $2605. The proceeds of these several sales, amounting, in the aggregate, to $9866, were distributed by the auditor among the respective lien creditors in their order as they stood at the time of the sales. Out of the fund realized from the sale of Morris's real estate he appropriated $574.07 to the payment of a judgment in favor of McGregor to use of Gillespie against Couch and Morris, entered October 18, 1875, on the joint and several note of the defendants. There was nothing upon the face of the record to indicate that the relation of the defendants to each other was not that of joint debtors; and assuming, as creditors were bound to do, that they were both principals in the debt secured by the judgment, the correctness of the distribution made by the auditor cannot be questioned. It was, however, shown *aliunde* on the hearing, that Morris was merely surety for Couch, and on this ground it was claimed that the amount thus taken out of the Morris fund to pay Couch's proper debt, should, on the principle of equitable subrogation, be given to Morris's creditors, thereby diminishing, to that extent, the fund to which appellant, as a lien creditor of Couch, looked for payment. The auditor refused to recognize the principle of substitution thus contended for by the creditors of Morris, but the Court, adopting the opposite views, reversed the auditor in this particular, awarded the $574.07 to Morris's creditors and deducted the same from the distributive share of the appellant; this action of the Court is substantially the only matter assigned for error.

As was held in Douglass's Appeal (12 Wright, 223), the rights of those claiming to participate in the proceeds of a sheriff's sale are to be determined by their status as shown by the record at the time of the sale. All liens then on the land, except first mortgages and other fixed liens, are divested by the sale and the lien holders are turned over to the proceeds. No lien upon the fund, and consequently no right to participate in its distribution can ordinarily be acquired afterwards. It was on this principle that the learned auditor proceeded in distributing the funds, and we are satisfied he was right. The only safe guide that lien creditors can have in bidding at sheriff's sale of real estate, in which they are interested, is the record as it stands at the time of the sale.

An examination of the records after the first sheriff's sales would show that the proceeds of those sales, applied to the judgments in their order would nearly satisfy all the liens that were ahead of appellants' second judgment, so that when the sale of Couch's property took place in December following, appellant would have a right to assume that the proceeds of that sale, with the exception of a small amount, would be applicable to its second judgment which was nearly reached by the first sales; and thus relying upon the state of the record at that time, might well be governed by it in bidding at the last sale. As we have already seen there was nothing on the face of the record to indicate that any right of subrogation existed, and in fact none did exist. Morris as surety of Couch might have paid the debt before the sales, and upon satisfying the Court as to the proper facts, might have been subrogated to the rights of the plaintiff in that judgment, but he did not do so then or at any other time; and the last sale took place without anything to warn appellant or other creditors that the proceeds of the sale would not be applicable to the judgments in their order as they then stood on the judgment docket. Under such circumstances it would be inequitable to permit Morris or any of his creditors, claiming through him, to displace a creditor, who, as the record stood at the time of the last sale, was entitled to the proceeds. We think the principle upon which the auditor distributed the funds was correct and his report should have been confirmed.

Decree reversed; report of the auditor confirmed, and it is ordered and decreed that the funds be paid out in accordance therewith; the costs of this appeal to be paid by the appellee.

Opinion by STERRETT, J.

Quarter Sessions.

April, 1880.
Commonwealth v. Moreland.

Criminal law—An assault and battery upon a constable, who had forcibly opened an outer door of a house, is justifiable, even though he went there to conduct a sale under a previous levy.

The indictment charged Kate Moreland with an assault and battery upon one George Hook, a constable, on the 8th day of March, 1880. Plea, *Not guilty.*

Upon the trial, said Hook testified that the defendant was the tenant of one West; that rent being in arrear, he had previously made a levy in the regular way, and on the morning of the assault had gone to the house to conduct a sale; that in the parlor the defendant flew at him with a hatchet, struck him with her hands, and bit him severely.

On cross-examination, it appeared that at the time of Hook's arrival at the house the front door was locked, and that he had opened it with a false key.

Hampton L. Carson, for the defendant, admitted the regularity of the levy, but asked the Court to instruct the jury to acquit the defendant, on the ground that the officer was a trespasser; that he had no right to make a pound of the premises, and then break into the house in order to preserve his custody of the goods.

Dallas Sanders, for the Commonwealth.

As the officer had previously made a levy upon the premises, he had a right to be there. The defendant was guilty of resisting legal process.

FINLETTER, J., directed an acquittal, remarking that the officer was a trespasser, and that the assault and battery was justifiable.

The jury accordingly rendered a verdict of not guilty.

Common Pleas—Equity.

C. P. No. 2. Sept. 21, 1880.
Ewing v. The Wilcox and Gibbs Sewing Machine Company.

Agreements in restraint of trade—Agency—Whether parties may terminate agreement where no limitation of time is expressed—When an appointment as exclusive territorial vendor is such an agreement in restraint of trade as equity will enforce.

Sur demurrer to bill.

The bill set out that the plaintiff had acted as an exclusive territorial vendor for defendants for several years prior to Oct. 15, 1874, and that on that date the following agreement was made between them:—

The first party (the defendants) hereby appoints, subject to conditions hereinafter expressed, the second party (the plaintiff) its exclusive vendor for its sewing machines, parts, and attachments, in and for the following named territory, to wit: the city of Philadelphia, Pa., and the adjacent country lying within a radius of ten miles from the City Hall of said city. The second party hereby accepts said appointment. The first party will sell for the present to second party its sewing machines and parts thereof at 60 per cent. discount from its present New York retail price list; and its needles, attachments, silk, and cotton at its lowest wholesale rates. In the event of a change (the liberty to effect which is not herein intended to be restricted) in retail prices, or of a general revision of discounts by first party, the second party is to be as favorably considered then in the readjusting and fixing of discount rates to him as is extended to him on present basis of prices. . . . The first party will not knowingly supply its goods at a discount to go within the limits of territory hereby assigned. But the first party reserves the right always to sell its sewing machines, parts, and accessories at full retail rates to go anywhere. . . . Second party will be allowed to fill orders from any locality at full list rates; but trade must not be solicited by his connivance or consent in the territory of other agents; and discounts or any equivalent device therefor must not be allowed in any form, on articles herein specified, permitted to go out of his own territory. . . . It is hereby agreed that his time, attention, and abilities must primarily be devoted to the forwarding of the interest of party of the first part. If for any reason, at any time, the connection hereby formed shall cease, the first party shall have the right to buy back of its goods sold to second party, all such goods as first party may select, first party to pay therefor the same price as charged second party. Second party agrees to purchase from first party during the year 1875 at least $20,000 net worth of machines, parts, and accessories, to be taken in equal monthly parts, and to be paid for as stated herein. Violation of the spirit of this agreement shall be sufficient cause for its abrogation. Permission is granted second party to trade in all former territory occupied by him until such time as first party shall form other connections for occupying the territory not contained in that designated herein as belonging to second party. And it is agreed and understood that this appointment or agency is not salable or transferable by second party without obtaining the written consent of first party; but such consent is to be given, providing the purchaser or other person is acceptable to said first party. . .

In witness whereof, etc.

Further that large amounts of money had been put into the business by the plaintiff, and that he had entered into contracts and agreements for the purpose of carrying on and enlarging this business, which was in a very prosperous condition; that the defendants, "without any legal right, and without cause," had notified plaintiff that they would not supply him with any more machines and had refused to fill his orders therefor. The bill then averred that defendants were about establishing an agency in this city, and prayed, *inter alia*, an injunction to restrain them from so doing.

Demurrer for want of equity.

G. W. Thorn, for demurrer.

There is no time fixed in the agreement for its continuance, and it may therefore be terminated at any time.

J. G. Johnson, contra.

This is not the ordinary case of an appointment of an agent, as an examination of the contract shows, but one of those agreements in partial restraint of trade which equity will enforce by injunction. The usual agreements disposing of exclusive rights in patents are similar to this.

Thorn, in reply.

A partnership agreement for a definite period may be dissolved during that period by any partner without subjecting himself to anything more than an action at law. An agreement in restraint of trade which equity will enforce must contain a covenant not to exercise the trade in question.

[HARE, P. J. Is not such a covenant to be implied here from the use of the word "exclusive?" I now recollect a decision of Judge STRONG, as to the duration of an indefinite employment. Coffin *v.* Landis, 10 Wr. 426.]

THE COURT. Demurrer overruled.

Common Pleas—Law.

C. P. No. 3. October 23, 1880.

Bank v. Castner et al.

Promissory notes—Liability of an alleged member of a firm on an indorsement made by another member of it—Affidavit of defence law—Particularity of averments.

Rule for judgment for want of a sufficient affidavit of defence.

Assumpsit on promissory notes drawn by D. J. Cutter, A. C. Wellington, and other parties to the order of Castner, Stickney & Wellington, and by them indorsed in blank to plaintiffs.

About one-half the amount of said notes had been paid when the present suit was brought. Castner filed an affidavit of defence setting forth that the—

"Indorsement on which he is sought to be charged is that of a firm, to wit, Castner, Stickney & Wellington. The person who made that indorsement was Jonas C. Wellington, who traded in Massachusetts under that firm. Defendant was not a member of that firm or partnership, and had no interest in the business, nor was he directly or indirectly interested in the proceeds of said indorsement or in the transaction in which it was given or in which the notes were taken by the plaintiffs. The defendant is informed and believes and expects to prove that the plaintiffs have received on the claim from the drawer 65 per cent. of the amount of the notes on the notes drawn by Cutter, and 32 per cent. of the amount of the notes on those drawn by Austin C. Wellington."

T. D. Mowlds, for the rule.

Though a man have no interest in a firm, yet if he suffer himself to be held out to the world as a member of it, he thereby authorizes those to whom he has been so held out to treat him as a partner.

Byles on Bills, page 50.
Parsons on Partnership, page 36.
3 Kent's Com., pages 32 and 33.
Story on Partnership, page 104, sec. 64.

The averments of the affidavit are insufficient in that matters necessary to the defence are left to inference; and the incomplete averments must be construed against the maker.

R. C. McMurtrie, contra.

THE COURT. Rule discharged.

C. P. No. 3.   Nov. 20, 1880.

Kiker v. Weightman et al.

Practice—Interpleader—Filing of narr. and bond by claimant nunc pro tunc—When it will be permitted.

Rule to show cause why claimants should not be permitted to file their narr. and their own bond *nunc pro tunc*, and that the order to sheriff to proceed to sell be rescinded, proceedings to stay meanwhile.

The depositions in support of the rule set forth that claimants, acting on the advice of their father, one of the defendants in the execution, filed with the sheriff their affidavits, claiming as their own property the goods taken in execution as the property of their father and brother; that they supposed the filing of the affidavit was all that was required, until the sheriff posted bills announcing the sale of the goods, when they consulted a lawyer; that their father and brother never had any title to or in the goods, but that claimants had purchased them with their own earnings, and further that they had never received any notice of the rule for an interpleader.

Counsel for plaintiff in the execution stated that four weeks had elapsed since the rules for an interpleader had been made absolute, and no bonds or *narrs.* had been filed; and further that notice of the rules had been mailed by the sheriff to the house of the father of the claimants.

J. M. West, for the rule.
J. J. Broadhurst, contra.

THE COURT. Rule absolute.

C. P. No. 4.   Oct. 11, 1880.

Martzinger v. Smith.

Jurisdiction—Practice—The Court of Common Pleas cannot entertain any question in a cause after the record has been removed to the Supreme Court by writ of error.

Rule on plaintiff to show cause why defendant should not be allowed to pay money into Court sufficient to cover judgment, interest, and costs in above case, and that the real estate be released from the lien of said judgment.

The defendant's petition alleged that judgment had been obtained against him as executor, etc., for $1092, and that thereupon a writ of error was taken, which is now pending in the Supreme Court; that the petitioner as executor and trustee had sold and was about to sell real estate of the decedent, which he was desirous of having released from the lien of the said judgment; and that the plaintiff had refused his request that sufficient money to cover the judgment, interest, and costs should be paid into Court, and that thereupon the real estate should be released.

Kinsey, for the rule.
Wetherill, showed cause.

There is no authority for the granting of this petition; and the Court has no longer jurisdiction over the case.

THE COURT. The record having been removed by writ of error, we cannot entertain any question in this case, or make any order therein. (Cox's adm'r *v.* Henry, 12 Casey, 445.)

Rule discharged.

Per THAYER, P. J.

Orphans' Court.

November 27, 1880.

Steel's Estate.

Decedents' estates—Act of April 14, 1851—Exemption of $300 in favor of widow or "children" of decedent—Minor children only are entitled to the benefit of the Act.

Sur petition of children to retain $300 in personal property.

The petitioners, a son and married daughter of decedent both over twenty-one years of age, averred that the wife of decedent died before her husband, and petitioners constituted his family at the time of his decease; they prayed to retain and have set apart for their use, according to the Act of April 14, 1851, the articles of personal property enumerated in the inventory and appraisement annexed to their petition.

The petition was duly advertised according to the rule of Court, and no exceptions were filed thereto.

William S. Price, for petitioners.

Dec. 4, 1880. THE COURT. It appears from the petition that decedent left no widow surviving, but at the time of his decease his family consisted of two children, a son and daughter; the latter married, and both more than twenty-one years of age. They now claim to retain and have set apart to their use personal property late of decedent, to the value of three hundred dollars, by virtue of the Act of April 14th, 1851. This, however, cannot be allowed. While the Act provides that "the widow or the children of any decedent" may retain either real or personal property to the value of three hundred dollars, and the same shall not be sold, but suffered to remain for the use of the widow and family, yet it has never been construed to include adult children of a decedent, although they may have resided with him as a part of his family. The object of the Act was primarily to provide for the immediate wants of a widow deprived by death of her husband, the natural provider and protector of herself and infant children, and was a beneficent provision of the law for their urgent necessities. And if the decedent leaves both a widow and children surviving, the former is alone entitled to the exemption, to the exclusion of the children. (Nevin's Appeal, 11 Wr. 230.) But it is not every decedent who is contemplated by the Act; it only applies to the case of a deceased husband or father. Where a wife and mother dies, leaving a separate estate, the children cannot, after her decease, claim the exemption out of her estate. (King's Appeal, 3 Norris, 345.) If a decedent dies leaving no widow, but minor children, they are entitled to the benefits intended by the Act, and the proper practice is to claim the exemption through their guardian regularly appointed. But it cannot be said that adult children, married, perhaps, and having adequate maintenance and means of livelihood, are included within the spirit and meaning of the Act. And as said by STRONG, Justice, in Nevins's Appeal (*supra*), "The Act was not designed as a statute of distribution. It has always been construed rather according to its spirit than its letter." And in the same case where adult children claimed to be entitled together with the widow, to the exemption, it was refused, STRONG, Justice, saying, they are not the beneficiaries intended, for "if they are, then in cases where there is no widow, $300 may be taken from the creditors of a decedent by his children, who are above want, who were independent of any assistance from their father in his lifetime, and who have families of their own. Such could not have been what was intended by the Legislature."

Being of the opinion that the petitioners are not entitled to the exemption provided by the Act, their petition is dismissed.

Opinion by HANNA, P. J.

Oct. 19, 1880.

Cassady's Estate

Where legacies are charged upon land, the legatee is entitled to partition in order to apply for the sale of real estate—Where the petition does not in terms apply for partition, and the lands cannot be sold for the payment of legacies without it, the Court will afford the proper relief—Act of Feb. 24, 1834—Practice.

Sur petition for order to sell real estate and answer.

This was a petition by the American Baptist Publication Society and others, legatees under the will of Park Hill Cassady for an order on the executrix to sell real estate for the payment of legacies, the particulars of which are set forth in the opinion of the Court. The answer set forth that it was the intention of the executrix forthwith to sell so much of said real estate as may be needed to carry out the provisions of testator's will with reference to legacies presently payable, but that a forced public sale of the whole of testator's real estate would prejudice her right under the will, as widow, to two-thirds of said estate for life.

E. Coppée Mitchell and *Edward Olmsted* for petition.

H. C. Thompson and *George Junkin* contra.

October 30, 1880. THE COURT. The will of the testator gives to his widow for life two-thirds of his real estate, and to the American Baptist Publication Society, his residuary devisee, one-third, with remainder in the two-thirds given to the widow. Legacies amounting to $25,400 are given. These are charged upon the real estate—power of sale being given to the executors for their payment—with the proviso that if the estate (that is, that portion not so given to the widow) shall be insufficient for the purpose, certain of them amounting to $13,000, shall be postponed until the widow's death.

The personal property applicable to the payment of legacies has proved wholly insufficient, and since the testator's death, which occurred in October, 1874, eight of the thirty-six pieces of real estate of which he died seized, all of which are set out and fully described in the present petition, have been sold by the widow, who is also executrix, under the power conferred by the will. Of the purchase money two-thirds remain upon mortgage during her lifetime, and one-third, amounting to about $5000, has been applied or is applicable to the payment of legacies.

At the rate at which sales have thus been made, it will require over twenty years to dispose of the properties still remaining, if they also are to be sold successively at such times as the widow may deem expedient. And, one-third of the proceeds only being applicable to the payment of legacies, it is evident that all will have to be sold before it can be determined whether the contingently deferred legacies are payable during her lifetime or not. If they are, interest is accumulating upon them, as, under any circumstances, it is upon those which are given absolutely. In the mean time, the widow, it is said, is in the exclusive occupancy of the estate, and receipts of the rents; and thus, while it is true there is the right to an account against her, the estate of the residuary devisee may become so burdened as to be of very little value.

We think that such a result could not have been intended by the testator. It is clear that the legatees in whose favor the lands are charged are entitled to the order of sale, now asked for; but before it can be granted we must ascertain what it is that is to be sold. The widow's two-thirds cannot be touched while she lives, and the sale of an undivided third of twenty-eight separate properties is impracticable.

The third now chargeable must be set apart in severalty. There is no difficulty with regard to this. The Acts of 11th April, 1835 (P. L. 199); 29th March, 1832, § 46 (P. L. 204), and 20th February, 1854, § 1 (P. L. 89; Purd. Dig. p. 1117, pl. 29), make provision for partition in case of a life estate in one or more of the purparts; and the Act of 24th February, 1834, hereinafter referred to, makes the course very clear.

It is objected that the petition does not in terms ask for partition. But it does ask for a sale of that which cannot be determined without it, and it also asks for general relief. Moreover, it is a familiar principle of equity jurisprudence that where all the parties and the subject matter are before the Court, it will afford the proper relief even if they have failed in appropriate terms to ask for it. In Danzeisen's Appeal (23 Smith, 65), where the Court of Nisi Prius had dismissed a bill alleging a trust and asking for an account and reconveyance, the evidence failing to establish a trust, the Supreme Court being of opinion that the facts set out showed a mortgage, though the bill contained no allegation to that effect, reversed the decree in order to "do equity and reach the justice of the case," saying, "we cannot turn the plaintiff out of Court by reason of the inappropriate terms used in the bill, indicating a trust instead of a mortgage." That this principle is equally applicable to the Orphans' Court, whose jurisdiction is administered in the forms of a Court of Equity, is well settled (Woodward's Appeal, 2 Wright, 328; Postlethwaite's Appeal, 18 Smith, 477). In the latter case, in affirming the decree of the Court below granting relief not prayed for by the petition, SHARSWOOD, J., says: "It is evident that the jurisdiction of the Court having attached by the presentation of the petition, it had entire control of the subject as a Court of Equity would have. Having all the parties before it, it can and ought to make such decree as law and equity would require, and which will be binding upon all."

But we need not consider the case upon general principles. Our right to direct this partition as a preliminary to an order for the payment of the legacies out of the real estate is conferred almost in explicit terms by the Act of 24th February, 1834 (P. L. 84)—the Act upon which the present proceeding is founded—which provides that, "When a legacy is or shall be hereafter charged upon or payable out of real estate, it shall be lawful for the legatee to apply by bill or petition to the Orphans' Court having jurisdiction of the accounts of the executor of the will by which such legacy was bequeathed, whereupon such Court, having caused due notice to be given to such executor, and to the devisee or heir, as the case may be, of the real estate charged with such legacy, and to such other persons interested in the estate as justice may require, may proceed according to equity to make such decree or order touching the payment of the legacy out of such real estate as may be requisite and just."

It is certainly "requisite and just," before making the order of sale, that we should ascertain the portion of the estate which alone can be sold during the lifetime of the testator's widow. A partition for this purpose is an essential preliminary.

Under this Act and that of March 14th, 1857, § 1 (P. L. 97), it is probable that we have the power to refer the cause to a Master to make the requisite partition, but upon the whole we prefer that it shall be made in the manner usually practised in this Court. We will therefore award an inquest, with leave to the parties to apply for further order.

Counsel will prepare the necessary decree.

Opinion by PENROSE, J.

November 16, 1880.

Goldsmith's Estate.

Practice—Executor not liable to attachment for default of decedent.

Sur petition for rule for attachment.

The petition of the administrator *d. b. n. c. t. a.* of decedent, set forth, that the account of Charles Eckhardt, deceased, executor of the will of this decedent, as filed by his executrix, had been adjudicated and confirmed, by which it was decreed that the estate of the deceased executor was indebted to the estate of testatrix in the sum of $1384.59. That no part thereof had been paid to the petitioner.

On September 27, 1880, an order was issued commanding the executrix of the deceased executor to pay said amount to the petitioner. The order having been served, but not complied with, on October 19, 1880, a rule was granted on the executrix to show cause why an attachment should not issue against her for not complying with the order to pay. To this an answer was filed by the executrix, that she was unable to pay said amount, because her husband died suddenly, leaving her in almost total ignorance of his affairs, and especially as to said estate. That "she has strenuously exerted herself to find where or how he deposited the funds he became possessed of as executor," and "is still seeking to obtain this knowledge." She therefore prayed that an attachment be not granted against her.

Bowers & White, for petitioner.
John J. Hargadon, contra.

November 20, 1880. THE COURT. The error in this proceeding is in supposing a personal liability was imposed upon the executrix of the deceased executor. She was not decreed to pay the amount ascertained to have been in his hands at the date of his death, but his *estate* was declared the debtor. The petitioner therefore represents simply a creditor of the deceased executor, and must obtain a speedy settlement, in the mode prescribed by law, of his estate. Accordingly the proper practice is, to require the executrix to file an account at the expiration of the year, and then present petitioner's claim for payment.

The attachment is refused, the order to pay vacated, and the petition therefore dismissed.

Opinion by HANNA, P. J.

U. S. Circuit Court— Equity.

May, 1879.

Lathrop and Taylor v. The Junction R. R. Co. and The Pennsylvania R. R. Co.

Railroad—Ownership of track forming part of the line of another railroad in which it is a stockholder—Right of way of latter road—Manner of enforcement—Obligation to transport freight under general railroad law— Stockholders' bill—Preliminary injunction.

Motion for a preliminary injunction.

Bill in equity, filed by Francis L. Lathrop and Lewis H. Taylor, citizens of the State of New Jersey, for themselves and other stockholders of the Junction Railroad Company, against the Junction Railroad Company and the Pennsylvania Railroad Company, corporations incorporated and doing business under the laws of Pennsylvania. At the same time that this bill was filed similar bills were filed by the Baltimore and Ohio Railroad Company and the Central Railroad Company of New Jersey against the same defendants.

The complainants each owned one share of stock of the Junction Railroad Company.

The bill and affidavits set forth the following facts:—

On May 3, 1860, an Act of Assembly was passed (P. L. 1860, p. 780) incorporating the Junction Railroad Company, the capital to consist of 5000 shares of $50 each, subject to the General Railroad Law of February 19, 1849. The company was authorized to construct a railroad, commencing at a point upon the Philadelphia and Reading Railroad, at or near the bridge of said company, near Peters Island, in the river Schuylkill, thence by the best route to a point upon the line of the Pennsylvania Railroad, thence by said railroad by the most direct and practicable route to a point upon the line of the Philadelphia, Wilmington, and Baltimore Railroad. The company was authorized to borrow money to the amount of $300,000, which was subsequently increased to $800,000. By a supplement passed March 23, 1861 (P. L. 177), the company was authorized to use the roadway of the Pennsylvania Railroad and of the West Chester and Philadelphia Railroad, or either of them, with the consent of such companies respectively, or to construct the whole or such parts of their railroad as may be needful, with or without the use of one or both of the roads of the companies aforesaid.

The Junction Railroad Company was formed by a combination entered into by the Pennsylvania Railroad, the Philadelphia, Wilmington, and Baltimore Railroad, and the Philadelphia and Reading Railroad Companies, and all the stock was subscribed for by them except a few shares subscribed for by individuals. The company was organized, and proceeded to construct a railroad from a point on the Philadelphia and Reading Railroad to Haverford Street, and also from the north side of Market Street to a point on the Philadelphia, Wilmington, and Baltimore Railroad at or near Gray's Ferry. The ground between the north side of Market Street and Haverford Street belonged to the Pennsylvania Railroad Company, being part of what is now called the company's yard. The road on this portion of the line was actually made by the Pennsylvania Railroad Company, they paying the cost of materials, labor, and all cost of construction. Bonds were issued by the Junction Railroad Company to the amount of $800,000, secured by a mortgage of the entire road.

Proceedings were afterwards instituted by the Junction Railroad Company, in the State Courts of Pennsylvania, against the Pennsylvania Railroad Company, to determine the rights of the said companies in the portion of road lying between Market Street and Haverford Street, and the decree of the Supreme Court of Pennsylvania declared the ownership of the strip to be in the Pennsylvania Railroad Company, without prejudice, however, to any rights of the Junction Railroad Company relating to the use of said portion. (Pennsylvania Railroad Company's Appeal, 30 Sm. 265.)

By the General Railroad Law of 1849, it is provided that upon the completion of any railroad, the same shall be esteemed a public highway for the conveyance of passengers and the transportation of freight, provided that the said company shall have exclusive control of the motive power, and may establish such rates of toll as to the president and directors shall seem reasonable; provided, however, nevertheless, that said rates of toll, when the cars used for such conveyance are owned or furnished by others, shall not exceed two and one-half cents per mile for each passenger; three cents for each ton of 2000 pounds of freight; three cents per mile for each passenger or baggage car; and two cents per mile for each produce or freight car.

The Baltimore and Ohio Railroad Company proposed to send its cars over the Junction Railroad in course of transmission to New York City, and to bring them back again for transmission to the West; the Philadelphia and Reading Railroad Company, and the Philadelphia, Wilmington and Baltimore Railroad Company were ready and willing to receive and haul these cars, respectively, over their roads to and from the Junction Railroad, but the Junction Railroad Company refused to furnish the motive power to haul the said cars over the portion of their road belonging to the Pennsylvania Railroad Company; permitting the Pennsylvania Railroad Company to furnish exclusively the motive power. The Pennsylvania Railroad Company were requested to furnish the motive power, but returned no answer.

The prayer of the bill was, *inter alia*, (1) That the Junction Railroad Company be enjoined from refusing to furnish motive power to transport over their road freight or passengers shipped by the Philadelphia, Wilmington, and Baltimore Railroad Company, or the Reading Railroad Company. (2) That the Pennsylvania Railroad Company be enjoined from interfering with the Junction Railroad Company in the performance of their corporate duties, and in the transporting of freight and passengers.

The Pennsylvania Railroad Company, in their answer, denied that they had ever surrendered any of their rights to the Junction Railroad Company over that portion of the Junction Railroad which belonged to them, and ran through their yard; and denied that the Junction Railroad Company had violated its duty by refusal to transport passengers or merchandise over said strip of land, or that they were themselves required so to transport said cars.

Samuel Dickson and *John C. Bullitt*, for the motion.

If the owner of an estate stand by and see another expend money upon an adjoining estate, the latter relying upon an existing right of easement in the other estate, without which such expenditure would be useless, and do not interpose to prevent the work, he will not be permitted to interrupt the enjoyment of such easement.
Brooks *v.* Curtis, 4 Lans. 283.

This is a right in the nature of a right of way of necessity.
Washburn on Easements, 31.
Cro. Jac., pp. 170-189.
Bacon's Abr., vol. 4, 688, '9.
Morris *v.* Edgington, 3 Taunt. 31.

When two or more persons have a common interest in property, equity will not allow one to appropriate it exclusively, or impair its worth to the others.
Jackson *v.* Ludeling, 21 Wall. 616.
Green's Brice's Ultra Vires, 565, etc.
D. L. & W. R. R. *v.* Erie R. R., 6 C. E. Green, 307.
Jersey City H. H. R. Co. *v.* Jersey City R. R. Co., 6 C. E. Green, 550.

Adequate relief can be given on an interlocutory application.
Oxlade *v.* N. E. R. Co., 1 C. B. n. s. 454.
Garton *v.* B. & E. R. W. Co., 6 C. B. n. s. 639.
Baxendale *v.* West. R. W. Co., 3 Giff. 650; 7 L. T. n. s. 297.
Att'y Gen. *v.* G. N. R. C., 1 Drew & S. 154.
Lane *v.* Newdigate, 10 Vesey, 192.
Robison *v.* Byron, 1 Bro. C. C. 588.
Rankin *v.* Huskesson, 4 Sim.
Hervey *v.* Smith, 1 K. & J. 392.
Att'y Gen. *v.* Met. Board of Works, 1 Hem. & M. 312.
Hepburn *v.* Lordan, 2 Hem. & M. 345.
Beadel *v.* Perry, L. R., 3 Eq. 465.
Cooke *v.* Chilcott, L. R., 3 Ch. Div. 694.
Audenried *v.* Phila., 68 Pa. St. 375.
Cole Silver Mining Co. *v.* Virginia, 1 Sawyer, 685.
Baptist Congregation *v.* Scannel, 3 Grant, 49.
Manhattan Manf. Co. *v.* N. J. Stock Yard Co., 8 C. E. Gr. 161.

Wayne McVeagh, Chapman Biddle, and *John Scott*, for the Pennsylvania Railroad Company, respondents.

This is not a case for the issue of a preliminary injunction. There is no precedent for using a preliminary writ to take the subject of the litigation from a party who has always heretofore enjoyed it, and give it, *pendente lite*, to a party who has never heretofore enjoyed it—that being the function of a final decree only. There is "not only a current but a torrent of authorities" to the contrary.
Child *v.* Douglas, Kay's Ch. R. 578.
Turner *v.* Spooner, 1 Dr. & Sm. 467.
Durell *v.* Prichard, L. R., 1 Ch. 244.
Gale *v.* Abbot, 8 Jurist, n. s. 988.
Camblos *v.* R. R. Co., 9 Phila. 411.
Farmers' R. R. Co. *v.* Reno O. C. & P. H. R. R. Co., 53 Pa. St. 224.
Mammoth V. C. C. Co.'s App., 54 Pa. St. 183.
Murdock Case, 2 Bland, 469.
University *v.* Green, 1 Mary. Ch. 97.

N. Y. Printing & Dyeing Est. *v.* Fitch, 1 Paige, 97.
Bosley *v.* Susquehanna Canal, 3 Bland, 65.
Att'y Gen. *v.* New Jersey R. R. & T. Co., 2 Gr. Ch. 136.
Att'y Gen. *v.* City of Paterson, 1 Stockton, 624.

But even if a preliminary injunction were a proper remedy the complainants in this case are not entitled to the relief sought. Although they sue as nominal stockholders (having purchased one share each), the bill is not filed in good faith for the protection of the stockholders' interests, but is in aid of the other bills filed by the Baltimore and Ohio and the N. J. Central Railroad companies, two *foreign corporations* of which the complainants are officers. Even in the case of *bona fide* stockholders' bills, the complainants must aver that they had appealed to the company to protect itself, and that it had refused. This bill contains no such allegation.

Dodge *v.* Woolsey, 18 Howard, 331.
Sparhawk *v.* P. R. R. Co., 4 Sm. 401.
Forrest *v.* R. W. Co., 7 Jurist, n. s., 887.

The stockholders cannot have this relief upon any other grounds than that the directors of the Junction Railroad Company are guilty of a breach of trust. They are not guilty of that breach of trust, because the relation in which they stand to the Pennsylvania Railroad Company for the use of this mile of track is in effect and in law a contract made in pursuance of the terms of their charter and exercise of their discretion; and unless this Court will undertake to put itself in the place of the directors, reversing their discretion, and say that the mile must be run in some other mode than under this contract, there can be no injunction.

1 Potter on Corp's, § 84.
Green's Brice's Ultra Vires, 183.

James E. Gowen, for the Junction Railroad Company.

C. A. V.

Oct. 28, 1880. THE COURT. It is no part of my present purpose to notice any other than the main question in this case. It is sufficient for me to say, as to several other questions discussed by counsel at the argument, that, in my opinion, the Court has power to grant the preliminary relief prayed for, and that the alleged impending injury to the interests of the complainants is of such a character as to entitle them to invoke the intervention of the Court.

The Junction Railroad Company is a corporation created by a special Act of the Pennsylvania Legislature, dated May 30, 1860, whereby it was authorized to "construct a railroad commencing at a point upon the Philadelphia and Reading Railroad, at or near the bridge of said company, near Peters Island, in the river Schuylkill; thence by the best route to a point upon the line of the Pennsylvania Railroad, within one mile east of George's Run, at the village of Hestonville; thence by the line of the Pennsylvania Railroad, by the most direct and practicable route, to a point upon the line of the Philadelphia, Wilmington, and Baltimore Railroad."

By a supplement to this charter, passed in 1861, the Junction Railroad Company was authorized to "make a complete line of railway from a point on the Philadelphia and Reading Railroad, at or near the bridge at Peters Island, to a point on the Philadelphia, Wilmington, and Baltimore Railroad, at or near Gray's Ferry Bridge, by the most convenient and practicable route."

By further legislation the company was authorized to borrow $500,000 upon mortgage of its property and franchises, and upon this security a loan of that amount was negotiated upon the authorized guaranty of it by the three companies named.

The stock of the company was taken and is now held by the Pennsylvania Railroad Company, the Philadelphia and Reading Railroad Company, and the Philadelphia, Wilmington, and Baltimore Railroad Company, except a few shares which are held by individuals.

At the organization of the company in 1861, the President of the Pennsylvania Railroad Company was elected its president, and occupied that position until 1867, during which time the whole line of its road was located definitely between its prescribed termini; under his direction a large sum, to wit, about $870,000, was expended in its construction, and the whole of the road, except that part between Market and Thirty-fifth streets, was completed by it.

This intervening part was constructed by the Pennsylvania Railroad Company, and was held by the Supreme Court of Pennsylvania to be the property of that company, and this decision must be regarded as conclusive, so far as the legal ownership of that link is concerned. But in view of the admission that the Junction Railroad may have rights touching the use of the section of road referred to, the decree was entered without prejudice to such rights, or to the assertion of them in an appropriate proceeding.

Various other facts are alleged in the bills of complaint, and are verified by the accompanying affidavits, which, all together, constitute a "strange, eventful" history of the construction of the road.

Enough of them have been here stated to indicate the vital object, and the essential importance to the public, of the construction of the road.

The Pennsylvania, the Philadelphia and Reading, and the Philadelphia, Wilmington, and Baltimore Railroads terminate at Philadelphia. They were unconnected with each other, and so the immense traffic requiring transfer from the one to the other, was necessarily conducted with great expense, inconvenience, and embarrassment. These difficulties could be almost entirely avoided by the construction of a continuous line only about four miles long from Gray's Ferry to Peters Island, and accordingly the Junction Road was projected and made. A broken line with a gap in the middle of it would not answer the purpose; its continuity was absolutely essential to effectuate the object of its creation, as well as to meet the just expectation of its stockholders and the public. So, in the annual report of the Pennsylvania Railroad Company, February 3, 1862, it is said: The Philadelphia, Wilmington, and Baltimore Railroad Company, the Philadelphia and Reading Railroad Company, and the Pennsylvania Railroad Company have organized the Junction Railroad Company, under a charter procured from the Legislature of 1860, and amended at the last session. The object of this line is to connect these three railroads by a *continuous* line along the west bank of the Schuylkill River, from the Reading Railroad, near Peters Island Bridge, to the Philadelphia, Wilmington, and Baltimore Railroad, at Gray's Ferry, *intersecting the Pennsylvania Railroad, near the Wire Bridge, at Fairmount,* so that an interchange of freight between these lines may be effected without passing through the populous portions of the city. In apparent accordance with this declaration were all the acts and declarations of the Pennsylvania Railroad Company during the progress of construction until the controversy arose as to the ownership of the middle section, and they may, therefore, be fairly regarded as, in a great measure, inducing the expenditure of the large sum laid out by the Junction Railroad on its line.

Any other hypothesis must assume that the Junction Railroad Company was willing to imperil the chief object of the enterprise and the value of its investment, by making itself entirely dependent upon the arbitrary will of the owner of the middle section for the profitable use and enjoyment of the two other sections of the line.

Ought the Pennsylvania Railroad Company, then, to be permitted so to control the section of the road of which it is the proprietor, as to exclude the Junction Railroad Company from participation in its use as part of a continuous line? I think not. It must be treated, in equity, as having agreed to such reasonable use of the section owned by it, as is necessary to effectuate the common object of those who furnished the means of constructing the Junction Road as a continuous line; and, to that extent, to a modification of its proprietary rights. It would certainly be unwarrantable in the Junction Company to exclude the Pennsylvania Railroad Company from the beneficial use of the northern and southern sections of the Junction Road, either by denying it altogether, or by imposing burdensome restrictions upon it. Why ought not a like measure of justice be meted out to the other interests associated with the Pennsylvania Company, in reference to the middle section of the Junction Road, when it induced these interests to make large expenditures of money and incur large liabilities upon the faith that this middle section should constitute an indispensable constituent of a joint enterprise? There is no just ground for any discrimination.

While I am of opinion that the Junction Railroad Company may have the right to employ its own motive power over the whole line between its termini, yet, I think, the operations of the road should be conducted with as little friction as possible, and without any avoidable abridgment of the proprietary rights of the Pennsylvania Railroad Company. The injunction granted, therefore, will not restrain that company from operating its own portion of the line with its own motive power.

The following decree was entered;—

(1) And now, October 28, 1880, it is ordered and decreed that an injunction be granted until further order of this Court, enjoining and restraining the said Junction Railroad Company, its officers, servants and agents from declining or refusing or in any manner failing to perform the duties required of them by the charter of said company, and especially from declining or refusing to furnish motive power, haul, receive, ship or transport over its road freights or passengers arriving in cars by the Philadelphia, Wilmington, and Baltimore Railroad destined for the Philadelphia and Reading Railroad or its connections, or from declining or refusing to furnish motive power, haul, receive, ship or transport freight or passengers arriving in cars by the Philadelphia and Reading Railroad, destined for the Philadelphia, Wilmington, and Baltimore Railroad or its connections.

(2) That the said Pennsylvania Railroad Company, its officers, agents, and servants be enjoined and restrained from interfering with or in any manner hindering the said Junction Railroad Company from performing its said corporate duties and transporting freight and passengers as aforesaid.

(3) This injunction shall not be taken to restrain the said Pennsylvania Railroad Company from furnishing exclusively the motive power to transport the cars aforesaid over and upon that portion of the Junction Line which is situated between the north side of Market and Thirty-fifth streets in the city of Philadelphia.

Opinion by McKENNAN, Cir. J.

Supreme Court.

July, '79, 67.   March 5, 1880.
Pennsylvania R. R. Co. v. Bock.

Negligence—Contributory negligence—Suit for death of minor child—Pleading—Declaration—Joinder of common law and statutory claims—Joinder of parties suing in different rights.

In an action against a railroad company for negligence, the defendant requested the Court to charge: "That the plaintiff being about to drive a team, with two mules and a horse on the lead, across a railroad track, with a loaded wagon, having placed his son, seven years of age, on the lead horse, over which he, the father, had no control, was guilty of negligence in placing his son in such a dangerous position; and cannot recover for the loss of his son or his horse killed by the passing train." To which the Court answered: "This point assumes a fact, the existence or non-existence of which is a question for your consideration, to wit: whether plaintiff placed his son on a horse *over which he had no control.* This is for you and we cannot assume it. *If it were true it would be strong evidence of negligence.* It is for you to find under all the evidence in the cause whether there was negligence either on the part of the plaintiff or of his son who was killed, which contributed to the production of the accident. If there was such contributing negligence the plaintiff cannot recover." The verdict was for the plaintiff:

Held, that the assumption in the point forbade its affirmance, and that it could have been well refused without qualifying remarks.

Held, further, that there was error in the remark that if the assumed fact were true, it would be strong evidence of negligence, for on the verity of the facts as assumed, without reference to other proofs, it would be contributory negligence *per se;* and as it was not certain that the error did the defendant no harm, the judgment must be reversed.

Where the form of the declaration shows no inconsistency in the rights sued upon, nor an apparent misjoinder of the claimants thereunder, an actual misjoinder of rights or parties must be taken advantage of on trial and not by motion in arrest of judgment.

A claim for statutory and common law damages admitting of the same pleas and judgment may be joined in the same action.

In an action against a railroad company for the death of plaintiff's minor child, in which was joined a claim for the loss of personal property, it was agreed on the trial that the action should be tried as if the mother were a party, and she should be precluded by the verdict. The verdict was for the plaintiff:

Held, that no such error was apparent on the record as could be taken advantage of by motion in arrest of judgment.

Error to the Common Pleas of Bucks County.

Case, by Anthony Bock against the Pennsylvania Railroad Company, to recover damages for the loss occasioned by the death of his son Anthony Bock, Jr., and also for the loss of a horse killed at the same time by a train on defendant's track at a crossing in the borough of Bristol.

At the trial, before WATSON, P. J., it was agreed that the action should be tried with the same effect as if the plaintiff's wife had been a party plaintiff and that she should be concluded by the verdict. The evidence showed that on the morning of May 31, 1875, the plaintiff was engaged in hauling manure in the borough of Bristol with a team consisting of a hay wagon, two mules, and a lead horse. He had crossed the track, which ran through a well-built up portion of the town, earlier in the day with the wagon and mules only, and proceeded to load up, at a stable not far distant from the track, while his son, a lad of seven years, but remarkably intelligent and well-grown, and accustomed to assist his father in this and other ways, brought the horse round by another road, leading under the track, but which at that time was impassable for the wagon. There was no line attached to the horse, the boy, who rode upon his back, controlling him by the bridle. While the plaintiff was loading the wagon the boy geared the horse to the wagon and when ready to start jumped upon the horse's back and the team started off, the plaintiff taking the near mule by the bridle and walking beside him. At the foot of a slight rise leading to the track and about 60 feet from it plaintiff stopped the team. From this point, owing to the houses, the track is only visible for a few feet in the westerly direction; from a point about eleven feet from the track it can be seen in the same direction for about 468 feet, and from the middle of the track the view is clear for 1500 feet. At the crossing planks are laid down making an even surface. Plaintiff, after stopping the team, walked ahead to the middle of the track, from which place he looked in both directions and listened for about half a minute; not hearing any train he called to the boy to come on, and returning to meet the wagon took the near mule by the bridle as before; just as the horse was about to step across the first rail plaintiff heard a train approaching; he shouted "Oh!" and jerked the mule back but the horse had already got his forefeet on the track and was struck by the locomotive of an east-bound train. The horse was instantly killed; and the boy was thrown upon the engine and received serious injury from which he died within a few hours.

A witness who was present testified that so soon as he saw the train both he and the plaintiff shouted, but within three seconds from the time that the train was in sight the accident happened. There was conflicting evidence as to the rate of speed of the train, which plaintiff alleged was in excess of that permitted by ordinance, the testimony variously estimating it at from eight to twenty-five miles an hour; there was also conflicting testimony as to whether the whistle was blown or the bell rung.

Defendant requested the Court to charge, *inter alia*, as follows: "(5) That the plaintiff being about to drive a team, with two mules and a horse on a-lead, across a railroad track, with a loaded wagon, where trains were running propelled by steam, having placed his son, seven years of age, on the lead horse over which he, the father, had no control, was guilty of negligence in placing his son in such a dangerous position; and cannot recover for the loss of his son or his horse killed by the passing train. *Answer.* This point assumes a fact, the existence or non-existence of which is a question for your consideration, to wit: whether plaintiff placed his son on a horse over which he had no control. This is for you and we cannot assume it. If it were true it would be strong evidence of negligence. It is for you to find under all the evidence in the cause whether there was negligence either on the part of the plaintiff or of his son who was killed, which contributed to the production of the accident. If there was such contributing negligence the plaintiff cannot recover."

Verdict "in favor of plaintiff for the sum of $2176 for horse and funeral expenses included and six cents costs."

Defendant moved in arrest of judgment, upon which motion the Court delivered the following opinion: "It is almost unnecessary to say we can arrest the judgment only for error apparent on the face of the record. Is there such error here? The wrong complained of in the narr. is negligence resulting in (1) the killing of the plaintiff's minor son whereby he lost his services and was put to expense in taking care of and burying his body. (2) The killing of his horse.

"When the jury was about to be empanelled it was agreed by the parties that 'this action shall be tried in the same manner and with the same effect as if Linda Bock, wife of plaintiff, had been a party plaintiff thereto, and that the recovery, if any is had, shall include all her demands against the defendant, and that she shall be concluded by the verdict should it be in favor of the defendant.' We do not regard this as making the wife a party to the suit. We look upon it rather as an agreement that the entire damages should be determined and recovered in the suit by the husband, and that in consideration thereof the defendant should not thereafter be molested for any claim by or for the wife.

"But suppose we consider that agreement as placing her as a party plaintiff on the record. How does this render an error apparent on its face? The effect would be to join her as a plaintiff on every count and upon every statement of ownership or claim. Instead of a separate cause of action in the husband for separate injuries to him we should have a statement of a joint cause of action for injury to joint property in the horse, joint expenses in the burial of the son, and joint loss by reason of his death. The declaration would still be a consistent whole. There would be nothing there to show that the several items of the demand were in different rights. The error, if any, in this respect would be on the trial and not on the face of the record.

"We see no reason why the common law claim for the loss of the horse and the statutory claim for the loss of the son may not be joined in the same declaration. They are of the same nature, admit of the same pleas and are followed by the same judgment. (1 Ch. Pl., 197; Martin *v.* Stille, 3 Wh., 337.)

"These views apply to all the reasons in support of the motion in arrest of judgment."

Judgment was entered on the verdict, and defendant took this writ of error, assigning for error, *inter alia*, (3) the answer to the fifth point presented as above, and (4 and 5) the overruling of his motion in arrest of judgment, and entering judgment on the verdict.

G. & H. Lear, for plaintiff in error.

On the facts as stated in the point submitted the Court should have charged absolutely that there was contributory negligence.

Glassey *v.* Hestonville, M. & F. P. R. W. Co., 7 Sm. 172.
Smith *v.* O'Connor, 12 Wr. 218.
Pittsburgh, All. and Man. R. W. Co. *v.* Pearson, 22 Sm. 169.
Smith *v.* R. R. Co., 8 WEEKLY NOTES, 165.

The action for the boy's death is a statutory right and cannot be joined with the common law remedy for the loss of the horse.

North Pa. R. Co. *v.* Robinson, 8 Wr. 178.
2 T. & H. Pr. 83.
1 Chitty, ¿ 200.

The wife had no cause of action for the loss of the horse; there was therefore a misjoinder of her and her husband's right with his alone.

1 Chitty, ¿ 75 and ¿ 205.

B. F. Gilkeson (with whom were *Geo. Ross* and *L. L. James*), contra.

It could not be said as matter of law that plaintiff was guilty of contributory negligence. In the position in which the father was he could control the movements of the whole team. The position of the driver of a team of four or three horses is always upon the back or at the bridle of the near tongue horse; and under the instruction of the Court the jury so found; it was properly left a question for them.

Catawissa R. R. Co. *v.* Armstrong, 2 Sm. 282.
Oakland R. R. Co. *v.* Fielding, 12 Wr. 320.
Phila. P. R. R. Co. *v.* Hazzard, 25 Sm. 367.

Defendants took their chances on the trial and ought not to unravel the case here, when the defect, if any, might have been taken advantage of by a *non pros.* on the counts for the horse and the funeral expenses.

March 29, 1880. THE COURT. The defendant's fifth point was, "That the plaintiff being about to drive a team, with two mules and a horse on the lead, across a railroad track, with a loaded wagon, where trains were running, propelled by steam, having placed his son, seven years of age, on the lead horse, over which he, the father, had no control, was guilty of negligence in placing his son in such a dangerous position, and cannot recover for the loss of his son or his horse killed by the passing train." *Answer.* "This point assumes a fact, the existence or non-existence of which is a question for your consideration, to wit: Whether the plaintiff placed his son on a horse over which he had no control? This is for you, and we cannot assume it. If it were true, it would be strong evidence of negligence. It is for you to find, under all the evidence in the case, whether there was negligence of the plaintiff, or of his son who was killed, which contributed to the production of the accident. If there was such contributory negligence, the plaintiff cannot recover."

The point must be considered with reference to the facts which the testimony would have warranted the jury in finding. From that they could have found that the train was running through the borough at the rate of twenty miles an hour, and no bell was rung nor whistle blown till after the accident; that the deceased was a remarkably stout and intelligent boy for his age, and was in the habit of working with his father; that he had often rode the lead horse in the team; had, on the day he was killed, taken the horse by a way under the railroad to the place of loading, and geared him to the wagon, while his father put on the load; that he got on the horse, and the team was driven near to the railroad, and stopped; that the plaintiff went upon the track, looked both ways, listened, and neither seeing nor hearing an approaching train, started back, telling the boy to come ahead; that the team was started before the plaintiff reached it; he took the mule by the head, the horse got his forefeet on the track, and was struck within three seconds from the time a witness, who was standing by, saw the cars; that as soon as said witness heard the train, he hallooed, the plaintiff hallooed, but the train was too fast. Not a witness saw anything that could have been done to save the horse or boy between the time of hearing the train and the accident. It cannot be pretended that any evidence shows the horse could have been got out of the way had a man sat in the place of the boy, or if the plaintiff had had a line on the horse.

The assumption in the point forbade its affirmance. It was earnestly argued that the testimony authorized the Court to assume the fact. Perhaps in all the farming and mining portions of the State there is not a Judge or juror who would say a man could have no control of the lead horse unless he has a line on him. Be this as it may, it is not a question of law for the Court to say, where there is no line there is no control.

The point could have been well refused without qualifying remarks, and had it been there would have been no cause of complaint. Its assumed facts are but a fraction of the story, and the part omitted shows the plaintiff's care, before his attempt to cross the track, and that he was caught too suddenly for escape. In the light of the evidence, the Court could not say the plaintiff was negligent, unless it is negligence in itself for a teamster to cross a railway track with his little son riding the lead horse—a proposition which has not been advanced.

Excepting one remark, the instructions to the jury were accurate, adequate, and applicable to the proofs, enabling them to intelligently dispose of the questions submitted. That remark was in the answer to the fifth point, the Court saying, if the assumed fact were true, it would be strong evidence of negligence. As an abstraction, we think that was error; for on the verity of the facts as assumed, without reference to the other proofs, the plaintiff was guilty of negligence. Had the point been differently framed, submitting its isolated facts to the jury, it should have been affirmed; but the Court would have reminded them, as it did, that they were to consider all the facts established by the testimony.

Unless it be certain that the error did the defendant no harm, the judgment must be reversed, and the cause sent back for another trial. This is doubtful. The jury judge of the credibility of witnesses, and possibly they may have found the facts as contended for by the defendant; and, if so, the error was hurtful. The opinion of the learned Judge of the Common Pleas, on the motion in arrest of judgment, comprises all that need be said respecting the fourth and fifth assignments.

Judgment reversed, and *venire facias de novo* awarded.

Opinion by TRUNKEY, J. MERCUR and GREEN, JJ., absent.

May, '80, 85.   May 11, 1880.

Russell et al. v. Baughman et al.

Ejectment—Specific performance—Estoppel—Laches—What amounts to such laches as will bar a right to specific performance.

Ejectment is in Pennsylvania an equitable action, and when a plaintiff seeks by it to enforce specific performance of a contract to convey, he must show that he has himself been ready, prompt, and desirous of performance on his part; if he has slept on his rights, and by conduct long persisted in, conveyed the idea that he had abandoned them, he cannot, after there has been a material change of circumstances affecting the rights of the parties, obtain redress.

Although this rule is not held so strictly against a defendant in possession, it is generally by reason of his equities, but when they are so weak as to present no substantial ground for protection, they must yield to the general rule.

By writing made in 1856, A. contracted to convey to B. & C. certain mining rights, the purchase-money to be paid in instalments; the hand money was paid, but no deed was made, nor were any of the instalments ever paid; in 1871 A. conveyed the land, by a deed making no reference to the prior grant of the mine, to D. & E., who, in 1878, brought ejectment against B. & C. On the trial B. & C. tendered the unpaid purchase-money, and sought to obtain specific performance of the contract of 1856:

Held (affirming the judgment of the Court below) that they were barred by lapse of time.

Error to the Common Pleas of Bedford County.

Ejectment, by Baughman & Barndollar, against S. L. Russell, Thomas A. Scott, J. H. Sigmoun, Reese D. Fell and wife, and the heirs of Robert H. Gratz, deceased, to recover a tract of land, including the iron ore and minerals upon and under it, with the exclusive right to mine, take, and carry away the same.

On the trial, before HALL, P. J., the following facts appeared: On the 8th of February, 1856, Frederick Mench being the owner of about 222 acres of land in West Providence Township, Bedford County, Pa., executed an agreement with Samuel H. Tate and Wm. P. Schell, conveying "the right to dig, take, and carry away all such iron ore and other minerals as may be on, in, and under" said lands, "supposed to contain one hundred acres more or less," . . . "for one dollar and fifty cents per acre payable in four instalments—one in hand and the remainder in annual instalments—the deed to be made on the first of May following." This paper was not signed by the wife of Frederick Mench. Twenty dollars was paid Feb. 8, 1856, according to agreement. The agreement was not recorded until Sept. 7, 1865. By divers conveyances the title of Tate and Schell became vested in the defendants.

On Nov. 4, 1871, Mench and wife sold the whole tract of 222 acres to the plaintiffs, Baughman and Barndollar, by a deed containing a general warranty, for $4400. No reference was made in the deed to the mining rights conveyed to Schell and Tate. Afterward the lands greatly increased in value, and Mench obtained a release from all responsibility to Baughman and Barndollar, "on account of the clause of general warranty contained in their deed so far as the same applies to any damage or loss they might sustain on account of the ore or mineral lease to Tate and Schell."

By a lease dated May 30, 1872, the defendants granted several tracts of lands to the Kemble Coal and Iron Co. for a period of eleven years from April 1, 1872. The tract now in dispute was included in this lease, which was delivered and recorded July 13, 1872. Baughman and Barndollar notified the company in June, 1872, that they were the owners of the land and minerals in the Mench tract, and afterward, on March 6, 1873, executed to the Kemble Company an agreement allowing the company to mine on the Mench tract. This license was acknowledged by Baughman and Barndollar, and recorded April 23, 1873. In September 1872, the Kemble Company commenced mining, worked about one year, then ceased operations and notified their landlords accordingly. Nothing was ever expended upon, nor was there any ore taken from the Mench tract. In November, 1878, Baughman and Barndollar applied to the Kemble Company for a revocation of the license granted by the agreement of March 6, 1873. More than five years had elapsed and nothing was being done—they received no rent from the Kemble Company. The contract was rescinded by the Kemble Company. Subsequently this action was brought.

The defendants tendered plaintiffs, on the trial, $325.00, the balance of the purchase-money and interest in full, and they refused to take it.

Defendants submitted to the Court below, *inter alia*, the following points:—

(5) . . . If the jury believe . . . that the vendees of Tate and Schell exercised acts of ownership by leasing said property to the Kemble Coal and Iron Company, of which Baughman and Barndollar had notice; that Baughman and Barndollar sold ten acres of ground to said lessees, and stood by when the money was being laid out and expended by said lessees in attempting to open the ores in said ground, then they are estopped from setting up a claim to the land, and the verdict can only be for the plaintiffs, the land in dispute to be released upon the payment of the unpaid purchase-money owing by defendants on the articles of agreement between Mench and Tate and Schell. *Refused.* (2d assignment of error.)

(6) That an action of ejectment is a possessory

action, and by it possession is conceded in the defendant; that Tate and Schell having paid part of the purchase-money and taken possession, which is conceded by this action, their vendees, the defendants, are entitled to hold the land upon payment of the balance of the purchase-money, and the verdict must be for the plaintiffs for the land in dispute, to be released upon the payment of the balance of the said purchase-money. *Refused.* (3d assignment of error.)

In the general charge his Honor said, *inter alia*: "If a party seeking a specific performance has been guilty of gross *laches*, or if in the intermediate period there has been a material change of circumstances affecting the rights, interests, and obligation of the parties a court of equity will refuse a decree. An ejectment is a substitute for a bill in equity to enforce a performance. A party cannot call upon a court of equity to enforce a specific performance unless he has shown himself ready, desirous, prompt, and eager."

Verdict "for the plaintiff," and judgment thereon. The defendants took this writ, assigning for error, *inter alia*, the refusal of their points, as above.

Russell and *Longenecker* (*W. H. Koonts* with them), for plaintiffs in error.

Baughman and Barndollar are estopped from denying the validity of the lease to the Kemble Company, both because they stood by and saw money expended upon the faith of it, and because they ratified it by their subsequent agreement.

Troxell *v.* Lehigh Crane Co., 6 Wr. 514.

In the contract between Mench, of the one part, and Tate and Schell, of the other, the covenants were mutual, and it was as much the duty of Mench to tender a deed and demand the balance of the purchase-money, as it was of Tate and Schell to tender a performance on their part.

Williams *v.* Bentley, 3 C. 301.

Then, too, the defendants below were in possession of the minerals under said land. This is conceded by the form of action, which is a possessory action and admits the possession in the defendants; and being in possession, and having paid part of the purchase-money, and being ready and willing to pay the balance, we were entitled to have specific performance of the contract decreed.

Dixon *v.* Oliver, 5 W. 509.
Caldwell *v.* Fulton, 7 C. 480.

John Cessna, for defendants in error.

It is not alleged that there was any actual possession taken by Tate and Schell, or the grantees; they rely upon the technical plea that our bringing an action of ejectment admits their possession. It is difficult to see how the action brought in 1878 can affect the state of facts in 1856.

Conceding all they ask, they are far too late in asking for specific performance.

Porter *v.* Dougherty, 1 C. 405.
Callen *v.* Ferguson, 5 Id. 247.
Churcher *v.* Guernsey, 3 Wr. 84.
Alley *v.* Deschamps, 13 Ves. 225.
Peters *v.* Delaplaine, 49 N. Y. 362.
Roby *v.* Cossitt, 78 Ill. 638.

May 24, 1880. THE COURT. Ejectment in Pennsylvania is an equitable action. (Peebles *v.* Reading, 8 S. & R. 484.) When brought to enforce the execution of an agreement to convey, it is a substitute for a bill in equity. When a party calls upon a court of equity to enforce specific performance he must show that he has himself been ready, prompt, and desirous of performing on his part; if he has been guilty of gross laches, and unreasonable delay, if he has slept on his rights, and by conduct long persisted in conveyed the idea that he had abandoned them, he cannot, after there has been a material change of circumstances affecting the rights, interests, and obligation of the parties, move a Chancellor to decree specific performance. (Parrish *v.* Koons, 1 Pars. 79; Patterson *v.* Martz; 8 Watts, 374; Callen *v.* Ferguson, 5 Casey, 247, Du Bois *v.* Baum, 10 Wright, 537; Miller *v.* Henlan, 1 P. F. Smith, 265; Cadwalader's Appeal, 7 Id. 158.) It is true the rule is not held so strictly against one who is in possession defending. It is, however, generally by reason of his equities. When they are so weak as to present no substantial grounds for protection, they must yield to the general rule. If possession be taken, and improvements be made and expenditures be incurred, they will create a substantial equity.

The agreement under which the plaintiffs in error claim was executed in February, 1856. It was for a mineral right in consideration of $150, to be paid therefor. One-fourth of the purchase-money was to be paid by the first of May following, when the deed was to be executed, and the residue in three annual instalments thereafter. Twenty dollars, part of the first instalment, was paid at the execution of the agreement, and nothing more was ever paid. There was evidence indicating a willingness on the part of the vendor to convey on payment according to the contract; but no subsequent payment was made nor deed demanded. Neither the vendee, nor those claiming under him, took any visible possession of the premises, they made no expenditure on them, they took no ore from them. After a lapse of nearly fifteen years, the defendants in error elected to consider the plaintiffs in error in the constructive possession, and brought this action of ejectment. In the mean time the lands had become of very great value, and the plaintiffs in error sought to revive equities which they

had suffered to sleep for so many years. It was too late. The time to assert them had passed. Judgment affirmed.
Opinion by MERCUR, J. SHARSWOOD, C. J., and GREEN, J., absent.

July, '78, 43.   March 15, 1880.
Hartley v. White.

Partnership—Fraudulent transfer of firm property in payment of individual debts of a partner—Attachment execution—Rights of firm creditors—Practice—Judgment—Defective form of entry of judgment amendable.

A partner, who sells firm property without the knowledge and consent of his copartner, and with intended fraud on the rights of creditors of the firm, to pay his own individual debts, gives the purchaser no title as against creditors of the firm

The entry of a form of judgment containing a reference to an Act of Assembly and to a case in the Reports, is not a fatal error, but may be amended by striking out such references.

Error to the Common Pleas of Susquehanna County.

Attachment execution, by Norman White and D. K. Morss, assignee of Norman White, against M. J. Decker and Andrew Halstead, defendants, and Silas Hartley, garnishee. Returned "served" as to Halstead and Hartley, and "*non est inventus*" as to Decker. A rule was taken on the garnishee to answer interrogatories, who afterwards pleaded "*nulla bona*."

On the trial, before MORROW, P. J., the following material facts were in evidence: In 1870 M. J. Decker and Andrew Halstead, who were trading as Decker & Halstead, in the milling and lumber business, borrowed $2000 from Norman White, for the use of the firm in their business. White entered judgment against them on the note given for this loan, July 27, 1872. After the sale of their property at sheriff's sale, White assigned to Morss one-half of the above judgment and costs, under a stipulation that White's part of the judgment was to be paid out of the proceeds of the sheriff's sale, and if anything remained over it was to be applied to the part of the judgment assigned to Morss. Under the auditor's report, Morss received $206.57, and on the rest of the judgment which remained unpaid, he issued in June 24, 1875, this attachment execution against Hartley as garnishee, on the ground that he had in possession property belonging to the firm of Decker & Halstead.

On December 2, 1872, Hartley bought from Halstead notes and judgments taken by the firm of Decker & Halstead in their business, amounting to $2050, for which he paid him $753, $35.21 of which was a debt due him by the firm, and the rest was in notes he held against Halstead individually, excepting the sum of $225, which he paid on a note of Halstead's held by Stewart. These notes were bought while the firm was deeply in debt, and without the knowledge and consent of Decker, who had sold out his interest in the firm to Halstead. Some time after the sale of the notes, the firm became insolvent. Hartley, as he alleged, collected about $700 of the notes, the most of which were surrendered to Hartley, and new notes given Hartley in place of the same.

The Court, in the general charge to the jury, said, *inter alia:* "Hartley claims he purchased of Halstead about Dec. 2, 1872, notes and judgments owned by Decker & Halstead, amounting to $2050, and paid him therefor $753, of which $35.21 was a debt held against them, and the rest was in notes he held against Halstead alone, except $225, which he paid on a note one Stewart had against Halstead. He swears that he considered many of these notes almost or entirely worthless, others he made the purchase, but that the purchase was made with the knowledge and express consent of Decker. This Decker denies *in toto* except as to the Gifford note, as you will recollect his evidence in regard to that in connection with Mrs. Gifford's evidence. The plaintiff claims to recover the amount yet unpaid on his judgment against Decker & Halstead, $1250.20, if the jury find the notes in the possession of Hartley are of that value. If not of so great value then to recover an amount equal to their value. He bases his right to recover on the ground that the transfer of the notes assigned to Hartley was fraudulently made, the fraudulent purpose being to pay the individual debts held against Halstead out of the firm property and to prevent the same from being applied to firm debts. If the jury find the transfer was fraudulent, and was made for the purpose stated, and Hartley colluding with Halstead or with Decker & Halstead obtained the notes, etc., knowing they were the property of the firm, it was void, and the plaintiff may recover whatever they were worth. This for the reason that Hartley acquired no title as against the creditors of Decker & Halstead. They may follow and seize them in his hands as firm property. Or if the jury find that Hartley obtained the notes and judgments from Halstead in payment of the debts against Halstead without the knowledge or consent of Decker, knowing them to be firm property, the plaintiff may recover their value. This for the reason that by the action of Halstead the firm were not deprived of their title to this property and could maintain suit therefor; this being the fact, the creditors of Decker & Halstead could reach and hold them upon attachment execution.

"One partner cannot use the property of the firm to pay individual debts, even if the act is honest and in good faith, if his copartners had no knowledge of the transaction, if such transfer prevents the creditors of the firm from collecting their debts. A different rule prevails if both parties consent *bona fide* to the transfer. You will recollect that Hartley swears Decker did consent to it.

"Fraud is not presumed, the burden is on the party alleging fraud to establish it by satisfactory evidence."

The Court directs the jury to find a special verdict, and stated to them all the facts their finding should cover, calling their attention to evidence bearing upon each proposition they were to determine and find in their verdict.

The jury found the following special verdict: "We find that the money for which the note entered in No. 715, Aug. T., 1872, was borrowed by Decker & Halstead, copartners, and used in their partnership business, of $1250.20 remain unpaid. Attachment execution served July 24, 1875. That Silas Hartley, garnishee, obtained from Andrew Halstead about the 2d day of December, 1872, notes and judgments amounting to about $2000, face value; that the notes and judgments belonged and were the property of Decker & Halstead when so assigned and transferred. That he has collected on these notes $700, and has given up other notes to the makers, and included in notes taken in his own name to the amount of $723. That the interest on the $700 is $210, and on the $723 is $216.90, computed by us for five years. We find that the notes and judgments not collected, surrendered, were of the value of $125 when they transferred to Hartley interest on same for five years $37.50. We further find that the value of the notes surrendered by Hartley to the makers, and new notes taken by him, and now uncollected, were of the value of $578.40, interest thereon for five years, $173.50. For all the notes and judgments which Hartley received from Halstead he paid Halstead $493.53, by delivering to him his notes and accounts he held against Halstead individually, also paid a note of about $225 which one Stewart held against Halstead. He also applied payment of a debt he had against Decker & Halstead of $35.21, making a total of $753.74.

"We further find that the transfer of these notes adjudged was fraudulent, and intended by Halstead and Hartley to be in payment of Halstead's private debts, and to prevent the same from being used and applied in the payment of the firm debts of Decker & Halstead, and the transfer was in the absence and without the knowledge or consent of M. J. Decker, except as to the Gifford note, and that at this time Decker & Halstead were largely in debt, and soon after became insolvent and unable to pay their debts, the debt of the plaintiff being one.

"We find also that about five years ago Hartley borrowed a pair of platform scales, property of Decker & Halstead. At the time he borrowed them they were of the value of $65; that on being required to return them he refused, unless Decker & Halstead paid an individual debt he owed him, said Hartley, and he still has them in his possession.

"We find for the plaintiff such sum as the Court may be of opinion he has a right to recover under these facts, verdict to be moulded by the Court and judgment entered thereon in such manner and amount as the Court may deem legal and proper. If the Court be of opinion he cannot recover under the facts found by us, then our verdict is for the defendant."

A rule was afterwards granted to show cause why judgment should not be entered for $1250, which the Court made absolute, in the following entry of record:—

"And now, April 27, 1878, rule absolute, judgment in favor of plaintiff and against the said garnishee, for $1250.20 and costs. Under the Act of Assembly and the cases (*vide* Bonaffon *v.* Thompson, 4 WEEKLY NOTES, 210), execution is restricted first as to the goods and effects in the garnishee's hands, or so much thereof as may satisfy the plaintiff's demands, and secondly against him as of his proper debt if he refuses to produce such goods and effects. BY THE COURT."

The garnishee took this writ, assigning for error, *inter alia*, the charge of the Court, the form of the special verdict, and the entry of judgment thereon.

Little & Blakeslee, for plaintiff in error.

The priority of firm over individual creditors is admitted where both have acquired liens on the partnership assets before a sale. It is the specific lien before a sale which enables a firm creditor, through the equity of the other partner, to enforce his priority. But a general creditor of the firm has no such lien, and cannot restrain an individual partner from selling his interest.

Young *v.* Frier, 1 Stockton, 468.
Mittnight *v.* Smith, 2 C. E. Green, 259.

The right of a firm creditor is subordinate to the power of a partner to make a *bona fide* disposition of his interest before the creditor has acquired a lien.

Field *v.* Hunt, 24 Howard's Pr. 463.

The lien of a partnership creditor is in time if acquired before a sale.

Coover's Appeal, 5 Casey, 15.

After the sale and delivery of a chose in action

to a third party a firm creditor cannot follow it.

Teal *v.* Bogue, 8 Harris, 234.

The insolvency in this case was subsequent to the sale of the notes. By the agreement of July 20, 1872, Decker was to pay Halstead's half of the firm indebtedness. He thus became the principal and Halstead the surety. Decker having no equity the firm creditor is without remedy.

Colgrove *v.* Tallman, 67 N. Y. 95.

The equity is in the partners and not in the creditors. If the partners waive or extinguish it, it cannot be set up by firm creditors.

Taggart *v.* Keys, 3 Phila. 97.

The firm's title to the notes passed to Hartley because (1) a partner may sell a chose in action, and (2) a partner may, without his copartner's assent, pay a firm debt.

Mere preference of individual debts over firm debts is not such fraud upon partnership creditors as will be set aside by a court of equity.

National Bank *v.* Sprague, 5 C. E. Green, 30.

A special verdict must contain all the facts upon which the judgment of the Court is to rest.

P. R. R. *v.* Evans, 53 Pa. 250.

Nothing can be supplied by the charge nor from the evidence.

Craven *v.* Gearhart, 1 WEEKLY NOTES, 257.
Commonwealth *v.* McDowell, 6 Id. 74.

The special verdict is fatally defective, because it does not state the amount of the Gifford note, and does not find the dissolution of the firm.

Bentley and *E. Robinson*, for defendant in error.

A partner cannot make a valid transfer of firm property in payment of his individual debts without the assent of his copartner.

Todd *v.* Lorah, 25 Sm. 155.

Such a transaction with a partner, with full knowledge of the circumstances, is *mala fides* and a nullity.

Leonard's Ex'rs *v.* Winslow, 2 Grant, 139.

A partner cannot divest the title of the firm to partnership property by fraudulent delivery to a third party, as security for his separate debt, nor for his own benefit in any way.

Porter *v.* Miller, 1 WEEKLY NOTES, 240.

An attaching creditor takes the property in the hands of the garnishee, with all its legal incidents, and is entitled to the fund produced by such property.

Fessler *v.* Ellis, 2 Grant, 472.
Fitzsimmon's Appeal, 4 Barr, 248.
Fox *v.* Foster, Id. 119.

The equity of Decker could in no way be defeated by Halstead's fraud. The argument on the other side, showing the right of a partner to sell *bona fide* his interest in the firm property before a lien was attached, is wholly inapplicable to this case.

The special verdict, though admittedly defective, yet contains all the facts necessary for the Court to base its judgment upon. There is no more reason why the amount of the Gifford note should be mentioned than that that of any other note should be.

May 3, 1880. THE COURT. This judgment was entered on a special verdict. It does not present the facts in a clear and methodical manner. It is not a model to be followed. It may, however, be sufficient to sustain a judgment. The plaintiff in error was served as garnishee of Decker and Halstead, copartners. The jury found that in fraud of the creditors of the firm, and without the knowledge or consent of Decker, except as to one note (shown by evidence to be about $40), Halstead assigned and transferred judgments and notes, the property of the firm amounting to about $2000 to the garnishee; that the transfer of this property was fraudulent and intended by Halstead and the garnishee to be in payment of Halstead's private debts, and to prevent the same from being used and applied in the payment of the firm debts of Decker and Halstead; that the firm was at the time largely in debt, and soon after became insolvent. They further found that out of the claims thus assigned to the garnishee, he had collected a specific sum in cash, and that he had surrendered to the makers notes, and taken new ones therefor for a sum certain and of sufficient value added to the cash received, to exceed by several hundred dollars the sum due to the attaching creditor, or for which judgment was entered against the garnishee.

It is well settled that one partner cannot make a valid transfer of firm property in payment of his individual debt, without the consent of his copartner (Todd *v.* Lorah, 25 P. F. Smith, 155). Such act is a fraud on his copartner, and the right of property in the firm does not pass to the individual creditor. The present case goes still further. Not only was the attempted sale a fraud on the copartner, but it was intended and operated as a fraud on the creditors of the firm. It is then clear, under these facts, the purchaser cannot hold the property against the creditors intended to be defrauded. He has no reason to complain of the amount for which judgment was entered against him. It is for a sum less than he has realized out of the property.

It is further objected that the form of the judgment is wrong. It must be conceded that the reference to the Act of Assembly, and to the case of Bonaffon *v.* Thompson, might more appropriately have been made in an opinion of the Court than be interwoven in the judgment. This, however, is not a fatal error. The form of the judgment can be amended. It is now done by striking out those references so that it shall stand—judgment in favor of plaintiff below, and against said garnishee for twelve hundred and fifty dollars and twenty cents and costs, to be levied on the goods and effects of Decker and Halstead in his hands, or, in case he fails or refuses to produce such goods and effects, sufficient to satisfy the execution, then to be levied against him as his own proper debt. Thus amended the Judgment is affirmed.

Opinion by MERCUR, J.

Jan. '80, 141.   February 18, 1880.

Armstrong's Estate.
Philadelphia Trust Company's Appeal.

Trusts and trustees—Dry trust—Statute of Uses—Sole and separate use—Estate tail.

When there is a dry trust for the sole and separate use of a woman neither married nor in contemplation of marriage, the mere fact that on a certain contingency, which might never happen, the trustee was directed to execute a conveyance after the death of the cestui que trust will not change the dry character of the trust and make it active.

The words "heirs of the body lawfully begotten," are the proper and technical words to create an estate tail, and where nothing in the will qualifies or changes their import, they must have their legal effect whatever the testator may have intended.

Appeal from the Common Pleas No. 2. of Philadelphia County.

Bill in equity, filed by Henrietta Armstrong against The Philadelphia Trust, Safe Deposit, and Insurance Co., trustees under the will of Thomas Armstrong, et al.

The bill set out the following facts: Thomas Armstrong, late of the city of Philadelphia, died in 1842, having first made his last will and testament in writing, duly proved and registered, wherein he devised, after the death or marriage of his widow, unto his son Edward, certain real estate, upon the following trusts:—

"I give and devise to my son Edward all that house and lot of ground, with the appurtenances, adjoining the south side of my said dwelling-house, to hold to him, his heirs, and assigns, to and for the uses, intents, and purposes hereinafter expressed and declared of and concerning the same, that is to say, in trust, that he shall and will permit my daughter Henrietta to receive the rents thereof for her sole use during her lifetime, to the intent that the same shall not be liable to the contracts, or control of any husband with whom she may intermarry, and from and immediately after her decease, then to the heirs of the body of the said Henrietta lawfully to be begotten. But in case the said Henrietta should not marry, or marry and have no such issue, then upon trust that he, the said Edward, and his heirs, executors, or administrators shall and will grant and convey the fee simple inheritance of the before-described premises unto such person or persons, in such manner as the said Henrietta, whether she be married or sole, by her last will and testament, in writing, signed, sealed, and attested in the presence of two credible witnesses, may order and direct. But if she should die without making such disposition, then in trust for my two daughters, Mary McKeen and Emeline Bent, and their heirs and assigns forever; and it is my will and request, that the said Edward pay off the ground-rent and mortgage on the before-mentioned premises, that the same may be free from encumbrance at the time my said daughter may be entitled to receive the rents thereof, as aforesaid, or as soon afterwards as he may be able to discharge the same."

The testator left surviving him a widow, since deceased, and four children. His son Edward, the trustee, having died, The Philadelphia Trust, Safe Deposit, and Insurance Company was appointed trustee in his stead by the Orphans' Court. The testator's daughter, Henrietta, the complainant, was neither married nor in contemplation of marriage at the death of testator, and has remained single.

By virtue of a decree of the Orphans' Court, the said real estate was lately sold at private sale, under the Act of April 18, 1853, all interested parties consenting thereto. A deed was also executed by the complainant, duly recorded, etc., which was intended to bar and dock the entail. The purchase-money was received by the Philadelphia Trust Company, and is held upon the same trusts as heretofore.

The bill averred that the trust is not now, and never was an active one, and that the complainant took a legal estate in fee tail, and that said entail is now barred; and that the oratrix is therefore absolutely entitled to the securities in the hands of the present trustee, and prays accordingly.

The answer admitted the facts averred in the bill, and submitted to the judgment of the Court in respect to the questions of law involved, etc.

Upon hearing, on bill and answer, the Court (HARE, P. J.), entered a decree in accordance with the prayer of the bill, directing the Trust Company to transfer absolutely the property in its hands to Henrietta Armstrong. The Trust Company took this appeal, assigning for error the entering of the decree as above.

L. L. Eyre (*R. L. Ashhurst* with him), for the appellant.

The devise created an active trust in favor of the daughter for life, with alienative limitations over in fee. The operation of the rule in Shelly's case must be in abeyance until the intention of the testator is discovered.

An estate tail cannot be implied from the context, because (1) the particular estate is given as a sole and separate use, and (2) the words determining the estate must, of necessity, mean a definite failure of issue.

This case is decided by—

Ingersoll's Appeal, 6 WEEKLY NOTES, 125.

Rowland Evans, for the appellee.

The trust is a dry trust, and there is nothing to prevent the operation of the Statute of Uses. It being given as a sole and separate use, and the cestui que trust not being in contemplation of marriage, or married at the time of its creation, the trust falls.

McBride *v.* Smith, 4 Sm. 250.

An estate tail is expressly created here, the words "heirs of her body," being apt, technical ones of limitation, not to be construed otherwise except upon the direct express intention to the contrary on the part of the testator.

Bender *v.* Fleurie, 2 Gr. 345.
Linn *v.* Alexander, 9 Sm. 43.
Taylor *v.* Taylor, 13 Sm. 486.

This case is clearly distinguishable from Ingersoll's appeal; there the trust given was an active one, and the gift was in fee simple.

May 3, 1880. THE COURT. This contention arises under the will of Thomas Armstrong. It declares "I give and devise to my son Edward all that house and lot of ground with the appurtenances adjoining the south side of my said dwelling house, to hold to him, his heirs and assigns, to and for the uses, intents, and purposes hereinafter expressed and declared of and concerning the same, that is to say, in trust, that he shall and will permit my daughter Henrietta to receive the rents thereof for her sole use during her lifetime, to the intent that the same shall not be liable to the contracts or control of any husband with whom she may intermarry, and from and immediately after her decease, then to the heirs of the body of the said Henrietta lawfully to be begotten; but in case the said Henrietta should not marry, or marry and have no such issue, then upon trust, that he, the said Edward, and his heirs, executors, and administrators, shall and will grant and convey the fee simple inheritance of the before-described premises unto such person or persons, in such manner as the said Henrietta, whether she be married or sole, by her last will and testament in writing, signed, sealed, and attested in the presence of two credible witnesses, may order and direct. But if she should die without making such disposition, then in trust for my two daughters, Mary McKeen and Emeline Bent, and their heirs and assigns forever."

Edward, the trustee named, having died, the appellant was appointed in his place by the Orphans' Court. The real estate, by virtue of a decree of said Court, was sold at private sale under the Act of Assembly. The record of the proceedings declared that the purchaser should take an estate in fee simple, discharged of all trusts, contingent remainder, and executory devise limited thereon. Henrietta, the appellant, also executed to the purchaser a deed intended to bar the entail. On motion in open Court, it was duly entered of record in the Common Pleas of said county. The purchase-money was received by the appellant. The appellee filed this bill, praying for a decree that, under the will, she took an absolute legal estate in fee, in the real estate; and that the appellant be required to assign and pay over to her the proceeds of the sale thereof. The Court decreed in accordance with her prayer.

We will first consider the character of the trust created by the will. Its language, substantially, is in trust, that the trustee shall permit Henrietta to receive the rents thereof for her sole use during her life, and the intent of the trust is declared to be, that the property shall not be liable to the contracts or control of any husband she may thereafter have. No care or duty was imposed on the trustee in regard to the management or protection of the property, nor as to the collection or payment of the rents. He had no active duties to perform. It was a dry trust. The purpose was to create a separate use in Henrietta. She was *sui juris*. She took the whole beneficial interest devised to her. Her estate, as well as that given in remainder, were both legal, for the trust was executed under the statute. (Physick's Appeal, 14 Wright, 128; Nice's Appeal, Id. 143; Ogden's Appeal, 20 P. F. Smith, 501; Megargee *v.* Naglee, 14 Id. 216; Kinsel *v.* Ramey, 6 Norris, 248.) The mere fact that on a certain contingency, which might never happen, the trustee was directed to execute a conveyance after her death, to her devisees, did not change the dry character of the trust and make it active. (Bradley's Appeal, 36 Leg. Int. 38.) Still further, Henrietta was neither married nor contemplating marriage at the death of the testator. She never married. The expressed purpose of the trust being solely to protect against any husband she might have, it cannot be sustained. A separate use for a woman cannot be created unless she is covert or is in immediate contemplation of marriage. (McBride *v.* Smythe, 4 P. F. Smith, 245.) The trust therefore failed to take effect. What estate then did Henrietta take? It was given to her for life, and the remainder expressly limited to the heirs of her body lawfully begotten. These are the proper and technical words to create an estate tail. They must have their legal effect, whatever the testator may have intended. (Bender *et al. v.* Fleurie, 2 Grant, 345; Linn *v.* Alexander, 9 P. F. Smith, 43; Taylor *v.* Taylor, 13 Id. 481.) No words in the will changed or qualified the legal import of this language. An estate tail was thereby created. It was duly barred by the conveyance, and the learned Judge correctly decreed in favor of the appellee.

Decree affirmed, and appeal dismissed at the costs of the appellant.

Opinion by MERCUR, J.

Quarter Sessions.

December 4, 1880.

Commonwealth v. Wilson.

Criminal law—"Ticket scalping"—Acts of May 6, 1863, and April 10, 1872, forbidding the unauthorized selling of railroad tickets—Constitutionality of—Practice—Demurrer to evidence in criminal trial—Effect of.

Sur demurrer to evidence.

The defendant, Albert Wilson, a railroad ticket broker doing business in the city of Philadelphia, was indicted under the Act of May 6, 1863 (Purd. Dig. 220), and the supplement thereto of April 10, 1872 (P. L. 51), for that on July 28, 1880, he sold to one George G. Bishop an unused portion of an unlimited contract or ticket entitling the holder to one first-class passage from Altoona to Pittsburgh by way of the Pennsylvania Railroad, contrary to the provisions of the said Acts, etc. The ticket, with coupons attached, was originally sold by the company's agent in Boston, and was so stamped on its back.

The Act of May 6, 1863, as amended by the Act of April 10, 1872, provides as follows—

Sect. 1. It shall be the duty of the owner or owners of any railroad, steamboat, or other conveyance for the transportation of passengers, to provide *each agent who may be authorized to sell tickets, or other* certificates entitling *the holder* to travel upon any railroad, steamboat or other public conveyance, with a certificate, setting forth the authority of such agent to make such sales; which certificate shall be duly attested by the corporate seal, if such there be, of the owner of such railroad, steamboat, or other public conveyance, and also by the signatures of the owner, or officer whose name is signed upon the tickets or coupons, which such agent may sell.

Sect. 2. It shall not be lawful for any person, not possessed of such authority, so evidenced, to sell, barter, or transfer, for any consideration whatever, the whole, or any part of any ticket or tickets, passes, or other evidences of the holder's title to travel on any railroad, steamboat or other public conveyance, whether the same be situated, operated, or owned within or without the limits of this Commonwealth.

Sect. 3. Any person or persons violating the provisions of the second section of this Act shall be deemed guilty of misdemeanor, and shall be liable to be punished, by a fine not exceeding five hundred dollars, and by imprisonment not exceeding one year, or either or both, in the discretion of the Court in which such person or persons shall be convicted.

Sect. 4. It shall be the duty of every agent who shall be authorized to sell tickets, or parts of tickets, or other evidences of the holder's title to travel, to exhibit to any person desiring to purchase a ticket, or to any officer of the law who may request him, the certificate of his authority thus to sell and to keep said certificate posted in a conspicuous place in his office for the information of travellers.

Sect. 5. It shall be the duty of the owner or owners of railroad, steamboat, and other public conveyances, to provide for the redemption of the whole, or any parts or coupons of any ticket or tickets, as they may have sold, as the purchaser, for any reason, has not used, and does not desire to use, at a rate which shall be equal to the difference between the price paid for the whole ticket, and the cost of a ticket between the points, for which the proportion of said ticket was actually used; and the sale by any person, of the unused portion of any ticket, otherwise than by the presentation of the same for redemption, as provided for in this section, shall be deemed to be a violation of the provisions of this Act, and shall be punished as hereinbefore provided. *Provided,* That this Act shall not prohibit any person who has purchased a ticket from any agent authorized by this Act, with the *bona fide* intention of travelling upon the same the whole distance between the points named in the said ticket, from selling the unused part of the same to the company that sold the same: and it shall be the duty of the said company to pay for such unused portion of ticket, the difference between the actual fare to point used, and the amount paid for such ticket.

The defendant first demurred to the indictment, and this demurrer having been overruled *pro forma* by the Court, the trial proceeded and upon the close of the Commonwealth's case, the defendant demurred to the evidence.

W. Horace Hepburn, for the demurrer.

The Act under which the defendant is indicted is unconstitutional and void, in that it violates the several provisions of the Constitution of the United States, which declare that no citizen shall be deprived of his privileges or immunities, life, liberty, or property, without *due process of law*; that no law shall be passed impairing the obligation of contracts; and that Congress shall have power to regulate commerce among the several States.

Constitution of U. S., Art. I., §§ 8, 10, Art. V. Amendments thereto, Art. XIV., sect., 1.

Further it is void because it creates a monopoly in a lawful business, and it assumes power not legislative in its nature.

The ticket in question was originally sold, and the contract of which it is the evidence was made by the railroad company in Massachusetts, where no such law exists. On its face the ticket and coupons entitled *"the holder"* to passage from Boston to Pittsburgh. It contained no restrictions on transferability. The railroad company contracted with the purchaser to pass the *holder* of the ticket; the purchaser therefore bought the right either to travel himself, or to give away, or to sell the ticket. This he might do in Boston, or *en route* until he reaches Pennsylvania, where he finds this law, which impairs the obligation of his contract by limiting its sale *to the company that sold it, for a specified price,* under penalty of forfeiting his property (for the vendor's benefit) and fine and imprisonment; this without "due process of law."

This phrase *due process of law* has a well-defined legal meaning. It is derived from Magna Charta, and was originally styled *law of the land.* "By the law of the land is most clearly intended the general law which *hears before it condemns*, and proceeds upon inquiry and renders judgment only after trial."

 Webster's definition.   Dartmouth College Case, 4 Wheaton, 519.

"The Legislature has no power to deprive one of his property and transfer it to another, for private use, *by enacting a bargain between them.*"

 In re John and Cherry Sts., 19 Wend. 676.
 Westervelt *v.* Gregg, 12 N. Y. 209.
 Taylor *v.* Porter, 4 Hill, 147.
 Embury *v.* Conner, 3 N. Y. 517.

The right of property includes the right of using and *disposing* of a thing as one's own. The power of alienation is a necessary incident to the right of property. In the right of transfer there is value, and value is property. A law which extinguishes or changes rights of property without due legal process comes directly in conflict with the Constitution.

 Wynehamer *v.* The People, 13 N. Y. 434.
 2 Kent Comm. 326.
 2 Bouv. Law Dict. 346.

This Act extinguishes the right of transfer, (unless the owner accepts a special bargain made for him by the Legislature) without a trial, or other process of law.

The Act further prescribes that none but the railroad company shall engage in the business of selling tickets, and thus unlawfully creates a *monopoly in a lawful business.* Any person may *buy* with impunity, but cannot *sell* his acquisition. No one can obtain by legislation an exclusive right to sell, except by virtue of the patent or copyright laws.

 Live Stock Ass. *v.* Crescent City Co., 1 Abb. C. C. 388.
 Slaughter House Case, 16 Wallace, 122.

It is true that the Legislature may prescribe what are called "police regulations," but this Act does not come within the scope of this power. The preamble, reciting the reasons of the Act, has no reference to any subject within the police power of the State, but starts with the unwarrantable assumption that the legal holder of a railroad ticket has no right to sell it, and then draws from this false premise the questionable conclusion that a re-sale by the purchaser would be a fraud on the railroad company and on the public. The police power includes the right to make *restrictions* upon otherwise legitimate business for the prevention of calamities, diseases, or offenses; for purposes of charity, for registration, etc.; but Acts *prohibiting* a business not *per se* immoral or illegal, to the prejudice of the many and the benefit of the few, are unconstitutional. Part of the citizen's right of natural liberty, is the liberty to choose his occupation, and a law which summarily deprives a class from adopting a lawful employment deprives them of both their liberty and their property, without due process of law.

 Mayor of Hudson *v.* Thorn, 7 Paige, 261.
 Gaslight Company's Case, 25 Conn. 19.
 Slaughter House Case, *supra*, opinion by FIELD, J., p. 83.
 Arrowsmith *v.* Burlingim, 4 McLean, 497.
 Cooley's Const. Lim. 487, 493.
 1 Bl. Comm. 125.
 Dorsey *v.* Allen, 11 Rep. 84.
 Burlemaqui's Political Law, sec. 15.
 Locke on Civil Government, sec. 142.
 Calder *v.* Bull, 3 Dall. 388.

Suppose a purchaser in Boston buys a ticket entitling the holder to travel to San Francisco over a designated route, via Philadelphia, and on arriving in Philadelphia desires to change his route, how is he to get his money? The company from which he purchased would only redeem (if at all) the unused portion *over their own line*, and that for less than its value. But this portion may have been all used. The Act prohibits the sale of tickets on all railroads both in and out of the State; but it is ridiculous for the Legislature to legislate beyond their jurisdiction.

The Act thus operates as a burden on interstate commerce, for passenger travel is commerce.

 R. R. Co. *v.* Husen, 5 Otto, 465.
 Chy Lung *v.* Freeman, 92 Id. 275.

Finally, the Act in question is an assumption of power not in its nature legislative or constitutional, in that it deprives the citizen of his liberty, his property, his right to travel; it impairs the obligation of a lawful contract, and makes another bargain for him; it creates an unlawful monopoly; it imposes an excessive penalty by fine and imprisonment; all without trial before a magistrate, court, jury, or other *due process of law.* The Act is obnoxious alike to the natural, constitutional, and social rights of a freeman.

William W. Ker, Assistant District Attorney, and *Wayne Mac Veagh* (with them *Robert W. Lesley*) contra.

On principle and authority the Act in question is constitutional. Its subject does not fall within any of the powers delegated by the several States to the United States. The Constitution of the United States must be strictly construed. Even on general subjects delegated to the United States, the States may legislate so far as relates to the safety, health, morals, and domestic order of their citizens. The delegation to Congress of the right to regulate commerce was not a surrender of the "police power" of the State, on that subject.

 R. R. Co. *v.* Husen, 5 Otto, 465.
 Slaughter House Case, 16 Wallace, 83.

Thus the constitutionality of State Laws relating to the following commercial subjects has been admitted or judicially affirmed, viz., Acts prohibiting the export from the State of uninspected beef, pork, biscuit, bark, butter, lard, pot and pearl ashes, flour, meal, flaxseed, leather, lumber, and tobacco; prohibiting the import into the State of coal, lime, grain, salt fish, and marble unless inspected; prohibiting the sale of adulterated provisions; the storage of explosives within city limits, etc.

So, on the subject of personal liberty, the State has passed valid laws authorizing the summary arrest, conviction, and imprisonment of tramps, and professional pickpockets when found in crowds; articles of apprenticeship may, on the death of the master, be sold by his executor without the consent of the apprentice; it is a misdemeanor, for a cashier of a bank to engage in any other occupation; to employ female waiters in a theatre or concert saloon; for a physician or apothecary to practise without a diploma; to sell bread otherwise than by weight, or butter in lumps less than a pound; to sell liquor to, or buy scrap iron from minors, etc. Other Acts prescribe licenses as requisites to engaging in certain kinds of business, as, *e. g.*, by agents of foreign insurance companies, owners and pilots of steamboats, engineers, auctioneers, etc. Other Acts might at first seem to impair the obligation of contracts. Thus notes, bills, and obligations falling due on holidays must, by Act of Assembly, be paid the day previous.

The Act now in question clearly falls within the scope of a police regulation, and is much less stringent than many of those above cited. Its lawful object is to prevent frauds, by diminishing the temptation offered to employés of railroad companies to omit to punch, and to steal and sell travellers' tickets, and by discouraging thieves from stealing tickets from emigrants and others.

This Act is also in the nature of a license Act. It is objected that the licensing power is not vested in a public official, but in a private corporation; we answer, physicians, apothecaries, and attorneys-at-law receive their diplomas from colleges.

But the Act does not in any degree impair a contract or deprive one of his property without "due process of law." The purchaser knows when he buys the ticket that it is to be surrendered to the company on arriving at his destination, just as a baggage check is surrendered. If he does not complete his journey, the law provides a full remedy, viz., that the company shall, on application, redeem the unused portion, for its proportionate value. Thus a due process of law is provided, whereby honest ticket holders are protected from loss. The purchaser was bound to know of the Act when he bought his ticket, and its provisions were virtually written in the contract.

Acts similar to this, relating to the unauthorized sale of railroad tickets, have been declared constitutional in Indiana and Illinois; and we are informed that the courts of Dauphin and Allegheny counties have declared our own Act to be constitutional.

Fry *v.* State, Sup. Court of Indiana, vol. 63 (1878), 552.
18 Am. Law Register, N. S. 425.
People *v.* Walser, Criminal Court of Cooke County, Ill., Chicago Leg. News, vol. 11, Sept. 28, 1878, p. 12.

THE COURT. (LUDLOW, P. J.) The defendant was indicted for the violation of the following Act of Assembly, passed May 6, 1863, and amended by the Act of April 10, 1872. [His Honor here quoted the Act, *ut supra*.]

A demurrer was filed to the indictment, which was overruled *pro forma*, by the Court. The trial then proceeded in the usual way, and when the District Attorney closed the Commonwealth's case the defendant demurred to the evidence. The legal effect of this demurrer was to admit the truth of every fact proved by the Commonwealth, and of every fair inference to be drawn from the facts, and the only question now presented to us, is the question of the constitutionality of the Act of Assembly under which this indictment is framed. If the decision of the Court is against the defendant, the demurrer is overruled and judgment may at once be entered upon the record for the Commonwealth. It is as well to notice this effect of a demurrer to the evidence.

A demurrer to the indictment only, if decided against the defendant, is always followed by an order giving the defendant leave to plead over, because he has had no trial by a jury. I know of but one instance in which this practice in a criminal court was ever departed from. In the Circuit Court of the United States for the District of New York, a judgment was entered upon a demurrer to an indictment only, but Congress settled the question promptly by an Act which gives to the defendant in such cases a right to a trial by jury. Where, however, the demurrer is to the evidence, the cause has been heard upon its merits, and such a demurrer admits the truth of every fact proved, and the defendant stands alone upon the constitutionality of the Act of Assembly. If the evidence is clear, and the law applies to the case, and is constitutional, the judgment follows as a matter of course.

Demurrers to evidence are rare in Pennsylvania, but Commonwealth *v.* Parr (5 W. & S. 345), established the law, and the question is no longer an open one.

This demurrer stands then only upon the decision of the question of the constitutionality of this Act of Assembly, and wherever such a question arises it becomes the Court to approach the solution of it with caution. While the judicial department of the government may destroy a law, every Court in the Commonwealth, and especially a subordinate tribunal, will only pronounce such a decision, having such an effect, where the law is clearly unconstitutional, and, therefore, void. Had the Legislature of this State the right to enact this law?

In the view which we take of this case and of the facts proved, it is unnecessary to decide how far the Legislature may restrict the right of an individual to sell a single ticket bought here or in another State, and make it criminal for that individual so to do; much of the reasoning which follows may apply to such a case, but that is not the case developed by the evidence, for here the testimony produced presents the case of one who has established a business in Philadelphia, the whole object of which is to trade in railroad tickets; he is in fact a "ticket broker."

This law is attacked because it violates the provisions of the Constitution of the United States, in that it deprives a person of his property without due process of law, abridges the privileges and immunities of citizens of the United States, interferes with the right of Congress to regulate commerce with foreign nations and among the several States, and impairs the obligation of contracts.

And the Act is, as is argued, unlawful under our own and the Federal Constitution, in that it creates a monopoly in lawful business, and is an assumption of power not legislative in its nature.

It is not true that this Act of Assembly deprives a person of his property without due process of law, for by the very terms of the Act the unused portion of any ticket may be sold to the company which issued it, "and it shall be the duty of said company to pay for such unused portion of the ticket the difference between the actual fare to the point used and the amount paid for such ticket." Here the owner of the ticket is simply limited in the sale of the ticket to the company from which he bought the same, and is not deprived of it or his property in it, and if the Legislature may upon any valid ground (a point to be hereafter considered) thus limit a right, the law sins not against the clause in the Constitution referred to. But it is said that this law abridges the privileges and immunities of citizens of the United States. Upon the facts admitted here, what privilege or immunity of this defendant has been abridged? His right to establish a certain business, which the Legislature has declared to be, in the preamble, the cause of "numerous frauds," has been curtailed, and it may be destroyed, but is this an abridgment of "immunity or privilege" with the meaning of the Constitution of the United States? In a state of nature a man may establish any business injurious to health he pleases; he may, unless restrained somehow, destroy at will all who deal with him. In a state of nature men may store gunpowder in dangerous places, sell tainted meat, liquor without inspection and license, set up gambling houses and houses of ill-fame, and do numerous other acts which any thinking man may imagine; but civilized men, living under a benign government, easily recognize the principle that rights and duties are reciprocal, and that these may grow out of the very fact that men surrender a portion of their natural rights in order that they may live together in civilized countries under a common rule of action called the law.

This principle was embodied in an authoritative declaration of the law by the Court, in Corfield *v.* Coryell (4 W. C. C. 371), where the meaning of the words now under consideration claimed and received the attention of the Court: "We feel no hesitation in confining these expressions to privileges and immunities which are fundamental. . . . Among these are protection by the Government of the right to acquire and possess property of every kind, and to pursue and obtain happiness and safety, *subject, nevertheless, to such restraints as the Government may prescribe for the general good of the whole.*"

If the clause in the Constitution is to receive the construction contended for in this case, then all the laws above referred to, and many others which might be named, which, under a well-known principle (to be hereafter specified), have been sustained, must be in conflict with the Constitution of the United States, because the citizen's privileges and immunities have been destroyed or "abridged," and are void. To state such a result is to answer the argument made in this case upon this point. But it is argued that the Act of Assembly impairs the obligation of a contract. The ticket sold in this case was simply, at best, the evidence of a contract, and not the contract itself. For convenience these tickets have been introduced, and the person who presents the ticket exhibits a card in the nature of a receipt; before this ticket was sold the Act of Assembly was passed, and when, therefore, the contract itself was made, this defendant must be presumed to have known that to contract with any one who was not an authorized agent of the company which had sold the ticket was a criminal act.

The question in my mind is, not what was the contract made by the original holder of the ticket with the company in Boston, but what was the contract made in this jurisdiction. Was or was not that a contract prohibited by law? If the State can, for any legal reason, limit or restrain the sale of these receipts, then any contract made is illegal and void, and no obligation is "impaired" under the Constitution of the United States, for none legally existed or could exist.

The last point made and ably argued by the learned counsel for the defendant, Mr. Hepburn, will develop the true principle upon which this law must be sustained, and will moreover develop and illustrate the admirable manner in which, upon a true interpretation of the law, the Constitution of the United States, and the sovereign authority of the individual States may not only be harmonized, but made effective under our delicate and complicated system of government.

By Art. X. of the Amendments to the Constitution of the United States, it is expressly provided: That "the powers not delegated to the United States by the Constitution, nor prohibited by it to the States, are reserved to the States respectively or to the people."

In the case of Railroad Co. *v.* Husen (5 Otto, 465), the Supreme Court of the United States declares: "We admit that the deposit in Congress of the power to regulate foreign commerce, and commerce among the States, was not a surrender of that which may properly be denominated police power. What that power is it is difficult to define with sharp precision. It is generally said to extend to making regulations promotive of domestic order, morals, health, and safety. . . . It may be admitted that the police power of a State justifies the adoption of precautionary measures against social evils. Under it a State may legislate to prevent the spread of crime, pauperism, or disturbances of the peace."

No State Legislature may with impunity interfere with the power which Congress possesses "to regulate commerce with foreign nations and among the several States." Why? Because this power has been directly vested in Congress by the several States and the people thereof.

Any obstacle to commerce or burden laid upon it is, by the authority of the Supreme Court of the United States, from the leading case of Gibbons *v.* Ogden (9 Wheaton, 1), to the present time, unconstitutional and void. To fall, however, within the prohibition the law must be an obstacle or a burden within the meaning of the decision of the Supreme Court of the United States.

Can it be contended that a law which prohibits that which has become a fruitful source of crime is an obstacle or burden to commerce between the States?

The law in effect declares that the railroad companies as common carriers shall exercise their franchises subject to a duty, to wit: the repurchase of unused tickets, but for reasons of public policy no unauthorized agent shall sell these tickets to any one. How does this limitation or restriction hinder transportation of either men or things, and transportation (as has been said) is essential to commerce, or rather it is commerce itself. (See Railroad Co. *v.* Husen, *supra*.)

The law does not prohibit the sale of tickets at all, but only admits the right to authorized agents of the company, and compels the common carrier, that is the company, to repurchase. To prove that the power exercised in this instance by the Legislature of Pennsylvania is in no just and legal sense such a regulation of "commerce between the States" as to impinge upon any provision in the Constitution of the United States, is not only to answer the last objection made to this Act, but to develop the principle which sustains this and kindred laws.

We have already adverted to the fact that there resides in every Commonwealth a fundamental right to protect her citizens.

In Railroad Co. *v.* Husen, *supra*, it was said, "We admit that the deposit in Congress of the power to regulate foreign commerce and commerce among the States was not a surrender of that which may properly be denominated police power."

The principle thus admitted is founded, under the Constitution of the United States, in the rights reserved to the States and the people, and it has not only received the sanction of the highest Court under the Government of the United States, but that sanction has been emphasized in the Slaughter House case (16 Wall. 83), where the majority of the Court firmly maintained the right of the State under the Constitution.

The power to create a police regulation then resides in the State, and in the State alone. Has the Legislature of Pennsylvania exercised her right to declare what shall become a constitutional police regulation with reference to the sale of unused railroad tickets as a business to be transacted by brokers throughout the Commonwealth, or has a law been enacted which establishes a monopoly?

It would be useless to refer to a multitude of Acts, already upon the statute book, in which this power has been used.

The learned Assistant District Attorney, Mr. Ker, referred in detail to at least fifteen or twenty laws, all of them analagous in principle to the law now under consideration. It would also be a mere affectation of learning to cite from the reported decisions of the United States Supreme Court, case after case, in which the right of a State to enact laws in principle identical with the law now before the Court, has been affirmed. Already we have in this opinion referred to opinions which, in our judgment, rule this cause.

It is enough now to say, that in the case reported as the Slaughter House case, and cited *supra*, the doctrines pronounced by the Supreme

Court of the United States not only embrace a cause like the one now before this Court, but go much beyond it. That great cause did not decide that a monopoly might be created, but that a Commonwealth might do that which was demanded for the public welfare.

Even Mr. Justice FIELD, one of the dissenting Judges, declared that this "power extends to all regulations affecting the health, good order, morals, peace, and safety of society, and is exercised in a great variety of subjects, and in numberless ways."

In the argument of this cause it was publicly stated, by the learned gentleman, Mr. McVeagh, who assisted the District Attorney, that large numbers of tickets had been stolen from emigrants, going West, before the trains had passed Harrisburg; other tickets, which had expired by limitation of time, had been sold to ignorant and unsuspecting victims, while the conductors upon the road were daily importuned by the agents of brokers to sell to them unused tickets, thus presenting a temptation to otherwise honest men to become plunderers of the stockholders of this road.

I do not take for granted these facts, and express no judgment upon them, but I have a right to assume, that reasons based upon such facts were presented to the Legislature, and that, influenced by these reasons, thus presented, the Legislature intended to destroy a business detrimental to good morals, and as bad in its effects as gambling itself. Viewed in this light, the preamble to this Act of Assembly has an incisive force. That preamble reads thus:—

"Whereas, Numerous frauds have been practised upon unsuspecting travellers by means of the sale by unauthorized persons of railway and other tickets, and also upon railroads and other corporations, by the fraudulent use of tickets in violation of the contract of their purchase," etc.

Upon the trial of this very cause it appeared in evidence that, in addition to the ticket purchased from Altoona, west, this defendant sold a pass, which had been given to an employé of the road to enable him to travel from Altoona to Philadelphia *and return*. This employé, finding his services wanted here, sold the return pass to this defendant, who in turn sold it to the purchaser, who testified in the cause.

A double fraud was thus perpetrated—one by this defendant, who knew exactly what he bought, and afterwards sold, and the other by the employé, who might have been saved from this perpetration of a fraud upon the stockholders of this company but for the temptation held out to him by this defendant. We have nothing to do with the wisdom of this Act of Assembly. With the facts, however, before me, it is not difficult to understand why the legislative department of the Government determined that the time had arrived when a business which produced results such as have been specified, should be utterly destroyed, and, by a police regulation, it has been declared to be a criminal act to establish a brokerage business in the sale of "the whole or any part of any ticket or tickets, passes, or other evidence of the holder's title to travel on any railroad, steamboat, or other public conveyance."

This Act of Assembly is, under the evidence in this cause, constitutional, and judgment will be entered upon the demurrer to the evidence for the Commonwealth.

His Honor then sentenced the defendant to four months' imprisonment, and to pay a fine of $200.

Common Pleas—Law.

C. P. No. 1.   Nov. 27, 1880.

Reis v. Junker.

Foreign attachment—Practice—In foreign attachment a bond may be given by the garnishee to the sheriff with surety to be approved by the Court, conditioned for the return of the goods attached, or payment of the debt, under the Act of June 13, 1836, sec. 50, and the sheriff shall thereupon withdraw from possession of the goods—The bond should be given to the sheriff, and not to the plaintiff.

Rule to show cause why the garnishee in a foreign attachment should not give a bond to the sheriff, conditioned for the return of the goods attached or payment of the debt, the sheriff thereupon to withdraw, etc.

Under the Act of March 17, 1869, two attachments had issued and certain goods in the hands of John Junker attached as the property of Chas. Junker, the defendant.

John Junker claimed the goods as his individual property, and sheriff's rule of interpleader was taken, pending which rule a writ of foreign attachment was issued and the same goods again attached. Whereupon the present rule was taken by the garnishee.

George Sergeant, for the rule, relied on the Act of June 13, 1836, sec. 50 (Purd. Dig. 718, pl. 11).

O. A. Law, contra, contended that under the Act the bond should be given to the plaintiff in the foreign attachment and not to the sheriff.

Winship and *Gilpin*, for the sheriff.

THE COURT. Rule absolute.

WEEKLY NOTES OF CASES.

Vol. IX.]   THURSDAY, DEC. 30, 1880.   [No. 19.

Supreme Court.

Jan. '79, 237.   March 19, 1880.
Brandon v. Fritz.

Ejectment—Interfering surveys—Presumption of authority to make a re-survey—Effect of granting patents—Sale of land assessed in a mixed list as "unseated land"—County Commissioners' deeds—Tax sales.

In July, 1793, James Sillyman obtained eighteen warrants, of 400 acres each, previously applied for by him in his own name, and in the names of others, as warrantees. These warrants called for land on the "north side of Mahanoy Mountain, supposed to be in Berks County." Surveys were made under these warrants in July, 1793, by Henry Vanderslice, Deputy Surveyor of Berks County, whose location was subsequently found to have been made upon territory in Northumberland County. Vanderslice's surveys were returned 16th July, 1793. On the 18th July, 1793, a caveat was filed against granting patents thereupon, for the reason that the location interfered with older warrant rights. No citation ever issued upon this caveat. In October, 1793, a re-survey of fourteen of the eighteen warrants was made by William Gray, Deputy Surveyor of Northumberland County, partly upon the same ground previously occupied by Vanderslice, though avoiding the interferences complained of. Gray's surveys were returned 15 March, 1794. Five patents were granted upon tracts of the Gray location in 1806; two in 1808; one in 1813, and three in 1865. Upon tracts in the Vanderslice location a patent was granted in 1833, and one in 1870. John Bitler obtained a warrant for 100 acres of land in 1827, and caused a survey under it to be made by George Reber, D. S., in June, 1829. The Bitler survey, as located by Reber upon the ground, interferes with the Gray surveys in the warrantee names of Christian Troxel, Christian Immel, Casper Thiel, and John Shomo.

The Thiel tract was sold to the county for non-payment of taxes in 1834, and sold by the commissioners at public sale in 1843. The Immel and Troxel tracts were sold to the county for non-payment of taxes in 1844, and sold by the commissioners at public sale in 1849. The Bitler tract was sold to the county for non-payment of taxes at the same time with the Immel and Troxel tracts, in 1844, and sold by the commissioners at the same time with the said tracts, by public sale, in 1849. The deed from the commissioners to the purchaser of the Bitler tract was not delivered, nor the purchase-money paid by him, until five years after payment of the purchase-money and delivery of the commissioners' deeds to the purchasers at the same sale of the Immel and the Troxel tracts. In an ejectment by plaintiffs claiming under the Bitler warrant and survey:

Held (affirming the judgment below), that the eighteen warrants applied for and issued at the same time were intended to form a block of surveys, and that they were so located is clearly shown by the return of Vanderslice July, 1793. There was nothing to show that the Vanderslice surveys were ever accepted. A patent was issued by the Commonwealth for the Anna Maria Shomo tract, as located by Vanderslice; this, if done understandingly, would be some evidence of the acceptance of his surveys. But it was clearly shown that the patent was issued by mistake, and contrary to the intention of the party in interest.

Held, further, that the caveat, although never acted upon, afforded sufficient grounds for refusing to accept the Vanderslice returns. Another reason for not accepting them was the fact that the surveys were not within his proper district; though the latter fact would not have invalidated the title if his returns had been accepted and patents issued in pursuance thereof:

Held, further, that the acceptance of Gray's surveys, as well as his authority to make them, may be inferred from the fact that nearly all the tracts included in his block of surveys have been patented. Granting a patent according to a return of survey, is virtually an acceptance of the return.

Held, further, that the plaintiffs' claim was properly restricted to the Christian Troxel tract, as located by Gray, and does not embrace any portion of the Casper Thiel, John Shomo, or Christian Immel tracts.

Error to the Common Pleas of Schuylkill County.

Ejectment, brought in 1863, by Nelson Brandon and Henry Snyder against Andrew Fritz, Henry Fermier, *et al.*, to recover a tract of land in Union Township, Schuylkill County, containing two hundred acres, or thereabouts, bounded by land surveyed to James Smith, Christian Immel, John Klinger, and others. Plea, not guilty. Edward S. Silliman and James B. Boylan were subsequently added as plaintiffs.

The case came before the Supreme Court on a previous writ of error. (See Fritz *v.* Brandon, 28 Sm. 342; S. C., 2 WEEKLY NOTES, 164.)

The case was tried 20th January, 1879, before PERSHING, P. J. The plaintiffs asserted their title to the land in controversy by an application of John Bitler, dated 16th of March, 1827, for one hundred acres of land; a warrant dated 21st March, 1827, to John Bitler, for one hundred acres of land, "being unimproved, adjoining land surveyed for James Smith on the east, and on the south, west, and north vacant," situate in the township of Union, in the county of Schuylkill; and a survey made under this warrant by George Reber, Deputy Surveyor, dated 22d June, 1829, for 199 acres 63½ perches, and allowance for roads; and the return, indorsed: "Accepted the 17th of October, 1829." . . . . They then introduced, under objection and exception, parol evidence that John Bitler took up this land in trust for his two daughters, Hannah and Elizabeth, and that they furnished him with the money with which to pay for the survey and the fees of the land office; also that John Bitler executed a deed of conveyance of the same to Hannah and Elizabeth in 1829 or 1830, and that this deed is lost; that Hannah Bitler sold her interest in the John Bitler tract to her sister, Elizabeth Bitler. Also, under objection and exception, parol evidence that Elizabeth Bitler paid the taxes upon this tract from the year 1829 to 1841; and tax receipts of the supervisor of Union Township to Hannah and Elizabeth Bitler for 38 cents for road-tax in 1834, and for 4⅞ cents for the year 1840, dated Union Township, 1839. . . . They then gave in evidence, under objection and exception, the transcript-book of triennial assessments for Union Township, with assessments to Hannah and Elizabeth Bitler, as follows: for the years 1832, 1833, and 1834, "100 acres mountain land, 50 acres do.;" for 1835, 1836, and 1837, "60 acres unseated land;" for 1838 and 1839, "Bitler, Elizabeth, 103 acres land; Bitler, Elizabeth and Hannah, 30 acres land on the Green Mountain;" and for 1840, "Bitler, Elizabeth and Hannah, 30 acres land on the Green Mountain;" for 1841, "30 acres unseated land;" for 1842, "300 acres land unseated;" for 1843, "Bitler, Elizabeth, 103 acres of land; Bitler, Elizabeth and Hannah, 300 acres unseated land." The plaintiffs alleged that these assessments to Hannah and Elizabeth Bitler refer to the land in controversy; also that this land was assessed as seated land until the year 1841, after which date it was transferred to the unseated list without notice to Hannah and Elizabeth Bitler, the owners. They introduced, under objection and exception, the testimony of a clerk in the office of the County Commissioners, to prove that the list of assessments given in evidence was a seated list; it appeared, however, upon cross-examination, that the list was a "mixed list," in which there were assessments both of seated and of unseated land.

They then gave in evidence, under objection and exception, a deed dated 18th December, 1858, Elizabeth Bitler to Nelson Brandon, for "all her right, title, and interest of, in, and to any and all real estate in the County of Schuylkill to which she may be entitled;" a deed dated 16th April, 1860, Elizabeth Bitler to Henry Snyder, for "the undivided one-half part of a certain tract in Union Township, Schuylkill County, containing 199 acres 63½ perches, and a release dated 17th April, 1860, Nelson Brandon to Henry Snyder, for the same. Then also two deeds, conveying respectively undivided interests in this tract, the one dated 16th January, 1872, from Henry Snyder to James B. Boylan, and the other dated 23d December, 1872, from Nelson Brandon to Edward S. Silliman. They introduced, under objection and exception, testimony of witnesses to prove that Nelson Brandon had exercised acts of ownership upon the John Bitler tract; that he had built a log house upon it, and had shafted for coal there.

They then gave in evidence the receipt of Henry S. Magraw, State Treasurer, dated 9th August, 1856, to Nelson Brandon, for $73.40, purchase-money and interest due to the Commonwealth upon 199 acres 63½ perches, surveyed in the name of John Bitler, and $10 for patent fees. Also transcript of Union Township, from 1854 to 1860, with divers assessments of seated and unseated lands, to John Bitler, deceased, Nelson Brandon, and Hannah and Elizabeth Bitler, and, under objection and exception, Treasurer's extract book, to show payment of taxes upon the John Bitler tract from 1854 to 1857, inclusive. The plaintiffs then rested.

The defendants gave in evidence an application of James Sillyman, in his own name and in the names of others, dated 1st July, 1793, for eighteen tracts of land, of 400 acres each; eighteen warrants dated 1st July, 1793, each for 400 acres of land, "on the north side of Mahanoy Mountain, supposed to be in Berks County," in the warrantee names of James Sillyman, Susannah Sillyman, Casper Thiel, Mary Thiel, Henry Thiel, Christian Immel, George Rose, Catharine Rose, Jacob Kelchner, Maria Kelchner, Ann Maria Shomo, John Shomo, Christian Troxel, John Klinger, John Witman, Mary Witman, Jacob Yeager, and Wm. Witman; and surveys made in October, 1793, by William Gray, Deputy Surveyor of Northumberland County, under fourteen of these eighteen warrants; among them those in the warrantee names of Christian Troxel, Christian Immel, Casper Thiel, and John Klinger. Upon each survey was the indorsement, "Another return on this same warrant made by Henry Vanderslice, D. S. of Berks County, located in another place." They gave in evidence the old purchase-money voucher and a copy of the purchase-money blotter, "J. Sillyman, etc., July 1, 1793, 18 w'ts of 400 each; 7200 acres, paid in specie £180. Fees £9," and an official connected draft of these fourteen surveys; also a certified copy of the entry of the commission of William Gray, dated 22d April, 1785, to be Deputy Surveyor of all that part of Northumberland County lying east of the river Susquehanna. They proved, by a certified list of returns, that these fourteen surveys were returned to the land office in a block by William Gray, on the 15th March, 1794.

They gave in evidence patents to John Meyer, dated 10th December, 1806, for each of the tracts respectively, as surveyed by Gray, in the warrantee names of James Sillyman, Susannah Sillyman, Henry Thiel, Mary Thiel, and George Rose; patents dated 13th January, 1808, to John Meyer, for the Catharine Rose and the Jacob Kelchner tracts respectively, as surveyed by Gray; and a patent dated 25th January, 1813, to Jacob Trout, for the Casper Thiel tract, also conforming to the survey of William Gray; these, as tending to show the completion of title to the Gray block of surveys and the acceptance of them by the land office. They then proved assessments for Union Township, Schuylkill County, for the years 1841, 1842, and 1843, in the names of Christian Troxel, Christian Immel, and John Klinger respectively, "400 acres unseated land;" a sale by the County Treasurer to the County Commissioners of the Troxel, Immel, and Klinger tracts, for non-payment of taxes, on the 10th June, 1844, and gave in evidence a deed for each of them, dated respectively 13th July, 1844, from the Treasurer to the Commissioners; they proved a sale of the said three tracts by the Commissioners, on the 16th July, 1849, to John W. Roseberry, B. Nehff, and H. Krebs, and gave in evidence deeds for the same from the Commissioners to Roseberry, Nehff, and Krebs, dated respectively 13th August, 1849. The plaintiffs objected to the Commissioners' deeds, that they do not show that the prerequisites of the Acts of Assembly relative to the sale of unseated lands had been complied with; and also that the deed of the Klinger tract was irrelevant, as not referring to land in dispute. The Court admitted the deeds in evidence, and sealed a bill of exceptions for the plaintiffs. The defendants further gave in evidence assessments of Union Township for 1832 and 1833, in the name of Casper Thiel, "400 acres unseated land," a treasurer's sale of the Thiel tract to the Commissioners, for non-payment of taxes, 9th June, 1834, and a deed for the same dated 17th June, 1834, from the Treasurer to the Commissioners; a sale of the Thiel tract on the 13th February, 1843, by the Commissioners, to Benjamin F. Taylor and John Clayton, and a deed for the same from the Commissioners to Taylor and Clayton, dated 15th March, 1843. The plaintiffs objected to this deed of the Commissioners, as to those previously offered. The Court admitted it, and sealed a bill of exceptions. The defendants then proved that the title of Roseberry, Nehff, and Krebs to the Immel and the Troxel tracts and the northern half of the Klinger tract, and the title of Taylor and Clayton to the Thiel tract, have vested, by sundry mesne conveyances of the same, in John H. Brown. They then gave in evidence, under objection and exception, a sale of the Casper Thiel tract by the Sheriff of Northumberland County, and deed poll from him dated 22d August, 1806, for the same to John Meyer, and showed that the title of John Meyer to the said tract has become vested, by mesne conveyances, through Jacob Trout and others, in John H. Brown. Also a lease dated 13th April, 1863, John H. Brown to Henry Fermier, for the Christian Troxel, Christian Immel, and Casper Thiel tracts, and the northern half of the John Klinger tract, under the Gray survey, with renewals of this lease every year, the last renewal from 13th April, 1878, to 13th April, 1879. They then proved assessments and payment of taxes upon the Casper Thiel, Christian Immel, Christian Troxel, and John Klinger tracts from the date of the Commissioners' sale of the same respectively to the year 1860; also a treasurer's sale for non-payment of taxes for 1860 and 1861, of the Thiel, Immel, Troxel, and Klinger tracts to Lewis Reeser, on the 9th June, 1862, and gave in evidence deeds for the said four tracts, dated respectively 1st September, 1862, from the Treasurer to Lewis Reeser; also patents for the Immel, Troxel, and the northern half of the Klinger tracts, to Lewis Reeser, dated respectively 28th January, 1865. The plaintiffs objected to these patents that they were executed after suit brought. The Court admitted them, and sealed a bill of exceptions. The defendants then showed that the title of Lewis Reeser in the Immel, Troxel, and the northern half of the Klinger tracts has vested in John H. Brown; this to show the claim of title in the defendants to the land in controversy, and that the title held by the patentee to these tracts is not an outstanding title. They then proved assessments to Hannah and Elizabeth Bitler in 1841, 1842, and 1843, upon 300 acres of unseated land in Union Township, alleged by the plaintiffs to refer to the land in controversy, also a sale of the same for non-payment of taxes by the Treasurer to the Commissioners on the 10th June, 1844, and a sale thereof by the Commissioners on the 16th July, 1849, to C. M. Straub. They proved that Straub did not pay the purchase-money and take his deed until 1854, five years subsequent to the payment of the purchase-money to the county by Roseberry, Nehff, and Krebs for the Christian Troxel tract. They proved that this tract was conveyed by Straub to Elizabeth Bitler, "as tending to show that she claimed the land in controversy under a worthless tax title to Straub, and that it was this title that she subsequently conveyed to Brandon and Snyder in 1858 and 1860." They introduced the testimony of surveyors that the lines of the block of Gray surveys are clearly defined by marks still existing upon the ground, which conform to the calls of the original returns made by Gray, as also to the official location of eleven older surveys adjoining the Gray block, of which the defendants gave in evidence a certified connected draft. The surveyors testified that the John Bitler tract interferes with the Christian Troxel, the Christian Immel, the Casper Thiel, and the John Shomo tracts as located by Gray. It appeared from the testimony of surveyors that the lines had been skilfully shortened in the official return of the John Bitler survey, so as to conform to the quantity of land returned, 199 acres 63½ perches, though that tract, as actually located, embraces 299 acres 63½ perches of land. It also appeared that the territory upon which the surveys of Vanderslice and those of Gray were made was ascertained to have been in Northumberland County by the line run for the purpose of defining the limit of that county, in accordance with the Act of 1795, and that this territory became a part of Schuylkill County in 1818. Defendants rested.

In rebuttal, the plaintiffs offered certified copies of eighteen surveys, made in July, 1793, by Henry Vanderslice, Deputy Surveyor of Berks County, and returned by him 16 July, 1793, under the same warrants issued upon the application of James Sillyman, dated 1 July, 1793, given in evidence by the defendants. To be followed by evidence of the location of these surveys, of their return into the Land Office, and of their having been filed without objection. To be followed by evidence that the Commonwealth granted patents upon the John Shomo survey, as made by Vanderslice, and rejected the John Shomo, Ann Maria Shomo, and the Casper Thiel surveys, as made by Gray, but subsequently adopted the Gray Casper Thiel, pursuant to a warrant of acceptance issued by the Surveyor-General in 1813, before the patent granted thereon to Jacob Trout; that such patent was only in pursuance of such warrant of acceptance and upon payment of the whole purchase-money, as if no original warrant had been issued; that, in 1812, the Board of Property declared the Gray Casper Thiel survey void, because made upon a warrant exhausted by reason of the Vanderslice survey of the same; that neither Christian Immel, Christian Troxel, Casper Thiel, John Klinger, John Shomo, or James Sillyman ever asserted any claim of title to the surveys made by Gray in their names respectively as warrantees, or ever paid taxes thereon. To be followed by evidence from the Land Office that the Board of Property never granted any authority either to make, or to accept, the Gray surveys; that the Land Office does not show a list of *accepted* surveys applicable to those of Gray; there is no express evidence that it ever adopted the Gray surveys except as to the tracts patented in 1806 and 1808; and that it has treated them, ever since, as void against those of Vanderslice. To be followed by evidence that the Christian Troxel tract was first assessed in 1818, was sold to the county in 1822 for non-payment of taxes, and that in 1827 or 1828 the county entered upon its records that there was no land to satisfy the assessment of the Christian Troxel tract.

The defendants objected to this offer, which, after argument, the Court rejected, and sealed a bill of exceptions for the plaintiffs. But, subsequently, upon suggestion by the defendants that they were "willing the evidence should go upon record, and the legal effect of the testimony be pronounced by the Court at the conclusion of the case," the Court allowed the plaintiffs to introduce the evidence as set forth in their offer. The plaintiffs then introduced the testimony of a clerk in the Department of the Interior to prove, from the record, that the certificate shown by the defendants is not a certificate of *accepted* surveys. It appeared, however, upon cross-examination, that it was not the practice in the Land Office, before the year 1800 or 1801, to make a note of acceptance upon the survey itself. It further appeared that these two sets of surveys have been kept together, upon the files, a Gray survey inside a Vanderslice survey, or *vice versa*. The plaintiffs followed this testimony by certified copies of the returns made by Vanderslice, in July, 1793, upon the eighteen warrants issued on 1 July, 1793, to James Sillyman, as contained in their offer, and a certified connected draft of these eighteen tracts of land "situate on the branches of the Catawissa on the north side of Mahanoy Mountain, county of Berks." Eleven of these surveys bear the indorsement: "See another return on the same warrant by William Gray, D. S. of Northumberland County," and similar indorsements are upon the others, except the John Witman, Jacob Yeager, William Witman, and Mary Witman, which were located and returned by William Wheeler, D. S., in 1837. They then gave in evidence a patent, dated 11 December, 1833, for the John Shomo tract, as surveyed by Vanderslice, and a patent dated 19 April, 1870, for the Ann Maria Shomo tract, as surveyed by Vanderslice. It appeared, however, from the testimony of the patentees of the Ann Maria Shomo tract, that they claimed this tract, as surveyed by Gray, and lived upon it, and that the patent they obtained from the Commonwealth was not what they wanted, but related to land they never claimed. The plaintiffs then gave in evidence a certified copy of the proceedings of the Board of Property, dated 13 November, 1812, which recites that there was "an irregularity" in the second return (*i. e.*, the Gray return) of the Casper Thiel survey, and directs the Secretary of the Land Office to issue a warrant to the Surveyor-General to accept the said survey, made the 23 October, 1793, "inasmuch as the said Casper Thiel, and those claiming under him, have held the land from that date to the present time; and that a patent issue thereon to Jacob Trout, he paying the purchase-money and interest due from the 1st July, 1793." They gave also a certified copy of the order from the Secretary of the Land Office to Andrew Porter, Surveyor-General, directing him to accept the Gray survey of the Casper Thiel tract; this to show that the Board of Property treated the Gray survey as void, and for the purpose of rebutting the defendants' general offer of patents as tending to show acceptance of the Gray surveys prior to the date of such patents. They gave further the Gray returns of the surveys made by him upon the warrants to Ann Maria Shomo and John Shomo respectively, with indorsement upon the former: "This return rejected by the Board of Property as not lying in the same county called for by the warrant;" and upon the latter: "This return rejected by the Board of Property, there being another return on the same warrant for lands in the county of Berks." They then gave in evidence a warrant to John Bitler, dated 9 April, 1811, and a survey upon the same, dated 11 May, 1811, to John Bitler, for 243 acres 25 perches, and allowance; the survey calls for John Bitler, in the right of George More, of John Klinger, of Mary Thiel, of George Rose, of Catharine Rose, and of Maria Kelchner. Plaintiffs allege that this tract, called "the long John Bitler tract," interferes with the Gray surveys of the Christian Immel and the Maria Kelchner tracts. Several surveyors testified, however, that the interference alleged arises from a location of this tract with reference to a line called "Meyer's line," or "the line of 1806," which locates the southern boundary of the Gray block of surveys eighty perches north of the lines of older surveys adjoining the Gray block, which are called for in the original returns made by Gray, and in the patents granted to John Meyer. It also appeared that "the line of 1806" is not an official line, and that "the long John Bitler tract" will not interfere, as alleged, if located by its calls in connection with the official lines as run and marked by Gray. The plaintiffs then gave in evidence, under objection, the Court reserving the legal effect of the offer for future discussion, assessments of Union Township to show that the Christian Immel tract was not assessed from 1811 until 1841, also that the Christian Troxel tract was first assessed in 1819, and a sale of the Troxel tract by the Treasurer to the Commissioners in 1822 for nonpayment of taxes, and a sale by them to John Wickersham in 1831, with a deed, dated 23 March, 1831, from the Commissioners to Wickersham for the Christian Troxel tract. The deed was acknowledged, but never delivered; this to show that the assessments of 1841, 1842, and 1843 were void, and the sale thereunder by the Treasurer to the Commissioners passed no title. They also showed that the Christian Troxel tract was not assessed from 1827 until 1841.

In sur-rebuttal the defendants gave in evidence, under objection and exception, a caveat dated 18 July, 1793, filed by John Kunckel and Aaron Bowen, against granting patents for lands situate in Catawissa Valley, Northumberland or Berks County, granted by eighteen warrants dated 1 July, 1793, in the warrantee names of James Sillyman, Susannah Sillyman, etc.: "The said Kunckel and Bowen alleging that they have warrants dated 19th May, 1792, in the names of Charles Shoemaker, George Raver, etc., for a part of the same land;" offered, under objection and exception, as a caveat filed against issuing patents upon the surveys made by Vanderslice. The defendants also gave in evidence files of newspapers published under date of June 7 and June 8, 1849, as also for five consecutive weeks following those dates respectively, to show affirmatively, by the advertisements contained in them, that the Commissioners' sale of the Bitler, Immel, Troxel, and Klinger tracts, held July 16, 1849, was a public sale, and was duly advertised.

This was followed, upon the part of the plaintiffs, under objection and exception, by a certificate from the office of the Surveyor-General, dated 26th November, 1873, that there is no record of any citation ever having been issued upon the caveat given in evidence by the defendants, or of any proceedings upon the same by the Board of Property.

The Court below (PERSHING, P. J.), charged, *inter alia :* "You have the evidence in regard to the location of these fourteen Gray surveys. Mr. Hawley (a surveyor), says: 'I have not a particle of doubt the Gray surveys were located where claimed. The east line is well marked, extraordinarily so, after this lapse of time.' This is the testimony of Mr. Hawley, a very intelligent witness, produced upon the part of the plaintiffs, and it is the testimony of all the surveyors, with the exception of Stauffer, who did not examine it. There does not appear to be any controversy as to the location of these fourteen Gray surveys. The effect of the confirmatory act of the Commonwealth in granting patents on part of these Gray surveys, extends to the whole block, and is not confined to those only for which the patents were issued. (Fritz *v.* Brandon, 28 P. F. Smith, 351.) One effect of a patent is to merge all previous proceedings and to waive, upon the part of the Commonwealth, whatever informalities may have occurred, so that, upon the granting of it, the title of the patentee as against the Commonwealth becomes complete both in equity and in law. They (the plaintiffs), have offered in evidence the same warrants offered by the defendants, with returns upon them made by Henry Vanderslice, in July, 1793, about three months before the surveys were made by Gray, with evidence of the return of these surveys into the land office some eight months prior to the time that Gray made his return. Here arises what is, perhaps, the main controversy in this case. Which of these surveys, those made by Gray or those made by Vanderslice, are the valid surveys? They cover to some extent the same ground. When this question was before the Court the last time, we ruled, as a question of law, that the Vanderslice surveys were the valid surveys, for the reasons that they were the first made and returned into the land office; that the rule of law was that, a survey having once been made upon a warrant and returned, the warrant was exhausted and the second survey upon the same was simply void. We, therefore, instructed the jury squarely, that the Gray surveys were void and that the Vanderslice surveys were valid. The Supreme Court has, just as squarely, decided that we were in error in that instruction, and that the Gray surveys are valid and that the Vanderslice surveys were abandoned. It has been pressed very strongly upon the Court what our duty is under the circumstances of this trial. It has been urged that the validity of the Gray and the Vanderslice surveys is a question that should be submitted to the jury upon the facts as they now stand. It is claimed that new facts have been presented, the effect of which should be to change the decision of the Supreme Court, rendered, it is said, under a misapprehension of the facts as they actually existed. It has been repeatedly said in your hearing, that the Chief Justice not only misapprehended the facts of the case, but stated, in his opinion, matters which the evidence showed were not facts at all, and that, therefore, the decision of the Supreme Court should not bind us in this case. It strikes us that there has been very little new evidence introduced into this trial upon this particular question. Stress has been laid upon the fact that, in the paper-book of the defendants presented to the Supreme Court, their reference to the certificate of the land office as to the Gray surveys, contained in it the words "*accepted surveys.*" It has been argued that the Supreme Court was misled by this word *accepted*. The fact is that both the Gray and the Vanderslice certificates are alike in their language. The plaintiffs, however, directed the attention of the Supreme Court to the fact that the word *accepted* did not appear in the certificate, and also that the surveys made by Vanderslice were first returned, and that the evidence of their acceptance was precisely that which the defendants offered of the acceptance of the Gray surveys. The patent to Trout, of the Thiel tract, and the proceedings preliminary to granting it, were before the Supreme Court. So also, the fact that two of the Gray surveys were rejected. The John Shomo and Ann Maria Shomo surveys were rejected, and the reasons for their rejection were printed in the paper-book of the defendants. The caveat was also before the Supreme Court, and was printed just as it was read here. It is alleged that it was a mistake to assert that the Vanderslice surveys interfered with any of the lands mentioned by the caveators, and that the Supreme Court was misled by the allegations of this caveat. It does, however, appear in evidence that the Vanderslice surveys interfered with older warrants in the names of Martin, Rutherford, and others, warrants which were located upon the ground prior to the making of the Vanderslice surveys. We do not think that the Supreme Court were misled by the caveat when they disposed of this case on the writ of error taken from the former judgment of this Court. Our error was not the taking of this question from the jury, but it consisted in ruling that the Gray surveys were invalid. This the Supreme Court corrected, by ruling that the Vanderslice, and not the Gray, were the invalid surveys. This is repeated so often, and with such emphasis, throughout the opinion of Chief Justice AGNEW, that is impossible for me to come to the conclusion that I should, in the discharge of my duty, under the evidence as it is now presented, submit to you, as a question of fact, whether the Gray or the Vanderslice surveys were the valid surveys.

Following the evidence of the defendants, we come to the question of the tax-sales. The requisites of a tax-sale are: That the land must be unseated at the time of the assessment; that a tax appears to have been, and in fact was, assessed by the proper officer; that it was due for one whole year and remained unpaid. Unseated lands assessed are the debtor for the taxes; it is immaterial in what name they are assessed, if it is the same land that is taxed and sold, and was at the time unseated. The sale in the name of a younger warrantee will pass the title, it not being assessed at all in the name of the first warrantee. Upon this subject, as bearing upon some of the questions introduced, it has been held by the Supreme Court that, 'the constructive possession of land, not actually occupied, follows the legal title;' that is, in contemplation of law, every man is in possession of the land he owns, until ousted by an intruder, and abandonment of title is not presumed from non-entry nor from neglect to pay taxes. The law does not limit a man's title to the *possessio pedis*. Inchoate rights may be abandoned, but abandonment is scarcely predicable of perfect titles. And though it is an owner's duty to pay taxes, what if he does not? The law, instead of presuming his title abandoned, seizes it and sells it to the highest bidder. (Mayor of Phila. *v.* Riddle, 1 Casey, 263.)

"It appears that, in 1841, 1842, and 1843, the Christian Troxel, Christian Immel, and John Klinger tracts were assessed with road, State, and county taxes, and that, by the Treasurer's sale of the 10th June, 1844, these tracts were sold to the county, and deeds delivered in pursuance of the Act of Assembly. It further appears that the Commissioners held them for five years, as required by the Act of Assembly, and that, upon the 16th of July, 1849, they were sold by the Commissioners of the County to John W. Roseberry, Benjamin Nehff, and Henry Krebs, who paid their purchase-money and received their deeds upon the 1st September, 1849. A question has been raised as to the validity of this sale. It appears from the evidence, that there was a sale of the Christian Troxel tract, in 1822, to the county, and it is claimed that it could not be assessed for taxes during the time it was the property of the county, only to the extent of the five years limited by the Act of Assembly, during which time the county held the land for redemption. The subsequent assessment, no doubt, was an irregularity, which possibly may be explained as a similar transaction, to some extent, is explained in Goodman *v.* Sanger (4 Norris, 42). Russel *v.* Werntz (12 Harris, 347) is a case where the county taxed land held by itself. It was there held that 'whilst the title was in the county, it could not be prejudiced by the payment of taxes other than those for which it had been sold. If the county taxed lands the title of which was in itself, and parties paid the taxes in ignorance of the fact, they may, perhaps, have an equitable right to reclaim their money; but they cannot invalidate that title in the hands of a *bona fide* purchaser from the county.' It is claimed upon the part of the plaintiffs, that they have a right to recover for that portion of the John Bitler survey which interferes with the Casper Thiel, amounting to about thirty-six acres. They claim for that portion of the Bitler, included within the Thiel survey, that the taxes were paid by Hannah and Elizabeth Bitler, in 1831 and 1832, and that, therefore, the sale to the county in 1834, and afterwards by the county to Taylor and Clayton, conveyed no title to that portion of the land on the Thiel survey included within the lines of the Bitler survey. The rule upon this subject appears to be this: 'Proof of the actual payment of the tax avoids the sale.' (Hunter *v.* Cochran, 3 Barr, 105; Reading *v.* Finney, 23 P. F. S. 472.) They, the plaintiffs, claim that the sale of the Thiel was invalid, because the Act of Assembly was not complied with. In the case of Lee *v.* Jeddo Coal Co. (3 Norris, 74), the Supreme Court held that 'the recitals in the deeds of County Commissioners made in pursuance of a sale of land for taxes, *prima facie*, raise a presumption that the Commissioners did their duty and made the sale according to law.' (McCoy *v.* Michew, 7 W. & S. 386.) I am inclined to think, from the evidence, it is a fair presumption after the lapse of thirty years or more, that these public officers did their duty. In Lee *v.* Jeddo Coal Co. (*supra*), the question as to the conclusiveness of such a presumption is left open. Here, in the absence of evidence to overthrow it, we think the maxim *omnia præsumuntur* has proper application. With regard to the assessments, the question has been raised and argued, that the sale of the Troxel tract as unseated, was void because it was upon the seated list. From the books in evidence and the testimony of Mr. Aregood, it would seem that it was upon what was called 'the mixed list;' a list which contained both seated and unseated lands. It was assessed upon this list as unseated. We say to you, that if this land was entered on what is called 'the mixed list,' if there found assessed as unseated and sold as unseated, the taxes not having been previously paid, it would convey a good title." (The Court cited in this connection: Laird *v.* Hiester, 12 Harris, 452; Thompson *v.* Chase, 2 Grant, 367; and Russel *v.* Werntz, 12 Harris, 337.) "That the taxes for 1841, 1842, and 1843 were not paid, is not disputed.

"There is another question of importance in this case, which was not raised at the former trial: What have the plaintiffs sued for? What land is embraced in their præcipe and writ? The land described in the præcipe is 'a tract of land situate in Union Township, containing 200 acres or thereabouts, bounded by land surveyed to James Smith, Christian Immel, John Klinger, and others.' In the survey the call is for the Casper Thiel on the north. In the præcipe, reference is made to the deed from Elizabeth Bitler to Snyder, which, it is claimed, is also a part of the description. The adjoiners called for by the præcipe, including the deed, are James Smith, Casper Thiel, Christian Immel, and John Klinger, all older surveys, and all located upon the ground by the testimony of the surveyors. It is claimed, upon the part of the plaintiffs, that they have a right to run beyond the Immel. The land they claim cuts into the Thiel and runs beyond the line of the Immel some on to the Shomo. It is claimed that the survey upon the ground is the true survey, without regard to the calls for adjoiners. The official distance for the east and west line between the Thiel and the Troxel is 320 perches, and the distance as given on the Bitler is 310. Commencing at the Smith and running 310 perches toward the Immel will not reach the Immel tract. But plaintiffs claim the right to run 350 perches and thus run upon the Immel and the Shomo tracts and include 299 acres. It is argued that, these being the lines upon the ground, of the John Bitler survey, they must control the calls for the adjoiners, and that the adjoiners cannot control the lines upon the ground.

"It is to be remembered that the James Smith is an older survey and its place is well established. The Casper Thiel is an old survey, patented in 1813; while the survey of the Bitler was only made in 1829 and calls for the Thiel. The fact that the Thiel was patented in 1813, was notice to Bitler where the lines of the Thiel survey were located and, of course, he would have no right to run upon any portion of the Thiel in making his survey. The line of 1806, known as 'the Meyer line' was introduced in this connection. This line, under the testimony of the surveyors, makes great changes in the location of many tracts and interferes with a large body of surveys. It is only a matter of conjecture for what purpose the line was run, but we think it has nothing to do with, and could not change the location of these surveys as originally returned to the land office. The position taken by the plaintiffs in this case, in reference to 'the Meyer line' of 1806 is like that taken by the plaintiffs in Wagner *v.* Wagner (18 P. F. S. 392). Whatever was the purpose in running this line, it is not claimed it was done by any official authority. We instruct you, therefore, that it can have no weight in deciding the present litigation. But, as bearing directly upon this question of what is included in the plaintiffs' description, we have a decision of the Supreme Court where it is distinctly held that: 'It is a principle of construction, that, where land is described by courses and distances and also by calls for adjoiners, the latter, where there is a discrepance, invariably govern; and it is applicable to conveyances as well as to official surveys.' (Cox *v.* Couch, 8 Barr, 154. This has been followed in other cases. Petts *v.* Gaw, 3 Harris, 222.) If our construction is correct, this controversy is narrowed to the interference of the John Bitler with the Christian Troxel survey. For, following the description contained in the plaintiffs' præcipe and deed, and beginning at the James Smith and running along the Casper Thiel to the Immel and then, by courses and distances, back to the Smith, would not interfere with the Thiel, the Immel or the John Shomo. We are constrained to say to you that, upon the whole evidence in this case, the defendants have a right to a verdict at your hands. In saying this, we negative the points of the plaintiffs."

Exception taken by plaintiffs and bill sealed.

Verdict for the defendants as directed by the Court, and judgment thereon. The plaintiffs took this writ, and filed twenty-six assignments of error, among which were the following:—

(5) The Court erred in negativing the plaintiffs' third point, which was: That if the jury believe that the assessment to Hannah and Elizabeth Bitler from 1832 to 1840 inclusive, embraced the John Bitler survey of 1829, and that the said assessment was in the seated list and claimed by Elizabeth Bitler to be so assessed, then the assessment of the same land by any name in the unseated list without notice to her, the then owner, was void and the treasurer's sale of 1844, based on such changed assessment, was void as to her and passed no title to the purchasers at the commissioners' sale of 1849.

(12) The Court erred in negativing the plaintiffs' twelfth point, which was: That the defendants have shown no title to the Casper Thiel at the time they entered upon the land in suit and when this suit was brought, that the alleged sale and conveyance by the Commissioners to Taylor and Clayton, by the deed, dated 15 March, 1843, pursuant to sale made 13th February, 1843, does not recite any advertisement or notice of the sale, or that the sale was a public one, or made according to law, nor has any evidence been given to show any such advertisement or notice, or that the sale was not a private sale; and that a sale so made would not divest any title of the owners of the John Bitler warrant and survey in suit so far as it interferes with the Casper Thiel.

(13) The Court erred in negativing the plaintiffs' thirteenth point, which was: That the defendants have given in evidence the assessments, in the names of Hannah and Elizabeth Bitler, and a treasurer's sale, in 1844, by the county treasurer to the county of Schuylkill, and a sale, in 1849, by the county to C. M. Straub; then, if the Court hold the sale of 1849 valid against the county, such deed vested in C. M. Straub so much of the Casper Thiel as the defendants admit to have been interfered with by the John Bitler survey in suit, and the title having been vested in the plaintiffs before suit brought, they are entitled to recover that part of the land in suit which the defendants admit to be interfered with by the Gray location of the Casper Thiel.

F. W. Hughes and *F. W. Bechtel*, for plaintiffs in error.

The Vanderslice surveys were regularly made and returned, with the consent of the warrantees, and the title of the warrantees to land in these surveys, not previously appropriated, was complete against everybody but the Commonwealth, who held the legal title as security for patent fees.

Drinker *v.* Holliday, 2 Yeates, 87.
Porter *v.* Ferguson, 3 Yeates, 60.
Hunter *v.* Meason, 4 Yeates, 107.
Adams *v.* Jackson, 4 W. & S. 78.
Bunting *v.* Young, 5 W. & S. 188.

These lands lie in the old purchases. The 15th Section of the Act of April 8, 1785, and the 6th Section of the Act of April 3, 1792

(Purd. Dig. 898-902), apply only to the new purchases or to purchases from the Indians after 1768.

> Smith v. Wells, 1 Yeates, 286.
> Shields v. Buchanan, 2 Id. 219.
> Funston v. McMahon, 2 Id. 245.
> Harris v. Monks, 2 S. & R. 557.
> McNamara v. Shorb, 2 Watts, 288-292.
> Prout v. Bard, 10 Watts, 379.
> Goddard v. Gloninger, 5 Watts, 222.

The Act of 1795, which provided for a commission to mark the line between Northumberland County and Berks County, rendered valid all surveys previously made by any deputy surveyor. That Vanderslice was out of his district, does not invalidate the surveys made by him in 1793.

The caveat filed by Kunckel and Bowen was not directed against the *surveys* made by Vanderslice, but against the granting of patents to Sillyman and the other warrantees, for the lands granted them by warrants dated 1st July, 1793. The reason assigned by the caveators is, that they had other *warrants* for a part of the same land; they do not allude to any *surveys*, whether of Vanderslice or of any other person. No subsequent survey upon the land called for in the Sillyman warrants could remove this objection; hence Gray's surveys were nugatory. The opinion of the learned Chief Justice, reversing the judgment of the lower Court, at the former hearing of this case, is predicated upon an erroneous assumption of facts. (Fritz v. Brandon, 28 P. F. S. 350.)

A second survey, made without a previous warrant of re-survey from the Surveyor-General or the Board of Property, is void.

> Drinker v. Holliday, *supra*.
> Porter v. Ferguson, *supra*.
> Deal v. McCormick, 3 S. & R. 343.
> Oyster v. Bellas, 2 Watts, 397.
> Cassidy v. Conway, 1 Casey, 240.
> Bellas v. Cleaver, 4 Wr. 260.
> Hughes v. Stevens, 7 Wr. 202.
> Improvement Co. v. Munson, 14 Wallace, 442.

At the end of twenty-one years after a survey has been made and returned into the Land Office a presumption of law arises that it was regularly made on the ground; but it is denied that this presumption extends to the authority to make it.

The Gray surveys, being unofficial, were not notice to subsequent appropriators.

> Barton v. Smith, 1 Rawle, 403.
> Manhattan Coal Co. v. Green, 23 P. F. S. 320.

Where a survey is removed, or shifted to lands not described in the warrant, title begins from the time the survey is *returned and accepted.*

> Lauman v. Thomas, 4 Binney, 58.
> Moore v. Shaver, 6 S. & R. 133.

The Immel and Troxel tracts were sold by the Commissioners for non-payment of taxes, under different assessments, *on the same day.* These sales were to effect a payment of the taxes by each claimant under his own assessment, and left each claimant's title just where it was before.

> Hunter v. Albright, 5 W. & S. 423.
> Diamond Coal Co. v. Fisher, 7 Har. 267.
> Fritz v. Brandon, 28 P. F. S. 356.

Though a patent conveys the legal estate, as against the Commonwealth, it will not prevail over a prior estate by warrant and survey.

> Maclay v. Work, 5 Binney, 154.
> Gonzalus v. Hoover, 6 S. & R. 118.
> Woods v. Wilson, 37 Penn. St. 379.

A patent inures to the benefit of the owner of the title, though issued to another.

> Urket v. Coryell, 5 W. & S. 60.

A patent obtained through ignorance of the Land Office, does not legalize an unauthorized survey.

> Burd v. Seabold, 6 S. & R. 137.

Land that has been assessed upon the seated list, upon which taxes have been paid as upon seated land, cannot be transferred to the unseated list, assessed and sold as unseated land, without notice to the owner.

> Larimer v. McCall, 4 W. & S. 133.
> Milliken v. Benedict, 8 Barr, 169.
> Com. Bank v. Woodside, 2 Har. 404.
> Stewart v. Trevor, 6 P. F. S. 374.
> Bechdle v. Lingle, 16 P. F. S. 38.

James Ryon and *George R. Kaercher* (with them *S. H. Kaercher, John W. Ryon,* and *C. Tower, Jr.*), for the defendants in error.

Vanderslice located the warrants involved in this controversy wholly out of his district. His surveys were the acts of a private person, and without legal authority.

> Lessee of Hubley v. Chew, 2 Sm. Laws, 257.

This principle is not shaken by the ruling in Shields v. Buchanan (*supra*), and Funston v. McMahon (*supra*); for the surveys in those cases were made and returned by persons who never had commissions as deputy surveyors.

Every survey made by a deputy surveyor out of his proper district is void.

> Act 1792, sect. 6, 3 Sm. Laws, 70.

A deputy surveyor, without a special authority, cannot go beyond the known lines of his district to make a survey.

> Harris v. Monks, 2 S. & R. 557.

The Vanderslice surveys were returned as located in Berks County; the acceptance of them cannot be construed as a ratification by the Surveyor-General of an irregular act; for the limits of the county were not defined until two years later.

It is not denied that, after a survey has been made and returned, no new survey can be made on the same warrant without a new authority; but this rule presupposes the first survey to have been made by the regular deputy within his district.

Gray's surveys were returned upon lands in

his own 'district, and accepted immediately by the Surveyor-General; they were surveyed and returned as a block, the property of James Sillyman; five of them were patented in 1806, two in 1808, and one in 1813; the warrants surveyed by Gray at the same time upon a portion of Vanderslice's location abandoned by the re-survey were accepted, and some of them patented in 1794; the title under the Gray location was sold to actual settlers, who have occupied and improved the land; these lands have been assessed and have paid taxes since the territory became a part of Schuylkill County; no one ever claimed under the Vanderslice surveys, and they were never taxed; Gray's returns were accepted more than thirty-five years before the John Bitler warrant was located. These facts justify the presumption that the Surveyor-General gave a special authority for a re-survey.

Goddard v. Gloninger, 5 Watts, 221.
Creek v. Moon, 7 S. & R. 330.
Bellas v. Levan, 4 Watts, 294.
Caul v. Spring, 2 Id. 390.
Collins v. Barclay, 7 Barr, 67.
Nieman v. Ward, 1 W. & S. 68.
Lambourn v. Hartswick, 13 S. & R. 113.
Brock v. Savage, 10 Wr. 83.

If a re-survey abandon the lines of the original survey, and the parties subsequently claim by the re-survey, the land thrown out by it is abandoned, and left open to re-appropriation.

Sabins v. McGhee, 12 Casey, 453.

So, where a warrantee has two surveys of different tracts made on the same warrant, and accepts a patent for one of them, the other is subject to appropriation by a settler.

Coxe v. Woolbach, 2 Casey, 122.

Ever since the case of Drinker v. Holliday (*supra*), the rule has been, in Pennsylvania, that where a survey has been made, returned, and accepted, a new one cannot be made without the assent of those representing the Commonwealth, and not even then so as to affect intervening rights.

Cassidy v. Conway, 1 Casey, 240.

The Courts of this State have uniformly refused to go back more than twenty-one years to settle difficulties about the issuing of warrants or patents, or the making or returning of surveys, or payment of the purchase-money to the Commonwealth.

Stimpfler v. Roberts, 6 Harris, 283.

The plaintiffs do not claim title under the Vanderslice surveys, or in any manner connect themselves with that title. It is worthy of consideration whether they were in a position to make use of those surveys to defeat the defendants' possession and claim under the re-surveys.

Balliot v. Bauman, 5 W. & S. 150.
Hull v. Campbell, 6 P. F. S. 154.
Glass v. Gilbert, 8 P. F. S. 266.

The authority of Gray was just as great to make the survey of these fourteen tracts as it was to make a survey of a single one of them. The Commonwealth has granted patents upon seven of the tracts; if Gray's act was valid as to these seven, it was so as to the whole block. After a lapse of eighty years, and after the settlement of this whole country, the presumption is one of *law* that these surveys were made under competent authority.

Caul v. Spring, 2 Watts, 394.
Stimpfler v. Roberts, 6 Harris, 299.
Ormsby v. Ihmsen, 10 Casey, 462.
McBarron v. Gilbert, 6 Wr. 279.
Stephens v. Cowan, 6 Watts, 515.
Malone v. Sallada, 12 Wr. 425.
Darrah v. Bryant, 6 P. F. S. 73.

In reply to the plaintiffs' 5th assignment of error. The assessments to Hannah and Elizabeth Bitler of 30 acres as unseated land, on the mixed list, for 1838, 1839, and 1840, and of 60 acres so assessed for 1835, 1836, and 1837 were frauds practised upon the county by the owner of the land, if they referred to the John Bitler tract of 300 acres, and no correction and placing of the tract upon the proper list by the proper officer, at the lawful time appointed for making the triennial assessments would prevent a valid sale of the land for non-payment of taxes, either upon that assessment or upon the assessments in the names of Christian Troxel and Christian Immel.

Clarke v. Dougan, 2 Jones, 87.

As to the validity of the tax sales of the Immel and Troxel tracts, see—

Laird v. Hiester, 12 Harris, 453.
Arthurs v. Smathers, 2 Wr. 40.
Bechdle v. Lingle, 16 P. F. S. 38.
Stewart v. Trevor, 6 P. F. S. 374.
Thompson v. Chase, 2 Grant, 367.
Russel v. Werntz, 12 Harris, 337.

In reply to the plaintiffs' 12th assignment of error. A deed from the County Commissioners, in fee simple, duly acknowledged, conveys effectually the county's title.

Act of 29th March, 1824, Purd. Dig., p. 1452, sec. 51.

The plaintiffs cannot object to the sale of the Casper Thiel tract that the Commissioners did not recite, in their deed, advertisement, and notice of sale, etc.; for, excepting the single requirement that the sale shall be public—and the defendants have shown *affirmatively* in their evidence that the sale of the Thiel tract to Taylor and Clayton was a public sale—the provisions of the Act of 1824, in regard to the sale of lands by the Commissioners after title has become absolute in the county, are simply directory.

Huston v. Foster, 1 Watts, 477.
Kirkpatrick v. Mathiot, 4 W. & S. 251.
Jenks v. Wright, 11 P. F. S. 410.
Hess v. Herrington, 23 P. F. S. 438.
Lee v. Jeddo Coal Co., 3 Norris, 74.
McCoy v. Michew, 7 W. & S. 386.

In reply to the plaintiffs' 13th assignment of

error. All taxes due on the Thiel tract prior to 1843 were discharged by the sale to Taylor and Clayton; the sale in 1844 of so much of the Thiel tract as may have been interfered with by the Hannah and Elizabeth Bitler 300-acre tract was void; no title passed to the county and it had no title to sell to Straub in 1849. The absence of the requisites of a valid sale renders the sale void. If the tax be not due and unpaid one whole year, there is no authority to sell.

Laird *v.* Hiester, 12 Harris, 453.
McReynolds *v.* Longenberger, 25 P. F. S. 13.
Rogers *v.* Johnson, 17 Id. 43.
Breisch *v.* Coxe, 31 Id. 336.

The county owned the Thiel tract in 1843, hence it could levy no tax upon it for that year. There is no authority to levy tax for a portion of a year, nor can a tax be apportioned by the county so as to assess part of it to its vendee and assume the other part itself.

The land described in the plaintiffs' præcipe and writ would not cover any part of the Thiel, Shomo or Immel tracts; but it would lie entirely upon the Christian Troxel tract. The defendants never claimed the John Shomo tract. Their plea of not guilty was only, *prima facie*, evidence of their being in possession of the land described in the writ, which did not include any part of the John Shomo tract, and it was competent for the defendants to show that they were not in possession of that tract.

The contest before the Court and the jury was, as to whether the plaintiffs or the defendants have a better title to that portion of the Christian Troxel tract with which the John Bitler survey interferes.

The doctrine of abandonment of the valid title, by warrants and surveys, to the Immel and Troxel tracts under the Gray location, in favor of the void survey to John Bitler, has no foundation in the law of Pennsylvania. If an abandonment is to be presumed, it is one in favor of the owners of the tax title to the Immel and the Troxel tracts, and not in favor of the void survey to John Bitler.

Bunting *v.* Young, 5 W. & S. 197.
Foust *v.* Ross, 1 Id. 506.

October 4, 1880. THE COURT. The controlling questions presented by this record are substantially the same that were fully considered and determined when the case was here on the former writ of error, and if we adhere to the principles upon which that decision is based, the present judgment should be affirmed, and but little, if anything, need be added to what is said in the elaborate opinion of the Court by Chief Justice AGNEW, reported in 28 P. F. Smith, 350, in which all the authorities are collected and the questions involved fully discussed. Even if there should be doubt as to the soundness of some of the conclusions there reached, the doctrine of *stare decisis* forbids that the former decision, by which the Court was guided in the last trial, should be virtually overruled.

The claim of the plaintiffs was founded on the John Bitler warrant of 1827 and survey made, returned and accepted in 1829, and it may be assumed, for the present, that the verdict should have been in favor of the plaintiffs, unless the defendants succeeded in showing an older and better title, which it is contended they did. They claimed under the warrants of July 1, 1793, and surveys thereunder made and returned in 1794 by William Gray, Deputy Surveyor of Northumberland County, in whose district the lands were situated; and then connected themselves with these warrants and surveys by tax titles.

The main question on the last as well as the former trial, was whether the Gray surveys were valid appropriations of the land in dispute. The plaintiffs contended that they were not, for the reason that surveys under the same warrants were previously made and returned by Henry Vanderslice, Deputy Surveyor of Berks County, within a few weeks after the warrants were issued; that the Gray surveys were made under exhausted warrants, without an order of re-survey and therefore void, and that they were never accepted. It cannot be doubted that the eighteen warrants which were applied for and issued at the same time and on which the purchase-money appears by the entry to have been paid in a gross sum, were intended to form a block of surveys; and that they were so located is clearly shown by the return of Vanderslice, made July 16, 1793. There was nothing to show that the Vanderslice surveys were ever accepted. It is true that about nine years ago a patent was issued by the Commonwealth for the Ann Maria Shomo tract, as located by Vanderslice. This, if done understandingly, would be some evidence of the acceptance of his surveys, but it was clearly shown that the patent was issued by mistake and contrary to the purpose and intention of the party in interest. The tract thus patented by mistake was covered by surveys of the Gray location under which it was patented more than three-quarters of a century ago, and occupied for about the same length of time. It may therefore be said, with substantial accuracy, that there was no evidence of acceptance of the Vanderslice surveys; on the contrary, satisfactory reasons for their non-acceptance were disclosed.

On July 18, 1793, two days after the Vanderslice returns were made to the Land Office, a caveat was filed on behalf of persons claiming under prior warrants with which there was an alleged interference. While it does not appear that the caveat was ever acted on or any citation issued, it still afforded sufficient grounds for refusing to accept the Vanderslice returns; and to this, perhaps, may be added as a further reason, the fact that the surveys were not within his proper district. This latter fact, however, would not have invalidated the title if his returns had been accepted and patents issued in pursuance thereof. Shortly after the caveat was filed, the same warrants found their way into the hands of William Gray, Deputy Surveyor of Northumberland County, who, in October, 1793, located fourteen of them in a single block, partly on the same ground covered by the former survey, but so as to avoid any interference with older rights. These surveys were returned in March of the following year, and while the records of the Land Office fail to furnish any direct evidence of Gray's authority to make the re-survey or of the acceptance of his returns, they do show that nearly all the tracts included in his block of surveys were from time to time patented; from which latter fact the acceptance of his surveys as well as his authority to make them may be inferred. Granting a patent according to a return of survey is virtually an acceptance of the return. Patents were granted to John Meyer in 1806 for the James Sillyman, Susanna Sillyman, Henry Thiel, Mary Thiel and Gorge Rose tracts, reciting deeds poll from the warrantees, dated July 14, 1793; in 1808 patents were issued to the same person for the Catherine Rose and Jacob Kelchner tracts, reciting deeds poll from the warrantees dated July 10, 1793, and in later years patents were issued for other tracts in the same block. When these patents were issued the fair presumption is that the proper officers of the land department had before them satisfactory evidence of the regularity of the Gray surveys. This presumption is strengthened by the fact that the Vanderslice surveys were never recognized either by the Commonwealth or the warrantees as the foundation of title; and after so great a lapse of time, under the leading and undisputed facts of the case, the presumption should be regarded as conclusive that the Vanderslice surveys were not accepted, and that the re-surveys made by Gray were authorized and his returns accepted. The reasons and authorities in support of this presumption are so fully given in the opinion referred to, that nothing more is now required. The learned Judge of the Common Pleas adhered strictly to the principles of law therein recognized, and as we think, correctly held that there was not sufficient additional or different testimony introduced at the last trial to justify any other course. As remarked in the outset, the controlling questions are the same as in the former trial, and the facts upon which they must be determined are substantially the same.

Those portions of the charge which relate to the tax titles given in evidence and relied on by the respective parties are unobjectionable and require no further notice.

Under the construction correctly put upon the præcipe by the Court, the plaintiffs' claim was properly restricted to the northerly portion of the Christian Troxel tract, as located by the Gray survey, and did not embrace any portion of the Casper Thiel, John Shomo, or Christian Immel tracts. The charge of the learned Judge on this point is quite clear and conclusive.

We discover nothing in any of the assignments of error to justify a reversal of the judgment.

Judgment affirmed.

Opinion by STERRETT, J.

May, '80, 69. May 6, 1880.

Rudy's Appeal.

Sheriffs' sale—Distribution—Lien creditors—A judgment revived against defendant, but not against terre-tenant cannot participate in distribution—Parol agreement by terre-tenant to pay such judgment does not estop him from claiming balance of fund, as owner.

Creditors whose claims were liens on the land at the time of a sheriff's sale, and were discharged, and the owner of the land sold, can alone participate in the distribution of the proceeds.

Real estate of H. was sold as the property of K. his vendor. The fund was awarded to a judgment creditor of H., and the balance to H. as owner. R., a judgment-creditor of K., whose judgment had not been revived as against H., claimed the fund, on the ground that when H. purchased the property, he was permitted by K. to retain sufficient of the purchase-money to pay R.'s judgment, and he had, by a parol contract with K., expressly assumed the debt and promised to pay it:

Held (affirming the decree of the Court below), that R. had no standing to participate in the distribution.

Appeal from the decree of the Common Pleas of Lancaster County, distributing the proceeds of a sheriff's sale of real estate.

The premises were sold March 8, 1879, as the property of Michael Kauffman, under two judgments in favor of Benjamin L. Rudy, executor of John Rudy, viz.: (1) judgment for $100, entered to January Term, 1874, and duly revived to March Term, 1879, against Kauffman, defendant, and C. F. Hearing, terre-tenant; (2) judgment for $800 entered to January Term, 1873, and revived to January Term, 1878, by amicable sci. fa. against Kauffman, but not against Hearing the terre-tenant. This amicable revival was executed by Kauffman in the presence of Isaac L. Landis, a claimant on the fund as mentioned below. There was no dispute as to the priority of the judgment for $100 first above mentioned.

The payment of the $800 Rudy judgment was contested, because at the time of its revival against Kauffman the premises were owned by said Hearing, who had purchased them from Kauffman in 1877, and the judgment was not revived as against Hearing. Isaac L. Landis, a judgment-creditor of Hearing claimed payment of his judgment (after payment of the $100 Rudy judgment), and Hearing claimed the balance of the fund.

It appeared in evidence, that in November, 1876, Kauffman agreed to convey the land to Hearing on April 1, 1877, for $1250. Hearing went into possession in January, 1877, and on April 2, 1877, Hearing paid $300, and $50 more in June, 1877, when the deed was delivered. It was not recorded, but Rudy knew of the sale. Hearing borrowed the $350 from Landis to whom he confessed judgment to November Term, 1878. At the time of the delivery of the deed, the two Rudy judgments of $100 and $800 respectively were liens on the land.

The auditor (Wm. Aug. Atlee) reported: "These sums ($100 and $800) with the $350 paid in cash made up the sum of the purchase-money, $1250, and it was agreed between Kauffman and Hearing that Rudy was to get the balance; this was their agreement as Kauffman testifies; Hearing testifies that his bargain with Kauffman was that he was to pay the $900 judgments to Rudy; the testimony all shows that the land was bought subject to these judgments."

The auditor held that the $800 Rudy judgment was not a lien at the time of the sheriff's sale, because not revived against the terre-tenant, and that Landis's judgment against Hearing was discharged by the sale and payable out of the proceeds. He then awarded the balance of the fund towards the payment of the $800 Rudy judgment, on the ground that Hearing had agreed to pay it, had kept its amount back out of the purchase-money, and that his parol agreement, while it could not affect subsequent judgment-creditors, did affect Hearing's claim to the balance, as owner. "It undoubtedly gives Rudy a right of action against him, and, in the auditor's opinion, gives him a right to interpose here and claim the balance of the money made out of the land specifically devoted by Hearing to the payment of the debt; it is an equitable lien, good between the parties. Hearing having by contemporaneous parol agreement, for sufficient consideration (as he only paid the balance), agreed to pay it, and having made the land, so far as he was concerned, subject to the debt, and therefore the particular fund out of which it was to be paid, is he not precluded from participating in the fund until it is paid? Is he not estopped from claiming any of the proceeds of this land until all the debts for which he made it liable are paid? This judgment was duly kept alive against Kauffman; Hearing had agreed that the land should be subject to it; and the auditor decides that he cannot come upon this fund until the judgment is paid, and that the balance must be awarded to Benjamin Rudy, executor of John Rudy, deceased."

Rudy filed exceptions, because the auditor awarded payment of the Landis judgment in preference to his $800 judgment; and Hearing excepted, because the auditor awarded the balance of the fund to the Rudy $800 judgment instead of to him as owner.

The Court, in an opinion by LIVINGSTON, P. J., overruled Rudy's exceptions, and sustained Hearing's exceptions, saying: "We think, that although the learned auditor has presented the matter in the strongest possible light, he has erred in awarding the balance remaining after the payment of the $100 Rudy judgment and the Landis judgment, to Benjamin Rudy, executor of John Rudy, deceased, to wit: $77.17. He has reported, and in our judgment very properly, that Rudy's executor has no right by lien in law to claim priority over the judgment of Landis as to this fund. He should have gone further, and decided and reported that Rudy's executor could have no claim as a lien-creditor on the money for distribution. The judgment which he held was at one time a lien on the land sold by Kauffman to Hearing, but he had revived it after the sale to Hearing against Kauffman alone, and did not include Hearing, the purchaser and terre-tenant. By this proceeding the judgment became a lien on the remaining land owned by Kauffman only, and the land sold to Hearing was entirely relieved therefrom.

"It does not appear that at the time the agreement between Kauffman and Hearing was written, anything was said or any agreement made with reference to the payment of the Rudy judgments. There is nothing stated in either agreement or deed with reference to these judgments. It is true, that when he came to pay for the property and get his deed, Hearing had not money enough, and he then agreed, after paying $350 of the purchase-money, to pay the Rudy judgments, and upon this agreement or arrangement Kauffman delivered him the deed. Hearing afterwards stated to Rudy, or his executor, that he had promised Mr. Kauffman to pay, and he would pay, the Rudy judgments, but this did not and could not revive the lien or continue the old lien, nor did it create a new lien, nor did it make Rudy's executor a lien-creditor, so as to enable or entitle him to participate in the funds for distribution. These judgments at the time of the sale to Hearing were a lien on all the real estate of Kauffman situate in Lancaster County, including that sold to Hearing. But at the time of the sale of Hearing's real estate by the sheriff the judgment held by Rudy's executor was a lien on Kauffman's real estate only, and no lien or encumbrance on the property sold by the sheriff. The executor was not even a general creditor (viewed from a legal point) of Hearing, whose property was sold. He had, as the learned auditor states, promised to pay to Rudy's executor this debt of Kauffman, but it may well be doubted whether this promise could, under the Statute of Frauds, have been enforced.

"There was no lien, therefore, held by either Kauffman or Rudy's executor against Hearing or the real estate owned by him and sold as Kauffman's at the time of the sale by the sheriff, and neither of them can, so far as the claim of Rudy's executor against Kauffman is concerned, participate in this distribution.

"The exceptions filed by counsel for Mr. Hearing are, therefore, sustained, and the report of the auditor reformed accordingly.'

Rudy's executor thereupon took this appeal, assigning for error the decree awarding payment of the Landis judgment, and awarding the balance of the fund to Hearing.

Wm. R. Wilson, for appellant.

A positive agreement by Hearing to pay Kauffman's judgments, as a condition of the sale to him, of which Landis had notice, being proved and found as a fact by the auditor, why shall it not be enforced in this distribution? It was Hearing's own debt that he promised to pay, because the Rudy judgments were part of the purchase-money. Kauffman's lien for purchase-money became vested in Rudy. That the agreement was not made an express covenant in the deed is not fatal as between the parties and the claimants having notice of it. That the $800 judgment had lost its legal lien against Hearing is immaterial, in the light of his contract to pay it out of the purchase-money.

M. Brosius and *A. E. Hostetter*, for appellees.

The case is ruled by Fickes's Appeal (21 Sm. 447). A parol agreement by Hearing could not create a lien on the land and on the proceeds; it could not keep alive a judgment, annul the statutes, and dispense with a revival as against the terre-tenant.

June 19, 1880. THE COURT. Whenever the real estate of a debtor is sold by the sheriff, the proceeds must be distributed among the lien creditors, and the surplus, if any remaining, must be paid to the debtor. (Act of 16 June, 1836, Pamph. L. 777.) That is precisely what the Court below did here. The appellant, however, is not satisfied with the decree, hence this appeal. The difficulty which the appellant has to meet is that the lien of his testator's judgment has expired. It was revived against the original defendant without joining the terre-tenant. After the lien was lost by this omission, Hearing, the terre-tenant, confessed a judgment in favor of Landis. The property was sold on a judgment against Kauffman, Hearing's vendor, and it was contended by appellant that because the real estate was sold as the property of Kauffman and not of Hearing, the proceeds must go to Kauffman's lien creditors; that is to say, to the appellant's judgment, the lien whereof has expired. We need not discuss this proposition. That there is nothing in it is settled by a host of authorities. I will only refer to Fickes's Appeal (21 P. F. Smith, 447).

It was said, however, that even if the lien of appellant's judgment had expired, he was entitled to the fund for the reason that Hearing had made a prior promise to Kauffman to pay this judgment, and that he kept back so much of the purchase-money. This would be wrenching the recent "under and subject" cases out of all manner of shape. The most that can be said is that Hearing may have made himself liable to an action on the part of the holder of the judgment. That such a promise could galvanize into life this dead lien so as to entitle it to claim the proceeds of a sheriff's sale is a proposition exceedingly difficult to sustain.

After paying the liens the Court below awarded the balance of the fund to the owner of the land sold. This was in strict conformity to the Act of Assembly. But here again the applicant interposes, and says it is true I have lost my lien, but Hearing promised to pay my judgment, and he has that much of the purchase-money in his hands. The applicant seems to forget that a mere contract creditor has not even a right to be heard upon a question of distribution, nor can he take a writ of error. This is settled law (Smith *v.* Reiff, 8 Harris, 364). The promise to pay the judgment was at most an agreement to indemnify the vendor; it was not a promise to pay out of the land, nor did the promise run with the land; it created no estate upon condition which would revert to the vendor upon breach of condition. To create such estate the intention must be expressed by apt words in the deed (Hiester *v.* Green, 12 Wright, 96; Bortz, Id. 382; Perry *v.* Scott, 1 P. F. S. 119).

Nor is there any equitable lien for the purchase-money. After the legal title has passed the lien must be expressly charged upon the land (Kauffelt *v.* Bower 7 S. & R. 64; Strauss's Appeal, 13 Wright, 353; Trinity Church *v.* Watson, 14 Id. 518).

There is no room for estoppel; the appellant's testator parted with nothing, and did nothing by

May, '80, 82.   May 11, 1880.

Kensinger v. Smith, to use of McClain.

Equitable ejectment—Parties—Equitable plaintiff—Cestui que trust—When one not a party to a deed may maintain ejectment against the grantee to enforce a charge or condition expressed in the deed in his favor—Practice—Conditional verdict—When defect will be supplied in Supreme Court.

Where a deed from A. to B. contained a clause that the land was conveyed subject to the payment of a balance of purchase-money "for which a judgment had been entered in the name of C.," and the habendum was "subject to the payment of the sum . . . as aforesaid;"
Held, that C. could maintain ejectment against B., either in his own name or in the name of A. to his use, to enforce payment of said sum.

Where a conditional verdict and judgment for plaintiff in ejectment omitted to fix a time for the payment of the sum upon which the verdict was to be released, the Supreme Court, on error, amended the judgment by inserting a date before which payment should be made.

Error to the Common Pleas of Bedford County.

Ejectment, by Esther Smith, for the use of Samuel McClain, against Samuel Kensinger and Nancy Kensinger, his wife, for two tracts of land in Woodberry Township, Bedford County.

The facts were as follows: Jacob K. Smith died seized of the land in controversy. His widow, Esther Smith, purchased the tracts at an Orphans' Court sale for the payment of debts for the consideration of $2216.69. At the time of sale $1410 was paid by Nancy Kensinger, mother of Esther Smith. Of this sum of $1410 $350 was borrowed from Samuel McClain, brother of Nancy Kensinger. The sale was confirmed by the Court November 18, 1872; but the deed from the administrator was not delivered until the balance of the purchase-money was paid, November 12, 1873.

On October 30, 1873, Esther Smith, by articles of agreement under seal, agreed to sell and convey to Nancy Kensinger the land in controversy for "the sum of $2214 in manner following, to wit: $1515 cash, and the balance the said Nancy Kensinger to pay to the administrator of Jacob K. Smith, to get the deed which was made to the said Esther Smith by the administrator of Jacob Smith, deceased, when the said Esther Smith will make the same over to the said Nancy Kensinger." On the same day Nancy Kensinger paid the $1515; and on November 12, 1873, she borrowed from Samuel McClain the further sum of $773.41, and with $100 she had herself, paid off the balance of the purchase-money due from Esther Smith to Jacob K. Smith's administrator, whereupon he, the administrator, delivered the deed to Esther Smith. On the same day Esther Smith conveyed the same land to Nancy Kensinger in pursuance of their agreement. A settlement was then had between Samuel McClain and Nancy Kensinger, and it was found that the latter was in debt to McClain for $1378.09, for which he took her individual judgment note, and had judgment thereon entered against her the same day. The consideration named in the deed from Esther Smith to Nancy Kensinger was $1108.35. This deed was in the usual form, and after the description of the land contained the following clause:—

"The said real estate is conveyed subject to the payment of the sum of one thousand three hundred and seventy-eight dollars and nine cents, being the balance of purchase-money due, for which a judgment has been entered in the name of Samuel McClain." . . . .

Habendum, etc., ... "subject nevertheless to the payment of the sum of one thousand three hundred and seventy-eight dollars and nine cents, as aforesaid."

On December 1, 1879, Esther Smith filed her petition praying for a rule on Samuel McClain, for whose use and at whose instance this action of ejectment was brought, to show cause why the use of her name as legal plaintiff should not be prohibited, and the same stricken from the record. This application was not disposed of until the trial, when its substance was embodied in defendants' points.

Upon the trial, before HALL, P. J., the defendants requested the Court to charge—

(1) That ejectment, in its present form, cannot, under all the evidence, be sustained in this case. *Refused.*

(2) That ejectment, by Samuel McClain for his use against the consent of Esther Smith, cannot be maintained. *Refused.*

(3) That Esther Smith having parted with all her right, title, and interest in the land by conveyance to Nancy Kensinger, and all the purchase-money due her or her predecessors in title having been paid, Samuel McClain is a stranger to the deed and to the title, and therefore has no such right or title at law as would enable him to recover in this form of action. *Refused.*

(4) That the undisputed evidence being that the purchase-money due Esther Smith and her predecessors in the title was all paid when the conveyance was made to Nancy Kensinger, she

---

reason of Hearing's promise to pay his judgment. If the money is lost it will be by reason of his laches in not reviving his judgment so as to hold the terre-tenant.

The decree is affirmed and the appeal dismissed, at the cost of the appellant.

Opinion by PAXSON, J. SHARSWOOD, C. J., and GREEN, J., absent.

stood in no other relation to Samuel McClain than as a debtor for the amount advanced by McClain to satisfy the purchase-money owing by Nancy Kensinger on the conveyance to her, and upon a breach of the conditions in said deed to Nancy Kensinger, he has no right of entry for condition broken, nor any right to enforce the performance of the condition by this action of ejectment. *Refused.*

The Court directed the jury to render a "verdict for the plaintiff for the land in dispute, to be released on payment of $1573.30." Verdict accordingly, and judgment thereon. The defendants took this writ, assigning for error the refusal of their points, and the direction to the jury, as above stated.

John Cessna and *J. M. Reynolds,* for plaintiffs in error.

Before this action of ejectment can be sustained plaintiff must show either legal or equitable title to the land which he seeks to recover.

Westenberger *v.* Reist, 1 Harris, 597.
Reed *v.* Murray, 1 Jones, 334
Megargel *v.* Saul, 3 Wh. 19.
Thompson *v.* Adams, 5 Sm. 482.
Kenege *v.* Elliott, 9 Watts, 262.

There being in this case neither a trust to execute nor a conveyance sought to be enforced, the courts of this State will not by instrumentality of a jury direct a recovery in ejectment.

Peebles *v.* Reading, 8 S. & R. 491.

Parties to deeds of conveyance may by clear and express words create liens upon land either for purchase-money or for the performance of collateral conditions, which will be binding on themselves and their privies; but *strangers* to the deed can create no such lien. It is a rule of the common law that no one can take advantage of a breach of condition expressed but parties and privies in right and representation, as heirs, executors, or administrators of natural persons, and the successors of a body politic. No assignee or stranger can enter.

Strauss's Appeal, 13 Wr. 353.
Kiester *v.* Green, 12 Id. 96.
Hepburn *v.* Snyder, 3 Barr, 72.
Campbell *v,* Shrum, 3 Watts, 60.
Taylor *v.* Preston, 29 Sm. 436.
Crabb on Real Property.
Hamilton *v.* Elliott, 5 S. & R. 385.

The verdict of the jury must be set aside, because it is not in proper form. A period should have been stipulated in which payment was to be made in order to release the land under the verdict.

Dixon *v.* Oliver, 5 Watts, 509.

Russell & Longenecker, G. H. Spang, and *R. B. Petriken,* for defendants in error.

The intention of the parties, gathered from their acts and the language of their deed, shows that the land was to be a security to McClain for the payment of his money, and it matters not whether it was a charge, condition or equitable lien.

Sheppard's Touchstone, 121.
Bear *v.* Whisler, 7 Watts, 144.
Washburne on Real Property, 467.
Hamilton *v.* Elliott, 5 W. & S. 381.
Westenberger *v.* Reist, 1 Har. 598.

The payment of any lien, condition, or charge on land may be enforced by ejectment, where there is a clear intent to make the real estate chargeable with the money.

Bear *v.* Whisler, 7 Watts, 144.
Perry *v.* Scott, 1 Sm. 124.
Soper *v.* Guernsey, 21 Id. 223.
Watters *v.* Bredin, 20 Sm. 235.
Galbraith *v.* Fenton, 3 S. & R. 361.
Ripple *v.* Ripple, 1 Rawle, 386.
Simpson *v.* Ammons, 1 Binney, 176.
Smith *v.* Shuler, 12 S. & R. 243.
Knaub *v.* Essieck, 2 Watts, 282.
Fluck *v.* Replogle, 1 Har. 406.

The Court properly overruled the point that the action could not be maintained in the name of Esther Smith, against her consent. The suit was brought in the name of the right plaintiff, and her consent was not necessary.

1 Chitty on Pleading, 2.
Ins. Co. *v.* Smith, 1 Jones, 124,
Riley *v.* Vandyke, 1 Phila. 180.
Montgomery *v.* Cook, 6 Watts, 238.

Any interested party in the performance of a condition may enforce it by ejectment.

Strauss's App. 13 Wr. 355.

May 14, 1880. THE COURT. A *cestui que trust* may maintain ejectment in his own name. (Kennedy *v.* Fury, 1 Dall. 76.) If entitled to possession he may maintain it against his trustee. (Presbyterian Congregation *v.* Johnson, 1 W. & S. 9.)

Esther Smith was unnecessarily named as the legal party, but she was powerless to prevent McClain from enforcing his right for the unpaid purchase-money. It is expressly declared in the deed made to the plaintiff in error, and under which she holds that the land is conveyed "subject to the payment of the sum of one thousand three hundred and seventy-eight dollars and nine cents, being the balance of purchase-money due for which a judgment has been entered in the name of Samuel McClain." In the *habendum* it is declared she shall hold subject nevertheless to the payment of the said sum "as aforesaid."

In this State ejectment is an equitable action. (Russell *et al. v.* Baughman *et al.* just decided [reported *ante* p. 284] and cases there cited.) It lies to enforce unpaid purchase-money clearly shown in the conveyance to be a part of the consideration on which the deed is made and declared to be subject to its payment. The fact that a judgment note, recited in the deed to be for the same purchase-money, was also given, will not defeat ejectment, which would otherwise lie, brought to enforce payment of the purchase-money. We think the remedies are cumulative and either may be pursued.

The only error we discover is an omission to fix a time for the payment of the sum found to be due. We therefore amend the judgment so that it shall read, judgment in favor of the plaintiff below for the land in dispute to be released on payment of the sum of fifteen hundred and seventy-three dollars and thirty-seven cents with interest thereon from the 22d December, 1879, and costs, on or before the 15th November, 1880; and, thus amended,

Judgment affirmed.

Opinion by MERCUR, J. SHARSWOOD, C. J., and GREEN, J., absent.

May, '80, 161.   May 14, 1880.

Mortimer's Appeal.

Divorce—Errors and appeals—Limitation of appeal in divorce—Appeal entered after statutory limitation will be quashed—No appeal lies to a refusal of the Court below to open or vacate a decree in divorce.

Sur motion to quash appeal.

Appeal of Betsy Mortimer from a decree of the Common Pleas of Perry County.

The record showed the following facts: On January 10, 1876, Frank Mortimer filed his bill in divorce, praying for a divorce *a vinculo matrimonii* from his wife Betsy Mortimer; no service was made on her, but on the return of an order of publication, and on the report of a Commissioner appointed to take testimony, the Court, on January 12, 1878, entered a final decree as prayed for by the libellant. On Jan. 8, 1880, the said Betsy Mortimer, by her next friend and brother, presented her petition, praying the Court for a rule on the libellant to show cause why the said decree should not be reversed and cancelled, on the ground, *inter alia*, that the said Betsy, at the time of the said proceedings in divorce, was insane and confined in a lunatic asylum, where she had been placed by her said husband, which facts had not been referred to in the testimony, and that she had had no notice of the proceeding; and further, because the testimony showed no sufficient ground for divorce *a. v. m.*

The Court refused to grant a rule to show cause, and dismissed the petition, whereupon the petitioner took this appeal, assigning for error the decree of divorce *a vinculo matrimonii* on the testimony, and the dismissal of her petition.

When the case was called in the Supreme Court, counsel for the appellee moved to quash the appeal, on the following grounds, viz.:—

"(1) That the decree in divorce from which this appeal is taken was made on the 12th Jan. 1878, and no appeal was taken therefrom until 7th April, 1880, more than two years thereafter. The statute limits the time for appeal to one year from date of decree, and, therefore, this appeal was taken too late.

"(2) That the refusal of the Court below to entertain a motion to vacate this decree, made two years before, is not a final decree, and no appeal lies.

"(3) That the refusal of the Court below to entertain this motion to vacate this decree was a matter purely within its own discretion, and not reviewable by this Court.

"(4) That as an appeal from the final decree of 12th January, 1878, is barred by the Act of 13 March, 1815, and that as any matter contained in appellant's paper-book, other than that on the record, is new matter of fact, therefore, as to it, this Court would have to be a Court of original jurisdiction to enable it to consider it."

W. N. Seibert and *J. E. Junkin*, for the motion.

H. D. Russell and *Chas. A. Barnett*, contra.

May 24, 1880. THE COURT. No appeal lies from a refusal of the Court to open or vacate the decree. The 13th section of the Act of 13th March, 1815, declares, "No appeal shall lie from the final sentence or decree of the Court of Common Pleas, or other Court, having competent jurisdiction in cases of divorce, after the expiration of one year from the time of pronouncing the said final sentence or decree." In this case the final decree of divorce was made on the 12th January, 1878. More than two years thereafter, this application was made to set aside the decree, and after that was refused, this appeal was taken. The right to an appeal was, therefore, barred by the statute. The power of the prothonotary to administer the oath to the libellant is clearly given by the Act of 22d March, 1859.

Appeal quashed.

PER CURIAM. SHARSWOOD, C. J., and GREEN, J., absent.

Quarter Sessions.

November, 1880.

Commonwealth ex rel. Ellen Barron v. The Keeper of the County Prison.

Magistrate's judgment in trover and conversion against husband and wife—Ca. sa. against the wife improper—Habeas corpus—Practice.

A *capias ad satisfaciendum* cannot be lawfully issued against a married woman upon a judgment obtained against her and her husband for a joint conversion of personal property during her coverture.

Where it appeared that a married woman was imprisoned under such circumstances by virtue of a *capias ad satisfaciendum* issued upon a judgment obtained before a magistrate, that the twenty days allowed by law for a writ of certiorari or appeal had elapsed, and that no means existed of reviewing directly the legality of the *capias ad satisfaciendum* under which she was taken, she was discharged on *habeas corpus*.

Ellen Barron asked to be discharged on a writ of *habeas corpus*. She had been committed by a magistrate on a charge of trover and conversion. On the return to the writ, the following facts appeared: She had been induced by an agent of the Singer Manufacturing Company to exchange a sewing machine she had for one of the company's make. She signed an agreement of lease of the machine, the difference in price of the machines to be paid by instalments. She paid all but a small sum, when the company, in default of that payment, issued a summons case against her and her husband for the amount, and obtained judgment before a magistrate for $30. An execution was issued upon this judgment, the return to which was "no goods." Finally, an action of trover and conversion was brought before the magistrate, judgment obtained, and writs of *fieri facias* and *capias ad satisfaciendum* were issued against Ellen Barron and her husband, and upon the latter writ the relator was committed to prison.

T. Warren O'Neill, for relator.

The writs of fi. fa. and ca. sa., having been issued together, nullified each other. By a provision of the Act of 1819, re-enacted by the Act of 1836, women were exempted from imprisonment for debt. This proceeding of trover and conversion is really founded upon a debt, and the relator being a married woman cannot be imprisoned in such a proceeding, the husband being the party responsible to the plaintiff company.

Nathan H. Sharpless, contra.

This commitment was made in a civil proceeding in which the magistrate had jurisdiction. The Court of Quarter Sessions has no jurisdiction and cannot review the magistrate's action upon a writ of *habeas corpus*. In this case a well-established practice has been followed, and the exemption of females from imprisonment by the provisions of the Acts quoted do not apply to torts or civil wrongs, but only to ordinary cases of indebtedness.

Nov. 30, 1880. THE COURT. It appears by the return to the writ and the certified transcript of the magistrate that James Barron and his wife Ellen were jointly sued before a magistrate by the Singer Sewing Machine Company in an action of trover for a sewing machine, that judgment was obtained against them, upon which a *capias ad satisfaciendum* was issued against Mrs. Barron, under which she was arrested and lodged in jail. She has sued out the present writ of *habeas corpus* to be relieved from this imprisonment.

The general rule that females are liable to arrest and imprisonment by civil process for torts committed by them does not, I apprehend, admit of question. I speak, of course, of "torts simpliciter;" that is, of torts pure and simple, and not of such as have a contract for their basis, or such as, in the language of the Court, in Keen *v.* Hartman (12 Wr. 499) are founded upon duties growing out of contracts. But it is very old law that the condition of married women is, in this respect, better than that of single women. "If judgment be recovered," says Sir WILLIAM BLACKSTONE, "against husband and wife for the contract, nay, even for the personal misbehavior of the wife during her coverture, the capias shall issue against the husband only, which is one of the many great privileges of English wives" (3 Com. 414). Even upon a judgment against husband and wife for a battery by the wife the capias shall be against the husband only (Cro. Car. 513; 1 Vent. 51). In an action against husband and wife the husband alone is liable to be arrested (Tidd's Pr. 26). And so Chancellor KENT, "where the remedy for the tort is only damages by suit, the husband is liable with the wife; but if the remedy be sought by imprisonment on execution, the husband alone is liable to imprisonment" (2 Kent's Com. 149, Lec. 28). And in Hawk *v.* Harman (5 Bin. 45), the law was laid down by YEATES, J., in the very words of BLACKSTONE. The Act of 8th of February, 1819 (7 Smith's L. 150), re-enacted by the Act of 13th of June, 1836, § 6 (P. L. 573), declared, it is true that no female shall be arrested or imprisoned on any civil process for any *debt* contracted after the passage of the Act. But surely we are not to infer from that an intention to abrogate the well-known privilege of married women to be exempt from arrest upon civil process, whether for debts contracted or torts committed during coverture. Such an inference would be altogether unreasonable.

This being, as I apprehend, the law, it is apparent upon the face of these proceedings that the *capias ad satisfaciendum* against Mrs. Barron is unlawful and void, and that her imprisonment under it is an unlawful imprisonment, for the judgment was against husband and wife for a joint conversion during coverture.

Then the question arises whether, that being so, this Court ought to relieve her upon *habeas corpus*. There can be no doubt that the writ of *habeas corpus* lies not only to relieve a person from imprisonment upon unfounded criminal charges, but from every species of unlawful imprisonment. It is a great constitutional remedy, which extends to every case of illegal confinement. The Habeas Corpus Act extends to commitments under civil process as well as criminal. The 13th section of the Act of 1785 is very express upon this subject, and in Respublica *v.* Arnold (3 Yeates, 263), and Hecker *v.* Jarret (3 Binney, 404), it was so decided. It has been determined, however, that whenever the process under which a person has been committed emanates from a Court of competent jurisdiction, whose proceedings may be reviewed, so that redress may be had by appeal, writ of error or any other direct means of review, a Judge is not justifiable in giving relief upon *habeas corpus*, for that would be to bring different tribunals into collision, and to produce endless confusion. In such a case, therefore, the party aggrieved will be left to those direct methods of redress provided by a writ of error or appeal. Upon this ground the Supreme Court refused to discharge a prisoner from a commitment under a *capias ad satisfaciendum* issued out of the Common Pleas of Allegheny County (Commonwealth *ex rel.* Davis *v.* Lecky, 1 Watts, 66). In that case a writ of error had actually been taken, and was then pending in the Supreme Court.

In the case now before me the *capias ad satisfaciendum* under which Mrs. Barron was taken in execution, was not issued by a court of record. I do not know that that circumstance would make any difference in the application of the rule to which I have just referred, if any means existed by which the legality of the writ could be reviewed. But no such means exist. The twenty days allowed by law for a certiorari or an appeal to the Court of Common Pleas have gone by. The 21st section of the Act of 1810 expressly enacts that no execution shall be set aside, upon a certiorari, unless it has been issued and served within twenty days after the execution issued. And the 24th section of the same Act prohibits the Supreme Court from issuing writs of certiorari to justices of the peace in any civil suit or action whatever. If the relator could remove the proceedings into the Court of Common Pleas by certiorari or otherwise for review, I might well abstain from interference with the capias under which she is imprisoned; but it is manifest that she cannot do so, and that she is absolutely without remedy for an imprisonment which is clearly unlawful, unless she can be relieved by the writ of *habeas corpus*. Under these circumstances, I entertain no doubt of her right to this writ, or that it is my duty to discharge her. It is accordingly ordered that she be discharged.

Opinion by THAYER, P. J.

Dec. 10, 17, 1880.

Commonwealth ex rel. Charles Hegler v. Edward Schladensky.

Parent and child.— Custody of minor child— Habeas corpus— When father's right to custody may be denied.

Coram YERKES, J.

Habeas corpus, issued at the relation of Charles Hegler, to recover the custody of his minor son Henry.

On the hearing of the return, the testimony disclosed the following facts: The boy was thirteen years of age, his mother had been dead for about ten years, and subsequently his father had married a second time and been divorced, and about six years previous to the hearing had been married a third time, and by the third wife had three children one of whom was dead. On May 30, 1880, the boy ran away from home to the house of his maternal grandfather, Henry Rieser, alleging that he had been badly treated and beaten by his stepmother. The relator visited Rieser shortly after for the purpose of obtaining the boy, but offered some violence to him, whereupon he was arrested at Rieser's instance and held in $300 bail to keep the peace. After the hearing before the magistrate, at which the boy was present, his stepmother told the relator that she would not live with him if he took the boy home, and he was left in the office of the magistrate, who advised the grandfather to take the boy and report the facts to the Society to Protect Children from Cruelty; this he did, and on June 8, 1880, under the advice of the society, the care of the boy was assumed by the respondent, who was a son-in-law of Rieser. At this time the boy showed some bruises upon his head, and there was testimony as to there being some such evidences of blows at other times previously, and generally as to cruelty and neglect by his father and stepmother, but the testimony as to his treatment was conflicting; within a day or two after the respondent took charge of the boy the relator called at the office of the society and expressed satisfaction at the disposition made of the boy, stating that he could do nothing with him; he also expressed himself to the respondent as satisfied, and told him to call for his clothes, but afterwards, when he called, declined to give them up, and said that he would have the boy back. The relator and his wife said that the boy was lazy, impudent, disobedient, and utterly untruthful, and generally a very bad boy, which fact they ascribed to the influence of the Rieser family, who, they alleged, had been unfriendly to the relator since his last marriage; this the respondent's witnesses denied. The respondent and his wife both said that they found no difficulty in managing the boy. It appeared that he had theretofore spent a great portion of his time with his grandfather, sometimes at the direct request of his father.

After hearing on the return day the case was continued for one week.

Goldbeck, for the relator.
N. D. Miller, contra cited—
Comm. *v.* Ashton, 8 WEEKLY NOTES, 563.

Dec. 17, 1880. THE COURT. I gave counsel additional time to secure evidence as to the treatment of the boy, and some testimony upon that point has been adduced. I am not sure, however, that I should consider it sufficient to justify me in taking the boy away from his father were it not that both his father and stepmother give the boy a very bad character, calling him lazy, impudent, disobedient, and untruthful. There is a memorable precedent for giving the child to that one of the claimants who loves it most, and since both the respondent and his wife give the boy a good character ever since he has been with them, I cannot but think that with them he finds such treatment as will best educate him.

The writ is dismissed, and the boy remanded to the custody of the respondent, with leave to the relator to renew this application in the future, when additional facts may be brought to the notice of the Court.

Opinion by YERKES, J.

Common Pleas—Law.

C. P. No. 3.   Jan., 1878.
Huston v. Clark et al.

Arbitration and award—Reference under statutes —Rule of Court—Submission, when revocable before award.

Rule to cancel agreement of submission, and to strike from the record said agreement of submission and award of arbitrators, together with all docket entries relating to the same.

On February 16, 1877, an agreement was made between Samuel Huston, the plaintiff, and Edward W. Clark, William Sellers, and John Sellers, the defendants, reciting that sundry controversies and differences had arisen between them, growing out of their business relations with each other, in connection with the Midvale Steel Works, and naming three gentlemen as referees or arbitrators to settle the matters in dispute between them. This agreement or submission stipulated, *inter alia*, as follows:—

The said parties have agreed, and do hereby agree, to submit said controversies and differences to the award or umpirage of Israel H. Johnson, John C. Bullitt, and E. A. Rollins; and they do further agree that this said reference or agreement shall be made a rule of the Court of Common Pleas in and for the City and County of Philadelphia, which for the time may have jurisdiction of the case, that they and each of them shall and will submit to and be finally concluded by the arbitration, umpirage, and award which shall be made by said arbitration or by any two of them in pursuance of this submission, and that neither of said parties shall except to or appeal from said award for any cause, act, matter, or thing whatever. And it is further agreed by and between said parties that in case of the death of either party this agreement or submission shall not be revoked, or in any wise affected, but the executors or administrators of such deceased party shall be forthwith made parties, and the reference proceed against them with like effect as if their testator or intestate had not died.

Subsequently these arbitrators entered upon the discharge of their duties, and held several meetings, at which they heard the evidence offered by the respective parties. On the 28th of November, 1877, a majority of the arbitrators, Messrs. Bullitt and Rollins, filed their award of record, in accordance with the terms of the agreement, and thereby originated the present proceeding.

Plaintiff took this rule to cancel the agreement of submission, and to strike it from the record, together with the award, and all docket entries relating to it, principally upon the ground that the submission had been revoked by the plaintiff before the award had been made.

The depositions taken disclosed the following additional facts: The meetings before the arbitrators continued until the summer of 1877, when the testimony was practically closed, and they had several conferences in regard to a decision of the case. Some time in June, a form of award, expressing the conclusions of Messrs. Bullitt and Rollins, was drawn by Mr. Bullitt, and submitted at a meeting of all the referees. This paper, Mr. Bullitt testified, embodied the substance of the award finally filed. Mr. Johnson dissented from this report, and the papers were handed to him to examine, with the request that he would submit his views in writing to his colleagues. At the next meeting, some time in

September, Mr. Johnson presented his written view of the case, the main points of which were not concurred in by the other arbitrators. Several other meetings were held without any agreement having been reached, when it was finally concluded that a majority award, substantially similar to the draft submitted in the preceding June, should be presented by Messrs. Bullitt and Rollins, and a minority report by Mr. Johnson. These papers, when finally prepared, were to be filed, or otherwise disposed of. Some time in November, Mr. Bullitt's draft was re-copied, with some alterations as to figures, and signed by Mr. Rollins and himself. This was a few days before the notice of revocation of their authority was served upon them.

On the 24th of November, a notice was served upon each of the arbitrators by Mr. Huston revoking the agreement of submission. The meeting at which the final award was signed was held two or three days after this notice of revocation had been received. Mr. Johnson's minority report had been in Mr. Bullitt's possession some days before this time. Mr. Bullitt had no doubt that the paper first signed by himself and Mr. Rollins was signed before they had notice of the revocation, but said that it was not used as the final award; some of its figures were altered, and the language changed in places in the award finally made, but no substantial changes were made in the findings. Notices of a meeting to be held on the 28th of November were dictated by Mr. Bullitt to his stenographer on Nov. 23, which, through neglect of the latter, were not delivered until Nov. 26, two days after the date of the alleged revocation. A final meeting, of which all the parties in interest were notified, was held on Dec. 1, at which the award, as filed, was for the first time made public.

It further appeared from the testimony, that Mr. Huston had been informed by Mr. Johnson, the arbitrator appointed by him, of the status of the case prior to his giving the notice revoking the submission.

E. Spencer Miller and *George M. Dallas*, showed cause.

In former times, when Courts were unfavorable to references, it was the rule, perhaps, that all submissions might be revoked by either party at any time before award, and this upon the ground that all naked powers might be revoked; but the policy of the law upon this subject has changed, and this rule has been very materially modified and restricted. Where, as in this case, the submission is more than a naked power, and amounts to a contract, for which there is a valuable consideration in the time, labor, and money expended, as well as in the delay in the proceedings at law already instituted, etc., the rule established by McGheehen *v.* Duffield (5 Barr, 497), Shisler *v.* Keavy (25 Sm. 79), and Paist *v.* Caldwell (25 Sm. 161), is that the power of revocation does not exist.

And this is particularly so where the reference is, by the submission, made a rule of Court under the Acts of Assembly. Equity will not, in cases of this character, interfere to cancel the submission, but will leave the parties to their remedy under the statutes, viz., by exceptions.

Pope *v.* Duncannon, 9 Sim. 177, and 16 Eng. Ch Rep., Dunlap's Ed., decided upon the statute o 9 and 10 Wm. III., which was reported as in force in this State.

But even if revocation were allowable, it has come too late. The decision of the referees had been made and signed before the revocation; the re-signing resulted wholly from unsubstantial changes in the opinions only.

Oxley *v.* Olden, 1 D. 453.
Pollock *v.* Hall, 3 Y. 42.

Mr. Huston, in revoking the submission, acted upon information from the dissenting arbitrator that the award was against him. This is of itself sufficient to defeat the attempted revocation.

Robinson *v.* Bickley, 6 Cas. 384.

Affidavits to the submission having been filed with the award, give to the proceedings the same effect, for every purpose now involved, as if they had been filed and entered at the date of the agreement of submission.

Massey *v.* Thomas, 6 Bin. 333.
Wall *v.* Fife, 1 Wr. 394.

A. Sydney Biddle and *Geo. W. Biddle* (with them *F. C. Brewster*), contra.

Parties cannot, by contract, oust the ordinary Courts of their jurisdiction.

Scott *v.* Avery, 5 H. of L. Cases, 846.
Monongahela Co. *v.* Fenlon, 4 W. & S. 211.

Is the contract in this case a release of all existing liabilities, and the taking in lieu thereof the new one to be named by third parties, or is it that the authorized agents of the parties shall settle disputes? If the former, it comes within the principle of McGheehen *v.* Duffield (5 Barr, 497), and Paist *v.* Caldwell (25 Sm. 161), where valuable rights were released on both sides, and revocation consequently prohibited. The reason of this is obvious. All that remains after the execution of the agreement is a new obligation, and the agreement, if properly executed, by which the original rights have been lost, cannot be rescinded, because it is a conveyance, and the original obligations to the releasor have terminated and passed out of existence by the act of conveyance. His only right then is to enforce from the other party the consideration provided in the contract. This is the real explanation of that class of cases in which it is said that a contract cannot be revoked. The question then is no longer one of ability to terminate an agency, but of power to reinstate one's self in *statu quo* after conveyance made.

The submission in this case is not of this character. There is no allusion made in it to the equity suit then pending, and there is no release of any existing rights. Mr. Huston's position is precisely similar to that of a party to a written contract, upon which there had been a breach by the other party, in which there was an independent covenant to arbitrate, and falls within the principle of the cases referred to in Dawson *v.* Lord Otho Fitzgerald (L. R. 1 Exch. Div. 257). There JESSEL, M. R., stated the law to be that a defence to an action on an agreement to arbitrate on the ground that no arbitration had occurred, could only be made in two cases: First, where the action can only be brought for the sum named by the arbitrator; secondly, where it is agreed that no action shall be brought until there has been an arbitration, or that arbitration shall be a condition precedent to the right of action. In all other cases where there is, first, a covenant to pay; and, secondly, a covenant to refer, the covenants are distinct and collateral, and the plaintiff may sue on the first.

The rule here taken is a proper one. It is not to strike off the award *qua* award, but to remove from the records of the Court an impertinent paper filed without authority, and is in no sense an appeal to the equity powers of the Court.

The Act of 1836 allows exceptions to be made to awards for the following causes only: viz., misbehavior of the arbitrators; that they committed a plain mistake of law or fact, or that the award was procured by corruption or other undue means (Purd. Dig., page 78). Hence revocation could not be taken advantage of in that way.

Again, there is a fatal defect in the proceedings in this that the arbitrators were never sworn or affirmed as required by law.

Acts 21 March, 1806, P. L. 1805–6, p. 559.
Acts 20 March, 1810, P. L. 1809–10, p. 145.
Acts 16 June, 1836, P. L. 1835–36, p. 715.

The fact that the arbitrators had agreed on what terms or principles the award should be made, before the revocation was communicated to them, will not sustain the award. The agreement of the majority was not final, and did not settle conclusions or amounts. Robinson *v.* Bickley, *supra*, was an entirely different case; there an award had been drawn up and signed by two of the arbitrators, under circumstances which obviated the necessity of obtaining the signature of the third, before the revocation was attempted. That the reference was made a rule of Court does not alter the law upon this subject.

Power *v.* Power, 7 Watts, 212.
Johnson *v.* Andress, 5 Phila. 8.

January 26, 1878. THE COURT. The parties to this case agreed to submit certain controversies to the umpirage of three men, that the reference should be made a rule of Court, and that the award of the referees, or any two of them, should be final, and without the right of exception or appeal. There was no suit pending. The reference was not made a rule of Court by filing the agreement until after an award was made, and there does not seem to have been any other consideration than the mutual agreement to refer.

The first question that arises is, whether either of the parties to such an agreement can revoke it before the referees have agreed upon their award. The case of Johnson *v.* Andress (5 Phila. Rep. 8), expressly decides that they can. That case was approved in Keavy *v.* Shisler (8 Phila. Rep. 54, afterwards affirmed in the Supreme Court; 25 P. F. Smith, 79.)

We can find no Pennsylvania case that overrules or shakes the authority of Johnson *v.* Andress; but can find many where the reasoning and *dicta* of Judges sustain it. Cases where there were other considerations than the naked agreement are not in point. We decide that this agreement was revocable before the award was agreed upon.

Many careful readings of the testimony leave us in doubt as to whether an award was agreed upon before the revocation by plaintiff. There are some expressions in the evidence sustaining the affirmative and others the negative of this question. The award must have been agreed upon at a meeting of the referees. Does the evidence establish that satisfactorily? It is clear that radical differences were apparent in July, 1876, and that the majority at that time put their views in writing. One of the arbitrators, after alluding to meetings in September, says: "We finally concluded that Mr. Rollins and myself would sign a report substantially such as I had submitted in June, and that Mr. Johnson would make a separate report." Again, he says, on page 43: "It was understood that we would prepare a majority report, and he would prepare a minority report." The fact that at a meeting it was agreed that the majority should unite in a report does not establish that an award was agreed upon. Such an agreement clearly establishes the fact that the principles that were to guide in the award were agreed upon; but an award is the exact result deduced from principles. The law upon this point is clearly enunciated in Johnson *v.* Andress, *supra*. "Nor can the award be sustained on the ground that the arbitrators had agreed on what terms or principles the award should be made before the revocation was communicated to them. An agreement to agree is obviously not a final agreement, particularly when, as here, it merely ascertains or fixes principles or data, and does not settle or arrive at conclusions or amounts."

There is in the evidence the expression that the report agreed upon was substantially such as had been drafted in June. Does this reference to that paper make it certain that the agreement for a majority report established results as well as principles. The paper of June was never considered more than a presentation of the views of the majority. After its preparation, meetings were held and evidence heard as to an item of $20,000 and another of $200 per week. It seems to have been modified as to one of these items. In alluding to this paper, the writer of it says, on page 42: "That paper was only stating the general principles involved, and yet I should say that the alterations from that paper were not in any sense substantial." This paper, was not intended as an award. We cannot find from the evidence that it embodied results. We doubt whether it was more than a mere construction of the agreement of May 13, 1873. To agree to make such a paper substantially the basis of a majority report does not mean an agreement to an award.

We are not satisfied that an award *qua* award was agreed upon at any meeting of the referees before November 28th, 1877. Doubtless the award was the inevitable and logical result of the principles which the majority had agreed upon; but this result should have been deduced and agreed upon by the majority at a meeting of the referees. The testimony on page 45 describes the later meetings of the referees. It is as follows: "We had one or more meetings at which the parties were present for these purposes. Afterwards we had several meetings during October for the purpose of considering an award. At one of these meetings Mr. Johnson submitted a second report, which we discussed. Subsequently he sent me the report in November, to which I have referred. These meetings took up the greater part of October, and the delay, to which I have referred as being due to my engagements, occurred." This extract sustains the view we have taken, that the testimony does not establish that an award was agreed upon before November 28th. The calling of a formal meeting upon that day is presumptive evidence that at no meeting had the referees agreed upon an award.

It seems clear that no meeting of the referees was held in November, between the beginning and the 28th. Between November 16th and 20th, the paper called the second paper was prepared and signed by two of the referees. It was never presented at any meeting, and therefore was the act of the two referees as individuals. We cannot, therefore, hold that it was an award.

It follows that the revocation upon November 24th was in time, and therefore the award must be stricken off.

Rule absolute.

Opinion by YERKES, J.

Dissenting opinion by LUDLOW, P. J.

Under the submission the parties agreed that the reference or agreement should be made "a rule of the Court of Common Pleas in and for the City and County of Philadelphia, which, for the time being, may have jurisdiction of the case."

In McAdam's Executors *v.* Stilwell (1 H. 98) BELL, J., declares: "I think all the prior determinations show this authority (Benjamin *v.* Benjamin, 5 W. & S. 562) to be inapplicable when there are actions in court to which the submission refers, or a simultaneous agreement to commence one, for then there is a plain implication of an intended rule.

The Court, and not the parties, had the control of this case, and without its sanction the submission could not be revoked.

Taking another view of the subject, it is contended, as a sound principle of law, that where a cause has been fully heard, and the elements of an award agreed upon, and one arbitrator dissents therefrom, and gives the others so to understand, the proceeding is not vitiated by the fact that the award was afterwards drawn up and executed. (Robinson *v.* Bickley, 6 C. 390–7.)

In the case before us, the "elements" had been considered and agreed upon; the figures, in what may be considered as a report, and which in no way disturbed the result, were only to be reconsidered.

It is difficult, and I think impossible, to resist the conclusion, that two of the arbitrators had agreed to find for defendant. The other arbitrator took the papers to prepare a report of his view of the case, and while he did not, in terms, inform the plaintiff what the award would be, it is impossible, from the testimony, not to believe that the plaintiff was informed by implication of the result.

The conclusion arrived at was never changed, and the "elements" of the award appear in the final action of the arbitrators.

I have no hesitation in saying, that under the circumstances surrounding this case, I would strain every principle to its utmost legal endurance, before I would permit parties who have agreed in good faith to abide by the award of their own tribunal, and have made that agreement substantially a rule of Court, to escape the result of their own action by the baldest of technicalities.

There are several other reasons which might

Orphans' Court.

November 15, 1880.

Hook's Estate.

Practice—Examination of witnesses before examiner—A witness is bound to attend before an examiner at the instance of either party, until his deposition has been finally closed by signing—Practice to compel attendance.

Sur petition for an order on proponents of a will to produce a witness for further cross-examination before the examiner appointed to take testimony under an appeal from the Register of Wills, and answer.

The petition of George W. Hook, contestant of the alleged will of Henry Hook, deceased, set forth that a witness had been produced and examined by proponents, and cross-examined by petitioner's counsel. The meeting was then adjourned at the request of proponent, in order that his counsel might prepare their re-examination. At the next meeting it was announced that there would be no re-examination. Counsel for petitioner then desired to ask the witness further questions by way of cross-examination, and requested counsel for proponents to recall him. This proponents refused to do, and the petitioner declined to proceed with the examination of other witnesses.

The petitioner prayed for an order upon proponents to produce the witness at the next meeting before the examiner.

The answer alleged that the petitioner's counsel having closed their cross-examination, the proponents had exercised their discretion of re-examining him or not, and declined to do so; that there was no promise to re-examine, and that they having finished with the witness, he had passed out of their control.

It was admitted on the argument that the witness had not yet signed his deposition.

Washington and *Wiltbank,* for the petitioner.

The question is not *how* shall a certain witness be made to appear; but must the petitioner, in further cross-examining him, be held to have made him his own witness.

Apart from the equity founded on the belief that the witness would be reproduced, the request would not have been refused in a common law trial, *à fortiori* not in proceedings before an examiner.

The exercise of the most liberal discretion in favor of justice has been enjoined even where the evidence has closed, and the cause has been opened to the jury.

2 Dan. Chanc. *1104.
Alldred *v.* Halliwell, 1 Starkie's Rep. 95.
Brown *v.* Giles, 1 Carr. & Payne, 118.
3 Chitty's Gen. Prac. 901, § 12.
Browne *v.* Molliston, 3 Wh. 137.
Devall *v.* Burbridge, 6 W. & S. 530.
Koenig *v.* Bauer, 7 Sm. 172.

And in like circumstances to this case the Supreme Court has examined the decision of a lower Court, and directed the granting of a request for the recall of a witness. So there are exceptions to the general principle that a decision as to the recall of a witness is an exercise of discretion of the Court, and not subject to appeal.

Covanhovan *v.* Hart, 9 H. 495.

E. C. Mitchell, contra.

The petitioner having closed his cross-examination, or having no re-examination, has dismissed the witness. We should not be compelled to be at the burden of reproducing him.

Nov. 20, 1880. THE COURT. After spending four meetings before the examiner in the cross-examination of the witness, and after having announced that they had closed, we do not think that the petitioners can require the respondents to produce the witness for further cross-examination; nor can the expectation of counsel that at the next meeting the opposite side would recall the witness for re-examination, confer such right.

But the witness is bound to attend at the instance of either party, until his deposition has been actually closed by signing. (Daniell's Ch. Pr. 973.) If he refuses to attend to be cross-examined, an application may be made to Court, and he will then be compelled to do what the party has a right to require of him. (Courtenay *v.* Hoskins, 2 Russ. 253; Daniell's Ch. P. 922.)

As yet, the witness is in no default, for it does not appear that his attendance has been requested. The proper practice, we think, would be that the examiner should give notice to the witness to attend before him, at a day to be appointed, for the purpose of further cross-examination. Should he fail to attend, upon certificate to the Court from the examiner, the necessary process will, on motion, and at the expense of the witness, be granted. (1 Dan. Ch. Pr. 891.)

The order made November 8, 1880, is rescinded, and the petition dismissed without prejudice.

Opinion by PENROSE, J.

Supreme Court.

Oct. & Nov. '79, 304. Oct. 25, 1880.

Metz v. Hipps et al.

Taxes—Treasurer's sales of unseated lands for—Act of March 13, 1815 (6 Sm. L. 299)—Redemption—Saving clause in 4th sect. of said Act as to persons under disability does not extend to sales under 5th section and redemption therefrom under 6th section.

The saving clause in sect. 4 of the Act of March 13, 1815 (6 Sm. L. 299), relative to the sale of unseated lands for taxes, whereby minors and insane persons whose lands have been so sold are entitled to two years after removal of their disability wherein to redeem the same, does not extend to cases of sales made under the 5th sect. of said Act to the County Commissioners, and to the redemption therefrom as provided in the 6th sect.

Plaintiff was born in 1851. Her title to the land in question accrued in 1854. In 1862 said land was sold for taxes in arrear in accordance with the provisions of the Act of March 13, 1815 (6 Sm. L. 299), sect. 1, relative to the sale of unseated lands for taxes. Said land was bought in by the County Commissioners in pursuance of sect. 5 of said Act, and by them sold to one of the defendants in 1868. In 1874 plaintiff, within two years after coming of age, paid to the treasurer of the county the full amount necessary to redeem her interest in the said land. In ejectment against those claiming under the conveyance from the County Commissioners:

Held, that the attempted redemption by the plaintiff was too late, and was, therefore, inoperative to divest the defendants' title.

Error to the Common Pleas of Cambria County.

Ejectment, by Thomas J. Metz and Jennie McM., his wife, in right of the said Jennie, against John Hipps and Uriah Lloyd, for an undivided fourth part of a certain tract of land in Chest Township.

On the trial, before ORVIS, A. L. J., it appeared, that the said Jennie was born September 10, 1851, that her title to the land in dispute descended upon her in 1854, upon the death of her mother, who had previously been seised thereof; that the whole tract, whereof the said Jennie owned one undivided fourth part, was regularly assessed for taxes for the years 1860 and 1861, and on June 13, 1862, was sold by the treasurer of the said county for default in payment of the said taxes, in pursuance of the Act of March 13, 1815 (6 Sm. L. 299), sect. 1, regulating the sale of unseated lands for taxes; that, in pursuance of the provisions of sects. 5 and 7 of the said Act, the said land not bringing at said sale the full amount of taxes assessed thereon and costs, the same was bought in by the Commissioners of the said county, and by them held until September 8, 1868, when the same was sold by them at public sale, and conveyed to John Hipps, one of the defendants; and that on August 25, 1874, within two years after said Jennie came of age, she paid to the county treasurer the full amount necessary to redeem her interest in the said tract of land.

Notice had been given by the plaintiff of a claim for mesne profits, and evidence was introduced in support of the claim.

The Court directed a verdict for plaintiff, reserving the question whether the redemption made by the said Jennie on August 25, 1874, was good and valid in law so as to divest the defendants' title acquired under the sale by the Commissioners, September 8, 1868. Verdict for plaintiff accordingly, and damages assessed at $3508.

The Court subsequently entered judgment for the defendants on the reserved point, *non obstante veredicto*. The following was the opinion of the Court, delivered by ORVIS, A. L. J., after stating the facts of the case:—

. . . If the plaintiff has the right to redeem this land any time within two years after attaining her majority, judgment should be entered upon the verdict for the plaintiff. If her right to redeem terminated at the end of five years from the treasurer's sale to the Commissioners, judgment should be entered for the defendants, *non obstante veredicto*. The decision of this question depends upon the proper construction of the Act of March 13, 1815, regulating the sale of unseated lands for taxes.*

---

* The following are the material provisions of the Act of March 13, 1815 (6 Sm. L. 299):—

Sec. 1. The treasurers of the several counties in this Commonwealth shall be and they are hereby respectively authorized and directed . . . at the expiration of every two years . . . to make public sale of the whole or any part of such tracts of unseated lands situate in the proper county as will pay the arrearages of the taxes, any part of which shall then have remained due and unpaid for the space of one year before, together with all costs necessarily accruing by reason of such delinquency, and to make and execute a deed or deeds, in fee simple, in the manner directed by the Act to which this is a further supplement . . .

Sec. 4. If the owner or owners of lands sold as aforesaid shall make or cause to be made, within two years after such sale, an offer or legal tender of the amount of the taxes for which the said lands were sold, and the costs, together with the additional sum of twenty-five per cent. on the same, to the county treasurer, who is hereby authorized and required to receive and receipt for the

Does the *proviso* to the 4th section, extending the time during which certain classes of persons under disability may redeem their lands sold by the treasurer, extend to sales made under the 5th section to the County Commissioners, and to the redemption therefrom as provided for in the 6th section? It seems somewhat strange that this question has not arisen and been settled by the Supreme Court long ago, when we remember the date of the Act under which it arises. After the most careful examination of our books of reports, we are unable to find that the question has ever before even been mooted. It is true that in Sidle *v.* Walters (5 Watts, 389), and in some other cases, it is said that unseated land, the property of minors, sold for taxes, is subject to be redeemed at any time within two years after they respectively come of age. But wherever this or similar language occurs it is in the decision of cases where the land was sold to individuals and not to the county. It is equally true that in Steiner *v.* Coxe (4 Barr, 13), and in many subsequent cases, the Supreme Court has held that after the lapse of five years from a treasurer's sale to the Commissioners the title of the county becomes absolute. But in all these cases the former owner was under no disability, and of course the Judges delivering the opinions had not in their minds the question raised in this case. From the fact that this question seems never to have been before raised, we at first were inclined to infer that it was so clear and plain that all lawyers agreed about it; but to our surprise, on submitting the question to several eminent and learned land-lawyers, we found they divided nearly equally in their construction of the Act in this particular. We are therefore left to come to the best conclusion we may, after as thorough consideration as we have been able to give the subject.

A literal reading of the proviso of the 4th section of the Act would make it apply only to the redemption provided for in the body of the section. . . . This would look as though the *proviso* referred only to the kind of sales from which the owners not under disability had to redeem within *two years* by paying the taxes, costs, and twenty-five per cent. on the same.

The counsel for the plaintiff, however, contend that this would be too narrow and technical a mode of reading the statute—that it is to be considered as a whole, and the words of this proviso should have the same force and effect as though they were in a section by themselves at

---

same and to pay it over to the said purchaser on demand . . . said owner or owners shall be entitled to recover the same by due course of law. . . . And it is hereby declared that no . . . irregularity in the assessment or in the process or otherwise shall be construed or taken to affect the title of the purchaser, but the same shall be declared to be good and legal: *Provided,* That, where the owner or owners of lands *sold as aforesaid* shall at the time of such sale be an orphan or orphans or insane, and residing within the United States, two years after such disability is removed shall be allowed such person or persons, their heirs or legal representatives, to bring their suit or action for recovery of the lands so sold; but where the recovery is effected in such cases, the value of the improvements made on the land so sold, after the sale thereof, shall be ascertained by the jury trying the action for recovery and paid by the person or persons recovering the same before he, she, or they shall thereupon obtain possession of the lands so recovered.

Sec. 5. If any tract of unseated land hereafter to be sold for taxes due at this time or which shall hereafter be imposed shall not have bidden for it a sum equal to the whole amount of taxes for which it shall have been advertised, and the costs accrued, then and in that case it shall be the duty of the Commissioners of the proper county, or any of them, to bid off the same, and a deed shall thereupon be made by the treasurer to the Commissioners for the time being and to their successors in office, to and for the use of the proper county, and it shall be the duty of the Commissioners to provide a book wherein shall be entered the name of the person as whose estate the same shall have been sold, the quantity of land, and the amount of taxes it was sold for, and every such tract of land shall not thereafter so long as the same shall remain the property of the county be charged in the duplicate of the proper collector, but for five years next following such sale, if it shall so long remain unredeemed, the Commissioners shall, in separate columns in the same book, charge every such tract of land with reasonable county and road tax, according to the quality of the said land, not exceeding in any case the sum of six dollars for every hundred acres.

Sec. 6. That the right of redemption shall remain in the real owner of such land for five years after such sale, and on paying the treasurer of the county all the taxes and costs due thereon at the time of sale, and interest therefor for the same time, and also the taxes which shall have been assessed thereon from year to year after the sale, and interest of each assessment to be counted from the time it ought to have been paid, and on production of the treasurer's receipt, the Commissioner shall, by deed poll, endorsed on the back of the treasurer's deed to them, convey to the person who shall have been the owner of the land at the time of sale, or his legal representative, all the right and title which the county may have acquired under such sale as aforesaid; the moneys so received for road taxes shall be paid to the supervisors of the roads of the township.

Sec. 7. That, if the owner of any such land shall not redeem the same within the period aforesaid, it shall thereafter be lawful for the Commissioners to sell any such lands by public sale, and make a deed therefor to the purchaser, which shall be available in law, as well against the county as against the person or persons as whose estate the same had been sold, but no tract shall be sold for a sum less than the amount of taxes, costs, and interest, which shall be due at the time of such sale by the Commissioners, and such land shall thereafter be charged by the township assessors in the name of such last purchaser or redeemer, and shall again be liable to be assessed and sold for taxes, agreeably to this Act and the Act to which this Act is a supplement.

N. B.—By the Act of April 25, 1850, § 30 (P. L. 574), it is enacted that the words "orphan or orphans," in the 4th section of the above Act, shall be taken and construed to mean "minor or minors."

the end of the Act; in which case they would undoubtedly apply to all sales made in pursuance of any section of the Act. That the general purpose of the law was to enforce the payment of taxes, and not to forfeit or confiscate the estates of citizens; that the right of redemption is an equitable and beneficial one, and should not be narrowed by construction. (Patterson *v.* Brindle, 9 Watts, 98; Dubois *v.* Hepburn, 10 Peters, 1; Jenks *v.* Wright, 11 P. F. Smith, 410; Lynch *v.* Brudie, 13 Id. 206.) That the general policy of our law has been to preserve and protect the rights of minors and others under disability, especially from all species of forfeiture by reason of *laches.* That no good reason can be assigned for denying the same privileges to minors when their lands are sold to the county, which the Act undoubtedly gives them if the same lands were sold to individuals. That the provisions of the 4th section of the Act, which cures all defects in the form of sales of unseated lands for taxes, has been repeatedly held by the Supreme Court to apply to sales made to the Commissioners under the 5th section. (Peters *v.* Heasley, 10 Watts, 208; Lee *v.* Jeddo Coal Co., 4 WEEKLY NOTES, 231; Huston *v.* Foster, 1 Watts, 477; Laird *v.* Hiester, 12 Harris, 452; and many other cases.) That, if the provision curing defects in the forms of sales of unseated lands contained in the 4th section applies to all sales made in pursuance of the Act whether made to individuals or to the Commissioners, *a fortiori* the provision in favor of minors in the same section should apply to all sales under the Act, even though made to the county.

We have given these several arguments due consideration, and though many of them might be sufficient if addressed to the Legislature to induce that body to change the law so as to preserve the rights of minors when their lands are sold to the county, yet we are not convinced by them that the Legislature by the enactment of March 13, 1815, did so make the law. A careful reading of the entire Act brings our mind to the opposite conclusion. . . . It would be difficult to imagine what words the Legislature could have used to limit the right of redemption to five years in cases of land bought by the commissioners, regardless of the age and condition of the former owner, if the language . . . is liable to a different construction. 'The right of redemption shall remain in the real owner of such land for five years after such sale,' is as clear and conclusive as if the words *and no longer* had been added; and as no exception is made in favor of minors or insane persons in respect to this right of redemption, we must presume the Legislature intended there should be none. It must be borne in mind that the rights of all parties under tax sales in Pennsylvania, including the right of the owner to redeem, is purely statutory, and while we may not abridge or narrow the right of redemption by construction, neither can we extend it to any cases in which the Legislature has not seen fit to give it. It is not pertinent to say that the minor is as much entitled to it in this case as if the land had been sold by the treasurer to an individual. Why the Legislature gave it in the one case and did not give it in the other, we may not be able at this late day to ascertain. But if it were necessary to give a reason, one might be found in the fact that as to all lands bought by the Commissioners, the terms of redemption were made easier by not requiring the twenty-five per cent. additional to the taxes and costs to be paid, but only simple interest, and the time for redemption was extended from two to five years, which the Legislature may have thought was sufficient for persons under disability, they generally having guardians or committees to look after their estates; especially as the lands that would be thus bought by the Commissioners were only those of so little value that no individual would bid the taxes and costs for them.

If any further argument than that found in the words of the Act were necessary to show that the Legislature did not contemplate that the right to redeem from a treasurer's sale to the Commissioners could exist in any owner beyond the period of five years, it may be found in the absence of all provisions in the Act which would be necessary if such right survived. If the infant or insane owner of a tract of land sold to the Commissioners has the right to redeem after the expiration of five years, one of two consequences must necessarily follow : either, first, the Commissioners may not sell such tract at all as long as the right of redemption exists, viz. : until the former owner shall have arrived at the age of twenty-three if he was a minor, or until he recovered his reason if he had been insane ; or secondly, the Commissioners may sell at the expiration of five years after their purchase, in which case their vendee would take the land subject to the right of the former owner still to redeem. If we assume the first to be true, it would then clearly be the duty of the County Commissioners, whenever they purchased a tract of land at treasurer's sale, to make inquiries and ascertain the age and condition of the former owner in order that they might know when his right of redemption would expire. In many instances this would be impossible for them to do, as the land might not have been assessed in the name of the real owner, who may be a non-resident of the county and his title deeds may not have been placed on record. Besides, this duty would be entirely foreign to the ordinary official duties of County Commissioners. It is, however, sufficient to say that no such duty was imposed on them by the Act either in express words or by necessary implication, for they are clearly authorized to sell every tract of unseated land 'if the owner of any such land shall not redeem the same within the period aforesaid,' *i. e.*, within five years after the treasurer's sale.

If, therefore, the right of redemption in any case survives this period, the Commissioners may sell, but the purchaser takes the land subject still to the right of the former owner to redeem from the treasurer's sale. If a redemption should be made under such circumstances, to whom would the redemption money belong? Not to the county and supervisors of the roads, for they have already received all that was due the public from the proceeds of the Commissioners' sale. It may be said that in equity it belongs to the purchaser at the Commissioners' sale, as he has already paid the same taxes and costs into the county treasury; but the county treasurer is not authorized or required to pay this redemption to him, as he is to pay the redemption money to the purchaser at treasurer's sale under the 4th section of this Act. But, even if we concede that the vendee of the county would be entitled to this redemption money, it might not compensate him for the amount he paid the county for the land. In consequence of the restriction in the 7th section he could not purchase it for *less* than the taxes, costs, and interest; he might pay much more. . . . Clearly this Act does not require the county to refund the money; the former owner is only required to pay the taxes, costs, and interest, and yet the purchaser at Commissioners' sale loses his title by a redemption without having the money which he paid refunded to him. It may be said that he purchased at his own risk, and if he gets no title it is his own loss. It is true that in all Commissioners' sales the rule of *caveat emptor* applies. The purchaser necessarily runs the risk of the existence and value of the tract and the validity of the title. He simply purchases and pays for the title which the county has; if he gets that he must be satisfied, whether it is valuable or not. But surely the law will not provide to take that title from him by a subsequent redemption without at the same time providing to restore to him the consideration which he paid for it. The very absence of all provisions in the Act for adjusting the equities between the former owner, the county, and the purchaser at Commissioners' sale, in case a tract of land was redeemed from the sale by the treasurer to the Commissioners after the Commissioners had regularly re-sold the same, is conclusive to our mind that the Legislature never intended any such right of redemption to exist. As long as the county continues to own lands purchased by the Commissioners at treasurer's sales, the owner may redeem with the consent of the Commissioners, although more than five years may have elapsed since their purchase. (Steiner *v.* Coxe, *supra;* Coxe *v.* Wolcot & Smith, 3 Casey 154.) But after the Commissioners have regularly sold the land at public sale, no act of theirs or of the county treasurer in receiving redemption money can defeat the title of the county's vendee. (Diamond Coal Co. *v.* Fisher, 7 Harris, 267.)

We are, therefore, brought to the conclusion that the redemption by the plaintiff of the undivided one-fourth of the James Hunter tract on the twenty-fifth day of August, A. D. 1874, more than twelve years after the treasurer's sale to the County Commissioners, and nearly six years after the Commissioners had sold to John Hipps, one of the defendants, was without legal warrant or authority, and therefore inoperative to divest the defendants' title. . . .

Plaintiff took this writ, assigning for error the entry of judgment for defendants *non obstante veredicto*.

Samuel S. Blair, for plaintiff in error.

W. Horace Rose (with him *F. A. Shoemaker*), for defendants in error.

Nov. 8, 1880. THE COURT. It seems scarcely necessary to add anything to the clear and able opinion of the learned Judge of the Court below, which we adopt as the opinion of this Court. Limitations of remedies are purely statutory. While it may well be doubted whether the Legislature could enact an immediate bar to any existing right, yet it is clearly settled that to prescribe the period within which any right may be enforced is within their power. They may or may not except disabilities, according to their pleasure. If they omit to say anything upon the subject, there is no power in the Courts to supply what may have been an accidental or intentional omission. The case of Warfield *v.* Fox (3 P. F. Smith, 382) strongly illustrates this doctrine. There it was expressly ruled that a saving from the operation of statutes for disabilities must be expressed, or it does not exist. It is true that some pains was taken to show, in the opinion, that the statute there in question did not purport to be a supplement to the general Act of 1785, but that was merely an answer to the argument that the disabilities of that Act were impliedly incorporated with it. We do not understand from it that if it had been a supplement to the Act of 1785, the determination would have been different. All Acts of limitation are *in pari materia*, and the same principles of construction are to be applied. If they were to be consolidated into one statute, it would not follow that a saving of disabilities specially enacted as to one class of subjects would be applied as to all others. If the first section of such a statute related to limitation of actions for lands, and contained a saving of disabilities, it would not follow that such a saving would be implied as to personal actions. Each subject-matter must be considered as distinct. Had the seventh section of the Act of April 22, 1856, been a subsequent section of such a statute, it would not be a sound construction to import into it the saving of disabilities contained in the first, unless there was some reference to it. The argument of the learned counsel of the plaintiff in error, that the fourth and seventh sections of the Act of 1815, being part of the same statute, are to be construed as if the seventh section was a mere supplement to the fourth, is, therefore, more ingenious than sound. They relate to different subjects; the one to sales by the treasurer to individuals in which a period of two years is allowed for redemption, the other a sale to the Commissioners in which the period is extended to five years. In the fourth section the saving of disabilities is expressly limited to sales *as aforesaid* made by the treasurer. In the seventh section, there is no saving of disabilities. It is useless to speculate as to what may have been the reason of this distinction. If there were no reason, or a bad one, it would make no difference. It is enough to say that such was the will of the law-makers. Besides the incongruities pointed out in the opinion of the learned Judge below, it is enough to say that they may have meant that, to secure a full price for lands held by the county, the purchasers should have a clear and indefeasible title, and thus the public treasury be benefited.

Judgment affirmed.
Opinion by SHARSWOOD, C. J.

Jan. '80, 235. March 31, 1880.
James v. National Building Association.

Principal and agent—Representations of agent— When binding upon principal—Building associations—Maxim Qui sentit commodum sentire debet et onus.

Where one through the representations of a secretary of a building association is induced to become a surety upon a promissory note, the association cannot set up a want of authority in the secretary to make the contract as against a defence made under the terms of the agreement. It cannot have the benefit of the security and at the same time repudiate the contract by means of which it was obtained.

Error to the Common Pleas of Lackawanna County.

Feigned issue, framed between the National Building Association plaintiff, and David L. James and David T. Jones defendants, to determine the liability of the latter as surety upon a promissory note given by James to the association.

In May, 1870, David L. James borrowed from the building association, which was then unincorporated, the sum of $680, giving his note for $1000, the difference in amounts being the premium which, under the regulations of the association, he paid for the use of the money. David T. Jones became surety upon this note, upon the verbal assurance of the secretary of the association that he would only be held liable for two or three months, or until James could obtain a policy of insurance on his house and deposit it with the association. The policy was subsequently obtained and deposited with the association, whereupon Jones demanded a release from the secretary, who said he would give it to him, but never did so. Subsequently, Jones again demanded to be released, stated that he considered himself free from his obligation, and notified the association that it must look to Mr. James for its money. Judgment had been previously entered up upon the note against James maker, and Jones as surety. Upon a *scire facias* to revive the same, Jones obtained a rule to open the judgment and let him into a defence, which rule was made absolute and this issue framed, which was referred to a referee (Jas. H. Torrey), who found the facts substantially as above set forth, and reported the following conclusion of law : That, as Jones and James were members of the unincorporated association, "D. T. Jones, the surety, is estopped to set up as a defence to this action the fraudulent representations of the agent of the association." He therefore found for the plaintiff.

No exceptions were filed to the referee's finding of facts, and on exceptions to his conclusion of law, as above stated, the Court (HAND, J.) confirmed the finding of the referee, and entered judgment against D. T. Jones. The defendant took this writ, assigning for error the overruling of the exceptions and the confirmation of the auditor's report as above set forth.

D. L. James and *David T. Jones*, for plaintiff in error.

Lemuel Amerman, for defendant in error.

May 3, 1880. THE COURT. The learned referee found as matter of fact, that, at the time the note in controversy was executed, J. M. C. Ranck, the secretary of the building association, represented to David T. Jones, the surety in said note, that he would only be security on the loan for about three months, or until Mr. James, the principal, could get an insurance policy on his house and deposit it with the association; that, about ten weeks after, Mr. James procured a policy of insurance on his house and deposited it with the association, and that soon after Mr. Jones demanded of Mr. Ranck, a compliance with his agreement and a release of his (Jones') obligation as surety, and that Mr. Ranck again assured him that he should be released.

The referee's finding of the law is not so satisfactory. It was, "That D. T. Jones, the surety, is estopped to set up, as a defence to this action, the fraudulent representations of the agent of the association." The Court below sustained the finding of the referee upon the law. No exceptions were filed to his finding of facts.

The contention on the part of the association plaintiff is, that the secretary had no authority to make the representations by which Jones was induced to sign the note as surety; that it was, therefore, a fraud and not binding on said association. That is to say, the latter would repudiate the fraud, and yet hold on to its fruits. This cannot be done. Common honesty and the law of the land alike forbid it. Whether the association was incorporated or unincorporated; whether the secretary was or was not authorized to make the representations to Jones, it is clear the association cannot have the benefit of the security and at the same time repudiate the contract by means of which they obtained it. No principle of law is better settled than that a man cannot reap the fruits of his agent's fraud. (Musser *v.* Hyde, 2 W. & S. 314; Hunt *v.* Moore, 2 Barr, 105; Mundorff *v.* Wickersham, 13 P. F. S. 87; Keough *v.* Leslie, 8 W. N. 172.) The association took this security *cum onere*, and the maxim *qui sentit commodum sentire debet et onus* applies.

The judgment is reversed as to David T. Jones, the surety.

Opinion by PAXSON, J. GREEN, J., absent.
[See next case.]

May, '80, 144.   June 8, 1880.

Gass v. Citizens' Building and Loan Association.

Building associations—When not bound by agreements of their agent—Parol agreement to vary written contract—Sufficiency of evidence to establish.

Where a surety on a bond to a building association attempts to set up a defence thereto by virtue of an agreement, made with the agent of the association, to the effect that upon the happening of a certain contingency he should be released from liability, he must establish that the agreement existed within the knowledge of the officers of the association, or that the agent was acting at the time within the scope of his authority, or that his declarations were made in the course of business which he was authorized to transact, and that the contingency has occurred.

In this case the evidence was insufficient to support such a defence.

Error to the Common Pleas of Northumberland County.

Feigned issue, between Martin Gass, plaintiff, and the Citizens' Building and Loan Association of Centralia, defendant, to determine whether a certain judgment of the Association against Gass has been paid or satisfied, or whether he has been released or discharged from the payment of the same.

The following were the facts upon which the issue was framed:—

In February, 1873, J. J. Hoagland applied to the Citizens' Building and Loan Association of Centralia, the defendant in this issue, for ten loans of $200 each, amounting in the aggregate to $2000; when the board of directors decided to grant him four loans, or $800 thereof, upon the security of his own property in Columbia County, and, inasmuch as there was at that time a prior lien in favor of the Centralia Mutual Saving Fund Association, against Hoagland's property, the loan association requested him to give them additional security for the remaining "six loans" or $1200. Hoagland thereupon offered his father-in-law, Martin Gass, as his surety, and the association, after examining his property, accepted him, and a bond and mortgage was duly executed, with Hoagland as principal and Gass as surety, thereon. Judgment was subsequently entered upon the bond by virtue of a warrant of attorney contained therein.

On November 21, 1877, Martin Gass presented his petition to the Court, asking that this judgment should be stricken off, or opened, and he be let into a defence. The Court, upon hearing, opened the judgment and made the rule absolute.

Upon the trial of the issue, before ROCKEFELLER, P. J., Martin Gass offered to prove a parol agreement, contemporaneous with the execution of the bond, of the following nature: that, when he agreed with J. J. Hoagland to become his surety, he was informed by him that the association had agreed to hold him liable as surety only until the lien of the Centralia Mutual Saving Fund Association against Hoagland's property expired, or when the "Old Fund," as it was called, ran out. In support of the agreement he offered in evidence a certified copy of the record of the Common Pleas of Columbia County, by which it appeared that the judgment in favor of the Saving Fund against J. J. Hoagland, entered March 13, 1871, was not revived, and that therefore the lien thereof against the property of Hoagland expired on March 13, 1875. J. J. Hoagland, a witness for plaintiff, testified as follows:—

"Mr. Gass was to be released when the old fund ran out; the last payment on the old fund ran out in January, 1874; it has not run out; they are trying to make an assessment now; I am secretary of the company now; the old association had run out in January, 1874, as we supposed; there are debts now standing that we are trying to collect, and there is some property to be sold; the old association has issued notices to members to pay in one or two payments to pay off the shares. . . . I would not consider the old association finally settled until all the judgments and property had been sold and collected in; . . . I told Gass they agreed to release him when the old fund ran out; all the information Gass had about this matter he received from me; I presume that this last loan was made on the strength of Gass going bail."

J. P. Hoagland, also a witness for the plaintiff, testified as follows: "I was secretary of the association at the time the loan was made to my father, J. J. Hoagland; I think there was ten shares loaned to him, $2000; Martin Gass was offered as bail on six shares, or $1200 of the $2000; the board of directors decided to give J. J. Hoagland a loan of $800 upon his own security, and for the balance $1200 (six shares) he was to give Martin Gass as security; that was the only thing that was embodied in the motion, though there was a general conversation taking place in the room that if the old saving fund should expire he would be released; Martin Gass was to be released; that was not embodied in the regular motion for the loan; that was the conversation through the room by the board of directors, directors of the Citizens' Building and Loan Association; the old fund was called, I believe, the Centralia Mutual Saving Fund Association. . . . The board of directors did not authorize me to inform Mr. Gass on the subject of release at any time; I had no authority whatever from the board to go to him; I went at the request of their attorney, who was called out of town; J. Harry James was their attorney at that time; I did not communicate to the other members of the board of directors at a meeting what my father had told me relative to the conversation he had with Mr. Gass; I don't think my father was a member of the board at the time of this conversation relative to the release."

The plaintiff testified as follows: "I was asked to execute the bond as bail for J. J. Hoagland; J. P. Hoagland came there for me to sign that bond and mortgage; I understood him to say that the board (some of them) had sent him; he told me he was 'secretary of the association;' I asked him whether the understanding was that I was to be released when the loan on the old saving fund expired, and he told me, 'Yes, if the old saving fund against J. J. Hoagland expired;' and he said 'that was the understanding by the board;' that he 'heard them say so.' I told him 'under that arrangement that I was to be released I would sign it if that was the case;' I think them was the words I used, 'if that is the case I'll sign it.'"

The Court charged the jury, *inter alia*, as follows: "It is not as a matter of law necessary that the alleged agreement of Gass should appear upon the books of the association; but it is necessary for Gass to show you clearly and satisfactorily that there was such action on the part of the board of directors. A mere talk without coming to any conclusion or agreement between them would amount to nothing at all. Whether there was such a conclusion and agreement or not on their part we leave to you to determine from all the facts and circumstances in evidence. . . . If you find from all the evidence in the case that at their meeting, *while they were an organized board of directors, they agreed with Mr. Gass*, that if he became bail for Hoagland he should be released upon the conditions he stated, and that after such agreement amongst themselves it was afterwards communicated by John P. Hoagland to Mr. Gass, and Mr. Gass acted upon it, then it would be binding upon the association. . . .

"The counsel for Mr. Gass ask us to say to you as a matter of law, that the mere fact that John P. Hoagland went there with the bond and mortgage for the purpose of procuring its execution by Mr. Gass, if he made the representations as stated by him to Mr. Gass, without any authority, still Mr. Gass would be released. I do not charge you that this is the law."

The defendant presented, *inter alia*, the following points:—

(4) That no authority has been shown by the plaintiff to have ever been given by the defendant, either to the committee of investigation or to J. P. Hoagland, to represent to Martin Gass, that he would be released as bail of J. J. Hoagland when the old fund ran out or was paid, and without authority from the board of directors such representations, if made, could not bind the defendant. *Affirmed.*

(8) That by plaintiff's own showing any representation made by J. P. Hoagland, who took the bond and mortgage to Gass for execution, was made without authority, and could not be binding on the defendant. *Affirmed.*

Verdict and judgment for the defendant. Plaintiff took this writ, assigning for error those portions of the charge of the Court and the affirmation of defendant's points above quoted.

William C. Packer, for the plaintiff in error.

L. H. Kase and *S. P. Wolverton*, for the defendant in error.

October 4, 1880. THE COURT. The verdict in favor of the defendant in the feigned issue, if not demanded, was fully justified by the uncontradicted testimony of the plaintiff's principal witnesses, and there appears to be nothing in the instructions complained of that could have unduly prejudiced the plaintiff's case. His contention was that, as surety for his son-in-law, Hoagland, he executed the bond on which judgment was entered, with the verbal understanding or agreement that he should be released from all liability as soon as the loan of the Centralia Mutual Savings Fund Association to Hoagland, or "old fund," as it is termed, ran out or was paid. To maintain the issue on his part it was necessary for him to prove not only that the alleged understanding or agreement existed, and that he became a party to the bond on the faith of it, but that the Savings Fund loan had, by its terms, expired, or was fully paid; and, if either of these essential facts was not clearly established by the testimony, the issue was justly determined against him. It is very evident from an inspection of the testimony that he not only failed to show that the loan referred to was paid, or in any manner satisfied; but, on the contrary, he actually proved that it was still unsettled, and payment of additional instalments had been demanded by the company. His son-in-law, Hoagland, for whom he became surety in the bond held by the defendant, testified that the loan from the Centralia Mutual Savings Fund Association was not fully paid. Speaking of that association, he says: "It has not run out; they are trying to make an assessment now. I am now secretary of the company. The old association had run out, as we supposed, in January, 1874; but there are debts that they are now trying to collect, and there is some property to be sold." He further testified in substance that formal demand had been made on the members, of which he was one, for additional instalments to pay off the shareholders, and they would be compelled to pay, unless a sufficient amount was realized from collections and sales of property; and that he did not consider the association finally settled until all the judgments are collected and property sold. It was impossible for the jury, with such testimony before them, to escape the conclusion that the condition on which the plaintiff claimed he was to be released, as surety, had not yet been fulfilled.

The plaintiff's testimony, tending to prove the alleged understanding or agreement on the faith of which he became surety for Hoagland, was received and submitted to the jury with appropriate instructions. The learned Judge charged in substance that it was necessary for him to show clearly and satisfactorily that the board of directors had assented to the condition on which he proposed to become surety; that a mere talk on the subject among members of the board, without arriving at any conclusions or agreement among themselves, would amount to nothing; that if, from all the facts and circumstances in evidence, they found that the board of directors did agree that, in case he should become surety for Hoagland, he should be released upon the condition alleged; and if this consent of the board was communicated to him, and he acted on it, the association would be bound thereby. This instruction was certainly quite as favorable to the plaintiff as he had a right to ask. Indeed, the Court, with great propriety, might have instructed the jury that, upon his own showing, the plaintiff was not entitled to a verdict.

The only persons with whom the plaintiff appears to have had any communication on the subject of the suretyship, prior to the execution of the bond, were his son-in-law, J. J. Hoagland, and J. P. Hoagland, the secretary of the association defendant. It is not pretended that the former, by his acts or declarations, could bind the association, but it is claimed that it was bound by the statements of J. P. Hoagland, alleged to have been made at the time plaintiff signed the bond. This might have been so if it had been shown that, at the time the declarations were made, Hoagland was acting within the scope of authority confided to him by the board of directors, or that they were made in the course of business which the board authorized him to transact; but such was not the case. He himself testifies that he was not authorized by the board of directors to make any statement to plaintiff on the subject of the loan or his release as surety, and that he had no authority from them to call upon him for any purpose. This is the only testimony on the subject of his authority to make any statement to plaintiff or transact any business with him on behalf of the board. It cannot be pretended that corporate rights may be thus frittered away, or liabilities created by loose and unauthorized declarations made by persons who, at the time, are not authorized to represent the corporation in relation to the subject concerning which the declarations or representations are made.

There is nothing in any of the assignments of which the plaintiff has any just reason to complain.

Judgment affirmed. Opinion by STERRETT, J.

[See preceding case.
From some expressions in the above opinion it might at first seem as if there was a conflict between this and the preceding case, but an examination will show that in this case the question of the authority of the agent was not vital to the decision, the conclusion reached resting upon the insufficiency of the evidence to establish either that the alleged agreement existed, or that the contingency had happened.]

May, '80, 1.   May 7, 1880.

Brown's Appeal.

Husband and wife—Married women—Powers over their separate personal property—Executed contract, when irrevocable — Distribution.

A married woman, who had loaned money to her husband out of her personal estate, and taken a judgment in the name of a trustee to secure the loan, being willing to facilitate him in effecting a new loan from a stranger, certified in writing, with her husband's consent, that the judgment to be entered to secure the new loan should be entitled to precedence over her judgment. This certificate was entered on the docket, and the new loan and judgment were thereupon created. On distribution of the proceeds of a sheriff's sale of the husband's real estate:

Held, that the certificate constituted an executed contract, and operated as a voluntary and unconditional release of lien in favor of the second judgment creditor, which the wife could not subsequently repudiate, on the ground that she was a feme covert.

Appeal from the decree of the Court of Common Pleas of Lancaster County, distributing the proceeds of a sheriff's sale of real estate.

The fund in controversy was produced by the sale of the real estate of Kirk Brown, under a judgment entered to April Term, 1873, No. 613, in favor of T. Haines, trustee for Mrs. Emeline Brown, the wife of the said Kirk Brown. Before the auditor (Geo. M. Kline) Mrs. Brown claimed that the fund should be applied to the payment of her (Haines) judgment for $5000, the validity of which was not disputed. The fund was also claimed by Mrs. Levis (formerly Mrs. Heister) under a subsequent judgment, which, however, she averred, was entitled to *priority* over Mrs. Brown's judgment, by reason of a writing signed by Mrs. Brown, under the following circumstances: In 1877 Kirk Brown desired to borrow $3000 from Mrs. Heister (now Levis), who declined to lend it to him unless his wife would agree to postpone the lien of her judgment for $5000, whereupon Mrs. Brown indorsed the following on her bond:—

"April 2, 1877. This is to certify that I give my consent for the judgment bond of Mary J. E. Heister, amounting to $3000, to have precedence over mine.
"EMELINE H. BROWN."
"Witness, KIRK BROWN."

This agreement having been entered upon the appearance docket, Mrs. Heister lent Kirk Brown the $3000, and took his judgment bond therefor, which was entered to Jan. T. '77, No. 819.

The auditor reported, *inter alia,* as follows: "Two facts distinctly appear. (1) The consent of Mrs. Brown was voluntarily given, and attested by her husband. (2) Without this consent of preference of lien Mrs. Heister would not have loaned this money to Kirk Brown.

"Mrs. Brown insists that the lien of her judgment is not to be postponed by any act of hers, because (1) she was and is a married woman. (2) The contract is executory and cannot be specifically enforced against her. (3) She received no consideration for her act.

"These antagonistic positions present the question, Can a married woman, holding a judgment against her husband's real estate, surrender, with his consent, her preference of lien in favor of a junior judgment creditor, when the loan of this junior judgment creditor was made upon the faith of her act of surrender, and without which it would not have been made?

"The Act of 11th April, 1848, is restraining and protective. While it gives her no powers that she did not possess before it does not deprive her of any that she had previously enjoyed, it protects the wife's estate from the encroachments of the husband or his creditors. But her power of disposition, either for her own use or for his benefit, continues as it existed prior to this enactment.

"If it be to dispose of her real estate by conveyance, or make a special pledge of it by mortgage, the husband must join in the act, and all the requisite forms of the Act of 1770 be carefully observed. If it be to dispose of her personal estate, that requires no separate acknowledgment. She may give her money or other personal effects to her husband or to a stranger, with his knowledge and consent; she may assign her choses in action, her husband joining in the act or assenting to it; and having the power to do so, the instrument employed will be construed so as to carry out the intention of the parties. She may let her husband have the effect of the benefit of her separate estate, "and whether she has made a prudent or imprudent, a good or bad disposition of the estate, is not to be made a test, whereby the validity of such disposition, whatever it may be, is to be determined." (Towers *v.* Hagner, 3 Wh. 48; Hoover *v.* The Samaritan Society, 4 Wh. 445.)

"In this case Mrs. Brown made no contract, creating a personal liability or a charge upon her estate. All that she did was to execute and deliver an instrument intended to control an incident to her judgment in relief of her husband, and with his assent.

"Suppose she had assigned this judgment *in toto* to her husband, or to a stranger with his consent, is there any principle of law or equity, outside of fraud or duress, or mental incapacity, by which she could be relieved from her voluntary act? Or suppose, for the purpose of raising money to promote the advantage or benefit of her husband, she had assigned $3000 of her judgment to Mrs. Heister, and then loaned the money received to her husband, who lost it by the misfortune of trade, or squandered it by profligacy, could she repudiate her assignment and demand the whole sum represented by her judgment for her own use? This would be a fraud so gross as to offend every sense of right. Or suppose Mrs. Brown, with her husband, had released this judgment for the purpose of giving Mrs. Hiester the first lien, and after that a new judgment for the old debt was entered in Mrs. Brown's favor, upon a distribution following a judicial sale, could there be any pretence of claim made to transpose these judgments, and give to Mrs. Brown the first lien?

"If this married woman, with her husband's consent, could have assigned or released, in whole or in part, this judgment, thereby extinguishing to either extent her estate represented by this security, why cannot she, under like circumstances, do a lesser act, which does not destroy the debt, but only affects the lien thereof to a limited extent? The husband was the actor through whom the wife acted. Can she bind herself by acting with her husband in an arrangement of this character? The language of the Court in M'Cullough v. Wilson (9 Harris, 442) is so tersely applicable to this case that it is here quoted: 'True, she did not bind herself by a separate acknowledgment, but that form of proceeding does not apply to such an act. True, also, a door is here open through which the wife may be imposed upon by her husband; but we find it open and would not shut it, for it is opened by the very confidence that ought to exist between husband and wife.'"

"With these views the auditor appropriates the fund: 1st. To the payment of the judgment of Mrs. Hiester, now Levis. 2d. The balance on the judgment held for the use of Mrs. Brown."

Exceptions filed to this report by Mrs. Brown were overruled by the Court, PATTERSON, A. L. J., and the report confirmed, whereupon Mrs. Brown took this appeal, assigning for error the action of the Court.

H. M. North and *J. Henry Brown*, for the appellant.

Mrs. Brown, being a married woman, had no power to make the agreement giving up her right of priority. She received no consideration for it, and her agreement cannot be enforced. The auditor reasoned that as the result might have been effected in another manner, *form* was unimportant, and he decided the case on what he supposed to be abstract justice. This doctrine of the offence to the moral sense was repudiated in Schlosser's Appeal (8 Sm. 493). The single exception where a married woman can bind herself by bond is her obligation to the vendor of real estate to secure the purchase-money, but even then as a personal obligation it is void.

W. W. Brown and *B. F. Eshleman*, for appellee.

There was no contract between Mrs. Brown and Mrs. Heister, of which specific performance is sought. What was done was between Kirk Brown and his wife. She could have forgiven him the whole debt, and it follows she had the right to cede a lesser right, viz., her lien or right of priority over a debt to be incurred by him to another. This gift was executed by delivery of the bond and placing the endorsement on record. As an executed gift it required no consideration. Mrs. Brown created no liability. She used her separate estate as she had a right to do, and is estoppped by what she did.

May 17, 1880. THE COURT. Prior to the Act of April 11, 1848, a married woman could dispose of her personal estate to her husband by gift or otherwise, and, with his consent, to a stranger. That Act took from her no rights in regard thereto which she had previously possessed. Its main purpose was to protect her property, both real and personal, from levy and execution for the debts of her husband. It prescribed a mode by which she might convey her real estate, but did not restrain her freedom in disposing of her personal property. While she may not be liable on a contract to sell and deliver her personal property at some future time, yet she cannot repudiate a gift, nor a contract fairly made, under which she had delivered the possession of the property. (Haffey *v.* Carey, 23 P. F. Smith, 431; Bond *v.* Bunting, 28 Id. 215; Fryer *v.* Rishell, 3 Norris, 521; Dando's Appeal, decided at the present term, 9 WEEKLY NOTES, 5.)

The auditor has found that her consent was voluntarily given and executed, and attested by her husband, and without this the appellee would not have loaned the money to her husband. It was not an executory contract. It was executed and delivered with the bond. Nothing remained to be done by the appellant. It operated as an immediate and unconditional release of her prior right of lien to the extent of three thousand dollars in favor of the appellee, and induced the latter to part with that sum. Having thus executed and delivered the release upon sufficient consideration, she cannot revoke it to the prejudice of the appellee.

Decree affirmed, and appeal dismissed at the costs of the appellant.

PER CURIAM. SHARSWOOD, C. J., and GREEN, J., absent.

May, '79, 5.　　　　　　　　May 27, 1879.

Hamaker v. Blanchard.

Lost chattels—Title of finder as against all but true owner—Place of finding—Innkeeper may not claim possession of lost personal property, found by servant in a public room within the inn—Distinction between property lost and property intentionally deposited in a place and forgotten.

The finder of lost property has a valid title to it against all but the true owner.

It seems that the place where the article was found does not affect the rule, provided it appears that the article was *lost*.

But property is not lost, in the sense of the rule, if the surroundings evidence that it was intentionally deposited where found, and forgotten by the owner; in such case the proprietor of the premises where it was found is entitled to its custody as against the finder.

When money is found on the floor of a room in a hotel, common to all classes of persons, no presumption arises that it is the property of a guest, and the innkeeper cannot claim possession from the finder.

A domestic servant in a hotel, while cleaning the public parlor, found a roll of bank notes, which she reported to the proprietor, and upon his stating that he thought they belonged to a guest who had transacted business in the parlor, gave them to him to restore to the supposed owner. The guest had not lost the money, and the owner remained unknown:

Held, that the servant could recover the money from her employer.

Error to the Common Pleas of Mifflin County.

Assumpsit, brought in April, 1877, by James Blanchard and Sophia Blanchard, for her use, against W. W. Hamaker. The narr. was in the common counts.

On the trial, before BUCHER, P. J., the following facts appeared: The plaintiff, Mrs. Sophia Blanchard, was a domestic servant in the employ of the defendant, in a hotel kept by him in Lewistown. On September 6, 1876, while engaged in dusting the hotel parlor, on pushing back a table, she found and picked up a small roll of bank bills, consisting of three $20 notes. She immediately went to the defendant, and after asking if he had lost anything, or knew of any one who had, to which he answered no, showed him the money, which he took, saying that it probably belonged to one Wiley, a guest, who had transacted some business in the parlor, and if so he would restore it. This proved not to be the fact, and it was admitted on the trial that the owner was unknown. Hamaker, however, retained the money, being advised that he, as proprietor of the hotel, was trustee for the owner, or was responsible for its protection, and was entitled to keep it till the owner was found.

The Court charged, *inter alia*, as follows: "If the evidence is believed, it seems clear that this money was lost money—at all events no owner has appeared as yet who the proof shows is entitled to this fund as against this woman . . . [If you find that this was lost money—Hamaker did not lose it,—and that it never belonged to him, but that it belonged to some one else who has not appeared to claim it, then you ought to find for the plaintiff, on the principle that the finder of a lost chattel is entitled to the possession and use of it as against all the world except the true owner.] (1st assignment of error.)

"[The counsel for the defendant asks us to say that as the defendant was the proprietor of a hotel, and the money was found therein, the presumption of law is that it belonged to a guest, who had lost it, and that the defendant has a right to retain it as against this woman, the finder, to await the demand of the true owner. I decline to give you such instructions; but charge you that under the circumstances there is no presumption of law that this money was lost by a guest at the hotel and that the defendant is entitled to keep it as against this woman for the true owner.] I repeat, if you find this was lost money that never belonged to the defendant, and that it was found by the plaintiff, who delivered it to the defendant upon his declaration that it belonged to the whip man, and he would hand it to him; and that this was false, and the defendant never did deliver it, you ought to find for her." (2d assignment.)

Verdict for the plaintiff, and judgment thereon. The defendant took this writ, assigning for error the portions of the charge within brackets, as above.

H. J. Culbertson, for the plaintiff in error.

The rule that the finder of a lost chattel is entitled to it as against all persons but the owner, is modified by the exception that where the place in which it is found gives rise to a responsibility and duty of protection by another person than the finder, the latter is entitled to its custody. Thus, in the case of a stranger finding a pocketbook accidentally left by another on a table in a shop, the shopkeeper is bound to claim it, for the purpose of protection and restoration to the owner when found.

McAvoy *v.* Medina, 11 Allen (Mass.), 549.

It is only where the circumstances show that the shopkeeper has no duty of protection that the finder may retain it.

Bridges *v.* Hawkesworth, 7 Eng. L. & E. Rep. 430.

An innkeeper is responsible for the goods of his guests, including money brought within his inn, and is also responsible for the honesty of his servants.

Houser *v.* Tully, 12 Sm. 92.

To hold that servants may retain for their own

use whatever money or chattels they may find within the inn would encourage dishonesty, at the proprietor's risk. It has been said that even in a private house servants who find lost articles, of which the owner is unknown, may not retain them against their employer's consent.

Mathews *v.* Hersell, 1 E. D. Smith (N. Y.), 394, per WOODRUFF, J.

If no owner is found, he should have the money who bears the responsibility.

J. A. McKee, for defendant in error.

The proprietor of a hotel is not liable to a guest who negligently loses money in a public parlor. But *non constat* that the money was lost by a guest, and if lost by a stranger, or casual visitor, no responsibility could attach to the proprietor, and he could not retain it as against the finder.

June 9, 1879. THE COURT. It seems to be settled law that the finder of lost property has a valid claim to the same against all the world except the true owner, and generally that the place in which it is found creates no exception to this rule. But property is not lost, in the sense of the rule, if it was intentionally laid on a table, counter, or other place by the owner, who forgot to take it away, and in such case the proprietor of the premises is entitled to retain the custody. Whenever the surroundings evidence that the article was deposited in its place, the finder has no right of possession against the owner of the building. (McEvoy *v.* Medina, 11 Allen, Mass., 548.) An article casually dropped is within the rule. Where one went into a shop and as he was leaving picked up a parcel of bank notes which was lying on the floor, and immediately showed them to the shopman, it was held that the facts did not warrant the supposition that the notes had been deposited there intentionally, they being manifestly lost by some one, and there was no circumstance in the case to take it out of the general rule of law, that the finder of a lost article is entitled to it as against all persons except the real owner. (Bridges *v.* Hawkesworth, 7 Eng. Law & Eq. R. 424.) The decision in Mathews *v.* Harsell (1 E. D. Smith, N. Y. 393) is not in conflict with the principle, nor is it an exception. Mrs. Mathews, a domestic in the house of Mrs. Barmore, found some Texas notes which she handed to her mistress to keep for her. Mrs. Barmore afterwards entrusted the notes to Harsell for the purpose of ascertaining their value, informing him that she was acting for her servant for whom she held the notes. Harsell sold them and appropriated the proceeds, whereupon Mrs. Mathews sued him and recovered their value with interest from date of sale. Such is that case. True, WOODRUFF, J., says: "I am by no means prepared to hold that a house servant who finds lost jewels, money, or chattels, in the house of his or her employer, acquires any title even to retain possession against the will of the employer. It will tend much more to promote honesty and justice to require servants in such cases to deliver the property so found to the employer for the benefit of the true owner." To that remark, foreign to the case, as understood by himself, he added the antidote: "And yet the Court of Queen's Bench, in England, have recently decided that the place in which a lost article is found, does not form the ground of any exception to the general rule of law, that the finder is entitled to it against all persons except the owner." His views of what will promote honesty and justice are entitled to respect, yet many may think Mrs. Barmore's method of treating servants far superior.

The assignments of error are to so much of the charge as instructed the jury that, if they found the money in question was lost the defendant had no right to retain it because found in his hotel, the circumstances raising no presumption that it was lost by a guest, and their verdict ought to be for the plaintiff. That the money was not voluntarily placed where it was found, but accidentally lost, is settled by the verdict. It is admitted that it was found in the parlor—a public place, open to all. There is nothing to indicate whether it was lost by a guest or a boarder, or one who had called with or without business. The pretence that it was the property of a guest to whom the defendant would be liable, is not founded on an act or circumstance in evidence.

Many authorities were cited in argument touching the rights, duties, and responsibilities of an innkeeper in relation to his guests. These are so well settled as to be uncontroverted.

In respect to other persons than guests, an innkeeper is another man. When money is found in his house, on the floor of a room common to all classes of persons, no presumption of ownership arises—the case is like the finding upon the floor of a shop. The research of counsel failed to discover authority that an innkeeper shall have an article which another finds in a public room of his house, when there is no circumstance pointing to its loss by a guest. In such case the general rule should prevail. If the finder be an honest woman, who immediately informs her employer and gives him the article on his false pretence that he knows the owner and will restore it, she is entitled to have it back, and hold it till the owner comes.

A rule of law ought to apply to all alike. Persons employed in inns will be encouraged to fidelity by protecting them in equality of rights with others. The learned Judge was right in his instructions to the jury.

Judgment affirmed.

Opinion by TRUNKEY, J. MERCUR, J., dissents.

Common Pleas—Law.

C. P. No. 1.   Oct. 23, 1880.
Loftus v. Corles.

Landlord and tenant—Surety on lease—Affidavit of defence—Insufficiency of by surety—What will amount to a discharge of surety—It is not necessary to file the lease if the contract of suretyship, with an averment of the material facts, is filed.

Rule for judgment for want of a sufficient affidavit of defence.

Covenant against the surety on a lease. Plaintiff filed, together with the contract of suretyship, the following averment: "That in consideration of the surety's contract, he had leased certain premises to one J. W. Hellings, at an annual rent of one thousand dollars ($1000), payable in monthly instalments; that the said Hellings failed to pay the rent which became due on the first day of June, and had removed his goods from the said premises in order to avoid such payment; that the plaintiff had endeavored to collect the rent due on June 1st by distress, but was unable to do so by reason of said removal; and that there was due him on the first day of July one hundred and sixty-six dollars and sixty-seven cents ($166.67)."

The affidavit of defence set forth: That the contract of suretyship filed by the plaintiff was not such an instrument as to entitle him to judgment for want of an affidavit of defence; that at the time of leasing said premises plaintiff was warned by defendant to proceed immediately to distrain in the event of Hellings not paying the rent on June 1st; that on June 2d defendant had received a letter from plaintiff stating that Hellings had asked for fifteen days' time, and asking defendant to assent thereto, which assent, however, defendant had refused to give; and that in consequence of this indulgence and plaintiff's failure to promptly use his right of distress, Hellings removed his goods and plaintiff lost his chance of collecting said rent; that Hellings had left on the premises bar and gas fixtures, of which plaintiff has taken possession, and which are worth more in value than the amount of rent due.

D. W. Dougherty, for the rule.

Copy of bond signed by the surety, with an averment, is such an instrument as will entitle plaintiff to judgment for want of a sufficient affidavit of defence.

Montague v. Carey, 1 WEEKLY NOTES, 311.
Flanigan v. Rossiter, 7 Ibid. 180.
Dickson v. Wolf, 5 Ibid. 37.

A creditor is not bound to resort to the principal for the collection of his debt in the first instance, nor is he bound first to resort to a lien for its security, but may sue and recover from the surety.

Geddis v. Hawk, 1 Watts, 280.
Richards v. Commonwealth, 4 Wright, 146.

An affidavit that lessor did not use due diligence to collect the rent from the tenant, is insufficient to discharge the surety.

Miller v. Keller, 1 WEEKLY NOTES, 27.
Poorman v. Goswiler, 2 Watts, 69.

The tenant having failed to remove the fixtures put in by him during his term, they become the property of the landlord.

Overton v. Williams, 7 Casey, 159.
White v. Arndt, 1 Wharton, 95.

P. A. Cregar, contra.

                             C. A. V.

Oct. 30, 1880. THE COURT. The lease was not filed, but the undertaking of the defendant was set out in full, along with an averment which is very complete, and contains all the substantial points of the case. This is sufficient. It has, however, been argued that the conduct of the plaintiff was such as to discharge the surety, but it appears from the averment that the goods were removed before the change in the surety's liability. This point is not contradicted in the affidavit, so we must take it as a fact. On all grounds, therefore, we must decide the affidavit insufficient.

Rule absolute.

Oral opinion by ALLISON, P. J.

C. P. No. 1.   June, 1880.
Grayson v. Hangstorfer.

Execution—Sheriff's sale—Fraud—In distribution by an auditor, a judgment confessed to defendant's mother, partly in consideration of moneys advanced to defendant while a minor, and partly for a debt barred by the Statute of Limitations, cannot be impeached on the ground that it was intended to defeat the claimant under a subsequent judgment—Costs—Where the judgment on which the sale is made is not entitled to share in the proceeds, the costs of the judgment will not be allowed out of the fund—Costs of audit—When in part imposed on creditor unsuccessfully claiming to participate in the distribution.

Sur exceptions to auditor's report, distributing the proceeds of a sheriff's sale.

The fund in controversy was produced by an execution on a judgment, entered upon a verdict, recovered October 31, 1878, by Richard H. Grayson *et al.* against Frederick Hangstorfer. The premises were purchased, at the sheriff's sale, by Barbara E. Hangstorfer, mother of the defendant, for $700, and the sheriff made a special return that he had received the amount of the taxes, costs, etc., viz. $198.97, and that, the purchaser being a judgment-creditor under a prior judgment entered October 29, 1878, he had taken her receipt for the balance. Exceptions to this return were filed by Grayson, the only other lien creditor, alleging that the judgment note on which Mrs. Hangstorfer's judgment was entered was given by the defendant without consideration, for the purpose of defeating his (Grayson's) judgment, and was therefore fraudulent. The matter was thereupon referred to an auditor (J. Davis Duffield) to report distribution. By consent of the parties the fund was not paid into court.

The material facts, as found by the auditor, were as follows: "On the day on which the suit of Grayson *et al. v.* Frederick Hangstorfer was set down for trial, October 28, 1878, and three days before the verdict was rendered, the defendant gave a judgment note for $1000, to his mother, the said Barbara, payable one day after date, on which judgment was entered the next day, Oct. 29, 1878. The auditor reported that the judgment note was given without any fraudulent intent for a valuable consideration, viz. various sums advanced to or paid for defendant by his mother at different times from the year 1863, when defendant was but twenty years of age, down to the year 1876 inclusive. He further reported that defendant had the right to give a preference to his mother, and that the transaction was not invalidated as to creditors by the fact that a portion of the consideration was paid to defendant during his minority, or by the fact that a portion of it could not have been enforced on account of the bar of the Statute of Limitations.

The auditor also reported that, as both judgment-creditors consented, he could, under the Act of June 28, 1871, sec. 1 (Purd. Dig. 658, pl. 11), make distribution of the entire proceeds of sale although not paid into court; and awarded to Barbara E. Hangstorfer the balance of the fund after payment of taxes and costs.

With regard to the costs, the auditor, upon the authority of Fry's Appeal (26 P. F. Smith, 82), and Malone's Appeal (29 P. F. Smith, 481), held that only the costs connected with the sheriff's sale, and not the costs incident to the judgment, were payable out of the fund.

As to the costs of the audit he held that their allowance out of the fund was a matter entirely within the discretion of the Court, and he therefore imposed one-half upon the exceptants to the sheriff's return and the other half upon the fund.

Exceptions were filed by Grayson for sustaining the validity of the judgment note, for refusing to allow the costs of the exceptants' judgment and imposing upon exceptants one-half of the costs of the audit.

J. D. Bennett, for exceptants.
Frederick Gaston and *John E. Faunce*, contra.

C. A. V.

July 3, 1880. THE COURT. Exceptions dismissed and report confirmed.

Orphans' Court.

November 16, 1880.

Burnell's Estate.

Debts of decedent—Interest on, only allowed where the estate is solvent—Subrogation—Appropriation of payments by creditors—Rents collected by the decedent's executor are not assets for the payment of debts—Interest on mortgages, taxes, etc., accruing after the death of decedent, not to be paid out of the principal of the estate.

Sur exceptions to adjudication.

At the audit of the second account filed by the executors of W. W. Burnell, the decedent, the facts were substantially as follows:—

The decedent, Henry Wheeler, and Anthony Pope, were copartners, trading as Wheeler & Pope. The decedent in his lifetime sold his interest in the firm to Henry Wheeler, who assumed the debts of the old copartnership, and continued the business. Henry Wheeler afterwards died.

On the audit of the first account of the executors of Burnell's estate 24.68 per cent. was awarded to Powers & Weightman upon a claim against the old firm of $1535.24. This did not include interest. Afterwards upon the audit of the first and second accounts of the executors of Wheeler's Estate, Powers & Weightman proved the same claim, and also a claim against Henry Wheeler, for $855, without interest, and were awarded dividends amounting to 45.93 per cent.

Upon the audit of the second account in Burnell's Estate, the Auditing Judge found that

Powers & Weightman and other creditors had received from the above dividends, 70.79 per cent. of their claims against the decedent's estate, and at the same time awarded another dividend of 29.21 per cent. which the Auditing Judge found would pay them in full, holding : "that upon the payment of the said 29.21 per cent. their claims became the property of the accountants to collect them."

As stated above both in Burnell's and Wheeler's Estates, counsel for Powers & Weightman did not at the audit of the first account, on the presentation of their claims, make any demand for interest, there being a deficiency of assets. At the audit, however, of the last account in Burnell's Estate, additional assets having come into the accountant's hands, interest was asked for, but refused by the Auditing Judge, because not included in the claim as originally submitted.

To this finding, exceptions were filed in behalf of Powers & Weightman, and V. R. Elliot.

The Auditing Judge also refused to allow Powers & Weightman to appropriate the dividends received from Wheeler's estate, on account of the joint debt of Wheeler and Burnell, towards the payment of Wheeler's indebtedness and afterwards to apply the balance, if any, towards the payment of the aforesaid joint debt of Burnell and Wheeler. This, counsel claimed, would pay Wheeler's individual debt in full, and about 16 per cent. of Burnell and Wheeler in addition to the 24.68 per cent. already received.

To this refusal exceptions were also filed.

As to an error in the account in reference to rents and interest on mortgages the matter is sufficiently set out in the subsequent correction of these charges as in the opinion below.

J. C. Stillwell, for Powers & Weightman, as to right to appropriate payments, cited—
Ege *v.* Watts, 5 Smith, 321.
Foster *v.* McGraw, 14 Ibid. 464.

The fact that interest was not demanded at the time the claim was proved should not estop creditors from claiming it now.

Judgments carry interest, and an adjudication is in the nature of a judgment.

L. W. Barringer, for V. R. Elliot.

November 20, 1880. THE COURT. There can be no doubt that it is the well settled rule of law in this State that the creditor of a decedent is entitled to lawful interest upon his claim, unless prevented by the terms of the contract or the estate proves insolvent. In this estate the decedent died possessed of both realty and personalty. But upon the audit of the first account of the executors, the personal estate in their hands was insufficient to pay in full the debts proved. A *pro rata* distribution was accordingly made among all the creditors, paying a certain dividend only upon the face or principal of their claim.

The executors afterwards collected other personal estate, and this forms the present or second account. Now, if this fund proves sufficient to pay the creditors in full, it certainly could not be successfully contended that they would not be entitled to the whole amount of their claims with interest thereon from the date on which they respectively matured, that is, the date they were payable by the decedent, less the amount awarded upon the settlement of the first account of the executors, otherwise the creditors could not be said to be paid in full.

But it appears that the balance of personal estate included in this second account is insufficient to pay in full, that is, the balance of the principal of the claims and the interest thereon, supposing the estate to be solvent, which is alleged by the creditors. The only course, then, to be adopted is to declare another dividend upon the principal of the claims, thus exhausting the funds in the hands of the accountants, and, as the personal estate is still insolvent, that is, insufficient to pay the claims with interest thereon, the executors must mortgage or sell real estate to liquidate the balance due. It follows that it was erroneous to find in the adjudication that the claims presented were paid in full and became the property of the accountants, who will thereupon be entitled to collect them, "that is, from the estate of Henry Wheeler, deceased, who was the copartner of this decedent." This decedent, as a surety for his late copartner, would only be entitled to reimbursement for the amount he had been obliged to pay in order to discharge said claims in full, and not the portion or dividend paid by his deceased copartner's estate. These accountants would only, therefore, be entitled to collect from Wheeler's estate the dividends paid out of this estate, and not the whole amount of the claims, as erroneously stated in the adjudication. In regard to the exceptions filed by Messrs. Powers & Weightman, it is only necessary to state that their claim was against the firm composed of this decedent and his late copartner, Henry Wheeler, also deceased. For this the estate of each copartner was of course liable. After the creation of the debt the firm was dissolved, this decedent retiring; but Henry Wheeler continued the business, and assumed the indebtedness of the firm. The exceptants continued to deal with him, and at his death he was indebted to them. The exceptants then were creditors of decedent and his deceased copartner, jointly and severally, and of the deceased copartner alone as to his separate debt. The first mentioned claim was proved to be $1535.24 at the dissolution of the firm, exclusive of interest, and the indebtedness of Wheeler alone was $855.68, without interest. Out of the estate of this decedent, the claimants, it is evident, could collect no more than their joint and several claim, and upon this they have been awarded *pro rata* dividends out of the estate of each deceased copartner. Therefore, out of the fund now for distribution they can only be awarded a dividend upon the claim for $1535.24, and, with other creditors, will be entitled to receive the balance uncollected from Wheeler's estate, out of the real estate of this decedent.

An error is also apparent upon the account which must be corrected. Rents accruing since the death of decedent are not assets for the payment of debts; they belong to the devisees, and should not be brought into the account. So interest upon mortgages, water rents, and taxes, since the death of decedent, are not to be paid out of the *principal* of the estate, but by the heirs or devisees out of the rents. All these items must be stricken from the account.

The adjudication is, therefore, recommitted for amendment in accordance herewith.

Opinion by HANNA, P. J.

November 15, 1880.

Bauer's Estate.

Dower—Act of March 29, 1832—An amendment to correct an error apparent upon the ace of the record, affecting intervening rights, will not be allowed after the lapse of seven years.

Sur petition for decree that certain premises were subject to the dower of the widow of decedent, and answer.

The petition of Catharine Bauer, widow of John A. Bauer, the decedent, set forth that Henry A. Bauer, executor of decedent, by virtue of an order of sale in partition, wherein the petitioner was mentioned as the widow of decedent, on July 13, 1870, sold certain property (describing it) to Augustus Karstien, for $1330, which sale was confirmed and a deed executed to the purchaser on Oct. 1, 1870. That though the petitioner was mentioned in the petition for an inquest as the widow of decedent, and as such was entitled to have her dower or thirds secured upon the premises, no direction was given in the order of sale that her dower was to remain secured thereon, nor was it so secured, but a deed absolute upon its face was made to Karstien, the whole purchase-money was paid to the executor, and the petitioner never released her dower, nor agreed that the premises should be sold free therefrom.

That the said Karstien has since died intestate, leaving a widow and three children, to whom the said property descended.

That the petitioner had demanded of the said parties the payment of her dower, but they have refused to acknowledge her right to have the same out of the said premises.

The petitioner prayed for a citation to the said widow and children of Augustus Karstien, deceased, to show cause why a decree should not be entered that the sale of the premises and deed therefor conveyed them charged with the payment of the sum of $26.60 per annum to the petitioner for life, as, and for her dower or thirds.

The answer of Elizabeth Karstien set forth that the order of sale was prayed for by all the parties interested, and that the deed to her deceased husband conveyed the property freed and discharged of all liens, encumbrances, and dower interest.

J. E. Bowers and *John White*, for the petitioner.

G. W. Arundel, contra, cited—

Act of March 29, 1832, Purd. Dig. 437, pl. 158.

Nov. 20, 1880. THE COURT. If seven years after a final decree a bill of review will not lie to correct an error apparent upon the face of the record (Littleton's Appeal, 9 WEEKLY NOTES, 188) it seems clear that the same thing cannot be done by mere amendment, which is in effect what is asked in this case. It may be, as has been argued in this case, that the widow's rights under preceedings in partition are preserved to her by the Act of Assembly, and are not affected by the form of the proceedings or of the deed made thereunder; in that case an amendment is unnecessary; while in any other case it would now, after the lapse of nearly ten years, and after rights have intervened, be improper.

Petition dismissed.

Opinion by PENROSE, J.

WEEKLY NOTES OF CASES.

Vol. IX.] THURSDAY, JAN. 13, 1881. [No. 21.

Supreme Court.

May, '80, 151.   June 16, 1880.
Baker et al. v. Allegheny Valley Railroad Company.

Master and servant—Relative duties of—Negligence—Contributory negligence—Unsafe tools and machinery—Knowledge and notice of defect—Declarations, when not binding on master.

It is a general principle that the duty which the master owes to his servant, to provide him with safe tools and machinery, does not involve the engagement that they will always continue in the same condition.

It is not negligence in the master if the tool or machine break from an internal original fault, not apparent when the tool or machine was first made or provided, or from an external apparent fault; for it is the duty of the servant to observe and report to his master apparent defects.

But a different rule applies if the tool or machinery be perishable; the employer is bound to know that fact, and it is his duty to renew such instruments at proper intervals.

The constructive knowledge of the servant does not relieve the master from acting on the constructive knowledge which is chargeable to him, nor impose upon the servant the duty of notifying the master of that which he ought to know.

Declarations as to the defectiveness of an instrument, made immediately after an accident by a delegate of the master, are not binding upon the master unless accompanied by an admission of knowledge of the defect existing before the accident.

Error to the Common Pleas of Clearfield County.

Trespass on the case, by Bridget Baker *et al.*, wife and infant children of Bartley Baker, against the Allegheny Valley Railroad Co., to recover damages for the death of the said Bartley Baker, ensuing from the alleged negligence of the defendant. Plea, "Not guilty."

Upon the trial, before Orvis, A. L. J., the plaintiffs' evidence showed the following facts: Baker was one of a gang of men working on a gravel train, and on September 15, 1876, the day of the accident, was engaged, with others, in hoisting heavy stones upon the cars of the gravel train. In loading the stones, the men used a derrick, which consisted of an upright wooden mast, about twelve inches in diameter at the ground, and about fifty feet in height, and held in place by four guy ropes attached to the top of the mast, the other end of the ropes being anchored to posts in the ground. To the mast of the derrick was attached a crane with pulley-blocks, tackle, etc. On the morning the accident happened the men had loaded two or three stones. Baker was standing on one of the cars, in the act of obeying an order of the man in charge of the work, and a heavy stone was being raised, when one of the guy ropes gave way on account of the rottenness of the rope, and the mast of the derrick fell with great force, striking Baker across the breast, from the effects of which he died within an hour after he was hurt. At the time Baker was hurt, he was working under the direction of Daniel Nolan, who then had, under the defendant company, the exclusive charge and direction of the gravel train and men connected with it, and had authority from the company to hire and discharge the men who worked in his crew. William McGregor was superintendent of the work at Summit Tunnel, where Baker was killed.

The derrick was furnished by the defendant, and had not been used for some time previous to the day of Baker's death. It was an old structure, erected in 1873, and the guy ropes, although originally sufficiently strong, had been exposed constantly to the weather, without change, for a long time. There was evidence that they were old and decayed, and were unsafe and unfit for the purpose for which the derrick was used at the time it fell. There was also expert testimony that such ropes, after being exposed to the weather for a year, were unsafe and unfit to sustain a heavy weight.

The plaintiffs proposed to prove that Daniel Nolan, the superintendent of the gravel train, a few minutes before the accident happened, said to this witness, or in his hearing, that one part of the men should go to one side of the derrick, as it was not safe; this order not being given to Bartley Baker, or in his hearing, to the witness's knowledge. Objected to, because the offer is immaterial and irrelevant; because no order there given by Daniel Nolan could affect the defendants or make them liable in damages to the plaintiffs, he being a co-employé; and because such order may have been given, and the witness not have heard it, and the testimony does not show such order was not given to Baker, if it was material to prove that it was not. Objections sustained (1st assignment of error).

Plaintiffs' second offer was as follows:—

Q. What did Mr. McGregor say at the time the rope was examined, immediately at the time of the accident, as to its cause, if anything? Objected to, because it is immaterial and irrelevant under the proof in this stage of the cause; and because the plaintiffs have not shown that McGregor held such a relation to the defendants as would make his declarations admissible to affect the defendants. Objection sustained (2d assignment of error).

The plaintiff having closed, the Court, on motion of defendant, entered a compulsory nonsuit, and the Court in banc subsequently refused a motion to take it off; whereupon the plaintiffs took this writ, assigning for error the rejection of their offers, and the refusal to take off the nonsuit.

Frank Fielding and *George A. Jenks*, for the plaintiffs in error.

The evidence of the declarations of Nolan was admissible as part of the *res gestæ*. Nolan was in charge, and held authority from the defendant. His agency was established, and made his acts and knowledge those of the defendant.

The same rule applies to the declarations of McGregor, the superintendent.

Woodwell *v.* Brown, 8 Wr. 121.
Mullan *v.* Phila. & Southern M. S. S. Co., 28 Sm. 25.
Hanover R. R. Co. *v.* Coyle, 5 Id. 396.
Wharton on Negligence, ₴ 1173.

It was the duty of the company to supply its employés with safe and efficient instrumentalities.

Ardesco Oil Co. *v.* Gilson, 13 Sm. 146.
Caldwell *v.* Brown, 3 Id. 453.
Frasier *v.* Pa. R. R., 2 Wr. 104.
Patterson *v.* P. & C. R. R., 26 Sm. 393.
1 American Rw. Rep. 573.
O'Donnell *v.* Allegheny Valley R. R., 9 Sm. 248.
Johnson *v.* Bruner, 11 Id. 61.
Mullan *v.* P. & So. M. S. S. Co., 28 Id. 25.
Oak Ridge Coal Co. *v.* Reed, 5 WEEKLY NOTES, 3.
Addison on Torts, ₴ 254, and notes.
Noyes *v.* Smith, 28 Vt. 59.
Bessex *v.* C. & N. W. Rw. Co., 1 Wis. Leg. News, 62.
Smith *v.* R. R. Co., 42 Wis. 520.
Craker *v.* R. R. Co., 36 Id. 657.
Ryan *v.* Fowler, 24 N. Y. 410.
Laning *v.* N. Y. C. R. R. Co., 49 Id. 521.

It does not matter that the defendant may not have known of the condition of the ropes; it was its duty to know. Baker could not be chargeable with contributory negligence in not examining the ropes; his duty was obedience.

Nor were Dolan and McGregor co-employés. So to hold would relieve corporations of liability for their negligence.

Clarke *v.* Holmes, 7 H. & N. 943.
Wedgwood *v.* C. & N. W. Rw., 41 Wis. 478.
Wharton on Negligence, ₴ 222.
Corcoran *v.* Holbrook, 59 N. Y. 517.
Flike *v.* B. & A. R. R., 53 Id. 549.

H. T. Beardsley and *Wallace & Krebs*, for the defendant in error.

Nolan and McGregor were co-employés with Baker; the difference in grade did not change this relation. Neither of the former possessed the ultimate authority of the company, and the case is therefore distinguishable from Mullan *v.* S. S. Co. (*supra*). Hence their declarations could not affect the company.

Patton *v.* Minesinger, 1 C. 393.
Wood's Law of Master and Servant, 809.
Lehigh Valley Coal Co. *v.* Jones, 5 N. 432.

The company was not bound to warrant the continuing safety of the derrick. Baker had the better opportunity of examining the condition of the ropes, and if they were defective, it was his duty to inform the company of the fact.

Ryan *v.* Cumberland Valley R. R. Co., 11 Har. 384.
Wood on Master and Servant, 755, 800.
Wharton on Negligence, ₴ 212, 217.
Mad River and Lake Erie R. R. *v.* Barber, 5 Ohio St. 541.
Mansfield Coal and Coke Co. *v.* McEnery, 37 Leg. Int. 28.
Frasier *v.* Pa. R. R., 2 Wr. 104.

October 4, 1880. THE COURT. The deceased, to recover damages for whose death this action was instituted in the Court below, was a laborer employed by the defendants in hoisting stones upon the cars of a gravel train. For this purpose a derrick was used, or upright wooden mast held in place by guy ropes; and, while in the act of raising a heavy stone, one of the ropes broke, and the mast of the derrick fell with great force on the deceased, inflicting an injury from the effects of which he died within an hour.

Whether the defendants were *prima facie* liable was the question: in other words, did the evidence adduced by the plaintiffs make out such a case as ought to be submitted to the jury? The learned Judge below thought not, and accordingly nonsuited the plaintiff.

The facts in regard to the rope may be briefly stated: It was about two inches thick, and there was every reason to believe that it was originally sufficiently strong for the purpose for which it was used. But there was evidence that the derrick was an old structure, and the ropes at the time of the accident had been in use two or three years, perhaps more. During this time they had been exposed to the weather. Several witnesses who examined the rope immediately after the accident testified that at the place where it had broken it was rotten and unsafe, and there was evidence that such was commonly the result of the exposure of such a rope to the weather, for that or a much shorter period of time.

There is no dispute as to the law applicable to such a case. It has been long and well settled. A servant assumes all the ordinary risks of his employment. He cannot hold the master responsible for an injury which cannot be traced directly to his negligence. If it has resulted from the negligence of a fellow servant in the same employment, he must look to him and not to the master for redress. The master does not warrant him against such negligence. The duty which the master owes to his servants is to provide them with safe tools and machinery, where that is necessary. When he does this he does not however engage that they will always continue in the same condition. Any defect which may become apparent in their use it is the duty of the servant to observe and report to his employer. The servant has the means of discovering any such defect which the master does not possess. It is not negligence in the master if the tool or machine breaks, whether from an internal original fault, not apparent when the tool or machine was at first provided, or for an external apparent one produced by time and use, not brought to the master's knowledge. These are the ordinary risks of the employment which the servant takes upon himself. (Ryan *v.* The Cumberland Valley Railroad Co., 11 Harris, 384.)

But do these rules apply to such an instrument as a rope used in a derrick which is employed in raising heavy weights? No doubt a perfectly new rope, and one to all appearance sound, may break, and the master would not be responsible for the consequences, having furnished a rope of the proper size for the purpose, to all appearances sound. But there was evidence in this case, sufficient certainly to make a question for the jury, that such a rope, after having been used for a year or more, and exposed during that time, as the one in question seems to have been, was no longer a safe rope, even though it did not outwardly exhibit any signs of decay. The master is bound to know that a rope under such circumstances will only last a limited time. It will not do for him to furnish a sound rope and then fold his arms until by actually breaking it is demonstrated to be insecure. It will not do to say that the servant is bound to know this as well as his master, and to warn him that after such a time he ought to procure a new rope. Is the servant bound to notify the master of that which he knows or ought to know himself without such information? He knows how long the rope has been in use. The servant may not know. In this case the deceased did not know. It appears to have been the first day that he worked on the derrick. There was nothing to attract his notice in the outward appearance to show how long it had been in use. It is the duty of employers to renew instruments of this character at proper intervals. The expense would certainly not be great, and a due regard to the lives of their servants imperatively demands it.

The order given by Nolan just before the accident was rightly excluded. It did not show that he knew of the defect in question, but was a caution given to the men to keep out of the way of an accident which might happen to the best rope. He was a competent witness, and might have been examined on the part of the plaintiffs. As to the declaration of McGregor, it did not sufficiently appear that his relations to the work were such as to make his declarations evidence. As the case goes back to another trial, it can be shown what his office and duties were. Besides, it would appear that the declarations proposed were made after the accident, and were not of such a character as to show that he had previous knowledge of any defect of the rope. After seeing the broken rope his opinion that it was an unsafe one would not be binding on the company more than the declaration of the opinion of any other witness. Unless the declaration was to the effect that he knew before the accident that the rope was unsafe, it could not fall within the cases of Hanover Railroad Company *v.* Coyle (5 P. F. Smith, 396), and Mullan *v.* Philadelphia and Southern Mail Steamship Company (28 Ibid. 25).

Judgment reversed, and *procedendo* awarded.
Opinion by SHARSWOOD, C. J.

May, '80, 54.   Jan. 11 & 12, 1880.

Books, Administrator, etc., v. Borough of Danville.

Constitutional law—Art. III., Sec. 21—Survival of actions for death caused by negligence—Who may sue—Personal representatives of deceased cannot—Acts of April 15, 1851, and April 26, 1855.

Under Art. III., Section 21, of the Constitution, which provides that "in case of death from injuries the right of action shall survive, and the General Assembly shall prescribe for whose benefit such actions shall be prosecuted," no right of action survives to the personal representatives of the deceased, but (in the absence of any new legislation) such right is vested in the relatives who, by the Act of April 26, 1855, were entitled to sue, namely, parents for the loss of children, children for the loss of parents, and reciprocally in husband and wife.

No right of action for damages for negligence causing death existed, or could exist in the deceased; the right was given to, and first existed in the relatives entitled by statute to sue therefor.

Mann *v.* Wieand, 4 WEEKLY NOTES, 6, followed.

In a suit by an administrator against an incorporated borough, to recover damages for the death of his intestate (his wife), caused by the defendant's negligence:

Held, that the plaintiff was properly nonsuited. The action should have been in his own right as surviving husband.

Error to the Common Pleas of Columbia County.

Case, by Curtis S. Books, administrator of Charlotte Books, deceased, against the borough of Danville, to recover damages for the death of his wife, the said Charlotte Books, caused, as alleged, by the negligence of the defendant in permitting the abutment of a bridge on a public street to remain unguarded, whereby the said Charlotte, on a dark evening in October, 1878, missed the entrance to the bridge, fell from the abutment into the canal below, and was drowned.

The action was originally brought in the Common Pleas of Montour County, and the venue was changed to Columbia County.

On the trial, before ELWELL, P. J., the plaintiff proved the legal duty of the borough to maintain the street and bridge in safe condition, under its Act of incorporation and other Acts of Assembly relating to or extended to said borough. He also proved the circumstances of the accident, showing a *prima facie* case of negligence on the part of the defendant, and rested.

The defendant moved for a nonsuit, on the ground that the action was brought in the name of the plaintiff as administrator of his deceased wife, and as such he had no right of recovery.

The Court granted the motion, and subsequently discharged a rule to take it off, ELWELL, P. J., delivering the following opinion:—

"The Acts of the 15 April, 1851, and of the 26 April, 1855, confer new rights unknown to the common law. For injuries by unlawful violence or negligence, causing death, the former Act gave a right of action to the widow of the deceased, and in case there be no widow, then to the personal representative. The Act of 1855 changed the law, so far as regards the personal representative, and conferred the right of recovery *only* upon parents for the loss of children, and upon children for the loss of parents, and reciprocally upon husband and wife. The right of action was given by the Act of 1851, and the Act of 1855 defines who may sue. The damages are given, not to the *estate* of the deceased, but in express terms to specially enumerated relatives, as compensation for the pecuniary loss which *they* sustain by the death.

"Conceding this to be the correct construction of the Acts of Assembly, it is contended that the right of action is extended to the personal representatives of the deceased by the twenty-first Section of Art. III. of the Constitution of 1873. That section provides that in the case of "death from injuries, the right of action shall *survive*, and the General Assembly shall prescribe for whose benefit such action shall be prosecuted. Since the adoption of the Constitution, no law has been passed upon this subject, for the reason, no doubt, that the Legislature was satisfied with the law already in force.

"The Act of 1855, which gave a right of action to the relatives named, was continued in full force by the second section of the Schedule to the Constitution. It provides that 'all laws in force in the Commonwealth at the time of the adoption of this Constitution not inconsistent therewith, and all *rights, actions*, prosecutions, and contracts shall continue as if this Constitution had not been adopted.'

"The provisions in the Constitution, that the right of action shall *survive*, and that of the Act of 1855, that the relatives named shall have that right, are not inconsistent. The constitutional provision was for the purpose of preventing the passage of any laws by which the common law would be restored, and all right of action taken away. It declared that the right of action shall survive, but submitted to the law to say to *whom*. By continuing the former law in force, it, in effect, declared that no person but the husband, *as such*, shall maintain an action for injuries by negligence, causing the death of his wife. As administrator he has no right of action. The nonsuit was, therefore, properly ordered. Motion to strike it off overruled."

The plaintiff thereupon took this writ, assigning for error the refusal of the Court to take off the nonsuit.

Joshua W. Comly (with whom were *Charles R. Buckalew* and *Leander K. Mowrer*), for plaintiff in error.

We contend that, under Sect. 21 of Art. III. of the Constitution, an action for the cause therein declared to "survive" can only be brought by the executors or administrators of the deceased. The husband could, no doubt, also maintain his action in his own right under the Act of 1855, but the right of action declared by the Constitution to "survive" is a totally different right, viz., that which the deceased had in his lifetime for the injuries sustained, and which, when the injuries are followed by death, "survives" to his administrator. No one is expressly mentioned in the section, but the words "injuries to persons" and "in case of death from such injuries," necessarily imply a person suffering such injuries, and by reason of them succumbing to death, and it is his cause of action which the Constitution says shall not die with him, but shall survive. There is no word in this section of the Constitution relating to the domestic relatives of the deceased, or to the pecuniary damages to those relatives to whom the Act of April 26, 1855, gives an action for their recovery. Nor does the Constitution give expressly an action to recover damages for the death of the deceased, as did the 19th Section of the Act of April 15, 1851, though we think that the intention clearly appears that the action shall survive to recover compensation for all that the deceased suffered or lost by means of the injury to his person.

Actio personalis moritur cum persona is the rule of the common law, and in case of the death of either the plaintiff or the defendant, a personal action always abated. Where, however, the right of action arose *ex contractu*, it generally survived the death of either party, and whenever it did survive it always descended to the personal representatives of him who had it in his lifetime. (3 Bl. Com. 302.) There is no reason why such rights should vest in any one else. Where the Constitution in this section, therefore, says "the right of action shall survive," it vests the right in the personal representatives of the deceased.

Had the first sentence ended with the words "the right of action shall survive," it is probable that no one would have thought of arguing that the right of action thus surviving was not vested by the Constitution in the legal representatives of the deceased. But the sentence proceeds, saying, "and the General Assembly shall prescribe *for whose benefit* such actions *shall be prosecuted*," and it was these latter words, which the learned Court below construed as authorizing the Legislature to *transfer* the *legal right of action* from the legal representatives of the deceased to her surviving husband. We are unable to assent to this construction. The section has no relation to the legal parties or to the legal form of the action, but only to what might be recovered by it. The Constitution fixed the *legal party*, and authorized the Legislature to designate the *use party*. There is a legal congruity in requiring that a right of action which survives the deceased, shall be prosecuted in the name of his legal representative, and it certainly cannot be said in Pennsylvania that there is any legal incongruity in requiring an action to be brought in the name of a legal plaintiff for the use and benefit of another person. Besides this, there was strong reason why the Constitution should fix the parties, and give a complete and perfect right of action itself, inasmuch as the object and purpose of this section was to restrain and control the Legislature, as otherwise this object and purpose would be defeated by the Legislature, simply by omitting the action required of them to perfect the right of action. The Legislature, in fact, has not attempted to prescribe for whose use these actions shall be prosecuted.

The Act of 1851 gave an action to the widow, or if there was no widow, to the personal representatives, to recover damages for the death of the deceased, and left it to the jury to place a money value on the life in the same manner as in other cases they estimate the value of health and reputation.

Penna. R. R. Co. *v.* McCloskey's Adm'r., 11 Har. 526.

The Act of 1855 changed this, and substituted as the measure of damage the pecuniary loss suffered by the husband, wife, children, or parents, plaintiffs in the action, or for whose use it was brought. This was an entire change of the cause of action, and in a suit under the Act of 1855 nothing can be recovered for any suffering borne or loss sustained by the deceased, but only for the pecuniary loss which his said surviving relatives may have sustained by reason of his death.

Penna. R. R. Co. *v.* Zebe, 9 Cas. 318.
Same *v.* Vandever, 12 Cas. 298.
Same *v.* Butler, 7 P. F. S. 335.
Mansfield Coal & Coke Co. *v.* McEnery, 8 WEEKLY NOTES, 81.

By these cases it is established that the cause of action, under the Act of 1855, is the pecuniary loss of the deceased's *surviving family;* but that cause of action which *survives* by the Constitution is for the suffering and loss which the *deceased* sustained in his lifetime, and for which he could have recovered damages if he had lived to bring suit and obtain judgment. There is no resemblance between these two distinct causes of action. The difference is recognized and asserted in—

Penna. R. R. Co. *v.* Henderson, 1 P. F. S. 315.

There is no conflict between the Constitution and the Act of 1855; they regard different rights, and if the Act had been passed immediately after the adoption of the Constitution of 1873, instead of more than eighteen years before, it could, with no propriety or justice, be considered an execution of the power given to the Legislature by the twenty-first section of the third article of the Constitution. It does not affect the Constitution, nor is it thereby affected. It was not unconstitutional when it was passed in 1855, and is not so now. Its vigor is unimpaired by the Constitution of 1873, and there are no provisions in the latter which can prevent the passage by the Legislature of a supplement extending the provisions of the Act to other relatives than those therein named, or to any other persons whatever. There is nothing to prevent the two actions, the one for the injury to the deceased, the other for the pecuniary loss sustained by the family of the deceased, from being maintained at the same time, and both pursued to judgment and execution.

The chief purpose of this section of the Constitution was to protect lives from destruction by negligence, by making such deaths expensive to those whose faults should occasion them; and these actions for damages for injuries resulting in death, are the means adopted to effect that purpose. The Act of 15 April, 1851, was passed for the same purpose, and made nearly the same provisions. The members of the Constitutional Convention saw its provisions frittered away by the Act of 26 April, 1855, and a further effort in that direction made by the Act of 4 April, 1868 (P. L, 58, Purd. Dig. 1094). This was supposed to have been done by the Legislature under the influence of certain corporations. These corporations were certainly in the minds of the members of the Constitutional Convention, for they are mentioned in this very section, and the Legislature is therein prohibited from favoring them with a special Statute of Limitations.

The object being to fix permanently the law relating to these injuries and rights of action by a constitutional provision, which would be beyond the power of legislative meddling, it is absurd to suppose that the framers of this provision designed to empower the Legislature, intended thereby to be restrained, to prevent its ever going into effect, simply by omitting to do anything.

William J. Baldy and *John G. Freeze*, for defendant in error.

The sole object of the constitutional provision was to restrain the Legislature from returning to the common law rule, and taking away all right of action. The framers did not otherwise interfere with the Acts of 1851 and 1855, either as to the basis of damages, or as to the distinction between parties entitled thereto. The constitutional right of action is not additional to the one already existing. The Constitution provides that but one action shall be brought, in which all proper parties shall appear of record, but on the theory of the plaintiff in error two different actions, in different rights, can be maintained, and damages recovered twice for the same negligence. We submit that no argument can read that result into the Constitution.

Oct. 4, 1880. THE COURT. The maxim *Actio personalis moritur cum persona* was abrogated in Pennsylvania, in cases of injuries resulting in death, by legislation prior to the adoption of the Constitution of 1873. The Act of April 15, 1851, gave a right of action for such injuries to the personal representative of the deceased. The effect of that Act was to make the damages recovered in such actions general assets of the deceased in the hands of the representatives, and, of course, they were available to creditors in the first instance. It followed that in all cases of insolvent estates of such deceased persons, where the victim of the injury was a husband and father, the widow and children derived little or no advantage from the action, although they were the persons most directly and severely injured. Hence it was that a change was made, and by a new Act, passed April 26, 1855, the right of action for such injuries was taken away from the personal representatives of the deceased, and conferred only upon parents for the loss of children, and children for the loss of parents, and reciprocally upon husband and wife. So far as the subject is concerned this was the condition of the law in 1873 when the present Constitution was adopted. Of course as this right of action was derived from legislative enactment, it might, in the same mode, be taken away. To prevent this being done a special provision was incorporated in the organic law, declaring that in cases of death resulting from injuries "the right of action shall survive, and the General Assembly shall prescribe for whose benefits such actions shall be prosecuted." Since the adoption of the Constitution no new legislation has been enacted on this subject. It is plain, therefore, that the Act of 1856, prescribing the persons "for whose benefits such actions shall be prosecuted," is still the law. No other persons have been clothed with the right, and hence no other persons can sustain such actions.

The present action is brought by an administrator to recover damages for injuries resulting in the death of the intestate. But the Legislature has not declared that such a person may maintain such an action, and hence the right to do so does not exist. The designation of the persons for whose benefit such actions shall be prosecuted is expressly referred to the action of the Legislature by the language of the Constitution. No such law has been enacted, and hence the inference is irresistible that the persons who may now exercise the right are those, and those only who could do so at the time of the adoption of the Constitution.

It is argued, however, that such a right exists in the personal representative because of the provision in the Constitution that "the right of action shall survive." The argument submitted in support of this position is ingenious, but, in our judgment, it is entirely fallacious. The provision of the Constitution, coupled as it is in the same sentence with the direction that the Legislature shall declare who shall exercise the right, would be conclusive that the right itself is a limited one, to be put in force only for certain persons to be prescribed by the legislative body. Hence the inference is not warranted that the right of action is a general one to exist independently of, or without the appropriate legislation.

This conclusion is much strengthened by another consideration of still greater force. The argument is, as it must be, that the personal representatives may recover for the injuries to the person of the deceased, and other persons may recover for the death. Unfortunately for that position it is not the fact that two separate and independent rights of action are given. The language is, "and in case of death from such injuries the right of action shall survive," etc. What right of action? Manifestly the right to recover damages for the death of the person killed. No other cause of action is created. It is one right, not two, and its very existence, as a right of action at all, is absolutely dependent upon the fact of death.

For the injuries preceding the death and independently of it, no right of action is given, and hence there is none to survive. The opposing argument *assumes* that it exists, and upon the basis of that assumption infers the survival. But the assumption is unwarranted, and therefore the inference cannot be made. Moreover it is too plain for argument that the deceased person never had or could have a right of action in advance of his death for damages resulting only from his death, and therefore again as the right in him never existed, it could not survive to his representative. In the case of Mann *v.* Wieand (4 WEEKLY NOTES CASES, 6), we held that the right of action for damages from death by negligence never existed in the deceased—that it was given to and first existed in the widow, and hence the defendant was a competent witness in his own behalf in an action against him by the widow. The same principle applies here. We are of opinion that the nonsuit in the Court below was properly entered.

Judgment affirmed.
Opinion by GREEN, J.

March 5, 1880.
Koch & Balliet's Appeal.

Equity jurisdiction—Adequate remedy at law—Mining lease reserving royalty—Implied covenant to prosecute development—Alleged breach by stopping work—Bill in equity will not lie to compel development, or cancellation of contract, and for damages.

Where a right to mine is granted in consideration of a royalty reserved, the law implies a covenant by the grantee to work the mine with diligence so that the grantor may receive the contemplated compensation; but, in the absence of special grounds of equity jurisdiction, such covenant will not be specifically enforced in equity, an action at law for damages being an adequate remedy.

A. and B. covenanted that A. should have the exclusive right to mine the iron ore upon B.'s lands, and should annually pay one-sixth thereof to B., and that he should be absolutely entitled to the remaining five-sixths. After working for some years A. suspended operations, and B. brought a bill in equity, praying for a decree that defendants should proceed with the mining or deliver up the contract to be cancelled. A decree was made as prayed for, and damages were awarded:

Held (reversing the decree of the Court below), that an action at law for breach of covenant would clearly lie, and that there was no jurisdiction in equity.

Appeal from the Common Pleas of Lehigh County.

Bill in equity, by Benjamin Guth *et al.*, heirs and administrators of Daniel A. Guth, deceased, against John Koch, Sr., Lewis B. Balliet, executor of Stephen Balliet, deceased, and Edward H. Balliet *et al.*, heirs of said Stephen Balliet, deceased.

The bill, filed March 3, 1873, alleged:—

(1) That on August 23, 1842, Daniel A. Guth, since deceased, entered into an agreement with Christian Pretz and others, of which the material parts were as follows:—

"For the consideration hereinafter mentioned the said party of the first part [Guth] hereby covenants, grants, and agrees to and with the said party of the second part, that he, the said party of the first part, will and does hereby grant, permit, and allow the said parties of the second part, their heirs, executors, administrators, and assigns, the exclusive right and privilege to open pits, sink shafts, mine, and make all necessary work for mining and for mining purposes in and upon all or any part of all that tract or parcel of land owned by said party of the first part, situate in the township of South Whitehall aforesaid . . . for the purpose of digging and mining iron ore, and all other kinds of minerals and ores, and to mine, dig, take away from said land, sell, use, and dispose of iron ore, and all other kinds of minerals and ores. The said parties of the second part, their workmen and laborers, to do as little damage to the land, wood growing thereon, and premises, as the nature and proper prosecution of the proposed undertakings will permit.

"In consideration whereof, the said parties of the second part promise and agree to give and to deliver to the said party of the first part, or to his heirs, executors, administrators, or assigns, the one-sixth part of all the iron ore, and of all other ores and minerals, which they, the said parties of the second part, their heirs, executors, administrators, or assigns, may mine, dig, or cause to be mined or dug from, in, or upon the said land, the one-sixth part to be delivered at the mouth or mouths of the pit or pits, free and clear of all expenses to him, the said party of the first part, his heirs and assigns. The remaining five-sixths parts of all the aforesaid ores and minerals to belong to and be the property of the said parties of the second part, their heirs, executors, administrators, and assigns. And the said party of the first part further agrees that the parties of the second part may, if they deem necessary, erect one or more buildings for the accommodation of those employed in the mines upon said land, provided, that if at any time the said parties of the second part, their executors, administrators, or assigns shall finally abandon the working of said mines, the said party of the first part shall have the first chance to purchase such buildings, and if the price cannot be agreed upon, then said building or buildings shall, at the expense of the said parties of the second part, their executors, administrators, or assigns, be removed from said lands. And it is further agreed that, if limestone shall be mined or quarried upon said land by the said parties of the second part, their executors, administrators, or assigns, they may sell the same, paying one-sixth part of the proceeds of sale to said party of the first part, his heirs or assigns."

(2) That on various subsequent dates the several parties of the second part had assigned and transferred to John Koch, Sr., and Stephen Balliet, deceased, their rights and privileges under the said contract. (3) That in pursuance of their rights under the agreement Koch & Balliet built and maintained extensive machinery and im-

provements, sunk pits and shafts, and for thirty years or more mined large quantities of iron ore, paying one-sixth thereof to the persons entitled, averaging about $3000 annually. (4) That on or about April 1, 1872, the respondents, without any cause, suspended, and abandoned the mining of the ore and the delivery to the complainants, and had so continued. (5) That, although repeated offers had been made, by responsible parties, to the respondents, to work and operate the said mines, on reasonable terms, all such offers had been refused, and, notwithstanding frequent requests from the complainants to resume mining operations, or surrender or rescind the contract, the respondents refused; and that the complainants were informed, and believed, that the respondents did not intend to carry out the purposes of the contract. (6) That there is on the said tract a large and valuable bed of iron ore which can be profitably worked.

The complainants prayed for a decree that the respondents should "proceed to dig, mine, and raise iron and other ores and minerals upon said land, and deliver the one-sixth part thereof to" the complainants "according to the spirit and intent of the said contract or agreement, or in default thereof to cancel, rescind, and deliver up unto" the complainants "the aforesaid contract or agreement," and further relief.

The respondents filed a demurrer to the bill, upon the ground that the complainants had an adequate remedy at law, which demurrer was overruled by the Court. Thereupon respondents filed an answer admitting the first and second paragraphs of the bill to be substantially true, but alleging that on March 2, 1848, there was made a supplemental agreement between Daniel A. Guth and Pretz, as agent and partner of the Guth Mining Company, by which it was agreed that, as the Mining Company had built certain buildings on the land, the taxes should be divided and each pay one-half; that the company should pay Guth for the rent of the land on which the buildings stood and the gardens attached to them; and in case the ores should become exhausted or the company should at any time see fit to surrender, and it should happen that they could not agree upon the price at which Guth should take the houses, etc., a method of appraisement should be resorted to; and the answer further alleged that this supplemental agreement was included in the transfers mentioned in paragraph (2) of the bill. The answer admitted the mining and raising of ore, but denied that it had been for so long a time, or produced so large an annual average as alleged in the bill; it denied the abandonment of the mines, and alleged the recent completion of a new lease to the Bethlehem Iron Company; it denied the allegations of the 5th and 6th paragraphs of the bill, and all other allegations not referred to, and made technical objection to one of the parties.

Complainants filed the usual replication, and the case was referred to a Master (T. B. Metzger), before whom a large amount of testimony was taken to support the allegations of both the bill and answer.

The Master filed a report recommending a decree dismissing the bill, upon the ground that the complainants had an adequate remedy at law. After argument upon exceptions filed by complainants, the Court referred the case again to the Master, "with instructions to entertain the complainants' bill, to consider and marshal the testimony, and report the findings of facts as required by the rules of equity practice, to determine and assess the damages, and to report a form of decree."

The Master thereupon filed a second report finding that the allegations in paragraphs (1), (2), and (3) were proven: he also found that the complainants had proved a refusal to extend the lease of the Crane Iron Company, but had not proven "that the respondents neglected, refused, or were indifferent to a leasing of these same premises to parties other than the Crane Iron Company;" that the measure of damages was the price of ore per ton from November, 1872, which was from $3.50 to $4, and that the yield continued during this time about the same as it had been; but he again recommended the decree recommended in his previous report.

The complainants and the defendants both excepted, and the Court (LONGAKER, P. J.) filed an opinion, in accordance with which a decree was drawn requiring the defendants within thirty days to pay to the complainants $8615.10, with interest from January 1, 1877, retaining therefor 1833 tons of ore; and that they proceed to mine and raise ore with diligence and deliver one-sixth of the proceeds to the complainants, and in case of default within five days to cancel and deliver up the agreement. From this decree the defendants appealed, assigning for error, *inter alia*, the overruling of their demurrer and the entry of this decree.

John D. Stiles and *Morris L. Kauffman*, for appellants.

The jurisdiction could only have been acquired in this case under Article 6, section 2, of the Act of 1836: "The affording specific relief when a recovery in damages would be an inadequate remedy." This does not confer universal equity powers; there must be no adequate remedy at law. The chancery powers of our Courts extend only to prevent acts contrary to law, and this refusal to carry out the terms of a contract is not one of them. Equity cannot be used merely for the purpose of obtaining damages.

Hagner v. Heyberger, 7 W. & S. 104.
Kauffman's Appeal, 5 Sm. 383.

To justify the cancellation of a contract requires a stronger case than is required to resist a specific performance. Equity will not order an instrument to be delivered up or cancelled except in a very clear case.

Brainard v. Holsaple, 4 Green (Iowa), 485.
Stewart's Appeal, 28 Sm. 88.

The rescission of an executed contract will not be decreed except for fraud or palpable mistake.

Graham v. Pancoast, 6 C. 89.
Geddes's Appeal, 30 Sm. 442.

The agreement of 1842 was a grant of the coal in place.

Caldwell v. Fulton, 7 C. 480.
Clement et al. v. Youngman et al., 4 Wr. 345.
Barker v. Dale, 3 Pitt's R. 190.

R. E. Wright & Son and *Edward Harvey*, contra.

Where there is a lease of an ore mine or the grant of a right to mine ores, and the consideration of the grant or the rental reserved is a certain proportion of the ores mined, or a royalty thereon, the law implies a covenant upon the part of the lessee to work the mines with diligence and in a proper manner, so that the grantor may receive the return contemplated in the lease or grant.

Sharp v. Wright, 28 Beav. 150.
Bainbridge on Mines, 1st Am. ed., p. 214.
Shrewsbury v. Gould, 2 B. & Ald. 487.
Lyon v. Miller, 12 Il. 393.
Brainerd v. Arnold, 27 Conn. 617.

The jurisdiction of equity attaches not only where there is no remedy at law, but where there is not an *adequate* remedy, where the damages recovered would not be a complete compensation and the amount could not be certainly fixed, and in order to set at rest a source of constant litigation and prevent a multiplicity of suits.

Brainerd v. Arnold, 27 Conn. 617.
Finley v. Aiken, 1 Gr. 84.
Brightly's Eq., 247, 609.
Bank of Kentucky v. Schuylkill Bank, 1 Pars. 180.
Bank v. Adams, 1 Pars. 537.
Campbell's Appeal, 30 Sm. 311.
Masson's Appeal, 20 Sm. 26.

And since these defendants persistently refused to work the mine, in fraud of the complainants' rights, the contract under which they claim the exercise of this right ought to be cancelled, which can only be enforced in equity.

Wilson et al. v. Getty et al., 7 Sm. 266.
Duncan's Appeal, 7 Wr. 67.
Hetrick's Appeal, 8 Sm. 477.
Lippincott v. Whitmore, 3 WEEKLY NOTES, 314.
Souder's Appeal, 7 Sm. 498.
Wilhelm's Appeal, 29 Sm. 121.

May 3, 1880. THE COURT. The agreement which forms the basis of claim in this case was made in August, 1842, by and between Daniel A. Guth, of the one part, whose interest therein is now represented by the appellees, plaintiffs below, and Christian Pretz and others, parties of the second part, to whose rights, duties, and obligations the appellants succeeded by virtue of sundry assignments of the agreement. Guth, being then the owner of the land, covenanted and agreed with the "parties of the second part, their heirs, executors, administrators, and assigns, to furnish and allow them . . . the exclusive right and privilege to dig, mine, and take away all iron ore and all other minerals which are or may be found in or upon the land" described in the agreement, "and for that purpose to open pits and shafts, and to make and erect all necessary works for the purpose of digging and mining said ore and minerals, and taking the same from said land," etc. In consideration whereof the parties of the second part covenanted and agreed "to deliver to the said party of the first part, or to his heirs and assigns, the one-sixth part of all the iron ore and of all other ores and minerals which they . . . may mine or dig, or cause to be mined or dug in or upon said land. The said one-sixth part to be delivered at the mouth or mouths of the pit or pits free and clear of all charges and expenses to the said party of the first part," etc. "It being agreed and understood by all the parties that the remaining five-sixths part of all said ores and minerals shall belong to and be the property of the said parties of the second part, their heirs, executors, administrators, and assigns." This was followed by a supplemental agreement made in March, 1848, by which it was provided that each party should pay one-half of the taxes; that the grantees should pay a certain rent for land occupied by their houses, stables, etc.; and in case the mines should become exhausted, or the grantees should "for any other cause see fit to surrender and give up their lease of said mines;" provision is also made for valuing and disposing of the houses, stables, etc.

The bill charges that in pursuance of the agreement the mines had been successfully worked for many years, and yielded a large income to the plaintiffs; that on or about April 1, 1872, the defendants, 'without any cause whatever, and in violation of the terms and spirit of the aforesaid contract and agreement, entirely ceased, suspended, and abandoned, or caused to be suspended and abandoned, the digging, mining, and raising of iron ore and other ores and minerals upon the said premises . . . and have persistently and without cause ever since continued their abandonment and suspension of the mining, digging, and raising of said iron ore and other minerals;" and then concludes with a prayer for a decree that the defendants shall within a reasonable time proceed to work the mines, and deliver one-sixth of the ores and other minerals mined to the plaintiffs according to the spirit and intent of the agreement, or in default thereof cancel, rescind, and deliver up the contract; and for "such further relief in the premises as may seem agreeable to equity and good conscience."

The master very properly found that the mines had not been actually abandoned by the defendants, nor had anything been done that amounted to an abandonment. While it was shown that they had declined to extend the lease of the Crane Iron Company before it expired, and did not afterwards work the mines themselves, the master finds that immediately after the expiration of that lease, they made diligent, but unsuccessful, efforts to lease the mines for the purpose of mining. They may, and perhaps did, fail to comply with the terms of the agreement according to its true intent and meaning, but there was nothing done, or omitted to be done, that would justify a cancellation of the agreement. At most they rendered themselves liable to damages for neglect to work or cause the mines to be worked. While the rights granted are without limit as to time, and the agreement contains no express covenant as to how the mines shall be worked, or that any specified amount of ore shall be taken out, it does not follow that the appellants were at liberty to operate the mines or not as they saw fit. It was evidently the intention of the parties that they should be worked with reasonable diligence, and that would depend largely on the circumstances. The quantity and quality of the ore, and the demand that existed from time to time, would necessarily enter more or less into the question of due diligence. If the ore proved to be abundant, and of good quality, and the demand was such as to justify a vigorous prosecution of the work, the spirit of the agreement manifestly required that it should be so worked.

Where a right to mine iron ore or other minerals is granted in consideration of the reservation of a certain proportion of the product. to the grantor, the law implies a covenant on the part of the grantee to work the mine in a proper manner, and with reasonable diligence, so that the grantor may receive the compensation or income which both parties must have had in contemplation when the agreement was entered into. This principle appears to be recognized in Watson *v.* O'Hern (6 Watts, 362) and Lyon *v.* Miller (12 Harris, 392). In the former a lease of a stone quarry, in consideration that the lessee should pay a certain price per perch for all the stone taken out, was held to be a contract on his part that he would work the quarry, and upon his failure to do so the lessor might maintain covenant, and recover damages. It is there said, "If the defendants had any excuse, legal or equitable, from the responsibility thus assumed by their agreement, it lay upon them to show it. The plaintiff was not bound to prove the extent of their capacity to fulfil the contract. The lease presupposes they would work the quarry, and gives them the entire control over the premises; and being themselves acquainted with their own business and concerns, they were better prepared to show the extent to which they were able to work it; or, if not worked at all, the reasons for their inability. Not having done so, it was for the jury to give such damages as they might deem a compensation for the loss of rent."

Assuming, then, that appellants neglected and refused to work the mines with reasonable diligence, it is very clear that the appellees had a complete and adequate remedy at law for the recovery of such damages as they may have sustained.

There was no allegation of fraud, accident, or mistake in the procurement or execution of the agreement, nor was there anything alleged or shown that would justify a mandatory order on the appellants, requiring them to proceed and prosecute the work of mining within a specified time, on pain of forfeiting their rights under the agreement. Nor could it be justly claimed that by proceeding in equity a multiplicity of suits would be avoided. While the agreement remains in force, the right of action must necessarily depend on breaches of its provisions, and *non constat* that any will occur hereafter. The only claim that has been made, and sustained with any degree of success, is the demand for damages resulting from a breach of the agreement, and for that there was no doubt an adequate remedy at law. Where proper ground for equitable relief is laid and sustained, and jurisdiction has thus attached, courts of equity will proceed to award compensation or damages when they are incidental to such relief, but not otherwise. We think the conclusion reached by the master, in both of his reports, that the bill should be dismissed, was correct.

Decree reversed and set aside, and it is now ordered and decreed that the bill be dismissed, and that the appellees pay the costs, including the costs of this appeal.

Opinion by STERRETT, J.
MERCUR and GREEN, JJ., absent.

Jan. '80, 388.   Jan. 8, 1881.
Kaufman v. Hirsch.

Practice—Bail in error—Justification of sureties—Vacation thereof by the Supreme Court for cause—Order for substitution of sufficient bail.

Rule to show cause why the approval of Joseph Kaufman, as surety, should not be vacated.

Error to Common Pleas No. 1, of Philadelphia County.

From the record, and the depositions taken under the rule, the following facts appeared: The action was begun by a capias in case; and was so proceeded in that, in March, 1880, the plaintiff recovered a verdict and judgment against the defendant for $1165. A new trial having been refused, the defendant took a writ of error, and offered as bail in error, one A. H. Siegle and Joseph Kaufman, son of plaintiff in error. On exceptions, the prothonotary declined to accept the said sureties. The principal objection to Kaufman was that certain real estate owned by him was encumbered by a mortgage held by a building association. Another surety was offered and accepted in place of Siegle, and soon afterwards, on April 28, 1880, Joseph Kaufman again appeared before the prothonotary, informed him that he had paid off the mortgage on his property, and produced the mortgage itself, with a certificate of satisfaction indorsed thereon by the recorder of deeds. The prothonotary then accepted him as bail.

The depositions showed that this mortgage was paid off out of money advanced to said Kaufman by one Gegenheimer, and that, at the time, it was expressly agreed and understood between them that the latter should be secured by a conveyance, or a mortgage of the premises. An absolute conveyance was accordingly executed to him on May 20, 1880, but was not recorded until Sept. 18, 1880, and plaintiff some time afterwards discovered these facts. He then applied to the prothonotary to vacate the approval, but he declined to act, deeming his authority exhausted by the former approval. This rule was then taken.

Bispham, for the rule.

Although there is no reported precedent in this State, there can be no doubt that this Court will, in a proper case, supervise and control the taking of security on writs of error. The Act of June 16, 1836, § 7 (Purd. Dig. 605, pl. 16), requires the plaintiff in error to give recognizance, with *sufficient* sureties, etc.; and the Rule of this Court of Feb. 18, 1878 (5 WEEKLY NOTES, 81), provides for the justification of sureties before the prothonotary.

The transaction here was simply a substitution of one encumbrance for another, and the approval of the prothonotary was obtained by concealment of the secret agreement to convey the real estate. That amounted to fraud against the party, the prothonotary, and the Court, and we are entitled to have sufficient surety. Courts have, on general principles, the right to vacate the approval of sureties for cause, and to order sufficient or additional security to be entered, even where no fraud exists—*a fortiori*, where the approval was obtained by a trick. Such jurisdiction has been exercised by the U. S. Supreme Court, sitting in banc, in regard to sureties who had been approved by a single justice.

Jerome *v.* McCarter, 21 Wall. 31.

W. J. Budd, contra.

The depositions do not show any fraud in the transaction. When a man becomes security on a writ of error, it is a personal obligation, and his property is not thereby tied up. There is no lien, nor covenant against alienation, and to hold that a surety cannot mortgage or sell his property without disqualifying himself as surety will introduce a new principle in the law.

C. A. V.

Jan. 10, 1881. THE COURT. Rule absolute, with leave to substitute other sufficient bail within ten days.

PER CURIAM.

Common Pleas—Law.

C. P. No. 3.   December 11, 1880.
City to use v. Wood, owner, etc.

City claim—Notice to city solicitor of rule to issue scire facias—Sufficiency of such notice.

Rule to strike off lien.

Claim for $317.36 for curbing and grading against a lot of ground situate on the northwesterly side of Woodland Avenue, etc.

On November 10, 1880, a rule was taken on claimants to issue a sci. fa. to the first Monday of December next, and on November 20, 1880, said rule was made absolute.

Nov. 10, 1880, the owner of the premises left at the office of the city solicitor a notice in the following form:—

"City ⎫ C. P. No. 3.
 v.   ⎬ J. '79, 424.
 Wood ⎭ M. L. D.

Dear Sir:—

Please notice rule entered this day upon claimant to issue sci. fa. in above case, returnable 1st Monday of December next, sec. reg.

Yours, etc.,
JAMES R. BOOTH.

To W. N. West, Esq., City Solicitor."

Dec. 9, 1880, the present rule was taken.
Booth, for the rule.
Osbourn, for the city, argued that the city solicitor was not bound to notice the copy of the rule so served, as it was not in accordance with the terms of sec. 1 of Act of February 21, 1862 (Purd. Dig., vol. 2, p. 1091, pl. 38).
C. A. V.
THE COURT. Rule absolute.

C. P. No. 4. Dec. 20, 1880.
City to use v. Lukens.
Taxation of "rural or suburban" property in proportion to benefits received—Unconstitutional assessments—Lien for continuous work—When it should be filed.

Rule for a new trial. Scire facias by the city to the use of E. Peters against Lukens on a municipal claim for curbing and paving 200 feet on Orthodox Street, north of Peirce Street, in Frankford, Twenty-third Ward. The curbing was commenced in the fall of 1873; the paving was finished the ensuing spring; the lien was filed October, 1874, more than six months after the completion of the curb. The defence was that the property described in the lien was rural and assessed as such. On the trial it was shown that the value of the property had been greatly increased by the improvement, and the Court charged, as requested by the plaintiff, that if the jury believed from the evidence that the property in question was benefited to the extent of the expense of the paving, it would not be in violation of the Constitution to hold it responsible, and the verdict should be for the plaintiff. The jury gave a verdict for the plaintiff, whereupon, the defendant having obtained this rule—

Wm. Hopple, Jr., showed cause.
The pleading raised a question of fact properly left to the jury.
City *v.* Rule, 8 WEEKLY NOTES, 244.
Craig *v.* Philadelphia, 8 Norris, 265.

Assessment in cities in proportion to benefits received is constitutional.
Washington Avenue, 19 P. F. S. 352.

Seely *v.* Pittsburgh (1 Norris, 360) was a case stated, and the fact of the rural or suburban character of the property was not questioned. So in City *v.* Rule, *supra*.

Walter J. Budd, for the rule.
The improvement of the property is not the test, but its character as suburban.
City *v.* Rule, 8 WEEKLY NOTES, 244.

The city is bound by the assessment and classification of the Board of Revision.
Act of 24 March, 1868, P. L. 444.

No notice was given for the laying of the curb, as is required by a fair construction of the city ordinance of May 3, 1855.

Admitting the claim for paving, that for curbing was not good. The plaintiff should have filed his lien for the curb within six months and afterwards suggested his claim for the paving. His lien for the former work is gone.
December 23, 1880. THE COURT. Rule absolute.

C. P. No. 4. December 11, 1880.
Griffiths v. Stadtmüller.
Discontinuance—Attachment execution—Costs of garnishee—Attorney fee.

Rule to set aside fi. fa. issued by the garnishee against plaintiff for costs.

This was an attachment execution issued upon a judgment recovered by the plaintiff in an appeal from a magistrate. After the attachment was at issue the plaintiff discontinued, paying the prothonotary's costs, but not the costs of the garnishee. After the discontinuance, the garnishee filed his bill for witness fees, and subsequently issued a fi. fa. against the plaintiff for costs, which were the garnishee's bill, the attorney's fee of $3.00, and the costs of issuing and serving the fi. fa.

Sprogell, for the rule.
Wm. B. Lane, contra.

Upon a discontinuance, an execution may issue against the plaintiff for costs, if they have not been paid.
Gibson *v.* Gibson, 8 Harris, 9.
Musser *v.* Good, 11 S. & R. 247.
C. A. V.

December 18, 1880. THE COURT. The only question in this case is whether a garnishee in an attachment execution is entitled to an attorney's fee as part of his costs, upon a discontinuance entered by the plaintiff. In Magruder *v.* Adams (determined in the District Court in 1850, and reported 1 Troub. & H. Pr., § 925, note 1), it was decided, that, when the plaintiff fails in his attachment against the garnishee, the costs of the latter are to be taxed precisely as they are in an original suit. "It is clear," says SHARSWOOD, P. J., delivering the opinion of the Court, "that the attachment occupies, in respect to the garnishee, the same place that a separate *scire facias* does against a garnishee in a foreign attachment, and it is not to be doubted that such a *scire facias* is a suit, costs in which are recoverable as in the case of a suit commenced by original process." It follows that a garnishee is as much entitled to an attorney's fee as a defendant in an original action. As to him it is an original action. Upon a discontinuance the defendant's costs are to be taxed as upon a nonsuit. A discontinuance is allowable only on the payment of costs. By the 8th Eliz., c. 2, § 2, in force in Pennsylvania (3

Binney, 621), the defendant is entitled to costs where the plaintiff "shall not prosecute his suit with effect, but shall willingly suffer his suit to be delayed or shall suffer the same *to be discontinued*, or be otherwise nonsuited therein."

Rule discharged.

Opinion by THAYER, P. J.

C. P. No. 4.   Dec. 16, 1880.

Hirst v. Randall.

Practice—Amendment of record after verdict—Parties—Substitution—Waiver of formal defects by pleading in bar—After issue joined, and verdict found, a mere formal defect in the narr. cannot be taken advantage of by motion in arrest of judgment.

Motion in arrest of judgment.

Assumpsit, by the payee against the maker of a promissory note drawn to the order of Wm. L. Hirst by Robert E. Randall. The original summons issued in the name of Lydia B. Hirst, executrix of William L. Hirst, dec'd, to the use of James F. Wood, and was returned nihil habet. Before the alias issued the removal of Lydia B. Hirst, as executrix, and the appointment of the Philadelphia Trust Company in her stead, as administrator *d. b. n. c. t. a.* were suggested. The alias summons followed the original and the declaration was in the name of Lydia B. Hirst, but after plea in bar the jury was sworn to try the issue between the Philadelphia Trust Company, administrator, etc., and Robert E. Randall.

Chase & Lawrence, for the motion.

Husband, contra.

The defendant should have taken advantage of the alleged defect in the narr. before plea pleaded. Having waived his right to plead in abatement he cannot move in arrest of judgment. No injustice is done the defendant and the Court has power to amend the record.   C. A. V.

Dec. 23, 1880. THE COURT. Ordered that the declaration be amended in accordance with the record by substituting as the plaintiffs therein the Philadelphia Trust, Safe Deposit, and Insurance Company, administrator *d. b. n. c. t. a.* of William L. Hirst, deceased, to the use, etc., in lieu of Lydia B. Hirst, executrix of the last will and testament of Wm. L. Hirst, deceased, to the use, etc.

Eo die. Motion in arrest of judgment overruled.

Orphans' Court.

Oct. 1880.

Dunlap's Estate.

Commissions—The amount of commissions allowed to an accountant is regulated by the circumstances of each case.

Sur audit of the account of the executor of Ann W. Dunlap, deceased. *Coram* ASHMAN, J.

The only question which arose concerned the amount of commissions charged by the accountant, and the facts are fully set forth in the adjudication, which was as follows:—

The fund embraced by the account amounted to $32,960.83. It was composed of the proceeds of sale of two pieces of real estate and of certain corporation bonds and stocks and of three other small items. Commissions at the rate of three per cent. on the proceeds of realty and five per cent. on the personalty were deducted by the executor, and their allowance was objected to by the counsel for three of the legatees.

The securities in question were investments owned in her lifetime by the testatrix, and were undistributed assets remaining over at the settlement of the first account, in May, 1879. They were sold in November, 1879, by the accountant, under the advice of counsel, by M. Thomas & Sons, at public auction. Formal notice of the sale was given to all the legatees, and special permission was granted by the Court to the wife of the executor, to bid for all or any part of the securities. The circumstance that they were actually purchased by an agent selected by some of the legatees does not alter the fact of the sale nor the fact that the price obtained was the market value of the stock at that time. When appraised in December, 1878, the 480 shares of Allentown Iron Company were valued at $1 per share, or $480. They were bought in at the sale for $30 per share, or $14,400. Mr. Flanders objected that the executor's commissions should have been based upon the value of the securities at the date when a sale could first have been had, and that the delay in selling until the stock had risen in value afforded no ground for increased commissions.

Stated without any qualifying circumstances, this objection would seem plausible. But the commissions were charged upon the actual amount realized, thirteen months after the issuing of letters testamentary. The force of the objection was further broken by the testimony of Richard Wood, J. Vaughan Merrick, Edward Samuel, and Charles Chauncey. It was abundantly proved at the audit that the rise in value of the securities was largely due to the exertions of the accountant himself. In February, 1879, the Allentown Iron Company was deeply in debt, was doing business at a loss, and was threatened with immediate suit by its creditors. A meeting of stockholders was called, and as a result of the meeting a committee was appointed to raise subscriptions and to devise a plan of settlement. The committee failed to secure an amount sufficient for the emergency, and asked to be discharged. Mr. Conarroe, who had appeared at the meetings, strenuously objected to the discharge of the committee, and insisted that its number should be enlarged and that it should be instructed to continue its work. He was thereupon, with two other gentlemen, placed on the committee, and, to use the language of a witness who was himself a member, devoted half his time during several months to the work of resuscitating the company. His efforts were so far successful that within the current year stock which was valued when the committee first met at $1 per share was sold for $40 per share. This immense rise was undoubtedly accelerated by the improved tone of the iron market; but all the witnesses were emphatic in declaring that the revival in business did not manifest itself until after the company had fully recovered its footing, and that this recovery alone enabled it to take advantage of the revival.

These facts are an essential element in any inquiry into the compensation which should be awarded to the accountant. In the nature of things, no rule can be framed which will meet with mathematical precision the circumstances of every case. The nearest approach to a formula is to be found in the language used in various cases, that a Court of Equity will require in an executor only common skill, prudence, and caution, and that in fixing his compensation regard will be had to the amount and character of the trust estate, and to the labor, skill, and success attending its administration. (Heckert's Appeal, 12 Har. 482.) In estates of moderate amount, whose settlement has been attended with ordinary labor and responsibility, the minimum rate of commissions has been definitely fixed at five per cent. on the sum total of the personalty. No legal obligation compelled the accountant in this case to put forth extraordinary efforts to rescue the estate of his decedent from loss. Compliance with the routine of official duty required simply a sale of the stocks for whatever they would bring and a distribution of the proceeds. The law cannot do more than exact the performance of formal duties, although the latter may often fall short of the demands of conscience. But it does reserve in certain cases a discretion to reward meritorious service, and this is one of those cases. An executor, for instance, may not seek the trust for profit, but he may nevertheless be adequately paid for unusual labor and responsibility. It is of the highest moment to the estates of decedents in particular that they should be managed with skill and integrity, and these qualities cannot always be secured for nothing.

It is no answer to the demand of the accountant, to say that he gave his services to the company, and through it to the estate, voluntarily, and that the estate is not called upon to pay, because the company was not charged. The accountant served the company only in order to serve the estate. It is true that his wife, as a distributee under testatrix's will, was interested in the safety of the stock, but her interest was only one of several equally benefited, and she pays her proportion of the expenses. Without further elaboration, the auditing Judge is of opinion that the rate of commissions charged upon the value of the stocks, as determined by the sale, may be taken as a fair and even moderate standard for compensation. There was no evidence for the assertion that the sale was postponed by the accountant in the hope of personal profit. He waited until a favorable season should arrive for the sale of the real estate, and he sold the stocks and bonds fully six months before he disposed of the land. In proof of this the following agreement, which appeared as part of the account filed in May, 1879, may be quoted: "From this (balance) must be deducted amount of railroad bonds and stocks which are at present unsalable, and for which no reliable quotation can be given, *and which are desired by distributees not now to be divided.*" And then follows a list which includes the securities in question. This was signed by the counsel who now makes the objection.

The objection to the charge of commission at three per cent. on the proceeds of sale of the realty must be dismissed. Ordinarily, when the proceeds amount, as here, to $12,000, the commissions would be fixed at two and one-half per cent. But in view of the extraordinary service rendered by the accountant, and of the right of the Court to award a gross sum by way of compensation, the commissions charged by the accountant, viewed as a total, must be accepted as entirely reasonable and considerably below what the witnesses testified his services were worth.

And now, October 30, 1880, it is ordered and decreed that the account, upon payment of clerks' fees, be confirmed nisi, and that payment and distribution be made of the balance in accordance with the will of the testatrix, and that a schedule of such distribution be attached by counsel to this adjudication.

Henry Flanders, for the exceptants.
Geo. W. Biddle, for the accountant, cited—
Robb's Appeal, 5 Wr. 45.
Duval's Estate, 2 Id. 125.

November 20, 1880. Confirmed absolutely.

U. S. Circuit Court—Admiralty.

April 28, 1879.
Schmidt v. Steamship Pennsylvania.

Vendor and vendee—Stoppage in transitu—Liability of carrier to vendee's assignee holding indorsed bill of lading, for refusal to deliver the goods, under shipper's order of stoppage in transitu—Measure of damages—Loss of profit on contract of sale, made by such assignee and prevented by non-delivery—When recoverable against the carrier.

Appeals by both libellant and respondent from a decree of the United States District Court.

Libel, by Henry Schmidt against the Steamship Pennsylvania, to recover damages for the refusal of the master of the steamship to deliver goods shipped under a bill of lading of which Schmidt was the holder.

The facts of the case were as follows: Bresch at Trieste shipped goatskins to Philadelphia *via* Liverpool, on a through bill of lading to the order of the shipper, the bill being signed by the respondent's agent in Trieste. Bresch indorsed the bill to Havemann & Poleman, who sold the goatskins and indorsed the bill of lading to Schmidt, who afterwards, and before the arrival of the goods, made a sale of the skins to Keene. The contract of sale by Schmidt to Keene was in form an order for the skins accepted by Keene and signed by Schmidt as broker. Before the arrival of the skins at Philadelphia Bresch's agents telegraphed respondent's agents at Philadelphia to stop the goods. The vessel arrived February 3, 1878. On Feb. 6, Schmidt presented the bill of lading and demanded the delivery of the skins, in order to enable him to complete his contract of sale, which demand was refused. Keene then threw up the contract with Schmidt, and refused to accept the goods. On Feb. 12, 1878, Schmidt filed a libel against the vessel. On February 19 the order to stop was withdrawn, and respondents offered to deliver the goods, and requested a discontinuance of the suit, offering to pay the costs. On March 5, 1878, the goods were delivered to Schmidt, without prejudice to his right to claim damages for loss sustained by non-delivery on arrival.

For a more detailed statement of the facts see the report of the case in the District Court, 7 WEEKLY NOTES, 98.

On November 23, 1878, the District Court entered a decree for libellant. The Judge having intimated upon the argument that in his opinion the damages should be based upon the decline in value of the goods to the date of the offer to deliver and not to the date of actual delivery, a pro forma assessment of damages was entered in accordance with this intimation, and both parties then appealed to this Court.

Morton P. Henry, for the Steamship Company.

No liability exists on the part of the shipowner for obeying the order of the shipper to stop delivery of goods to the consignee or assignee of a bill of lading. It is to be observed that mere indorsement of a bill of lading does not necessarily imply that it is for value.

Benjamin on Sales, ₴ 862, note.

As between the original parties to a bill of lading the receipt of it by the purchaser or consignee merely establishes the vesting of the property in him. It cannot be said to defeat the right of stoppage in transitu, but rather gives occasion for its exercise.

Stanton v. Eager, 16 Pick. 467.

The law does not throw on the master as bailee the duty of determining whether the indorsement has passed the title to the goods as between the shipper and consignee.

The contract is with the shipper, not with the consignee, and the ship-owner is bound to obey the orders of the shipper.

Rosenfield v. The Express Co., 1 Woods, 131.
The Tigress, Browning & Lushington's R. 38.

If the steamship company had undertaken to deliver the goods to Schmidt after Bresch's order to stop, they would have assumed the duty of proving Schmidt's title against Bresch.

The Idaho, 11 Blatchford, C. C. R. 218.

An indorsement of a bill of lading does not imply that it is for value; it is the form which would be used if the consignee were a mere agent to receive the goods for the shipper. It passes the property if so intended, but not necessarily so.

Dracachi v. The Anglo-Egyptian Nav. Co., L. R. 3 C. P. 190, and cases cited.

The following additional cases on the right of stoppage in transitu illustrate our position.

(1) Master refusing to allow vendor to retake on the ground that he had signed bills of lading deliverable to another, guilty of conversion.

Thompson v. Trail, 6 Barn. & Cres. 36.

(2) Before notice to stop, purchaser may bring trover; after such notice, seller may.

Litt v. Cowley, 7 Taunton, 169.

(3) Bill of lading for goods purchased by bankrupt's correspondent filled up to order of bankrupt; stoppage in transitu sustained.

Feise v. Wray, 3 East R. 93.

As to measure of damages of consignee or vendee, if the carrier is liable for obeying the shipper's orders to stop goods. This is decided,

by two cases in the Circuit Courts of the United States, to be the difference between the value of goods when demanded, February 6, and the day when tendered, February 19.
The Success, 7 Blatch. C. C. R. p. 552.

The rule of damages was held to be the difference between a fair market value of cargo at the port of destination when the cargo ought to have been delivered, and the value when vessel was in readiness to make such delivery. "It can hardly be claimed, I think, that the loss of that special contract (of sale) furnished a rule of damages." Per WOODRUFF, J.
Chauncery Page v. G. C. Munro, 1 Holmes C. C. R. 233 (first Judicial Circuit).

Both cases reject the loss of sale as a measure of damages. The same rule obtains in England.
Simmons v. The South Eastern Railway, 7 Hurlst. & Norman, 1002.
British Columbia Saw Mill Co. v. Nettleship, L. R. 3 C. P. 499.

Schmidt had no interest in this matter except as earning his commission, and that he received from Havemann & Polèman.

If there had been any danger of a loss of sale to Keene, Schmidt could have obtained the goods by replevin and delivered them. Stoppage in transitu does not rescind a sale.
2 Kent's Comm. p. 541.
Newhall v. Vargas, 13 Maine Rep. 93.

The rules which govern the transaction are set out in Jones v. U. S., 6 Otto, 24.

Schmidt's measure of damages, if any, was the same as Keene's, and that was the decline in price between Feb. 6th and Feb. 19, 1878.

If the principle of the District Court is sustained Schmidt and Keene by agreeing to annul the sale can recover the fall in the market since Nov. 30, 1877.

E. G. Platt and *S. Dickson*, for libellant.

The Court below found that a liability existed on the part of the shipper for not delivering the goods to the holder of the bill of lading. The libellant was a bona fide holder for value of the bill of lading, and the cases and text-books are all to the effect that in such a contingency the right of stoppage in transitu is defeated. The right of property is in such case absolutely vested in the consignee, which gives him the right to maintain an action of trover or replevin.
Lickbarrow v. Mason, 2 T. R. 63.

Lord TENTERDEN, in his work on shipping, says: "It is now the admitted doctrine of our Courts that the consignee may (by assignment of bill of lading) confer an absolute right of property upon a third person indefeasible by any claim on the part of the consignor."
Thompson v. Dominy, 14 Mees. & Wels. 403.

The sole question is, Can the owner of a vessel escape liability on the plea that he is between conflicting claimants and as such not answerable for any damages caused by his action?
Benjamin on Sales, p. 719.
Abbott on Shipping, pp. 338, 540.

The holder of a bill of lading has a threefold remedy for the non-delivery of goods—against the master, the owner, and the vessel *in rem*.
Leonidas Olc. p. 12.
The Thames, 14 Wall. 98, cases cited.

As to the rule of damages. The actual delivery was March 5th, the tender of Feb. 19 was qualified; by accepting it the libellant would have waived all claims to any damages, and that he was clearly not compelled to do. The libellant gave notice of his contract of sale to Keene, and it was claimed that, under the circumstances and in view of the notice, the respondent would be liable for difference between the contract price and actual value of goods at the time of delivery. This view was taken by the late Judge CADWALADER in his opinion (7 W. N. C. 100).

This is the view we are now endeavoring to support, and it seems to be supported by common sense and common justice, and by all the authorities from Hadley v. Boxendale down.

C. A. V.

October 28, 1880. THE COURT. The opinion of the late District Judge, who decided this cause, so concisely and accurately states the law by which it must be governed, that I do not propose to add anything to it.

The ordinary measure of damages, between vendor and vendee, for breach of a contract for the sale of goods, is the difference between the contract price and the market price at the time and place of delivery, for the reason that this is the actual loss sustained by the vendee. But here the respondent was in possession of the libellant's goods, which were wrongfully withheld from him, whereby he was disabled from performing a contract for the sale of them, and the sale of them was defeated. Of this sale the respondent was duly notified, when a delivery of the goods was demanded, and by its refusal to deliver them took the risk of a renunciation of the purchase by the complainant's vendee. Whatever sum the complainant would have realized by this contract in excess of the market price of the goods at the time of their delivery, when he had the power to dispose of them, is clearly the amount of his actual loss which was caused by the respondent's act. The goods were withheld from the complainant until the 5th of March, 1878, and for the difference between their market price at that time and the price for which they had been sold to Keene, he is entitled to a decree. This difference amounts to $1916.57, for which sum, with interest from March 5, 1878, and costs, a decree will be entered in favor of the libellant.

Opinion by MCKENNAN, Cir. J.

Weekly Notes of Cases.

Vol. IX.] THURSDAY, JAN. 20, 1881. [No. 22.

Supreme Court.

May, '79, 81.
May 16, 1879.
Harlan v. Maglaughlin.

Fraudulent conveyances as against creditors, under Stat. 13 Eliz. Cap. V.—Subsequent creditors can avail themselves only of fraud intended against them—Requisites of voluntary settlements.

A voluntary conveyance to wife or children cannot be impeached by subsequent creditors as fraudulent, under the Stat. of 13 Eliz. Cap. V., unless they show that the settlement was intended to defraud or hinder them.

It is not enough for subsequent creditors to show an intent to delay or defeat existing creditors.

A man about to make a voluntary settlement, if indebted, or if contemplating indebtedness, must provide for such existing and future indebtedness; but he need not provide for future indebtedness which he does not anticipate and which may never occur.

Snyder *v.* Christ, 3 Wr. 499, and Monroe *v.* Smith, 29 Sm. 459, followed.

Thomson *v.* Dougherty, 12 S. & R. 448, dissented from. Other cases commented upon by Gordon, J.

Error to the Common Pleas of Cumberland County.

Ejectment, by M. & W. R. Maglaughlin, by their guardian, W. A. Coffey, against Anne Harlan and David Sipe, for two lots of ground in Carlisle, Pa.

The plaintiffs claimed as heirs of their father, Charles E. Maglaughlin, who died in April, 1874, and showed title in him as follows: Judgment, Sept. 22, 1869, Christian Kindler against John B. Noble for $129.47, on note dated March 5, 1869; fi. fa. and vend. ex., under which the premises in question were sold at sheriff's sale, in January, 1870, as the property of John B. Noble, and were purchased by the said Charles E. Maglaughlin, to whom the sheriff executed a deed therefor, duly recorded.

At the time of the said judgment and sheriff's sale, the title to the premises stood in the name of Isabella Noble, wife of the said John B. Noble, to whom they were granted and conveyed by two deeds, for the respective lots, one dated March 31, 1859, from John Mell, for the consideration of $50, recorded Aug. 27, 1859; the other, dated March 20, 1865, from William Blair, in consideration of $200, recorded March 28, 1868.

The plaintiffs claimed that these deeds were fraudulent and void as against existing and subsequent creditors, under the Stat. 13 Eliz., and alleged that the lots were purchased and paid for by John B. Noble, at a time when he was indebted, and that he caused the deeds to be made out in his wife's name for the purpose of defrauding and hindering creditors.

On the trial, before Herman, P. J., the evidence showed that John B. Noble had paid the purchase money of the lots, and the cost of the houses built thereon. The evidence as to his indebtedness was as follows: On March 31, 1859, when the first deed was made, he was indebted to different parties in the sums of $3.67, and $60; in 1859, after March 31, he contracted sundry small debts, viz., May 10, $18.09; May 20, $45; Nov. 29, $39; on which judgments were obtained, and executions in two cases returned "no goods." In 1860, he contracted debts as follows: Jan'y 13, $60, judgment obtained, and money made; April 13, $21.92, judgment obtained, and execution returned "no goods;" this judgment paid May 4, 1861; April 14, 1860, judgment, $5, for penalty for use of borough scales. In 1862—May 14, $4.02, paid May 28, 1862; Nov. 26, judgment, $6.50, on claim originally for $65. In 1869—Sept. 22, judgment $129.47, being the Kindler judgment under which the property was sold as above mentioned.

The assessment books for 1857 and 1858 showed that John B. Noble was assessed for taxes on a valuation of his real and personal estate of $700, and that his wife, Isabella Noble, was not assessed.

The only evidence relating to fraudulent intent was as follows: A witness, George Foote, testified: "I put a cistern on the lot. John paid me for it. I had a good bit of conversation with John. He told me before the war, in 1859, that he was in a good bit of trouble, and that he was going to put what he had, his property, over into his wife's hands."

The defendants proved that the said Isabella Noble, wife of John B. Noble, died intestate in June, 1875, without having conveyed the premises in dispute, and they claimed title as purchasers under an Orphans' Court sale for the payment of debts, and a deed from her administrator dated Nov. 1, 1877, duly recorded.

The plaintiffs requested the Court to charge *inter alia*: (6) If the jury believe that John B. Noble was indebted at the time the Mell lot was purchased, and that he paid for it, and had the conveyance made to his wife for the purpose of putting his property beyond the reach of his creditors; and that afterwards he increased his indebtedness until 1865; and then purchased the Blair lot, and caused the deed to be executed in the name of his wife, but did not record it till 1868; and that up to the time he contracted the debt to Kindler (under which the property was sold to the plaintiffs) he continued to contract debts, which remain unpaid, then they would be justified in finding that both said lots were conveyed to his wife for the purpose of hindering and defrauding his existing, as well as all his future creditors, and the sheriff's sale to Maglaughlin conveyed a good title, and the verdict should be for the plaintiffs. *Affirmed.*

The defendants presented, *inter alia*, the following points:—

(1) To render a voluntary conveyance void as to subsequent creditors, it must appear that it was made in contemplation of future indebtedness, and until this was shown the plaintiffs could not call upon the defendants to prove the consideration for the conveyances to Isabella Noble through whom he derives title. *Answer.* This would be so, if, at the time of the voluntary conveyance, no debts of the grantor existed, the recovery of which would be thereby delayed, hindered, or defeated. Where there are debts existing at the time, and the conveyance has delayed, hindered, or defeated their recovery, this circumstance raises a suspicion of fraud from which an intent to defraud subsequent as well as existing creditors may be inferred.

(2) Of the deeds under which defendants claim, one was made 31st March, 1859, and recorded 27th August, 1859, and the other was made 20th March, 1865, and recorded 23d March, 1868, while the debt, which was the foundation of the sheriff's sale, was not contracted until 5th March, 1869, nearly ten years after first conveyance, and nearly three years after second conveyance, and there being no evidence that the said deeds were made in contemplation of future indebtedness, the plaintiff cannot recover. *Answer.* The principle invoked in this point would be correct in its application to this case if no indebtedness prior to the dates of the deeds existed to raise the suspicion of fraud. Whether the deeds were made in contemplation of future indebtedness or not is a question for the jury under all the evidence, and we submit it to them. If the deeds were made to defraud subsequent creditors, then they would be fraudulent and void, and the defendants, claiming title through Mrs. Noble, would have no title whatever.

(3) Even if the conveyances to Mrs. Noble were void as to existing creditors of John B. Noble at the dates of the said conveyances, they were not fraudulent and void as to subsequent creditors, unless the conveyances were intended to defraud them, or unless Noble at that time was about engaging in some hazardous business which would necessarily involve the capital, credit, or labor of others; and no such circumstances have been shown by plaintiffs which would raise such a presumption. *Answer.* We cannot charge you exactly as requested in this point, but say to you, that, even if the conveyances to Mrs. Noble were void as to existing creditors of John B. Noble at the dates of the said conveyances, they were not therefore necessarily void as to Kindler, whose debt it seems was not contracted until 5th March, 1869, unless the conveyances were intended to defraud future as well as existing creditors, or unless Noble at the time was about engaging in some hazardous business which would necessarily involve the capital, credit, or labor of others. Does the evidence satisfy your minds that the conveyances were made with the intention of defrauding future creditors? We submit the question to the jury.

(4) There could be no legal fraud except as to creditors at the time of conveyances and such subsequent creditors as might have been contemplated by Noble at those times, and as there is no evidence shown from which it can be inferred that he was about engaging in a hazardous business or had in contemplation future indebtedness, the plaintiffs cannot recover. *Answer.* There can be no legal fraud except as to existing or subsequent creditors. To be a fraud as to subsequent creditors there must have been an intention in the mind of Noble at the time of the conveyances to defraud his future creditors. We cannot say to you that there is no evidence in the case from which it can be inferred that he had in contemplation his future indebtedness. There is some evidence on the question, and it is for the jury. We cannot withdraw the case from their consideration. But unless the evidence satisfies the jury that the conveyances were made for the purpose of defrauding the future creditors of Noble, the deeds to Mrs. Noble would not be fraudulent and void as to Kindler, on whose execution the property was sold by the sheriff; and if not fraudulent and void as to him the plaintiffs cannot recover.

Verdict and judgment for the plaintiffs. The defendants took this writ, assigning for error, *inter alia*, the answers to points as above given.

W. Trickett, J. W. Wetzel, and *W. F. Sadler*, for the plaintiffs in error.

The Statute of 13 Eliz. Cap. V. avoids a deed made with intent to defraud a creditor "*only as against that person . . . whose actions*, suits . . . by such devices, are, shall, or might be in any wise disturbed, hindered, delayed, or defrauded." It cannot be said that, by the deeds of 1859 and 1865, Kindler was defrauded, when his debt was not contracted until 1869. Even if Noble intended to delay the few creditors for small amounts that existed at the dates of the deeds (the most of whom were subsequently paid in full), it is not the law that a subsequent creditor, whose debt was not contracted until long after the deeds were recorded, can take advantage of such fraudulent intent, to set aside the deeds in his favor.

Sexton v. Wheaton, 1 Am. L. Cas. 43.
Snyder v. Christ, 3 Wr. 499.
Monroe v. Smith, 29 Sm. 462.
Williams v. Davis, 19 Id. 29.
Nippes's Appeal, 25 Id. 478.
Black v. Nease, 1 Wr. 433.
Byrod's Appeal, 7 Cas. 241.
Miner v. Warner, 2 Gr. Cas. 449.

The case of Thomson v. Dougherty (12 S. & R. 448), relied on by the other side, has been practically overruled in Mateer v. Hissim (3 P. & W. 161), and subsequent cases. The answers to the plaintiffs' and defendants' points, with respect to future creditors, were misleading, and erroneous. They were told, that, where any existing debts were delayed, a *suspicion* arose of an intent to defraud all subsequent as well as the existing creditors. But the legal and laudable purpose of all voluntary settlements on wives or children is to *protect* the beneficiary against the settlor's possible reverses. If reasonable in amount, if not impeached as fraudulent by existing creditors, and if the settler does not show fraudulent intent by soon afterwards contracting large debts, or entering into a hazardous business, such settlements cannot be set aside as fraudulent by creditors whose debts were contracted long afterwards. In this case the deeds were recorded long before the Kindler debt was created, and it must be assumed that credit was not based on the ownership of the property. The existing creditors did not complain, and subsequent creditors certainly cannot.

S. *Hepburn, Jr.*, and S. *Hepburn*, contra.

Noble paid for the property, and occupied it; he was indebted at the time, and executions for small amounts were returned, "no goods." It was not a voluntary settlement, but a purchase by him, and although the property was put in the name of his wife, it was his; it remained his, was liable to sale as his, and the sale vested the title in the purchaser.

Garrison v. Monaghan, 9 Cas. 234.

"I consider it an undeniable position that subsequent creditors are let in, . . . where they can impeach the settlement as fraudulent by reason of the prior indebtedness."

Thomson v. Dougherty, 12 S. & R. 448, per DUNCAN, J.
Anderson v. Roberts, 18 John. 526, per SPENCER, C. J.

The question of fraudulent intent was properly left to the jury, and they have found the deed void on that account. And if void at the time, it is void as to subsequent as well as existing creditors.

Conley v. Bentley, 6 WEEKLY NOTES, 338.

Black v. Nease, 1 Wr. 438.
Mullen v. Wilson, 8 Id. 416.
Winter v. Hartman, 1 Id. 161–2.

October 6, 1879. THE COURT. The Court below fell into an error which pervades every part of this case. A single point and answer will serve to develop this error and determine the material questions involved in this controversy. The counsel for the defendants below, plaintiffs in error, asked the Court to say to the jury that "to render a voluntary conveyance void, as to subsequent creditors, it must appear that it was made in contemplation of future indebtedness, and, until this was shown, the plaintiffs could not call upon the defendants to prove the consideration for the conveyance to Isabella Noble, through whom they claim title." The Court answered: "This would be so if, at the time of the voluntary conveyance, no debts of the grantor existed, the recovery of which would thereby be delayed, hindered, or defeated. Where there are existing debts at the time, and the conveyance has delayed, hindered, or defeated their recovery, this circumstance raises a suspicion of fraud from which an intent to defraud subsequent as well as existing creditors may be inferred."

This language is borrowed from the case of Thomson v. Dougherty (12 S. & R. 448), where it is applied, as in the case in hand, to debts contracted after the execution of the voluntary grant. It is, however, mere *obiter dicta*, not called for by facts in the case, and not true in law. Notwithstanding the many loose declarations in the books to the contrary, the Statute of 13th Elizabeth does not make voluntary conveyances void as to future creditors unless there is some evidence to indicate that the grantor intended to withdraw his property from the reach of such creditors (Snyder v. Christ, 3 Wr. 499); and it is properly said in Williams v. Davis (19 P. F. S. 21), that even an expectation of future indebtedness will not render a voluntary conveyance void when there is no fraud intended by such conveyance; and so, also, in Thomson v. Dougherty, Mr. Justice DUNCAN, citing Sexton v. Wheaton (8 Wheat. 229), says: "Chief Justice MARSHALL decided that a post-nuptial settlement on a wife and children by a man who is not indebted at the time, was valid against subsequent creditors, and that the statute does not apply to such creditors if the conveyance be not made with a fraudulent intent." A similar ruling will be found in Townsend v. Maynard (9 Wr. 198), and in Greenfield's Est. (2 Har. 489). In the latter case, which involved a deed of trust of all the grantor's property, it was alleged by Mr. Justice BELL, to be a sound rule of law that subsequent indebtedness cannot be invoked to invalidate a voluntary settlement made by one not indebted at the time, or who reserves sufficient to pay all existing debts, unless there be something to show that the settlement was made in anticipation of future indebtedness. It is further said, that, though some doubt was thrown on this principle by Thomson *v.* Dougherty, it was afterwards dissipated by Mateer *v.* Hissim (3 P. & W. 161). Furthermore, the case of Snyder *v.* Christ, above mentioned, which is very like the case in hand, settled any doubts that may previously have existed as to the effect of subsequent indebtedness. For though it seems to have been generally admitted that the statute is not operative as to such indebtedness, yet the admission has been so beclouded by apparently inconsistent *dicta* and qualifications as to render its meaning obscure and unintelligible. The settlement is good against after-contracted debts, if the settlor is unindebted at the time, or if he has made provision for existing debts, and so on. But how if there be existing debts not provided for, and how if the settlement is fraudulent as to such debts? Will the settlement in such case be void as to all future indebtedness? Is there no place for repentance and atonement by the after-payment of existing debts, or may after-creditors, notwithstanding such payment, avoid the debt? Justice DUNCAN answers these questions by saying: "If the jury find a prior indebtedness, and any of that class of creditors is defeated by the settlement, then my opinion is, that the property conveyed is to be considered as part of the estate of the debtor for the benefit of all his creditors. I know no midway. When a statute declares a matter void, it thrusts all to destruction, like a tyrant; while the common law, like a nursing father, makes that void where the fault is, and preserves the rest." In this, singularly enough, the fact is overlooked that the statute makes the gift or deed void *only* as to those who may be hindered, delayed, or defrauded thereby, and that in this it follows the common law. This oversight, however, would seem to be accounted for by the fact that the opinion of SPENCER, Chief Justice, in Anderson *v.* Roberts (18 John. 526) is adopted, wherein it is said, that the Statute of 13th Elizabeth protects creditors whose debts accrue subsequently to the fraudulent conveyance equally as those whose debts were due when it was made.

It would seem to be on this that Justice DUNCAN founds the assertion, already referred to, that the existence of prior debts creates a suspicion of fraud which can only be repelled by showing that the subsequent creditors were provided for in the settlement. This, as it stands, is unintelligible; for one cannot provide for what he does not anticipate; if he has no future debts in contemplation, how is it possible to make provision for them? It, in fact, simply amounts to saying, that the statute is operative upon subsequent as well as present indebtedness. In like manner, it has been said, the settlor must not only retain property enough to satisfy present debts, but also to answer the reasonable probabilities of the future. But this rule is unreasonable in this, that it prevents men of limited means from making any settlement whatever upon their wives and children; a result certainly not contemplated by the statute. Besides this, the attempt to keep men and women in judicial leading strings all their lives, to direct what they shall or shall not do with their own property, is a matter which commends itself neither to sound legal reason nor to common sense. If a man is in debt he may not give away his property until he has paid or provided for such debt; the reason for this is found in the principles of common honesty. If he contemplates future indebtedness, he must, for a like reason, provide for it, but he must not provide for what he does not anticipate, and for what may never occur. And if, without concealment, a man chooses to give away all his estate, or settle it upon his wife and children, what right has a subsequent creditor to complain? It did him no harm; he gave the grantor no credit because of such property; he is, therefore, neither cheated nor impoverished by such gift. Furthermore, if A, by a voluntary conveyance defrauds B. this year, how is C., whose debt has no existence until ten years after, defrauded by that same conveyance? It certainly will not do to say, that because B. was cheated, therefore C. is cheated, for between B. and C. there is no possible connection or privity. But if C. has not been defrauded by this grant, then, if the statute means what it most expressly says, he cannot impeach it.

We turn, therefore, with satisfaction to the case of Snyder *v.* Christ, where we have the plain and unambiguous declaration that the subsequent creditor can avail himself only of that fraud which is practised against himself. The doctrine thus announced is made the more positive in that it is said, if the creditor knew of the voluntary conveyance when he gave the credit, he could not be defrauded thereby, and hence could not impeach it. This case, not only from the direct manner in which the principal subject of discussion is treated, but also by reason of the facts upon which it depends, must be regarded as a final determination of the question in hand. These facts are briefly as follows: John Snyder, being the owner of a tract of one hundred acres of land, conveyed it to one John Reyer in trust for the use of himself and wife for their joint lives and the life of the survivor of them, with remainder to two children of the wife, and to such children as the grantor might have. This was all the real estate Snyder owned, and it was in proof that, at the date of the deed, his debts amounted to some two hundred dollars, and that his personal property did not exceed in value one hundred and fifty dollars. Furthermore, he had expressed apprehension of a claim for damages for a breach of a promise of marriage, and, within a few days after the making of the deed, he had borrowed two hundred dollars, and had also contracted the debt on a judgment for which the property in suit was sold.

Here then, we have every element necessary for a test case. A voluntary deed in trust of all the grantor's real estate, providing, *inter alia*, for himself for life, existing debts unprovided for, and, as to which, this deed was undoubtedly fraudulent; no property reserved for the reasonable probabilities of the future, an immediate contraction of subsequent debts, and an expressed apprehension of a pending claim for damages. It was nevertheless held, that of these facts the subsequent creditor could not avail himself, unless he could further show that a fraud was intended against himself. In other words, these facts, standing alone, did not make for him even a *prima facie* case.

Snyder *v.* Christ was followed in Monroe *v.* Smith (29 P. F. S. 459), in which it was said that a deed, void as to existing creditors, by reason of the grantor's fraud, is not necessarily void as to subsequent creditors; that it is bad only as to those it is intended to defraud.

It is scarcely necessary to say, that these cases rule the one now under consideration. The deed of John Mell to Isabella Noble was executed on the 31st of March, 1859, and was recorded in August of the same year. The deed of William Blair to Mrs. Noble was made March 20th, 1865, and was recorded 28th of March, 1868. The judgment of Kindler *v.* John B. Noble, upon which the property in dispute was sold, was founded on a note dated March 5th, 1869, ten years after the date of the first deed, and nearly three years after the date of the second. When, in addition to this, we reflect that Noble's debts at no time were large, that the testimony of Foote relates to declarations made by Noble ten years before Kindler's debt had an existence, that there is not one particle of evidence, direct or indirect, that a fraud was intended on future creditors, we must certainly conclude that the plaintiffs had no case, and that the Court should have instructed the jury so.

The judgment is reversed, and a *venire facias de novo* awarded.

Opinion by GORDON, J.

[See following cases.]

May, '78, 148.　　　　　　　　　June 15, 1880.

Kimble v. Smith.

Voluntary settlements—When not fraudulent as against subsequent creditors—Stat. 13 Eliz.

It is now settled, that, in order to avoid a voluntary conveyance, under the Statute of 13th Eliz., a subsequent creditor must show a fraud against himself, and not merely a fraud as to existing creditors.

Harlan *v.* Maglaughlin, *ante*, p. 353, followed.

Error to the Common Pleas of Columbia County.

Ejectment, by Daniel Smith against John B. Kimble, to recover a house and tract of land containing about eighty acres, in Franklin Township.

On the trial, before ELWELL, P. J., the plaintiff gave in evidence the record of a judgment obtained by Kostenbader's administrators against John B. Kimble, on February 25, 1874, for $5.33, upon a claim originally for $15.40, arising in 1870, and an execution thereunder, by virtue of which the premises were taken in execution as the property of the said John B. Kimble, and sold at sheriff's sale to Daniel Smith, the plaintiff, for $185. The full value of the tract was about $600.

The defendant claimed that at the date of the judgment and sheriff's sale John B. Kimble had no title to the land, but that the same was the separate estate of Mrs. Hannah Jane Kimble, wife of John B. Kimble, to whom it was conveyed by the following deeds, put in evidence, viz.:—

1862, Jan. 25. Deed. John B. Kimble and wife to William O. Wolverton and his heirs, for the tract in question (being the same premises which William Rohrbach and wife, by indenture dated March 29, 1860, not recorded, conveyed to the said John B. Kimble in fee). Acknowledged same day. (Not recorded.)

Same date. Deed. William O. Wolverton to Hannah Jane Kimble and her heirs, for the same premises. Acknowledged same day. Recorded same day.

The plaintiff's evidence in rebuttal, so far as material, was substantially as follows: That the conveyances in 1862, vesting the title in the defendant's wife, were made without consideration; that John B. Kimble was at that time indebted to the amount of $291.41 (subsequently reduced to $166.40); that he had not then sufficient property, liable to execution, to satisfy his existing debts; that, after the conveyances, a witness said to Kimble that the witness "believed he had put his property out of his hands to cheat his creditors," and Kimble replied: "What else would I have done it for?;" and that Kimble continued to reside on the farm after the conveyances. It did not appear that any of the existing creditors in 1862 had ever impeached the validity of the settlement of 1862.

The defendant presented, *inter alia*, the following points:—

(2) That the creditors of John B. Kimble, whose claims were subsequent in date to 1862, had due record notice of Mrs. Kimble's title, and, not having extended credit upon the faith of his ownership of the land, cannot impeach the conveyances of 1862, as voluntary and void. They had and have no rights to be affected thereby. *Answer.* I decline to affirm that point, and refer you again to the instruction that I have already given, to the effect that subsequent creditors may impeach a conveyance provided they can show it was made with intent to defraud creditors; though in what I have said I have instructed you that the mere fact that Mr. Kimble was indebted at that time does not, of itself, show that his intent was fraudulent. The amount of his indebtedness and his means of payment are to be taken into consideration in ascertaining whether his intent was fraudulent or not.

(3) That the small debts of John B. Kimble, shown to have existed in 1862, not being debts upon which the sheriff's sale was made to the plaintiff, their existence furnishes no ground for the plaintiff's recovery in this action. *Answer.* I decline to charge, as a matter of law, that the debts of John B. Kimble, in 1862, furnish no ground for a recovery by the plaintiff; but I submit to you, as in the general charge, whether under all the facts, considering the amount of debts unpaid and the value of the property still retained, the conveyance on the 23d of January, 1862, was designed and intended to defraud creditors; that is, I repeat, submitted for your consideration.

The Court, in the general charge, said, *inter alia*: "Now if you find that Kimble was merely making a transfer of title, expecting to pay off his debts, and not really intending to defraud his creditors, then subsequent creditors (those whose claims accrued quite a number of years afterwards) could not complain. But if he was in debt, and if he intended to defraud creditors (although they were then existing creditors), and if subsequent creditors can show that the conveyance was made *with that view*, then they may take advantage of it—in other words, if the transaction was attended with fraud at the time it occurred, there would be nothing occurring afterwards to condone that fraud; and if the subsequent creditors can show that the conveyance was without consideration, that it was voluntary, and that it was made with the intention of defeating creditors, then they, the subsequent creditors, could overturn the whole transaction by causing judgment to be entered against Mr. Kimble and by the sale of the property. The case therefore must turn upon the intention of John B. Kimble at the time he made that conveyance."

Verdict and judgment for the plaintiff. The defendant took this writ, assigning for error, *inter alia*, the answers to points and the portion of the charge above quoted.

C. R. & W. J. Buckalew and *John M. Clark*, for plaintiff in error.

Samuel Knorr (with him *Wm. H. Abbott*), for defendant in error.

The intent to defraud existing creditors is prima facie evidence of intent to defraud subsequent creditors.

Bump on Fraudulent Conveyances, 326–7.
Clarke *v.* French, 23 Me. 221.
Thomson *v.* Dougherty, 12 S. & R. 448.
Shantz *v.* Brown, 3 Cas. 128.
Preston *v.* Jones, 14 Wr. 66.

June 19, 1880. THE COURT. Hannah Jane Kimble, the wife of the defendant below, acquired her title to the land for which this ejectment was brought on the 25th of January, 1862. It consisted of a deed from William O. Wolverton, to whom the defendant and Mrs. Kimble had executed a deed the same day. William Rohrbach and his wife had conveyed the land to Kimble on the 29th of March, 1860. The deeds from Rohrbach and wife to Kimble, and from Kimble and wife to Wolverton, have never been placed on record. That from Wolverton to Mrs. Kimble was recorded immediately after its execution. The judgment in favor of the administrators of Jacob Kostenbader, amounting to $5.30, and costs, under which the property was sold to the plaintiff below, was recovered on the 25th of February, 1874.

At the trial of the cause, the allegation of the plaintiff was that the defendant had procured the conveyance to his wife to be made in order to hinder and delay his creditors. The existence of a number of unpaid simple contract debts, amounting to about $117, was proved. In addition to these, three judgments, aggregating about $33, were standing open against him on dockets of justices of the peace.

There was an interval of nearly twelve years between the date of the deed from Wolverton to Mrs. Kimble and the date of the recovery of the judgment of Kostenbader's administrators. During the entire interval the deed had been upon record. The creditors whom Kimble owed had acquiesced in the settlement he had made upon his wife. Most, if not all, of his simple contract debts had been barred by the Statute of Limitations, and the judgments obtained before the justices of the peace had not been pursued. The Kostenbader judgment was in no manner connected with any of the original debts, with any transaction that had grown out of those debts, or with any business relations formed by Kimble immediately or shortly after the settlement.

May a creditor travel back to inquire into the

details of an adjustment of property made without concealment twelve years before the adjustment could have interest or concern to him, and which parties having existing adversary interests had made no effort to disturb? The Court in submitting the question of fraud to the jury instructed them, in substance, that, if the conveyance was made by Kimble with intent to defraud existing creditors, it was not only void as to the creditors intended to be defrauded, but also as to subsequent creditors. Under this ruling the jury found the defendant's intention to have been fraudulent.

That the Court below erred in its view of the law is conclusively shown by the case of Harlan *v.* Maglaughlin, decided by this Court since the trial in the Court below [reported *ante*, p. 353]. The opinion, delivered by Mr. Justice GORDON, contains a careful review of the authorities. As a result of such examination the doctrine is there laid down—following ·Snyder *v.* Christ (3 Wright, 499), Monroe *v.* Smith (29 P. F. S. 459), and other cases—that, in order to avoid a conveyance under the Statute of 13 Elizabeth, a subsequent creditor must show a fraud against himself, and not merely a fraud as to existing creditors. This is entirely reasonable and in harmony with the statute which avoids such conveyances only as to the parties intended to be defrauded.

The application of this principle to the case in hand is eminently proper. Here we have the sale of the property under a petty judgment of $5.30 recovered upon a debt contracted years after the settlement was made, and after the title stood in Mrs. Kimble's name upon the record. The trifling debts existing at the time of the settlement were paid or barred by the statute; if any wrong had been contemplated as to existing creditors, it had been condoned or forgotten, at least it had not been followed up by adversary proceedings. We are unable to see any evidence in the cause that a fraud was intended by the defendant as to subsequent creditors, and the learned Court should have so instructed the jury.

Judgment reversed.

Opinion by PAXSON, J. SHARSWOOD, J., absent.

[See preceding and following cases.]

May, '80, 95.　　　　　　　　May 4, 1880.

Reehling v. Byers et al.

Fraudulent conveyances—Stat. 13 Elis.— To impeach deed from a debtor to a creditor for property worth more than the debt, the difference being paid in money, fraud must be proved on the part of the grantee as well as of the grantor—Near relationship of parties does not afford presumption of fraud.

A father, for the purpose of securing a debt of $550, due him by his son, who was in embarrassed circumstances, purchased from the latter certain real estate of the value of $1350, and, after deducting his debt, paid the balance in cash to his son, who immediately used it to pay certain other debts. A few days later, another creditor recovered an award, and subsequently a judgment against the son, under which the realty was sold in execution as the property of the son. The purchaser obtained possession, and, the father having subsequently made an assignment for the benefit of creditors, his assignee brought ejectment:

Held, that, in the absence of any evidence of fraudulent intent on the part of the father, the Court should have directed a verdict for the plaintiff. That the son alone conveyed with an intent to defeat creditors is immaterial.

Per GORDON, J. If the father's motive was to secure his own debt, his purchase cannot be impeached because he paid the difference between the amount of his debt and the price agreed upon, in money. In this we must look to the motive of the creditor; if that was honest and lawful, the intent of his debtor does not enter into the question. One man cannot be prejudiced by the fraud of another of which he has no notice.

Business dealings between parents and children, and other near relatives, are not *per se* fraudulent; they must be treated just as are the transactions between ordinary debtors and creditors.

Error to the Common Pleas of York County.

Ejectment, by C. F. Reehling, assignee for the benefit of creditors of Isaac Taylor, against W. R. Byers, tenant, and the widow and heirs of Joel Brinton, deceased, for certain real estate in York County.

On the trial, before WICKES, J., the following facts appeared: On June 23, 1876, William H. Taylor, being then the owner of the premises in dispute, conveyed the same to his father, Isaac Taylor, in consideration of $1350. A few days afterwards, on June 27, Joel Brinton recovered an award, before arbitrators, against the said William H. Taylor for $1174, on a note dated April 1, 1873, signed by Wm. H. Taylor as surety for one Kurtz. This award was, on appeal, affirmed and entered as a judgment in the Common Pleas, and, under a fi. fa. and vend. exp. issued thereon, the premises in question were taken in execution as the property of W. H. Taylor, and were purchased at sheriff's sale, June 2, 1877, by the said Joel Brinton, the plaintiff in the execution. Under proceedings before two Justices, William H. Taylor, who had remained in possession as tenant of Isaac Taylor, was ejected, and possession was delivered to the said Joel Brinton. On Dec. 28, 1877, Isaac Taylor made an assignment for the benefit of creditors, to C. F. Reehling, who brought this action January 25, 1878.

The defendants alleged that the deed of June

23, 1876, from Wm. H. Taylor to Isaac Taylor, was fraudulent and void as against Joel Brinton. The evidence showed that this deed was executed under the following circumstances: On April 15, 1868, William H. Taylor borrowed from his father $1420, and gave him his note therefor. On April 1, 1874, the debt had been reduced by payments to $550, when a new note was given for this balance. W. H. Taylor was also indebted to his sister, Mrs. Sarah Meredith, in the sum of $589.64, for which he had given her his note dated April 1, 1873. In January, 1876, Mrs. Meredith notified W. H. Taylor that she required the money due her by him. His father, Isaac Taylor, also demanded additional security for his note of $550. To meet these demands W. H. Taylor agreed to sell to his father the premises now in dispute, for $1350, their full value, the note of $550 with accrued interest to be taken in part payment, and the balance to be paid in cash. At the time of consummating this arrangement, June 23, 1876, Isaac Taylor, not having sufficient cash to pay the balance, borrowed from his daughter, Mrs. Meredith, $219.25, and thereupon paid to W. H. Taylor the said purchase money, to wit: note and interest $591.25, and cash (or bonds equivalent to cash) $758.75, and received a deed for the premises. Out of the money thus received, W. H. Taylor, the same day, paid his note due to his sister Mrs. Meredith, with interest amounting to $704.75, and applied the balance $54, to the payment of his other debts.

The defendants offered to prove declarations by W. H. Taylor, after the conveyance, to the effect that he "would not have sold his property to his father except to get out of paying Brinton;" that he wanted to compromise with Brinton so as to get the property back, for without it he could do no business; to be followed by evidence that Isaac Taylor had notice of such fraudulent intent. The evidence was admitted, under objection and exception, but it was not followed by any direct evidence of knowledge or collusion on the part of Isaac Taylor. There was no evidence of indebtedness by W. H. Taylor, at the time of the execution of the deed, other than that to his father, his sister, and to Joel Brinton, as above mentioned. At the close of the defendants' case, the plaintiff asked the Court to instruct the jury that there was no evidence of fraud, and that they must render a verdict for the plaintiff. *Refused.* The plaintiff, after producing testimony in rebuttal, presented, *inter alia*, the following points: (1) That under all the evidence in the case the verdict should be for the plaintiff. *Refused.* (6) That there is no sufficient evidence in this case, either to implicate Isaac Taylor in any purpose or design, collusion or conspiracy, by purchase of the real estate from W. H. Taylor, to delay, hinder, or defraud Joel Brinton or any other creditor or creditors of W. H. Taylor, or to charge Isaac Taylor with notice or knowledge of such purpose or design, to authorize the jury to find a verdict for the defendants; and the verdict must be for the plaintiff. *Refused.*

The defendants requested the Court to charge (1) That, if the jury believe, from the evidence, that W. H. Taylor sold and conveyed the premises in dispute in this suit, for the purpose of hindering, delaying, and defeating Joel Brinton in the recovery of his debt, and that Isaac Taylor knew of such purpose, then the deed of William H. Taylor to Isaac Taylor is fraudulent and void as against Joel Brinton, and those claiming under him, and their verdict must be for the defendants. *Answer.* The principle of law is correctly stated. For its application to this case the jury is referred to the general charge, and to our answer to defendants' second point.

(2) If the jury believe, from the evidence, that W. H. Taylor sold and conveyed the premises in dispute in this suit to Isaac Taylor, his father, for the purpose of hindering, delaying, or defeating Joel Brinton in the recovery of his debt, and that Isaac Taylor had any manner of knowledge or notice of such purpose and intent of his son, W. H. Taylor, then the deed of W. H. Taylor to Isaac Taylor is fraudulent and void as to Joel Brinton, even though Isaac Taylor had actually paid a full price for the property; and these defendants claiming through Joel Brinton are entitled to their verdict. *Answer.* In the purchase of property from an insolvent debtor, a volunteer stands upon a different footing from a creditor. A volunteer who purchases with notice that the sale is made to hinder, delay, or defraud the creditors of the vendor, is a participator in the fraud, and the conveyance is void under the Statute of 13 Eliz. But a creditor has a right to secure his debt although he knows that some other creditors must lose in consequence, and that the object and purpose of the debtor is to secure and prefer him. Such knowledge would not render the conveyance void under the statute. But it is for the jury to say whether Isaac Taylor was a *bona fide* creditor of his son W. H. Taylor to the extent of the note he held, and whether the balance of the purchase money was honestly paid.

The Court, in the general charge, instructed the jury, that, in order to avoid the deed as against the defendants, claiming under Joel Brinton, they must find that the conveyance was intended by both grantor and grantee to hinder or delay Joel Brinton in the collection of his debt; or they must find such facts, clearly and conclusively proven, as would justify them in presuming the existence of such joint fraudulent intent. His Honor further charged as follows:

"In transactions of this character, the Courts have placed creditors and volunteers upon different footings. A volunteer who buys with notice of the intended fraud cannot hold the property against the creditor whose debt has been delayed or hindered, even although he may have paid its full value. But when a creditor takes the property to secure his debt, the transaction is not void, although he may have full notice that the debtor prefers him to his other creditors, and that other creditors must lose in consequence of such preference. [Indeed where the property conveyed is not worth more than the existing indebtedness, it would be difficult to conceive a case in which fraud, under the Statute of 13th Eliz., could be established. But when, as in the case before us, a note is held by the vendee and applied only in part payment for the property, and cash is paid for what is due in excess of the note, and the jury is of opinion that the cash payment is not *bona fide*, but made only to deceive, and cover up a fraud upon the creditors of the vendor, what is the effect? I instruct you that it would render the whole transaction void, because fraud vitiates everything it touches, and although you may be of opinion that the *note* was honestly held, yet if you shall further believe from the evidence that the *money* was not honestly paid, then the purchase would be fraudulent and void against the creditors of W. H. Taylor.]"

Verdict for defendants, and a new trial having been refused, judgment was entered thereon. The plaintiff took this writ, assigning for error, *inter alia*, the admission of the evidence objected to, the answers to plaintiff's and defendants' points, and the portion of the charge quoted in brackets.

Edward W. Spangler and *Cochran & Hay*, for plaintiff in error.

There was no evidence of fraudulent intent. Even if the alleged subsequent declarations of William had been admissible to charge him, there was absolutely nothing to affect Isaac Taylor with fraudulent intent or knowledge, and it was the permission given to the jury, by the submission of the case, to "deduce fraud from that which the law presumes honest," of which we complain. Isaac Taylor had an undoubted right to receive a conveyance of the property to protect his debt; and the fact that his note against W. H. Taylor did not amount to the entire purchase money—the balance of which was applied to Mrs. Meredith's debt—did not constitute him a volunteer. The purchase was ancillary to the main object, viz., the realization of his debt.

Bear's Estate, 10 Sm. 430.
Craver *v.* Miller, 15 Ibid. 456.
Uhler *v.* Maulfair, 11 Har. 481.

Wm. C. Chapman, for defendant in error.

There was ample evidence to submit to the jury, from which they might infer fraud—the large indebtedness of W. H. Taylor to Brinton; the fact that the conveyance was made only three days before the award of the abitrators in favor of the latter, and that it comprised all his real estate; the declarations of W. H. Taylor that he had sold the property "to get rid of paying the bail money to Brinton;" the intimate relationship between father and son; the insolvency of the father not very long after the transaction; the retention of possession by W. H. Taylor, though nominally as tenant of his father; the borrowing of money by Isaac from Mrs. Meredith to pay William, and its immediate transfer back to Mrs. Meredith—all these circumstances were badges of fraud to go to the jury. It is a stronger case of collusion between father and son than Ferris *v.* Irons (2 Nor. 179), where this Court reversed for the withdrawal of evidence less forcible than that in this case.

This case is ruled by Forsyth *v.* Mathews (2 Har. 100), in which LOWRIE, J., says: "An assignment of all a man's property when he is largely in debt naturally excites suspicion of fraud, and it is therefore evidence of fraud. *If there be a judgment just ripening for execution at the time of the assignment*, this increases the suspicion and adds weight to the evidence. That the transaction is between a father and son makes it still more suspicious, because the father is supposed to be better acquainted than other people with the embarrassed circumstances of the son." See also—

Ferris *v.* Irons, *supra.*
Gans *v.* Renshaw, 2 Barr, 34.
Babb *v.* Clemson, 10 S. & R. 419.
Kaine *v.* Weigley, 10 Har. 183.

May 17, 1880. THE COURT. "A volunteer," says the learned Judge of the Court below, "who buys with notice of the intended fraud, cannot hold the property against the creditor whose debt has been delayed or hindered, even although he may have paid its full value. But when a creditor takes the property to secure his debt, the transaction is not void, although he may have full notice that the debtor prefers him to his other creditors, and that other creditors must lose in consequence of such preference; indeed, where property conveyed is not worth more than the existing indebtedness, it would be difficult to conceive a case in which fraud, under the Statute of 13th Eliz., could be established; but when, as in the case before us, a note is held by the vendee and applied only in part payment for the property, and cash is paid for what is due in excess of the note, and the jury is of opinion that the cash payment is not *bona fide*, but made only to deceive and cover up a fraud upon the creditors of the vendor, what is the effect? I instruct you that it would render the whole transaction void, because fraud vitiates everything it touches, and although you may be of opinion that the note was honestly held, yet, if you shall further believe, from the evidence, that the money was not honestly paid, then the purchase would be fraudulent and void against the creditors of W. H. Taylor."

With the above, as a general statement of the law governing cases of fraud arising under the Statute of 13th Elizabeth, no fault can be found; the difficulty arises in its application to the case in hand. It does not seem to be questioned that Isaac Taylor was a *bona fide* creditor of his son W. H. Taylor, and, as such, the learned Court concedes, his son might have preferred him over other creditors, even though he had full notice of such preference.

It follows, if Isaac Taylor's motive in the purchase of the property in controversy was the security of his own debt, his purchase cannot be impeached, though he may have paid the difference between the amount of the note and the price agreed upon for the property, in money. In this we must look to the motive of the creditor; if that was honest and lawful the intent of his debtor does not enter into the question. As was said by Mr. Justice COULTER, in Scott *v.* Heilager (2 Harris, 238): "One man cannot be prejudiced by the fraud of another of which he has no notice nor opportunity of receiving notice."

It is true, indeed, if the intention of the parties was not only to secure the note due to the father, but also to put the balance of the property into such a shape that it could not be reached by the son's creditors, then, as to such creditors, the whole transaction would be void. But of such intention we can find no evidence; the defendants offered to prove, and did prove, that William H. Taylor said: "I wouldn't have sold it," that is, the property in controversy, "only to get out of paying the bail money to Brinton." This was all very well, in order to show the motive by which Wm. H. was actuated in the transfer of his property, but it does not affect Isaac unless he knew of this fraudulent design at the time of the consummation of the sale. So well did the counsel of defendants know that this evidence standing alone would come to nothing, that the offer, under which it was admitted, was supplemented by a proposition to prove a fraudulent collusion between W. H. Taylor and his father. No effort, however, was made to fulfil this proposition; hence, the proof adduced was but an isolated link in a proposed chain of evidence which was never completed, and, therefore, utterly worthless, and so the Court should have treated it. (Battles *v.* Laudenslager, 3 Nor. 446.) Not only was there no evidence that this alleged fraudulent intention of William H. Taylor had been communicated to his father, either before or after the sale, but it was not even shown that the father knew that his son had been sued on the Brinton note, in which he was surety for A. B. Kurtz; indeed, for aught that appears, he was wholly ignorant of the claim, which it is now said, he colluded with his son to avoid. But, as we have already intimated, had he known the fact of his son's suretyship for Kurtz, and that Brinton was about to obtain judgment, that would not have rendered his purchase void, if in making it his intent was to secure his own debt, and not to hinder, delay, or defraud Brinton. That Isaac Taylor borrowed part of the money to pay the balance of the purchase money from his daughter, Mrs. Meredith, was of no kind of significance. What if this money were that which she had just received from her brother, and was part of that which he had that day received from his father? Her claim was an honest one; no one doubts that fact; one on which she had a right to receive the money paid to her, and there surely was nothing wrong in her loaning it to her father. It is a mere trifling with the principles of justice to allow a circumstance such as this, in itself so fair and proper, to be used to stamp a transaction otherwise honest and lawful with the character of fraud. Business dealings between parents and children, and other near relatives, are not *per se* fraudulent. They must be treated just as are the transactions between ordinary debtors and creditors; as, in the latter case, where the *bona fides* of such transactions is attacked, the fraud alleged must be clearly and distinctly proved, so likewise in the former. We have but to say, in conclusion, that, as there was in this case not even a scintilla of evidence tending to involve the assignor of the plaintiff in the alleged fraud, the Court should have affirmed the plaintiff's first point, that is: "That, under all the evidence given in this case, the verdict should be for the plaintiff."

The judgment is reversed, and a new venire ordered.

Opinion by GORDON, J.
SHARSWOOD, C. J., and GREEN, J., absent.
[See preceding and following cases.]

May, '80, 22.   May 10, 1880.

Mowry's Appeal.

Fraudulent conveyances—Stat. 13 Eliz.—Existing and subsequent creditors—Estoppel—Declarations upon the faith of which a debt is contracted—Distribution by Auditor of surplus funds in hands of assignee for benefit of creditors—Who may participate.

Creditors, whose debts were contracted, subsequently to a fraudulent conveyance, expressly on the faith of declartions made by both grantor and grantee, that the grantor retained his interest in the property conveyed, may, as against the grantee, avoid the conveyance as a fraud against them.

D. lent money to M., the grantor of certain real estate, upon the faith of declarations by the grantee that the deed to him was intended to defraud the grantor's then existing creditors; and that (this indebtedness having been satisfied) the grantor retained his interest in the land. The grantee then assigned the land for the benefit of certain creditors. Afterwards S., upon the faith of declarations by the grantee similar to the above, loaned money to M. the grantor. The assignee for creditors sold the land for more than enough to pay all the debts for which it was assigned. Upon distribution by an Auditor of the surplus, it was claimed by A. as assignor, and by D. and S.:

Held, that A. was estopped by his declarations from claiming the fund as against D. and S. The latter, as creditors of M.—whose interest had passed to the purchaser at the assignee's sale—were entitled, under the circumstances, to be paid out of the fund.

Appeal from a decree of the Common Pleas of Bedford County, dismissing the exceptions to the report of an Auditor distributing the surplus of a fund in the hands of an assignee for the benefit of creditors, and confirming the report.

The material facts, as found by the Auditor, were as follows: Andrew Mowry and John R. Mowry, brothers, were tenants in common of certain real estate. John R. Mowry died March 13, 1864, intestate, leaving to survive him a widow and four sons, viz., Josiah, Nathaniel, Zachariah, and Isaiah, to whom the said real estate descended in equal shares, subject to the widow's interest.

By indenture dated August 30, 1864, duly recorded, Josiah Mowry conveyed his undivided interest in his father's estate to his uncle, the said Andrew Mowry.

In January, 1873, Andrew Mowry and the sons of John R. Mowry, deceased, except Josiah, executed deeds of assignment of the aforesaid real estate for the benefit of the creditors of Andrew Mowry and John R. Mowry, deceased, and in trust, as to the surplus after paying the said debts, if any, to retransfer the same to the assignors. The assignee sold the real estate, paid all the debts, and in 1879 filed his final account, showing a balance remaining in his hands of $5947.36, and an Auditor was appointed to make distribution.

Before the Auditor (Moses A. Points) the only contest related to that portion of the fund which represented the interest of Josiah Mowry, which had been conveyed, as above mentioned, to Andrew Mowry. The same was claimed, on the one hand, by Andrew Mowry, by virtue of the said conveyance to him; and, on the other hand, by Samuel Dubbs and Mrs. Susannah Mowry, wife of Josiah Mowry, as creditors of Josiah Mowry, whose debts were contracted in 1871 and 1877, respectively. They averred that, although their debts were contracted after the date of the deed from Josiah to Andrew, of which they had knowledge, they loaned moneys to Josiah expressly on the faith of assertions, by both Andrew Mowry and Josiah Mowry, but especially by Andrew, that the said conveyance was made without consideration, and for the sole purpose of fraudulently defeating the then existing indebtedness of Josiah Mowry; and that, such indebtedness having been since paid or satisfied (in 1869), the said Josiah Mowry retained his interest in the said property. Much evidence on this point was taken before the Auditor, who reported the facts to be as alleged by Samuel Dubbs and Mrs. Susannah Mowry.

The Auditor, therefore, reported, as matter of law, *inter alia*, that Andrew Mowry, by reason of his said declarations, "is now estopped from setting up, in this distribution, a contrary state of facts, and for him to do so would be inequitable to the creditors who advanced moneys to Josiah upon the strength of these representations, and a fraud upon them. That, so far as the creditors of Josiah Mowry, viz., Samuel Dubbs and Susannah Mowry, are concerned, . . . the interest of Josiah Mowry in the estate of John R. Mowry to its full extent was affected with a trust in favor of these creditors, and, the land being now converted into money, the proceeds for distribution are affected with a like trust, and his share should be distributed to said creditors."

He therefore awarded payment to Samuel Dubbs and Mrs. Mowry of the amount of their claims.

Exceptions to the Auditor's report, filed by Andrew Mowry, were dismissed by the Court (HALL, P. J.), and the Auditor's report was confirmed; whereupon Andrew Mowry took this appeal, assigning for error the said action of the Court.

John Cessna (with him *J. W. Lingenfelter* and *John H. Jordan*), for appellant.

Admitting that the deed was fraudulent as to the existing creditors, in 1864, it is not possible that it was intended to defraud creditors whose debts were not contracted until 1871 and 1877. The existing indebtedness was wiped out in 1869, and with it the fraud against the existing creditors. It is not alleged that Josiah became again indebted until he contracted the Dubbs debt in 1871. But the subsequent creditors base their equity on the declarations made in 1871 and 1877. These might afford ground for an action, but could not infuse fraud into a deed made in 1864, when these debts were not contemplated.

Beck *v.* Parker, 15 Sm. 263.
Monroe *v.* Smith, 29 Ibid. 459.
Byrod's Appeal, 7 Cas. 241.
Snyder *v.* Christ, 3 Wr. 499.

But this proceeding, in distribution by an

Auditor of the surplus of an assigned estate, is not one for investigating the questions of title and of fraud in the deed. The appellees' debts were contracted not with the assignors, before the assignment, but with a stranger, and after the assignment. How then can they claim the fund raised by the assignment? The usual and proper mode would be for them to sell Josiah Dubbs' supposed interest in the land at sheriff's sale, when the questions would be settled before a jury, in an ejectment by the purchaser.

Stewart *v.* Coder, 1 Jones, 90.

Moreover, the appellees are attacking the very title that produced the fund, and they cannot do this and come in for a share. If Josiah's share is in court for distribution, it came here by virtue of the deed made by him to Andrew, and through the deed of assignment made by Andrew. Josiah was no party to the assignment. Unless his interest passed by his deed to Andrew, it still remains unsold, and would be liable for his debts. If title passed by Josiah's deed, then his interest must go to Andrew, because there was no reconveyance. Creditors cannot assail this deed on the ground of fraud, and at the same time participate in the distribution of a fund brought into court by reason of the deed.

Bush, Bunn & Co.'s Appeal, 15 Sm. 363.
Helfrich's Appeal, 3 Har. 382.

J. M. Reynolds (with him *Russell & Longenecker*), for appellees.

May 24, 1880. THE COURT. In March, 1864, John R. Mowry died intestate, seized of the undivided moiety of real estate which he and his brother Andrew purchased and held as tenants in common. He left surviving him a widow and four sons. In August of the same year, Josiah, one of the sons, executed and delivered to his uncle, Andrew Mowry, a deed for all his right, title, and interest in his father's real estate. Several years thereafter Andrew Mowry, and the other three sons made deeds of general assignment, conveying the property in trust for creditors, etc., to Joseph Ickes, who subsequently sold the assigned estate; and after paying the creditors, there remained a surplus to be divided among the assignors, or such persons as might be entitled thereto. It was conceded that Andrew Mowry was entitled to one-half and each of the three nephews to one-eighth of the surplus, and it was accordingly appropriated to them respectively. The present contention arose in regard to the remaining one-eighth, which was claimed, on the one hand, by Andrew, as purchaser of the interest formerly owned by Josiah, and, on the other, by the appellees, as creditors of Josiah, who alleged that their respective debts had been contracted solely on the faith of declarations made by Andrew to the effect that, notwithstanding the conveyance to him, Josiah was still the rightful owner of the interest he originally had in his father's estate. The single question, therefore, was whether Andrew or these creditors of Josiah were entitled to that portion of the surplus.

The Auditor found that the conveyance from Josiah to his uncle was without consideration, and for the purpose on the part of both vendor and vendee of defrauding the creditors of Josiah; that Andrew subsequently declared to Samuel Dubbs and Susannah Mowry, the appellees to whom the fund was awarded, that Josiah still retained his interest in the property thus fraudulently conveyed, and that they loaned the money and became creditors of Josiah solely on the faith of the representations made by Andrew. These facts were fully established by the testimony.

The legal title to Josiah's interest in his father's estate appeared by the record to have been regularly conveyed to Andrew, by his deed of assignment, passed the same to his assignee. Under these circumstances, in the absence of actual or constructive notice that the conveyance from Josiah to Andrew was fraudulent, the purchaser from the assignee took a good title, unaffected by the fraud.

The interest of Josiah being thus converted into money, the surplus of all the interests, after paying debts of the assignors, was *prima facie* payable to them according to their respective interests in the assigned estate; but the appellees, who had become creditors of Josiah on the faith of appellant's representations, interposed and asserted their right to that part of the fund, in preference to him; and why were they not entitled to it? It is difficult to see upon what principle of equity he could be permitted to take the fund, as against those who gave credit to Josiah on the faith of the representations that the interest he had in his father's estate still belonged to him. As between the parties to the fraudulent conveyance, neither law nor equity would lend its aid to either of them; and thus, while the appellant might as against Josiah claim and hold the surplus, he stands in a very different relation to the appellees, who were induced solely by his representations to do that by which they will be greatly prejudiced if they are excluded from participation in the fund. In view of the facts found by the Auditor, he is estopped from claiming the fund as against them. There would be no equity in permitting him to take it to their exclusion.

It is contended, that, inasmuch as the claims of the appellees arose after the assignment, and are not debts against either of the assignors, they have no interest in the funds arising from sale of the assigned estate; this would be true if it were not for the important fact that they gave credit to their debtor solely on the faith of appellant's representations, and he is the only one who is resisting their claim to the fund. As general creditors of the assigned estate, without more, they would have no standing, but upon the facts found by the Auditor their right to the fund in question is superior to that of the appellant.

Decree affirmed and appeal dismissed at the costs of the appellant.

Opinion by STERRETT, J.
SHARSWOOD, C. J., and GREEN, J., absent.

[See preceding cases.]

Common Pleas—Equity.

C. P. No. 3. December 13, 1880.

Skelly v. Ogden and Wife.

Equity—Bill to compel extinguishment of ground-rents—Deed—Construction of—Deed executed by trustee and cestui que trust reserving ground-rent—Effect of subsequent decree that the trust was invalid—Proviso in the deed postponing extinguishment during a life in being—Act of April 22, 1850, § 21, prohibiting irredeemable ground-rents.

Bill in equity, filed by Thomas Skelly *v.* Gouverneur M. Ogden and Harriet V. his wife, in her right, to compel the defendants to extinguish certain ground-rents upon payment of the principal. The material facts, stated in the bill and admitted by the answer, were these :—

(1) Cadwalader Evans, by his will, proved in 1841, devised one-eighth of his residuary real estate to trustees, in trust for the sole and separate use of his daughter Harriet V. Evans (now Mrs. Ogden) for and during her life, and after her death in trust for the uses therein set forth ; and the testator directed that the said trustees might, with his daughter's consent in writing, grant and convey said real estate, reserving ground-rents, which should be redeemable at any time *after the death of said Harriet,* but not during her lifetime.

(2) By six several indentures, dated June 23, 1868, duly recorded, Manlius G. Evans, sole substituted trustee under the said will, and Gouverneur M. Ogden and Harriet V. his wife (formerly the said Harriet V. Evans) granted and conveyed unto Thomas Skelly, the complainant, six lots of ground, part of the said trust estate, reserving thereout respectively six yearly ground-rents, unto the said Manlius G. Evans, in trust for the purposes set forth in the will of the said testator. And it was in the said deeds provided :

"That, if the said Thomas Skelly, his heirs or assigns, shall and do, at any time *after the decease of the said Harriet V. Ogden,* pay or cause to be paid to the said Manlius G. Evans, sole trustee aforesaid, his heirs or assigns," the principal moneys therein named, amounting to $4666.66, and all arrears due, "then the same shall forever thereafter cease and be extinguished, and the covenants for the payment thereof shall become void, and then he, the said Manlius G. Evans, sole trustee aforesaid, his heirs or assigns, shall and will, at the proper costs and charges in the law of the said grantee, his heirs or assigns, seal and execute a sufficient discharge" of the said ground-rents to the said Thomas Skelly, his heirs and assigns forever.

(3) The bill then recited certain proceedings in equity in the Court of Common Pleas of Philadelphia County, to March Term, 1871, wherein the said Gouverneur M. Ogden and Harriet his wife were plaintiffs, and the said Manlius G. Evans, trustee, was defendant, instituted for the purpose of having the said trust, under the will of Cadwalader Evans, for the sole and separate use of the said Harriet, declared passive, executed, and void, on the ground that at the death of the said testator the said Harriet was a minor, unmarried, and not in contemplation of marriage; wherein the Court of Common Pleas decreed that the bill be dismissed, but, upon appeal, the Supreme Court reversed the said decree, and decreed, *inter alia,* "that the said Manlius G. Evans, as such alleged trustee, make a valid transfer and conveyance to the said Harriet V. Ogden, in fee tail general, of the real estate which he holds now for her sole use and benefit." (See Ogden's Appeal, 20 Sm. 501.)

Manlius G. Evans, trustee, accordingly, by indenture dated Oct. 4, 1872, granted and conveyed the said six yearly ground-rents unto the said Harriet V. Ogden, in fee tail general; and, by indentures of the same date, executed for the purpose of barring the entail, the said Gouverneur M. Ogden and Harriet his wife conveyed the same to George W. Morris, who reconveyed the same to the said Harriet V. Ogden and her heirs.

(4) That the complainant, being desirous of redeeming the said ground-rents, tendered to the defendants the principal moneys thereof at par, with a deed of extinguishment, which the defendants refused to receive and to execute, alleging that, under the proviso in the ground-rent deeds, above recited, the same were not redeemable during the lifetime of said Harriet, except at the defendants' option; but the defendants offered to extinguish the same upon payment of a premium on the principal thereof.

Wherefore the complainant prayed that the defendants be compelled, upon payment of the principal sum of $4666.66, with arrears of ground-rent due to date of tender, to execute and deliver to the complainant, at his cost, a sufficient deed of extinguishment of the said yearly ground-rents.

The respondents in their answer averred that the proviso in said ground-rent deeds, postponing the time for the redemption of said ground-rent until after the decease of the said Harriet, formed a part of the consideration moving the respondents for the conveyance of the land to Thomas Skelly, and that the object of said condition was to save said Harriet from the annoyance, inconvenience, and anxiety of reinvestment, and the loss of interest, and perhaps principal, that would probably result. And they insisted, that the benefit of this condition is a right of property in said Harriet that cannot lawfully be taken from her without her consent.

J. Carroll McCaffrey, for complainant.

The proviso in the deeds that the ground-rents should not be redeemable until after Mrs. Ogden's death was inserted by the trustee to carry out the supposed intent of the settlor. When the Supreme Court struck down the trust, it in effect struck out from the deeds the name of the trustee, leaving them as though executed only by Mrs. Ogden and her husband to the grantee, reserving the rents to Mrs. Ogden. This virtually strikes out also the proviso, for it cannot be said that *these parties* had any *intention* to provide for a state of facts not contemplated. The proviso stipulates for extinguishment by the *trustee* after Mrs. Ogden's death. To strike out the trustee and leave the proviso would provide for extinguishment by Mrs. Ogden after her own death, which is absurd. Such redemption being impossible, the ground-rents would be irredeemable. But this would be in contravention of the Act of April 22, 1850, § 21 (Purd. Dig. 748, pl. 2).

Rowland Evans, for defendants.

The proviso in the deeds does not contravene the Act of 1850, for the ground-rents do not thereby become perpetual on failure to pay the redemption money within any specified period, but it is expressly provided that they shall be redeemable upon the happening of an event that is certain to occur, within the period allowed by the rule against perpetuities, viz., the end of a life then in being. There is no reason why the proviso shall not stand, for on Mrs. Ogden's death the rents will be extinguishable by her heirs, on payment of the redemption money.

December 27, 1880. THE COURT. The Act of Assembly of April 22, 1850, sec. 21 (Purd. Dig. p. 748), was intended to destroy irredeemable ground-rents, but the covenants contained in a deed must be so construed, if possible, as to carry out the intention of the parties. It seems to us very clear that Mrs. Ogden was only to enjoy a life estate in the rents, and that when she died the rent itself might be extinguished by payment of the principal.

A decision of the Supreme Court has destroyed the trust, but the intention of the parties was evidently, not that the ground-rents should perish upon the happening of an event not contemplated, but upon the death of Mrs. Ogden. This bill must be dismissed.

Opinion by LUDLOW, P. J.

Common Pleas—Law.

C. P. No. 2.　　　　　　　　December 6, 1882.

Irvine et ux. v. Dowling.

Married woman—Authorising attorney to sue when husband does not join in letter of attorney.

Rule to strike off warrant of attorney filed by plaintiffs' attorneys.

Assumpsit, by James Irvine and Mary his wife, in right of said Mary Irvine, against William Dowling, to recover money loaned by the said Mary Irvine out of her separate estate to the defendant.

The plaintiffs' attorneys, having been ruled to file their warrant of attorney, filed a warrant of attorney signed by Mary Irvine only, whereupon this rule was taken.

Daniels, for the rule.

The Act of 25 April, 1850, § 39 (Purd. Dig. 1007, pl. 20), took away the separate right of action recognized in Goodyear *v.* Rumbaugh (1 Harris, 480).

Ritter *v.* Ritter, 7 Casey, 400.

This suit should not be sustained, as it would make the non-consenting husband liable for costs.

Harrity (with whom was *Gordon*), contra.

Since the Act of April 11, 1848, a married woman may sue for her own property in her own name alone, and, if suit is brought in name of the husband and wife, that forms no objection to it.

Goodyear *v.* Rumbaugh, *supra.*

In such a suit the husband is merely joined for conformity.

1 Daniels' Chancery Prac. 111.

A warrant of attorney signed by the wife alone is sufficient.

Bowler *v.* Titus, 2 WEEKLY NOTES, 184.

HARE, P. J. In the present state of the law it may be difficult to avoid the dilemma of making an unwilling husband liable for costs in a suit he has not consented to; or, on the other hand, allowing him unreasonably to prevent his wife from asserting her rights by a suit to which his name is necessary. Perhaps the difficulty may be avoided by allowing her to use his name for conformity, upon securing him against costs.

THE COURT. Rule discharged, upon plaintiff entering security for costs.

[*Cf.* Thompson *v.* Hibbard, 8 WEEKLY NOTES, 254; Wireman *v.* Ervin, Ibid. 237; Darlington *v.* Ervin, 7 Ibid. 456.]

C. P. No. 2.   Nov. 27, 1880.

City to use of Cunningham & McNichol v. Tyson.

Practice—Consolidation of actions—When two municipal claims have been filed, each against a separate portion of the same lot, by the same plaintiff against the same defendant and for the same work, the Court will, on motion of defendant, compel the plaintiff to consolidate.

Rule to show cause why certain actions should not be consolidated.

The facts were as follows: Two municipal claims for paving were filed by the City to the use of Cunningham & McNichol; one against a lot of ground at the northwest corner of 52d and Spruce Streets, containing twenty feet on Spruce Street and extending northward along 52d Street eighty-five feet; and the other against a lot of the same dimensions immediately adjoining the first to the north on 52d Street.

The affidavit of Tyson, the owner of the land, upon which this rule was granted, set forth that he had purchased the premises in question as one lot, containing in front on Spruce Street twenty feet, and extending along 52d Street one hundred and seventy feet; that the same had never been divided, and were still registered in the Survey Department as a single lot; that the division into two was entirely the arbitrary act of the plaintiff, and, if allowed to stand, would entail double and unnecessary costs on the defendant.

McGlathery, for the rule.

THE COURT. Rule absolute.

C. P. No. 2.   Dec. 8, 1880.

Curran et al. v. Elliot.

The sheriff is not liable for false return to parties other than the parties to the suit—Terre-tenant not named in the writ cannot recover against sheriff for false return of service on the original covenantor, in covenant sur ground-rent deed.

Motion for a rule to show cause why a nonsuit should not be taken off.

The suit was brought by Curran and another against ex-sheriff Elliot for a false return to a summons in an action of covenant sur ground-rent deed, wherein Thomas W. Webb was plaintiff and Patrick Fitzpatrick defendant.

The return complained of was as follows:—

"Served Patrick Fitzpatrick by leaving a true and attested copy of the within writ at his dwelling-house, 1210 Ellsworth Street, with an adult member of his family, December 6, 1875."

Judgment was entered for want of an affidavit of defence, and under an execution issued thereon the premises out of which the rent issued were sold at sheriff's sale for the sum of $225. The premises are worth $1200. The plaintiffs, as tenants in common, are the present owners of two-thirds of the premises, Fitzpatrick having sold them in 1855, subject to the ground-rent.

On the trial, before HARE, P. J., it appeared that Fitzpatrick did not live at 1210 Ellsworth Street, and had not been served; though he admitted "that his grandchildren told him that he had been sued by Mr. Webb." The plaintiffs testified that they had received no notice of the suit.

The Court entered a nonsuit on the grounds (1) that the sheriff was not responsible to persons other than parties to the suits, and (2) that the plaintiffs, having failed to pay the ground-rent for which suit was brought, were guilty of concurrent negligence, and could not recover.

Brightly, for the motion.

The liability of the sheriff for official misconduct is to the Commonwealth and to any individual showing actual loss or damages.

Act April 3, 1860, Purd. Dig. 1307, pl. 15 and 17.
Commonwealth *v.* McCoy, 8 W. 154.
Commonwealth *v.* Contner, 9 H. 266.
Commonwealth *v.* Allen, 6 C. 49.
Thayer *v.* Roberts, 44 Me. 247.

If the sheriff had made a true return of "nihil habet," it would have been his duty under the Act of April 8, 1840, § 1 (Purd. Dig. 751), upon the issuing of the alias summons, to have served a copy on the terre-tenant or person in possession, or to have posted and published, and we should have thus been protected. We were entitled, as terre-tenants, to a strict compliance with the Act.

The concurrent negligence of the plaintiffs cannot affect the liability of the sheriff; the suit against him is for official misconduct, not for negligence.

THE COURT. Rule refused.

C. P. No. 4.   December 14, 1880.

Monaghan v. Ferry Co. [No. 1.]

Negligence—Carrier—Steamboat—Boat striking slip with violence—Contributory negligence—Passenger leaving seat before boat is ready to land.

Sur exceptions to decision of referee appointed under Act of May 14, 1874 (P. L. 166).

The testimony taken before the referee showed the following facts: The defendant owned a line of steam ferry boats plying between Camden and Philadelphia. On the evening of March 20, 1880, the plaintiff was a passenger on one of the defendant's boats; as the boat neared the ferry slip, the plaintiff stood up to get ready to land, and shortly afterwards the boat struck the slip with such violence that the plaintiff was thrown down and suffered serious injury, the lower end of her fibula being fractured and her ankle-joint sprained.

The referee (Francis Rawle) found that the defendant was negligent in allowing the boat to strike the slip with violence, and awarded the plaintiff $3200 damages.

The referee's report having been filed in this Court, the defendant filed exceptions thereto.

Wayne MacVeagh, for the exceptions.

The jar was inevitable and one of the unavoidable incidents of steamboat travel, hence it did not constitute negligence. The plaintiff was guilty of contributory negligence in leaving her seat before the boat landed.

T. C. Patterson, contra.

The plaintiff's act was not negligent, but if so it was a remote and not a proximate cause of injury. Where a passenger is injured and no negligence appears on his part, negligence on the part of the carrier is to be presumed.
Sullivan v. R. R. Co., 6 C. 238.

Care on the part of one injured in an accident is presumed by law in the absence of proof to the contrary.
R. R. v. Hall, 11 Sm. 361.
Canal Co. v. Bentley, 16 Ibid. 30.
R. R. v. Rowan, Ibid. 393.
R. R. v. Weber, 26 Ibid. 167.

It is the duty of a carrier to carry and set down passengers safely.
Rwy. Co. v. Hassard, 25 Sm. 367.

Unless the plaintiff's case shows want of care, the defendant must prove it.
Weiss v. R. R., 2 WEEKLY NOTES, 214.

As to measure of damages see—
Canal Co. v. Graham, 13 Sm. 299.
R. R. v. Books, 7 Ibid. 339.
R. W. Co. v. Donahue, 20 Ibid. 119.
R. R. v. Dale, 26 Ibid. 49.
McLaughlin v. Corry, 27 Ibid. 109.
R. R. v. Allen, 3 Ibid. 276.

C. A. V.

December 22, 1880. THE COURT. Exceptions dismissed.

C. P. No. 4.   January 8, 1881.

Monaghan v. Ferry Co. [No. 2.]

Submission of cause to referee, by agreement, under Act of 14 May, 1874—Jurisdiction of Court of Common Pleas to review referee's judgment, on exceptions—Writ of error—When not a supersedeas.

Rule to set aside *fi. fa.*

Upon an agreement of reference under the Act of May 14, 1874 (P. L. 166), the referee awarded in favor of the plaintiff, and filed his report in this Court on October 19, 1880. Exceptions on behalf of the defendant were filed, and after argument were dismissed by the Court. (See preceding case.)

The plaintiff having issued a *fi. fa.*, the defendant took a writ of error on December 31, 1880, within twenty-one days of the decree of the Court dismissing the exceptions.

Wayne MacVeagh, for the rule.

This Court has jurisdiction to review the referee's decision, and the writ of error, having been taken within twenty-one days of its judgment, is a supersedeas.
Collins v. City, 8 WEEKLY NOTES, 409.

T. C. Patterson, contra.

The referee's report was filed Oct. 19, 1880, and under the Act of 14 May, 1874, the award became a final judgment on Nov. 18, 1880, and the writ of error, in order to act as a supersedeas, should have been taken out within twenty-one days from that date.

This Court has no jurisdiction over the judgment of the referee, which is final under the Act of reference. The writ of error goes directly to the referee's judgment.
Act of May 14, 1874, Purd. Dig. Sup., 1940.
Linnard v. City, 8 WEEKLY NOTES, 453.
Eyster v. McCulla, 3 Ibid. 219.
Adleman v. Steele, 34 Leg. Int. 134.
McDowell v. Ackley, 8 WEEKLY NOTES, 465.
Smith v. Ins. Co., 7 Ibid. 365.

Aside from this, there are only questions of fact involved, which are not reviewable.
Lee v. Keys, 7 N. 177.

THE COURT. If we have power to review the finding of the referee, the time within which the taking out of the writ acts as a supersedeas, runs from the date of our decision upon the exceptions. The question of power has not yet been considered by the Supreme Court, but only by our co-ordinate Courts. We think, and have held, that we have power, at any rate, to review the decision of the referee upon questions of law.

Rule absolute.

Oral opinion by THAYER, P. J.

[See Collins v. City, 8 WEEKLY NOTES, 409, note.]

Supreme Court.

Oct. & Nov. '80, 308. Nov. 20, 1880.

Commonwealth ex rel. Attorney General v. Dumbauld and Roberts.

Constitutional law—Art. V. Sec. 5, relating to the erection of separate judicial districts—Associate Judges of Fayette County—Act of April 9, 1874, providing that the fourteenth judicial district shall be composed "of the county of Fayette, to which the county of Greene is hereby attached"—Construction of—Quo warranto—Original jurisdiction of Supreme Court to issue quo warranto to Judges of Common Pleas—Judges and Associate Judges of Common Pleas are officers of the Commonwealth whose jurisdiction extends over the State.

Art. V. Sec. 5, of the Constitution, which provides, "Whenever a county shall contain 40,000 inhabitants it shall constitute a separate judicial district," does not execute itself, but merely declares the basis on which judicial districts may be created by the Legislature.

The provision in the same section, that "The office of Associate Judge not learned in the law is abolished in counties forming separate districts," applies to those counties only which the Legislature has constituted separate districts.

The language of the Act of April 9, 1874 (P. L. 54, Purd. Dig. 1835), that "The Fourteenth District [shall be composed] of the county of Fayette, to which the county of Greene is hereby attached," although not aptly chosen, manifestly intends to declare that the county of Greene is for judicial purposes attached to the same district with Fayette, and that the two counties thus united form the fourteenth district.

Hence it follows that the county of Fayette does not constitute a separate judicial district, and the office of Associate Judge not learned in the law is not abolished in said district.

Judges and Associate Judges of the Courts of Common Pleas are "officers of the Commonwealth whose jurisdiction extends over the State." Hence, under Art. V. Sec. 3, of the Constitution, the Supreme Court and the Judges thereof have exclusive original jurisdiction to issue writs of quo warranto to Associate Judges of the Common Pleas.

In the Supreme Court of Pennsylvania.

Quo warranto, issued by the Supreme Court, at the relation of the Attorney General, commanding the sheriff of Fayette County to summon David W. C. Dumbauld and Griffith Roberts to appear and show by what authority they or either of them claim to exercise the office of Associate Judge in and for the county of Fayette.

The case was heard on demurrer to the respondent's return to said writ. The several facts and averments set forth in the suggestion and return are fully recited in the opinion of the Supreme Court, as follows:—

"This writ of quo warranto was issued on information and suggestion of the Attorney General that said defendants were elected Associate Judges in and for the county of Fayette, at a general election held in said county on the first Tuesday of November, 1876; that afterwards, on the 8th of December, 1876, they were commissioned as Associate Judges in and for said county, to have and to hold the said office, and to exercise the power thereof, by the Governor of Pennsylvania, for a period of five years, from the first Monday of January, 1877; that they did thereupon assume the duties of the said office and take upon themselves to exercise all the rights, powers, and privileges thereof, and have so continued to do ever since; that the fifth section of the fifth article of the Constitution of this Commonwealth provides that, 'whenever a county shall contain forty thousand inhabitants, it shall constitute a separate judicial district,' and that 'the office of Associate Judge not learned in the law is abolished in counties forming separate districts.' That in April, 1874, the said county of Fayette contained forty thousand inhabitants, whereupon the Legislature of said Commonwealth, on the 9th day of April, 1874, enacted a law that the said county of Fayette should be a separate judicial district; that the said county did, in November, 1876, and still does, contain forty thousand inhabitants; that the said defendants are not learned in the law, and that, therefore, they do usurp, intrude into, and unlawfully hold and exercise the said office of Associate Judges.

"On the return day of the writ the defendants pleaded that the action and cause of action were not within the jurisdiction of this Court; wherefore they prayed judgment, etc. This plea was overruled *pro forma*, and the defendants directed to answer, whereupon for answer thereto they say, they admit what is alleged in the suggestion filed as to their election, commission, and service as Associate Judges in and for the county of Fayette, and they also admit that in April, 1874, Fayette County had a population of over forty thousand inhabitants. But they deny that the Legislature of Pennsylvania, on the 9th of April, 1874, enacted a law that the said county of Fayette should be a separate judicial district. And they aver that the Legislature, by the Act aforesaid, did enact that the fourteenth judicial district of the Commonwealth should be composed of 'the county of Fayette, to which the county of Greene is hereby attached,' and they aver that the fourteenth judicial district is composed of the counties of Fayette and Greene, and deny that the office of Associate Judge not learned in the law was abolished in the said county of Fayette by the fifth section of the fifth article of the Constitution of Pennsylvania. They therefore deny that they usurp, have intruded into, or unlawfully hold and exercise said office.

"To this answer the plaintiff demurred."

Art. V. Sec. 5 of the Constitution reads as follows:—

"Whenever a county shall contain forty thousand inhabitants, it shall constitute a separate judicial district, and shall elect one Judge learned in the law, and the General Assembly shall provide for additional judges as the business of the said district may require. Counties containing a population less than is sufficient to constitute separate districts shall be formed into convenient single districts, or if necessary may be *attached to contiguous districts*, as the General Assembly may provide. The office of Associate Judge not learned in the law is abolished in counties forming separate districts, but the several Associate Judges in office when this Constitution shall be adopted shall serve for their unexpired terms."

The Act of April 9, 1874 (P. L. 54, Purd. Dig. 1835), provides as follows:—

"The judicial districts of the Commonwealth shall be numbered, composed, and designated as follows: . . . The fourteenth district, of the county of Fayette, to which the county of Greene is hereby attached."

Edward Campbell (with whom was *Henry W. Palmer*, Attorney-general), for the relator.

Under the Constitution and the Act of 1874, the office of Associate Judge not learned in the law has no existence in Fayette County. The Constitution provides that "counties containing a population less than sufficient to constitute separate districts . . . may be attached to contiguous districts, as the General Assembly may provide." The General Assembly has provided, by the Act of 1874, in the same identical terms, for the county of Dauphin, the twelfth district, to which the county of Lebanon is attached, and for the county of Franklin, the thirty-ninth district, to which the county of Fulton is attached. It is a little singular that in Dauphin and Franklin these provisions of the Constitution and Act of 1874 should by common consent be understood as dispensing with Associate Judges, while in Fayette they should be interpreted as having no effect upon them.

Authorities in the case are not to be found. No such case has ever arisen. It is altogether a question of the interpretation of the Constitution, and a single Act of Assembly.

C. E Boyle (*Mestrezat* with him), for respondents.

Jan. 3, 1881. THE COURT (after stating the facts *ut supra*):—

Two important constitutional questions are thus presented for consideration. They arise for the first time under the Constitution of 1874. One relates to our power to issue the writ of quo warranto against the defendants, the other to their right to the office.

We will first consider the question of jurisdiction. Art. V. Sec. 3, declares the jurisdiction of the Supreme Court shall extend over the State, and the Judges thereof shall have original jurisdiction . . . "of quo warranto as to all officers of the Commonwealth whose jurisdiction extends over the State." Thus the original jurisdiction of this Court in cases of quo warranto is limited to the class of officers named. It will be observed the language does not declare that those over whom jurisdiction is given shall be "State officers," but those "whose jurisdiction extends over the State."

Although Judges are elected within a county or a district, that fact does not make them county officers. They receive their compensation from the State. They are subject to impeachment by the Legislature, or, on the address of two-thirds of each house, may be removed by the Governor. When the Court is composed of a President Judge and two Associate Judges, any two of them constitute a quorum. These two may be the Associate Judges in every case except when they compose a court of Oyer and Terminer, then the President Judge must be one. In the exercise of the general jurisdiction given to the Court, the president and his associates, as a general rule, are put on a footing of equality as to their powers and duties, whenever two of them act together; while thus sitting they are on the same constitutional footing, and when acting individually their powers are coextensive within the limits of their jurisdiction. (Leib v. Commth., 9 Watts, 200.) It was, therefore, expressly held in this case that the Court of Common Pleas of each county is a State court, and the office of an Associate Judge is a State office. It is true that case was decided under the Constitution of 1838, yet there is nothing in the present Constitution changing the legal status of an Associate Judge not learned in the law. Still further, although elected in and for a county or district, the Judges constitute a Court which for many purposes has jurisdiction "over the State." Thus they may issue subpœnas for witnesses in any part of the State, and attachments to compel the attendance thereof. So under section three of the Act of 13th June, 1836 (P. L. 572), and its supplement, the Act of 4th March, 1862, section one (P. L. 79), they may send their process into any county of the State and the sheriff of their county to execute it, in any action for the recovery of damages, for a trespass or nuisance committed on real estate by a nonresident of the county wherever such real estate is situated. Under section one of the Act of 24th April, 1857 (P. L. 318), in certain cases against an insurance company, the Court of the county in which the property insured shall be ocated may direct its process to the sheriff of any county in the Commonwealth, and it is made his duty to execute it. It follows that each Judge of a Court of Common Pleas is an officer of the Commonwealth whose jurisdiction extends over the State. Neither the Constitution nor any Act of Assembly authorizes a Court of Common Pleas to inquire by writ of quo warranto into the title of an Associate Judge. As we have shown, this power is expressly given by the Constitution to the Supreme Court; we, therefore, committed no error in overruling the plea to our jurisdiction.

The remaining question is the validity of the defendants' title to the office.

Although Art. V. Sec. 5 of the Constitution declares that "whenever a county shall contain forty thousand inhabitants it shall constitute a separate judicial district," yet that provision does not execute itself so as to establish a separate district, whenever a county attains that number; but merely declares the basis on which, at a proper time and in a proper manner, judicial districts may be created by the Legislature. (Commonwealth *ex rel.* Chase *v.* Harding *et al.*, 6 Norris, 343.) To hold otherwise would work irreparable mischief and confusion, and be substantially impracticable to carry into effect. The same section declares: "The office of Associate Judge not learned in the law is abolished in counties forming separate districts." Giving due effect to each part of the section, and making them harmonize, it is manifest that Associate Judges not learned in the law are abolished in those counties only which the Legislature has constituted separate districts.

This brings us to a consideration of the question, whether under the Act of 9th April, 1874, the county of Fayette does form a separate district, or whether the counties of Fayette and Greene together form a district. The answer to this depends upon the effect to be given to the language, that the fourteenth judicial district shall be composed "of the county of Fayette, to which the county of Greene is hereby attached."

The Constitution is not to receive a technical construction like a common law instrument, nor like an Act of the Legislature. It must be so interpreted as to give effect to the great principles of government which it is intended to secure. (Commonwealth *v.* Clark, 7 W. & S. 127.) No such prominence should be given to any one part as to prevent giving reasonable effect to every other part, or to destroy the harmonious purpose of the whole. It gives to the Legislature power to make one county a separate judicial district, and to put any number of counties not exceeding four into one district. The question, therefore, is not whether the Legislature had power to constitute Fayette County a separate district, but whether that power has been so exercised.

It should never be assumed that any Act of the Legislature was intended to be in conflict with the Constitution, or that it would be violative of any of its provisions. If a statute is alleged to be unconstitutional, the burden of establishing the truth of the allegation is on him who alleges it. While in considering the validity of a legislative Act we may not look beyond the Constitution (Sharpless *v.* Philadelphia, 9 Harris, 147), yet in arriving at the intention of the Legislature we may consider the mischief that would arise from giving too literal effect to the language of the Act.

Let us then briefly consider the condition of the people of Greene County. That county is either within or without the fourteenth district. If without, what is its position? It is not a part of any other district. The Constitution gives to the people a right to vote in the election of their Judges. Have the people of Greene County such a right? If so, is it to vote for a Judge in a district of which their county forms a part, or is it to vote for a Judge in another district? If the view of the plaintiff be correct, the latter is the only course open to a citizen of the county of Greene. Again, for whom must the elector vote? Must he be a resident of Fayette, or may he be a resident of Greene? If a resident of the latter, must he take up his residence in Fayette to comply with the requirements of the Constitution? Suppose, in case of several candidates, the vote cast in Greene should elect the President Judge, is that vote competent and valid to elect him, and yet its soil legally disqualified from giving him a residence? These, and other objections which might be stated, show the difficulties in adopting the view of the plaintiff. The whole spirit of the Constitution, and of the Acts of Assembly, is that the people of each county shall be permitted to vote for a President Judge, and that they shall vote in the election of one for their district only. The doctrine that a county can be made a kind of a territorial appendage to a judicial district, and the people therein shorn of their rights, finds no warrant in the Constitution.

Although the language of the Act of 9th April, 1874, may not be aptly chosen, yet it manifestly intends to declare that the county of Greene is, for judicial purposes, attached to the same district with Fayette, and that the two counties thus united form the fourteenth district. It follows that the county of Fayette does not constitute a separate judicial district, and the defendants do lawfully hold and exercise the offices of Associate Judges therein.

Writ dismissed.

Opinion by MERCUR, J.

SHARSWOOD, C. J., absent.

May, '80, 98.   June 21, 1880.

Welch et al. v. Emerson.

Ejectment—Articles of sale of real estate—Vendee's equity—Re-entry by vendor for non-payment of purchase-money—Conditional verdict—What is a sufficient taking possession to extinguish an equity of redemption—Proviso that vendor, after re-entry, may sell to another—Effect of.

W. covenanted, by articles of agreement, to sell to E. a tract of land for $800, and to execute a deed of conveyance for the same whenever the purchase-money should have been paid in the following manner, to wit: $300 on a day certain mentioned in the agreement, and $100, with interest upon the whole of the balance, annually, until the whole should be paid. The articles of agreement also contained a provision that, in case E., the vendee, failed to make the payments as therein stipulated, W., the vendor, should have the right to take possession of the premises and to sell the same to any other person, upon giving notice to E. of twenty-four hours. E. entered and held possession of the land, according to the agreement, though he never made any of the payments therein provided for; but he alleged, as his reason, that there were certain judgments of record against W., his vendor, that were liens upon the land, and asserted his readiness to pay the purchase-money when such liens should be discharged. After the date at which, in accordance with the agreement, the final payment of purchase-money should have been made, the liens having meanwhile been discharged, G. M., the assignee of W., the vendor, served notice of twenty-four hours upon E., that he thereby took possession of the land, and that he would expose the same for sale at 10 o'clock A. M. on the second day thereafter on the premises. Following this notice, he sent his agent on to the premises, who, during a stay there of less than fifteen minutes, sold the same to a third person, and then, being ordered off by E., retired, with the purchaser, leaving E. still in undisturbed possession.

The purchaser at this sale then brought this ejectment against E. to recover the land. Upon a special verdict, in which the jury found that there had been a mere going upon the premises, the Court directed judgment to be entered for the plaintiffs, to be set aside and entered for the defendant upon payment by the latter of the purchase-money and interest within thirty days from the entry of judgment:

Held (affirming the judgment of the Court below), that the equity of the defendant was not extinguished by the entry and sale, and he was entitled to the conditional verdict.

Held, further, that a mere going upon the premises, and a sale in pursuance of the notice, was not a "taking possession," according to the terms of the contract.

Error to the Common Pleas of McKean County.

Ejectment, brought in April, 1879, by George K. Welch and A. I. Wilcox against Enos Emerson, to recover a tract of land situate in Keating Township, McKean County, containing forty-nine acres, more or less.

Upon the trial, October 22, 1879, before WILLIAMS, P. J., the following facts appeared in evidence: James M. Welch and Enos Emerson entered into articles of agreement, dated November 23, 1872, by which Welch covenanted to sell to Emerson the land now in controversy, and to execute a deed in fee simple of the same to the said Emerson whenever the purchase-money should be paid as therein agreed upon, that is to say: Emerson covenanted to pay to Welch the sum of $800 in the following manner, "$300 on the 1st day of April then next, and $100, together with the interest on the whole of the balance annually, until the whole is paid." Emerson also agreed to pay all taxes levied upon the said land. The articles of agreement contained this further provision:—

"And the said Emerson further covenants and agrees that, in case of failure to make the payments aforesaid at the times hereinbefore stipulated, with interest and taxes, then the party of the first part shall have the right and privilege to take possession of the premises, and to sell the same to any other person, on a notice given to said Emerson of twenty-four hours."

Emerson entered into possession of the land, and made a judgment-note for $300 to Welch as security for so much of the purchase-money due and payable upon the 1st day of April next following. He never made any other payment under the articles of agreement, though he remained in possession when this suit was brought. In September, 1873, judgment was entered against Emerson upon his note of $300, given to secure the first payment of purchase-money, and a writ of fi. fa. subsequently issued. But, upon a petition of Emerson, in which he set forth that there were judgments of record against Welch, in amount much beyond that of the purchase-money under the articles of agreement, and that the said judgments remained liens upon the land, by reason of which he, Emerson, could not pay the purchase-money and receive his deed of conveyance, as agreed, the Court directed execution upon the said writ to be stayed.

It appeared in evidence, also, that in the autumn of 1873 Emerson made a tender to Welch of the whole amount of purchase-money due under the agreement, provided all liens were removed from the land and a clear title to the same were given to him. This was not done, however, nor was there any further transaction between the parties to the agreement until 1878. In the mean time James M. Welch, party of the first part, conveyed to George K. Welch, on December 2, 1873, certain tracts of land situate in McKean County, among which were the forty-nine acres then in the possession of Emerson; though the latter had no notice of this sale, nor was the deed to George K. Welch recorded until June, 1874. George K. Welch, the grantee in that conveyance, then executed a deed to Emerson for the land in controversy, and caused it to be tendered to him with a demand for the residue of the purchase-money. Emerson refused to accept this deed, upon the ground that his grantor was James M. Welch, and not George K. Welch, with whom he had made no contract.

Upon February 17, 1879, by which time the liens formerly charged upon the land had been removed, the following notice was served upon Emerson:—

"To Enos Emerson. Take notice that, under the provisions of the contract made by you with J. M. Welch, dated Nov. 3, 1872, I hereby notify you that, as you have failed to perform the stipulations therein, I hereby take possession of the land mentioned in said contract, and notify you that I will expose the same for sale, on the premises, on the 19th of Feb. 1879, at 10 o'clock A. M.

"HENRY BOYER,
"Attorney in fact for J. M. and G. K. Welch."

Boyer, the agent of James M. Welch, drove by Emerson's house on the morning of the 19th February, 1879, accompanied by A. I. Wilcox, the agent of George K. Welch, and stopped before the barn, upon the premises, distant about sixty feet from the house, where he and Wilcox remained, as it appeared from the testimony of witnesses, from five minutes to fifteen minutes, during which time Boyer, as agent of James M. Welch, sold the land for $1200 to Wilcox, as agent for George K. Welch. There was a conflict of evidence as to whether the sale was cried loud enough to have been heard by one approaching the barn from the house, and also as to whether Boyer and Wilcox remained seated in the sleigh by which they had come upon the premises, or whether they descended and stood upon the ground. While they were upon the premises Emerson came out of his house and ordered them away; they thereupon retired, leaving him still in possession. George K. Welch, the purchaser at this sale, with A. I. Wilcox, to whom Welch, by deed dated 11 June, 1879, conveyed the undivided one-half part of the land in controversy, then brought this action of ejectment to recover possession from Emerson.

The Court directed a special verdict for plaintiffs, finding the facts as above stated, and reserving these questions: "If the Court be of the opinion, upon these facts, that a mere going upon the premises in pursuance of such notice is a sufficient taking possession by the vendor under the contract, that it was made by the proper person and at the proper time to enable the vendor to extinguish the vendee's equity, then we find for the plaintiff the land described in the writ. If the Court be of opinion that such entry was not a sufficient taking of such possession, or that it was not made by a proper person, or at the proper time, then we find for the plaintiff the land described in the writ, to be set aside and entered for the defendant on the payment of the sum of one thousand and eighty-six dollars and forty cents, within thirty days from entry of judgment herein.

The Court subsequently entered judgment for the plaintiff to be set aside and entered for the defendant upon payment made by the latter within thirty days, as provided in the special verdict. WILLIAMS, P. J., delivered the opinion of the Court, after reviewing the facts of the case, as follows: "The question raised by the special verdict is whether he (the plaintiff) shall recover, according to the terms of the contract of 3d November, 1872, a conditional verdict for the possession, to be released on payment of the purchase-money; or, adversely and absolutely. This depends upon the construction to be given to the clause in the contract under which this proceeding was had, and the effect of what was done on the premises on the 17th and 19th days of February, 1879. The contract of November 3d, 1872, was a contract of sale which vested an equitable title to the land described therein in Emerson, the vendee. He went into possession under this contract. Now, the law provides two well-defined methods by which such an equity may be extinguished,—an action of ejectment to compel specific execution of the agreement, and a sale by the sheriff upon a judgment obtained for the purchase-money. But the parties to this contract sought to provide still another method, and one that might be made use of by the vendor himself without the necessity of recourse to the machinery of the Courts. They accordingly provided, in express terms, that on failure by the vendee to make the payments, the vendor should "have the right and privilege to take possession of the premises and sell the same to any other person on a notice given to the said Emerson of twenty-four hours." Upon failure by the vendee to make the payments, the vendor had an election of remedies. He might proceed upon his contract in the Courts, or he might proceed by his own act to "take possession of the premises." If he chose his remedy at law, the law would extinguish the equity of the vendee and put him back into possession. If he chose the remedy provided for his own enforcement, he could retake the possession and so extinguish the vendee's equity. Being in possession and holding the title, he might of course sell, and "to any other person," just as he could have sold if this contract had never been made. But so summary a mode of extinguishing the equity is relieved by the provision that this proceeding should be had only "on a notice being given to Emerson of twenty-four hours." Of what is Emerson to have this notice of twenty-four hours? The plaintiff says, of the time and place of sale. But suppose the vendor does not choose to sell. Having exercised his "right and privilege to take possession of the premises," he may choose to remain in possession and occupy them himself. Holding the legal title, he enters upon the land and ousts the holder of the equity, in accordance with the provisions of the contract. He thereby becomes the holder of the equity which his vendee acquired under the contract. The legal and equitable titles are united in him, and the vendee's equity is extinguished. Having thus the title and the possession, he may never sell, the land may descend to his heirs like any other land held in fee simple.

We think it more reasonable to construe this clause as requiring a twenty-four hours notice of the intent to adopt this remedy. The vendee is in possession, he has not paid the purchase-money, the vendor elects to take the mode provided by this clause in the contract. He must give his vendee twenty-four hours notice that he intends to "take possession of the premises" and so oust him and extinguish his equity. If, within the twenty-four hours, the vendee pays the purchase-money, the right of the vendor to "take possession of the premises" is gone and the title of the vendee saved. If he does not pay the purchase-money, his days of grace are gone, and the vendor may come and "take possession of the premises," and so end the contract and the equitable title created by it.

But, suppose the notice to be served in accordance with our construction of the contract, what must the vendor do, in order to entitle himself to the benefit of this remedy? We reply, in the language of the contract, he must "take possession of the premises." A mere going on the land for a few moments is not enough. The "possession of the premises" must be taken by the vendor—it must be an actual visible possession, an ouster of the vendee. But, it is argued, such a construction of this contract puts it in the power of the vendee to defeat his vendor by a successful resistance of the effort to take possession. What effect forcible resistance to an actual effort to "take possession of the premises," might have upon the rights of the vendor, it is not now necessary to determine. The special verdict finds that the plaintiff made an entry, merely, upon the premises. The evidence showed that he drove upon the land, near the barn, and after a few moments drove away again. No effort was made to take actual possession; and, without such an effort forcibly resisted, the question suggested is not raised.

The real position of the plaintiff is, after all, this: That the entry upon the premises and sale made by Boyer to Wilcox, as agent of the plaintiff, Welch, extinguished Emerson's equity, though he was left in actual possession. The equity being thus extinguished, this action of ejectment is brought to obtain the possession, and the plaintiff insists that the defendant cannot reply his contract in defence of his possession, because the rights acquired under it were divested by the entry and sale. The reply to this seems to be, that the contract provided for no such means of divesting the vendee's title. The words of this clause, "shall have the right and privilege to take possession of the premises," contemplated an actual taking of possession. The vendee did not agree that an entry upon any part of the premises should divest his title, nor that, upon notice that the possession was wanted or claimed by the vendor, his right to the possession should be at an end. He did agree, however, that if he failed to pay, the vendor need not wait for the law to give him back the possession, but might come and take it. That such stipulations are capable of enforcement, when it can be done without a breach of the peace, has been frequently held. Such, in effect, is the ruling in Rich v. Keyser (4 P. F. S. 86), and in Overdeer v. Lewis (1 W. & S. 90). If it cannot be done without a breach of the peace, by reason of the vendee's resistance, the remedy is, probably, by action upon the covenant, to recover damages for its breach, as in any other case of breach of covenant (Rich v. Keyser, supra). But, our question does not reach the case of forcible resistance. It is, in substance, whether an entry upon land of which the defendant remains in the peaceable and undisputed possession, is taking "possession of the premises" in accordance with the terms of the contract of 3d November, 1872. We have sufficiently indicated the construction which we put upon the contract, and our opinion that the vendor did not avail himself of his "right and privilege to take possession of the premises." It then follows that the vendee, being called upon, by this action of ejectment, to defend his possession, may do so under the contract of sale.

The plaintiffs then took this writ, and assigned as error the entry of judgment upon the special verdict, as above mentioned.

J. R. Clark and *C. H. Noyes* (with whom were *A. G. Olmstead* and *C. B. Curtis*), for plaintiffs in error.

There is no question that what has been done, upon the part of the plaintiffs, was done by the proper person and after proper notice; the only doubt is, whether this was sufficient to extinguish the defendant's equity. The parties to the agreement intended, by the clause as to re-entry, that in case the vendee failed to pay the purchase-money as he had agreed, and continued to do so after notice, then they should occupy respectively the positions occupied by them before the contract, and that the vendor might take possession and sell to any other person. This would leave no equity in the vendee; its effect would be the same as if the parties had agreed that, in such case, the contract should be totally rescinded.

This vendee received twenty-four hours notice, the period of grace provided by his own agreement, instead of the time that might have been granted him by a court of equity or allowed him by a jury. When he permitted this time to pass by without making payment, his equity expired, because he had so agreed.

Stone v. Sprague, 20 Barb. (N. Y.) 509.

Specific performance is matter of equitable discretion when demanded by one who himself is in default.

Miller v. Henlan, 1 Sm. 265.

The right to take possession, without more, is perhaps not inconsistent with the vendee's equity. The vendor has this right after default by the vendee, without special agreement, and, if he exercises it, the latter may tender payment and demand performance. It may be doubted whether mere possession obtained under this clause in the agreement would extinguish the vendee's equity.

Youst v. Martin, 3 S. &. R 432.

But the right to sell to any other person, is plainly inconsistent with any such equity. Its exercise implies complete termination of the vendee's rights.

Berry & Elliott (with whom were *N. B. Smiley, David Sterrett,* and *W. M. Boggs*), for defendant in error.

In order to divest the defendant of his title under the provision of re-entry contained in the contract, everything thereby required to be done by the vendor must be performed with exactness. This clause required the vendor, besides giving the vendee notice of his intention to re-enter, to take actual possession of the land and to turn the vendee out. A mere going upon the land, without disturbing or attempting to disturb the defendant, who was occupying the same, cannot be such a taking possession as was contemplated by this contract. Nor can it be maintained that giving notice of an intention to perform an act is equivalent to performance of the act itself.

Neither the vendor nor his assignee had a right, under the facts in this case, to take possession of the land in February, 1879, and to sell it, under the provision in the contract. The vendor had such a right at the time when the payments fell due; but as he gave the vendee no notice of his intention to exercise it until nearly a year after the last payment fell due, he thereby waived his right to proceed under that provision in the contract.

Oct. 4, 1880. THE COURT. We concur in opinion with the learned Judge in the Court below, that, upon the special finding of the jury, the equity of the defendant was not extinguished, and that he was entitled to a conditional verdict in his favor. The vendor undertook, it would seem, to provide a summary remedy for himself, and he must not be disappointed if he is required strictly to pursue the course prescribed. The jury have found that there was a mere going upon the premises, and a sale in pursuance of the notice. Surely this was not a "taking possession" according to the terms of the contract.

But really the clause in the article gave the vendor no right or remedy which he did not possess without it. It is horn-book law that the legal owner can take possession if he can do so without a breach of the peace. If an action of trespass is brought against him, he can justify under the plea of *liberum tenementum*. He cannot be dispossessed by an ejectment except by some one suing on a better title. If it be, as in this instance, a vendor who has regained possession peaceably, his vendee can eject him only by showing that he has paid the purchase-money and has a right to call for a conveyance. What was there in the clause of the article in question to show that it was intended by the parties that the equity of the vendee should be entirely extinguished and gone? Nobody doubts that the vendor could maintain ejectment on his legal title without any formal entry or taking possession. The learned counsel for the plaintiff in error very candidly concedes that it may be doubted whether possession obtained under this clause in the agreement would extinguish the vendee's equity. There can be no doubt, that, if the vendor had recovered in ejectment and been placed in possession by the sheriff, the equity of the vendee would not be affected. He would still have a right to recover back the possession upon tender or payment of the whole purchase-money unless a conditional verdict, taking the place of a decree in equity, had limited a time for its payment. The recovery in ejectment by the mortgagee certainly does not foreclose the mortgage and extinguish the equity of redemption. Neither does the recovery by the vendor. But the learned counsel contend that the right after taking possession to sell to any other person, is plainly inconsistent with any equity to the vendee. Why so? The article does not expressly say nor necessarily imply that the sale shall be discharged of the equity, and ought we to import such a provision into the contract without some word on which to found it? We have seen that the bare agreement that he should take possession gave the vendor no right he did not possess without it; why then should the agreement that he might sell to any other be construed to give him any power which he did not possess before? He might without it have sold his legal title. What is there in the contract which says he shall do more? The purchaser took with notice of the defendant's equity, and, of course, subject to it.

Judgment affirmed.

Opinion by SHARSWOOD, C. J. PAXSON, J., absent.

May, '80, 119.   June 8, 1880.

County of Luzerne v. Trimmer.

Contested election—Emoluments pending contest—Certiorari—Effect of—Act of July 2, 1839.

Pending a contested election of a county officer, and until its final determination on the merits, the fees belong to the last incumbent.

The decision of the Common Pleas in a contested election, on the merits, is final. A certiorari to the Supreme Court brings up only the record, and if its regularity is affirmed, the decision of the Court below takes effect from its date.

A commission issued to a county officer pending a contest of his election is irregular, but not void. Upon the determination of the contest in his favor the commission takes effect. No second commission is necessary.

B. was elected prothonotary, and his election was contested. Pending the contest a commission was issued to him. The Common Pleas dismissed the contesting petition on June 30, 1877, and, on certiorari, the decree of the Court below was affirmed March 25, 1878. In a proceeding by the previous incumbent to recover from the county the fees of office, paid into the County treasury, pending the contest, and until the date of the decision of the Supreme Court:

Held, that the decision of the Court below, on June 30, 1877, was final, on the merits, and that the plaintiff was not entitled to any fees after that date.

In re Contested Election of Barber, 5 Nor. 392; S. C., 5 WEEKLY NOTES, 350, explained.

Error to the Common Pleas of Columbia County. The suit was originally brought in Luzerne County, and the venue was changed to Columbia County.

Assumpsit. Case stated, between S. W. Trimmer, plaintiff, and The County of Luzerne, defendant, setting forth the following facts: In 1873, the plaintiff was duly elected and commissioned prothonotary of the county of Luzerne, to hold office until the first Monday of January, 1877, and until his successor should be duly qualified. In November, 1876, his successor, A. P. Barber, was elected; and, on December 7, 1876, the thirtieth day after the election, was commissioned. On December 6th, the twenty-ninth day after the election, a petition contesting his election was filed; which was dismissed by the Court of Common Pleas, on June 30, 1877.

On January 3, 1877, a writ of quo warranto was issued against Trimmer, at the suggestion of Barber; on the same day, judgment of ouster was entered thereon, and Trimmer was removed from the office and Barber placed therein. On March 25, 1878, the judgment in the quo warranto was reversed by the Supreme Court, and upon the same date the decree in the contested election case, on certiorari, was affirmed. (See 5 Nor. 392.)

Between January 3, 1877, and March 25, 1878, Barber, while acting as prothonotary, collected and paid into the county treasury, $26,569.12, and the county paid out of the treasury for the current expenses of the said office, clerk hire and salary of the prothonotary, $15,800.27.

After the decision of the Supreme Court on March 25, 1878, reversing the judgment of ouster, viz., on April 12, 1878, Trimmer demanded, from the county of Luzerne, the fees of the office, between Jan. 3, 1877, and March 25, 1878, which demand being refused this action and case stated was brought.

If the Court be of opinion that the plaintiff is entitled to the said fees, or any part thereof, judgment to be entered for the plaintiff; otherwise judgment for the defendant.

The Court held, that Trimmer was entitled, under the law, to fifty per cent. of that portion of the fees collected by Barber and paid into the county treasury, over and above the amount paid out of the treasury for current expenses of the office, between January 3, 1877, and March 25, 1878 (the date of the final decree of the Supreme Court), with interest, and the Court entered judgment in his favor for $5956.50, with costs.

The county took this writ, assigning for error the judgment of the Court, in holding that the plaintiff was entitled to any fees after June 30, 1877, the date of the determination of the contested election by the Common Pleas.

Thomas H. Atherton (with him *Allan H. Dickson* and *Henry W. Palmer*, Attorney General), for the plaintiff in error.

The decision made by the Court of Common Pleas on June 30, 1877, was final. The certiorari merely brought up the record, to determine whether the proceedings were had before competent authority and in proper form.

Act of July 2, 1839, P. L. 566; Purd. Dig. 1181, pl. 68.

Ewing *v.* Thompson, 7 Wr. 372.

Election Cases, 15 Sm. 20.

The commission issued to Barber pending the contest was not void; the right to the office under the same was merely suspended, and the commission simply did not take effect until the legal qualification of the plaintiff's successor, which was, at the latest, on June 30, 1877.

Act of July 2, 1839, § 3, *supra*.

In re Election of A. P. Barber, 5 Nor. 392; s. c., 5 WEEKLY NOTES, 350.

Ewing *v.* Thompson, *supra*.

John Lynch and *C. R. Buckalew*, for the defendant in error.

The effect of the certiorari was to suspend all claims and all action under the decree of June 30, 1877, until the final decision of the Supreme Court, in March, 1878. Until then the contest was "pending," and the plaintiff is entitled to fees until that date.

Ewing v. Thompson, *supra*, per WOODWARD, J.

The Act of July 2, 1839, provides that no commission shall issue within thirty days after the election, nor pending a contest for the office. The commission to the plaintiff's successor was, therefore, null and void.

In re Contested Election of Barber, *supra*.
Cromelien *v.* Brink, 5 Casey, 522.
Marks's Ex'rs *v.* Russell, 4 Wr. 372.
In re Election of A. P. Barber, *supra*.
Mayfield *v.* Moore, Bright. El. Cas. 605.

October 4, 1880. THE COURT. The right of the defendant in error to the emoluments of the office ended when it was judicially decided that Barber was duly elected and entitled to the office. The decision in favor of Barber was made by the Court of Common Pleas on the 30th June, 1877. Inasmuch, however, as a certiorari was taken to that judgment, and it was not affirmed in this Court until the 25th March, 1878, the learned Judge held the defendant in error entitled to the emoluments of the office until the latter date. In so holding there was error. Due effect was not thereby given to the judgment of the 30th June, 1877. The merits of that decision were not reviewed in this Court. The certiorari brought up the record only. Although our affirmance of the decree was on the 25th March, 1878, yet the effect thereof was to confirm the decree as of the 30th June, 1877. That was the final decree on the merits of the controversy. (Election Cases, 15 P. F. Smith, 20.) Barber was thereby declared to be the prothonotary *de jure*. Thenceforth the defendant in error was merely an officer *de facto*. His acts were good as to third persons who have an interest in the act done, but he could not recover the fees given for the official services. (Riddle *v.* County of Bedford, 7 S. & R. 387; Commonwealth *ex rel.* Bowman *v.* Slifer, 1 Casey, 23.)

It is contended that Barber was not duly qualified when the decree of the 30th June was made in his favor. This argument rests on the fact that the Act of Assembly declares no commission shall issue within thirty days after the election, nor pending a contest for the office. The petition contesting his election was filed on the twenty-ninth day thereafter, and, without notice thereof, the Governor issued the commission on the thirtieth day after the election. It is therefore urged that the commission was wholly invalid, under the authority of *In re* Contested Election of Barber (5 Norris, 392). Such an inference might be drawn from the generality of the language used in that case. It should, however, be interpreted in view of the question then presented. The contention was whether the effect of the commission was such as to authorize Barber to take possession of the office, and to hold the same during the pendency of the contest. It was held to give no such power. It issued irregularly, but was not void. Its operative power was suspended during the pendency of the contest. When it was decided that Barber was entitled to the office, then the commission took effect. No second commission was necessary. This conclusion is in harmony with that part of the third section of the Act of 2d July, 1839 (Purd. Dig. 1181), which declares, when a commission is suspended by reason of a contest, it shall take effect from the time of the legal qualification of the officer under the same. To the same effect is Ewing *v.* Thompson (7 Wright, 372). In case the defendant in error had yielded up the office to Barber at the time the Court decided in favor of the latter, his right thereto would have been clear. He had taken the oath of office, and held a commission from the only authority competent to issue it. The defendant in error is not entitled to recover any portion of the fees after the 30th June, 1877. The learned Judge therefore erred in entering judgment for any fees received after that date. It must therefore be modified so far as to give the defendant in error a judgment for the sum of two thousand six hundred and eighty-seven dollars and ninety cents, with interest from the time payment was demanded.

And now, to wit, October 4, 1880, judgment reversed and set aside, and judgment is hereby entered in favor of the defendant in error for $3087.50, as of this date.

Opinion by MERCUR, J.

Common Pleas—Equity.

C. P. No. 1.   Oct. 30, 1880.

Albrecht v. Lane et al.
Garretson v. Same.
Stoesslein et al. v. Same.

Equity—Injunction—Bill to restrain the collection of taxes—Billiard tables—The Recorder of Philadelphia has no jurisdiction of a suit to collect the license fees upon billiard tables—Acts of April 18, 1878, and April 14, 1851.

Motion for preliminary injunctions.

These were bills in equity against David H. Lane, Recorder, John G. Franklin, Deputy Recorder, and Joseph G. Martin, Treasurer of the City of Philadelphia, to restrain defendants from issuing execution on a judgment for the tax upon certain pool tables owned by complainants.

The bills set forth that suits had been brought against complainants by the City Treasurer before the Recorder and Deputy Recorder, for non-payment of licenses for keeping billiard rooms, under the Act of April 14, 1851 (P. L. 570, Purd. Dig. 729), wherein judgments had been obtained for the amount of the license fee and cost of suit, and that executions therefor were about to issue; that complainants were licensed tavern keepers, and kept in their saloons, for the gratuitous amusement of guests, tables upon which was played a game called "pool;" that such tables were known as "pool tables" and not as "billiard tables," and were of different construction from the latter; that the game of pool was dissimilar to the game of billiards; wherefore complainants were not bound to pay a license as if for keeping a billiard saloon, under the Act of April 14, 1851. They further set forth that the Recorder had no jurisdiction of suits for the non-payment of licenses for keeping billiard saloons, and no authority to demand costs; that the Recorder would not allow complainants to appeal from the judgments aforesaid without prepayment of costs; and that the Act of April 18, 1878 (P. L. 26), investing the Recorder with judicial authority, is unconstitutional.

The bills prayed that the judgments aforesaid be declared null and void; that an injunction be granted to restrain defendants from issuing execution as aforesaid; and that Sections 6 and 7 of the Act of April 18, 1878 (P. L. 26), entitled "An Act to define the term of office and enlarge the duties of Recorders of cities of the first class," be declared unconstitutional, null, and void.

Joseph T. Ford, for the motion.

The Recorder has no legal authority to demand costs. In this case, he has followed the schedule of fees allowed to aldermen of Philadelphia by the Act of Feb. 3, 1868 (P. L. 62); for which he has no authority. The statute not having fixed the amount of his fees, the complainants cannot offer a "legal fee."

The Act of April 18, 1878 (P. L. 26), gives the Recorder jurisdiction in suits for the non-payment of tavern and mercantile licenses. The tax upon billiard tables is not such a tax. The Act of April 14, 1851 (P. L. 570), established the tax upon billiard tables, and provided that it should be collected as in the case of tavern licenses. At that time, tavern licenses were collected by suit before an alderman or a justice of the peace, according to Section 9 of the Act of April 16, 1849 (P. L. 660) and Section 2 of the Act of March 4, 1824 (P. L. 33). The suits should have been brought before a magistrate, since magistrates in the city of Philadelphia have succeeded to the office and duties of aldermen.

Sections 6 and 7 of the Act of April 18, 1878, in effect create another Court with such powers as are vested by the Constitution in the Courts of Common Pleas. They are therefore contrary to Sections 1 and 26 of Article V. of the Constitution.

Brewster, contra.

The Act is constitutional, the Legislature having power to provide for the collection of taxes in any way it deems proper, and the tax-payer is not thereby deprived of his right to trial by jury. The collection of a tax will not be enjoined unless there is clearly no authority for its levy.

Campbell *v.* Campbell, 26 Leg. Int. 261.
Lackawana Coal Co. *v.* Osterhout, 2 Luz. L. Obs. 84.
Gorrell *v.* Murphy, 1 Leg. Gaz. R. 495.
Crist *v.* Morris, 2 W. N. C. 620.
Wharton *v.* Directors, 6 Wright, 358.
St. Clair School Board's Ap., 24 Sm. 252.
Truesdell's Appeal, 8 Sm. 148.
Livingston *v.* Moore, 7 Peters U. S. 478.
Smith *v.* Nicholson, 4 Yeates, 6.

The complainants cannot evade payment of the tax by a fine-drawn distinction between pool tables and billiard tables. In the technical language of billiard players "pool" is a different game from "billiards," but a pool table is a billiard table, within the meaning of the Act. There are several kinds of games of billiards, some of which are played on the same tables on which pool is played.

Nov. 6, 1880. THE COURT. We take a view of this case which makes it unnecessary for us to decide whether Sections 6 and 7 of the Act of April 18, 1878 (P. L. 28), are constitutional or not. Neither do we undertake to say that a pool table is or is not identical with a billiard table. We hold that, in any event, the Recorder has no jurisdiction. According to the Act of April 14, 1851 (P. L. 570), billiard licenses are to be collected in the same manner as tavern licenses were then collected. The Act of April 16, 1849 (P. L. 660), provides that tavern licenses shall be collected in the same manner as the duty upon retailers of foreign merchandise. By Act of March 4, 1824 (P. L. 33), the duty upon retailers of foreign merchandise was collected by suit before an alderman or justice of the peace. In Philadelphia County, magistrates have succeeded to the office and duties of aldermen. Suit to collect this tax should therefore have been brought before a magistrate.

Injunction granted.

Oral opinion by PEIRCE, J.

Common Pleas—Law.

C. P. No. 2.   Dec. 13, 1880.
Schassberger v. Staendel et al.

Equity — Unincorporated associations — Beneficial society — Rights over members — Provisions in Constitution and by-laws for trial of member should be strictly followed — Right to fine or expel, given by a clause of the Constitution, does not include right to suspend.

Sur exceptions to Master's report.

Bill in equity, filed by Schassberger (who died pending the suit, and for whom his executrix was substituted) against Staendel, secretary, and Pancker, treasurer of the Arbeiter Unterstutzungs Verein, No. 2, an unincorporated beneficial society, setting forth: That the defendants were officers of said Verein, and the plaintiff, a member thereof, had always paid his dues; that he was sick during a long time, and entitled to sick benefits at the rate of $4 per week, but that the association and its officers had refused to pay him the said allowance; and prayed a decree that the treasurer pay the same to the plaintiff.

The defendants answered, setting up that, believing the plaintiff was imposing upon it, the association caused an investigation to be made in accordance with the following provisions of its Constitution and by-laws:*—

CONSTITUTION.—Art. III. § 3. The association reserves the right to expel members for immoral conduct. In order to expel a member a charge must be made in writing, which must be referred to an investigating committee. Said committee must consist of 12 members and 3 substitutes, who must be drawn by lot. If a majority of the committee shall be of the opinion that the member shall be expelled, they shall report the same to the association for their action. The order to expel a member shall only be legal when two-thirds of the members present vote to that effect.

BY-LAWS.—Art. III. A sick member, who is caught working before he has reported himself well, shall be fined not less than $3, and not more than $30, or be proceeded against according to Art. III. § 3 of the Constitution.

Further, that in accordance therewith it suspended the plaintiff from membership for two years, during which time the benefits claimed accrued.

The matter was referred to an examiner and master. The master found that the charge against the plaintiff was that of receiving sick benefits when able to work, and actually working; that in point of fact the plaintiff was very sick, and that the "work" alleged consisted in such trifling acts of assistance to others as not to fall within the meaning of the Constitution of the association. That the trial alleged in the answer was conducted by members not chosen by lot, but elected by the association, that the accused was not confronted with the only witness examined, but was called in after the testimony closed, and asked what he had to say, and that no opportunity of appeal to the society at large was given.

The master further reported, as matter of law, that the power to expel or fine given by the Constitution did not include the power to suspend, that the so-called trial or investigation was void for its irregularity, and that the plaintiff was not guilty of fraud on the association; and reported a decree for plaintiff for the amount of benefits at the rate of $4 per week to the date of Schassberger's death, to be paid out of present or future funds of the Verein.

The defendants excepted.

C. Davis, for exceptions.

The power to expel implies the power to suspend, on the principle that the greater includes the less. It was an act of mercy in the Verein not to expel Schassberger. Even if the proceedings were irregular, the evidence shows Schassberger guilty.

Staendel, the secretary, should not have been joined; the bill should have been solely against the treasurer, who, as custodian of the funds, is alone liable under the Act of April 28, 1876 (P. L. 53).

[MITCHELL, J. There is no decree asked against the secretary.]

H. Budd, Jr., contra.

HARE, P. J. The quasi-judicial powers of associations like this should be exercised in exact conformity to law. The proceedings in this case were irregular in several respects. The power to expel cannot justly be held to include a power to suspend, for the latter might work great injustice, by depriving a member of the right to benefits while leaving him subject to the payment of dues, etc.

THE COURT. Exceptions dismissed, and decree for complainant.

C. P. No. 3.   Dec. 21, 1880.
Mills v. Slook.

New trial — Lunacy — Scire facias sur mortgage — Effect of subsequent inquisition finding that at the time of the execution of the mortgage the mortgagor was a lunatic — Want of notice and absence of fraud.

Rule for a new trial.

Scire facias sur mortgage.

On the trial, the defence was insanity. The

---

* The Constitution and by-laws are in the German language. The extract here given is a translation.

plaintiff put in evidence a mortgage by defendant to him, dated Dec. 22, 1874, and duly recorded, and rested. The defendant then offered in evidence, as conclusive proof of the defendant's incapacity to execute the mortgage, the record of proceedings in lunacy begun to Dec. term 1874, whereby the defendant was found to have been a lunatic without lucid intervals from March 3, 1871. Objection being made to the offer, the evidence was excluded. Defendant then offered to prove that the appearance, actions, and conduct of defendant, at the time offered execution of the instrument, were such as to put a prudent man upon inquiry and guard. Objected to and excluded.

The Court charged the jury that it was incumbent upon defendant to show fraud, or notice to plaintiff of defendant's mental incapacity at the time of execution of the mortgage, before other evidence of defendant's mental unsoundness can be admitted; and defendant having failed to do this, the verdict should be for plaintiff. Verdict accordingly for $3821, the amount of the mortgage with interest.

This rule having been obtained—

W. J. Budd showed cause.

The inquisition is but *prima facie* evidence of insanity, and is not conclusive. They were bound to show fraud on our part, or bring home to us notice of defendant's incapacity.

Kneedler's Appeal, 8 WEEKLY NOTES, 97.

Husbands, contra.

Our offer to avoid the mortgage by showing that defendant was *non compos mentis* at the time of its execution, should have been admitted.

Bensell *v.* Chancellor, 5 Wharton, 371.
Bank *v.* Moore, 28 Sm. 407.

C. A. V.

Dec. 23, 1880. THE COURT. Rule absolute.

Orphans' Court.

Dec. 21, 1880.

Davis's Estate.

Partition—Jurisdiction of Orphans' Court to determine questions of kinship—Requisites of an answer.

Sur petition for partition and answer, and exceptions to answer.

The petition of certain heirs of Eliza T. Davis, deceased, set forth:—

That the decedent died intestate on or about August 15, 1880, seised in fee of certain real estate in the City of Philadelphia, leaving to survive her as her heirs and next of kin, children, and uncles and aunts of the whole blood and of the half blood. The petitioners prayed for an inquest to make partition.

Elizabeth D. Kiegel, a niece of decedent, filed an answer to the petition, of which the following is the material portion: "While this respondent cannot directly deny that the persons named as petitioners in the said petition as heirs at law and next of kin are such, nevertheless she does not in any wise admit such relationship to the said decedent as is therein set forth, or any other relationship whatever of the said parties or any o them. This respondent, though well acquainted with the said decedent in her lifetime, has no knowledge whatsoever of the relationship of the said persons or any of them, nor did she so much as hear of their claim of such relationship, or even of their existence, until very recently; and she prays that all the allegations in the petition may be strictly proved."

The respondent also suggested that the Court had no jurisdiction to try the question of title to real estate, or make partition thereof among claimants thereto when the title of any of them is in dispute.

To this answer the petitioners filed exceptions.

Gormley and *Thorn*, for petitioners.

In this case it is conceded that the estate is the estate of the decedent. The only question is: "Who are the heirs at law?" The power of the Court to decide who are the heirs of a decedent entitled to the real estate is commensurate with its power to decide who are the distributees of the personal estate.

McBride's Appeal, 22 S. 484.
Braman's Appeal, 7 WEEKLY NOTES, 304.
In re Snyder's Appeal, 12 Casey, 166.
Herr *et al. v.* Herr, 5 Barr, 428.
Merklein *v.* Trapnell, 10 Casey, 42.

The cases of *In re* Eell's Estate (6 Barr, 457), Flaherty's Estate (5 Phila. 477), and McMasters *v.* Carothers (1 Barr, 324), have no application to the present case. To bring herself within these authorities the respondent must disclaim her interest as heir and make herself a stranger by setting up an adverse title.

Mehaffy *v.* Dobbs, 9 Watts, 363.

The answer is insufficient because it neither traverses nor confesses and avoids the petition. The respondent does not state the facts contained in the answer on her information and belief. She simply denies any knowledge of the relationship of the petitioners to the decedent. This is not sufficient to put the petitioners to proof.

E. F. Pugh, contra, as to the jurisdiction of the Court, cited—

Eell's Estate, 6 Barr, 457.
Flaherty's Estate, 5 Phila. 477.

McMasters's Appeal, 1 Barr, 324.
The respondent is not bound to admit, deny, or state her belief, since she asserts her ignorance of the subject.
Morris *v.* Parker, 1 Johns. Ch. 297.
Norton *v.* Warner, 3 Edw. Ch. 106.
Amhurst *v.* King, 2 Sim. & St. 183.
Utica Ins. Co. *v.* Lynch, 3 Paige, 210.

Dec. 27, 1880. THE COURT. The jurisdiction of the Orphans' Court in partition is confined to cases in which the decedent died seised of the estate in respect of which it is asked. If, therefore, his ownership is denied, if a holding adverse to him is set up, it necessarily follows that his title must first be established at law, before further proceedings can be had here. (Eell's Estate, 6 Barr, 457; McMasters *v.* Carothers, 1 Barr, 324.)

But a very different case is presented where his seisin is admitted, and all that is questioned is whether the person asking for partition is or is not an heir. There is no reason to deny the jurisdiction of the Court upon this point. The right "to determine any question of kindred" is among the powers expressly conferred upon the Register's Court (which have now passed to the Orphans' Court) by the Act of 15th March, 1832, § 25. The power to decide all questions necessary to a proper distribution of a fund, said Judge LEWIS in Kittera's Estate (5 Harris, 416), "follows the power of distribution in the Orphans' Court as a necessary incident to its jurisdiction. That Court is as competent to determine all questions of *law* as the Common Pleas . . . and it has ample power to send an issue to the Common Pleas for the trial of facts by the jury.'

This, it is true, was said with reference to a distribution of personal estate; but the same section of the same Act, which gives the Court the right "to make distribution of the assets of the estates of decedents," confers in equally explicit terms the right "to make partition of the real estate of intestates among the heirs." (Act of 16th June, 1836, § 19, P. L. 792.)

The method of determining the question of kindred must be the same in either case, and it is not easy to conceive why the power should exist in one case and be denied in the other. The power to make partition, equally with the power to make distribution, under the maxim *quando aliqua mandatur, mandatur et omne per quod ad id pervenitur*, implies a power to decide all questions necessary to a proper division and distribution. To hold otherwise would enable any one of the heirs to oust the jurisdiction expressly given by the statute, and which, until the Act of 21st of April, 1846, was, in cases of intestacy, exclusive.

A very different view with regard to the authority and jurisdiction of the Orphans' Court is held now from that entertained so lately even as the date of some of Chief Justice TILGHMAN's decisions. (Seider *v.* Seider, 5 Whart. 208; Thomas *v.* Simpson, 3 Barr, 60.) "It was not until the able and exhaustive opinion of Judge DUNCAN, delivered in 1824, in McPherson *v.* Cunliff (11 S. & R. 422)," says Judge AGNEW in Mussleman's Appeal (15 Smith, 485), "which settled the proper position of the Orphans' Court, that it reached its true dignity, and the way was prepared for the revision of the Orphans' Court system, its jurisdiction, powers and practice, contained in the Acts of 29th March, 1832, 24th February, 1834, and 16th June, 1836. Under these laws, the Orphans' Court came up to the full measure of a Court of record, standing upon an equality with the others. At first the true extent of the work was not perceived, especially by those who disliked to unlearn what they knew, and who took with difficulty to a new system. But its powers have grown clearer to the professional vision, as its utility increased in appreciation."

Accordingly, it was declared in Dundas's Estate (23 Smith, 474) that the "Orphans' Court, in a proceeding to distribute an estate among legatees, next of kin *and heirs*, has ample power to inquire into and determine *all* questions standing directly in the way of a distribution to these parties." (See also Otterson *v.* Gallagher, 7 Norris, 355.)

We have no doubt, therefore, as to our power to determine any dispute upon the question of heirship in the case now before us.

But is there "a dispute"? The respondent makes no claim to hold adversely or to the exclusion of the other heirs of the decedent. She even "cannot directly deny" the right of the other parties to the proceeding. All that she avers is that she has no *knowledge* of their relationship, and that, "until very recently," she had never heard of their existence; and she wholly omits to state her *belief* on the subject.

This neither traverses, nor confesses and avoids the allegations of the petition. It is text-book law that one who undertakes to answer a bill or petition, at all, must answer fully. The answer must confess and avoid, deny or traverse all the material parts of the bill or petition. The respondent must answer not only as to his knowledge and information, but also as to his belief. And while it is not essential that the precise words "knowledge, information, and belief" should be used, some equivalent expression is required. (Story's Eq. Pl., § 854; Utica Insurance Co. *v.* Lynch, 3 Paige, 210; Morris *v.* Parker, 3 Johns. Ch. R. 297; 2 Daniell's Ch. Pr. 256; Amhurst *v.* King, 2 Sim. & Stu. 183.)

The answer is clearly insufficient in this respect. If the relationship is admitted, as set forth in the petition, we shall be in a position to consider the rights of the half blood. If it should be traversed, we can appoint an examiner, or, if necessary, award an issue.

It may be well to remark that the records of the court show that the relationship of these parties to the decedent was fully established upon testimony produced, and not contradicted, upon the proceedings on the account filed by the respondent as administratrix ; and that the decree of distribution based thereon was not excepted to or appealed from. How far such decree will be conclusive between the same parties in any other proceeding, is a question which is not now before us. It is at least probable that upon the question of costs, should the proceedings assume such a shape as to require the same facts to be re-established, it may have a very material bearing.

The exceptions to the answer are sustained, leave being given to file a sufficient answer on or before January 6, 1881, otherwise the petition to be taken *pro confesso*.

Opinion by PENROSE, J.

December 21, 1880.

Fell's Estate.

Decedents' estates — Jurisdiction — Land purchased by an executor on the foreclosure of a mortgage held by the decedent is treated, for purposes of distribution, as personal property— The Orphans' Court has jurisdiction to confirm a sale of real estate purchased on foreclosure of a mortgage and subsequently sold by an executor—Relief will be afforded where the Court has jurisdiction over the subject matter, notwithstanding the use of inappropriate terms in the petition.

Sur exceptions to Master's report.

The petition of the executors of J. Gillingham Fell, deceased, set forth that the decedent had died, seised of an equitable interest in two certain mortgages made by one Stewardson to James A. McCrea, to secure certain loans made by the decedent together with A. E. Borie, Charles L. Borie, and others to said Stewardson. By his will the equitable interest of the decedent in these mortgages passed to his executors. The mortgages were foreclosed, and the properties purchased by C. L. Borie. After this purchase Borie entered into an agreement with the petitioner and other equitable owners, by which he was to sell the property purchased by him as aforesaid, and, after deducting the costs incurred by him at the sheriff's sale, to divide the purchase money, in proportion to their respective interests in the mortgages foreclosed, between the executors of the decedent and the other creditors of the mortgagor who were equitably interested in the mortgage.

A sale was effected and a good price obtained, but the purchaser refused to take title unless the Orphans' Court would authorize the executors of the decedent to join in a conveyance of their interest. The executors then petitioned the Orphans' Court, setting forth the facts recited, and also that, the decedent having died within five years, his real estate was subject to the lien of his debts not of record, and prayed the Court for leave to join the other parties in interest in a sale and conveyance of the premises in question.

The petition was referred to an Examiner and Master, who reported that the sale was a desirable one, and that the prayer ought to be granted if the Court had jurisdiction, but as to the jurisdiction of the Court the Master found that the mortgage and the land purchased on the foreclosure must be treated as personal property, and therefore a petition to sell the land to remove the lien of debts would not lie, and further that the Act of 27 April, 1855, section 5 (P. L. 369), which enacts that, "wherever the estate shall be derived partly by deed and partly by descent or will, either the Court of Common Pleas or the Orphans' Court may entertain jurisdiction of the proceedings to make sale or lease thereof," does not apply, because the estate was derived entirely by the sheriff's deed; also that the Court could have had jurisdiction in this case, if the executors had petitioned for leave to bid at the sale, but that subsequently to the purchase it was too late for the Court to acquire jurisdiction.

To this finding of the Master, exceptions were filed on behalf of the petitioners.

Hanris, for exceptants.

The jurisdiction of a Court cannot be acquired or lost by the act or omission of a party. It stands on a more stable footing. If it be once conceded that the Orphans' Court has jurisdiction over that mortgage in the hands of the executors, then their jurisdiction continued until the proceeds of that mortgage, in whatever shape they might be, were distributed under its order. If the Court could have entertained jurisdiction on a petition to bid at the sale, the Court can regain its jurisdiction by approving of the purchase *nunc pro tunc*.

As to the jurisdiction of the Court see—
Act of June 16. 1836, § 19.
Otterson *v.* Gallagher, 7 Norris, 355.
Schollenberger *v.* Ins. Co., 5 WEEKLY NOTES, 366.
Ingersoll's Estate, 1 Id. 417.

The Orphans' Court within its jurisdiction is a court of equity, and, when it has jurisdiction at any stage of a proceeding over a fund, it retains its jurisdiction until final distribution.

The petitioners were entitled to have the sale approved by the Court, to protect them from a subsequent attempt to surcharge them when they brought in the proceeds for distribution, as in Dundas's Appeal (14 Sm. 325). The purchaser was entitled to have the sale approved, whereby the propriety of the purchase at sheriff's sale would be ratified.

(No counsel appeared contra.)

December 31, 1880. THE COURT. It must be conceded that the petitioners have mistaken the grounds upon which their application should have been based. The lands as to which it is asked the executors may make private sale, discharged of the lien of their testator's debts, were purchased by them at a sheriff's sale, under proceedings upon a mortgage held by them as part of his estate. These lands never having belonged to him were, of course, as such, never subject to the lien of his debts; and our right to permit the sale cannot be derived from the provision of the Act relative to the discharge of such lien.

A purchase so made by executors is considered, not as a conversion of money into land, but simply as a temporary investment; and for administration and distribution, and for all other purposes of the testator's estate, the lands are treated as personalty. Nor can it be doubted, under the authorities cited by the Master in his very able and elaborate report, that the executor has full power to dispose of lands thus acquired, just as he may of the personal estate which has retained its natural form and character, without the intervention of the Court; and that the title which his deed confers upon his vendee is perfectly valid and free from objection. (Billington's Appeal, 3 Rawle, 47; Oeslager *v.* Fisher, 2 Barr, 467, etc.)

It appears, however, in the present case, that the purchaser is unwilling to take the title without the approval of this Court and the protection of its decree; and it is necessary to consider whether, upon any ground, we have jurisdiction, and whether, if we have, it is proper that we should exercise it.

That the petitioners have based their application upon incorrect grounds, is immaterial. The Court having all the parties before it, if they have jurisdiction of the subject matter, will afford the proper relief, notwithstanding the use of inappropriate terms in the bill or petition. (Wilhelm's Appeal, 29 Smith, 120; Danzeisen's Appeal, 23 Smith, 65; Postlethwaite's Appeal, 18 Smith, 477; Cassady's Estate, 9 WEEKLY NOTES, 275.)

We cannot doubt our jurisdiction. The Act of 18th of April, 1853, provided, among other things, that a sale might be decreed "whenever real estate shall have been purchased, . . . and be held by any person acting in a trust or fiduciary capacity:" but, as under that Act the jurisdiction of the Orphans' Court was expressly limited to "cases of real estate acquired by descent or last will," it was clear that the sale of land purchased by a fiduciary could, so far as the Act was concerned, be ordered by the Common Pleas only.

But then came the Act of April 27th, 1855, § 5, which provided that either the Court of Common Pleas or the Orphans' Court should have jurisdiction in cases arising under the Act of 1853, "whenever the real estate shall have been *derived* partly by deed and partly by descent or will." The present case comes literally within the terms of this Act; for certainly the estate of the executors in these lands is derived in part from the will of their testator and in part from the deed from the sheriff. The Act is a remedial one, and should not be so construed, contrary to its letter, as to abridge the jurisdiction of the Orphans' Court with regard to matters peculiarly cognizable by it, viz., the estates of decedents. Even if the question were more doubtful than it is, our doubts should be resolved in favor of, and not against our own jurisdiction, under the maxim, *est boni judicis*, &c.

We need not, however, consider this question, because we are of opinion that, irrespective of these Acts, and treating the lands as personalty, we have, by virtue of our general powers as a Court of Equity, having complete jurisdiction under the Act of 16th June, 1836, § 19, "in all cases . . . wherein executors, administrators, guardians, or trustees may be possessed of, or *in any way accountable* for any real or personal estate of a decedent," ample authority to decree the sale now asked for. The Master has found that the price offered is a proper one, and that it would be to the advantage of the estate that the sale should be made. If, by our decree, we can facilitate the restoration of the assets of the estate to their natural form, and thus make them available for administration or distribution, why should we not make it? It is our duty to protect both the estate of the testator and the executors personally from the effects of acts done by them in good faith and in the proper discharge of their duties. (Woodward's Appeal, 2 Wright, 322.)

That we do not share the doubts of the purchaser as to the right of the executors to make title, and that we regard his apprehensions in this respect as groundless, is not sufficient to cause us to refuse the decree. On the contrary, the removal of a supposed cloud upon the title may, of itself, be a sufficient reason to induce action on the part of a Court of Equity. (Kay *v.* Scates, 1 Wright, 31.)

Upon another ground it is clear that we should

grant permission to make this sale. The purchase of the lands by the executors being regarded merely as a temporary investment (Oeslager *v.* Fisher, *supra*), the petition is to be treated as an application to permit a sale for the purposes either of administration or reinvestment. Our power in this respect cannot be questioned, and it is one which we are constantly called upon to exercise.

It is conceded by the Master that if the investment by the executors had been made under the Act of 13th of April, 1854, which provides that it shall be lawful for any person acting in a fiduciary capacity to invest, with leave of the proper Court, trust moneys in ground rents or other real estate, where the Court shall be of opinion that such investment will be for the advantage of the estate, the jurisdiction of the Court having thus attached would continue, so as to permit the direction of the subsequent sale. But the same Act, § 3, provides, and, in this respect, it is simply declaratory of a well-settled principle (Mussleman's Appeal, 15 Smith, 480), that in all cases of sale or conveyance, etc., made without leave of the Court, it shall be lawful for the Court, if approving of such sale, conveyance, etc. etc., "to approve, ratify, and confirm the same, with the same effect as if such decree had preceded," etc.

Ratification is always retroactive, and equivalent to a precedent authority; and as it is clear, under the circumstances of this case, as detailed by the Master, that the Court would have permitted the purchase of the mortgaged lands by the executors had application been made for that purpose, we now ratify the investment, and grant permission to sell and dispose of the security thus purchased.

As the effect of the sale is merely to restore personal estate of the testator to the custody of his executors, we are of opinion that no security should be required from them.

To the extent that the Master's report recommends that the petition be dismissed, on the ground of want of jurisdiction, we sustain the exceptions, and grant permission to make private sale of the lands upon the terms offered.

Counsel will prepare a decree in accordance with the principles of this opinion.

Opinion by PENROSE, J.

December 21, 1880.

Wunder's Estate.

Decedents' estates—Where a bequest is immediate to children in a class, children in existence at the death of a testator alone are entitled.

Sur petition for citation and answer.

The petition of Andrew Tyler Wunder set forth: that Lydia Johnson, by her will, after making certain bequests, provided as follows:—

"The residue of my estate, real and personal, is to be divided as follows: My sister is to have the interest of one thousand dollars so long as she lives, and the remainder of my estate, real and personal, to go to Andrew Tyler Wunder's children, to be managed to the best advantage for their benefit and education."

The petitioner, at the time of the decease of the testatrix, had two children, and the Court made an order, directing their guardian to pay to them the income resulting from the funds passing under the residuary clause above quoted. The petition prayed for a citation to the Pennsylvania Co., the guardian, to show cause why the order cited should not be modified, and they be directed to admit a child born subsequently to the death of testatrix to a share of the income.

The answer of the Pennsylvania Company admitted the facts of the petition, but averred that the child subsequently born was not entitled to participation in the fund.

J. D. Yocum, for the petitioner.
J. G. Johnson, contra.

Dec. 27, 1880. THE COURT. Where a bequest is immediate to children in a class, children in existence at the death of the testator (a child *in ventre sa mere* being regarded as in existence) alone are entitled. But where the division of the fund is deferred until a future period, as at the termination of a prior life estate, any child who falls under the description at the time fixed for such division, though born after the death of the testator, is entitled to participate (Roberts *v.* Higman, 1 Bro. Ch. C. 532, note; Davidson *v.* Dallas, 14 Vesey, 576; Barrington *v.* Tristram, 6 Vesey, 345; 2 Williams on Executors, *935.)

In the present case the child who claims a share of the estate in the hands of the guardian was born after the death of the testatrix, and it does not appear that there was any prior life estate which had not expired before the birth of such child.

The petition must, therefore, be dismissed.

Opinion by PENROSE, J.

Supreme Court.

Oct. & Nov. '80, 202.　　　　　　　　Oct. 4, 1880.
Fahnestock v. Wilson.

Mechanic's lien—Amendment of—Act of June 11, 1879—Construction of.

The Act of June 11, 1879 (P. L. 122), entitled "An Act relating to Mechanics' Liens, and authorizing the amendment of the same," is not retroactive.

Per TRUNKEY, J. The Act confers an important right on the claimant, and subjects the building to additional liabilities and its owner to increased risks. To this extent it is more than remedial.

Error to the Common Pleas No. 2, of Allegheny County.

Scire facias sur mechanic's lien, filed October 13, 1876, by R. H. Wilson, a sub-contractor, against B. L. Fahnestock, owner, and A. J. Fair, contractor, for "paint and materials done and furnished within six months past, for and about the erection and construction" of one of three certain described buildings.

The bill of particulars annexed to the claim was as follows:—

ALLEGHENY CITY, Oct. 6, 1876.
Mr. A. J. Fair, for B. L. Fahnestock,
　　　　　　　　　　　　To R. H. Wilson, Dr.
July 26. To painting and glazing warehouses
　　on Fourth Avenue, for B. L. Fahne-
　　stock, by contract $880 00
" "　11 lights of glass extra, 12x36, 50 cts. 　5 50
" "　To painting three skylights, extra, $3
　　each . . . . . . 　9 00
　　　　　　　　　　　　　　　　$894 50

On April 18, 1877, the defendant, Fahnestock, filed an affidavit of defence denying the validity of the first item in the bill and admitting the two other items, tendered judgment for $4.84, with interest from October 1, 1876. Thereafter he moved to strike off the said item of $880 for insufficiency of description, which motion the Court refused. A scire facias was then issued, and on December 20, 1878, in response to a rule to plead, Fahnestock demurred to the item of $880, "because the same does not set out the nature or kind of work done, or the kind and amount of materials, nor the time when the same were furnished;" and again tendered judgment as before, with costs up to that time. The demurrer was overruled, and the defendant pleaded specially, setting forth the insufficiency of the item objected to.

On June 19, 1879, the case being at issue, the Court made the following order, which was entered on the mechanics' lien docket: "On motion of A. C. Patterson, attorney of the plaintiff, leave is granted to the plaintiff to amend his bill of particulars in lien filed in above case, and more fully itemize work embraced in the lien in the above case." PER CURIAM.

The defendant then filed the following paper, viz.:—

Supplemental bill of items, as authorized to be filed by leave of Court granted in No. 30, July Term, 1877, under the Act of Assembly of 1879.

July 26, 1876.　　　　　　A. C. PATTERSON,
　　　　　　　　　　　　　Attorney for Plaintiff.
Mr. A. J. Fair, for B. L. Fahnestock's Buildings,
　　　　　　　　　　　　To R. H. Wilson, Dr.
1876.
July 26. 21 panes of plate-glass, for building . $625 00
" "　Pittsburgh glass, for skylight . 　.35 00
" "　Paints, oils, etc. . . . 　165 00
" "　To 18¼ days' work . . 　55 00
" "　To reglazing 11 lights of glass, 50 cts.
　　each . . . . 　5 50
" "　To painting old skylights . . 　9 00
　　　　　　　　　　　　　　　　$894 50
" "　Cr. By 500 lbs. white lead . 　50 00
　　　　　　　　　　　　　　　　$844 50

Before the trial the defendant moved to strike off the supplemental bill, as having been filed without authority of law. The motion having been denied, counsel agreed upon a special verdict, in favor of the plaintiff, for $350.22, subject to the opinion of the Court upon the following questions:—

(1st) Was it competent for the Court to allow the supplemental bill of items, filed June 27, 1879, and provided for by order of June 19, 1879, to be filed?

(2d) Whether said amendment, if allowed, is sufficient to entitle the plaintiff to recover?

The jury found accordingly.

The Court, EWING, P. J., decided both questions in favor of the plaintiff, and directed judgment to be entered on the verdict. To which the defendant excepted and took this writ, assigning the said action of the Court for error.

Oliver and *Rodgers*, for the plaintiff in error.

The amendment, as allowed in this case, is not within the purview of the Act of June 11, 1879 (P. L. 122). That Act is not retroactive.

McCay's Appeal, 1 Wr. 125.
Sutton *v.* Clark *et al.*, 7 W. N. C. 437.
Ashman *v.* McIlvaine, 8 Id. 309.

The Act can only be construed as retroactive by reading into it words referring to past time;

thus doing violence to the rules of construction and to the constitutional rights of the defendant.
Lambertson et al. v. Hogan, 2 Barr, 22.
Potter's Dwarris on Statutes, 162.
McCabe v. Emerson, 6 Har. 111.
Becker's Appeal, 27 Pa. St. 55.
W. Br. Boom Co. v. Dodge, 31 Id. 285-8.
Bates v. Koch, 6 Barr, 476.
Ogle v. S. & Mt. P. T. Co., 13 S. & R. 256.
The amended specification is insufficient.
Lee v. Burke, 16 P. F. S. 336.
Russell v. Bell, 8 Wr. 47.
Shields v. Garrett, 5 W. N. C. 120.

A. C. Patterson, contra.
The preamble and the language of the whole Act in question indicate the design of the Legislature to extend the rights of the claimants in mechanics' liens, just as it did of parties in other cases when it enacted the Statute of Amendments, in 1806. The former Act being remedial, it should receive the same liberal construction that has been given to the latter.
Com. v. Dillon, 11 Smith, 488.

Oct. 18, 1880. THE COURT. The claim was filed Oct. 13, 1876, and was defective. Therefore, by the terms of the statute which created the lien, it expired at the end of six months from the time the work was done and materials were furnished. More than two years after the lien died, an attempt was made to restore it to life by an amendment. Whether it was competent for the Court to waive the lien, is the first question reserved.

A mechanic's lien on a building is entirely statutory, a privilege not of common right, and is in addition to the common law remedies which belong to all citizens. While the lien continues, and after it falls, the claimant, notwithstanding his special boon, is entitled to the same remedies as other laborers and vendors, for recovery of his debt. The remedies remain whether the claim filed be perfect or faulty, or none be filed at all. The favor is not merely a remedy by suit, it is a lien on property from the commencement of the work, a valuable right, preferring the claimant before other creditors, and often compelling one man to pay another's debts. Its enforcement is by proceeding *in rem.* Where the claimant is a sub-contractor, it is no defence for the owner of the building to show that he has fully paid the party with whom he contracted. Such a right existing at the time the work was done or materials furnished cannot be taken from the claimant by repeal of the statute, nor impaired by pretence of changing remedies. It has been repeatedly held that the Legislature has no power to take away vested rights. Like principle forbids imposing the corresponding liability on specific property or its owner, where they are free. A defunct lien drops from the property, leaving it free as if the lien had never attached.

Prior to the Act of June 11, 1879 (P. L. 122), no contract was made with reference to its provisions; since, of course, it is altogether different. That Act is now a part of the Mechanic's Lien Law. In one sense it is remedial, in another it confers an important right on the claimant, and subjects the building to additional liabilities, and its owner to increased risks. Just to the extent of these rights and liabilities, is the Act more than remedial. If applicable to claims which existed before its enactment, this case illustrates its operation, namely, the resurrection of a lien and placing it upon a building and appurtenant land, so that the owner must lose his property or pay a debt he never contracted. Aside from any constitutional question, the Act comes within the rule, "that a statute shall always be interpreted so as to operate prospectively, and not retrospectively, unless the language is so clear as to preclude all question of the intention of the Legislature." "Retrospective laws generally, if not universally, work injustice, and ought to be so construed only when the mandate of the Legislature is imperative." (Taylor v. Mitchell, 7 P. F. S. 209.) A statute will not be held unconstitutional if it admit of an interpretation not in conflict with the Constitution. Were this Act purely remedial, it might be held applicable to cases pending at its passage. Its language is by no means imperative that it shall be retroactive, and without violence may be construed to operate prospectively only. This must have been the legislative intent.

The first reserved question, being decided in the negative, disposes of the case, and we express no opinion upon the second.

Judgment reversed; and now judgment in favor of the plaintiff for $5.86 with interest from date of verdict and costs accrued up to April 18, 1877.

Opinion by TRUNKEY, J.

Oct. & Nov. '80, 128.   Oct. 4, 1880.

Lehman et al. v. Howley.

Practice—Power of Courts to make rules—Ejectment—Rule of Court requiring defendant to file abstract of title, in default of which plaintiff may have judgment if his abstract, duly filed, shows a good prima facie title—Validity of.

It is within the general powers of the Courts of Common Pleas to provide by rule, that, upon failure of a defendant in ejectment to file within a certain time an abstract of title or a statement of facts upon which he relies, the plaintiff shall be entitled to a judgment such as is warranted by the facts set out in the abstract and statement which he is also by the same rule required to file.

To entitle the plaintiff to such a judgment his abstract of title or statement of facts must make out a good *prima facie* case.

Accordingly, where the plaintiff's abstract traced his title back to a deed of partition, but did not show title in the parties to such deed, and the Court entered judgment against the defendant in default of his filing the necessary statement:

Held, to be error.

Error to the Common Pleas No. 2, of Allegheny County.

Ejectment, brought Dec. 31, 1879, by Martin Howley against Henry Lehman and T. H. B. Patterson, for a tract of land in the possession of Lehman as tenant of Patterson.

The writ was duly served on the defendant Lehman, for whom an appearance *de bene esse* was entered, and a return of *non est inventus* made as to Patterson. The præcipe contained a description of the premises, and averred "the right of possession or title to be in the plaintiff," who, in pursuance of a rule of Court, filed, within proper time, an abstract of title, deducing title to him, by mesne conveyances and judicial proceedings, starting with the following deed of partition, viz.:—

Deed of partition, between William Philipps, C. B. M. Smith and John Brown, dated August 14, 1858. Acknowledged August 17, 1858. Recorded August 23d, in Deed Book, vol. 134-357, in Recorder's Office of Allegheny County, in which deed the property described in præcipe is allotted to William Philipps.

The rule of Court is as follows:—

Rule 89, Sec. 1. "In all actions of ejectment hereafter brought, it shall be the duty of the plaintiff, either by himself, his agent or attorney, to file in the office of the prothonotary of this Court, on or before the first day of the term to which the writ is returnable, a statement containing a description of the land, together with the number of acres and the proportion thereof which he claims, and an abstract of the title on which he relies for his recovery, whether the same be in writing or otherwise; and, where the same is matter of record, a reference thereto. And the defendant shall plead not guilty, and enter his defence, if any he hath, for the whole or any part thereof before the next term; and at the time of entering his plea he shall by himself, his attorney or agent, file a statement containing an abstract of the title or facts on which he relies for his defence, whether the same be in writing or otherwise; and where the same is matter of record, a reference thereto, together with a specification of so much of the plaintiff's title as he denies, and so much thereof as is not denied shall be deemed admitted, and at the trial the evidence shall be confined to the facts respectively denied by the parties."

Sec. 2. "On failure of the plaintiff to file an abstract and statement, as required by the first section of this rule, judgment of *non pros.* shall be entered by the prothonotary on præcipe of defendant's attorney, or the like judgment may be entered on motion in open court. The failure of the defendant to file the abstract and statement required by this rule shall be deemed a confession of the truth of the facts set forth by the plaintiff, and that he has no defence thereto. And thereupon, on motion in open court, the plaintiff shall be entitled to such judgment as may be warranted by the facts set out in the abstract and statement filed by the plaintiff."

The defendant having failed to file the abstract or statement required by the same rule, the plaintiff moved for judgment, whereupon the Court made the following order, viz.: "And now, to wit, April 17, 1880, it appearing to the Court that the defendant has failed to file an abstract of title and statement of defence, as required by the rules of Court, and it further appearing to the Court, from the abstract of title and statement filed by the plaintiff, that the plaintiff is entitled to recover the premises described in the writ from the defendant, it is ordered that judgment be entered in favor of the plaintiff and against the defendant for the premises described in this writ with costs. PER CURIAM."

The defendant then took this writ, and assigned for error the above action of the Court.

W. S. Wilson and *J. S. Ferguson*, for the plaintiff in error.

The judgment is erroneous, because it does not appear upon the plaintiff's own showing that he was entitled to the possession of the premises in dispute. The mere issuing of the writ implies an adverse possession in the defendant. The plaintiff has not alleged that he or any of those under whom he claims were ever seised of the land in dispute. He does not aver that he and the defendant claim under the same title, and does not trace his title back to a common source. He does not show title out of the Commonwealth and vesting regularly in him. He does not allege the defendant to have been a mere intruder. He did not, therefore, upon his own abstract, make out such a title as would entitle him to recover. The plaintiff must recover upon the strength of his own title, and not the weakness of the defendant's.

Covert *v.* Irwin, 3 S. & R. 288.

No Act of Assembly authorized the Court to enter judgment by default against a defendant in ejectment who had appeared. While the Act of March 21, 1806, directs that "the defendant shall enter his defence if any he hath . . . before the next term," it provides no penalty for not so doing.

The Act of Dec. 5, 1860 (P. L. of 1861, Appendix, 844), limits the power of the Court where an appearance has been entered.

J. W. Over, contra.

The plaintiff below, in his abstract, shows the title to have been in the parties under whom he claims for more than twenty-one years prior to the bringing of the suit, and, in the præcipe and statement filed, he averred that the right of possession or title to the premises was in him and not in the defendant. The Court below adjudged that the facts set forth by the plaintiff were sufficient to entitle him to judgment under the rule, and this Court will not interfere, as the Common Pleas Courts are the most proper judges of the extent and application of their own rules.

Snyder *v.* Bauchman, 8 S. & R. 336.

In addition to the general powers of the Court to make the rule in question, express authority is conferred by Acts of Assembly.

Snyder *v.* Bauchman, *supra.*
Vanatta *v.* Anderson, 3 Binney, 417.
Act of June 16, 1836, Purd. Dig. 233, pl. 136.
Act of May 24, 1878, P. L. 135.

The Act of Dec. 5, 1860, does not limit the power of the Court in the premises. The Act is not mandatory, and it leaves it optional with the Court to direct a plea to be entered in default of an appearance.

Oct. 18, 1880. THE COURT (after quoting the rule, *supra*). The power of the Court to make and enforce such a rule as this cannot be doubted. The right to make rules for the regulation of their practice is included in the general powers of the Courts of Common Pleas. (Vanatta *v.* Anderson, 3 Bin. 417; Snyder *v.* Bauchman, 8 S. & R. 336.) But in addition to this inherent authority, express power is given by the Acts of June 16, 1836, and May 24, 1878, the former of which provides that the Courts of Common Pleas shall have full power and authority to establish such rules for regulating the practice thereof respectively, and for expediting the determination of suits, causes, and proceedings therein, as in their discretion they shall judge necessary and proper, *provided* that such rules shall not be inconsistent with the Constitution and laws of this Commonwealth; and the latter declares that said Courts shall have full power to make all necessary rules and regulations for the transaction of all business brought before them.

The rule under consideration is clearly not in conflict with any of the provisions of the Constitution, or the law relating to actions of ejectment, or any other Act of Assembly. It follows, therefore, that the Court had full power and authority to adopt the rule. Its provisions are just and reasonable, and their enforcement will greatly expedite and facilitate the administration of justice by eliminating matters about which there is really no dispute, and thus narrowing the controversy to such questions as are actually involved in the case. When, as is frequently the case, the plaintiff in ejectment is required to show title out of the Commonwealth, and then trace it down to himself through numerous mesne conveyances, judicial proceedings, etc., much time is often consumed to no good purpose, and frequently technical difficulties unexpectedly arise and impede a fair and speedy trial on the merits. The rule contemplates that the plaintiff's abstract will present facts, which if true, will warrant the Court in adjudging that the right of possession or title is in him and not in the defendant; and if the latter appears but fails to file the required abstract, the facts properly averred by the plain-tiff are taken to be true. The fact that the writ was properly served on the defendant Lehman, and so returned by the sheriff, gave the appearance *de bene esse* by his attorney, full effect as a general appearance, and he was clearly in default, in not filing the abstract and statement required by the rule. This entitled the plaintiff to judgment, provided it was warranted by the facts set out in his abstract and statement.

The contention of the plaintiff in error is that a *prima facie* case, entitling the plaintiff to judgment, was not presented, and in this we think he is right. Upon his own showing, it does not appear that the plaintiff below is entitled to possession of the premises in dispute. No principle is better settled than that a plaintiff in ejectment must recover, if at all, on the strength of his own title, and not upon the weakness of the defendant's. (Covert *v.* Irwin, 3 S. & R. 283.) The foundation of plaintiff's title, as exhibited by his abstract, is a deed of partition dated August 14, 1858, between William Phillips, C. B. M. Smith, and John Brown, by which the property in dispute was allotted to William Phillips, who in December of the same year conveyed the same to Jacob Daniel, who in 1874 mortgaged the same to Isaac M. Pennock, who subsequently assigned the mortgage to the plaintiff below. It is further shown by the abstract, that by proceedings on the mortgage, judgment was obtained, and the premises were sold by the sheriff, and duly conveyed to the plaintiff on Oct. 11, 1879. Proper references are given to the records of the deed, mortgage, and judicial proceedings which form the several links in the chain of title thus presented; but it does not appear from anything contained in the abstract, how or from whom the parties to the deed of partition acquired title, or that they, or any of the parties under whom the plaintiff claims, were ever seised of the land in dispute, or at any time in possession thereof; nor does it appear that the defendant below claims under the same title as the plaintiff, or that their titles have a common source. In short, assuming all that is presented by the abstract to be true, it fails to show title out of the Commonwealth, and in the plaintiff or any of those under whom he claims. It is very clear that if all the facts set forth were proved on the trial of his action, he would not be entitled to a verdict.

It is contended, however, that the statement in the præcipe, that the right of possession or title is in the plaintiff, and not in the defendant, is a sufficient averment. It is certainly an unqualified assertion of title in himself, but it is a legal conclusion, and not a statement of facts from which the Court could say that the right of possession was in him and not in the defendant. The rule of Court contemplates a brief statement of facts upon which the Court may base its judg-

Oct. & Nov. '80, 152.   Oct. 15, 1880.

Scott Township v. Montgomery.

Negligence—Roads, highways, and bridges—Failure of township authorities to provide proper guards along the roads—Damages—Measure of.

Townships, as well as other municipalities, are bound to keep their public roads in a safe condition.

If a public road, running through a township, is so dangerous by reason of its proximity to a precipice, that common prudence requires extra precaution in order to secure safety to travellers, the township is bound to use such precaution, and the omission to do so is negligence.

Even if a township is not a corporation proper, such as a city or borough, nor invested with power to tax for road purposes beyond one *per centum* on the county valuation, it is, nevertheless, bound to erect walls or barriers along the sides of its roads, if that is necessary to the safety of travellers.

The Court below affirmed the following point: "If the jury find for the plaintiff, they should allow, in estimating damages, not only for the direct expenses incurred by the plaintiff by reason of the injury, but also for the privation and inconvenience he is subjected to, and for the pain and suffering he has already endured, bodily and mental, and which he is likely to experience, as well as the pecuniary loss he has sustained, and is likely to sustain during the remainder of his life, from his disabled condition?"

Held, that the measure of damages was correctly stated.

Error to the Common Pleas No. 1, of Allegheny County.

Case, by John M. Montgomery against the township of Scott, to recover damages for injuries suffered by the plaintiff through the alleged negligence of the township officers.

Upon the trial, before COLLIER, J., the following facts appeared: On July 5, 1872, the plaintiff was driving in a buggy along a public road in Scott Township, Allegheny County, when his horse shied, from some unknown cause, and ran off the road, down the hillside, taking the buggy and its occupants along, and permanently injuring the plaintiff. The road at the place where the accident occurred runs along the side of a hill, and is bounded on one side by a fence inclosing a cultivated field; on the other side, where the accident occurred, is a precipitous descent of about 40 feet, and it was admitted that there was no fence or barrier of any kind along the edge of this side of the road. The road had been opened as a public road under an order of Court in 1836, and, at the time of the accident, was otherwise in good condition. It did not appear that it had ever been fenced at this point, and there was evidence that no accident had ever before happened there.

That part of Allegheny County, south of the Ohio and Monongahela rivers, including Scott Township, is broken, uneven, and very hilly, so that fully one-fourth of the 40 miles of public roads in the township is laid out along hillsides and declivities, and it has never been the custom to construct barriers along the side of these roads.

Plaintiff's counsel requested the Court to charge, *inter alia* :—

(1) If the jury find that the public road, where the accident occurred, was so dangerous by reason of its proximity to a precipice that common prudence required extra precaution, in order to secure safety to travellers, the township was bound to use such precaution, and the omission to do so was negligence. *Answer.* Affirmed as a general proposition.

(7) If the jury in view of all the evidence find for the plaintiff, they should allow in estimating the damages not only for the direct expenses incurred by the plaintiff by reason of the injury, but also for the privation and inconvenience he is subjected to, and for the pain and suffering he has already endured, bodily and mental, and which he is likely to experience, as well as the pecuniary loss he has sustained, and is likely to sustain during the remainder of his life, from his disabled condition. *Affirmed.*

The defendant's counsel requested the Court to charge, *inter alia:* That Scott Township, not being a corporation proper, such as a city or borough, nor invested with power to tax itself for road purposes beyond one per centum on the county valuation, is not bound to erect walls or barriers along the sides of its road. *Answer.* Refused and reserved.

Verdict for the plaintiff for $7000, subject to the point reserved. Afterwards the Court entered judgment for the plaintiff upon the reserved point, whereupon the defendant took this writ, assigning for error, *inter alia,* the answers to plaintiff's points, and the entering of judgment for plaintiff on the question of law reserved.

Malcolm Hay and *Jacob H. Miller* (with them *W. D. Porter* and *A. McBride*), for plaintiff in error.

Townships are only liable for the condition of their public roads by and under the Act of June 13, 1836 (P. L. 555). That Act was intended as a certain guide for the supervisors, most of them plain and unlearned men, and specifies their duties with great detail and particularity. It requires only that the roads be "effectually opened and constantly kept in repair," and "clear of all

---

ment. In other words, the plaintiff must exhibit in his abstract, a *prima facie* case, based upon facts distinctly averred.

Judgment reversed and a *procedendo* awarded. Opinion by STERRETT, J.

impediments to easy and convenient passing and travelling." The statute did not require fencing as an element of original construction, and it is not required as repair. *Repair* here means that the road-*bed* must be kept in proper condition, not that costly barriers must be erected along the sides of the roads. In all of the cases in which townships have been held liable, the facts show that the road-bed itself was out of repair, and not clear of impediment, as the statute required.

A very different measure of duty is imposed upon townships from that which is imposed upon cities and boroughs; the one being only a *quasi*-corporation, with very limited powers and duties, and the others being corporations of vastly larger, though differing, powers, and having jurisdiction and control over their streets, enabling them to construct and supervise them much more efficiently, and containing population and possessing means which impose larger responsibilities.

Dillon on Mun. Corp., sec. 761, 762, 763, 786.
Borough of Pittston *v.* Hart, 8 Norris, 389.
Perry Township *v.* John, 29 Sm. 412.
Graffius *v.* Comm., 3 Pa. 504.

When the Court below instructed the jury that they should allow in estimating the damages not only for the mental pain which plaintiff had already endured, but also for that which he was likely to experience during the remainder of his life, it left the whole matter, without possibility of evidence, open to their unlimited imagination.

H. Weir (*R. M. Gibson* with him), contra.

There is no distinction, either in reason or authority, between cities, boroughs, and townships, or between streets, bridges, and roads. It makes no difference from what cause the dangerous condition arose, whether from the want of repairs to the bed of the road or street, or from the want of protection in case of close proximity to dangerous precipices. The meaning of the Act is that they shall be kept in such condition as may be necessary for the safety of the travelling public. Having failed in their duty in this regard, the township is liable.

Lower Macungie Township *v.* Merkhoffer, 21 Sm. 276.
Mahanoy Township *v.* Scholly, 3 Nor. 136; S. C., 4 WEEKLY NOTES, 134.
City of Scranton *v.* Dean, 2 WEEKLY NOTES, 467.
Hey *v.* Philadelphia, 31 Sm. 44; S. C., 2 WEEKLY NOTES, 465.

October 25, 1880. THE COURT. We think this case was rightly tried and submitted to the jury. Under the numerous decisions of this Court on the liability of municipalities for injuries resulting from negligence in not having dangerous places on roads properly guarded, the learned Judge could not have answered the points presented to him otherwise than he did. Many of these cases were cases of townships. We see nothing in the point made and reserved as to the taxable ability of the defendants. Judgment was rightly entered upon it for the plaintiff.

The measure of damages was correctly stated. (Pennsylvania and Ohio Canal Co. *v.* Graham, 13 P. F. Smith, 290.)

PER CURIAM. Judgment affirmed.

GREEN, J., absent.

[*Cf.* Act of May 25, 1878, Purd. Dig., Supplement, 2163. As to measure of damages, *J.* Mansfield Co. *v.* McEnery, 8 W. N. C. 81.]

May, '80, 6.   May 24, 1880.

Union Township v. Gibboney.

Township supervisors—Their powers and duties —When one of several supervisors may bind the township—Roads, highways, and bridges —Status of townships as municipal corporations.

One of several township supervisors may bind the township in merely ministerial matters, within the scope of his duty; but the consent of a majority, given at a regularly convened meeting of the board, is necessary in all matters requiring deliberation, consultation, and judgment.

The ordinary repairs of roads and bridges are classed with ministerial duties, but the law contemplates that this work shall be paid for by the road tax which the taxpayers may work out.

Whether a debt should be contracted for such ordinary repairs, is a matter for deliberation and judgment, and the joint action of the supervisors, acting within their very limited power to contract debts, is necessary to bind the township.

Two supervisors divided their township into sections, each assuming the repairs of the roads of one section; one supervisor issued to road laborers orders on a storekeeper for "goods," to be charged to the township, to the extent of several hundred dollars, which orders were honored by the storekeeper, who afterwards brought suit thereon against the township:

Held, that it was error to admit the orders in evidence, and to instruct the jury that the orders were binding on the township.

The corporate status of counties and townships, their powers and duties, and the powers of road supervisors, considered by TRUNKEY, J.

Error to the Common Pleas of Mifflin County. Assumpsit, by Gibboney and Nelson against the township of Union, to recover the amount of certain orders for merchandise and laborers' supplies, issued to them on the credit of said township by one of the supervisors of said township.

The material facts were as follows: William F. Stroup and J. N. Yoder were supervisors of Union Township for the years 1874 and 1875. By an arrangement between themselves the township was divided into two sections, each supervisor assuming charge of the roads in the section where he resided. The roads in Stroup's division were in need of repair, and Stroup employed laborers to do the work, but, not being then in funds from the receipt of road taxes, Stroup arranged with the plaintiffs, who were storekeepers, to furnish the men with materials, provisions, etc., upon orders to be issued by him upon the credit of Union Township. The plaintiffs furnished, upon such orders, lumber and material for the repair of the roads to the amount of $36.76, and provisions and personal supplies for laborers to the amount of about $950, reduced by payments to $444.89. This suit was brought to recover the said sums of $36.76, and $444.89, with interest thereon. Payment was not resisted of the orders amounting to $36.76, representing material furnished for and used in the repair of the roads.

Upon the trial, before BUCHER, P. J., the plaintiffs offered in evidence the "laborers" orders, which were in the following form:—

"GIBBONEY & NELSON:—Let Charles Bennet have goods to the amount of two dollars, and charge to Union Township.
$2.00   W. F. STROUP, Sup."

Objected to by defendant, on the ground, *inter alia*, that one supervisor had no power to charge the township by such a contract. Objection overruled; exception.

The defendant produced evidence, under objection and exception, showing that the township Auditors had a settlement with the supervisors, in which the latter were allowed credit for the work done on the roads covered by certain orders mentioned in the settlement, and that at the time of the settlement it was stated to the Auditors that there were other orders outstanding and unpaid.

The Court charged, *inter alia*: "The defendant insists that these orders are not binding upon the township, for want of authority in the supervisors to draw them. For the present we instruct you that these orders are valid and binding upon the plaintiffs, and you ought to find for the plaintiffs, unless indeed the defendant has shown that they have been paid. We permitted the defendant to give evidence that the township authorities had a settlement with the supervisors, and that they were allowed a credit for the work done on the roads covered by the orders in the settlement. It is also in proof that at the time this settlement was made it was proven to the township Auditors that there were outstanding orders unpaid. Now we instruct you that this settlement, which was made in the absence of the plaintiffs, and without notice to them, cannot defeat a recovery."

Verdict for plaintiffs, and judgment thereon. The defendant took this writ, assigning for error the admission of the orders, and the charge of the Court as above quoted.

A. Reed, *G. W. & R. C. Elder*, for plaintiff in error.

The powers of township supervisors are limited by statute, and parties dealing with them are bound by those limits. The issuing of orders is but another form of borrowing money on the credit of the township, which it is doubtful if even the township itself can do: much less can the supervisors, and still less can one supervisor.

Cooper *v.* Lampeter Township, 8 Watts, 125.
1 Potter on Corporations, 478.
Williamsport *v.* Com'th, 3 Nor. 487.
Addis *v.* Pittsburgh, 4 Id. 379.
Com'th *ex rel.* Middleton *v.* Commissioners, 1 Wr. 241.

The township paid Stroup for the work in the settlement with the supervisors, and to sustain the power of a supervisor to bind the township by orders given to a stranger would encourage frauds.

D. W. Woods, for defendants in error.

The repair of roads was within the scope of the supervisors' duty, and their authority to bind the township for the expense thereof is clear.

Cook *v.* Deerfield Township, 14 Sm. 445.
Dauphin Co. *v.* Bridenhart, 4 Har. 458.

In all matters which the township was bound to perform, one supervisor may bind the township even where the other refuses his consent.

Pottsville *v.* Norwegian Township, 2 Harris, 543.

One supervisor may bind the township by a mere ministerial act—such as the employment of hands and giving due-bills for the amount of work done on the roads.

Dull *v.* Ridgway, 9 Barr, 272.
McNeal *v.* Allegheny Township, 1 Am. L. Reg. 124.

Where supervisors agree, as in this case, that each shall take charge of a certain portion of the township, the action of each within the limits assigned is binding on the township.

Commonwealth *v.* Supervisors of Colley Township, 5 Casey, 121.
Hopewell Township *v.* Putt, 2 WEEKLY NOTES 46.

June 22, 1880. THE COURT. Counties and townships are involuntary civil divisions of the State, incorporated by general laws to aid in the administration of government. Their powers all relate to matters of State as distinguished from local concern, such as the administration of justice and the establishment and repair of public highways. The statutes confer upon them all the powers they possess, prescribe all the duties they owe, and impose all liabilities to which they are subject. Considered in respect to the limited number of their corporate powers, they rank low down in the scale or grade of corporate existence, and hence have been frequently termed *quasi* corporations. This designation distinguishes them from private corporations aggregate, and from municipal corporations proper, such as cities or towns acting under charters or incorporating statutes, and which are invested with more powers and endowed with more functions and a larger measure of corporate life. (Dillon on Munic. Corp. § 10 *a*.) It is a statutory duty of townships to open, construct, and keep in repair all public roads within their limits, and they may make such contracts as shall be necessary and proper for the execution of that purpose. By the general statutes, supervisors are enjoined and required to open and constantly keep in repair all public highways, making sufficient causeways on marshy and swampy ground, and bridges over small creeks and rivulets, for which they may purchase, at the expense of the townships, all necessary materials and employ and direct a sufficient number of laborers. They may lay an assessment not exceeding one cent on the dollar on real and personal estate, which may be paid in work on the roads; and they have no power to issue a warrant for the collection of said tax until after they shall have given the tax-payers notice and full opportunity to work out their respective taxes. Nor have they power to make a contract the effect of which would be to deprive the tax-payers of that privilege.

Power is given to lay an additional assessment for the purpose of paying any just debt due a former supervisor. Townships have no express authority to borrow money, and they have none, unless by necessary implication, for carrying out the duties imposed upon them. They cannot give negotiable securities which would preclude defence on the merits against any holder. One supervisor cannot bind the township for performance of a contract, the propriety of entering into which is the subject of deliberation and the exercise of judgment, but he may in matters purely ministerial. When the business requires deliberation, consultation, and judgment, all should be convened, because the advice and opinions of all may be useful; though they do not unite in opinion, a majority may act when there is more than two. Before constructing a new bridge they must meet and act as a board, for this can only be done on deliberation and consultation and with the assent of both or a majority. But the ordinary repairs of roads and bridges and opening roads authorized by the Courts of Quarter Sessions are classed with ministerial duties, and may be performed by one. In Cooper *v.* Lampeter Township (8 Watts, 125) the Court say: "It is conceded that one supervisor cannot levy a tax to pay the debts contracted and the expenses incurred in the township. The consent of both is required, because it is a deliberative and not a ministerial duty. For the same reason such contracts cannot be made by less than a majority of the board, as this would enable the one to involve a township in expenses which would render a tax inevitable. They are not permitted to do indirectly what they cannot do directly. When damage is done to a road or bridge by a freshet or other accidental cause, or when it needs repair from the natural progress of decay, there can be no objection to the necessary expenditure being authorized by less than a majority. This is an absolute duty which calls neither for deliberation nor consultation." The sound doctrine of that case has not been overruled by the later cases relied on by the plaintiffs below.

In Pottsville Borough *v.* Norwegian Township (2 Har. 543), a bridge over a creek, the dividing line between the borough and township, had become ruinous and dangerous, and the borough, having requested the township to join in rebuilding, and the latter having neglected its duty, constructed a new bridge: it was held, the actor could recover one-half the costs of such a bridge as was reasonably necessary, but not half the cost of the one which was built, if more expensive than was necessary, having reference to the wealth of the township. There the necessity for a bridge had been settled, it was a legal duty of the borough and township to rebuild, and the law fixed the township for half the expenses. It was held in Dull *v.* Ridgway Township (9 Barr, 272), that, when a supervisor gives a due-bill to a laborer which shows on its face it was for work done for a certain road, it is valid; for that is in the line of his ministerial duty in employing laborers to open or repair a road. The laborer could recover for his work without the due-bill, it adds not a tittle to his right; and though *prima facie* entitling him to recover, it would not bar any meritorious defence. Opening a road in obedience to an order of the Quarter Sessions is a ministerial duty, for the supervisor cannot interpose his judgment to avoid it. Hence it was ruled in Hopewell Township *v.* Putt (2 W. N. C. 46), that, when one supervisor awarded a contract for building a new road, a person who paid money on the contract, at the request of the supervisor, could recover the same from the township. Certainly, making the contract, though for work authoritatively commanded, went to the verge of the power of a single supervisor if not beyond; and one of the Judges dissented.

Undoubtedly a county or township may be legally liable for a debt, without the active agency of the commissioners or supervisors. A county is liable for expenses of a jury in a capital case, and for the expenses of Courts. (Commissioners *v.* Hall, 7 Watts, 290; McCalmont *v.* Allegheny, 5 Casey, 417.) But these and like cases throw no light on the question whether one commissioner, or one supervisor, has power by contract to subject the county or township to liability for money or merchandise furnished to himself.

The supervisors divided the township, each taking charge of the roads in his part. Their respective duties were repairing old roads and keeping them in order. The law contemplates that this should be done by the road tax, which the tax-payers may work out under the directions of the supervisors. If they refuse to work they must pay the tax in money, and it is the supervisors' duty to collect it and properly apply it for road purposes. Except when some extraordinary expenditure is required, it is not contemplated that debts shall be contracted to be paid by an additional assessment. Whether a debt should be contracted for the ordinary repairs of roads and bridges is a matter for deliberation and judgment, and the township cannot be bound for borrowed money save by the joint action of the supervisors; nor even then in all cases, for their power to contract debts is very limited. "Those who deal with such agents must take care to have the express consent of all to whom the law has entrusted the transaction of the public business. The inhabitants of the township whose interest must be protected have a right to the counsel and judgment of all to whom such trusts are committed." Per ROGERS, J.

Stroup as supervisor employed laborers to repair the roads, and could have given them orders on the township treasury or evidence of the amount of their work in the form of a duebill. Within such limit there is comparatively little room for abuse. He made a contract with the plaintiffs for credit to an indefinite amount, he to give his laborers orders on them, which they would accept and give goods therefor on the credit of the township. These aggregate the sum of $952.50, and are in the following form: "Gibboney & Nelson: let Charles Bennet have goods to the amount of two dollars, and charge to Union Township. W. F. Stroup, Sup." A more vicious method of contracting indebtedness against a township could scarcely be imagined even if it were by the joint act of the supervisors. The parties to this transaction were honest, it is said, yet the supervisor who did the work and gave the orders settled his accounts with the auditors and was allowed for the whole amount of labor done. The taxes nearly covered all the work which was done by both supervisors. The learned Judge of the Common Pleas was entirely right in ruling, "that this settlement, which was made in the absence of the plaintiffs and without notice to them, cannot defeat a recovery." It is illustrative of the wisdom of the law in withholding power from one supervisor to contract the debt. Stroup and the plaintiffs were honest, and the attempt is to hold the township liable for hundreds of dollars already paid to Stroup in his settlement. If this contract binds the township, what may be done by a dishonest officer? On its face it is a barter, wherein lurk temptations to excessive wages, excessive prices for goods, and favors of some sort between merchant and officer. Were the orders payable in money the danger to the interest of the township would be nearly as great. Such a contract as is set up here ought never to be made by supervisors; when it is the act of one only, for that reason the township is not bound, and, at present, it is unnecessary to say whether, if the act of both, it would be void on the ground of public policy. We are of opinion it was error to admit the orders in evidence and to rule that they were binding upon the township.

That part of the plaintiff's claim which is for materials furnished for repairs of the roads, at request of one of the supervisors, rests on a different footing, and no objection has been made to its recovery.

Judgment reversed and *venire facias de novo* awarded.

Opinion by TRUNKEY, J.

May, '79. 60. May 27, 1880.

Donaldson v. Commonwealth.

Court of Oyer and Terminer—Legal requisites to constitute—Full complement of jurors, directed by Act, an essential element—Certificate of case from Quarter Sessions to Oyer and Terminer—May be filed after trial, nunc pro tunc—Criminal Law—Rape—Duty of district attorney to call physician who attended prosecutrix.

It is an essential element of the legal constitution of a Court of Oyer and Terminer that not less than forty-eight persons shall be summoned to serve as petit jurors, as directed by the Act of April 14, 1834, § 113 (P. L. 362).

Where the precept and venire issued from the Quarter Sessions for less than that number, a trial, although conducted in other respects according to the forms of the Oyer and Terminer, is erroneous and void for want of jurisdiction. That the number of jurors actually returned was not exhausted by challenges, is immaterial.

The failure to summon and return the full number of jurors directed by law is not such a "defect or error in the precept or venire or in drawing, summoning, or returning" jurors, as will, after a trial on the merits, be cured by force of the Act of March 31, 1860, § 53 (P. L. 443).

Semble, that a certificate from the Quarter Sessions, certifying a case into the Oyer and Terminer, may be filed after the trial, *nunc pro tunc*, provided the trial was had in a legally constituted Court of Oyer and Terminer.

Per GREEN, J. In a trial for rape, the physician who examined the person of the woman soon after the alleged offence, should have been called to testify by the district attorney. Whether his evidence tended to acquit or convict, it was demanded equally by the cause of humanity on the one hand, or of justice on the other.

Error to the Oyer and Terminer of Warren County.

Irvine Donaldson was indicted in the Quarter Sessions for rape. The Court made an order, which was entered on the Quarter Sessions docket, that "this case is certified to the Court of Oyer and Terminer," but no certificate was filed among the records of the Oyer and Terminer until some time after the trial, when a certificate in due form was filed *nunc pro tunc*. No separate Oyer and Terminer docket was kept among the records, but the proceedings of that Court were by custom entered in the docket of the Quarter Sessions. The Judges of the Quarter Sessions are also, by virtue of their commission, the Judges of the Oyer and Terminer.

On the trial, before WETMORE, P. J., and CONNELY and ACOCKS, A. JJ., a number of witnesses were examined, but the physician who attended the prosecutrix, a girl thirteen years of age, and examined her person soon after the alleged offence, although present during the trial, was not called by either party to testify.

The defendant requested the Court to charge, *inter alia:* (2) There can be no conviction in this case where the alleged violence was committed on a girl only thirteen years of age, and the physician who examined her the next day was in Court during the trial till the prosecution closed their evidence in chief, and was not called by the Commonwealth to prove that violence had been done to the prosecutrix. *Refused.*

The jury found a verdict of guilty.

After the trial, it was discovered that the precept and venire had issued for 38 petit jurors, returnable to the Court of Quarter Sessions, whereas, it is required by the Act of April 14, 1834, § 113, that the number of petit jurors summoned to serve in a Court of Oyer and Terminer shall not be less than forty-eight. On this ground, and because no certificate to the Oyer and Terminer had been filed, the defendant's counsel moved in arrest of judgment and for a new trial. A rule to show cause was granted, and after argument, discharged, the Court holding that although the venire was irregular, yet, after a trial on the merits, without objection, the defect was cured by virtue of the Act of March 31, 1860, § 53 (re-enacting the Act of February 21, 1814), which provides as follows:—

"No verdict in any criminal Court shall be set aside, nor shall any judgment be arrested or reversed, nor sentence delayed, for any defect or error in the *precept* issued from any Court, or in the *venire* issued for the summoning or returning of jurors, or for any defect in drawing, summoning or returning any juror or panel of jurors, but a trial or an agreement to try on the merits, or the pleading guilty, or the general issue, in any case, shall be a waiver of all errors and defects in or relative or appertaining to the said *precept, venire,* drawing, summoning and returning of jurors."

The Court, in an opinion discharging the rule, after citing Commonwealth *v.* Smith (2 S. & R. 300), Jewell *v.* Commonwealth (10 Har. 94), and Fife *v.* Commonwealth (5 Cas. 429), said: "If the defendant had declined to go to trial, or moved to quash the array, the trial would probably have been postponed, or the array quashed. But going to trial, by the forms and with the challenges allowed in the Court of Oyer and Terminer, we are constrained to the conclusion, from the letter of the statute and judicial construction given to the same, that after verdict it is too late for this objection to prevail."

The Court further held, upon the authority of Brown *v.* Commonwealth (28 Sm. 122), that the filing of the certificate to the Oyer and Terminer, *nunc pro tunc*, was sufficient.

The defendant took this writ, assigning for error, *inter alia:* (1) There was no Oyer and Terminer jury, and the Court, thus constituted, had no jurisdiction to try the case; (2) There being no certificate transferring the case from the Quarter Sessions to the Oyer and Terminer, it was tried in the Quarter Sessions which had no jurisdiction to try such an offence. (5) The refusal of the defendant's point, as above quoted.

R. Brown, for plaintiff in error.

The Act of March 31, 1860, § 53, which remedies *defects*, cannot apply to this case, where neither precept nor venire for an Oyer and Terminer jury was issued at all. The venire was issued for a Quarter Sessions jury of 38, a totally different thing from an Oyer and Terminer jury of not less than 48. The case was really tried in the Quarter Sessions. None of the cases of irregularity, cited by the Court below, apply, nor has any precisely similar case been found. But it is analogous to the case of People *v.* McKay (18 Johns. 218), where no venire had ever been issued, and it was held that there was entire absence of authority in the sheriff, and not any default which could be termed an irregularity.

Under the Act of March 31, 1860, § 35, a formal certificate is a condition precedent to jurisdiction of the Oyer and Terminer. This cannot be waived, even by express consent.

Dougherty *v.* Comth., 19 Sm. 286.
Mills *v.* Comth., 1 Har. 627.

The rule in England seems to be that there is not sufficient proof of penetration to constitute the offence, unless there be positive medical evidence of some sort of violence to the person.

2 Whar. & Stil. Med. J., sec. 279, 3d.

The fact that a physician did examine the prosecutrix, the next day after the offence was committed, in the presence of and at the instance of her mother, after she accused the defendant of the act, and the physician was present in Court during the trial and was not called by the Commonwealth, ought under the English rule to have acquitted the defendant, and the Court should have affirmed the second point.

S. P. Johnson, for defendant in error.

The case was tried and concluded without the question of jurisdiction once occurring to the Court, the District Attorney, or the defendant's counsel. The panel was not exhausted in the selection of the trial jury, and no talesmen were called. The defendant made all the challenges he desired, and there were plenty more regularly summoned jurors in attendance from whom further selections could have been made. The objection is purely technical; no allegation is made that anything was either omitted or committed prejudicial to the rights or safety of the defendant. The defect was merely a harmless oversight, which, if noticed in time, the defendant might perhaps have taken advantage of to postpone the trial. Even this is not certain under the ruling in—

Foust *v.* Commonwealth, 9 Cas. 338.

Being a "defect in or appertaining to the venire," the trial on the merits was, under the Act, a waiver of it. If this defect in the venire and shortage of jurors is not within the spirit and letter of the Act, it has failed to accomplish what it aimed at.

The power to amend by filing a certificate *nunc pro tunc*, to the Oyer and Terminer, was settled by Brown *v.* Commonwealth (28 Sm. 127, per AGNEW, C. J.), and the fact that the amendment was duly made and entered of record, disposes of the second assignment of error.

The physician was present and equally accessible to either party. When the Commonwealth closed, the district attorney informed the defendant's counsel that he did not intend to examine him. Yet after full opportunity to ascertain what his testimony would be, the defendant also omitted to call him, for the reason, presumably, that his testimony was valueless to either side. There is no more reason to presume that our not calling him was suggestive of defendant's innocence, than to presume that defendant's omission to call him was suggestive of his guilt. The English rule never obtained in this country, nor anywhere else since rape ceased to be a capital crime.

June 14, 1880. THE COURT. We are of opinion that the first assignment of error is sustained, and the judgment must therefore be reversed. The defendant was tried in the Court of Quarter Sessions for an offence of which that Court had no jurisdiction. This alone, however, would not have constituted a sufficient objection to the validity of the trial and sentence, after verdict and after a certificate of the cause into the Oyer and Terminer. Had there been a legal and actual Court of Oyer and Terminer in session at the time the case was tried, we should have held the subsequent certificate of the cause into that Court, *nunc pro tunc*, as sufficient, upon the authority of Brown *v.* Com'th (28 P. F. Smith, 122). But in point of fact there was no legally constituted Court of Oyer and Terminer in session, or capable of sitting at the time of the trial. The Act of April 14, 1834, § 113, provides that "the number of persons who shall be summoned and returned as aforesaid to serve as petit jurors in any Court of Oyer and Terminer shall not be less than forty-eight nor more than eighty, and in any other Court of criminal jurisdiction not less than twenty-four nor more than sixty." Now to summon thirty-eight jurors to serve in a Court of Oyer and Terminer is not a mere defect or irregularity in the venire. Without a panel of forty-eight jurors summoned and returned for service, an essential constituent of that Court is wanting. If a panel of thirty-eight would be a sufficient compliance with the law, we see no reason why a number still less would not suffice. The defect, or omission rather, is fatal to the constitution of the Court, and hence the certificate of a cause from the Quarter Sessions into a Court so composed is inoperative to effect the transfer. This consideration distinguishes the present case from all those cited by the learned Judge of the Court below. We hold, therefore, that there was no valid trial and sentence, and must reverse the judgment for that reason.

This decision makes it unnecessary to consider the other errors assigned. We cannot forbear, however, remarking that, in our opinion, the physician, who on the day after the occurrence examined the person of the girl upon whom the offence was alleged to have been committed, should have been called as a witness and required to testify by the district attorney. Whether his evidence tended to acquit or convict, it was demanded equally by the cause of humanity on the one hand, or of justice on the other. We say this, more especially, because there was no direct evidence of the *factum* of the crime, and no proof of actual penetration, the prosecutrix having testified that she was insensible and had no knowledge of what took place. We do not reverse for this reason, and do not sustain the fifth assignment of error which raises the question, but merely express our opinion as to what should have been done in the peculiar circumstances of this case.

Judgment reversed and venire facias de novo awarded.

Opinion by GREEN, J. SHARSWOOD, C. J., and PAXSON, J., absent.

May, '80.   May 11, 1880.
Colvin v. Beaver.
In re Contested Election of J. E. Colvin.

Constitutional law—Annexation of lands in one township to another township or borough for school purposes—Special Act of April 8, 1867—Constitutionality of—General Act of April 13, 1867—Construction of.

A school district is not strictly a municipal corporation.

The special Act of April 8, 1867 (P. L. 934), which provides that certain lands in Napier Township shall be attached to the borough of Schellsburg for school purposes, and the occupants thereof shall pay their school taxes to and be entitled to school privileges—including the right to vote for school directors—in said borough, is not in violation of the provision of the Constitutions of 1838 and 1874, that electors shall reside in the election district in which they vote.

Under the general Act of April 13, 1867 (Purd. Dig. 237), which authorizes the Court of Quarter Sessions by decree to annex lands in one township to another township or borough "for educational purposes," a resident on lands so annexed is brought within the new school district for all purposes for which it is formed—including the right to vote for school directors—although he remains connected with his township or former district for all other purposes.

Certiorari to the Quarter Sessions of Bedford County.

The petition of more than twenty-five qualified electors of the borough of Schellsburg, in Bedford County, Penna., set forth that it appeared by the returns of an election held on the 17th of February, 1880, for two persons to fill the office of school directors of said borough, that Charles W. Colvin received 51 votes, and was duly elected; that J. E. Colvin received 44 votes, and William H. Beaver received 43 votes; and that the said J. E. Colvin was returned as elected. The petitioners averred that William H. Beaver should have been returned as elected, and not J. E. Colvin, on the ground that a large number of qualified voters who had offered to vote for said Beaver were refused, and their votes rejected and not counted in the return—among others, the votes of persons included in the two following classes, viz.: (1) Persons residing on certain farms in Napier Township particularly named and annexed to the school district of said borough, for school purposes, by the special Act of April 8, 1867 (P. L. 934), which provides as follows:—

"Sect. 1. That the following named lands and tenements, situate in Napier Township, Bedford County, near the borough of Schellsburg, are *hereby attached to said borough, for school purposes,* to wit: The farms of Charles W. Colvin, the one known as the Reiley farm, and the other as the Hillegas farm; also the farm of George W. Bowser, and that of Reuben Colvin, all in Napier Township; and that all persons who now, or may hereafter, reside on said farms and properties, shall *pay their school taxes to,* and be entitled to all *school privileges, including the right to vote for* and serve as *school directors, in said borough: Provided,* that said persons shall not be liable to taxation for any purposes except school tax, in said borough."

(2) Persons residing on lands in Napier Township which had been annexed to the school district of said borough, for educational purposes, by a decree of the Court of Quarter Sessions, under the general Act of April 13, 1867 (Purd. Dig. 237), which provides as follows:—

"The several Courts of Quarter Sessions of this Commonwealth shall have authority, within their respective counties, to annex the land, or parts thereof, of persons resident in one township or borough, to another township or borough, for school purposes, so that when so annexed, the applicant shall pay his school taxes and be included within the school district to which it is so annexed, for educational purposes, and remain connected with the district or township of his residence, for all other purposes; and the said Court shall, upon the petition of any one desiring such change, proceed by views and reviews, in the manner, and under the restrictions, provided under the Act of General Assembly approved April 15, 1834, with its supplements, in regard to the alteration of the lines of any two or more adjoining townships: *Provided,* That all the costs of such proceedings shall be paid by the person or persons applying for such change."

The answer of J. E. Colvin admitted the facts set forth in the petition, but denied the right of the persons embraced in the said two classes to vote at said election for school directors, on the grounds (1) that the special Act of April 8, 1867, is unconstitutional, in that it contravenes Art. III., Sect. 8, of the Constitution of 1838, and Art. VIII., Sect. 1, of the Constitution of 1874, requiring that electors shall reside in the election district in which they vote. (2) That the general Act of April 13, 1867, authorizing the Court to annex lands to a school district "for educational purposes," does not contemplate annexation for any other purpose than that of paying taxes and sending children to school in the borough school district, and does not confer the right to vote for school directors therein.

After argument, the Court, HALL, P. J., held that the special Act of April 8, 1867, was not unconstitutional before the Constitution of 1874, and that it was not repealed or affected thereby; that the persons residing on said farms in Napier Township, above mentioned, were entitled to vote at the said election in the borough of Schellsburg ; and decreed that the return of the election of J. E. Colvin was illegal, and that W. H. Beaver was duly elected. The Court did not decide the question arising under the general Act of April 13, 1867, deeming it unnecessary for the determination of the case.

J. E. Colvin took this writ, assigning for error (1) the decree of the Court, deciding that the said special Act was constitutional. (2) That the Court should have decided that the said general Act does not confer on persons residing on lands annexed to a school district by the Court the right to vote for school directors in the township or borough to which they are so annexed.

Russell & Longenecker, for plaintiff in error.

The Legislature cannot extend the privileges of voters beyond their constitutional qualifications. The Constitution requires that electors shall reside in the election district in which they vote; the special Act of April 8, 1867, authorizes residents of one election district to vote in another. It is true that such right is only as to one set of officers, but the evil is greater than if the voter's whole power were transferred, because it opens the door to fraudulent voting by the same person in two districts.

The general Act of April 13, 1867, does not in terms give the *right to vote* to persons residing on the annexed lands, but provides that the lands shall only be annexed "for educational purposes," and the occupant "remains connected with the district of his residence for all other purposes."

Page *v.* Allen, 8 Sm. 338.
McDaniel's Case, Brightly's Elec. Cas. 238–242.
Williams *v.* Whiting, Ibid. 107.
Fry's Case, 21 Sm. 308.

J. M. Reynolds, for defendant in error.

The school system is a system peculiar to itself, and outside the general constitutional and legislative provisions relating to the election of purely municipal officers. School districts are territorial divisions rather than municipal corporations.

The Legislature has general power, with respect to school districts, to fix any boundaries it deems proper; to provide in what manner, in what place, and by whom school directors shall be elected.

Wharton *v.* School Directors, 6 Wr. 363.

The Legislature has always exercised, without question, the right to erect *independent* school districts out of parts of several municipal election districts, and has provided for holding elections for school directors therein. The constitutionality of such Acts has never been questioned.

Act of May 8, 1855, Purd. Dig. 237.
Act of April 11, 1862, Ibid. 239.

Prior to the new Constitution there was no prohibition against a special Act making a single school district by annexing a borough and a township, or two townships, for school purposes, and providing that the election for directors shall be in either; and the annexation of particular lands to an adjoining school district, for school purposes, by a special Act, or by the Court under a general Act, is similar in principle. Under the special Act, the right to vote for school directors in the district to which the lands are annexed is expressly given; under the general Act, it is an incident of the annexation; the privileges and obligations accruing thereby are correlative and coextensive.

May 24, 1880. THE COURT. This contention is as to the effect to be given to the special Act of 8 April, 1867 (P. L. 934), and the general Act of 13 April, 1867 (Purd. Dig. 237). The former declares that all persons residing on certain lands therein named, situate in the township of Napier, are attached to the borough of Schellsburg for school purposes, and shall pay their school taxes and be entitled to all school privileges—including the right to vote for and serve as school directors—in said borough. The general Act declares that, when the land of a resident of a township or borough shall be so annexed to another township or borough, the applicant shall pay his school taxes and be included within the school district to which it is so annexed for educational purposes, and remain connected with the district or township of his residence for all other purposes.

The language in the general Act shows a slight change from that used in the prior special Act, yet, we think, the substantial purpose and intent are the same. The later Act manifestly uses the more comprehensive words "for educational purposes," with the view of expressing in fewer words the same rights and obligations given and imposed in the previous Act. A person residing on the land thus annexed is brought within the school district for all purposes for which it is formed. There he pays his taxes towards the support of its schools and the erection of its school-houses. There he sends his children, and there he resides for all "educational purposes."

It is clearly within the true intent and spirit of the statute, that, where a person assumes those obligations and enjoys those benefits, there he shall have a voice in the election of school directors, and, if possessing the other necessary qualifications, be eligible as a director. It is not the design of the Act that he should be denied the exercise of those rights and privileges in the only place where he has such a direct interest. It would be an anomaly in the law to hold that he can exercise such rights in another school district where he pays no school taxes, can derive no special benefit from the schools, and within the bounds of which, for educational purposes, he does not reside. He does remain connected with his township or former district "for all other purposes," so as to give due effect to that clause in the statute. There he must continue to pay all his other municipal taxes, and there he retains all his other rights as a resident and an elector. A school district is not strictly a municipal corporation. (Wharton *et al. v.* School Directors, 6 Wright, 358; Commonwealth *v.* Beamish, 31 P. F. Smith, 389.) There was no constitutional prohibition against such a school district when it was formed. There is none now against forming such by a general law. Like independent school districts, they may wholly disregard township lines.

Judgment affirmed.
Opinion by MERCUR, J.
SHARSWOOD, C. J., and GREEN, J., absent.

July, '79, 75.   March 29, 1880.

Roth's Appeal.
Roth v. Riegel.

Execution—Attachment execution—Real estate —Acts of June 13, 1836, June 16, 1836, April 13, 1843, and April 10, 1849—Debtor's interest in the real estate of an intestate—Insufficiency of process to attach—"Legacies given"—"Lands devised."

Where on its face a writ of attachment embraces nothing but the defendant's interest or his distributive share in the personal assets of the decedent in the administrator's hands, and the return of service shows no attachment of land or interest therein, the administrator being admittedly not in possession of the land, the writ and service do not bind the defendant's interest in the real estate of the decedent.

PER TRUNKEY, J. The statutes of June 13, 1836, June 16, 1836, April 13, 1843, and April 10, 1849, have not confounded legacies and devises, nor the respective interests of one in the realty and personalty of an intestate, but have made each liable to attachment upon execution in satisfaction of a judgment. "Legacies given" and "Lands devised" are artistic phrases, neither of which includes the other. An interest in the goods and chattels of an intestate is quite different from an interest in his lands.

Neely *v.* Grantham (8 Sm. 433), and Straley's Appeal (7 Wr. 89), commented upon.

Appeal from the Common Pleas of Northampton County.

Appeal of Jeremiah Roth, trustee for Barbara Harwi, from a decree of the Court confirming the report of a commissioner appointed to distribute the fund arising from a sheriff's sale of the interest of Jacob Harwi, Jr., in the real estate of his father, Jacob Harwi, Sr.

The following material facts were found by the commissioner (Richard Brodhead) to whom the case was referred: Jacob Harwi, Jr., made a general assignment for the benefit of creditors in May, 1877. On the judgment docket of Northampton County there were recorded against him at the time of the assignment the following judgments:—

Samuel Riegel, No. 556, Sept. T. 1875, entry Nov. 29, 1875, $4500.

Jeremiah Dundore, No. 392, April T. 1876, entry May 5, 1876, $900.

The real estate assigned was duly sold by the assignee, but the judgment-creditors above were not reached.

Jacob Harwi, Sr., died in 1877 intestate, leaving considerable real estate, and personal property amounting to $16,000. The defendant, Jacob Harwi, Jr., was one of eight children of the decedent. John Harwi, one of the decedent's sons, took out letters of administration in January, 1878.

Riegel and Dundore issued writs of attachment Nos. 54 and 57 of February Term, 1878. The præcipe of Riegel was as follows:—

"Issue writ of attachment directed to the sheriff of Northampton County, commanding him to attach all moneys, property, legacies, or right, title, and interest of the defendant in the hands of John Harwi, administrator of Jacob Harwi, Sr., deceased, and summon him as garnishee."

Dundore's præcipe was substantially the same, concluding with "summon the said John Harwi, administrator, as garnishee." The writs were served in each case on January 7, 1878, to which the sheriff made the following return:—

"Attached, as within commanded, all the goods and chattels, debts, credits, effects, legacies, and distributive share of the defendant, Jacob Harwi, Jr., in the hands, possession, or custody of John Harwi, administrator of Jacob Harwi, Sr., deceased, and summoned him as garnishee by giving him a true and attested copy of this writ personally on Feb. 7, 1878."

Both the above judgments were transferred to Lehigh County, January 22, 1878, and on the same day attachments were issued upon the interest of the defendant, Jacob Harwi, Jr., in the estate of his father, Jacob Harwi, Sr., in the hands of the administrator. The præcipes and returns were substantially the same as those in Northampton County. Interrogatories to John Harwi, administrator, were filed in Lehigh County in the cases of Riegel and Dundore, which were served March 23, 1878, and answers were filed by the administrator, in which it appeared that the defendant was entitled to a distributive share in the real and personal estate of Jacob Harwi, Sr., deceased.

On February 27, 1878, Jacob Harwi, Jr., confessed judgment to Jeremiah Roth, in trust for Barbara Harwi for $8600, which was entered in the Common Pleas of Northampton County as of February Term, 1878, No. 269, and on which execution was issued March 4, 1878, No. 547, April Term, 1878. A fi. fa. was thereupon issued by Roth, trustee, etc., to April Term, 1878, and a vend. ex., under which the interest of Jacob Harwi, Jr., in the real estate, was sold on August 17, 1878, for $1800, to the plaintiff in the writ, and the fund, less the costs, was ruled into Court for distribution.

In his supplemental report the commissioner found the following facts: that the occupants of the realty of the decedent's estate were not served with process under the attachments, that the sheriff omitted to file a description of the realty alleged to have been attached within five days after service of the writ, that the judgment index did not show that the attachments were a lien on the realty, and that the personal estate of the defendant would be more than sufficient to pay his debts. Before the commissioner Riegel and Dundore claimed the fund by virtue of the lien created upon the interest of the defendant in the estate, both real and personal, of his father, by the attachment executions issued under the Act of April 13, 1843, upon their judgments. This claim was resisted by Roth because the præcipe, writs, and sheriff's return were not in accordance with the mode of procedure set forth in the above Act, for the reason that they did not specifically describe the real estate in which the defendant's interest was sold under the subsequent judgment of the plaintiff, and further that the said attachment executions were invalid against the said Roth, because the requirements of the Acts of Assembly were not complied with.

The commissioner allowed the claims of Riegel and Dundore, and awarded them the fund in Court. To this report Jeremiah Roth filed exceptions, which the Court (MEYERS, P. J.) overruled, on the authority of Straley's Appeal (7 Wright, 90) and Neely *v.* Grantham (8 Sm. 433), and confirmed the report absolutely. Jeremiah Roth took this appeal, assigning for error the action of the Court in dismissing his exceptions and confirming the report of the commissioner.

Edward Harvey and *M. C. Kline*, for the appellant.

The real estate in this case was not in the possession or occupancy of the administrator. Nor were the occupants served with process under the attachments. No description of the realty was filed with the præcipe, no real estate was attached or described in the return, nor was any reference to realty to be found in the judgment index. The Act of 1843 merely enlarged the writ of attachment so as to include legacies, land, or interest in real or personal estate, while they were in the hands or possession of some one other than the defendant. An analysis of the several Acts shows clearly that the writ must be issued against legacies, lands, or interests, real or personal estate held by the defendant or by some one whether he be executor or administrator, and the person holding or occupying must be summoned as garnishee. If land is attached, it is essential that the person holding or occupying be garnisheed. The proceeding is *quasi* in rem, in which the thing against which the process is directed must be levied upon.

The property must be actually and potentially under the control and within the possession of the garnishee.

Kase *v.* Kase, 10 Casey, 130.

It is admitted here that the personal estate is more than sufficient to discharge all debts. True, lands are assets for the payment of debts, but only when the personal estate is insufficient. But until the administrator takes the necessary steps to make the land available for that purpose, the land descends to the heir, who is entitled to the rents.

Bishop's Estate, 10 Barr, 471.

The administrator had no actual possible interest in the undivided one-eighth interest of the defendant in the lands of his father. Having no such interest, and not holding the land for the defendant, no lien was acquired on the land under the attachments, and, as no lien was acquired, the plaintiff is entitled to the fund in Court. But, further, the law requires service of the writ on the party in possession, a levy and description by metes and bounds, a return as having been so levied upon, and a description of the land, which must be filed with the prothonotary within five days, who is directed to note it on the judgment index.

Land is not mentioned either in the writ or the return. The prescribed form of serving the writ must be strictly pursued.

Hayes *v.* Gillespie, 11 Casey, 156.

The first thing is to "serve" the property, and then the person in whose hands it is found.

Lambert *v.* Challis, 11 Casey, 146, in notes.

The return must show on its face a legal service.

Lehigh Valley Ins. Co. *v.* Fuller, 31 Sm. 398.

In Straley's Appeal (7 Wr. 90), cited on the other side, the land was within the actual control of the administrator, and the personalty was insufficient to pay the debts. In Neely *v.* Grantham (8 Sm. 433) there was a conversion, and the Court was not unanimous.

W. E. Doster and *B. F. Fackenthall*, for appellees.

There is here no dispute as to our priority in point of time, and the question is, were the attachments of Riegel and Dundore liens upon the defendant's interest in his father's estate? It is submitted that a specific description of the realty is not necessary in a case like this, where the interest of the defendant in the estate of the decedent is sought to be charged. If the subject of attachment were the land of a living person, the case would be different. By the Foreign Attachment Act of July 27, 1842, three things may be attached: (1) legacies, (2) lands devised, and (3) any interest in the real or personal estate of any decedent. The subject matter claimed to be attached is any interest of the defendant in the real or personal estate of the decedent. The Act of April, 1843, is substantially similar in its provisions. The interest of the debtor in the real and personal estate of the decedent is attachable no matter in whose hands it may be, and the interest is not any defined or specific property, but is analogous to the interest of a partner in the partnership. But the interest, if it were in doubt, is plainly described in the words "distributive share." It is submitted that no especial degree of certainty is required in such writs if the object is fairly indicated, so that the garnishee may know how to frame his answer, and the Court to make a decree.

The case is ruled by--
Neely v. Grantham, 8 Sm. 433.
Straley's Appeal, 7 Wr. 89.

May 3, 1880. THE COURT. Section 10, Act of April 13, 1843 (P. L. 235), subjects all legacies given, and lands devised to any person, and any interest which any person may have in real or personal estate of any decedent, by will or otherwise, in the hands or possession of the executor or administrator, or in whosesoever hands the same may be, except legacies and distributive shares due married women, to attachment and levy in satisfaction of any judgment, in the same manner as debts due are made subject to execution by the 22d section of the Act of June 16, 1836 (P. L. 765). Said twenty-second section makes debts due to any defendant liable to execution like other goods and chattels. As debts cannot be taken in the same mode as a horse, or leasehold, the thirty-fifth section declares "the same may be attached and levied in satisfaction of the judgment in the manner allowed in the case of a foreign attachment." In the case of personal property, a foreign attachment is served by the officer going to the person in whose hands or possession the defendant's goods or effects are supposed to be, and then and there declaring, in the presence of one or more credible persons of the neighborhood, that he attaches the said goods or effects. (Act June 13, 1836, § 48, P. L. 580.) The forty-ninth section declares how the writ shall be executed; and the fiftieth, what the sheriff shall do after the service, in case of real estate. By Act of 1849, § 11 (P. L. 620), process in the nature of attachment may be issued at any time after the interest of the defendant in the real or personal estate shall have accrued by reason of the death of the decedent.

The statutes have not confounded legacies and devises, nor the respective interests of one in the realty and personalty of an intestate, but have made each and all liable to attachment upon execution in satisfaction of a judgment. "Legacies given". and "lands devised," are artistic phrases, meaning different things, and neither includes the other. And so an interest in the goods and chattels of an intestate is quite different from an interest in his lands. Immediately after the death of a decedent, his heir takes the real estate in possession, and, as if he held by purchase, he may sell and convey or encumber it, or his judgment creditor may cause it to be seized in execution. The administrator of an intestate has no right of possession or custody of his lands. The possibility that the primary fund may be insufficient for payment of the decedent's debts does not prevent possession and control of the land by the heir until adjudication and conversion by proceedings in the proper Court. One who acquires the title of the heir stands in his place and holds subject to liability for debts of the intestate, if there be not enough personalty to pay them. Here the præcipe directed an attachment of the moneys and interest of the defendant in the hands of the administrator, and the writ rightly followed the præcipe. Obeying this writ, the sheriff attached "all the goods and chattels, debts, effects, credits, legacies, distributive shares of the defendant" in the hands, possession, or custody of the administrator of Jacob Harwi, deceased. Upon the admitted facts the administrator was not in possession of the lands, and no service was made on the occupants. The personal estate of the decedent is more than sufficient for payment of his debts, but this fact matters little, if anything. On its face the writ embraces nothing but the defendant's interest, or his distributive share, in the personal assets in the administrator's hands, and the return of service shows no attachment of lands or interest therein.

Clearly the writ and service did not bind the defendant's interest in the real estate, and it is unnecessary now to decide how the writ for such purpose should be executed. The record fails to show an attachment or levy on lands or interest therein, and consequently there is not a semblance of notice to subsequent purchasers or encumbrancers.

The decree of the Court below seems to rest mainly on the authority of Straley's Appeal (7 Wr. 89) and Neely v. Grantham (8 P. F. S. 433). The former was not referred to in the latter, though at variance with the views of a majority of the Court. In Neely v. Grantham, two of the five Judges dissented, holding that the writ, not having been served in the manner directed in a foreign attachment, did not create a lien, and the present Chief Justice agreed in the judgment expressly upon the ground that the interest of the defendant in the estate was personalty; but if realty, the strong inclination of his mind was to unite with the dissenting Judges. Therefore, the case cannot be regarded as ruling that the defendant's interest in the real estate of the decedent is bound by an attachment of his interest only in the personal estate, or that the real and personal estates are so blended in the statute that words exclusively applicable to one include the other.

Decree reversed, and it is now considered and decreed that the fund $1549.32 be appropriated to the judgment in favor of Jeremiah Roth, trustee for Barbara Harwi, No. 269, Feb. Term, 1878, costs to be paid by appellees.

Opinion by TRUNKEY, J.

May, '79, 122.
May 27, 1879.

Lehr v. Taylor.

Trover—When not maintainable—Joint owners—Right of possession in defendant—Landlord and tenant—Equitable defence in the nature of set-off in actions ex delicto.

Trover is not maintainable when the right of possession is in the defendant.

Semble, per PAXSON, J. Even in actions ex delicto, an equitable defence in the nature of set-off, as to matters growing out of the same transaction, may be admissible.

Error to the Common Pleas of Mifflin County.

Trover, by Matthew P. Taylor against Henry Lehr, to recover damages for the conversion of one hundred and sixty-five bushels of wheat. Plea, the general issue.

The evidence disclosed the following facts: In 1871, the plaintiff went into possession of certain premises under a lease from the defendant. The lease was for one year, but the plaintiff had been permitted to remain on the property for five years, without any other agreement. The lease provided that the plaintiff should sow such portion of the farm as the defendant might designate, and receive from him one-half of the produce. And it was further stipulated—

"that the right of possession of the crops of grain and hay in the fields, or in the barn, shall be in the first party [the defendant] until the same is divided, and the first party's share is delivered to him."

At the expiration of his term in the spring of 1876, the plaintiff removed from the premises and the defendant resumed possession. During the summer, the plaintiff cut and put into the barn the wheat crop in question, which had been sown in the previous fall, and demanded of the defendant his share or its equivalent in money. The defendant refused to comply with this request until the plaintiff accounted for the defendant's portion of a corn crop alleged to have been fraudulently retained by the plaintiff. The defendant subsequently sold the entire crop of wheat and kept the proceeds.

On trial, before BUCHER, P. J., the defendant submitted the following points:—

(1) That under the article of agreement, the plaintiff cannot sustain his suit in this form of action, and the verdict must be for defendant. *Refused* (1st assignment of error).

(2) That if the jury believe, from the evidence, that the plaintiff did not deliver to the defendant, of the crop of the last year of his tenancy, his full share of the corn crop, but fraudulently withheld a part thereof, and that defendant offered to plaintiff that he could thresh the wheat and have his part of it, if he would comply with the article of agreement and give defendant his share or part of the corn crop withheld, then plaintiff cannot recover, and the verdict must be for defendant. *Refused* (2d assignment).

(3) If the Court refuses to answer the first and second points as requested, the Court is requested to charge the jury that the defendant is entitled to deduct from the plaintiff's claim the value of whatever corn of defendant's share plaintiff withheld and did not deliver to him, in mitigation of damages. *Refused* (3d assignment).

The Judge charged, *inter alia,* as follows: "This is an action ex delicto, and the set-off here claimed cannot be allowed . . . . . We admitted this evidence with hesitation, and have come to the conclusion that this set-off cannot be allowed. If you believe, then, that there has been a conversion of this wheat by the defendant, you ought to find a verdict for the plaintiff."

Verdict and judgment for the plaintiff. The defendant took this writ, assigning for error the refusal to affirm the points presented, and the charge of the Court as above quoted.

D. W. Woods, for the plaintiff in error.

The right of possession of the wheat being in the defendant, trover cannot be maintained.

Given v. Kelly *et al.,* 4 WEEKLY NOTES, 433.
2 Tr. and H. Prac., 5 ed., § 1561, p. 51.

Even admitting that the action is in the proper form, the defendant should have been allowed to show, in mitigation of damages, that the plaintiff had fraudulently withheld the defendant's share of other crops.

Romig's Adm'r v. Romig, 2 Rawle, 241.
Saam v. Saam, 4 Watts, 432.

A. Reed, for the defendant in error.

Trover may be maintained between joint owners, where the common property has been destroyed, converted, or misappropriated.

Addison on Torts, § 420.
2 Hilliard on Torts, 296.
Agnew v. Johnson, 5 Harris, 373.

The stipulation in the lease, that the defendant should retain the right of possession of the grain until divided, gave him no more than a lien thereon until he should receive his share. It did not vest him with authority to sell it and convert it to his own use.

Stafford v. Ames, 9 Barr, 343.
Adams v. McKesson's Ex'r, 3 Sm. 81.

Set-off is only allowable in actions ex contractu.
Romig's Adm'r v. Romig, *supra*.
Kater v. Steinruck's Adm'r, 4 Wr. 501.

October 6, 1879. THE COURT. The plaintiff worked the defendant's farm upon shares. By the terms of the lease he was to have half the grain, but the right of possession thereof in the fields or in the barn was to be in the defendant until divided, and his share delivered to him under the terms of the lease. The plaintiff moved off the farm in the spring of 1876. The wheat which is the subject of the present contention was sown the previous fall and harvested during 1876. It was therefore one of the crops of the year 1875. The defendant refused to allow plaintiff to take his share thereof, upon the allegation that the plaintiff had fraudulently withheld a portion of the corn and other crops for the year 1875. Thereupon the plaintiff brought this action of trover and conversion to recover the value of one half the wheat crop. Upon the trial in the Court below the defendant contended: (1) That the action of trover and conversion would not lie; and (2) That, if it were the proper form of remedy, the defendant could show in mitigation of damages that the plaintiff had fraudulently withheld a portion of the crops, and could recover the value thereof in this proceeding. Both these points were ruled against the defendant, the learned Judge holding that in an action in form *ex delicto* no set-off can be allowed.

We are of opinion that the plaintiff has mistaken his form of action. The possession and the right of possession of the grain were in the defendant until divided as stipulated in the lease, not as to the wheat crop alone, but as to all the crops of grain and hay in the fields or in the barn. If therefore the plaintiff has appropriated the corn and other crops to his own use in fraud of the rights of his landlord under the lease, would he also be entitled to demand a division of the wheat, and sue the latter in trover and conversion upon a refusal? We need not argue such a plain proposition. The possession being in the defendant, the action of trover cannot be sustained. Nor does it matter that the defendant sold the wheat and recovered the entire proceeds, if, as he alleges the plaintiff has in his hands more than the amount unlawfully withheld from him. Had the plaintiff brought his action upon the lease, all questions arising under it could have been properly adjusted. The attempt to settle only so many of them as suits his convenience is ingenious, but carries with it the penalty of failure by reason of a mistake in the form of action.

As this view is decisive of the case, we need not discuss at length the question raised by the 2d and 3d assignments. The general rule is, as stated by the Court below, that in an action *ex delicto* a set-off is not admissible. But the evidence offered here was not by way of set-off, but of equitable defence as to matters growing out of the same transaction. There is a line of cases which go very far towards establishing its competency. (See Heck v. Shener, 4 S. & R. 249; Romig v. Romig, 2 Rawle, 241; Saam v. Saam, 4 Watts, 432.) There is a growing disposition to favor every principle that avoids circuity of action. There is always a saving of expense, and sometimes a great gain to the cause of justice, by having one jury to pass upon the whole case.

Judgment reversed.
Opinion by PAXSON, J.

Quarter Sessions.

Oct. 30, 1880.
Commonwealth v. McGurk.

Indictment for murder—Act of 1785, providing for discharge of untried prisoner, on bail, after second term of Court—Not applicable where, after trial, a new trial has been granted as matter of grace, and the second trial has been delayed more than two terms.

Motion for discharge.

The prisoner was tried at the January Term, 1880, and convicted of murder in the first degree. Upon his motion a rule for a new trial was granted, and, on Saturday, May 1, 1880, the last day of the April Term, made absolute. Four terms having elapsed at which Courts of Oyer and Terminer were held, without the second trial taking place, the prisoner now moved for his discharge under the Act of 1785.

E. B. Morris and *Walter G. Smith*, for the motion.

The new trial having been granted, the verdict in the first trial is wiped out, and defendant is now in the position of never having been tried, so that the two-term rule should run, in his favor, from the date of the rule being made absolute for new trial, as though that had been his commitment.

The motion for new trial was based wholly on errors of law. The new trial was therefore matter of right, and the prisoner should not be made to suffer for what was not his fault. The Act is imperative, and as the prisoner's case does not fall within either of the exceptions mentioned therein, he is entitled to a discharge.

MITCHELL, J. The object of the Act of 1785 was to prevent oppression of a prisoner in confinement by undue delay in bringing him to trial. Notwithstanding the general language of the Act, it has been held that the provision for a discharge at the end of the second term does not apply where the trial has been prevented by any circumstances of moral, physical, or legal necessity. Most of the exceptional cases which had then arisen (1875) are referred to in Comm. *v.* Brown (32 Leg. Int. 430; 2 WEEKLY NOTES, 153); and in Comm. *v.* Hale (7 WEEKLY NOTES, 359) it was further held that where the prisoner had been a fugitive and had surrendered, he had put himself outside of the protection of the Act, and could not now complain if the Commonwealth chose its own time to try him.

The present case is new, but is strongly analogous to Comm. *v.* Hale. The Commonwealth did its whole duty in trying the prisoner at the proper time. The result was his conviction; and now that a new trial has been granted to him upon his own motion and as matter of grace, it would be unreasonable to allow him to dictate when the Commonwealth shall be ready to try him the second time. Having asked and received the favor of the Court, he must take it *cum onere.*

It is not necessary to decide what would be the effect of a new trial granted by the same Court for error in law, or a reversal of judgment by the Supreme Court for the same reason. I have read carefully the opinion of Judge ELCOCK, and think it sets forth clearly that the new trial is granted solely as matter of grace, and out of tenderness for the prisoner in a case involving his life.

The motion must be refused.

Common Pleas—Law.

C. P. No. 1.   December 11, 1880.

Backer v. Saurman.

Practice—Attachment execution—A motion to dissolve an attachment is too late after plea filed.

Motion to dissolve attachment execution.

The plaintiff Saurman, having obtained a judgment against one Knabe, attached certain music plates belonging to defendant, which were in the possession of Backer, a printer, having been left with him for the purpose of being printed from. Backer pleaded *nulla bona,* and afterwards moved to quash the writ.

N. Dubois Miller, for the motion

The attachment was improvidently issued under the Act of June 16, 1880 (P. L. 767), because the goods were neither pawned, pledged, nor demised by defendant.

Troubat & Haly's Prac. § 1181.

Price, contra. After plea filed it is too late to move to set aside the attachment.

Poor *v.* Colburn, 7 Sm. 415.
Troubat & Haly's Prac. § 1198.

THE COURT. Rule discharged.

C. P. No. 4.   Dec. 6, 1880.

In re St. Nicholas Coal Co.

Lost certificate of stock—Corporation—Dissolution of—Evidence of ownership of stock as between corporation and stockholder — The stock ledger and stock certificate book are the evidence of the ownership of stock—The certificate need not be produced to entitle the owner to receive an amount awarded him upon a final distribution of the assets of the corporation.

Rule to show why accountants should not pay the amount awarded by the auditor, without production of certificate of stock.

The affidavit of E. S. Stagers, upon which the Court granted the rule, set forth that on May 1, 1880, the St. Nicholas Coal Company, a corporation, was dissolved by a decree of the Court in a proceeding for dissolution and distribution under the Act of April 9, 1856 (P. L. 293); that the assets were converted into cash, and the known debts of the company paid by the directors, who then filed their first and final account, showing a balance in their hands of $28,553.42; that the account was referred to an auditor, who reported that, no creditors appearing, the fund must be awarded *pro rata* amongst the stockholders upon producing their certificates of stock to the accountants; that the auditor reported that the deponent's name appeared upon the stock ledger and stock certificate book as the owner of 208 shares of stock, and awarded to him $94.12 as his share of the balance in the hands of accountants. The affidavit further set forth that, though he had made diligent search, the deponent had been unable to find the certificate for 200 shares of said stock, that the same had been mislaid or lost by him, that he had so informed accountants, and that he had at no time assigned or sold the same or any of said shares. The accountants, however, refused to pay him the amount awarded him by the auditor without the production of the lost certificate.

M. H. Todd showed cause.

A rule to show cause, in a statutory proceeding of this character, is not a proper method of obtaining payment of a lost instrument. There should be some formal proof of loss, filed of record, other than the mere affidavit on which the rule was granted. A petition or bill should be filed, and, upon answer, the matter should be referred to an examiner to take testimony. But even if relief can be granted by rule, indemnity should be required to protect the accountants, who under the Act are trustees, against subsequent *bona fide* claimants.

Wm. A. Redding, for the rule.

As between a corporation and corporator the stock ledger and stock certificate book are evidence of the ownership of the stock; the certificate is only secondary evidence, and it is not necessary to produce it.

Bank of Commerce's Appeal, 23 S. 59.

THAYER, P. J. The affidavit may be treated as a petition, and the facts set forth not being denied must be taken to be admitted. The distribution being made in a judicial proceeding after public notice to all parties in interest, no responsibility can attach to the accountants. I do not think indemnity is necessary in this case.

THE COURT. Rule absolute.

[The jurisdiction of a Court of Equity to compel the payment of lost obligations has always been recognized in England. Where the instrument is negotiable or transferable by delivery, or where a title would pass to a bona fide holder for value without the necessity of such inquiry as would develop the fact of the loss, indemnity is a condition precedent of payment. The jurisdiction is classed under the general head of "Accident." (Haynes's Outlines of Eq. 131-2; Story Eq. Jur. §§ 81-83; Bispham's Eq. § 177 *et seq.*) The original ground of jurisdiction in equity appears to have been the impossibility of making *profert*, which was necessary at law, and also the superior machinery of a Court of Equity to protect the defendant by requiring indemnity against subsequent claimants. Although it is believed that no reported case can be found where this equity jurisdiction has been exercised in Pennsylvania, there is no doubt that it exists, by virtue of the Acts extending to the Common Pleas Courts equity jurisdiction "in all cases over which Courts of Chancery entertain jurisdiction on the grounds of fraud, *accident*," etc. (Acts of June 13, 1840, § 39; April 16, 1845, § 3; and Feb. 14, 1857.) The jurisdiction has been exercised in Vermont and North Carolina. (Miller *v.* R. R. Co., 40 Ver. 399; Carter *v.* Jones, 5 Iredell Eq. 196; Deans *v.* Dortch, Id. 331.)

Apart from the separate equity practice, there are several instances, in Pennsylvania, where the equitable remedy has been administered in actions at law. Thus, in Meeker *v.* Jackson (3 Yeates, 442), the plaintiff in assumpsit recovered the amount of a lost bill of exchange, the Court requiring that "the plaintiff must indemnify the defendant against the bill." So, in Snyder *v.* Wolfley (8 S. & R. 328), the plaintiff in an action of debt was permitted to recover the amount of a prize drawn by a lost lottery ticket, upon giving indemnity against future claims founded upon it. In Bisbing *v.* Graham (2 Har. 14), a recovery was had in assumpsit on a promissory note lost after suit brought upon it, the Court holding that execution should be restrained until indemnity was given. Again, in Fitchelt *v.* R. R. Co. (5 Phila. 132), the District Court of Philadelphia, per HARE, J., held that the same principle applied to lost coupons of railroad bonds.

In the case reported above, the relief was afforded by rule, in a statutory proceeding, of an equitable character, by petition, etc., for the dissolution of a corporation, as provided by Act of Assembly.]

C. P. No. 4.   Dec. 20, 1880.

Mayberry v. Railway Co.

Street railways—Liability for negligence—Duty to keep in repair streets occupied by them—Husband and wife—Suit by wife alone—Release by wife—Feme sole trader—What necessary to entitle wife to immunities of Act of 1855.

Rule for a new trial.

Case, by Mary A. Mayberry against The Second and Third Streets Passenger Railway Co.

On the trial, before ELCOCK, J., it appeared that the plaintiff was a married woman but not living with her husband and was supporting herself and family; that she with her mother and some of her family took passage upon one of the defendant's cars to go to Meadow St., Frankford; that she was carried safely to the place of her destination; that at the place where the plaintiff and her party were landed the street was crossed at right angles by a deep gutter, which was covered by large iron plates over which passed all the travel of the street; that it was dark at the time in question, and one of the plates was so displaced or turned that, as the mother of the plaintiff stepped upon one end of the plate, it tilted up and fell back upon the foot of the plaintiff, who was following, inflicting serious injury.

The defendant offered in evidence, *inter alia*, a release executed by the plaintiff to the defendant in consideration of the sum of $20. It was admitted not as a bar to the action, but as evidence affecting the measure of damages.

The jury gave a verdict for the plaintiff, and assessed the damages at $702.

George W. Thorn, for the rule.

The release given by the plaintiff was a bar to the action. She became by the desertion of her husband a feme sole trader so far as to permit her to sue for or release a claim of which she was the meritorious object. The claim against the defendant, if any, was her separate property, and as such she could release it as if she were unmarried.

Act 4 May, 1855, Purd. Dig. 692.

Black *v.* Tricker, 9 Sm. 13.

Elsey *v.* McDaniel, 9 WEEKLY NOTES, 269.

The contract of the defendants was ended when the plaintiff was safely landed, after that there was no further liability. She had no right of action against them for any injury which happened to her by reason of the street being out of repair. The statute which requires the company to keep the streets in repair imposes no pecuniary liability upon the company to a party injured, whatever may be its effect as to the municipality.

Phila. and Reading R. R. *v.* Ervin, 8 Nor. 71.

J. Newton Brown, for plaintiff, contra, cited, Act 10 April, 1858 (P. L. 240), incorporating the company, and City Ordinances of April 1, 1859 (Ordinances, p. 138), and of May 6, 1876 (Ibid. p. 98), as to the obligation of the company to keep the streets in repair.

The evidence does not make out a case coming under the Act of 1855, as construed in—

D'Arros's Appeal, 7 WEEKLY NOTES, 125.
King *v.* Thompson, 6 WEEKLY NOTES, 241.

January 22d, 1881. THE COURT. By the Act of Assembly of April 10th, 1858 (P. L. 240), incorporating said company, "it is provided that the company shall keep the streets and avenues traversed by the said railway in perpetual good repair, at their own expense." This is the usual stipulation in the railway Acts of incorporation of this city, and obliges the company to maintain the highway in safe repair its whole width, from curb to curb, and in fact this company did construct this gutter and covering agreeably to the ordinance of Counsels, and under the supervision and plan of the Commissioner of Highways. For any defect in the plan or mode of construction the company are not liable, but, constructed as it is, they are bound to keep it in proper order and repair and safe for travel. Of course the company should be allowed a reasonable time, in case of its becoming out of repair or deranged, to restore it to its proper condition. What would be a reasonable time, under the circumstances, would be a question for the jury. That the jury have passed upon, and the remaining question is whether, by the release signed by plaintiff without the joinder of her husband, she is estopped in her action. It has been determined, in R. R. *v.* Burson (11 Sm. 369), that a release by a married woman, her husband not joining, of land damages, was void. In this case it is but her chose in action, but as she could not sue or recover without the joinder of her husband, therefore she cannot release. In Black *v.* Tricker (9 Sm. 13), it is held that where the circumstances mentioned in the Act of February 22d, 1718, and the Act of May 5th, 1855, have been established in any controversy in the ordinary way by proofs, the privilege of being a *feme sole* trader results to the married woman. It has been contended, in argument before us, that, as the plaintiff at the time was separated from her husband, and supporting herself and family, she was entitled to the damages happening to her, and, being so entitled, could release them by a written instrument, under seal, and thus bar her action within the ruling of the case last cited. In this case the evidence was simply the testimony of the plaintiff, who said: "I have not always gone by the name of Mayberry. He was my second husband. I sometimes signed my name just as it came handy. At other times I signed my name Hague. This was my first husband's name. I was not living with Mr. Mayberry on August 24, 1878; have not been living with him for six or seven years up to the present time. I only lived with him four months from the day we were married. I was married to him on the 10th day of November, 1873. After I left him I supported myself. In these four years he did not support me at all: went mostly by the name of Hague." This does not make out a case within the Act of Assembly cited, for a simple failure to support the wife, without drunkenness or other cause, will not deprive the husband of his right to the wife's personal property on her death without issue. (See D'Arros's Appeal, 7 W. N. C. 125.)

There must be a desertion or a neglect or refusal on the part of the husband—something that involves the wilful non-performance of a duty on his part. (King *v.* Thompson, 8 W. N. C. 241.)

Here there is no evidence of desertion by the husband, and for aught that appears, they may have agreed amicably to separate, or in fact the wife may have deserted the husband. Unless the evidence shows that the wife would be entitled to a decree as a *feme sole* trader, she cannot be regarded within the benefits of the Act, and her release, therefore, cannot amount to an estoppel. It is evidence against her as a declaration of what she estimated her damages at the time, and as against her oral testimony upon the subject matter, and for such purpose it was admitted.

There was some evidence in the cause affecting the *bona fides* of the release, which the verdict also settles in favor of the plaintiff, which, irrespective of the legal questions involved, might determine the cause.

Upon the whole, we see no reason to disturb the verdict, and the rule for a new trial is discharged.

Opinion by ELCOCK, J.

Orphans' Court.

Nov. 16, 1880.

Connell's Estate.

Decedent's estate—Distribution—Surcharge of executors—Issue to try validity of voluntary conveyance to wife (and executrix) alleged to be fraudulent as to subsequent creditors—When not granted—Effect on fraudulent conveyance of grantor's discharge in bankruptcy—Limitations.

Sur exceptions to the report of an auditor recommending that an issue be awarded.

The account of Elizabeth Connell, widow of the decedent, and C. C. Haffelfinger, executors of George Connell, deceased, was referred by agreement to an auditor to audit and report distribution of the balance, before whom evidence was submitted, tending to show the following facts:—

In 1862 the said George Connell, being insolvent, for the purpose of defeating creditors, conveyed, for a nominal consideration, certain real and personal estate, being all his property, to one Pennock, who executed a declaration of trust, not recorded, to the effect that he held the same as security for present and *future* indebtedness of Connell to him, and, as to the excess, in favor of the grantor's wife. Connell became a bankrupt in 1868, and was discharged in 1869. He died in 1871, and in 1872 Pennock conveyed the property to his widow. Both before and since the decedent's death, Mrs. Connell received large sums of money, being the proceeds of sales of parts of the property so conveyed.

Before the auditor, one Watts claimed payment of a judgment obtained by him against the decedent in his lifetime, in 1869, after the discharge in bankruptcy, and, the fund being insufficient, he alleged that the said voluntary conveyance of 1862 was fraudulent and void as to him, and that the property and proceeds held by the widow, one of the accountants, was property of the decedent's estate, with which she should be surcharged.

At his request, the auditor filed a report recommending that an issue be awarded to try, substantially, the validity of the said conveyance of 1862, to which report the accountants excepted.

John G. Johnson, for the exceptants.

Even if subsequent creditors could impeach the deed, which they cannot, they are concluded by the discharge in bankruptcy. The assignee alone could have inquired into its validity.

F. P. Prichard and *A. M. Burton,* contra.

Subsequent creditors can always impeach a voluntary conveyance intended to defraud them. And such fraudulent intent is sufficiently shown, under the authorities, to warrant an issue in this case, by the following facts, viz.: total insolvency at the time of the conveyance; want of consideration; the property was all the grantor's estate; a secret trust for *future,* as well as alleged existing indebtedness; no reconveyance to the wife until after the grantor's death.

Bump on Fraud. Conv. 327, 83-84.
Ridgeway v. Underwood, 4 W. C. C. R. 129.
Ammon's Appeal, 13 Sm. 289.
Thomson v. Dougherty, 12 S. & R. 448.
Smith v. Carlisle, 17 N. H. 417.
McCulloch v. Hutchinson, 7 Watts, 434.
Johnston v. Harvy, 2 Pa. Rep. 82.
Mackason's Appeal, 6 Wr. 330.
Serfoss v. Fisher, 10 Barr, 184.
Barringer v. Stiver, 13 Wr. 129.

The failure of the assignee in bankruptcy to impeach the deed does not conclude us, as the secret trust was a continuing one, and void as against future creditors. The discharge of prior debts cannot affect the question here raised, which is whether the property is that of the decedent's estate, with which the accountant shall be surcharged. See

Elliott's Appeal, 14 Wr. 75.
Crunkleton v. Wilson, 1 Browne, 361.

November 27, 1880. THE COURT. To what extent a voluntary conveyance may be attacked by subsequent creditors, has been very elaborately considered by the Supreme Court, in the recent case of Harlan *v.* Maglaughlin (37 Legal Intelligencer, 16; reported *ante,* p. 353.) . . .

Under the principles thus enunciated, it is, perhaps, not easy to see how issues can be awarded in the present case at the instance of the parties now asking for them, who did not become creditors of the decedent until long after the date of the conveyances which they seek to impeach, and who have shown no fact, certainly none stronger than in Snyder *v.* Christ (3 Wr. 400), indicating an intention to commit a fraud against them.

We need not, however, inquire whether it would not be possible to distinguish the case before us from the authorities referred to, because an insuperable obstacle in the way of the subsequent creditors is found in the proceedings in bankruptcy which followed the conveyance and preceded the creation of the indebtedness now existing.

Under the Bankrupt Act of 1867, § 14 (Revised Statutes, § 5046), it was expressly provided that "All property conveyed by the bankrupt in fraud of his creditors, all rights in equity . . all debts due him or any person for his use, and all liens and securities therefor, and all his rights of action for property or estate, real or personal . . . and all his rights of redeeming such property or estate, together with the like right, title, power, and authority to sell, manage, dispose of, sue for and recover or defend the same, as the bankrupt might have had if no assignment had been made, shall, in virtue of the adjudication of bankruptcy and the appointment of his assignee, . . . be at once vested in such assignee."

The property and rights thus vested in the assignee became a fund for the payment of the debts of the bankrupt then existing, the debts which, so far as concerns after-acquired property, were discharged by the discharge granted to the debtor under the proceedings in bankruptcy. The fund belongs exclusively to them, and neither in whole nor in part can it be diverted from them.

It is clear, therefore, even if it be conceded that the conveyances made, directly or indirectly, by the decedent to the accountant, his wife, were expressly designed to defraud future as well as existing creditors, that those who did not become creditors at all until after the bankruptcy, and who, therefore, can have no interest in the property conveyed, have no right to inquire into the transaction.

Such right can only be exercised by the assignee, and that for the benefit of the then existing creditors.

That the assignee did not, within two years after the property or right of action vested in him, bring suit to enforce his right, cannot avail subsequent creditors or confer the right upon them. The provision in the Act, that, if the property was held by one claiming adversely, the assignee shall be barred in two years if he shall not bring suit, was intended, like all other statutes of limitation, for the purposes of quiet and repose. As the right of action was vested exclusively in the assignee, if he should not exercise it, the title of the person holding adversely becomes absolute as against the world, just as in the case of real estate held adversely against the real owner for twenty-one years. (See Munshower *v.* Patton, 10 S. & R. 334.) Certainly the bankrupt could not afterwards assert ownership, and his subsequent creditors must claim through him.

On the other hand, if the property has not been held adversely, the assignee has not been barred, and he alone can assert ownership or maintain a suit.

We therefore sustain the exceptions to the Auditor's report, and decree accordingly.

Opinion by PENROSE, J.

Dec. 21, 1880.

Rankin's Estate.

Accounts of executors and administrators—Statement of principal and income to be separate—Allowance for stating an account—When counsel fee allowed to executors and trustees in an issue devisavit vel non—Duty of executors to require indemnity for costs and expenses of litigation from parties interested in maintaining the will.

Sur exceptions to adjudication.

At the audit of the account of the executors and trustees of Eleanor Rankin, deceased, before ASHMAN, J., the following facts appeared :—

By her will the decedent devised to her sons, Abraham G. M. Rankin and Alexander M. Rankin, the dwelling-house in which she resided at the time of her decease. All the residue of her estate she devised to her executors in trust to pay over the income to her daughters, Marcella F. Rankin and Ellen F. Rankin, making certain provisions in case of their death or marriage. The daughters contested the validity of this will, and offered for probate a will of prior date, which they contended had been republished after the date of the instrument in question.

An Examiner was appointed, and the executors and trustees retained counsel to sustain the will. In their account the accountants claimed credit for a counsel fee of $500, for legal expenses in maintaining the will. Credit was also claimed for a counsel fee of $100, for services in connection with the audit, and $15 for preparing the account. In regard to these claims the Auditing Judge found that the executors must be surcharged with the counsel fee of $500, as the expense of the contest must be borne by those interested in the issue. He also reduced the credit of $100 for services in connection with the audit to $50, and disallowed the claim of $15 for preparing the account, surcharging the executors in the amount of $565.

To this finding exceptions were filed on behalf of the daughters.

H. M. Dechert, for exceptants.

Costs accrued in proceedings to maintain a will, which result successfully, and in defending the interests of the estate, are a proper credit in the account of the executor.

Sterrett's Appeal, 2 Pa. R. 426.
Geddis's Appeal, 9 Watts, 284.
Koppenhaffer *v.* Isaacs, 7 Watts, 170.
Scott's Est., 9 W. & S. 98.
Royer's Appeal, 1 H. 569.
Price's Est., Martin's Appeal, 3 W. N. C. 320.
Jacobs *v.* Bull, 1 Watts, 370.

J. R. Welsh and *Zane*, contra.

Dec. 31, 1880. THE COURT. The first error apparent upon the face of the account is in combining principal and income in one account. They should always be separated. The labor of both Auditing Judge and counsel would thus be lessened, and the condition of the estate and its management by the accountants rendered intelligible to the parties interested. . . . It is also erroneous to claim a credit for preparing the account, when the same was prepared by the trustee personally, himself a member of the bar. It is usual for a reasonable allowance to be made to an executor, administrator, or other trustee, who is unable to state his account by reason of unfamiliarity with bookkeeping or accounting, and is consequently obliged to employ another to perform that duty, but never where he undertakes the clerical or professional labor himself. It is a part of his duty to keep a book or books, showing the receipts and expenditures of the estate, and to prepare his account personally, unless from the unusual labor and skill required he would be justified in employing an accountant or bookkeeper. And it is always presumed that the commissions or compensation granted by the Court is in part a recompense for whatever clerical labor may be thus rendered. This item of credit must be disallowed.

The first exception is in disallowing a credit claimed for five hundred dollars, paid to the counsel of accountants for professional services in successfully resisting an appeal by the *cestuis que trust*, from the decision of the Register, in admitting to probate the will of testatrix. In view of the long-continued contest, and the services performed by counsel both before the Examiner and the Court, and upon comparison with the amount expended by the contestants for services of counsel in their behalf, the Auditing Judge concludes that the sum paid by accountants for professional services in upholding the will, is not excessive, but disallows the expenditure as an improper credit, for the reason that the expenses of the contest should have been borne by the parties immediately interested in the issue. That the accountants as executors were mere stakeholders, and their duty, before taking part in the contest, was to call upon the parties interested in the establishment of the will, to indemnify them against the costs and expenses to which they might be subjected. This view of the law is entirely correct, and fully sustained by the authorities, among which may be cited Mumper's Appeal (3 W. & S. 441), Geddis's Appeal (9 Watts, 284), Royer's Appeal (13 Penna. St. Rep. 569), and Landis's Estate (1 Phila. Rep. 528). And an administrator *pendente lite* cannot charge the estate with the expenses of an issue to try the validity of a will (Dietrich's Account, 2 Watts, 332).

But the rule of law so well settled is inapplicable to the present case. Here the contestants were the *cestuis que trust*, and the proponents of the will both executors and trustees. They were made respondents by the act of the *cestuis que trust*, in their effort to destroy the trust declared by testatrix, and it became their duty to defend and uphold the will. This they did, not merely as executors, but as testamentary trustees, and were successful. In such case we think the estate should justly pay the expenses incurred. In Landis' Estate, *supra*, THOMPSON, P. J., says, *inter alia:* "An executor cannot claim the expenses of such a proceeding, unless, in endeavoring to sustain the will, he acts for the benefit of the estate. If it is of no advantage to the estate or to those entitled to the fund that such litigation should be carried on, the executor cannot claim allowance in his account for expenses so incurred. If the executor acts to sustain a trust, and is successful, his expenses would be fairly chargeable upon the trust fund; but where no such fund exists, and the supposed trust is a nullity, the real owners of the estate cannot be made liable." This exception is sustained.

In addition to the above expenditure for the services of counsel in the appeal from the Register, the accountants also ask an allowance of one hundred dollars for the advice and services of counsel during the continuance of the trust, and rendered in the settlement and adjudication of their account. The trust extended through a period of more than five years prior to the filing of the account, and is still continuing. During all this time, from the character of the trust estate, mainly realty, and the litigious and hostile disposition and attitude of the *cestuis que trust*, it frequently became necessary for the trustees to consult counsel to aid them in the care and management of the estate. Then, upon the filing of the account, the trustees were met with objections and attempts to surcharge, which have been found without foundation. These hearings before the Auditing Judge and the Court all required the labor and services of counsel, and for which no additional compensation is requested. We therefore think that the allowance asked by the trustees is reasonable and proper. This exception also is sustained. . . .

The adjudication is re-committed for correction, in accordance with this opinion.

Opinion by HANNA, P. J.

WEEKLY NOTES OF CASES.

Vol. IX.]   THURSDAY, FEB. 10, 1881.   [No. 25.

Supreme Court.

Oct. & Nov. '80, 188.   Oct. 5, 1880.
Stabler v. The Commonwealth.

Criminal law—Section 82 of Act of March 31, 1860—Attempt to poison—What constitutes an "attempt" within the meaning of the Act—Distinction between "attempt" and "intention."

Merely delivering poison to a person, and soliciting him to place it in the spring of another, is not an "attempt to administer poison" to the latter, within the meaning of the 82d section of the Act of March 31, 1860 (Purd. Dig. 340, pl. 128). The Act recognizes a distinction between intent and attempt.

Error to the Quarter Sessions of Allegheny County.

Indictment of Alois Stabler. The first count charged that the defendant, on the 3d day of July, 1879, etc., "feloniously did attempt to administer a certain poison, commonly called Paris green, etc., to one Richard F. Waring, with intent to commit the crime of murder, and to feloniously kill and murder the said Richard F. Waring," etc. The sixth count charged that the defendant solicited one John Neyer, a servant of the said Richard F. Waring, to administer a certain poison, etc., to the said Waring, etc. The defendant was convicted on both counts. No complaint was made of the conviction under the sixth count.

There having been no official notes of testimony taken on the trial of the case in the Court below, it was agreed by counsel that the Supreme Court shall treat the following as being all the testimony bearing on the first count of the indictment.

"The only witness sworn was John Neyer, who testified, that he had a conversation with Alois Stabler, over a year before the information was made against him, in which Stabler stated his grievance against Waring, and stated his (Stabler's) determination to be revenged, and then solicited Neyer to put poison in Waring's spring, so that he and his family would be poisoned, and offered the witness a reward therefor, and gave him directions how to administer the poison, and gave him the poison to administer. That the witness refused to administer the poison, and said he would not have anything to do with it, and handed the poison back to Stabler. That the witness had his coat off when the two were talking together. Three or four days after this conversation the witness, upon putting on his coat, found a package in his coat pocket, which he believed was the same package that Stabler had handed him. That the witness shortly after left the city of Pittsburgh and went to Toledo, Ohio, where he remained several months. That he again returned to Pittsburgh, about a year after the conversation with Stabler, and then, for the first time, told a party about what had taken place, and handed this party the package of poison.

"That the witness never had any intention of administering the poison, and never did anything towards it, and never had any other conversation with Stabler about the matter except the one stated."

The Court, EWING, J., charged that if the jury believed the evidence of John Neyer, in substance as above given, it constituted an attempt, and they might find the defendant guilty on the first count.

The jury found a verdict of guilty on both counts. The defendant moved for a new trial and in arrest of judgment, which motion was overruled by the Court, and separate sentences were pronounced. The defendant took this writ, assigning for error, *inter alia*, the charge of the Court, that the testimony of Neyer was sufficient to sustain a verdict of guilty on the first count.

W. C. Moreland (*N. C. Cook* with him), for plaintiff in error.

An attempt to commit a crime is an endeavor to accomplish it, carried beyond mere preparation, but falling short of the ultimate design. Acts, directly tending to the end in view, are necessary to constitute an attempt. Mere intent is not enough.

Kelly v. Commonwealth, 1 Grant, 488.

The proof in this case does not sustain the allegation. The Act of 1860, § 82 (P. L. 403), under which the indictment is drawn, follows the Stat. of 1 Vic., c. 85, sec. 3, which has been construed as we now contend in—

Regina v. Williams & Rees, 1 Car. & Kirwan, 589; s. c., 1 Denison's Crown Cases, 40.

Where a foreign statute agrees with our own, a judicial construction of the former will have weight in construing the latter. The case of People v. Bush (4 Hill, 134), on which the Court below relied, was decided on a statute of New York, differing materially in some of its language from the Act of 1860.

John S. Robb, District Attorney, contra.

October 15, 1880. THE COURT. This indictment contains six counts. A conviction was had on the first and sixth, and sentence was pronounced on each separately. The first charged a felonious attempt to administer poison to one

Waring, with intent to commit the crime of murder, and feloniously to kill and murder him; the sixth with wickedly soliciting one Neyer to administer poison to said Waring. No error is now alleged to the conviction and judgment on the sixth count. The conviction on the first and the judgment thereon are assigned for error.

This count is framed under § 82 of the Act of 31st March, 1860 (Purd. Dig. 340). It declares: "If any person shall attempt to administer poison or other destructive thing, or shall attempt to cut or stab or wound or shall shoot at any person, or shall, by drawing a trigger or in any other manner, attempt to discharge any kind of loaded arms at any person, or shall attempt to drown, suffocate, or strangle any person, with intent, in any of the cases aforesaid, to commit the crime of murder, he shall, although no bodily injury be effected, be guilty of felony, and be sentenced to pay a fine of one thousand dollars, and undergo an imprisonment, by separate or solitary confinement, not exceeding seven years."

All the testimony to prove the first count was the evidence of Neyer. He testified to a conversation which he had with Stabler more than a year before the information was made against him. His testimony is substantially this: Stabler stated his grievance against Waring, and a determination to be revenged. He solicited witness to put poison in Waring's spring, so that the latter and his family would be poisoned, offering him a reward for so doing. He handed witness the poison, and directed how it should be administered. Witness replied he would have nothing to do with it, and handed the poison back to Stabler. While they were conversing the coat of witness was off; on putting it on, three or four days thereafter, he found a package in the pocket, and believed it to be the one Stabler had handed him. Soon after this witness left the State, and did not return until about a year thereafter. He then, for the first time, related the conversation to a person, and handed him the package of poison. He further testified that he never had any intention of administering the poison, and never did anything towards it, and had no other conversation with Stabler about the matter.

Is this evidence sufficient, within the meaning of the statute, to prove an attempt on the part of Stabler to administer the poison? The Act recognizes a distinction between *intent* and *attempt*. The former indicates the purpose existing in the mind; the latter an act to be committed. Merely soliciting another to do an act is not an attempt to do that act. (Rex *v.* Butler, 6 C. & P. 368; Smith *v.* Commonwealth, 4 P. F. Smith, 209.) In this last case it was said: "In a high moral sense it may be true that solicitation is attempt; but in a legal sense it is not." In some cases it has been held, although a solicitation to commit a misdemeanor does not constitute an attempt to commit the misdemeanor, yet a solicitation to commit a felony does constitute an attempt to commit the felony. This view does not appear to have been adopted in Pennsylvania. The case of Kelly *v.* The Commonwealth (1 Grant, 484) was an indictment for murder charged to have been committed in an attempt to commit a rape. It was held that acts were necessary to constitute an attempt. That an attempt to commit a rape was an ineffectual offer by force with intent to have carnal knowledge. If such acts, with such intent, were not proved, the prisoner could not be convicted of the attempt; that it should be an actual, not a constructive attempt. An intent to commit fornication was not sufficient.

In the present case it is contended that putting the poison into the pocket of the witness was an act sufficient to constitute the attempt if Stabler expected and believed it would be used as he had requested. The uncontradicted evidence is, that it was so put without the knowledge of the witness, and after his positive and unqualified refusal to use it. He swears he never used it, or attempted to use it, or had any intention of so doing. To submit to the jury to find that Stabler expected and believed the witness would administer it, was not only without evidence, but against the evidence. If, however, it was actually delivered with that intent, we do not think it constituted an attempt to murder under the 82d section of the Act of 31st March, 1860. This section is substantially a copy of the 3d section of the Act of 1 Victoria, chapter 85. In an indictment under that Act in Regina *v.* Williams *et al.* (1 Car. & Kirwan, 589), it was held that the delivery of poison to an agent, with directions to him to cause it to be administered to another, was insufficient to establish an attempt to murder. So, on an indictment under the same chapter for attempting to discharge loaded firearms at a person, it was held in Regina *v.* Lewis (9 C. & P. 523), that some act must be shown to prove the person did attempt to discharge the firearms, and merely presenting them was not sufficient. Upon an indictment for attempting to discharge a pistol loaded with powder and ball, with intent to murder, a witness testified: "The prisoner took out a small pistol, and said, 'I will settle you,' or 'I will do you,' and either half or full-cocked the pistol, and pointed the muzzle at my brother," with his finger on the trigger. Yet it was held the charge of felony could not be supported, as it was not proved that the prisoner drew the trigger. (Reg. *v.* St. George, Idem, 483, 38 E. C. L. R.) PARKE, B., said: Here a trigger was to be drawn, and it is not drawn. It seems to me that the object of the Act was to punish proximate attempts—that is, those attempts which immediately lead to the discharge of loaded arms." It is true, in People *v.* Bush (4 Hill, 133), a conviction was sustained for an attempt to commit a felony where the act proved was as remote from the crime intended to be perpetrated as the act proved is in the present case. That ruling, however, rests on a statute of New York, which contains language not in the Act of 1 Victoria cited, nor in our own statute. It has additional words, "and in such attempt shall do any act toward the commission of such offence." In giving construction to a statute containing such language, a conclusion may well be reached that would be forced and unjust in construing our statute, which is so different. The conduct of the plaintiff in error, as testified to by the witness, undoubtedly shows an offence for which an indictment will lie without any further act having been committed. He was rightly convicted, therefore, on the sixth count. We, however, think all that occurred at the interview with the witness, and the legal inference deducible therefrom, followed by no other act, is not sufficient to justify a conviction for an attempt to commit the felony as charged. The act proved did not approximate sufficiently near to the commission of murder to establish an attempt to commit it within the meaning of the statute. The second and third assignments are sustained, and, on the first count, judgment reversed.

Opinion by MERCUR, J. STERRETT, J., dissents.

Jan. '80, 70.   Jan. 7, 1881.
Dick v. Stevenson.

Mechanic's lien law—Validity of claim filed for materials delivered at the shop of the contractor before the commencement of the building—Under what circumstances the omission to name all the contractors not fatal.

In the absence of fraud, materials furnished for a building on its credit, delivered at the shop of the contractor, may be made the subject of a lien, although they were delivered before the commencement of the building.

Where one of two joint contractors dies during the progress of the work, a claim filed against the other alone, not naming him as survivor, is good; the proceeding being *in rem*, it would be improper to substitute the personal representatives of the deceased.

Error to the Common Pleas No. 3, of Philadelphia County.

Scire facias sur mechanics' claim filed by Hugh Stevenson and John Stevenson, trading as Stevenson & Co., against Walter B. Dick, owner, and Albert J. McLaughlin, contractor, for lumber furnished to premises on Sixteenth Street and Jefferson Street.

Defendant filed an affidavit of defence of the following nature: (1) That Albert J. McLaughlin, named in the claim filed as contractor for said building, was not the contractor thereof. That the building was erected under a contract in writing, dated the 18th of December, 1877, between John McLaughlin, Jr., and Albert J. McLaughlin, of the one part, and affiant, of the other part, and that the said Albert J. McLaughlin had no authority to make contracts for labor or materials, in the construction of said building, except such as he acquired under said written contract, in conjunction with the said John McLaughlin, Jr. That the building was begun and continued by said contractors, until the 24th of August, 1878, when John McLaughlin, Jr., died. And that claimant is not entitled to a claim against the building for lumber furnished, during the lifetime of John McLaughlin, Jr., under a contract with Albert J. McLaughlin, alone, without the conjunction of John McLaughlin, Jr. (2) That the building was not commenced until 23d February, 1878, when the cellar digging was begun. That the items of lumber charged in said claim, prior to that time, were not delivered at the said building, or upon the lot of ground upon which the same is erected, but at the shop of Albert J. McLaughlin, and that as to those items, amounting, in the aggregate, to the sum of $137.65, the claimant is not entitled to a claim against said building.

A rule for judgment for want of a sufficient affidavit was made absolute, LUDLOW, P. J., delivering the following opinion: "It has been frequently decided, that materials furnished for a building, though not used or delivered at the building, may be made the subject of a lien, and, in the absence of any allegation of fraud in the affidavit of defence, there seems to be no reason why, in this instance, a judgment should not be entered. It is a matter of common practice for building materials to be prepared long before a house is commenced; and to strike down this lien for the reason assigned would be to destroy a right incident to the very nature of the business, which it is the avowed object of the lien law to protect.

"We are also of the opinion that the contractor is properly named. After the death of one of the contractors, as the proceeding is *in rem*, it would be improper to substitute the personal representatives of the deceased contractor; and while it would possibly have been better to have named the living contractor as the survivor, yet we do not think the omission is fatal to the validity of the lien."

The defendant took this writ, assigning for error the action of the Court in entering judgment for want of a sufficient affidavit of defence.

John M. Thomas, for the plaintiff in error.

Part of the lumber furnished was delivered before the commencement of the building; that part therefore could not have been sold upon its credit. There is no lien where materials are not furnished upon the credit of the building.

Hills *v.* Elliott, 16 S. & R. 59.

In the cases which decide that there is a lien for materials delivered at the shop of a contractor, the building was in process of erection.

White *v.* Miller, 6 Har. 52.

The objection is not that the contractor, Albert J. McLaughlin, was not described as the survivor, as stated in the opinion of the Court below, but that Stevenson & Son, by a sale of materials to Albert J. McLaughlin alone, during the lifetime of John McLaughlin, Jr., could not acquire a lien against the building, by reason of the owner's contract with John McLaughlin, Jr., and Albert J. McLaughlin jointly.

Charles C. Lister, for the defendant in error.

The time and place of delivery are not important, provided the materials are furnished upon the credit of the building. The Act of Assembly gives a lien for materials furnished "*for* or about the erection or construction of the building." Hence the price of materials furnished *for*, but not used *in* the building, can be recovered.

Hinchman *v.* Graham, 2 S. & R. 170.
Church *v.* Allison, 10 Barr, 416.
Odd Fellows' Hall *v.* Masser, 12 Har. 507.
Parrish's Appeal, 2 Norris, 111.

The lien of plaintiff below complies strictly with the Act of Assembly, which requires "the name of the contractor to be set out when the contract of the *claimant* is made with such contractor." This has been done here.

The proceeding is *in rem.* "The object of naming the parties connected with the structure is a designation of the thing, not of the person."

Knabb's Appeal, 10 Barr, 186.

January 17, 1881. THE COURT. The survivor of two joint contractors is rightly named as sole contractor in the claim filed. He had the power, as such survivor, to bind the building, and so far as the owner was concerned, it mattered not whether the materials were furnished at the shop of the contractor, before or after the building was begun, provided they were furnished on its credit. We think the opinion of the learned President of the Court fully sustained both on principle and authority.

PER CURIAM. Judgment affirmed.

Oct. & Nov. '80, 147.   Nov. 10, 1880.

Faas v. Warner, Controller, etc.

Constitutional law—Legislative power—Special Act directing a county to pay the personal debt of its ex-sheriff—Unconstitutionality of—Mandamus.

An Act of Assembly requiring a county to pay the personal debt of its ex-sheriff, contracted for bread for jail prisoners, is void.

A sheriff of Allegheny County, having agreed with the county to board all jail prisoners at a specified price for each per day, contracted with one F. to furnish the necessary bread. After F. had furnished bread to a large amount, the sheriff died insolvent, largely indebted to F. The county paid all that it owed the sheriff to his administrator, and F. received a portion of his claim from the administrator. Afterwards by a special Act of Assembly, the controller of the county was required to ascertain the balance due from A. to F., and to certify the amount to the commissioners for payment. Upon petition for a mandamus to compel the controller to comply with the requirements of the Act:

Held, that the debt being the personal debt of A., the Act of Assembly was unconstitutional and void.

Error to the Common Pleas No. 1, of Allegheny County.

This cause arose in the Court below upon a petition by J. M. Faas for a mandamus to Henry Warner, Controller of Allegheny County. It was subsequently agreed that the petition should be regarded as a writ of alternative mandamus and the answer as a return to that writ. The plaintiff demurred to the answer.

The petition set forth that the late Harry Woods, while sheriff of Allegheny County, contracted with the petitioner to furnish bread for the prisoners in the county jail, and that, under this contract, Woods at the time of his death was largely indebted to the petitioner. That the petitioner had received from the estate of Woods a portion of his debt, but that there was still due him $855.48, which the estate was insufficient to pay. That in view of this insufficiency, by a special Act of Assembly, approved March 30, 1870 (P. L. 673), the controller of said county was authorized and required to ascertain the balance due the petitioner, with interest, and to certify the same to the commissioners, whose duty it should be to direct the same to be paid as other claims against the county are paid. That the controller has refused to examine the claim, or to certify it in accordance with the Act, and, therefore, the petitioner prayed for a mandamus directing him so to do.

The answer of the controller set forth: that the County of Allegheny did not contract the debt, and never was liable to pay it; that Woods was commissioned sheriff on November 27, 1861, and on that day made a contract with the county by which he agreed to board all jail prisoners at a specified price for each per day, said board necessarily including bread as well as other food, and that in pursuance of this contract, the county had paid Woods during his lifetime, and after his death in August, 1863, to his administrator, and before the passage of the said Act of Assembly, in full for boarding said prisoners; that the said Act of Assembly is unconstitutional and void; and that petitioner's claim was barred by the statute of limitations before the passage of said Act, and is not revived thereby.

The petitioner having demurred to the answer, the Court, after argument, refused the mandamus. Whereupon the petitioner took this writ, assigning for error the refusal of the mandamus.

Geo. Shiras, Jr., for plaintiff in error.

The Act, if otherwise legal, clearly waives the statute of limitations in this particular case. The State itself, as a sovereign political entity, may waive the benefit of such a statute, and it follows that a county, which is territorially a part of the State, and as far as legal and political powers and obligations are concerned is merely possessed of such powers and obligations by way of delegation, cannot claim a vested right under a statute of limitations, or complain if the State think fit to declare in any particular case, that the county shall not have the advantage of such a statute.

Can the validity of the Act be more successfully assailed on the ground that it undertakes to devolve upon the county the debt of Harry Woods? It may be conceded that the State could not legislatively throw such a burden upon a county regardless of the question whether the municipality had received any benefit amounting to a consideration for such a burden, but here the county has received such benefit. It was bound to provide bread for its prisoners. The plaintiff furnished the bread, and has not been paid. Why may not the State give the plaintiff a remedy against the county? It is no answer to say that the county has paid the debt to Woods's estate. She was bound to know of and provide for the debts contracted for her benefit, and cannot relieve herself of the liability to pay for the sustenance of her prisoners by a private and secret contract with one of her officers. She is not asked to pay a second time. It must be presumed that all the money paid to Woods's estate on account of bread was properly applied. The plaintiff gives credit for all he received, and only asks payment of the balance.

S. H. Geyer, contra.

While the county is legally bound to furnish bread for her prisoners, she may make the contract, for that purpose, with whomsoever she pleases. She made the contract with Woods, and did not know Faas in the matter. The plaintiff cannot recover, because there is no privity between him and the county, and the Legislature would no more have the power to compel a county to pay a debt it did not owe, than it would to compel a private individual to pay a debt he did not owe.

Sharpless v. Mayor of Philadelphia, 9 Harris, 147.

Nov. 22, 1880. THE COURT. This case is heard on petition and answer, and, of course, as the answer is demurred to, we must accept the facts therein set forth as true. The answer alleges that the County of Allegheny did not contract the debt mentioned in the petition, and was never liable for the payment of it. It avers, on the contrary, that the county contracted with Woods, the sheriff, for a stipulated sum, for the support of the convicts, and that this compensation necessarily included bread as well as all other articles of food necessary for their support. The answer further avers that the entire contract price was paid to Woods and his administrator in various sums and at different dates aggregating $7333.25, which sum it says was "more than ample to pay for all the food (including bread) furnished" to the prisoners. The petition itself avers that Woods, personally, contracted the debt in question, and that a considerable part of it was received from his estate in payment. It thus appears that the petitioner's claim was a purely personal one, by himself against Woods, and further that there was not even a shade of obligation, legal or moral, on the part of the county to pay this debt. In such circumstances an Act of the Legislature, directing the county to pay it, is of no more validity than would be an Act directing the county to pay the debt of any private citizen. Such legislation is void for want of constitutional power to enact it. No authority has been shown in support of the claim of the plaintiff, and we are clearly of opinion that the Court below was right in refusing the writ of mandamus prayed for.

Judgment affirmed.

Opinion by GREEN, J.

May, '8c, 158.   May 10, 1880.

Himes's Appeal.
Anderson's Estate.

Decedents' estates—Act of April 14, 1851—Exemption of $300 in favor of widow or children of "decedent"—Minor child of a widow is entitled to the benefit of the Act.

The decedent was a widow before and at the time of her death. Her entire estate, real and personal, was appraised at less than $300. This the only surviving child, a minor, claimed to have set apart for her use, under the Act of April 14, 1851:

Held, that the property was rightly set off to the minor child.

King's Appeal, 3 Norris, 345, distinguished.

Appeal from the decree of the Orphans' Court of Bedford County, approving the appraisement setting apart $300 worth of property of Susan Anderson, deceased, for the use of Frances Anderson, a minor child of said decedent, under the Act of April 14, 1851.

The following facts were found by the auditor (John H. Jordan): Susan Anderson died intestate, leaving to survive her one child, Frances Anderson, a minor. The decedent's husband had deserted her, and had not been heard of for more than seven years. At the time of her death, Susan Anderson owned personal property, and a tract of land comprising about twenty-six acres. The whole of this property was appraised at less than $300, and set apart for the use of the surviving child of the deceased, under the Act of April 14, 1851. Among the debts owed by the decedent was a claim of $75 made by Catharine Himes, the appellant, for services rendered the former during her last illness.

The appellant filed exceptions to the appraisement when it was presented to the Court for approval, which exceptions were sustained by the auditor. Exceptions to the report of the auditor were subsequently sustained by the Court, and the appraisement approved.

Catharine Himes thereupon appealed, assigning for error the decree of the Court setting apart the property to the minor child.

Alexander King, for appellant.

The provisions of the Act of April 14, 1851, are limited to the property of a husband or father.

King's Appeal, 3 Norris, 345.
Nevins's Appeal, 11 Wr. 230.

Spang & Cessna, for appellees.

The *decision* in King's Appeal is not authority for the plaintiff's argument. And, under the facts of this case, the appellee is clearly entitled to the benefit of the exemption.

Burrell Township *v.* Pitts. Guard. of the Poor, 12 Sm. 472.
Sipes *v.* Mann, 3 Wr. 414.
Terry's Appeal, 5 Sm. 344.
Hettrick *v.* Hettrick, Id. 290.

May 24, 1880. THE COURT. This contention is as to the right of the appellee to have the property of her deceased mother, in value less than three hundred dollars, set off to her under the Act of 14th April, 1851.

The appellee is a minor, and her mother, before and at the time of her death, was a widow. It is contended that the appellee is not entitled to it under the authority of King's Appeal (3 Norris, 345). In seeking to ascertain the true ruling in any case, due regard must be had to the facts on which it was decided. The contention there was between the husband of the deceased wife and her children. The children of the wife sought to claim it against the rights of her surviving husband. Here there was neither husband nor wife. It was the property of a widow, and the contention is between a creditor and her only child. No marital rights of a husband are invoked, and the child does not claim property derived from a wife, but from a widow. The facts are so essentially different that the rule declared in King's Appeal does not apply. We adhere to the correctness of that ruling whenever applicable. To strain the principle there declared so as to control the present case, would do violence to its spirit and defeat the humane provisions of the statute.

The learned Judge was clearly right in distinguishing that case from the present, and committed no error in ordering the property to be set off to the minor child.

Decree affirmed and appeal dismissed at the costs of the appellant.

PER CURIAM. SHARSWOOD, C. J., and GREEN, J., absent.

[*Cf.* Steel's Estate, *ante*, 274.]

Jan. '81, 69.   Jan. 14, 1881.

Brady v. The Delaware and Raritan Canal Company.

Negligence—What is not, on part of a canal company—Duties of canal company beyond line of canal.

A canal company propelled, by a stationary engine, plaintiff's barge from the mouth of their canal into the Raritan River on a falling tide, towards a wharf where the barge was to be tied up until made up into a tow to be towed by the company's tugs to New York. The barge, while under the charge of her owner's crew, ran upon a snag in the river and sank. It was, in the opinion of several boatmen, dangerous to shove boats out upon the river in such a state of the tide, and boats had before grounded in that neighborhood. In an action by the owner against the canal company for the injury to his barge:

Held, that the above state of facts presented no evidence of negligence to go to a jury, and that, in default of evidence that defendant's agent had knowledge of the existence of the obstruction, a nonsuit was properly granted.

Error to Common Pleas No. 3, of Philadelphia County.

Case, by John Brady against the Delaware and Raritan Canal Company, the Pennsylvania Railroad Company, lessee, to recover damages for injury done to the plaintiff's barge.

On the trial, before YERKES, J., the plaintiff proved, that, on the day when the alleged injury was done, plaintiff's barge, laden with coal, was being forwarded by the company defendant to New York. The barge was manned by a crew of two men in the employ of the plaintiff. On reaching the outlet lock of the Delaware and Raritan Canal, it was discovered that one of the lock gates was broken. Between half and three quarters of an hour was required to repair the gate. Meantime, defendant's barge was detained in the lock, and the tide in the Raritan River outside continued to fall, until, when the repairs were concluded, it was very near low water. Immediately after the repair of the gate plaintiff's barge was, together with some others in front of her, discharged from the mouth of the canal, and by a stationary engine of defendant propelled towards the snubbing place about a thousand feet further down the Raritan River, where the barges were usually secured until made up into the tow to be towed to New York by defendant's tug boats. No barge was propelled out of the canal after the plaintiff's. As soon as plaintiff's barge left the canal, or cast off from the stationary engine, she was duly steered by her captain towards the snubbing place; but, about two or three hundred feet from the mouth of the canal, and some one hundred feet from the point where she cast off the lines from the stationary engine, she ran upon a snag, and stuck there till the obstruction pierced through her bottom and she sank, notwithstanding all reasonable efforts were made by her crew to get her off. Plaintiff also showed by several boatmen who knew the locality, that in their opinion it was dangerous to send boats out from the canal into the Raritan River when the tide was from one-half to three-quarters down, that the bottom was bad for boats to rest on, and that boats had before got aground in that neighborhood on a falling tide. The plaintiff then closed.

Counsel for defendant asked for a nonsuit, which the Court granted. This nonsuit the Court in banc subsequently refused to take off. Plaintiff took this writ, assigning for error the entry of judgment of nonsuit.

J. Warren Coulston, for plaintiff in error.

The defendant was negligent in discharging the plaintiff's boat on too low a tide, into a portion of the river over which defendant had assumed control.

The company was bound to provide a safe bed for its canal, and for the entrance thereto and exit therefrom.

Parnaby *v.* Lancaster Canal Co., 11 Ad. & Ell. 223.
Thompson *v.* N. E. Railway Co., 2 Best & S. 106.
Nelson *v.* Phœnix Chemical Works, 7 Ben. 37.
Sawyer *v.* Oakman, 1 Lowell, 134.

The question should have been left to the jury as to whether defendant's negligence was not the proximate cause of the injury to plaintiff's barge.

Milwaukee R. R. Co. *v.* Kellogg, 4 Otto, 474.
Penna. R. R. Co. *v.* Hope, 30 Smith, 377.
Penna. & N. J. Canal & R. R. Co. *v.* Lacey, 8 Norris, 458.

David W. Sellers, for defendant in error.

The duty of canal companies arises under their charter, and is only to the work which constitutes the franchise.

Canal Co. *v.* Manning, 6 Norris, 242.

No evidence was given to show that defendant's agents knew of the obstruction, nor that any duty was imposed on them relative to the navigation of the Raritan River. The plaintiff therefore gave no evidence of negligence, and a nonsuit was rightly awarded.

Hoag and Algee *v.* Railway Co., 4 Norris, 293.
King *v.* Thompson, 6 Norris, 367.
Railroad Co. *v.* McClurg, 6 Smith, 294.
Ashmore *v.* Transportation Co., 9 Vroom, 13.

January 21, 1881. THE COURT. We see no evidence of negligence in the defendants below. Even if the stump had been in the bed of their canal, it is very doubtful whether they could be held responsible, without express knowledge or notice; but for obstructions in the bed of Raritan River, of which they knew nothing, we think they were certainly not liable.

PER CURIAM. Judgment affirmed.

PAXSON, J., absent.

July, '80, 116.   Jan. 14, 1881.

City to use, etc., v. Donath et al.

Municipal claim — City Ordinance authorising paving — Notice — Construction of such Ordinance as to time and method of serving notice to pave.

An Ordinance of the City of Philadelphia for the paving of the footway of a street, passed January 29, 1870, directed the Chief Commissioner of Highways to notify the owners of property on said street to pave their footways in front of their properties on or before April 1, 1870, and in case they refused so to do said Commissioner was thereby directed to contract for the said paving, and collect the costs thereof from the owners of the property in front of which the same should be done. A notice in pursuance of the terms of this Ordinance was served on the tenant in possession of defendant's premises in February, 1870, and a notice to pave within twenty days was served on one of the defendants in April, 1874. The defendants refusing to pave, the work was done by a contractor with the city in July, 1874. In a scire facias by the city to use, etc., on a claim filed against defendants' property :

Held, that neither of the notices had been served in accordance with the terms of the Ordinance, that there was, therefore, no authority by law to pave said footway, and that a nonsuit was properly awarded.

Error to Common Pleas No. 1, of Philadelphia County.

Scire facias sur municipal claim by the City of Philadelphia to use, etc. *v.* Theresa Donath and others, owners, etc., for paving the footway of the defendants' property on Nicetown Lane, on July 23, 1874.

The pleas were nil debet, payment with leave,

set-off, and, *inter alia*, two special pleas averring that Councils had never ordered the paving of the cartway or footway, and that the defendants had not been duly and legally notified to pave said footway.

The first trial of the case resulted in a verdict for plaintiff. Defendants moved for a new trial, and for judgment *non obstante veredicto*. The rule for a new trial was made absolute, and the rule for judgment *non obstante veredicto* was discharged in the following opinion by PEIRCE, J.:—

"This was an action on a municipal claim for paving a footway on Nicetown Lane. By an Act of Assembly of May 2, 1871, the Councils of the City of Philadelphia were directed to have placed on the public plans of said city Nicetown Lane, of the width of fifty feet from Germantown Avenue to Ridge Road, in the Twenty-eighth Ward; and the Department of Highways of the City of Philadelphia was directed to order the opening, curbing, and grading of said street, between the points therein named; and when the majority of owners, for the whole or part of the distance, should ask the same to be paved or macadamized, the Department of Highways of the City of Philadelphia should enter into a contract for the same.

"This Act seems to be limited to paving or macadamizing the cartway, which it directed the Department of Highways to enter into a contract for when the majority of owners should ask; but it does not direct the paving of the footway. If it was intended to include the footways, it did not direct the owners to pave them, nor that it should be done at their expense.

"The cartway of Nicetown Lane was paved and curbed under this Act. In the fall of 1873 and spring of 1874, the Commissioner of Highways issued notices to the owners to pave the sidewalk in question, and in default of the owners doing so, he awarded a contract to the claimant in this case to pave it. He did the work and filed the claim, which is the subject of this suit.

"It is claimed that the right to give this notice and award the contract for paving the footway, in default of the owners doing so, was by virtue of the City Ordinance of May 3, 1855, which directs, that, 'whenever the cartway of any public street, or portion thereof, shall be by Councils ordered to be paved, or whenever they may order the paving, grading, and curbing of the footway of any street, every owner of ground fronting on such street shall, without delay, at his own cost, cause the footway in front of his ground to be graded, paved with brick or flat stone, and supported by curbstones; and if the owner of such ground shall neglect to grade, pave, and curb as aforesaid . . . for the space of twenty days after he shall have been thereto required by the Commissioner of Highways, . . . the said Commissioner, or proper authority, shall cause the same to be graded, paved, and curbed, or repaired, as the case may be, and the charge thereof shall be paid by such owner.'

"This Ordinance gives authority to the Commissioner of Highways to award a contract to do the paving of the footway, in default of the owner doing it, in two cases, viz., whenever the cartway of any public street, or portion thereof, shall be by Councils ordered to be paved, or whenever they may order the paving, grading, and curbing of the footway of any street.

"It is further claimed, that by special Ordinance of January 29, 1870,* notice was to be given the property owners to grade and pave their footwalks on Nicetown Lane, on or before April, 1870, and should they refuse to do so, the Chief Commissioner of Highways was directed to enter into a contract for the work. No notice was given under this Ordinance, nor was any notice whatever given until 1873 or 1874. The defendants claim that this Ordinance is *functus officii*, and that no notice could be given by virtue of it after April, 1870.

"The case then stands thus: An Act of Assembly [1871] directed the opening, curbing, and grading of Nicetown Lane, and when the majority of the owners should ask it, to pave or macadamize the roadway, but gave no direction to pave the footway.

"Councils passed no Ordinance directing the footway to be paved, except the Ordinance of January 29, 1870, which directed notice to be given to the property owners to grade and pave the footwalks on or before April, 1870. No notice was given under this Ordinance. The notices of 1873 and 1874 were not a compliance with it, and there being neither an Act of Assembly nor Ordinance directing the footwalks to be paved, except the Ordinance of January 29, 1870, which became null by want of action under it, it follows that there was no authority of law for the paving of the footwalks, nor giving notice to the owners to do it.

"In the case of The Bank *v.* Lefever (24 P.

---

* The following is the Ordinance of January 29, 1870: "Resolved, by the Select and Common Councils of the City of Philadelphia, That the Chief Commissioner of Highways is hereby directed to notify the owners of property on Nicetown Lane, from Germantown Avenue to the Philadelphia and Germantown Railroad, to grade and pave sidewalks on Nicetown Lane, in front of their respective properties, on or before the first day of April, 1870, and should they refuse to do the same, the Chief Commissioner of Highways is hereby directed to enter into a contract with a competent person or persons to grade and pave the same, and collect the cost thereof from the owners of property, respectively, before which the work shall be done."

F. Smith, 49, the Supreme Court has said: "That where no question has been reserved, the Court which has tried the case cannot enter judgment *non obstante veredicto*. As no question was reserved in this case, the rule for judgment *non obstante veredicto* is discharged, and the verdict is set aside."

On the second trial of the case, the plaintiff offered in evidence the Act and Ordinances referred to in the above opinion, and also the claim filed, which averred that "the said owner or reputed owner of said premises having, in accordance with existing ordinances of the city of Philadelphia, and agreeably to the several Acts of Assembly of the Commonwealth of Pennsylvania, been duly and legally notified by the Commissioner of Highways to grade and pave the footway on Nicetown Avenue, in front of said lot, within twenty days from the date of said notice." He then further proved that such a notice had, about the end of February, 1870, been served on the tenant in possession of the premises, and that one of the defendants had had a notice to pave within twenty days served on him about the end of April, 1874.

The Court thereupon granted a nonsuit, which the Court in banc subsequently refused to take off. Plaintiff took this writ, assigning for error, *inter alia*, the entering judgment of nonsuit.

Henry C. Titus (with him *Wm. Nelson West*, City Solicitor), for plaintiff in error.

The claim avers that notice was served on defendants. The evidence showed that such notice was served on their tenant in 1870. The presumption was, therefore, raised that such notice reached the owner through the tenant. The averments of the claim, when offered in evidence, are conclusive until disproved.

Act of March 11, 1846, Purd. Dig. 1089, pl. 27.
Watson v. The City, 8 WEEKLY NOTES, 275.
Lea v. The City, 1 WEEKLY NOTES, 189.

At any rate, defendants had notice in 1874. This was in time. The provisions of the Ordinance as to when the notice was to be given were merely directory, and raise a question exclusively between the city and the Highway Department. Defendants can take no advantage of the delay.

City v. Brooke, 31 Smith, 23.
City v. Coursin, 24 Smith, 400.
Magee v. Commonwealth, 10 Wright, 358.
Hutchinson v. The City, 22 Smith, 320.
Schenley v. Commonwealth, 12 Casey, 29.
City v. Burgin, 14 Wright, 539.
City v. Wistar, 11 Casey, 427.
Bladen v. The City, 10 Smith, 464.
People v. Allen, 6 Wend. 487.
Jackson v. Young, 5 Cow. 269.
Pond v. Negus, 3 Mass. 232.

Notice of a municipal matter to one tenant in common is notice to all.

Darlington v. Commonwealth, 5 Wright, 73.

Rowland Evans and *Richard L. Ashhurst*, for defendants in error.

The notice of 1870 was not served upon the *owners*, as required by the Ordinance, and was, therefore, of no effect.

Simons v. Kern, 8 WEEKLY NOTES, 257.
Wistar v. City, 5 Norris, 215.

Nor can the plaintiff rely on the averment of the claim. That was merely in general terms. He was obliged to prove *aliunde* compliance with the particular provisions of the Ordinance.

The terms of the Ordinance require notices to be served on the property holders to pave on or before April 1, 1870. A service of notice in 1874 could not be a compliance with this stipulation. The Ordinance must be strictly followed. Exact compliance with its terms was a necessary prerequisite to the jurisdiction to pave defendants' footway.

Commissioners v. Keith, 2 Barr, 219.
Pittsburgh v. Walter, 19 Smith, 368.
City v. Edwards, 28 Smith, 62.
Fell v. The City, 31 Smith, 58.
City v. Sanger, 5 WEEKLY NOTES, 335.
Reilly v. City, 10 Smith, 469.
O'Rourke v. Railroad Co., 7 Norris, 83.

The plaintiff cannot recover on the general Ordinance of 1855, because it only confers authority on the Commissioner to order the paving of the sidewalk after Councils have ordered the paving of the cartway. This event never happened. The cartway was paved here under an Act of Assembly.

January 24, 1881. THE COURT. We affirm this judgment upon the opinion of the learned Judge of the Court below, on the motion for a new trial, on the first trial.

Judgment affirmed.
PER CURIAM. PAXSON, J., absent.

Commonwealth ex rel. Attorney General v. Dumbauld and Roberts.

(*Reported ante, p. 369.*)

Feb. 7, 1881. TRUNKEY and STERRETT, JJ., dissent from the opinion and judgment in this case.

Common Pleas—Equity.

C. P. No. 3.   Dec. 13, 1880.

Dill v. Haugh.

Injunction—Nuisance—Action at law—Right to a well of water in a part of the city in which there is a supply of water from the city waterworks.

Sur exceptions to master's report.

Bill in equity filed by Matthias Dill against

Marcus Haugh, to March Term, 1876, to enjoin him from using a certain cesspool which had been dug by said Haugh on his own premises adjoining the premises of said Dill.

The bill set forth that complainant purchased his property in April, 1845; that at the time of the said purchase there was, and had been for a long time a well thereon, furnishing a supply of the purest water, and, until the commission of the acts of the respondent complained of, this well continued to supply complainant with all the water needed for household purposes. That respondent entered into possession of the neighboring premises a year or more ago, and after entering therein, dug a well to be used as a privy at a distance of about three feet from complainant's land, and the same has been used for the purpose ever since. That in the early part of the digging of said cesspool, complainant warned respondent that one of the possible effects of the location of said well would be to injure or destroy the use of complainant's well, which respondent denied. That afterwards by percolation of the water and filth from respondent's cesspool, the water in complainant's well was affected, and from the same cause still remains unfit for any use whatever, for which damage respondent, on being requested, refused to provide a remedy. The bill prayed that respondent and all persons under him be perpetually enjoined from using said cesspool as long as the water or filth therefrom shall percolate into and injure the water in complainant's well.

The answer denied any injury to complainant by respondent's use of said well. The examiner and master to whom the cause was referred (J. Howard Gendell) found the facts as complained, and reported a decree in favor of complainant, with costs, enjoining respondent from permitting any water or filth to run or percolate into plaintiff's premises from the privy on his own, and requiring him within thirty days from the entry of decree to thoroughly cleanse his privy well, and enjoining him from using said well or permitting the same to be used until it is thoroughly cemented and otherwise rendered watertight. To this report respondent excepted.

George W. Arundel and *B. H. Brewster,* for exceptant.

There is an adequate remedy at law.
Kerr on Injunctions, 199.

The well, under the present facility of obtaining water from the sources provided by the public authorities, is a luxury, whereas the cesspool is a necessity. The one should therefore give way to the other. The well owner in putting down his well took the risk of his neighbors being compelled through necessity to construct a cesspool. The mischief from these causes is not irreparable.

Fletcher *v.* Rylands, 1 Law Rep. Exch. 265.
Losee *v.* Buchanan, 51 N. Y. Ct. App. 476.
Acton *v.* Blundell, 12 M. & W. 324.
Greatrex *v.* Hayward, 20 Eng. Law and Eq. Rep. 377.
Fishmonger Co. *v.* East India Co., 1 Deck. 164.
Broadbent *v.* Ramsbotham, 34 Eng. Law and Eq. 553.
Greenleaf *v.* Francis, 18 Pickering, 117.
Roath *v.* Driscoll, 20 Conn. 533.
Wheatley *v.* Baugh, 1 Casey, 528.

J. Alexander Simpson, Jr., contra.

The objection to the equity proceedings can only be taken advantage of by demurrer.
Adams *v.* Beach, 1 Phila. Rep. 178.
Finley *v.* Aiken, 3 Pittsburgh Leg. J. 1.

Equity will restrain a trespass of a continuing and permanent nature, an action for damages in such cases not being adequate remedy.
Masson's Appeal, 20 Sm. 26.
Allison's Appeal, 27 Sm. 221.
Scheetz's Appeal, 11 Cas. 88.
Sunderland *v.* Whitesides, 7 Phila. Rep. 335.
Pittinger *v.* Kennedy, 3 Leg. Gaz. 277.
Brightly's Equity, ₴ 291.
Story's Equity, ₴ 925.
Minnig's Appeal, 1 Norris, 373.

Where a subterranean flow of water has become so well defined as to constitute a regular and constant stream, the owner of land above through which it flows may not divert or destroy it to the injury of the person below on whose land it issues in the form of a spring.
Wheatley *v.* Baugh, 1 C. 528.
Jacobs *v.* Worrall, 15 Leg. Int. 139.
Shuter *v.* City, 3 Phila. 228.
Wood on Nuisances, pp. 556, 559.
Gas Co. *v.* Murphy, 3 Wr. 257.
Cooley on Torts, p. 567, ed. 1879.

December 23, 1880. THE COURT. Exceptions dismissed and report confirmed.

Common Pleas—Law.

C. P. No 3.   Jan. 22, 1881.

Lea v. Brown.

Mortgage—Taxes—Acts of Assembly relating to the lien of mortgages—Effect of a sheriff's sale under a subsequent judgment upon a mortgage prior to which was a lien for unpaid taxes.

Rule for judgment for want of a sufficient affidavit of defense.

Sci. fa. sur mortgage made by Christian Brown to M. Carey Lea, on March 29, 1877, for $2000, secured on premises No. 1819 Gratz Street. The affidavit of defence set forth substantially that on June 25, 1877, Brown conveyed the premises subject to this mortgage to one McNeill, who thereupon executed a second mortgage to the Rhein Building Association. That subsequently proceedings were instituted by the said Building Association on this second mortgage on May 24, 1880, and at the sheriff's sale which followed the property was bought in by the Association. That at the time of the sheriff's sale taxes due to the city on said premises for the year 1875 remained unpaid, which taxes had been registered on January 1, 1876, and for which a lien had been filed in the Court of Common Pleas No. 2, to March term, 1880.

M. H. Stutsbach showed cause.

This mortgage was discharged by the sheriff's sale of the premises by reason of the taxes for the year 1875 remaining unpaid at the time of the said sale.

Price on Limitations and Liens, p. 293, 294.
Parker's Appeal, 8 W. & S. 449.
Perry v. Brinton, 1 Harris, 208.

J. G. Johnson, contra.

C. A. V.

Jan. 29, 1881. THE COURT. Prior to the Act of April 6th, 1830, all mortgages were discharged by any judicial sale, and this in case of taxes, because under the Act of February 3, 1824, "taxes thereafter assessed shall be a lien on said real estate for which they were assessed, and that said lien shall have priority to, and shall be fully paid and satisfied before, any . . . mortgage, which said real estate may become charged with."

The Act of 1830 did not, however, accomplish the end for which it was designed, and hence it was provided by the Act of April 11th, 1835, that "no lien by virtue of the Act passed the 3d of February, 1824, . . . shall be construed within the meaning of the Act of Assembly of April 6th, 1830."

Again, upon the 16th of April, 1845 (Purdon, 479, pl. 108), it was enacted, "that the lien of a mortgage upon any real estate situate in the city and county of Philadelphia shall not be destroyed or in any way affected by any sale of the mortgaged premises, under a subsequent judgment (other than one entered upon a claim which was a lien on the premises prior to the recording of such mortgage), by reason of the prior lien of any tax, charge or assessment whatsoever; but the same shall continue as if such prior lien did not exist, where, by existing laws, the lien of such mortgage would otherwise continue: provided, that the continuance of the lien of such mortgage shall not prevent the discharge of such prior lien for taxes, charges, or assessments, by such sale, or the satisfaction thereof, out of the proceeds of such sale."

is now contended, notwithstanding this legislation the Act of April 21st, 1858 (P. L. 385, § 2), in effect repeals the Acts of Assembly above referred to, because it is therein declared, that "in the month of January, annually, the said receiver shall, in books to be called 'The Register of unpaid taxes on real estate,' register all unpaid taxes (except occupation taxes) of the preceding year; *and the said taxes are hereby declared to be a lien on all real estate, in accordance with the provisions of the Act of 3d of February, 1824.*"

We cannot take this view of the subject. Among other reasons, the following may be stated: The Act of April 21st, 1858, in which this section occurs, was in terms "a supplement to the Act incorporating the city of Philadelphia." The Act is of a general nature, and was, as a whole, designed to perfect previous legislation by which the city had been incorporated. Many very important provisions are contained in this law, and, among others, this section, which was designed to create a system of registration, and to preserve the lien of taxes so registered. It never entered into the mind of the Legislature that the security designed by the Acts of 1835 and 1845, in so far as the lien of first mortgages was concerned, was to be swept away by the general language used in the statute, but only that the lien of registered taxes, *subject to the whole preceding legislation*, should be preserved beyond cavil or doubt.

Taking this view of the subject, we must, of course, enter judgment for want of a sufficient affidavit of defence.

Opinion by LUDLOW, P. J.

C. P. No. 3. Dec. 13, 1880.

Winkler v. Pemberton.

Married women—Practice— Act of June 11, 1879—Right of a married woman who has been deserted by her husband to bring suit in her own name.

Sur demurrer to amended declaration.

Assumpsit, by Mary Winkler, a married woman, in her own name, for the breach of an alleged contract of defendant to employ plaintiff as a domestic servant.

To the original declaration defendant pleaded in abatement the coverture of plaintiff, and, after argument, the Court sustained the plea, but allowed plaintiff to amend her declaration by the insertion of the following: "wife of Edward Winkler, the said Edward Winkler having deserted the said Mary Winkler heretofore, to wit, on the first day of April, A. D. 1879," under the Act of June 11, 1879 (P. L. 126).

To the declaration, as amended, the present demurrer was filed.

Dever (with him *Ransford*), for demurrer.

Plaintiff cannot maintain her action at all, the

right of action being in her husband, unless secured to her by Act of April 3, 1872.
Purd. Dig. 1010, pl. 38, 39.
There is no allegation in the narr. that plaintiff has taken advantage of the last-mentioned Act. The Act of June 11, 1870, is but an enabling Act, authorizing a married woman, entitled by law to her separate earnings, to sue for the same in her own name.

Sobernheimer, contra.

Dec. 30, 1880. THE COURT. Demurrer overruled, with leave, etc.

C. P. No. 3.   Dec. 14, 1880.

Catharine Shoemaker, administratrix of Charles Shoemaker v. The Kensington National Bank.

Decedent's estate—Debtor and creditor—Insolvency—Right of bank to set off a note discounted against moneys deposited—Death of insolvent depositor before maturity of discounted note.

Case stated, showing the following facts:—

Charles Shoemaker was, in his lifetime, a depositor in the defendant bank. On Nov. 14, 1879, the bank discounted for plaintiff a note for $400, which fell due Feb. 18, 1880; and on Jan. 27, 1880, one for $250, which fell due May 1, 1880; the amount of the notes, less discount at the rate of six per cent. per annum, being placed to plaintiff's credit. These two notes were the last of a series of renewals of two notes, one for $475, and the other for $575, discounted by the bank for Shoemaker (the endorser), in October, 1877, and renewed from time to time after the maker's insolvency, upon representations made by Shoemaker to the bank, that he was solvent. Shoemaker died February 13, 1880, insolvent, before either of said notes became due, having standing to his credit on the books of the company the sum of $539.29. Upon the maturity of the $400 note, the bank charged the amount to Shoemaker's account, the bank at this time knowing of plaintiff's death, but not of his insolvency. Subsequently, the bank, learning the fact of the plaintiff's insolvency, charged the $250 note to his account; there resulting a balance due the bank of $114.81.

If the Court should be of opinion that the bank had no right to retain any part of the balance on its books due plaintiff at his death, then judgment to be entered for plaintiff for $539.29, with interest from Feb. 19, 1880, etc.

J. M. Gibb, for plaintiff, relied on—
Bosler's Adm'x v. Bank, 4 Barr, 32.
Appeal of F. & M. Bank, 12 Wr. 57.
Jordan et al. v. Sharlock, 3 Norris, 366.

F. J. Gowen (with him *A. D. Campbell*), for defendant, cited—
Dougherty et al. v. Bank, 9 WEEKLY NOTES,

Jan. 8, 1881. THE COURT. This case falls within the rulings of the Supreme Court in Bosler v. Ex. Bank (4 Barr, 32), and Appeal of The Farmers' and Mechanics' Bank (12 Wr. 57).

Judgment for plaintiff for $539.29, with interest from February 19, 1880.

Opinion by LUDLOW, P. J.

Orphans' Court.

ADDITIONAL RULES.

And now, January 29, 1881, it is ordered that the following additional Rules be adopted:—

1. The Rules of Equity Practice, adopted by the Supreme Court of Pennsylvania, May 27, 1865, are, so far as they are applicable to the practice and proceedings therein, adopted by this Court, subject to the provisions of the Acts of Assembly regulating such proceedings and practice.

2. So much of Rule VIII., Section 3, heretofore adopted, as requires the issuing and personal service of a rule to show cause, etc., before awarding an attachment to enforce obedience to a peremptory order to pay, or other order or decree, is hereby repealed. And hereafter, upon proof of personal service of a certified copy of such order to pay, or other order or decree, if the same be not complied with within ten days thereafter, an attachment will be forthwith awarded.

WILLIAM B. HANNA, P. J.

Jan. 17, 1881.

Whitaker's Estate.

Decedents' estates—Retention of securities to meet contingencies of litigation—Legal investments—Practice.

Sur petition of executors to sell securities and re-invest, and answer.

The petition of William Overington and Edward J. Robinson, acting executors under the will of Robert Whitaker, the decedent, represented that in June, 1880, an adjudication of their accounts was made, and a balance reported for distribution ($450,000), leaving the residue of the estate in their hands to provide against the contingencies of certain claims in litigation, and believing that the litigation concerning said claims against the estate, and other matters connected with the distribution, would consume much time, the petitioners expressed their desire to make some disposition of the present assets, in view of their fluctuating character, as none of them are legal investments.

To the petition were appended exhibits containing a list of the securities which constituted the above-mentioned residue in the petitioners' hands; also copies of letters addressed to the various distributees, intimating petitioners' wishes concerning a sale and re-investment of the aforesaid securities, and certain answers thereto.

The prayer of the petition was for authority to separate the assets into two equal parts, to sell one, and re-invest in legal securities such as the Court should direct, upon the understanding that said moiety, less a moiety of debts and expenses in any future distribution which might be ordered, should be paid to the executors of Mary G. Whitaker, decedent's widow (said executors coinciding in petitioners' views), and the other moiety to remain unconverted, and to be paid to the other distributees, under the same conditions, at the time of final distribution.

Then followed a prayer for a citation to the parties in interest (decedent's nephews and nieces, and the issue of those deceased, some thirty-four in all), a suggestion of the minority of same, and a prayer for the appointment of a guardian *ad litem* to accept service of citation.

Henry Cartwright, and fifteen others, filed an answer which set forth their belief that the securities of which the residue of the estate consisted, were judiciously selected by the testator himself, being for the most part good and safe investments, and "looking, therefore, to the expense of conversion and re-investment, also the probable loss upon principal of new securities, and certain loss upon the rate of income, these respondents are of opinion that it is injudicious to make such conversion and re-investment, and would prefer, as far as practicable, to have, at the time of final distribution, a division of the securities in kind, or have the estate so divided that the portion of the securities to which they would be entitled may be set apart, and credited with its own proper income, and charged with its own proper share of debts and liabilities, as in the manner indicated in executors' petition."

John G. Johnson and *Chas. S. Pancoast*, for the executors.

Samuel Dickson, John C. Bullitt, W. R. Smith, and *John M. Collins,* for respondents

Geo. W. Biddle, and *Geo. W. Thorn,* for executors of Mary E. Whitaker.

January 22, 1881. THE COURT. In this matter we discover no reason for departing from the usual and well recognized practice. The executors, in the care and disposition of the assets of the estate, being investments by testator, should have in view the directions contained in his will, and act according to their best judgment and discretion, guided by the advice of counsel. If from their knowledge of all the circumstances, a further distribution can now be made, they should file a second account, embracing the securities directed to be retained by them, and the proceeds of any since converted. Then at the audit a re-appraisement should be made, whereupon the legatees may agree to a distribution in kind, or a sufficient amount directed to be sold to pay the legacies or distributive shares of those who prefer to receive the same in money. And should it still be desirable to retain any sum to meet existing or probable litigation, those who would be entitled to such balance, upon the final determination of the litigation, are fully competent to agree that its equivalent in securities may be thus set apart. But if no such agreement be made, the executors, to be relieved from responsibility, should, at such time as they deem most advantageous, convert such assets, and re-invest in investments recognized by law.

The petition is accordingly dismissed.

Opinion by HANNA, P. J.

December 21, 1880.

Hilles's Estate.

Removal of trustee—Acts of May 1, 1861, and April 9, 1868—Trustee removed where his continuance in office, though not jeoparding the trust, might probably work disadvantage or inconvenience to the cestuis que trustent.

Sur petition for removal of trustee.

The petition of Samuel Hilles and Mary his wife set forth: that the decedent, William Hilles, by his last will and testament bequeathed to his son Nathan Hilles, and his son-in-law Thomas Lippincott, $10,000 in trust for the said petitioners during their lives, and upon the decease of the survivor of them, the principal to vest in their children. That upon a former petition by these petitioners, Nathan Hilles was discharged from the trust; that a petition was then presented by them, praying that the Guarantee Trust and Safe Deposit Company should be appointed in his place, to which last petition Thomas Lippincott filed an answer refusing his consent to such appointment. Further, that the petitioners have been engaged in adverse litigation with Thomas Lippincott in the settlement of his accounts as trustee, and upon adjudication thereon, a balance in favor of the said trust was adjudged to be due, to which finding Thomas Lippincott filed exceptions, which are not yet settled. That by reason of said adverse litigation, unpleasant relations existed between him and the petitioners, and they averred that the care and management of said trust funds would be best served by a change of the trustee, and prayed the removal of Thomas Lippincott from the trust, and the appointment of the Guarantee Trust and Safe Deposit Company in his place.

An answer was filed by Thomas Lippincott.
C. S. *Pancoast*, for petitioners.
J. L. *Kinsey*, contra.

December 31, 1880. THE COURT. The petition in this case is drawn under the provisions of the Act of 9th of April, 1868, § 1, and prays for the removal of a testamentary trustee, and the appointment in his place of a trustee who is nominated by the *cestuis que trustent*. The Act gives to the *cestuis que trustent*, or a majority of those having the life estate, the right to choose a trustee, and directs the Court, upon petition of said parties in interest, to remove the acting trustee, and to appoint the person selected by the *cestuis que trustent*. In Stevenson's Appeal (18 P. F. Sm. 101), the Act was held to be so far directory as to permit the Court to judge of the existence of cause for removal, and the petition was dismissed in that case because it set forth no cause whatever. Under the Act of 1st of May, 1861, § 1, the Court had already power to remove a trustee whenever it should be made to appear that for any reason the interests of the trust estate were likely to be jeoparded by the continuance of such trustee. We are of opinion that the Act of 1868 was intended to enlarge the discretion of the Court, and to permit the removal of a trustee whose continuance in the office, while it might not imperil or jeopard the trust, would probably work positive disadvantage or inconvenience to the *cestuis que trustent*. The petition and answer in this case show that hostile relations exist between the petitioners and the respondent. Exceptions to the account of the latter as executor and trustee were presented by the *cestuis que trustent*, and since the filing of this petition have been determined against the respondent. His co-trustee had been previously removed for cause, and the trustee now suggested by the petitioners was not appointed, owing to the strenuous opposition of the respondent. The evils which are inevitable from this condition of affairs seem to be reached by the Act of 1868. That Act evidently recognizes a distinction between the case of creditors and that of *cestuis que trustent*. While nothing less than actual mismanagement, or such other conduct as jeopards the estate would justify the removal of a trustee upon the petition of a creditor (Parsons' Estate, 1 Nor. 465), there may yet be circumstances calling for such removal less grave, and with which creditors have no concern, but which directly affect the comfort of the *cestuis que trustent*. In such case, upon the petition of the latter or a majority of them, the Act authorizes the intervention of the Court. We think that the record discloses a case for relief which is needed, and which we are empowered to administer, and the prayer of the petition is accordingly granted.

Opinion by ASHMAN, J.

U. S. Circuit Court—Law.

Jan. 19, 1881.
Norrington v. Wright.

Severable contract—Partial performance—Acceptance of—Right to rescind on subsequent default.

Under a contract for 5000 tons of rails to be shipped in about equal quantities in February and four succeeding months, the whole to be delivered by August 1, the purchaser may rescind on failure to ship the stipulated quantity in February.

A severable contract may be severed for the purpose of enforcing rights as they accrue, but a party in default cannot insist on its being treated as severed to avoid a right to rescind for non-performance of any one portion.

Partial performance, accepted and retained in ignorance of any default of the seller as to the residue, does not prevent the right of rescission for such residue when the contract furnishes an exact measure of compensation for the partial performance.

Motion to take off nonsuit. The action was assumpsit on the following contract :—

PHILADELPHIA, Jan'y 19, 1880.
Sold to Messrs. Peter Wright & Sons, for account of Messrs. A. Norrington & Co., London, five thousand (5000) tons old T iron rails, for shipment from a European port or ports at the rate of about one thousand (1000) tons per month, beginning February, 1880, but whole contract to be shipped before August 1, 1880, at forty-five (45) dollars per ton of twenty-two hundred and forty pounds custom-house weight, on ship "Philadelphia." Settlement cash, on presentation of bills accompanied by custom-house certificates of weight. Sellers to notify buyers of shipments, with vessels named, as soon as known by them. Sellers not to be compelled *to replace* any parcel lost after shipment. Sellers, when possible, to secure to buyers right to name discharging berth of vessels at Philadelphia.

Three counts set out the contract and averred performance in its terms, *i. e.*, a shipment of about 1000 tons in January, February, etc., with averment of arrival, tender, and refusal to accept. The fourth count it was admitted was not proved.

On the trial, the plaintiffs proved shipments were made in February, 395 tons; March, 897 tons; April, 1349 tons; May, 1099 tons; June, 991 tons; July, 306 tons.

The 395 tons shipment arrived, was delivered, and paid for. In May, the defendants, having ascertained the amounts that had been shipped in February and March, thereupon gave notice of rescission, and declined to accept any shipments as they arrived and were tendered.

At the close of the plaintiffs' case, the Court, MCKENNAN and BUTLER, JJ., stated their opinion that the defendants had the right of rescission if, at the time of their acceptance of the 395 tons, they were not aware that there had been a default in shipping the stipulated February parcel. The defendants then called witnesses to negative this knowledge.

At the conclusion of this testimony, the plaintiffs admitted that they could not ask a verdict on that evidence, and they elected to suffer a nonsuit, with leave to move, etc. Plaintiffs moved to take off the nonsuit.

Samuel Dickson (*J. C. Bullitt* with him), for the motion.

The right of rescission does not exist when the contract is, as this, severable. The remedy is confined to a reduction of the price by the damages for the failures to ship. As iron had fallen during the whole time for performance, there were none.

There being six months to ship, 833 tons per month would have satisfied the terms. The right to ship in the six months shows that time was not material, and the exclusion of the duty to replace cargoes lost shows that complete performance was not material. Then each cargo is to be taken and paid for separately, and this is the real meaning of Pordage *v.* Cole (1 Wms. Saund. 320), that the covenant is substituted for exact performance. The rule is stated in 2 Parsons on Contracts, 29–31, that such contracts as these are to be treated as distinct to each parcel. This is cited with approval in Lucesco *v.* Brewer (16 P. F. Smith, 351), and it lies on the other side to show reasons for treating the contract as entire.

Graver *v.* Scott, 30 P. F. Smith, 88.

The weight of authority is to treat them as severable.

Scott *v.* Kittanning Coal Co., 8 Norris, 231. Note of Mr. Arthur Biddle, 19 Am. Law Reg. 418, July 18, 1880.
Morgan *v.* McKee, 27 P. F. Smith, 229.
Perkins *v.* Hart, 11 Wheat. 237.

And the exceptions prove the rule.

Quigley *v.* De Haas, 1 Norris, 267.
Carmalt *v.* Platt, 7 W. 318.

The rule contended for is borne out by—

Benjamin on Sales, 426.
Stoddart *v.* Smith, 5 Binney, 355.

Reybold *v.* Voorhees (6 Casey, 116) was put on the ground that the articles were perishable. In New York, contracts of this kind have uniformly been held divisible.

Tipton *v.* Feitner, 20 N. Y. 423.
Snook *v.* Fries, 19 Barb. 313.
Lee *v.* Beebe, 13 Hun, 89.

As to the English courts, the cases establish and the other side admits the rule to be as we contend.

Jonassohn *v.* Young, 4 Best & Smith, 296.
Simpson *v.* Crippin, L. Rep., 8 Q. B. 14.
Roper *v.* Johnson, L. R., 8 C. P. Div. 169.
Freeth *v.* Burr, L. R., 9 C. P. 208.
Bloomer *v.* Bernstein, Id. 588.
Ex parte Chalmers, 8 Ch. App. 289.
Morgan *v.* Bain, L. R., 10 C. P. 15.
Houck *v.* Miller, The London Times, Dec. 18, 1880. Opinion of Mr. Benjamin stating the present state of rule and commenting on the decisions.

It is of importance that we should have a rule in construction of contracts uniform with the rule now settled in England. The English rule has, we contend, become the rule of construction. We admit that, under the circumstances, the partial performance did not preclude the defendants from rescission.

R. C. McMurtrie, contra.

It is true that the rule, as it has existed in England since Simpson *v.* Crippin, excludes the right to rescind. But it is admitted to be new, and is inconsistent with prior English decisions, and wholly at variance with the American decisions. Oxendale *v.* Wetherell (9 B. & Cress. 386) is express, that there is this remedy by rescission in such a contract. It is inconsistent with recent English decisions, for it turns the contract into as many contracts as there are severable performances.

Brandt *v.* Lawrence, 1 Q. B. Div. 344.

Yet this new rule concedes that these can be sued for in one count, which can only be when the contract is entire, and allows a deduction from the price of one for injury on another, which can never be done there with distinct contracts.

The deductions seem to be a *demonstratio ad absurdum*, for in the last case one shipment is called the *first* contract, though the only severance was the optional right to ship by *steamer or steamers;* moreover, the plaintiff had elected to treat this as an entire contract, and cannot, under these counts, treat each of the shipments as independent contracts.

2 Wms. Saunders, 97[b], cited by TINDAL, C. J., in Bushell *v.* Beavan, 1 Bing. N. Cases, 120.

The American cases have always assumed the rule as laid down in Hoare *v.* Rennie (5 Hur. & Norm. 19). The citation from Parsons is supported by one authority only, and that was a contract for two lots of ground at different times. The passage that follows shows that the rule does not apply to commercial contracts. The cases in Pennsylvania are mere *dicta*, and utterly uncalled for; one of them was merely the case of Boone *v.* Ayre. The authorities recognizing the right are—

Johnson *v.* Johnson, 3 B. & Pull. 162–70.
Oxendale *v.* Wetherill, *supra*.
Smith *v.* Lewis, 40 Indiana, 98.
2 Chitty, Contracts, 923, note by American Editor.
Hoare *v.* Rennie, 3 H. & Nor. 19.
Coddington *v.* Paleologo, L. R., 2 Ex. 193.
McMillan *v.* Vanderlip, 12 Johnston, 165.
Catlin *v.* Tobias, 26 N. Y. 217.

In Shinn *v.* Bodine (10 Sm. 182), the whole argument of the Court is based on the existence of the rule. Reybold *v.* Voorhees (6 Cas. 116) is admittedly so, unless the quality of the goods can make a difference in the effect of the contract to exclude this remedy.

Bradley *v.* King, 44 Illinois, 339–41.

And this new rule seems to be going back to the reasoning in Pordage *v.* Cole, that performance is not the consideration for the promise, if there is an express promise, while it is if there is only an implied promise, and thus rendering the promises not dependent on conditions precedent, which has certainly been abandoned for a century in entire contracts.

Rescission is a remedy as much as the right to sue, and a most important one; and the effect is to eliminate it because merely of severability in performance, while it is admittedly retained, though the subject is capable of severance (Benj. on Sales, 689); and really, under Brant *v.* Lawrence, *supra*, it comes to this, that the permitting the delivery of any parcel, which is capable of being used alone, precludes any rescission for further non-delivery.

The better rule is that deducible from Grant *v.* Johnson (1 Seldon, 252), Dox *v.* Dey (3 Wend. 361), and expressly decided in Bradley *v.* King (44 Ill. 339–44), that, as each severable performance is executed in whole or in part, that is no longer subject to the remedy by rescission, but that remedy exists as to all future shipments or acts to be performed.

As to the rule allowing the right to rescind notwithstanding the partial performance retained and its reason, see—

3 Best & Smith, 751; Chitty on Cont. 1094, add. by American Editor.
Hill *v.* Crew, 1 Metcalfe, 268–72.
Haines *v.* Tucker, 50 N. H. 309.
Dwinel *v.* Howard, 30 Maine, 258.
Miner *v.* Bradley, 22 Pick. 459–60.
Boone *v.* Ayre, as stated in 6 T. R. 573.

C. A. V.

January 24. BUTLER, J., discharged the rule for a new trial, saying: To justify an allowance of the motion we must be convinced that our ruling at the trial was wrong. We are not so convinced. The motion must, therefore, be dismissed.

For myself, however, I may say that I regard the point as involved in serious doubt; not so much when considered on general principles, as when viewed in the light of modern decisions. The right to rescind a contract for non-performance is a remedy as old as the law of contract itself. Where the contract is entire—indivisible—the right is unquestioned. The undertakings on the one side, and on the other, are dependent, and performance by one party cannot be enforced by the other without performance, or a tender of performance, on his own part. In the case before us the contract is "severable." But to say it is "severable," does not advance the plaintiffs' argument. A "severable" contract, as the language imports, is a contract *liable* simply to be severed. In its origin, and till severed, it is entire—a single bargain, or transaction. The doctrine of severableness (if I may be allowed to coin a word) in contracts is an invention of the Courts, in the interests of justice, designed to enable one who has partially performed, and is entitled on such partial performance to something from the other side, to sustain an action, in advance of complete performance—as where goods are sold to be delivered and paid for in parcels, to enable the seller to recover for the parcels delivered, in advance of completing his undertaking. But this equitable doctrine should not be invoked by one who had failed to perform, for the purpose of defeating the other's right to rescind, and thus to protect himself against the consequences of his own wrong. As against such a party the contract should be treated, and enforced, as entire. To say, therefore, that the contract is "severable," does not, I repeat, advance the argument. To render the plaintiff's position logical, it is necessary to take a step forward, and hold that such a transaction (it would not be accurate in this view to call it a *contract*) constitutes *several distinct, independent contracts*. Then, of course, it follows that a failure, as respects one of several successive deliveries, affords no right to rescind in regard to those yet to be made. And this step, after much apparent doubt and hesitation, the English Courts have taken. It was the necessary outgrowth of the decision in Simpson *v.* Crippen, which overruled Hoare *v.* Rennie. In our own country the cases are inharmonious, and the question unsettled. After a careful examination of what has been said on the subject, I shall not be surprised if the Courts here finally adopt the present English rule, and thus substitute compensation in damages for the remedy by rescission, to the extent there done. I say this, however, not because I think it wise to adopt this rule, but because of an apparent leaning in that direction.

The question, however, as here presented, is properly for the Supreme Court, to which I hope it may be carried, and the rule thus be settled.

MCKENNAN, J. I concur even more decidedly. I am not satisfied that the weight of the opinions, even in England, is with these decisions. So far as this country is concerned it cannot be said there is any such rule. I have such doubt of the justice of the rule that I am not willing to take this step forward. It is more respectful to remit this to the Supreme Court, and, therefore, I do not feel disposed to take the advanced step.

Rule discharged.

WEEKLY NOTES OF CASES.

Vol. IX.] THURSDAY, FEB. 17, 1881. [No. 26.

[The question of the right to rescind after the partial breach of a severable contract, involved in Norrington v. Wright (reported in the preceding pages), was elaborately argued. The report gives the substance of the oral arguments, to which may be added the following extract from the printed brief of plaintiff's counsel, explaining, *arguendo*, the application of the case of Pordage v. Cole, as intended by BLACKBURN, J., in the case of Simpson v. Crippin (*supra*). It was urged, among other considerations tending to show that the contract in this case was severable, that "the provision in the fourth clause, 'Sellers not to be compelled to replace any parcel lost after shipment,' shows that the buyers did not attach importance to a complete performance as being of the essence of the bargain. The contract looked to successive shipments from any European port, and provided for 'Settlement cash on presentation of bills accompanied by custom-house certificates of weight.' Each cargo was to be taken and paid for by itself; and this is the recognized and decisive test. The uncertainty in the time of arrival, the exemption from liability to replace lost shipments, and the prolonged time for deliveries, all show that it was not vital to the contract that the whole should be delivered.

"The parts *may* be so related to each other that the failure to deliver one may render the balance useless, or defeat the whole object of the bargain. In such case, the completeness or regularity of delivery goes to the entire consideration, or the failure to deliver each and every parcel as stipulated, defeats the whole purpose of the contract; and it is in this sense that the doctrine of Pordage v. Cole is applicable. It is, of course, competent for the parties to contract, and their intention may be gathered from the nature of their dealing as well as from express language; but in contracts practically identical with this, between vendor and vendee, the courts have uniformly said a contrary intention appears."

This line of argument refers to a different class of considerations from those suggested by Lord COLERIDGE in Freeth v. Burr (L. R. 9 C. P. 208), who gives this explanation of the authorities: "In cases of this sort, where the question is whether the one party is set free by the action of the other, the real matter for consideration is whether the acts or conduct of the one do. or do not amount to an intention to abandon and altogether to refuse performance of the contract. I say this in order to explain the ground upon which I think the decision in these cases must rest. There has been some conflict amongst them. But I think it may be taken that the fair result of them is as I have stated, viz.: that the true question is, whether the acts and conduct of the party evince an intention no longer to be bound by the contract. Now, non-payment on the one hand, or non-delivery on the other, may amount to such an act, or may be evidence for a jury of an intention wholly to abandon the contract and set the other party free."

The opinion of Mr. Benjamin, referred to in the report, was one taken on the contract in suit, in which, after stating, in his judgment, that "under the law of England, as now conclusively settled (though the decisions at one time were somewhat conflicting), the plaintiffs have a good cause of action, and the defence set up would not be regarded as serious," he says: "At the time when I wrote the second edition of my book on Sales, the cases of Hoare v. Rennie and Simpson v. Crippin were regarded by the profession here as hardly reconcilable, and Hoare v. Rennie, though regarded with distrust, was not considered to be finally overruled; but I ventured at pages 737-8 to point out that in Roper v. Johnson, the case of Simpson v. Crippin was treated *as settling the law on this point*. Subsequently, in Freeth v. Burr, the decision of Lord Coleridge so far reconciled the case of Hoare v. Rennie with all the other cases, as to point out that the partial breach of an agreement *may* take place under circumstances which show that the party committing the breach intended to abandon the contract, and no longer to continue to execute his part of it. In such a case, a partial breach might justify the opposite party in saying: 'Well, if you don't intend to go on with the contract, I also withdraw from it, and give notice that it is rescinded.' In general, as in this very case, there is not the least difficulty in determining at once what the real intention is. It would be absurd even to suggest that the plaintiffs, by failing to send the full instalments of one thousand tons each in February and March, intended thereby to abandon the contract, inasmuch as they continued the shipments in April, May, etc. If, in any particular case, the conduct of the party committing the partial breach were such as to render his purpose doubtful, the question like any other disputed issue would be determined by the jury."]

Supreme Court.

Jan. '80, 136.   Feb. 24, 1880, and Jan. 4, 1881.

Girard Life Insurance, Annuity, and Trust Company, Administrator of Edward Magarge, v. Mutual Life Insurance Company of New York.

Life insurance—Proofs of death—Proofs of death filed with a company available upon as many policies as the company may have issued upon the life of the deceased—Whether a company which claims that a policy is forfeited may demand proofs of death under such policy —Forfeiture for non-payment of premium— Waiver—Custom of receiving over-due premiums—What sufficient evidence is—Effect of custom upon express condition of policy—Stipulation attached to policy—When not considered part of the contract—Mutual companies— Dividends—When a company is bound to appropriate an accrued dividend in payment of an accruing premium.

Where an insurance company issues two policies upon the life of the same person, it is not necessary for the representatives of the insured to furnish separate proofs of death under each policy.

Per PAXSON, J. The assured was dead not under one policy but under both, and the facts had been communicated to the company with the cause of death and all the surrounding circumstances connected therewith which they desired to know.

In such a case if the contract had called for separate proofs under each policy, or if the different policies demanded a different character of proof, the rule might be different.

Even if the circumstances are such as to justify a company in refusing proofs of death upon the faith of which they had already paid one policy, they must make their objections promptly, and where they fail to do so until after a case has been before three juries, and has once been argued before the Supreme Court, they are too late.

Where an insurance company resists the payment of a policy on the ground that it has been forfeited for non-payment of premiums, there is, according to the contention of the company, no policy in existence, and it cannot, therefore, fairly demand proofs of death under a non-existent policy

Where a mutual life insurance company has in its possession dividends standing to the credit of a policy-holder more than sufficient to pay an accruing premium at the time it falls due, it is bound so to appropriate the money, and may not declare the policy forfeited for an alleged failure to pay the premium in question.

Where a premium upon a policy of life insurance fell due on Saturday, Jan. 14, 1871, and payment was tendered on the following Monday morning:

Held (reversing the ruling of the Court below), that evidence to prove a custom of life insurance companies, doing business in Philadelphia, to receive premiums within a reasonable time after they fall due, provided the assured remains in usual health, notwithstanding a forfeiture clause in the policy, is admissible.

Girard Trust Co. *v.* Mutual Life Ins. Co. of N. Y., 5 WEEKLY NOTES, 173; s. c., 5 Nor. 236, followed.

It is competent for a life insurance company to stipulate that premiums received after the day on which they fall due are received as acts of grace, and do not control the future action of the company, but where such a clause is obscurely printed at the top of a blank page, and there is nothing to show at what time it was placed there, it cannot be regarded as a condition of the policy, but is, at most, a qualification of receipts to be thereunder written; and in a case where no receipts were written upon the policy, evidence to show the previous course of dealing with the insured as to the receipt of over-due premiums is admissible.

Per PAXSON, J. "The foregoing [opinion in this case] may appear inconsistent with my dissent in 5 Norris, 236. The case differs in many of its essential features from the case there decided, and as to others my views have been modified."

Error to the Common Pleas No. 3, of Philadelphia County.

Case, by the Girard Life and Trust Company, administrator of Edward Magarge, deceased, to the use of Sarah R. Magarge, against The Mutual Life Insurance Company of New York, upon a policy of life insurance issued by the defendants upon the life of plaintiff's intestate on April 14, 1863, for $10,000.

The case was originally tried before LYND, J., on September 20, 1875, and the plaintiffs were non-suited; after a motion to take off the non-suit had been denied, a writ of error was taken, and the Supreme Court, on February 25, 1878, reversed the judgment and awarded a *procedendo* (reported 5 WEEKLY NOTES, 173, and 5 Nor. 236).

A jury was again called, before YERKES, J., on Oct. 30, 1878, and on Nov. 7 following a verdict for the plaintiff for $14,358.50 was rendered. Subsequently a rule for a new trial was made absolute, and the case was again called for trial Nov. 25, 1879.

The policy in suit was numbered 28,735, and was for $10,000; it provided for the payment of a quarterly "premium of $51, to be paid on or before the 14th days of April, July, October, and January in each year during the continuance of the policy," and contained a provision that—

"If the said premiums shall not be paid on or before the days above mentioned for the payment thereof, at the office of the company, then and in every such case the company shall not be liable for the payment of the sum assured or any part thereof, and this policy shall cease and determine."

On the previous trials the defence had been the failure of the assured to pay the premium due on Jan. 14, 1871.

At the head of the two inside pages, and over a column prepared for receipts of premium, on which, however, no receipts had been written, was the following indorsement, in small type, occupying about two lines:—

"Receipts heretofore by the company, of premiums after the day on which they fell due, were by the assured and the company considered acts of grace or courtesy, and as forming no precedent in regard to future payments of premiums on the policy; and all future receipts by the company of premiums after due, are viewed and understood by the parties in interest as acts of courtesy of the company, and in no case to be considered a precedent or a waiver of the forfeiture of the policy, according to the condition expressed therein, if any future payment of premium be omitted on the day it falls due."

It appeared that the company had issued another policy upon Magarge's life, being No. 73,712, for $5000. After his death blanks for proofs of death to be filled by the oaths of the doctor and undertaker in attendance, etc., were furnished by the company, and were properly filled up and filed with the company, who immediately paid the $5000. These proofs were used without objection on the former trials, and the usual *subpœna duces tecum* for their production on this trial was issued. The circumstances attending the failure to produce them are sufficiently detailed in the opinion of the Supreme Court (*infra*). John J. Ridgway, Jr., counsel for the plaintiff, then took the stand, and offer was made to prove by him that he furnished the company with proofs of Magarge's death. Objected to, unless the proofs are shown to be connected with the policy in suit. Objection sustained. The witness then testified that he had caused copies of the proofs furnished to the company to be prepared, and had compared them with the originals, and identified the papers shown him as the copies that he had compared. The papers offered were, on objection by the defendant, excluded.

The exceptions to the rulings on this branch of the case are covered by the assignments of error, from numbers 1 to 6, inclusive, and numbers 17, 18, and 19.

The plaintiff's testimony disclosed that the company had invariably sent notices to the assured a few days before the premiums fell due, and that they had omitted to do so in January, 1871; that Magarge's bookkeeper tendered payment in full on the Monday following the Saturday on which the premium fell due, and it was refused, and the policy declared forfeited.

Magarge then filed a bill to enjoin the company from declaring it forfeited, and whilst the cause was being argued before a Master Magarge died. It was shown that Magarge was in good health in January, 1871.

Counsel then asked George E. Wagner, a witness for plaintiff: Q. What is the custom among life insurance companies doing business in Philadelphia with regard to receiving premiums after they are due, if tendered within a reasonable time, and the insured is in good health, notwithstanding they are policies containing a clause of forfeiture for non-payment on the very day they are due?

Objected to; objection sustained; exception to plaintiffs. (11th assignment.)

Plaintiff then offered to prove the custom of the company with relation to receiving over-due premiums on the policy in suit. Offer overruled; exceptions. (Assignments 7th to 10th.)

Plaintiff then offered to prove that when the premium of $51 fell due on Jan. 14, 1871, there was due by the company to Magarge $67.72, as his share of the surplus earned during the preceding year, and to be divided among the policy holders, and offered in evidence a book issued by the defendant, and produced on call by their agent, entitled "Mutual Life Rates," to show that such was their custom. Offers overruled; exceptions. (20th and 22d assignments.)

After the plaintiff had closed, the Court entered a compulsory nonsuit, which the Court in banc subsequently refused to take off (23d assignment). Plaintiff then took this writ, assigning as error, *inter alia*, the rulings on evidence, and the refusal to take off the nonsuit, as above indicated.

The case was argued in the Supreme Court February 24, 1880, and the Court ordered a reargument, which was had Jan. 4, 1881.

John J. Ridgway, Jr. (*Daniel Dougherty* with him), for plaintiff in error.

The view of the Court below on the question of the proofs of death was clearly erroneous; all that the company could in reason have demanded was reasonable certainty of the death of Magarge, and that the proofs with which they were furnished were sufficient is amply evidenced by the fact that they paid one policy upon the faith of them.

Walsh *v.* Marine Ins. Co., 32 N. Y. 427.
Mason *v.* Harvey, 8 Exch. 819.
Taylor *v.* Ins. Co., 13 Gray, 434.
Bliss on Life Ins. § 254.

But the action of the company in this case obviated the necessity of furnishing proofs of death at all; for they had, more than a year before Magarge's death, declared the policy forfeited. It would certainly have declined proofs of death "under this policy," as it claimed no such policy was in existence. A refusal to pay a policy of life insurance on other grounds, is a waiver of the right to proofs of death before suit.

McMasters *v.* Fire Insurance Co., 25 Wend. 379.
Rogers *v.* Insurance Co., 6 Paige, 583.
Lewis *v.* Fire Insurance Co., 52 Me. 492.
Miller *v.* Life Insurance Co., 2 E. D. Smith, 268.
Vos *v.* Robinson, 9 Johns. 192.
Savage *v.* Insurance Co., 4 Bosw. 1.
Blake *v.* Fire Insurance Co., 12 Gray, 265.
Bumstead *v.* Fire Insurance Co., 2 Kernan, 81.
Tayloe *v.* Fire Insurance Co., 9 Howard, 390.
O'Niel *v.* Fire Insurance Co., 3 Comst. 122.
Francis *v.* Fire Insurance Co., 1 Dutch. 78.
Schenck *v.* Fire Insurance Co., 4 Zab. 447.
Fire Insurance Co. *v.* Coates, 14 Md. 285.
Angell on Fire and Life Insurance, § 244.

From the testimony on this branch of the case it sufficiently appeared that the original proofs of death were out of the jurisdiction of the Court, and this was sufficient to make the copies admissible.

Carland *v.* Cunningham, 1 Wr. 228.
Starkie on Evidence, 571.
Ralph *v.* Brown, 3 W. & S. 395.

The refusal of the Court below to allow evidence of the previous dealing between the company and the insured as to the receipt of overdue premiums, in spite of the ruling of this Court on the former writ of error (5 Nor. 239), was based on the notice (for it cannot be called a condition) printed across the inside of the policy so nearly illegible that it seems to have escaped the attention of the learned counsel for the company until this trial. It is doubtful whether this Court would sustain this ruling now on account of the delay in making the point.

Ins. Co. *v.* Schreffler, 8 Wr. 269–272.

But it is objectionable on the ground that the statement in question, by its position, can have formed no part of the contract between the company and the insured.

Kingsley *v.* Ins. Co., 8 Cush. 393.
Brittan *v.* Barnaby, 21 How. 536.

Nothing can be more pointed than the language of this Court upon this very case. "If the notices were courtesies with forfeit warning *prods*, other acts of the company were opiates. They should not give him a notice with one hand and lull him to sleep with the other."

Girard Co. v. Ins. Co., *supra*.

The question as to evidence of the custom of insurance companies doing business in Philadelphia has been expressly ruled in our favor.

Girard Co. v. Ins. Co., *supra*.
Helme v. Ins. Co., 11 Sm. 107.

That the company should be allowed to declare a policy forfeited for non-payment of a premium of $51, when there was due by the company to the insured $67.72, would be to give judicial sanction to an act of harshness that would quite abrogate the settled principle that equity abhors a forfeiture. It is no answer to say that the company did not know, by the 14th of January, the amount of the dividend declared on the 1st of January which would ultimately be appropriated to the Magarge policy; the facts and figures were in their possession, and if they were lax in making their calculations they cannot expect that others should thereby be made to suffer. Our contention is supported in—

Hull v. Ins. Co., 39 Wis. 397.
Russam v. Ins. Co., 5 Big. 243.
Ohde v. Ins. Co., Id. 145.

Henry J. McCarthy and *Wm. A. Porter*, for defendant in error.

A great many unnecessary questions in regard to the proofs of death were asked, but the pertinent question "Where are the 'proofs?'" seems to have been overlooked, and it is submitted that there was, therefore, no such proof of their loss or destruction as to render the copies admissible.

The stipulation in the policy that receipts of overdue premium should be considered acts of grace took the case out of the line of Girard Co. v. Ins. Co. (*supra*) and Helme v. Ins. Co. (*supra*), and rendered the evidence offered as to the previous dealing of the company inadmissible; and that this stipulation was part of the contract is abundantly sustained.

Kensington Bank v. Yerkes, 5 Nor. 227.
Fire Association v. Williamson, 2 Cas. 196.
Desilver v. Ins. Co., 2 Wr. 130.
Trask v. Ins. Co., 5 C. 198.

The testimony of Wagner would have been insufficient to fix the custom of receiving overdue premiums upon this company in such a manner as to satisfy the rulings of this Court.

Burger v. Ins. Co., 21 Sm. 424.
Adams v. Ins. Co., 26 Id. 414.

Finally, the company had no right to assume that Magarge desired to have his dividend applied to the payment of his premium; the money was his to appropriate, and the company would not have been justified in doing so for him.

January 24, 1881. THE COURT. This record presents some questions which were not considered when the cause was here upon a former writ of error (see 5 Norris, 236). The assignments are too numerous to be discussed in detail, without extending this opinion to an unreasonable length. I will endeavor, as briefly as is consistent with the importance of the case, to indicate the principles upon which it should be ruled.

The first question relates to the proofs of death furnished the defendant. It is necessary to a proper understanding of this matter, that the facts, as they occurred at the trial, should be stated. The defendant was a foreign corporation, having its principal place of business in the city of New York. It had a branch office in the city of Philadelphia, and an agent there. It had issued two policies upon the life of Edward Magarge, deceased, one of them No. 73,712 for the sum of $5000, the other No. 28,375 for $10,000. The former policy was paid soon after Mr. Magarge's death; payment of the latter was resisted, and forms the subject of the present contention. The defence was the non-payment of the premium on the day it became due. The facts are, that a quarterly premium of $51 fell due upon January 14, 1871, which was neither paid nor tendered on that day; that on the 16th of the same month, the full amount of said premium was tendered in cash, refused by the company, and the policy declared forfeited.

Upon the trial in the Court below, the plaintiff, after giving in evidence the policy in suit, called upon defendant's counsel to produce the "notice and proofs of death of Edward Magarge given to defendant and filed in defendant's office." To this call defendant's counsel replied "there are no proofs of death under this policy." The plaintiff then called William N. Lambert, agent of the defendant, who admitted that a subpoena *duces tecum* had been served upon him, to produce the books and papers relating to this case; that he informed the person who served the subpoena, that he would produce the papers; that the proofs of death had been furnished under policy No. 73,712, which had been paid, that the proofs were filed by us (the agents), in the office of the company in New York, and were brought on here for the trials of this case; that the witness did not know where the proofs were, but supposed them to be in the hands of the counsel of the company. The plaintiff then called the defendant's counsel to the stand, and the result of his somewhat extended examination may be embodied in a single question and answer.

Question. Have you in your possession proofs of the death of Edward Magarge, that were filed with the defendant company?

Answer. I have not in my actual possession,

nor had I when the subpœna was served upon me within a few minutes, any proofs of death of Edward Magarge, and I never have had in my possession any proofs of the death of Edward Magarge, which purported to relate to the policy now in suit." Some other questions were then asked of the counsel, a portion of which it would have been in better taste to have omitted, and then we have this inquiry: "Where are those papers and those proofs of death you had at the last trial?" This question was objected to, and, according to the bill of exceptions, remained unanswered. The plaintiff then called John J. Ridgway, Jr., whose testimony is so important that I give it *in extenso.*

"I knew Edward Magarge. I knew of his death on the 21st of February, 1872. I called at the company's office, and informed them of Magarge's death. They gave me three blanks to have filled up and sworn to by a friend of Magarge's, the doctor who attended him in his last illness, and the undertaker who buried him. I either filled them up or caused them to be filled up, but they were filled up and returned in proper form to the company, sworn to by the parties as directed.

"*Question.* Did you ever obtain the original proofs of death from Judge Porter?

"*Answer.* I did, and had a copy made of them. I can swear that those (witness here points to the papers) are true copies, made by Mr. McAdam, who is in my office, and compared by me, of the proofs of death of Edward Magarge, furnished to defendant. There have been some papers attached."

I quote further from the bill of exceptions.

"Copy of proof of death of Edward Magarge offered in evidence as identified by witness (marked Exhibit A). Objected to. Objection sustained, because the paper itself shows that it referred to another policy. Exception to plaintiff.

"Plaintiff now offers in evidence, the identified copies containing statements of doctor, friend, and undertaker, all certified under oath, being copies of the proofs of death of Edward Magarge, sworn to by doctor March 6, 1872, by the friend on March 9, 1872, and the undertaker's statement sworn to February 29, 1872." Papers Nos. 1, 2, and 3 of Exhibit A. "Offer overruled unless it be shown they were furnished under the special policy in suit. Exception to plaintiff."

It will be observed the Court below placed the exclusion of this evidence upon the sole ground, that the proofs were not furnished under the policy in suit.

No evidence appears to have been offered upon this point. Mr. Ridgway, who furnished the proofs, does not say under which policy they were made. There is nothing upon the face of the papers, copies of which are printed in the paper-book, to indicate under which policy the proofs were furnished, except a reference in the "friend's statement" to the number and amount of the policy which the company paid, and an indorsement, evidently by an officer of the company, of the number (73,712) on the back of the papers.

It appears to have been assumed by the company and the Court below, that it was necessary for the plaintiff to have made separate proofs of death under the policy in suit, notwithstanding the admitted fact that such proofs had been furnished, which the company had accepted, and under which it had paid the $5000 policy.

It is undoubtedly competent for a company to contract with the assured, that, in case they issue more than one policy on his life, separate proofs shall be furnished under each policy in case of his death. There was no such contract here. The policy provides for the payment of the sum thereby insured "in sixty days after due notice and proof of the death of the said Edward Magarge." Upon the death of the insured, the company were entitled to notice and due proof thereof. The plaintiff having once made such proof, there was no object in proving it again, and the company had no right to demand second proofs. The assured was dead, not under one policy, but under both: the fact had been communicated to the company, with the cause of death, and all the circumstances connected therewith they desired to know, and as to which it was important they should be informed. A demand that all this should be repeated, merely because two policies had been issued upon Mr. Magarge's life, is as unreasonable as it is foreign to the contract between the parties.

Had the different policies called for different modes of proof, there would have been more force in the demand for proofs under each policy. Such is not the case, however, and if it were, it was too late for the company to insist upon this point. Mr. Magarge had been dead for years; the case had been tried three times before in the Court below, and once here. Upon the previous trials, these same proofs of death had been produced by the company, and used without objection. If for any reason the proofs were defective, or were not in conformity with the policy in suit, it was the duty of the company to have so notified the plaintiff. The rule in this respect was accurately laid down by Chancellor WALWORTH in Ætna Fire Ins. Co. v. Tyler (16 Wend. 385). "Good faith on the part of the underwriters requires that, if they mean to insist upon a mere formal defect of this kind in the preliminary proofs, they should apprise the insured that they consider them defective in that particular, or to put their refusal to pay upon that ground, as well as others, so as to give him an opportunity to supply the defect before it could be too late; and if they neglect to do so, their silence should be held a waiver of such defect in the preliminary proofs, so that the same shall be considered as having been duly made according to the condition of the policy." (To the same effect are Ins. Co. v. Schreffler, 6 Wright, 188; McMasters v. Ins. Co., 25 Wend. 379, 16 Id. 401; Ins. Co. v. Lawrence, 10 Peters, 507; Rogers v. Ins. Co., 6 Paige, 583; Lewis v. The Ins. Co., 52 Maine, 492; Miller v. Ins. Co., 2 E. D. Smith, 268; Savage v. Ins. Co., 4 Bosworth, 1; Blake v. Ins. Co., 12 Gray, 265; Noyes v. Ins. Co., 30 Vermont, 659; Norwich v. The Ins. Co., 6 Blatchford C. C. R. 241; Francis v. The Ins. Co., 6 Cowen, 404; Angell on Fire and Life Insurance, § 244; O'Niel v. The Ins. Co., 3 Comst. 122; Francis v. The Ins. Co., 1 Dutch. 78; Schenck v. The Ins. Co., 4 Zabriskie, 447; Vos v. Robinson, 9 Johnson, 192.)

Aside from this, the proofs referred to were not essential. The plaintiffs had proved the death of Mr. Magarge. Further they were not bound to go. The defendant company denied all liability under the policy. They had declared it forfeited months before the death of the assured. Their position was, that as to the assured there was no policy. It was precisely as if they had denied ever having issued one. How then could they call upon the representatives of the assured, to furnish proofs of death "under the policy?" It was held, in the Franklin Insurance Co. of Philadelphia v. Coates (14 Md. 285), that "the refusal of an insurance company to pay the amount of the loss, upon the ground that they were not upon the risk, is a waiver of the preliminary proofs required by the policy." The same doctrine was held by the Supreme Court of Missouri, in McComas v. The Ins. Co. (56 Mo. 573), where it was ruled that, "In a suit on a policy of life insurance, where the company in its defence denied all responsibility, and refused to pay anything, such defence amounts to a waiver of notice and proof of death, and where such defence is interposed to a suit on a policy, which requires the insurance to be paid within sixty days after notice and proofs of loss, the same will be held due at that period after his death." We regard this as settled law.

Another important question is, the right of the company to forfeit the policy. This is raised by the 20th assignment, and as it underlies some of the other points involved I will consider it out of its order.

The plaintiff offered to prove, "that upon January 1, 1871, the surplus of defendant company for the year 1870 was divided among the policy holders of the company, and that this policy now in suit was then entitled to the sum of $67.72, which appears by the books produced by the witness to the credit of that policy; and that the previous divisions of surplus or annual dividends due to this policy were more than the quarterly premiums due in January of each year; also to show how Magarge was in the habit of using those dividends in payment of his premiums.'

As before stated, a quarterly premium fell due January 14, 1871. It was tendered on the 16th, and refused, whereupon the company declared the policy forfeited by reason of its non-payment. Had the company a right so to declare? In considering this point, I throw out of the case all question of the right of the assured to pay within a reasonable time, after the maturity of the premium by reason of the previous course of dealing with him by the company.

This is a matter of exceeding importance to life insurance, in its bearing upon the rights of each of the contracting parties. The consideration of such contracts is the payment of premiums by the assured, annually or otherwise, as may be agreed upon. Without it, the company would not have the means or the power to indemnify the family of the assured in case of his death. It is a contract that calls for the exercise of the highest good faith on both sides. The assured pays his money for indemnity in case of death. The company agrees to indemnify in case the premiums are paid as stipulated in the policy. It will readily be seen that time is of the essence of such a contract. It is entirely competent for the parties to stipulate that, in case the payments are not made on the days and times agreed upon, the policy shall be forfeited, nor has the assured who neglects to pay a right to complain if the terms of the policy are enforced against him. The law, however, does not favor forfeitures; it never enforces them cheerfully, and will decline to enforce them where they are against equity and good conscience. Was it conscionable for the defendant company to forfeit this policy when it had in its hands more than enough of the assured's money to pay the quarterly premium due on the 14th of January?

To state the proposition most favorably to the company: suppose the assured on the 14th of January had been mortally ill, and for that reason had not paid his premium, and instead of tendering it on the 16th had died upon that day. Would a chancellor have permitted a forfeiture of the policy, if it appeared the company had more than enough of the assured's money in its possession to have paid the premium? What is the ground of the forfeiture? It is that the assured, by withholding from the company the money which he agreed to pay, prevents the latter from performing its contract of indemnity with others. It is therefore just that it should not perform it with the defaulting assured. If, however, the company has in its possession money of the assured sufficient to cover the default, and which it has the right to apply, it has the means to keep its covenants with others, and why not keep them with the assured? This brings us to the question, had the company the right to apply the surplus belonging to Mr. Magarge to the payment of the premium which became due on January 14th? If it had such right, equity will compel such application to prevent the forfeiture. Upon this point we have not been furnished with much information by the paper-books, and must take the record as we find it. The evidence referred to in the 22d assignment would have given us some light upon this subject, and it was error to exclude it. That the book was issued and published by the company after the date of the policy in suit is not material. It was not pretended that it did not apply to all policies theretofore issued. Taking the record as it stands, and conceding the truth of the offer in the 20th assignment, it is clear the company had in its possession on the 14th of January the sum of $67.72 in cash belonging to the assured. It was urged that it could not have been applied to the payment of the premium without his consent. No sufficient reason had been advanced in support of this proposition. Suppose the company had so applied it, could the assured have recovered it back? Could not the company have set off the unpaid premium in any suit that he could have brought for such purpose? It is true, mutual demands do not necessarily extinguish each other, but that is not the question here. The true point is the power of the company to make the application, and the right to set off the premium against a suit for the dividend. It was urged that the application of such a rule to the affairs of a large insurance company may seriously embarrass its business. On the other hand, the forfeiture of policies for non-payment of premiums, when the company has in its possession money sufficient to pay them, may seriously embarrass the unfortunate assured. The argument, *ab inconvenienti*, is certainly as strong on the one side as the other. As a matter of fact, the consent of the assured to the appropriation may be presumed. That he would object to it and thereby forfeit his policy is a proposition too absurd to be seriously considered.

It may be urged that the amount of dividend had not been ascertained on the 14th of January. If this be so, it does not help the company. The dividend had been declared on the first of that month, and if its precise amount had not been determined by the 14th, it was no fault of the assured. It could not have been difficult for the company, with its past experience and knowledge of the previous year's business, to have measured the dividend with reasonable accuracy. And if doubt existed upon this point, or as to the willingness of the assured to apply the dividend to the payment of the premium, equity and a just regard to his right would require the company to seek information as to these matters, before proceeding to the harsh measure of forfeiting the policy. The plaintiff offered to show that Mr. Magarge had used previous dividends in payment of premiums. The company had therefore reason to believe from its prior dealings with him, that he would have desired such application.

While a Court of Equity will sustain a forfeiture under some circumstances, it will scrutinize the transaction and require that all the rights of the assured shall be respected. It is quite possible, there may be facts which in the judgment of the officers of the defendant company justified them in declaring the policy forfeited in this case; yet we are constrained to say, that it is inequitable and against the policy of the law to permit an insurance company to forfeit a life policy for non-payment of a premium, when such company has in its possession the money of the assured to an amount covering the premium, and which it has the power to apply to its payment.

The Court below excluded evidence on behalf of the plaintiff offered for the purpose of showing the previous course of dealings between the defendant and the insured, as to the payment of overdue premiums. This point was squarely decided, when the cause was here before. It was said by Justice TRUNKEY, "no vestige of reason is discoverable for refusing the premium tendered the second day after it became due." Under this ruling, the evidence referred to in the 7th, 8th, 9th, and 10th assignments of error ought to have been received. The learned Judge would doubtless have permitted it, had not his attention been called to two lines printed upon the policy, declaring in substance that all receipts of overdue premiums are acts of grace and courtesy on the part of the company, and shall in no case be considered a precedent or waiver of forfeiture.

This clause is peculiar, whether we regard its position on the policy, or its phraseology. It does not appear on the face of the policy, nor does the policy refer to it in any manner, as is usual where printed conditions annexed are made a part of the contract. Nor does it appear upon the back of the policy, where it would readily meet the eye, but upon the inside, being two lines of printed matter at the top of the second or inside page, over the ruled columns intended for the entry of the payment of premiums from time to time. No such entries were ever made, and the entire page is a blank, save the two printed lines referred to, and the printed headings. The phraseology is peculiar in this, that it refers to "receipts *heretofore* by the company of premiums after they fell due," as well as all future receipts of premiums, etc. Whether this clause was upon the policy when it was issued, does not appear. The learned Court below treated it as a supplemental agreement. I quote its language:—"It is evident that it was written after premiums had been received which were overdue, and before the 16th of January, 1871, when the last tender of premium was made." Had it been written as the learned Judge states, there would have been much force in this suggestion, in view of its phraseology. But the words are printed, and there was absolutely nothing in the case to show when they were placed there. Not the least remarkable feature of this matter is the fact, that no one, not even the defendant or its counsel, appears to have had any knowledge of this clause until the case was brought into this Court upon a second writ of error, when for the first time it was set up in the Court below as an answer to the plaintiff's allegation, that the defendant had lulled the assured into security by the acceptance of overdue premiums from time to time.

It is settled that the conditions annexed to a policy are as much a part of the contract as though incorporated in the instrument. (1 Hen. Black. 254; 6 T. R. 710; 6 Cowen, 576; Fire Ins. *v.* Williamson, 2 Casey, 196; Trask *v.* The State Mutual, 5 Id. 198; Inland Ins. Co. *v.* Stauffer, 9 Id. 379; Desilver *v.* The Ins. Co., 2 Wright, 130; Ins. Co. *v.* Gottman, 12 Id. 151.)

While this line of decisions relates almost exclusively to fire policies, the reason of the rule would apply equally well to life policies. In the former, however, as is well known, it is the invariable practice for the policy to contain a reference to the conditions, and the insurance is made "according to the tenor of the conditions hereto annexed." While the cases cited do not disclose the fact, it is safe to assume it existed in all of them. The policy in suit contains upon its face a condition, authorizing a forfeiture of the policy in case of the non-payment of the premium; and refers to no condition or stipulation outside of its four corners, excepting the declaration of the assured made in his application for the policy. It was said by Mr. Justice SWAYNE in Brittan *v.* Barnaby (21 Howard, at page 536): "In the first place, as loose, indefinite, and dangerous as some of the decisions in the English and American Reports are, concerning memorandums of this kind, no case can be found in either in which effect has been given to any memorandum which was not on the face or the margin of the policy." This, however, is not authority, for it was not the point decided; but we must regard the effect of a memorandum, not purporting upon its face to be a condition upon which the insurance was effected, printed in an obscure place on the policy and in no way referred to in the policy itself, as an open question. There are reasons why it is not necessary to decide it in this case.

This memorandum can hardly be regarded as a condition of the policy. It is more in the nature of a qualification of the receipts for the premiums, which were intended to be indorsed on the policy from time to time. This was its manifest object. But no such receipts were indorsed; there was nothing to qualify and nothing to which it could attach. In point of fact, the receipts, if any were given, were loose receipts. Did they contain any such qualification? We have no evidence upon this point. If they did not, the act would be too equivocal to hold the assured to notice that the acceptance of overdue premiums would not be drawn into precedent. Nothing could be better calculated to lull the assured into security than the giving of receipts for overdue premiums without such warning had, even though the attention of the assured had been specially called to the memorandum in question.

If the defendant company relied upon this clause to enforce its forfeiture of the policy and prevent a recovery in this suit, the point should have been made at an earlier stage of the proceedings. Having failed to set it up until after at least two trials in the Court below and a hearing in this Court, we must regard it as having been waived. It is no answer to this, to say that neither the defendant nor its counsel knew of the existence of this memorandum until the last trial in the Court below. That it was placed upon the policy by the company or its authorized agent is too plain to be disputed; it cannot now be permitted to say it did not know of its own act, and good faith to the assured required that, if intended as a defence, it should have been set up at the earliest moment. To spring it upon the plaintiffs now, after all these years of litigation, would be unfair to them. To admit such alleged want of knowledge on the part of the defendant company as an excuse for this delay, would be especially inequitable in view of the fact that it is sought to charge the assured with knowledge of the memorandum from its inception. We do not think it was a sufficient ground for the rejection of the evidence referred to.

We are unable to see any error in the exclusion of the evidence referred to in the 10th assignment. The offer was not broad enough to give it any value as evidence. The mere fact that the witness received no notice of the premium falling due on January 14 amounts to nothing. Had there been an offer to show that previous notices had been sent and this one purposely omitted with the design of forfeiting the policy, it would have been clearly admissible. "Forfeitures are odious in law . . . and there must be no cast of management or trickery to entrap the party into a forfeiture." (Helme *v.* The Ins. Co., 11 P. F. S. 107.)

The last question to be noticed relates to the exclusion of the evidence offered by the plaintiff to show a custom or usage among life insurance companies in Philadelphia to receive overdue premiums. (See assignments 11th to 16th inclusive; also 21st.) That such a custom may be shown was ruled in Helme *v.* The Ins. Co., *supra*, and in this case, upon the former writ of error, where it was said by Justice TRUNKEY: "Upon the verity of the testimony of Mr. Ashbrook, the jury would have been warranted in finding, that it is a custom among life insurance companies to receive premiums if tendered at any time within thirty days of the time they fall due, provided the insured is in good health, and that this custom includes policies stipulating for forfeiture in case of non-payment of premium on the day." Mr. Ashbrook was not called at the last trial in the Court below, but another witness, George E. Wagner, was called to prove the custom. Several of the questions put to this witness were objectionable, and their exclusion was not error. But we are unable to see any sufficient reason why the question referred to in the 15th assignment should have been excluded. It was as follows: "Does the custom apply to policies containing a clause of forfeiture for non-payment of premium on the day it is due?" Of course the custom sought to be proved must be applicable to contracts of insurance, such as the one in suit. But applicable in what respect? Manifestly in the matter of forfeiture, which was the only point the custom had reference to. The question was carefully framed to meet this view, and it was error to exclude the evidence.

What has been said sufficiently covers the various assignments of error.

The foregoing may appear inconsistent with my dissent in 5 Norris, 236. The case as now presented differs in many of its essential features from the one there decided, and as to others my views have been modified.

The judgment is reversed and a *procedendo* awarded.

Opinion by PAXSON, J.

GORDON and GREEN, JJ., being members of the defendant company, by having insured therein, did not sit.

Vol. IX.—28

May, '80, 71.   May 13, 1880.

Spahr v. Farmers' Bank, Carlisle.

Corporations—Defective organization—De facto exercise of franchise under charter by special Act—Ultra vires—When not a defence by one who has dealt with a de facto corporation.

One who has dealt with a corporation, as such, will not be permitted to deny his liability on a contract by alleging that the corporation has no legal existence, and therefore no right to sue.

The "Farmers' Bank" was chartered, in 1868, and did business under the provisions of the Free Banking Act of 1861. In 1871 it ceased to act under its charter, and thenceforth acted under a new charter granted to its officers by a special Act of the Legislature, which gave other corporate powers, under the title of the "Farmers' Bank, Carlisle." The stock and assets of the old bank were treated as belonging to the new, and the business was continued without interruption. Renewal notes were taken for the unpaid portion of certain notes discounted by the old bank at a higher rate than six per cent., and new notes and renewals were made, also at a usurious rate of discount. In a suit by the "Farmers' Bank, Carlisle," against the indorser on the series of notes and renewals:

Held, that the defendant could not set up as a defence the invalidity of the change from the old charter to the new.

Error to the Common Pleas of Cumberland County.

Assumpsit, by the Farmers' Bank, Carlisle, against Peter Spahr, on certain promissory notes indorsed by the defendant.

By agreement filed, the case was tried without a jury, before HERMAN, P. J., who found substantially the following facts: The "Farmers' Bank," of Carlisle, Pa., was organized and incorporated by letters patent issued by the Governor, October 28, 1868, as a bank of discount, deposit, and circulation, under the provisions of the Free Banking Act of May 1, 1861, with a paid-up capital stock of $50,000, and continued to do business under said charter until May 1, 1871. On March 15, 1871, the persons who were officers and directors of the Farmers' Bank procured from the Legislature a special Act (P. L. 1871, 366), incorporating them under the title of the "Farmers' Bank, Carlisle," with certain powers prescribed by the Act, differing materially from the powers granted by the former charter. By resolution of the directors, and with the consent in writing of the stockholders (except the holders of fifteen shares, who did not dissent), the said bank, on May 1, 1871, ceased to use and act under the charter of 1868, and thenceforth used the charter of March 5, 1871, and conducted its business under its provisions in the name of the "Farmers' Bank, Carlisle." A notice of this change was sent by the cashier to the Auditor-General. The assets of the old corporation were treated as assets of the new, the requisite verbal changes were made in the old books, and the business was carried along by the same officers without interruption and in the same manner as before, except in the discounting of paper. Under the old charter, notes on which a greater rate than six per cent. was taken were made payable at some place other than the bank, and the excess was entered in the books as exchange; but under the new charter all notes were made payable at the bank, and when a greater rate than six per cent. was taken it was entered as discount. Under the new charter the capital stock was $100,000, but the bank was authorized to do business when $50,000 was paid up. The $50,000 paid-up capital of the old bank was carried as the paid-up portion of the capital stock of the new bank, without the issue of new or additional certificates (except in cases of transfers), and dividends were regularly paid thereon.

Prior to the reorganization the bank had discounted certain notes, and renewals, on which Peter Spahr was accommodation indorser, at the rate of eight per cent. A portion of these notes was renewed, at the same rate, after the reorganization, and new notes and renewals were taken and discounted at the same rate, the notes in suit being the last renewals in these several series.

The defendant pleaded, specially, that the "Farmers' Bank, Carlisle," plaintiff, never completed its organization according to law, and had no legal corporate existence; that its acts in discounting the said notes were *ultra vires;* that the old "Farmers' Bank" of Carlisle was, and is still, in existence; but under the provisions of the Banking Act of 1861, it had no right to discount the said notes for a higher rate than six per cent. under penalty of forfeiting the whole debt.

The plaintiff presented several points, to the effect that the facts showed practically and legally a determination and ending of the first charter so far as the subsequent acts of the corporators are concerned under the second charter; that usury taken in discounting notes under the second charter could be set off, but did not defeat the plaintiff's claim; that the discount by the plaintiff of the renewal notes which originated in the "Farmers' Bank" was a novation, founded on a sufficient consideration, and plaintiff took them free from any prior existing taint of usury; that the acceptance and use of the new charter rendered the same valid and binding on all parties dealing and contracting with the bank, and unimpeachable, except, perhaps, by the commonwealth or a corporator; and that the defendant, being a debtor to the bank, cannot deny its legal existence, or set up as a defence to the notes any irregularities or omissions in the organization of the new corporation, or in the acceptance of its charter—all which points were affirmed by the Court.

The defendant presented a number of points, to a contrary effect, which were refused.

HERMAN, P. J., filed an opinion, in which he said, *inter alia:* . . . . "These being the facts of the case, I am of the opinion that the 'Farmers' Bank, Carlisle,' is a corporation duly organized, doing business, and having its legal existence under and by virtue of the charter of 15th March, 1871, and that it is entitled to recover from Peter Spahr, the defendant, the amount of the notes in suit, after deducting the sum of $384.35, being the excess over the legal rate of interest taken and received by the bank, on all the different series of notes represented by the notes in suit, and also allowing a credit of $1000, paid on account of these notes, by him, on 17th January, 1876. . . . . I think it cannot be seriously doubted, that the charter of 1871 was granted by the Legislature with the intention that it should be accepted and used by the "Farmers' Bank" in lieu of the old charter of 1868, and that the bank has practically done precisely what it was thus intended it should do. The corporators named in the charter of 1871 cannot complain of what was done, for they recommended it; neither can the stockholders complain, for they assented to it. There are no creditors to complain, for all the liabilities of the bank incurred under the old charter have been fully discharged and paid. No person has been hurt or prejudiced by the change, certainly not this defendant, for the bank's money was procured on the faith of his indorsements, and full value given therefor, excepting only in the taking and reserving the excess over the legal rate of interest, and for this he can and will now be fully compensated by deducting it from the amount of the notes in suit. And if the bank owes any duty to the State which it has failed to perform, this defendant cannot take any advantage of that; it will not relieve him of his duty to pay his debt to the bank.

"The bank having, since 1st May, 1871, been a corporation existing and operating under the charter of 1871, and not under that of 1868, it has not since then been subject to the charter of 1868, and all the notes in suit having been given and discounted in the years 1874 and 1875, the taking and reserving of a greater than the legal rate of interest thereon does not operate as a forfeiture of the debt represented by any of the notes. . . . . The decision of the Court is rendered in favor of the plaintiff for the sum of $5587.40."

Exceptions filed to this decision were overruled by the Court, and judgment entered for, the plaintiff; whereupon the defendant took this writ, assigning for error, *inter alia*, the answers to points, and the judgment of the Court as above given.

S. Hepburn, Jr., and *S. Hepburn*, for plaintiff in error.

This is not an attempt to set up a mere defective organization as a defence to an honest debt. The plaintiff's right to recover depends on its legal existence as a corporation. The defendant, as indorser, had rights secured under the charter of 1868, which the plaintiff sought to evade by setting up a pretended new charter, in violation of all law as to the dissolution of one corporation and the creation of a new one. It is a new principle to admit acts done by one corporation to prove the creation of another, when none of the conditions precedent, required by law, have been complied with. The manner in which corporations may be dissolved and charters surrendered is fixed by statute.

Act of April 9, 1856, sec. 1, Purd. Dig. 285, pl. 21.
Com'th *v.* Slifer, 3 Sm. 71.
Green's Brice's Ultra Vires, 651, and note.
Potter on Corporations, sec. 703.

The special Act of 1861 was not a re-charter, nor a supplement or amendment of the existing charter. It contemplated the organization of a bank in the usual way, and the intention of the corporators could not affect the intention of the Legislature. It directed the capital of $100,000 to be divided into 2000 shares, to be paid in such instalments as the bank should by its by-laws direct. There having been no bona fide organization under the new charter, it was invalidated by the Constitution of 1874, Art. xvi., Sect. 1. The plaintiff failed to show that it was a legally organized corporation, but did show that the old "Farmers' Bank" is in existence, and that that bank, by violating its charter in taking usurious discount, by the terms of its charter forfeited the whole debt and interest.

W. F. Sadler and *L. Todd*, for defendant in error.

Where a charter is granted to named corporators by a *special Act* of the Legislature, creating a corporation *in presenti*, they become a corporation immediately on the passage of the Act, and the production of the charter is proof of incorporation. The omission to do certain acts directed by such Act, though possible cause for dissolution by the commonwealth or the courts, does not, *ipso facto*, affect the corporate status, and cannot be inquired into collaterally. The omissions here were of directory provisions only, and would not support a quo warranto.

Potter on Corp., sec. 66.
Talladega Ins. Co. *v.* Landers, 43 Ala. 115.
Brouwer *v.* Appleby, 1 Sandf. 158.
People *v.* Manhattan Co., 9 Wend. 383.
Fire Dep. *v.* Kip, 10 Wend. 266.
Rathbone *v.* Tioga Nav. Co., 2 W. & S. 74.
Hughes *v.* Parker, 20 N. H. 58.
Newcomb *v.* Reed, 12 Allen, 362.
Irvine *v.* Bank, 2 W. & S. 190.

The defendant dealt with the corporation as such, and is estopped from denying its existence.

Cong. Soc. *v.* Perry, 6 N. H. 164.
Dutcher's Manf. Co. *v.* Davis, 14 Johns. 238.
Jones *v.* Bank, 8 B. Monroe, 122.
Angell and Ames on Corp., § 94.
Bigelow on Estoppel, 425, and note 4.

May 24, 1880. THE COURT. A corporation is the mere creature of the law. It can exercise no powers which are not expressly conferred or necessarily implied in furtherance of the object of its creation. (Diligent Fire Co. *v.* Com'th, 25 P. F. Smith, 295.) When, however, a charter has actually been granted to certain persons to act as a corporation, and they are actually in the possession and enjoyment of the corporate rights granted, such possession and enjoyment will be valid against one who has dealt with them in their corporate character. (Angell and Ames on Corp., § 80.) He cannot be permitted to prove, in a collateral proceeding, that a condition precedent to its full corporate existence has not been complied with. As against him, the charter and a user of rights claimed to have been conferred by it, are sufficient. When there is a *de facto* corporation, and the State does not interfere, its corporate existence and its ability to contract cannot be questioned in a suit brought upon an evidence of a debt given to it. (Commissioners *v.* Bolles, 4 Otto, 104.) It is well settled, that although a charter may be declared null and void by the proper authority, yet the violation thereof cannot be determined in a collateral suit. (Irvine *v.* Lumberman's Bank, 2 W. & S. 190.)

The facts show the bank has professed to carry on all its business under the Act of 15th of March, 1871. On the 1st of May, 1871, it reported to the Auditor-General that it had ceased to act under its former charter, and commenced operations under the Act of 15th of March, 1871. It transferred all the stock and assets of the former corporation to the present one. It gave up the exercise of all powers under the old charter, and has continuously used and exercised the powers given by the new charter. Although it has been done in an irregular manner, yet it lies not with the plaintiff in error to question its powers in this transaction and in this suit. Judgment affirmed.

Opinion by MERCUR, J.
SHARSWOOD, C. J., and GREEN, J., absent.

Jan. '80, 118.   May 14, 1880.
Duncan's Appeal.
Duncan v. Pennsylvania Railroad Co.

Preliminary injunction—When properly refused—Bill to restrain Pennsylvania Railroad Company from building railroad in a public street in Philadelphia.

Appeal from a decree of the Common Pleas No. 2, of Philadelphia County, refusing a preliminary injunction.

This cause was fully reported, in the Court below, 7 WEEKLY NOTES, 551, *q. v.* The Court having refused to grant a preliminary injunction, this appeal was taken, under the provisions of the Act of June 12, 1879 (P. L. 177), and on motion the record (with the record of two similar cases) was certified to the Middle District for argument at the May Term (see 8 WEEKLY NOTES, 340). The only assignment of error was the refusal to grant a preliminary injunction.

M. Hampton Todd and *D. T. Watson,* for appellant.

Wayne MacVeagh and *John Scott,* for appellee.

May 24, 1880. THE COURT. Decree refusing preliminary injunction affirmed, and appeal dismissed at the costs of the appellants.

PER CURIAM.

SHARSWOOD, C. J., and GREEN, J., absent.

Common Pleas—Law.

C. P. of Montgomery Co.   Nov. 30, 1880.
Bradfield v. Union Mutual Insurance Co.

Mutual insurance companies—Dual relation of insured member to the company—Contract rights under the policy, and liabilities as corporator—A by-law, authorising company to rebuild, passed subsequently to date of policy, binds one in his relation of corporator, but does not affect his rights under the policy to recover the amount insured in cash.

Sur demurrer to replication.

Covenant, on a policy of insurance issued by the company defendant to the plaintiff, insuring the plaintiff's barn and other buildings against loss by fire. At the date of the policy, August 23, 1876, the 18th section of the by-laws provided as follows:—

"Damage by fire shall be valued by the committee appointed for that purpose at the actual damage sustained, without reference to that which was not destroyed, provided it does not exceed the whole amount of insurance thereon."

Subsequently to this, at an annual meeting of the board of directors on January 14, 1878, at which the plaintiff was not present, the above by-law was amended by the enactment of the following additional clause:—

"The company always reserves the right to repair or rebuild the property injured or destroyed by fire."

On October 17, 1879, the plaintiff's barn was destroyed by fire, and at or about the expiration of the ninety days which the company had, under the by-laws, within which to settle the loss, the defendants claimed the right to rebuild, and proceeded, against the plaintiff's consent, to deposit materials, etc. on plaintiff's premises for that purpose, and began work. The plaintiff claimed the insurance money in cash, and on refusal of his demand brought this suit. The defendants filed a plea in abatement, alleging that they were rebuilding as provided for by said amended by-law. The plaintiff replied that said amendment was passed more than a year and a half after the policy was issued; that plaintiff was not present at the time of its passage, and never subsequently consented that said by-law should change, modify, or forfeit his rights under the said contract. To this replication defendants demurred, and joinder.

N. H. Larzelere, for plaintiff.

H. K. Weand, for defendant.

Jan. 15, 1881. THE COURT (after reciting the facts). The question presented by this record is, whether the defendant corporation has the right, under the 18th section of the by-laws, as amended, to rebuild the burnt premises. It resolves itself into another inquiry, which is, whether a mutual fire insurance company can, by an amendment to their by-laws, change or alter the contract made with one of their members, in pursuance of the charter and by-laws existing at the time the contract was made?

To answer the question correctly, it must be carefully borne in mind that one insured occupies a dual relation to the association: (1) as a member of the company—a corporator; (2) as a contracting party with the corporation. (Ins. Co. *v.* Connor, 5 Harris, 142; Rosenberger *v.* Fire Ins. Co., 6 Norris, 207; Revere *v.* Boston Copper Co., 15 Pickering, 363.) As a corporator simply, he is bound by the acts of the majority, and his corporate rights are subject to the authority of the corporation. As one insured by contract with the company his rights stand entirely free from such control.

The distinction is well drawn by TRUNKEY, J., in Rosenberger *v.* Fire Ins. Co. (6 Norris, 212). It is there said: "They are, as members, subject to liabilities, and entitled to privileges; a member may participate in its benefits; is presumed to know its rules and regulations; its books are evidence against him; and he shall bear his proportion of burden. His corporate rights may be subject to the control of the corporation; *but his rights as a party insured rest upon the contract.*" " Assurer and insured are alike bound by the charter; and neither can do what it does not authorize; *nor can either change a by-law so as to modify the contract without the other's consent.*" To the authorities already cited may be added Flanders on Insurance, 20, 218; and it seems to be clear, that no by-law can be made which will abrogate the contract, or by its effect forfeit the rights of a corporator in his contract relations.

This being true, the next question that presents itself is, whether the alteration and amendment of the by-law in the case at bar is within the rule laid down. It does not present a forfeiture such as was worked by the operation of the amendment in Insurance Co. *v.* Connor; and, in the Supreme Court, that case was ruled by LEWIS, C. J., upon the distinct ground that a forfeiture was wrought by its operation. There is no case in Pennsylvania where the point raised here is decided, though TRUNKEY, J., *arguendo*, declares, in the opinion already cited, "nor can either change a by-law so as to *modify* the contract, without the other's consent," and refers to Ins. Co. *v.* Connor as the authority for this statement of the law.

The question, being an open one, must be determined either by an application of principles or by rulings upon kindred questions in other States. Tested first, by the former, it would seem that if contract rights are altered or greatly modified by the amendment, it ought not to affect the holder of a prior insurance. If it can, then contract rights are altered or greatly modified or destroyed by what, in fact, is *ex post facto* legislation.

This is well illustrated by the reasoning of C. J. LEWIS in Ins. Co. *v.* Connor (5 Har. 143), who says: "What security is there in a policy of insurance which is liable to be declared forfeited by one party without the consent of the other? The chances of indemnity against loss would be diminished by such an uncertain provision. If this be established as the law which is to govern contracts with mutual insurance corporations, it will be destructive of all business transactions with them. Its tendency would be to defeat the chief object of the party who effects an insurance. The recognition of the power claimed in this case by the plaintiff in error would be injurious to the interests of insurance companies, contrary to the principles upon which they are founded, and dangerous to the just and equal rights of the citizen."

It is difficult to distinguish, under this reasoning, the difference between a forfeiture of the contract and a material alteration or modification of it. But if it is said that the object of the insurance is to protect the insured against loss, and that, if the burnt building be replaced, he is made whole, and the object intended to be provided for is substantially attained. But if one contracts with a tailor for a suit of broadcloth, and in fulfilment he has given to him a suit of Lyons velvets of equal or greater value, it cannot be pretended that the contract is executed. An insurance to be paid in money is almost totally different from an insurance to rebuild. It changes the rights of the insured, and directs a value for which he contracted as an indemnity to a special purpose, when, by the terms of the agreement, it was to be at his absolute disposal. It compels him to accept a similar structure upon the same site, with materials partly new and partly old; whereas, by this contract, he could have either devoted the money to another purpose, selected a different site, 'and remodelled his building in accordance with his own taste, or the existing architectural fashion. It seems clear, therefore, upon general reasoning, that the amendment involves a material alteration and modification of the original contract, short, it is true, of forfeiture, but changing the contract essentially.

This is at once contrary to law and against public policy. But the question is not without the guiding light of authority. In Flanders on Fire Insurance, p. 20, it is laid down as elementary law, "that where the assured has duly become the member of a mutual insurance company, and the company subsequently make by-laws without his consent, which are in conflict with the charter, and which would, in fact, change and impair his rights under the contract, such by-laws are void as to him." (Citing Ins. Co. *v.* Harvey, 45 N. H. 292.) Here the by-law, it is true, is not in conflict with chartered rights, but it does change and impair his rights. The same doctrine is again succinctly declared by the same author, page 218 (citing Mutual Fire Ins. Co. *v.* Butler, 34 Maine, 451); and the very question at bar seems to have been ruled in Wallace *v.* Ins. Co. (4 La. 289). Flanders, in citing the case, p. 569, states its conclusion as follows: "An insurance company has no right to rebuild, or replace the articles lost, unless the right is expressly given in the policy; otherwise they would have the right to change the contract, and substitute one mode of performance for another." The case cited by the author will be found in 1 Bennett's Fire Ins. Cases, 414.

The whole doctrine of the right to make by-laws is to be determined by the fact that it is purely a legislative power, and is restricted and limited by the constitutional and statute law of the State in which it is established, as well as by the general principles and policy of the common law as it is there accepted. (Angell and Ames on Corp., chap. x.; Revere *v.* Boston Copper Co., 15 Pick. 363; Bank *v.* Baker, 4 Metc. 176; Savings Institution, 1 Wh. 468; Ins. Co. *v.* Harvey, 4 Am. Law Reg. N. S. 508; Slee *v.* Bloom, 19 Johns. 456.)

It is, therefore, concluded by the Court, that this by-law, while it controls the plaintiff as a corporator, and in that relation is binding upon him, does not and cannot affect his contract relations under his contract as evidenced by his policy: (1) because, being passed without his assent, it is, as to him, *ex post facto;* (2), because it materially modifies and changes his contract rights. This being true, it follows that judgment upon the pleadings must be entered in favor of the plaintiff and against the defendant *quod respondeat ouster.*

Opinion by Ross, P. J.

C. P. No 4.   Dec. 17, 1880.

Johnson v. Black.

Landlord and tenant — Distress — Replevin — Failure to appraise goods distrained where no sale has been made — Act of March 21, 1772.

Motion for judgment *non obstante veredicto.*

Edward P. Johnson leased certain premises from John Black, by lease dated October 1, 1878. On June 1, 1879, the tenant was four months in arrears for rent. On June 17, 1879, distress was made for the rent due. On June 23, the tenant waived an appraisement of goods. On June 27, the goods were replevied by John J. Johnson, the present plaintiff. On the trial it was proved that the goods were the property of the plaintiff at the time of the levy; that notice of said ownership was given by the tenant to the bailiff at the time the levy was made, and that the tenant waived an appraisement of the goods.

The jury rendered a verdict for defendant, the Court reserving the following points: "The landlord having notice at the time that the distress was made that the ownership of the goods was in a stranger and not in the tenant, was he not bound to make an appraisement according to the terms of the Act of Assembly of March 21, 1772, and did not his failure to appraise the said goods render him a trespasser so far as the property of the stranger was concerned?"

W. M. Mervine, for plaintiff.

The landlord, failing to make an appraisement of the goods in question, became a trespasser *ab initio;* the tenant, being a bailee of the goods, had no authority to waive an appraisement. The landlord had no authority to enter upon the premises unless under the authority of the law which regulated the manner of taking a distress. The Act of 1772 makes it imperative that an appraisement be made after five days.

We contend that it was our right to have the goods appraised, that in the event of other and sufficient goods belonging to the tenant being found on the premises, the landlord could have satisfied his claim for rent without depriving us of our property. The tenant could not, as agent for the owner, have either waived the appraisement, or given the landlord permission to leave the goods on the premises.

Briggs *v.* Large, 6 Cas. 287.
McKinney *v.* Reader, 6 Watts, 39.
Waitt *v.* Ewing, 7 Phila. 195.

Alexander Simpson, Jr., for defendant.

The goods being such as could be distrained for rent, and the distraint having been made, he who takes them by replevin must answer in their value to the landlord. Here the goods were properly distrained upon. Notice to the tenant was sufficient, he could waive the appraisement, and a sale would pass a good and sufficient title.

Henkels *v.* Brown, 4 Phila. 299.

Besides, in this case, no sale was had, and complaint cannot be made as to the waiver of appraisement, for the plaintiff was not injured thereby. The waiver of appraisement did not and could not vitiate the distraint, but at the most would have vitiated a sale thereunder.

McKinney *v.* Reader, 6 Watts, 40.

Non constat but that, before the sale had been made, there would have been an appraisement. The fact that the landlord evinced an intention to proceed and sell does not affect the matter.

C. A. V.

January 22, 1881. THE COURT (after stating the facts). It is now contended that the tenant could not waive the appraisement as to the goods of a stranger, and, as the landlord did not appraise the goods before the replevin, he has no claim thereon for his rent. The first of these propositions is undoubtedly correct (see Briggs *v.* Large, 30 Penna. St. 287); but we do not see that there is anything in either the statute or the common law which requires a landlord to appraise the goods distrained within any period save a reasonable time, and at least six days before sale of them under his warrant. By the Act of Assembly of 21st March, 1772, it is provided: "Where any goods or chattels shall be distrained for any rent reserved upon any demise, and the tenant or owner shall not, within five days after such distress, replevin the same, then, on the expiration of said five days, the person distraining shall and may cause the goods and chattels so distrained to be appraised, and after such appraisement shall or may, after six days' public notice, lawfully sell the goods and chattels." There can be no necessity for an appraisement where the goods are replevied, the object of the appraisement being that the tenant may know the sum at which he can redeem his goods. Our Act of Assembly follows that of

2 Wm. & Mary, § 5, and under that it has been decided that the landlord, upon the expiration of the five days, is allowed a reasonable time afterwards for the appraisement and sale (Pitt *v.* Shew, 4 B. & A. 206). The cases which determine that the landlord becomes a trespasser for a failure to appraise the goods, arise solely when he has made a sale of the property. Judgment is, therefore, ordered in favor of the landlord (the defendant) on the point reserved.

Opinion by ELCOCK, J.

Orphans' Court.

Dec. 22, 1880.

Stokes's Estate.

A promise in aid of a charity will not be sustained by the moral obligation alone—A joint voluntary promise may be retracted at any time before the requisite fund is secured, unless some responsibility upon the faith of the pledge has been incurred in the mean while.

Quære, Whether a promise inter vivos in writing to pay money to a charity at a future date is avoided by the death of the promisor within a month of the date of the promise, and before the date of payment—Act of April 26, 1855.

Sur exceptions to adjudication.

Mary G. Stokes, the decedent, died in December, 1878. Upon the audit of the account of her executors a claim on the estate was presented by the First Baptist Church of Philadelphia, upon a note or instrument in writing signed by the decedent and reading as follows:—

"$500. Phila., Nov. 13, 1878.
I hereby subscribe to the Building Fund of the Grace Baptist Church *Five hundred dollars.* Payable to the treasurer of First Baptist Church on or before May 1, 1879. MARY G. STOKES."

The date, amount, and signature were written in lead pencil, the rest being a printed form.

The Grace Baptist Church of Philadelphia was organized in 1872, and in 1874 had partially erected an edifice on Berks and Mervine Streets at a cost of $22,000 when it was compelled to stop operations from want of funds. The building stood in 1878 under a temporary roof, and was subject to a mortgage of $6000. In order to finish the building, an appeal was made to the First Baptist Church, and a circular was issued in that congregation with blanks inclosed, reading as the above instrument.

Mr. Parker, acting as treasurer of the Building Fund, called on Miss Stokes after the circular had been issued, and told her that a friend of hers had given him $6000.

Miss Stokes gave Mr. Parker the above note for $500. Miss Stokes died within one calendar month after making the subscription. No work was done or contract made for the completion of the building till August, 1879.

The claim of the church was disallowed, to which finding exceptions were filed.

A. F. Custis, for the exceptions.

A moral obligation is a sufficient consideration to support an express promise, and will sustain an action. A subscription to erect a church raises such a moral obligation.

Caul *v.* Gibson, 3 Barr, 416.
Chambers *v.* Calhoun, 6 Harris, 13.
Ryerss *v.* The Congregation, 9 Cas. 114.
Edinboro' Acad. *v.* Robinson, 1 Wr. 210.
Shober's Admrs. *v.* The Park Asso., 18 Sm. 429.
Helfenstein's Est., 27 Sm. 331.
Hart's Est., 7 WEEKLY NOTES, 162.

The subscription in question was not a solitary but a mutual one, and a consideration therefor was the subscription of previous subscribers.

Hart's Est., *supra.*
Helfenstein's Est., *supra.*
Edinboro' Acad. *v.* Robinson, *supra.*

The offer or promise of the decedent had been accepted by those authorized to receive the same, and thereby became irrevocable.

Helfenstein's Est., *supra.*

This case does not fall within the rule laid down in Phipps *v.* Jones (8 Harris, 260), and Baird's Est. (7 WEEKLY NOTES, 439). In these cases no organization had been effected, no subscription paid, and nothing done at the time of the death of the promisor. In this case an organization had been perfected, and $6000 had been paid by one of the subscribers before the death of Miss Stokes.

The provisions of the Act of 26 April, 1855, do not make void the act of the promisor in this case. That Act has reference to dispositions by will or deed, to take effect after the decease of the testator or alienor.

E. L. Perkins, contra.

There was no consideration to support the subscription. The note was dated November 13, 1878; the decedent died December 12, 1878. The subscription list was not then full, and no contract was made for the work till August, 1879. The death of the decedent under this state of facts worked a withdrawal and revocation of the subscription. No acceptance was made before her death.

Phipps *v.* Jones, 8 Har. 260.
Helfenstein's Est., 27 Sm. 330.
Baird's Estate, 7 WEEKLY NOTES, 439.

The testimony shows that the payment of $6000 was independent of the subscription list. It was to relieve the church from prior pecuniary difficulties. Neither decedent nor others subscribed to the subsequent appeal for aid on the faith of this gift. The testimony also shows that nothing had been done by the church nor any subscriptions been obtained in consequence of decedent's note.

The subscription contravenes the spirit of the Act of April 26, 1855, sec. 11 (Purdon Dig. p. 208), the note being dated within one calendar month of Miss Stokes's death.

This case does not fall within the purview of the decisions in Caul *v.* Gibson and Chambers *v.* Calhoun (*supra*), and similar rulings elsewhere. In those cases work had been done, and something accomplished on the faith of the promises.

January 8, 1881. THE COURT. A promise in aid of a charity will not be sustained by the moral obligation alone which underlies it. Like any other voluntary undertaking, the question of its performance rests wholly with the conscience. A legal consideration attaches only when work is begun or responsibility incurred upon the faith of the promise, or when it becomes the basis of similar engagements by others, and in either case it must be made to a party capable of enforcing it. Any obscurity which may appear in the cases touching these very plain principles, probably arises from the hold which the objects of these promises have obtained upon our sympathies, and not from any difficulty in applying the ordinary rules governing contracts. For if the violation of a promise, purely voluntary, to aid in a project of benevolence, carries with it greater turpitude than would attend the breach of a similar undertaking in a business enterprise, the law at least cannot recognize the distinction. The single question to be determined in this case is, whether the promise of the decedent was founded upon a legal consideration. The decedent died before her subscription had matured, and nothing was attempted by the promisees, in furtherance of the scheme which she had favored, until some months after her death. It is clear that her promise could not be enforced on the ground that work had been begun on the faith of its fulfilment, because, until the actual commencement of such work, the decedent could have revoked her subscription, and her death was a revocation. This was expressly ruled in Helfenstein's Estate (27 P. F. Smith, 328). Was there then such mutuality between the engagement of the decedent and that of the other subscribers, as has been held to constitute a consideration for the joint promise? (See 2 Kent's Com. 465.) The auditing Judge has found that there was not, and the only witness who was examined on the point testified that, so far as he knew, no person was induced to subscribe by the fact that the decedent had promised to contribute. The witness, however, declared that the subscription of the decedent was made known to at least one subsequent subscriber. If we accept this circumstance as proof that the promise of the decedent induced the later subscriptions, we shall still raise a consideration which would be complete only when the fund was full or when operations were begun under it. At any time short of either event, as it might first happen, the decedent could withdraw her offer, and her death within the period worked a withdrawal by which her personal representatives were bound. In Phipps *v.* Jones (8 Har. 264), LOWRIE, J., says: "It is generally essential that there be something more than a moral duty as the bond of the relation and basis of the promise. An engagement to subscribe for the benefit of an association is necessarily a mere proposal, and therefore revocable until the association is formed. It is a promise of each for the benefit of the associate whole, and remains unattached and incomplete until the association is complete. In this case it was withdrawn by the death of the subscriber before its acceptance." The right to retract, before the stipulated sum was raised, was also recognized in Edinboro' Academy *v.* Robinson (1 Wr. 213). In Limerick Academy *v.* Davis (11 Mass. 113), upon a joint subscription towards the erection of an academy, SEWALL, C. J., said: "It is a promise to give, connected with a similar promise by others to give to the same appropriation and purpose; but these promises are not mutual among the subscribers, so as to make the promise of one, or the performance of it, a consideration for the promise of another. At the most it was a donation to come into operation at the will of each subscriber, which has not been confirmed by any act of the party charged." From these and parallel cases, the principle is clearly deducible, that, in a joint voluntary promise, the promisor may retract his offer at any time before the requisite fund is secured, unless some responsibility, upon the faith of his pledge, has been incurred in the mean while.

The circumstances under which voluntary promises have been held binding, and hence irrevocable, are reported in Caul *v.* Gibson (3 Barr, 416); Ryerss *v.* Congregation (9 Cas. 114); Shober *v.* Park Association (18 P. F. Sm. 429); McAuley *v.* Billenger (20 Johns. 89); Homes *v.* Dana (12 Mass. 190); Amherst Academy *v.* Cowls (6 Pick. 427); Bryant *v.* Goodnow (5 Pick. 228).

An interesting inquiry might be started whether the decedent's promise to pay, executed, as it was, within one calendar month of her death, is not within the Act of April 26, 1855, making void all dispositions of property to religious or charitable uses, contrary to the provisions of the Act. This case, however, we think falls so clearly in the line of well-settled legal principles, that such a discussion would be unnecessary, and therefore unprofitable.

The exceptions are dismissed and the adjudication is confirmed.

Opinion by ASHMAN, J.

WEEKLY NOTES OF CASES.

Vol. IX.] THURSDAY, FEB. 24, 1881. [No. 27.

Supreme Court.

July, '80, 180.　　　　　　　　　January 6, 1881.
Moxey's Appeal.

Unincorporated associations—Constitution and rules—Philadelphia Stock Exchange—Character of seat—Rights of members—Sale of seat of, and distribution of proceeds—Suspension of members for insolvency.

The constitution and articles of a voluntary association, such as the Philadelphia Stock Exchange, are law as to its members.

Where there is a provision in the constitution of such an association for the suspension of members upon their insolvency, if the insolvent person admits to the association his insolvency, it is not necessary that he should have a formal hearing and trial; he, in effect, pleads guilty.

It is perfectly competent for such an association to make a regulation to the effect that, if a suspended member fails to comply with all his contracts within a year, his seat shall be sold, and the proceeds of the sale be distributed among his creditors, members of the association. Such a regulation may give the members an advantage over other creditors, but they have a right to stipulate for it, and all members are parties assenting to the law.

Appeal from the Common Pleas No. 4, of Philadelphia County.

Appeal by E. P. Moxey from a decree of the Common Pleas No. 4, of Philadelphia County, dismissing his bill in equity filed against the Philadelphia Stock Exchange, Abraham Barker, President thereof, *et al.*

From the bill, answer, and proofs, the following facts appeared: The plaintiff, E. P. Moxey, purchased, in 1875, a seat in the Philadelphia Stock Exchange, was duly elected a member of the Board of Brokers, and transacted business as such until July 29, 1876. At or about that time, the firm of Bond, Moxey & Co., of which plaintiff was a member, had purchased in the Board about 51,000 shares of the capital stock of the Hestonville, Mantua, and Fairmount Passenger Railway Company; some of these shares were deliverable, and payment therefor due July 29, and some July 31 (Monday); others were already settled for and held by Bond, Moxey & Co. The whole capital stock of the company was about 39,900 shares. After the adjournment of the Board of Brokers on July 29, a rumor got abroad that plaintiff's firm was unable to meet its contracts; whereupon a special meeting of the Board was called, and a committee appointed to inquire into the matter. To this committee the firm handed a letter addressed to the President of the Stock Exchange, saying that they were unable to meet their cash-contracts that day, but hoped to do so on Monday, and that they would on Monday, at 9.30, announce their ability or inability to do so. On Monday the committee reported to the Board that they had waited on the firm, who informed them that they were unable to meet their contracts. Plaintiff's firm was then, on August 7th, suspended from the Board, under Section XIII. of their Constitution, which provides as follows:—

"SECTION XIII. *On Insolvency.*—Any member who fails to comply with his contracts, or who becomes insolvent, shall immediately inform the president of the Exchange of the fact, whose duty it shall be to give notice forthwith of the failure of such member; and in case of the refusal or neglect of such delinquent to make such report to the president, it shall be the duty of any member having a knowledge of the fact to report the same forthwith to the Standing Committee or the president, who shall thereupon appoint a committee of three members to inquire into the fact and report thereon without delay; and if said committee report the charge to be true, and no appeal from the said report be taken within seven days, or where an appeal having been taken, the report shall have been confirmed by the Stock Exchange, said member shall be suspended. . . . And in case of the insolvency of any member, he shall within three (3) days make good to the full amount thereof all friendly loans of cash or stocks from members, or any over-draft on any bank. But seven (7) days shall be allowed him in which to settle stock contracts."

A subsequent paragraph of Section XIII. provides as follows:—

"If any suspended member fails to settle with all his creditors within one year from the time of his suspension from the Stock Exchange, his seat shall be sold by the secretary, and the proceeds shall be paid *pro rata* to his creditors in the Stock Exchange."

On January 15, 1877, the plaintiff went into voluntary bankruptcy, and obtained his discharge on Dec. 21, 1877. On Jan. 15, 1878, plaintiff wrote to the secretary of defendants that he had obtained his discharge in bankruptcy, and he received an answer that, if he desired to apply for re-admission, under the rules of the Stock Exchange, the matter would be immediately referred to the standing committee, and investigated. The letter also notified plaintiff that as more than a year had elapsed since his suspension, the Exchange considered itself entitled to sell his seat at any time. No notice was taken of this letter, and on July 5, 1878, plaintiff's seat was sold, on demand of his creditors, at public sale of the Board, after posting and notice in accordance with the rules. At the time plaintiff joined the Stock Exchange a Gratuity Fund existed, payable on the death of a full member (whether suspended or not) to his nominee, widow, child, or legal representative. On Nov. 15, 1877, this was altered so that any suspended member, who failed for three months to pay in full all gratuity dues and assessments, should cease to be a full member for the purposes of the Gratuity Fund. Plaintiff was notified of the passage of this provision, but failed to pay his dues, and on March 7, 1878, was notified that he was debarred from participating in the benefit thereof. The bill alleged that by far the greater part of the indebtedness of Bond, Moxey & Co. was merely fictitious, being founded on contracts for the sale and delivery of certificates of stock which had no real existence; that, therefore, the payment of these debts would be in violation of the Bankrupt Act; but that, nevertheless, the proceeds of the sale of plaintiff's seat will be distributed *pro rata* to the unreal as well as the real creditors in the Board. The bill prayed (1) an injunction to restrain defendants from interfering with plaintiff's right and privilege of using his seat in the Board; (2) an account of his actual indebtedness in the Exchange; (3) an account of the property of the Exchange, and that plaintiff's share therein might be paid him; (4) general relief.

The Court, after hearing, dismissed the bill, in an opinion by ELCOCK, J. (reported 37 Leg. Int. 82), whereupon plaintiff took this appeal, assigning for error the said action of the Court.

N. H. Sharpless, for appellant.

It was not shown that plaintiff's firm failed to comply with any contract on July 29; nor was he given any hearing, to which he was entitled as a matter of right.

Evans *v.* Phila. Club, 14 Wr. 107.

The suspension was not under the bankrupt proceedings, as the regulations in that matter apply only to members, and the contention of defendants, from the first, has been that the plaintiff ceased to be a member from August 7th. Such a power as that claimed here has been held to be ground for refusing a charter, when the proposed charter authorized such action.

In re Butcher's Beneficial Association, 11 Casey, 151.

The advantages which the Stock Exchange tries to secure to its own members over other creditors are in direct contravention of the Bankrupt Act; and, in this very case, debts will be paid which could not be recovered at law, while other creditors will remain unpaid.

A. S. Biddle, for appellees.

Appellant was a party to the regulations of the Stock Exchange, and therefore cannot object to them. His suspension was in strict accordance with their rules, upon his own admission of insolvency. The right to distribute the proceeds of the sale of plaintiff's seat, as they are being distributed, is settled.

Thompson *v.* Adams, 7 WEEKLY NOTES, 281.
McDowell *v.* Ackley, 8 Ibid. 464.

January 17, 1881. THE COURT. The firm, of which the appellant was a member, admitted inability to fulfil their contracts, and under the by-laws of the association, the membership of the appellant was immediately suspended. Surely no trial is necessary in the case of a man who pleads guilty. The bankruptcy had the same effect, and we see nothing unreasonable in the rule that before such a party can be re-admitted, he must settle with his creditors, who are members of the company. It may give them an advantage over other creditors, but they have a right to stipulate for it, and the appellant was a party assenting to the law.

Decree affirmed and appeal dismissed at the costs of the appellant.

PER CURIAM.

July, '78, 102, 109, 110, 111, and 112. Feb. 16, 1880.

Appeal of Alden et al.
Appeal of Ferguson et al., executors.
Appeal of Ferguson et al., executors.
Appeal of Brooke et al., executors.
Appeal of White et al., executors.

Mines and mining—Ore-right reserved—Construction of reservation in deed of "a sufficient quantity of iron ore for the supply of any one furnace at the election of the grantor, his heirs or assigns at all times hereafter"—Measure of ore—Extent of grantor's right—Practice—Pleading—Bar of the statute of limitations, when too late to plead—Equitable jurisdiction of the Court.

In May, 1786, Peter Grubb, Jr., conveyed to Robert Coleman, Sr., an undivided sixth part of the Cornwall ore banks, subject to the following reservation: "saving and excepting unto the grantor, his heirs and assigns forever, the right, liberty, and privilege at all times hereafter of entering upon the premises granted and released, with his and their horses, carts, carriages, and servants, and of digging, raising, and hauling away a sufficient quantity of iron ore for the supply of any one furnace at the election of the said grantor, his heirs or assigns at all times hereafter." The grantees claimed that under the reservation the grantor or his assigns were entitled to no more ore than was sufficient for the supply of a furnace such as was known in Pennsylvania at the time of the execution of the deed, and filed a bill for an account of the amount of ore unlawfully taken:

Held, that a court of equity has jurisdiction to entertain the bill and grant relief.

Held further (affirming the decree of the Court below), that the reservation carried with it the right to use or sell as much ore as would supply any one furnace, constructed and operated with the modern improvements in general use for the time being, to be selected by the grantor or his assigns; and that the right to select was not exhausted by its exercise in a single instance.

Held further, that the measure of quantity of ore must be interpreted to mean so much ore and no more as a given furnace would use in the course of a year, taking into consideration the wear and tear, and the necessity of going out of blast for repairs at stated periods.

Held further, that the defendants had an absolute right of property in the ore the moment it was taken out of the ground, subject only to the single qualification that it must be measured by the capacity of one furnace.

Held further, that the defendants could not take in one year ore they might have taken the previous year but had omitted to take.

Held further, that interest was properly chargeable on the ore taken or sold in excess.

It is too late for executors to avail themselves of the plea of the bar of the statute of limitations, who did not suggest it at the time they were made parties to the suit six years after their testator's death, nor set it up in their answer to the amended bill six years later.

Grubb's Appeal, 9 Nor. 228; s. c., 7 WEEKLY NOTES, 349, distinguished.

Appeals from the Common Pleas No. 4, of Philadelphia County, of July term, 1878.

No. 102. Appeal of Anne C. Alden, Margaret C. Freeman, and Sarah H. Coleman; of A. Wilhelm, surviving administrator *d. b. n.* of Robert W. Coleman, deceased; of Anna C. Coleman, by her guardian Samuel Small; of Robert H. Coleman; and of A. Wilhelm, surviving administrators *d. b. n.* of William Coleman, deceased.

No. 109. Appeal of Nathaniel Ferguson and William R. White, Henry P. Borie, and J. Henry Hentz, executors of William R. White, deceased.

No. 110. Appeal of Nathaniel Ferguson, and William R. White, Henry P. Borie, and J. Henry Hentz, executors of William R. White, deceased, and Sarah D. Robeson, executrix of Henry P. Robeson, deceased.

No. 111. Appeal of Edward Brooke, surviving executor of Clement Brooke, deceased, and Sarah D. Robeson, executrix of Henry P. Robeson, deceased.

No. 112. Appeal of William R. White, Henry P. Borie, and J. Henry Hentz, executors of William R. White, deceased, and Sarah D. Robeson, executrix of Henry P. Robeson, deceased.

The above were appeals from a final decree of said Court in a suit in equity in which Robert and George Dawson Coleman were complainants, and Robert W. Coleman, William Coleman, Henry P. Robeson, and Clement Brooke were defendants.

All of the defendants to the original bill died during the progress of the suit, and their executors and devisees were brought in by supplemental bill.

The bill, which was filed July 15, 1856, in the Supreme Court at Nisi Prius, set forth: that Peter Grubb, Jr., on May 9, 1786, conveyed to Robert Coleman, Sr., *inter alia,* an undivided sixth part of the Cornwall mine hills and ore banks, in the county of Lebanon, subject to the following reservation in the deed:—

"Saving and excepting unto the said Peter Grubb, the grantor, his heirs and assigns forever, the right, liberty, and privilege at all times hereafter of entering upon the premises hereby granted and released, with his and their horses, carts, carriages, and servants, and of digging, raising, and hauling away a sufficient quantity of iron ore for the supply of *any one furnace* at the election of the said Peter Grubb, his heirs or assigns at all times hereafter, anything hereinbefore contained to the contrary thereof in any wise notwithstanding."

That Robert Coleman, Sr., afterwards acquired other four-sixths of the premises, of which the title by divers mesne conveyances was vested in the complainants and the defendants Robert W. and William Coleman, in certain proportions: that on May 7, 1788, Peter Grubb, Jr., for the consideration of £3000, in gold and silver, conveyed his reserved ore right to George Ege in fee, who was then seized of the Reading furnace estate, on which was erected a furnace for the manufacture of iron called the Reading Furnace, situated in Berks County, at which Ege, during his life, manufactured iron from ore obtained by him from the Cornwall ore banks, and so elected that furnace as the one to be supplied with ore, by which election his right became fixed, and could not afterwards be in any way altered or enlarged; that the Reading furnace so elected was constructed for the manufacture of iron by the use of charcoal as fuel, with a cold blast from bellows driven by water-power, the utmost capacity of which, for the production of iron, being fifty tons per week; that by improvements in machinery, the introduction of the hot blast, and the use of anthracite coal as fuel, the capacity of furnaces of the present time of the best description is tenfold that of the best furnace worked in the most approved method known until long after the election of the Reading furnace; that the legal effect of the reservation was to vest in Peter Grubb, Jr., in fee, a right to dig, take, and haul away, for the purpose of being converted into iron, such a quantity of iron ore as could be so converted by one furnace, this quantity to be determined by the capacity of one furnace then erected, or to be erected, and by Peter Grubb, Jr., or by his heirs or assigns elected as the furnace to be supplied under the reservation; that the quantity of ore to be taken was at all times thereafter limited to the amount which the furnace at the time of election was capable of, converting into iron; that the Reading furnace was not until the year 1845 capable of using more than 2000 tons of ore annually, but that in that year the defendants, Brooke & Robeson, pulled down the Reading furnace and erected a new furnace in its place of larger dimensions, and with new appliances, by means of which the present capacity of the Reading furnace has been made one hundred and sixty tons per week; that since the erection of the new furnace the defendants have taken away a large quantity of ore in excess of what they are entitled to take; that Brooke & Robeson have built a second furnace, claiming to take the ore, under the reservation in the deed, for the supply of both, using one while the other is out of blast, so that the consumption of ore is continuous, and that the defendants, under a pretended claim of right by virtue of the reservation, have carried away and sold large quantities of ore from the Cornwall banks.

The bill prayed (1) for a discovery of the amount of ore used at the old Reading furnace, the amount necessary for the new furnace, and of the amount of ore used and sold; (2) that the extent of the right reserved under the deed of May 9, 1786, might be defined; (3) for an account of all the ore unlawfully taken away, used, sold, or consumed otherwise than as the defendants were lawfully entitled to take; and (4) for general relief.

In their answer the defendants claimed that under the reservation in the deed of May 9, 1786, they, as assignees of Ege, had a right to a sufficient quantity of ore for the supply, not of a particular furnace, but of any one furnace at their election at all times thereafter; that they had a right from time to time to elect any one furnace, as the measure of that quantity, having the largest known capacity now or hereafter in use; that for the supply of a furnace which they at present elected 20,000 tons of ore were yearly required; that at the time of the execution of the deed furnaces were known to be of different sizes and capacities, some being constructed with one, some with two, and some with three tuyères, and using mineral coal or charcoal; that by reason of the vast quantities of ore which have been taken from the mines, the use of anthracite and the hot blast have become a necessity, owing to the exhaustion of ores suitable to consumption in charcoal furnaces using the cold blast; they denied that the right reserved by the deed was first exercised at the Reading furnace, but averred, on the contrary, that that furnace was not erected until 1793, and that the first supply of ore was to the Berkshire furnace, under an arrangement between Peter Grubb and the owners; that since May 9, 1786, the construction of furnaces has been improved by enlarged boshes, increased height, and by the hot blast; that since the introduction of anthracite a much greater quantity of ore is required for a furnace; they admitted that the Reading furnace was a cold-blast charcoal furnace, worked by water power, and that on May 9, 1786, cold-blast furnaces alone were in use in Pennsylvania, but they denied that the greatest average capacity of such furnaces was twenty tons of iron a week, or that it was believed to be impossible to produce a greater quantity. The answer concluded with an averment, that it was never denied by Robert Coleman, Sr., and his successors, that furnaces might be improved from time to time, or that the right of election, under the ore right, extended to such improved furnaces and a claim to take ore sufficient to supply a furnace of the best construction. In the answers to the interrogatories in the bill, they alleged that the Reading furnace was completed in 1793 by Ege: that before its completion ore was taken under the reservation, and used at the Berkshire furnace; that they pulled down the old furnace and erected a new one in 1848, which was called Robesonia Furnace No. 1; that the furnace completed in 1855 was called the Robesonia Furnace No. 2; that it required two tons of Cornwall ore to make one of iron; and they had also sold some 5000 tons of ore.

The case was referred to an examiner and master (Peter McCall), who reported the following facts:—

(1) That on September 26, 1785, articles of agreement were entered into between Peter Grubb the younger and Robert Coleman, by which Mr. Grubb, in consideration of £8500 to be paid him, covenanted to grant and assure to Mr. Coleman by May 1, 1786, all the estate which his father Ceutes Grubb had conveyed to him, "except and specially reserving unto the said Peter Grubb, Junior, his heirs and assigns, the liberty of digging, raising, and hauling away a sufficient quantity of iron ore to supply the furnace which he purchased of John Patton, or any other furnace which he may erect elsewhere: provided there is not more than one furnace blowing at the same time."

(2) That in the interval of time between the article and the deed the contract for the purchase of the Patton furnace was annulled.

(3) That on May 9, 1786, the deed containing the reservation (already quoted) was executed and delivered. The consideration was £8500. This deed contained for further assurance of the premises, "saving and excepting always thereunto the right, liberty, and privilege hereinbefore reserved unto the said Peter Grubb, his heirs and assigns, of a sufficiency of iron ore for the use of one furnace forever."

(4) That Mr. Grubb exercised this ore-right by supplying the Berkshire furnace, situate about four miles from the Reading furnace; that he sold the ore-right in 1788 to Peter Ege for £3000, and that Ege continued to use it for the supply of the Berkshire furnace till 1793, when the Reading furnace was finished, and that from that time it was used to supply the Reading, now called the Robesonia furnace.

(5) That the average yield of furnaces in the Cornwall region was about 30 tons in 1800, and the maximum yield about 35 tons per week; that the mode of producing the blast in Penna., in 1786, was by a wooden bellows worked by water power; that the steam-engine was not applied to this purpose till 1839 in Pennsylvania, although it had been used by Watt as early as 1774 in England; that the only fuel used here in 1786 was charcoal, anthracite coal not having been used until 1840; that the blast was a cold blast; and that the furnaces of 1786 had only one tuyère.

(6) That the defendants, the owners of the ore right, had used iron ore in two furnaces, running one while the other was out of blast; that they had sold iron ore; and that the amount they had used annually was largely in excess of the capacity of furnaces in Pennsylvania in 1786.

Upon these facts the Master reported, *inter alia:* "On the whole I am of opinion, and so report, that the owners of the ore-right reserved by the deed of 9th May, 1786, are not restricted to the quantity of ore used by Mr. Ege at the time he elected the Reading furnace; but that they have a right to a sufficient quantity of iron ore to supply any one furnace, from time to time to be selected by them, although of larger capacity than the Reading furnace elected by Mr. Ege, and using anthracite as fuel, the hot blast, and other modern improvements in the manufacture of iron, not known and in use at the time of the election of the Reading furnace.

"I am also of opinion, and so report, that they can use the ore taken under this ore-right in one furnace only elected by them, and not part of the time in one furnace and part of the time in another furnace, as they have done in No. 1 furnace while No. 2 furnace was out of blast.

"The owners of the estate out of which the ore-right was reserved have a right to any benefit that may arise from the furnace elected being out of blast for purposes of repair or other cause.

"I further report that under this ore-right they can use the ore taken by them only to supply the furnace elected by them, and that they have no right to sell or otherwise dispose of the ore."

To this report exceptions were filed by Anne C. Alden *et al.*, which the Court overruled, and sustained the report of the Master, THAYER, P. J., delivering the following opinion :—

". . . After the most attentive consideration of everything that has been urged by the learned counsel against the correctness of the master's conclusions, we are unable to see that he could have reached any other result than that at which he has arrived, consistently with the plain language of the deed of May 9th, 1786, and the other evidence in the cause. We agree with him in both propositions upon which his report is based, viz.: First, that the evidence shows that it was not the intention of the parties to limit the extent of the ore-right reserved, by the capacity of any particular furnace then existing, or by the capacity of furnaces made and used at the date of the reservation; and secondly, that the words 'at all times hereafter,' in the second place in which they occur in the deed, refer to the right of selection of the furnace to be supplied, and not to the perpetual character of the reservation.

"In regard to the first proposition, without repeating the argument of the master, a few additional considerations may properly be mentioned in support of his conclusion. If it be true, as is assumed by the plaintiffs (we think without sufficient ground to warrant it), that neither of the parties contemplated the great improvements which have been made in the smelting of iron and the operation of furnaces since the deed of 9th of May, 1786, it would be manifestly inequitable (unless, indeed, the words of the deed require it and present no other alternative) to put such a construction upon that instrument as would enable one of the parties to avail himself of these improvements while the other is precluded. If the plaintiffs may draw upon the ore banks, either for their own use or for sale to others, as they clearly may, to any extent rendered possible by the increased capacity of furnaces throughout the country, and the consequently greatly increased demand for the ore, and the defendants may not supply their one furnace according to the same increased capacity, it must be manifest that the right reserved by Peter Grubb is immensely diminished in value by those changes in the condition of the business which neither party is said to have foreseen. For that right will, by reason of the greatly increased quantity drawn from the ore banks and consumed and sold by the plaintiffs in consequence of those improvements, be exhausted at a much earlier day than it otherwise would be. This consideration, while it may amount to a hardship, is of course no answer to the plaintiffs' claim if that claim be supported by clear and unambiguous language in the deed. But if the words used do not necessarily lead to such a result, or if there be any ambiguity in the language used, it is a consideration of some weight in determining the true interpretation.

"But we agree with the master that on the face of the deed there is no ambiguity, that it neither indicates nor expresses an intention to fix the furnaces of that day as a certain and unvarying standard of quantity. The words of the reservation are 'the right of digging, raising, and hauling away a sufficient quantity of iron ore for the supply of *any* one furnace at the election of the said Peter Grubb, his heirs or assigns, at all times hereafter.' It is not said in the deed 'any one furnace then built,' nor 'any one furnace of the capacity of furnaces as then made and used.' It would have been easy to have said this if this was intended. But the words are without any such limitation or qualification. The language used has a much broader sweep. It is '*any* one furnace *at the election of Peter Grubb*, his heirs or assigns, *at all times hereafter*.'

"And this brings me to remark briefly upon the second proposition of the master, that these words '*at all times hereafter*' refer to the right of selecting the furnace to be supplied, and are not words introduced in this place to indicate the perpetual character of the reservation. As is pointed out by the master, the same words had already been used for that purpose in the previous part of the same sentence, and there was no occasion to use them again in another part of the sentence for the same purpose. They had already said 'saving and excepting unto the said Peter Grubb, his heirs and assigns forever, the right *at all times hereafter* of entering and digging, etc.' When the phrase 'at all times hereafter' is used a second time in the same sentence, it is used after the words 'at the election of the said Peter Grubb, his heirs or assigns.' The phrase was plainly intended to qualify those words, and not to qualify over again the words in the remoter part of the sentence. Such a construction as that contended for by the plaintiffs appears to us to be a construction at once unnatural, ungrammatical, and arbitrary. Undoubtedly words may be transposed if it be necessary to do so in order to give effect to the evident intent of the parties. Parkhurst *v.* Smith (Willes's R. 332), cited by the plaintiffs, is an instance of this, and in our own reports Mutter's Estate (2 Wright, 314). But no rule of interpretation would justify us in transposing words to create an intent which does not otherwise appear in the instrument, nor to destroy the natural sense which the words of the instrument and the connection in which they are used plainly convey. We can see no warrant for taking these words out of the position to which they have been assigned in the deed by the parties themselves, and putting them somewhere else where they will mean something totally different, or where they would produce a meaningless tautology; nor any warrant for dropping them out of the deed entirely. When the parties to this deed have said 'any one furnace at the election of the said Peter Grubb, his heirs or assigns, at all times hereafter,' we cannot see that they intended anything else than that which they have said, viz.: that Peter Grubb, and his heirs or assigns, should have the liberty of exercising that right of election at all times thereafter.

"Too much stress has, we think, been placed in the argument upon the use in the deed of the word 'election.' The word in its technical signification means an obligation imposed upon a party to choose between two inconsistent or alternative rights or claims, in cases where there is a clear intention of the person from whom he derives one, that he should not enjoy both. It is of the nature of an election used in this sense that when once made it is final, and cannot be exercised again. But the word is not used in any such technical sense in this deed, but rather in the sense of 'selection' or 'choice,' and in no other sense. What the grantor, his heirs and assigns, are to do is, not to elect between two inconsistent rights (there is but one right), but to elect from time to time the particular furnace with reference to which the right is to be exercised. What was reserved was a perpetual right to take from the ore banks a sufficient supply for '*any* one furnace,' and a perpetual right to select from time to time the one furnace to be supplied. It is as if the parties had said 'the grantor excepts and reserves out of this grant, to himself, his heirs and assigns forever, the right at all times hereafter of entering, digging, and hauling away a sufficient quantity of iron ore for the supply of any one furnace, the said one furnace to be selected or designated by him, his heirs or assigns, at all times hereafter;' that is, from time to time hereafter as often as their interests or wishes may lead them to select or designate the one furnace which is to be supplied. 'At all times hereafter' means as often as the grantor, his heirs and assigns, may choose to exercise the right of designating the one furnace to be supplied. These words are totally inconsistent with the proposition that the right of designating the furnace to be supplied is exhausted by a single exercise of it. Such a proposition cannot be successfully maintained without striking these words out of the deed in the place where they stand, and so making a new contract for the parties instead of the one which they made for themselves. Looking at the whole deed and at the particular words which are the subject of dispute, and gathering the intent from the natural sense of those words and the order in which they stand, we cannot see that any other meaning can by any fair or legitimate method of interpretation be extracted from them than that which the master has found in them, and it is needless to add anything further upon this point to the reasons which he has assigned with so much perspicuity and force, in his report, for the conclusion at which he arrived.

"It is quite plain that the ore-right reserved cannot be used to supply two furnaces alternately, that is that the two furnaces cannot be operated at the same time and the ore supplied alternately to the one or the other of them as one or the other of them may be out of blast. The supply can only be taken for one furnace, and that furnace must be designated. The designation may be changed from time to time, but not so as to enable the owners of the right to supply two furnaces alternately during the same general period of time, or so as to enable them to evade the restriction which is fastened upon the right.

'With regard to the ore sold by Robeson & Brooke, in 1855 and 1856, it does not appear from the master's report under what circumstances that ore was sold—whether it was surplus ore, remaining unused at the furnace, or ore sold directly from the banks. It is perhaps immaterial, for as the defendants had no right to mine ore for the purpose of sale, neither could they sell what was mined for the supply of their furnace. If any such supply remained on hand at any time unused by reason of the furnace being out of blast temporarily, it was their duty to have kept it on hand to go toward the supply of the furnace when work was resumed. Otherwise it is clear that the quantity to be taken from the ore banks to keep up the supply of the furnace when in blast again, would be increased by just the quantity they had sold. They have thus taken not only a sufficient supply to supply the furnace while running (which is the meaning of the reservation), but a certain other quantity which they have sold, and for this they must account.

"It was objected by the defendants' counsel on the argument, that, as it appears by the evidence that one-sixth of the Cornwall ore banks and mine hills belong to Clement B. Grubb, and the heirs of Edward B. Grubb, as tenants in common with the Coleman family, these persons ought to be made parties to the present proceedings, before any account is decreed. Certainly they would be very proper parties to participate in the account which is to be taken partly for their benefit, but as no objection to their omission was taken by the defendants, either in their answer or by way of plea or demurrer, and as the defendants have not excepted to the master's report upon this ground, we must decline to delay a decree for this reason. To do so would be to open afresh, and perhaps to commence again from the beginning, a litigation which has already endured for more than twenty years.

"Therefore let the decree reported by the master stand as the decree of this Court."

The case was then referred back to the master to state the accounts and to report what sums were due by the defendants to the plaintiffs for ore taken by them.

The master in his supplemental report charged the estates respectively represented in Appeals Nos. 109, 110, 111, and 112, with the amount of ore unlawfully taken from the Cornwall ore banks, and with interest on the value of the ore from the time it was taken.

To this report Anne C. Alden and others excepted because the master did not report a decree in conformity with the prayer of their bill.

The parties represented in No. 111 excepted because the master disallowed the defence of the statute of limitations to claims for ore sold during the lives of the decedents, and because he had allowed interest upon the claims, and because he had charged for the use of ore taken and used in one furnace while the other was out of blast.

The parties in No. 112 excepted for the last-mentioned reason alone.

The Court dismissed the exceptions and confirmed the report.

Anne C. Alden and others took this appeal (102), assigning for error the action of the Court in overruling their exceptions to the master's report and confirming the report.

The other appellants took separate appeals, as above stated.

George W. Biddle and *F. W. Hughes* (with them *S. S. Hollingsworth* and *James L. Reynolds*), for the appellants.

The main question in controversy is the extent of the reservation in the deed of May 9, 1786. The undoubted intention of the parties to that deed was to lay down a measure of quantity which should be fixed and determinate for all time to come. That fixed measure of ore to be taken annually under the reservation, was the capacity of a furnace in operation in Pennsylvania at the time of execution of the deed. The standard furnace of that day in the United States was a charcoal furnace, which went out of blast every autumn. It was furnished with ordinary wooden bellows for blowing and was run by water power. The blast was applied through a single open tuyère, the only fuel was charcoal, and the average production was about thirty tons a week.

The reservation in the articles of agreement was measured by the capacity of the furnace of that day. The change in the language of the reservation in the *deed* from that in the *articles* was to enable Grubb to sell it without first building a furnace. In the interval between the execution of the articles and the deed, the purchase of the Patton furnace had fallen through, and he was in doubt whether he would build a furnace. The reservation in the articles was for iron ore to be used at the Patton furnace, or a furnace to be erected by Mr. Grubb. Such a right would not be salable, and the broader language in the deed was inserted to meet what had occurred after the articles were executed, the consideration being the same.

The reservation is for the supply of a machine known then as a *furnace*. The machine now known as a *furnace* is a different thing, and cannot be included within the reservation because called by the same name.

Bridge Proprietors *v.* Hoboken Co., 1 Wall. 116.

The language of the deed is not unambiguous. There is room for interpretation, and all the circumstances must be looked at.

Sheppard's Touchstone, 1, *86.
Moorhead *v.* Snyder, 7 C. 514.
Carney *v.* Brook, 23 S. 80.
Galloway *v.* Wilder, 26 Michigan, 97.
Clement *v.* Youngman, 4 Wr. 341.

The words "at all times hereafter" in the deed are mere conveyancing surplusage, and add nothing to extent of the grant.

Williams on Real Property, 135.
Brookman *v.* Smith, L. R. 6 Exch. 291–306.

The owners of the ore-right are not entitled to increase the extent of the reservation because they see fit to enlarge the size of their furnace. The reservation is analogous to a grant of estovers for a house, of water for a mill, and of a way over land. None of these can be increased by a change in the manner of using the thing granted.

Luttrel's Case, 4 Rep. 86.
2 Vernon, 646.
Allen *v.* Gomme, 11 Ad. & E. 759 (39 E. C. L. R.) 215.
Sharpe *v.* Hancock, 7 M. & G. (49 E. C. L. R.) 354.
Viner's Abridgment, Grant II. 13.
Wood *v.* Saunders, L. R. 10 Ch. Ap. 582.
Johnson *v.* Ryan, 6 N. Hamp. 22.
Carlisle *v.* Cooper, 6 C. E. Green, 576.
Wakely *v.* Davidson, 26 N. Y. 387.
Kirkham *v.* Sharp, 1 Wh. 323.
Jameson *v.* McCurdy, 5 W. & S. 129.
Moore *v.* Schuylkill Nav. Co., 2 Wh. 477.
Cress *v.* Vanesy, 5 H. 496.
Commonwealth *v.* Erie & N. E. R. Co., 3 Casey, 339.
Soohan *v.* City, 9 Casey, 9.

Senhowser *v.* Christian (1 T. R. 560), Daud *v.* Kingscote (6 M. & W. 174), and Bishop *v.* North (11 Ibid. 418) do not establish any different principle, but only decide that, in construing the extent of easement, of necessity the growth of the art must be taken into consideration. They do not decide that it is when the extent of a grant, not of necessity, is the question to be determined.

Bostick *v.* Sidebottom, 18 Ad. & Ellis, N. S. 813 (83 E. C. L. R. 812).
S. C. in Exchequer Chamber, 18 Ad. & Ellis, N. S. 829.

The jurisdiction in equity rests—
On the power to prevent destructive waste.

Dernoy *v.* Bronson, 5 Casey, 382.
Bonaparte *v.* C. & A. R. R. Co., 1 Bald. 205.
Tarden *v.* P. W. & B. R. R. Co., 3 Wh. 502.
Thomas *v.* Oakley, 18 Ves. 185.

Unangst's Appeal, 5 Sm. 128.
Gass's Appeal, 23 Sm. 39.
Allison & Evans's Appeal, 27 Sm. 221.

On power to prevent multiplicity of suits.

Sheetz's Appeal, 11 Casey, 88.
Mosson's Appeal, 20 Sm. 26.

On power to grant relief when, from complication of interests and number of parties, the remedy at law is inadequate.

Townsend *v.* Ash, 3 Atkyns, 337.
Magic Ruffle Co. *v.* Elen City Co., 14 Blatch. 109.
Walker *v.* Cheever, 35 N. Hamp. 339.

James E. Gowen, for the appellees.

This case is not within the equitable jurisdiction of this Court, for there is no averment of irreparable mischief in the bill, or allegation that there is no remedy at common law.

Grubb *v.* Grubb, 7 WEEKLY NOTES, 349.

The construction we contend for is clearly founded upon the language of the deed, which is unambiguous, and in the plainest English. No extrinsic evidence is required to make the deed intelligible, or to give effect to every word, clause, and sentence. The intention of the parties is to be sought for in the deed. This case is governed by the cardinal canon of construction—*quoties in verbis nulla est ambiguitas, ibi nulla expositio contra verba fienda est.*

Harvey *v.* Vandegrift, 7 WEEKLY NOTES, 481.
Wusthoff *v.* Dracourt, 3 W. 240.
Hannum *v.* West Chester, 20 Sm. 372.

The parties to the deed were intelligent iron men, and it is inconceivable that they did not anticipate improvements in the reduction of ore when they knew that great advance in its production had been made in the past. If they had intended to put in the deed a fixed number of tons of ore, why did they not plainly so insert it in the deed? According to the language of the reservation, the furnace to be supplied was to be "at the election of the said Peter Grubb, his heirs or assigns." If the construction contended for on the other side is correct, it is difficult to understand how the heirs and assigns are to elect in the future from the furnaces of the past. If a right of election is given to A. and his heirs and assigns, the heirs and assigns have the right to elect as well as A. The election is exercisable "at all times hereafter," which the other side very ingeniously propose to explain by disregarding that right, and then to suppose that the grantor did not intend to use the words as he did, or that he did not intend them to convey their evident meaning. There is no possible right to alter their collocation, or to strike them out as the verbiage of conveyancing.

If there be ambiguity, it is patent, and not explainable by evidence *dehors* the deed.

Addison on Contracts, vol. 1, 339.

The rule "*contra proferentem verba fortius accipiuntur*" is to be resorted to only when all other rules of exposition fail. The modern and

most reasonable rule is to give the language its just sense.
Taylor *v.* Corporation of St. Helens, L. R., 6 Ch. 270.
2 Kent Com. 556.

The cases cited on the other side as to estovers, etc. turn upon the terms of the grant creating them, and are inapplicable to this case. It is not pretended that Peter Grubb might not have made the ore-consuming capacity of some one particular furnace the measure of the ore right; but it is denied that he did so.

James E. Gowen, for appellants in 109, 110, and 112.

The appellants were charged with the value of ore consumed in Robesonia Furnace No. 1, on several occasions when No. 2 was out of blast. It is contended that so long as the quantity taken did not exceed the measure prescribed in the reservation of the ore right, the disposal of the ore was within their discretion. That measure was the quantity required to supply a furnace. The right reserved by Peter Grubb was not an easement, license, or privilege exercisable upon the land of another, but an estate itself in the land, and every presumption is in favor of unrestricted enjoyment. The appellants have a right to the unrestricted use of the ore taken by them under the ore right.
Luttrel's Case, 4 Rep. 86.
Hall *v.* Swift, 33 E. C. L. 382.
Cress *v.* Varney, 5 Harris, 497.
Tourtellot *v.* Phelps, 4 Gray, 370.

Even if the ore must be used in an elected furnace, it can be used in a temporarily elected furnace during the temporary suspension of another furnace which had been elected, and is intended to be elected again. Assuming the right of election, why may not the owners use Furnace A when Furnace B is out of blast? If Furnace No. 2 were destroyed by fire or storm, could not the supply of ore have been immediately diverted to Furnace No. 1? For the right of election is a continuous and ever-existing right. Did not the proviso that "not more than one furnace should be blowing at the same time" mean, that the grantee could keep one of the two furnaces blowing all the time?

James W. Paul, for the appellants in No. 111.

The lapse of time relieves the appellants from all liability to account for ore sold in 1856, and that used in Furnace No. 1 before March 1, 1860.

They were made parties to these proceedings more than six years after the deaths of the original defendants, and the account was carried back to a date more than eleven years before they were made parties.

The Court, it is submitted, should not allow interest as an element of damage for taking property which was taken under the firm belief that a legal right was being exercised. It is inequitable that the unaccountable delay of the plaintiffs should be visited upon the estates of decedents in the form of such a heavy penalty. Interest is not an incident to damages in actions of tort.
Lykens Valley Coal Company *v.* Doak, 12 Sm. 236.

George W. Biddle and *F. W. Hughes* (with them *S. S. Hollingsworth* and *James L. Reynolds*), for appellees in Nos. 109, 110, 111, and 112.

There is no doubtful question so far as the disposal of the ore is concerned. Under the reservation it is clear the ore cannot be used in any other way than in a furnace. The supply was for a furnace, which went out of blast every autumn, and continued so for three months, and there is no possible right to an alternative use of the ore in two or more furnaces during the same period of time. In order to avail themselves of the Statute of Limitations they should have pleaded it, as there is nothing on the face of the bill to show the statute has run.
Angell on Limitations, § 295.

Acquiescence without objection is a waiver.
2 Daniell's Chancery Practice, 1542.

After waiting ten years, and contesting the suit at every step, it is too late, after the entry of a decree to account, to attempt to set up the Statute. Continuing the case without objection estops them from afterwards setting it up.

In cases of trover, etc., interest on the value of the property is assessed by way of damages for the purpose of indemnification. It is recoverable as a matter of law.
Sedgwick on Damages, p. 491.
Parrott *v.* Ice Company, 46 N. Y. 361.
Andrews *v.* Durant, 18 Id. 496.

May 3, 1880. THE COURT. The above appeals are all from the same decree. They may properly be discussed in one opinion, and will be considered in the order above stated.

ALDEN'S APPEAL, No. 102. The underlying question in this, as well as the other appeals, is the proper construction of the reservation in the deed from Peter Grubb, Jr., to Robert Coleman. In this appeal the particular question is, whether the appellees in whom are now vested the rights reserved by the said Peter Grubb, Jr., in said deed, are entitled to a full supply of ore for a modern furnace, with all the recent improvements of the hot blast, the use of anthracite coal for fuel, of steam engine for power, and with three tuyères instead of one, or whether they are to be restricted to sufficient ore for the charcoal furnace as it existed at the time of the reservation. The question is important, as it affects the parties, for the reason that the modern furnace will make ten times as much iron as the old charcoal furnace with its cold blast admitted by a single tuyère, the uncertain power of water, and the certain blowing out of the furnace in the fall to enable the men to chop wood and make charcoal in the winter.

The learned Court below held, affirming the master, that the appellees were entitled to a supply of ore for a modern furnace, that they had a right to elect what furnace should be supplied, and that the right of election was not exhausted by its exercise upon a single occasion. In other words, they could change the furnace from time to time, as the exigencies of their business or their convenience might require. Both the master and the Court below have so well vindicated their respective rulings upon this branch of the case, that there remains little to add. We see no ambiguity in the reservation, nothing which extrinsic evidence is required or would even be permitted to explain. Where such is the case, no more unsafe rule could be adopted than to search for a meaning of the parties that is not doubtful, and to write into their agreements matters which they have left out. It would have been very easy for Peter Grubb and Robert Coleman when they contracted in 1786 to have placed a fixed limit upon this reservation. They were both ironmasters and men of intelligence, and knew, or must be presumed to have known, just what they were about. They could have limited their supply to a fixed number of tons, and, knowing, as they did the capacity of the furnaces of their day, they could have agreed that the annual consumption of one of them at that time should be the maximum beyond which the reservation should not go. It is no part of our duty to speculate as to why they did not limit the amount of ore by a fixed standard; it is enough for us to know that they have not done so. Yet if it were necessary, it would not be difficult to find excellent reasons why they adopted a shifting standard. We must assume that in contracting they mutually contemplated future improvements in the manufacture of iron, or else deny them average intelligence. Prior to 1785 a marked advance had been made in England. There Smeaton's cylindrical blowing machine had already supplanted the rude wooden bellows, worked by water power here up to and later than 1786. While it is true that the steam engine was not applied to driving blast in Pennsylvania until 1839, yet it had been known in England many years before, and was in practical, successful operation prior to 1785. So as to the use of mineral coal as fuel for making iron. It was not introduced here until 1839, but in England it had been used in blast furnaces since 1750. It may be that the great abundance and cheapness of wood in this country delayed for some time the introduction of mineral coal for such uses.

The reservation was of sufficient ore for one furnace at all times thereafter forever. This was a perpetual reservation, or at least for so long a time as the ore banks should remain unexhausted. This reserved to Peter Grubb, his heirs and assigns, a certain interest in the ore in common with the owners of the ore banks. At the time of the reservation, other furnaces were being operated in the same manner as the Berkshire furnace and using the ore in substantially similar quantities. The ownership of the Cornwall ore banks has since that time become further subdivided by death and conveyances. Other furnaces have been constructed, and all are being operated with the modern improvements and are using a correspondingly increased amount of ore. To allow them to thus increase consumption, and yet to confine the heirs or grantees of Peter Grubb to the quantity consumed in the old charcoal furnace of 1786, would be a forced and arbitrary construction of the reservation, and instead of carrying out the probable intention of the parties, would in our opinion be doing violence to any reasonable view of what they contemplated at the time. It is but just to suppose they expected Peter Grubb, his heirs and assigns, should operate this one furnace as other owners were operating theirs. There was no essential difference at the time of the reservation. Why should there be now? It was manifestly the intention that the reservation should be of a certain proportion of the ore. By allowing to the appellees the same improvements in the manufacture of iron as are enjoyed by the appellants, this proportion can be maintained, and it can be done in no other way. These furnaces may be compared to so many candles, all lighted and consuming this ore at the same time. Peter Grubb's candle burns no faster than the others, and while this is the case the appellants have no just cause of complaint. If the appellants may draw upon these ore banks without limit, with the use of all the modern improvements by means of which the manufacture of iron is so rapidly multiplied, and yet hold the grantees of this reservation to the supply of the antiquated charcoal furnace, it is manifest the reservation itself is immensely diminished in value, and it is only a question of time, depending upon the extent of the ore banks, when it will be entirely defeated.

We need not pursue this branch of the case further. We are of opinion that the reservation gives the appellees the right to as much ore as will supply any one furnace to be selected by them, and that the right to select was not exhausted by its exercise in a single instance. This appeal is not sustained.

FERGUSON'S APPEAL, No. 109. This was an appeal by the executors of William R. White, deceased. The learned Court below held, that, under the reservation of said deed of May 9, 1786, from Grubb to Coleman—1st. That the appellants are only entitled to a supply of ore for one single furnace selected, and cannot, while such furnace is undergoing repairs, use it in another furnace. 2dly. That the appellants must use ore in the furnace so selected, and have no right to sell the same or any part thereof; and that for ore so used they were liable to account to the appellees. A decree was accordingly made against Nathaniel Ferguson and the estate of the said William R. White, that they pay to the appellees the sum of $912.06 for ore used in Robesonia Furnace No. 1, from June 5, 1867, to June 25, 1867, and a further decree against the same parties of $32,773.55, for ore used in Robesonia Furnace No. 1, from March 13, 1873, to May 24, 1874. So far as the above decrees were for ore used in Robesonia Furnace No. 1, while No. 2 was undergoing repairs, we think they are correct. Regarding the words in the reservation, "a sufficient supply of ore for any one furnace," as a measure of quantity, we must interpret them to mean so much ore, and no more, as a given furnace would use in the course of a year, taking into consideration the wear and tear, and the necessity of its going out of blast for repairs at stated periods. No furnace can continue in blast forever; hence, when parties fix the capacity of a certain furnace as a measure of the quantity of ore, they must be presumed to have had in view the fact that every furnace must stop at times, not only for ordinary repairs, but for other accidents and contingencies to the business. The use of Furnace No. 2 from time to time pending repairs to No. 1, the selected furnace, was using more ore than any one furnace was capable of doing; and hence cannot be presumed to have been in the contemplation of the parties, as it certainly is not within the terms of the reservation. That portion of the decree, however, which charges the appellants with the ore used in Robesonia Furnace No. 2, from December 31, 1873, to May 28, 1874, rests upon different footing. During all of this last period No. 1 was in repair, and could have been put in blast. That this was not done was due to the belief of the appellants, as we gather from the offer of evidence rejected by the master, that they had a right to use No. 1 instead of No. 2. That they had no such right is manifest. If, however, there had been an honest mistake here, the appellees have no right in equity to take advantage of it unless they can show that they have been injured. They have not shown any such injury. The appellants had the right to use the ore in No. 2; had they done so, the consumption of ore, according to the offer, would "have been much larger than was consumed in No. 1." It is true, by using No. 1 for five months, it enabled the appellants to operate No. 2 just that much longer without stopping for repairs, and to that extent, perhaps, the appellees may claim to have been injured. But this injury, if not within the rule *de minimis*, is capable of being defined in extent by the master, and may have been more than compensated by the lesser quantity of ore consumed by No. 1. The appellees must remember that they are appealing to the conscience of a Chancellor, as well as seeking the enforcement of legal rights, and that, before they can ask for a decree in their favor for this particular ore, they must show some equity which would make it unjust to withhold it. We are of opinion that the master ought to have heard and considered the evidence referred to in the seventh assignment of error, and to this extent we sustain this appeal. The right to sell ore will be considered in the next appeal.

. APPEAL OF NATHANIEL FERGUSON et al., executors of William R. White, deceased, and of Sarah D. Robeson, executrix of Henry P. Robeson, deceased, No. 110. This appeal raises two questions, distinct from those already discussed, viz.: 1. The right of the appellants, or owners of the ore right, to sell or dispose of the ore so taken by them otherwise than in the supply of the selected furnace; and, 2d, on behalf of the estate of said Henry P. Robeson, the liability to interest on the amount charged, as the value of the ores taken between November 6, 1861, and March 31, 1862.

Upon the question of the sales of ore there is an obscurity as to the facts both in the history of the case and in the report of the Master. Nor is any additional light thrown upon this subject in the opinion of the Court. The learned Judge says: "With regard to the ore sold by Robeson and Brooke in 1855 and 1856, it does not appear from the Master's report under what circumstances that ore was sold,—whether it was surplus ore remaining unused at the furnace, or ore sold directly from the banks. It is, perhaps, immaterial, for, as the defendants had no right to mine ore for the purpose of sale, neither could they sell what was mined for the supply of their furnace."

We do not assent to the broad proposition, that the appellants had no right to sell ore under any circumstances. It is conceded they could not supply the elected furnace, and at the same time sell additional ore from the banks. This would extend the reservation beyond its terms, and make it as broad as the grant itself. It would be using more ore than was requisite for the supply of one furnace. But the appellants claimed, and so aver in their answer, that a portion of the ore sold was to make up the ores used by them from other mines, and the schedules in their answers give the data upon which this claim is founded. If, as they assert, ores from other mines were mixed with the Cornwall ores, and so used in their furnace to improve the quality of the iron, they would have a right to sell a corresponding amount of Cornwall ore. To illustrate: if the elected furnace consumed ten thousand tons of ore in any one year, all of which the appellants were entitled to take under the reservation, and it was found that a better quality of iron could be obtained by the mixture of twenty per cent., say two thousand tons of other ore, they would have a right to exchange that number of tons of Cornwall ore for such purpose, or to sell the same and with the proceeds purchase the same quantity of other ores. This results from two causes: 1st. The right to take a full supply for the selected furnace; and, 2d. Their right of dominion or absolute property in the thing taken. The reservation of the ore right was not necessarily connected with the use of the furnace, except so far as it is necessary to measure the quantity. The appellants are under no obligation to operate the furnace which they may select. They are entitled to select a furnace, and to sell to the proprietor thereof a sufficient supply from the Cornwall ore banks. They may not sell to different furnaces, nor more than a supply to the selected furnace, for that would exceed the reservation. But the ore, when taken out under the reservation, and to the extent it authorizes, is as much the property of the appellants as the ore remaining in the banks is the property of the appellees. To impose such a restraint upon the use and alienation of property, as is here claimed by the appellees, would require the clearest language in the deed. Yet there is not a word in that instrument to justify such a claim. The appellants have an absolute right of property in the ore, the moment it is taken out of the banks, subject to the single qualification that it must pass through some one furnace to be selected by them for the purpose of measuring the quantity. It, therefore, becomes of the highest importance to know under what circumstances the ore in question was sold, and for this purpose the case must go back to the master. The master finds sales by Brooke and Robeson from the Cornwall ore banks of over six thousand tons. The answer avers the use by appellants of other ores at the Reading Furnace of over one thousand tons. To this extent, at least, they were entitled to sell Cornwall ore. The claim of the appellants to make up the deficiencies of former years is not sustained. They cannot take in one year what they might have taken the previous year, but neglected to do so. The right, if not exercised, or only partially exercised for any one year, is gone with the expiration of that year. We are unable to see any sufficient reason why interest should not be charged against appellants upon whatever is found against them for excess of ore. They have sold it and received the money. For the purpose of complete indemnity the interest is as essential as the value itself. This point does not need elaboration. To the extent indicated this appeal is sustained.

APPEAL OF EDWARD BROOKE et al., No. 111, July T. 1878. APPEAL OF WM. R. WHITE et al., No. 112. These appeals present but a single question not already disposed of. The appellants have interposed the Statute of Limitations. This bill was filed July 15, 1856. The answer of Messrs. Robeson and Brooke was filed on the 13th of October of the same year. The former died March 8, 1860; the latter May 18, 1861. The appellants, the executor and executrix of said parties, respectively, were not made parties to the bill until September, 1867. This was more than six years after the death of their respective testators, and if the appellants had set up the Statute by plea or answer when they were first brought in, they would have a stronger case. But they answered the amended bill in 1873, and did not suggest the bar of the Statute. The record shows no step taken by the executors objecting to the revival of the suit on the ground of lapse of time. It is too late to do so now. These appeals are however sustained for other reasons sufficiently set forth in the other cases.

The question of jurisdiction alone remains. This is common to all the appeals. A motion to quash was made upon this ground, and Grubb v. Grubb (7 W. N. C. 349) was cited in support of said motion. We need not extend this already protracted opinion by a discussion of this question. The distinction between Grubb v. Grubb and the case in hand, is palpable. The motion is denied. We have not considered it necessary to refer to the numerous authorities cited on either side. Few of them have any bearing upon the case. We have been led to our conclusions more from the terms of the reservation and its surrounding circumstances, than from the authority of decided cases which are not in point.

This cause came on to be heard and was argued by counsel at the last term of this Court, held in the city of Philadelphia, whereupon, May 3, 1880, it is ordered and adjudged that the decree be affirmed as to Anne C. Alden et al., appellants in No. 102, July Term, 1878, and their appeal is dismissed as to them with costs; and that said decree be reversed as to Nathaniel Ferguson et al., appellants in No. 110, July T. 1878; Edward Brooke et al., appellants in No. 111, July T.

1878; and William R. White et al., appellants in No. 112, July T. 1878, and that the record be remitted to the Court below for further proceedings, in accordance with the principles indicated in this opinion.

Opinion by PAXSON, J. GORDON and TRUNKEY, JJ., dissent to the affirmance of Alden's appeal.

May, '80, 55.   May 13, 1880.
Comp v. Carlisle Deposit Bank.

Banks and banking—Bailment—Depositum—Liability of bailee without reward—Negligence—Agency—How far representations of cashier may bind bank—Evidence—When parol evidence not admissible to vary terms of written contract.

A bank, whose affairs were conducted by a board of directors, and whose cashier was elected by such board, was accustomed to receive deposits of bonds in its vaults gratuitously at the risk of the depositors. Plaintiff deposited bonds therein at the solicitation and request of the cashier, and received a receipt stipulating that the bonds should be at the owner's risk. The cashier had no power from the authorities of the bank to solicit deposits or make representations as to their safe keeping, nor were the authorities of the bank proved to have any knowledge of this specific transaction. The bonds were afterwards lost:

Held, that parol evidence of representations made at the time of the transaction by the cashier, to the effect that the bank took as good care of depositors' bonds as of its own, and that plaintiff was all right, except in case of fire or burglary, was not sufficient to change the effect of the written receipt so as to affect the bank.

The bank was in the habit of paying the interest on such bonds to depositors, and of collecting the amount thereof by detaching the coupons, sending them to other banks, and obtaining credit at such banks for a fund equal to the value of the coupons. On these amounts interest was sometimes paid, and upon them the bank drew drafts, charging a small commission. It was necessary to have such credits to accommodate its customers with drafts, but the whole amount realized from this branch of business was insufficient to compensate for the trouble of forwarding the coupons:

Held, that the bank was, notwithstanding this state of facts, a bailee of the bonds without hire.

Bonds so deposited with the bank were placed in a fireproof safe, securely guarded. The cashier was a person of good repute, and the authorities of the bank had no knowledge of any misconduct by him:

Held, that the bank were not bound to examine packages so left on deposit, and that there was no evidence of such negligence on the part of the bank, in the care of such deposits, as to make it liable in case of loss occurring by reason of the cashier's dishonesty.

Error to the Common Pleas of Cumberland County.

Assumpsit, by Samuel Comp against The Carlisle Deposit Bank, to recover the value of certain United States bonds deposited by plaintiff in defendant's keeping, and lost while in its custody.

On the trial, before M'CLEAN, P. J., the following facts appeared: The corporation defendant was in the habit of receiving and keeping bonds for the convenience of its customers and others without receiving compensation from the depositors. These bonds were placed in a tin box inside of a burglar-proof safe, almost always locked, to which access could be had only by the cashier or the authorities of the bank. The defendant was in the habit of paying the interest on these various bonds directly to the various depositors. As the instalments became due the cashier would cut off the coupons, send them to banks in New York or Philadelphia, obtain credit at such banks for the fund represented by such coupons, and then use such fund to draw drafts upon, charging the drawees a small commission. It was of advantage to the bank to have such funds to draw on that they might accommodate their customers; but little or no interest was paid thereon, and no indirect profit derived therefrom compensated the bank for the trouble involved in forwarding the coupons. Under the charter of the bank the directors had power to manage its affairs and appoint its cashier. From 1863 or 1864 until 1876 one Hassler was the cashier. He was a well-known man, and was esteemed an honest and upright one by the community. On January 28, 1868, Hassler wrote nine letters to the Treasury Department at Washington, inclosing a number of U. S. 7-30 bonds, which he wished to exchange for U. S. 5-20's of 1867. These transactions were expressed in the letters to be for private parties, but not as regards any of them for Hassler himself. The authorities of the bank defendant had no knowledge of them, nor does any trace of them appear on their books, except copies of Hassler's letters, which remain in their letter-book. The 5-20's desired were received and receipted for by Hassler, on February 14, 1868.

On the following day, February 15, plaintiff entered the bank and asked Hassler whether the defendant exchanged 5-20's for 7-30's. Hassler replied they did, whereupon plaintiff produced $2200 in 7-30's and asked to have them exchanged for four $500 5-20's and two $100 5-20's. Hassler obtained the bonds desired, which were some of those received by him from Washington on the 14th instant, and handed them to plaintiff, asking him what he was going to do with them. Plaintiff replied he was going to deposit them in a bank near his home. Hassler then asked why he did not leave them on deposit there, and insisted on his doing so, which plaintiff finally consented to do. Hassler then drew up and gave plaintiff the following receipt:—

CARLISLE DEPOSIT BANK.

CARLISLE, PA., Feb. 15th, 1868.

Received of Samuel Comp, Esq., New Bloomfield, Perry Co., Pa., for deposit in the vault of this Bank at the risk of the depositor, the following bond packages, &c., to be delivered on return of this ticket.

1 U. S. 5-20 Bond	145289	100
1 " " "	145288	100
1 " " "	78359	500
.. .. ..	78358	500
	78360	500
	78359	500
		$2200

Int. due July and Jan'y.

J. P. HASSLER, *Cas.*

Plaintiff then said he would run no risk; he would take the bonds. Hassler replied, "You stand no risk without there's burglars break in and rob the bank, or fire should take place and burn up the bank. The bank takes as good care of their depositors' money as they do of their own." He then took plaintiff into the vault, showed him the deposits, and importuned him to leave the bonds, which plaintiff finally agreed to do. No special authority was proved to have been given to Hassler by the authorities of the bank to ask particularly for such deposits, nor to make any representations as to their safe keeping. The transactions was not entered on the books of the bank defendant, nor did it enter into their working operations.

The 5-20 bonds of 1867 were redeemed by the Government in 1870, but the interest on plaintiff's bonds was duly paid him up to and including the instalment accruing in July, 1876. These payments were by cashiers' or tellers' checks on the bank defendant, all of which were duly honored. The amounts of these checks were charged on the books of the bank defendant. The teller who signed some of these checks was Louis A. Smith, a reputable and esteemed member of the community. In September, 1876, Smith died, and Hassler then admitted that he had conspired with deceased to defraud the bank, and made various fraudulent entries in the books. He was dismissed from office, prosecuted for embezzlement, and finally committed suicide.

In January, 1877, plaintiff went to the bank to collect his interest. The new cashier told him that the bank had no such bonds, but on sight of his receipt concluded that they must be mislaid, and paid him his instalment of interest. On searching, however, no such bonds were found. Hassler, who was then alive, was summoned, and stated that there had been such bonds on deposit, but he could not tell what had become of them. Plaintiff thereupon brought this suit against the bank defendant to recover the value of the bonds. Subsequently the two $100 bonds were found in an open envelope between some books stowed away in a corner of the bank's safe. These were tendered to and accepted by plaintiff, and a certificate to that effect filed of record in the case.

The plaintiff presented, *inter alia*, points substantially as follows:—

(1) "If the jury believe that the officers of the bank were in the habit of receiving Government and other bonds, for safe keeping, with the knowledge of the directors, and the plaintiff, Comp, left the bonds in question with the bank for safe keeping at the special instance and request of the cashier, and upon his solicitation, and the officers of the bank were grossly negligent, in the care taken of said bonds, the plaintiff may recover the value thereof together with interest thereon from January, 1877." *Answer.* "There being no evidence in the case that the cashier had any authority to make such special request and solicitation as is embraced in this point, and in view of the peculiar circumstances of the deposit in this case, the point is not affirmed."

(2 and 3) If the jury believe that plaintiff bought said bonds, either of the bank or cashier, and was induced to leave them on deposit by the cashier's solicitations and representations, and that they were lost neither by burglary nor fire, the plaintiff may recover. *Refused.*

(4) "If the jury believe that the bonds in controversy were left with the bank for safe keeping on the 15th of February, 1868, and were purchased by the United States Government in October, 1870, and the loss of the bonds was not made known to the plaintiff until January, 1877, a period of over six years, during all of which time the bank continued to pay the coupons and premium, these are facts for the consideration of the jury in determining the question of gross negligence." *Answer.* "There being no evidence showing knowledge on the part of the directors or any officers of the bank, except Hassler the cashier, and Smith the teller, of or concerning those four lost or stolen bonds in their use proper or improper, this point is not affirmed."

(5) "If the bank received the bonds in question with the understanding that they were to collect the coupons in Philadelphia for the plaintiff, and did collect them, and thus obtained credit in city banks, upon which they sold checks and drafts at a premium, the bank would not be a bailee without compensation, but if it solicited the deposit, for its own special accommodation, it would be responsible for ordinary neglect, and if the jury so believe, they should find for the plaintiff." *Answer.* "Under the evidence in this case this point is not affirmed."

(6) "If the jury believe that the defendant did not take the same care of the plaintiff's bonds

as it did of its own, then the defendant is guilty of such negligence as will entitle the plaintiff to recover." *Answer.* "If the jury find that the four missing bonds were lawfully purchased by the plaintiff from Mr. Hassler, the cashier, on the 15th of February, 1868, and were deposited according to the practice of the defendant corporation, it was not bound to take the same care of them as it did of its own."

(7) "If J. P. Hassler, the cashier, spontaneously and officiously proposed that the bank would keep the bonds of plaintiff, the defendant is responsible in such case for ordinary neglect." *Answer.* "Any such spontaneous and officious act of the cashier being unauthorized by the bank, it is not responsible for ordinary neglect."

The defendant presented, *inter alia*, the following points:—

(1) "The course of business shown as regards collecting interest on the bonds does not imply any consideration for keeping them. The defendant is, therefore, only liable for such gross negligence as led directly to their loss." *Affirmed.*

(2) "The uncontradicted evidence in this case being that the bonds of the plaintiff never belonged to the bank, that they never entered into its working, and that they were kept where the bank kept its money and valuables, repels any presumption of such gross negligence as to render the defendant liable for the plaintiff's bonds." *Answer.* "If the jury find that the four missing bonds never belonged to the bank, but were the lawful property of the plaintiff, and never entered into the working of the bank, and that they were kept where the bank kept its money and valuables, this would repel any presumption of such gross negligence as to render the defendant liable for such bonds, but the measure of the care is slight diligence."

(3) "There being no evidence in the cause to show gross negligence on the part of the officers of the bank, and the uncontradicted testimony being that Mr. Hassler was of high standing in the community until the discovery of his fraudulent conduct, and that he had the confidence of the community as well as of the directors of the bank, the verdict of the jury should be for the defendant." *Affirmed.*

(4) "No solicitation by Mr. Hassler to Mr. Comp, to leave his bonds in the bank, in the absence of all evidence showing any authority to Mr. Hassler to make any such solicitation, and in the absence of all evidence of any custom so to do known to and acquiesced in by the directors of the bank, will suffice to alter or change the terms of the receipt accepted and produced by the plaintiff, which must be taken as the contract of the party." *Affirmed.*

The Court charged, *inter alia*. "The first inquiry of fact to be determined by you is, who had the ownership of the bonds that Mr. Hassler professed to sell or exchange. . . . Were they the property of the bank? Were they the property of Mr. Hassler, the cashier? It is argued that his solicitude and importunity in having Mr. Comp leave the bonds in the bank is some evidence of a dishonest and fraudulent design on the part of Mr. Hassler in dealing with Mr. Comp in the transaction, that Mr. Hassler had not the right to offer and to appear to pass them to Mr. Comp, if they were the special property of some of the private customers of the bank. The argument of the defendant further is, that the four $500 bonds may have been restored to the parties rightfully owning them, and that Mr. Hassler appropriated to himself the 7-30 notes which the plaintiff passed to him. And that the subsequent acts and conduct of Mr. Hassler in sending the plaintiff the semi-annual returns of the coupons and gold premium after the four bonds had passed back into the treasury of the United States and were redeemed as far back as the 20th of October, 1870, are convincing evidence of the fraud practised by him on Mr. Comp as well as upon the bank, and that Smith, the teller, was cognizant of and participated in this guilty conduct. . . .

"[I must instruct you then at the threshold of the case, that, if you find the bargain of February 15, 1868, tainted with fraud on the part of Mr. Hassler in disposing of property not his own, nor the bank's, it is a vicious thing, upon which the defendant cannot be held liable. You need not proceed to make the next inquiry in the case if the first is determined by you against the plaintiff. It is a question of fact, and the testimony would seem to be strong in support of the defendant's position upon this stage of the case, but the inquiry is to be answered by you from the evidence, and you must not be controlled by any opinion I may have expressed or may express upon the facts.] . . .

"[To conclude, gentlemen, if you find from the evidence that the transaction of the 15th of February, 1868, was a fraud and trick on the part of Hassler, that he had not then the lawful control of the four missing bonds, but that his act was a sham and deception, your verdict will be for the defendant.]"

Verdict and judgment for defendant. Plaintiff took this writ, assigning for error, *inter alia*, the refusal of plaintiff's points above cited, the affirming of defendant's points above cited, and those portions of the charge of the Court quoted above within brackets.

H. Newsham and *W. A. Sponsler* (with them *Graham and Son*), for plaintiff in error.

The bank defendant is bound by the representations of the cashier. The principal is liable for the acts and declarations of his agent when made in the discharge of an act the agent is authorized to perform, although he may exceed the limits of his express authority.

Lancaster Bank *v.* Irvine, 3 P. & W. 250.
Chestnut Hill Turnpike Co. *v.* Rutter, 4 S. & R. 11.
Steamboat Co. *v.* McCutcheon, 1 Harris, 15.
Penna. R. R. Co. *v.* Titusville Plankroad Co., 21 Smith, 355.
Bissell *v.* First National Bank of Franklin, 19 Smith, 419.
Merchant's Bank *v.* State Bank, 10 Wall. 645.
First Nat. Bank *v.* Graham, 8 WEEKLY NOTES, 361.

Parol evidence was admissible to vary the terms of the written contract.

Thompson *v.* White, 1 Dallas, 427.
Irwin *v.* Shoemaker, 8 W. & S. 75.
Overton *v.* Tracey, 14 S. & R. 311.
Hultz *v.* Wright, 16 S. & R. 345.
Oliver *v.* Oliver & Bell, 4 Rawle, 141.
Campbell *v.* McClenachan, 6 S. & R. 172.
Green *v.* Scott, 30 Smith, 88.
Chalfant *v.* Williams, 11 Casey, 212.
Mundorff *v.* Wickersham, 13 Smith, 87.
Caley *v.* Phila. & ' Chester R. R. Co., 2 WEEKLY NOTES, 313.
Lippincott *v.* Whitman, 2 Norris, 244.
Greenawalt *v.* Kohne, 4 Norris, 369.
Eilenberger *v.* Mutual Ins. Co., 7 WEEKLY NOTES, 363.
Spencer *v.* Colt, Ibid. 333.

The use by the bank of the cut off coupons made the deposit with them of advantage to them. They were, therefore, bailees for hire, and liable for ordinary negligence.

Bank *v.* Graham, 29 Smith, 116.

The officious soliciting by its officer of the deposit makes the bank liable for ordinary negligence.

2 Kent's Comm. 564.
Jones on Bailment, 54.

The bonds being purchased by the government in 1870, the paying of interest on them until 1876 was itself evidence of gross negligence on the part of the bank authorities, which should have been submitted to a jury.

No fraud was practised by Hassler on the bank in giving Comp the 5-20 bonds. The bank cannot, therefore, take advantage as against Comp of any fraud practised upon Comp by Hassler. The bonds were received or deposited by their accredited agent, and they became responsible for the safety of them.

John Hays and *Lemuel Todd*, for defendant in error.

The defendant could not be bound by the cashier's representations. By the charter he was the agent of the directors, not of the corporation. Bissell *v.* First National Bank of Franklin (19 Smith, 419) is not, therefore, applicable. The cashier was an agent acting outside the scope of his authority, and could not, therefore bind his principal.

Wharton on Agency,
Maul *et ux. v.* Rider, 9 Smith, 167.
Speer *v.* Evans, 11 Wright, 141.

Ins. Co. *v.* Robinson, 6 Smith, 256.
Butcher *v.* Yocum, 11 Smith, 168.
Fechley *v.* Barr, 16 Smith, 196.

Parol evidence was incompetent to show a different contract from that contained in the receipt.

There was no evidence of sufficient compensation to the bank from their course of business in reference to the coupons to make them bailees for hire and liable for ordinary negligence, and there was no evidence of gross negligence to go to the jury. The fact of allowing payments of interest to continue until 1876 was not such evidence. The immediate cause of loss was the cashier's fraud, and the bank's confidence in him was apparently justifiable.

Scott *v.* National Bank, 22 Smith, 479.

The charge of the Court was right. If the 5-20's given by Hassler to plaintiff belonged neither to Hassler nor the bank, but to private parties, the whole transaction was a fraud and sham, and plaintiff could not call the bank to account for the fraud perpetrated on him.

May 24, 1880. THE COURT. When the plaintiff left these bonds, he took a receipt therefor, in which it was declared they were received " for deposit in the vault of this bank at the risk of the depositor."

The parol evidence of the declaration of the cashier was not sufficient to change the effect of the written receipt, so as to affect the bank. There was no evidence that it was accustomed to receiving bonds for safe keeping, except at the risk of the owner, nor that the directors had any knowledge that bonds were left at the instance, request, or solicitation of the cashier. We are unable to discover any negligence in the manner in which the bank kept the bonds. They were placed in the vault. They were not lost by outside robbery, but by inside larceny. Whether kept in paper envelope or small tin box, in either case the cashier might readily have had access to them. He was of good repute, and no negligence can be imputed to the directors for retaining him in his position. Having full confidence in his integrity, they trusted him with the property of the bank. They had no knowledge of any misconduct on his part. They were not bound to examine packages left on deposit without reward, to see if the contents remained. The bank was a bailee without hire.

It is not necessary to consider the assignments in detail. We discover no error.

Judgment affirmed.

PER CURIAM. SHARSWOOD, C. J., and GREEN, J., absent.

May, '80, 179.   May 6, 7, 1880.
Porter's Appeal—Eberle's Estate.

Advancements—Intention of testator to convert debt into advancement—Interest—Construction of will—Technical words.

In the absence of a clear intent to the contrary, technical words in a will are presumed to have been used by the testator in their technical sense.

This presumption will be less easily overcome in an artistically drawn will than in one bearing on its face the evidence that it was drawn by an ignorant testator.

The legal meaning of a technical word will not be affected by a direction in the will which is capable of a construction consistent with that meaning.

A testator declared in his will (which was artistically drawn) that two notes, given to him by a son and a married daughter, respectively, bearing interest on their face, were "deemed by him as advancements to the respective drawers thereof," and he directed, further, "that the said notes be valued and appraised at their full amounts as assets of my estate in the hands of my executors, and to be respectively paid and accounted for, by the respective drawers thereof, out of their respective shares" in the distribution of testator's estate:

Held (reversing the decree of the Court below), that this direction did not indicate that the term advancement was used by the testator in other than its technical signification; and that it was, therefore, error to charge interest on the note of the daughter in the distribution.

Appeal from a decree of the Orphans' Court of Lancaster County, dismissing the exceptions to the report of an auditor, in the matter of the distribution of the estate of Henry Eberle dec'd, and confirming the said report.

The material facts were as follows: Henry Eberle died Feb. 22, 1876, leaving to survive him five children. By his will, dated Oct. 15, 1875, he directed, *inter alia*, as follows:—

"The note of four thousand dollars ($4000) dated August 6, A. D. 1861, bearing interest at the rate of five (5) per cent. per annum, which I hold against my daughter Mary, and the one of three thousand dollars ($3000), bearing date the same day, at same rate of interest, which I hold against my son, Benjamin F. Eberle, are deemed by me as advancements to the respective drawers thereof, and I order and direct that they be valued and appraised at their full amounts, as assets of my estate in the hands of my executors, and to be respectively paid and accounted for, by the respective drawers thereof, at the first distribution of the residue of my estate, out of their respective shares therein."

The following is a copy of the note of Mrs. Mary C. Porter, above referred to:—

One year after date I promise to pay to Henry Eberle, Sen., or order, Four Thousand Dollars, without defalcation, for value received, with interest at five per cent. per annum until paid. Witness my hand and seal this sixth day of August, One Thousand Eight Hundred and Sixty-one.

    MARY C. PORTER. [SEAL.]
Witness: A. M. HERSHEY.

The testator directed his executors, John H. Zeller and his son Benjamin F. Eberle, to sell his real and personal property, and directed the proceeds of his residuary estate, real and personal, to be divided in equal shares among his said five children. The executors included in the inventory the said two notes, with interest to date of filing the inventory. Subsequently Benjamin F. Eberle paid or accounted for the amount of his note, $3000, with interest thereon, to date of filing the executor's account, $2347.91; and the executors charged themselves with the total sum of $5347.91.

Mary C. Porter claimed that the principal of her note was, by the will of her father, converted into an advancement, and that, while the principal was to be deducted from her share, she was not chargeable with interest thereon.

Before the auditor, to whom the executors' account was referred, it appeared that at the time this note was given Mary C. Porter was a married woman, and that she gave the note to her father, at his request, to secure certain indorsements made by him for the accommodation of her husband, George W. Porter, who died in 1863. The testator subsequently learned that the note was void, by reason of Mrs. Porter's coverture. Parol evidence was offered of declarations by the testator in his life time to the effect, that, as his daughter had not received the money, which was paid for her husband, he did not wish to charge her therewith, but that to give satisfaction among his children he would charge her share of his estate with the principal, but not with interest. The testimony was taken, but was subsequently excluded by the auditor as inadmissible.

The auditor reported, *inter alia*, as follows: "The note of Mrs. Mary C. Porter, having been executed during the lifetime of her husband, was void, and being therefore entirely valueless as an asset of the estate, there was no mode in which the payment of the debt for which it was given could be secured, but by providing in the will for its deduction from her share of his estate. The testator has provided for such a deduction, but has he done so in such terms as to make it inclusive of interest upon the principal?

"The provision on that subject constitutes the fourth item of the will, which has already been recited, and need not now be repeated. After describing the notes, it states that 'they are deemed by me (the testator) as advancements to the respective drawers thereof;' and if this were all that was said upon the subject, there could unquestionably be no charge of interest upon them. The item, however, does not so end, but proceeds further to provide 'that they (the notes) shall be *valued and appraised* at their *full amounts*, as assets of my estate in the hands of my executors, and to be respectively paid and *accounted for* by the respective drawers thereof at the first distribution of the residue of my estate out of their respective shares therein.'

"Now, an advancement being, as we have already seen, an irrevocable gift of the money or property which is its subject, that money or property ceases definitely thereafter to belong to the donor, and of course upon his death is neither to be included in the inventory of his estate, nor appraised as a portion of its assets. It is evident, therefore, that the testator has here used the term without any distinct perception of its technical meaning; and that his intention in the provision is to be determined, not from its use alone, but from the general scope and effect of the phraseology employed to express that intention.

"Whatever the testator chose to call these notes, he had unquestionably a right so to dispose of his estate, that the presumptive shares therein of the respective drawers of the notes should be diminished by the amounts for which they were severally given. That he so intended as to the principal, is certain, and observing the particularity with which, in the final clause of the item under consideration, he has directed the notes to 'be valued and appraised at their *full amounts as assets of his estate*, in the hands of his executors, and (so appraised) to be respectively paid and accounted for by the respective drawers thereof,' it has seemed to the auditor impossible to escape the conclusion, that the diminution of the shares of the drawers of the notes was intended to include interest as well as principal.

"In this distribution, therefore, the share of Mrs. Mary Porter will be merely her fifth part of the residue of this estate, after deducting therefrom the principal of her note of August 6, 1861, with interest thereon from that date to the time of the filing of this report."

Exceptions filed to the report by Mrs. Porter were dismissed by the Court, LIVINGSTON, P. J., saying: "We have examined the authorities cited, the will of the decedent, the able report of the learned auditor and minutes of audit, and have felt obliged (though reluctantly) to arrive at the same conclusions presented to the Court by the learned auditor. The Court therefore overrules the exceptions, and confirms the report of the auditor."

PATTERSON, A. L. J., dissented from the foregoing opinion, holding that the $4000 to the daughter of testator, Mrs. Porter, was an advancement, and did not carry interest.

Mary C. Porter took this appeal, assigning for error the above decree of the Court.

S. H. Reynolds (with him *H. C. Brubaker*), for appellant, cited—

Hawkins on Wills, Prop. 111, *4, 5, 7.

Doebler's Appeal, 14 Sm. 15.
Green *v.* Howell, 6 W. & S. 203.
Hail *v.* Davis, 3 Pick. 450.

N. Ellmaker, D. G. Eshleman, and *H. M. North,* for appellees, cited—

Miller's Appeal, 4 Wr. 57.
Oller *v.* Bonebrake, 15 Sm. 338.
High's Appeal, 9 Har. 283.
Roland *v.* Schrack, 5 Cas. 125.
Yarnall's Appeal, 20 Sm. 335, 340.
Provenchere's Appeal, 17 Sm. 463.
Gilbert's Appeal, 4 Nor. 347.

May 17, 1880. THE COURT. The intention of the testator is the prevailing consideration in applying all rules of construction. It is the intention of the testator expressed in the will that is to govern. And this is to be judged of exclusively by the words of the instrument, as applied to the subject matter, and surrounding circumstances. Parol evidence to show what were the actual testamentary intentions, such as his declarations of what he had done, or meant to do, is inadmissible, but it is competent to determine which of several persons or things were intended under an equivocal description. In construing the autograph will of an illiterate man, the meaning of technical language may be disregarded, but no word which has a clear and definite object may be struck out. Technical words and phrases, although prima facie to be taken in their true sense, will not be construed so as to defeat any obvious general intention of the testator, since wills are often prepared by persons wholly unacquainted with the precise technical force of legal words and formulas. In seeking for the expressed intention of the testator, his words are to receive that construction and interpretation, which a long series of decisions has attached to them, unless it is very certain they were used in a different sense. These oft-repeated rules are recalled by the question now presented.

This will is artistic, and evinces an accurate use of technical terms. Hence the presumption that the testator employed them in their legal sense will not be so easily overcome as if the will bore on its face evidence that it was drawn by an ignorant man. Here is no exhibition of such illiteracy as calls for a departure from the actual meaning of its words to a real or supposed popular sense, but rather such skill as induces belief that its words which have been judicially defined were understandingly employed.

An advancement is an irrevocable gift, by a parent in his lifetime, to a child, on account of such child's share in the parent's estate. It is valued as of the time of the gift. Therefore interest is not chargeable thereon, unless there be clear expression that it shall carry interest, as was the case in Fickes *v.* Wireman (2 Watts, 314).

Statutory provisions respecting advancements are applicable only to the children of intestates.

When the parent giving money to a child takes a note for its repayment, it is a debt. If such note be void because the maker was a married woman, the money is not an advancement. But a parent has power, by his will, to turn a debt into an advancement, and when he does so he gives it all the usual incidents, one of which is that it shall be valued as of the date the child received the money. It will not continue a debt as regards interest, and a gift as regards principal, unless he plainly says so. (Green *v.* Howell, 6 W. & S. 203; Hutchinson's Appeal, 11 Wright, 84.)

In this case the testator declared that he deemed the note he held against his daughter Mary as an advancement, and directed that it be valued and appraised at its full amount, as assets of his estate in the hands of his executors, and to be paid and accounted for by her, at the first distribution of the residue of his estate, out of her share therein. In unmistakable phrase he turned the debt into a gift, to be valued at the date of the note. The word advancement occurs nowhere else in the will, nor is there anything to show it was not used in its legal sense. The advancement is directed to be valued and appraised at its full amount, as assets for distribution, and to be deducted from her share. Of what date shall it be valued? Giving every word its proper meaning, at the date of the gift. Its full amount is the face of the note, without interest. To "be valued and appraised" has no significance as showing inclusion or exclusion of interest; for even if the note were a debt, mere appraisement means its amount, either with or without interest, according to the contract. A debt on interest by contract or overdue, converted into an advancement, and directed to be appraised as part of the assets, is taken without interest, unless otherwise expressed. No case has been found to the contrary.

We are of opinion that the testator's intention, expressed in his will, is not doubtful : but if it be, no rule of interpretation requires or permits the well-settled meaning of an apt word to be set aside by a direction which admits of a construction consistent with that meaning. It was error to charge Mrs. Porter any interest on the principal sum of $4000, which was made an advancement to her.

Decree reversed, and it is ordered that the record be remitted to the Orphans' Court for further proceeding. Costs of this appeal to be paid by the executors out of the moneys of the estate.

Opinion by TRUNKEY, J.

SHARSWOOD, C. J., and GREEN, J., absent.

Jan. '80, 330.　　　　　　　　　January 6, 1881.

Jones v. Caldwell.

Will—Equitable conversion, what will effect—Absolute direction by testator to sell—Effect of provision that heirs may agree to a division among themselves—Surplusage.

An absolute direction by a testator to his executors to sell real estate and divide the proceeds among the heirs, works an equitable conversion; and the addition of a provision that the heirs may agree to a division among themselves, and that the executors need not then sell, does not operate to prevent a conversion.

Per PAXSON, J. Such provision is mere surplusage, and may be stricken from the will without altering its legal effect. It merely gives the heirs a right which the law secures to them independently of the will.

A testator provided that, after his own and his widow's death, his executors should sell his real estate, and that the proceeds should be divided among his heirs; "but my executors shall not be bound to make such advertisement and sale, if all the legal heirs or their legal representatives shall agree to a division of said estate among themselves." After the death of the testator and his widow, and before sale of the property, a judgment was recovered against one of the heirs; a sale was subsequently made by the executor in accordance with the provision in the will; upon a case stated, setting forth the above facts:

Held (reversing the judgment of the Court below), that a conversion had been worked, and that the judgment had not attached as a lien upon the land, and, therefore, was not entitled to be paid out of the proceeds.

Laird's Appeal, 4 WEEKLY NOTES, 473, followed.
Neely *v.* Grantham, 8 Sm. 433, distinguished.

Error to the Common Pleas No. 2, of Philadelphia County.

Case stated, wherein J. C. Caldwell was plaintiff, and T. C. Jones, administrator *d. b. n. c. t. a.* of M. Andress, deceased, was defendant, setting forth the following facts: Michael Andress died June 28, 1865, seised in fee, *inter alia,* of premises No. 139 Noble St. He left surviving him his widow, five sons, and three daughters, among whom was Mary B., intermarried with Edward Durrell. By his will, duly admitted to probate, he provided, *inter alia,* as follows:—

Item. After my own and my wife's decease it is my will that my executors shall dispose of all my property, real, personal, and mixed, without any application to Orphans' Court, or make return to any court of this Commonwealth, other than where collateral inheritance tax might occur, and I hereby authorize my said executors to make legal deeds to the purchasers of any of my real estate, provided nevertheless, that they shall publish in two daily newspapers, one month daily, showing the time and place when the same is to be disposed of, which shall be at public auction, but my executors shall not be bound to make such advertisement or sale, if all the legal heirs or their legal representatives shall agree to a division of said estate amongst themselves, notwithstanding the above provision for a sale, but this will shall nevertheless be recorded in the Register of Wills' Office in the City of Philadelphia.

He then provided for an equal distribution of

his estate among his children, after the decease of himself and wife. Sophia Andress, his wife, survived him and died July 5, 1878. On Sept. 10, 1874, J. C. Caldwell, the plaintiff here, recovered a judgment for $229 against Mary B. Durrell, who had since become and still remained a widow. Mary B. Durrell died Oct. 31, 1876. On Nov. 26, 1878, T. C. Jones, administrator *d. b. n. c. t. a.* of Michael Andress, sold the testator's real estate at public sale, under the authority contained in the will; and the plaintiff released the lien of his judgment upon the house and lot in Noble Street, upon an agreement made by the administrator to retain out of the proceeds enough to pay plaintiff's debt, interest, and costs, provided that Mary B. Durrell's interest in her father's estate was, on Sept. 10, 1874, such that plaintiff's judgment, recovered on that day, attached thereto as a lien. If the Court should be of opinion that on the above facts the plaintiff is entitled to judgment, then judgment for plaintiff for $229 and interest, etc.

The Court entered judgment for plaintiff for $304.50; whereupon defendant took this writ, assigning for error the entry of said judgment.

J. A. Abrams (with him *J. L. Tull*), for plaintiff in error.

The law of Pensylvania is that a positive direction to sell realty works an equitab conversion, and, therefore, a judgment is not a lien.

Allison *v.* Wilson, 13 S. & R. 333.
Brolasky *v.* Gally's Execrs., 1 Sm. 509.
Evans's Appeal, 13 Sm. 183.

The provision that the heirs might take the realty as such, makes no difference.

Laird's Appeal, 4 WEEKLY NOTES, 473.

(No counsel appeared, nor was any paper-book furnished, on the other side.)

January 24, 1881. THE COURT. The portion of the will of Michael Andress which is the subject of the present contention is as follows: [His Honor then set forth the provision of the will *ut supra.*] The will then directs the proceeds of such sales to be divided among his eight children, share and share alike.

The single question for our consideration is, whether the will works a conversion of the real estate. If it does, the judgment obtained by the defendant in error against Mary B. Durrell, one of the testator's children, was not a lien upon the real estate, and the judgment entered by the Court below upon the case stated must be reversed.

An absolute direction to sell lands after the death of the testator's widow, and to divide the proceeds among his children, effects an equitable conversion thereof into personalty, and the interest of one of the children is not bound by a judgment against him, before a sale, as real estate. (Allison *v.* Wilson, 13 S. & R. 330; Morrow *v.* Brenizer, 2 Rawle, 185; Burr *v.* Sim, 1 Wh. 252;

Allison *v.* Kurtz, 2 Watts, 185; Gray *v.* Smith, 3 Ibid. 289; Simpson *v.* Kelso, 8 Ibid. 247; Hess *v.* Shorb, 7 Barr, 231; Willing *v.* Peters, Ibid. 287; Silverthorn *v.* McKinster, 2 Jones, 67; Parkinson's Appeal, 8 Casey, 455; Wilson *v.* Shoenberger, 10 Ibid. 121; Brolasky *v.* Gally's Exrs., 1 P. F. S. 509; Evans's Appeal, 13 P. F. S. 183; McClure's Appeal, 22 Ibid. 414.) In order to work a conversion, however, the direction to sell must be positive and explicit. It must not rest in the discretion of the executor, nor depend upon contingencies. A direction to sell upon a future contingency does not effect an equitable conversion until an actual sale. (Nagle's Appeal, 1 Har. 260; Bleight *v.* The Bank, 10 Barr, 131; Stoner *v.* Zimmerman, 9 Harris, 397; Anewalt's Appeal, 6 Wright, 417; Chew *v.* Nicklin, 9 Ibid. 84.)

The direction in the will of Michael Andress to sell his estate is as explicit as language can make it. Does the subsequent provision, that, if his heirs shall agree to a division of the estate among themselves, the executor shall not be bound to sell, operate to prevent a conversion? We are of opinion that it does not, for the reason, that the provision referred to is surplusage and may be stricken from the will without altering its legal effect. It merely gave the heirs the right to elect to take the property as real estate. The law gives them this right independently of the will. It is well settled that where real estate is ordered to be sold, the parties interested in the proceeds may elect to take the land as such. (Smith *v.* Starr, 3 Wharton, 262; Rice *v.* Bixler, 1 W. & S. 445.)

The testator must have intended a conversion even in the event of a division of the estate among the heirs by agreement. There were eight heirs, and there appear to have been but five separate properties of unequal values. Be that as it may, to have divided them would have required either a sale between themselves or partition according to law. The latter would have necessarily involved an appraisement and sale, and hence a conversion. It was held in Laird's Appeal (4 W. N. C. 473), that a provision by a testator in his will, that any of his sons may take his real estate at an appraisement, does not prevent equitable conversion under an explicit direction that his real estate be sold and converted into money.

The foregoing views are not in serious conflict with Neely *v.* Grantham (8 P. F. S. 433). The facts of that case are essentially different. A testator directed that his wife should have his mansion farm for life, and further ordered : " it is my will, that, if any one or two of my children wish to hold the mansion property, after two of them is of age, they can do so by agreeing among themselves; if they cannot agree, they can get three disinterested persons to divide and agree for them, the eldest to have the first choice, and each of my children's share remaining in the property, until they arrive at twenty-one years. If in case none of my children purchase the old mansion, it must be sold to the best advantage for the use of my children, and not until after the decease of my wife." An attachment in execution was issued against the son and served on the executors as garnishees. It was held, that the attachment bound the proceeds of the sale of the lands in the hands of the executors: THOMPSON, C. J., and READ, J., being of opinion that there was no conversion, but that the land was bound as such by the attachment; SHARSWOOD, J., that the order to sell worked a conversion, and it was bound as personal estate; and STRONG and AGNEW, JJ., dissented. It will thus be seen that, while three of the Judges concurred in the judgment, though for different reasons, four were of opinion there was no conversion.

It must be conceded that the distinction between Neely *v.* Grantham and the later case of Laird's Appeal, *supra,* is very slight. Yet there is a difference. In Laird's Appeal the provision was that *any* of the testator's sons might take the real estate at the appraisement. This required an agreement between the sons, as to *who* should take. They could have so agreed, and the property could have been taken without the provision of the will. In either event there would have been a sale and a conversion of the estate into money, which is precisely what the testator intended. In Neely *v.* Grantham, the provision was, " that, if any *one or two* of my children wish to hold the old mansion property, after two of them is of age, they can do so by agreeing among themselves; if not agreeing, they can get three disinterested persons to divide and agree for them, the oldest to have the first choice, and each of my children's share remaining in the property." This clause of the will could not be stricken out without essentially changing its legal effect. The right is not given to all the children to take; it is to one or two only, and the eldest to have the right of choice. It is true that the children might have dispensed with all this by agreement; nevertheless, rights are given to a portion of them, to the exclusion of others. It is not, as in the case in hand, a provision which confers upon the children just what the law gives them without the will.

Neely *v.* Grantham does not seem to have been called to our attention when Laird's Appeal was decided. It was not cited so far as the report shows, nor is it referred to in the opinion of the Court. It appears, however, to have been rightly decided, and does not need qualification. The principle we regard as sound, that where there is a positive direction in a will to sell real estate, and it is coupled with no qualification as to a division of the property between the heirs other than that which the law gives, such direction to sell works an equitable conversion. I do not see that that this interferes with Neely *v.* Grantham; if it does, that case must give way to this extent to the later case of Laird's Appeal.

The judgment is reversed, and judgment for the defendant below upon the case stated.

Opinion by PAXSON, J.

Common Pleas—Law.

C. P. No. 1. Jan. 29, 1881.

Hurst v. Smith.

Practice—Capias ad respondendum—Direction of counsel indorsed upon writ—When sheriff need not regard—A capias against the wife charged with slander should include the husband.

Rule to quash *capias ad respondendum.*

The writ issued regularly against James Smith and Sarah Smith, his wife. The counsel for plaintiff indorsed upon the writ, in writing, a direction to the sheriff: "Take only the body of Sarah Smith."

Winship, for the rule.

The writ should be quashed, on the ground that the direction on the writ, "Take only the body of Sarah Smith," is irregular, as it should have been directed against both husband and wife.

Hawk *v.* Harman, 5 Bin. 45.
Commonwealth *ex rel.* Helen Barron *v.* Keeper of County Prison, 9 WEEKLY NOTES, 314.

Meany, contra.

THE COURT. The writ issued regularly from the prothonotary. What was added by counsel did not vitiate the writ. The sheriff should disregard it.

Rule discharged, with direction that the wife be discharged on common bail.

PER CURIAM.

C. P. No. 4. Feb. 5, 1881.

O'Connor v. Weeks's Executor, etc.

Actions against executors—Practice—Pleading —When plea of plene administravit will be stricken off.

Rule to show cause why plea of *plene administravit* should not be stricken off.

Assumpsit, against defendant as executor of

Mary B. Vandyke, deceased. The plaintiff filed a narr. containing the common counts, and declared specially (1) for work and labor, and (2) for wages for services rendered to decedent. The narr. did not aver a *devastavit*.

The defendant pleaded non assumpsit, payment, set-off with leave, etc.; and for a further plea, *plene administravit*.

Wm. Herbert Washington, for the rule.

The plea of *plene administravit* involves the personal liability of the executor; but since the Act of Feb. 24, 1834, where the narr. does not charge a *devastavit*, the plea is irregular, and should be stricken off.

Act of Feb. 24, 1834, ₴ 37, 1 Purd. Dig. 426.
Sergeant's Executors *v.* Ewing, 6 C. 75.

Horace J. Weeks, contra.

The plea is necessary for the personal protection of the executor.

THE COURT. We think that *plene administravit* is a bad plea to this declaration; for if a judgment is obtained, it will not be against the executor personally, but against the estate.

Rule absolute.

Per THAYER, P. J.

C. P. No. 4. Jan. 22, 1881.

Evans *v.* Fries.

Landlord and tenant—Confession of judgment under warrant in lease—Conditional forfeiture—Covenant of forfeiture for non-payment of rent runs with the land.

Rule to open judgment, etc.

On September 23d, 1878, the Fidelity Trust and Safe Deposit Company leased the premises No. 2302 Chestnut Street to the defendant for the term of one year. The lease provided that the rent should be payable monthly in advance, which said rent the lessee agreed to pay regularly as it fell due, or within five days thereafter, and that in default of payment the lessor might re-enter, or at his option enter judgment against the lessee in an action of ejectment, . . . without appeal, writ of error, or stay of execution, and that for confessing judgment the lease should be the warrant. Subsequently the Trust Company sold the premises to the plaintiff. On Saturday, Jan. 1, 1881 (the day on which the rent was due), plaintiff's agent called at the defendant's house, when he was informed by defendant's daughter that her father and mother were absent, and that they would send the rent on the following Monday. The depositions showed a conflict of testimony as to whether a demand had been made by the agent for the rent. On January 7, 1881, judgment was entered under the warrant in the lease, and subsequently on the same day a tender of the rent was made and refused.

L. R. Fletcher, for the rule.

This lease was made between the Trust Company and defendant. The covenant is a personal one, and does not run with the land.

Spencer's Case, 1 Sm. Lead. Cas.

The Court will relieve a tenant from a forfeiture when it is the result of accident or mistake. In this case there was not such a demand as the law requires. This covenant is an authority to a particular person (the lessor), and confers a right on no other person.

J. H. Sloan, contra.

The warrant of attorney authorizes any person to confess judgment, and the entering up of the judgment is but the enforcement of a legal right.

Adam *v.* Clark, 2 WEEKLY NOTES, 429.

THAYER, P. J. This may be a hard case, but there is an express stipulation for a forfeiture in case of a default for five days.

THE COURT. Rule discharged.

C. P. No. 4. Nov. 20, 1880.

Brooke *v.* Harman.

Judgment-note—Forgery—Adoption of forged instrument—What acts of adoption estop from defending on ground of forgery.

Rule to strike off judgment.

Judgment was entered December 11, 1876, on single bill, under seal, dated December 4, 1876, for $717.29.

The depositions taken under the rule showed the following facts: Harman, the defendant, being indebted to the plaintiff for groceries, his daughter brought to the plaintiff a judgment-note purporting to be signed by Harman. The plaintiff, thinking some acknowledgment necessary, went with the daughter before an alderman, and to the questions of the latter she swore that she had seen her father sign the note. In May, 1877, the defendant called upon the plaintiff and informed him that he had just learned of the existence of the note. "It seemed to be a transaction, that is, the judgment-note, he seemed to know nothing about; he gave that as an excuse." He then said that he was raising some money on a house, and requested the plaintiff to release the house from the lien of the judgment, promising to pay $250 when he got the money on the mortgage, and the balance as soon as possible. The plaintiff assented, and the release was filed of record in June, 1877. A few days later the defendant paid the plaintiff $200 on account of the judgment-note, and in August, 1877, $50 more. From that time he took no action until the taking of this rule. The daughter confessed to the forgery.

Andrew Zane, Jr., for the rule.

A. M. Beitler, contra.

There is no irregularity apparent on the face

of the record; the rule, therefore, should be to open the judgment, and let the defendant into a defence.

O'Hara v. Baum, 1 N. 420.
Mitchell on Motion and Rules, 74.

The acts of the defendant contradict the testimony of forgery. But assuming the note to have been forged, the defendant has, by those acts, ratified the instrument.

Garrett v. Goner, 6 Wr. 143.

THE COURT. The acts of the defendant, as shown by the depositions, constitute a ratification of the instrument, and by the operation of the doctrine of estoppel, establish its validity as clearly as if a new instrument had been executed.

Rule discharged.

Oral opinion per BRIGGS, J. THAYER, P. J., absent.

C. P. No. 4.   Jan. 29, 1881.

Howell v. Bateson.

Practice—Ground-rent in arrear—Concurrent remedies for—Distress—Covenant.

Rule for judgment for want of a sufficient affidavit of defence.

Covenant sur ground-rent deed.

The affidavit of defence set forth that the plaintiff had distrained upon the premises for rent in arrear, but had abandoned the distress and then brought this action against the terre-tenant, and further that there were sufficient goods on the premises at the time of making the distraint to satisfy the arrears due.

Cattell, for the rule.

The remedy is cumulative. It is in the plaintiff's option to abandon the distress, and proceed against the terre-tenant.

Royer v. Ake, 3 P. & W. 461.

Bickel, contra.

The plaintiff, having begun the distress, cannot abandon it without showing it to be unproductive.

Quinn v. Wallace, 6 Wharton, 467.

THE COURT. Rule absolute.

Orphans' Court.

Dec. 21, 1880.

Lindsay's Estate.

Bill of review—Act of Oct. 13, 1840—Limitations.

Sur petition for review and answer.

The petition of Elizabeth B. Craige, administratrix *d. b. n.* of the estate of J. Lindsay Craige, set forth: that John Lindsay died in 1842, leaving a will appointing Evans Rogers and Charles Waters executors, and by it bequeathed, *inter alia*, a legacy of $500 to J. Lindsay Craige. Charles Waters having died, Evans Rogers, surviving executor, filed three accounts of administration of Lindsay's estate: the first in February, 1847, confirmed absolutely in August, 1847; the second, in January, 1865, was referred to an auditor, whose report was duly confirmed; and the third in April, 1870, and confirmed in May, 1870, on the statement of Maria H. Waters, the residuary legatee, that she was the only person interested in the decedent's estate, and that she was satisfied of the correctness of the account, which statement was supported by the affidavit of one of the accountants; whereas the legacy of $500 to J. Lindsay Craige had never been paid. This misrepresentation arose from the fact that Craige had been long missing, and from the belief that he had died in the lifetime of John Lindsay, the testator, and therefore the gift had lapsed. The balance was accordingly awarded and paid over to the said Maria H. Waters, residuary legatee, by the surviving executor, Evans Rogers, and on petition he was duly discharged. Evans Rogers died in 1870.

The petition prayed in substance for a citation to show cause why the decree should not be opened, and the matter of the said legacy be passed upon.

An answer was filed by the executors of Evans Rodgers, deceased, suggesting that as more than five years had elapsed since the confirmation of the last account filed by Evans Rogers, surviving executor, by force of the Act of October 13, 1840, this Court has no jurisdiction to entertain a bill of review; and further, that even if the five years had not elapsed, the balance being actually paid over and discharged by the executor, this case was brought within the said Act.

H. M. Dechert, for petitioner.
R. L. Ashhurst, contra.

December 31, 1880. THE COURT. This application sets forth an error upon the face of the record, resulting from alleged fraud or negligence, whereby a decree of confirmation and distribution was procured without any audit of the account. The fraud consisted in a statement by the residuary legatee that she was the only person interested in the decedent's estate, and that she was satisfied of the correctness of the account, which statement was fortified by the affidavit of one of the accountants; whereas a legacy of $500 due to the petitioner's intestate had never been paid. This legacy was payable on the death of the life tenant, which took place July 5, 1869. The final account of the executors was confirmed May 20, 1870. It was not shown that the legatee was under any disability at the time of the vesting of the legacy, nor that access to the knowledge of the gift was not as open to him then as afterwards, while it was shown that the misrepresentation arose from the circumstance that he had been long missing, and from an apparently well-founded belief that he had died in the testator's lifetime.

The Act of 13th October, 1840, § 1, which gives a rehearing in five years after the final decree confirming the account of an executor, administrator, or guardian, upon a petition specifically setting forth errors in such account, concludes with the proviso, "That this Act shall not extend to any cause when the balance found due shall have been actually paid and discharged by any executor, administrator, or guardian." It declares that "such relief shall be given as equity and justice may require," and hence, as was said in Green's Appeal (9 P. F. Sm. 235), the rules of construction which have been applied to it, are such as have governed as to bills of review in the Court of Chancery ever since the time of Lord Chancellor BACON. The purpose of the Act was twofold, to make as a matter of right what had been before a matter of favor, and to limit the time within which the Court might act. The errors whose correction is a matter of right are errors of law apparent on the face of the record, or which are shown by new matter arising since the decree. The correction of errors disclosed by newly discovered proofs which could not have been used at the hearing, is a matter of discretion with the Court. (Riddle's Estate, 7 Har. 431; Hartman's Appeal, 12 Cas. 70; Green's Appeal, 9 P. F. Sm. 235; Kinter's Appeal, 12 P. F. Sm. 318.)

Three things may be observed of this Act: (1) That while it compels relief for the errors which have been specified, it does not exclude the discretion of the Court in granting relief for errors which are not apparent upon the face of the record, or where no new matter is averred. This is sufficiently shown in George's Appeal (2 Jones, 260); Bishop's Appeal (2 Cas. 470); Whelen's Appeal (20 P. F. Sm. 410). In the first of these cases, it is said: "Where it is shown an injurious mistake exists, though in part ascribable to the party averring it, we do not think the Orphans' Court ought to be deterred from its correction by the sole fact that it is not apparent in the unassisted record." "A bill of review is never allowed to stand on strict law and against equity." (Stevenson's Appeal, 8 Cas. 324.) (2) That the correction, whether as a matter of right or of favor, can be made only within five years after the date of the decree. (Kinter's Appeal, *supra*, 322; Neill's Appeal, 37 Legal Intel. 148.) (3) That "the balance found due" must be of an account which has been actually litigated. Under this heading may be grouped the cases in which it has been held that the confirmation by the Orphans' Court of an administration account is not conclusive as to matters of distribution, nor as to debts with which the accountants had charged themselves as assets of the estate. Thus, in Rittenhouse *v.* Levering (6 W. & S. 190), a distributee, who was charged as a debtor in the account and inventory, was allowed, in an action brought to recover his share of the estate, to prove that he was not so indebted. In Foulk *v.* Brown (2 W. 214) it was held that the decree of the Orphans' Court could have no bearing on the question, in another court, as to the amount due to a legatee. But these and kindred cases, which are collected in Keech *v.* Rinehart (10 Barr, 240), were decided upon the ground that the administration account simply ascertains the net balance of the administered estate which remains in the hands of the accountant, and that the usual method of enforcing distribution was by an action at common law. Under the present practice of the Orphans' Court, however, this reasoning and these authorities do not apply. It cannot now be said, as in Rittenhouse *v.* Levering (*supra*), that "the Court do not undertake to ascertain who are the heirs, or what proportion each is entitled to," because the work of distribution is now assumed by that Court and necessitates such inquiry. Even under the old methods, it was admitted, in the case last cited, that if, upon petition, the Court had proceeded to award distribution, and had given notice to the parties, the result would have been different. This was repeated in Flory *v.* Becker (2 Barr, 472).

But an accountant is not protected by the Act of 1840, where the balance in his hands has been fixed and the distribution made solely upon the agreement of the parties. It cannot, in that case, be said that the balance has been "found due," yet it is only to such a balance that the proviso of the Act relates. (Whelen's Appeal, *supra*.) We have felt this to be the difficulty in the present case. We think, however, that, outside of the Act of 1840, we have a safe standard in the limitation of seven years formerly prescribed for the issuing of writs of error, and which, by analogy, was held to govern bills of review where no positive rule was laid down by the Legislature. (See Baggs's Appeal, 7 Wr. 512; Story's Eq. Pl., sec. 410.) The effect of the disallowance of her prayer will be simply to relegate the petitioner to her action upon the refunding bond taken by the executors, which will afford her an ample remedy. (Given's Estate, 6 W. N. C. 434.)

The petition is dismissed.
Opinion by ASHMAN, J.

WEEKLY NOTES OF CASES.

Vol. IX.] *THURSDAY, MARCH 3, 1881.* [No. 28.

Supreme Court.

Jan. '80, 356.   January 7, 1881.

Owen v. Western Saving Fund.

Statute of Limitations—Time from which it begins to run—Recorders of Deeds—Liability for giving a false certificate of search—When the statute will be a bar to an action for.

In an action upon the case against a Recorder of Deeds for negligently giving a false certificate of search, where no fraud is alleged, the Statute of Limitations begins to run from the time when the search was given, and not from the discovery of its falsity.

As far as the running of the statute is concerned, there is no distinction between torts arising from contract, and those which arise from official malfeasance.

Error to the Common Pleas No. 3, of Philadelphia County.

Case, by the Western Saving Fund Society of Philadelphia against Joshua T. Owen, late Recorder of Deeds for the city and county of Philadelphia, for negligently and carelessly certifying that there were no unsatisfied mortgages of record in his office on certain premises on Arch Street in said city. Pleas (1) Not guilty. (2) *Actio non accrevit infra sex annos.*

The following was agreed upon as a case stated for the opinion of the Court: By indenture of mortgage, dated the 13th day of August, 1836, one Jacob S. Rose, being the owner of the property hereinafter mentioned, conveyed to Brittain Cooper in mortgage, to secure the payment of six thousand dollars in one year, with interest, certain premises described as being situated on the south side of Mulberry Street, at the distance of one hundred and forty feet west of Eleventh Street, in the city of Philadelphia, containing in front twenty feet, and extending in depth one hundred and forty-one feet. This mortgage was on the same day duly recorded at Philadelphia, in Mortgage Book S. H. F. No. 2, page 283, etc.; and by four assignments, duly recorded in the same office, the said mortgage subsequently became vested in Caspar W. Pennock.

By an ordinance of Councils of the City of Philadelphia, approved the 8th day of December, 1853, Section 1, it is enacted, "That Cedar Street, High Street, Mulberry Street, and Sassafras Street, shall be hereafter named and called respectively, South Street, Market Street, Arch Street, and Race Street."

By deed dated January 2, 1855, duly recorded in the same office, the said premises became vested in Robert McGrath.

In the month of November, 1867, the plaintiffs, being so requested by McGrath, agreed to loan him the sum of $12,000 on the security of a first mortgage, to be executed by him, of the premises.

The plaintiffs thereupon applied to the defendant, who was the Recorder of Deeds of Philadelphia County (and whose term extended from November 29, 1866, to November 29, 1870), to certify any unsatisfied mortgages upon the premises, given by the said Jacob S. Rose, from August 1, 1836, to September 1, 1844, the said premises being described as situate "on the south side of Arch Street, one hundred and forty feet west of Eleventh Street, containing in front twenty feet, and extending in depth one hundred and forty-one feet."

Upon receipt of the fee demanded therefor, the defendant's clerk did, on the 4th of November, 1867, certify under the defendant's seal of office, that there were no unsatisfied mortgages of the above premises. On the faith of this certificate, the said sum of $12,000 was loaned to McGrath on the security of his supposed first mortgage, which was executed to the plaintiffs and duly recorded.

The defendant's certificate was based on a search made from a private working index, compiled for the convenience of a former Recorder of Deeds, wherein the mortgagor's name appears as Jacob S. Ross. The official index, however, correctly discloses the mortgage by Jacob S. Rose.

The interest upon the plaintiffs' mortgage of $12,000 was regularly paid until the year 1876, when, default being made, proceedings were instituted by the plaintiffs on the said mortgage, the premises exposed to sale, and purchased by them on the 3d of December, 1877, for $5000, and a sheriff's deed therefor duly acknowledged and delivered.

After the plaintiffs had thus acquired title, they were notified by the holders of the Rose mortgage, that six months' interest thereon was unpaid. This was the first notice that the plaintiffs had of the existence of the prior mortgage.

It subsequently appeared, that up to that time interest had been regularly paid upon this Rose mortgage, and its existence concealed from the plaintiffs. Proceedings were then instituted on the same against Jacob S. Rose, defendant, and the present plaintiffs, terre-tenants, in which judgment was, on March 19, 1878, obtained for $5003.20, and a *levari facias* issued, under which the premises were to he sold on the 1st Monday of May, 1878, and to avoid such sale the present plaintiffs, on the 23d day of April, 1878, paid to the attorney for the plaintiffs in such suit the sum of $5051.26.

On May 4, 1878, this writ was issued, and the defendant pleaded, *inter alia,* the Statute of Limitations.

If, upon the above facts, the Court should be of opinion that the plaintiffs are entitled to recover in this form of action, then judgment to be entered in their favor, and damages assessed at $5051.26. Otherwise, judgment to be entered for the defendant. Either party to be at liberty to take a writ of error to the judgment of the Court upon this case stated.

After argument the Court entered judgment for the plaintiffs, LUDLOW, P. J., delivering the opinion (reported 8 WEEKLY NOTES, 358, *q. v.*). The defendant took this writ, assigning for error the entering of judgment as above.

George Northrop, for the plaintiff in error.

The Act of Assembly, passed March 27, 1713 (Purd. Dig. 930, 931), is as follows:—

"All actions of trespass, *quare clausum fregit;* all actions of *detinue, trover,* and *replevin,* .... all actions of account and *upon the case,* .... all actions of debt without specialty, ... all actions of trespass, etc., shall be commenced and sued within six years next after the cause of such actions or suits, and not after."

Where there is no fraud on the part of the defendant, the statute begins to run from the date of the negligence or other breach of duty, and not merely from the consequences or discovery of it.

Howell *v.* Young, 5 Barn. & Cress. 259.
Downey *v.* Garard, 12 H. 53.
Barton *v.* Dickens, 12 Wr. 523.
Marsteller *v.* Marsteller, 8 WEEKLY NOTES, 553.

Where there is no fraud on the part of the defendant, the statute begins to run from the time the right of action accrues without regard to the want of knowledge of such right by the plaintiff, and not from the time when the damage was developed or became definite. To make it apply to the latter is to alter the statute.

The right of action accrued when the certificate was given.

Howell *v.* Young, *supra.*
Campbell *v.* Boggs, 12 Wr. 525.
Glenn *v.* Cuttle, 2 Gr. 275.
Miller *v.* Wilson, 12 H. 121.

Where there is no fraud on the part of the defendant it does not matter whether the action is in assumpsit, debt, or case; the statute is equally a bar, and begins to run from the same period, *i. e.*, from the time of the negligent act.

Battley *v.* Faulkner, 3 Barn. & Ald. 292.
Short *v.* McCarthy, 3 Barn. & Ald. 626.
Howell *v.* Young, 5 Barn. & Cress. 259.
Wilcox *v.* Extrs. Plummer, 4 Peters, 181.
Moore *v.* Juvenal, 7 WEEKLY NOTES, 375.

The case of Hanna *v.* Holton (28 Sm. 338), relied on by plaintiffs, is misapplied; there was there a continuing duty down to a certain time, and the Court held that as the right of action could not accrue until the happening of that time, the statute did not begin to run until then; here there is no continuing duty, the rights of the parties being fixed at the time of the delivery of the certificate.

William Henry Rawle, for the defendant in error.

It is well established that "until the cause of the *particular action,* which the defendant sets up the statute to bar, has arisen—until the right is *complete* to institute *that* action—the statute does not begin to run."

Wickersham *v.* Russell, 1 P. F. Smith, 71, 74.
Marsteller *v.* Marsteller, 8 WEEKLY NOTES, 553.

The defendant has been guilty of no laches. Its first notice of the falsity of the certificate arose at the time of the sale. Until that time, it was not only without knowledge of the prior encumbrance, but was, in fact, not injured. *Non constat* that it ever would be injured. For (1) the owner might pay off the first mortgage. (2) He might pay off our mortgage. (3) We might assign our mortgage. (4) The property might bring enough at sheriff's sale to cover both mortgages.

So that, even if, in 1867, we had discovered our position, these four contingencies would have barred our right of recovery. For to have mulcted the defendant in damages when we might never be injured, would have been most unjust. Hence the action is not for *giving* a false certificate, but because of injury happening by reason of its falsity, and without injury the action is not maintainable.

Kimball *v.* Connolly, 3 Keyes, 57.
Planck *v.* Anderson, 5 Term Rep. 37.
Williams *v.* Mostyn, 4 Mees. & Wells. 145.
Bank *v.* Waterman, 26 Conn. 324.
Hanna *v.* Holton, 28 Sm. 334.

The defendant below was Recorder of Deeds, and, as such, was a public official clothed with the performance of special duties, among which is giving searches to the public at large.

McCaraher *v.* Com., 5 Watts & Serg. 26.
Ziegler *v.* Com., 2 Jones, 227.
Com. *v.* Harmer, 6 Phila. Rep. 90.
Siewers *v.* Com., 6 W. N. Cases, 17.

Hence, his duty being to furnish a true certificate, he is *prima facie* liable for damages caused by its falsity.

The distinctions which underlie this case are familiar, and are based upon the difference existing between torts arising from contract, express or implied, and torts for injuries occasioned by official misfeasance.

In the former line of cases the statute is held to run from the breach of the contract, as full damages can be immediately recovered, while, on the other hand, in actions for injuries resulting from the misfeasance of public officials, the cause of action occurs when the damage is complete, and the statute runs from that time, as prior thereto the injured party has no right of redress.

Bank *v.* Waterman, 26 Conn. 324.
Harriman *v.* Wilkins, 20 Maine, 97.
Lytle *v.* Mehaffy, 8 Watts, 267.

In actions upon the case for consequential injuries, the Statute of Limitations only commences to run from the time the damage is developed. This doctrine is laid down in Hanna *v.* Holton (28 Sm. 334), which decision should govern this case, and also in—

Campbell *v.* Boggs, 12 Wr. 524.
Ludlow *v.* Hudson River Co., 6 Lansing, 133.
Hancock *v.* Wilhoite, 1 Duvall, 313.
Polly *v.* McCall, 37 Alabama, 20.
Thornton *v.* Turner, 11 Minn. 336.
Foster *v.* Marsh, 25 Iowa, 300.
Angell on Limitations, section 304.

January 31, 1881. THE COURT. This case may be certainly and readily determined by mere attention to and following of the language of the Act of March 27, 1713, which prescribes, *inter alia,* "That all actions of account and upon the case shall be commenced and sued within six years next after the cause of such actions and suits, and not after." The action now in hand is "upon the case," brought by the plaintiff against the defendant, for the recovery of damages, alleged to have resulted from a false certificate of search issued by him, when Recorder of Deeds of the county of Philadelphia, to the plaintiff.

As fraud is not charged against the defendant, the case is not complicated by that element, and the action is founded on negligence alone. Under the statute then, the question is, What was the cause of action, and when did it arise? Undoubtedly the cause was the issuing the false certificate, and the right of action accrued to the plaintiff just as soon as it parted with its money on the faith of it, and, as a consequence, from that period, the statute began to run. But, answers the counsel for the plaintiff, *non constat,* that there was at any time any special damage. This may be true; but special damage is a result, not a cause, and, as was said in Howell *v.* Young (5 Barn. & Cress. 259), the gist of the action being the misconduct of the defendant, omitting wholly the allegation of special damage, the plaintiff would, nevertheless, be entitled to nominal damages. And, in this same case, it was held, that special damages, resulting from a breach of duty, do not constitute a fresh ground of action, but are merely the measure of the injury resulting from the original cause. This same doctrine was held in Wilcox *v.* Plummers, executors (4 Pet. 172), which was an action for a loss resulting from the neglect or unskilful conduct of an attorney; also in the Bank of Utica *v.* Childs (6 Cowen, 245), where the action was founded on the default of a notary in not giving notice of the non-payment of a promissory note; in Miller *v.* Adams (16 Mass. 456), where the suit was against a deputy sheriff, for a breach of official duty in making a defective return to an original writ. In our own Court we have this very doctrine restated by our brother, Mr. Justice STERRETT, only about one year ago, in Moore *v.* Juvenal (8 W. N. C. 411), which was a suit brought to recover damages, arising from the negligence of an attorney in prosecuting a claim. To the same purpose are Campbell's Executors *v.* Boggs (12 Wr. 524), Downing *v.* Garard, and Miller *v.* Wilson (12 Har. 52 and 114). All these authorities, and many more which might be cited, only serve to illustrate that which the statute of itself makes plain enough; namely, that the commencement of the limitation is contemporaneous with the origin of the cause of action.

And we see also, from the cases stated, that the distinction, which the counsel for the plaintiff has attempted to draw, between torts arising from contracts and those which arise from official misfeasance, cannot be sustained. Such a distinction is not found in the statute, and it is clearly opposed to reason; for why should a duty imposed by the Legislature be obligatory rather than one which is involuntarily assumed? Nay, a man might the rather be excused from the performance of an obligation forced upon him than from one which, of his own will, he took upon himself. Indeed, the two become equal, and all distinction disappears, only, when we consider that the statutory duty is assumed as part of the office which incumbent undertakes to fulfil. Moreover, the officer having thus assumed the duty, and being paid therefor by the party who requires its performance, the transaction, to all intents and purposes, becomes a personal contract, as much so as though it were wholly voluntary, and not statutory.

The judgment of the Court below is now reversed and set aside, and it is ordered that judgment be entered, on the case stated, for the defendant, with costs.

Opinion by GORDON, J.

Jan. '80, 336.   January 7, 1881.

Germantown Passenger Railway Co. v. Walling.

Negligence—Contributory negligence—Passenger railway companies—Duties and liabilities of, as regards passengers—Whether it is contribu-

tory negligence for a passenger to ride upon the front platform of a horse car, a question for the jury.

Where the measure of duty on the part of a passenger is ordinary and reasonable care, and the standard shifts with the circumstances of the case, the question of contributory negligence is for the jury.

Standing on the step of the front platform of a street railway car, with the implied assent of the conductor and driver, is not contributory negligence *per se*.

W., having hailed a street car which stopped for him went to the rear platform, but was unable to get on because of the crowd; he then went to the front platform, and, although that was crowded, he succeeded in getting on the step and maintained himself there by holding on with either hand to the iron bars at the sides. Through some mischance several passengers were thrown against him, forcing him off the car in front, where he was run over and killed:

Held, that, having been accepted as a passenger, it was not contributory negligence *per se* for him to ride on the front platform as he did.

Held further, that, as the facts of this case showed that the measure of duty on the part of the deceased was ordinary and reasonable care, it was properly left to the jury to say what that duty was, and whether the deceased had complied with it.

Error to the Common Pleas No. 2, of Philadelphia County.

Case, by Jane R. Walling and Joshua Clendennon, guardian of Grace M. Walling, against the Germantown Passenger Railway Company, for negligently causing the death of Bernard Walling, husband of the said Jane R. Walling. Plea, "Not guilty."

Upon the trial, before MITCHELL, J., the following facts appeared: On the morning of Oct. 2, 1876, Bernard Walling hailed one of defendant's cars at Nineteenth and Girard Avenue, going westward. The car stopped, and he first tried to get upon the rear platform, but, being unable to do so by reason of the crowd, he went to the front platform, got upon the step, and maintained his position there by holding on to the iron of the dasher with one hand and with the other to the iron under the front window. The car proceeded for some distance without incident, when, upon rounding a curve formed by the track in running from Girard Avenue to Poplar Street, several passengers were precipitated against Walling, and, forcing his hold from the iron bar under the window, he clung on for a moment by the iron of the dasher, was carried some distance, then fell off in front of the car, was run over by it and instantly killed. Several other passengers who were standing on the front platform were also thrown off. The testimony was conflicting as to whether the passengers were forced against Walling by reason of a tinsmith who with his furnace and tools was attempting to get off the car, or by a jolt which occurred at that point by reason of a defect in the track, and also by reason of the speed of the car in turning the curve.

The defendant presented the following points:

(1) The jury must find for the defendant on the evidence.

(3) As the plaintiff's own evidence shows that Bernard Walling, husband of the plaintiff, Jane R. Walling, got on the front platform of the car and stood while the car was in motion, with one foot on the step of the platform, and that the platform was so crowded that it was necessary for him to hold one hand to the dasher, and the other to the iron bar under the window of the car in order to retain his position on the car, and that his occupancy of this position in this manner was a contributory cause of his death, the plaintiff cannot recover.

(4) If the jury believe that Bernard Walling, husband of the plaintiff, Jane R. Walling, got on the front platform of the car and stood while the car was in motion, with one foot on the step of the platform, and that the platform was so crowded that it was necessary for him to hold with one hand to the dasher and with the other to the iron bar under the window of the car, in order to retain his position on the car, and that his occupancy of this position in this manner was a contributing cause of his death, the plaintiff cannot recover.

(5) The plaintiff's own evidence showing that the death of Bernard Walling, husband of the plaintiff, Jane R. Walling, resulted from the jolt of the car concurring with the crowded condition of the front platform of the car, and that Bernard Walling contributed to the crowding of the platform, the plaintiff cannot recover.

(6) If the jury believe that the death of Bernard Walling, husband of the plaintiff, Jane R. Walling, resulted from the jolt of the car concurring with the crowded condition of the front platform of the car, and that Bernard Walling contributed to the crowding of the platform, the plaintiff cannot recover.

The Court declined to answer these points except as answered in the general charge, and charged the jury, *inter alia*, as follows:—

"Now it is the duty of the carriers of passengers, such as the horse-car companies, or any other carrying company, such as railroad companies, to take the highest possible care of their passengers which the circumstances permit; and when they allow a passenger to get on at an unusual place, that is an assurance to him that he will be taken care of, and that they will guard him against accident as far as the circumstances will permit. On the other hand, it is the duty of the passenger to go into the proper, usual, and safe place, if it is possible to do so. When Mr. Walling, therefore, stopped the car at Nineteenth

Street, it was his duty to get inside the car if he could, and, if not, to take a place on the rear platform as the next best place, and not until he failed to get into the car or on the rear platform would he have been justified in going to the unusual and somewhat dangerous place of the front platform. If, however, as I have said, he could not get in the body of the car, or could not get upon the rear platform, he was permitted to go upon the front platform, then he had a right to take that as an assurance that the company would take all reasonable and proper precautions to avoid injury to him even in that place.

"As I have said, the testimony is that at Nineteenth Street Mr. Walling stopped the car, and the testimony of some of the witnesses is that he went toward the rear platform, and then came forward and tried to get on the front platform. It is for you to say whether there is sufficient evidence to show that he could not get on the rear platform. If so, then he was justified in getting upon the front. He did not succeed in getting upon the front platform, however, but he got only upon the step upon the left-hand side of the car as it was going out, and he there held on with one hand by the rail under the window in front of the car, and with the other to the iron of the dasher." . . . .

"Upon the cause of the accident it is for you to consider all the evidence on it—the condition of the car, the speed at which it was going, the fact of the turning of the curve, whether or not there was any jolt, and to what extent it influenced the accident, the action of the tinsmith, and all the other facts in the cause—to make up your minds according to your best judgment upon all of the facts as to what was the cause of the accident. If you find it was through the negligence or fault of the defendant company, then you will find a verdict here for the plaintiff; but if you find it was not from the defendant's negligence, or if it was by the joint negligence of defendant and Mr. Walling himself, then, no matter how unfortunate the accident may have been in its results to the plaintiff, the defendant cannot honestly and legally be compelled to pay for it.

"As you find in one or the other way, gentlemen, you will find a verdict either for the plaintiff or defendant. If you find a verdict for the plaintiff upon the grounds that I have stated, you would then have to consider the question of damages. That, as has been said to you by counsel for plaintiff, is allowed by law to be damages simply for pecuniary loss. Injuries to feelings and suffering by the deprival of companionship are not capable of compensation in money. The law does not undertake to place an estimate upon these considerations; but the law does permit, where the loss has resulted from the negligence of defendant, that the plaintiff shall be put in a reasonable and, as nearly as may be, in the same pecuniary condition that she would have been had no such accident occurred."

Verdict and judgment for the plaintiff for $5000. Defendant took this writ, assigning for error the refusal of the Court to affirm the points above set forth.

C. H. Gross (*T. J. Barger* with him), for plaintiff in error.

The conduct of Walling in getting upon a car so crowded that in order to remain upon the car he was forced to occupy the position that he did is negligence *per se*, and the Court should have so instructed the jury.

This case is distinguished from Pass. Railway Company *v.* Boudrou (8 WEEKLY NOTES, 241) and kindred cases in New York, in that there the injuries resulted from causes too remote to be foreseen; here the position of the plaintiff made him liable to be tumbled off at any time, and by remaining upon the car he took that risk upon himself.

R. P. White, for the defendant in error.

There was no such state of facts presented here as would have justified the Court in instructing the jury that the actions of the plaintiff constituted negligence *per se*. The habit of riding upon platforms is one continually indulged in by all passengers, without reproof by the railway companies, and as long as companies accept passengers to ride on the cars, the latter have a right to assume that the limit of safety has not been reached, and that they will be carried properly.

If the crowded state of the platform is the standard of negligence, it shifts with the numbers upon it, and consequently is for the jury.

It has been decided that it is not conclusive evidence of the want of due care, where a passenger stands upon the front platform, although there was room inside.

Walton *v.* R. R., 107 Mass. 108.
Maguire *v.* R. R., 115 Mass. 239.

The question was properly left to the jury to say whether, in the position he was forced to occupy, the plaintiff acted negligently in remaining on the platform.

Ginna *v.* R. R., 8 Hun, (N. Y.) 494.
Meeser *v.* R. R., 8 Allen (Mass.), 234.
Burns *v.* R. R., 50 Mo. 140.

January 24, 1881. THE COURT. At the outset the defendant (plaintiff in error) claims but two questions are presented in the assignments. (1) Was Bernard Walling guilty of contributory negligence *per se*, so as to make it the duty of the Court below to instruct the jury that he could not recover? And (2) was the evidence of damage too vague under the requirements of the Act of April 4, 1868, to justify a verdict for the plaintiffs below?

In fact the second question is not raised in the record. As a general rule, where specific instructions were not requested by a proper point, and no exceptions were taken to such as were given, there is no error for correction. Complaint is not now made of the charge respecting damages; the only errors alleged are the refusal of the defendant's points, and they were upon another branch of the case. Surely if the decedent's death, without fault in him, was caused by the defendant's default, the plaintiffs were entitled to recover. In a charge of marked accuracy and fairness the questions of defendant's negligence and of the decedent's concurrent negligence were submitted to the jury. It is not pretended that the Court could have refused to submit to them to decide whether the defendant was negligent, and it is conceded that fact is settled by the verdict. If it was the duty of the Court to determine there was contributory negligence by the decedent, all the defendant's points should have been affirmed. This is the sole question now for consideration—the one first stated by defendant.

The facts, claimed to reveal want of due care in the decedent, are not in dispute. "He voluntarily got upon a car so crowded that he was obliged to take a position on the step of the front platform of the car, occupied at the time by two other men, between whom he squeezed into a position, where, for the purpose of retaining his place, he was obliged to hold fast with one hand to the dasher and the other to the iron bar, under the window of the car," so says the defendant. In addition the car stopped and received him as a passenger. The driver testifies he knew the car was so full a man could not go through to the back platform. Crowded as it was, the conductor says there was room for more, both inside and on the rear platform. But Walling first tried to get on the rear platform, and failing went to the front.

Conductor, driver, and passengers acted as if there was room, so long as a man could find a rest for his feet and a place to hold on with his hands. Nor was that action exceptional. Notoriously, it was very common in 1876, and, perhaps, is not infrequent at this day. The companies do not consider such practice dangerous, for they knowingly suffer it, and are parties to it. Their cars stop for passengers when none but experienced conductors could see a footing inside or out. The risk in travelling at the rate of six miles an hour is not that when the rate is sixty or even thirty. An act which would strike all minds as gross carelessness in a passenger, on a train drawn by steam-power, might be prudent if done on a horse car. Rules prescribed for observance of passengers on steam railroads, which run their trains at great speed, are very different from those on street railways. In absence of express rules, every passenger knows that what might be consistent with safety on one would be extremely hazardous on the other. Street railway companies have all along considered their platforms a place of safety, and so have the public. Shall the Court say that riding on a platform is so dangerous, that one who pays for his standing there can recover nothing for an injury arising from the company's default?

Meesel *v.* Lynn and Boston R. Co. (8 Allen, Mass. 234) was a case much like this in its facts. The Court said: "It is well known that the highest speed of a horse railroad car is very moderate, and the driver easily controls it, and stops the car by means of his voice, his reins, and his brake. In turning round an angle, from one street to another, passengers are not required to expect that he will drive at a rapid rate, but, on the contrary, might reasonably expect a careful driver to slacken his speed. The seats inside are not the only places where the managers expect passengers to remain; but it is notorious that they stop habitually to receive passengers to stand, inside, till the car is full, and then to stand on the platforms till they are full, and continue to stop and receive them, after there is no place to stand except on the steps of the platforms. Neither the officers of these corporations, nor the managers of the cars, nor the travelling public seem to regard this practice as hazardous; nor does experience, thus far, seem to require that it should be restrained on account of its danger. There is, therefore, no basis upon which the Court can decide, upon the evidence reported, that the plaintiff did not use ordinary care. It was a proper case to be submitted to the jury upon the special circumstances which appeared in evidence." These remarks are quite applicable to the case in hand.

Standing on the front platform of a horse car when there is room inside, is not conclusive evidence that the person injured by the driver's default was not exercising due care. (Maguire *v.* Middlesex R. Co., 115 Mass. 239.) A street railway company has the right to carry passengers on the platforms, and, if a passenger be injured while standing there without objection by the company's agent, whether the injury was with his contributory negligence is for the jury to decide, under all the facts and circumstances detailed in evidence. (Burns *v.* Bellefontaine and St. L. R. Co., 50 Mo. 139.)

It has also been decided in other States, that, if a passenger be injured while standing on the platform of a street or horse car, the question of his contributory negligence is one of fact for the jury.

So little danger exists in riding on the platforms, accidents to passengers while thus riding are so rare, that this is the first time the question raised has been presented in Pennsylvania. We think the decisions in other States above referred to are sound. They accord with well-settled principles. What is and what is not negligence in a particular case, is generally a question for the jury and not for the Court. It is always a question for the jury when the measure of duty is ordinary and reasonable care. When the standard shifts with the circumstances of the case, it is, in its very nature, incapable of being determined as a matter of law. When both the duty and the measure of its performance are to be ascertained as facts, a jury alone can determine what is negligence, and whether it has been proven. (West Chester and Philadelphia R. Co. v. McElwee, 17 P. F. S. 311.)

It is the duty of Courts, in cases of clear negligence arising from an obvious disregard of duty and safety, to determine it as a question of law. This principle was applied in the numerous cases cited by defendant. It should always be when the admitted facts, or the proofs adduced by a party, conclusively show his negligence.

The undisputed facts in this case show, that the measure of duty on the part of the deceased was ordinary and reasonable care, and what that was, and whether he complied with it, could only be determined by the jury.

Judgment affirmed.

Opinion by TRUNKEY, J.

Jan. '81, 21. Jan. 25, 1881.

Machette's Administrator v. Cuyler's Administratrix.

Survival of actions—Scire facias to bring in administrator of deceased party—"Action depending," what is—Act of February 24, 1834.

The mere issuing of process against a defendant, and its return *tarde venit*, or *nihil habet*, does not constitute an "action depending" within the meaning of the Act of February 24, 1834 (P. L. 77), providing for a writ of scire facias to bring in the personal representatives of a deceased "party" to an action.

Plaintiff issued a summons against a defendant, which was returned *tarde venit*. This was followed by an alias, which was returned *nihil habet*, and by a pluries, which was returned *tarde venit*. Five years afterwards plaintiff's counsel suggested on record the death of both plaintiff and defendant, substituted their administrators, and issued a sci. fa. against defendant's administratrix, under the Act of February 24, 1834:

Held, that, as the defendant was not served in his lifetime, no action was "depending" at the time of his death, and that the Court below properly quashed the writ of sci. fa.

Error to the Common Pleas No. 3, of Philadelphia County.

Scire facias, by F. V. Machette, Jr., administrator c. t. a. of E. V. Machette, deceased, against Mary De Witt Cuyler, administratrix of Theodore Cuyler, deceased, issued in pursuance of the Act of Feb. 24, 1834 (P. L. 1833–34, p. 77), to require the said defendant to become a party to a certain action depending in said Court, wherein the said E. V. Machette was plaintiff and the said Theodore Cuyler defendant. "Made known."

From the record the following facts appeared: On July 16, 1873, E. V. Machette issued a summons case against Theodore Cuyler, in the Old District Court for the City and County of Philadelphia, returnable the first Monday of August, 1873. This writ was returned *tarde venit*. On September 13 or 15, 1873, the plaintiff issued an alias summons case, returnable the third Monday of September then instant. (The writ was tested the 15th day of September; the entry in the docket was "exit September 13." The 15th was the return day.) This writ was returned *nihil habet*. On October 4, 1873, the plaintiff issued a pluries writ, summons *debt*, returnable the first Monday of October, then instant. This writ was returned *tarde venit*.

After the erection of the Courts of Common Pleas, under the Constitution of 1874, the cause was transferred, under the rules, to the Court of Common Pleas No. 3, but nothing further was done in the case until December 20, 1878, on which date, by writing filed, the deaths of the plaintiff and defendant were suggested on the record, and the respective administrators of said parties were substituted as plaintiff and defendant. On the same day the above-mentioned writ of scire facias was issued, and was subsequently returned "made known."

On January 30, 1879, counsel for defendant (without entering an appearance) obtained a rule to show cause why the said writ of scire facias should not be quashed, which rule the Court, on March 22, 1879, made absolute. The plaintiff thereupon took this writ, assigning for error the order quashing the writ.

E. *Hunn, Jr.*, for plaintiff in error.

The order quashing the sci. fa. being in the nature of a final judgment, a writ of error lies thereto.

Good v. Ziegler, 8 WEEKLY NOTES, 190.
Beale v. Dougherty, 3 Bin. 432.
Com'th v. The Judges, Id. 273.

The Act of February 24, 1834, re-enacting the Act of April 13, 1791, § 8, authorizes a scire facias to bring in the executor or administrator of a person who, at the time of his death, was a party in any action "depending in any court." The Act of 1791 was a rescript of the Act of Congress of September 24, 1789, ch. 20 (1 U. S. L. 90). Under all these Acts the uniform course of decision has been that the mere issuing of a writ comes within the intent and meaning of the words "action depending."

2 Troubat & Haly's Pr. (Ed. 1868) 708.
1 Dane's Abr. Ch. 29, Art. 7, ₴ 3, ₴ 5.
Hatch v. Eustis, 1 Gallison, 164.
Pennock v. Hart, 8 S. & R. 380.
Gemmill v. Butler, 4 Barr, 233, per COULTER, J.

The cause was kept alive by the alias and pluries writs, though service was not made, and the running of the Statute of Limitations was tolled.
Hemphill v. McClimans, 24 Pa. St. 367.
Curcier's Est., 28 Pa. St. 261.

According to the contention of defendants in error a return of *tarde venit* or *nihil habet* to a first or alias summons ends the case, and is conclusive that no action is depending. This theory would destroy our well-established system of alias and pluries writs founded on an original returned without service.

Wm. Herbert Washington and C. Stuart Patterson, for defendant in error.

The writ of error should be quashed. The order of the Court below quashing the sci. fa. was not a final judgment; it would not be pleadable in bar by defendant to a new suit for the same cause of action.
Miller v. Spreeher, 2 Yeates, 162.
Brown v. Ridgway, 10 Barr, 42.
Wellock v. Cowan, 16 S. & R. 318.
Bossler v. Hostetter, 2 P. & W. 331.
Com'th v. The Judges, 3 Bin. 273.

The action was not "depending" at the time of defendant's death. A return of *tarde venit* to a summons will not support an alias or pluries to bind the defendant. The case is not analogous to that of an alias sci. fa. to revive a judgment, which may relate back to an original sci. fa. issued before the expiration of the five years, though not served; the reason in this case being that the Act authorizing such writ was passed for the protection of purchasers, and the first writ, though not served, performed the office of notice equally well as if it had been.
Pennock v. Hart, 8 S. & R. 369.

Here there is no question of notice to third parties, and to bind the defendant's estate it must be shown that the defendant had been made a "party" by a return of service. Without jurisdiction had over the decedent there can be no substitution of his personal representatives.
Harris v. Woolford, 6 Term Rep. 617.
Stratton v. Savignac, 3 Bos. & Pul. 330.
Atwood v. Burr, 7 Mod. 5.
Weston v. Fournier, 14 East. 491.
Gregory v. Hurrill, 5 B. & C. 341.
Borden v. The State, 11 Ark. 558.
Shaefer v. Gates,.2 B. Monroe, 455.
Penobscot R. R. Co. v. Weeks, 52 Me. 463.
McKee v. McKee, 2 Har. 237.
7 Robinson's Pr. 116, and notes

February 7, 1881. THE COURT. We are of opinion that there was no suit depending, upon which this scire facias could be issued to bring in the personal representatives of the defendant, within the provisions of the Act of February 24, 1834 (Pamph. L. 77). As the writ had not been served, no step could have been taken in it without new process and service on the defendant. How, then, can it be said to be depending? Even in the antiquated process of a writ of journey's account, which was allowed when a suit abated without the fault of the plaintiff or demandant, it was required to be sued within a reasonable time in the discretion of the justices. (Com. Dig., Abatement P.; Bacon's Abridg., Abatement Q.)

It is not necessary to say what would have been the case if there had been ordinary diligence to effect service on the original defendant. The first writ, issued July 16, was returned *tarde venit;* the alias, issued Sept. 13, was returned *nihil habet;* the pluries, issued Oct. 4, 1879, was returned *tarde venit:* then the plaintiff let the matter drop. It was not until five years after that the death of the defendant was suggested, and this scire facias sued out. We think the proceeding cannot be revived under the circumstances, and the plaintiff must be put to suing out a new original.

Judgment affirmed.
PER CURIAM.

Oct. & Nov. '80, 153.   Nov. 18, 1880.

National Bank of Fayette County v. Dushane et al., Admrs.

National banks—Usury—Suit to recover balance due on last note of a series of renewals on which usury had been taken—Set-off.

Usurious interest actually received by a national bank in the renewals of a series of notes cannot be set off in a suit brought by the bank on the last renewal note in the series. The forfeiture of the interest only occurs where illegal interest has been stipulated for but not paid.

The only remedy of the defendant is by an action of debt against the bank, under the National Bank Act, to recover the penalty therein prescribed.

Lucas v. The Bank (28 Sm. 228), Overholt v. The Bank (1 Nor. 490), and kindred cases, overruled, so far as they hold that illegal interest taken by a national bank can be used by way of set-off on payment.

Error to the Common Pleas of Fayette County.

Assumpsit, by the National Bank of Fayette County against Dushane et al., administrators of the estate of Martin O. Tinstman, deceased, to recover the balance alleged to be due by Tinstman's estate on a promissory note made by said Tinstman Oct. 19, 1872, for $5000, payable four months after date to the order of Overholt & Co., and by the latter indorsed. Plaintiff admitted the payment of interest on said note to Jan. 1, 1875, and also credits on the principal amounting to $2519.12. Pleas, non-assumpsit, payment, and payment with leave, etc.

Upon the trial, before STOWE, P. J., May 22, 1879, the only defence made was that of usury, to establish which the defendants showed that the note in suit was the last of a series of notes given in renewal of a loan of $5000, originally obtained by said Tinstman from said bank on March 3, 1870, which notes the bank had regularly discounted at the rate of ten per cent. per annum. The dates, length of time, and discount of each note were as follows:—

Date.	Time.	Discount paid.
March 3d, '70,	90 days,	$130 55
June 4th, '70,	6 months,	259 72
Dec. 7th, '70,	4 "	173 60
April 10th, '71,	6 "	257 66
Oct. 13th, '71,	6 "	259 72
April 16th, '72,	6 "	259 72
Interest and discount paid on note in suit to Jan. 1, '75,		744 45
Credits on principal as aforesaid		2519 12
Total amount paid on loan		$4604 54

The defendants presented the following point: (1) That, if the jury find from the evidence that the plaintiff has charged and received a rate of interest over six per cent. on the note in suit, and the several notes of which it is a renewal, the interest-bearing quality of said notes is thereby destroyed, and no interest can be allowed; and the defendant is entitled to a credit against the face of the note of all payments made. *Affirmed.*

Verdict for plaintiffs for $395.46, being the difference between the face of the note and the sum total of all the discounts and payments made on the loan from the beginning of the series. Judgment having been entered on the verdict, the plaintiff took this writ, assigning for error the affirmance of defendant's point.

Nathaniel Ewing, for plaintiff in error.

When this case was tried, the recognized authority, on such questions of usury as were raised here, was Lucas *et al. v.* Government National Bank of Pottsville (28 P. F. Smith, 228); and the Court below followed the principles there laid down in affirming the point submitted by the defendants. But since that time both the Supreme Court of the United States and this Court—the former in Barnet *et al. v.* Muncie National Bank (8 Otto, 555), and the latter in National Bank of Clarion *v.* Gruber (8 W. N. C. 119), have placed a different construction upon the National Banking Act. These later cases decide that the usurious interest or discount cannot be applied by way of off-set or payment to the note in suit, as was done in this case; but that where such illegal interest has been paid, twice the amount so paid can be recovered in a penal action of debt. The Court, therefore, erred in permitting the defendants to defalk from the face of the note in suit the whole amount paid as interest or discount on the loan from the beginning.

As the interest was actually paid in this case, and not merely stipulated for, it is not embraced in the first category defined by the United States Supreme Court in the case of Barnet *et al. v.* The Bank, above referred to, where the interest-bearing quality of the note is destroyed and only the sum lent, without interest, can be recovered. Hence we are entitled to recover the amount of the note *with* interest, less the credits admitted.

Mestresat (with whom was *Boyle*), for defendant in error.

By the Act of Congress of June 3, 1864, sect. 30, the entire interest is forfeited whenever usury has been taken, reserved or charged. This being a renewal note, the last in a series on all of which usury had been taken, all interest was forfeited; the several amounts taken by the plaintiff were payments on the note, and plaintiff was only entitled to recover the face of the note, less these payments.

An analysis of the decisions of the Supreme Court of the United States, and of this Court, relied on by the plaintiff in error, will show that they do not conflict with the ruling of the Court below in this case.

In Barnet *v.* National Bank (8 Otto, 555) the *second* ground of defence was precisely similar to our defence here, viz., that the bill in suit was the last of eight renewals; that illegal interest was taken upon the series, all of which, it was claimed, should be applied as a payment upon the bill in suit. The Circuit Court, while sustaining the demurrer to the *first* and *third* defences (which do not touch this case), *overruled it as to the second;* no exception was taken to this ruling, and it was not reviewed in the Supreme Court, although the opinion refers to it without indicating any objection.

In First National Bank of Clarion *v.* Gruber (8 W. N. C. 119) the question was not similar to the case in hand. That was an action of debt against the bank to recover, under the National Bank Act, double the amount of certain payments of usurious interest made to the bank within two years prior to the beginning of the action, and also the excess of interest over six per cent. on certain other payments of usurious interest, made more than two years previous to and within six years of the time of suit brought. The defendant requested the Court below to charge that there could be no recovery except for the penalty, but the Court held that the plaintiff could recover payments of interest or discount in excess of six per cent. The Supreme Court, reversing the Court below, on the au-

474 WEEKLY NOTES OF CASES.

thority of Barnet *v.* The Bank, held that only the penalty could be recovered. What was said as to set-off, in an action brought by the bank, was *obiter dicta*, and not warranted by Barnet *v.* The Bank. This Court will not overrule a long line of decisions unless compelled thereto in explicit terms.

January 3, 1881. THE COURT. This case, on the authority of the recent decision of the Supreme Court of the United States, Barnet *v.* The National Bank (8 Otto, 555), must be reversed. It was there held that usurious interest previously received by a national bank, though taken in the renewals of a series of bills, of which the one in suit was the last, could not be pleaded by way of set-off, and that the only remedy was by an action of debt founded on the penal clause of the Act of Congress. This case, of course, overrules Lucas *v.* The Bank (28 P. F. S. 228), Overholt *v.* The Bank (1 Nor. 490), and cases of a similar character, at least so far as they hold that illegal interest taken by a national bank can be used by way of set-off or payment. In a transaction like the one in hand, from the case above cited, it will be found that the defendant's only remedy was by a penal action for double the illegal interest paid, and that the forfeiture of the interest upon the note only occurs where illegal interest has been stipulated for but not paid. It follows that the plaintiff should have been permitted to recover the full amount of the note in suit, with interest.

Judgment reversed and a new venire ordered.
Opinion by GORDON, J.

Oct. & Nov. '80, 79.   Oct. 18, 1880.

Galbraith et al. *v.* Walker.

Practice—Costs—Interest not allowed in suit by sheriff for.

In an action by the sheriff for costs due him for services in a cause, interest will not be allowed on the amount due the plaintiff.

Baum *v.* Reed, 24 Smith, 322, and Rogers *v.* Burns, 3 Cas. 528, approved and followed.

Error to the Common Pleas of Erie County.
Assumpsit, by Thomas M. Walker against William A. Galbraith and Charles Brandes.

The following case stated was filed by agreement of the parties as though on appeal from the judgment of an alderman.

"The claim of the plaintiff is as follows: In No. 169, May term, 1873, of said Court, the defendant had issued a summons in partition. The plaintiff was at that time sheriff of said county, and served the writ and alias summons No. 7, September term, 1873.

His fees for service, travel, mileage, and advertising were $24 21
Interest from September 1, 1873, to February 1, 1879, 5 years and 6 months.   7 97
                                        $32 18

"The defendants deny their liability for interest.

"If the Court be of opinion that the fees of the sheriff bear interest, they shall enter judgment for the plaintiff for $32.18 with costs. If they be of the opinion that the plaintiff is not entitled to interest on his fees, they shall enter judgment for the plaintiff for $24.21 without costs."

The Court (McDERMITT, P. J.) was of opinion that the plaintiff was entitled to interest, and entered judgment on the case stated for the plaintiff in the sum of $32.18. Defendants took this writ, assigning for error the entry of the judgment for $32.18 instead of $24.21.

L. S. Norton, for plaintiffs in error.
It has never been the custom in Pennsylvania to allow interest on costs.
Rogers *v.* Burns' Admr., 3 Casey, 525.
Baum *v.* Reed, 24 Smith, 322.

John P. Vincent (with whom was *J. W. Wetmore*), for defendant in error.
The only reasons why in the ordinary issuing of a fi. fa. no interest is allowed on costs are, (1) inconvenience, (2) the rule "*de minimis*."

But when an officer becomes an actor and brings suit to recover payment for his services, he is like every other laborer entitled to interest on his demand.
Cone *v.* Donaldson, 11 Wr. 363.

November 8, 1880. THE COURT. In the case of Rogers *v.* Burns (3 Cas. on p. 528), we said: "But the Court below allowed interest on the judgment for costs. By the common law of England, this is not allowed. (14 Viner's Abr. 457; Sweatland *v.* Squire, Id. 458; Butler *v.* Burk, 2 Salk. 623; 2 Jacob's Law Dic., tit. Interest.) In Pennsylvania the same rule prevails, and the statute allowing interest on judgments is held to apply to the debt alone, and not to the costs. (2 Dall. 105, note; McCausland's Administrator *v.* Bell, 9 S. & R. 388.)

In Baum *v.* Reed (24 P. F. S., on p. 322) we said: "It is certainly the settled general rule in this State that costs do not bear interest. The best evidence of this is the universal practice of indorsing executions. On the fi. fa. or other writ, the debt is stated, followed by the date from which interest is to be computed, and then come the costs, without date of interest. Such is the mode of indorsement, no matter how many years have elapsed from the entry of judgment. Even after a revival of the judgment, the same practice is pursued, the first costs being marked as on the original, and the second as on the scire facias." We see no reason for changing the rule thus laid down. We understand it to be the uniform practice in all parts of the State, not to allow interest on costs, to the officers to whom they are due. There is no statute, course of decision, or practice, authorizing or justifying such allowance, nor is interest a natural or necessary incident to costs in any view of the subject. Of course we except from these remarks, the case of an actual payment of costs by a party. There, interest may be allowed as on money paid and expended. But that is not this case. This is an ordinary case of a claim by a sheriff for costs due him for services in a cause. The Court below allowed interest on the costs, and in this there was error.

Judgment reversed, and judgment is entered here, on the case stated, in favor of the plaintiff, for twenty-four and $\frac{21}{100}$ dollars.

Opinion by GREEN, J.

Jan. '80, 80. Jan. 25, 1881.

Bondbright's Appeal. Hough's Estate.

Bequest—Condition in restraint of marriage—When void—Limitation over—When not invalid—Distinction between statutory heir and heir at common law, as affecting validity of limitation over on breach of condition subsequent.

A bequest to the widow of personalty for life, coupled with a condition subsequent in restraint of marriage, is *in terrorem*, and void; and the widow takes an absolute estate.

But the condition is validated by a limitation over in the event of remarriage; for such limitation shows that the condition was not intended as a menace, but as the basis of a distinct gift.

Such limitation over is none the less valid because to one upon whom the law itself casts the property,—but

Semble, that this rule, as enunciated, applies only to bequests; although, what would be the case where the limitation over is to one upon whom the property would be cast by descent or intestacy at common law, not decided.

Parsons *v.* Winslow, 6 Mass. 169, distinguished.

Appeal from the Orphans' Court of Philadelphia County.

Appeal of Mrs. Elizabeth Bondbright from the decree of the Orphans' Court dismissing her exceptions to the adjudication, upon the trust account of the executors of Phineas Hough, Jr., deceased.

The facts of this case and the opinion of the Court below are reported in full in 7 WEEKLY NOTES, 559, *q. v.*

Mrs. Bondbright took this appeal, assigning for error (1) the dismissal of her exceptions. (2) The Court erred in not deciding that the limitation over in the will of Phineas Hough, Jr., was void, and that Elizabeth L. Bondbright was entitled to the income of the fund, $20,000, notwithstanding her remarriage. (3) The Court erred in not awarding the income of the balance in the hands of the accountants to Elizabeth L. Bondbright (formerly Hough) for life. (4) The Court erred in awarding the balance in the hands of the accountants to the executors of the will of Phineas Hough, Sr., deceased.

Isaac D. Yocum, for the appellant.

Furman Sheppard, for the appellees.

February 7, 1881. THE COURT. The decree is affirmed upon the opinion of the learned Court below.

Decree affirmed, and appeal dismissed at the costs of the appellant.

PER CURIAM.

Common Pleas—Law.

C. P. No. 3. Dec. 13, 1880.

Sharp v. Robb.

Contract by several owners, one of whom is a minor, to sell lands—Contract by agent without written authority—Payment of part of consideration—Subsequent sale at a higher price to another party—Tender of deed—Statute of Frauds—Measure of damages—Suit against adult vendors.

Case stated, as follows:—

On January 29, 1875, the defendants, Maria M. Robb, Ella Jane Robb, and Jane E. J. Robb, guardian of Ambrose M. Robb, with one John H. Robb, now deceased, were the owners of the store and dwelling, with the lot attached, situate at the northeast corner of Passyunk Avenue and Carpenter Street. Ambrose M. Robb, who, through his guardian Jane E. J. Robb, was a party to the present action, was at that time a minor, and was entitled to one-fifth undivided interest in the premises mentioned above. Defendants, through their attorney G. T. Bispham, Esq., had previously employed G. A. Coursault, a real estate agent, to obtain for them a purchaser for the property in question. On Jan. 29, 1875, O. C. Coursault, acting for his brother G. A. Coursault, as agent, agreed, after consultation with defendant's attorney, to sell to the plaintiff the premises above mentioned for the sum of $3400; and thereupon plaintiff paid to O. C. Coursault, on account of the purchase-money, the sum of $75. The paper given to plaintiff by O. C. Coursault reads as follows:—

PHILADELPHIA, January 29, 1875.

Received of Victor A. Sharp the sum of seventy-five dollars as security for the sale of house N. E. corner of Passyunk Avenue and Carpenter Street, the full consideration of which is to be thirty-four hundred dollars, clear of all encumbrances, in cash when the title is made complete and satisfactory to the said V. A. Sharp, he to take the same, or if not, to forfeit the above seventy-five dollars, the title to be made within two months.

$75.   O. C. COURSAULT,
216 S. 4th St.   for G. T. BISPHAM.

About one week afterwards an offer of four thousand dollars was made by another party, to wit, Mrs. Sedwith, for the same property, being an advance of six hundred dollars upon the offer of Mr. Sharp. This fact, in the opinion of the said G. T. Bispham, would have prevented the Orphans' Court, which had charge of the interest of the minor, Ambrose M. Robb, from decreeing a sale of the property in question, so far as said interest was concerned, for any sum less than that offered by Mrs. Sedwith. At or shortly after this second offer was made, O. C. Coursault informed the plaintiff of said second offer, as well as of the fact that one of the owners of the property in question was a minor. The defendants were advised by their attorney, G. T. Bispham, that it would be impossible to get the Orphans' Court to confirm the sale of the minor's interest when there was a higher offer outstanding, and that the sale to Sharp could not therefore be consummated.

The Orphans' Court, as to said minor, confirmed the sale to the second party, who had offered a higher price.

No deed was ever tendered to the plaintiff in this action. No further money was demanded of him at any time, and no deed was ever tendered by him for execution, and no tender of the purchase-money was ever made. No written authority to sell the property in question was ever given by the defendants to Mr. Bispham, their attorney, or to any other person; nor was any such written authority given by Mr. Bispham either to G. A. Coursault or to O. C. Coursault. Defendants have on several occasions tendered to plaintiff, and are still ready to pay to him the sum of $75, that being the sum paid by plaintiff to O. C. Coursault on account of the purchase-money mentioned in the paper signed by O. C. Coursault.

If the Court should be of opinion that under the above facts the defendants, Jane E. J. Robb, Maria M. Robb, and Ella J. Robb, are liable to plaintiff for their proportion of the difference between the contract price with him and the price at which the property was subsequently sold, as well as for a return of the deposit-money, judgment to be entered in favor of the plaintiff against the said defendants for $137 each. If the Court are of opinion that the defendants are liable only for a return of the deposit-money, judgment to be entered for $75.

William H. Browne, for plaintiff.

The sale of the property to another party obviated the necessity of a tender by plaintiff to the vendors of either deed or money.

Kerst *v.* Ginder, 1 Pitts. 314.

The acquiescence of defendants in the written contract of sale of their agent, together with their virtual acceptance through such agent of a portion of the purchase-money, estops them from denying such agent's power to contract for want of written authority to him, and places plaintiff in the virtual position of dealing directly with defendants as principals by their adoption of the written contract with him, and thus takes the case out of the Statute of Frauds.

The adult defendants cannot escape the consequences of their contract with the plaintiff under the plea that they can convey to him but four-fifths undivided interest in the property. The vendee can decline such fractional title, but the vendors cannot take advantage of their own wrong, and refuse to convey what they possess.

Burk's Appeal, 25 Sm. 141.
Story's Equity, sect. 779.
Harding *v.* Parohall, 56 Ill. 227.
Waters *v.* Travis, 9 Johnson, 450.

The sale to a third party by defendants, in violation of their contract with plaintiff, renders them liable to the latter for the proportionate difference between the contract price of their interests in the property and the amount actually received by them from such third party.

D. Holsman (*Bispham* with him), for defendants.

When the vendor of an estate is, without fraud on his part, incompetent to make out a title, the purchaser is not entitled to recover damages for the loss of his bargain. This is the rule even when the contract conforms to the requisites prescribed by the Statute of Frauds.

Flureau *v.* Thornhill, 2 Wm. Bl. 1078.
Johnson *v.* Johnson, 3 B. & P. 167.
Walker *v.* Moore, 10 B. & C. 100.
Pounsett *v.* Fuller, 17 C. B. 660.
Sugden on Vendors, chap. ix. § 3, note (14th Engl. ed., 8th Am. ed.).
Sedgwick on Measure of Damages, p. 184, note.
Bitner *v.* Brough, 1 Jones, 127.
Dumars *v.* Miller, 10 C. 322.
McNair *v.* Compton, 11 C. 28.

Where the contract, as in this case, is within the prohibition of the Statute of Frauds, there is additional reason for limiting the plaintiff's damages to his actual expenses, with interest thereon. To give him damages for the loss of his bargain would be tantamount to a repeal of the statute, for although the vendee might not recover the land for which he had bargained, of what avail would be the statute if he could recover the value in money? Such recovery would be equivalent to specific performance.

Thompson *v.* Sheplar, 22 Sm. 165.
Hertzog *v.* Hertzog, 10 C. 418.
Harris *v.* Harris, 20 Sm. 174.
Meason *v.* Kaine, 17 Sm. 126.
McClowry *v.* Croghan, 1 Grant, 307.
Sausser *v.* Steinmetz, 8 WEEKLY NOTES, 100.

C. A. V.

Dec. 23, 1880. THE COURT. Undoubtedly damages may be recovered in this case; but upon the facts admitted and in the absence of fraud, the measure of damages must be the amount expended by the plaintiff, with the interest thereon. Judgment for plaintiff for $75.

Per LUDLOW, P. J.

C. P. No. 3.   Jan. 1881.

Bank v. Huston.

Promissory note — Accord and satisfaction — Agreement to receive in satisfaction of a promissory note cash and new notes to a less amount.

Rule for new trial.

Assumpsit upon a promissory note for $1265.

At the trial defendant gave evidence to show that after the maturity of the note the plaintiff agreed to accept in satisfaction 75 per cent. in cash and new notes, and upon the cash and new notes being received to surrender the old notes. In pursuance of this agreement defendant sent the cash and notes to plaintiff at Harrisburg. Plaintiff never returned the new notes, nor did he repudiate the agreement until some months afterwards, when he refused to surrender the old note. The Judge charged the jury, that, if the alleged agreement was made and the defendant fully and exactly carried it out, and if the plaintiff did not return the notes, or repudiate the agreement within a reasonable time, it was good by way of accord and satisfaction, and plaintiff could not recover upon the old note.

Verdict for defendant.

G. T. *Bispham*, for rule, relied on—
Cumber *v.* Wane, 1 Sm. L. C. 439.
D'Olier *v.* Bank, 4 Leg. Gaz. 66.

George H. *Earle* and R. P. *White*, contra.

C. A. V.

January 22, 1881. THE COURT (after reciting the facts as above stated). At one time it was the law of Pennsylvania that the acceptance of part of the money due in satisfaction of the whole debt was a good accord and satisfaction. (Milliken *v.* Brown, 1 Rawle, 391.) In their note to Cumber *v.* Wane (1 Sm. L. Cas. 439) Messrs. Hare and Wallace say: " This case may be considered, so far as Pennsylvania is concerned, as overthrowing the old common law rule." In Hall *v.* Warrick (2 Am. L. J. 186), decided in 1845, Judge BURNSIDE says, this has always been the law of Pennsylvania. However, in Diller *v.* Brubaker (2 P. F. S. 498), Judge THOMPSON, and in Savage *v.* Everman (20 P. F. S. 315), Chief Justice SHARSWOOD, allude to the old common law rule as the law. But the exact point does not arise until Bank *v.* D'Olier (4 Legal Gazette, 66, 1872), and there the rule of Milliken *v.* Brown, and Hall *v.* Warrick, is overthrown.

In our case it is not. But this rule has been frequently criticised, and is not extended beyond its exact terms. The acceptance of any chattel in satisfaction is held as good, no matter how unequal to the debt it may appear. In the present case the jury found that partly cash and partly notes were received in satisfaction. The case of Sibree *v.* Tripp (15 M. & W. 23) is almost identical with this. The old note, however, was not to be surrendered until the new ones were paid, although it was alleged the new ones were received in satisfaction. It was there distinctly held, that the giving of the debtor's own negotiable paper, and its acceptance in full satisfaction of a larger liquidated demand, is good by way of accord and satisfaction. And among the conclusions arrived at by the English annotators on Cumber *v.* Wane, in Smith's Leading Cases (1st vol., bottom of page 439), " 3. An overdue demand, whether liquidated or unliquidated, may by agreement be discharged . . . by a negotiable instrument binding the debtor or a third person to pay a smaller sum."

On this authority the rule for the new trial is refused.

Opinion by YERKES, J.

C. P. No. 4.   Dec. 1880.

Coller v. Frankford and Southwark Railway Co.

Street railways—Duty of passenger railway to passengers—Liability of company for refusal to stop when signalled—Negligence—Degree of care required of a child of twelve years—Agency—Brakeman has no authority to change a rule of the company, and it cannot be affected thereby—Volunteers—Statements of one without authority cannot bind the company.

Rule for a new trial.

This action was by a boy aged twelve years, to recover damages for injuries sustained by the alleged negligence of the defendants. On the trial the following facts appeared. The plaintiff resided at Frankford, 23d Ward, and was in the habit of riding on the defendants' road each morning by a six o'clock train to Bromley's

Mills, at Germantown Avenue and York Street, at which place he was employed. The defendants use in that section of the city a dummy engine and two of the ordinary passenger street cars as a train. The defendants' train had stopped at Unity Street, Frankford, to take on passengers, and had started again, when the plaintiff states he signalled the engineer to stop, and as he did not stop, he ran towards the train, and in attempting to get on the platform of the middle car his foot slipped and he fell under the wheel, and his leg was so crushed and injured that it had to be amputated. As an excuse for attempting to get on the car, the plaintiff testified, that on a former occasion one of his fellow workmen at Bromley's Mills, who was allowed by the company defendants to act as brakeman on the six o'clock train in the morning, in consideration of a free ride, said to him as he got on the car that he was young, and should run and jump on the car. This was denied by the witness on the other side, and witnesses were also produced who testified that they had warned the boy against jumping on the car while in motion.

All the facts were left to the jury, who found in favor of the plaintiff, $4500.

Edward Olmsted, for the rule.

The invitation given by the brakeman who was not an employé of the company could not bind it. The question whether such an invitation was given should not have been left to the jury, and as there was no evidence of negligence on the part of the defendant a verdict should have been rendered in its favor.

R. P. White, contra.

The question of negligence depends upon the circumstances of the case. It was for the jury to determine what degree of care was demanded on the part of the plaintiff, a child of tender years, and what duty the defendant owed him.

Crissey *v.* R. R., 25 P. F. S. 86.
Nagle *v.* R. R., 7 Nor. 35.

Jan. 22, 1881. THE COURT (after reciting the facts *ut supra*). The degree of care required of a child of tender years is always a question of fact for the jury, and what is negligence *per se* in an adult might not be so in one of tender years. But an important question in this case is, what duty was owing by the defendant to the plaintiff. They were bound to stop on his signal, and on failure to do so, would be liable in damages resulting therefrom, if loss of employment or otherwise; but it would be irrational to say that a failure on the part of those in charge of the train to stop would justify any one old enough to travel alone in attempting to get on a moving train as a passenger. The duty to the plaintiff did not, therefore, extend to his personal safety when not on the train as a passenger, nor to his safely getting on unless the train had stopped.

The question, therefore, whether an invitation was given by the officers or agents of the company to the boy to get on, became the turning point of the case. If, on the occasion in question, the agents of the defendants, having charge of the train, had invited the boy to get on while the train was in motion, it would be a fair question for the jury whether he was justified in taking such a risk.

But here the statement made to the boy, that he was young, and could run and jump, was made at a different time, and under different circumstances. It can hardly be supposed that such an invitation would extend to getting on the cars without regard to the rate of speed, or the time or place.

But was the invitation given by any one having authority to bind the company? The brakeman, who is said to have given the instruction alluded to by the plaintiff, was not a regular brakeman on the cars, but was a fellow employé in the mill with the plaintiff, and well known to him. By the ordinary duties of brakeman he has no authority over the management of the train, or to regulate the loading or unloading of the train, or to direct the conduct or ingress or egress of the passengers. His simple duty is to attend to the brake. To permit the idle remarks of one without authority, or a mere volunteer, to bind the company would be unreasonable. Thus, in Flower *v.* Penna. R. R. (19 Sm. 210), a fireman had invited a boy of tender years to get on the tender of the engine at a station, and the boy was killed by thus acting, by the negligence of the employés of the road in allowing the balance of the train to run into the engine; it was held that the engineer or fireman had no authority to invite any one on the engine, and that the company consequently was not liable.

The brakeman had no authority to change any rule of the company or to waive any legal rights they may have in regard to regulating their mode of receiving or discharging their passengers. It was not within the scope of his authority. The train was in charge of a regular conductor and engineer, who had the lawful control of it. The question was not raised upon the trial, and the whole subject went to the jury upon the question whether any invitation was given by the brakeman. The jury, therefore, we think, had too much latitude; and, as the evidence does not establish a case of negligence on the part of defendants, a new trial must be granted.

Rule absolute.

Opinion by ELCOCK, J.

Orphans' Court.

Jan. 1881.

Davis's Estate.

Partition in equity— Intestacy — Descent— Collaterals —Half blood—Real estate —Among cousins, those of the half blood inherit real estate equally with those of the whole blood— Acts of April 8, 1833, and April 27, 1855.

Sur petition for inquest to make partition, and answer.

The petition set forth that Eliza T. Davis, the decedent, died in August, 1880, intestate, unmarried, and without issue, leaving to survive her, as heirs-at-law and next of kin, certain first cousins, some of the half, and others of the whole blood. That the decedent died seised in her demesne as of fee, *inter alia*, of certain real estate therein described, part of which she acquired by purchase, and part by descent from her brother Samuel Davis, who had purchased it and died intestate, unmarried, and without issue. The petition was filed by certain of said cousins of the half blood, and prayed that an inquest be awarded to make partition of said real estate.

Elizabeth D. Kiegel, a first cousin of the whole blood on the father's side, filed an answer to the petition, admitting the facts averred in the petition, but denying that the persons except herself named therein as heirs-at-law were such, and, without denying the alleged relationship, prayed they might be required to prove it, and further alleging, that, even if true that certain persons therein named as cousins of the half blood were of said relationship, yet they, being of the half blood, were not entitled to any share in the estate of the decedent.

Exceptions to the answer as insufficient were sustained by the Court (9 WEEKLY NOTES, 380), with leave to respondent to make further answer, which she failed to do, and an order was made that the petition be taken *pro confesso* as to the matters of fact, and that the question of law raised by the answer, as to the right of the half blood, be heard by the Court.

G. W. Thorn and *S. Gormley*, for petitioners.

The question turns upon the construction to be given to the intestate Act of April 8, 1833, and the Act of April 27, 1855.

The Act of 1833 provides, that on failure of lineal descendants the real estate of the intestate shall descend to the brothers and sisters of the whole blood and the children of such deceased brothers and sisters, and upon failure of brothers and sisters of the whole blood and their children then to the next of kin being the descendants of brothers and sisters of the whole blood. On failure of such descendants, after providing for the father and mother, it provides that the real estate shall descend to the brothers and sisters of the half blood and their issue, and in default of these, the real and personal estate shall descend to and be distributed among the next of kin to such intestate.

Thus in Sec. 7 of the Act, the personal estate, as to which the Act makes no distinction of blood, is blended for the first time with the real, and this fact, together with the omission to make any distinction, is conclusive evidence that none was intended.

Danner *v.* Shissler, 7 Cas. 289.

In Brenneman's App. (4 Wr. 115), affirmed in Hayes's App. (8 Nor. 256), it was decided that the Act of 1855 created a special class of heirs, who take in all instances as representatives of their parents.

As the parents of the half blood in the present case, being uncles of the intestate, would have taken equally with uncles of the whole blood, it follows under this construction that their shares descend to their children. Lane's App. (4 Cas. 487) is not in conflict with this conclusion. There it was said that the words in the Act of 1855, "when by existing laws entitled to inherit," were intended to preserve the distinction of blood as it existed in the Act of 1833. In that Act it existed only in the case of brothers and sisters and their descendants, and these words were not intended to extend the distinction to any other class of collaterals.

The real estate in question was partly purchased by the intestate and partly derived by descent from her brother. All the persons named in the petition are of the blood of the brother as well as of the sister. Had he died seised, they would have inherited from him as they now inherit from the intestate.

He who is to inherit an estate which descended to the intestate must be also heir to him from whom it descended.

Maffit *v.* Clark, 6 W. & S. 261.
Lewis *v.* Gorman, 5 Barr, 164.

The word blood, in its technical and its natural sense, includes the half blood.

Baker *v.* Chalfant, 5 Whart. 477.
Dorsey *v.* Vanhorn, 9 WEEKLY NOTES, 95.
1 Sharswood's Black. 220, note.

E. F. Pugh, contra.

At common law first cousins of the half blood could not inherit real estate.

Black Com. *224.

And the right must be conferred by Act of Assembly. While it has been decided that under the Act of 1833 an uncle of the half blood is such *next of kin* as to take equally with those of the whole blood (Danner *v.* Shissler, *supra*), yet the whole drift of the Acts of Assembly shows the intention to preserve the distinction between the whole and half blood whenever any degree is mentioned in the Act. Whenever there are relations of the whole blood, who are named in the Act, they take, as to real estate, in exclusion of the half blood of the same degree.

The Act of 1855 is to be taken as if it had been passed as part of the Act of 1833, with Secs. 7 and 8 of that Act following it. Viewed in that light, it will be seen what the Court means in Lane's App. (4 Cas. 487), Brenneman's App. (4 Wr. 115), Graham's Est. (7 WEEKLY NOTES, 11), Illigs's Est. (3 Luz. Leg. Obser. 102), in speaking of the cousins (or grand-nephews) being created by the Act additional *classes* of heirs, as distinguished from *next of kin*, and deciding directly, that the words, "when by existing laws entitled to inherit," are intended to preserve the distinction between the whole and the half blood.

Two new classes of heirs are established, to wit, grand-nephews and first cousins of the whole blood. In default of these, the estate descends to next of kin, under Secs. 7 and 8 of Act of 1833.

January 22, 1881. THE COURT. The expression in the Act of 8th of April, 1833, of the preference given to the whole blood, being confined to the case of the inheritance of real estate by brothers and sisters and their descendants, the familiar rule of construction excludes the implication that, in any other case, such preference was intended; while the fact that, in providing for inheritance by the next of kin, personal estate, as to which there is, concededly, no distinction of blood, is blended with real estate—the latter being subject only to the provision that no estate of inheritance therein shall pass to one not "*of* the blood" (that is, either of the whole or half blood, Baker *v*. Chalfant, 5 Whart. 477) of the first purchaser—shows, conclusively and affirmatively, that the omission in the case of next of kin was not accidental. It was accordingly held in Danner *v*. Shissler (7 Casey, 289), that where the next of kin of an intestate were uncles and aunts, they took under the Act without distinction of blood.

In the case before us, the parties claiming are all children of deceased uncles and aunts of the whole and of the half blood; and, under the Act of 1833, being the next of kin, both alike would clearly be entitled.

But it is contended by the respondent that a different rule has been introduced by the Act of April 27, 1855, which provides, that "among collaterals, when, by existing laws, entitled to inherit, the real and personal estate shall descend and be distributed among the grandchildren of brothers and sisters, and the children of uncles and aunts by representation; such descendants taking equally among them such share as their parent would have taken if living."

It is not easy to see upon what principle such a result as that now claimed can take place. Under Section 8 of the Act of 1833, which declared that "no representation shall be admitted amongst collaterals after brothers' and sisters' children," a living nephew or niece took to the entire exclusion of the children of all deceased nephews or nieces; and a living uncle or aunt to the exclusion of the children of all deceased uncles or aunts. This was decided in 1853, in the case of Parr *v*. Bankhart (10 Harris, 291); and it was doubtless to remedy the hardship of such a case that the Act of 1855 was passed.

It is a primary canon of construction "that it is not to be presumed that the Legislature intended to make an innovation upon the existing law, further than the case absolutely required. For the law rather infers that the Act did *not* intend to make any alteration *other* than what is specified, and besides what has been plainly expressed; "for if the Parliament had held that design, it is naturally said, they would have expressed it." (Dwarris on Stat. 43.) We are not left to mere interpretation, however, upon this point, since the Act, in express terms, says that the persons taking by representation under its provisions shall do so (in all cases) "when, by *existing* laws," collaterals shall be "entitled to inherit." By the laws then existing brothers and sisters of the whole blood, and their descendants, took to the exclusion of brothers and sisters of the half blood and their descendants; and by the same existing law uncles and aunts of the whole blood had no preference whatever over uncles and aunts of the half blood. In either case, the persons taking by representation under the new Act could only have what "their parent would have taken if living." Hence, a nephew or niece of the half blood, and consequently their children, could take nothing should there be a nephew or niece of the whole blood or their children, while an uncle or aunt of the half blood, and consequently their children, would take equally with an uncle or aunt of the whole blood or their children; provided, in both cases alike, that the parties claiming were of the blood of the first purchaser.

This is said by the Court below in Danner *v*. Shissler, *supra*, to be clear since the Act of 1855, and the judgment was affirmed without remark upon the point.

We have no doubt, therefore, that the children of deceased uncles or aunts of the half blood are entitled to share with those of the whole blood in the case before us.

Under the construction given to the Act of 1855 by the Supreme Court, the distribution must be made *per stirpes*, notwithstanding the fact that the parties entitled stand in the same degree of consanguinity to the intestate.

Inquest awarded.

Opinion by PENROSE, J.

WEEKLY NOTES OF CASES.

Vol. IX.] *THURSDAY, MARCH 10, 1881.* [No. 29

Supreme Court.

January, '80, 28.　　　　　　January 24, 1881.
Lanigan, to use etc., v. Kille.

Lessor and lessee—Covenant for quiet enjoyment—Eviction by paramount title—Improvements erected by lessee—In suit against lessor on implied covenant for quiet enjoyment, damages cannot be recovered for value of improvements, which lessee had right to remove.

In case of an eviction of a purchaser or lessee of real estate by paramount title, his measure of damages, under the ordinary covenants of title express or implied, in the absence of fraud on the vendor's or lessor's part, is the consideration paid.

K. leased to L. for fifteen years, in consideration of a royalty, certain ore-lands, L. covenanting to erect forthwith good and approved machinery to take out the ore, and K. covenanting that the lessee should have full privilege of erecting all buildings necessary to working the ore, and that, at the end of the term, he should have the right to take down and remove all buildings put up by him. The lease contained the usual words "demise and let," but no express covenant for title. L. was subsequently evicted in an ejectment-suit founded on a paramount title. In an action by L. against K. to recover damages for the eviction:

Held (affirming the judgment of the Court below), that the measure of damages was the consideration paid, and that the damages in this case, therefore, could only be nominal.

The plaintiff offered to show the value of machinery erected by him and standing at the time of eviction, as a portion of the damages he was entitled to; and in order to fix the value thereof, offered to show that, in an action for mesne profits brought against the defendant, he had fixed the value of said improvements at $9600, and reduced the verdict by that amount:

Held (affirming the judgment of the Court below), that the evidence was inadmissible.

Per PAXSON, J. As to improvements put up by permission merely of the lessor, there could be no question; and the machinery covenanted to be put up was merely that which was necessary to work the mine; without it, the lessee could not make the rent. He would have been obliged to put it up, if the covenant were not in the lease. It is to be observed that in no case were any improvements to belong to the lessor, after the termination of the lease; the lessee had the right to remove them. The covenant formed no part of the consideration paid for the lease; at most it merely increased the lessor's security for the rent. If the improvements were to become the lessor's property, the question would be different.

Per PAXSON, J. In ordinary short leases, an examination of title by the lessee may be unusual, but in leases of such a character as this one, title is so important that no one but a very careless man would think of renting without a careful examination. When a lessee seeks to improve demised premises, the rule caveat emptor applies; he should examine his lessor's title or protect himself by apt words in an express covenant.

Bender *v.* Fromberger, 4 Dall. 407; McClowry *v.* Croghan's adm'r, 1 Grant, 307, followed.

Error to the Common Pleas No. 2, of Philadelphia County.

Covenant, brought by J. Lanigan, to the use of H. P. Stichter, against J. T. Kille, to recover damages for an eviction from certain ore-land demised for a term of years by defendant to plaintiff. Pleas, covenants performed, covenants performed *absque hoc*, performance with leave, etc.

On the trial, before MITCHELL, J., the following facts appeared: By lease dated August 1, 1871, the defendant Kille leased to J. Lanigan certain ore-lands in Cumberland County for the term of fifteen years, in consideration of a certain royalty. The lease contained the following material provisions:—

. . . Witnesseth that the said lessor doth hereby demise and let unto the said lessee, etc. . . . The said lessee hereby covenants and agrees to and with the said lessor that he will forthwith procure and set up good and approved machinery to take out and work said ore, and that he will work and mine the same in a good, workmanlike manner, and as an open bank, and that he will mine and take away not less than four thousand tons of ore in each and every year of this agreement; . . . The said lessor covenants and agrees, to and with the said lessee, that he shall have the full privilege of building houses and erecting all necessary machinery for developing, working, and taking out the ore upon said tract, and that at the expiration of the hereby demised term, or in case ore shall not be found in sufficient quantity upon the said tract, *he shall have the right to take down and remove all buildings and machinery so put up or erected.*

The lease contained no express covenant for title. The lessee entered upon the premises and erected certain improvements. Subsequently judgment was recovered against Kille (the lessor) in an action of ejectment, founded upon a paramount title (Kille *v.* Ege, 29 Sm. 15; S. C., 1 WEEKLY NOTES, 500); and the lessee was, accordingly, put out of possession by the sheriff under a writ of *hab. fac. poss.* (See Ege *v.* Kille, 3 Norris, 339.) Subsequently Lanigan assigned his lease to H. P. Stichter. An action for mesne profits was then brought by Ege (the successful party in the above-mentioned ejectment) against Kille, and the defendant in that suit was allowed to set off against the plaintiff's claim the improvements erected by Lanigan on the property. (See Kille *v.* Ege, 1 Norris, 102; S. C., 3 WEEKLY NOTES, 443.)

The plaintiff made the following offers of evidence: (1) To show the value of the improvements as affixed to the freehold, erected by plaintiff upon the land under his lease from defendant, at the time of the eviction. Objection sustained and exception. (1st assignment of error.) (2) To prove that the defendant, in an action against him for mesne profits by the claimant in the ejectment suit, fixed the value of said improvement at $9600, and used the same as a set-off to the claim for mesne profits, and was allowed for the same. Objected to; objection sustained and exception. (2d assignment of error.)

The Court instructed the jury to find for the plaintiff for nominal damages. (3d assignment of error.)

Verdict for plaintiff for $6, and judgment thereon; whereupon the plaintiff took this writ, assigning for error the above rulings on evidence, and the charge of the Court to the jury.

S. E. Cavin and *F. C. Brewster* (with them *F. E. Brewster*), for plaintiff in error.

A. S. Biddle and *Geo. W. Biddle*, for defendant in error.

(For opinion of MITCHELL, J., and argument of counsel, see report of the case on a rule for a new trial, 7 WEEKLY NOTES, 293.)

February 21, 1881. THE COURT. This was an action of covenant brought by the lessee of certain ore-lands in Cumberland County, against the lessor, to recover damages for an eviction from the demised premises. The lease was for a term of fifteen years, and some time prior to its expiration the lessee was evicted under ejectment proceedings upon a paramount title.

It is settled by abundant authority that the word *concessi* or *demisi* in a lease implies a covenant for quiet enjoyment during the term. It is sufficient to refer to Hemphill *v.* Eckfeldt (5 Wharton, 274), Maule *v.* Ashmead (8 Harris, 482), Schuylkill and Dauphin Improvement and Railroad Company *v.* Schmoele (7 P. F. S. 271), Nokes's Case (4 Rep. 80 *b*), Line *v.* Stephenson (35 E. C. L. R. 77), Smith's Landlord and Tenant, 263; Rawle's Covenants for Title (4th ed.), 464.

So much is conceded. Nor is it denied that, for a breach of the covenant implied from the use of the word *let* or *demise*, an action can be maintained. The only contention is, as to the proper measure of damages. The plaintiff offered to prove in the Court below (see first specification), the value of the improvements which he had erected upon the demised premises, as a means of ascertaining the damages which he had sustained by reason of the eviction. The Court below ruled out the offer, and instructed the jury to find nominal damages only.

The eviction here, as before stated, was by a paramount title. It is not the case of an eviction by a landlord in disaffirmance of his own act, or by a fraud perpetrated upon the tenant. It is important to bear this distinction in mind, as the measure of damages is different in the two classes of cases.

It may be conceded to be settled law in England, that the measure of damages for the breach of an express covenant for quiet enjoyment is the value of the property at the time of the eviction. (Williams *v.* Burrell, 50 E. C. L. R 401; Lock *v.* Furze, 115 Id. 94; Rolph *v.* Crouch, 3 L. R. Exchequer, 44.) These cases hold that the rule in Flureau *v.* Thornhill (2 W. Black. 1078), that, where a contract of sale of real estate goes off in consequence of a defect in the vendor's title, the vendee is not entitled to damages for the loss of the bargain, does not apply to the case of a lease granted by one who has no title to grant it.

In this State it is settled that, as between vendor and vendee, the measure of damages is the consideration paid. Bender *v.* Fromberger (4 Dallas, 441), which expressly ruled the point, has never been questioned, but, on the contrary, has been followed in a number of later cases, which it is needless to cite. While the contrary doctrine has been asserted in a few of the States, the principle of Bender *v.* Fromberger has been recognized in a large majority of them, and by the Supreme Court of the United States. The cases will be found collected by Mr. Rawle in his Covenants for Title at page 235.

The question which immediately concerns us is whether the same rule applies as between lessor and lessee. In England, as we have seen, it does not, and the measure of damages is the value of the property at the time of the eviction. Upon this point the authorities are meagre, and by no means uniform. The true rule, however, would appear to be, that in an action by a lessee against his lessor for an eviction by a paramount title, the measure of damages is the consideration paid, and such mesne profits as he has paid or may be liable for. The consideration for a lease is usually the rent reserved. If the tenant has enjoyed the possession of the demised premises, he has had the precise equivalent for the rent; if he has paid the rent in advance, he is entitled to recover it back in the form of damages for the eviction. This is substantially the rule laid down in Mack *v.* Patchin (42 N. Y. 167), where it was said by EARL, C. J. "In an action by the lessee against the lessor for breach of covenant for quiet enjoyment, the lessee can ordinarily recover only such rent as he has advanced, and such mesne-profits as he is liable to pay over; and in cases where the lessor is sued for a breach of contract to give a lease or to give possession, ordinarily the lessee can recover only nominal damages and some incidental expenses, but nothing for the value of the lease. These rules, however much they may be criticised, must be regarded as settled in this State." The learned Chief Justice then proceeds to say, that, "at an early day, in England and in this country, certain cases were declared to be exceptions to these rules, or, more properly speaking, not to be within them: as, if the vendor is guilty of fraud; or can convey, but will not, either from perverseness or to secure a better bargain; or if he has covenanted to convey when he knew he had no authority to contract to convey; or where it is in his power to remedy a defect in the title and he refuses or neglects to do so; or when he refuses to incur expenses which would enable him to fulfil his contract; in all these cases, the vendor or lessor is liable to the vendee or lessee for the loss of the bargain, under rules analogous to those applied in the sale of personal property." Mack *v.* Patchin came within the exception noted above. The tenant in that case was evicted under proceedings to foreclose a mortgage upon the demised premises, which mortgage antedated the lease. The foreclosure was evidently procured by the lessor. The collusion of the latter appears in the report of the facts of the case, in the opinion of the Court, and is specially referred to in the concurring opinion of Mr. Justice SMITH, who said, "the plaintiff (tenant) was clearly evicted from the premises by the act, procurement, and fault of the defendant (lessor). He expedited, if he did not instigate, the foreclosure of the mortgage under which the eviction was had. He became a joint purchaser, on the mortgage sale, of the demised premises, and a joint petitioner with Dorsheimer for the writ of assistance under which the plaintiff was evicted from the premises." Under these circumstances, it is not surprising that the Court permitted the lessee to recover, not nominal damages merely, but the value of the lease, less the rent stipulated to be paid.

The case in hand does not come within either of the exceptions noted. Neither fraud nor bad faith was imputed to the lessor. He demised the premises under the belief that he had a good title. The lessee leased the premises under a similar belief; both were mistaken. The lessor loses what he paid for the property, unless he is protected by apt covenants in his title, and is liable to his lessee to the extent of the consideration paid by the latter. Is he liable beyond this? The lessee contends that he is also liable for the improvements made by said lessee upon the property.

The liability of a lessor under the implied covenant for quiet enjoyment, for improvements made upon the demised premises by the lessee, may depend upon circumstances. A tenant, who, upon his own motion and for his own purposes, erects a building or other improvement upon a leasehold, certainly cannot recover the value thereof from the lessor in event of an eviction. In such case the rule of *caveat emptor* would apply. It was his own folly to build upon another's land. It was contended that the case in hand does not come within such rule, however, for the reason that the lessee covenanted with the lessor to erect the improvements in question. The lease does contain such a covenant, as to a portion of the improvements. It provides that the lessee shall "forthwith procure and set up good and approved machinery, to take out and work said ore," and the lessor "covenants and agrees, to and with the said lessee, that he shall have the full privilege of building houses and erecting all necessary machinery for developing, working, and taking out the ore upon the said tract, and that at the expiration of the hereby demised term, or in case the ore shall not be found in sufficient quantity upon the said tract, he shall have the right to take down and remove all buildings and machinery so put up or erected."

So far as the improvements which were put up by permission merely of the lessor are concerned, there can be no question. There was no obligation to put them up, and there can be no recovery. But it is said, that as to the machinery, there was a covenant to erect it, and therefore the lessee may recover its value in this proceeding. It will be observed that in no event was it to become the property of the lessor. The lessee was expressly authorized to remove it at the close of his term, or sooner, if ore shall not be found in sufficient quantity upon the tract. We are, therefore, unembarrassed with the question that would arise had the covenant required the improvements to be left upon the premises at the expiration of the term. The improvements were primarily for the use and benefit of the lessee in his business. He leased the premises for the purpose of mining iron ore. This necessarily involved the use of the machinery and appliances usual in such business. Without them, the tenant could not possibly have made the rent which he had covenanted to pay. The lessee having covenanted to mine the ore, the covenant to erect the necessary machinery added nothing to its strength, for the reason that such erection was an essential incident of such mining. He might as well have covenanted to put on the mules, carts, picks, and tools ordinarily used in mining. The lessor had neither title nor interest in the machinery. He could not be said to have derived any benefit from it, except incidentally, as it enabled the lessee to pay the rent. The most that can be said is that it increased the lessor's security for his rent. The payment of the rent upon the days and times stipulated would have been so far an answer to a suit by the lessor against the lessee for a breach of the covenant of the latter to erect the machinery, that nominal damages only could have been recovered. If, then, the machinery was the property of the lessee, was erected for his own convenience for the prosecution of his business, it cannot be said to have been a part of the consideration paid for the lease. Not any more than in the ordinary case of landlord and tenant, when the latter for his own convenience and without a covenant erects a building or puts up machinery for the purposes of trade. In either case, the lessor has increased security for his rent, to the exact amount that property of this description is placed upon the premises.

There was evidently a mutual mistake in regard to the title. Why should the lessee throw the consequences of that mistake wholly upon the lessor? He was neither deceived nor misled by the latter. He probably examined the lessor's title, at least he might have done so, and the omission of such examination would be negligence under the circumstances. While it may be and doubtless is true, that in ordinary short leases, an examination of title is neither usual nor necessary, the same cannot be said in regard to leases of valuable ore-lands, having fifteen years to run, and when from the necessities of the business costly improvements are required. The lessee of a small tenement has little occasion to concern himself about the title. If he is evicted, the rent ceases, and that is the end of it. But in leases of the character of the one we are considering, title is of such supreme importance, that no one but a very careless man would ever think of renting without a careful examination. However careless a man may be as to title in ordinary leases, it is well to understand that, when a lessee seeks to improve demised premises, the rule of *caveat emptor* applies, and he would do well to see that his lessor has title. And if not satisfied therewith, he may further protect himself by apt words in an express covenant.

There is no case in this State which is in conflict with this view. Hemphill v. Eckfeldt (5 Wh. 274) is not in point. The question of the measure of damages in an implied covenant for quiet enjoyment, was not before the Court. In Maule v. Ashmead (8 Harris, 482), the eviction was not by title paramount, but by the act of the lessor, and comes within the exceptions noted in Mack v. Patchin, *supra*. In Schuylkill and Dauphin Railroad Co. v. Schmoele (7 P. F. S. 271), the measure of damages was not even adverted to. Kille v. Ege (1 Norris, 102) was an action of mesne profits, and raised no such question as the one we are considering. McClowry v. Croghan's Adm'rs (1 Grant, 307) is an authority the other way. That was an action to recover damages for the breach of a contract to renew a lease, and it was held the plaintiff could not recover for the loss of his bargain; that the value of the contract was not the measure of damages for its breach.

We are of opinion the Court below committed no error in excluding the offer to show the value of the improvements referred to in the first specification.

The second specification alleges that the Court erred in excluding plaintiff's offer to prove "that the defendant, in an action against him for mesne profits, by the claimant in the ejectment suit, fixed the value of said improvements at the sum of $9600, and used the same as a set-off to the claim for mesne profits and was allowed for the same." There was no error in rejecting this offer. Under no circumstances, as we view the case, would such evidence have been admissible. If we concede the right of the plaintiff to recover more than nominal damages, it is manifest he could only claim the value of the machinery after its removal, whereas the offer is to show its value in place. It is not to the purpose that years afterwards, the defendant, in an action against him for the mesne profits, succeeded in reducing the damages by showing that the value of the property was enhanced by the improvements. He would have had the same right, had they been placed there by a stranger or even by a trespasser. His defence in that suit was that the plaintiff had gotten back his property increased in value; he was not using Lanigan's property, nor his own as a set-off, but merely reducing the plaintiff's claim to what *ex aequo et bono* he was entitled to recover. Had the suit been against Lanigan for the mesne profits, he could in like manner have set up the value of the improvements as a defence *pro tanto*. Had there been a verdict against him, I have no doubt, under all the authorities, he could have recovered it back in this proceeding as a part of his damages for the eviction. But he would have been limited to the amount of the verdict, not the verdict plus the improvements by which its amount has been reduced. As, however, the action for the mesne profits was against Kille, Mr. Lanigan has no further concern in that matter, and it is referred to only by way of illustration.

The third specification has been sufficiently answered by what has been already said.

The judgment is affirmed.

Opinion by PAXSON, J.

January, '79, 179. Jan. 13, 1881.

Amanda Martin's Appeal

Distribution of proceeds of sheriff's sale by auditor—Demand for issue—Where facts in dispute are immaterial, issue is properly re-

fused—Successive conveyances of lots bound by a common mortgage—Lots chargeable by mortgagee in inverse order of conveyance—Effect of release of lot last conveyed on lot previously conveyed—Notice.

A demand for an issue of fact, under the Act of April 20, 1846, in a distribution by an auditor, is properly refused if the disputed facts are immaterial.

Three lots of ground, Nos. 841, 839, and 837, subject to a mortgage, were conveyed in the order given. Nos. 841 and 837 having been released from the mortgage-debt, it was sought to charge the entire debt upon 839. The auditor found as a fact that No. 837 was of sufficient value, at the time of its release, to pay the mortgage-debt:

Held (affirming the decree of the Court below), that No. 837, the last parcel aliened, having been released, No. 839 was released also.

Appeal from a decree of the Common Pleas No. 2, of Philadelphia County, confirming the report of an auditor appointed to distribute the proceeds of a sheriff's sale.

The fund was produced by the sheriff's sale of a house and lot of ground, No. 839 North Broad Street, sold under an execution on a judgment obtained in an action of covenant sur ground-rent deed. The sheriff paid the execution-creditor the amount of his judgment, and the balance of the purchase-money constituted the fund for distribution. Before the auditor the portion of the fund in dispute was claimed, on the one hand, by Amanda Martin, executrix and legatee of Edward D. Martin, deceased, under a mortgage of said premises, hereinafter mentioned, and, on the other hand, by one Sarmiento, as terre-tenant and owner, and by Mrs. Susan L. Morris under a second mortgage executed by Sarmiento.

The contention arose on the refusal by the auditor of a demand for an issue by Amanda Martin, based on disputed questions of fact arising out of the state of the title to the premises in question (No. 839), and the lots adjoining on either side, Nos. 837 and 841, and depended principally upon the legal effect of a release of Nos. 837 and 841 from the lien of the said mortgage.

The paper title may be stated, in abstract, as follows:—

1849, May 2. THREE DEEDS. McCloskey to Grimstone for said three lots, Nos. 837, 839, and 841, reserving a ground-rent from each.

1849, May 25. MORTGAGE. Grimstone to Farrington, of said three lots for $2000.

Assigned Nov. 17, 1851, to Spink; and by Spink assigned Dec. 12, 1851, to Edward D. Martin, the appellant's testator. This mortgage was the foundation of Amanda Martin's claim.

1849, May 26. DEED. Grimstone to Fitch for the said three lots.

1850, June 12. DEED. Fitch to Foust for No. 841.

1850, Aug. 21. DEED. Fitch to Charter for No. 839.

Sarmiento, terre-tenant and appellee, claims under this deed through Charter.

1851, Nov. 7. DEED. Fitch to Bitmeyer, for No. 837.

1851, Nov. 10. RELEASE OF MORTGAGE. Farrington to Fitch and Foust, releasing from the lien of $2000 mortgage lots No. 837 (Bitmeyer), and No. 841. Reserving lien on 839 (Charter-Sarmiento).

On April 4, 1868, Sarmiento executed a (second) mortgage on No. 839, to Susan L. Patrick (now Morris) for $1666.67.

On Sept. 6, 1876, E. D. Martin issued a sci. fa. on the $2000 mortgage against Grimstone, mortgagor, and Sarmiento, terre-tenant, but this proceeding was not prosecuted to judgment.

On June 21, 1877, a summons covenant sur ground-rent deed of No. 839 was issued against Grimstone, covenantor, and Sarmiento, terre-tenant, on which judgment was obtained, and the premises sold at sheriff's sale, as aforesaid, for $3600.

Conflicting testimony was taken before the auditor tending to show that no interest was ever paid on the $2000 mortgage since its execution, and that the assignment thereof to Martin was without consideration and invalid. At the conclusion of the hearings before the auditor, but before the filing of his report, Amanda Martin presented an affidavit and a demand for an issue to try the question of the validity of said mortgage, and whether interest had been paid thereon, but the auditor disregarded the request, and subsequently filed his report, stating therein that he deemed the facts, averred to be in dispute, to be immaterial to the question of distribution. He reported that the purchasers of the three lots, subject to the general mortgage, were in equity to be charged in the inverse order of alienation. As No. 837 was last in order of alienation, it should bear the mortgage encumbrance, and this burden could not be shifted to or retained upon No. 839 by a reservation in the release of the mortgage as to Nos. 837 and 841, the owner of 839 not being a party or privy thereto; that the claim of Amanda Martin was, therefore, not a lien upon the fund produced by 839, and he, therefore, awarded to Susan L. Morris the amount due on her (second) mortgage, and the balance of the fund to Sarmiento, as terre-tenant and owner.

Exceptions having been taken by Amanda Martin to this report, it was referred back to the auditor to report "whether Farrington, the releasor, had notice of the conveyance of No. 839 at the time of the release of Nos. 837 and 841, and if so, what was the value of No. 837 at the time it was released." The auditor filed a supplemental report to the effect that Farrington, the releasor, had no knowledge of the conveyance of No. 839 at the time of the release of Nos. 837 and 841, but that such knowledge was unnecessary, as the auditor found as a fact that William Spink was the purchaser and equitable owner of all the lots from the time of their nominal conveyance to Grimstone, in 1849, until their separate conveyance by Fitch in 1850 and 1851, and of the mortgage in question from the date of its creation. Mary Farrington, therefore, having no beneficial title to the mortgage, had no interest to be protected; and William Spink was, of course, aware of all conveyances of the properties, as he directed and procured the release of the mortgage.

The auditor also found that the value of lot No. 837 was sufficient to pay the mortgage at the time of the release of it. No change was made in the distribution as formerly reported.

To the first and supplemental reports exceptions were filed by Amanda Martin on the grounds, *inter alia*, that the auditor erred in proceeding to make his report after application for an issue; in not awarding the amount of the $2000 mortgage, with interest, to the exceptant; in stating that the notice was immaterial to Mrs. Farrington, and that she had no interest in the mortgage, and in putting an excessive value on premises No. 837.

The Court below dismissed the exceptions and confirmed the report (no opinion filed), whereupon the exceptant took this appeal, assigning for error the action of the Court in refusing the application for an issue pending the audit, and in dismissing the exceptions to the auditor's report.

Aaron Thompson, for appellant.

The Act of April 20, 1846 (Purdon Dig. 656, pl. 108, 109), relating to distribution, declares that the Court *shall,* at the request in writing of any person interested, direct an issue to try such facts as shall, by affidavit, be alleged to be material and in dispute. A lien creditor has a right to an issue, and it is not too late to make application therefor after the evidence has been heard, and the case argued.

Reigart's Appeal, 7 W. & S. 267.
Bischel v. Bank, 5 W. 140.
Dickerson's Appeal, 7 Barr, 255.
Souder's Appeal, 7 Sm. 498.
Christophers v. Selden, 4 Cas. 165.
Trimble's Appeal, 6 W. 133.
Myers's Appeal, 2 Barr, 463.

A formal release of one of several tracts of land from the lien of a mortgage, under the circumstances of this case, will not discharge the other lands from the encumbrance.

Act April 2, 1822 (Purdon, p. 480.)
Culp v. Fisher, 1 W. 494.
Crawford v. Crawford, 2 W. 339.
Mevey's Appeal, 4 Barr, 82.

William L. Marshall, for Sarmiento, appellee.

The facts upon which the demand for an issue is based must be material. A mere naked allegation cannot constitute a dispute within the meaning of the law. In this case the facts alleged, if disputed, were immaterial.

Biddle v. King. 1 Phila. 394.
Knight's Appeal, 7 Harris, 493.
Brinton v. Perry, 1 Phila. 436.
Battin v. Meyer, 5 Ibid. 73.
Robinson's Appeal, 12 C. 81.

Whenever the mortgagor has made successive sales of distinct parcels of the mortgaged premises, the mortgagee shall sell the mortgaged land in the inverse order of its alienation by the mortgagor.

Nailer v. Stanley, 10 S. & R. 450.
Cowden's Estate, 1 Barr, 267.

January 31, 1881. THE COURT. If a mortgagor or judgment-debtor has a lot or parcel of land, say of ten acres, and of this he sells five to B., the remaining five acres, if of sufficient value, must sustain the whole charge, and the part sold to B. cannot be made to contribute until that remaining in the debtor or mortgagor has been exhausted; and this rule extends to purchasers of the encumbered premises, and in an order inverse to the date of their several titles. The burthen falls first upon the last purchase, and it is only after the fund arising from this source has been consumed, that resort can be had to that which is antecedent, and so on in regular order, until the land of the first purchaser is reached, which is the last to be called on for contribution, and then only to the amount of what remains of the original charge after the lands post-dating it in title have been exhausted. And this, it is said in Mevey's Appeal (4 Barr, 80), because it cannot be in the power of the debtor, by the act of selling or assigning his remaining land, to throw the burthen of the payment or a ratable part of it back on the first purchaser. It is true, that in the Presbyterian Church Corporation v. Wallace (3 Rawle, 165) a different doctrine was held, but that case was in terms overruled in Cowden's Estate (1 Barr, 267), and the former ruling of Nailer v. Stanley (10 S. & R. 450) restored.

Precisely the same rule applies to the release of the lien of a mortgage or judgment from the land of one of several vendees of the mortgagor or debtor. Thus if A.'s land is mortgaged to B., and A. afterwards divides that land into three several parts, and at successive periods of time sells such parts to C., D., and F., and B. releases D., this also releases C., unless indeed the values of the purparts of both F. and D. should be insufficient to satisfy the mortgage, in which case C. may be called upon for the balance.

This is the doctrine of Paxton v. Harrier (1 Jones, 312), and Lowry v. McKinney (18 P. F. S. 294). In the case last cited, it was said, that the land of the first purchaser was surety for the debt upon the whole land, and by payment of it this purchaser would be entitled to subrogation, and of this fact the creditor with knowledge was bound to take notice, hence he could not release any of the primary securities and expect to hold the secondaries.

The application of this principle renders the solution of the case in hand easy. Grimstone on the 25th of May, 1849, owned the lots Nos. 837, 839, 841, and on that day executed the mortgage now owned by the appellant to Alonzo Farrington. On the next day after the execution of this mortgage Grimstone conveyed to Robert M. Fitch, and Fitch afterwards conveyed as follows; June 12, 1850, No. 841 to Robert M. Foust: August 21st of the same year No. 839, the lot in controversy, to Henry A. Charter, under whom F. Sarmiento, one of the appellees in this case, now claims; November 7, 1851, No. 837 to Peter Bitmeyer. Then, on the 10th of November, 1851, Mary Farrington, as administratrix of Alonzo Farrington's estate, released the lien of the above-mentioned mortgage from lots No. 837 (Bitmeyer) and 841 (Foust), attempting, without the consent of Charter, to reserve the lien on 839, which of course was nugatory. Finally, on the 17th of November following, she assigned the mortgage to Wm. Spink, who afterwards transferred it to Edward D. Martin, now deceased, the estate of whom is represented by the appellant. Now, as we have before us no question of notice or of the entire sufficiency of the Bitmeyer lot, No. 837, to have paid the mortgage in full, the application for an issue not having raised either of these questions, and the Master having found that the value of said lot was ample for that purpose, it is very clear that the release of 837, the subsequent purchase, released also 839, the prior purchase. It follows that the Court below properly awarded the money arising from the sheriff's sale of this property, after payment of the costs and mortgage of Mrs. Morris, to Sarmiento.

It is furthermore thus made apparent, that the demand for an issue of fact was properly refused, since, if to the appellant all that she proposes to establish thereby is admitted, her case is made no better, since the writings themselves exhibit a condition of affairs under which she cannot recover, and from which the proposed facts would not relieve her.

The decree is affirmed with costs.

Opinion by GORDON, J. PAXSON, J., absent.

Oct. & Nov. '79, 61.　　　　　　Nov. 21, 1879.

Campbell v. Braden.

Ejectment—Title by parol gift and by adverse possession—Statute of Frauds—What evidence of gift followed by possession sufficient to be submitted to the jury.

Plaintiff in ejectment showed title in himself under an Orphans' Court sale for the payment of debts of C., the defendant's father. The defendant showed that he had entered into possession in 1854, claiming under an alleged parol gift from his father, who was then unembarrassed, and that he had enjoyed uninterrupted possession for more than twenty-one years prior to his father's death. The Court charged that the evidence on behalf of defendant was insufficient to take the case out of the Statute of Frauds, and directed a verdict for plaintiff:

Held (reversing the judgment of the Court below), that even though the evidence of the alleged parol gift were insufficient to establish a good title, the evidence of adverse possession should have carried the case to the jury. Even as to the gift, there was evidence enough to go to the jury, except as explanatory of how the defendant went into possession.

Per GORDON, J. The real question is not so much what was intended by the donor, as what the donee's understanding was; what he claimed and did. Did he consider the gift absolute, and under that idea did he hold adversely to his father for the period of twenty-one years?

Error to the Common Pleas of Greene County.

Ejectment, by Daniel W. Braden against Benjamin F. Campbell, for a house and lot of ground in the borough of Waynesburg, Greene County, Pa., being one-half of lot No. 146, in the original town plan. Plea, Not guilty.

On the trial, before WILLSON, P. J., both parties claimed under Benjamin Campbell, deceased, father of the defendant. The plaintiff showed a good *prima facie* title in himself, by virtue of his purchase of the premises in question at an Orphans' Court sale, for payment of debts, duly confirmed by the Court, and a deed to him from the executors of said decedent.

The defendant claimed under an alleged parol gift from his father in 1853, by virtue of which he, the defendant, had entered into possession in 1854; and had enjoyed uninterrupted possession, by himself or his tenants, ever since. The testimony of R. K. Campbell, defendant's brother, and other witnesses was to the following effect: that Benjamin Campbell, the father, had purchased the entire lot No. 146, on the town plan, in 1848, with the intention of giving it to his two sons, R. K. Campbell and the defendant, both of whom had recently been married, and with the purpose of building a house apiece for them. The house on the lot in dispute was built partly at the expense of the father and partly of the defendant. At the time of the gift the father was in good circumstances, worth about $20,000 or $30,000, but he became embarrassed about 1875-1876, and died Aug. 17, 1876, owing the debts to pay which the property was sold at Orphans' Court sale. No deed was executed by the father to either of the sons at the time of the gift, and the witness R. K. Campbell testified on this subject that the arrangement was that the father would make deeds when they were wanted; that the witness subsequently sold his lot, and received the purchase-money, his father and mother making the deed to the purchaser. The property was assessed to the father down to 1862, and to the defendant since that date. It appeared that the taxes were generally paid by the defendant, or paid by the father and charged to defendant.

The plaintiff presented the following point: "Taking into consideration the whole of the evidence introduced by the defendant, and the proper inference deducible from it, the defendant has failed to establish such a gift as takes his case out of the Statute of Frauds and Perjuries." *Affirmed.*

Verdict and judgment for the plaintiff. The defendant took this writ, assigning for error the affirmance of plaintiff's point.

Downey (with whom were *Purman* and *Black*), for plaintiff in error.

The question is not whether the defendant made out such a case as would entitle him to a decree of specific performance, but whether he has shown enough to prevent the disturbance of his possession by the legal title—a possession taken under a parol gift, and enjoyed without dispute for over twenty-five years. In affirming the plaintiff's point, the Court necessarily admitted the competency and credibility of all the testimony on behalf of the defendant.

That there may be a valid parol gift of real estate, from a parent to a child, properly executed by possession and improvements, notwithstanding the Statute of Frauds and Perjuries, cannot be disputed. From Syler *v.* Eckhart (1 Binn. 378) to Sowers' Admr's *v.* Weaver (3 Nor. 262) this principle is uniformly held.

Aitkin *v.* Young, 2 Jones, 15.
Reed *v.* Reed, Id. 117.
Hugus *v.* Walker, Idem, 173.
Moore *v.* Small, 7 Harris, 468.

It may be that the Courts have sought to restrain rather than enlarge the application of the rule, yet all agree that in a proper case such equitable title will prevail; and when such case is presented, it is just as much the duty of the Court to submit the facts to the jury as it would be to withhold them when such facts are manifestly insufficient. In this case they were amply sufficient to be submitted.

Buchanan (*Wily* and *Walton* with him), for defendant in error.

To establish a title by gift, the evidence must be clear and positive not only of the gift, but of acceptance and possession taken thereunder. The defendant's evidence was not up to this standard.

Jan. 5, 1880. THE COURT. It may be conceded that the parol gift to Benjamin F. Campbell, the defendant below, by his father, Benjamin Campbell, was neither sufficiently definite in its terms, nor sufficiently executed to vest in him a good title to the premises in dispute; but it must be remembered, that in this State, twenty-one years' adverse and uninterrupted possession does much to cure infirm titles. Such possession is, indeed, without more title of itself.

If the defendant's testimony is to be credited, he entered into the possession of the house and lot in dispute some time in the spring or early part of the summer of 1854, claiming the property under a parol gift from his father; he finished the house, partially erected for him by his father, and has since that time, without interruption, occupied and claimed the premises as absolute owner, unchallenged by the donor or any one else. Now, Benjamin Campbell died in 1876, something over twenty-one years after he had put his son into the possession of this property, and that he did not interfere in any manner with his son's claim of title, and that he did not disturb his possession during all this time, is of itself evidence of the absolute character of his gift. But, as we have before intimated, the gift of itself is of little account, though, even as to that, there was evidence enough to have gone to the jury, except as explanatory of how the defendant went into possession, that his claim was in his own right, and not as a mere tenant at will under his father. For the real question is not so much what was intended by the donor, as what the donee's understanding was; what he claimed and did. Did he consider the gift absolute, and, under that idea, did he hold adversely to his father for the period of twenty-one years? If he did, that is a full answer to, and an end of this question of title. In that event, the defendant's right is good as against any and every claimant whatever.

The judgment is reversed, and a *venire facias de novo* awarded.

Opinion by GORDON, J. STERRETT, J., absent.

[*Cf.* Ewing *v.* Ewing, next case.]

Oct. & Nov. '80, 157.   Nov. 20, 1880.
Ewing v. Ewing.

Evidence—Act of April 15, 1869—Proviso to Sect. 1—"Assignor of thing or contract in action," who is—Supplements to Act of 1869.

Plaintiff in ejectment showed title to the premises in question in her husband, who died seised thereof, having by his will devised the same to the plaintiff. The defendant, a son of the testator, was admitted under objection to testify in his own behalf, in support of a claim of title by adverse possession during his father's lifetime. On cross-examination he also testified to the circumstances of an alleged parol gift by his father to himself:

Held (reversing the ruling of the Court below), that the testator was, in the statutory sense, the "assignor of the thing in action," and that the defendant was, therefore, incompetent to testify as to any matters or things relating to his alleged title, occurring in the lifetime of the deceased.

The provisions of the Act of April 15, 1869, and its supplements, and the decisions thereunder, reviewed by STERRETT, J.

Error to the Common Pleas of Fayette County.
Ejectment, by Ann L. Ewing against John K. Ewing, for a lot of ground in Uniontown, Pa.

On the trial, before STOWE, P. J., the plaintiff proved title to the premises in question, in Nathaniel Ewing, her husband, who died seised thereof, having by his will, duly proved and admitted in evidence, devised the same to the plaintiff. The defendant had filed an abstract showing title in himself by adverse possession against his father, the said Nathaniel Ewing deceased since 1848, and also claiming title by parol gift from his said father. (This abstract was lost before the record was removed to the Supreme Court, and no copy of it was produced or printed.) The defendant was offered as a witness in his own behalf, and was objected to, on the ground that, Nathaniel Ewing being dead, he was incompetent to testify as to any matters or transactions which occurred between him and his father during the lifetime of the latter. The objection was overruled, and the defendant admitted to testify. The substance of his testimony, so far as material, is recited in the opinion of the Supreme Court, *infra.* After this testimony had been given, the plaintiff moved to strike out the testimony objected to, relating to matters which occurred prior to the death of said Nathaniel Ewing. This motion was overruled. The foregoing rulings of the Court constituted the first, second, and third assignments of error.

The plaintiff presented, *inter alia,* the following points:—

(9) The defendant was not a competent witness in this case to any matter or thing occurring in the lifetime of his father—and the jury will disregard all of his testimony as to any matter or thing occurring prior to his death. *Refused.* (4th assignment.)

(7) That all the testimony of John K. Ewing, the defendant, in respect to his taking and holding the premises in dispute, during the lifetime of Nathaniel Ewing, deceased, is withdrawn from the jury, and is not to be considered by them in making up and rendering their verdict. *Refused.* (5th assignment.)

(8) That all the testimony of the defendant, John K. Ewing, with respect to improvements on the property during the lifetime of his father, Nathaniel Ewing, is withdrawn from the consideration of the jury. *Refused.* (6th assignment.)

(2) That the occupancy by this son, of a house owned by his father, is perfectly consistent with his father's title, and twenty-one years' possession would give no title under the statute of limitations unless the possession was held after the assertion of an independent right in himself. *Refused.* (7th assignment.)

(3) The fact that the son allowed his father to pay the taxes under assessments made to him, was a tacit acknowledgment upon the part of the son, that the title was in the father, and the statute did not commence to run while the taxes were being so paid. *Refused.* (8th assignment.)

(10) The jury should disregard the evidence of the witnesses, given as to declarations of defendant made in ordinary conversation, simply speaking of the house as "his house," or "his home," without more, and without any evidence that the conversation related to any question or subject of ownership or title to the same, as such declarations refer to the occupancy rather than ownership or title. *Refused.* (9th assignment).

(11) That, the defendant having shown by his own testimony that the alleged gift was a promise by his father, made him prior to May, 1847, to give him (the defendant) the property at a future time, and that his father, subsequently acquired title to the property, to wit, August 12, 1847, and that he (the defendant) went into the occupancy of the property without any evidence of any further promise or arrangement with his father, but with his permission, on the 1st of April, 1848, and remained in the property thereafter with his father's permission, and his father paying the taxes, he is in law presumed under this state of facts to have held the possession under his father. *Refused.* (10th assignment.)

The defendant presented no points.
The Court charged the jury that, if they believed the testimony of defendant, the verdict should be for the defendant.

Verdict for defendant, and judgment thereon. The plaintiff took this writ, assigning for error the admission of the defendant as a witness, and the answers to points as above stated.

W. H. Coldren and *M. A. Woodward*, for plaintiff in error.

All the material testimony of the defendant related to what was done by or between himself and his father, during the latter's lifetime. His claim rests on the double ground of a parol gift and adverse possession under it. He claims adversely to the devisee under his father's will. All the facts testified to would have been capable of explanation or contradiction by his father were he alive. Under all the authorities the defendant was within the proviso to the first section of the Act of April 15, 1869 (P. L. 30), which declares that parties shall not be permitted to testify (*inter alia*), "where the assignor of the thing or contract in action is dead." The "assignor," etc., in the statutory sense, is judicially defined to be, "he whose rights therein or thereunder, at or before the time of his decease, passed by his own act or by law to a party in the action," and Nathaniel Ewing clearly comes within this definition.

Karns *v.* Tanner, 16 Sm. 297.
Hess *v.* Gourley, 8 Nor. 195.
Hanna *v.* Wray, 27 Sm. 27.
Gardner *v.* M'Lallen, 29 Sm. 403.
Taylor *v.* Kelly, 30 Sm. 95.
Evans *v.* Reed, 3 Nor. 254.
Long *v.* Spencer, 28 Sm. 303.
Standbridge *v.* Catanach, 2 Nor. 368.

The Court should have affirmed our 2d, 3d, and 9th points (7th, 8th, and 9th specifications of error).

Poorman *v.* Kilgore, 2 Cas. 372.
Cox *v.* Cox, 2 Cas. 375.
Harris *v.* Richey, 6 Sm. 398.
Ackerman *v.* Fisher, 7 Sm. 459.
Collins *v.* Collins, 2 Grant, 120.
Bishop *v.* Lee, 3 Barr, 217.
Bannon *v.* Brandon, 10 Cas. 267.

It was error also to refuse our 11th point. Where a parol gift of land can be supported, it must be a positive, absolute, and present gift, to take effect at once, and possession must be taken because of and upon the gift. A possession taken in subordination to the title of another is presumed to continue.

Hood *v.* Hood, 2 Grant, 229.
Hart *v.* Carroll, 4 Nor. 510.
McClure *v.* McClure, 1 Barr, 378.
McKowen *v.* McDonald, 7 Wr. 444.
Moore *v.* Small, 7 Har. 467.

W. H. Playford (*Edward Campbell* with him), for defendant in error.

The defendant was properly admitted to testify to the facts of his *adverse possession*, which was no more adverse to his father than it was to all the world. No evidence *in chief* was given by him as to anything that occurred between him and his father; all such testimony was forced out by the plaintiff on cross-examination, against the wish of defendant and his counsel. A party may not compel a witness to testify to incompetent evidence in the hope of hearing something to his satisfaction, and when he finds it to his disadvantage assign the admission for error. The plaintiff thereby waived objection, and made the witness competent.

Pattison *v.* Armstrong, 24 Sm. 476.

The refusal of plaintiff's 11th point was correct under—

Campbell *v.* Braden, O. & N., '79, 61 [*ante*, p. 487].
Sumner *v.* Murphy, 2 Hill (S. C.), 488.

January 3, 1881. THE COURT. The contention involved in several of the specifications of error is, that the defendant was an incompetent witness to prove anything that occurred in the lifetime of his father, respecting the possession or ownership of the lot in controversy. It is claimed that in the statutory sense of the term, his father, under whose will the plaintiff claims title, was her assignor, and therefore defendant was incompetent.

The Act of April 15, 1869, declares in general terms that "no interest nor policy of law shall exclude a party or person from being a witness in any civil proceeding." The rule thus established, as a substitute for that of the common law, is undoubtedly broad enough to embrace the defendant; but the Act, restrained as it is by the terms of the *proviso*, does not apply to certain persons and actions therein particularly designated, and hence the common law rules of evidence are still in force as to the persons and actions thus excluded from the operation of the Act. It is provided that the Act shall not alter the then existing law so as to allow husband and wife to testify against each other, nor counsel to testify to the confidential communications of his client, and that it "shall not apply to actions by or against executors, administrators, or guardians, nor where the assignor of the thing or contract in action may be dead, excepting in issues and inquiries *devisavit vel non*, and others respecting the right of such deceased owner, between parties claiming such right by devolution on the death of such owner." Some of these provisions have been somewhat modified by subsequent legislation. The Act of March 4, 1870, authorizes both husband and wife to testify "in his or her own behalf in any proceeding for a divorce, in every case where personal service of the subpœna is made on the opposite party, or said party appears and defends." By the Act of April 9, 1870, it is provided that "in all actions and civil proceedings . . . by or against executors, administrators, or guardians, or in actions where the assignor of the thing or contract in action may be dead, no interest or policy of law shall exclude any party to the record from testifying to matters occurring since the death of the person whose estate, through a legal representative, is a party to the record." The supplement of June 8, 1874, enlarges the scope of the proviso, by declaring that the Act "shall not apply to actions by or against committees of lunatics, except as to matters occurring after the appointment of said committee; and the Act of May 25, 1878, provides, "That in all civil proceedings in law and equity, . . . by or against surviving partners, no interest or policy of law shall exclude any party to the record from testifying to matters having occurred between the surviving partners and the adverse party on the record."

Several of these provisions have no direct bearing on the precise question under consideration, but they are here noticed for the purpose of better bringing into view the general scope and spirit of the Act. While the legislative purpose to establish a new rule of evidence is clearly expressed, the intention to exclude from its operation certain persons, disqualified on grounds of public policy, and cases in which inequality and consequent undue advantage would otherwise result, is equally manifest.

One of the evident purposes of the proviso was to exclude certain cases in which it was impossible for the opposing parties to be placed on a footing of substantial equality in regard to testifying. In general, where parties have dealt together, or have sustained relations to each other out of which rights and obligations have sprung, each may be supposed to have an equal knowledge of the transaction or of the relations existing between them, and both, if living and of sound mind, are permitted to testify; but if death or insanity has precluded one of them from testifying, the other is not entitled to the undue advantage of being a witness in his own case. The spirit of equality which pervades the Act, forbids the application of the new rule in actions where the rights of a deceased person or a lunatic are represented by one of the parties, except as to matters occurring since the death of such person, or the appointment of the committee of such lunatic, and matters between surviving partners and the adverse party on the record. (Hess *v.* Gourley, 8 Norris, 195.) In that case it is said: "In determining the competency of a witness to prove a matter which occurred during the life of a decedent, the inquiry is whether the action is within the statute. This is not difficult when the suit is by or against an executor, administrator, or guardian in his representative capacity. Nor is it in other cases, if the spirit of the statute be kept in view, and the persons intended by the word *assignor* be learned from the context rather than its technical definition."

The defendant was undoubtedly competent to prove anything that occurred after the decease of his father, the plaintiff's testator; but, was he competent to prove what occurred before? He undoubtedly was, unless the action was one of those to which the *proviso* declares the Act shall not apply, for example, "where the assignor of the thing or contract may be dead." If, in the statutory sense, the plaintiff's devisor was her assignor of the lot in controversy, then by the very terms of the proviso the Act did not apply, and the defendant was therefore incompetent to prove any fact or circumstance that occurred in the lifetime of his father, tending to show that he acquired and held possession of the lot, either adversely to him, or as his donee. This must be determined by the nature and character of the claim and defence, as disclosed by the testimony. The plaintiff, claiming as devisee under the will of her husband, proved that he acquired the title by deed of conveyance from Benjamin Hayden, in August, 1847, and in connection therewith gave in evidence the will, duly probated in February, 1874, by which the property was devised to her in fee. The chain of title thus exhibited gave her a clear *prima facie* right of possession. On the other hand, the defendant, not questioning the goodness of the title acquired by his father in 1847, claimed under the Statute of Limitations, alleging "that he went into possession of the lot in dispute in the spring of 1848, claiming it as his own; that he occupied and held it as such from that time until the bringing of this action in 1879; that from time to time he made valuable improvements, and in the mean time his ownership had never been disputed by any one." He was called as a witness in his own behalf, and under a general objection and exception to his competency, on the ground that the plaintiff's devisor was dead, he was permitted to testify substantially as above stated. In doing so, he refrained from testifying in chief to any understanding or transaction between himself and his father in relation to the property; but, on cross-examination, the fact was elicited that he went into possession in 1848, in pursuance of a parol gift from his father, and ever since had claimed the property as his own. His testimony as to the inception of his claim, and the character of his possession for a period of nearly thirty years, was clear and positive, and under the charge of the learned Judge must have satisfied the jury that his title under the statute, by adverse possession, was complete. If, under a proper construction of the Act, he was incompetent to prove what occurred in the lifetime of his father, it may be his misfortune; but the real or supposed hardship of any particular case cannot be considered in construing the statute.

In view of the evidence, showing distinctly the position in which the parties stood with reference to the title, the language of the proviso, as well as the spirit of the Act, and the construction it has heretofore received, we are clearly of opinion that the testator must be regarded as the assignor of the plaintiff within the fair intendment and meaning of the Act. As was said in Hess *v.* Gourley, *supra:* "In the statutory sense the assignor of the thing or contract is he whose rights therein or thereunder, at or before the time of his decease, passed by his own act, or by law, to a party in the action." The title which the testator had to the lot in controversy, at the time of his decease, passed then by his will to the plaintiff, by whom the same title is now represented in this action. He was, therefore, in the proper sense of the term, the assignor of the thing in action. The case was one of the class which is excepted from the operation of the general rule of evidence prescribed by the Act of 1869, and the defendant was therefore clearly incompetent to prove the facts and circumstances to which he testified as having occurred in the lifetime of his father, in relation to the ownership and possession of the lot. He was adversary to the deceased assignor, whose title, represented by the plaintiff in the action, his testimony tended strongly to defeat. The first six specifications of error are sustained.

In view of the nature of the defence that was interposed, we cannot say there was error in refusing to charge as complained of in the remaining assignments. The defendant did not rely on the alleged parol gift, except for the purpose of establishing the adverse character of his possession. His defence was that he went into possession in 1848, claiming the property in his own right, and not in subordination to his father's title, and continued so to hold it until his title under the Statute of Limitations was complete. Any fact or circumstance tending to show that defendant's possession was adverse, was proper for the consideration of the jury. As was said in Campbell *v.* Braden [reported *ante,* p. 487], "The real question in such case is, not so much what was intended by the donor, as what the donee's understanding was; what he claimed; what he did. Did he consider the gift absolutely to his father?" This was substantially the question that was submitted to the jury, under the defendant's testimony and other evidence in the case. The learned Judge instructed them, that, if the evidence as to the nature and character of the possession claimed by the defendant was so clear and satisfactory as to convince them of its truth, their verdict should be in favor of the defendant. The error, as we have seen, was in permitting defendant to testify to what occurred during his father's lifetime, and in submitting this testimony to the jury. If he had been a competent witness generally, there would have been no error of which the plaintiff would have had just reason to complain.

Judgment reversed, and a *venire facias de novo* awarded.

Opinion by STERRETT, J. SHARSWOOD, C. J., absent.

Jan. '81.   March 3, 1881.
Dietrich v. Addams.

Errors and appeals—Practice—Assignments of error to the admission or rejection of evidence—Rules XII. and XXIV.—Failure to assign errors in accordance with—Non pros, when entered.

The requisites of Rule XXIV. of the Supreme Court, in relation to the proper assignment of errors to the admission or rejection of evidence, must be complied with, and upon failure to do so, the Court will of its own motion enter a non pros.

Error to the Common Pleas of Berks County.
Scire facias sur mortgage.

Plaintiff in error (the defendant below) filed of record *seriatim* the various offers of evidence made by him, which were objected to, and rejected by the Court upon the trial of the cause; he also filed the following as his specifications of error.

1. The Court erred in rejecting the evidence contained in defendant's first offer.
2. The Court erred in rejecting the evidence contained in defendant's second offer.
3. The Court erred in rejecting the evidence contained in defendant's third offer.
4. The Court erred in rejecting the evidence contained in defendant's fourth offer.
5. The Court erred in directing the jury to give a verdict for the plaintiff for the whole amount of the mortgage.

The offers of evidence were printed in full in the paper-book of plaintiff in error, and also the specifications of error as above set forth.

The Court, on examination of the paper-book, declined to hear counsel, and of its own motion entered a non pros. Counsel for plaintiff in error asked leave to amend at bar, which was not granted.

SHARSWOOD, C. J., in entering the judgment said: The assignments of error are not in the form required by our rule. The offers of testimony, which were the subject of the rulings of the Court below now complained of, are simply referred to, instead of being quoted at length, in the specifications of error. We have frequently overlooked such irregularities, and permitted amendments at bar, but it is bad practice. Apart from the inconvenience to the Court of having to hunt through the paper-book for the testimony excepted to, there would remain nothing upon the record of this Court, when the record is returned to the Court below, to show the real questions raised for our decision. We think the time has come when we must insist upon compliance with our rules relating to assignments of error and to the preparation of paper-books.

[RULE XII. In all cases brought into this Court by writ of error, the counsel for the plaintiff in error shall, on or before the third day of the term to which the writ is returnable, specify in writing the particular errors which he assigns, and file the same in the prothonotary's office; and on failure so to do, the Court may non pros the writ.

RULE XXII. Each error relied on must be specified particularly, and by itself. If any specification embrace more than one point, or refer to more than one bill of exceptions, or raise more than one distinct question, it shall be considered a waiver of all the errors so alleged.

RULE XXIII. When the error assigned is to the charge of the Court, or to answer to points, the part of the charge or the points referred to must be quoted *totidem verbis* in the specification.

RULE XXIV. When the error assigned is to the admission or rejection of evidence, the specification must quote the full substance of the bill of exceptions, or copy the bill in immediate connection with the specification. When error is to the admission or rejection of a writing, a full copy of the writing must be printed in the paper-book. Any assignment of error not according to this and the last rule will be held the same as none.

See Rules of Supreme Court, 2 WEEKLY NOTES, 249.]

Jan. '79, 197.   March 5, 1880.

Naftzinger v. Roth.

Equity—Equitable remedies through common law procedure—Conditional verdict—Specific performance of verbal agreement to convey land—When not enforced in assumpsit for the value of improvements—Burden of proof on plaintiff to show performance and breach by defendant.

Plaintiff in assumpsit is not entitled to a conditional verdict to enforce specific performance of a verbal agreement to convey land unless he clearly proves a strict compliance with all of the terms of the agreement on his own part.

Assumpsit will not lie to recover the value of improvements made upon the defendant's land when the plaintiff is in the uninterrupted enjoyment of the improvements and land appurtenant thereto.

In assumpsit by A. against B. to recover the value of improvements made upon B.'s land, A.'s evidence showed that he had entered into a verbal agreement with B. to erect a dwelling-house and blacksmith shop upon B.'s land for his (A.'s) use, and to board and lodge B., and to pay him the interest upon $1500; in consideration of which B. was to convey or devise the land to A. in fee so that it should vest in him after B.'s death; all of which agreement was to be reduced to writing. B.'s version of the agreement differed materially from this. After some time B. notified A. to quit all of the land except that necessary for the use of the buildings, but A. remained in possession of the improvements and profits on the land up to the time of trial; and had paid no interest to B. who had refused board and lodging. Neither party had ever tendered or demanded a written agreement;

Held, that the jury should have been directed to find for the defendant.

Error to the Common Pleas of Berks County.

Assumpsit, by Daniel Roth against Philip Naftzinger for breach of a verbal contract by the defendant to convey certain land to the plaintiff.

Upon the trial, before SASSAMAN, J., the plaintiff testified : " I am a blacksmith, am nephew of defendant. He lived in the spring-house upon his property. I made an agreement with Naftzinger in the spring of 1871. He said he was old : could no longer work ; I should move to his property; build house, barn, and blacksmith shop; he wanted to live on the premises and if I lived longer than he I should have the property ; he said he must live on the land, but if we could not live together and were quarrelsome, he would move away and I must pay him the interest of $1500 as long as he lived.

"This was the agreement and upon this I built. In the first place the agreement was he should not live with me because it would cost too much for building for the first few years. He had money himself, and it cost me too much to build ; then I should board him. He had reserved for him a room in the new house. Under this agreement I built on the premises and I wanted to give him the board right away ; he didn't take it long. I built house, stable, and blacksmith shop ; made garden fences, put lime on land, and planted trees. . . . . If I had to pay for boarding to work hands and money expended it would be about $3000. . . . In November, 1872, I went into possession of this new house, November 13th ; I commenced building in the spring of 1872. . . . Naftzinger lived with me one and one-half years, as near as I can say; so long I furnished the boarding. He left in October, 1874, I think, as near as I know. He said the boarding was not good enough for him. . . . . In the beginning it was said there should be papers made. After I had the house up partly, the people got talking about my putting up the house without papers; I told him, he said he would have it written ; but he would not die that week and asked me to see Esquire Haak. I saw Esquire Haak ; he did not do it ; then after that he said no more about it ; this was before I lived there ; he boarded with me ; the papers were not begun to draw up."

On cross-examination he said, "The understanding was that Naftzinger was to board with me and have the interest from me of $1500 at the same time. . . . . I paid no interest on the $1500. Until the agreement is finished I do not think I owe any ; since October, 1873, I had the income of the place ; . . can't say when we first spoke of a writing, but it was during the winter before building. After the building was up and under—I think the plasterers in—I spoke to him about the writing. . .

During the winter it was often spoken of, perhaps three or four times spoken about putting it in writing; but it was never done."

The defendant testified: "I was 72 years old July 15th, 1876; I meant I was too old to live alone; I thought I wanted help; . . . they wanted to come to me; I told the wife it might make a good deal of trouble; we then talked about it till we came to my house; then I said they might tear down the old house and might build a new one; I told them I wanted to live with them but perhaps it was too late for that year. . . . There was a bargain he must pay me interest of $1500, but I would board with him when one could . . . the $1500, I said he must pay me as I needed it, until I had enough, and I must be buried at the end; I was to have part of this money when I needed it; I was to have the interest of the money till I needed more; then after I had needed more I wouldn't get the interest any more in full. . . Before the building was torn down we both thought we were too smart, we needed no writing. . . . When they were plastering he came down and asked me for the writing, the deed; . . . . I then said I would not give up my deed yet; I would not die yet; I wanted a bond to lay on the land; some one to read it first. I would lay it on the land. . . . For allowing Roth to have the land and build on I wanted this bond so that I was safe; I wanted to live on the land; he was to give me the interest every year for my clothes, and if it was not enough some of the principal."

There was also put in evidence a notice dated December 4, 1874, served upon the plaintiff by the defendant to quit all of the land "except such as may be necessary to the use of the buildings thereon and next adjacent to said buildings."

The defendant requested the Court to charge, *inter alia*, as follows: (9) "From the whole evidence shown in this case, the plaintiff has shown no cause of action, and no recovery can be had." *Refused.*

The jury were instructed to bring in a special verdict, and found as follows:—

"Jury returns that they find in favor of the plaintiff the sum of $2955.78. The judgment to be released if within thirty days after final judgment on the verdict Philip Naftzinger tenders and files in this suit a deed from himself to Daniel Roth, his heirs and assigns, for a tract of land in Upper Bern Township, adjoining lands of Benjamin Stitzel, George Wagner, William Sell and others, containing 30 acres, more or less, and subject to the following conditions: That Philip Naftzinger shall have the use, during his natural life, of the back room of the new house, and that Daniel Roth, his heirs and assigns, shall, and will, furnish Philip Naftzinger all necessary food, victuals, and board and attendance; and if the said Daniel Roth and Philip Naftzinger cannot agree together, in lieu of board, food victuals and attendance, the said Daniel Roth shall pay to Philip Naftzinger, annually, the interest on fifteen hundred dollars ($1500) during his (Naftzinger's) natural life."

Judgment was entered thereon, the Court saying in its opinion, "When this case was on trial we were considerably perplexed about it. It was evident to us that the parties to this suit had got themselves into a condition by their contract relations which they hardly understood themselves at any time, and by which after an attempt to execute it they only got into a worse state of understanding, in fact into actual misunderstanding. From the demeanor of the parties towards each other, one would have really supposed that there was no comprehensible contract relation between the parties. . . . As matter of law, we are now of the opinion, upon reflection, that this suit was maintainable, and the only remedy which the plaintiff had."

The defendant took this writ of error, assigning for error, *inter alia*, the refusal of the Court to charge as requested in the 9th point.

On March 26, 1879, the judgment was affirmed by the Supreme Court, but on April 3d, following, upon petition of plaintiff in error, a re-argument was ordered.

A. G. Green (with whom was *William P. Bard*), for plaintiff in error.

Roth could not remain in possession of the land, enjoying the rents and profits, and at the same time maintain an action at law for the value of the improvements.

Cornell Ex. *v.* Vanartsdalen, 4 Barr, 372.

There is no evidence of breach of contract on the part of Naftzinger; the only act which can possibly be construed as a breach of contract is the service of the notice to quit; but it especially excepted that portion of the land necessary for the use of the buildings, and even if it had included everything, since it did not alter the enjoyment of the land, and the plaintiff remained just where he was before, it would not have operated as a breach of contract. Supposing plaintiff's version of the contract to be correct, the only remedy that he could have would be a bill to perpetuate testimony. To enforce specific performance of a sale of land the precise terms and nature of the contract must be distinctly proven.

Sage *v.* McGuire, 4 W. & S. 228.
Ackerman *v.* Fisher, 7 Sm. 457.
Harris *v.* Richey, 6 Sm. 395.

If the party invoking the remedy is in *statu quo*, and sustains no loss by remaining so, and the circumstances are so altered as to work great injustice to the other, it will be denied.

Miller *v.* Henlan, 1 Sm. 265.

George F. Baer (with whom was C. H. *Schaeffer*), contra.

Roth could have waited until after Naftzinger's death, and then have sued his representatives in assumpsit, and received the money expended.

Ewing *v.* Thompson's Adm'r's, 16 Sm. 382.

Where a parol contract of sale is precise as to the terms and subject matter, and the vendee has taken possession in pursuance of it, and made valuable improvements with the assent of the vendor, it is not within the Statute of Frauds; and in such case if the vendor brings ejectment the jury ought to find a conditional verdict.

McGibbeny *v.* Burmaster, 3 Sm. 332.
Farley *v.* Stokes, 1 Pars. 422.
Milliken *v.* Dravo, 17 Sm. 232.

Specific performance has been decreed in this State in actions of covenant, debt, ejectment, and assumpsit.

DeCamp *v.* Feay, 5 S. & R. 323.
Haverstick *v.* Gas Co., 5 C. 254.
Huber *v.* Burke, 11 S. & R. 238.
Irvine *v.* Bull, 7 W. 323.

May 3, 1880. THE COURT. Roth testifies, "I made an agreement with Naftzinger in the spring of 1871. He said he was old, could no longer work; I should move to his property, build house, barn, and blacksmith shop; he wanted to live on the premises, and if I lived longer than he, I should have the property; he said he must live on the land, but if we could not live together and were quarrelsome he would move away and I must pay him the interest of $1500 as long as he lived. This was the agreement, and upon this I built. . . . He had reserved for him a room in the new house. Under this agreement I built on the premises, and I wanted to give him the board right away; he did not take it long." According to his testimony, he put up buildings, and made improvements at a total cost of $3000; he commenced building in the spring of 1872; still has possession, and has had the income to his own use; after his house was partly built, had talk with Naftzinger about papers, none were drawn up; in the beginning it was said there should be papers; he and Naftzinger quarrelled, the latter told him he would not live there longer than five years; quit boarding with him, and gave him notice to quit possession, except so much of the ground as necessary for use of the buildings. Roth has paid no interest, has demanded no writing, and has not been disturbed in the actual possession of any part of the premises. Since the spring of 1872 he has possessed and enjoyed all to which he was entitled by the contract as proved by himself.

Naftzinger's testimony differs materially as to the consideration, he saying that the $1500 were to be paid when he should require. Neither says they agreed as to writings; both say they were talked of; both agree that Roth should have the property, if he survived; but whether Naftzinger was to secure it to him by deed or will is as uncertain in the proof as in the pleadings.

The plaintiff being in the enjoyment of all that came within the contract, as he stated it, abandoned his claim for damages merely, and set up a claim for specific performance, to be enforced by a conditional verdict and judgment. He has as little right to maintain this suit for specific execution of the contract—without showing precisely what the contract was, his own performance, and breach by defendant—as to recover the value of the improvements of which he has not been dispossessed. In this State there is no doubt that in a proper case the rights of the parties under a parol contract for sale of land, may be settled in assumpsit; but the plaintiff must show that his right of action had accrued before its commencement. A defendant sued by the holder of the legal title may plead his equity to defeat recovery, or to secure a condition to the recovery, though not in position to maintain suit himself. Roth has a heavier burden than he would have if sued by Naftzinger for recovery of the land.

The learned Judge of the Common Pleas says, "When this case was on trial we were considerably perplexed about it. It was evident to us that the parties to this suit had got themselves into a condition by their contract relations, which they hardly understood themselves at any time, and by which, after an attempt to execute it, they only got into a worse state of understanding; in fact into actual misunderstanding. From the demeanor of the parties toward each other one would really have supposed that there was no comprehensible contract relation between the parties."

Such was the Chancellor's first impression of the case. Reflection and the verdict changed his views of the character of the evidence. Whether it was sufficient to warrant a decree for specific execution of the contract we shall not consider, for we are of opinion that it should clearly appear that the plaintiff had performed or offered performance on his part before bringing suit in assumpsit, in order to obtain a verdict equivalent to such decree. He failed not only to show the kind of writing, if any he was to have, but he proved no offer of writing to secure payment of the consideration and request of Naftzinger to execute either a deed or will. The defendant's ninth point ought to have been affirmed.

Judgment reversed.

Opinion by TRUNKEY, J. MERCUR and GREEN, JJ., absent.

Orphans' Court.

January 17, 1881.
McCloskey's Estate.

Decedent's estate—Direction for maintenance and support—Allowance for support of lunatic made in 1873, not reduced by reason of shrinkage of income of estate.

Sur exceptions to Examiner's report.

By the report of the Examiner the following facts appeared:—

Michael McCloskey, the decedent, died in 1860. Some time before, he had brought to this country a nephew and niece, Michael and Mary McCloskey. The latter, being of feeble mind, resided in testator's family until his death. By his will he provided as follows:—

"I direct that the children of my brother John shall be maintained, and supported, as long as they shall live, and charge my executors therewith, out of the rents, issues, and profits of my estate, and should they survive the distribution of my estate, I charge my grandchildren with their support."

In May, 1873, Mary McCloskey, by her next friend, Susan McVey, presented a petition to this Court, praying for an allowance out of the estate. On June 10 of the same year the Court granted the prayer of the petition, and made an order on the executors for the payment of seven dollars a week, said order to be subject to modification, proceedings in lunacy then pending. On the 28th of February, 1880, Catherine Mansfield, decedent's daughter, filed a petition for a citation to the said Susan McVey, next friend, etc., to show cause why the order of June 10, 1873, should not be modified. An answer and replication were also filed, and the matter referred to an Examiner, who reported the income of the estate as being reduced more than thirty per cent. since 1873. He also found that the petitioner could be maintained on a less sum than that ordered in June, 1873, the cost of living being since then somewhat reduced, and reported that the sum of five dollars and fifty cents a week was sufficient under the circumstances.

To this finding exceptions were filed in behalf of both petitioner and respondent. Mrs. Mansfield's exceptions were at the argument withdrawn.

Samuel E. Cavin, D. C. Harrington, and *F. C. Brewster,* for Susan McVey, next friend, etc.

William Henry Lex and *Benj. Harris Brewster,* for Mrs. Mansfield.

Jan. 22, 1881. THE COURT. The exceptions to the weekly allowance of $5.50, fixed by the Master, for the support of the legatee, on the ground that it was excessive, were properly withdrawn.

This leaves for consideration the exceptions by the respondent to the finding that any deduction should be made from the original order for the payment of seven dollars per week. The Master based his conclusion partly upon the testimony of several witnesses who declared that board and lodging could be had for three dollars per week. As this is the rate charged at the almshouse to inmates who are able to pay, it may be regarded as sufficiently economical, and as acquitting the Master of any leaning to the side of prodigality. The Master also reported that the cost of living in 1880 was about twenty-five per cent. less than it was in 1873, when the order now appealed from was made. No testimony having been heard upon this point, the statement appears to have been made as an historical fact, for which, however, our own reading does not supply an authority.

We think that the error of the Master lay in assuming that the support and maintenance directed by the will, were intended to be graduated to the estate taken by the life tenant. Nothing can be plainer, however, than that the two gifts were independent of each other. The testator directed that the children of his brother should be maintained and supported as long as each of them should live, and he charged his executors with the duty of providing the funds for this purpose out of the rents, issues, and profits of his estate. The residue of his estate, after a life interest which has fallen, he gave to his daughter, the petitioner, for life. Until, therefore, the payment of this charge should be secured, the petitioner would take nothing. The respondent had indeed a peculiar title to the sympathy of the testator. She was old, and mentally unfitted to earn a livelihood, and she had come to this country at his solicitation. After his death, she was adjudged, upon proceedings instituted by the petitioner, to be a lunatic. The testator had recognized the double claim of kinship and misfortune by making her one of his family up to the time of his death, and by providing for her needs beyond that period. This action on his part does not comport with the theory that he intended, for the object of so much solicitude while living, a maintenance after his death which should be only one step removed from pauperism. It is matter for regret that the net income of the estate should have fallen from $4680 in 1873 to $2864 in 1880. But it is possible that by a wise application of the economy which is sought to be enforced by this proceeding, even this reduced amount may be found able to bear the strain of the charge in question.

We do not perceive in the evidence any substantial reason for the reduction recommended by the Master. The respondent's exceptions are therefore sustained, and the order for the payment of seven dollars per week is continued in force.

WEEKLY NOTES OF CASES.

Vol. IX.] THURSDAY, MARCH 17, 1881. [No. 30.

Supreme Court.

July, '78, 35.   Feb. 12, 1880, and Jan. 17, 18, 1881.
Phila. & Reading R. R. Co. v. Boyer.

Common carriers—Collision between street car and steam train—Rights and duties of a non-carrying company to a passenger of another company—Negligence and contributory negligence—Law and facts—Province of Court and jury—Effect of Act limiting pecuniary responsibilities of a railroad company upon a company that has not formally accepted its terms.—Effect of Article III. Sec. 21, of the Constitution.

The duty of a carrier company to its passengers is to use the greatest possible care; hence, to enable a passenger to recover for injuries from a company whose train came into collision with the car upon which he was travelling, it must appear that the carrier company did not fail in its duty to him.

In such a case the duty of the non-carrying company is merely ordinary care, according to the circumstances.

Where the track of a horse-car company crosses the track of a steam railroad company at grade, the duty of the conductor or driver of the horse-car company to "stop, look, and listen," and use whatever other precautions were reasonably in his power, is not excused by the fact that the flagman of the steam railroad company motioned him to come on, or failed to warn him not to come on.

In a suit by the representatives of one who was killed by the collision of the street car upon which he was travelling with the steam train of another company, in which the latter company are defendants, it is error to charge the jury, that, if they are satisfied that the carrier company was not guilty of negligence, they must find for the plaintiff, because it withdraws from the jury the question of the defendant's negligence.

B., a passenger on a one-horse street car, was killed by a collision of a train of the P. G. & N. R. R., with the horse car, at the point in the line of Broad St., above Huntingdon St., where the street railroad crosses the steam road. In a suit by the representatives of B. against the lessees of the P. G. & N. road, the testimony was conflicting as to whether the flagman of the steam road did or did not motion to the driver not to come on; one witness, however, did testify positively that he, a passer-by, gave warning of the danger:

Held (reversing the ruling of the Court below), that the attempt of the driver to cross under the circumstances was the result either of criminal carelessness or gross stupidity.

Held, further, that no conduct on the part of the flagman would excuse the driver from the exercise of the necessary precautions before crossing the track.

Vol. IX.—32

An ordinance of the City of Philadelphia provides, that all passenger railways, whose track crosses any steam railroads at grade, shall, before their cars cross such road, compel their conductors to stop all cars, and cross such steam railroads in advance of the cars, under a penalty:

Held, that this ordinance did not apply to a car in the charge of one man, who acted both as conductor and driver.

The effect of the Act of April 4, 1868 (P. L. 58), limiting the pecuniary responsibility of railroad companies for death by negligence, upon a company which never accepted its provisions, and the effect of Article III. Sect. 21, of the Constitution upon this Act, not decided.

Error to the Common Pleas No. 4, of Philadelphia Court.

Case, by the widow and minor children of Jacob P. Boyer, against the Philadelphia and Reading Railroad Company, for negligence. Plea, "not guilty," and specially that the accident was caused by the negligence of the Thirteenth and Fifteenth Streets Pass. R. R. Co.

On the trial, before BRIGGS, J., the following facts appeared: Jacob P. Boyer, a policeman of Philadelphia, was a passenger on one of the one-horse cars of the Thirteenth and Fifteenth Streets Railroad on Broad Street, on the morning of March 6, 1877, between 6.30 and 7 o'clock. The only other occupants of the car were four other policemen and the driver. The car was going north. At the point where the Phila., Germantown, and Norristown Railroad, operated by the Phila. and Reading R. R. Co., defendants, crosses Broad Street, between Huntingdon Street and Lehigh Avenue, at an acute angle, a train going northwestwardly toward Germantown struck the car, and Boyer and one other of the passengers were killed. There is a flagman stationed by the Reading R. R. Co. at the intersection of their road with Broad Street on the east side of the track. The track of the Thirteenth and Fifteenth Streets Pass. Railway Co. runs along the east side of Broad Street, and crosses the Reading track immediately at the flagman's watchbox.

The testimony of the surviving passengers of the horse car was, that the horse car was coming very slowly and the train approaching very rapidly; that the flagman gave no signal, but came sauntering out of his box with his flag under his arm, that the passengers on the car did not know of the approach of the train until instantly before the horse car was struck, that no whistle was blown, nor other notice given by the Phila. and Reading Company, and that just before the collision occurred the flagman turned round and went into the box.

Martin V. Spencer, a colored man, who was present at the time of the accident, testified, that he saw no flagman, and "seeing no flagman out I called the attention of the driver—that is, the driver of the car. I think that after the second call he recognized my signal, and he came out in front of the car. I cannot say positively that he was inside the car. When he began winding the brakes he was about four or five lengths of his horse from the train. I was standing on the steam car track and saw both the train and the car approaching. After I had hallooed a second time, the flagman came out. I then stepped off the track and down toward the curb of the street, and the engine struck the car about three feet from the rear platform. The driver had room to stop when I first called, but the flagman said, 'let him come on,' and motioned with his rolled-up flag to him to come on."

The driver testified: "We left Broad and Norris Streets; had the five officers in the car; both doors were shut. I was on the front of my car all the way up, and had the lines in one hand and the brake in the other. I continued on up Broad Street, until I came to the watchman's box. I came opposite to his box. The watchman came out, with his hands in his pockets and the flag under his arm. The flag was rolled up. I brought my horse down to a walk, and I heard no noise of an approaching train. I then continued on my course. As my horse struck the south track, I heard the colored man hallooing. I paid no attention to him, thinking, when I saw the watchman, that everything was all right. I continued on my course, and I struck the north track. I paid no attention to him, thinking, from seeing the watchman, that there was no train approaching. When the horse struck the north track, I seen the colored man jump for my horse. I happened to cast my eye down the track, and then I see the train. I let go of my brake, and catched hold my lines on a short hold, and hollered to the colored man, 'What the hell are you doing? look out there!' I then struck the horse with the short end of the lines, and I knew no more until somebody picked me up out of the car."

There was no conductor on the horse-car.

The testimony on behalf of the defendant company was, that the train was approaching on time, and at the usual rate of speed, about nine miles an hour, that the usual whistle for Broad Street was blown, and immediately thereafter a danger whistle, accompanied by the ringing of the bell; that the flagman gave the signal of danger by waving the car back, but that he was not seen because the driver was not in his place. The employés of the railroad were corroborated by a woman who was in the upper window of a house on the south side of the track, just east of Broad Street. The flagman testified that he did not turn back to the watch-box until the horse had gotten upon the track, and he saw that an accident was inevitable, and that he only did so then to avoid seeing the accident.

The defendant requested the Court to charge, *inter alia*:—

(3) That it was the duty of the driver of the passenger-car to stop before reaching the railroad, and to look and listen for approaching trains; and if the jury believe from the evidence that he failed to do so, the plaintiff cannot recover in this action, and the verdict must be for the defendants. *Answer*. In view of the testimony that the flagman beckoned to the driver to come on, this point is declined. (Ninth assignment of error.)

(4) That it was the duty of the conductor, who was also the driver of the passenger-car, to stop the car and cross the tracks of the railroad company in advance; and if the jury believe from the evidence that he failed to do so, the plaintiffs cannot recover in this action, and the verdict must be for the defendants. *Answer*. This point is declined, for the same reason as is given in the last answer. (Tenth and eleventh assignments of error.)

In the general charge, the Court said, *inter alia*:—

[If you find, however, from the evidence before you, in its entirety, that there was no negligence on the part of the Thirteenth and Fifteenth Streets Passenger Railway Company, then you have no trouble, and should, without a moment's hesitation, reach the conclusion that it is your duty to find a verdict against these defendants.] For it is, beyond all peradventure, a conceded fact, from every aspect of the case, and by both counsel in the case, that Mr. Boyer was killed by the passenger railway car being thrown violently from its track by the Reading Railroad train. And there is no evidence whatever in the case for me to submit to you that there was any negligence on the part of Mr. Boyer himself; that is frankly and manfully conceded by the counsel of the Reading Railroad Company also.

[If the story of the driver is true, then, gentlemen, he had no signal. If the story of Spencer, the colored man, is true, then the flagman, on whom, gentlemen, as great a responsibility as can rest upon any human being rested, was guilty of the grossest negligence.]

But I say to you unqualifiedly, advisedly, feeling keenly the responsibility that rests upon me, in view of the importance of the case to us in the relation it occupies to this dense centre of population and the geographical position of th intersection, known to me, and of which I a bound by law to take notice, and that people ar constantly passing that point during the busine hours of the day [that the highest degree of care responsibility, vigilance, and observation rested upon that flagman that could possibly be exercised by a man possessing care, vigilance, and observation, under the same circumstances].

[The law as to him is not ordinary care, it is extraordinary care. It is that care springing from the fact that human life may be imperiled if he does not exercise it, and as the law values human life, so does it tax him with the exercise of his utmost faculties to protect human life. There he stood, a sentinel of this character, and if he did not come up to the full measure that the law affixes to his office, then this defendant-company was not only guilty of negligence, but it was guilty of negligence of the grossest kind.]

Now, gentlemen, I define the law sharply, and I do it advisedly. I mean what I say, and there must be no shrinking by you nor by me; for servants occupying the relation that this flagman did to this deceased man must be taught that human life is worthy the exercise of the utmost of human vigilance. . . . .

[But if the driver was beckoned on by the flagman, or told to come on by the flagman, then, gentlemen, that flagman being stationed there especially for the purpose of giving warning, the driver was justified in responding in action to the invitation by going on. And if you find that to be so, there is no negligence on the part of the passenger railway company, and the verdict in that aspect should be against the Reading Railroad Company].

Verdict for plaintiffs for $12,000, subsequently reduced by the Court in banc to $10,000, and judgment thereon. The defendants took this writ, assigning for error the answers to their points, and the portions of the general charge inclosed in brackets.

The case was argued in the Supreme Court on Feb. 12, 1880, and, a re-argument having been ordered, it was again heard on Jan. 17th and 18th, 1881.

James E. Gowen, for plaintiff in error.

In charging that the accident was the result of negligence, and that the jury, if they found that there was no negligence on the part of the horse-car company, must find against the railroad company, the Court withdrew a material question of fact from the jury. This was error.

Madara *v.* Eversole, 12 Sm. 160.
Huston *v.* Barstow, 7 Har. 169.
Tenbrooke *v.* Jahke, 27 Sm. 392.

In charging the jury that, if the testimony of the driver was true, he had no signal, his Honor gave rise to an inference that it was incumbent on the R. R. Co. to give a signal; this is not warranted by the law.

D. L. & W. R. R. *v.* Toffey, 9 Vroom, 525.

The duty of the flagman was ordinary, not extraordinary care.

R. R. Co. *v.* Fries, 5 WEEKLY NOTES, 545.
Frankfort and Bristol Turnpike Co. *v.* P. & T. R. R., 4 Sm. 345.
Adams Express Co. *v.* Sharpless, 27 Sm. 516.
R. R. Co. *v.* McTighe, 10 Wr. 316.

The proposition embodied in the fourth point of the defendant is drawn from an ordinance of the city councils; and as their right to impose such a duty is undoubted, the failure of the horse-car company to comply with its provisions is negligence.

Ordinance of December 31, 1875.
Penna. Canal Co. *v.* Bentley, 16 Sm. 30.
Johnson *v.* Bruner, 11 Id. 58.
Ins. Co. *v.* Marsh, 5 Wr. 386.

That the failure of the driver to "stop, look, and listen," was contributory negligence is settled by a host of authorities.

Schultz *v.* R. R., 6 WEEKLY NOTES, 69.
R. R. *v.* Beale, 23 Sm. 504.
Haven *v.* The Railway Co., 41 N. Y. 296.
Railroad Co. *v.* Houston, 5 Otto, 697.
Dascomb *v.* The R. R. Co., 27 Barb. 221.
Wilcox *v.* The R. R. Co., 39 N. Y. 358.
Butterfield *v.* The R. R. Co., 10 Allen, 532.
McCall *v.* The R. R. Co., 54 N. Y. 642.
Gorton *v.* The Railway Co., 45 N. Y. 660.
R. R. Co. *v.* Hunter, 33 Ind. 335.
O'Brien *v.* The R. R. Co., 3 Phila. 76.
Dodge *v.* The R. R. Co., 34 Iowa, 276.
Railway Company *v.* Mathias, 50 Ind. 65.
Skelton *v.* The Railway Company, Law Repts. 2 C. P. 631.

Rufus E. Shapley (*Wm. C. Gross*, with him), for defendant in error.

That one invited to cross a railroad by signals from a flagman is justified in doing so, is sustained by numerous decisions.

Borst *v.* Lake Shore R. R. Co., 4 Hun, 346.
Cleveland R. R. Co. *v.* Crawford, 24 Ohio, 631.
Kennayde *v.* Pacific R. R. Co., 45 Mo. 255.
Tabor *v.* Missouri Valley R. R. Co., 46 Mo. 353.
Newson *v.* N. Y. Cen. R. R. Co., 29 N. Y. 383.
Beisiegel *v.* Same, 34 N. Y. 622.
Brown *v.* Same, 32 N. Y. 597.
Sweeny *v.* Old Colony R. R. Co., 10 Allen, 368.
Spencer *v.* Illinois Cen. R. R. Co., 29 Iowa, 55.
Warner *v.* N. Y. Cen. R. R. Co., 45 Barb. 299.

Flagmen or other servants of a railroad company are presumed to act as its agents, and hence a person who, in compliance with a notice that he can cross, crosses the track, though it be in view of an approaching train, may recover of the company in case of injury.

Wharton's Law of Negligence (ed. 1874), § 387.

Although it is not negligence for a railroad company to omit to keep a flagman at a crossing, yet, if one is employed, his neglect to perform the usual and ordinary functions of the place may be sufficient to charge the company. If one approaching a crossing where there is a flagman does not hear the bell of an approaching train, and the flagman neglects to give any warning, and an injury happens, solely produced by such negligence, it is sufficient to make the company liable.

Kissenger v. N. Y. & Harlem R. R. Co., 56 N. Y. Court of Appeals, 538.
Reading R. R. v. Killips, 8 WEEKLY NOTES, 526.

January 31, 1881. THE COURT. Jacob P. Boyer, to recover damages for the loss of whose life this action has been brought by his widow and children, was, on the 6th day of March, 1877, a passenger on a car of the Thirteenth and Fifteenth Streets Passenger Railway Company, and, as this car was moving across the tracks of the Philadelphia and Reading Railroad, it was struck by a passing locomotive; the result was the wreck of the car and the loss of two lives, that of Boyer being one of them.

The success of this action depends upon the establishment of two assumptions : (1) That the death of Boyer resulted directly from the carelessness of the defendant's servants; (2) That the person in charge of the street car was chargeable with no negligence. It is only on this hypothesis that the suit can be maintained, for the rule is, that, where a passenger on a carrier vehicle is injured by a collision resulting from the mutual negligence of those in charge of it and another party, the carrier alone must answer for the injury. (Lockhart v. Lichtenthaler, 10 Wr. 151.) On this theory the case was tried, and the principal point on which it turned was the question, whether the driver of the horse-car was or was not guilty of contributory negligence. This, of course, was exclusively for the jury, and it was error for the Court to assume as true any fact upon which that body had to pass. (Elkins v. McKean, 29 P. F. S. 493.) When, therefore,—in answer to the defendant's third point, asking instruction, that it was the duty of the driver of the passenger car to stop before reaching the railroad, and look and listen for approaching trains, and, if the jury believe from the evidence he failed to do so, the plaintiffs cannot recover,—the Court said : " In view of the testimony that the flagman beckoned the driver to come on, this point is declined ;" the rule as above stated was violated, for the Court assumed as true, the very fact of all others upon which the case turned, since the only possible excuse of the driver for his neglect in not stopping his car was the fact, if fact it was, that the flagman did beckon him to cross the track. His duty to the passengers under his care was of the highest order, whilst that of the flagman as an employé of the railroad company was but secondary. He was bound to but ordinary care. The learned Judge, however, seems to have inverted this order, for he says : " The highest degree of care, responsibility, vigilance, and observation rested upon the flagman, that could possibly be exercised by a man possessing care, vigilance, and observation, under the same circumstances." Had he applied this language to the driver of the horse-car, it would have been unexceptionable, but to apply it to the flagman was erroneous. It is true that that care, called ordinary care, must vary according to circumstances. What would be ordinary care in handling building sand would be gross negligence in handling gunpowder; so, the care to be exercised in running a locomotive through a crowded city is something very different from that required in driving the same kind of vehicle through the open country ; nevertheless, in both cases the care required is that only which a man of ordinary prudence would exercise under like circumstances. All this, the Court might and ought to have told the jury. But it had no right to impose upon the company the duty of extraordinary care; that was the obligation resting upon the driver of the street car, and upon him alone. From what has been said, it follows that the defendant's second point should have been affirmed without qualification, except, perhaps, to explain what ordinary care under the circumstances would be.

Furthermore, the learned Judge erred in the following instruction: "If you find, however, from the evidence before you in its entirety, that there was no negligence on the part of the Thirteenth and Fifteenth Streets Railway Company, then you have no trouble, and should, without a moment's hesitation, reach the conclusion that it is your duty to find against the defendants."

Here, again, is an assumption in which the Court ought not to have indulged. From the evidence such a conclusion might possibly follow, but it was for the jury to draw it, not the Court.

Again, the Court said: "If the story of the driver is true, then, gentlemen, he had no signal. If the story of Spencer, the colored man, is true, then the flagman on whom, gentlemen, as great a responsibility as can rest upon any human being rested, was guilty of the grossest negligence." But if the driver had no signal; if the flagman, as the driver himself says, came sauntering out of his box with his flag rolled up, under his arm, giving no heed to the railroad or what was upon it, what, under such circumstances, was the driver's duty? Under his care was the safety of his passengers; upon him rested the superior duty. Surely he ought to have stopped, looked for himself, or asked the flagman so to do; and this the more so, as Spencer was doing all in his power to warn him of the coming danger. The fact is, resting the case wholly upon his own and Spencer's testimony, the driver did not exercise that care which, under the circumstances, was required of him. He had the lives of five men under his charge. He was approaching a place of known danger. Had he stopped for one moment, he would have heard the noise of the approaching train. Spencer was directly in front of him, shouting and gesticulating in order to induce him to stop, and, instead of heeding this warning, with a curse he orders Spencer out of the way, and drives on. Now, suppose the flagman did beckon him on; tell him to go on: what was his duty as a prudent man? How could he help knowing that a train was coming? He was not only warned of the fact, but, had he used his eyes, he might have seen it. It is, therefore, well nigh certain that his attempt to cross the tracks at that time, even under the supposition that the flagman signalled him to do so, was the result either of criminal carelessness or gross stupidity. One man told him to stop, another to go on; was he not to pause and judge between them, by the sure witness of his eye-sight? Surely this is a proposition of easy solution, and one, had it been properly submitted, that ought not to have given the jury much trouble. Again, the answer to the defendant's fourth point was wrong, because it assumes the fact, as in the answer to the third point, that the flagman actually did beckon the driver on. The Court might have refused this point. It was not necessary for the driver to cross the tracks in advance of his car. This would have been proper had there been a conductor in charge of this vehicle, but as there was only a driver, this could not be done. Had he stopped, where he could have had a proper view of the road, and looked and listened, he would have discharged his whole duty. This point embodies the city ordinance, regulating the passage of railroad tracks by street cars; an excellent regulation, and one that should be strictly enforced; but, as we have said in the case of the Railroad Co. *v.* Ervin (36 Leg. Int. 244), a municipal ordinance creates no new liability in favor of one injured by the negligence of another; hence, had the driver of the car observed the proper precautions, though they might not have conformed strictly to the directions of the ordinance, that would have been sufficient to have thrown the responsibility of the accident on the defendant, if its servants were negligent; nevertheless, the Court, having undertaken to answer this point, should have done so in a proper manner, and not by an assumption of the prerogative of the jury.

We do not deem it proper now to discuss the exception to the entry of judgment in excess of five thousand dollars, the limit prescribed by the Act of 1868. It does not appear that the Philadelphia and Reading Railroad Company ever formally accepted the provisions of that Act so as to make them part of its charter. Under such circumstances, whether the Act applies at all to non-accepting companies, is an important question, and a still more important question is, admitting it thus to apply as a general law, though not part of the company's charter, what effect has the Constitution of 1874 upon the Statute by way of repeal? Should the case ever come before us again, which is not likely, it may be presented in a better shape for the discussion of these questions, but for the present we pass them.

The judgment is reversed, and a new venire is ordered.

Opinion by GORDON, J.

Jan. '80, 341.　　　　　January 6, 1881.

Knight v. The Mutual Life Insurance Company of New York.

Life Insurance—Declaration of insured forming basis of contract—Guaranty that insured will not contract habit of intemperance—Violation thereof—Meaning of word guaranty—Pleading—Matter of estoppel—When inadmissible—Powers of general agent.

In an application for a policy of life insurance, a *guaranty* by the insured that he will not contract any pernicious habit, is equivalent to a warranty; and, in case of violation of such guaranty, the policy is properly forfeited under a stipulation that, if any of the statements in the application are false, the policy shall be forfeited.

Matter of estoppel *in pais* is not admissible in evidence, when the question of estoppel has not been raised on the pleadings.

It is not within the power of the general agent of an insurance company, by declarations that the insured has complied with his contract, and that his policy is good, to estop the company from setting up, as against one who purchased the policy on the faith of such assurance, that the policy is void because of misrepresentations on the part of the insured at the time of issue of the policy.

Error to the Common Pleas No. 4, of Philadelphia County.

Assumpsit, by W. A. Knight against the above-named company, upon a paid-up policy for $3500 issued upon the life of W. P. Beatty.

The material facts of this case were as follows: In 1866, W. P. Beatty insured his life in the defendant company for $10,000. Before the policy was issued, the applicant filed an application with the company, which contained, *inter alia*, the following questions: Are your habits of life correct and temperate? Have they always been so? Both these questions were answered in the affirmative. The following declaration, signed by the insured, was appended to the declaration as a part thereof:—

And it is hereby expressly stipulated and agreed that the above application and this declaration shall form the basis of the contract between the above-named persons and the said The Mutual Life Insurance Company of New York, and that if any misrepresentations or fraudulent and untrue answers have been made, or if any facts which should have been stated to the Company have been suppressed therein, or if any violation of the covenants, conditions, or restrictions of the policy (should one be issued), shall occur, or any omission or neglect to pay any of the premiums on or before the days on which they shall fall due shall take place, that then in either event the said policy shall become and be null and void, and all moneys which shall have been paid, and also all dividends which may have accrued thereon, shall be forfeited to the said Company for its sole use and benefit. And the said William Penn Beatty further declares that he is not now afflicted with any disease or disorder, and that he does not now nor will he practise any pernicious habit that obviously tends to the shortening of life.

In 1871, Beatty allowed his policy to lapse, and on May 19, 1871, took from the company a new paid-up policy (the one in suit) for $3500. Before this policy issued, he signed a declaration, whereby he agreed that the said declaration and his application for the original policy should be part of his contract with the company; this declaration contained, *inter alia*, the following terms:—

And I do hereby declare that the several answers given by me, or in my behalf, to the questions on pages 1, 2, and 3, of the original application for a policy of life insurance, which was dated February 21, 1866, and signed by the above-named, and which this is intended to replace, were true and correct when made; and I guarantee that he does not and will not practise any bad or vicious habit that tends to the shortening of life.

The policy contained a clause to the effect that "agents of the company are not authorized to make, alter, or discharge contracts, or waive forfeitures."

Beatty subsequently failed and made an assignment, owing the plaintiff Knight a large sum. The policy in suit was sold at public sale after due notice by the assignee, and bought by the plaintiff for $1510. On Feb. 9, 1878, Beatty died, and the company declining to pay the policy, this suit was brought.

The defendant pleaded specially (1) that the insured had given false answers to the questions in his original application, and (2 and 3) that he had violated his declaration and guaranty that he did not and would not practise any pernicious habit obviously tending to shorten life, wherefore, by the terms of the policy, it was null and void. The plaintiff filed two replications to each plea, one traversing the fact of intemperance, and the other setting up matter of estoppel (see offer below). A demurrer having been filed on the ground that the replications made two issues to each plea, plaintiff amended by withdrawing the replications setting up matter of estoppel.

On the trial, before ELCOCK, J., plaintiff offered to show that, before he purchased the policy, he went to the office of the general agents of the insurance company, and was assured by the general agents that the policy was good and would be paid without any delay, and that upon this assurance he made the purchase. Objected to; objection sustained, and exception.

The Court charged the jury, *inter alia*, as follows: The insured warranted that he would not contract any pernicious habit obviously tending to shorten life; the *guaranty* is the same as a warranty; and if the jury believe that, afterwards, the insured practised the pernicious habit of intemperance, the policy became null and void.

Verdict and judgment for defendant, whereupon the plaintiff took this writ, assigning for error, *inter alia*, the overruling of his offer of evidence and the charge of the Court as above set forth.

E. D. McLoughlin (with him *W. K. Shryock*), for plaintiff in error.

Estoppel *in pais* need not be pleaded; formerly, it would have been error to plead it, as it would be setting forth on the record mere matter of evidence.

Bank *v*. Wollaston, 3 Har. (Del.) 90.
Duchess of Kingston's Case, 2 Smith's L. Cas. *611, *683.
Kilheffer *v*. Herr, 17 S. & R. 319.
Man *v*. Drexel, 2 Barr, 208.

The guaranty contained in the declaration did not amount to a warranty; the Courts have never yet gone so far. If the company intended to extract a warranty, they should have used that word. See—

Reichard *v*. Ins. Co., 31 Mo. 518.
Horton *v*. Life Ass. Co., 2 Big. Cas. 108.
Knecht *v*. Ins. Co., 7 WEEKLY NOTES, 297.

The only distinction between this case and Knecht *v*. The Insurance Co. (*supra*) is that here the word guarantee is used instead of declare. The word is insensible here, as a guaranty is really a collateral undertaking in relation to another person. It would seem that it can mean nothing here except declare.

W. W. Porter (with him *W. A. Porter*), for defendants in error.

Evidence of estoppel could not be introduced under the pleadings, which involved only the question of intemperance.

Stephen on Pleading, *83 and *162.
R. R. Co. *v*. Howard, 13 How. 335.

The cases cited show that where the *general issue* is pleaded, the evidence of estoppel is admissible; here there was no general issue pleaded.

The evidence was also inadmissible on the ground that the agent had no authority to make the statement; the policy expressly provided against such a thing.

Mentz *v*. Ins. Co., 29 Sm. 475.
Martin *v*. Berens, 17 Sm. 459.
Lloyd *v*. Farrell, 12 Wr. 73.
Hain *v*. Kalbach, 14 S. & R. 159.

The *guaranty* was more than a declaration, and brings the case within the very exception pointed out in Knecht *v*. Ins. Co. (*supra*). See—

Holterhoff *v*. Ins. Co., 3 Am. L. Record, 272.

January 24, 1881. THE COURT. The question of estoppel did not arise on the pleadings. If it had, however, it is clear that the company could not have been estopped by the declarations of the general agent, as to the performance of the conditions of the contract. Nor were they admissible as evidence, under the clause of the policy that "Agents of the Company are not authorized to make, alter, or discharge contracts, or waive forfeitures." We agree in opinion with the learned Judge below, that the word "guarantee" means "warrant," and in this respect the case is distinguishable from Knecht *v.* Ins. Co. (7 W. N. C. 297).

Judgment affirmed.

PER CURIAM.

GORDON and GREEN, JJ., absent.

July, '80, 127.   January 6, 1881.

Lennig's Appeal.

Attachment-execution—Act of June 16, 1836, §§ 23 and 35 (P. L. 767)—Goods pawned, pledged, or demised, what are—In order for attachment to lie, garnishee must have fixed title to goods.

Goods of a defendant left for storage with a warehouseman at a stipulated sum per month, cannot be made the subject of an attachment-execution.

PER CURIAM. In order for goods to be liable to an attachment, the party in whose possession they are must have such a fixed title or interest that they cannot be taken from him. Such has been the uniform construction of the Act in the lower courts since 1849.

Appeal of G. C. Lennig from a decree of the Court of Common Pleas No. 3, of Philadelphia County, dismissing his exceptions to and confirming the report of the auditor appointed to distribute the fund produced by a sheriff's sale of certain personal property of H. Worrell.

The following are the material facts of the case: G. C. Lennig, having obtained a judgment against H. Worrell, issued an attachment-execution thereon, making one Wm. B. Collins and others garnishees, and attached certain casks of black lead belonging to defendant, and stored with the garnishees, next door to defendant's place of business. The statement of the garnishees, which was accepted in place of the usual interrogatories and answers, was to the effect that Worrell was in the habit of storing in the garnishees' warehouse articles of merchandise for a certain sum per month, and that the articles here attached were stored in accordance with that custom. While this attachment was pending, one P. C. Tomson issued a fi. fa. on a judgment he held against Worrell, and sold thereunder these casks of lead and other goods. The proceeds of the sale were ordered into Court, and, before the auditor appointed to make distribution thereof, G. C. Lennig claimed that his attachment was entitled to priority over the judgment of Tomson, so far as regarded the proceeds of the casks of black lead. The auditor found otherwise, and awarded the fund to Tomson. G. C. Lennig filed exceptions to this award, but they were dismissed, and the auditor's report confirmed; whereupon Lennig took this appeal, assigning for error the said action of the Court.

H. C. Brown, for appellant.

The words "as aforesaid" in the 35th section of the Act of June 16, 1836, refer back to the 23d section. These two sections provide as follows:—

SECTION 23. Goods or chattels of the defendant in any writ of *fieri facias*, which shall have been pawned or pledged by him as security for any debt or liability, or which have been demised, or in any manner delivered or bailed for a term, shall be liable to sale upon execution as aforesaid, subject, nevertheless, to all and singular the rights and interests of the pawnee, bailee, or lessee, to the possession or otherwise of such chattels or goods, by reason of such pledge, demise, or bailment.

SECTION 35. In the case of a debt due to the defendant or of a deposit of money made by him, or of goods or chattels pawned, pledged, or demised, *as aforesaid*, the same may be attached and levied in satisfaction of the judgment in the manner allowed in the case of a foreign attachment . . . .

The words of the 23d section are as broad as they can be made, and clearly cover this case. The word "delivered" is used, and this case certainly falls within that word. The warehouseman here held the goods on storage at a fixed compensation, and could have refused to give them up until paid. This would make the fi. fa. and attachment concurrent, and creditors could then ascertain from the garnishee's answers, what they often cannot learn otherwise, whether certain goods belong to the defendant or not.

J. W. Patton, for appellee.

The attachment is restricted by the 35th section to goods "pawned, pledged, or demised," and cannot be extended to a case of mere storage like this. The appellant should have issued a fi. fa. The Act has been uniformly construed as we claim it should be.

Good *v.* Obertauffer, decided in the District Court in 1849 (note to 1 Tr. & Ha. Pr. 5th ed. 1880, § 1182).
Buckner *v.* Croissant, 3 Phila. 219.
Hall *v.* Fitler, 2 WEEKLY NOTES, 154.

January 17, 1881. THE COURT. Giving all the force to the words "as aforesaid" in the 35th section of the Act of June 16, 1836, contended for by the learned counsel of the appellant, it will not avail him, for still to authorize an attachment, the goods must have been pawned or pledged, demised, or in any manner delivered or bailed *for a term.* That is, the party in whose possession the goods are must have such a fixed title or interest that they cannot be taken from him. Such has been the uniform construction, in the lower courts at least, since Good *v.* Obertauffer was decided in 1849. (Brightly's Tr. & Haly, sect. 1182, note.)

Decree affirmed, and appeal dismissed at the cost of the appellant.

PER CURIAM.

Oct. & Nov. '79.   Oct. 24, 1879.

Duff v. Allegheny Valley R. R. Co.

Railroad Company—Negligence—Injury to trespasser—Who is a trespasser.

A railroad company owes no duty to a trespasser riding on a train.

The conductor of an accommodation train, at the request of a brakeman, permitted a lad of fifteen to ride free daily on the train to sell newspapers. Under the company's rules this was beyond the scope of the conductor's authority. After this practice had continued five or six months, the boy was killed in an accident to the train, caused by the alleged negligence of the company. In an action by the boy's mother to recover damages:

Held (affirming the judgment of the Court below), that under the evidence the boy was neither a passenger nor an employé, but was a mere trespasser, to whom the company owed no duty, and the plaintiff could not recover.

Error to the Common Pleas of Venango County.

Case, by Thomas H. Duff and Mary his wife, formerly Mary Cordell, in her right, to recover damages for the death of her son James Cordell, a minor, caused by the alleged negligence of the defendant.

On the trial, before CHURCH, P. J., the evidence showed that on February 10, 1873, an accommodation or mixed train, consisting of a number of freight, coal, and oil cars, with one passenger car in the rear, parted from the engine, and ran off the track, while rounding a curve; several cars, including the passenger car, were precipitated into a shallow part of the river, where the cars took fire, and the boy James Cordell, who was in the passenger car, was killed. The boy had been permitted by the conductor at the request of the brakeman, who was the boy's half-brother, to ride free on the train daily for five or six months, to sell newspapers. He occasionally made up the fire or lighted the lamps for the brakeman. The rules of the company showed that the conductor had no authority to permit the boy to ride free. The superintendent while travelling, had occasionally seen the boy on the train, but it did not appear that he either knew of, consented to, or objected to the boy riding free. The exact cause of the accident did not clearly appear. An axle of one of the cars was found to be broken, and the track and ties were badly damaged. Much conflicting testimony was taken tending to show that the track at this point was in bad condition.

The plaintiff presented, *inter alia*, the following points:—

(3) If the jury believe that the plaintiff's son was allowed by the conductor to ride on the train, and that his death was caused by defendant's negligence, plaintiff's right to recover would not be affected by want of express authority to the conductor to make such arrangement, in the absence of knowledge by the boy or his parents of such defect of authority, and in the absence of negligence on the part of the boy contributing to the accident. *Answer.* That we refuse to answer under the facts in this case.

(5) The same standard of conduct cannot be applied to boys as to men. If the jury believe that at the time of the accident the plaintiff's son was exercising the same degree of care usually exercised by boys of his age, and that he was killed through defendant's neglect to maintain its road-bed or rolling stock in good condition, or in attaching petroleum cars to the train, the plaintiffs are entitled to recover, even if the jury believe the boy was not properly on the car; provided he was not a wilful trespasser, and his wrongful act was not the proximate cause of the accident by which he lost his life. *Answer.* That we refuse under the facts in this case.

The defendant presented the following points:

(1) That under the evidence in this case James Cordell was neither a passenger upon the Allegheny Valley Railroad, nor an employé in its service at the time of his death. *Answer.* That we answer in the affirmative, that he neither was a passenger nor an employé.

(2) That under the evidence, the conductor of the train upon which James Cordell was found at the time of his death had no authority to permit him to travel upon the train in the manner stated in the evidence, and that his presence upon the train for the purpose of making profit for himself by the sale of newspapers, in violation of the company's rules and the conductor's duty, would not make the railroad company liable in damages for his death. *Answer.* That we answer in the affirmative.

The Court charged the jury, *inter alia:* "If the boy was there by the invitation of the brakeman, permitted by the conductor, for the purpose simply of pursuing his own employment, and without the authorization of the company's superior officers, then he was an intruder and stranger upon the train, and the company came under no obligation to him, and his mother cannot recover in this action. . . . . . .

"Now, if this be the case, we say to you that this deceased boy was neither a passenger, for he did not come within that category by having paid his fare, having a ticket or free pass, nor was he an employé of the defendant; but being on that train as stated he was an intruder or trespasser—not, of course, that he was a wilful trespasser, in that he had used force, but that he was an intruder or trespasser upon the train in that he was a stranger to it, and was where he had no lawful business to be; and we say to you that if this boy was on the train as a trespasser without permission from any one having power to give it, plaintiff cannot recover damages, except for intentional injury or very gross negligence, and then probably not from the company, but from the person causing the damage.

"If we are right in this case, the plaintiff is not entitled to recover."

Verdict and judgment for defendant. The plaintiffs took this writ, assigning for error, *inter alia*, the answers to points, and the charge of the Court.

Isaac Ash (with whom was *Jas. D. Hancock*), for plaintiff in error.

The conductor of a train has supreme control of it as to all travellers. If his control is limited by private rules, as between the company and himself, strangers without notice are not to be affected thereby. The invitation and permission of the conductor to the boy to travel free, in consideration of the accommodation to passengers by selling newspapers, lighting fires and lamps, etc., constituted him a passenger. One travelling daily on a particular train with the knowledge and permission of the superintendent and conductor, and performing service, may be considered either a passenger or an employé, according to circumstances, but it is absurd to say that he is a trespasser. The evidence should have been fairly submitted to the jury. If they found him to be a passenger, the defendant was liable on the implied contract to carry safely; if found to have been a stranger merely, or upon the cars by invitation of the conductor, without fault on his own part contributing to the accident, the defendant was liable on account of its negligence in running oil cars and a passenger car on the same train; if, by reason of the Act of 1868 (Purd. Dig. 1094, pl. 5), the plaintiffs' right to recover should be limited to the same extent as if for death of an employé, we say that in such case the defendant would be clearly liable for negligence in not maintaining a sufficient track and roadbed.

Patterson *v.* Connellsville R. R. Co., 26 Smith, 389.
O'Donnell *v.* Allegheny Valley R. R. Co., 9 Smith, 239.
Coal Co. *v.* Reed, 25 Pitts. L. J. 82, Jan. 9, 1878.

Osmer (*E. S. Golden* with him), for defendant in error, relied on—

Flower *v.* Penna. R. R. Co., 19 Sm. 213.
Kirby *v.* Penna. R. R. Co., 26 Sm. 506.
Toledo R. R. Co. *v.* Brooks, 81 Ill. 292.

Nov. 3, 1879. THE COURT. This was an action by a parent to recover damages for the death of her son on account of the alleged negligence of the defendant. It is clear from the evidence that the boy was on the train from day to day—not as a passenger or employé of the company—but by the connivance of the conductor, in order to sell newspapers. It is not like a person allowed by the conductor to ride in a car as a passenger without paying fare. In that case there is a legal liability to the company for the fare. This is the case of a mere trespasser, and the company owed him no duty. We are of opinion that the rulings of the learned Judge below were right.

Judgment affirmed.

PER CURIAM. GREEN, J., absent.

[See Cauley *v.* R. R. Co., next case.]

Oct. & Nov. '80, 110, 197.   Oct. 11, 1880.

Cauley v. Pittsburgh, Cincinnati and St. Louis R. W. Co.

Railroad companies—Right to a clear track—Injury to child of tender years trespassing on railroad — Negligence — Contributory negligence of parent—Errors and appeals—Practice—One writ of error cannot be taken to the judgments in two cases tried together.

One writ of error cannot be taken to separate judgments in two actions arising out of the same facts, and tried together on the same evidence. In such case the writ of error will be quashed.

Except at street crossings, where the public has a right of way, a railroad company has the right to a clear track, and it owes no duty to trespassers, whether they be adults, minors, or children of tender years. (Per PAXSON, J.)

It is contributory negligence *per se* in parents to suffer their children to trespass on the cars or track of a railroad company. The fact that the trespass was committed without the knowledge or consent of the parent is immaterial. (Per PAXSON, J.)

While boys were playing on a sand-laden car standing on a switch within the city limits, the train was moved, and while in motion the conductor ordered the boys off. The youngest, a boy of seven years, in jumping off fell under the wheels and was injured. In actions brought by the father of the child, and by the child, against the company, the plaintiffs offered to prove the above facts, and others showing negligence by defendant's servants:

Held, that the Court below properly refused to admit the plaintiffs' offers, and properly directed verdicts for the defendant. (PAXSON, J.)

TRUNKEY and STERRETT, JJ., dissent.

Error to the Common Pleas No. 2, of Allegheny County.

These were two actions on the case, one brought by John H. Cauley, a minor, by his father and next friend John Cauley, and the other by the said John Cauley, the father, against the above-mentioned railway company, to recover damages for injuries to said minor, and loss of service, etc., caused by the alleged negligence of defendant's servants. Plea, not guilty. The docket entries in both cases were the same, and both were tried together.

When the causes came on for trial, before KIRKPATRICK, J., the plaintiffs offered to prove substantially the following facts: On the morning of Sept. 20, 1879, John H. Cauley, a boy of seven years of age, was, without his parents' consent, playing with older boys on a flat car loaded with sand, that was standing upon a switch of the defendant's railroad, at a point within the city of Pittsburgh, adjacent to a street crossing, in a thickly populated district near rolling mills and factories, and near the residence of plaintiffs' family; while so playing, the defendant's servants caused the said car with others to be shifted by a locomotive, and while the train was in rapid motion the conductor, who was on the ground near by, ordered the boys off, and at the same time a brakeman on the train approached the boys in a threatening manner, when the boys jumped off the train, and the plaintiff, John H. Cauley, in so doing fell and was run over, suffering injury which required the amputation of his leg below the knee; the mother of the boy seeing the danger, had called to the conductor protesting against his ordering her boy off the train while it was in motion, to which remonstrance he paid no attention, but with oaths repeated his orders to the boys to get off, while the cars were in motion.

Offers objected to as irrelevant, and because they disclose the fact that the boy was a trespasser at the time of the injury, and they fail to disclose such negligence on the part of the defendants as would entitle plaintiffs to recover. Objection sustained, and offers excluded.

There being no other evidence, the Court charged, as requested by defendant, that the verdict should be for the defendant, adding, at plaintiff's request, that the reason in so charging was because the Court ruled out the plaintiffs' offers of evidence.

Verdict and judgment in each case, for defendant. The plaintiffs took this writ of error to said judgments, assigning for error, the exclusion of plaintiffs' offers of testimony.

A. M. Watson, for plaintiffs in error.

The Court below treated the child as if he were an adult, overlooking the distinction between the legal responsibility of adults and infants of tender years, and the corresponding distinction in the duty of the railroad company to the two classes. The car loaded with sand, standing on a switch in a populous district, not fenced off from the street, offered an irresistible temptation to boys to play in the sand, and the company in failing to provide a watchman to warn them off, tacitly encouraged the trespass, and were guilty of negligence in inhumanly ordering the boys off while the train was in rapid motion, when, by waiting a few minutes, the train would have stopped, and no harm would have been done to the company or to the boys. "A defendant is liable to an infant seven years old for injury resulting from negligence, though the plaintiff was a trespasser and contributed to the mischief by his own act."

Smith v. O'Connor, 12 Wr. 221.
Penna. R. R. Co. v. Lewis, 29 Sm. 33.
Phila. and Reading R. R. Co. v. Long, 25 Sm. 257.
P. & M. Pass. R. W. Co. v. Donahue, 20 Sm. 119.
R. R. Co. v. Spearen, 11 Wr. 300.
Pa. R. R. Co. v. Morgan, 1 Nor. 134.
Lynch v. Nurdin, 1 Ad. & E. 422.
Robinson v. Cone, 22 Ver. 224.

Dalzell (*Hampton,* with him), for defendant in error.

The Court ruled out the plaintiffs' offers, not on the ground of contributory negligence, but because the boy was a trespasser. A distinction may be taken between the suit by the father and that by the minor. There could be no recovery by the former, under any of the authorities. It is the duty of parents to prevent their children from trespassing on a railroad track, and a failure to do so is contributory negligence *per se.*

Smith v. Hestonville, Mantua, and Fairmount Pass. R. W. Co., 8 WEEKLY NOTES, 166.

Nor is the case really doubtful as to the latter. The company owes no duty to trespassers, without regard to age.

Duff v. A. V. R. R. Co. [*ante* p. 504], 27 Pitts. Leg. Journ. 58, Nov. 26, 1879.
Flower v. Pa. R. R. Co., 19 Sm. 214.
Cunningham v. Pa. R. R. Co., Oct. & Nov. T. 1859, unreported.
Knight v. Abert, 6 Barr, 472.
Phila. & Read. R. R. Co. v. Yeiser, Id. 366.

In this case the question of negligence was for the Court.

Goshorn v. Smith, 8 WEEKLY NOTES, 290.

Nov. 8, 1880. THE COURT. It was said by Mr. Justice STRONG, in Philadelphia & Reading R. R. Co. v. Hummell (8 Wright, at page 378): "It is true it should be understood in this State that the use of a railroad track, cutting, or embankment, is exclusive of the public everywhere, except where a way crosses it." The same doctrine has been reiterated again and again, in subsequent cases. In Mulherrin v. Delaware, Lackawanna & Western Railroad Co. (31 P. F. S. 366), it was said: "Except at crossings, where the public have a right of way, a man who steps his foot upon a railroad track, does so at his peril. The company has not only a right of way, but it is exclusive at all times and for all purposes," and Railroad *v.* Norton (12 Harris, 465) was cited in support of this rule.

Many other cases might be referred to were it necessary. We live in an age of steam and rapid development. The world demands quick transportation. Increased speed necessarily involves increased danger. Holding, as we do, such corporations to a strict responsibility for negligence, it is our duty to give them a clear track. This rule is not only proper in itself, but is necessary for the preservation of life. Its propriety is no longer a subject for discussion.

It ought also to be equally well understood that parents who permit their children to trespass upon the track of a railroad are guilty of negligence. It is not only gross, but culpable negligence, as it imperils the lives of the children so trespassing, as also the lives of the travelling public. A similar view was taken in Railroad Company *v.* Hummell, *supra*, where it was said that children "cannot be upon the railroad without a culpable violation of duty by their parents or guardians." It is very clear, therefore, that as to the suit brought by John Cauley, in his own right, for the injury to his son, he cannot recover. The child was upon the car, where he ought not to have been, by the negligence and want of care of his father. Nor does the offer of evidence ruled out by the Court below tend to rebut the presumption of negligence on the part of his parents; on the contrary, it strengthens it. Assuming the offer to be true, it shows that the child was not only playing upon the car on the occasion when he received the injury, but that he had done so before. The location was near his parents' house, probably in sight, as his mother saw the accident, and called to the conductor. That the child was there without his father's consent, is not to the purpose. "To suffer a child to wander on the street has the sense of permit. If such permission or sufferance exist, it is negligence." (Phila. & Reading R. R. Co. *v.* Long, 25 P. F. S. 265.) I apprehend few parents would consent to a child's playing upon a railroad track, or any other known place of danger. But many parents might neglect the precautions necessary to prevent it. In some instances it would require more than merely to caution a child against it. Positive prohibition, followed by punishment for violation, may sometimes be necessary. It too often happens that boys are allowed to wander about the streets, and trespass upon railroad tracks, with very little care or supervision of their parents. Whilst so engaged, injuries of this character are likely to happen. Much as they are to be deplored, and however much our sympathies may be aroused for one so injured, it would be unjust to compel a corporation or individual to make a pecuniary compensation for such accident, when it was the result of the lawful pursuit of a lawful business by such corporation or individual. Aside from this, the defendant-company owed the father of this child no duty. The father owed his child the duty of protection. The company did not. The evidence was properly rejected.

In regard to the suit brought for the child by his father, as his next friend, it is sufficient to say that the child being unlawfully upon the car, the defendant company owed it no duty, and is not liable for the injury. This was the principle upon which Railroad Co. *v.* Hummell was ruled. In the recent case of Duff *v.* Allegheny Valley R. R. Co. (Pittsburgh Legal Journal of Nov. 26, 1879; s. c., *ante*, p. 504), it appears that a conductor of a train, in violation of the rules of the company, permitted a boy to sell papers on the train. By the alleged negligence of the company the boy was killed. The right of his mother to recover was denied upon the ground that the boy was a mere trespasser, and the company owed him no duty. It is useless to multiply authorities. The rule is well settled, and is sustained by reason and authority. Moreover, it is demanded by humanity. There are many unfeeling parents, who not only neglect, but maltreat their children. It would be cruel to such children to lay down a rule which would make it an object for unprincipled parents to expose them to injury and death, upon a railroad track.

Upon the merits, these judgments ought to be affirmed. But we notice that one writ of error has been taken to the two cases. There is no authority for this. It is a practice that we will not encourage. Besides, the Commonwealth loses the tax upon one writ. There should have been a separate writ of error to bring up each case. We have expressed our opinion upon the merits to avoid having our time occupied with the cases again. But we will not enter judgment.

Writ quashed.

Opinion by PAXSON, J.

TRUNKEY and STERRETT, JJ., concur in quashing the writ, but not in the opinion, from which they dissent.

July, '78, 74.   June 25, 1878.

Matthews v. City of Scranton.

Municipal corporations—Cities of the third class—Taxes—Powers of Board of Appeal and Revision—Bonds.

The taxes, for the year 1877, in the City of Scranton were not levied at the time directed by law. The Board of Appeal and Revision made numerous changes in valuations, without appeal from individual taxpayers. On a taxpayer's bill for an injunction to restrain collection of the tax:

Held (reversing the decree of the Court below), that the tax levy was not thereby invalidated, and that a special injunction was improperly awarded.

Whether bonds issued without a statement filed as required by Sec. 2, Act of April 20, 1874 (P. L. 65), are illegal, not decided.

Appeal from the Common Pleas of Luzerne County.

The bill, filed by Matthews *et al.*, taxpayers, etc., set forth that the city of Scranton is a city of the third class, having accepted the Act of 1874 (P. L. 230), and the supplement of 1875 (P. L. 15). By the latter Act it is provided that the taxes shall be levied and the duplicates placed in the hands of the treasurer on or before the first day of July of each year. In 1877, this was not done until October. The Board of Appeal and Revision provided for by the Act of 1875, also made changes in valuations without appeal by the individual taxpayers. The bill averred that this was without authority of law, and that the board had no jurisdiction in the matter of changing valuations except where taxpayers had appealed.

The bill also alleged that part of the debt was illegal, the bonds having been issued without a statement filed as required by Sec. 2, Act of April 20, 1874 (P. L. 65); and prayed that the city and her officers be restrained by injunction, special until hearing, and final thereafter, from collecting said taxes, and from payment of interest on said bonds.

The Court (HANDLEY, J.) granted a special injunction as prayed. From this decree the city took this appeal, assigning the decree as error.

I. H. Burns and *Samuel Dickson*, for appellants.

The time of levying a tax is directory.
Gearhart *v.* Dixon, 1 Barr, 228.
Ins. Co. *v.* Yard, 5 Har. 331.
Parker's Appeal, 8 W. & S. 449.

The Act of March 18, 1875 (P. L. 15), gives the Board of Appeal and Revision power to lower and raise valuations.

The bonds bear on their face the declaration that they are issued in pursuance of law, and the city is bound by this recital.
Knox County *v.* Aspinwall, 21 Howard, 539.
Coloma *v.* Eaves, 2 Otto, 484.
County of Warren *v.* Marcey, 10 Chicago Leg. News, 291.

J. H. Campbell and *Alexander Farnham*, for appellees.

The Act of March 18, 1875, under which taxes are levied in Scranton, is mandatory in its provisions as to time, and must be strictly complied with. The lapse of a day is fatal. See—

Williamsport *v.* Kent, 14 Ind. 306.
People *v.* McCreery, 34 Cal. 432.

The Board of Appeal and Revision could make no changes in valuations, except upon appeal by a taxpayer.
Act of March 18, 1875, P. L. 15.

June 25, 1878. THE COURT. It is ordered that the special injunction in this case be dissolved so far as to permit the Councils and officers of the city of Scranton to collect the taxes laid for the year 1877, and to levy and collect the taxes for 1878, and to perform their ordinary and necessary duties, including therein the payment of the necessary expenses of the Police, Fire, and Highway Departments, and to enable the treasurer of said city to pay the interest on so much of the debt of the said city as is not contested by the city. As to all other matters, including the creation of new debts, and payment of money to members of Councils, the injunction is continued, and the same is ordered to be remitted for further proceedings in due course of procedure.

PER CURIAM.

Jan. '81, 35.   January 6, 1881.

Wiser's Appeal.

Equity — Injunction — Want of jurisdiction — When advantage may be taken of — Injunction not grantable to restrain sale of real estate in which a creditor avers his debtor has an interest.

Filing an answer and proceeding to proof is not a waiver of objection to the jurisdiction of a Court of Equity; such objection may be taken advantage of, even at final hearing.

It is well settled that a Court of Equity has no jurisdiction to restrain by injunction a creditor from levying upon land in which he avers that his debtor has an interest.

Appeal, by Catharine Wiser, from a decree of the Common Pleas No. 2, of Philadelphia County, dismissing her bill for want of jurisdiction.

Bill in equity, filed by C. Wiser against J. Dorff and Wm. H. Wright, Sheriff, averring that the plaintiff was the owner of certain premises in the city of Philadelphia, to which she had obtained title, in the year 1875, by deed duly recorded, from one J. W. Matthews *et ux.*; that, on February 19, 1878, J. Dorff had obtained a judgment against J. W. Matthews on a judgment note, on which judgment he had caused to be issued a writ of fi. fa. and subsequently a vend. exp. against J. W. Matthews, by virtue of which writs the sheriff had taken in execution and was proceeding to sell as the property of J. W. Matthews the above-mentioned premises, conveyed in 1875 to the plaintiff, notwithstanding that the said judgment was no lien thereon; and that great and irreparable damage would be done plaintiff if said sale was allowed to go on; wherefore the plaintiff prayed for an injunction, special until hearing and perpetual thereafter, to restrain defendants from proceeding with said writs and sale. The Court refused to grant a special injunction, and this decree was affirmed on appeal. (Wiser's Appeal, 8 WEEKLY NOTES, 354.)

Subsequently an answer was filed, denying the averments of the bill that the properties belonged to plaintiff, and that J. W. Matthews had no interest therein. A replication was filed joining issue and an examiner appointed, before whom much testimony was taken. When the case came up to be heard on the bill, answer, and proofs, the question of jurisdiction was raised, and the Court dismissed the bill for want of jurisdiction, whereupon the plaintiff took this appeal, assigning for error this action of the Court.

Hennershots (*De F. Ballou* with him), for appellant.

The defendants voluntarily submitted themselves to the jurisdiction, and cannot at this late day object to it. Their consent induced the long proceedings before an examiner, in all of which they took part. It is too late now for them to raise the point.

Bank *v.* Bank, 1 Pars. 222.
Underhill *v.* Van Cortlandt, 2 Johns. Chan. R. 369.
Wilhelm's Appeal, 29 Sm. 141.

J. H. Campbell, for J. Dorff, was not called upon.

January 17, 1881. THE COURT. Nothing is better settled than that a Court of Equity has no jurisdiction to restrain, by injunction, a creditor from levying upon land in which he avers that his debtor has an interest. It is supposed, however, by the learned counsel for the appellant, that the defendant is bound to take the objection *in limine*, and that he waives it by answer and proceeding to proof. It is true that a party may now waive a trial by jury in any civil case, but that is under a special Act of Assembly in proceedings at common law. The waiver in such case must be by express agreement. It is clear that the objection to the jurisdiction in equity may be taken on final hearing.

Decree affirmed and appeal dismissed at the costs of the appellant.

PER CURIAM.

Common Pleas—Law.

C. P. No. 2. Dec. 7, 1880.
Bell v. Bell.

Practice—Proceedings in divorce—Cross-interrogatories, how they should be framed, and when put to witness—Examination other than on the interrogatories filed—Explanation of interrogatories.

In divorce proceedings the cross-interrogatories must be cross-examination strictly, and should be put immediately after the witness has answered the direct interrogatories; there is no right of examination outside of the interrogatories filed, and in case explanation of the interrogatories is necessary, it should be made by the Examiner.

Sur interlocutory report of Examiner in divorce, for instruction.

The report set out that at a meeting duly held "the libellant was produced and examined, and her testimony reduced to writing, as to the interrogatories filed by the libellant, and the examination being concluded, Mr. Perkins, counsel for the respondent, requested your Examiner to propound the cross-interrogatories filed by the respondent; whereupon Mr. Randall, counsel for the libellant, objected to the cross-interrogatories being propounded to the witness until libellant's case is closed, Mr. Randall stating the counsel for the respondent is at liberty to cross-examine witness orally, if he choose, subject to the question of relevancy and competency, reserving the right to himself, as counsel for the libellant, to re-examine the witness *orally*, subject to the same question of relevancy and competency; whereupon Mr. Perkins declined, insisting that the examination of the witness should be confined to the interrogatories and cross-interrogatories filed."

E. Randall, in support of his position, contended that the cross-interrogatories were not limited to cross-examination, and that they should not be put until the libellant's case had been closed, and cited—

Zane *v.* Zane, 1 WEEKLY NOTES, 123.

S. C. Perkins, contra, referred to the Rules of Court on the subject of divorce, and contended that the proper practice was to confine the examination to the interrogatories and cross-interrogatories filed; that the cross-interrogatories should be cross-examination strictly, and should be put immediately after the direct interrogatories; and that oral examination or cross-examination before an Examiner in divorce was not permissible; it was the duty of the *Examiner* to see that the witness stated the matter inquired of in detail.

HARE, P. J. On the ground that the opposite party's witnesses may not be obtainable at a future day, we think that the cross-interrogatories may be propounded immediately after the witness has answered the direct interrogatories. Further, that as any witness may be called and examined by the opposite party in chief, the cross-interrogatories must be cross-examination strictly, and may be excepted to if they are not. The Examiner should explain the interrogatories when explanation is necessary.

C. P. No. 2.   Dec. 27, 1880.

Commonwealth ex rel. Fawkes v. Lynd and Gannon.

Official bond—Suit on, against principal and surety—A sum greater than the face of the bond may be claimed—Interest.

Sur demurrer to narr.

This was an action brought on the official bond of James Lynd, a constable, against him and Thomas Gannon, his surety.

The bond was in the sum of $1000.

The narr. recited that the defendant Lynd had permitted a certain defendant to remove his goods after they had been levied upon and advertised for sale, and claimed damages in the sum of $1200.

Defendant demurred on the ground that the damages claimed were greater than the penalty of the bond.

Gimber, for the demurrer.
Cardesa, contra.

A sum sufficient to cover interest may be claimed in addition to the penal sum of the bond.
N. Y. Ins. Co. v. Seckel, 8 Phila. 92.
Hughes v. Hughes, 4 Sm. 240.

THE COURT. Demurrer overruled.

C. P. No. 2.   Feb. 19, 1880.

Brittin v. Shloss.

Practice—Amendment—New defendant cannot be substituted in action begun by capias.

Rule to amend by changing the name of the defendant from Joseph Shloss to Abraham Shloss, the pleadings to be withdrawn, and the new defendant to be brought into court by an alias writ.

Action of trespass on the case for slander, capias ad respondendum issuing against Joseph Shloss.

The affidavit of plaintiff made in support of the motion disclosed the following facts: That the plaintiff was misinformed as to the name of the defendant; that Joseph Shloss himself conspired to deceive the plaintiff as to the proper defendant, and knowing that he was the wrong party, appeared by attorney and went to issue.

Hoffman, for the rule.

The plaintiff asks leave to amend his præcipe, file a withdrawal of his pleadings in the issue between himself and Joseph Shloss, and bring the proper defendant into court by an alias writ. As to his right to do this see—
Dusenberry v. Bradley, 6 WEEKLY NOTES, 413.

Ledyard, contra.

THE COURT. The proper remedy is to discontinue present action, and to commence action anew by issuing a writ against the true defendant.

Rule discharged.

Per MITCHELL, J.

C. P. No. 2.   March, 1880.

Zanssig et al. v. Telegraph Co.

Practice—Letters rogatory—Execution thereof in foreign language.

Sur exceptions to execution of letters rogatory.

This was an action of trespass on the case for negligence in the transmission of a telegram by the Western Union Telegraph Company from the plaintiffs, Adolf Zanssig & Co., of Philadelphia, to the firm of Alexander & Co., of Gablong, in the empire of Austria.

Letters rogatory had been taken out by the plaintiffs for the purpose of taking the testimony of Moritz Zanssig, who was the managing clerk of the firm of Alexander & Co., in Gablong, Austria.

The return or execution of the letters rogatory was in a foreign language, and stated that the letters rogatory had been adopted or taken up by the R. I. District Court, that there were present at the examination the Judge Associate of the District Court, a sworn secretary, and the witness, Moritz Zanssig; that the witness had been sworn according to custom.

The return was signed by the Judge Associate and the sworn secretary, and there was appended a certificate of the R. I. District Court that the Associate Judge was empowered to execute or practice in the office of a Judge.

The exceptions were chiefly that the letters rogatory had not been executed by a Judge or tribunal having jurisdiction of civil causes, and authorized to administer oaths; that the return was in a foreign language unknown to the defendants; and that the translation was incorrect.

B. H. Brewster, for the exceptions.

THE COURT. Exceptions dismissed.

C. P. No. 2.   Feb. 19, 1881.
Phillips, to use, v. Quigley.

Practice—Sheriff's interpleader—Bond—What facts sufficient to entitle claimant to file his own bond.

Rule to show cause why claimant in interpleader should not be permitted to file his own bond.

On May 24, 1880, judgment was obtained in the Court of Common Pleas of Lebanon County by Phillips against Mrs. A. M. Quigley. This judgment was assigned to N. B. Desch, and, Mrs. Quigley having removed to Philadelphia, a transfer of the judgment was made to the Common Pleas of Philadelphia County. Execution issued, and a levy was made by the sheriff upon the furniture and fixtures in the house of Mrs. Dahl (formerly Mrs. Quigley), No. 208 Spruce Street. The property levied upon was claimed by Hans J. Dahl, and a rule of interpleader was entered by the sheriff to determine its ownership.

The affidavit of the claimant stated the following facts: The stock and fixtures of the premises No. 208 Spruce Street, levied upon by the sheriff under the fi. fa. issued on the transferred judgment, were not the property of the defendant, but his own individual property, having been purchased by him. That he had, at various times, deposited money with the defendant to enable her to furnish and stock the place No. 208 Spruce Street, and to carry on business there for him during his absence; and had taken from her receipts worded to that effect. With this money the defendant had purchased the furniture, etc., taken in execution by the sheriff. The money was not given to the defendant for her own use.

The receipts given by the defendant to the claimant, stating the objects to which the money was to be applied, were also produced.

R. C. *Winship*, for the rule.

When the claimant's case is, *prima facie*, very clear, as where he avers that he does not derive title from or through the defendant, the Court will not require security from him other than his own bond.

R. M. *Shick*, contra.

THE COURT. Rule absolute.

C. P. No. 4.   Feb. 12, 1881.
City v. Wagner.

Municipal claim—Amendment—Act 21 April, 1858, sect. 9—Misdescription of property—An amendment of municipal claim cannot affect intervening rights.

Sur rule to amend city claim.

The claim for curbing and paving was filed March 26, 1879. The sci. fa. had issued. Through a mistake of the District Surveyor the lien was described as against property situate on the east side of Germantown Avenue, 69 feet 5 inches south of Venango Street, "instead of 69 feet 5 inches south of Ontario Street. Plaintiff asked to amend so that the claim should appear to be filed against property on the east side of Germantown Avenue 69 feet 5 inches south of *Ontario* Street." Notice of this rule had been given defendant.

Pierce Archer, for the rule.

The Act of April 21, 1858 (Pur. Dig. 1088, pl. 22), provides that municipal claims . . . may be amended at any time before or at the trial on notice given to defendant under rule of Court.

[BRIGGS, J. We cannot allow this amendment if it will affect an innocent purchaser for value.]

The property has not changed owners since the lien was filed.

THE COURT. Rule absolute, saving all intermediate rights.

Orphans' Court.

Dec. 22, 1880.
Bucknor's Estate.

Review—Petition for modification of decree thereon—Jurisdiction—Practice—Reference back to auditing judge, after final decree and decree on review thereof.

Sur petition for modification of decree on petition for review.

In this case, reported in 7 WEEKLY NOTES, 470, (where all the facts are fully stated), it appeared that the prayer of the petition to amend the adjudication was granted. In pursuance of the opinion then filed, the following decree was subsequently made by the Court in October 1879:—

"It is ordered that said adjudication is not conclusive as to the amount which said A. J. Bucknor, Jr., deceased, or his representatives are entitled to receive, but that whether there is a set-off, or advancement, and if so the amount thereof, and whether there is any balance remaining after deducting the same, are left to be determined in said attachment suits."

F. F. *Milne* now filed a petition, which averred that the issues in said attachment suit came on duly for trial, when all the evidence was submitted, when the jury were directed to render a verdict for the plaintiff (the present petitioner) reserving the question of law as to whether the Common Pleas had jurisdiction, also that a motion for a new trial was made by counsel for the garnishee, and the Court of Common Pleas, being of opinion that it had no jurisdiction as to the question whether the due-bill was a loan or advancement by decedent to his son, directed petitioner to apply to this Court for a modification of so much of its decree, as given above, as included that question.

The petitioner also alleged that there never were any advancements made and charged by the said Bucknor to his son, nor any pretension thereof, until the word *advancements* was introduced into the decree.

The prayer was for an amendment and modification of this decree, by striking out the word *advancement* and as much as relates thereunto.

William A. James, the accountant, filed an answer, to the effect that the decree should not be modified as prayed for, because it represented what this Court intended to decide, and because if so modified, this Court alone having jurisdiction of said question of advancement, the Common Pleas cannot pass upon the same, and injustice will be done the estate by depriving it of the deduction from the share of A. J. Bucknor, Jr., on account of such advancement.

M. Arnold, for the petitioner.
S. Gustine Thompson, contra.

January 29, 1881. THE COURT. When the account in this estate was before the Auditing Judge, counsel were under the impression that all questions relating to the distributive share of A. J. Bucknor, Jr., could be determined under the attachment sur judgment then pending in the Court of Common Pleas. Nothing was said, therefore, with regard to the loans, etc., alleged to have been made to him by the decedent; and, as a necessary consequence, the adjudication awarded to him, subject to such attachment, an aliquot part of the estate, without any deduction whatever.

Subsequently counsel, apprehending that the decree thus entered would be conclusive, upon the trial of the attachment as to the amount of the share, presented a petition alleging the existence of claims on the part of the estate against the distributee, and asking that the adjudication might be opened so far as to leave the question of amount unembarrassed by any technicality when the matter should come before the Court of Common Pleas—the attachment in that court having preceded the adjudication.

The allegations of the petition having been admitted by demurrer (see report, 7 W. N. C. 470), we were of opinion, that, while the application did not come within the Act of 1840, it would be inequitable to permit a decree of distribution so made to preclude proof of the facts, and an ascertainment of the amount actually due the distributee. The prayer of the petition was therefore granted, and a decree, prepared by counsel for the accountants, and not objected to by counsel for the attaching creditors, was entered, no point being made as to the exclusiveness of our jurisdiction with regard to the matters involved.

This question is now presented for our consideration.

So far as advancements are concerned, it is clear that the jurisdiction of the Orphans' Court is exclusive. At one time the law was supposed to be otherwise (Earnest *v.* Earnest, 5 Rawle, 219), but the point was settled in Holliday *v.* Ward (7 Harris, 485).

The reasoning which led to this decision is equally applicable to matters of set-off. The Orphans' Court is the tribunal required to make distribution of the estates of decedents, and clothed with full power to determine all matters relating thereto. The amount withheld from a distributee's share by reason of his debt to the estate, equally with amounts advanced, must go into the balance for general distribution, and be divided among all the parties entitled. This would be impracticable in any other Court than the Orphans' Court; and the only effect of a determination by the Common Pleas that a distributee was not to receive his share because he was indebted to the estate in a sum which exceeded it, would be, so far as other distributees were concerned, to require the filing of a new account by the executor or administrator, and a redistribution to be made by the Orphans' Court. (See Springer's Estate, 5 Casey, 208; Hughes's Appeal, 7 Smith, 181; Achford *v.* Ewing, 1 Casey, 213.) The two cases last cited, in terms, assert the exclusiveness of the jurisdiction as to all matters affecting the question of distribution.

As we are now asked to modify our former decree, so far as it relates to the alleged advancements, we have concluded, instead of thus confining the correction, to do what we should have done when the adjudications were opened, viz., refer the accounts back to the Auditing Judge for the purpose of hearing the allegations and proof with regard to the share of A. J. Bucknor, Jr., and of ascertaining what amount, if any, was due to him in respect of such share at the date of the original adjudication, or at any time prior thereto after the death of the decedent.

Decree accordingly.
Opinion by PENROSE, J.

Supreme Court.

Jan. '80, 162. January 31, 1881.

Horstmann et al. v. Kaufman.
Horstmann's Appeal.

Constitutional law—Debtor aud creditor—Attachment—Act of June 11, 1879, relative to the appointment of a commissioner to take testimony of fraudulent debtors—Unconstitutionality of—Art. I. Sec. 9 of the Constitution—Affidavit, sufficiency of—Acts of July 13, 1842, March 27, 1865, and March 17, 1869—Evidence—Arbitrary compulsion and duress by Courts.

The Act of June 11, 1879 (P. L. 129) is unconstitutional and void, because it proposes on its face to force a debtor to forego his constitutional right under Art. I. Sec. 9, of the Constitution, of not being compelled to give evidence against himself, with which the Legislature has no power to interfere.

Per GORDON, J. Arbitrary compulsion and duress by Court stand on no higher ground than the duress and compulsion of natural persons. In either case because of the wrong done to the witness, the evidence thus produced cannot afterwards be used against him.

Certiorari to and appeal from Common Pleas No. 3, of Philadelphia County.

The case came before the Court below on a rule to show cause why a commissioner should not be appointed under the Act of June 11, 1879 (P. L. 129,) to take the testimony of the defendant and others. Charles J. Horstmann, Otto Von Hein and Gustavus Walter, trading as Horstmann, Von Hein & Co. obtained a judgment, September 20, 1879, against Charles Kaufman of June Term, 1879, No. 850, on which a fi. fa. issued upon the same day, to which the sheriff returned *nulla bona*. An affidavit was then filed by the plaintiff as follows:—

"Gustavus Walter, being duly sworn according to law, deposes and says, that he is a judgment-creditor of Charles Kaufman, the defendant in the above cause, and that he is a member of the firm of Horstmann, Von Hein & Co., the plaintiffs therein, and that he has reason to believe that the said defendant has property, rights in action, stocks, moneys or evidences of debts, which the said defendant fraudulently conceals and refuses to apply to the payment of his debts.

Sworn to and subscribed before me this 10th day of November, A. D. 1879. } GUSTAVUS WALTER.

A. H. NONES,
Notary Public, 486 Broadway, N. Y.

On November 12, 1879, on motion of counsel for the plaintiff, a rule on the defendant returnable on the 15th, was granted to show cause why a commissioner should not be appointed to take testimony. After a hearing the Court discharged the rule, FINLETTER, J., delivering the following opinion:—

"The very able argument of the counsel for defendant has left scarcely a doubt on our minds as to the unconstitutionality of the Act. We are not, however, called upon to decide this question, inasmuch as we are compelled to refuse the rule on other grounds. The Act must be construed in conformity with the construction given to the Act to which it is a supplement. The affidavit should, therefore, set out the facts which warrant the belief that the defendant has property, etc., and also the facts which warrant the averment of fraudulent concealment." (Reported 8 WEEKLY NOTES, 73.)

The plaintiff took this certiorari and appeal, assigning for error, the order of the Court discharging the rule.

Sharp (*Alleman*, with him), for the appellant.

The title of the Act of June 11, 1879, complies with the requirements of Art. III. Sec. 3, of the Constitution. The Act of 1879 is entitled "A *supplement* to an Act approved March 17, 1869, entitled 'An Act relative to fraudulent debtors.'"
The subject of the Act of 1879 is germane to the subject of the original Act, and, therefore, within the article of the Constitution.

In re Petition of First Presbyterian Church of Pittsburgh, 6 WEEKLY NOTES, 421.
State Line R. R. Co.'s Appeal, 27 Sm 429.
Allegheny County Home's Appeal, Ib. 77.

The Act of 1879 is not in violation of Sec. 8 of the Declaration of Rights, which was aimed at an abuse of power entirely different from the power given by this Act. The Declaration of Rights is nearly identical in words and quite identical in meaning with Art. IV. of the Constitution of the United States, the purpose of which was to prevent the issue of general criminal warrants, under which in England parties were arrested without being named therein.

Story on the Constitution, § 1895 (ed. 1833).

The process given by the Act of 1879 is the common law writ of subpœna. The objection that the Act violates Section IX. of the Bill of Rights which provides that "in criminal prosecutions the accused cannot be compelled to give evidence against himself" is without force because :—

(1) The witness has his common law privilege of refusing to answer where such answer will have a tendency to expose him to a penal liability, to any kind of punishment, or to a criminal charge.

1 Greenleaf on Evidence, sec. 451.
Regina v. Garbett, 1 Dennis C. C. 236.

Where the answer is made under a compulsory statute requiring the witness to disclose his crime, such disclosures cannot be used against him in a criminal prosecution, and therefore he cannot decline to answer.

U. S. v. Prescott, 2 Dillon C. C. 405.
In re Brooks, 5 Pac. L. R. 191.

(2) He has ample protection under the Act July 22, 1842, Sec. 22 (Purd. Dig. 53, pl. 70), which provides in substance that no person shall be excused from answering as a witness in relation to the fraudulent concealment of property, *but no answer given by him shall be used against him in any other suit or prosecution.*

The constitution does not protect a man from giving evidence affecting his property rights, or the Act of March 27, 1865, Sec. 1 (Purd. Dig. 624, pl. 13) would be unconstitutional. This no one would claim. The argument of the other side is fully answered by the practice under the Bankrupt Act of 1867 where there was no provision that disclosures made by a bankrupt upon his examination should not be used against him in a criminal prosecution, and yet it has been held that the bankrupt could not refuse to answer any question concerning fraudulent concealment of property.

This Act has been held to be constitutional in Loewi v. Haedrick, 8 WEEKLY NOTES, 70.
Dorf v. Matthews, 36 Leg. Int. 372.
Cox v. Walton, 8 WEEKLY NOTES, 360.

The Court below discharged this rule on the express ground that, in conformity with the practice under the Act of March 17, 1869, to which this Act is a supplement, the affidavit must set out the facts upon which the plaintiff has reason to believe that defendant has acted fraudulently. But this Court has since decided that an affidavit in the words of the Act of 1869 is sufficient.

Sharpless v. Ziegler, 8 WEEKLY NOTES, 190.

Mayer Sulzberger, for the appellee.

The Act of June 11, 1879, is unconstitutional because—

(1) It does not clearly express its subject in its title, as required by Art. III. Sec. 3, of the Constitution. It is not a supplement to the Act of March 17, 1869, as its title professes, for that Act was only to authorize the commencement of an action by attachment instead of by summons, and it is not germane to that object. It is rather a supplement to the Act of 1836 providing for bills of discovery.

(2) Because it is in violation of Art. I. Sec. 9 of the Constitution, which provides that "a man cannot be compelled to give evidence against himself."

The authorities cited on the other side to show the constitutionality of the Act are not judgments of Courts of last resort. It is well established that a statute making parties witnesses against themselves cannot be construed to compel them to disclose facts which would subject them to criminal punishment.

Cooley on Constitutional Limitations, § 394.
Broadbent v. The State, 7 Md. 416.

In order to compel a man to testify against himself the statute must exempt him from criminal prosecution.

Wharton's Criminal Law, § 808.

If the Act is constitutional, it involves the abandonment of our present system of procedure and the adoption in lieu thereof of the inquisitorial system of the civil law. It enables a plaintiff to compel a defendant to criminate himself and others in an *ex parte* proceeding.

To the contention that a perfect analogy is to be found in the practice under the bankrupt Act of 1867, it is a sufficient answer to say that practice under that Act was not uniform. On the contrary, it was held in two cases that a bankrupt could not be compelled to answer when his answer would criminate himself.

In re Koch, 1 B. R. 549.
In re Patterson, 1 Id. 125.

The Acts of 1842 and 1879 are not at all analogous, because the proceeding under the former is a judicial act, whereas in the latter the discretion of the plaintiff sets the procedure in motion. It is fatal to the constitutionality of the Act that the answers of the defendant may expose him to a criminal prosecution, for the alleged acts of the defendant are the very acts made misdemeanors by sections 130, 131, and 132 of the Penal Code of 1860.

Henry Emery's Case, 107 Mass. 172.
Galbraith v. Eichelberger, 3 Yeates, 515.

While it is true that an affidavit in the words of the Act of 1869 has been held valid, yet that affidavit swears to a *fact*, and not to an *opinion* or *mere belief*, and gives security for any injustice done under it.

This appeal is in effect an application to this Court to issue a mandamus to the Court below commanding it to appoint a commissioner.

February 14, 1881. THE COURT. In Sharpless v. Ziegler (8 W. N. C. 190), we held that under the Act of 17th of March, 1869, where the affidavit followed in general terms the wording of the statute, it was a sufficient warrant to the prothonotary to issue the writ of attachment, and that the Court had no power to quash such writ, though it might, on proper cause shown, dissolve such attachment so far as it affected the goods of the debtor seized under it. We also called attention to the obvious distinction in this respect, between this Act and that of July 13, 1842, in that, whilst the attachment directed by the latter can be issued only after judicial consideration, the writ authorized by the former issues from the prothonotary as a ministerial act.

The Act under consideration, June 11, 1879 (P. L. 129), would seem in this respect to be of the same character as that of 1869. All that is required of the Court is, that upon filing the prescribed affidavit, it shall appoint a commissioner, an act purely ministerial. Indeed, even this may be dispensed with, if there be a standing commissioner, for the Act does not require that such officer be appointed specially for the case in hand.

Whilst, therefore, the correctness of the decree in this case is admitted, we cannot agree with the Court below that, admitting the validity of the Act, the affidavit was insufficient to support the motion to appoint a commissioner. The affidavit is in the words of the statute, which is all that seems to be required; no such thing as judicial discretion is left to the Court, it is made the mere minister of the creditor. The plaintiff in the execution is clothed with the sole, unrestrained, and unlimited power to call before himself and his commissioner the defendant with his books and papers, and then and there at his own good pleasure examine him and them without rule, restraint, or supervision, and without limitation as to time or manner. What questions shall be asked, how they shall be asked, what books and papers shall be produced, and, how they shall be examined, how long the unfortunate debtor may be detained and when discharged, of all these the creditor is made the sole judge, and the Court of Common Pleas is but his minister to enforce his behests by subpœnas and attachments.

With all this power the execution-plaintiff clothes himself by the mere act of filing an affidavit "that he has reason to believe that said judgment debtor has property, rights in action, stocks, moneys or evidences of debt, which he fraudulently conceals and refuses to apply to the payment of his debts." And when he is so clad with this power, whether he will use it discreetly and properly, or arbitrarily and improperly, rests altogether with himself. A more ingenious inquisitorial device to squeeze the last farthing from the wretched debtor was never before devised, and for its complete perfection it needs but the boot and thumbscrew.

Dropping, however, the question whether the Legislature can constitutionally invest one citizen with a power so arbitrary and so irresponsible as that found in this statute, over a fellow-citizen, and whether a Court may be so far disrobed of its judicial functions as to be made the mere tool of the creditor, there are, nevertheless, some rights possessed by the debtor, which even the law-making power is bound to respect.

One of these rights is, that he shall not be compelled to give evidence that may be used against him in a criminal prosecution, in other words, he may not be compelled to do that which may criminate himself. The framers of the Act of 1842 were careful to provide that no answer which the defendant was required to make as a witness should be used against him in any other suit or prosecution. But this Act of 1879 makes no provision of that kind, and yet, as has been well shown by the learned counsel for the defendant, the initial proposition is to compel the debtor to reveal that which is made a misdemeanor by the Crimes Act of 1860. This cannot be done. (Galbreath v. Eichelberger, 3 Yeates, 515). And as this enactment proposes on its face to force the debtor to forego a constitutional right, with which the Legislature has no power to interfere, it is utterly void and worthless. No such attempt has ever heretofore been made in Pennsylvania, and it is to no purpose to refer to the Act of 1842, for that Act leaves the option with the defendant. He may verify his allegations by his affidavit, but, if he does so, he submits himself as a witness and may be examined by the complainant. Even then, when he thus voluntarily submits himself, the Act protects him in that it not only prohibits the use of the evidence so given from being used in any prosecution, but, also, in any suit against him. (Uhler v. Maulfair, 11 Har. 481.) The Act of 27 March, 1865, is still less to the point, for it certainly does not follow, that because a party in a civil suit may use his adversary as a witness, he may therefore compel him to testify to that which would criminate himself. His rights as a witness remain, though the right to refuse to testify, which he formerly had as a party, is taken away. The argument, therefore, based on this Act is not sound; but, the counsel for the plaintiff argues, and cites a number of authorities to prove, that where a witness answers under a compulsory order of the Court, such answers cannot be used against him, and hence without a statutory provision he is sufficiently protected. This is true, and for the very reason that he answers under an arbitrary compulsion, to which he ought not to have been subjected. (Regina v. Garbet, 1 Denison's Cr. C. 236.) In this case it was held, that statements made by a witness after he had appealed to the Court to be excused from making such statements, cannot be admitted to prove him guilty of a crime; that such statements must be regarded as given under compulsion and duress, upon the same principle that confessions not free and voluntary cannot be received to affect the defendant.

It is thus manifest, that arbitrary compulsion and duress by a Court, stand on no higher ground than the duress and compulsion of natural persons. In either case because of the wrong done to the witness, the evidence thus produced cannot afterwards be used against him.

As then the Act of 1879 contravenes an important principle of the Bill of Rights, it must be regarded as unconstitutional and void.

The order of the Court below discharging the rule for a commissioner is affirmed.

Opinion by GORDON, J.

Oct. & Nov. '79, 337.   Oct. 7, 1880.

Travellers' Insurance Company of Hartford, Conn., v. Heath.

Reversal of judgment after money paid under execution—Subsequent final judgment for defendant—Right of defendant to recover the money back in assumpsit—Right not barred by refusal of order of restitution, on reversal—Recognisance of bail in error, where writ of error was non prossed, effect of.

The rule that money collected by execution cannot be recovered back, though not lawfully due, does not apply where the judgment on which the execution issued was subsequently reversed on writ of error, and a second trial resulted in a judgment for the defendant. In such case assumpsit will lie to recover back the money so paid.

The fact that the Supreme Court in reversing the judgment refused to award an order of restitution, is not a bar to such action.

Error to the Common Pleas No. 1, of Allegheny County.

Assumpsit, by John Heath, against the above-named corporation, to recover back money paid under an execution upon a judgment which was subsequently reversed by the Supreme Court.

The facts of this case were as follows: In July, 1870, the Travellers' Insurance Company of Hartford, Conn., a corporation incorporated by the Legislature of Connecticut, appointed one Thorne, of the city of Pittsburgh, to be their agent for the west part of the State of Pennsylvania during the pleasure of the officers of said company, and said Thorne gave bond to the company in $5000, with the plaintiff Heath, and another, as sureties thereon, conditioned for the prompt payment by Thorne to the company of all premiums and other moneys of the company to be received by him, and for the due performance of his duties as agent. Thorne having subsequently failed to pay over moneys so collected by him, the company, in January, 1873, brought suit on the bond against him and the sureties, in the Common Pleas No. 2, of Allegheny County, and recovered a verdict and judgment against said defendants for $1847.08. The principal ground of defence in said action was that the corporation-plaintiff had not complied with the statute law of Pennsylvania relating to foreign insurance companies, and therefore had no status to maintain the action. The Court below declined so to hold, and the cause was removed to the Supreme Court by writ of error, the defendants entering a recognizance in order to effect a supersedeas. This writ of error was non prossed to October and November Term, 1874, and, upon the return of the record to the Court below, a fi. fa. was issued against the defendants, to which the sheriff returned, "Money made; paid by John Heath." Subsequently another writ of error was sued out, to October and November Term, 1875, upon which the Supreme Court, holding that the company had no status to maintain the action, reversed the judgment of the Court below, and awarded a *venire facias de novo*. (Reported 30 Sm. 28.) Heath thereupon presented a petition to the Supreme Court, asking for an order of restitution, which was refused by the Court. On the second trial the Court below ruled, in accordance with the opinion of the Supreme Court, that the company could not recover, and a verdict and final judgment were entered for defendants.

Heath thereupon brought this action of assumpsit against the Insurance Company to recover back the sum so paid by him, and declared in the common counts for money had and received, etc. Upon the trial, before COLLIER, J., the defendant offered to prove that the money for which this suit was brought was paid by Heath on account of moneys belonging to the defendant received by Thorne as their agent and not paid over by him, for which Heath was liable as surety under the condition of his bond. Objected to; objection sustained. (10th assignment of error.)

The defendant presented the following points:
(1) That a payment without compulsion is a voluntary payment, and if they find the alleged payment by Heath to have been made without compulsion they must find for defendant. *Affirmed.*

(2) That compulsion in this case under the evidence would be a levy upon the property of said Heath, and a payment by him to relieve his property from the levy; and if no such levy was made, and he, without that, paid the debt, your verdict must be for defendant. *Refused.* (1st assignment of error.)

(3) That the return of the sheriff, "Money made; paid by John Heath," implies a voluntary payment, and that the return of the sheriff

being of record is conclusive, and John Heath cannot recover in this case. *Refused.* (2d assignment of error.)

(4) That by the bond dated July 25, 1870, the said plaintiff, John Heath, in equity and good morals, undertook to pay to the Travellers' Insurance Company the very moneys that he has paid, to wit: such moneys as Robert Thorne should *receive* as their agent after the date of said bond, and *not pay over*, and if the jury find that the moneys paid by John Heath are such moneys, then he cannot recover. *Refused.* (3d assignment.)

(5) That the entering into the recognizance for writ of error to Supreme Court by John Heath was a voluntary undertaking by him; and, according to the condition thereof, he agreed to pay if the writ was not prosecuted with effect; and I now instruct you that as that writ was not prosecuted with effect, and the money he subsequently paid was the condemnation money, and costs as therein provided, he cannot in this action recover the money so paid. *Refused.* (4th assignment.)

(6) That if the jury find the moneys paid by Heath to have been paid after the first writ of error in Supreme Court was non prossed, the reversal of the judgment and all subsequent proceedings cannot aid Heath in recovering the money back. *Refused.* (7th assignment.)

(7) The plaintiff, John Heath, having failed to prosecute this writ of error with effect, in pursuance of the recognizance taken June 17, 1874, in No. 177, October and November Term, 1874, of the Supreme Court of Pennsylvania for the Western District of Pennsylvania—which recognizance, and the records of the case in which it was taken, are now in evidence—the said John Heath became liable to pay the condemnation money and costs, and having done so cannot recover in this action for said money so paid. *Refused.* (5th assignment.)

(8) The said John Heath, at No. 9, October and November Term, 1875, of the Supreme Court of Pennsylvania, having applied for a writ or order of restitution as per his petition in evidence, which order of restitution against the defendant company was refused, and it being for the same money for which this action was brought, the plaintiff cannot recover. *Refused.* (6th assignment.)

(9) Under all the evidence in the case the plaintiff cannot recover. *Refused.* (8th assignment.)

The Court charged the jury, *inter alia,* as follows: "Now, if Mr. Heath paid that money voluntarily, without any execution having been issued against him, or without any threat of execution, he could not recover it back here; but if he knew the execution was issued, and that his property was bound, and there might be a levy made, and he be forced to pay the money, then if he should go and pay it. that would not be a voluntary payment; it would be compulsory." (9th assignment.)

Verdict and judgment for the plaintiff. The defendant took this writ, assigning for error the rejection of its offer of testimony, the answers to points, and the portion of the charge quoted, as above indicated.

D. T. Watson and *S. M. Raymond*, for the plaintiff in error.

Assumpsit cannot be maintained in this case. The record does not show that the payment was a compulsory one; the return "money made; paid by John Heath," does not show that a levy was made, and it is consistent with a voluntary payment. The mere fact that a fi. fa. issued is insufficient to shift the burden of proof, which was on plaintiff, to show that the payment was compulsory.

Colwell *v.* Peden, 3 Watts, 327.
Allentown *v.* Saeger, 8 Har. 421.

But if it were compulsory, money paid on execution cannot be recovered back in assumpsit, though not lawfully due.

Federal Ins. Co. *v.* Robinson, 1 Nor. 359.
Finnel *v.* Brew, 2 WEEKLY NOTES, 622.

The refusal by the Supreme Court of the writ of restitution, on the reversal of the judgment, was conclusive against the plaintiff's claim to recover back the payment.

Breading *v.* Blocher, 5 Cas. 349.
Harger *v.* Commissioners, 2 Jones, 251.
Thorne and Heath *v.* Ins. Co., 30 Sm. 28.

Our offer should have been admitted to show that the money was *ex æquo et bono* the money of the insurance company, which they had an equitable right to *retain*, as against the plaintiff, after they had once received it from him, although, owing to a technicality, they were incompetent to sue for it.

Barr *v.* Craig, 2 Dal. 151.
Haldane *v.* Duche, Ibid. 176.

We also had the right to retain the money, under the terms of the plaintiff's recognizance, as bail in error, on the first writ of error which was not "prosecuted with effect," but non prossed.

W. S. Purviance and *H. W. Weir*, for defendant in error.

Assumpsit will lie where money has been received under a judgment which has been reversed, or where the Court had no jurisdiction.

Duncan *v.* Kirkpatrick, 13 S. & R. 294.
Newdigate *v.* Davy, 1 Raymond, 742.
Marriott *v.* Hampton, 2 Esp. N. P. Rep. 546–48, note.

October 18, 1880. THE COURT. After reversal of the judgment obtained by the present plaintiff in error against Robert Thorne and his sureties, it was finally determined, on the second trial, in accordance with the judgment of this Court (reported in 30 P. F. Smith, 15), that the insurance company had no right to recover the amount of the premiums, etc., for which suit was brought, for the reason that the company, during the time that Thorne, acting as its agent, collected the same, was doing business within this Commonwealth in direct contravention of the law relating to foreign insurance companies. It was held in that case that the Legislature had a clear right to prescribe the conditions under which foreign corporations may do business in this State, and the mode of appointing and qualifying their agents; and that actions based upon transactions prohibited by the statute cannot be maintained in our courts. The general principle underlying the decision is that courts will not aid a party in an action grounded on an immoral or illegal act; and it is right that it should be so, because if foreign insurance companies were aided by our courts in gathering the fruits of their illegal acts, done in palpable violation of the statute, it would soon become practically a dead letter as to many of them.

For the reasons stated, it was thus definitely settled that the Travellers' Insurance Company had no legal claim upon the bond against either Thorne or his sureties for the premiums collected by him; and it is difficult to understand upon what principle of equity or sound morality the company could claim to collect and retain, as against one of the sureties, money which represented the fruit of illegal transactions.

The first writ of error, sued out by Thorne and his sureties, was non prossed by this Court in 1874, whereupon the record was remitted and an execution was issued, upon which, according to the sheriff's return, the money was collected from John Heath, one of the sureties. An alias writ of error was then purchased, and upon it, in 1875, the judgment was reversed, and a *venire facias de novo* awarded. The new trial resulted in a verdict and final judgment in favor of Thorne and his sureties, as above stated. The present action was then brought by John Heath to recover back the money which he was compelled to pay on the execution, and to which, according to the final judgment of the Court, the defendant-company had no legal claim.

The first assignment of error is the refusal of the Court to charge—"That compulsion in this case under the evidence would be a levy upon the property of Heath and a payment by him to relieve his property from the levy; and if no such levy was made, and he without that paid the debt, the verdict must be for the defendant." The second is the refusal of the Court to charge —"That the return of the sheriff, 'money made, paid by John Heath,' implies a voluntary payment, and that the return of the sheriff being of record is conclusive, and John Heath cannot recover in this case."

The substance of the contention in these two assignments, together with the ninth, is that, inasmuch as it does not appear that a levy was actually made on the property of Heath before he paid the money to the sheriff, the payment was voluntary, and therefore he could not recover. We cannot assent to this proposition. The first writ of error, by which the execution had theretofore been restrained, was non prossed, the execution was issued, and at once became a lien on all of Heath's personal property in the county from the time it was placed in the sheriff's hands. Heath had no alternative but to pay the money or submit to the seizure and sale of his property. Under these circumstances, payment of the money to the sheriff on the execution was not, in any proper sense of the term, a voluntary payment; on the contrary, it was under stress of the execution, and therefore compulsory. The learned Judge had affirmed defendant's first point—"That a payment without compulsion is a voluntary payment, and, if the jury find the alleged payment by Heath to have been made without compulsion, they must find for the defendant." The question was thus by defendant's request submitted to the jury; but, in any aspect of the case, there was no error in refusing to affirm the second and third points, or in charging as complained of in the ninth assignment.

The third, fourth, and fifth assignments are not sustained. The principle involved in the third was broadly settled in Thorne *et al. v.* The Insurance Co. (*supra*); nor does his recognizance, entered into when he took the first writ of error, or the *non pros* of the suit stand in the way of his recovery. The money which he seeks to recover back was not collected under the recognizance, but on the execution issued on the original judgment.

The contention in the sixth assignment is that the refusal of the Court to grant a writ of restitution immediately upon the reversal of the first judgment is a bar to this action. We do not think so. Restitution is not always of right; it is frequently a matter of grace; and the refusal to grant the writ before the second trial was had, and the right of the insurance company to recover the amount of premiums collected finally determined, cannot be a bar to the present suit instituted after the first was ended. In Harger *v.* Commissioners of Washington Co. (2 Jones, 251), it is said: "Restitution is not of mere right; it is *ex gratia;* resting in the exercise of a sound discretion; and the Court will not order it where the justice of the case does not call for it." In refusing the order of restitution, the

Court may have been influenced by the fact apparent on the record, that the plaintiff in error was guilty of laches in not prosecuting his first writ of error, and permitting the same to be non prossed, whereby he lost the benefit of his writ as a supersedeas; but, on whatever ground it may have been refused, we are of opinion that the refusal at the time and under the circumstances is not a bar to the present action.

What has already been said is a sufficient answer to the seventh and eighth assignments, both of which present the general question of the right of the plaintiff below to recover. The general principle undoubtedly is that money collected or paid upon lawful process of execution cannot be recovered back, though not justly or lawfully due by the defendant in the execution to the plaintiff. Cases in which the principle is recognized are numerous, but in none of them is the reason more clearly and forcibly stated than in Federal Insurance Company *v.* Robinson (1 Norris, 359). They are cases in which the judgment on which the execution issued was never reversed or vacated. Whereas in the case before us—the judgment which supported the execution has not only been reversed, but, on a re-trial, final judgment has been entered in favor of the opposite party, the principle does not apply. In Duncan *v.* Kirkpatrick (13 S. & R. 292), Chief Justice GIBSON remarks "that assumpsit is the proper action when the money has been received under a judgment which has been reversed;" but he restricts its application to cases of reversal without any order of restitution.

The offer which is the subject of complaint in the last assignment was properly rejected.

Judgment affirmed.

Opinion by STERRETT, J. GORDON, J., did not sit.

Jan. '80, 134.   Jan. 4, 1881.

Boughton *v.* The American Exchange National Bank.

Bills and notes—Usury—Affidavits of defence—Law of another State—Question of fact—Precision of averment—Practice.

The laws of another State, a member of the Union, must be proved as matters of fact, hence an averment in an affidavit of defence of the law of another State must be made with the same precision as the averment of any other fact.

In a suit upon two promissory notes by the indorsee against the maker, the affidavit of defence averred that the notes though dated at Philadelphia were in fact made in New York, that the notes included usury, and that, "under the statute of New York and the decisions thereon, the said notes are usurious and void even in the hands of third persons:"

Held, that the averment was insufficient to prevent judgment.

Error to the Common Pleas No. 3, of Philadelphia County.

Assumpsit, by the American Exchange National Bank against John W. Boughton, upon two promissory notes drawn by Boughton to the order of one Hussey and by him indorsed. The notes were dated Philadelphia, and payable in New York.

The affidavit of defence set forth "that the two notes copies of which are filed in this case, were delivered to the payee Hussey, doing business in New York, and by him there indorsed. That they were executed by the defendant, and delivered to the said Hussey in New York simply as a matter of accommodation to said Hussey, and for the purpose of renewing two preceding accommodation notes given to said Hussey, and in the hands of Samuel S. Harris, banker, at 658 Broadway, New York. That the said Hussey, in receiving the two notes now sued upon, and before the maturity of the same, delivered them to said Harris in New York City in renewal of the two preceding notes and paid him therefor legal interest at seven per cent., and the further sum of twenty-five dollars on each of said notes as usurious interest.

"The defendant suggests to the Court that, under the statute of New York and the decisions thereon, the said notes are usurious and void even in the hands of third persons."

A rule for judgment for want of a sufficient affidavit of defence having been made absolute, the defendant took this writ, assigning for error the action of the Court.

Thomas Greenbank, for plaintiff in error.

The law which governs the contracts in this case is the *lex loci contractus.*

Brewster *v.* Lyndes, 2 Miles, 185.

Under the Act of Assembly of New York of May 15, 1837 (Dig. Laws N. Y., 2 Fay, 371), the notes in suit are void.

Kent *v.* Walton, 7 Wend. 257.
Eastman *v.* Shaw, 65 N. Y. 522.
Bank *v.* Potter, 1 Clark Ch. 432.
Powell *v.* Waters, 8 Cowen, 670.
Bennet *v.* Smith, 15 John. 355.

Besides these New York cases, this Court has construed the statute in question favorably to our contention.

Vantine *v.* Wood, 1 H. 272.

William W. Montgomery (*Samuel Wagner* with him), for defendant in error.

The question of usury is one affecting the remedy, and therefore the *lex fori* should govern.

January 24, 1881. THE COURT. The defendant in this case claims, that, although the notes in suit are dated at Philadelphia, they are payable in New York, and he argues that they are to be governed by the law of New York. He further contends, that, by the law of that State, such securities as these, although on their face they purport to be ordinary business paper, may be shown to be accommodation paper, and, such being the fact, that they are void by the statute law of New York as interpreted by the Courts of that State. He argues that this consequence follows, even as against innocent third parties, who take them in the regular course of business, before maturity, for full value actually paid and without notice of any taint, if, in point of fact, as between the original parties, they were in any manner affected with usury. It is needless to say, that in this Commonwealth such a defence would not be listened to, in any Court of justice, if the transaction were a Pennsylvania contract. Of course, in order to maintain such a defence in our Courts upon the ground that it is a good defence by the law of New York, it is absolutely essential, in an affidavit of defence, to aver, and on the trial to prove by competent testimony, that the law of New York is in accordance with the contention. The question, what is the law of another country or State, when that law is set up in a litigated cause, is a pure question of fact. "The established doctrine now is, that no Court takes judicial notice of the laws of a foreign country, but they must be proved as facts." (Story, Confl. of Laws, § 637. See also 1 Whart. Law of Evid. § 300, and §§ 304 to 312 inclusive.) As to the necessity and kind of proof required in such cases see Ripple *v.* Ripple (1 R. 386). The laws of another State, a member of the Union, are to be proved, as the laws of a foreign country. It is well settled, that in the absence of proof, the law of the State where the contract was made will be presumed to be the same as the *lex fori*. (20 P. F. S. 257-8, and cases cited.)

The defence in the present case is brought before us in an affidavit of defence. The only averment in the affidavit upon this subject is in the following words: "The defendant suggests to the Court, that, under the statute of New York and the decisions thereon, the said notes are usurious and void in the hands of third persons." If this mode of stating facts were to be used as to any ordinary matter of fact, it would not be tolerated as a sufficient statement. The averment under consideration is, at the best, a mere suggestion and not an assertion of anything. Even if it were an assertion, it should be very much more specific than it is. No statute is quoted either in words or by any statement of its substance. No decisions of any Courts are described or even referred to, as establishing any particular rule of law. It is very certain that no statute and no decisions of New York ever declared "that said notes are usurious and void even in the hands of third persons," and yet this is the whole of the averment. It cannot be anything more than the opinion of the affiant, that, under some statute of New York and the decisions thereunder, the particular notes upon which this suit is founded are void. But this is altogether inadequate. In Peck *v.* Jones (20 P. F. S. 83) we held, that an affidavit of defence should aver distinctly every fact necessary to constitute a defence; nothing should be left to inference. There are many other cases to the same effect. An affidavit of defence should state specifically and at length the nature and character of the defence relied on, and should set forth such facts as will warrant the legal inference of a full and legal defence to the plaintiff's cause of action. (Bryar *v.* Harrison, 1 Wr. 233; Woods *v.* Watkins, 4 Wr. 458.) How could the Court below, or how could we determine from the *facts* set out in this affidavit, whether the said notes are usurious and void even in the hands of third persons? We are asked to make a solemn decree to that effect, but upon what information can we be permitted to found such a judgment? Absolutely none. It is too plain for argument, that no indictment for perjury could be maintained for the falsity of the averment we are considering. It alleges no fact, and the opinion which it expresses may, for aught else contained in the affidavit, be entirely erroneous. The affidavit of defence is insufficient, and the Court was right in entering judgment for the plaintiff. The excessive payments made by Hussey, the payee, to Harris, the bill broker, constitute no defence in favor of the maker, Boughton, against the plaintiff, an innocent holder.

Judgment affirmed.
Opinion by GREEN, J.

July, 1880, 123.   Feb. 10, 1881.

Appeal of the Trustees of the University of Pennsylvania.

Will — Abatement — Annuity — Legacy — No abatement when founded on valuable consideration or in pursuance of contract — Lapse — When substitutionary words will prevent — "Representatives," construction of word.

In case of a will, where there is a deficiency after payment of debts, expenses, and specific legacies, to pay the other legacies, the rule is generally that the loss shall be borne entirely and proportionally by those pecuniary legacies which are in their nature general. An annuity charged on the personal estate is a general legacy, and in case of such deficiency must abate ratably with the other general legacies.

per TRUNKEY, J. Where there is any valuable consideration for a testamentary gift, or any right or interest is relinquished in consideration thereof, such legacy will be entitled to payment over other general legacies which are mere bounties.

A general legacy to a volunteer will not be entitled to exemption from abatement on the ground of its being applied to any particular object or purpose, unless there be clear and unequivocal evidence from the terms of the will that the testator intended to give it a priority. The presumption is against such intent, and the onus lies upon the party seeking such priority to make out his case by clear and conclusive proof.

In order to prevent a legacy from lapsing by the death of the legatee before the testator's death, such testator must in his will declare either expressly or in terms from which it can be collected with sufficient clearness what person or persons he intended to substitute for the legatee dying in his lifetime.

A testator provided as follows: "I give and bequeath $7500 unto A. B., but it is my will that whatsoever amount her son C. D., shall owe me, principal and interest, shall be taken to have been so much paid on account of said legacy, and his notes shall be handed over to her or her representatives:"

Held, in the absence of any other evidence as to the testator's intent, that this clause did not contain sufficient to prevent a lapse of the legacy to A. B. by reason of her death during the testator's lifetime.

Appeal of the Trustees of the University of Pennsylvania from a decree of the Orphans' Court of Philadelphia County, dismissing their exceptions to and confirming the adjudication of the Judge auditing the account of the executors of Dr. George B. Wood, deceased.

The facts of this case as they appeared at the audit, together with the adjudication of PENROSE, J., thereon, the exceptions filed thereto, and the opinion of HANNA, P. J., dismissing said exceptions, are reported at length, *ante*, page 170, etc. The Trustees of the University of Pennsylvania took this appeal, assigning for error—

(1) The action of the Court in holding that the annuity of $2500 and the legacy of $50,000 to appellants were not given in pursuance of a binding contract made by testator, but that the same were voluntary gifts, and decreeing that they should abate ratably with the general legacies.

(2) The action of the Court in holding that the legacy of $7500 to Mrs. Chamberlin did not lapse by reason of her death before testator's death, and in decreeing the same to her administrator for the use of her next of kin.

J. B. Townsend (with whom was *Eli K. Price*), for appellants.

To arrive at the true meaning of testator's contract with the appellants, the subject matter, situation, and relation of the parties, and all the attendant circumstances may be taken into consideration.

2 Kent's Comm. 733.
Addison on Contracts (Am. ed.), vol. 1, § 220.
Shore *v.* Wilson, 9 Cl. & Fin. 555.
McDonald *v.* Longbottom, 29 L. J. (Q. B.), 256.
Mumford *v.* Gething, 29 L. J. (C. P.), 110.
Carr *v.* Montefiore, 33 L. J. (Q. B.), 256.

Viewing all these circumstances, and comparing them with the will, it is clear that testator agreed to furnish, even after his death, $2500 annually to the appellants; and it was in pursuance of such contract that the legacies in dispute were left to appellants.

This contract was a binding one on testator. Where expense or liability is incurred on the faith of a voluntary subscription, this constitutes sufficient consideration to bind the promisor.

Everhart *v.* West Chester R. R. Co., 4 Casey, 339.
Plank Road *v.* Brown, 1 Casey, 156.
R. R. Co. *v.* Echternacht, 9 Harris, 230.
R. R. Co. *v.* Bowser, 12 Wright, 29.
Garrett *v.* R. R. Co., 28 Smith, 465.
Edinton Academy *v.* Robinson, 1 Wright, 210.
Shober *v.* Park, 28 Smith, 429.
Steamship Co. *v.* Murphy, 6 Phila. 224.
Caul *v.* Gibson, 3 Barr, 416.
Chambers *v.* Calhoun, 6 Harris, 13.
Phipps *v.* Jones, 8 Harris, 260.
Rogers *v.* Church, 9 Casey, 264.
Landis *v.* Royer, 9 Smith, 95.
Cunningham *v.* Garvin, 10 Barr, 366.
Riddle *v.* Stevens, 2 S. & R. 537.
1 Hilliard on Contracts, 251.

These legacies being, therefore, given in satisfaction of a debt, do not abate ratably with other general legacies.

Burridge *v.* Bradyl, 1 P. Wms. 126.
Blower *v.* Morret, 2 Ves. Sr. 420.
Davenhill *v.* Teitchen, Amb. 244.
Sarah Zane's Will, Bright. 347, note.
Helfenstein's Estate, 27 Smith, 328.

But independent of the footing of a debt or contract there is enough to show that the testator considered certain of his property impressed with a trust to furnish the appellants the amount of $2500 a year.

Ex Parte Pye, 18 Vesey, 140.
Ellison *v.* Ellison, 6 Ves. 656.
Richardson *v.* Richardson, L. R. (3 Eq. Cas.) 686.
Morgan *v.* Malleson, L. R. (10 Eq. Cas.) 475.

Funds so impressed with a trust cannot lose their character by being bequeathed by will and will be saved from lapse or abatement.

Williams on Exec. (6 Am. ed.), 1176.
Theo. on Cons. of Wills, 459.
Blower *v.* Morret, 2 Ves. Sr. 420.
Davies *v.* Bush, 1 You. 341.
Stahlschmidt *v.* Lett, 1 Sm. & G. 421.
Williamson *v.* Naylor, 3 Y. & C. 208.
Philips *v.* Philips, 3 Hare, 282.

The intention to give priority to these legacies over others is clear from the terms of testator's will.

Edmonson *v.* Nichols, 10 Harris, 79.
Mutter's Estate, 2 Wright, 314.
Schott's Estate, 28 Smith, 40.

Quain's Appeal (10 Harris, 510), and Williams's Appeal (11 Wright, 283), can have no bearing. They only take away one remedy of a ground landlord, for whom sufficient protection already otherwise exists.

The legacy to Mrs. Chamberlin lapsed by her death. To save such a lapse a clear intent to make an alternative or substitutionary gift to another party as legatee, in place of the first named legatee, must appear in the will.

Dickinson *v.* Purvis, 8 S. & R. 71.
Patterson *v.* Hawthorn, 12 S. & R. 112.
Ralston *v.* Waln, 8 Wright, 279.
Gibbons *v.* Fairlamb, 2 Cas. 217.

The words of the will are not sufficient to indicate such intent.

Sloan *v.* Hanse, 2 Rawle, 28.
King *v.* King, 1 W. & S. 205.
Reed *v.* Buckley, 5 W. & S. 517.
Buckley *v.* Reed, 3 Harris, 83.
McGill's Appeal, 11 Smith, 46.
Comfort *v.* Mather, 2 W. & S. 450.
Weishaupt *v.* Brehman, 5 Binn. 115.
Sword *v.* Adams, 3 Yeates, 34.

The legacy therefore lapsed and fell into the residue.

Woolmer's Estate, 3 Mart. 477.
Nyce's Estate, 5 W. & S. 260.
Loxley's Estate, 6 W. N. C. 529.

R. Francis Wood and *George W. Biddle* (with them *George Biddle*), for the executors of Dr. George B. Wood.

There was no evidence of any binding contract on the part of testator to pay appellants the sum of $2500 a year. The testator was by the terms of the gift to be at liberty whenever his personal convenience required it to discontinue his bounty, and of the propriety of so doing he was the necessarily sole judge.

Nelson *v.* Von Bonnhorst, 5 Casey, 352.

There is, in any case, no evidence of any contract of the testator to extend beyond his death.

The legacy and the annuity are therefore merely voluntary gifts, and will abate ratably with the other general legacies.

Creed *v.* Creed, 11 Cl. & Finn. 1844.
Heath *v.* Weston, 3 DeG. M. & G. 606.
Gaskin *v.* Rogers, L. R. (2 Eq.) 291.
Simmons *v.* Vallance, 4 Bro. C. C. 349.
Apreece *v.* Apreece, Ves. & B. 365.
Ashburnham *v.* Ashburnham, 16 Sim. 188.
Crowder *v.* Clowes, 2 Ves. Jr. 449.
Fidelity Ins. Co.'s Appeal, 37 Leg. Int. 2
Leacroft *v.* Maynard, 1 Ves. 279.
Fisher *v.* Brierley, 30 Beav. 267.
Earl of Shaftesbury *v.* Duke of Marlborough, 7 Sim. 237.

Thorn, for the administrator of Hannah Chamberlin.

The will of the testator shows a clear intent that the legacy to Mrs. Chamberlin should not lapse. In the same clause he bequeathed a legacy to one grandchild of Mrs. Willis, and it is probable that he intended other grandchildren (children of Mrs. Chamberlin) to take also. This proposition is strengthened by the provision as to David Edwards's debts to testator.

The authorities are clear that the testator meant by the word "representatives," next of kin, according to the Statute of Distributions.

Baines *v.* Ottey, 1 Myl. & K. 465.
Walker *v.* Makin, 6 Sim. 148.
Cotton *v.* Cotton, 2 Beav. 67.
Styth *v.* Monro, 6 Sim. 49.
Blagge *v.* Miles, 1 Story, 449.
Bulmer *v.* Jay, 4 Sim. 48.
Bridge *v.* Abbot, 3 Bro. C. C. 187.
Long *v.* Blackall, 3 Ves. 487.
In Re Crawford's Trusts, 2 Drewry, 234.
Cotton *v.* Cotton, 2 Beav. 67.
Ware *v.* Fisher, 2 Yeates, 578.
Stook's Appeal, 8 Harris, 349.
Gibbons *v.* Fairlamb, 2 Casey, 217.
Hodge's Appeal, 37 Leg. Int. 264.

February 28, 1880. THE COURT. Whether Dr. Wood, was legally bound to pay the University of Pennsylvania the sum of twenty-five hundred dollars annually, during his life, is unnecessary to determine. Did he contract for such payments to be made after his death? He proposed to appropriate out of his income the annual sum of twenty-five hundred dollars to be applied by the trustees to the support of an Auxiliary Faculty of Professors in the medical department, stating he did so with some diffidence, as he had no right to suppose that the board could "have so much confidence in his disinterestedness or stability of purpose, as to justify them in commencing an enterprise, any misdirection or failure of which might in some measure compromise the dignity of the board," that he made " the appropriation conditional on his future ability to maintain it, without material personal inconvenience;" and pledged himself, should they accept, that no trifling cause should interfere with its due fulfilment on his part. The trustees gratefully accepted, organized the faculty, and provided that the professors be appointed for one year, and reappointed annually during satisfactory service, "so long as the plan for the establishment of the Auxiliary Faculty of Medicine now adopted shall continue in operation." They elected other professors for an indefinite period, but for this Auxiliary Faculty for one year. They understood that he intended himself to judge of his future ability to make the annual payments without inconvenience. His purpose was to make such payments. The trustees believed he would; and he did during his life. Both parties acted in accord with the promise contained in the proposition; but not a word in the proposition or resolutions tend to establish an agreement, that he would provide for the payment of that sum, or any other, annually after his decease.

The nature of Dr. Wood's pledge is shown by a written evidence, and that is the "engagement" and "agreement" referred to in his will. If nude or for good consideration, on its face, he was under no moral or legal obligation to provide an annuity, or an endowment fund. Probably he contemplated making the University a chief beneficiary of his estate; he did not promise this, and held out no reason for the trustees to expect it, other than continuous acts of generosity. His declarations in the will are evidence of his own understanding of the writings. In section 27, after reciting that the trustees established the faculty at his bequest, which he had aided by an annual payment, and that it is his "desire that said faculty and professorships shall be permanently established," he says: "Therefore, for that purpose I give and bequeath unto the Trustees of the University of Pennsylvania fifty thousand dollars." This reveals that the testator deemed the "establishing" and "founding" of the faculty and professorships temporary, and that he desired they should be permanent. To that end he made the bequest. Here is his first expression for a permanent endowment, not in performance of an obligation, but to accomplish a desire. In section 16 of a codicil of same date as the will, he enjoined his executors to pay no legacies except those less than five thousand dollars, and except also the payments necessary to continue those annual payments which he had for some years made by agreement with certain institutions, in the interval before getting the principal of their legacies, until the accomplishment of his directions for putting a tract of land under cranberry culture. He says in section 30 of the will "having heretofore engaged to pay and paid to the trustees" twenty-five hundred dollars a year, I direct my executors to continue such payments until said legacy shall be paid, which will be without deduction from the legacy. The words "agreement" and "engaged to pay and paid," following section 27, would fairly apply to the proposition for the temporary establishment of the faculty, and the direction to continue the yearly payments until the legacy of fifty thousand dollars shall be paid, is a bounty in furtherance of the permanent establishment he desired. It seems very clear that the testator was not bound by a contract for such payments to be continued after his decease.

Neither the acts of the testator in his lifetime, nor the declarations in his will, recognize equitable rights in the appellant to pay any part of his estate standing in his name. He paid all he promised; he gives legacies for specified purposes. We have carefully considered the able argument of appellant on this point, sound in its statement of the law, but we fail to discover any evidence of property held in trust by the testator for the University, nor had the University had an equitable interest in any property held in the testator's name.

The rule is, that where there is deficiency after payment of debts, expenses, and specific legacies, the loss shall be borne entirely and proportionally by those pecuniary legacies which are in their nature general. A general legacy to a volunteer will not be entitled to any exemption from abatement, on the ground of its being applied to any particular object or purpose, as where the bequest is to a wife or child, or to a charity. But if there be any valuable consideration for the testamentary gift, or the relinquishment of any right or interest, such legacy will be entitled to preference of payment over other general legacies which are mere bounties. An annuity charged on the personal estate is a general legacy, and in cases of deficiency all annuities and legacies abate ratably, for since they cannot all be paid in full, they shall all abate ratably, on the principle of the maxim, "equality is equity" or "equity delighteth in equality." This rule is subject to exceptions, for there are cases, where some annuities and legacies are to be paid in priority to others; but the onus lies on the party seeking priority to make out that such priority was intended, by clear and conclusive proof. In absence of such proof, the testator must be deemed to have considered that his estate would be sufficient, and, consequently, not to have thought it necessary to provide against a deficiency, by giving priority to some of the objects of his bounty. If the chances of deficiency are anticipated and provided for by the terms of the will, then the directions of the testator will govern. It is always a question of intention, and when the intent of the testator is manifest to give one general legatee priority over others, that intention shall prevail. As between legacies which are in their nature mere bounties, the presumption of intended equality exists and governs, unless overcome by unequivocal evidence to the contrary. No priority will be allowed where the expressions of the will are ambiguous. (Towle v. Swasey, 106 Mass. 100; Miller v. Huddleston, 3 Mac. & G. 513; Attorney General v. Hudson, 1 P. Wms. 675; Attorney General v. Robins, 2 Ibid. 23; 2 Williams on Exrs. 1364–1371.)

Applying these principles to this case, the Orphans' Court was clearly right in ruling that the legacy of fifty thousand dollars, and until its payment, the sum of twenty-five hundred dollars per annum, to the Trustees of the Auxiliary Faculty, must abate ratably with the other pecuniary legacies. It seems plain that no conclusive proof can be furnished from the language of the will, of intent to give these legacies priority over others; if there be expressions which tend to favor priority, they are much too ambiguous to be relied on in support of a preference. Indeed the intention as to all pecuniary legacies is that they shall stand on equal footing. The testator anticipated the possibility of a deficiency, and made this provision: "Should my estate prove deficient to pay all the legacies, then the pecuniary legacies will abate ratably;"—precisely what the law would have declared had he given no such direction. He made numerous bequests to near relatives and friends, as well as to charities, and as he expressed no particular intent as to any one of the pecuniary legacies or annuities, and all are to volunteers: they must abate proportionally, in accord with the general intent. We discover no sufficient evidence of an intended priority in favor of the appellant.

The second question presented is, Did the legacy of $7500 to Hannah Chamberlin lapse by reason of her death before the testator?

This legacy is given as follows: "I give and bequeath seventy-five hundred dollars unto Mrs. Hannah Chamberlin, a daughter of Mrs. Willis, aforesaid; but it is my will that whatsoever amount her son David Edwards shall owe me, principal and interest, shall be taken to have been so much paid on account of said legacy, and his notes shall be handed over to her or her representatives."

The word representatives may mean next of kin, or descendants, or executors, or administrators, according as the intention of the testator is manifested in the will. It has been held to mean the husband of a deceased legatee. (Gibbons *v.* Fairlamb, 2 Casey, 217.) In all cases where it is apparent in the context of the will that a word is not used in its ordinary sense, if the intention can be ascertained, it shall govern rather than a technical definition, or the usual sense. In this will there is little room for interpretation; the testator seems to have been at no loss for an intelligent use of words. When he intended to give the interest of a sum to one for life, and at the death of the legatee the principal to his legal representatives, he said so, as in the bequest to John Garrison. If he meant a legacy should not lapse, in case of the decease of the legatee before himself, he so directed, as when he added to the bequest to James Quinn, "if he deceased to go to his children." Evidently, he was mindful of collateral inheritance taxes, and gave certain legacies clear of taxes. He closed the codicil of even date with his will, thus: "And should any provision of my will fail by lapse or otherwise, it is my will that all dispositions so failing shall fall into and become part of the residue of my estate, and as such to vest in the residuary legatee, under the residuary clause of my will." Surely, he contemplated the probability of lapse of some of the numerous legacies.

There is not a substitutionary word applied to the legacy of $7500 to Mrs. Chamberlin. The clause directs that her son's indebtedness, whatsoever it may be, shall be so much paid on account of said legacy, and the notes handed to her or her representatives.

What is there in this will to show the words were not used in their usual sense? Is it the general and particular accuracy of language in every other part? A testator may prevent a legacy from lapsing; but to effect this object, he must declare, either expressly or in terms from which it can be collected with sufficient clearness, what person or persons he intended to substitute for the legatee dying in his lifetime. (2 Williams on Ex'rs, 1210.) This legacy is to Mrs. Chamberlin, not to her son, or her representatives. An advancement on account of the legacy, made in her lifetime, will not prevent a lapse. We are of opinion that the terms of this will, instead of showing the testator's intention to prevent a lapse of the legacy to Mrs. Chamberlin in case of her death before his, show that in such event he intended said legacy, or so much of it as had not been advanced, should fall into and become a part of the residue of his estate.

So much of the decree as directs payment of money on the legacy to Hannah Chamberlin is reversed, and record remitted for further proceedings. Costs of appeal to be paid by the executors out of moneys of the estate.

Opinion by TRUNKEY, J. SHARSWOOD, C. J., absent.

Quarter Sessions.

Q. S. of Erie Co. Feb. 28, 1881.

Commonwealth v. Willard.

Libel—Publication in newspaper without publisher's knowledge—Indictment against publisher.

It is no defence to an indictment against one who is the editor and publisher of a newspaper that the libellous article complained of was written and inserted by the local editor of the journal, without the knowledge of the defendant, and in violation of a general order forbidding the publication of any article of a libellous nature without first submitting it to the publisher for his approval.

Rule for a new trial.

James R. Willard was indicted and tried on a charge of libel, the alleged offence being the publication in the *Erie Dispatch,* of which paper the defendant is the editor and publisher, of a ridiculous and libellous article concerning one Müller, a resident of the city of Erie. The fact of publication, and the libellous character of the article was not denied. The defence set up was that the publication was not the act of the defendant but that of a subordinate, the local editor, and that the defendant did not know that the article had been published in his paper until arrested on the charge of publishing a libel. It was proved that the defendant had previously given to his employés a general instruction "never to publish nor allow to be published any article of a libellous nature without first submitting the same to him for his approval."

The jury found a verdict of guilty, whereupon this rule was obtained.

H. Souther, for the rule.
S. A. Davenport, contra.

March 9, 1881. THE COURT. The defendant's counsel did not deny on the trial that the article complained of was libellous. It was not pretended that there was the slightest foundation in fact for the narrative in which the prosecutor was made to figure, or that such occurrences ever took place. But it was urged as a sufficient legal exculpation that the offensive publication was made without the knowledge of the defendant and against his instructions, previously given, "never to publish nor allow to be published any article of a libellous nature without first submitting the same to him for his approval." It was held by the Court as a matter of law and the jury were so charged that this was not a sufficient defence. It is now claimed as ground for a new trial, that this instruction was erroneous, and also that the Court erred in charging that the publication was libellous, instead of leaving that question to be decided by the jury.

As to this latter position, it is sufficient to say that the jury were only told what had already been admitted by the counsel for the defence in their presence, and moreover the propriety of the course taken in this particular was determined by the Supreme Court in the case of Pittock *v.* O'Niell (63 Pennsylvania State Reports, 257), where it was held that "there can be no doubt that both in criminal and civil cases the Court may express to the jury their opinion as to whether the publication is libellous."

As to the remaining question—Can the publisher of a newspaper relieve himself from criminal liability for a libel appearing in his paper, by proof that it was written by an employé and published without his knowledge and against a general order forbidding libellous publications?

The Pennsylvania statute defining the offence of libel not only includes those who write, print, or exhibit libels, but those also who *publish* them. Aside from the incalculable damage that may and often does result to the innocent from a misuse of the press in the hands of reckless or malicious persons, and the consequent caution proper to be exacted from those managing newspapers as to the selection of the subordinates in whose hands they intrust this dangerous power, there is the peculiarity incident to the profession of a publisher that the publication of a journal or a magazine or a book is not the visible, manual act of the publisher himself, but is made up of the labors of many different persons, in no one portion of which he may have an actual part. He may not be present at or witness any single one of the various processes of work by which the completed book or newspaper is finally produced; he may not even see it when done and issued to the public, and yet the publication is his act. This is in part, no doubt, the reason why the law of libel forms an apparent exception to the usual rule that one can only be liable criminally for his own individual acts.

That such is the law, whatever may be the reason for it, there would seem to be no question. It was established by a long line of cases in England, decided by such Judges as HALE, MANSFIELD, RAYMOND, KENYON, .POWELL, FOSTER, ELLENBOROUGH, and TENTERDEN, and which will be found fully stated in a note in Starkie on Slander, first American edition, vol. 2, pages 30 to 34. It is found clearly recognized in all the leading text-books on criminal law, and has also been recognized and affirmed by the Courts in many of the States of the Union. In Roscoe's Criminal Evidence, sixth American edition (edited by GEORGE SHARSWOOD, now Chief Justice of the Supreme Court of Pennsylvania), on page 621, under the head of "Constructive Publication," the rule is stated as follows: "It is now well established that in order to render a party guilty of publishing a libel it is not necessary that he should be the actual publisher of it, or that he should even have a knowledge of the publication; not only is a person who procures another to publish a libel himself guilty of the offence, but a bookseller or publisher whose servant publishes a libel is criminally answerable for that act, though done without his knowledge. This rule, which is an exception to those which govern the other branches of criminal law, appears to be founded upon a principle of policy, and to have been arbitrarily adopted with a view of rendering publishers cautious with regard to the matters to which they give general circulation."

And in Wharton's Criminal Law (seventh American edition, published in 1874), section 2564, the same law is thus tersely stated by the eminent Pennsylvania lawyer and law writer, Francis Wharton: "Evidence of the libel having been purchased in a bookseller's shop, or at a newspaper office, or the office of a news-vender of a servant thereof, in the course of business, will maintain a count charging the master with having published it, although it be proved that the master was not privy to it."

In a celebrated English case, the King v. Gutch (1 Moody & Malkin, 433) where it was urged that the rule respecting the liability of publishers in libel was contrary to the principle which prevails in all other cases, Chief Justice TENTERDEN, in summing up the case to the jury, thus reasoned as to the justice and propriety of the law: "The rule seems to me to be conformable to principle and to common sense. Surely a person who derives profit from and who furnishes means for carrying on the concern, intrusts the conduct of the publication to one whom he selects and in whom he confides, may be said to cause to be published what actually appears, and ought to be accountable, although you cannot show that he was individually concerned in the particular publication. It would be exceedingly dangerous to hold otherwise, for then an irresponsible person might be put forward and the person really producing the publication and without whom it could not be published might remain behind and escape altogether."

Among the many American cases in support of this rule, a leading and quite recent one is that of Commonwealth v. Morgan (107 Massachusetts Reports, 199), in which it was held after a full argument and review of the cases, English and American, that "The publisher of a newspaper in which a libel appears is *prima facie* presumed to have published the libel, and this presumption is not rebutted by evidence that he never saw the libel and was not aware of its publication until it was pointed out to him, and that an apology and retraction were afterwards published in the same newspaper, and the exclusion of such evidence at his trial on an indictment for the libel gives him no ground of exception."

Another quite recent case in which the liability of newspaper publishers was very carefully considered, is that of Perret v. the New Orleans Times (25 Louisiana, 170). Certain irresponsible persons, whose residence was unknown, published in the defendant's journal an advertisement severely reflecting on certain public men. The publication was admitted, but the defence was that it was received at a late hour of the night and during the absence and without the knowledge of the proprietor of the paper. It was denied that the defendant had any malicious intent, and, as proving an absence of malice, it was shown that as soon as the injury was brought to the notice of the defendant, an editorial article was inserted explanatory of the publication. The defendant was, however, held liable.

This last was a civil suit, but the only difference between a suit for damages and a criminal prosecution, so far as the evidence is concerned, as shown by all the authorities, is that in the former, such proof as that proposed in this case goes to the jury in mitigation of damages, while in the latter it is for the Court only in mitigation of sentence.

But it is needless to occupy further time in referring to the numerous authorities bearing on this question. They are remarkably uniform and consistent in one direction. Only a solitary case was cited by defendant's counsel in which the opposite rule was held, Smith v. Ashley (11th Metcalf Mass. Reports), 367, and this has been overruled by the case of Commonwealth v. Morgan, already cited, and which was decided twenty-three years later, and in a note by Mr. Wendell, editor of the first American edition of Starkie on Slander, vol. 2, page 34, this same case of Smith v. Ashley is severely criticized, and he says of it, "With all respect, it is conceived that this decision may be questioned as not warranted by the authorities cited in the case."

By a recent English statute (6 and 7 Victoria) a defendant in a suit or prosecution for libel is there permitted to prove in his defence that the publication was made without his knowledge and did not arise from a want of due care and caution on his part. But no such statute has been enacted here, and the Pennsylvania Constitutional Convention in 1873, where the whole subject of the responsibilities of publishers was most ably and elaborately debated, the press being represented by some of the first talent in the State, refused to make any change in the then existing laws so far as men not in official position were concerned, except to provide that where the matter was "proper for public investigation or information" no conviction should be had in any prosecution "where the fact that such publication was not maliciously nor negligently made shall be established to the satisfaction of the jury." An addition to this amendment, amounting in substance to the English statute, was proposed by Mr. Dodd, of Venango, but it was not adopted. (Debates in Constitutional Convention, vol. 5, page 596.)

The present case, it will be observed, is not that of a libel surreptitiously smuggled into a newspaper by an employé whose position did not authorize him to prepare or select matter for its columns, as was the fact in Goodrich v. Stone (11th Metcalf, Mass. Reports, 486), for the article was prepared by the local editor, employed for and entrusted with that branch of the business, and it was done in the usual course of his daily occupation. Nor is it the case of objectionable matter shown to the publisher and by him refused, nor was it a fraud or imposition practised upon a publisher, by which he was misled. It is not even the case of a publisher absent from the town, and obliged to trust the management to another during his absence. As shown by the testimony of the defendant himself, it was simply the case of an editor and publisher of a newspaper leaving his press and office to the sole control of a subordinate, and with such apparent indifference to the outcome of this confidence that up to the time of his arrest he had not even seen the publication complained of. It may be considered by judicious, thoughtful men, who are in favor of the freedom of the press, but opposed to its license, that this case furnishes in itself an illustration of and an argument for the wisdom of the rule, but be that as it may, it is my duty to enforce the law as it is, and not to theorize as to what it ought to be. When public opinion requires additional modification of the law of libel, that popular sentiment will doubtless be respected by the law-making power, the Legislature; until then the courts can only carry out the law as they find it.

The motion for a new trial is refused.

Opinion by GALBRAITH, P. J.

The defendant was sentenced to pay a fine of $25, and the costs of prosecution.

Common Pleas—Law.

C. P. No. 2.   Jan. 8, 1881.

Brass Co. v. Rudy.

Judgment for want of a plea—Conditions upon which it will be opened—Affidavit of defence.

Rule to open judgment entered for plaintiff for want of a plea.

Assumpsit. The docket entries were as follows:—

Nov. 12, 1880. Summons exit.
Dec. 16, 1880. Narr. and rule to plead filed.
Dec. 27, 1880. Affidavit of service of copy of narr. and of rule to plead filed, and judgment for want of plea entered.
Dec. 30, 1880. Rule to open judgment for want of a plea entered.

Scollay, for rule.
Edmunds, contra.

THE COURT. Rule absolute on condition that defendant file an affidavit setting forth his defence.

C. P. No. 4.   March 16, 1881.

In re Petition of Jacob Kohler.

Mortgages—Leave to pay money into Court and have satisfaction entered, when not granted—Act of 3 April, 1851, § 14—Where the Court has no jurisdiction to allow money to be paid into Court and decree satisfaction to be entered.

Sur petition for leave to pay principal of mortgage into Court and for a decree ordering the Recorder of Deeds to enter satisfaction of said mortgage.

The petition set forth that certain property had been conveyed to the petitioner, and a mortgage thereon executed May 3, 1879, for $2408.17, with interest, payable "in five years from the date thereof;" that the mortgage had been assigned, and that the petitioner had offered the assignee to pay the principal and interest of said mortgage and requested him to enter satisfaction of the same, and that the assignee had refused to accept the principal debt and to satisfy the mortgage of record.

The assignee filed a plea denying the jurisdiction of the Court as to the subject matter of the petition; averring that, by the terms of the petition, it did not appear that the mortgage debt was due and payable, and that, in any event, the costs of an adjudication of the question and the expenses of a review by the Appellate Court should be secured to the respondent.

M. H. Stutzbach, for the petitioner.

Under the Act of 3 April, 1851, § 14 (P. L. 871), the mortgagor is entitled to pay the money into Court and have satisfaction entered. The clause in the mortgage payable "*in* five years from the date thereof," should be read "*within* five years from the date thereof."

Horstman v. Gerker, 13 Wr. 282.

Jos. M. Pile, contra.

The statement in Horstman *v.* Gerker (*supra*) that the word "in" should be read "within" is *obiter dictum*. The Act should be construed strictly. Under it the Court have no jurisdiction. There must be a dispute as to whether the money has been paid, otherwise the Court cannot consider the petition.

THE COURT. It appears to us that this case does not fall within the Act, and, therefore, we have not jurisdiction.

Petition dismissed.

Per BRIGGS, J. THAYER, P. J., absent.

C. P. No. 4.   March 12, 1881.
Badger v. McKay.

Affidavit of defence—Sale of chattels—Warranty—Representations—When an express warranty is alleged in an affidavit, it is for a jury to say whether there was such a warranty—Defect in quality, when a defence.

Rule for judgment for want of a sufficient affidavit of defence.

Assumpsit on a promissory note.

The affidavit of defence set forth that the note in suit was given in payment of furniture bought by defendant from an agent of plaintiff's; that the furniture was purchased for shipment to South America, and, at the time of the sale, it was expressly warranted to be good furniture and suitable for the climate of South America; that, relying upon their representations, the furniture was purchased without examination by deponent, and delivered, covered with bagging, for shipment; that it was not until the arrival of the furniture in South America that it was seen and examined by deponent; that, when examined by deponent upon its arrival in South America, it was found, upon removing the bagging, that at least one-half of it was almost valueless, the joints having come apart, and that it was utterly unfit and unsuited for the climate for which it had been purchased; that, by reason of its condition, the deponent was obliged to sell it at public auction for whatever price could be obtained for it; that some of these sets which had cost $131, deponent was obliged to sell at $50 a set, and so on in that proportion; that the balance which was not sold deponent was obliged to ship back again to Philadelphia; that deponent therefore claimed a credit of at least $700.

Edward G. McCollin, for the rule.

Warranty is a matter of law, and an affidavit of defence which omits to state the exact language used by the plaintiff is insufficient.

Water Proof Co. *v.* Brunner, 1 WEEKLY NOTES, 514.

It is not sufficient to swear to a conclusion of law; all the facts must be set out in order that the Court may draw the proper conclusion.

Stitt *v.* Garrett, 3 Whart. 281.
Dewey *v.* Dupuy, 2 W. & S. 553.
Marsh *v.* Marshall, 53 Pa. St. 396.

Mere representations as to quality of the article sold do not constitute a warranty.

Wetherill *v.* Neilson, 8 Har. 448.

Chas. F. Corson, contra.

Where goods are bought for a special purpose, and are expressly warranted to be such as are suitable for the purpose, a breach of the warranty is a good defence to an action for the price.

Lehigh Coal Co. *v.* Link, 1 WEEKLY NOTES, 102.
Nagle *v.* Potter, 3 Ibid. 26.

Whether there was such an express warranty is a question for the jury.

McFarland *v.* Newman, 9 Watts, 60.
Nagle *v.* Potter, 3 WEEKLY NOTES, 26.

A warranty and breach may be shown without offering to return the goods.

Steigleman *v.* Jeffries, 1 S. & R. 477.
Borrekins *v.* Bevan, 3 R. 23.
Erriniger *v.* Miller, 3 Phila. 344.

THE COURT. Rule discharged.

C. P. No. 4.   March 7, 1881.
Steinbeisser v. Corbion.

Practice—Rules of Court—Filing affidavit denying partnership nunc pro tunc.

Sur rule to show cause why the defendants should not be permitted to file an affidavit and plea denying partnership *nunc pro tunc.*

The action was in case against George Corbion and George Corbion, Jr., trading as George Corbion & Son. The defendants had pleaded not guilty, and the cause was at issue. In support of the rule, an affidavit of the counsel who drew the plea was filed to the effect that, at the time of plea filed, he was unaware that the non-existence of a partnership between the defendants constituted part of the defence.

Rule I., § 2, of the Rules of Court provides that, "in all cases by or against partners, it shall not be necessary for the plaintiff at the trial to prove the partnership, but the same shall be taken to be admitted as alleged on the record, unless one or more of the defendants . . shall, at or before the time of filing his or their plea, file an affidavit denying the existence of the partnership," etc.

John Roberts, showed cause.

By allowing the affidavit to be filed *nunc pro tunc* the plaintiff would be obliged at the trial to prove the partnership. As the case stands, it amounts to an admission by the defendants of the partnership. The plaintiff should not be deprived of the benefit of that admission.

[ELCOCK, J. If the defendants are not allowed to file this affidavit *nunc pro tunc,* they cannot prove the non-existence of the partnership at the trial.]

William M. Mintzer, for the rule.

The rule of Court is intended to prevent surprise at the trial. There was no negligence, as the rule was taken as soon as the facts came to the knowledge of counsel.

THE COURT. There is no reason why the rule should not be enlarged in case of necessity. The plaintiff is merely relegated to the position in which he would have been had the defendants filed their affidavit within the prescribed time. No injustice is done to the plaintiff.

Rule absolute.

Per THAYER, P. J.

Supreme Court.

Oct. & Nov. '80, 308.   Feb. 25, 1881.

Commonwealth ex rel. Attorney-General v. Dumbauld and Roberts.

Constitutional law—Art. V. Sect. 5, relating to the erection of separate judicial districts—Associate Judges of Fayette County—Act of April 9, 1874, providing that the Fourteenth Judicial District shall be composed " of the county of Fayette, to which the county of Greene is hereby attached"—Construction of—Quo warranto—Original jurisdiction of Supreme Court to issue quo warranto to Judges of Common Pleas—Judges and Associate Judges of Common Pleas are officers of the Commonwealth, whose jurisdiction extends over the State.

Art. V. Sect. 5 of the Constitution secures to every county of over forty thousand inhabitants—
(1) The right to be a separate judicial district;
(2) The right to have a resident law Judge; and
(3) The right not to have Associate Judges.

This right not to have Associate Judges cannot be taken away from such a county by a legislative enactment *attaching* a contiguous county of less than forty thousand inhabitants thereto, in pursuance of the provisions of said Art. V. Sect. 5 of the Constitution.

A county so *attached* to a separate judicial district does not become a part of such district by virtue of such attachment. It has the right to have Associate Judges resident in the county, and to have the President Judge of the county to which it is attached preside in its courts.

MERCUR, GORDON, and GREEN, JJ., dissent.

Whether the inhabitants of a county so attached are entitled to vote at the election of the President Judge who is to preside in its courts, not decided.

Judges and Associate Judges of the Courts of Common Pleas are " officers of the Commonwealth whose jurisdiction extends over the State." Hence, under Art. V. Sec. 3 of the Constitution, the Supreme Court and the Judges thereof have exclusive original jurisdiction to issue writs of quo warranto to Associate Judges of the Common Pleas.

In the Supreme Court of Pennsylvania.

Quo warranto, issued by the Supreme Court, at the relation of the Attorney-General, commanding the sheriff of Fayette County to summon David W. C. Dumbauld and Griffith Roberts, to appear and show cause by what authority they or either of them claim to exercise the office of Associate Judge in and for the county of Fayette. The case was heard on demurrer to the respondent's return to said writ.

The pleadings and facts of this case, together with the former arguments of counsel and former opinion of the Supreme Court, filed January 3, 1881, are reported at length, *ante*, page 369.

SHARSWOOD, C. J., having been absent at the time of the argument, and TRUNKEY and STERRETT, JJ., having dissented from the opinion and judgment of the Court (see *ante*, page 417), a reargument was on Feb. 14, 1881, ordered on application of the Attorney-General.

Henry W. Palmer, Attorney-General, and *C. R. Buckalew* (with them *Edward Campbell*), for the Commonwealth.

Art. V. Sect. 5 of the Constitution secures to every county of 40,000 inhabitants the right, *inter alia*, to constitute a separate judicial district, have a resident President Judge, and have no Associate Judges. The duties of the Legislature as contained in this Article and in Sects. 13 and 14 of the Schedule, in reference to the designation of what are separate judicial districts, are merely ministerial. The Legislature has no right to refuse to act as required by the Constitution, nor to alter or take away any rights thereby secured. Hence, when, in accordance with the constitutional provisions, the Legislature *attaches* a county to a contiguous district, as in the Act of April 9, 1874 (P. L. 54), such action must be considered as simply binding or fastening it to such district, not as constituting it a part thereof, and not as varying or altering in any way the constitutional right secured to a county constituting a separate district to which it is attached. The attachment of Greene County to Fayette cannot, therefore, force the latter county to have Associate Judges.

If it be urged that such attached county will be in a position of hardship or inequality, because its electors have no right to participate in the election of the President Judge to preside in its courts, it may be answered : (1) The hardship is no greater than is frequently suffered when, upon the erection of new judicial districts or by transferring a county from one district to another, the courts of that county have been presided over for years by a Judge not chosen or voted for by its electors.

(2) The true construction of the Constitution may give the electors of said county the right to vote for such President Judge.

The construction contended for by the Commonwealth was evidently the intent of the Constitutional Convention, and has received the assent of the public. See—

Pike Co. *v.* Rowland, 9 WEEKLY NOTES, 241.

The Act of 1874 attached Lebanon County to

Dauphin, and Fulton County to Franklin, precisely as in the case at bar. In both these instances, it has been admitted that no Associate Judges should exist in the counties forming separate judicial districts.

(No counsel appeared contra, and no paperbook for respondents was furnished to the Court.)

March 21, 1881. THE COURT. This was a writ of quo warranto, issued at the relation of the Attorney-General, requiring the defendants to show by what authority they hold and exercise the office of Associate Judges of Fayette Co.

It appears, by the suggestion filed, that Fayette County has a population of forty thousand inhabitants; that by the Act of 9th April, 1874 (P. L. 54), it was designated as the Fourteenth Judicial District, "to which the county of Greene is hereby attached;" that the Associate Judges of Fayette County, in office at the time of the adoption of the Constitution, remained in office until the expiration of their respective terms, that the defendants were elected after such expiration, and have continued in office since that time under the belief that Fayette County is still entitled to Associate Judges.

We are met at the threshold of the case by a denial of our jurisdiction. Section 3 of Article 5 of the Constitution declares the jurisdiction of the Supreme Court shall extend over the State, and the Judges thereof shall have original jurisdiction in cases . . . of "quo warranto, as to all officers of the Commonwealth whose jurisdiction extends over the State." It is objected that the jurisdiction of a Judge of the Common Pleas does not extend over the State, but is confined to his judicial district, from which it is argued that he is not "an officer of the Commonwealth" whose right to hold his office can be inquired into by this Court upon a writ of quo warranto. If this position be sound, there would be no remedy in such cases, as neither the Constitution nor any Act of Assembly confers such jurisdiction upon the Courts of Common Pleas, and a person who had intruded himself into the office of President or Associate Judge of such Court could hold the office so usurped indefinitely. We are not driven to this unfortunate position, as we regard the question of our jurisdiction as free from difficulty. That Judges of the Common Pleas are State officers is not denied. (Leib v. Com., 9 Watts, 200.) While their jurisdiction for many purposes is confined to their respective judicial districts, it is equally true that for some purposes it extends over the State. Witnesses may be subpoenaed in any portion of the State, and their attendance compelled by attachment in any county of the State by the Court of Common Pleas of such county. In many instances, original process may issue from such Courts to other counties throughout the State. The 3d section of the Act of 13 June, 1836 (P. L. 572), the Act of 4 March, 1862 (P. L. 79), and the Act of 24 April, 1857 (P. L. 318), are cited as illustrations. Many similar Acts might be referred to were it necessary. We need not pursue this branch of the case further. It is too plain for argument. We are of opinion that a Judge of the Court of Common Pleas is an officer whose jurisdiction extends over the State, within the meaning of the 3d section of the 5th Article of the Constitution. It follows that this Court has jurisdiction to inquire upon quo warranto by what right the defendants hold the offices which they respectively claim.

We pass now to the main question in the case. Its solution must depend chiefly upon the construction which should be placed upon the 5th section of the 5th Article (Judiciary) of the Constitution. The language of said section is as follows: "Whenever a county shall contain forty thousand inhabitants, it shall constitute a separate judicial district, and shall select one Judge, learned in the law, and the General Assembly shall provide for additional Judges as the business of the said districts may require. Counties containing a population less than is sufficient to constitute separate districts shall be formed into convenient single districts, or, if necessary, may be attached to contiguous districts, as the General Assembly may provide. The office of Associate Judge not learned in the law is abolished in counties forming separate districts; but the several Associate Judges in office when this Constitution shall be adopted shall serve for their unexpired terms."

The Act of 1874, to which reference has been made, was passed to give effect to this constitutional provision, and designates the different judicial districts throughout the State.

It is clearly the right of Fayette County, having a population of forty thousand inhabitants, to be a separate judicial district. Hence it was entirely proper for the Legislature to designate it as the 14th district.

Counties having forty thousand inhabitants are entitled to three privileges under the 5th Article. They are: 1. The right to be a separate judicial district; 2. The right to have a resident law Judge; and 3. The right not to have Associate Judges. As these rights rest upon the fundamental law, it is not in the power of the Legislature to take them away. The designation in the Act of 1874 of Fayette County as the 14th judicial district is the equivalent of declaring it a separate district. To hold otherwise would convict the Legislature of a wilful violation of the Constitution.

It was urged, however, that by attaching Greene County to Fayette, under the provision of the 5th Article, Fayette lost its distinctive character as a separate district, and that Greene became a part of the district. This proposition cannot be sustained without writing something into the Constitution that is not there. It does not say that counties with forty thousand inhabitants shall be separate judicial districts, excepting where a county with a less population is attached thereto. There is nothing in the language of the Constitution to indicate that Fayette County loses any of its rights as a separate district by having Greene attached.

The word "attached" in the 5th Article, and in the Act of 1874, must be understood according to its popular meaning. It was well said in Monongahela Navigation Company *v.* Coons (6 W. & S., at page 114), that constitutions are for the million, not for the mere inspection of lawyers, and are expressed in terms that are most familiar to them, that they may discern their rights and duties. What would the citizen of average intelligence understand by the word attach? Precisely what the lexicographers defined it to mean, "to tie or fasten, to bind ; as to fasten one substance to another by a string or glue."—*Webster.* Surely he would never dream that when one thing is attached to another, the thing attached became a part of the thing to which it is attached. You may attach a chain to a watch, but it does not thereby become a watch, nor any part thereof. Nor does a small county attached to a separate judicial district become a part of such district by virtue of such attachment. To hold that it does, would require us to give a forced and unreasonable construction to the word attached, as well as to disregard the plain mandate of the Constitution, which declares that counties with a population of forty thousand inhabitants *shall* constitute a separate judicial district.

The Constitution having in language too clear to be misunderstood defined the rights of Fayette County as a separate district, I will consider for a moment the rights and position of Greene as an attached county. Among them are, 1st. The right to have Associate Judges resident in the county; and, 2d. The right to have the President Judge of Fayette to preside in her courts, and to attend to all such business as requires his action. For such purposes Greene is in the same position as if she were one of the counties of a single district.

In such case, however, it might fall to her lot, to have a resident President Judge, which can never be the case while attached to Fayette. If there is anything clear in the Constitution, it is that the mere attachment of Greene to Fayette does not change any of the rights of the latter county.

I grant that the position of an attached county is anomalous. It was probably intended to be so. It would have been very easy for the framers of the Constitution to have provided in that instrument that such a county should be a part of the judicial district to which it should be attached. But they carefully refrained from doing so, and we must presume for sufficient reasons. Its position at most is temporary. It may become a separate district by increase of population, or may be made a part of a single district, and I have no doubt this guarded language was used in the Constitution to prevent what has just occurred here, viz., an attempt on the part of Associate Judges to hold their offices in separate districts where, by reason of there being a resident law Judge, they are not needed. It is impossible to read the Constitution, or the Debates of the Convention which framed it, without coming to the conclusion, it was intended to abolish the office of Associate Judge in all counties where a President Judge is obliged to reside, that is in all "counties forming separate districts;" and in attaching a county to a separated district the separate character of the district is presumed, *so far as it concerns the office of Associate Judges not learned in the law.* Further than this it is not necessary for us to go. It may be that in some sense and for some purposes Greene County may be a portion of the Fourteenth District. It is certainly a portion of the territory over which the Judge of Fayette is required to preside, and in this sense the words "district" and "territory" may perhaps be considered as convertible terms. But it cannot be regarded as a part of the district in the sense of taking from Fayette County any of its rights as a separate district; it is not so written in the Constitution, nor do we see any good reason why we should give that instrument such a construction.

We have seen that Greene as an attached county has all the rights necessary for the holding of her courts and the proper administration of the law. It is said, however, that the construction we have placed upon the Constitution denies to her people the right to vote for President Judge; this does not necessarily follow. The 15th section of the 5th Article provides: "All Judges learned in the law, except the Judges of the Supreme Court, shall be elected by the qualified electors of the respective districts over which they are *to preside.* Speaking for myself, it may possibly be, that, in favor of the right of suffrage, and for election purposes, the word "districts" in this section may be construed to mean territory, so that in the case of an election for President Judge of the Fourteenth District, the voters of the entire territory over which he is to preside may vote at such election. This, however, is a mere suggestion, not even an opinion of my own. No such question is before us, nor can it be decided in this proceeding. Any attempt to do so would embarrass us in the future when such a case is brought before us, if it should be.

Even if there be a *casus omissus* in the Constitution in this respect, it would be no reason why we should deprive Fayette County of rights clearly given by the fundamental law. We can neither amend the Constitution nor make the law. If any remedy is needed, we leave it to the legislative department of the government, where it properly belongs.

This evil, if it exists, is not serious nor of a permanent character. It has often happened in the past that in the erection of new judicial districts or by transferring a county from one district to another, the courts of a county have been presided over for years by a Judge who was not voted for by its electors. And such instances may occur in the future under apportionments under the new Constitution. Such slight imperfection, in the working of that instrument in isolated cases, is no good reason for interfering with a general system which as a whole is commendable and may be found useful.

And now, March 21, 1881, after hearing and upon due consideration, judgment is entered for the Commonwealth; and it is further ordered and adjudged by the Court, that the said David W. C. Dumbauld and Griffith Roberts be and they are hereby respectively ousted from the office of Associate Judge of the Court of Common Pleas of Fayette County, and from the franchises, fees, and emoluments thereof, and that they pay the costs of this proceeding.

Opinion by PAXSON, J.

Dissenting opinion by MERCUR, J., in which GORDON and GREEN, JJ., concur.

Less than three months ago, after argument and ample time for consideration, we decided this case in favor of the defendants. Now, after a re-argument on the part of the plaintiff only, and without any substantial reasons not presented on the former argument, the judgment then entered is to be reversed. In this I cannot concur. Nothing less than clear error in the former judgment justifies the present judgment. This reversal is mainly based on that portion of Article 5, section 5, of the Constitution of 1874, which declares "whenever a county shall contain forty thousand inhabitants, it shall constitute a separate judicial district . . . . Counties containing a population less than is sufficient to constitute separate districts shall be formed into convenient single districts, or, if necessary, may be attached to contiguous districts, as the General Assembly may provide. The office of Associate Judge not learned in the law is abolished in counties forming separate districts."

As the clause relating to forty thousand inhabitants does not execute itself, but requires legislative action to give it effect (Com. *ex rel.* Chase *v.* Harding, 6 Norris, 343), and other parts of the Constitution relate to the same general subject-matter, no one should be interpreted by itself alone, but all should be made to harmonize so as to give due effect to the whole Constitution. It must be so interpreted as to carry out the great principles on which our government is based.

Section 15 of the same article declares "all Judges required to be learned in the law, except Judges of the Supreme Court, shall be elected by the qualified electors of the respective districts over which they are to preside." It is conceded that one President Judge presides in the counties of Fayette and Greene. It follows that he is the President Judge in each county, and the writs issued in each are tested in his name. Thus, in fact, the two counties constitute the district in which he presides. Then, in the language of the Constitution, he "shall be elected by the qualified electors" of that district.

Section 19 requires that Judges, "during their continuance in office, shall reside within the districts for which they shall be respectively elected."

Section 26 declares "all laws relating to Courts shall be general and of uniform operation."

The right of every male citizen of the Commonwealth, twenty-one years of age, to vote at all elections, under limited qualifications, is expressly declared in Article 8, section 1. This right of suffrage thus distinctly affirmed to exist in the great body of the people cannot be taken from them as long as the present Constitution stands, and it is not to be held subordinate to mere matters of convenience. It follows that the qualified electors of the county of Greene have a right to vote at every election of a President Judge to preside in that county. In case the vote in Fayette County should be divided between several candidates, and the whole vote of Greene County be cast for another candidate, whereby the latter received a plurality of all the votes cast, can it be contended that he is not thereby duly elected? It cannot be without ignoring one of the highly valued rights of the people. After a Judge shall be elected to preside in the two counties, it seems to me too clear for argument to try to prove he may reside in either county of the district, or that he may not at will change his residence from one county to another. He may reside in Greene every summer and in Fayette every winter. If the view is to prevail that the latter county shall be deprived of Associate Judges, the people thereof must at times suffer great inconveniences, at least when the Judge shall reside in Greene.

It is claimed, however, that the Constitution

declares a county or counties having a population insufficient to form a separate district may be attached to contiguous districts, and as Greene is attached to Fayette, the latter still remains a separate district. It is true the Constitution does permit a county to be attached to a contiguous district, yet there it stops. It does not profess to declare its legal *status*, nor the *status* of the citizens of the county thus attached. It certainly is not a forced presumption to say, that, when the people adopted the Constitution, they understood, whenever a county was "attached" to an existing district, it became a part of the district.

The very idea of territorial attachment is, that the two thus united became parts of one whole. It is but another word for annexation. Unless otherwise provided by the terms of annexation, it becomes an integral part of the enlarged territory.

The denial of Associate Judges to the county of Fayette is a distinct affirmation that in one county, in which the President Judge presides, he constitutes the whole Court. He may there hold a Court of Oyer and Terminer, and perform all the duties and exercise all the powers that he and Associate Judges not learned in the law jointly might do. In the county of Greene, where he also presides, it is admitted he has no such power. This is manifestly contrary to the whole spirit of the Constitution and the Act of Assembly creating the district. The idea that the presiding Judge has so much less power in one county of his district than in another, finds no warrant in the Constitution. It is conceded that this ground is wholly untenable, where the Legislature has in clear and express terms declared that two counties shall form a district.

It is therefore contended that the Legislature may make this discrimination, and make the clause applicable to Courts of the same grade of unequal operation, but this would seem to come in direct conflict with Section 26, which says: "All laws relating to Courts shall be general and of uniform operations." The construction contended for would be to recognize a law not general and not of uniform application.

This is not the case of a transfer of one county to a previously existing judicial district, for which the Constitution intended to provide. It is the formation of a new district by one and the same Act of Assembly, and in one line thereof.

After Judges were made elective in Pennsylvania, a question as to the power of the Legislature to transfer a county to another district, and thereby impose on the people thereof a Judge in whose election they had no voice, was somewhat mooted. To remove this doubt, and to bridge over the time intervening prior to the next election, this power to attach was expressly given. It cannot be that there was any intention to permanently take from the people of any one county substantial rights and powers enjoyed by the people of any other county. It is clearly wrong to say the people of Fayette County have a right to be deprived of Associate Judges. On the contrary, they have the right to enjoy all the conveniences resulting from having such Judges. They expressed such desire by electing these Judges. The Governor duly commissioned them. It cannot be presumed that he did so contrary to the advice of the then Attorney-General. Thus the action of the people of Fayette County had the sanction of the executive department.

Notwithstanding the words of the Constitution, that a county containing a population of forty thousand shall constitute a separate district, yet an Act of the Legislature is necessary to make it a district, and to set its machinery in motion. It is giving to that clause an undue effect when it is thus made to defeat other parts of the Constitution relating to the same subject-matter, and thus thwart the clear intent of the Legislature in uniting the two counties under one President Judge. To reach any other conclusion, is to assume it intended to violate a cardinal right of the people declared in the Constitution. The other view makes the Act harmonize with the different parts of the Constitution, so as to give a reasonable and practical effect to all of them.

Justices GORDON and GREEN concur in this opinion.

Oct. & Nov. '80, 211. Nov. 1, 1880.

Federal Street & Pleasant Valley Passenger Railway Company v. Gibson.

Negligence—Passenger railways—Injury to passenger caused by a passing vehicle—Burden of proof—Practice.

In many cases the mere fact of injury to a passenger on a railway car raises the presumption of want of care on the part of the railway company. Such is the case when the injury results from defective track, cars, machinery, or motive power. Per MERCUR, J.

But when a passenger on a railway car is injured by the act of a third party, over whom the railway company has no control, the burden of proof is upon him to show, not only that he was not guilty of contributory negligence, but that the company was guilty of negligence, and that its negligence was a cause of the injury.

G., a passenger on a street railway car, was sitting with his arm resting on the sill of an open window; the car-driver met and passed at a trot a load of hay, going in the opposite direction, when the hay brushed against the side of the car, and injured G.'s arm. In an action by G. against the railway company to recover damages:

Held (reversing the judgment of the Court below), that it was not sufficient, to entitle the plaintiff to recover, that he was free from fault, but that he must prove other facts, creating a presumption, at least, of negligence in the company, producing injury.

A point duly certified as a part of the record, showing that it was affirmed and bill sealed, although afterwards withdrawn, may be reviewed by the Supreme Court.

Error to the Court of Common Pleas No. 1, of Allegheny County.

Case, by A. J. Gibson against the Federal Street & Pleasant Valley Passenger Railway Company, to recover damages for an injury caused by the alleged negligence of one of defendants' drivers.

On the trial, before COLLIER, J., the following facts appeared: On the morning of July 8, 1879, the plaintiff, while riding down Federal Street, in the city of Allegheny, in one of defendants' cars, was sitting by an open window with his left arm resting on the window ledge. Whether or not his elbow projected outside of the window did not clearly appear from the evidence. A load of hay, passing up the street, rubbed along the side of the car, drew plaintiff's arm outside of the window, and, crushing it between the hay and the car, broke and otherwise injured it. The driver of the car testified that he saw the load of hay for some distance before meeting it; that he was going at a trot, and that when they passed he did not check nor stop the car, because he supposed he had room to pass.

The plaintiff submitted, *inter alia*, the following point: (1) If the jury believe from the evidence that the plaintiff, while a passenger on the defendants' street car, was injured, without his own fault, the plaintiff is entitled to recover, unless the defendant satisfies the jury by the weight of the evidence that the injury arose from an accident which could not be prevented by the utmost skill, foresight, and diligence on the part of defendants' driver. *Affirmed*. (First assignment of error.)

The defendants submitted, *inter alia*, the following point: (1) The Court is requested to charge the jury that there is no evidence in the case sufficient to show negligence on the part of the defendant. *Refused*. (Third assignment.)

The Court, in the general charge, said, *inter alia*: "If the plaintiff was injured without any fault on his part, then the burden is upon the company to show that the driver exercised the utmost degree of care and skill." (Fourth assignment.) "If you find that the plaintiff was injured without fault on his part, the defendant-company must satisfy you that the driver was not negligent, that he took the utmost care he could under the circumstances, otherwise your verdict must be for the plaintiff." (Fifth assignment.)

After plaintiff's points were read to the jury and answered, "Counsel for plaintiff withdrew his points."

Verdict and judgment for the plaintiff for $500. The defendants took this writ, assigning for error, *inter alia*, the answers to the plaintiff's and defendants' points, and the portions of the charge above quoted.

A. M. Brown (with him *C. C. Dickey*), for the plaintiffs in error.

The injury was not caused by defective machinery, cars, or road, or by anything that pertained properly to the business of the railway company, and, therefore, the burden of proving negligence in the carrier was upon the plaintiff.

P. F. W. & C. R. R. Co. *v.* Hinds, 3 Sm. 512.
McCully *v.* Clarke, 4 Wr. 399.
P. & R. R. Co. *v.* Hummell, 44 Id. 375.
Allen *v.* Willard, 57 Id. 374.
Waters *v.* Wing, 59 Id. 211.
P. R. R. Co. *v.* Goodman, 62 Id. 329.

J. W. Over, contra.

The first assignment of error is improperly made, as the points of plaintiff below were withdrawn, and the cause was submitted to the jury on the charge and the answers to defendants' points.

The *onus* of disproving negligence is upon the carrier "when the injury is caused by a defect in the road, cars, or machinery, or by a want of diligence or care in those employed."

Meier *v.* Penna. R. R. Co., 14 Sm. 230.

Jan. 3, 1881. THE COURT. This action was by a passenger to recover damages which he sustained while in a car of a street railway company, in being struck by a passing load of hay. The defendant in error sat near an open window with his arm so exposed that it was struck and injured by the hay on a passing wagon. Thus the proximate cause of injury, at least in part, was caused by the act of a third party, over which the railroad company had no control. If the injury was caused by contributory negligence of the passenger or by the sole negligence of the driver of the wagon, there should be no recovery against the company. The jury has found the passenger was without fault on his part. To enable him to recover he must also prove that the company was guilty of negligence, and its negligence was a cause of the injury. It is just here that the errors covered by the first, fourth, and fifth assignments appear. The learned Judge substantially charged, if the defendant in error was without fault, the company must prove that it was guilty of no negligence; thus shifting the burden of proof resting on the passenger, and throwing it on the company to disprove negligence. This was error. The duty rested on the defendant in error to prove negligence of the company. Without this, he established no cause of action against it. (McCully *v.* Clarke, 4 Wright, 399; Allen *v.* Willard, 7 P. F. Smith, 374; Waters *v.* Wing, 9 Id. 211.) It is true in many cases the mere fact of injury to a passenger raises the presumption of want of care on the part of a railroad company. Such is the case when the injury results from defective track, cars, machinery, or motive power. Here there was no privity between the company and the driver of the wagon. It was then not liable for the act of the wagon, on the principle of *respondeat superior*. (R. R. Co. *v.* Hinds, 3 Id. 512.) The car did not leave its track. It is not alleged that any of the property of the company was improperly constructed, or out of repair. If we correctly understand the complaint, it is as to the speed of the car. We see nothing in the case which relieved the defendant in error from proving negligence, or that threw on the company the burden of disproving it. It is not sufficient that he be free from fault; he must prove other facts, creating a presumption at least of negligence in the company producing injury. The question then is, in this branch of the case, whether, under the whole evidence, the jury is satisfied that the company did not use all just and proper care and diligence to prevent the injury.

It was urged on the argument, that the first assignment was improperly made, as the point covered thereby was withdrawn. It is, however, duly certified as a part of the record, showing that it was affirmed and bill sealed for defendant below. This creates a presumption, that it was read and answered in the hearing of the jury. It then had an effect not removed by its subsequent withdrawal, and may be reviewed. That question is of no practical importance now, inasmuch as substantially the same instructions are contained in the portions of the charge covered by the fourth and fifth assignments. The second and third assignments are not sustained.

Judgment reversed and a *venire facias de novo* awarded.

Opinion by MERCUR, J.
GORDON, TRUNKEY, and GREEN, JJ., absent.

[See Phila. & Reading R. R. Co. *v.* Boyer, *ante*, 497.]

Oct. & Nov. '80, 140.　　　　　　Oct. 7, 1880.

Palmer v. Gillespie.

Statute of Limitations—What is a sufficient admission of indebtedness to toll the running of—An actual or express promise to pay not necessary—Set-off.

In order to toll the running of the Statute of Limitations it is not essentially necessary that there should be an actual or express promise to pay. From an admission consistent with a promise to pay the law will imply a promise without its having been actually or expressly made.

Such an admission must be such a clear, distinct, and unequivocal acknowledgment of a particular debt as to remove hesitation in regard to the debtor's meaning.

Miller *v.* Baschore, 2 Norris, 356, commented upon and modified.

Error to the Common Pleas No. 1, of Allegheny County.

Debt, by John J. Gillespie against Robert H. Palmer.

Upon the trial, before COLLIER, J., the defendant admitted that he was indebted to the plaintiff in the sum of $750, but claimed to have a set-off to the whole claim as follows: About January, 1865, Gillespie was raising a fund to buy some oil land. The title to the property was to be taken in Gillespie's name, who should hold in trust for the contributors according to the amounts respectively contributed. Palmer, the defendant, contributed thereto $750 in two instalments, one of $500, the other of $250. One piece of property was purchased and held by Gillespie in his own name for several years. It did not clearly appear from the testimony how much, if any, of Palmer's money was invested. Palmer testified that about 1870 or 1871 he inquired of Gillespie about it, and that Gillespie said, "He didn't think I was in it at all. Said he would look at the papers. . . . He afterwards informed me that there was not enough to go around. I told him I wanted him to settle with me. . . . . He said he would settle it, but he thought he could buy me a share of equal value of a man that would come in. I let it go. I afterwards asked him about the man's coming in. He said that he hadn't come in, but he expected him, that he would settle it, would pay it, would see to it, that it was correct. First he said he didn't think the receipts were written by him, didn't think I had a receipt for it, and when I brought the receipts to him he said he would pay it, would settle it." Gillespie testified that he was not certain as to how much of Palmer's money had been invested; that the question had been referred to a third party but had never been decided; that more money had been paid in than was necessary for the purchase and that some had been paid back. He expressly denied the conversations testified to by Palmer.

The plaintiff submitted, *inter alia*, the following point: "That even if the jury believe from the evidence that Mr. Palmer, the defendant, gave to the plaintiff $750 to be invested, together with moneys of other parties, in real estate, which the said Gillespie was to hold in trust for said defendant and others, in proportion to the amounts of money by them respectively contributed to the purchase-money, and if the jury believe that the plaintiff took title to said property and recognized the interest of defendant therein, but that when making a subsequent conveyance to another trustee a dispute arose as to the quantum of interest in the property belonging to the defendant, such state of facts gave the defendant no right to recover back his purchase-money or any part thereof, nor is such defence available by way either of payment or set-off in this present action." *Affirmed.*

The Court in its general charge said, *inter alia*, as follows: "Then there is another matter, even if the proposition of the defendant is true. This transaction was more than six years before the bringing of this suit. It is necessary that Mr. Gillespie should make an actual promise to pay within the six years, should admit it, and say he would pay it before the defendant would be entitled to a verdict." . . . "Now, the transaction being more than six years old at the time of the bringing of this suit, unless there was a promise to pay, it would not avail."

Verdict and judgment for the plaintiff. The defendant took this writ, assigning for error the answer to plaintiff's point and the above portion of the charge of the Court.

West McMurray, for plaintiff in error.

If any portion of plaintiff in error's money was not invested, assumpsit for money had and received would lie, or it would be admissible as a set-off in this action.

Aycinena *v.* Peries, 6 W. & S. 244.
Jack *v.* Morrison, 12 Wr. 115.
Deysher *v.* Triebel, 14 Sm. 386.

For the purpose of taking the case out of the Statute of Limitations no actual promise to pay need be proved. An admission consistent with a promise to pay is enough. The jury might have found such an admission.

Suter *v.* Sheeler, 10 Harris, 308.
Patton *v.* Hassinger, 19 Sm. 311.
Senseman *v.* Hershman, 1 Norris, 85.
Johns *v.* Lantz, 13 Sm. 24.

John Dalzell (with him *John H. Hampton*), contra.

Under his plea of payment with leave the defendant proposed to revoke the trust committed to the plaintiff. The plaintiff was simply the treasurer of a fund contributed by a number of parties for a particular purpose. When the defendant's money was paid into the pool it lost its identity, and the surplus not invested would belong to all of the contributors, and they are all interested in its disposition. How then could it be settled in an action between the plaintiff and the defendant?

There was no clear, distinct, and unequivocal acknowledgment of the debt. At most it was a naked admission of indebtedness, without stating the amount or nature of the debt, or a promise to pay something without a reference to the sum to be paid. A promise to "attend to it," or "fix it," or "settle it," is not sufficient.

Miller *v.* Baschore, 2 Norris, 356; s. c., 3 WEEKLY NOTES, 402.
Emerson *v.* Miller, 3 Casey, 278.
Weaver *v.* Weaver, 4 Sm. 153.

The Court meant by actual promise simply a real promise, whether by words or acts, and not "express in terms."

Nov. 8, 1880. THE COURT. This contention relates to the allowance of a set-off claimed by the plaintiff in error. His right thereto is alleged to have arisen on this statement of facts. A purchase of oil lands was contemplated, in which both these parties and some others should be interested. The purchase was to be made in the name of the defendant in error; but in fact for the benefit of all who contributed towards the purchase-money, according to the amount subscribed by each respectively. The plaintiff in error testified that for this purpose, he put $750 into the hands of the defendant in error; but the latter did not so invest it, and afterwards promised to pay it back to him. Evidence was given tending to show that one piece of land was purchased by him and deed therefor taken in his name, and that he afterwards conveyed the same to one Hailman, without declaring any trust therein for the plaintiff in error. Whether any right of the latter in the land was then recognized to exist, is a question in dispute. It seems, however, if any was recognized, it was not equal to the whole $750. This sum had been advanced by the plaintiff in error in two instalments. The first of $250, the latter of $500.

This suit was brought more than six years after the money was thus advanced. To avoid the effect of the Statute of Limitations, the plaintiff in error relied on promises or admissions of indebtedness, alleged to have been made within the six years. The learned Judge charged substantially, that notwithstanding the defendant in error may have kept this money, and did not invest it in the oil property, yet as that was more than six years before suit brought, to make him liable, it was necessary that he "should make an actual promise to pay within the six years; should admit it, and say he would pay it" before he would now be liable therefor. Again he charged "now the transaction being more than six years old at the time of the bringing of this suit, unless there was a promise to pay it, it would not avail." In so charging, we think the learned Judge erred. It is not essentially necessary that the promise be actual or express, provided the other necessary facts are shown. A clear, distinct, and unequivocal acknowledgment of a debt is sufficient to take a case out of the operation of the statute. It must be an admission consistent with a promise to pay. If so, the law will imply the promise without its having been actually or expressly made. There must not be uncertainty as to the particular debt to which the admission applies. It must be so distinct and unambiguous as to remove hesitation in regard to the debtor's meaning. (Fries *v.* Boisselet, 9 S. & R. 128; Bailey *v.* Bailey, 14 Id. 195; Allison *v.* James, 9 Watts, 380; Gilkyson *v.* Larue, 6 W. & S. 213; Hazlebaker *v.* Reeves, 2 Jones, 264; Davis *v.* Steiner, 2 Harris, 275; Johns *v.* Lantz, 13 P. F. Smith, 324.) In this last case, it was said by the present Chief Justice, "No case, however, has ever gone the length of saying that there must be an express promise to pay in terms." Watson's Executors *v.* Sterm (26 Id. 121), and Senseman *et al. v.* Hershman *et al.* (1 Norris, 83), declare the rule to be as stated in the cases we have cited.

Miller *v.* Baschore (2 Norris, 356) was not intended to overrule the long line of preceding cases. The generality of the language therein used must therefore not be understood as requiring an express promise, but a promise that may be clearly implied. The rule as held in the other cases cited was approved and declared in Rider *v.* Kinger, decided last spring at Harrisburg.

Inasmuch as the jury might find under the evidence, that at least one part of the money was in fact never invested in land, the language covered by the first assignment may have been calculated to mislead them. It appears to assume that both sums should be held as one payment. The evidence bearing on each ought to be separately presented to the jury. This can be done on the next trial.

Judgment reversed, and a *venire facias de novo* awarded.

Opinion by MERCUR, J.

Oct. & Nov. '80, 104.   Oct. 26, 1880.

Montgomery v. Heilman.

Jurisdiction— Justice of the peace—Consent— Estoppel—When too late to take advantage of want of jurisdiction—Affidavit of defence law.

A justice of the peace has no jurisdiction in a suit instituted by a distributee in the Orphans' Court to recover from the executor his distributive share.

But where such a suit was instituted, and the defendant expressly agreed that the case should be tried before a justice, and the same was tried and resulted in a judgment for plaintiff, whereupon defendant took an appeal to the Common Pleas, and plaintiff afterwards, in accordance with a rule of Court, filed a sworn copy of his account, and took judgment for want of an affidavit of defence:

Held, that under the circumstances the defendant was estopped from interposing the objection of want of jurisdiction to destroy the validity of the judgment.

In the above case the rule of Court required plaintiff, before recovering judgment for want of an affidavit of defence, to "file, on or before the return-day of the writ, with his declaration or statement when necessary, or, in cases of appeal, on or before the first day of the term to which the appeal is entered, an affidavit stating the amount he verily believes to be due from the defendant, together with a copy of the book entries or instrument upon which the suit is brought; or where the claim is not evidenced by writing, a brief, setting forth a full and detailed statement of the same, verified as aforesaid." Plaintiff filed, in due time, a sworn calculation of the amount due him "per auditor's report" in the Orphans' Court:

Held, to be a sufficient compliance with the rule of Court, and that the plaintiff, upon failure of the defendant to file an affidavit of defence within the stipulated time, was entitled to judgment.

SHARSWOOD, C. J., PAXSON and TRUNKEY, JJ., dissent.

Error to the Common Pleas of Armstrong County.

Appeal from a judgment entered by M. H. Schall, Esq., a justice of the peace, in favor of Jacob Heilman, against Thomas Montgomery, for the sum of $8.57.

The suit was originally instituted against Montgomery, who was the executor of Jacob Heilman, Sr., on the following bill:—

THOMAS MONTGOMERY, Dr.
To JACOB HEILMAN,
Jan. 21, '79, amount of principal due per auditor's report of distribution of the estate of
Jacob Heilman, $95 57
         Cr. by cash paid,   87 00
                                                 ———————
                                                  $ 8 57

The defendant was duly summoned to appear. The transcript of the justice's docket contained the following: "Defendant appears in person, and claims that the above claim is on record in the Orphans' Court of Armstrong . . . . Defendant appears, and agrees to have the case tried before Justice Schall." The case was accordingly tried, and judgment entered for plaintiff. Defendant appealed to the Common Pleas, to June Term, 1879, filing a transcript of the justice's docket entries in said case. On June 2, 1879, plaintiff filed a sworn copy of his account as above, and on June 23, 1879, entered an office judgment for want of an affidavit of defence, in the sum of $9.03.

The rule of Court with reference to judgments for want of an affidavit of defence was as follows :—

"In actions on recognizances, judgments, mortgages, liens of mechanics and material men, municipal claims, transcripts from the Orphans' Court, book accounts, bonds, bills, notes, and other instruments of writing for the payment of money; and in all actions on express contract for the payment of money, and whether the same be in writing or not; and in appeals from the judgments of justices of the peace, if the plaintiff shall file on or before the return day of the writ, with his declaration or statement when necessary, or in cases of appeal, on or before the first day of the term to which the appeal is entered, an affidavit stating the amount he verily believes to be due from the defendant, together with a copy of the book entries or instrument upon which the suit is brought, or where the claim is not evidenced by writing, a brief, setting forth a full and detailed statement of the same, verified as aforesaid, he shall be entitled to judgment at any time after twenty days from the return day of the writ, or in case of appeal from the first day of the term to which the appeal is entered, unless the defendant shall have filed an affidavit of defence setting forth fully the nature and character of the same."

Defendant thereupon obtained a rule to show cause why the judgment should not be stricken off, on the ground that the record showed (1) That the claim was not within the affidavit of defence law. (2) That the justice of the peace had no jurisdiction of the cause of action. This rule the Court (NEALE, P. J.) subsequently discharged. Defendant took this writ, assigning for error the action of the Court in discharging the rule to show cause why the judgment should not be stricken off.

E. S. Solden, for plaintiff in error.

The plaintiff below was not entitled to judgment for want of an affidavit of defence.

He filed neither statement nor narr., as required by the rule of Court.

His case was not of such a kind that he could go to the jury, and recover on proof of the statement filed without more. This is the true test in every case.

Dickerson *v.* McCausland, 3 WEEKLY NOTES, 327.
Imhoff *v.* Brown, 6 Casey, 504.
Com. *v.* Pelletier, 8 WEEKLY NOTES, 516.
Mitchell on Motions and Rules, 63.

A distributee in the Orphans' Court cannot sue before a justice of the peace for his distributive share.

Loomis's Appeal, 10 Barr, 390.

Nor could consent give such jurisdiction.

Collins *v.* Collins, 1 Wright, 387.

(Defendant in error did not appear, and presented no paper-book.)

Jan. 24, 1881. THE COURT. It may be conceded that this cause of action was not within the jurisdiction of a justice of the peace. It is equally true that consent cannot give jurisdiction so as to prevent objection thereto being made in a future trial of the cause. It, however, is not obligatory on a party to interpose such objection. In this case, as appears by the record, after the claim was filed, the plaintiff in error appeared, and at first objected, but afterwards agreed that the case be tried before the justice, and it was so tried. On appeal to the Common Pleas, he made no allegation of want of jurisdiction. He put in no plea; made no affidavit of defence, as required by the rules of Court, and permitted judgment to be entered against him. Thus, by express agreement before the justice, and by his tacit consent afterwards, judgment was regularly entered. After this, the Court granted a rule to show cause why the judgment should not be stricken off, but subsequently discharged it. The alleged grievance of the plaintiff is, that "the Court erred in discharging the rule to show cause, and refusing to strike off the judgment for want of an affidavit of defence."

It is clearly shown by the rule of Court and the opinion of the Judge, that the requisite time had elapsed after the affidavit of claim was filed, to entitle the defendant in error to judgment for want of an affidavit of defence. It is urged, however, that, if the record showed want of jurisdiction, it dispensed with the necessity of putting in such an affidavit. The record did show a waiver of that question, and an agreement to try the case on its merits. A view of the whole record created no presumption, and gave no notice that any objection would be taken to the jurisdiction. As the case then stood, with jurisdiction agreed to, the action was subject to the same rule which applies to appeals from the judgment of a justice of the peace entered on a claim for money due. The attempt now is not to show want of jurisdiction in a pending action, nor that an affidavit of defence was not necessary, if under the showing of the record, the Court could entertain jurisdiction. Suppose, when judgment was moved for, the plaintiff in error, or his counsel, had risen in Court and said, "I interpose no objection by reason of want of jurisdiction. I expressly agreed to waive that, and that the case should be tried before the justice on its own merits, and it was so tried. I still adhere to that agreement, and desire the Court to pass upon the case as if there was undoubted jurisdiction,"—and the Court had thereupon ordered judgment; the case would have been no stronger than it is now. It would have been an oral assertion of what his declaration of record was asserting to the eye of the Court. Let us follow it a step further. Suppose he had suffered execution to issue on the judgment, and his property to be sold, could he then be permitted to question the validity of the judgment for want of jurisdiction in the justice? Could he maintain suit against the officer or purchaser resting on alleged want of jurisdiction? We think he would be estopped from so doing.

If, then, under any circumstances, he would be estopped from interposing want of jurisdiction to destroy the validity of the judgment, why not under the admitted facts in this case? With full knowledge of the law, by his express agreement he induced the defendant in error to incur the costs and expenses of a trial, and the justice and the prothonotary to render their services, for which the statute gives them fees. He invited the judgment to be entered against him. Can he thus trifle with two courts, and also escape the application of the doctrine of equitable estoppel? We think not. He now attempts to avoid the payment of costs, which he expressly induced the other party to incur. The judgment was regularly entered. His effort now is to contradict what he said of record before and at the time judgment was taken. He appealed to the sound discretion of the Court, either to open a judgment regular on its face, or to strike it off for a cause shown by the record to be waived. The learned Judge was right in refusing to disturb the judgment.

Judgment affirmed.
Opinion by MERCUR, J.

Dissenting opinion by TRUNKEY, J., in which SHARSWOOD, C. J., and PAXSON, J., concurred.

The plaintiff states his claim thus: "Amount of principal and interest due per Auditor's report of distribution of the estate of Jacob Heilman, Sr., dec'd, $95.57. Cr. by cash paid $87. Bal. due and unpaid $8.57." It is a reasonable inference that said report is in a proceeding in the Orphans' Court. It may issue execution to enforce its decrees for payment of money, and transcripts may be taken to the Common Pleas for purposes of lien and other proceedings. No statute gives a justice of the peace jurisdiction of decrees and judgments of the higher courts. The justice entered on his docket that the defendant, who appeared in obedience to summons, agreed to be tried before him; but consent cannot give jurisdiction save in one case, and in that the parties must voluntarily appear. The justice was not made an arbitrator, and had he been, there was no case in Court to authorize the judgment in default of an affidavit of defence. On the face of the record, the plaintiff had no right to the judgment, and it was the duty of the Court below to strike it off; it was against its rules as well as the law.

From the judgment of the justice, the defendant appealed. Before he was called on to plead or to defend the action in any way in the Common Pleas, the plaintiff filed a præcipe entering judgment in default of an affidavit of defence. The claim as stated showed the justice had no jurisdiction, and therefore no judgment could lawfully be taken against the defendant. Had the motion been made in open court, judgment would have been refused, of course, on the ground that the plaintiff was not entitled to recover. Moreover, the plaintiff did not comply with the rule of the Court. He did not file a copy of the Auditor's report, nor any part of it. He filed no reference to the place where it could be found of record. Hence he could not rightfully take judgment, even if the record had not shown want of jurisdiction. The judgment was not only against law, but was irregular and unauthorized by the rule. When the motion was made to strike it off, it was the imperative duty of the Court to grant it; the defendant demanded justice, he did not petition for grace. He is not barred of his right for not having filed an affidavit of defence, because the plaintiff had not a case for judgment in default. After his appeal he did nothing till he moved vacation of the wrongfully entered judgment, and to hold that he is estopped from asserting his rights is as novel as the action itself.

Common Pleas—Equity.

C. P. No. 3.   March 7, 1881.

Portuondo v. Faunce.

Equity pleading and practice—Discovery—Interrogatories—Plaintiff must establish his right to the subject-matter of the suit before he is entitled to discovery.

Sur demurrer and exceptions to interrogatories.

The bill in equity, as amended, filed by J. A. Portuondo against J. E. Faunce, set forth the following facts: The plaintiff is a son of the late J. F. Portuondo, a citizen of the United States, who was arrested and illegally put to death by the Spanish authorities in 1870, in Cuba; at that time plaintiff was a minor, and, at his request, his uncle, J. M. Portuondo, was appointed guardian of his person and estate by the Orphans' Court of Philadelphia County; the guardian prosecuted plaintiff's claim for damages for his father's death before the Commission of Claims of Citizens of the United States against Spain, under the treaty of February 12, 1871, and on May 31, 1879, recovered an award for $60,000, which sum has been paid over by Spain to the United States. In the prosecution of this claim the guardian employed as counsel Messrs. J. T. Oehlschlager (on whose death Mr. J. T. Owens took his place) and J. O'Byrne, who, as plaintiff is informed and believes, had sole charge of the prosecution of the case, and advanced all the funds necessary therefor. Plaintiff came of age March 15, 1876, and thereupon the said sum of $60,000 less $9000 due said counsel for their services, and for which they held the guardian's assignments, became due him. The bill as amended further averred that, under an assignment dated May 31, 1879, by the guardian to defendant Faunce, the sum of $12,000 of said award had been paid over to defendant by the Department of State of the United States, and that plaintiff was informed and believes that defendant never rendered any services in or about the prosecution of plaintiff's claim, and that said assignment of $12,000 is wholly without consideration and in fraud of plaintiff's rights, and was made subsequent to the time when plaintiff attained his majority; that defendant now alleges he has parted with and disposed of all the said sum of $12,000, to what persons your orator knows not, but believes them to be wholly irresponsible, and that the transfer was made without consideration, to hinder plaintiff from collecting what belongs to him; wherefore plaintiff needs discovery of the persons to whom and the amounts in which said payments were made.

The prayers were for discovery, a receiver to take charge of the sums so paid over, when the parties to whom such payments were made should be made parties to this suit, and further relief. Interrogatories were accordingly filed to aid in the obtaining of discovery as to said matters.

The answer of J. E. Faunce admitted the averments of the bill as to the claim and the fact of its recovery, but denied all its material allegations in regard to his connection or want of connection therewith, and set up affirmatively the following statement thereof: At the time of his father's death plaintiff was a minor, and without the funds necessary to prosecute a claim of the character of this one; the guardian was equally unable to do so, and accordingly entered into an agreement with Mr. T. H. Oehlschlager (on whose death Mr. Owens was taken into the case in his place), for him to take entire charge and pay all expenses incurred in efforts to secure a tribunal and prove plaintiff's case before it, and in compensation therefor to receive a contingent fee of 50 per cent. Mr. Oehlschlager being unable to furnish all the funds requisite, associated with himself Mr. O'Byrne. The guardian becoming dissatisfied with the conduct of the case desired defendant to take charge of it. Defendant did so, but, at his suggestion, the other counsel also were retained, and an agreement was then entered into between the guardian, Mr. Oehlschlager, Mr. O'Byrne, and the defendant, that 20 per cent. of the contingent fee of 50 per cent. should be paid to defendant, and the remaining 30 per cent. to the other counsel. From that time defendant bore his full share of the labor and expense of the suit. The assignment to defendant was drawn up in writing at the same time with the assignment to the other counsel. The answer averred that no part of the $12,000 which defendant had received in accordance with this agreement had been paid to the guardian; nor had he any interest whatever in its distribution.

Defendant, having been ruled to answer the interrogatories, filed a demurrer and exceptions to them, on the ground that plaintiff had no interest in the subject-matter of the suit, and no title thereto.

E. C. Mitchell (with him *F. Gaston*), for defendant.

Plaintiff is not entitled to discovery until he has shown his title to the property about which the suit is instituted. Here the defendant expressly denies all of plaintiff's right, and until plaintiff establishes his right, discovery would be merely an impertinent inquiry into a matter which does not concern him. An answer to the relief prayed for is an answer to the prayer for discovery.

Methodist Church *v.* Jaques, 1 Johns. Chan. 73.

F. E. Brewster (with him *E. R. Olcott* and *F. C. Brewster*), for plaintiff.

The bill prays for discovery as incidental to the relief sought, and defendant cannot in such a case demur to the discovery.

Wistar *v.* McManes, 4 Sm. 325.

We are entitled to discovery of all matters essential to the relief sought, and defendant cannot deprive us thereof by merely denying our right to relief.

Eo die. THE COURT having intimated its opinion that plaintiff was not entitled to discovery until he had established his right, an order was made as follows:—

Exceptions to interrogatories dismissed, and the rule to answer interrogatories stayed.

Common Pleas—Law.

C. P. No. 1.   Oct. 4, 1880.

Lukens v. Bryson.

Practice—Debt on recognizance of bail in error—Action must be brought in Court where suit originated—Want of jurisdiction can be taken advantage of on trial, after issue joined.

Sur motion, upon trial of cause, for nonsuit for want of jurisdiction.

Debt on recognizance of bail in error. The original suit was an action of covenant sur ground-rent deeds, in Common Pleas No. 2, against C. W. F. Calvert. Judgment was rendered for want of a sufficient affidavit of defence. Calvert took a writ of error, and the present defendant became bail. The judgment was affirmed by the Supreme Court, and Lukens brought suit against Bryson, one of the sureties, to recover his debt and costs. Plea, the general issue. On the trial, before ALLISON, J., the plaintiff produced recognizance, proved damages, and closed. Defendant then filed, by leave of Court, a special plea to the jurisdiction, under objection by plaintiff.

Harry J. Scott, for defendant, moved for a compulsory nonsuit.

This Court is without jurisdiction. An action of debt sur recognizance of bail in error, is an ancillary and not an independent action.

The original suit having been commenced in C. P. No. 2, this action should have been brought therein, and entitled of the same term and number.

Act of June 16, 1836, § 11, Purdon Dig. 606, pl. 21.
Troubat and H. Prac. (5th ed.), § 2039.
Smith v. Ramsey, 6 S. & R. 573.
Keyser v. Dialogue, 4 WEEKLY NOTES, 11.
Wahl v. Wanamaker, 8 Ib. 306.

Where two tribunals have concurrent and complete jurisdiction, the jurisdiction of that one which first has possession of the subject-matter is conclusive.

Slyhoof v. Flitcraft, 1 Ashmead, 171.
White v. Johnson, 2 Ib. 146.

In Bryan *v.* Dailey (37 Leg. Int. 332) ALLISON, P. J., says: "The result of these efforts to harmonize the practice in the several Courts and to retain jurisdiction of a suit throughout is, that all writs or processes of every kind that are founded upon and ancillary to some other action, and all proceedings ancillary, by execution or otherwise, are to be issued from the same Court, docketed in the same docket, and entitled in the same number and term as the original action or proceeding whereon they are founded."

The assignment of cases, under the new Constitution, by rule of Court requires ancillary proceedings to follow the original action.

Instructions to Prothonotary, 37 Leg. Int. 358.
Bank v. Parrish, 5 WEEKLY NOTES, 57.

Want of jurisdiction can be taken advantage of in any stage of the proceedings.

Borough of Little Meadows, 4 Casey, 256.
Black's Execrs. v. Id., 10 Ib. 354.
Capron v. Van Noorden, 2 Cranch, 126.
Mannhardt v. Soderstrom, 1 Binney, 142.
Ketland v. The Cassius, 2 Dallas, 368.

Where the Court is without jurisdiction, neither the laches of the defendant nor his consent can give jurisdiction.

Collins v. Collins, 1 Wright, 387.
Funk v. Ely, 2 P. F. S. 443.
Stroh v. Uhrich, 1 W. & S. 60.
Stoy v. Yost, 12 S. & R. 385.
McKee v. Sanford, 1 Casey, 105.
Van Dyke's Ap., 10 P. F. S. 481.
Peter v. Schlosser, 3 WEEKLY NOTES, 47.
Stearly's Ap., 3 Grant, 270.
Torrance v. Torrance, 3 P. F. S. 505.

Joseph M. Pile, for plaintiff.

THE COURT, ALLISON, J. Motion granted, and nonsuit entered.

[*Cf.* Montgomery v. Heilman, *ante*, 537; Wiser's Appeal, *ante*, 508.]

C. P. No. 2.   Feb. 26, 1881.

City v. Hitner.

Interpleader bonds—Where the city is a claimant it must enter its bond.

Sur rule to show cause why the sheriff should not vacate possession of the plant, machinery, etc., being used in the erection of the public buildings without requiring a bond from the city of Philadelphia, the claimant in the interpleader.

W. N. West, City Solicitor, for rule.

The Court, under the Act 10th April, 1848 (Purd. Dig. 644), has power to make such rules as shall appear to be just. The requiring a bond is within the discretion of the Court

Sharp, contra.

THE COURT. It would be inconvenient to allow the obligation of the city to remain in parol. There should be a bond if only to preserve evidence for the trial of the issue.

Rule discharged.

C. P. No. 3.   Feb. 26, 1881.

Heft v. Jones.

Practice—Bill of particulars—Lease—Covenant to surrender possession of premises in good order—Action for breach in permitting dilapidation—When bill of particulars not demandable.

Rule for bill of particulars.

Covenant for breach of covenants in a lease.

The narr. under which a bill of particulars was demanded, recited a lease by plaintiffs to defendants of certain premises, described "as the 'Dexter Mills,' Manayunk, together with the machinery, shafting, belting, tools, fixtures, and appurtenances thereto attached," as enumerated in schedule attached to the lease, and made profert of the lease.

The narr. further recited a covenant on the part of the defendants to surrender the premises in good order at the determination of the lease, and alleged a violation of this covenant by defendants in "permitting the said demised premises, with the appurtenances, to be and continue . . . . ruinous, prostrate, fallen down, and in great decay;" in yielding them up in that condition; and in permitting "a large quantity and number of the machinery, shafting, belting, tools, fixtures, and appurtenances, as well those mentioned in the schedule annexed to the said hereinbefore recited indenture of January 10, 1876, as also other parts and appurtenances of said machinery and demised premises, to wit, pattern chains, pattern pins, pinion wheels, belting, beam shuttles, and other appurtenances of said machinery and demised premises, to be ruined, spoiled, deteriorated, and wholly carried away from the said demised premises.

Ray W. Jones, for rule. We are entitled to a more specific enumeration of the damages, otherwise it is impossible for us to meet this claim.

Geo. Junkin, contra. The claim lies wholly within defendant's knowledge.

C. A. V.

March 8, 1881. THE COURT. Rule discharged.

C. P. No. 3.

Elliott, to use of Mackenthune, v. Kunszig.

Affidavit of defence law—Claim property bond filed in a replevin suit, not within the Act.

Rule for judgment for want of a sufficient affidavit of defence.

Debt on a claim property bond.

Plaintiff filed copy of the bond, the condition of which was that if the subject matter of the replevin suit should be adjudged to be the property of the plaintiff, and should not then be delivered to him by defendant in said suit, in such case the obligor in said bond should be liable to plaintiff in the sum of $500.

Plaintiff filed no averment, but, on argument, submitted a copy of the record in the replevin suit, showing that judgment had been given for plaintiff, and that to a writ of *fieri facias* issued on the judgment, the sheriff had made a return of "nulla bona."

An affidavit of defence was filed, alleging, *inter alia*, "that the writing filed is not such an instrument as entitles plaintiff to judgment for want of an affidavit of defence, and is not within any Act of Assembly relating thereto."

H. W. Tener, for the rule.

The condition upon which the bond was to be void having failed, the obligor has become absolutely liable to plaintiff for the value of the property in the replevin suit, which amount has been definitely ascertained.

Montayne v. Carey, 1 WEEKLY NOTES, 311.

This case is not distinguishable in principle from those in which the surety in a lease is held liable for lessee's failure to comply with the covenants; the bond is not for the payment of money in the first instance, but becomes so upon the tenant's default.

Audibert v. Young, 1 WEEKLY NOTES, 276.
Hohl v. Korn, 2 Ibid. 277.

Aldrich, contra.

THE COURT. The bond filed in this case is not within the affidavit of defence law. This has been decided by the Courts of this county before, and we see no reason to modify decisions heretofore made.

Opinion by LUDLOW, P. J. Rule discharged.

C. P. No. 3. March 14, 1881.

Biegenwald v. Winpenny.

Pleading—Sufficiency of plea—Replevin—Avowry for rent in arrear—Distraint upon goods in possession of the tenant in course of trade.

Sur demurrer to plea.

The narr. was in replevin, and the avowry alleged that the goods were distrained upon premises No. 1005 Arch Street, demised to T. W. Miller, for rent in arrear. To the avowry, the plaintiff filed a plea, setting up that the goods distrained were, at the time the distress was made, and now are plaintiff's, "and were by him in due course of business consigned and shipped as samples to said T. W. Miller, and put upon the premises in which, etc., in the way and for the benefit of trade," etc. Defendant demurred to the plea on the ground that it does not show to the Court that the goods were, for any good cause, exempt from distress.

John Dolman, for demurrer.

The plea should set forth a state of facts which will bring plaintiff within the exceptions to the general rule that all goods on demised premises are liable to distress for rent. It is not enough to aver that they were in due course of trade shipped as samples, for the landlord may not have leased the premises to be used for purposes of trade. The plea should show affirmatively that the case falls within one of the few exceptions to the general rule, and should state that the premises were used for purposes of trade, with the knowledge and consent of the landlord. We cannot traverse the fact of consignment as samples, for we cannot know whether it is true or false, and should be going off on an immaterial point.

[FINLETTER, J. The terms used in the have a fixed meaning in commerce, and if you can show on the trial that the state of facts differs from what those words import, it will be sufficient.]

Klinges, contra.

THE COURT. Demurrer overruled, with leave, etc.

C. P. No. 3. March 14, 1881.

Nass v. Winpenny.

Sur demurrer to plea.

The pleadings and the facts in this case were the same as in Biegenwald v. Winpenny, *supra*, except that the averment of the plea was that the goods, etc., were "the goods and chattels of the plaintiff in and upon the said premises in the way of trade, and as such privileged from distress." Defendant demurred to the plea on the ground that it does not show to the Court that the goods were for any good cause exempt from distress.

John Dolman, for demurrer.
W. H. Staake, contra.

THE COURT. Demurrer overruled, with leave, etc.

U. S. District Court—Admiralty.

March 10, 1881.

The Norman.

Maritime lien—Supplies furnished on order of charterers—Owner pro hac vice, what constitutes.

Libel, by the Consolidation Coal Company against the steamship Norman, to recover the price of 277 tons of coal furnished the ship while in New York. The answer denied that the coal had been furnished on the credit of the ship, but alleged that it had been furnished on the order of Murray, Ferris & Co., charterers of the vessel, who resided in New York. The testimony disclosed the following facts :—

By charter party, dated November 6, 1878, Murray, Ferris & Co., a firm residing in New York, and doing business there, chartered the steamship Norman from Henry Winsor & Co., of Philadelphia, agents of the owners, for a voyage from New York to Nassau, New Providence, Bahamas, and the south side of Cuba, and back to New York; Murray, Ferris & Co. engaging to pay the expense of manning, victualling, coaling, and running the said steamship. The right to appoint the captain and first and second engineers was reserved by Winsor & Co., but they were to be paid by Murray, Ferris & Co., the charterers. The charter party contained the usual covenants.

The Norman was described in the charter as "of Boston." She had a coasting license, and was owned by a Massachusetts corporation, composed of citizens of Massachusetts and Pennsylvania, and doing business in Boston and Philadelphia, at one of which ports she was enrolled. At the time of the charter, and in accordance with one of its stipulations, a foreign registry was taken out at New York.

Thomas J. Diehl and *J. Warren Coulston*, for libellants.

This is a proceeding *in rem*. The vessel was a foreign vessel, and the coal was delivered on the credit of the ship. A maritime lien, therefore, exists in favor of libellants. The onus of showing that supplies are furnished on *personal* credit is on the claimant of the ship.

The Lulu, 10 Wallace, 192.
The Kalorama, Id. 204.
The Custer, Id. 215.
The Patapsco, 13 Id. 329.
Ins. Co. *v.* Baring, 20 Id. 163–4.

To be a demise of the vessel the charter party must include a transfer of the command and possession of the vessel, and control over its navigation.

Hooe *v.* Groverman, 1 Cranch, 214.
Marcardier *v.* Ins. Co., 8 Cranch, 39.
Palmer *v.* Gracie, 4 Wash. C. C. R. 110.

The libellants had no knowledge of the charter party to Murray, Ferris & Co., and therefore there is nothing in the case to take it out of the ordinary rule of supplies furnished to a foreign vessel in a foreign port.

The Patapsco, 13 Wallace, 329, 333, 334, 335, per DAVIS, J.
The George T. Kemp, 2 Lowell, 477–9–80.

The charter to Murray, Ferris & Co. is a simple contract of hiring without change of possession. The general owners not having surrendered entire control and management of the ship to the charterers, but reserved the right of appointing certain officers, the latter under the law cannot be considered owners *pro hac vice*.

J. W. Brock and *Morton P. Henry*, for respondents.

The coal was furnished on the credit of Murray, Ferris & Co., not the credit of the ship, and no maritime lien will arise unless the repairs are made or furnished to the master in a foreign port.

The Lottawanna, 20 Wall. 219.
The St. Lawrence, 1 Black, 529.
The Harrison, 2 Abbott, D. & C. 78.
The Belfast, 7 Wall. 645.

Where a ship by contract is chartered for a voyage, the charterers to pay expenses of victualling, manning, etc., the possession is with the charterers, and they are owners for the voyage.

Drinkwater *v.* The Spartan, 1 Ware, 149.

Where the general owners charter a vessel to another party, giving him exclusive possession, to be used without charge, repairs, or expense to the owners, they will not be liable for any supplies or outfits procured by him.

Swanton *v.* Reed, 35 Maine, 176.
M'Lellan *v.* Reed, 35 Maine, 172.

By the terms of the charter party the charterers became owners *pro hac vice*, and neither the ship nor the general owners are liable for supplies furnished on the order of the charterers at the place where the latter reside.

The Golden Gate, 1 Newberry, 308.
Mott *v.* Ruckman, 3 Blatchford, 71.
The Secret, U. S. C. C., S. D. N. Y., Dec. 1, 1879 (unreported).
Beinecke *v.* The Secret, 3 Fed. Rep. 665.

March 15, 1881. THE COURT. The ordinary maritime lien for supplies is based upon an implied hypothecation of the ship; and this implication is founded on the ship's necessities and situation, the need of supplies, and the absence from home where the owner is without credit. As the master represents the owner with power to hypothecate, the law implies a hypothecation, whenever supplies are purchased by him under such circumstances. He is known everywhere as the owner's confidential agent. His character and position are, therefore, evidence of authority to represent him in all matters respecting the ship. His contract for supplies abroad raises an implication of lien, because of his power to pledge the ship, and the improbability of obtaining them without. "The master's contract imports an hypothecation." When at home, where the owner is presumed to have credit, and there is, therefore, no necessity for such pledge, none is implied. "To guard against misapprehension," says Mr. Conkling, "it is proper to remark that a lien is never implied from contracts of the *owner in person* [save in foreign ports?]. It is only the contracts which the *master enters into, in his character of master,* that specifically bind the ship, or affect it by way of lien or privilege." Conkling's U. S. Adm. 73, 78, 80; St. Jago de Cuba, 9 Wh. 417.

Were Murray, Ferris & Co. owners *pro hac vice?* If they were, then, the coal in question being purchased by such owners, when the ship was at home, no lien can be implied. Every circumstance necessary to the implication would be wanting. This was decided in "The Golden Gate," 1 Newb. Adm. 308. In the absence of authority, however, I think it could not be doubted. Did the charter party constitute Murray, Ferris & Co. such owners? In other words, did it, in effect, transfer the control and possession of the ship to them? They obtained the entire use and enjoyment, and bound themselves to furnish the men and supplies at their own expense. It is not important that the language is "to *pay* for manning, victualling," etc. The effect is as stated. That the parties so understood is shown by Murray, Ferris & Co.'s purchase of supplies, instead of looking to the general owners for them. The latter stipulated for the privilege of naming the captain and engineers, and the libellants consider this an indication that they retained control of the ship. On the other hand, I think it tends to show an understanding that the ship and her control were to pass to Murray, Ferris & Co. Otherwise, why insert such a provision? If she was not thus to pass, there could be no question of the general owner's right to appoint these officers, as well as the entire crew. The provision was, doubtless, intended to secure to these offices men in whose skill and care the general owners had confidence. I do not, however, deem it necessary to decide this question of ownership. There is another ground on which the case may, I believe, be rested with entire safety.

If the ship remained in the possession and control of the general owners (as libellants assert), no one but her master had authority to represent them. Murray, Ferris & Co. were not their agents, and could not by any act or contract bind them or their property. It would not be suggested that they could pledge the ship for supplies. How, then, can a pledge be implied from their purchase? Their relation to the ship (if libellants' view be accepted) was simply that of freighters. The fact that they were to furnish supplies in part payment is unimportant. And it is equally unimportant that the libellants may have trusted the ship. If they did, it was simply an act of folly, unwarranted and without effect. They cannot allege imposition; it was their duty to ascertain the purchaser's relation to the ship. They knew he was not the master. This officer had nothing whatever to do with the transaction. He saw the coal coming on board, and knew that Murray, Ferris & Co. procured it, as they were bound to do. The purchase was made exclusively by these people, of their own motion (so far as appears), on their own account, and for their own use and benefit. Both the master and engineer say *they* had nothing whatever to do with it. They neither kept a tally of the coal, nor receipted for it; the engineer saying that, when asked to sign a receipt, he referred the individual to Murray, Ferris & Co. Not only was the coal not purchased by the general owner's agent, but it was not even for their use or benefit. It was not important to them whether the ship went on her voyage or remained in port. The stipulated compensation for her use must have been paid, whether she sailed or remained idle. The charterers could not complain that she was without coal; they were bound to furnish it. In short, the libellants, if their view of the contract be adopted, are not creditors of the general owners, sold them nothing, and have no claim whatever on them, or their property in the ship. Beinecke *v.* The Secret, 3 Fed. Rep. 665, and Coal Co. *v.* The Secret, U. S. C. C., S. D. N. Y., Dec. 1, 1879 (not reported), closely resemble the case before me. There, however, the terms of the contract were somewhat different, leaving no room to doubt that the charterers were owners *pro hac vice;* and the decision might safely have been rested on this ground.

The libel must, therefore, be dismissed, with costs.

Opinion by BUTLER, J.

Supreme Court.

Vol. IX.] THURSDAY, APRIL 7, 1881. [No. 33.

Jan. '81, 3.
Jan. 13, 1881.

Borlin's Appeal.
Oct. & Nov. '80, 305.

Houston & Poultney's Appeal.

Conflict of jurisdiction—Testatum writs of execution—Powers of the sheriff in relation thereto—Construction of Act of June 16, 1836.

Judgment was obtained in the Court of Common Pleas No. 1, of Philadelphia County, against a corporation having its principal office in that city. A testatum writ of execution issued against lands of defendant in Westmoreland County. Upon a conflict of jurisdiction arising between the Courts of Common Pleas of Philadelphia and Westmoreland County, over the fund derived from the sale under the writ:

Held, that the sheriff to whom a testatum writ of execution is delivered, under the Act of June 16, 1836, must be ruled by the Court out of which process issued to return the writ, before proceedings in the nature of an attachment against him specified by said Act can be begun.

Application by the sheriff to the Court of the situs to take the acknowledgment of the sheriff's deed after a sale, is a condition precedent to the vesting of any power in that Court, but having thus acquired jurisdiction by virtue of the sheriff's application, it may proceed to inquire into the validity of the sale, etc. The authority given by the Act to the Court of the situs, does not in the least depend upon the permission of the Court whence the writ issues, or the consent of the parties in interest. The discretion to acknowledge the deed in the Court of the situs, and to pay the fund therein, lies entirely with the sheriff, and his exercise of it enables the Court of the situs to inquire into the validity of the sale and distribute the fund.

The sheriff is in no default if he defers making his return into the Court whence the writ issues, until his deed has been acknowledged in the Court of the situs.

(1) Appeal of James Borlin, Sheriff of Westmoreland County, from the decree of the Court of Common Pleas No. 1, of Philadelphia County.

(2) Appeal of Houston and Poultney from the decree of the Court of Common Pleas of Westmoreland County.

These two appeals, based on the same state of facts, were heard together.

A summons in debt by Henry H. Houston against the Youghiogheny Coal Hollow Coal Company, incorporated by Act of the Legislature of Pennsylvania, having its principal office in Philadelphia, issued out of the Common Pleas No. 1, of Philadelphia County, to June Term, 1879, on bonds of said Company secured by mortgage on their coal lands lying in Westmoreland County. Judgments were entered June 21, 1879, against defendant for want of an affidavit of defence, and damages assessed at $54,034.72. On July 12, 1879, upon said judgments a testatum writ of fieri facias issued out of said Court of Common Pleas No. 1 to James Borlin, the Sheriff of Westmoreland County, and upon the return of said sheriff that he had levied and condemned the lands of said Company in said county, a testatum writ of venditioni exponas on said judgments issued out of said Court of Common Pleas No. 1, November 8, 1879. Under this writ Borlin sold the lands December 6, 1879, for the sum of $115,050 to Wilson McCandless and Alexander King.

At the time of sale, there were various judgments in the Court of Common Pleas of Westmoreland County against the said company, also labor claims, and at least two mortgages, but there were no executions in the hands of the sheriff. On May 8, 1880, in the Court of Common Pleas of Westmoreland County, a rule was taken on the sheriff by one Fritchman, a judgment creditor, to pay the proceeds of sale into that Court. On the same day the sheriff filed his petition in the Court of Common Pleas of Westmoreland County, asking leave to acknowledge a deed to the purchasers, and accordingly the Court made an order fixing June 21 for taking the acknowledgment after notice to the parties to the execution and to the stockholders of the defendant.

On June 12, 1880, the Court of Common Pleas No. 1, of Philadelphia, on application of Houston, plaintiff in the execution, granted a rule on the said sheriff, Borlin, "to show cause why the moneys realized by him by his sale under the above writ shall not as soon as realized, be paid into this Court and not into any other Court." Pending the disposition of this rule, it is ordered that no payment shall be made by said sheriff of said proceeds of sale into any other Court." On June 26, the sheriff filed his answer in said Court of Common Pleas No. 1, setting up the proceedings which had been taken in the Westmoreland County Court, and declining to return his writ or pay the money into said Court of Common Pleas No. 1. Thereupon said rule was made absolute, and service of notice thereof duly made upon said sheriff.

In the mean time, on June 21, in the Court of Westmoreland County, the sheriff presented his deed for acknowledgment with a special return, setting forth that the purchasers were lien creditors to an amount exceeding fourteen thousand dollars, and that he had taken a receipt for said amount on account of their lien. The acknowledgment was deferred by the Court till July 3, and afterwards till July 12. On July 9, Houston filed exceptions to the sheriff's return, because not filed in the Court from which the vend. ex. issued, and because the Court of Common Pleas of Philadelphia County had ordered the money to be paid to it. Other lien creditors also filed exceptions to said return. On July 12, the Westmoreland County Court received the acknowledgment of the deed and appointed auditors to pass upon the exceptions filed to the return, as also to report the facts with a schedule of distribution. Thereupon Houston excepted to the jurisdiction of the Court in taking the acknowledgment and in making said order.

On July 31, the auditors filed their report and distribution, and on August 28, the Court approved of the finding of the auditors and ordered the sheriff to pay into Court the fund realized from the sale, fixing September 6 for the hearing of any questions arising upon the schedule of distribution reported by the auditors.

From this order Houston and Poultney *et al.*, other lien creditors, appealed, assigning for error the action of the Court in not entertaining the exceptions to the jurisdiction, in approving of the finding of the auditors, and in ruling the sheriff to pay the money into that Court.

Prior to this, the said sheriff not having obeyed the order of Common Pleas No. 1, of Philadelphia, nor having returned its writ of vend. ex. directed to him, a rule for an attachment for contempt of Court, was taken upon him out of said Court, which was made absolute July 22, 1880, the Court amercing him in the sum of $5000. On July 28, the sheriff filed a petition in said Court, setting forth that proceedings affecting the fund raised by the sale under the writ of testatum vend. ex., from Philadelphia County, had been begun in the Westmoreland County Court, and owing to these proceedings, the aforesaid writ had not been returned to the Court whence it issued ; that no rule to compel its return had been taken ; and that his official duties made it impossible for him to attend in Court at Philadelphia on the day on which the fine had been imposed upon him. That while the conflict of jurisdiction between the Common Pleas of Philadelphia County and that of Westmoreland County continued, his only security consisted in retaining the fund. In conclusion he disclaimed any intentional contempt, and prayed the Court to dissolve the attachment, or at least to stay execution thereof, until the question in dispute should be adjudicated, and to remit the fine.

At the same time the sheriff made return of the writ of vend. ex. to the said Court to the effect that he had sold the premises described in said writ to King and McCandless for $115,050, and held ready as commanded the amount so realized less $120.72 paid out for taxes by order of the Common Pleas of Westmoreland County, and less the sum of $14,006.98, which said purchasers as lien-creditors were entitled to receive and for which he had their receipt.

On the same day he made further return that the said King and McCandless had returned him the said $14,006.98, theretofore receipted for by them, and he therefore had the whole of said purchase-money ready as commanded, except the sum paid out for taxes as aforesaid.

Thereupon the Court ordered that upon a promise by said sheriff to make a return within five days setting forth that he held the whole sum realized by the sale, the amount of his fine should be reduced to $50.

From this order the said Borlin, sheriff, appealed, assigning for error the order of the Court directing him to return the moneys raised by the testatum vend. ex., and also the order amercing him for contempt.

H. P. Laird, for Sheriff Borlin.

Until the writ of vend. ex. was returned no order on the sheriff could be made by the Philadelphia Court to pay the money into Court. It was plaintiff's duty first to rule the sheriff to return the writ. Until this was done it was no contempt on the part of the sheriff merely to omit returning the writ.

1 Troubat & Haly's Pr. sec. 338.

The Act of June 16, 1836, sec. 100 (Purd. Dig. 664), not only empowers the sheriff to acknowledge the deed on a testatum process in the Court of the county where the real estate is situated, but also to pay the money made into that Court, and gives that Court power to set the sale aside, or if it is confirmed, to distribute the money. A rule, therefore, having been taken on the sheriff to pay the money into the Westmoreland Court on May 9, 1880, prior to the rule taken in the Philadelphia Court, it was his duty to obey where the jurisdiction first attached.

John G. Johnson and *William A. Porter*, for Houston *et al.*

A court whose execution raises the fund at the instance of one of its suitors cannot be deprived of its jurisdiction over the same without its assent. The 82d section of the Act of June 16, 1836 (Purd. Dig. 654, pl. 101), provides that if the sheriff to whom the testatum writ of execution is directed " neglects or refuses to execute and return the same according to the exigency thereof he shall be amerced in the Court where he ought to return it." Again, the 86th section of the same Act (Purd. Dig. 656, pl. 107) provides that where there are disputes concerning the distribution of the money arising from sales upon such execution "the Court from which the execution shall have issued shall have power, after reasonable notice given either personally or by advertisement to hear and determine the same according to law and equity." By the 99th section of the same Act (Purd. Dig. 659, pl. 124), it is made "the duty of the sheriff in any other Court than that in which the process issued, upon which the sale shall have been made, immediately thereafter to return the same into the office of the prothonotary or clerk from which it issued."

The jurisdiction of the Court which issues the writ to control the same, being duly fixed, it behooves those who seek to oust it to show the warrant of some clear statutory provision. This is not shown here. The 96th section of the Act of 1836 (Purd. Dig. 658, pl. 121), providing that the acknowledgment may be made in the Court of the city or county in which the real estate lies; and the 100th section of said Act (Purd. Dig. 659, pl. 125), providing that the Court to which application to take the acknowledgment of a deed for real estate may be made, shall have authority to examine the regularity and validity of such sale and set the same aside if there be cause, and may order the distribution of the proceeds, if they be paid into such Court in like manner as if such sale had been made by virtue of process issuing from such Court, are permissive and not obligatory provisions, and there is no direction that the acknowledgment or distribution is to be made in the county of the situs against the positive order of the Court whence the execution issued.

McKeown v. Craig, 8 Harris, 170.
18 Leg. Int. 349.

At best, the jurisdiction of the Court of the situs can only attach "if the proceeds of such sale shall be paid into it" (100th section, *supra*). There is no direction that the sheriff *must* pay into it such proceeds.

But the order of the Philadelphia Court to pay the money into its hands was made more than a month before the similar order of the Westmoreland County Court. In the absence of the fund, therefore, the latter Court had no jurisdiction.

February 14, 1881. THE COURT. There is no complaint as to the manner in which the testatum venditioni exponas directed to appellant as sheriff of Westmoreland County was executed. The proceedings against him in the Court below were grounded solely on neglect to return the writ and refusal to pay the purchase-money into Court. They were commenced June 12, 1880, by ruling him to show cause why the money, as soon as realized, should not be paid into Court, and ordering that it should not be paid into any other Court in the mean time. This rule was made absolute on June 26, 1880. Subsequently a rule was granted to show cause why he should not be attached for contempt in refusing to obey the foregoing order; and on the return thereof July 23, 1880, it was "ordered and adjudged that the said sheriff is in contempt of the Court in failing to return into this Court the writ of testatum venditioni exponas, in this cause, issued in accordance with its commands, and in further failing to obey said order of June 26, 1880, to pay into this Court the money realized by his sale thereunder. It is further ordered and adjudged that for these contempts the sheriff be attached, and that he be and is amerced in the sum of five thousand dollars." A few days thereafter a petition containing a detailed statement of what had been due was presented by the sheriff, setting forth, *inter alia*, that he had now received from the purchasers the whole of the purchase-money of the premises sold under the writ; and on the hearing of this petition July 28, 1880, it was ordered that, upon his making a return within five days that he had so received the whole of the purchase-money, the fine should be reduced to $50.

It will be observed that the sheriff was never ruled to return the writ, nor was it in fact returned until after the orders complained of were made. It is contended that, according to the usual course of practice in such cases, neither of the orders should have been made without first ruling the sheriff to make his return, and, if need be, enforcing it by attachment; that such a course of procedure is necessary for the protection of the officer as well as for the proper information of the Court.

The position thus assumed by the learned counsel for the sheriff is substantially correct. It is true the 82d section of the Act of 1836 provides: "If any sheriff to whom a testatum writ of execution shall be directed . . . shall neglect or refuse to execute and return the same according to the exigency thereof, he shall be amerced in the Court where he ought to return it, and also be liable to the action of the party aggrieved;" but it was never intended that the penalty thus prescribed should be summarily inflicted if the return was not made at the very day named in the writ; nor without first ruling him to make his return. While in general it is the duty of the sheriff to promptly execute and return all processes according to the commands thereof without being ruled, there are cases in which he is not required to do so. He is expressly authorized to sell real estate within six days after the return day; and, in testatum executions, he is invested with discretionary powers as to the acknowledgment of the deed and payment of the purchase-money into Court, the exercise of which may necessarily delay his return to the writ. After selling real estate on a testatum execution, he may, as was done in this case, elect to acknowledge his deed to the purchaser in the Court of the "county in which such real estate may be." (Purd. Dig. 658, pl. 121, 122.) It being made his duty to acknowledge the deed in open Court, he has the right to elect in which Court he will make the acknowledgment. It is an official right, of which, if properly exercised, he cannot be deprived; and the very fact of his application to the Court of the situs for that purpose may call into active exercise special powers of that Court which could not otherwise be invoked. The Act provides—" When application shall have been made to any Court to take the acknowledgment of a deed for real estate sold on the process issued by any other Court, the Court to which such application shall be made shall have power to examine the regularity and validity of such sale, and set the same aside if there be cause. And, if the proceeds of such sale be paid into the said Court, they may order the distribution thereof in like manner as if such sale had been made by virtue of process issued from such Court. (Purd. 659, pl. 125.)

It is evident from the phraseology of the Act that application to the Court of the situs to take the acknowledgment is a condition precedent to the vesting of any power in that Court; but, having thus acquired jurisdiction by virtue of the sheriff's application, it may proceed to inquire into the validity of the sale, etc. The power to distribute the proceeds of sale when paid into Court is also given in express terms; but it is, perhaps, not quite so clear as to how or by whom the money is to be paid. Inasmuch, however, as the sheriff alone is authorized to sell and receive the proceeds, we think it necessarily follows that he is the proper person to pay it into Court; and he may elect to pay it into the Court whence the writ issued or into the Court of his own county.

It is claimed by the learned counsel for the appellees that the provisions above referred to do not interfere with the jurisdiction of the Court whence the writ issues, but simply authorize that of the situs to act if the former be willing and the parties in interest consent. We find nothing in the Act, however, to warrant the conclusion that the authority given to the latter depends on the permission of the former Court or the consent of the parties in interest; on the contrary, it appears to have been the manifest intention of the Legislature to give the Court of the situs control over the sale whenever the sheriff offers his deed there for acknowledgment, and control over the proceeds whenever he elects to pay the same into that Court. These provisions were doubtless intended for the convenience of the sheriff as well as lien creditors; but, whatever may have been the object, the discretionary power, as to acknowledgment of deeds and payment of proceeds into Court, has been given to the sheriff, and the exercise of that discretion by him enables the Court to inquire into the validity of the sale and distribute the fund, as the case may be, under the circumstances specified in the Act.

When the deed is acknowledged in the Court of the situs, it is made the duty of the sheriff immediately thereafter to return the process, on which the sale shall have been made into the office of the prothonotary or clerk of the Court from which the same shall have been issued. (Purd. Dig. 659, pl. 124.) It follows from this that the sheriff is in no default if he defers making his return to the Court whence the writ issued until his deed has been acknowledged in the other Court. Prior to that time it would be impossible for him to make a full and final return.

Whenever it becomes necessary, in cases of neglect or unreasonable delay, to resort to summary proceedings against a sheriff, we think the correct practice is, first to rule him to make his return, so that the Court may be fully informed as to what has been done in pursuance of the writ, and thus be prepared to take such action as may be proper in the premises. This practice appears to be recognized in Com. *v.* McCoy (8 Watts, 153), where it is said "the sheriff may be called on by rule to return the writ, and if he neglect to do so, or to offer a reasonable excuse the Court will grant an attachment against him." It is applicable also to other than execution processes. "If the sheriff make no return to the writ, he may be proceeded against by attachment, after being first ruled to return the writ; the object of the rule being to bring him into contempt." (1 Troub. & H. Pract., sect. 325, 329, and 1157.) The Act of 1836 expressly authorizes, "rules on sheriffs and coroners for the return of all processes in their hands, and for the payment of money," etc., and provides for the enforcement thereof by attachment, limiting the time, however, in the case of ex-sheriffs and coroners, to two years after the expiration of their office.

The necessity for observing the rule of practice above stated, is more imperative in the case of testatum writs for the sale of real estate than in ordinary executions, for the reason that in the former the sheriff, as we have seen, is invested with important discretionary powers, which do not exist in the latter, the exercise of which may, in a greater or less degree, determine the action of the Court whence the process issues. In this case, before any action was taken by the Court below, the sheriff had elected to acknowledge the deed in the Court of Common Pleas of Westmoreland County, and the Court had fixed a day for that purpose, directed notice to be given as required by the Act, etc., but by continuances ordered by the Court the deed was not acknowledged until July 12, 1880, prior to which date the sheriff was not required to return the writ. If the first step in the proceeding against him had been a rule to return the writ, as we think it should have been, the pendency of his application to acknowledge the deed in the Court of Westmoreland County would have been a sufficient answer thereto. Until that application was acted on, and the deed acknowledged, the latter Court had at least concurrent power to set aside the sale. The peremptory order of the Court below to pay into it, and not into any other Court, the proceeds of sale as soon as realized was premature, and was also calculated to interfere with the right which the sheriff had to pay the money into the Court of Westmoreland County.

The proceedings of the Court below are reversed and set aside.

Opinion by STERRETT, J. PAXSON, J., absent.

Jan. '80, 240.   March 31, 1880.

County of Lackawanna v. First National Bank of Scranton.

Taxes and Taxation—Banks—Exemption from taxation—Act of March 31, 1870—Construction of—Constitutionality of—Constitution of Pennsylvania, Article IX. Sections 1 and 2.

The Act of March 31, 1870 (Purd. Dig. 143, pl. 97), provided that State and National banks upon the payment of a tax of one per centum upon all their capital stock at its par value, should be exempt from all other taxation upon their shares, capital, and profits:

Held, to be constitutional, and not repealed by the Constitution of 1874.

It is perfectly competent for the Legislature, where the State receives a fair equivalent, to commute for taxes upon property under its control.

In this case, the equivalent being reasonable, the question of commuting for a nominal tax amounting to an entire exemption not considered.

A national bank owning and occupying a bank building in which had been invested part of its capital and profits, having paid the amount of tax upon its capital stock, whereby the rest of its property was exempted from taxation, the fact that it rented out a portion of the bank building for other purposes than its own use will not subject those portions to a county tax.

Error to the Common Pleas of Lackawanna County.

The following facts were agreed upon as a case stated for the opinion of the Court in the nature of a special verdict.

On January 19, 1879, the First National Bank of Scranton, Pennsylvania, which is a banking association under the National Bank Act, paid into the State Treasury a tax of one per centum upon the par value of all the shares of said bank, having elected to collect the same from the shareholders of said bank, as provided in the Act of 31st March, 1870, paragraph 4.

Part of its capital and profits is invested in its bank building, situated on Lackawanna Avenue, in the city of Scranton, Lackawanna County. The said building is occupied as follows: The main or first floor is occupied by the said bank as its banking-room; in the rear of said banking-room are two small offices for rent. The second floor is divided into five offices, which are rented by the said bank. The third floor is used as a Masonic Hall. The basement of the same is occupied by the watchman of the said bank and his family, except a small room in the front part of the basement, which is occupied, under lease from said bank, as a shoe shop. The rents from the said offices and hall amount to $1100 per annum. The assessed valuation of the said bank building is $8000. The county tax against the said bank building for the year 1879 is $48.

If the Court shall be of opinion that the said building is liable to taxation for county purposes, then judgment for the plaintiff for $48, with costs; if not, then judgment for defendant, with costs. Either party to be at liberty to take out a writ of error.

Section 4 of the Act of Assembly of March 31, 1870 (Purd. Dig. 143, pl. 97), is as follows:—

" That in case any bank or savings institution aforesaid (*national banks located within this State and banks and savings institutions incorporated by this State*) shall elect to collect annually from the shareholders thereof a tax of one per centum upon the par value of all the shares of said bank or savings institution, and pay the same into the State Treasury on or before the twentieth day of January in every year, the said shares, capital, and profits shall be exempt from all other taxation under the laws of this Commonwealth."

The words in italics are in the first section of the Act.

The Court (HANDLEY, P. J.) entered judgment in favor of the defendants, exempting the building from taxation for county purposes.

The plaintiff took this writ, assigning for error the entry of judgment as above set forth.

Lemuel Amerman, county solicitor, for the plaintiff in error.

Art. IX. Sec. 2 of the Constitution provides that—

" All laws exempting property from taxation other than the property above enumerated (*public property used for public purposes, actual places of religious worship, places of burial not used or held for private or corporate profit, and institutions of purely public charity*) shall be void."

This repeals the Act of Assembly under which exemption is claimed, for if it does not the Legislature might place a nominal tax upon the property of any class of holders, and thus virtually exempt them from taxation, which would be entirely contrary to the provision of the Constitution.

In any event the Act must receive a strict construction, and upon this basis the exemption cannot be allowed, for Art. IX. Sec. 1 of the Constitution provides that "All taxes shall be uniform upon the same class of subjects within the territorial limits of the authority levying the tax;" if, therefore, an exemption is to be claimed under the Act, its extent must appear to be clear, well defined, and equal, but by its provision the bank by paying one per cent. upon the par value of all its shares has its buildings and other property exempted, while other property holders upon the same class of property are compelled by various county assessments to pay four and one-fifth per cent. upon its valuation. This is surely not "uniform taxation" within the meaning of the Constitution.

By the case stated the bank is shown to occupy only one floor of the building, the other portion being rented out by it for various purposes, but under the provisions of the United States statute the bank can hold as its capital and profits only "such real estate as shall be necessary for its immediate accommodation in the transaction of its business" (Rev. Stat. U. S., 2 Ed., Sec. 5137, p. 993); therefore, if the exemption is allowed, it can only be upon that portion of the building actually used for the purposes of the bank.

Lehigh Coal and Nav. Co. v. Northampton Co., 8 W. & S. 334.
N. Y. and Erie R. R. Co. v. Sabin, 2 Cas. 242.
Carbon Iron Co. v. Carbon County, 3 Wr. 251.

Whenever there is a charter or statutory exemption from taxation of the property of a corporation upon payment of a per centum upon the capital stock, it has been held to apply only to such property as is exclusively, undividedly, and necessarily used in the enjoyment of the franchise of the corporation. This is the rule of construction that the plaintiff asks shall be applied here.

State v. Commissioners of Mansfield, 3 Zab. 510.
State v. Hancock, 33 N. J. L. (4 Vroom), 315.
Cook v. Camden and Burlington County R. R. Co., 4 Vroom, 475.
Tucker v. Ferguson, 22 Wall. 527.

T. J. Post, for the defendant in error.
This Act is a contract between the State holding the taxing power and the defendant, and all banks of the State can accept, and become subject to, the provisions of the contract; it is not special or exclusive. It is express in its terms. Nothing is left to implication or to forced construction, and its intent clearly expressed is, that the capital and profits of the defendant shall be liable to no further taxation. Besides, the per centum fixed here is in no sense an exemption from taxation, but is rather a fair equivalent for all taxes.

The Legislature has the perfect authority to commute for taxes, receiving in exchange what it regards as an equivalent, and such action is in no sense such a privilege as would permit a strict rule of construction to be applied to such an Act.

Cooley on Taxation, pp. 137, 172.
Burroughs on Taxation, p. 66.
Kneeland v. Milwaukee, 15 Wis. 454.

Where the Legislature has exercised its power by taxing all the property of a corporation in a specified manner, and has intimated no design to subject it to further burdens, its property will be exempt from taxes imposed by general laws.

New York & Erie R. R. Co. v. Sabin, *supra*.
Wayne County v. Delaware and Hud. Canal Co., 3 Har. 351.
State v. Berry, 17 N. J. 80.
Camden and Amboy R. R. Co. v. Commissioners, 18 N. J. 11.
Gordon v. Mayor of Baltimore, 5 Gill, 231.
Farmers' Bank v. Long, 7 Bush, 327.
Commissioners v. Citizens' National Bank, 23 Minn. 280.

May 3, 1880. THE COURT. The fourth section of the Act entitled "An Act providing for the taxation of bank shares," passed March 31, 1870 (Pamph. L. 42), was not a law exempting property from taxation, within the provision of Art. IX. Sec. 2 of the Constitution. The tax which was thereby imposed, with the consent of the bank, was a commutation for all other taxes under the laws of the Commonwealth, upon a class of property entirely within the power of the Legislature. It was in no sense a mere nominal tax, and we need not consider what would be the effect of such a tax amounting to an entire exemption. The banking house was a part of the capital of the institution represented by its shares of stock, and a tax on the par value of the shares was a tax upon it. We do not see that the uses to which the building was applied in this case should subject any portion of it to taxation for county purposes.

Judgment affirmed.
PER CURIAM.

Oct. & Nov. '80, 265.   Oct. 26, 1880.

Truby's Appeal.

Constitutional law—Taxation—Constitution of Penna., Art. 9, § 1—Act of June 7, 1879, § 18 (P. L. 112)—Preliminary injunction—Appeals—Practice.

The Act of June 7, 1879, Sect. 18 (P. L. 112) enabling a bank to exempt its shareholders from all other taxation by collecting six-tenths of one per cent. upon the par value of all the shares and paying the same into the State treasury, was intended to take effect immediately and apply to the year of its passage. Said Act is valid and constitutional, and not in violation of Art. 9, Sect. 1, of the Constitution of Pennsylvania providing that "all taxes shall be uniform on the same class of subjects, within the territorial limits of the authority levying the tax."

Per SHARSWOOD, C. J. In appeals from preliminary injunctions, the Supreme Court do not usually pass on the merits of the case, but, except in those instances where it is very evident that the Court below has been in error, continue the injunction.

Appeal from the Common Pleas of Indiana County

Bill in Equity, between J. H. Kintner, John A. Stewart, and others, stockholders in the Indiana County Deposit Bank, complainants, and John Truby, Treasurer of Indiana County, defendant, setting forth the following facts:—

The Commissioners of Indiana County in assessing the rates and levies for county purposes for the year 1879, rated and assessed complainant's stock to pay five mills on the par value thereof for county purposes, and also a special tax thereon of three mills for the current year. Said taxes were assessed in pursuance of the Act of March 31, 1870 (Purd. Dig. 143, pl. 96), the material portions of which are as follows:—

"Section 3. All the shares of national banks, located within this State, and of banks and savings institutions incorporated by this State, shall be taxable for State purposes at the rate of three mills per annum upon the assessed value thereof; and for county, school, and local purposes, at the same rate as now is or may hereafter be assessed and imposed upon other moneyed capital in the hands of individual citizens of the State."

"Section 4. In case any bank or savings institution aforesaid shall elect to collect annually, from the shareholders thereof, a tax of one per centum upon the par value of all the shares of said bank or savings institution, and pay the same into the State treasury, on or before the 20th day of January in every year, the said shares, capital, and profits shall be exempt from all other taxation under the laws of this Commonwealth."

The said taxes so assessed being unpaid, said commissioners on or before May 1, 1879, placed the same in the hands of defendant for collection, which collection he was, by virtue of the Act of April 4, 1872 (P. L. 954), and the supplements thereto, duly authorized to make.

On June 7, 1879, an Act of Assembly was passed whereby it was provided, *inter alia*, as follows:—

"Sect. 17. That . . . . all shares of stock in any bank, banking or savings institution or company, now or hereafter incorporated by or in pursuance of any law of this Commonwealth . . . shall be and are hereby made taxable for State purposes, at the rate of four mills on every dollar of the value thereof annually; Provided, that . . . . in case any bank or savings institution incorporated by this State, or any national bank, elect to collect annually from the shareholders thereof a tax of six-tenths of one per centum upon the par value of all the shares of said bank or savings institution, and pay the same into the State treasury on or before the 20th day of June in every year, the shares, capital, and profits of such bank shall be exempt from all other taxation under the laws of this Commonwealth."

"Sect. 18. That this shall go into effect immediately. . . . . (P. L. 1879, 112, etc.)."

In pursuance of the provisions of said Act, said bank collected from the shareholders therein six-tenths of one per cent. on the par value of their stock, and on June 19, 1879, paid the same into the State treasury. The bill averred that in consequence thereof, complainant's shares were not liable to assessment for local or county purposes, but that the defendant nevertheless was by virtue of the powers conferred upon him by the Act of April 4, 1872, about to issue his warrant authorizing constables to levy and collect by distress and sale of complainant's goods the said taxes imposed by the Commissioners of Indiana County upon complainant's shares of stock for the year 1879, which said proceedings the bill averred would subject complainants to great expense and inconvenience, and do them irremediable injury. The bill therefore prayed for an injunction preliminary until hearing, and perpetual thereafter, to restrain defendant from taking any steps to collect said taxes.

The Court (HUNTER, P. J.) granted a preliminary injunction and subsequently continued the same until an answer or demurrer should be filed and a further hearing had. From this decree the defendant appealed, assigning for error the granting and continuing of the preliminary injunction.

J. A. C. Ruffner and *J. H. Banks*, for appellant.

[SHARSWOOD, C. J. "There is very little use in taking an appeal from a preliminary injunction like the present one. In deciding appeals from preliminary injunctions we usually do not pass on the merits of the case, but, except in those instances where it is very evident that the Court below has been in error, continue the injunction and make no final disposition of the case until a final decree is entered in the Court below and an appeal taken therefrom."

The counsel then agreed in writing at bar, by leave of the Court, that the preliminary injunction granted in this case should be taken and deemed to be final, and that the appeal therein should be considered as taken to said final decree.]

The appellees are not relieved from paying the taxes assessed for 1879. The Act of June 7, 1879, clearly did not refer to the then current year.

If it did so refer then it was unconstitutional, for the banks that neglected to pay in lieu of local taxes for 1879, the amount of one per cent. prior to Jan. 20, under the Act of 1870, could relieve themselves by payment of six-tenths of one per cent. before June 20, 1879, under the Act of June 7, 1879, thus making two different rates of taxation for the same class of subjects in the same year. This would be in violation of Art. 9, Sec. 1, of the Constitution of Pennsylvania. "All taxes shall be uniform on the same class of subjects, within the territorial limits of the authority levying the tax."

Moreover if any holders of bank stock in this county had paid the amount assessed on their shares for the year under the Act of 1870, then they would have been required to pay a different amount than those who might avail themselves of the new Act of 1879. This would also be in violation of the Constitution of Pennsylvania, Art. IX. Sec. 1.

[SHARSWOOD, C. J. Could any one take advantage of this but the taxpayers of amounts assessed under the Act of 1870 ?]

Silas M. Clark (with him *Harry White*), for appellees.

The Act of 1879 was by its express terms to go into effect at once. No question can be raised therefore as to the right of appellees to avail themselves of that Act, nor were its provisions in conflict with Art. 9, Sect. 1, of the Constitution of Pennsylvania. The taxes assessed under the Act of 1870 were uniform, and so were those assessed under the Act of 1879. The mere fact that an old uniform system gave way in the middle of a year to a new uniform system, thus enabling some persons to benefit by the provisions of the latter law beyond what was offered under previous laws, does not render the new law unconstitutional.

November 8, 1880. THE COURT. That it was the intention of the Legislature that the Act of June 7, 1879, should go into effect immediately, so as to include the year of its passage, is, we think, very plain upon the face as well as from a consideration of its object. This is indeed but faintly denied by the appellant, but it is earnestly contended that it was beyond their power, because they had already provided differently for that year. It is said, therefore, that it is wanting in the uniformity required by the Constitution. But the rate provided by the Act of 1879 is uniform. How can its constitutionality be affected by the fact that the Act of 1870 made a different provision, and that one or more banks may have availed themselves of its provision by paying one per cent. on their capital, to secure an exemption from all other taxation? These banks are not complaining. If the Legislature should, in the middle of a year, repeal totally a tax upon any particular class of subjects, would it be any objection to the constitutionality of making such a repealing Act go into effect at once, that one or more persons had already paid the taxes for that year which had thus been repealed? Their objections would not be heard to prevent the exercise of the legitimate authority of the Legislature in relief of the whole community. They might have an equitable claim on the government to have the taxes thus paid refunded, but could not insist that the old tax for that year should be collected. In principle we cannot see how this differs from the case in hand.

Decree affirmed and appeal dismissed at the cost of the appellant.

PER CURIAM.

Oct. & Nov. '80, 186, 187.   Nov. 11, 1880.

Keystone Bridge Company v. Newberry.

Same v. Kennedy.

Negligence—Master and servant—Co-employés —Who is a fellow servant for whose negligence the employer is not liable.

To take a case out of the rule that an employer is not liable for an injury to an employé caused by the negligence of a fellow-servant working in a common employment, it is not sufficient to show that the one whose negligence is complained of was a gang-boss, under whose orders the one injured was working.

If the gang-boss had no general power of control, but acted as foreman of workmen engaged by and furnished to him by a superintendent, whose orders he was bound to obey, the principle *respondeat superior* does not apply.

In an action by a servant against his employer, in the absence of evidence of knowledge by the employer of incompetency of the gang-boss, it is error to submit the question of negligence to the jury.

Error to the Common Pleas No. 2, of Allegheny County.

These were actions on the case by Newberry and Kennedy to recover damages for injuries resulting from alleged negligence of the said corporation.

The material facts, as developed on the trial before KIRKPATRICK, J., and not seriously disputed, were stated in the opinion of the Supreme Court, as follows:—

"The defendant was a corporation very largely engaged in the business of constructing and erecting iron bridges. They owned and used extensive works, and had erected an additional building about four hundred feet in length, and fifty feet in width. The walls were brick, and at the time of the accident they were already raised to their full height, and upon them an iron roof was being placed for purposes of ventilation. The plaintiffs were laboring men, who were working under the immediate direction of one William Wymond. An apparatus called a trussed plank was being used in putting on the roof, and while plaintiffs and some other workmen were engaged carrying an iron rafter over this plank, it gave way and they were precipitated to the ground, killing one man and injuring several, among them the plaintiffs. A large amount of testimony was taken, but so far as the principal questions are concerned, it was not at all contradictory. In regard to the position of Wymond, the undisputed testimony was to the following effect: Col. Piper was the general manager. He had supervision over the whole business of the company; employed and discharged the men, and gave general directions. His orders had to be obeyed by all except the President. Next to him in authority was Mr. Sheffler, the assistant manager, whose duties were the same as Col. Piper's, he giving attention to the details, and supervising the whole business in Col. Piper's absence. The next in authority was William Robinson. He was examined by the plaintiffs, and testified that he was the general foreman of the riveting and the laborers, and was under the control of Piper and Sheffler. He also said there were other foremen under him. It was he who detailed men to the various portions of the work, and directed what was to be done. Both the plaintiffs were engaged by Robinson, and were sent by him to Wymond to assist in putting on the iron roof. Wymond had charge of the men who were doing this particular work. The immediate orders to the men engaged in this work came from Wymond. Robinson testified, 'Mr. Wymond had control of the men as soon as I gave them to him ;' and again, 'I was instructed to furnish Mr. Wymond with men, by Mr. Sheffler.' Wymond's duties are thus described : 'I went on various kinds of work, moving machinery, repairing machinery, general repair work; sometimes he (Robinson) would give me three or four men to handle, and at other times only two; that was in the outside shops, but sometimes I would be ordered to go out and take a gang of men, and put up a roof or building, or bridges, as the case might be. Q. You were in charge of the work of the erection of ventilators on the new building, of which this is the model? Ans. Well, I suppose you might term it in charge; I was ordered to do the work. Q. State what your position was. Ans. I don't know that I held any commission position; I was put there by Mr. Robinson as near as I can remember. Q. To do what? Ans. To raise these trusses and to put up this building; and as for the men, he was to furnish me what men I wanted. Q. Did you employ the men? Ans. No, sir. . . . Q. Did you employ Mr. Kennedy or Mr. Newberry? Ans. No, sir. Q. How did they come to be under your control? Ans. I suppose Mr. Robinson sent them to me; he sent all the men that worked for me ; they would come there and tell me that Mr. Robinson told them that he wanted them to work there.' Both Kennedy and Newberry testified that they were employed by Robinson and sent by him to Wymond to work under his orders. Hurlston, a witness for defendant, testified that he was a foreman; had some men under him; was a gang boss; that Robinson had general charge of the works; that Piper was over Robinson, and was constantly going through the works, generally twice a day, giving orders and directions; that Wymond had charge of the erection of the structure, and was boss, and that Robinson was Wymond's boss. There was no contradiction of this testimony, and it establishes, in our opinion, that Wymond was in no manner the general representative of the company, or clothed with its powers. He simply had charge of a gang of men, of varying numbers, neither employed nor discharged by himself, but furnished to him by another who was his superior, and whose orders he was required to obey. Wymond, while he had charge of the work of putting up the ventilator, was himself a workman, and worked with the other men. It was testified by Wymond, Watkins, and Krekeler, that they three made the trussed plank which gave way and caused the accident."

The defendant presented, *inter alia*, the following points :—

Under the evidence in the case, Wm. Wymond was not such an officer in defendant company for whose act of negligence the company can be held responsible. *Refused.* We leave this to the jury from all the evidence, having, in our general instructions, and in answer to the plaintiffs' second and defendant's third points, shown what sort of a representative of the company he must be found by the jury to be. (Third assignment of error.)

There is no evidence of Wymond's incompetency or unskilfulness, and no evidence of any knowledge on the part of the company of any incompetency or unskilfulness of Wymond, and the verdict must therefore be for the defendant. *Refused.* This also we leave the jury to discover and determine. (Fourth assignment of error.)

That, even though the jury should find that Wymond was unskilful or incompetent, then the verdict should be for the defendant, because there is no evidence that the company knew of such unskilfulness or incompetency. *Refused.*

Even if the defendant company was guilty of negligence, yet if the plaintiffs, by any act of negligence, aided or assisted in bringing about the accident, they cannot recover. *Affirmed.* (Fifth assignment of error.)

The verdict in Newberry's case was for the plaintiff, for $2000; and in Kennedy's case, for the plaintiff for $4000. Judgments having been entered on the verdicts, the defendant took these writs, assigning for error, *inter alia*, the answers to points as above given.

S. Schoyer, Jr., and *West McMurray*, for plaintiffs in error.

Thomas M. Marshall, for defendant in error.

Jan. 3, 1881. THE COURT. Practically, these cases, as they come before us, turn upon two questions: 1. Was Wymond such an officer of the defendant-corporation as that it would be responsible for his act of negligence? and 2. Is there any evidence of Wymond's incompetency and unskilfulness, and that the company had knowledge of it? The learned Judge of the Court below left both these questions to the jury, in his general charge, and in his answers to the defendant's third and fourth points. It is claimed that he was in error in both. Taking the questions in their order, we will consider first the subject of the relation of Wymond to the company, on the one hand, and to the plaintiffs on the other. [His Honor here stated the facts, *ut supra*.]

It is quite clear to us that Wymond, and the men of whom he had charge, were engaged in one common pursuit, seeking to accomplish one common object, and that all of them were subject to the orders of another, who was their common superior. In these circumstances we think this case is ruled by the case of Lehigh Valley Coal Co. *v.* Jones (5 Norris, 433), and Delaware & Hudson Canal Co. *v.* Carroll (8 Norris, 374). In the former of these cases, Mr. Justice MERCUR, in delivering the opinion of the Court, said: "Who are fellow-servants in contemplation of law? To constitute such they need not at the same time be engaged in the same particular work. It is sufficient if they are in the employment of the same master, engaged in the same common work, and performing duties and services for the same general purpose. The rule is the same, although the one injured may be inferior in grade, and is subject to the control and direction of the superior whose act caused the injury, provided they are both co-operating to effect the same common object." Again, "Some of the employés were superior in the grade of their employment to Alexander Jones; others were inferior. Whether superior or inferior, they, as well as he, were all under one common superintendent; in his hands, and in his alone, was the entire charge of the business placed by the company. His negligence might be negligence of the company." In the case of Delaware & Hudson Canal Co. *v.* Carroll (*supra*), Mr. Justice PAXSON, in delivering the opinion of the Court, said: "There is no room for the allegation that a mining boss, under the mine ventilation Act of 1870, is an agent of the mine owner or a co-employer. He is clothed with no powers of engaging and discharging miners and laborers at pleasure. He is merely a fellow-servant with the miner. . . . He has no general power of control. His duties are confined to special matters. That they are different from those of others of his fellow co-laborers, or even that they are of a higher grade, does not matter." In the case of Caldwell *v.* Brown (3 P. F. Smith, 456), in which it was held that an engineer was a fellow-employé, for whose acts the employers were not liable, Judge READ, in the course of the opinion, quotes Gilman *v.* The Eastern Railroad Corp. (10 Allen, 233), in which it was held that, "In case of an injury to one servant by the negligence of another, it is immaterial whether he who causes and he who sustains the injury are, or are not, engaged in the same or similar labor, or in positions of equal grade or authority. If they are acting together, under one master, in carrying out a common object, they are fellow-servants." (See, also, Wright *v.* The N. Y. Central R. R. Co., 25 N. Y. 565; Morgan *v.* The Vale of Neath Railway Co., 35 L. J. Q. B. 23; and Weger *v.* The Penna. R. R. Co., 5 P. F. Smith, 463.)

We are clearly of opinion that Wymond, upon the undisputed testimony in the case, was not such a representative of the defendant as that they would be liable for his acts of negligence. A further consideration of this branch of the case leads us to the same result. The injuries of the plaintiffs, it is claimed, were occasioned by the breaking or giving way of a defective apparatus. Now, the apparatus in question was not furnished by the company at all. It was made by Wymond and two others of the workmen, and if it was defective, it was the result of the negligence of three fellow-workmen of the plaintiffs. No superior officer of the company gave orders that the particular materials used should be selected, or that the particular contrivance itself should be constructed. The workmen made such an apparatus as they deemed sufficient. If it proved insufficient, it was an error of judgment on their part, for which we can see no ground of liability as against the defendant for the injuries of the plaintiffs. It is quite uncertain, under the testimony, whether the accident resulted from overloading the truss plank, or from a defect in the iron rod which sustained it. No testimony was given as to whether there was a flaw in the iron, and it is not at all clear that the rod was too weak to sustain all the reasonable weight that should have been put upon it.

On the second question raised on the trial, to wit, whether the defendant employed Wymond knowing, or having reasonable cause to know, that he was an incapable and unskilful person, not fit to be put in charge of such work, we can find no testimony sustaining either allegation. The learned counsel for defendant in error alleges that Wymond was incompetent, but he does not refer to any testimony in support of that allegation. He does, indeed, contend that proof of Wymond's unfitness is found in his own testimony, but a careful examination of that and, other testimony proves quite the contrary. He testifies to a large experience in the business of building iron bridges, and bridges of iron and wood in combination, and he was engaged upon some of the largest and most important bridges in the country. He could not conduct that kind of work without acquiring much experience in the resisting powers of wood and iron when subjected to heavy pressure. There was actually no affirmative testimony of any want of skill or knowledge upon these subjects, and not a scrap of evidence that the company had the slightest knowledge of any want of capacity on his part to perform the work assigned to him. In the absence of any testimony on this subject, we think the learned Judge of the Court below was in error in submitting the question to the jury. We think the third, fourth, and fifth assignments of error are sustained, and on these the judgments are reversed, and writs of venire facias de novo awarded.

Opinion by GREEN, J.

July, '80, 47.   Jan. 27, 1881.

Gray v. Dick.

Mechanic's lien law—Sub-contractors—Certainty in claim—Act of 24 March, 1849, relating to Philadelphia and Chester Counties.

The Act of 24 March, 1849 (P. L. 675), relating to mechanics' liens in the city of Philadelphia and county of Chester, provides, *inter alia*, that "where the work shall be done by contract for a stipulated sum, it shall be lawful to file a statement of the time when the work was commenced and when finished, and of the aggregate price of the work and materials":

Held, that the Act, being local and limited to a favored class, is to be strictly construed as to the persons and subjects to which it relates.

Held further, that said Act includes contractors only, and not sub-contractors.

The reason which gives rise to the distinction, is that in the case of the sub-contractor, the agreement is not made with the owner himself, and it is therefore his right to know the particulars of the claim, so that he may satisfy himself that the building is bound for no more than the work done and materials furnished.

Error to the Common Pleas No. 2, of Philadelphia County.

This was a scire facias on a mechanic's claim for $265, filed by William Gray against Walter B. Dick, owner, and John McLaughlin and Albert J. McLaughlin, contractors, for marble furnished and stonework done towards the erection of a building on Sixteenth Street near Jefferson in the city of Philadelphia.

The facts were as follows: Plaintiff, a dealer in stone, on March 4, 1878, made an agreement in writing with John and Albert J. McLaughlin, contractors, to furnish the cut stonework for a house which they had contracted with Walter B. Dick, to erect on his premises. In this agreement it was stipulated that the stonework was to be furnished in accordance with plans and specifications prepared by the architect in charge of the building, J. K. Yarnall, and that the price of the work should be $1150, payable by instalments as the work progressed. Plaintiff completed his work and received two payments on account, leaving due him on account of the stipulated price $230.

On Feb. 12, 1879, plaintiff filed the claim in controversy for the balance due him, together with sundry small items aggregating $35.06, as set forth in the bill of particulars, of which the following is a copy:—

Philadelphia Jan. 31, 1879.
Messrs. J. & A. J. McLAUGHLIN,
Bought of WILLIAM GRAY.

1878.		To stonework of W. B. Dick's house, 1524 North 16th, above Jefferson, as per contract.	$1150 00
Mar. 8.		To 2½ hrs. man rubbing bricks on wheels @ $1 00	2 50
Apl. 2.		To 36 buff enam. bricks @ 8 cts.	2 88
		To 1⅞ hrs. man rubbing on wheel, @ 1 00	1 50
" 3.		To 2 rubbers, ½ day ea. on wheel, 1½ days @ 10 00	15 00
" 9.		To 21 enam. buff brick @ 8 cts.	1 68
		To 11½ hrs. of man rubbing on wheel @ $1 00	11 50
			$1185 06
1878.	Cr.		
Apl. 23.	By cash	600 00	
May 25.	"	320 00	
			920 00
			$265 06

Commenced Mar. 5, 1878.
Finished Sept. 14, 1878.

On the same day a sci. fa. issued in said claim, which being returned *served* as to Dick, owner, and *nihil habent* as to J. McLaughlin and A. J. McLaughlin, contractors, the defendant, owner, was ruled to plead. Dick, the said defendant, thereupon obtained a rule to show cause why the first item in the bill of particulars, to wit, "To stone-work of W. B. Dick's house, 1524 North 16th above Jefferson, as per contract, $1150," should not be stricken out. This rule was made absolute April 17, 1880.

On the same day the Court refused a motion

made by plaintiff to strike out of his claim all the items except the first. Thereupon plaintiff took this writ, assigning for error the action of the Court in striking out the first item of the claim, and in refusing plaintiff's motion to withdraw and strike out the remaining items.

M. Hampton Todd and *J. R. Booth*, for plaintiff in error.

The law as it now stands in Philadelphia protects all classes of material men and mechanics. The Act of June 16, 1836, gives a lien to the contractor and sub-contractor when there is no special contract. The Act of 1845 (Purd. Dig. 1027, pl. 19) gives the contractor a lien where he does the work under a special contract for a stipulated sum. And finally, the Act of March 24, 1849 (Purd. Dig. 1034, pl. 45), extends this lien to the sub-contractor in Philadelphia and Chester counties, by providing that it—

"shall be lawful for any mechanic or material man in the city or county of Philadelphia and county of Chester who performs work and furnishes materials, to include both in the same claim filed; and where the value or amount of the work or materials can only be ascertained by measurement when done, or shall be done by contract for a stipulated sum, it shall be lawful to file a statement of the time when the work was commenced and when finished, and of the aggregate price of the work and materials."

This claim complied with the requisites of this Act. The work was done, and the materials furnished "by contract for a stipulated sum."

Shields *v.* Garrett (5 WEEKLY NOTES, 120), relied on by defendant, is in our favor, since it recognizes a claim filed in accordance with the Act of 1849 as valid. In that case the lump charge was put under one date, and the statement of the beginning and ending of the whole work, including all the other items of the bill. In this case the lump charge has separate and independent dates for the commencing and finishing of the work under the special contract.

As to the second assignment of error, which raises the question as to our right to withdraw or strike out certain items of the claim, it would appear reasonable that if the defendant, by adverse motion, could strike out an item of the claim, the plaintiff could voluntarily renounce and withdraw one or more items, and this view would seem to be strengthened by the Act of 11 June, 1879 (P. L. 122), authorizing amendments to mechanic's claims in any stage of the proceedings "conducive to justice and a fair trial upon the merits."

John M. Thomas, for defendant in error.

Besides the first, neither the fourth nor seventh item has any date attached. The words "commenced March 5, 1878. Finished Sept. 14, 1878," might then refer to any one of these items.

The action of the Court below in striking out the lumping charge was under the authority of Shields *v.* Garrett (5 WEEKLY NOTES, 120), in which it was decided, notwithstanding there was a date given to the lumping charge, that where such a charge was one of a series of items, all of which had their appropriate dates, it was not a sufficient fulfilment of the conditions of the Act to state the times when the whole work was begun and finished.

The reasons given by the Court in Russell *v.* Bell (8 Wr. 47), and Lee *v.* Burke (16 Sm. 336), for holding that the Act of 1845 did not relieve sub-contractors from the provisions of the Act of 1836 with regard to itemizing their claims, hold good for a similar construction of the Act of 1849. The language of the former Act is quite as general as that of the latter. And it is fair to suppose that if, after the decision in Russell *v.* Bell, the Legislature had intended to change the law as laid down in that case, it would have said so in positive language, and not have left it to implication.

The Court had no power to strike out the items according to the plaintiff's motion, as more than a year had elapsed since the lien had been filed.

Russell *v.* Bell, *supra*.

The Act of 1879 not being retroactive, did not remedy the difficulty.

Sutton *v.* Clark, 7 WEEKLY NOTES, 437.
Ashman *v.* McIlvaine, 8 Ibid. 309.
Sparr *v.* Walz, 9 Ibid. 64.

February 7, 1881. THE COURT. A supplement to the Act of 1836, relating to mechanics' liens, provides: "It shall be lawful for any mechanic or material man in the city or county of Philadelphia and county of Chester, who performs work and furnishes materials, to include both in the same claim filed; and where the value or amount of the work or materials can only be ascertained by measurement when done, or shall be done by contract for a stipulated sum, it shall be lawful to file a statement of the time when the work was commenced and when finished, and of the aggregate price of the work and materials." (Act of March 24, 1849, P. L. 675.) The plaintiff submits that the claim filed complied with the requisites of this Act. It was a literal compliance, and the sole question is whether the plaintiff comes within the intendment of the statute.

The contract was not made with the owner, he was not a party to it, and presumably knew nothing of it. Such a contract would not be evidence of the sum which the owner ought to pay, nor of the amount of the claimant's lien on the building. The mechanics' lien laws have not invested contractors with power to obtain work and materials and bind the building for a larger sum than such work and materials are worth. As a general rule, the claim shall set forth the nature or kind of the work done, or the kind and amount of materials furnished, and the time when the work was done or materials were furnished, with reasonable certainty. This is the mode prescribed for giving the owner of the building information of the grounds of the claim; and, formerly, it had to be observed by contractors as well as by claimants with whom the owner had no contract relation.

The Act of 1845 (P. L. 538) provided for the case of a special contract made by a mechanic with the owner for the erection of a building or a part thereof; and in such case, it is not required to set out in the claim the nature or kind of work, or kind and amount of materials furnished, for there is no reason for application of the general rule. (Young *v*. Lyman, 9 Barr, 449.) Each party to the contract has knowledge of the claim under it, and the reason for furnishing particulars does not exist. That supplement declares that the Act of 1836 shall "extend to and embrace claims for labor done and materials furnished and used in erecting any house or other building, which shall have been or shall be erected, under or in pursuance of any contract or agreement for the erection of the same;" but, notwithstanding its general terms, it was decided that it did not place a sub-contractor on the same footing with the contractor: he continued bound to set forth particulars in his claim as directed by the Act of 1836, or his lien would fall. (Russell *v*. Bell, 8 Wr. 47; Lee *v*. Burke, 16 P. F. S. 336.) Among the reasons given in those cases for strict construction are: The sub-contractor is entitled to no more than the fair market value of the work done and materials furnished on the credit of the building, and hence the owner should be informed by the claim filed as to the particulars of the claim, that he may make the necessary inquiries to satisfy himself of its justice as a lien on his property. The agreement between the contractor and sub-contractor is not the measure of the owner's responsibility; his building is bound for no more than the value of the work done and materials furnished by the sub-contractor, and he has a right to insist on compliance with the requisites of the Act of 1836.

Every reason given for the distinction of the contractor under the supplement of 1845, applies in full force to the supplement of 1849. If the latter includes only those who contract with the owner, it harmonizes with the previous legislation, and wrongs nobody. But if it embraces sub-contractors, the owner of the building in this case has all the particulars he is entitled to, namely, the contract price which the contractor agreed to pay for stonework done by the claimant between March 5 and September 14, 1878. What light does that give one who is called on to pay a debt owing by another man? It is sufficient for the victim to see the amount demanded, but not to see that it is right. Unless imperatively required by the words of a statute, it should not be made an instrument of rank injustice. Not only is the right of lien a privilege to a favored class of creditors in addition to all remedies common to other creditors, but this supplement is local, limited to two counties. Therefore, by universal rules, it must receive a strict construction as to the persons and subjects to which it relates. Where a mechanic or material man contracted with the owner, and the value of the work or materials can only be ascertained by measurement, or is stipulated in the contract, it is enough to give the aggregate price with the dates of commencing and finishing. There is reason in that the parties stand equal. In such case, the contractor is within the words and intendment of the statute. Sub-contractors and persons who work for or sell materials to contractors are not necessarily included in the language of the statute, and we think are clearly without its intendment.

It is unnecessary to remark upon the question raised by the second assignment. If the motion to strike out was for the purpose of validating the claim under the alleged contract, it was rightly refused. (Fahnestock *v*. Wilson, 9 Pitts. L. J. 81.)

But for the special circumstances, this writ of error would be quashed, even without motion. Consent of parties will not induce review by piecemeal. However, we were satisfied that a decision, either way, would end the dispute, and consider the case as if the claimant's motion had been granted by the Court below.

Judgment affirmed.

Opinion by TRUNKEY, J.

Jan. '80, 248.　　　　　　　　　　　　January 18, 1881.

Yeager v. Fuss.

Errors and appeals—Practice—Assignments of error—Rules of Supreme Court concerning.

Where an assignment of error is to the admission of testimony, the specification must, in accordance with Rule XXIV. of this Court, quote the full substance of the bill of exceptions or copy the bill in immediate connection with the specification; and where the face of the bill of exceptions discloses no exception to the admission of the testimony complained of, a general exception at the end of the bill will be held not to apply to a ruling which does not appear to have been excepted to at the time of the admission. It is not sufficient that the bill of exceptions shows that an *objection* was made; it must also appear that an *exception* was taken at the same time.

Error to the Common Pleas No. 3, of Philadelphia County.

This was a proceeding under the Act of April 3, 1830, before Alderman Beitler, brought by John Fuss, landlord, against J. Henry Yeager, tenant, to obtain possession of the demised premises on the ground of non-payment of rent. Judgment having been given for the plaintiff by the alderman, the defendant appealed. Upon the trial, the defendant testified, that, when he went into possession, and for two or three months thereafter, he had possession of certain beer vats, but that afterwards he was evicted from them by the landlord. Plaintiff was then offered in rebuttal to prove that the lessee was informed that the vats in question were exceptions out of the lease. The bill of exceptions at this point read as follows :—

The counsel for the said J. Henry Yeager objected, and the evidence was admitted by the said Court on the ground that, as under the evidence of the said J. Henry Yeager there is an ambiguity in the lease, it is admissible: First, to explain the ambiguity; second, to contradict the evidence already given by the said J. Henry Yeager.

The only exception on the face of the bill was the usual general exception at the foot of the bill, that "the counsel for J. Henry Yeager did then and there except to the aforesaid opinion of the said Court."

The verdict and judgment were for the plaintiff. The defendant sued out this writ. The assignments of error were as follows :—

(1) The learned Court erred in admitting parol evidence of John Fuss to contradict or vary the terms of the lease executed between the parties on the 14th day of September, 1870.

(2) The learned Court erred in admitting proof of conversations between the parties as to what would go or pass under the lease in question to Yeager a day or two before its execution and in contradiction of its terms.

Leonard R. Fletcher (*C. F. Erichson* with him), for plaintiff in error.

D. W. Sellers, for defendant in error.

January 31, 1881. THE COURT. The assignments of error are not according to the rule, which requires that, when the error assigned is to the admission or rejection of evidence, the specification must quote the full substance of the bill of exceptions or copy the bill in immediate connection with the specification. On the face of the bill of exceptions, though there appears to have been an objection to the admission of the evidence complained of, there is no exception; and the general exception at the end of the bill cannot apply to a ruling which does not appear to have been excepted to at the time of the admission.

PER CURIAM. Judgment affirmed.

[See Dietrich *v.* Addams, 9 WEEKLY NOTES, 492.]

Common Pleas—Law.

C. P. No. 1.　　　　　　　　　　　March 5, 1881.

Prichett v. Moss.

Practice—Appeal from magistrate—Affidavit of defence law—In an appeal from a Magistrate's Court defendant is not bound to file an affidavit unless plaintiff puts something on the record showing his intention to ask for judgment for want of an affidavit of defence.

Rule for judgment for want of an affidavit of defence.

In January, 1881, plaintiff issued a scire facias out of a Magistrate's Court for the purpose of reviving a judgment obtained before Alderman Bonsall in 1867. The scire facias being properly served, judgment was duly revived with costs and interest to date; whereupon defendant took an appeal to this Court.

Plaintiff entered his appearance, and without filing any instrument of writing, or making any averment, asked for judgment for want of an affidavit of defence.

Carty, for the rule.

This case should be governed by the same rules and the same laws as if the scire facias to revive had issued out of this Court; hence plaintiff is entitled to judgment unless defendant files an affidavit of defence.

J. A. Abrams, contra.

The appeal removes the case from the Magistrate's Court for the purposes of review and retrial; the proceedings are *de novo*, and plaintiff is bound to take the initiative.

The scire facias issued out of the Magistrate's Court cannot be regarded in the same light as a scire facias issued out of this Court, because the former is not a court of record. This distinguishes the present case from the one where a judgment is transferred from one Court of record to another, in which case an affidavit of defence must be filed in answer to a scire facias to revive.

It cannot be argued that plaintiff intended to treat the transcript of the magistrate's docket as a scire facias issuing out of this Court, for to do this would require some positive act on his part. The transcript　　filed by defendant, and the affidavit annexed thereto shows that it was filed for the simple purpose of appeal.

Plaintiff must file a copy of such transcript, or put something upon the record which will entitle him to judgment before defendant can be compelled to defend

THE COURT. It has apparently never before been made a question whether a scire facias issued by a magistrate to revive a judgment, and upon which judgment is duly revived, and appeal taken, can be treated as if issued out of this Court. We think, however, that as plaintiff has failed to put anything upon the record which shows his intention to treat the scire facias in this light (he having not even filed a copy or transcript of the original judgment), the rule should be discharged.

Rule discharged.
Oral opinion by ALLISON, P. J.

C. P. No. 2. Jan. 29, 1881.

Vent et al. v. Pashley.

Sheriff's interpleader—Claim by partnership to goods levied on as the property of a member of the firm—Act of April 8, 1873—When claimants may give their own bond.

Since the Act of April 8, 1873, if partnership property is levied on under an ordinary fi. fa. against one of the partners for an individual debt, a feigned issue under the sheriff's interpleader Act, with the partnership as claimants, may be had:

But, in such a case, the partners will not be allowed to file their own bond, although the property levied on has not been derived from or through the defendant in the execution.

Rule to show cause why claimants should not file their own bond in a feigned issue under the sheriff's interpleader Act.

The goods claimed had been levied on under an ordinary fi. fa. issued on a judgment against Caroline White and George V. White, and were claimed by Frances Ann Vent, Edward Nicholay, and Caroline White, trading as Catharine Nicholay. The affidavit denied that the title of the partnership to the goods levied on came through the defendant.

I. S. Sharp, for the rule.

J. D. Yocum, contra.

THE COURT. Before the Act of April 8, 1873, this interpleader would not have been allowed, as the defendant, Caroline White, has an interest in the goods levied on; but since that Act, this interest could only be levied on by a special fi. fa. in accordance with it, so the interpleader is proper. The true rule in regard to allowing claimants to file their own bonds in interpleader cases is, that, where the goods are not derived from or through the defendant in the execution, the Court *may* allow the bond of the claimant only to be filed. Where the claimants say the defendant does not own the goods levied on individually, but is a tenant in common with the claimants, and the effect of the interpleader will be to put the goods again under the control of the defendant, we do not think the bond of the claimants alone sufficient.

Oral opinion by HARE, P. J.

Orphans' Court.

Feb. 23, 1881.

Somers's Estate.

Widow's exemption of $300—Act of April 14, 1851—Exemption not allowed where the petitioner neglects to demand an appraisement—Petition to vacate decree allowing exemption granted seven months after entry of decree.

Sur petition to vacate decree allowing the widow's exemption, and answer.

The petition of George L. Somers, one of the heirs and executors of Peter Somers, deceased, set forth: that the said Peter Somers died in June, 1864, leaving a will whereby he gave to his widow, Caroline, one-third of his estate real and personal, in lieu of dower, and the residue to his children; that in May, 1880, the widow filed a petition praying the Court to allow her to elect and retain for her own use the sum of $300, out of the estate under the Act of 14th April, 1851, and upon proof of advertisement, the Court granted the prayer of the petition; that the personal estate of the decedent was not sufficient for payment of debts, and the funds in the hands of the executors for distribution arose exclusively from sale of real estate and did not exceed $237.30. Further, that the widow's claim was made sixteen years after the testator's death, and not until the administration of the estate had been so entered upon and proceeded with as to leave a less amount in the hands of the executors than that claimed by the widow; that the entire personal estate had been disposed of in payment of debts, and the widow did not claim to have her exemption allowed either in real estate or the proceeds thereof.

The petition further averred that no notice or claim had ever been served upon the executors for the appraising of either personal or real property, for the use of the widow, and without such appraisement she was not entitled to claim out of the proceeds of realty. And the petitioner prayed that a citation be granted directed to the widow to show cause why the decree made in the behalf of the widow should not be vacated and the allowance of $300 so made to her be set aside.

To this citation Caroline Jacobs, lately Caroline Somers, filed an answer, representing that the decedent fully intended to provide for her by his will, but that she had never received a dollar of the estate; that she filed her petition for allowance of $300, just after she understood the said executors had converted the whole of the estate real and personal into cash, as required by the will; and before any lien claims against said property had been fully settled; that she had labored under the disadvantage of being without counsel and of not being able to read or write, and whilst she had made several demands of said executors for her rights and property as widow of said decedent, she did not know until about the time she filed her petition that she would be required to take legal steps to obtain her portion of the estate.

John Shallcross, for petitioner.
W. H. Waxler, contra.

MARCH 5, 1881. THE COURT. The claim of the widow to the exemption allowed by the Act of 14th April, 1851, was made and published after the sale of her husband's real estate, but before the resale which had become necessary, had been effected. The petition was in general terms to be permitted to retain $300 out of the husband's estate. No appraisement, either of the real or personal estate, was asked for or had. Under these circumstances, the allowance by the Court, of the exemption, was improvidently made. The mere delay in presenting the claim would not have availed to defeat it, if expense had not been already incurred by the executors in settling the estate and in the proceedings to effect a sale of the realty. (Baskin's Appeal, 2 Wr. 65; Davis's Appeal, 10 Cas. 256.) Nor would the fact that the widow had remarried. It is true that it was doubted in Burk *v.* Gleason (10 Wr. 297), whether a woman who had remarried after her husband's death, was a widow within the meaning of the Act. But it was afterwards assumed in Commonwealth *v.* Powell (1 P. F. Sm. 438) that the right of the wife, under the Exemption Act, having attached while she was yet a widow, could not be divested by her subsequent marriage.

The defect which we are compelled to regard as fatal in the application made by the widow, was her omission to demand an appraisement. By the Act of 1851, the property to be retained shall be appraised in the same manner as is provided by the Act of 9th April, 1849. Of the latter Act it was said in Neff's Appeal (9 Harris, 243), that "the object of the Legislature was to prevent the sale of the property; and every act or omission of the debtor which amounts to an acquiescence in or an affirmance of the sale is in direct contravention of that object.' The cases were reviewed in Hufman's Appeal (31 P. F. Smith, 329), and it was held that the appraisement was a necessary preliminary to the allowance of the claim. The distinction that the creditor in that case and the heir in this made the objection, is of no consequence where the question is one of compliance with a statutory direction. Were it not for that provision in the Act, we should hesitate to grant the prayer of the petition. The decree of confirmation was obtained in May, 1880, without exception on the part of the petitioner, who was executor as well as heir, and who now seeks to vacate it. The answer of the widow, which must be taken as verity, because it was not replied to, while it admits that the petition for the allowance was not filed until after the sale, declares that the claimant had made several demands upon the executors for her rights as widow. If the nature of these demands had been specifically set forth, it might appear that under them it was the duty of the executors to have caused an appraisement to be made, and that failing in that duty, they are liable in an action by the widow. (Compher *v.* Compher, 1 Cas. 31.) Such misconduct on the part of the executors would not, however, entitle the widow to impeach the sale nor to claim the proceeds. (Neely *v.* McCormick, 1 Cas. 255; Marks's Appeal, 10 Cas. 36.)

Seven months elapsed between the entry of the decree and the filing of the petition to annul it. In Metz's Appeal (11 S. & R. 204) the question was left untouched whether the Orphans' Court had the power to open and re-examine an administration account after the close of the term during which it was settled. The terms of that Court, by the Act of 14th April, 1834, § 57, are made to correspond with those of the Common Pleas. The Act of 13th October, 1840, however, compelled the opening of such accounts incertain cases, at any time within five years after their confirmation, and long before the passage of that Act, it had been the practice of the Court to grant relief where error was apparent, and no new rights had intervened, without much regard to the question of time. (George's Appeal, 2 Jones, 260) There is nothing therefore in the delay which has taken place, to prevent the vacation of the decree in this case.

The prayer of the petition is granted, and the decree confirming the widow's exemption claim is vacated.

Opinion by ASHMAN, J.

WEEKLY NOTES OF CASES.

Vol. IX.]   THURSDAY, APRIL 14, 1881.   [No. 34.

Supreme Court.

Jan. '81, 132.   Jan. 12, 1881.

Rutherford et al. v. Maynes.

Constitutional law—The Greenwich Island Meadow Company—Acts of 1760 and 1804, relating to—Assessments upon owners and possessors of land, under special Acts of Assembly, for making and repairing dams, embankments, etc.—Construction of special enabling Acts in their relations to the Bill of Rights—Powers under such Acts.

The Greenwich Island Meadow Company had authority, under the Act of April 12, 1760 (1 Sm. Laws, 227), and the supplement thereto, passed Jan. 30, 1804 (4 Sm. Laws, 109), to levy assessments upon the owners and possessors of certain marsh and cripple land in the City of Philadelphia, for the purpose of making dams, ditches, embankments, etc., to prevent overflow; the Acts directing the managers of the said company to ascertain the names of each possessor of every acre of the said land, and, having estimated the expenses for the year, to rate and assess each owner or possessor his proportionable part and to give a list thereof to the treasurer, who should demand and receive from every person in such list the sum wherewith such person is charged; and directing further, that, if any person should neglect or refuse to make payment within thirty days from the time of such demand, it should be the duty of the said treasurer to levy the said tax by distress and sale of the goods and chattels of the said delinquent, in the manner prescribed by the Act of April 11, 1799. In an action of replevin to recover certain goods of a tenant distrained under the provisions of the said Act of Assembly, to enforce payment of assessments:

Held (affirming the judgment of the Court below), that if the assessments were made before the tenant went into possession, he was not bound to pay them. The delinquent is he who is assessed and neglected to pay for thirty days after demand. One whose name is not on the list, and neither owned nor possessed the land when the assessment was made, is not within the terms of the statute.

Held further, that every statute of this character, which authorizes assessments upon the owners for improvement to their lands, ought to be strictly construed. If it admit of two constructions, one consistent with the Bill of Rights and the other repugnant, it should receive the former. The persons authorized to impose the assessments have just the powers, and no more, that are given expressly or by necessary implication.

Error to the Common Pleas No. 3, of Philadelphia County.

Replevin, by Charles Maynes, who was tenant under Elizabeth L. Devine, against William Rutherford, Treasurer of the Greenwich Island Meadow Company, and James J. Keating, for certain goods and chattels distrained by the Greenwich Island Meadow Company, for assessments levied upon the land of the said Elizabeth L. Devine, which were overdue and unpaid. The said Greenwich Island Meadow Company avowed, and James J. Keating made cognizance as bailiff, for taxes in arrear.

The facts of the case as they appeared upon the trial before LUDLOW, P. J., are fully reported, *ante,* 221, *q. v.* The Judge charged the jury, as follows: "I will bring this case down to a very narrow limit. It is somewhat complicated and involves questions of law too important for me to consider at this time. But there are two questions which I want you to decide. First, were these assessments made by this association of individuals before or after the tenant went into possession? If these assessments were made before the tenant went into possession, then your verdict will be for the plaintiff; for it would be a violation of the Bill of Rights that his property should be taken to pay the debt of another man. But if, on the other hand, you should find that the assessments were made after the tenant went into possession, then you may find for the defendants, provided notice was given as required by this Act. And this brings me to the second point, and it is an important question in this case. These Acts are highly penal and summary, and must be strictly construed. They require that thirty days' notice shall be given to the owner or possessor, or to his or her agent authorized to accept service of notice, and if no such notice was given to the owner, or to an agent authorized to accept service for him, then you will find for the plaintiff. But, if you find such notice was given, then you will find for the defendants, provided you further find that the assessments were made after the tenant went into possession."

Verdict for the plaintiff and judgment thereon. The defendant took this writ, assigning for error the charge of the Court as above.

J. M. Moyer (with whom was *R. P. Garsed*), for the plaintiffs in error.

The Greenwich Island Meadow Company is a *quasi* corporation, with powers limited by the object of its creation.

Fourth School District *v.* Wood, 13 Mass. 192.

Angel and Ames on Corp., sects. 25 and 30–41.

The grant by the Legislature to this Company was not alone for the improvement of private property, but because, in the language of the Act, it "is also of great benefit to the public."

Cooley on Taxation, 124.

To authorize the construction of levees and drains, and the reclamation of marsh lands, is an exercise of the police power of the State.

Sharpless *v.* Mayor of Philadelphia, 9 Harris, 147.

The assessment in question is not a lien upon the land, but a personal charge upon the owner or possessor. The language of the supplement to the Act makes it a personal charge. The land could not be sold to pay the tax thus imposed.

Sharp v. Speir, 4 Hill, 76.
Burd v. Ramsey, 9 S. & R. 109.

These assessments, being assessed by special grant of power by special legislation to a particular body, are not within the Act of 1854. They stand upon their own foundation, and independent of judicial decision, remain as when the Act was originally passed, not a lien upon the land but a personal charge.

Kilgore v. Commonwealth, 9 WEEKLY NOTES, 185.

If the Legislature had the authority to delegate to this company the right to lay assessments, it might also provide the means for their collection, whether by lien upon, and sale of the land, or by distress of the goods and chattels found upon the same.

Cooley on Taxation, 34.

The Act relating to county rates and levies, of April 11, 1779, has never been held unconstitutional because it authorized the seizure of the tenant's goods for taxes due prior to his tenancy.

Henry v. Horstick, 9 Watts, 414.

The remedy provided by the supplementary Act of 1804 is not in violation of the Bill of Rights. It is neither an exercise of eminent domain nor a taking of private property for public or corporate use. It is a species of taxation.

Potter's Dwarris on Statutes, 412.

There is in the Bill of Rights no limitation upon the right of taxation.

Sharpless v. Philadelphia, 9 Harris, 147.

Geo. W. Thorn, for the defendant in error.

This authority, even if rightfully conferred by the Act of 1760, is clearly in violation of the Bill of Rights, and has been repealed by the Constitution of 1790.

It is not every Act which the Legislature may call a tax law that is constitutional.

Sharpless v. City of Philadelphia, 9 Harris, 147.

Local assessments can only be constitutional when imposed to pay for local improvements, clearly conferring benefits upon the properties assessed, and to the extent of those benefits.

Hammett v. The City, 15 Smith, 155.
Washington Av., 19 Smith, 352.

There is nothing in the law to indicate that the owners of adjoining lands are under a common duty to drain their lands either by contract with each other, or by reason of a burden imposed by a common predecessor in an entire title under which all claim their several parts.

Rutherford's Case, 22 Smith, 82.

Some mode of determining the duty must be furnished. The process must be judicial in its nature.

City v. Scott, 31 Smith, 80.
City v. Field, 8 Id. 320.

A tax is a means of providing for a public burden. A tax law for the benefit of a private corporation, however meritorious, is of such very doubtful constitutionality that it will not be enforced by the Courts.

Phila. Ass'n v. Wood, 3 Wright, 73.

January 24, 1881. THE COURT. Greenwich Island, described in the preamble of the Act of 1760 as marsh, meadows and cripple land, partly drained and partly open to the overflowing of the tide, is the territory required by said Act to be embanked and drained for the common benefit of the owners. That it is divided into a number of farms, with several owners; that the lands would be almost, if not altogether unfit for cultivation without embankment and drainage, that the statute provides a just mode for making the general improvements and keeping up the same, and for levying the costs thereof as between the owners, are uncontroverted facts. After the lapse of one hundred and twenty years, during which time the land owners have enjoyed the benefits of the statute, it should not be declared void but for imperative reasons. Indeed, the Court below held it to be valid, and charged that if the assessments were made after the tenant went into possession, and the requisite notice had been given him, the jury could find for the defendant. But it was ruled that if the assessments were made before the tenant went into possession, he was not bound to pay them.

When any considerable tract of land, owned by different persons, is in a condition precluding cultivation by reason of moisture and overflow, which embankments and drains would relieve, the public have such an interest in the improvement, and the consequent advancement of the general interest of the locality, as will justify the levy of assessments upon the owners for the purposes of such improvements. (Cooley on Taxation, 424, and cases cited in note.) No doubt general taxation is admissible for this purpose, but the special benefits from enhancements of values must accrue mainly to the owners of the lands and legislation which imposes the costs upon those who, without the improvements, would be the principal sufferers, is probably in most cases wiser and better. (Ibid. 427.) When there is no consideration other than the improvement of land as property, the authority to levy such assessments is confined within limited bounds. In Pennsylvania, it can scarcely be measured by the necessities or laws of such States as Louisiana or California, where is but little land liable to overflow or swamp-land within her borders. As the facts are presented, we cannot say that the statute for improvement of Greenwich Island is without those limits of authority.

It widely differs from the Act of May 9, 1871, which was declared unconstitutional in Rutherford's Case (22 P. F. S. 82), and has been acquiesced in for several generations. Every statute which authorizes assessments upon the owners for improvement of their lands, ought to be strictly construed. If it admit of two constructions, one consistent with the Bill of Rights, the other repugnant, it should receive the former. It is said that the statute makes the owners of this island a *quasi* corporation. Be it so. The managers have just the powers, and none other, that are given expressly or by necessary implication. They claim the right to seize the goods of a tenant to satisfy an assessment laid prior to his possession. They must show the grant or their claim is false.

The Act of 1760 directed the managers to make a true list of the names of the owners or possessors, with the quantity of land held or possessed by each, with the sum per acre of the assessment for the current year; and in default of payment by any such person, judgment could be obtained against him, in satisfaction whereof his land should be levied and let for so long a time as the rents would pay the debt and costs. By the supplement of 1804, the managers shall ascertain the names of each owner or possessor of every acre of said island, and having estimated the expenses for the year, rate and assess each owner or possessor fairly and equally, his or her proportionable part, and give a list thereof, with their warrant, to the treasurer, who shall demand and receive from every person in such list, his or her legal representatives, the sum wherewith such person is charged. "And if any person shall neglect or refuse to make payment within thirty days from the time of such demand, it shall be the duty of said treasurer to levy, or cause to be levied, the said tax, and the costs attending such levy, by distress and sale of the goods and chattels, lands and tenements of the said delinquent, in such manner as is prescribed by the Act entitled 'An Act to raise and collect county rates and levies,' passed the eleventh day of April, Anno Domini, one thousand seven hundred and ninety-nine; such sum, if paid or recovered from a renter, to be deducted from his rent." In original and supplement, the assessments are required to be made on the owners or possessors. The possessor may be a renter, and if so, he may defalcate from the rent. Upon default, the property of the said delinquent may be seized. The delinquent is he who was assessed and neglected to pay for thirty days after demand. One whose name is not on the list, and neither owned nor possessed the land when the assessment was made, is not within the terms of the statute. The seizure and sale shall be in the manner prescribed by the Act of 1799, which manner is set forth in the 15th section. "It shall be the duty of the said collectors to levy the said tax by distress and sale of the goods and chattels of said delinquent, giving ten days public notice of such sale by written or printed advertisement." Nothing else in that Act relates to the manner of selling goods and chattels. Section 25 provides that the goods and chattels of tenants occupying lands, shall be as liable to be distrained for taxes, arising out of such lands, as though such tenants were the real owners thereof. This extends the liability to seizure to the property of other people, but does not affect the manner of sale. The treasurer of the managers of the Greenwich Island improvements is not vested with all the powers of tax collectors under the Act of 1879. In case goods of the owner or possessor cannot be found, he is not authorized to take the body of the delinquent to the county jail, as were collectors of county taxes, nor can he take the goods of a tenant who was not in possession when the assessment was laid.

It was said in Henry *v.* Horstick (9 Watts, 412), that the Act of Assembly will admit of a construction, which would authorize a distress of the goods of a party in possession of the land, though the tax was laid prior to his entering into possession; and that the Act in this respect being remedial, ought to be construed liberally in order to make the remedy provided by it effectual in all cases. This language was respecting the general laws for collection of taxes, and has no application to the construction of a private statute for local and special assessments.

It is not the intendment of the Greenwich Island enabling Act, or of its supplement, that the managers may suffer the assessments to remain unpaid for an indefinite time, finally to be collected from a new tenant, or an innocent purchaser. If it were, this case is illustrative of the result. The arrears exceed the value of the annual rent, and the tenant might lose all the excess. Cases would likely arise far worse than this; for here only the amount laid for three years is asked of the tenant. It is no answer to refer to the assessment of public taxes laid by public officers, and the case of obtaining information in the proper offices in regard to all such taxes. Prompt collection of the assessments from the proper parties is required by the spirit of the Act, rather than a loose and unwarranted construction for the enlargement of the powers of the managers.

Judgment affirmed.
Opinion by TRUNKEY, J. GREEN, J., absent.

July, '80, 118. Jan. 12, 1881.
Taney's Appeal.

Domicile — Residence — Non-resident guardians — Act of April 21, 1856 — Discharge of Pennsylvania guardian.

While a minor was emigrating with his parents from Pennsylvania to Kansas, he was deprived of both his parents by a railway accident, in the State of Michigan, and was left in the place of the accident, himself seriously injured. His maternal aunt went from Pennsylvania to Michigan to take charge of him, and she, having declared her intention to remain in Michigan, was duly appointed, by the Probate Court in that State, guardian of the person and of the estate of the said minor. Guardians of the minor's person and of his estate were also appointed by the Orphans' Court in Pennsylvania, who, upon petition of the Michigan guardian, were subsequently discharged:

Held (sustaining the decree of the Court below), that both the minor and his guardian appointed in Michigan were "non-residents" of Pennsylvania, within the purview of the Act of April 21, 1856 (P. L. 495).

Appeal of Ellen Taney from a decree of the Orphans' Court of Philadelphia County, discharging her as guardian of the person, and The Fidelity Insurance, Trust, and Safe Deposit Company as guardian of the estate, of William J. Rice, a minor.

The following material facts appeared in the petition and answer: The said minor, William J. Rice, was, at the time the petition was filed, in 1880, between three and four years of age; he was born in the city of Philadelphia, where he resided with his parents, who were citizens and residents of Philadelphia until the month of October, 1879. Upon the 10th day of that month, while the minor was travelling upon a railway train, in company with his parents, who had left Philadelphia and were upon their way to the State of Kansas, where it was their intention to remain, an accident happened upon the line of the Michigan Central Railway, at a place called Jackson, in the State of Michigan, by which his parents were instantly killed, and the said minor himself was seriously injured. In December, 1879, whilst the said minor was still detained in the city of Jackson by reason of his injuries, Mary C. Rogers, his maternal aunt, a resident of Philadelphia, went to Jackson, where, upon presentation of the facts of the case in a petition to the Probate Court of Jackson, and upon declaring her intention to remain in the State of Michigan, she was duly appointed by the said Court guardian of the person and of the estate of the said minor.

In January, 1880, Ellen Taney, an aunt of the said minor, was, upon petition of Michael Rice, his uncle, duly appointed by the Orphans' Court of the county of Philadelphia, guardian of the person, and the Fidelity Insurance, Trust, and Safe Deposit Company was appointed guardian of the estate of the said minor. In May, 1880, Mary C. Rogers made a petition to the Orphans' Court of the county of Philadelphia to have the guardians appointed by said Court discharged, under the provisions of the Act of April 21, 1856 (Purd. Dig., p. 412). This Act provides as follows:—

"In all cases where any guardian and his ward may both be non-residents of this State, and such ward may be entitled to property of any description in this State, such guardian, on producing satisfactory proof to the Orphans' Court of the proper county, by certificates, according to the Acts of Congress in such cases, that he has given bond and security in the State in which he and his ward reside in double the amount of the value of the property, as guardian, and it is found that a removal of the property will not conflict with the terms or limitations attending the right by which the ward owns the same, then any such guardian may demand or sue for and remove any such property to the place of residence of himself and ward."

"When such non-resident guardian shall produce an exemplification from under the seal of the office (if there be a seal) of the proper Court in the State of his residence, containing all the entries on record in relation to his appointment and giving bond, and authenticated, as required by the Act of Congress, as aforesaid, the Orphans' Court of the proper county in this State may cause suitable orders to be made discharging any resident guardian, executor or administrator, and authorizing the delivery and passing over of such property, and also requiring receipts to be passed and recorded, if deemed advisable," etc.

It appeared that the minor's estate consists almost wholly of his claim against the railway company for damages for the loss of his parents and for the injury to himself.

The Court below delivered no opinion, but entered the following decree: "And now, to wit, June 26, A. D. 1880, at an Orphans' Court held in and for the city and county of Philadelphia, it is ordered and decreed that the Fidelity Insurance, Trust, and Safe Deposit Company be discharged as guardian of the estate of William J. Rice, a minor; and further, that Ellen Taney be discharged as guardian of the person of the said William J. Rice."

Whereupon Ellen Taney took this appeal, and assigned as error the decree of the Court, as above.

Joseph C. Ferguson, for the appellant.

The operation of the Act of April 21, 1856, is expressly limited to cases where both guardian and ward are non-residents of this State. The Act cannot be invoked in this case, because both were domiciled and lived in Philadelphia until October, 1879, when the minor was left in Michigan by the chances of a railway accident. There is no distinction between the terms *residence* and *domicile,* so far as they apply to this case.

Cooper *v.* Galbraith, 3 W. C. C. R. 546.
United States *v.* Penelope, 2 Peters' Adm. 450.
State *v.* Daniels, 44 N. H. 383.

Jennison v. Hapgood, 10 Pickering, 77.
Allentown Contested Election Case, 8 Philada. 575.
2 Kent Comm. 431.
Frost v. Brisbin, 19 Wendell, 11.

In order to change a domicile, the intention to do so must be evident; clearly there was no intention in this case to change the domicile from Pennsylvania to Michigan. A man cannot be without a domicile, for he is supposed not to have abandoned his last domicile until he has acquired a new one.

Pfoutz v. Comford, 12 Casey, 422.
Reed's Appeal, 21 Smith, 383.

The father did not acquire a new domicile by his *intention* to change; he was prevented, by an accident, from carrying his intention into effect. His domicile was here, and consequently that of the infant is here; for an infant is incapable, until he is *sui juris*, of acquiring a domicile other than that of his father.

Guier v. O'Daniel, 1 Binney, 349, note.
School Directors v. James, 2 W. & S. 570.

E. A. *Anderson* (with whom was *John H. Fow*), for the appellee.

The only question here is whether or not this minor was such a non-resident of Pennsylvania as is contemplated by the Act of Assembly. The words domicile and residence are not synonymous, but there is a clear distinction between them; there may be a residence without a domicile, and a domicile without a residence.

The failure to distinguish clearly the meaning of the words *domicile* and *residence* has given rise to a confusion of terms, by which the two have been said to be synonymous. But, when an attempt is made to define domicile, it is found that residence is only an element of it, which, coupled with something else, namely, with the intention to remain permanently, goes to make up an actual domicile.

Dicey on Domicile, p. 1.
Guier v. O'Daniel, 1 Binney, 350.
Pearce v. State, 1 Sneed, 66.
White v. Brown, 1 Wall. Jr. 217.
Forbes v. Forbes, Kay, 359.
Mitchell v. United States, 21 Wallace, 350.

Persons have frequently left their native countries with the intention of residing abroad, and have actually resided abroad for years, passing the greater part of their lives away from their original domiciles; yet they have not become domiciled in the countries in which they were *residents ;* though there can be no question that they did acquire a *residence* in those countries.

Jopp v. Wood, 34 Law Journal, Ch. 625.
Moorhouse v. Lord, 32 Id. 295.
Bruce v. Bruce, 6 Brown, Par. Cases, 575.
Stratton v. Brigham, 2 Sneed (Tenn.), 421.
Bell v. Kennedy, Law Rep. 1 Scotch & Divorce App. 307, 320, 321.
Fuller v. Bryan, 8 Harris, 144.
Crawford v. Wilson, 4 Barr, 520.
In re Thompson, 1 Wendell, 43.

Residence is an intermediate term between *domicile* and *sojourn* or *visit*, having some of the elements of both, but is synonymous with neither; it has a less extended significance and effect than the former, though of larger import than the latter; and as a man may visit abroad without losing either his domicile or his residence, so he may abandon his residence and still retain his domicile. A residence is the place where a man has established his home, whether permanent or temporary; where he lives and transacts his business.

Long v. Ryan, 30 Grattan (Va.), 718.
Warren v. Thomaston, 43 Maine, 418.
North Yarmouth v. West Gardiner, 58 Id. 210.
Dicey on Domicile, p. 76.

It would seem the better doctrine, that a man may have but one domicile, the law of which shall regulate his personal succession, and the transmission of his property, while he may have a residence in another country, where he actually has his home, and the protection of whose laws he enjoys. Though it has been held that a man may abandon his domicile, and until he acquires another he may be without one.

Kilburn v. Bennett, 3 Metcalf, 199.
Hicks v. Skinner, 72 North Carolina, 1.
Wharton's Conflict of Laws, sec. 78.

There is no doubt that the father of the minor in this case did actually abandon his domicile in Pennsylvania when he emigrated with his family, and it can only be said, by a fiction of law adopted for the purpose of succession, that he retained his domicile here. He was a "non-resident," even though he had not acquired a new residence.

Exeter v. Brighton, 15 Maine, 60.
Inhabitants of Jefferson v. Inhabitants of Washington, 19 Id. 302.
Pfoutz v. Comford, 12 Casey, 422.

The minor was thus left homeless in Michigan, where he remains under the care of his aunt, now resident there. Such guardian may appoint the place of the ward's residence. A child may have a different residence from that of his parents.

Lyons v. Andrews, 12 La. An. 685.
Wells on Jurisdiction of Courts, p. 288.
School Directors v. James, 2 W. & S. 572.
Holyoke v. Haskings, 5 Pick. 26.
Cutts v. Haskins, 9 Mass. 543.

January 24, 1881. THE COURT. We are of opinion with the learned Court below, that both the guardian and ward were residents of the State of Michigan, and within the meaning and purview of the Act of April 21, 1856 (Pamph. L. 459). If the question regarded the law of succession to the ward's property the rule might be different. A clear distinction exists, as was shown in the able argument of the young gentlemen who argued this case for the appellee, between domicile and residence. Every reason of policy and convenience requires the application of the provision of the statute to a case of permanent residence in another State, though in strictness the domicile may remain unchanged.

Decree affirmed, and appeal dismissed at the costs of the appellant.

PER CURIAM. GREEN, J., absent.

July, '80, 77.   January 13, 1881.

Schively's Appeal.
Linnard's Estate.

Will—Construction of—Power of appointment—When well exercised.

A. bequeathed a fund in trust for B. for life, and after his death to such person or persons as he by last will should appoint; and in default of such appointment, to the heirs of B. who should be entitled under the intestate laws. B. bequeathed the fund to his wife "to be appropriated to clearing off, so far as it may, any encumbrance on any of my real estate; the remainder, if any, to be used in keeping up the repairs of the farm or other property." The appointee died in the lifetime of her husband, who himself afterwards died insolvent, all his property, both real and personal, being sold to pay his debts:

Held (reversing the Court below), that the appointment failed by reason of the death of the appointee and the absence of any property upon which it might be applied, and that the fund should be paid to B.'s heirs under the intestate laws, in accordance with the provisions of A.'s will.

Appeal of Charles Schively and Mary E. his wife, in right of the said Mary E., from a decree of the Orphans' Court of Philadelphia County in the matter of the account of Eugene Linnard, executor of Thomas M. Linnard, deceased.

The facts as found by the Auditing Judge were as follows: Thomas M. Linnard, the testator, died May 7, 1862, having first made a will whereby he bequeathed, *inter alia*, as follows:—

"From and immediately upon the death of my said wife I give and bequeath unto my executors hereinafter named, and to the survivor of them, the sum of sixteen thousand dollars in trust to invest the same in some safe and productive security and to pay the interest, income, and dividend of ten thousand dollars thereof to my son, William J. Linnard, during his life into his own hands, and whose receipt alone shall be a sufficient discharge, so that neither the principal nor income shall, under any circumstances, be liable for the debts or subject to the control or contracts of the said William J., or exposed or liable to execution or attachment, or any proceedings at law or in equity by any of his creditors, or for any of his debts, contracts, or liabilities, and from and immediately upon the death of the said William J., in trust, to pay over, deliver, and dispose of ten thousand dollars of the said principal sum of sixteen thousand dollars or the securities to that amount in which the same is invested to such person or persons, and for such purposes as the said William J., by any last will duly executed, may order and direct; and in default of any such last will, then, in trust to pay and deliver the same to the heirs of the said William J., who shall be entitled to the same by the intestate laws of this Commonwealth, and not to his administrators and assigns."

William J. Linnard died in the lifetime of the testator's widow, having first made his will whereby he bequeathed, *inter alia*, as follows:

"I likewise will and bequeath to my wife, Esther Elizabeth Linnard, the sum of ten thousand dollars left in trust by the will of my late father, Thomas Mifflin Linnard, of Philadelphia, said sum to be appropriated to clearing off, so far as it may, any incumbrance on any of my real estate: the remainder, if any, to be used in keeping up the repairs of the farm or other property."

Testator further nominated said Eugene Linnard as his executor. Mrs. Esther E. Linnard, wife of Wm. J. Linnard, died before her husband and without issue. William J. Linnard died May 21, 1875, leaving to survive him, his mother (since deceased), his brothers Eugene (the accountant), and James, his sister Mary E. wife of Charles Schively, and the issue of his brother Joseph T., deceased, viz., Eugene T., Kingston G., Joseph H., Theodore B., and Louis T. Linnard, and Adelaide J., wife of William T. Amies. He was at the time of his death possessed of both real and personal estate but was insolvent. His estate was settled and divided among his creditors, but was found insufficient to pay his debts.

Letters testamentary upon his estate were granted to Eugene Linnard, the executor named in his will.

The Auditing Judge awarded the aforesaid sum of ten thousand dollars, together with interest due thereon to the accountant as executor of the will of William J. Linnard on the ground that said Linnard had a vested interest in it upon the death of his mother, the legatee for life, the income and interest being payable to him; but as he died in the lifetime of the legatee for life, said legacy was payable by the executors of the will of his father to whomsoever he appointed by will; that he having exercised the power of appointment conferred upon him, but the appointee dying in his lifetime, said legacy lapsed and fell into the residue of his estate.

Exceptions to this adjudication were filed by Charles Schively and wife, in right of the said wife, and were sustained by the Court in an opinion by ASHMAN, J. (8 WEEKLY NOTES, 536). The Court was of opinion that the legacy to William J. Linnard was a vested interest in him, that consequently he had made a valid appointment of the amount thereof, that the gift so made by him to his wife was not absolute but in trust, and that the wife being dead, the Court would uphold the trust and appoint a new trustee. The fund was therefore decreed to be retained by the accountant as executor and trustee upon the trusts contained in the will of William J. Linnard, deceased.

Charles Schively and wife, in right of the said wife, took this appeal, assigning for error the decree entered by the Court below.

Silas W. Pettit (*John R. Read* with him), for appellants.

The general provisions of William J. Linnard's will were not an exercise of the power of appointment given him by the will of Thomas M. Linnard.

    Bingham's Appeal, 14 Sm. 345.
    1 Sugden on Powers, 385.
    4 Kent's Comm. 335.
    Lempriere *v.* Valpy, 5 Simons, 108.

As regards the particular provisions of William J. Linnard's will in favor of his wife, it is plain that where the donee of a power exercises it by appointing in favor of one who afterwards dies before him, the execution of it has failed to take effect, and the subjects of the power must be disposed of as though no attempt to execute it had been made.

    Williams on Executors, 1215.
    Sugden on Powers, 8th ed. pp. 639, 535.
    Ex parte Bernard, 6 Ir. Ch. Rep. 140.

If then his intention was to execute the power in favor of his wife and for her benefit, the interest lapsed and the power remained unexecuted by reason of her death during his lifetime.

If the intention was that she should hold in trust merely, the purpose of the trust has become impossible of execution. 1. Because the person is dead for whose benefit it was intended, and in whose discretion it was to be applied; and 2, there is no real estate of the testator to keep clear of incumbrance' or keep in repair. He having died insolvent, all his real estate has been sold to pay his debts. Consequently the power stands as if never executed and the fund should be distributed according to the directions of the donor's will in case of such non-execution.

It can hardly be supposed that William J. intended a trust for the benefit of his creditors, for he nowhere uses the words "in trust," and such an intention would have been in fraud of his father's purpose, who expressly provided that the sum in question should not be subject to his debts, etc. The decision of the Court below was gratuitous. The present owners of the real estate did not appear, nor ask that the fund be appropriated to the purposes of the trust. The effect of the decision is to withdraw the fund from the testator's family, and apply it for the benefit of strangers who have not asked for it.

The appointment was to his wife absolutely, and the words which follow are no more than the expression of a desire, which in Pennsylvania does not create a trust. Or, if considered in the light of a condition attached to the legacy, the performance of such condition is now impossible, and it is therefore void.

    Walker *v.* Walker, 2 DeG. F. & J. 255.
    2 Williams on Executors, 1264.
    4 Kent. Comm. 130.

(No counsel appeared contra.)

Jan. 31, 1881. THE COURT. We quite agree with the learned Court below, that the appointment in the will of William J. Linnard is not to be treated as an absolute gift to his wife, but as a trust. It is also clear that if the trustee had lived and there had been a subject upon which the trust could operate, the trust itself would have been enforced against the testamentary trustee, or in the event of her death, by means of a newly appointed trustee. But we encounter a practical difficulty in any attempt to enforce this trust. The trustee died before the testator who appointed her, and, as we understand the facts of the case, the subject of the trust has entirely disappeared, and is incapable of resuscitation. The power of appointment conferred upon William J. Linnard by the will of his father, Thomas M. Linnard, was exercised by the former in the following language of his will: "I likewise will and bequeath to my wife, Esther Elizabeth Linnard, the sum of ten thousand dollars, left in trust by the will of my late father, Thomas Mifflin Linnard, of Philadelphia, said sum to be appropriated to clearing off, so far as it may, any incumbrance on any of my real estate, the remainder, if any, to be used in keeping up the repairs of the farm or other property." We do not know whether any testimony was taken before the Auditing Judge of the Orphans' Court. None has been returned to us. The following finding, however, occurs in the adjudication. "It appeared that said testator died possessed of both real and personal estate, but insufficient to pay his debts. Mrs. Esther Linnard, his wife, died in his lifetime, and without issue." It is asserted in the appellant's history of the case, and nowhere contradicted, that W. J. Linnard was possessed of real and personal estate at the time of his death, but that he died insolvent, and that his estate has been settled and divided among his creditors. It was also asserted, and not denied, that the real estate of W. J. Linnard has long since been sold by or for the benefit of his creditors. There would arise a legal presumption from the facts found by the Auditing Judge, that the real and personal estate of the testator, W. J. Linnard, had all been appropriated by proper proceedings and in due course to the payment of his debts, and if so, there is no land left from which to lift encumbrances or which can be kept in repair. Against this presumption there is not a particle of proof and not even any allegation. It might well be, that if there were creditors having unsatisfied liens upon the land, they would be interested in the enforcement of the trust. But no such persons have appeared or preferred any claim. If there were such persons and they had claimed the fund, they would certainly have met with great difficulty in that clause of the will of Thomas M. Linnard, the donor of this fund, in which he both creates it and directs the manner of its disposition. He directs his executors "to pay the interest, income and dividends of ten thousand dollars thereof to my son, William J. Linnard, during his life, into his own hands, and whose receipt alone shall be a sufficient discharge, and so that neither the principal nor income shall under any circumstances be liable for the debts or subject to the control or contracts of the said William J., or exposed, or liable to execution or attachment, or any proceeding, either at law or in equity, by any of his creditors, or for any of his debts, contracts or liabilities." It is unnecessary to consider the question how far such a condition as this would be a restraint upon the power of appointment, subsequently conferred upon W. J. Linnard, even if he had directly ordered his executors to apply the fund to the payment of his debts, because that question is not before us. He made no such direction, and there is nothing on this record to show either that there is any real estate, to which the trust created by his will can possibly apply, or that there are any unsatisfied lien creditors, claiming the enforcement of the trust for their benefit. Such facts as these, we would be compelled to assume without evidence, and even against evidence, in order to sustain the decree of the learned Court below. We have neither the right nor the inclination to make any such assumptions. To award the fund, in these circumstances, to the executor of W. J. Linnard to retain the same upon the trust contained in the will of the latter, would be to award it to be held for an indefinite period and upon a mere barren trust, incapable of fruition now or hereafter. This we cannot do. We can only hold, as we do, that the power of appointment given to W. J. Linnard having been ineffectually exercised, so that its purpose can never be accomplished, is to be treated as never having been exercised at all. In other words, a default of appointment has arisen, and the fund must therefore be distributed in accordance with the will of the donor, Thomas M. Linnard. That instrument provides that in default of appointment by W. J. Linnard, the fund shall be paid to his heirs, "who shall be entitled to the same by the intestate laws of this Commonwealth."

These persons are ascertained by the Auditing Judge to be the brothers of the deceased to wit: Eugene and James Linnard, his sister Mary E. Schively, and the children of his deceased brother Joseph T. Linnard, to wit: Eugene T., Kingston J., Joseph H., Theodore B., and Louis T. Linnard and Adelaide J. Amies, and to these we award the fund.

Decree reversed and record remitted for further proceedings, and it is ordered, adjudged and decreed, that the sum of ten thousand dollars, together with interest thereon in the hands of the accountant, be paid and distributed in accordance with, and to the persons named in this opinion.

Opinion by GREEN, J.
PAXSON, J., absent.

Oct. & Nov. '80, 232.　　　　　　　Oct. 28, 1880.

The Baltimore and Ohio R. R. Co. v. The Sulphur Spring Independent School District.

Railroad companies—Negligence—Corporations—Agents—Lease—Admissions—Act of God—When negligence concurring with, a ground of liability.

In an action against the lessee of a railroad for damages caused by an alleged defective construction of defendant's road:

Held, that admissions as to such defective construction made to a third party by the resident engineer employed by the corporation originally constructing the road at the time of such construction, and before the lease to defendant, were inadmissible to bind the defendant in any way whatever.

In an action against a railroad company for injury to plaintiff's property occurring during an extraordinarily violent storm, which injury was alleged to have been brought about by reason of the defective construction of defendant's road, the Court charged substantially: "If there was negligence on the part of the defendant, concurring with the act of God, at the time plaintiff's loss was sustained, and if such negligence in any degree caused the loss, the defendant is liable, and the jury are not bound to inquire whether the loss would have happened if the defendant had not been guilty of negligence:"

Held to be error. The concurring negligence which, when combined with the act of God, produces the injury, must, in order to render the defendant responsible in damages, be such as is in itself a real producing cause of the injury, and not a merely fanciful or speculative negligence, which may not have been in the least degree the cause of the injury.

A railroad company in constructing its road and works is only bound to bring to their execution the engineering knowledge and skill ordinarily known and practised in such works. There is no liability on its part for not constructing a culvert sufficient to pass extraordinary floods.

Pittsburgh, Fort Wayne, and Chicago R. R. Co. v. Gilleland (6 Sm. 445), approved and followed.

Error to the Common Pleas of Westmoreland County.

Case, by the Sulphur Spring Independent School District of Sewickley Township, Westmoreland County, against The Baltimore and Ohio R. R. Co., lessee of the Pittsburgh and Connellsville R. R. Co.

On the trial, before HUNTER, P. J., the following facts appeared: That portion of the Pittsburgh and Connellsville Railroad passing through Sewickley Township was built in 1856. In order to pass at grade over a ravine known as Shaner's Hollow, it was necessary to erect a high embankment for the railroad, which embankment was pierced by three culverts serving as outlets for the waters running down the Hollow. For several years prior to the disaster one of these culverts had been choked up by a large stone. In 1876 the Pittsburg and Connellsville Railroad was leased by the Baltimore and Ohio Railroad Co., and has since been operated by the latter company. On July 23, 1879, a heavy rain occurred, which washed dirt and débris down the stream and filled up the two remaining open culverts. This was discovered the following day by the supervisor of that part of the road, and on the 26th inst. a gang of workmen was set to work to clean out the culverts. While they were thus employed, however, and before they had completed the job, a violent and extraordinary rain took place, the water rushed down the hollow, was dammed up behind the embankment, and finally carrying away the rails and road-bed of defendant, rushed over the embankment, lifted plaintiff's schoolhouse bodily off its foundation, and dashed it into the Youghiogheny River, where it was broken to pieces. The evidence was conflicting as to how far the stoppage of the culverts was the real cause of the injury. Several witnesses for the plaintiff testified that the culverts were of insufficient capacity to carry off the waters of even ordinarily violent storms. Others were of opinion that if the culverts had been open they would have been of sufficient capacity to carry off the water on July 26, 1879, without any injury to the neighborhood. There was evidence, on the contrary, for the defendant, that it would have required one hundred and twenty culverts similar to those already built, and that the bank would have had to have been perforated with culverts to insure safety against such a flood.

The plaintiff offered to prove by one Fulton "that he owned land on the line of the P. and C. R. R. Co. in 1856, and that he then notified the engineer who was employed by the P. and C. R. R. Co., and was engaged in the erection of the said barrels or culverts at Shaner's Station for the said company, that they were insufficient to receive and discharge the volume of water, and that the engineer replied he knew that they were not sufficiently large to receive the water." This offer was objected to by defendant as vague, incompetent, and irrelevant, because not showing a notice to any one in the P. and C. R. R. Co.'s service having plenary power and able to bind the same, and because the defendant could not be visited with notice given to the agent of another corporation.

Objection overruled and evidence admitted.

The witness then testified as follows: "At the time of the construction of the P. and C. R. R. along by Shaner's Station, I lived right beside the railroad, about two hundred yards from this particular point. I owned a house and lot there. When the engineer who had charge of the construction of these culverts came there . . . . I told the engineer that these culverts were too small at any rate. He said himself that they were not sufficient in that shape, from what he had seen of the floods there that summer. This was in 1856. He said the chief engineer would not change the culvert. He said that he had reported it to the chief engineer, but he thought it was sufficient, and would not change it." (Second assignment of error.)

Plaintiff presented, *inter alia*, the following points:—

(1) If there was negligence on the part of the defendant, concurring with the act of God at the time plaintiff's loss was sustained, then the defendant is liable, and the jury are not bound to inquire whether the loss would have happened had they not been guilty of negligence. *Affirmed.*

(2) It is not necessary to the plaintiff's recovery to show negligence on the part of the defendant, which contributed equally, or in a large degree, along with the act of God, to cause the loss; but if the defendant's negligence in any degree caused the loss, it would be liable in damages for the injury sustained by the plaintiff. *Affirmed.* (The affirmance of these two points constituted the fourth assignment of error.)

Verdict and judgment for plaintiff in the sum of $1525.88. Defendant took this writ, assigning for error, *inter alia*, the admission of the evidence above cited, and the affirmance of plaintiff's first and second points.

Markle and *McCullogh*, for plaintiff in error.

Fulton's evidence was improperly admitted. The resident engineer was a subordinate official, whose admissions could not bind the company. At any rate such declarations were mere hearsay as against the defendant. Notice to an employé of the P. and C. R. R. Co. could, under no circumstances, be evidence as against the B. and O. R. R. Co.

The defendant was only bound to ordinary care and diligence, and is not liable for damage done by extraordinary floods.

P., Ft. W., & C. R. R. Co. *v.* Gilleland, 6 Smith, 447.
Hey *v.* Philadelphia, 31 Smith, 44.
McCully *v.* Clarke & Thaw, 4 Wright, 399.

John F. Wentling (with him *Haslett* and *Williams* and *Jas. S. Moorhead*), for defendant in error.

A company is bound by the admissions of its official made at the time of the particular transaction which is the subject of inquiry, and while acting within the scope of his duty.

Huntingdon R. R. Co. v. Decker, 1 Norris, 123.
Dick v. Cooper, 12 Harris, 217.
Pa. R. R. Co. v. Books, 7 Smith, 399.
Danville Bridge Co. v. Pomroy et al., 3 Harris, 162.
Wharton on Evidence, § 1170.

The points of plaintiff were properly affirmed. The Court instructed the jury rightly as to the measure of defendant's duty.

Bell v. McClintock, 9 Watts, 119.
Livezey v. Philadelphia, 14 Smith, 106.
Knoll v. Light, 26 Smith, 268.

Nov. 22, 1880. THE COURT. On the trial of this cause the plaintiff made the following offer of proof by the witness, Alexander Fulton, viz. : "That he owned land on the line of the P. and C. R. R. Co. in 1856, and notified the engineer who was then employed by the P. and C. R. R. Co., and was engaged in the erection and construction of said barrels or culverts at Shaner's Station for the said company, that they were insufficient to receive and discharge the volume of water. That the engineer replied he knew they were not sufficiently large to receive the water." A similar offer, with a somewhat less precise designation of the character of the work in which the engineer was engaged, had been previously made and rejected under objections by the defendant, but when repeated in the form last offered, the objections were overruled, and the evidence was admitted. The witness then proceeded to testify that in 1856 he told the engineer who had charge of the construction of the culverts at Shaner's Station that they were too small, and that the engineer said in reply that "they were not sufficient in that shape from what he seen of the floods there that summer." We think this testimony was erroneously admitted. The witness did not name the person with whom he held this conversation, so that it could with certainty be determined whether he was correct in his supposition that he was the engineer in charge of the construction, or so that an opportunity for a possible contradiction would be afforded. Moreover the person, whoever he was, was not an agent of the defendant, but of another corporation which twenty-four years before had built the railroad and culvert. Again, the testimony itself was but the opinion of the witness as to the sufficiency of the culvert communicated to another, and that opinion he could give directly to the jury. Its communication to another, who was an entire stranger to the defendant, nearly a quarter of a century before the trial, certainly could not suffice to bind the defendant in any manner whatever. The second assignment of error is therefore sustained. We are also of opinion that the Court erred in their answers to the plaintiff's first and second points.

In affirming the first point the Court ruled that "if there was negligence on the part of the defendant, concurring with the act of God, at the time plaintiff's loss was sustained, then the defendant is liable, and the jury are not bound to inquire whether the loss would have happened if the defendant had not been guilty of negligence." As we understand this point, it practically declares that although the act of God alone, without any negligence of the defendant, would have caused the injury, the jury were not at liberty to consider that fact, if in reality there was negligence on the part of the defendant concurring with the act of God. In other words, no matter how terrible, extraordinary, and unprecedented were the storm and flood, so that they alone caused the injury, yet if there was concurring negligence of the defendant, although it did not produce the injury, and its absence would not have prevented it, still the defendant would be liable. The same idea is repeated in the plaintiff's second point, that if the defendant's negligence *in any degree* caused the loss, they would be liable. Now a small pebble in one of the culverts would *in some small degree* impede the course of the water, yet the doctrine of this point, which the Court affirmed, would make the defendant liable for the entire injury even though a huge avalanche of waters were suddenly launched upon the stream and hurled with irresistible force upon the embankment and culvert in question. Such is not the law. This is the very highest possible degree of care, greater even than is required of railroad companies in the carriage of passengers. The correct doctrine on this subject was expressed in the case of the Pitts., Ft. Wayne, and Chicago R. R. Co. v. Gilleland (6 P. F. S. 445), to wit: A railroad company in constructing its road and works is bound to bring to their execution the engineering knowledge and skill ordinarily known and practised in such works. There is no liability on the part of a railroad company for not constructing a culvert so as to pass extraordinary floods. On p. 452, AGNEW, J., delivering the opinion of the Court, says: "In the present case, then, if the culvert was so unskilfully and negligently constructed as to be insufficient to vent the ordinary high water of the stream, the railroad company building it would have been liable for the injury thereby caused. The apparent facts indicated the duty. The stream, though small, must find a vent or overflow the adjacent land and undermine the railroad. Its size, the character of its channel, and the declivity of the circumjacent territory which forms the water shed, indicated the probable quantity of water to be passed through. Proper engineering skill should observe these circumstances, and supply the means of avoiding the injury which would result from locking up the natural flow, or obstructing its passage, so as to cause a reflux in times of ordinary high water. Beyond this, prudent circumspection cannot be expected to look, and there is therefore no liability for extraordinary floods, those unexpected visitations whose comings are not foreshadowed by the usual course of nature, and must be laid to the account of Providence, whose dealings, though they may afflict, wrong no one." Here is a plain, easily understood, and carefully stated rule of duty and of liability. In the main, the Court below adhered to this rule, but in the answers to the plaintiff's first and second points they went beyond it, and in this there was error. We apprehend that the concurring negligence which, when combined with the act of God, produces the injury, must be such as is in itself a real producing cause of the injury, and not a merely fanciful or speculative or microscopic negligence which may not have been in the least degree the cause of the injury. In other words, if the act of God in the particular case was of such an overwhelming and destructive character, as by its own force, and independently of the particular negligence alleged or shown, produced the injury, there would be no liability though there was some negligence in the maintenance of the particular structure. To create liability, it must have required the combined effect of the act of God, and the concurring negligence to produce the injury. The present case affords a fair illustration of the reason for this distinction. The defendant's witnesses testified that the force and volume of the water were so very great that it would have required one hundred and twenty such culverts to pass it off. Hence, if the three culverts were in the most perfect condition, they would not at all have prevented the injury, and therefore the fact that they were somewhat obstructed might be quite immaterial. If the jury believed this testimony, it might have had a most important bearing upon their verdict, to the extent even of inducing them to find in favor of the defendant. But the case was not put to them in that way, and they had no opportunity of considering it in that aspect. For these reasons we sustain the second and fourth assignments of error. The other assignments are not material, and are not considered.

Judgment reversed and *venire facias de novo* awarded.

Opinion by GREEN, J.

Jan. '80, 183. Jan. 6, 1881.

Louchheim v. Henzey, Adm'r.

Errors and Appeals.—Where no injury worked by erroneous submission to jury, reversal not granted.—Practice.

Where there is no evidence of fraud, it is error to submit the question to the jury; but, if it does not appear affirmatively that the party complaining was injured by such submission, a reversal will not be granted.

Where the Court below has in the exercise of its sound discretion, refused a new trial, this Court will not review such decision.

Error to the Common Pleas No. 3, of Philadelphia County.

Trespass *de bonis asportatis* by Louchheim Bros. against E. M. Gregory (for whom his administrator, J. G. Henzey, was substituted), to recover damages for an alleged unlawful seizure and sale by defendant as U. S. Marshal for the Eastern District of Pennsylvania of certain goods of plaintiffs.

The facts of this case, as proved at the trial, were as follows: Louchheim Brothers recovered certain judgments against one N. Kahn and issued executions thereon, under which the sheriff on Jan. 5, 1870, sold Kahn's stock of goods; the goods were purchased at the sale partly by plaintiffs and partly by others, from whom plaintiffs subsequently bought. All the goods were left by plaintiffs in the charge of a son of Kahn for sale, and to carry on the business for plaintiffs. One of the Louchheims was a son-in-law of N. Kahn. Plaintiffs produced evidence tending to show that the defendant Gregory, as Marshal, seized these same goods, though described by the marshal in different words from the description in the sheriff's hand-bill, and disposed of them. This present action was brought to recover damages for this seizure. The present was the third trial of the case; the two prior trials had resulted in verdicts for defendant, which, on error, were reversed. (See Louchheim *v.* Henzey, 27 Sm. 305, S. C., 1 WEEKLY NOTES, 176, and 5 Norris, 350, S. C., 5 WEEKLY NOTES, 552.) At the two prior trials, the defendant had put in evidence the record of bankruptcy procedings against the above-named N. Kahn, the defendant in the judgments held by the Louchheims, begun within four months of the sheriff's sale of his goods, and some evidence of collusion between Louchheim and Kahn; and rested his defence on this ground. At the present trial, defendant offered no evidence.

The Court charged the jury, *inter alia*, as follows: "The questions are, (1) whether the title was a title which depended upon a *bona fide* sale, or a fraudulent collusion between Kahn and the creditors. (2) Whether the goods mentioned in the narr., or some of them, were the goods the defendant took possession of, either directly or indirectly; and in that event, you are to find the value of the goods at the time taken.

"In Pennsylvania, a man may not collude with creditors for the purpose of defrauding them. If, from the evidence in the cause, the jury are satisfied fraud exists, the sheriff's sale passes no title to the goods sold by him. It appears that Louchheim and Louchheim Bros. were creditors of Kahn, and in pursuance of suits of record, two separate judgments were obtained, and that the sheriff's sale took place under the executions thus issued. The only evidence to affect the question of fraud, is the testimony to show how that sale took place. In the absence of other proof, the mere fact that the suit was instituted by relatives, and that the goods were purchased by persons connected with Kahn, is not sufficient to destroy the sale's validity. If you can see anything else in the case, you are at liberty to do it. *There is no evidence of fraud submitted, which we have a right to look at, that I can see; but I leave the question to you, expressing my opinion as I have a right to do.*

"Were the goods specified in the narr. bought by these plaintiffs? It becomes necessary to look at the evidence bearing solely on that point. If they were not the identical goods, of course he cannot recover. If they have a good title, they have the right to the value of the goods thus taken. It is not alleged that the plaintiffs, except as to one bill, bought the goods directly, but it is alleged that they bought them afterwards from the persons who bought them. If the jury believe that fact, that part of the case is satisfied. If not, the title would fail at the outset."

Verdict for plaintiff for one cent damages, and judgment thereon. The Court having refused to grant a new trial, plaintiff took this writ, assigning for error the submission by the Court to the jury of any question of fraud or collusion invalidating the title of plaintiff to the goods in question, and its not charging the jury that the plaintiff's title to the goods was unassailed and made out by the evidence.

Geo. L. Crawford, for plaintiff in error.

The Judge, although charging that there was no evidence of fraud, erroneously submitted the question of fraud to the jury, and told them they were at liberty to discover fraud.

[SHARSWOOD, C. J. The verdict being for plaintiff, did not that negative fraud?]

That is illusory. The verdict for plaintiff for one cent is virtually a verdict for defendant. By using the plaintiff's name for the defendant's the jury, by a technicality, took the law out of the Court's province. It is practically equivalent to a verdict that there was fraud as to all the goods except one cent's worth. The defendant claimed, upon our evidence, that the goods seized by the marshal were not the same goods as had been sold by the sheriff. This was not so, but if it had been, it would be fatal to the defendant's case, for the allegation that the goods were sold at sheriff's sale to the plaintiff by collusion was the only foundation of the marshal's right to seize them on the ground of fraud in bankruptcy. Moreover, in this trial the defendant did not offer the bankruptcy proceedings in evidence, and without that evidence the marshal had no status and was a mere intruder. We were entitled to the value of all the goods or to nothing. The verdict was insensible, caused by the error of the Court in submitting the question of fraud, and the Court should have granted a new trial.

T. J. Diehl (with him *J. I. Doran* and *Samuel Dickson*), for defendant in error.

The charge of the Judge was quite as favorable as plaintiffs could expect. The burden was on them to satisfy the jury that the goods seized by the marshal were their property, and they failed to do this. This of course had to be submitted to the jury, and it cannot be reviewed here. The verdict for plaintiff negatived fraud, but the jury found that the evidence did not show any damages, because the plaintiff failed to show that the goods sold by the marshal were the same goods that the plaintiff had bought at the sheriff's sale, or had other title thereto. Under the previous opinions of this Court it was unnecessary for us to offer the bankruptcy proceedings in evidence.

January 31, 1881. THE COURT. The learned Judge below thought there was no evidence of fraud in the sheriff's sale, yet submitted the question to the jury. This was clearly an error, but how can we say that the plaintiffs were injured by it? The jury found in their favor, perhaps a verdict for a very inadequate amount. But it appears that there was a question as to the identity of the goods, under which the verdict may have been right, which question was submitted squarely by the Court and without exception. However wrong the verdict was, it is evident the plaintiff has no remedy in this Court. He made a motion for a new trial and was unsuccessful. The Court below was the best judge as to whether the verdict was right, and it would overturn the well settled law, were we to interfere with exercise of their sound discretion.

PER CURIAM. Judgment affirmed.

Jan. '80, 97. January 4, 1881.
Dutill v. Sully.

Affidavit of defence law—Executors and administrators—Sci. fa. sur mortgage—In a suit against a mortgagor judgment may be obtained for want of an affidavit of defence, notwithstanding the intervention of the representatives of a deceased terre-tenant.

The executor of a deceased terre-tenant, who was upon his own petition admitted to defend in a suit by the assignee of a mortgage against the mortgagor, does not come within the rule which declares that executors sued upon contracts of their decedents are not bound to file an affidavit of defence; and in such a case a judgment for want of an affidavit of defence against the defendant is regular.

The heirs or devisees of a deceased terre-tenant, who were not made parties to a suit, will, of course, not be precluded by the judgment; they have, therefore, no status to complain of any irregularity in the proceedings.

Error to the Common Pleas No. 3, of Philadelphia County.

Sophia H. Sully, executrix, etc., issued a sci. fa. sur mortgage against Henry A. Dutill, which was returned "made known." After the return-day, Enos Snyder, executor of Jacob E. Snyder, deceased, presented a petition setting forth, that Jacob E. Snyder had died seised of the premises upon which the mortgage was secured, and asking to be made a party to the suit *pro interesse suo*. A rule granted upon this petition, to permit said Enos Snyder, executor, etc., to become a party to the suit, was subsequently made absolute by the Court. Snyder then filed an affidavit setting forth, that he had been made a party to the suit, and that being sued in a representative capacity, he was not bound to file an affidavit of defence. The Court, however, gave judgment for want of a sufficient affidavit of defence. Snyder thereupon took this writ, assigning for error the above action of the Court.

De F. Ballou (*Hennershots* with him), for plaintiff in error.

The affidavit of defence law does not apply to suits wherein executors are defendants.

Leibert v. Hocker, 1 M. 263.
Vandusen v. Graham, 1 WEEKLY NOTES, 103.
Seymour v. Hubert, 3 WEEKLY NOTES, 423.

Rowland Evans (*R. L. Ashhurst* with him), for defendant in error.

In Pennsylvania a terre-tenant is not a necessary party to a suit upon a mortgage.

Mather v. Clark, 1 Watts, 493.
Mevey's Appeal, 4 Barr, 80.

The authorities cited by the plaintiff in error have no application, because no judgment was entered against any one but Henry Dutill, the defendant, who was personally served, and failed to file an affidavit of defence.

January 17, 1881. THE COURT. The executor of Snyder, the terre-tenant, as is alleged, of the mortgaged premises, was no party to the proceeding, and had no interest which entitled him to intervene. The heirs or devisees of the terre-tenant not having been made parties, will not be precluded by the judgment from showing that the mortgage was not a valid lien on the premises, in an ejectment by the sheriff's vendee. It is clear that the judgment was right.

Judgment affirmed.
PER CURIAM.

Common Pleas—Law.

C. P. No. 1. Oct. 2, 1880.
American Banking and Brokerage Co. (Limited) v. Donnelly.

Promissory note—Affidavit of defence—Allegation of fraud—Insufficiency of an affidavit which fails to aver that certain stock for which a note was given is worthless, nor any offer to return the stock.

Rule for judgment for want of a sufficient affidavit of defence.

Assumpsit by the holder against the maker of a promissory note, of which the following is a copy:—

$1000. Philadelphia, April 9, 1880.

Three months after date I promise to pay to the order of J. R. Muffly, one thousand dollars at ―――― without defalcation for value received.

JAMES DONNELLY,
2032 Columbia Ave.

Endorsement: Without recourse,
J. R. MUFFLY,
119 So. 4th St.

The affidavit and supplemental affidavit averred, that the defendant believes and expects to be able to prove that the plaintiffs are not the owners of the note for a valuable consideration before maturity, but that the same still belongs to the payee, and that the suit is brought in the name of plaintiffs only as a cover to preclude the deponent from setting up the defence of fraud and failure of consideration against the payee, Muffly; that the plaintiffs, or one of them, E. S. Records, was notified by defendant that he had a defence to the note, subject to which they would take it; that said note was given for 5600 shares of stock in the Western Mining Co., which Muffly represented as of great value, exhibiting specimens of ore as from the lands of said company, knowing that the lands were entirely unproductive, and that said specimens were not from such lands; that it was part of the consideration of the note that deponent should not be called on to pay it till he should be in funds from the sale of a property, as yet unsold, but the note was to be renewed from time to time.

Sylvester Gavitt, Jr., for the rule. An affidavit by a defendant that he believes and expects to be able to prove certain facts is not sufficient; he must state the grounds of his belief. And also, an affidavit is not sufficient where, merely on the defendant's belief, it denies the holder's title.

    Bank *v.* Gregg & Co., 29 Smith, 386.
    Gowen *v.* McPherson, 32 Leg. Int. 248.
    Salter *v.* Askin, 1 WEEKLY NOTES, 388.
    Williams *v.* Harding, Ibid. 344.

Nothing but clear evidence of knowledge and notice of fraud or *mala fides* can impeach the *prima facie* title of a holder of negotiable paper taken before maturity.

    Moorehead *v.* Gilmore, 27 Smith, 124.
    Phelan *v.* Moss, 17 Ibid. 59.
    Bardsley *v.* Delp, 7 Norris, 420.
    Lingg & Bro. *v.* Blummer, Ibid. 518.

Thos. J. Diehl, contra.

October 9, 1880. THE COURT. The affidavit sets out clearly the averment of fraud as between the original parties, as to the mine itself, but it says nothing about the stock. Now the mine might be worthless, and yet the stock have a market. Besides there is no averment of an offer to return the stock nor that defendant still retains it, but there was an averment by counsel, not disputed, that defendant had disposed of the stock for a higher figure than he had paid for it.

Rule absolute.

Oral opinion by PEIRCE, J.

C. P. No. 2.   June 26, 1880.

Fuller v. Bleim.

Payment of money into Court—Attachment of judgment.

Rule to show cause why money should not be paid into Court, and fi. fa. stayed.

A judgment in replevin for $250 had been obtained against Fuller, the plaintiff, by the defendant, Bleim, on May 21, 1880.

On June 9, 1880, an attachment execution was issued from Court of Common Pleas No. 3, against Bleim, defendant, and Fuller, garnishee. On June 15, 1880, a writ of fieri facias issued from Court of Common Pleas No. 2, upon the judgment obtained May 21, 1880.

The judgment in the replevin suit had, upon May 21, 1880, been marked to the use of W. G. Smith.

Fuller thereupon obtained this rule.

Benj. L. Temple, for the rule.

Peace, contra.

THE COURT. Rule absolute.

C. P. No. 3.   Jan. 15, 1881.

Hall v. Ritter.

Affidavit of defence law—Practice—Withdrawal of part of claim after filing of affidavit of defence.

Rule to show cause why leave should not be given to the plaintiff to withdraw from this suit his claim upon a certain due bill, without prejudice to his right to proceed for the same in another action. Also rule for judgment for want of a sufficient affidavit of defence upon the remaining items of his copy filed.

Assumpsit on two promissory notes and one due bill, amounting in all to $710.35.

The affidavit of defence set up, *inter alia*, that "it was expressly understood and agreed that the due bill, which amounts to $304.65, was not to be paid in cash, but was to be paid in merchandise; on account thereof eleven dollars have been paid in merchandise, and I am ready and willing to pay the balance of said due bill according to our agreement."

Henry F. Walton, for the rule.

The plaintiff may be allowed to withdraw disputed items without prejudice to his right to bring another action thereon, and take judgment for the balance.

    Brightly's Troubat & Haly's Practice, § 423.
    Burkhart *v.* Haviland, 7 WEEKLY NOTES, 486, 521.
    Johnson *v.* Bazin, 4 Ibid. 171.
    Richards *v.* Bisler, 3 Ibid. 485.

David Myers, contra.

THE COURT. Rules discharged.

C. P. No. 4.   March 21, 1881.

Lane v. Steinmetz.

Landlord and tenant—Right of distress—Distinction between boarder and renter of room.

Sur rule for a new trial.

Case, to recover damages for an alleged illegal distraint and sale of household goods.

On the trial, before THAYER, P. J., the facts appeared as follows: On September 21, 1877, the defendant leased to one Mrs. Hodges the premises at the northwest corner of Franklin and Race Streets "for a boarding-house."

On May 2, 1879, the plaintiff made the following arrangement with Mrs. Hodges: Mrs. Lane, the plaintiff, was to live in the house, furnish her room, pay Mrs. Hodges 25 cents for each meal she should take, and also pay $14 per month as rent for her room. Very few meals were eaten by Mrs. Lane under this arrangement, but she continued to rent the room at $14 a month, getting her meals elsewhere, or preparing them in her own room.

On August 19, 1879, the rent due by Mrs. Hodges to the defendant being in arrears, distraint was made upon the premises, and the furniture and goods of Mrs. Lane, in her own room, were distrained upon. Mrs. Hodges having fraudulently removed her goods from the premises, the goods of Mrs. Lane were sold under the distress, notwithstanding that she had given notice to the defendants and to the constable making the distress that the goods were hers, and of the arrangement under which she lodged.

THAYER, P. J., charged, *inter alia*, as follows: "If Mrs. Lane only rented these rooms and paid rent, the goods are liable to distress, and the defendants were right in what they did. . . . Mrs. Lane says that she rented these rooms at so much a month, and to have meals at twenty-five cents each, and fourteen dollars per month rent. This arrangement seems to have lasted a very short time. If it ceased before the rent accrued, and she became only a renter of the room, her goods were liable under the distress. . . . To constitute one a boarder he must get meals from the keeper of the boarding-house, that is, he must constitute one of the family of the boarding-house keeper; the goods of a person in that relation are exempt from the distress, but not the goods of a mere renter of rooms."

Verdict for defendant. Plaintiff obtained this rule on the ground of the alleged error in the instructions above cited.

Jenkins, for the rule cited—
Thompson *v.* Ward, L. R. 6 C. P. 360.
Allan *v.* Liverpool, L. R. 9 Q. B. 191.
Philip *v.* Henser, L. R. 3 C. P. 26.

Where the course of the business must necessarily put the tenant in possession of the property of his customers, it would be against the plainest dictates of honesty and conscience to permit the landlord to use him as a decoy, and pounce upon whatever is brought within his grasp, after having received the price of the exemption in the enhanced value of the rent.
Brown *v.* Sims, 17 S. & R. 138.

The goods of a boarder are not liable to be distrained for rent due by the keeper of the boarding-house.
Riddle *v.* Welden, 5 Whart. 9.
Cadwalader *v.* Tindall, 8 Har. 422.
Karns *v.* McKinney, 24 Smith, 396.
Howe Sewing Machine Co. *v.* Sloan, 6 Norris, 438.

J. R. Rhoads, contra.

The property of a stranger found on the demised premises left for no purpose of trade or other purpose requiring protection as a matter of public policy, is liable to distress for rent. It is true that a boarder's goods are exempt from distress.
Kleber *et al. v.* Ward *et al.*, 7 Norris, 93.
Erb *v.* Sadler, 8 WEEKLY NOTES, 13.
Jones *v.* Goldbeck, 8 WEEKLY NOTES, 533.

These cases follow Riddle *v.* Welden (5 Wharton, 9), in which case the distinction between a *boarder* and a *subtenant* is admitted, and the ground of the exemption of the goods of a boarder in a public boarding-house stated to be the public convenience. The *boarder* "pays for lodging, but *no rent.*" Compensation for use of his chamber is not a "separate charge, nor could his chattels be distrained for it, or anything be recovered from him in an action for use and occupation. : . . He has no interest or term in the place. . . Why, then, should not the *public* nature of the house protect his goods in it?" The question whether Mrs. Lane was a boarder was properly left to the jury as a question of fact.

March 23, 1881. THE COURT. Rule discharged.

C. P. No. 4.   Feb. 12, 1881.

Bowen v. Thornton.

Practice—Witnesses—Refusal to obey subpœna to testify before an examiner—Attachment—Upon the refusal of a witness to appear before an examiner the Court will issue an attachment.

Rule to show cause why an attachment should not issue against a witness to appear before an examiner.

A subpœna had twice been served upon the witness (the defendant), who refused to appear before the examiner. A certificate from the examiner showed that several meetings had been held, a reasonable time allowed for the witness to appear, and that, owing to his absence, it became necessary to continue the case.

Gangewer, for the rule.

THE COURT. Rule absolute.
[*Cf.* Assigned Estate of Hulburt, 8 WEEKLY NOTES, 254.]

Orphans' Court.

February 22, 1881.

Bauer's Estate.

Partition—Act of April 14, 1835—Citation to parties in interest—Although the proper practice is to issue such a citation, this is not essential where the names of the parties in interest appear in the petition, decree, and notices—Presumption that all requisite notices were given.

Sur petition to award a new writ of partition.

In Bauer's estate (reported *ante*, 336, *q. v.*) the Court refused to enter a decree, that premises sold by order of Court under proceedings in partition in 1870, should be charged with dower.

Catherine Bauer, the petitioner above, now presented a petition alleging that no citation issued before the award of the inquest in the partition, and consequently she was not a party thereunto. The prayer was for a citation on the widow and children of Augustus Karstien, to show cause why a new writ should not be awarded, so that by further partition being made between said parties and herself, her dower interest could be thus secured.

An answer *pro forma* was filed by Elizabeth Karstien, which set forth the sale of the premises to her husband, in October, 1870, which sale was duly confirmed by the Court, discharged from all lien of dower, and other encumbrance.

John White and *J. E. Bowers*, for the petition.

G. W. Arundel, for the respondent, cited the Act of April 14, 1835 (Purd. Dig. 435, pl. 147), and urged that when the name of a party in interest appears in a petition for a partition as directed by the above Act, it will be conclusively presumed in favor of the regularity of the proceedings, and that due and regular notice has been given, although not affirmatively shown on the record.

Richards *v.* Rote, 18 Sm. 253.

March 5, 1881. THE COURT. While it is undoubtedly the proper practice in proceedings in partition to issue a citation before awarding an inquest, it has long been settled that it is not essential to do so, and that the partition is not rendered invalid by reason of the want of preliminary notice to the parties. This was decided so long ago as Rex *v.* Rex (3 S. & R. 533) and so recently as Vensel's Appeal (27 Smith, 71).

It is true, as pointed out by Judge SHARSWOOD in Richards *v.* Rote (18 Smith, 253), Rex *v.* Rex was decided under the old Acts of Assembly, while, since the Act of 14th April, 1835, a partition will not divest the interest of one not named as a party in the petition, decree, and notices; but it was held in that case that as to parties who are so named, it is to be conclusively presumed, even though not affirmatively shown by the record, that all requisite notices were given; and hence, as afterwards decided in Vensel's Appeal, *supra*, as to such parties, the mere fact that a citation did not issue is immaterial.

In the case before us, a petition for partition was filed by Henry A. Bauer, in 1869, in which the widow of the intestate, who is the present petitioner, was named as a party, and her interest explicitly defined. There was no citation, but the petition was set forth at length in the writ which commanded the sheriff to give notice to "the parties aforesaid." His return showed affirmatively that such notice was given, and that the property, being incapable of partition, had been valued and appraised by the jurors.

The order of sale afterwards granted, recited that "all of the parties in interest had refused to take . . . at the valuation, and agreed that the order of sale be made absolute," which agreement, the record shows, was in writing, signed by the widow, as guardian of two of the heirs, though not by her separately as "widow." The return to the order of sale stated that the premises now in question were sold to Augustus Karstien for the sum of $1330, and the sale so made was confirmed September 8, 1870, security being ordered in double the amount of purchase-money.

It is now alleged that in making title to the purchaser no provision was made for securing to the widow her interest in the purchase-money, and that the whole amount was paid to the administrator, by whom, under the order of Court, the sale was made. For this reason, and because of the omission to issue a citation against her before the award of the inquest, it is supposed that the partition did not affect her, and we are asked to award a new writ in order that further partition may be made between her and the purchaser, and her interest thus charged upon the premises according to the provisions of the Act of Assembly.

That this cannot be done is clear. The partition already made was a legal conversion which bound the widow, and, as was decided in Vensel's Appeal, *supra*, divested her interest so far as the right to demand partition was concerned. How far the omission to have the widow's interest charged upon the premises can deprive her of her rights, or how far her own actions may have estopped her from asserting them, are questions not before us. Her remedies for collection are not within the jurisdiction of this Court.

Petition dismissed at the costs of the petitioner.

Opinion by PENROSE, J.

INDEX

OF

ALL THE CASES REPORTED IN THIS VOLUME.

BY

RICHARD C. DALE, Esq.

ABATEMENT, of legacies. See DECEDENTS' ESTATES. Appeal of Trustees of University, 520.
ACCORD AND SATISFACTION. An agreement to receive cash and new notes for seventy-five per cent. of an old note, in satisfaction of the same, is good as an accord and satisfaction. (C. P.) Bank v. Huston, 477.
ACKNOWLEDGMENT. See DEED.
ACTIONS. The mere issuing of process against a defendant, and its return *tarde venit*, or *nihil habet*, does not constitute an "action depending" within the meaning of the Act of February 24, 1834, providing for a writ of scire facias to bring in the personal representatives of a deceased "party" to an action. Machette v. Cuyler, 471.
ACTION ON THE CASE. Where an act of violence is committed by a servant in the ordinary course of his employment, but not by the direct command nor with the assent of the master, case and not trespass is the proper form of action in which to recover damages against the master. Drew v. Peer, 33.
Where a husband seeks to recover damages for an act of violence committed upon his wife, whereby he has lost her company and services, and suffered expense for medical attendance, case is the proper form of action. Ib.

ACTS OF ASSEMBLY.
1713' March 27. Limitations. 465.
1760, April 12. Taxes. 561.
1772, March 21. Distress 137, 438.
1794, April 22. Sunday. 200.
1798, February 27. Evidence. 169.
1804, January 30. Taxes. 561.
1813, March 22. Roads. 169.
1815, March 13. Tax Sales. 321.
1824, February 3. Sheriff's Sales. 418.
1832, March 15. Orphans' Court. 380.
1832, March 15. Wills. 207.
1832, March 29. Guardians. 255.
1832, March 29. Partition. 276.
1833, April 8. Wills. 209.
1833, April 8. Intestates. 95; 260, 479.
1833, April 9. Justice of Peace. 57.
1834, February 24. Decedents' Estates. 275, 471.
1834, April 14. Juries. 113.
1834, April 14. Crimes. 393.
1835, April 14. Partition. 276, 516.

ACTS OF ASSEMBLY—*Continued.*
1836, June 13. Townships. 389.
1836, June 13. Execution. 398.
1836, June 14. Actions. 131.
1836, June 16. Courts. 380, 386.
1836, June 16. Execution. 398, 503, 545.
1836, June 16. Mechanics' Liens. 157.
1839, July 2. Elections. 376.
1840, October 13. Orphans' Courts. 463.
1842, July 13. Evidence. 513.
'1843, April 13. Execution. 398.
1845, April 16. Sheriff's Sale. 418.
1846, March 11. Municipal Claims. 41.
1846, April 20. Decedents' Estates. 55.
1849, March 24. Mechanic's Lien. 555.
1849, April 10. Execution. 398.
1850, April 22. Ground Rents. 365.
1851, April 3. Mortgages. 14, 527.
1851, April 14. Decedents' Estates. 274, 559.
1851, April 14. Taxes. 377.
1851, April 14. Exemption. 413.
1851, April 14. Negligence. 339.
1853, April 14. Water Courses. 22.
1853, April 27. Orphans' Court. 382.
1854, February 20. Partition. 276.
1855, April 26. Negligence. 339, 440.
1855, April 27. Intestates. 95.
1855, May 4. Feme Sole Traders. 269.
1856, April 21. Guardians. 255, 564.
1857, March 14. Partition. 276.
1858, April 21. Amendments. 198, 511.
1858, April 21. Taxes. 418.
1859, April 12. Building Associations. 251.
1859, April 15. Building Associations. 83.
1860, March 29. Liquors. 170.
1860, March 31. Crimes. 61, 393, 409.
1861, May 1. Trustees. 421.
1863, May 6. Railroads. 291.
1865, March 27. Evidence. 513.
1866, March 23. Municipal Claims. 98.
1866, September 24. Warehouse Receipts. 49.
1867, April 8. School District. 396.
1867, April 13. School District. 396.
1868, April 4. Railroads. 497.
1868, April 9. Trustees. 421.
1869, March 17. Evidence. 513.
1869, April 15. Physicians. 31.

VOL. IX.—37 (577)

INDEX.

ACTS OF ASSEMBLY—*Continued.*

1869, April 15.	Evidence.	139, 249, 489.
1870, March 31.	Taxes.	549.
1870, April 9.	Evidence.	489.
1871, May 10.	Distress.	104.
1871, May 25.	Guardians.	255.
1871, June 6.	Streets.	43.
1872, April 3.	Licenses.	184.
1872, April 9.	Wages.	28.
1872, April 10.	Railroads.	291.
1873, March 27.	Railways.	233.
1873, April 8.	Execution.	559.
1874, April 9.	Courts.	369, 529.
1874, April 24.	Coal Companies.	74.
1874, April 29.	Corporations.	31.
1874, May 23.	Trustees.	110.
1874, May 23.	Municipal Corporations.	198.
1874, June 2.	Partnership.	92.
1875, April 12.	Licenses.	184.
1875, June 11.	Mechanics' Liens.	385.
1876, March 14.	Judgments.	246.
1876, April 28.	Beneficial Societies.	126.
1876, May 1.	Partnership.	92.
1877, March 24.	Physicians.	31.
1878, April 18.	Recorder.	377.
1878, May 24.	Rules of Court.	386.
1878, May 25.	Evidence.	489.
1879, May 19.	Attorneys.	145.
1879, June 7.	Taxes.	179, 550.
1879, June 11.	Amendments.	64.
1879, June 11.	Insolvent Debtors.	47, 513.
1879, June 11.	Mortgages.	89, 191.
1879, June 11.	Married Women.	419.

ACTS OF CONGRESS.

1802, April 14.	Naturalization.	169.
1824, May 26.	Naturalization.	159, 169.
1872, June 7.	Naturalization.	96.

ADMIRALTY. No maritime lien arises for supplies furnished to a vessel upon the orders of the charterers. Such charterers are not to be regarded as the agents of the owners for any such purpose. The master alone can pledge the vessel for supplies, and if supplies are furnished upon the order of any other person, the supply man must rely upon the credit of the person thus ordering. (U. S. D. C.) The Norman, 543.

ADVANCEMENTS. Distribution where shares of legatees are subject to advancements. (O. C.) Wolf's Estate, 260.

What words in will construed to create an advancement. See WILL. Porter's Appeal, 457.

AFFIDAVIT OF DEFENCE LAW.

Although ordinarily judgment cannot be entered against an executor for want of an affidavit of defence, the executor of a deceased terre-tenant who intervenes as a party defendant cannot claim the benefit of this rule. Dutill v. Sully, 573.

A rule upon the plaintiff to produce his books of original entry for the purpose of comparison with the copy filed is not a rule of course, the defendant must sustain his application by an affidavit that he is informed or has reason to believe that the copy filed is not a true copy. (C. P.) Burton v. McCully, 206.

Upon an appeal from a magistrate's court, defendant is not bound to file an affidavit of defence, unless the plaintiff puts something on the record showing an intention to ask for judgment for want of an affidavit. (C. P.) Prichett v. Moss, 558.

What a sufficient copy. A contract of suretyship for the payment of rent with an averment of all the substantial facts is sufficient without filing a copy of the lease. (C. P.) Loftus v. Corles, 333.

AFFIDAVIT OF DEFENCE LAW—*Continued.*

An acknowledgment that certain shares of building association stock are the property of the plaintiff, and that they will be paid in regular order of notice, is not a sufficient copy to entitle the plaintiff to judgment for want of an affidavit of defence. (C. P.) Newlin v. Building Association, 220.

A claim property bond in replevin is not a sufficient instrument. (C. P.) Elliott v. Kunzig, 542.

A plaintiff will not be permitted to withdraw a portion of his claim without prejudice to his right to proceed in another action and to take judgment for the balance. (C. P.) Hall v. Ritter, 574.

Affidavit, when sufficient. In an action for rent an affidavit setting up that the landlord by force and arms had ejected the tenant. (C. P.) Whitaker v. Read, 144.

In an action upon a promissory note, an averment that the note was obtained from the defendant by false representations, and fraudulently put into circulation is sufficient to prevent judgment. Smith v. Popular Loan Association, 168.

In an action for liquors sold, an affidavit that they were impure, vitiated, and adulterated is sufficient. (C. P.) Glenn v. Keenan, 170.

What a sufficient denial of partnership relation. (C. P.) Bank v. Castner, 273.

What a sufficient averment of defective quality in an action for goods sold and delivered. (C. P.) Badger v. McKay, 528.

What an insufficient averment of a set-off. (C. P.) Devenny v. Building Association, 127.

What an insufficient averment of defect in quality. (C. P.) Roebling v. Brown, 170.

In an action by a landlord against the surety of his tenant, an affidavit that at the time when the rent became due, there were upon the demised premises goods of sufficient value to pay the rent and that the landlord, although requested by the surety, failed to distrain, is insufficient to prevent judgment. (C. P.) Loftus v. Corles, 333.

In an action upon a promissory note made in New York, an averment that the notes included usury, and that under the statute of New York, and the decisions thereon, the notes are void even in the hands of third persons, is insufficient. Boughton v. Bank, 519.

An averment in an affidavit of defence of the law of another State must be made with the same precision as the averment of any other fact. Ib.

In an action upon a promissory note given in payment for stock sold, an affidavit of defence that the stock was worthless is insufficient unless accompanied by an averment of willingness to return the stock. (C. P.) American Banking Co. v. Donnelly, 573.

Affidavit of defence under rule of Court in Armstrong County. A plaintiff who files a sworn statement of the amount awarded him by an auditor upon the distribution of an estate in the Orphans' Court is entitled to judgment for want of an affidavit of defence. Montgomery v. Heilman, 537.

AGENT. See EVIDENCE. PRINCIPAL AND AGENT.

AGREEMENT. See CONTRACT.

AMENDMENT. A new defendant cannot be substituted by way of amendment in an action begun by a capias. (C. P.) Brittin v. Shloss, 510.

Under what circumstances the record may be amended after verdict by substitution of formal parties. (C. P.) Hirst v. Randall, 349.

Surplusage in judgment, when formal defects in, can be amended after the removal of the case to the Supreme Court. Hartley v. White, 286.

Where a conditional verdict and judgment for plain-

INDEX.   579

AMENDMENT—*Continued.*
tiff in ejectment omitted to fix a time for the payment of the sum upon which the verdict was to be released, the Supreme Court on error amended the judgment by inserting a date before which payment should be made. Kensinger *v.* Smith, 311.

A purely formal amendment, such as the insertion of the name of the legal plaintiff in a suit brought in the name of the equitable plaintiff, may be made even though a new suit would be barred by the Statute of Limitations. Clement *v.* Commonwealth, 131.

While a large discretion may be exercised by the Court below in permitting amendments to the pleadings, yet such an amendment to the narr. as substantially changes the cause of action, will not be allowed. Royse *v.* May, 104.

An amendment to correct an error apparent upon the face of a record of the Orphans' Court will not be allowed after the lapse of seven years, where intervening rights will be affected. (O. C.) Bauer's Appeal, 336.

Under the Act of April 21, 1858, a municipal claim may be amended at any time before or at the trial, provided intervening rights are not thereby prejudiced. Allentown *v.* Hower, 198. (C. P.) City *v.* Wagner, 511.

The Act of June 11, 1879, authorizing the amendment of mechanics' liens is not retroactive. Fahnestock *v.* Wilson, 385. (C. P.) Sparr *v.* Walz, 64.

ANNUITY. An annuity charged on the personal estate is a general legacy, and, in case of deficiency after payment of debts, expenses, and specific legacies to pay other general legacies, the annuity must abate ratably with the other general legacies. Appeal of the Trustees of the University, 520.

APPORTIONMENT of mortgage. See MORTGAGE. Amanda Martin's Appeal, 484.

ARBITRATION. An agreement for a reference, not made a rule of court for the filing of the agreement, is revocable until notice of the award is given to the parties by the arbitrators. (C. P.) Huston *v.* Clark, 316.

ARMSTRONG COUNTY. See AFFIDAVIT OF DEFENCE LAW. Montgomery *v.* Heilman, 537.

ASSIGNMENT FOR THE BENEFIT OF CREDITORS. An insolvent building associatio cannot be wound up under an assignment for the benefit of creditors. The members of the association, though quasi creditors, are not strictly so, and the equities of all interests can be best conserved by the appointment of a receiver. (C. P.) *In re* National Savings and Loan Association, 79.

Creditors who have lent money to the grantor of real estate upon the faith of declarations made by his grantee that the equitable interest in the land remained in such grantor, may share in the distribution of the proceeds of sale of such real estate by the assignee for the benefit of the creditors of the grantee, after payment of the debts for which the estate was specifically assigned. Mowry's Appeal, 362.

The commissions of an assignee for the benefit of creditors upon a fund of $16,535, produced by the sale of real estate, in the absence of evidence of any special trouble, were fixed at two and one-half per cent. Brice's Appeal, 227.

ASSUMPSIT. The rule that money collected by execution, though not lawfully due, cannot be recovered, does not apply where the judgment on which the execution issued was subsequently reversed on writ of error, and a second trial resulted in a judgment for the defendant. In such case assumpsit will lie to recover the money so paid. Travellers' Ins. Co. *v.* Heath, 516.

ATTACHMENT, EXECUTION. See EXECUTION.

ATTACHMENT, FOREIGN. See FOREIGN ATTACHMENT.

ATTACHMENT FOR CONTEMPT. See COURTS. Borlin's Appeal, 545. See PRACTICE. Bowen *v.* Thornton, 575.

ATTORNEY-AT-LAW. The office of an attorney is his property, and he cannot be deprived of it unless by the judgment of his peers or the law of the land. To deprive him of it summarily for the publication of a libel upon a man in a public capacity, or where the matter was proper for public investigation, would be an infraction of the spirit, if not of the letter of Art. 1, § 7 of the Constitution. *Ex parte* Steinman, 145.

A Court has the power, without any formal complaint or petition, upon its own motion to strike the name of an attorney from its roll, provided he is afforded an opportunity to be heard in his own defence. Ib.

There may be cases of misconduct not strictly professional which would clearly show a person not to be fit to be an attorney, *e. g.*, theft or forgery; but an attorney cannot, even in such a case, be summarily disbarred without a formal indictment and trial. Ib.

Attorney and Client. It is a well-settled principle that an attorney cannot make a profit out of his office to the prejudice of the rights and interests of his client. Hence where an attorney buys a title outstanding or adverse to that as to which he has been consulted or employed, he buys for the client, if the client should elect to take it. (C. P.) Lockhard *v.* McKinley, 11. (U. S. S. C.) Humphrey *v.* Baker, 13.

A commission of two per cent. is a reasonable figure for the collection of a mortgage of $2000, where the terre-tenant is a widow with a large family dependent upon her. (C. P.) Landis *v.* Aldrich, 192.

There is no definite standard of commission for the collection of a mortgage. In this case, a fee of $150 was allowed upon a mortgage of $4000. (C. P.) Reed *v.* Worthington, 192.

Upon a judgment for $2600 by warrant of attorney containing the clause, "with attorney's fees for collection," most of the debt was paid voluntarily, and the judgment was opened, and went to a jury upon a contested payment of $192. The jury decided in favor of the plaintiff, and the Court upon a reserved point allowed $103 attorney's commission on $2600, according to a fee bill agreed upon by members of the bar: *Held*, that this was not excessive, as there was litigation, and the labor of counsel would have been no greater had the verdict been for the whole face of the judgment. Imler *v.* Imler, 196.

AUTHOR. The performance of an uncopyrighted opera on the stage is not a publication, and gives no right to print the music from memory or otherwise. (C. P.) Gilbert *v.* Bacher, 14

BAIL, IN ERROR. A recognizance of bail in error, defective in form, may derive validity from the consent, expressed or implied, of the parties intended to be effected by it. Allen *v.* Kellam, 93.

The recognizance may be sustained as a voluntary personal contract, based on sufficient consideration, and if there be an election to accept one defective, and treating it as valid, to forbear to proceed by execution pending the writ of error, neither the principal nor the surety can evade liability on the ground of the defect. Ib.

But to treat the recognizance as a nullity, by issuing

580 INDEX.

BAIL IN ERROR—*Continued.*
execution and proceeding as if it had not been given, constitutes a good defence to an action upon it. Ib.

An action of debt upon the bond of bail in error should be brought in the Court where the original judgment was obtained. (C. P.) Lukens v. Bryson, 540.

Approval of bail in error, when vacated. See ERRORS AND APPEALS. Kaufman v. Hirsch, 347.

BAILMENT. In general terms, a bailment is the delivery of goods, or any other species of personal estate for use, keeping, or on some other trust, where the general property does not pass. Krause v. Commonwealth, 61.

A delivery of chattels upon a sale made on condition that the title shall pass on the payment of the purchase-money at a future day, does not constitute a bailment, but vests in the transferree a conditional title. Ib.

Difference of rights of innocent purchasers and creditors towards chattels held under bailment and under conditional sale, explained. Ib.

Liability of bank for loss of securities left with it for safe keeping as a bailee without hire. See BANKS AND BANKING. Comp v. Carlisle Deposit Bank, 453.

See COMMON CARRIERS.

BANKRUPTCY. Where one who conveys lands for the purpose of defrauding creditors, is subsequently adjudicated a bankrupt, the assignee in bankrupt alone can institute proceedings to set aside the fraudulent conveyance, and if he neglects to institute such proceedings for two years after his appointment, the title of the grantee becomes indefeasible. Creditors of the bankrupt, whose debts were contracted after the bankruptcy, have no standing to attack the conveyance. (O. C.) Connell's Estate, 406.

BANKS AND BANKING. A bank having opened a deposit account with a customer in the usual manner, cannot, in the absence of any claim by a third party, refuse to pay over on demand the balance standing to the credit of the account, on the ground that the moneys deposited were not the property of the depositor, but belonged to a third party, against whom the bank claimed a right of lien or set-off for an indebtedness due by the latter to the bank. First Nat. Bank of Lock Haven v. Mason, 265.

When a bank has extended its credit to a depositor by discounting his note, but learns of his insolvency before payment, or notice of any checks drawn upon the fund, the bank may withdraw the credit upon tendering the depositor the consideration, i. e., the notes and the amount of the discount. Dougherty v. Central National Bank, 1.

In case of the insolvency of the borrower before actual payment of the money by the lender, an equitable right analogous to the doctrine of *stoppage in transitu* may be exercised by the lender. Ib.

Where a bank depositor dies insolvent, the bank cannot set off against the amount standing to the credit of decedent, a note of the decedent discounted by the bank in his lifetime. (C. P.) Shoemaker v. Bank, 420.

A bank is responsible for the safe-keeping of the money of a depositor, and it cannot set up the fraud of its own officers as an answer to demand for repayment. Steckel v. First Nat. Bank of Allentown, 17.

The cashier is the executive officer of a bank, and authorized by the nature of his office to receive money on deposit; after receiving it no trick or fraud on his part, by means of which the money passes to a firm in which the bank officers are largely interested, can relieve the bank from its liability. Ziegler v. Bank, 19.

BANKS AND BANKING—*Continued.*
In an action by a bank upon a promissory note, evidence is admissible that the note was procured from the defendant by fraud on the part of the bank officers under the following circumstances: that the defendant went to the bank to receive payment of a certificate of deposit; that when the money was paid, he signed a paper represented by the bank officer to be a receipt for the money, but which afterwards turned out to be the note upon which suit was brought. Resh v. Bank, 21.

What a sufficient ratification of unauthorized acts of a bank president. Winton v. Little, 37.

Where bonds are left at a bank for safe-keeping without hire, the depositor taking a receipt stipulating that the deposit was made at his risk, the bank is not liable for their loss by the dishonesty of the cashier, even though it appear that the bank was in the habit of detaching the interest coupons, forwarding them for collection to corresponding banks, and by so doing obtaining a temporary credit at such banks, upon which interest was allowed. Comp v. Carlisle Bank, 453.

Evidence of loose declarations made by the cashier at the time of giving the receipt as to the safety of the bonds is not admissible to vary the effect of the written receipt. Ib.

National Banks. Real estate security may be taken by a national bank for present or future advances. Winton v. Little, 37.

Usurious interest actually received by a national bank in the renewals of a series of notes cannot be set off in a suit brought by the bank on the last renewal note in the series. The forfeiture of the interest only occurs where illegal interest has been stipulated for but not paid. National Bank of Fayette v. Dushane, 472.

The only remedy of the defendant is by an action of debt against the bank under the National Bank Act to recover the penalty therein prescribed. Ib.

Where the pledgee of stock has the shares transferred into his name upon the books of the company he is liable for all assessments made upon stockholders in the event of the bank becoming insolvent. But where the stock is put into the name of a third person to hold for benefit of the pledgor and pledgee, this liability does not attach. (U. S. C. C.) Anderson v. Philadelphia Warehousing Co., 262.

Where the stock is transferred into the name of the president of a corporation pledgee. the question should be submitted to the jury, whether such corporation consented to become shareholders, and whether the transfer to their president was with the understanding that it should be a transfer to them, or was subsequently recognized by them as such transfer. Ib.

Taxation of Banks. See TAXES AND TAXATION. Lackawanna v. First Nat. Bank of Scranton, 549. Truby's Appeal, 550.

BENEFICIAL SOCIETIES. A member of an unincorporated beneficial society cannot maintain an action for benefits against the officers of such society. The effect of the Act of April 28, 1876, is simply to exonerate the members from individual liability, and to confine the execution to association property. An action at law is still maintainable against the members as copartners with a liability thus limited. (C. P.) Kurz v. Eggert, 126.

See STOCK EXCHANGE.

BILLS AND NOTES. Parol evidence is admissible to show that the maker of a promissory note was induced to sign it under a belief caused by the representations of the payee, that the note was a receipt for money paid. Resh v. Bank, 21.

BILLS AND NOTES—*Continued.*

The moral obligation of a married woman to repay money borrowed by her, is a sufficient consideration for a note given by a third person to secure such indebtedness. Leonard v. Duffin, 155.

One who accepts a draft as treasurer is not liable personally, if the holder of the draft knew that the intention of the parties was that the defendant was not personally to be liable. (C. P.) German v. Moodie, 221.

In a suit against the indorser of a promissory note, in order to prevent judgment for want of a sufficient affidavit of defence, it is enough for the affidavit to show that the defendant's indorsement was obtained by misrepresentation, and that the note was negotiated in fraud of his rights. Smith v. Popular Building Association, 168.

Judgment for want of an affidavit of defence will not be entered against one who signs upon the face of a note below the maker adding to his name the word "indorser." (C. P.) Schwenk v. Yost, 16.

The payees of a check are not purchasers for value of negotiable paper so as to prevent the bank upon which the check is drawn from exercising a *quasi* right of stoppage in transitu upon the proceeds of a note of the drawer of the check constituting the only money in bank to his credit. Dougherty v. Central National Bank, 1.

What not sufficient averment of New York usury law in an affidavit of defence to a suit upon a promissory note made in New York. See AFFIDAVIT OF DEFENCE LAW. Boughton v. Bank, 519.

Usurious interest received by national banks upon a series of renewal notes, effect of. See BANKS AND BANKING. Bank v. Dushane, 472.

BILL OF PARTICULARS, when demandable in criminal case. See CRIMES. Williams v. Commonwealth, 113.

See PRACTICE.

BILL OF REVIEW. See ORPHANS' COURT.

BILLIARD TABLES, tax on. See TAXES. (C. P.) Albrecht v. Lane, 377.

BOND. In an action upon a bond for $1000, a narr. laying the damages at $1200 is not demurrable. A sum sufficient to cover interest may be claimed in addition to the penal sum of the bond. (C. P.) Commonwealth v. Lynd, 510.

Separate suits in the name of the Commonwealth may be maintained against the principal and each of the sureties upon the official bond of a prothonotary. The Act of June 14, 1836, only prohibits the bringing of separate suits by different plaintiffs upon the same bond. Clement v. Commonwealth, 131.

Where a suit upon an official bond has been brought in the name of the equitable plaintiff, the name of the Commonwealth as legal plaintiff may be brought in by amendment, even though at the time of the amendment, the original cause of action would have been barred by the statute. Ib.

A corporation which issues a coupon bond is in the position of a maker of a promissory note, not of the drawer of a check or bill of exchange. There is no obligation upon the holder to demand payment within a reasonable time. Williamsport Gas Co. v. Pinkerton, 97.

Whether municipal bonds issued without the filing of the statement required by the Act of April 20, 1874, § 2, are illegal, not decided. Matthews v. Scranton, 507.

BROKER. See STOCK EXCHANGE.

BUILDING ASSOCIATION. Building associations chartered under the general Act of April 15, 1859, must comply in all their operations with the provisions of that Act; they are required to loan moneys lawfully in the treasury to the highest bidder, in open competition, at a stated monthly meeting; they are not permitted to borrow money from banks or others for the purpose of loaning it to members at interest in excess of six per cent., nor can they fix a minimum rate of premium below which they will not receive bids. Stiles's Appeal, 83.

But a borrowing stockholder cannot complain of the action of the association in this respect unless he is injured by it, hence, if no bid was refused the borrower because it was below the minimum rate, but the loan was awarded to him upon a bid made by himself alone, or in consequence of competition with other bidders, at a premium above the minimum, he was not injured by the fact that an illegal rule had been established, and he is liable for the premium so bid. (C. P.) Orangeville Savings Fund v. Young, 251.

What not a sufficient averment of set-off in an action upon a building association order. (C. P.) Devenney v. Building Association, 127.

Payments on stock assigned as collateral security for a building association mortgage are not *ipso facto* payments on the mortgage. Economy Building Association v. Hungerbuehler, 218.

When such payments have been credited to the general account of the mortgagor, the testimony of the officers of the association that they considered the payments as upon account of the mortgage, is not admissible to prove that fact. Ib.

When a married woman having given a mortgage to a building association does not set up her coverture as a defence to the premiums contracted for, her next of kin after her death will not be permitted to do so. (C. P.) Building Association v. Roan, 15.

An insolvent building association cannot be wound up under an assignment for the benefit of creditors. In order to secure a fair and equitable distribution of its assets, among those entitled to receive them, a receiver should be appointed. (C. P.) *In re* Assigned Estate of National Building Association, 79.

BY-LAW. A by-law inconsistent with the constitution of an unincorporated society is void. (C. P.) Powell v. Abbott, 231.

CATCHING BARGAIN. See FRAUD.

COLLATERAL SECURITIES. See DEBTOR AND CREDITOR.

COMMISSIONS. See ATTORNEY-AT-LAW. ASSIGNMENT FOR BENEFIT OF CREDITORS. DECEDENTS' ESTATES.

COMMON CARRIER. Where a common carrier wrongfully refused to deliver goods to the assignee of a bill of lading, the measure of damages is the difference between the price at which such assignee sold them at the time when the goods ought to have been delivered, and the price realized at a sale after the delayed delivery. (U. S. C. C.) Schmidt v. The Pennsylvania, 351.

The duty of a carrier to its passengers is to use the greatest possible care, hence to enable a passenger to recover for injuries from a company, whose train came into collision with the car upon which he was travelling, it must appear that the carrier company did not fail in its duty to him. Phila. & Reading R. R. Co. v. Boyer, 497.

The driver of a horse car, whose tracks cross a steam road at grade, is bound to "stop, look, listen," and use whatever other precautions were reasonably in his power. His carelessness in this regard is not

COMMON CARRIER—*Continued.*
excused by the failure of the flagman of the steam road to give proper notice of an approaching train. Ib.

An ordinance of the city of Philadelphia providing that the conductors of all passenger railway cars shall in passing a steam road at grade, cross the track in advance of their car, does not apply to cars having no conductor, and attended only by a driver. Ib.

A boy permitted by a conductor of a train to ride upon the cars free of charge for the purpose of selling newspapers is not a passenger, and if he is killed while on the train, no action can be maintained against the company for his death. He is simply a trespasser, to whom the carrier owes no duty. Duff v. Allegheny Valley R. R. Co., 504.

Standing upon the step of a front platform of a crowded passenger railway car, with the implied assent of the conductor and driver, is not *per se* contributory negligence. Germantown P. R. W. Co. v. Walling, 467.

Where the measure of duty on the part of a passenger is ordinary and reasonable care, and the standard shifts with the circumstances of the case, the question of contributory negligence is for the jury. Ib.

A passenger railway is not liable for injuries to a boy injured while attempting to jump upon a "dummy" train, even though they fail to stop at his signal. (C. P.) Coller v. Frankford and S. R. W. Co., 477.

The fact that the boy was invited to jump on by a brakeman does not alter the case. Such an invitation was beyond the brakeman's authority, and does not bind the company. Ib.

Where injury to a passenger results from defective track, cars, machinery, or motive power, there is a presumption that the carrier has been negligent. But no such presumption arises when the passenger is injured by the act of a third person, over whom the carrier has no control. In such a case, in order to render the carrier liable, his negligence must be affirmatively proved. Federal Street P. R. W. Co. v. Gibson, 533.

Where a passenger on a ferry boat is thrown down, and injured by the boat striking the wharf with violence, the company is liable, and in a case where the lower end of a fibula was fractured, and an ankle-joint sprained, $3200 was awarded by a referee as reasonable damages. (C. P.) Monaghan v. Ferry Co., 368. (Affirmed. See 10 W. N. C. 46.)

See NEGLIGENCE.

CONDITION. A condition in restraint of marriage attached to a bequest in favor of a widow is *in terrorem* and void; but the condition is validated by a limitation over on event of remarriage, for such a limitation shows that the condition was not intended as a menace, but as the basis of a distinct gift. Bonbright's Appeal, 475.

Such a limitation over is none the less valid because to one upon whom the law itself casts the property. Ib.

CONFLICT OF JURISDICTION. See COURTS.

CONFLICT OF LAWS. The laws of another State, a member of the Union, must be proved as matters of fact. The Courts will not take judicial notice of them. Boughton v. American Exchange Bank, 519.

CONSTITUTION OF PENNSYLVANIA.

Art. I. § 7,	147.
Art. I. § 9,	513.
Art. III. § 21,	339.
Art. V. § 5,	369, 529.
Art. VII. § 1,	113.
Art. VIII. § 9,	113.
Art. IX. §§ 1, 2,	549, 550.
Art. IX. § 8,	241.
Art. XVI. § 8,	22.

CONSTITUTIONAL LAW. The constitutionality of the Act of April 22, 1794, known as the Sunday law, is now not open for argument. Seventh Day Baptists are as much subject to its provisions as other citizens. Waldo v. Commonwealth, 200.

The Act of June 11, 1879, relating to the examination of insolvent debtors is unconstitutional, because upon its face it proposes to force a debtor to forego his constitutional right under Art. I. § 9 of the Constitution, of not being compelled to give evidence which might render him liable to a criminal prosecution. Horstman v. Kaufman, 513.

To deprive an attorney summarily of his office for the publication of a libel on a man in a public capacity would be an infraction of Art. I. § 7 of the Constitution, which guarantees an immunity from punishment in all cases where the fact that publication of the alleged libel was not maliciously or negligently made shall be established to the satisfaction of the jury. *Ex parte* Steinman, 145.

The Acts of May 6, 1863, and April 10, 1872, punishing the sale of railroad tickets by unauthorized persons are not unconstitutional, but are a proper exercise of the police power of the State. (Q. S.) Commonwealth v. Wilson, 291.

These Acts do not trench upon the power of Congress to regulate inter-state commerce, nor do they impair the obligation of any contract. Ib.

A statute will not be held unconstitutional if it admit of an interpretation not in conflict with the Constitution. Hence the Act of June 11, 1879, authorizing the amendment of mechanics' claims is held not to be retroactive. Fahnestock v. Wilson, 385.

An Act of Assembly requiring a county to pay the personal debt of its ex-sheriff, contracted for the food of jail prisoners, is void. Faas v. Warner, 412.

Assessments for the expenses of draining meadow lands upon Greenwich Island cannot be enforced by distress against the goods of a tenant of the land against which the assessment is made, whose tenancy began after the assessment was laid. (C. P.) Maynes v. Rutherford, 221. Rutherford v. Maynes, 561.

A tax laid for a private purpose is unconstitutional. Ib.

Since the adoption of the Constitution of 1874, an action for consequential damages may be maintained against a corporation for acts done in the exercise of the right of eminent domain. Reading v. Althouse, 22.

Where a municipal corporation appropriates the water of a stream for municipal purposes, it becomes liable to all persons damaged by the diversion of the stream. Ib.

Under Art. III. § 21, of the Constitution, which provides that in cases of death caused by negligence the right of action shall survive, no right of action survives to the *personal representatives* of the deceased, but, in the absence of new legislation, the right of action is vested in the relatives who, by the Act of April 26, 1855, were entitled to sue. Books v. Danville, 339.

Quære, Whether the Act of April 4, 1868, limiting the pecuniary liability of railroad companies for negligently causing death can be taken advantage of by a corporation which never formally accepted its provisions. Phila. and Reading Railroad Co. v. Boyer, 497.

Quære, The effect of Art. III. § 21, of the Constitution of 1874, upon the Act of April 4, 1868. Ib.

The second clause of Art. IX. § 8, of the Constitution prohibits the creation of a new municipal debt or the increase of an existing debt of more than two per cent. of the assessed property valuation unless authorized by a public vote. It does not prevent municipal

CONSTITUTIONAL LAW—*Continued.*
officers from increasing existing or creating new indebtedness to an amount less than two per cent. without a public vote, provided the extreme limit of seven per cent. be not exceeded. Pike County v. Rowland, 241.

The Act of March 31, 1870, providing for the payment by banks of a tax of one per cent. upon their capital stock at par, and that upon such payment the other property of the bank should be exempt from taxation does not infringe upon the constitutional prohibition against exempting property from taxation. Lackawanna v. First Nat. Bank, 549.

The Act of June 7, 1879, reducing the tax upon national bank stock went into effect at once and applied to the tax of the current year. It does not violate the provision of Art. IX. § 1, of the Constitution that all taxes shall be uniform on the same class of subjects. Truby's Appeal, 550.

CONTRACT. An appointment as exclusive agent for the sale of a certain make of sewing machines within a prescribed territory is such a contract as a court of equity will restrain the breach of by an injunction. (C. P.) Ewing v. Willcox & Gibbs Sewing Machine Co., 272.

The moral obligation of a married woman to repay money borrowed by her is a sufficient consideration for a note given by a third person to secure such indebtedness. Leonard v. Duffin, 155.

An assignor for the benefit of creditors has sufficient interest in land assigned to support a guarantee given by him upon a sale of the land by his assignee that it contains a certain number of acres. Schriver v. Eckenrode, 161.

A note whose consideration is the stifling of a prosecution for forgery is void, and the entry of judgment thereon by virtue of a warrant of attorney does not make it an executed contract. Tebay & Bredin's Appeal, 151.

In such case public policy requires that the defendant be heard, and if the contract is void his relief is an incident. The principle depends on the public good, not on the merit of the defendant. But in a case of mere fraud between the parties, where the public is not interested, the law leaves the parties where they place themselves. Ib.

A promise in aid of a charity will not be sustained by the moral obligation alone, which underlies it. A legal consideration attaches only when work is begun or responsibility incurred upon the faith of the promise, or when it becomes the basis of similar engagements by others, and in either case it must be made to a party capable of enforcing it. (O. C.) Stokes's Estate, 439.

Quære, Whether a promise to pay money to a charity made within one calendar month of the death of the promisor is within the Act of April 26, 1855. Ib.

Where a contract between a mechanic and the owner of land for the erection of a house contained a covenant on the part of the mechanic that no mechanic's lien should be filed, and a covenant on the part of the owner that the building should be insured to a specified amount, these covenants are separate and independent and the breach of one does not justify a breach of the other. Long v. Caffrey, 25.

A severable contract may be severed for the purpose of enforcing rights as they accrue, but a party in default cannot insist on its being treated as severed to avoid a right to rescind for non-performance of any one portion. (U. S. C. C.) Norrington v. Wright, 422.

Under a contract for 5000 tons of rails to be shipped in about equal quantities in February and four suc-

CONTRACT—*Continued.*
ceeding months, the purchaser may rescind on failure to ship the stipulated quantity in February. Ib.

Under what circumstances time is not of the essence of a contract to pay for and take away merchandise purchased, within thirty days of the signing of the contract. (C. P.) Kitchen v. Stokes, 48.

Where one becomes surety for a consignee and in the contract of suretyship it is provided that the consignments are not to exceed in amount the sum of $5000 at any one time, and it appeared that several consignments were made exceeding the stipulated amount, the surety is discharged from all liability by reason of the variance in the terms of the contract. Brez v. Warner, 45.

A contract to pay a certain sum out of his income to the maintenance of a school, contingent upon the convenience of the promisor, of which he is to be the judge, is not binding upon his executors. (O. C.) Wood's Estate, 170. Appeal of Trustees of University; 520.

What sufficient evidence of performance of contract. (U. S. C. C.) Reading v. Texas & Pacific R. R. Co., 175.

Where one whose name is forged to a promissory note, after knowledge of the forgery ratifies the instrument by payments on account, he is estopped from denying the validity of the note. (C. P.) Brooke v. Harman, 462.

CONTRIBUTORY NEGLIGENCE. See NEGLIGENCE.

CONVERSION, equitable, what words in will work an equitable conversion. See WILL. Jones v. Caldwell, 459.

CORPORATION. A charter will not be granted to an institute for instruction in electricity as a curative agency with power to confer degrees, where the provisions of the charter as a prerequisite to the obtaining of a degree require in the applicant only a knowledge of electricity, galvanism, and magnetism. (C. P.) *In re* Electropathic Institute, 31.

By the Act of March 24, 1877, the standard qualifications for a practitioner of medicine are a good moral character, a thorough elementary education, a comprehensive knowledge of human anatomy, human physiology, pathology, chemistry, materia medica, obstetrics, and practice of medicine and surgery, and public hygiene. Ib.

A by-law must be neither inconsistent with nor repugnant to the charter of a corporation, nor can new and additional tests or qualifications be imposed by a by-law upon voters. (C. P.) Raynor v. Beatty, 201.

The Court of Common Pleas in equity has jurisdiction to supervise and control a corporate election, and in the exercise of this jurisdiction upon a bill filed anterior to an election at which it is alleged that difficulties may arise, it will direct the judges of election to return to the Court the votes cast together with the list of challenged votes which were received or ruled out. Ib.

In order to validate corporate action at a special meeting it is necessary that notice either actual or constructive be given to every corporator who is entitled to participate in such meeting. Pike County v. Rowland, 241.

Constructive notice may be given in any manner provided either in the charter or by-laws, but in the absence of such special provision, personal notice is requisite. Ib.

In the absence of due warning, any attempted corporate action at a special meeting is void. Ib.

The powers of a corporation are such as are conferred by their charters, whether express or fairly implied;

584 INDEX.

CORPORATION—*Continued.*
hence, in the absence of charter authority, a lease or contract by a railroad company to transfer all its rolling stock, etc., with all its rights and duties, is *ultra vires* and void. (U. S. S. C.) Thomas v. West Jersey R. R. Co., 65.

A mere recognition by the Legislature that such a lease has been made is not sufficient to operate as a legislative ratification of the same, nor can its invalidity be cured by the subsequent approval of the stockholders. Ib.

Any contract by which a corporation owing duties to the public disables itself from performing those duties without the consent of the State is void. Ib.

There are certain cases where good faith requires that the executed contracts of a corporation, though originally *ultra vires*, should be permitted to stand, but this principle does not prevent a Court from refusing to enforce such portions of an *ultra vires* contract as remain unexecuted. Ib.

The directors of a mutual insurance company have power to cancel a policy of insurance at the request of the insured upon payment of all assessments then made, and their action, if done in good faith, cannot be set aside by a receiver of the company subsequently appointed. Acker v. Hite, 99.

Public policy forbids that a bank should set up the fraud of its own officers as a defence to the repayment of money due depositors. Steckel v. Bank, 17.

The Legislature has the right to prescribe the conditions under which foreign corporations may do business in this State, and a corporation failing to comply with the requirements of the statute cannot maintain an action upon any contract in the Courts of this State. Travellers' Insurance Co. v. Heath, 516.

One who has dealt with a corporation as such will not be permitted to deny his liability on a contract by alleging that the corporation has no legal existence, and, therefore, no right to sue. Spahr v. Farmers' Bank, 433.

The mere fact that a corporation has adopted an illegal by-law does not absolve its debtors from compliance with their contracts unaffected by the objectionable by-law. (C. P.) Building Association v. Young, 251.

Where the charter of a cemetery company provides that its property shall be exempt from taxation except for State purposes, the land of the company is not liable for assessments for municipal improvements. Olive Cemetery Co. v. Philadelphia, 85.

The Act of April 24, 1874, relating to the taxation of coal mining companies applies to corporations authorized to hold and lease coal lands to be worked by others, although the corporation itself is expressly prohibited by its charter from mining. Big Black Creek Improvement Co. v. Commonwealth, 74.

For the purpose of assessing the stock of a corporation for taxation, under the Act of June 7, 1879, the actual cash value of the stock is to be ascertained by the prices at which it sold between the first and fifteenth days of November, and not by the average sales during the year ending on the first Monday of November. Penna. R. R. Co. v. Commonwealth, 179.

Where a railroad track crossing is in such a condition as to cause a dangerous obstruction to travel, the company may be indicted for maintaining a nuisance. Northern Central Railway Co. v. Commonwealth, 129.

A stockholder need not produce his certificate of stock in order to entitle him to receive the amount awarded to him upon a final distribution of the assets of a corporation. The stock ledger and stock certificate book are the evidence of the ownership of the stock. (C. P.) *In re* St. Nicholas Coal Co., 403.

CORPORATION—*Continued.*
Where the certificate of stock is lost, in such case, no indemnity need be offered by the stockholder. Ib.
See BANKS AND BANKING. INSURANCE. RAILROAD COMPANIES.

COSTS. Upon the discontinuance of an attachment execution, the garnishee is entitled to all his costs, including a $3.00 attorney fee. (C. P.) Griffiths v. Stadtmuller, 348.

In an action by the sheriff to recover costs, interest is not payable on the amount of his bill. Galbraith v. Walker, 474.

Where a defendant endeavors to set off the amount of his costs against the amount recovered by the plaintiff after a trial upon an appeal from a justice of the peace, upon the ground that before appeal the defendant tendered the amount recovered, it is necessary that the fact of such tender should appear upon the record. Driesbach v. Morris, 57.

Security for costs. Where a party to proceedings in the Orphans' Court desires to compel a non-resident party to enter security for costs, the proper practice is to apply for an order by petition. Until such an order is made, there is no stay of proceedings. (O. C.) King's Estate, 207.

COUNTY. An Act of Assembly requiring a county to pay the personal debt of its ex-sheriff, contracted for bread for jail prisoners, is void. Faas v. Warner, 412.

A board of county commissioners cannot perform any valid act at a special meeting, unless each member of the board has had personal notice of the time and place of such meeting. Pike County v. Rowland, 241.

Interpretation of Art. IX. § 8 of the Constitution, relating to the increase of county and municipal indebtedness. See CONSTITUTIONAL LAW. Pike County v. Rowland, 241.

Principles governing the settlement of the accounts of the treasurer of Allegheny County in reference to the collection of tavern licenses. Kilgore v. Commonwealth, 184.

Art. V. § 5 of the Constitution secures to every county of over 40,000 inhabitants (1) The right to be a separate judicial district; (2) The right to have a resident Law Judge; and (3) The right not to have Associate Judges. Commonwealth v. Dumbauld, 369, 417, 529.

This right not to have Associate Judges cannot be taken away from such a county by a legislative enactment attaching a contiguous county of less than 40,000 inhabitants. Ib.

A county so attached to a separate judicial district does not become a part of such district by virtue of such attachment. It has the right to have Associate Judges resident in the county, and to have the President Judge of the county to which it is attached preside in its courts. Ib.

Whether the inhabitants of a county so attached are entitled to vote at the election of the President Judge who is to preside in its Courts, not decided. Ib.

COURTS. It is within the general powers of the Courts of Common Pleas to make rules regulating their practice, which are not inconsistent with the Constitution and laws of the State. Lehman v. Howley, 386.

A rule is reasonable and valid that upon the failure of a defendant in ejectment to file within a certain time an abstract of title or a statement of facts upon which he relies, the plaintiff shall be entitled to a judgment such as is warranted by the facts set out in the abstract and statement which he is also by the same rule required to file. Ib.

INDEX. 585

COURTS—*Continued.*
A teller of a national bank, incorporated under the laws of the United States, may be convicted in a State Court upon an indictment charging him with fraudulently making false entries in the books of the bank. Such an offence is forgery at common law. Commonwealth v. Luberg, 4.

Judges and Associate Judges of the Courts of Common Pleas are "officers of the Commonwealth, whose jurisdiction extends over the State." Hence, under Art. V. § 3 of the Constitution, the Supreme Court and the Judges thereof have exclusive original jurisdiction to issue writs of quo warranto to Associate Judges of Common Pleas. Commonwealth v. Dumbauld, 369, 529.

Quære, How far the provisions of the Act of May 19, 1879, that the Supreme Court shall hear new testimony and decide *de novo* a case coming before them upon appeal from an order disbarring an attorney, are consistent with that article of the Constitution, which prohibits the Supreme Court from the exercise of original jurisdiction, except in specified cases. *Ex parte* Steinman, 145.

Where a testatum writ of vend. ex. is issued to the sheriff of another county, the Court of the situs of the land sold having acquired jurisdiction of the case by the acknowledgment of the sheriff's deed conveying the estate sold, may proceed to inquire into the validity of the sale, and also to distribute the proceeds. Borlin's Appeal, 545.

The Court issuing the writ thus loses its control over the execution, and the sheriff executing it is not liable to attachment for contempt if he declines to return the proceeds of sale to the Court issuing the execution. Ib.

A sheriff is not subject to attachment for failing to pay money into Court until a rule has been taken upon him to return the writ. Ib.

What counties are entitled to be separate judicial districts. See COUNTIES. Commonwealth v. Dumbauld, 369, 417, 529.

The Court of Common Pleas sitting in equity, not the Orphans' Court, is the proper form in which trustees, claiming under a will, should seek to compel a transfer to themselves of corporate securities belonging to the trust estate. (C. P.) Stockton v. Lehigh Coal and Navigation Co., 110.

Jurisdiction to compel opening of streets, whether in Common Pleas or Quarter Sessions. (C. P.) *In re* Volkmar Street, 169.

The Court of Quarter Sessions has no jurisdiction to revise a plan made by the Board of Surveyors of Philadelphia under the Act of June 6, 1871. *In re* Plan No. 166, 43.

It is an essential element of the legal constitution of a Court of Oyer and Terminer that not less than forty-eight persons shall be summoned to serve as petit jurors. Where the precept and venire issued from the Quarter Sessions for less than that number, a trial, although conducted in other respects according to the forms of the Oyer and Terminer, is erroneous and void for want of jurisdiction. Donaldson v. Commonwealth, 393.

Although a justice of the peace has no jurisdiction of a suit instituted by a distributee to recover from an executor his distributive share, yet if such a suit is heard before a justice, with the consent of the defendant, who subsequently takes an appeal to the Common Pleas, where judgment is entered against him by default for want of an affidavit of defence under a rule of Court, the defendant will be then estopped from raising the question of jurisdiction. Montgomery v. Heilman, 537.

COVENANT. A covenant of forfeiture for non-payment of rent runs with the land. (C. P.) Evans v. Fries, 462.

Breach of covenant for quiet enjoyment. See LANDLORD AND TENANT. Lanigan v. Kille, 481.

Action for arrears of ground-rent. See LANDLORD AND TENANT.

CRIMES, CRIMINAL LAW AND PROCEDURE. A State Court has jurisdiction to punish offences by national bank officers in the course of their employment as such, when such offences were punishable at common law. Commonwealth v. Luberg, 4.

The making of fraudulent entries in the books of a national bank by the teller is forgery at common law, and is punishable as such in the State Courts. Ib.

An indictment for such an offence laid under the statute, and not charging forgery in the technical manner required by strict rules of the common law, is good under the Criminal Procedure Act. Ib.

Merely delivering poison to a person, and soliciting him to place it in the spring of another, is not an "attempt to administer poison" within the meaning of the Act of March 31, 1860, which recognizes a distinction between intent and attempt. Stabler v. Commonwealth, 409.

An assault and battery upon a constable, who had forcibly opened an outer door of a house, is justifiable even though he went there to conduct a sale under a previous levy. (Q. S.) Commonwealth v. Moreland, 272.

In order to render one liable to indictment under § 108 of the Crimes Act of 1860 for larceny as a bailee, there must have been an obligation upon his part to return the identical property to his bailor. Krause v. Commonwealth, 61.

It is no defence to an indictment against one who is the editor and publisher of a newspaper that the libellous article complained of was written and inserted by a local editor without the knowledge of the defendant, and in violation of a general order forbidding the publication of any article of a libellous nature without first submitting it to the publisher for approval. (Q. S.) Commonwealth v. Willard, 524.

In order to warrant a conviction for perjury in taking the oath of office prescribed by Art. VII. of the Constitution, it is necessary that it should appear that the influence of an elector was purchased, or that he was induced to make interest at the election for the defendant by bribery, fraud, or other illegal means, or that he was to use wicked and corrupt arts in securing the election of the candidate. Williams v. Commonwealth, 113.

The Acts of May 6, 1863, and April 10, 1872, punishing the unauthorized sale of railroad tickets (commonly known as ticket scalping) are not unconstitutional. (Q. S.) Commonwealth v. Wilson, 291.

In a trial for rape, the physician who examined the person of the woman soon after the alleged offence should, if possible, be called by the District Attorney. Whether his evidence tends to acquit or convict, it is demanded equally by the cause of humanity on the one hand or of justice on the other. Donaldson v. Commonwealth, 393.

Upon an indictment containing several assignments of perjury, the Commonwealth is required to prove by two witnesses, or one witness and corroborative evidence, at least one of such assignments; and proof by one witness of a corrupt act is not corroborative evidence of another act which was proved by a different witness. Williams v. Commonwealth, 113.

An indictment which charges a crime substantially in the language of the Act prohibiting it, or, if at com-

INDEX.

CRIMES, CRIMINAL LAW AND PROCEDURE—*Continued.*
mon law so plainly that the nature of the offence may be easily understood by the jury, is sufficient under the Criminal Procedure Act of 1860. But the accused may apply to the Court or a Judge for an order that a bill of particulars be filed, and on the trial the Commonwealth will be restricted to proof of the item specified. Ib.

It is an essential element of the legal constitution of a Court of Oyer and Terminer that not less than forty-eight persons shall be summoned to serve as petit jurors. Where a precept and venire issued from the Quarter Sessions for less than that number, a trial, though conducted in other respects according to the forms of the Oyer and Terminer, is erroneous and void for want of jurisdiction. That the number of jurors actually returned was not exhausted by challenges is immaterial. Donaldson v. Commonwealth, 393.

The failure to summon and return the full number of jurors directed by law is not such a defect as will, after trial on the merits, be cured by the Act of March 31, 1860. Ib.

The Act of 1785, providing for the discharge of untried prisoners under the two-term rule, cannot be taken advantage of by a prisoner to whom a new trial has been granted as matter of grace, and the second trial has been delayed for more than two terms. (Q. S.) Commonwealth v. McGurk, 402.

CUSTOM. See EVIDENCE.

DAMAGES. The report of viewers appointed to assess damages for the construction of a railroad must set forth the material facts which constitute the elements of damage or advantage to the owner of land affected thereby. Phila. & Erie R. R. Co. v. Cake, 72.

A report is fatally defective which omits to state that the jury had made a fair comparison of the probable advantages and disadvantages likely to result to the land-owner from the new railroad, and had made allowance for the probable advantages. Ib.

A Court has power to set aside a report of viewers when the damages found are grossly excessive. Ib.

Consequential, when recoverable for destruction of a water course. See CONSTITUTIONAL LAW. Reading v. Althouse, 22.

Measure of damages. In an action for injuries caused to the plaintiff by the negligence of the defendant, he may recover, not only for the direct expenses incurred, but also for the privation and inconvenience which he is subjected to, and for the pain and suffering he has already endured, bodily and mental, which he is likely to experience during the remainder of his life. Scott Township v. Montgomery, 389.

In an action against a carrier for refusing to deliver goods to the assignee of a bill of lading, the plaintiff may recover the profits of a bargain which is lost by the refusal to deliver. (U. S. C. C.) Schmidt v. The Pennsylvania, 351.

In case of an eviction of a purchaser or lessee of real estate by paramount title, the measure of damages, under the ordinary covenants of title, express or implied, in the absence of fraud on the vendor's or lessor's part is the consideration paid. Lanigan v. Kille, 481. (C. P.) Sharp v. Robb, 475.

The lessee cannot recover the value of improvements placed upon the premises which he had the right to remove at the end of his term. Ib.

DEBTOR AND CREDITOR. The purchaser of chattels at a sheriff's sale may leave such chattels in the possession of the defendant in the execution by

DEBTOR AND CREDITOR—*Continued.*
way of bailment without thereby rendering the chattels subject to execution as the property of the defendant. Miller v. Irvine, 142.

A voluntary conveyance to wife or children cannot be impeached by subsequent creditors as fraudulent, unless they show that the settlement was intended to defraud or hinder them. Harlan v. Maglaughlin, 343. Kimble v. Smith, 357.

It is not enough for subsequent creditors to show an intent to delay or defeat existing creditors. Ib.

Where a parent takes a conveyance of real estate from a child, partly paying for it in cash, and partly taking it in payment for an antecedent debt, the fact that the child made the conveyance with an intent to defeat or delay his creditors will not impeach the title of the father, who was ignorant of the son's purpose, and who took the conveyance in good faith. Reehling v. Byers, 359.

Business dealings between parents and children and other near relatives are not, *per se*, fraudulent, they must be treated just as are the transactions between ordinary debtors and creditors. Ib.

Creditors whose debts were contracted subsequently to a fraudulent conveyance expressly on the faith of declarations made by both grantor and grantee that the grantor retained his interest in the property conveyed may, as against the grantee, avoid the conveyance as a fraud against them. Mowry's Appeal, 363.

Where an insolvent conveys his estate in fraud of his creditors, and is subsequently adjudicated a bankrupt, no one but the assignee in bankruptcy can avoid the conveyance. (O. C.) Connell's Estate, 406.

An insolvent debtor may confess a judgment to his wife for money justly due to her for the purpose of preferring her to his other creditors. Wingerd v. Fallon, 163.

The provision in the constitution of the Stock Exchange, that if a suspended member fails to comply with all his contracts within a year, his seat shall be sold, and the proceeds of such sale be divided among his creditors, members of the association, is valid. Moxey's Appeal, 441.

The voluntary payment of a secured debt by one who is a stranger is, *prima facie,* a purchase of the debt and the accompanying security, and the question is to be determined by the manifest intention and understanding of the parties at the time. Brice's Appeal, 227.

A corporation issuing a coupon bond is in the position of a maker of a promissory note, not of the drawer of a check or bill of exchange. There is no obligation on the holder to demand payment within a reasonable time. Williamsport Gas Co. v. Pinkerton, 97.

The mere fact that a corporation has adopted an illegal by-law does not absolve its debtors from compliance with their contracts unaffected by the objectionable by-law. (C. P.) Orangeville Savings Fund Association v. Young, 251.

A judgment bond given "as collateral security for sundry notes" given by the obligor, stands as security for notes given in renewal of the original notes, which the bond was intended to secure. Shrewsbury Savings Fund's Appeal, 166.

The Act of June 11, 1879, providing for the compulsory examination of insolvent debtors is unconstitutional. Horstmann v. Kaufman, 513.

If at the time of filing an affidavit upon which to obtain an order for the examination of a defendant under this Act, it appear upon the record that the plaintiff has the means of obtaining satisfaction of his

DEBTOR AND CREDITOR—*Continued.*
judgment, the proceedings will be quashed. (C. P.) Davis v. Mowbray, 47.

Relations of Bank and Depositor. See BANKS AND BANKING. Dougherty v. Central Nat. Bank, 1. (C. P.) Shoemaker v. Kensington Nat. Bank, 420.

DECEDENTS' ESTATES. Minor children only are entitled to the benefit of the Act of April 14, 1851, providing for an exemption of $300 in favor of the widow and children of the deceased. (O. C.) Steel's Estate, 274.

A minor child of a widow is entitled to have $300 of the mother's estate set apart for his use, under the Act of April 14, 1851, as against a creditor of the estate. Himes' Appeal, 413.

A widow's claim will not be allowed where she fails to demand an appraisement. And a decree improvidently granted without an appraisement will be vacated. (O. C.) Somers's Estate, 559.

Land held in trust under an unrecorded declaration of trust is not subject to the lien of the debts of such trustee. Roberts's Appeal, 118.

Sale of real estate for payment of debts. An issue to settle questions of fact arising in the distribution of the proceeds of sale must be tried in the county having jurisdiction of the sale. Gordon's Appeal, 55.

Although an executor is not the proper person to file the petition in proceedings to charge lands with a legacy, since the proceedings should be taken by the legatee himself, yet making the executor the petitioner does not avoid the proceedings for want of jurisdiction, if the legatees are in point of fact parties. Littleton's Appeal, 188.

Legacy, when chargeable on land. See (O. C.) Wolf's Estate, 260.

Where legacies are charged upon land, the legatee is entitled to partition in order to apply for the sale of real estate. Where the petition does not in terms apply for partition, and the lands cannot be sold for the payment of legacies without it, the Court will afford the proper relief. (O. C.) Cassady's Estate, 275.

Under what circumstances the Orphans' Court will compel executors to exercise a testamentary power. (O. C.) Fraley's Estate, 127.

An executor of a mortgagee has full power and authority to satisfy a mortgage held by his testator, who cannot, by his will, place restrictions upon this power of the executor which will embarrass the mortgagee in freeing his property from the lien of the mortgage upon payment of the debt. (O. C.) Becher's Estate, 128.

Power of administrator over corporation stock standing in the name of his intestate. Pike County v. Rowland, 241.

Under what circumstances an executor is justified in paying U. S. income tax. Littleton's Appeal, 188.

Right of bank to set off a note held by them against the account of a depositor dying insolvent. See BANKS AND BANKING. (C. P.) Shoemaker v. Bank, 420.

What not sufficient evidence of contract to bind estate of decedent. Appeal of Trustees of University, 520.

The mere issuing of process against a defendant and its return tarde venit, or nihil habet, does not constitute an "action depending" within the meaning of the Act of Feb. 24, 1834, providing for a writ of scire facias to bring in the personal representatives of a deceased party to an action. Machette v. Cuyler, 471.

In an action against an executor for a debt of his testator, a plea of plene administravit is bad, and will be stricken off upon motion. (C. P.) O'Conner v. Weeks, 461.

DECEDENTS' ESTATES—*Continued.*
Rents accruing after a decedent's death are not assets for the payment of his debts, nor should they be included in an administration account. (O. C.) Burnell's Estate, 334.

Nor are payments made by an executor for interest upon a mortgage, or taxes upon his testator's estate, proper items of credit, in an administration account. Ib.

A trustee should file in the Orphans' Court a separate account of the income and principal of the trust estate. (O. C.) Rankin's Estate, 407.

Interest upon claims against the estate of a decedent is allowed in the Orphans' Court only when the estate is solvent. (O. C.) Burnell's Estate, 334.

What is sufficient proof of a claim due by the estate of a testator to his executor. (O. C.) Droste's Estate, 224.

Under what circumstances a failure to present a claim at an audit will not debar claimant from presenting it after adjudication, and before final distribution. (O. C.) Callahan's Estate, 253.

Duties of executors, where distribution is delayed by pending litigation; petition of executors for leave to sell securities and re-invest in legal investments, when refused. (O. C.) Whitaker's Estate, 420.

Abatement of legacies. See LEGACIES. Appeal of Trustees of University, 520.

Among cousins those of the half-blood take real estate equally with those of the whole blood under the intestate laws. (C. P.) Dorsey v. Van Horn, 95. (O. C.) Davis's Estate, 479.

Under what circumstances an executor allowed expenses of employing counsel in an issue devisavit vel non. (O. C.) Rankin's Estate, 407.

What is a reasonable counsel fee for services rendered to executors as such. Ib.

DEEDS. A receipt signed by one who has taken the title of real estate in his own name, setting forth that one-fourth of the purchase-money has been furnished by another, and duly witnessed, is a sufficient declaration of trust, and may be recorded as such. Roberts's Appeal, 118.

The acknowledgment of a deed by a feme covert is not sufficient, unless it be expressed in the certificate of the magistrate who took the acknowledgment, that the contents of the deed were made known to her. Enterprise Trans. Company's Appeal, 225.

A grant of an ore-bank, reserving to the grantor the right to enter and take away "a sufficient quantity of iron ore for the supply of any one furnace at the election of the grantor, his heirs and assigns, at all times hereafter," entitles the grantor to use or sell as much ore as would supply any one furnace constructed with all the modern improvements in general use. Alden's Appeal, 442.

But in determining the quantity, allowance must be made for the time when a furnace would be out of blast for repairs. Ib.

The grantor could not in a subsequent year make up a deficiency in the quantity which he might have mined in the previous years. Ib.

Voluntary settlement, when not fraudulent as to creditors. See DEBTOR AND CREDITOR. Harlan v. Maglaughlan, 353. Kimble v. Smith, 357. Reehling v. Byers, 359. (O. C.) Connell's Appeal, 406.

DEPOSITIONS, formal requisites of. See PRACTICE. Winton v. Little, 37.

DESCENT. See INTESTATE LAW.

DISCOVERY. See EQUITY. (C. P.) Portuondo v. Faunce, 539.

DIVORCE. See HUSBAND AND WIFE.

DOMICILE. There is an important difference between change of residence and change of domicile. Taney's Appeal, 564.

Where the parents of a minor were killed while emigrating with him from Pennsylvania to Kansas, in Michigan, where the minor remained with an aunt, who went from Pennsylvania to Michigan to take charge of him, and declared an intention of remaining there, and was there appointed guardian by the proper court, such minor and guardian are non-residents within the meaning of the Act of April 21, 1856. Ib.

EJECTMENT. A husband and wife in possession of a tract of land may maintain ejectment against parties in possession of a portion of the tract claiming the right to operate oil wells under an invalid lease executed by the wife. Buchanan v. Hazzard, 267.

The saving clause in § 4 of the Act of March 13, 1815, relative to the sale of unseated lands for taxes, whereby minors and insane persons whose lands have been so sold, are entitled to two years after the removal of their disability wherein to redeem the same, does not extend to cases of sales made under the 5th section to the county commissioners, and to the redemption therefrom as provided in the 6th section. Metz v. Hipps, 321.

After the lapse of thirty years there is a presumption that the County Commissioners did their duty and that the recitals in their deed are true. Brandon v. Fritz, 297.

Interfering surveys in Schuylkill County discussed. Ib.

An ejectment for unpaid purchase-money is an equitable action. Kensinger v. Smith, 311.

Ejectment is an equitable action when the plaintiff seeks by it to enforce specific performance of a contract to convey, and he must show that he has been ready, prompt, and desirous of performance, and guilty of no laches. Russell v. Baughman, 284.

Although this rule is not held so strictly against a defendant in possession, it is generally by reason of his equities, but when they are so weak as to present no substantial ground for protection, they must yield to the general rule. Ib.

The Courts of Common Pleas have the power by rule to compel a defendant in ejectment to file an abstract of title or statement of facts upon which he relies, and in default thereof, to enter judgment against him, provided the plaintiff has previously filed a similar abstract. Lehman v. Howley, 386.

But to entitle the plaintiff to judgment his abstract or statement must present a good *prima facie* case. Accordingly it was error to enter judgment against a defendant by default, when the plaintiff's abstract traced the title back to a deed of partition, but did not state the necessary parties to such deed. Ib.

Under what circumstances a conditional verdict should be given for a defendant in ejectment. Welch v. Emerson, 372.

Where a conditional verdict and judgment for the plaintiff in ejectment omitted to fix a time for the payment of the sum upon which the verdict was to be released, the Supreme Court in error amended the judgment by inserting a date before which payment should be made. Kensinger v. Smith, 311.

The landlord of premises will be permitted to intervene *pro interesse suo* when an ejectment is brought against his tenant. (C. P.) Rittenhouse v. Fetters, 221.

ELECTIONS. A commission issued to a county officer pending a contest of his election is irregular, but not void. Upon the determination of the contest in

ELECTIONS—*Continued.*
his favor the commission takes effect. No second commission is necessary. Luzerne v. Trimmer, 376.

Pending a contested election of a county officer and until its final determination on the merits, the fees belong to the last incumbent. Ib.

The decision of the Common Pleas in a contested election is final on the merits. A certiorari from the Supreme Court brings up only the record, and if its regularity be affirmed, the decision of the Court below takes effect from its date. Ib.

An Act of Assembly attaching a portion of a township to a borough for school purposes, both of taxation and election, does not violate the constitutional provision that electors shall reside within their election district. Colvin v. Beaver, 396.

Power of Court of Equity to supervise corporate election. See CORPORATION. (C. P.) Raynor v. Beatty, 201.

Bribery at elections. See CRIMES. Williams v. Commonwealth, 113.

EMINENT DOMAIN. See DAMAGES.

EQUITABLE EJECTMENT. See EJECTMENT.

EQUITY. A bill to compel the extinguishment of a ground-rent, when dismissed. (C. P.) Skelly v. Ogden, 365.

Discovery. The plaintiff must establish his right to the subject matter of a suit before he is entitled to discovery. (C. P.) Portuondo v. Faunce, 539.

Account. A court of equity has jurisdiction to decree an account of iron ore unlawfully taken from the hands of the plaintiff. Alden's Appeal, 442.

Marshalling of securities. Where three lots of ground are subject to a common incumbrance, and are sold at different times, the lot last conveyed becomes primarily liable for the entire incumbrance, and if the holder of the encumbrance releases it from the lien of the encumbrance, the other lots are released by operation of law. Amanda Martin's Appeal, 484.

Subrogation. The voluntary payment of a secured debt by one who is a stranger is *prima facie* a purchase of the debt and the accompanying security, and is determined by the manifest intention and understanding of the parties at the time. Brice's Appeal, 227.

Where the separate real estate of A. and C. was sold by the sheriff in the order named, and judgment against A. and C. jointly, was awarded payment out of the fund produced by the sale of A.'s estate, the fact that it is shown by parol that C. was principal and A. surety, does not entitle A. or his judgment creditors to subrogation upon the fund produced by the sale of C.'s land. Indiana County Bank's Appeal, 270.

Unincorporated societies. A Court of Equity has power to restore a member unlawfully expelled from an unincorporated society. (C. P.) Schassberger v. Staendel, 379.

Fraud, Constructive. Confidential relation. See ATTORNEY AND CLIENT. (C. P.) Lockhard v. McKinley, 11. (U. S. S. C.) Baker v. Humphrey, 13.

A husband claiming to have been defrauded of his marital rights by an ante-nuptial settlement made by his wife, must act promptly, and cannot be permitted to make several experiments in litigation on different and inconsistent grounds. Hidell's Appeal, 212.

Specific performance. A plaintiff in assumpsit is not entitled to a conditional verdict to enforce specific performance of a verbal agreement to convey land, unless he clearly proves a strict compliance with all the terms of the agreement on his own part. Naftzinger v. Roth, 493.

A covenant to mine a certain quantity of ore will

EQUITY—*Continued.*
not be specifically enforced in equity, since an action at law for damages is an adequate remedy. Koch and Balliet's Appeal, 343.

Injunction. Although a Court of Equity may enjoin to stay waste, it cannot summarily appoint a receiver of an oil well. Enterprise Transportation Co.'s Appeal, 225. Emerson and Wall's Appeal, 227.

Injunction to restrain trade-mark, when granted. See TRADE-MARK. (C. P.) White v. Schlect, 77.

The performance of an opera upon the stage gives no right to print the music, and an attempt to print will be restrained by injunction. (C. P.) Gilbert v. Bacher, 14.

An injunction will be granted against one maintaining a nuisance in the shape of a privy well, the percolations from which corrupt a well of drinking water upon the plaintiff's premises. (C. P.) Dill v. Haugh, 417.

An injunction will not be issued against the maintenance of a powder magazine in an isolated spot, though it is in the neighborhood of a large city. Dilworth's Appeal, 133.

A Court of Equity has no jurisdiction in ordinary cases to enjoin the sale of real estate upon the ground that the defendant in the execution has no title in the same. Wiser's Appeal, 508.

An injunction will be issued to prevent the unlawful expulsion of a member of an unincorporated society. (C. P.) Powell v. Abbott, 231.

Injunction to restrain the collection of a tax. (C. P.) Albrecht v. Lane, 377.

Injunction when granted to protect a railroad in the use of a right of way over the road of another company. (U. S. C. C.) Junction R. R. Co. v. Pennsylvania R. R. Co., 277.

Injunction to restrain the Filbert Street extension of the Penna. R. R. Co. refused. Duncan's Appeal, 436.

A special injunction will be dissolved, where the plaintiff fails to prosecute the suit for more than a year after the granting of the injunction. (C. P.) White v. Schlect, 77.

A Court of Equity, not the Orphans' Court, is the proper forum in which a testamentary trustee, or an executor, should proceed to enforce a duty due to the estate of an equitable nature. (C. P.) Stockton v. Nav. Co., 110.

EQUITY PRACTICE. Filing an answer and proceeding to proof is not waiver of objection to the jurisdiction of a Court of Equity, such objection may be taken advantage of even at final hearing. Wiser's Appeal, 508.

Where a party in equity relies upon the statute of another State as the foundation of his right, such statute should be recited at length in the pleadings; a statement of its legal effect is not sufficient. (C. P.) Stockton v. Nav. Co., 110.

The effect of a demurrer to a bill as an admission of every fact well pleaded does not cure a defect such as this. Ib.

A witness is bound to attend before an examiner until his examination is completed by signing, and if he refuse his attendance will be compelled by appropriate process. (O. C.) Hook's Estate, 320.

In appeals from preliminary injunctions, the Supreme Court do not usually pass on the merits of the case, but except in those instances where it is very evident that the Court below has been in error, continues the injunction. Truby's Appeal, 551.

ERRORS AND APPEALS. Where the same party appeals from a decree of the Orphans' Court upon various claims against the estate of which he

ERRORS AND APPEALS—*Continued.*
is administrator, it is improper to take a separate appeal upon the subject-matter of each separate claim. As there is but one final decree, there can be but one appeal therefrom by the same party. Roberts's Appeal, 118.

One writ of error cannot be taken to separate judgments in two actions arising out of the same facts, and tried together on the same evidence. In such a case the writ will be quashed. Cauley v. Pittsburgh, C. & St. L. R. W. Co., 505.

An appeal taken from a decree in divorce proceedings more than one year after the entering of the decree will be quashed. Mortimer's Appeal, 313.

Bail in error. A recognizance of bail in error, defective in form, may derive validity from the consent, either express or implied, of the parties to be affected by it. Allen v. Kellam, 93.

Under what circumstances the approval of bail in error will be vacated. Kaufman v. Hirsch, 347.

What the subject of writ of error or appeal. No appeal lies to a refusal of the Court below to open or vacate a decree in divorce. Kepner's Appeal, 44. Mortimer's Appeal, 313.

A writ of error should not be taken to a judgment entered upon a single issue prior to a trial upon other issues of fact raised by the pleadings. Schriver v. Eckenrode, 161.

What cannot be assigned for error. The failure of a witness to sign his deposition cannot be assigned for error in the Supreme Court when no point was made upon it in the Court below. Winton v. Little, 37.

Where there is no evidence of fraud in a case it is error to submit the question to the jury; but if it does not appear affirmatively that the party complaining was injured by such submission, a reversal will not be granted. Louchheim v. Henzey, 571.

Where the Court below has in the exercise of its sound discretion refused a new trial, this Court will not review such decision. Ib.

Assignments of error. Form of. In conformity with Rule XXIII. of the Supreme Court, the points submitted to the Court below, and the answers of the Court must be quoted in *totidem verbis* in the specification of error. Monroe v. Monroe, 8.

Assignments of error which contain merely a memorandum of the names of witnesses whose testimony has been erroneously received or rejected are not in accordance with Rule XXIV., and will be disregarded. Royse v. May, 104. Yeager v. Fuss, 557.

Where the requisites of Rule XXIV. as to the form of assignments of error are disregarded, the Supreme Court of its own motion will enter a non-pros. Dietrick v. Addams, 492.

Other matters. In appeals from preliminary injunctions the Supreme Court do not usually pass on the merits of the case, but except in those instances in which it is very evident that the Court below has been in error, continues the injunction. Truby's Appeal, 550.

The decision of the Common Pleas in a contested election case upon the merits is final. A certiorari to the Supreme Court brings up only the record, and if its regularity is affirmed, the decision of the Court below takes effect from its date. Luzerne v. Trimmer, 376.

Appeal from an order of Court disbarring an attorney. See ATTORNEY-AT-LAW. *Ex parte* Steinman, 145.

Right of a defendant paying money under an execution to recover it back upon reversal of the judgment. See ASSUMPSIT. Ins. Co. v. Heath, 516.

ERRORS AND APPEALS—*Continued.*
In Philadelphia County an action of debt upon the bond of bail in error should be in the Court of Common Pleas where the original judgment was obtained. (C. P.) Lukens v. Bryson, 540.

ESTOPPEL. A mortgagee is not estopped from showing that a purchase-money mortgage was executed upon a day subsequent to its date in order that its lien may be preserved by its recording within sixty days of its execution. Parke v. Neely, 193.

Where a woman, upon the eve of marriage, makes a will with the consent of her intended husband, he is estopped from setting up the subsequent marriage as a revocation of its provisions. Lant's Appeal, 209.

A bank is estopped from denying the title of a depositor to moneys deposited in his own name. Lock Haven Bank v. Mason, 265.

The holder of the legal title to real estate who permits his grantor to obtain money upon the faith of statements that the equitable title is in such grantor, is estopped from setting up his legal title against such creditors of the grantor. Mowry's Appeal, 362.

Matters of estoppel *in pais* are not admissible in evidence when the question of estoppel has not been raised upon the pleadings. Knight v. Ins. Co., 501.

Under what circumstance parties will be estopped from questioning the jurisdiction of the Court. Montgomery v. Heilman, 537.

Where a feigned issue is awarded by an Orphans' Court to the Common Pleas of the wrong county, and there tried and the judgment upon the feigned issue affirmed in the Supreme Court, the parties are not thereby estopped from applying for an issue in the proper county. Gordon's Appeal, 55.

EVICTION. Measure of damages for. See LANDLORD AND TENANT. Lanigan v. Kille, 481.

EVIDENCE. Testimony taken under a commission is subject to the interpretation of the jury in the same manner as parol evidence, and is not to be regarded as an admission or estoppel of the party calling the witness. Moulor v. Ins. Co., 81.

Letters rogatory, what a sufficient execution of, answer of witness made in foreign language. (C. P.) Zanssig v. Telegraph Co., 510.

The laws of another State when different from those of Pennsylvania must be proved as a matter of fact. Boughton v. Bank, 519.

Witness, when not compelled to give evidence which might be used against himself in a criminal proceeding. Horstmann v. Kaufman, 513.

Matters of estoppel *in pais* are not admissible in evidence when the question of estoppel has not been raised on the pleadings. Knight v. Ins. Co., 501.

In divorce proceedings the cross-interrogatories must be cross-examination strictly, and should be put immediately after the witness has answered the interrogatories in chief, and in case explanation of the interrogatories is necessary it should be made by the examiner. (C. P.) Bell v. Bell, 509.

Rule for production of books and papers. See PRACTICE. (C. P.) Thompson v. Taylor, 169.

Evidence of intimacy of relation between parties to show motive for refusing confidence is not irrelevant. Wright v. Funck, 249.

Res Gestæ. In an action against a railroad for causing a fire through a defective spark-arrester upon an engine, evidence is admissible to show that the same engine had caused numerous other fires. Phila. & Read. R. R. Co. v. Schultz, 148.

Declarations of agent, when binding upon principal. A bank cashier's representations, made at the time of receiving bonds for safe-keeping, that the bank took as good care of securities so deposited as they did of their own securities, are not admissible to vary the effect of a written receipt given to the depositor. Comp v. Carlisle Bank, 453.

A railroad company is not bound by the declarations of a brakesman as to matters out of the line of his duty. (C. P.) Coller v. Pass. R. W. Co., 477.

In an action against the lessee of a railroad, declarations made by the resident engineer of the company constructing the road are not admissible to show the defective condition of the road. Balt. and Ohio R. R. Co. v. Sulphur Spring School District, 568.

Declarations as to the defective condition of a machine, made immediately after an accident by a servant, are not admissible in an action against the master, unless accompanied by an admission of knowledge of the defect existing before the accident. Baker v. Allegheny Valley R. R. Co., 337.

Under what circumstances the declarations of an agent exceeding his authority are not admissible against his principal. Whitney v. Lake, 137.

Custom, proof of. What a sufficient proof of a custom upon the part of life insurance companies to receive payment of premiums after the time of their falling due. Girard Life Ins. Co. v. Mutual Life Ins. Co., 425.

Parol evidence, when admissible to vary writing. Evidence is admissible to show that the defendant, an unlearned man, signed a judgment note, and subsequently agreements for amicable revivals of judgment, upon the faith of false representations of the nature of the instruments which he was signing made to him by the plaintiff. Monroe v. Monroe, 8.

Evidence is admissible to show, in an action upon a promissory note, that the maker, an unlearned man, signed the same upon the faith of representations made by the payee that the instrument was a receipt for money then paid to the defendant. Resh v. Bank, 21.

Parol evidence is admissible to show that a mortgage was executed upon a different day from that which it was dated, even though the effect of the evidence be to give the mortgage a lien which otherwise it would not have. Parke v. Neely, 193.

Under what circumstances parol representations made by a bank cashier, will not be admitted to vary the effect of a written receipt given by the bank for securities left for safe-keeping. Comp v. Carlisle Bank, 453.

Witnesses, competency of. A principal, when released from all liability growing out of an action against a surety, is a competent witness for the surety. Evans v. Jenks, 139.

A surviving partner and vendor of a chattel, when released by his vendee from liability, on his implied warranty of title, is a competent witness for the vendee in an action brought against the latter upon an adverse title. Wright v. Funck, 249.

Who is an "assignor of thing or contract in action" within the meaning of the Act of April 15, 1869. Ewing v. Ewing, 489.

EXECUTION. A Court of Equity has no jurisdiction to restrain by injunction a creditor from levying upon land in which he avers that his debtor has an interest. Wiser's Appeal, 508.

A capias ad satisfaciendum cannot be lawfully issued against a married woman upon a judgment obtained against her and her husband for a joint conversion of personal property during her coverture. (Q. S.) Commonwealth ex rel. Barron v. Keeper of County Prison, 314.

EXECUTION—*Continued.*
Where real estate is sold under a testatum fi. fa., the Court before whom the deed is acknowledged has jurisdiction over the distribution of the proceeds of sale. Borlin's Appeal, 545.

An execution may be issued in the Common Pleas against the personal estate of the defendant upon a transcript of a judgment of a magistrate. (C. P.) Weir v. Lawrence, 207.

Where goods are sold under a judgment waiving the benefit of the $300 exemption law, and the proceeds do not amount to $300, a landlord, whose lease contains no waiver of exemption, has no claim upon such proceeds. (C. P.) Frick v. McClain, 32.

Attachment-execution. Where on its face a writ of attachment embraces nothing but the defendant's interest, or his distributive share in the personal estate of the decedent in the administrator's hand, and the return of service shows no attachment of land or interest therein, the administrator being admittedly not in possession of the land, the writ and service do not bind the defendant's interest in real estate. Roth's Appeal, 398.

Goods of a defendant left for storage with a warehouseman at a stipulated sum per month, cannot be made the subject of an attachment-execution. Lennig's Appeal, 503.

In order to render goods liable to an attachment, the party in whose possession they are must have such a fixed title or interest that they cannot be taken from him. Such has been the uniform construction of the Act since 1819. Ib.

A motion to dissolve an attachment-execution, after plea filed, comes too late. (C. P.) Backer v. Saurman, 403.

Upon the discontinuance of an attachment-execution, a garnishee is entitled to full costs, including a $3.00 attorney fee. (C. P.) Griffitts v. Stadtmuller, 348.

Under what circumstances a garnishee will be permitted to pay money into court. (C. P.) Fuller v. Bleim, 574.

Interpleader. A title to goods held under an execution acquired subsequent to the levy for a full consideration and without notice, cannot be made the subject of an interpleader. (C. P.) Rodgers v. Douglass, 191.

Where there are several executions, the sheriff cannot postpone the sale without the consent of all the plaintiffs. If the sale be wrongfully postponed, the sheriff cannot claim the benefit of the Interpleader Act. (C. P.) Schofield v. Casselberry, 95.

The city of Philadelphia must file a bond when she claims articles levied upon by the sheriff. (C. P.) City v. Hitner, 541.

Under what circumstances a claimant will be permitted to file his own bond. (C. P.) Phillips v. Quigley, 511. (C. P.) Vent v. Pashley, 559.

When claimant will be permitted to file his bond and narr. nunc pro tunc. (C. P.) Kiker v. Weightman, 274.

Effect of sale. A purchaser of chattels at a fair sheriff's sale may leave them in the possession of the defendant in the execution without liability to be taken in execution by the creditors of such defendant. Miller v. Irvine, 142.

Distribution. In order that the claims of laborers may be a lien upon a fund under the Act of April 9, 1872, notice in writing of the claims must be given to the officer executing the writ before the sale of the property. It is incumbent upon the claimant to prove that such notice was given. Stichter v. Malley, 28.

A judgment entered in an amicable action for wages

EXECUTION—*Continued.*
due miners and laborers, and execution thereon, is not sufficient notice to the officer executing the writ. Ib.

A demand for an issue of fact under the Act of April 26, 1846, in a distribution by an auditor is properly refused if the disputed facts are immaterial. Amanda Martin's Appeal, 484.

While it is a general rule that a purchaser at sheriff's sale need not look beyond the records, the rule is not without exceptions. Parke v. Neely, 193.

It is the duty of a purchaser at sheriff's sale under a judgment obtained subsequent to the record of a purchase-money mortgage recorded more than sixty days after its date, and subsequent to prior liens of record, to ascertain *aliunde*, if necessary, that the mortgage was actually executed more than sixty days before the date of its record, particularly if there are facts appearing on the face of the record to put him on inquiry, otherwise he takes title subject to the mortgage. Ib.

Creditors whose claims were liens on the land at the time of a sheriff's sale, and were discharged by the sale, and the owner of the land sold, can alone participate in the distribution of the proceeds. Rudy's Appeal, 308.

Where the judgment upon which a sale is made is not reached in the distribution of the proceeds, the costs of the judgment will not be allowed out of the fund. (C. P.) Grayson v. Hangstorfer, 333.

Under what circumstances the costs of an audit will be imposed upon a claimant unsuccessfully demanding part of the fund. Ib.

Subrogation. See EQUITY. Indiana County Bank's Appeal, 270.

Marshalling of securities. See EQUITY. Amanda Martin's Appeal, 484.

EXEMPTION. See DECEDENTS' ESTATES. EXECUTION.

FEES, for tavern licenses in Allegheny County, when and how payable. Kilgore v. Commonwealth, 184.

FEME SOLE TRADER. See HUSBAND AND WIFE.

FEIGNED ISSUE. See EXECUTION. ESTOPPEL.

FINDER OF CHATTEL. The finder of lost property has a valid title to it against all but the true owner. But property is not lost in the sense of the rule, if the surroundings evidence that it was intentionally deposited where found, and forgotten by the owner; in such case, the proprietor of the premises where it was found is entitled to its custody against the finder. Hamaker v. Blanchard, 331.

Where money is found on the floor of a room in a hotel common to all classes of persons, no presumption arises that it is the property of a guest, and the innkeeper cannot claim possession from the finder. Ib.

FOREIGN ATTACHMENT. In foreign attachment a bond may be given by the garnishee to the sheriff, with surety to be approved by the Court, conditioned for the return of the goods attached or payment of the debt, under the Act of June 13, 1836, § 50, and it is the duty of the sheriff thereupon to withdraw from the possession of the goods. (C. P.) Reis v. Junker, 296.

FOREIGN GUARDIAN. See GUARDIAN AND WARD.

FORGERY. Ratification of. See RATIFICATION. (C. P.) Brooke v. Harman, 462.

See CRIMES.

FRAUD. Catching bargain. The purchase of a legacy payable at a future date at a usurious dis-

FRAUD—*Continued.*
count will be set aside in equity, notwithstanding the party imposed upon was of full age. (O. C.) Bogle's Estate, 256.

Confession of judgment by an insolvent husband in favor of his wife, when not evidence of fraud. Wingerd v. Fallon, 163.

It is not fraudulent for an insolvent son to confess a judgment to his mother for money due to her, although the debt was barred by the Statute of Limitations. (C. P.) Grayson v. Hangstorfer, 333.

Fraud, constructive. See EQUITY.

Rule in Twyne's Case. See DEBTOR AND CREDITOR.

FRAUDS, STATUTE OF. An action for breach of a parol contract concerning lands may be maintained, although specific performance of the contract could not be enforced. Schriver v. Eckenrode, 161.

What sufficient evidence of a gift followed by possession to be submitted to the jury. Campbell v. Braden, 487.

A plaintiff in assumpsit is not entitled to a conditional verdict to enforce specific performance of a verbal agreement to convey land unless he clearly proves a strict compliance with all the terms of the agreement on his own part. Naftzinger v. Roth, 493.

FRAUDULENT CONVEYANCES. See DEBTOR AND CREDITOR.

GIFT of land, parol, what sufficient evidence of, to take case out of the Statute of Frauds. Campbell v. Braden, 487.

Gift, from husband to wife, when not fraudulent as to creditors. See DEBTOR AND CREDITOR.

GROUND-RENT. See LANDLORD AND TENANT.

GUARANTY, meaning of word, in life insurance policy. See INSURANCE. Knight v. Ins. Co., 501.

GUARDIAN AND WARD. Under what circumstances a guardian appointed in a foreign State may interfere with his ward's estate in Pennsylvania. (O. C.) Rice's Estate, 255. Taney's Appeal, 564.

HABEAS CORPUS. Where a married woman was imprisoned under a ca. sa. issued upon a judgment obtained before a magistrate against her and her husband for a joint conversion of personal property during her coverture, and the twenty days allowed by law for a writ of certiorari or appeal has elapsed, and no other means exists of directly reviewing the legality of the ca. sa., the Quarter Sessions has jurisdiction to discharge her upon a habeas corpus. Commonwealth ex rel. Barron v. Keeper, 314.

See PARENT AND CHILD.

HALF-BLOOD. See DECEDENTS' ESTATES. INTESTATE LAW.

HIGHWAY. See ROADS, HIGHWAYS, AND BRIDGES.

HUSBAND AND WIFE. Where a woman upon the eve of marriage obtained her intended husband's verbal consent that she might dispose of her property by will or otherwise as she pleased, and executed a will the day before her marriage whereby she made a liberal provision for him, and gave the residue of her estate to her relatives, friends, and to charities; although the will was revoked by her subsequent marriage, yet nevertheless it might on her death take effect in equity as an ante-nuptial settlement. Lant's Appeal, 209.

Under what circumstances an ante-nuptial settlement will not be set aside upon the ground that it is in fraud of the marital rights of the husband. Hidell's Appeal, 212.

A man, indebted to his wife and other creditors,

HUSBAND AND WIFE—*Continued.*
may lawfully confess in her favor a judgment which will secure to her the money due her in preference to the other creditors. Wingerd v. Fallon, 163.

Under what circumstances a voluntary settlement by a husband in favor of his wife will not be decreed fraudulent as to creditors. See DEBTOR AND CREDITOR.

Right of dower, how affected by proceedings in partition in the Orphans' Court. (O. C.) Bauer's Estate, 336, 576.

In order to entitle a married woman to the privileges and immunities of being a feme sole trader under the Acts of 1718 and 1825, it is not enough to show that the husband is living separate from the wife and failed to support her; it must be shown that he has deserted her, or wilfully neglects or refuses to provide for her. (C. P.) Mayberry v. Railway Co., 404.

Where a married woman loans money to her husband and takes from him a judgment to secure the same in the name of a trustee, she has the power by writing made with the husband's consent in order to assist him in obtaining a new loan, to postpone the lien of her judgment to the lien of the judgment given to secure the new loan. Brown's Appeal, 329.

A release by a married woman of a right of action for injuries suffered by her through the negligence of a railway company, is not binding upon her, although she is living apart from her husband, unless it appear that she was strictly within the Acts of Assembly relating to feme sole traders. (C. P.) Mayberry v. Railway, 404.

Under what circumstances a married woman deserted by her husband can prosecute an action in her own name. (C. P.) Winkler v. Pemberton, 419.

Under what circumstances and conditions a married woman will be permitted to appoint an attorney to prosecute a suit in the joint name of husband and wife without the consent of her husband. (C. P.) Irvine v. Dowling, 366.

A married woman can pledge her personal estate to secure the debt of her husband, and will be bound by the terms of the contract under which the pledge was made as to sale and notice. Dando's Appeal, 5.

A married woman having the power to mortgage her lands to secure the future indebtedness of her husband may give the money raised by a mortgage of her separate estate directly to him. Daubert v. Eckert, 87.

Who has no status to contest the validity of a building association mortgage given by a married woman. (C. P.) Kingsessing Association v. Roan, 15.

The acknowledgment of a deed by a feme covert is not good unless it be expressed in the certificate of the officer who took the acknowledgment, that the contents of the deed were made known to her. Enterprise Transportation Company's Appeal, 225.

Where the original certificate of acknowledgment is defective, it cannot be cured by a subsequent certificate. Ib.

A deed or lease under seal of a married woman of her separate real estate in which her husband does not join is absolutely void, and cannot be validated by evidence of the husband's consent. Nor can the married woman be estopped by the receipt of the consideration, nor by any subsequent acts of ratification other than by a deed duly executed and acknowledged. Buchanan v. Hazzard, 267.

A married woman deserted and left unprovided for by her husband, may, by virtue of the Act of May 4, 1855, execute a deed efficacious to convey her real estate without the joinder of her husband, and without having previously obtained a decree authorizing her

HUSBAND AND WIFE—*Continued.*
to act as a feme sole trader. Elsey *v.* McDonald, 267.

As a personal obligation the bond of a married woman is void, but where given to secure the purchase-money of land sold to her, it may be enforced against such land. It makes no difference whether the bond be accompanied by a mortgage or not, or whether the judgment be by confession under a warrant of attorney or by suit, in either case the land may be charged. Shnyder *v.* Noble, 182.

A capias against a wife charged with slander, should also include the husband. (C. P.) Hurst *v.* Smith, 461.

A capias ad satisfaciendum cannot be lawfully issued against a married woman upon a judgment obtained against her and her husband for a joint conversion of personal property during her coverture. (Q. S.) Commonwealth *v.* Keeper, 314.

Where a husband acts for his wife in the ordinary management of her property with her knowledge and without any dissent on her part, he will be presumed to have acted as her duly appointed agent, and she will be estopped from subsequently claiming to recover interest moneys so received by him. Early *v.* Rolfe, 106.

Where a husband seeks to recover damages for an act of violence committed upon his wife, whereby he has lost her company and services, and put to expense for medical attendance, case is the proper form of action. Drew *v.* Peer, 33.

A husband is not liable upon a contract of his wife made before marriage for the lease of a house, which the wife continues to occupy after marriage, but in which the husband only visits her. Biery *v.* Ziegler, 154.

The moral obligation of a married woman to repay money borrowed by her is a sufficient consideration for a note given by a third person to secure such indebtedness. Leonard *v.* Duffin, 155.

Divorce. Under what circumstances a respondent in divorce will not be permitted to file an answer nunc pro tunc. (C. P.) Schneider *v.* Schneider, 253.

No appeal lies from the refusal of a Court below to open or vacate a decree in divorce. Mortimer's Appeal, 313. Kepner's Appeal, 44.

Examination of witnesses before an examiner, how to be conducted. (C. P.) Bell *v.* Bell, 509.

Cross Interrogatories, scope of. (C. P.) Bell *v.* Bell, 509.

INFANTS. Right of custody of. See PARENT AND CHILD. See GUARDIAN AND WARD.

INNKEEPER. When money is found on the floor of a room in an inn, common to all classes of people, no presumption arises that it is the property of a guest, and the innkeeper cannot claim possession from the finder. Hamaker *v.* Blanchard, 331.

INSURANCE. Fire. A policy upon a steam mill containing a provision, that if the insured should keep or have upon the premises any petroleum, benzine, etc., the policy should be avoided, is not vitiated by the fact that the insured having obtained permission to make repairs, used a small quantity of benzine for about two weeks in cleaning the machinery, and some weeks afterwards the mill was destroyed by a fire occurring from other causes. Mears *v.* Humboldt Ins. Co. 108.

Such a provision in a policy must have a reasonable interpretation, such as was probably contemplated by the parties at the time the contract was entered into. What was intended to be prohibited was the

VOL. IX.—38

INSURANCE—*Continued.*
habitual keeping or using of such articles, not their exceptional use for repairs, when permission to repair had been granted. Ib.

General words in a policy are to be limited in their application by reference to preceding particular words, and the Court will not take judicial notice that an article not specially prohibited in its nature comes within a general prohibition. The question is one of fact which must be submitted to a jury. Ib.

The right of a company to cancel a policy and thus terminate the contract for various acts of the insured is one which has constantly been recognized. Acker *v.* Hite, 99.

When the insured surrenders his policy and it is marked cancelled, from that moment he ceases to be a member of a mutual company, though he continues liable for assessments for losses which accrued while he was a member. Ib.

The relation of one insured in a mutual company is dual: (1) as a member of the company, a corporator; (2) as a contracting party with the corporation; as a corporator simply, he is bound by the acts of the majority, and his corporate rights are subject to the authority of the corporation. As one insured by contract with the company, his rights stand entirely free from such control. (C. P.) Bradfield *v.* Union Mutual Ins. Co., 436.

Hence a by-law authorizing a company to rebuild, passed subsequently to the date of a policy, binds one in his relation as corporator, but does not affect his rights under the policy to recover the amount insured in cash. Ib.

Life. Where an insurance company issues two policies upon the life of the same person, it is not necessary for the representatives of the insured to furnish separate proofs of death under each policy. Girard Life Ins. Co. *v.* Mutual Life Ins. Co., 425.

Even if circumstances existed which would justify a company in demanding separate proofs of death, such demand must be made without delay. Ib.

Where payment of a policy is resisted upon the ground of a forfeiture for non-payment of premiums, no proofs of death are demandable. Ib.

Where a mutual company has to the credit of a policy dividends more than sufficient to pay a maturing premium, it is bound so to appropriate the money in order to prevent a forfeiture for non-payment of the premium. Ib.

A custom to receive defaulted premiums within a few days after their falling due is good, if sufficiently proved. What sufficient proof of such a custom. Ib.

A guaranty, in an application for a policy, that the insured will not contract any pernicious habits is equivalent to a warranty; and, in case of violation of such guaranty, the policy is properly forfeited under a stipulation that, if any of the statements in the application are false, the policy shall be forfeited. Knight *v.* Mutual Life Ins. Co., 501.

It is not within the power of a general agent of an insurance company by declarations that the insured has complied with his contract, and that his policy is good to estop the company from setting up as against one who purchased the policy in the faith of such assurance, that the policy is void because of misrepresentations on the part of the insured at the time of issue of such policy. Ib.

The existence of a disease in one insured as contradistinguished from a predisposition or tendency to it, is a fact which it is error to withdraw from the jury. Moulor *v.* American Life Ins. Co., 61.

INTEREST. The mere absence of the creditor, or the death of a mortgagee without the appointment of an administrator, does not stop the running of interest nor exempt the mortgagor from its payment. His only remedy is by payment into court under the Act of April 3, 1851. (C. P.) Bouillou's Estate, 14.

Money received by one joint tenant for the sale of his co-tenant's interest in their joint estate is trust money; the rules therefore which forbid the charging of interest upon interest as between debtor and creditor have no application. Roberts's Appeal, 118.

Interest is not chargeable upon claims against the insolvent estates of decedents. (O. C.) Burnell's Estate, 334.

Interest is not chargeable on an advancement. Porter's Appeal, 457.

Interest is not chargeable on costs. Galbraith *v.* Walker, 474.

INTERPLEADER. See EXECUTION.

INTESTATE LAW. Among cousins those of the half-blood inherit equally with those of the whole blood. (C. P.) Dorsey *v.* Van Horn, 95. (O. C.) Davis's Estate, 479.

See DECEDENTS' ESTATES.

ISSUE. Demand for, when not granted. Amanda Martin's Appeal, 484.

Issue, feigned. See FEIGNED ISSUE.

JUDGES. See QUO WARRANTO.

JUDGMENT. Confessed judgment in favor of relative, when not fraudulent as to other creditors. See FRAUD.

While a judgment entered on warrant of attorney has the same effect as if on the verdict of a jury while t stands, such a judgment is not necessarily a waiver f the results of adjudication, and, where a defence is it up on the ground of public policy, the Court should open the confessed judgment and let the defendant into a defence. Tebay & Bredin's Appeal, 151.

A note whose consideration is the stifling of a prosecution for forgery is void, and the entry of judgment thereon by virtue of a warrant of attorney does not make the contract executed. Ib.

Under what circumstances a confessed judgment will be opened after two revivals, upon the ground of fraudulent imposition upon the defendant. Monroe *v.* Monroe, 8.

Under what circumstances proceedings will not be stayed upon a judgment entered upon a bond, although judgment in a suit on the accompanying mortgage has been refused for want of a sufficient affidavit of defence. (C. P.) Longstreth *v.* Thornton, 206.

The lien of a judgment when lost by lapse of time cannot be revived against a terre tenant by a parol agreement. Rudy's Appeal, 308.

The power of the Court under the Act of March 14, 1876, to decree the entry of satisfaction of a judgment upon due proof that it has been fully paid, is strictly limited to cases of actual payment in full. Gifford's Appeal, 246.

Where a judgment is satisfied upon the record by one who has the *prima facie* right to control it, one who subsequently advances money upon the faith of such satisfaction will be protected against the subsequent action of the Court in striking off such entry of satisfaction at the instance of the equitable assignee of the judgment. Harner's Appeal, 101.

JURISDICTION, conflict of. See COURTS.

When party estopped from objecting to want of. See COURTS. Montgomery *v.* Heilman, 537.

JUSTICE OF THE PEACE. A justice of the peace has no jurisdiction of a suit begun by a dis-

JUSTICE OF THE PEACE—*Continued.*
tributee in the Orphans' Court to recover from an executor his distributive share. Montgomery *v.* Heilman, 537.

But where the defendant expressly agrees that such an action should be tried before a justice, and the same was tried and resulted in a judgment for the plaintiff, from which the defendant appealed to the Common Pleas, it is too late for the defendant to raise the question of jurisdiction after judgment has been taken for want of an affidavit of defence. Ib.

Upon an appeal from a Magistrate's Court, the defendant is not bound to file an affidavit of defence unless the plaintiff puts something upon the record to show an intention to ask for judgment for want of an affidavit. (C. P.) Prichett *v.* Moss, 558.

When a defendant seeks to tax his bill of costs against the plaintiff's verdict, upon the ground that he tendered to the plaintiff before the justice of the peace as much or more than the plaintiff recovered after an appeal, it is necessary that the fact of such tender appear upon the record. Driesbach *v.* Morris, 57.

LACHES. What sufficient defence against action for specific performance. See EJECTMENT. . Russell *v.* Baughman, 284.

In applying for bill of review. See ORPHANS' COURT.

LANDLORD AND TENANT. An assault and battery by a tenant upon a constable, who had forcibly opened an outer door of a house, is justifiable even though he went there to conduct a sale under a previous levy. (Q. S.) Commonwealth *v.* Moreland, 272.

Breach of covenant for quiet enjoyment, measure of damages in action by tenant against landlord for an eviction. See DAMAGES, MEASURE OF. Lanigan *v.* Kille, 481.

If a tenant hold his lease at will or by the month, and his landlord grants that a lawful and necessary, yet offensive or dangerous factory or magazine may be erected, the tenant has not a right of action for its prevention. Dilworth's Appeal, 133.

Under what circumstances a husband is not liable for the rent of premises occupied by his wife. See HUSBAND AND WIFE. Biery *v.* Ziegler, 154.

A covenant of forfeiture of a lease for non-payment of rent, runs with the land. Confession of judgment when enforced. (C. P.) Evans *v.* Fries, 462.

A covenant in a mining lease to mine a certain quantity per annum, will not be specifically enforced in equity, but the parties will be left to their action at law. Koch & Balliet's Appeal, 343.

Where a right to mine is granted in consideration of a royalty reserved, the law implies a covenant by the grantee to work the mine with diligence so that the grantor may receive the contemplated compensation. Ib.

Distress. The goods of a stranger not exempt by some policy of law, who enters upon demised premises during the term of the tenant, without authority of the landlord, and thus remains in possession after the determination of the tenant's lease, are liable to distress for rent due by such tenant. Whiting *v.* Lake, 137.

What a sufficient averment that goods distrained for rent in arrear were upon the demised premises in the course of trade, and therefore exempt from distress. (C. P.) Blegenwald *v.* Winpenny, 542. Nass *v.* Winpenny, 542.

The goods of a renter of a room in a house are liable to distress for rent due by the tenant of the house. He is not a boarder within the exception exempting

LANDLORD AND TENANT—*Continued.*
the goods of a boarder from distress. (C. P.) Lane v. Steinmetz, 574.

Where no sale is made of goods distrained for rent, before they are replevied, it is not necessary that the constable should make an appraisement. (C. P.) Johnson v. Black, 438.

In an action against a constable for an excessive distress, the plaintiff (after an award of arbitrators in his favor and an appeal by the defendants), filed a narr. in trespass vi et armis, which set forth the tenancy, the amount of rent in arrear and the goods distrained; after this, upon the trial, the narr. could not be amended so as to deny the tenancy. Royse v. May, 104.

In such a case, the narr. not being under the Act of May 10, 1871, allowing double damages for distress where no rent is due, there can be no recovery under its provisions. Ib.

Ground-rent. In an action of covenant sur ground-rent deed, it is not a defence that the ground landlord had distrained and subsequently abandoned the distress, even though there were at that time enough goods upon the premises to have paid the rent. (C. P.) Howell v. Bateson, 463.

A ground-rent irredeemable during a life in being is not within the prohibition of the Act of April 22, 1850, § 21, prohibiting irredeemable ground-rents. (C. P.) Skelley v. Ogden, 365.

LEASE. Lease of railroad when ultra vires. See CORPORATION. (U. S. S. C.) Thomas v. West Jersey R. R. Co., 65.

LEGACY. A general legacy to a volunteer will not be entitled to exemption from abatement on the ground of its being applied to any particular object or purpose, unless there be clear and unequivocal evidence from the terms of the will that the testator intended to give it a priority. Appeal of the Trustees of the University, 520.

Where there is any valuable consideration for a testamentary gift or any right or interest is relinquished in consideration thereof, such legacy will be entitled to payment over other general legacies which are mere bounties. Ib.

Where there is a deficiency of assets after payment of debts, expenses, and specific legacies, to pay the other legacies, the rule is generally that the loss shall be borne entirely and proportionally by those pecuniary legacies which are in their nature general. An annuity charged on the personal estate is a general legacy, and in case of such deficiency, must abate rateably with other general legacies. Ib.

In order to prevent a legacy from lapsing by the death of the legatee in the lifetime of the testator, such testator must in his will declare either expressly or in terms from which it can be collected with sufficient clearness what person or persons he intended to substitute for the legatee dying in his lifetime. Ib.

Proceeding to charge a legacy upon lands. See DECEDENTS' ESTATES. Littleton's Appeal, 188.

When chargeable on lands. See DECEDENTS' ESTATES. (O. C.) Wolf's Estate, 260.

LIBEL. To deprive an attorney of his office summarily for the publication of a libel upon a man in a public capacity, or where the matter was proper for public investigation would be an infraction of the spirit, if not of the letter of Art. I. § 7 of the Constitution. *Ex parte* Steinman, 145.

See CRIMES. Commonwealth v. Willard, 524.

LICENSE. Fees for tavern licenses in Allegheny County. Kilgore v. Commonwealth, 184.

LIEN. For unpaid purchase-money, how preserved. See VENDOR AND VENDEE. Snyder's Appeal, 177.

See MECHANICS' LIENS. MUNICIPAL CLAIMS. ADMIRALTY.

LIMITATIONS, STATUTE OF. In an action upon the case against a Recorder of Deeds for negligently giving a false certificate of search, where no fraud is alleged, the Statute of Limitations begins to run from the time when the search was given, and not from the discovery of its falsity. Owen v. Western Saving Fund, 465.

As far as the running of the statute is concerned, there is no distinction between torts arising from contract, and those which arise from official malfeasance. Ib.

In order to toll the running of the Statute of Limitations, it is not essentially necessary that there should be an actual or express promise to pay. From an admission consistent with a promise to pay, the law will imply a promise without its having been actually or expressly made. Palmer v. Gillespie, 535.

Such an admission must be such a clear, distinct, and unequivocal acknowledgment of a particular debt as to remove hesitation in regard to the debtor's meaning. Ib.

The fact that a railroad crossing across a public highway has existed for twenty-four years, is no bar to an indictment for a nuisance, since the Statute of Limitations does not run against the Commonwealth. Northern Central Railway Co. v. Commonwealth, 129.

It is too late for executors to avail themselves of the plea of the Statute of Limitations, who did not suggest it at the time they were made parties to the suit six years after their testator's death, nor set it up in their answer to an amended bill six years later. Alden's Appeal, 442.

What not sufficient evidence of adverse possession to give a title to land. Campbell v. Braden, 487. Ewing v. Ewing, 489.

The saving clause in sect. 4 of the Act of March 13, 1815, whereby minors and insane persons whose unseated lands have been sold for taxes are entitled to two years after removal of their disabilities wherein to redeem the same, does not extend to sales made under sect. 5 of the Act to the County Commissioners, and to the redemption therefrom as provided in the 6th section of the same Act. Metz v. Hipps, 321.

Limitations of right to file bill of review. See ORPHANS' COURT.

LIMITED COMPANY. See PARTNERSHIP.

LUNATIC. Under what circumstances lunacy of the mortgagor is no defence to an action on a mortgage. (C. P.) Mills v. Slook, 379.

Allowance for support of lunatic, when not reduced because of diminution of income. (O. C.) McCloskey's Estate, 496.

MALICIOUS PROSECUTION. The advice of a detective is no defence to an action for malicious prosecution. (C. P.) Brietwiesser v. Stier, 112.

MANDAMUS. Where the Commissioner of Highways in the exercise of his discretion refused to grant an omnibus company a license for reasons which the Court deem unsubstantial, he will be compelled by mandamus to grant the license. (C. P.) Commonwealth v. Baldwin, 233.

MARITIME LIEN. See ADMIRALTY. (U. S. D. C.) The Norman, 543.

MARRIAGE. See HUSBAND AND WIFE.

MARRIED WOMAN. See HUSBAND AND WIFE.

MASTER AND SERVANT. In order that a receipt for goods on storage may be a warehouse receipt with the quality of negotiability, as contemplated by the Act of Sept. 24, 1866, the person issuing such receipt must be in possession of the goods in his own right and not merely an agent for a principal. Bank v. Gayley, 49.

When an act of violence is committed by a servant in the ordinary course of his employment, but not by the direct command nor assent of the master, case and not trespass is the proper form of action in which to recover damages against the master. Drew v. Peer, 33.

A master is not liable for an injury caused to his servant if a tool or machine break from an internal original fault not apparent when the tool or machine was first made or provided, or from an external apparent fault, for it is the duty of the servant to report to the master apparent defects. Baker v. Allegheny R. R. Co., 337.

But a different rule applies if the tool or machinery be perishable; the employer is bound to know that fact and it is his duty to renew such instrument at proper intervals. Ib.

The constructive knowledge of the servant does not relieve the master from acting on the constructive knowledge which is chargeable to him, nor impose upon the servant the duty of notifying the master of that which he ought to know. Ib.

A master is not liable for an injury caused to his servant through the negligence of a gang-boss, who had no general power of control but acted as foreman of workmen engaged by and furnished to him by a superintendent, whose orders he was bound to obey. Keystone Bridge Co. v. Newberry, 552.

In an action by a servant against his master in the absence of evidence of knowledge on the part of the master of the incompetency of the gang-boss, it is error to submit the question to the jury. Ib.

See PRINCIPAL AND AGENT; NEGLIGENCE.

MECHANICS' LIENS. The right to file a mechanic's claim may be waived by a stipulation in the contract under which the work was done. Long v. Caffrey, 25.

A claim for paving and curbing in front of a house is not within the mechanic's lien law. (C. P.) McIntee v. Thomas, 252.

A claim filed by a subcontractor must set forth specifically the time when and the nature and amount of materials furnished or work done; it is not sufficient to state the time of the beginning and ending of the work. Gray v. Dick, 555.

The Act of 24 March, 1849, relates only to claims filed by contractors, not to those of subcontractors. Ib.

The owner of a tract of land laid it out in ten building lots fronting on a street. Ten houses were built, in twos adjoining each other, making five blocks of two houses each, and between each block side-yards with a common partition fence. Between two of the blocks an additional space of ground of sixty feet frontage was left, with the intention of converting it into a street. This fact was not sufficient to prevent the filing of an apportioned claim against the entire lot, because at the time of beginning the work the street had not been dedicated to public use. Kline's Appeal, 26.

In the absence of fraud, materials furnished for a building on its credit, delivered at the shop of the contractor, may be made the subject of a lien, although they were delivered before the commencement of the building. Dick v. Stevenson, 411.

Where one of two joint contractors dies during the

MECHANICS' LIENS—*Continued.*
progress of the work, a claim filed against the other alone, not naming him as survivor, is good; the proceeding being in rem, it would be improper to substitute the personal representatives of the deceased. Ib.

A bill of particulars setting out the day and year of the first item, and the dates of the successive items in chronological order is a sufficient compliance with the Act of June 16, 1836. Scholl v. Gerhab, 157.

The validity of a mechanic's lien for materials is not put in issue by the pleas of non-assumpsit, payment with leave, etc., but it is a question to be taken advantage of by demurrer, or motion to strike off the lien. Ib.

The proper method of taking advantage of defects appearing upon the face of a claim is by demurrer or by motion to strike off the lien. Ib.

How long before the return-day a sci. fa. sur claim must issue in Delaware County. (C. P.) Miles v. Pleasants, 63.

The Act of June 11, 1879, authorizing the amendments of mechanics' claims is not retroactive. (C. P.) Sparr v. Walz, 64. Fahnestock v. Wilson, 386.

Alterations and repairs, lien for, when good. (C. P.) Shaffer v. Green, 144.

MINES AND MINING. Construction of reservation of right to mine. See DEED. Alden's Appeal, 442.

Mining lease construed and right to specific performance of covenant to mine a certain quantity annually considered. See EQUITY. Koch & Balliet's Appeal, 343.

MORTGAGE. Where a conveyance is accepted by a creditor in satisfaction and extinguishment of a debt, an agreement to reconvey cannot have the effect of turning the transaction into a mortgage. (O. C.) Callahan's Estate, 253.

Under what circumstances parol evidence is admissible to show that a purchase-money mortgage was executed subsequent to the day upon which it is dated for the purpose of preserving its lien. Parker. Neely, 193.

It is not material that a mortgage should appear on its face to be for purchase-money if the fact can be proved. Ib.

Effect of a sheriff's sale under a subsequent judgment upon a mortgage prior to which was a lien for unpaid taxes. (C. P.) Lea v. Brown, 418.

Power of a married woman to mortgage her separate estate and apply the proceeds of the mortgage. See HUSBAND AND WIFE. Daubert v. Eckert, 87.

The equity of a terre-tenant who has procured the payment of a mortgage, though not the possession of it, nor its satisfaction, is superior to that of the assignee for value of the mortgage, who upon the assignment made no inquiry of the mortgagor, who, by a recorded deed containing no reference to the mortgage, had sold the property to the terre-tenant. Sellers v. Benner, 88.

Under what circumstances the lunacy of the mortgagor is no defence to an action upon the mortgage. (C. P.) Mills v. Slook, 379.

A mortgagee cannot by will restrict the payment of the mortgage debt to his executors, or place upon the mortgagor an obligation to see to the application of the purchase-money. (O. C.) Becher's Estate, 128.

Payments on stock assigned as collateral security for a building association mortgage are not ipso facto payments on the mortgage. Economy Building Association v. Hungerbuehler, 218.

Who can set up invalidity of building association

MORTGAGE—*Continued.*
mortgage given by married woman. (C. P.) Kingsessing Building Association v. Roan, 15.

A terre-tenant cannot intervene in a sci. fa. upon a mortgage without leave of Court. (C. P.) Hobson v. Webster, 206.

In a suit against a mortgagor, judgment may be obtained for want of an affidavit of defence, notwithstanding the intervention of the representatives of a deceased terre-tenant. Dutill v. Sully, 573.

The heirs or devisees of a deceased terre-tenant who were not made parties to a suit are not precluded by a judgment obtained therein; they have therefore no status to complain of any irregularity in the proceedings. Ib.

Proceedings to compel satisfaction of mortgage under Act of June 11, 1879. Practice under. Sellers v. Benner, 88.

Where there is no one accessible who is authorized to enter satisfaction of a mortgage, the only method by which the mortgagee can relieve himself from the payment of interest is to pay the money into court. (C. P.) Bouillou's Estate, 14.

Under what circumstances leave will not be granted to pay money into court for the satisfaction of a mortgage under the Act of April 3, 1851. (C. P.) *In re* Kohler, 527.

Under what circumstances the Court will direct the satisfaction of a mortgage upon ex parte affidavits. (C. P.) *In re* John Gunther, 191.

Judgment upon bond pending proceedings upon accompanying mortgage when not stayed. (C. P.) Longstreth v. Thornton, 206.

Attorney's commission for collection. See ATTORNEY-AT-LAW.

MUNICIPAL CLAIMS. Lien for street improvement against suburban property. (C. P.) City v. Lukens, 348.

Assessments for street improvements are a species of taxation within the meaning of an Act of Assembly exempting a cemetery from taxation. Olive Cemetery Co. v. Philadelphia, 85.

Registration of lien for unpaid water tax containing neither location nor description of real estate is defective and insufficient to support a scire facias. Allentown v. Hower, 198.

To support a scire facias the property should be designated with such certainty as to enable the sheriff to execute the levari facias, but it is unnecessary to conform strictly to all the requisites of a mechanic's lien. The name of the contractor or material man need not be given, nor is a bill of particulars necessary. Ib.

The Act of April 21, 1858, is a general Act under which amendments are allowable when intervening rights are not prejudiced. Ib. (C. P.) City v. Wagner, 511.

What not sufficient notice to pave a footway. City of Philadelphia v. Donath, 415.

What a sufficient notice to the city solicitor of a rule to issue a sci. fa. sur municipal claim. (C. P.) City v. Wood, 347.

Where it appears from the sheriff's return to a sci. fa. sur municipal claim that the writ had not been posted upon the premises for two weeks as required by the Act of March 11, 1846, the return is fatally defective. O'Byrne v. Philadelphia, 41.

Under what circumstances proceedings upon municipal claims will be consolidated. (C. P.) City v. Tyson, 367.

Where a judgment has been reversed on account of a fatal defect in the sheriff's return to a writ of sci. fa.,

MUNICIPAL CLAIMS—*Continued.*
the effect is as if there had been no return at all, and the proper course is to issue an alias writ. Wistar v. Philadelphia, 98.

Where under such circumstances an alias writ is issued, it is not necessary to file a second affidavit that the defendant had been notified to make payment of the claim in order to entitle the plaintiff to a judgment by default. Ib.

Under what circumstances an entry of satisfaction of a claim made through mistake will be stricken off. (C. P.) City v. Thomas, 240.

MUNICIPAL CORPORATIONS. Power of the Councils of Philadelphia to provide by rule for the use of highways by omnibus lines. (C. P.) Commonwealth v. Baldwin, 233.

The taxes for the year 1877 in the city of Scranton, were not levied at the time directed by law. The Board of Appeal and Revision made numerous changes in valuation without appeal from individual taxpayers: held that the tax levy was not thereby invalidated, and that a special injunction to restrain its collection was improperly awarded. Matthews v. Scranton, 507.

Increase of debt of municipal corporations, how far restricted by the Constitution of 1874. Pike County v. Rowland, 241.

Action against municipality for negligently obstructing a highway. See NEGLIGENCE. Scranton v. Catterson, 59.

NATURALIZATION. The Act of Congress conferring the right of citizenship upon seamen who have served on board merchant vessels of the United States, does not extend to the United States naval service. (C. P.) *In re* Gormley, 96.

The Act of Congress of 1824 requires that an alien shall have declared at least three years before his admission, that it was *bona fide* his intention to become a citizen of the United States. (C. P.) *In re* Randall, 159.

Applicants must declare their intentions in such form as to show the time when the intention to become a citizen was actually formed. Ib.

A minor who has not declared his intention two years previous to his application nor proved a residence of five years, cannot be admitted to citizenship. (C. P.) *In re* Merry, 169.

NEGLIGENCE. A railroad company in constructing its road and works is only bound to bring to their execution the engineering knowledge and skill ordinarily known and practised in such works. There is no liability on its part for not constructing a culvert sufficient to pass extraordinary floods. Baltimore and Ohio R. R. Co. v. Sulphur Spring School District, 568.

The concurring negligence which when combined with the act of God produces the injury must, in order to render the defendant responsible in damages, be such as is in itself a real producing cause of the injury, and not a mere fanciful or speculative negligence, which may not have been in the least degree the cause of the injury. Ib.

Under what circumstances a canal company is not liable for the sinking of a barge while under their care near the mouth of their canal. Brady v. Delaware, etc., Canal Co., 414.

If a public road running through a township is so dangerous by reason of its proximity to a precipice that common prudence requires extra precaution in order to secure safety to travellers, the township is bound to use such precaution, and the omission to do so is negligence. Scott Township v. Montgomery, 389.

A municipal corporation is liable for injuries caused

NEGLIGENCE—*Continued.*
to one driving through its streets, whose wagon is upset by the iron head of a water plug. Scranton v. Catterson, 59.

If reasonable precautions are taken to provide locomotives with appliances best suited to the prevention of damage by fire, the railway company or persons using them cannot be made liable though they fire every rod of country through which they run. Phila. and Reading R. R. Co. v. Schultz, 148.

Evidence is not admissible to show that other engines of a company have defective spark arresters. Jennings v. Penna. R. R. Co., 150.

It is contributory negligence on the part of an owner of land along a railway to allow the accumulation of rubbish and brushwood on his property. A land-owner along a railway assumes the risk of fires necessarily following the proper and lawful use of locomotives, but there is no liability on his part to guard against their improper and unlawful use. Phila. and Reading R. R. Co. v. Schultz, 148.

A passenger railway liable under its charter to keep in good repair the streets which it traverses, is liable to a passenger, who in alighting from a car is injured through the defective condition of the street. (C. P.) Mayberry v. Railway Co., 404.

Except at street crossings, where the public has a right of way, a railroad company has the right to a clear track, and it owes no duty to trespassers, whether they be adults, minors, or children of tender years. Cauley v. P. C. and St. L. R. W. Co., 505.

It is contributory negligence *per se* in parents to suffer their children to trespass on the cars or track of a railroad company. The fact that the trespass was committed without the knowledge or consent of the parent is immaterial. Ib.

A railroad company owes no duty to a trespasser riding on a train. A boy riding free upon a train to sell newspapers is a trespasser, even though he had the permission of the conductor. To give such permission is beyond the conductor's powers. Duff v. Allegheny Valley R. R. Co., 504.

Liability of a railway company to the representatives of one killed while in the care of another carrier. Phila. and Reading R. R. Co. v. Boyer, 496.

Standing on the front platform of a street railway car with the implied consent of the conductor and driver is not contributory negligence *per se*. Germantown Pass. R. W. Co. v. Walling, 467.

Where the measure of duty on the part of a passenger is ordinary and reasonable care and the standard shifts with the circumstances of the case, the question of contributory negligence is for the jury. Ib.

What is contributory negligence *per se* in one about to cross a railway track with a pair of horses. Penna. R. R. Co. v. Bock, 281.

A husband as administrator of his wife cannot maintain an action against one who negligently causes her death. The action should be brought in his own right as urviving husband. Books v. Danville, 339.

A municipal ordinance cannot make that negligence which was not negligence without it. Phila. and Reading R. R. Co. v. Boyer, 497.

Sufficiency of narr. in action against municipality for negligently obstructing a highway. (C. P.) Kenyon v. City, 222.

A claim for statutory and common law damages admitting of the same pleas and judgment, may be joined in the same action. Penna. R. R. Co. v. Bock, 281.

Where the form of the declaration shows no inconsistency in the rights sued upon, but an apparent

NEGLIGENCE—*Continued.*
misjoinder of the claimants thereunder, an actual misjoinder of rights or parties must be taken advantage of on trial and not by motion in arrest of judgment. Ib.

Action against steamboat carrier for injury caused passenger by violently bumping against wharf. See COMMON CARRIER. (C. P.) Monaghan v. Ferry Co., 368.

Action against passenger railway company by passenger injured while attempting to get on car. See COMMON CARRIER. (C. P.) Coller v. Passenger Railway Co., 477.

Action against passenger railway company by passenger injured while in the car. See COMMON CARRIER. Federal St. Pass. Railway Co. v. Gibson, 533.

Action by servant against master. See MASTER AND SERVANT.

Limitation of action against recorder of deeds for negligently giving a false search. See LIMITATIONS, STATUTE OF. Owen v. Saving Fund, 465.

NEGOTIABLE INSTRUMENT. See BILLS AND NOTES.

NOTICE. What sufficient notice to put a party upon inquiry. Sellers v. Benner, 88.

When a purchaser of land will be charged with notice of encumbrances. Parke v Neely, 193.

NUISANCE. While the mere construction of a railroad track across a public highway, in pursuance of law, is no nuisance, it must be constructed in such a manner as not to impede travel. Northern Central Railway Co. v. Commonwealth, 129.

An indictment for maintaining a nuisance lies against a railroad company where the track crossing is such as to cause a dangerous obstruction to travel. Ib.

Bill in equity to restrain nuisance. See EQUITY. See LIMITATIONS, STATUTE OF.

OIL WELL, receiver of, power of Court of Equity to appoint. See EQUITY. Enterprise Trans. Company's Appeal, 225. Emerson & Wall's Appeal, 227.

ORPHANS' COURT. So far as advancements are concerned, the jurisdiction of the Orphans' Court is exclusive. It also has power to settle questions of set off against distributive shares, arising out of an indebtedness of a distributee to the decedent. (O. C.) Bucknor's Estate, 511.

When under the Act of April 20, 1846, a purchaser at an Orphans' Court sale of lands seeks to apply to the purchase-money a judgment originally entered in another county, but transferred to the county of the sale by exemplified copy, an issue to try the truth of an allegation that the consideration of the judgment has failed, can be tried only in the county having jurisdiction of the sale. Gordon's Appeal, 55.

Land purchased by an executor on the foreclosure of a mortgage held by the decedent is treated for the purposes of distribution as personal property. (O. C.) Fell's Estate, 382.

The Orphans' Court has jurisdiction to confirm a sale of real estate purchased on foreclosure of a mortgage, and subsequently sold by an executor. Ib.

Jurisdiction in Partition. See PARTITION.

Where the appellant from an order of the register of wills admitting to probate a certain will is a nonresident, he may, upon petition filed, be compelled to give security for costs. (O. C.) King's Estate, 207.

A witness is bound to attend before an examiner until his deposition is completed, and his attendance will be enforced by suitable process. (O. C.) Hook's Estate, 320.

ORPHANS' COURT—*Continued.*
Allowance for support, when not reduced. (O. C.) McCloskey's Estate, 496.

The executrix of a deceased executor is not liable to attachment for the default of such executor. (O. C.) Goldsmith's Estate, 276.

An amendment to correct an error apparent upon the face of the record will not be allowed after the lapse of seven years where intervening rights are to be affected. (O. C.) Bauer's Estate, 336.

Under what circumstances an adjudication and decree will be sent back to the Auditing Judge for review. (O. C.) Bucknor's Estate, 511.

Bill of Review, when too late. (O. C.) Lindsay's Estate, 463. Littleton's Appeal, 188.

Additional rules of Orphans' Court, 420.

PARENT AND CHILD. Under what circumstances a boy will be permitted to remain with his maternal grandparents, contrary to the will of his father. (Q. S.) Commonwealth v. Schladensky, 315.

PARTITION. Although in partition proceedings in the Orphans' Court the proper practice is to issue a citation to all the parties in interest, it is not essential where the names of the parties in interest appear in the petition decree and answer. There is a presumption that all requisite notices were given. (O. C.) Bauer's Estate, 576.

Where legacies are charged upon land, the legatee is entitled to partition in order to apply for the sale of the real estate. Where the petition does not in terms apply for partition, and the lands cannot be sold for the payment of legacies without it, the Court will afford the proper relief. (O. C.) Cassady's Estate, 275.

The jurisdiction of the Orphans' Court in partition is confined to cases in which the decedent died seised of the estate in respect to which it is asked. But when this element exists, the Court, for the purpose of making distribution, may determine all questions of kinship. (O. C.) Davis's Estate, 380.

PARTNERSHIP. A purchase by certain members of an unincorporated association, organized for the building, equipping, and operating of a certain railroad, of the entire stock of a competing road, was beyond the scope of their authority, and not binding upon unassenting members. Roberts's Appeal, 118.

Where it is sought to make a partner liable upon an alleged ratification of an unauthorized contract of some of his copartners, his assent to the precise provisions of the contract must appear. Roberts's Appeal, 118.

A partner who sells firm property without the knowledge and consent of his copartner, and with intended fraud on the rights of creditors of the firm to pay his own individual debts, gives the purchaser no title as against creditors of the firm. Hartley v. White, 286.

Limited Companies. Limited liability for partnership debts under the Act of June 2, 1874, and its supplements, is insured only by strict compliance with the Act. Maloney v. Bruce, 92.

The object of the provision requiring a schedule is to enable creditors to ascertain precisely of what the property consists, and to judge of its value. A general description or a lumping valuation is not the schedule required by that Act. Ib.

Effect of omission of word "limited" from the notes of a limited company. (C. P.) German v. Moodie, 221.

PASSENGER RAILWAY. See NEGLIGENCE.

PHYSICIAN, course of study required to entitle one to practise as a physician. (C. P.) *In re* Electropathic Institute, 31.

PLEADING. When trespass *vi et armis*, and when trespass upon the case should be brought. Drew v. Peer, 33.

A claim for statutory and common law damages admitting of the same pleas and judgment may be joined in the same action. Pennsylvania Railroad Co. v. Bock, 281.

Where the form of declaration shows no inconsistency in the rights sued upon, nor an apparent misjoinder of the claimants thereunder, an actual misjoinder of rights or parties must be taken advantage of on trial, and not by motion in arrest of judgment. Ib.

A plaintiff cannot recover the double damages for an unlawful distress allowed by the Act of May 10, 1871, unless the declaration be upon the statute. Royse v. May, 104.

When a narr. against a municipal corporation for negligence sufficiently states the duty of the corporation. (C. P.) Kenyon v. Philadelphia, 222.

Plea of plene administravit, when good. (C. P.) O'Conner v. Weeks, 461.

Sufficiency in replevin of plea to an avowry, that the goods were upon the demised premises in the course of trade. (C. P.) Biegenwald v. Winpenny, 542.

What evidence admissible under plea of non-assumpsit. Fisher v. Ball, 141.

POWDER MAGAZINE. Injunction to restrain. See EQUITY. Dilworth's Appeal, 133.

POWER. Deed of trust containing power of revocation, when revoked by will containing no reference to the power. (C. P.) Taylor v. Smiley, 30.

Power of appointment, when well exercised. Schively's Appeal, 566.

Power of attorney, when coupled with an interest not revoked by death. (O. C.) Droste's Estate, 224.

PRACTICE. An action of debt on recognizance of bail in error must be brought in Court where suit originated. (C. P.) Lukens v. Bryson, 540.

Service of sci. fa. upon municipal claim for taxes, when insufficient. See MUNICIPAL CLAIMS. O'Byrne v. Philadelphia, 41.

Effect of reversal of judgment upon municipal claim for defective service of the sci. fa. See MUNICIPAL CLAIMS. Wistar v. Philadelphia, 98.

A terre-tenant cannot intervene in an action upon a mortgage without leave of Court. (C. P.) Hobson v. Webster, 206.

In ejectment where the writ names a tenant as the defendant, the landlord may intervene to defend *pro interesse suo*. (C. P.) Rittenhouse v. Fetters, 221.

Under what circumstances the Court will order the consolidation of municipal claims. (C. P.) City v. Tyson, 367.

Under what circumstances a garnishee will be permitted to pay money into Court. (C. P.) Fuller v. Bleim, 574.

Capias. See HUSBAND AND WIFE.

Affidavit denying partnership, when permitted to be filed nunc pro tunc. (C. P.) Steinbeisser v. Corbion, 528.

Bill of particulars, when sufficient. (C. P.) Heft v. Jones, 541.

Under a motion to file an amended narr., the Court will not decide questions of pleading which ought to be raised by a demurrer. (C. P.) Spaulding v. Barber, 253.

Judgment for want of a plea, when opened on terms. (C. P.) Brass Co. v. Rudy, 527.

Under what circumstances a judgment for want of a plea will be stricken off, when a common appearance has been entered for the defendant. (C. P.) Bender v. Ryan, 144.

INDEX

PRACTICE—*Continued.*
Depositions, formal requisites of. Winton v. Little, 37.
Letters rogatory, what a sufficient execution of. (C. P.) Zanssig v. Telegraph Co., 510.
Examination of insolvent debtor under Act of 1879. (C. P.) Davis v. Mowbray, 47. Horstman v. Kaufman, 513.
An order of Court cannot be set aside without first taking a rule to show cause. (C. P.) Garver v. Ward, 192.
Rule for production of books and papers upon the trial under the Act of 1798, what not a sufficient answer to. (C. P.) Thompson v. Taylor, 169.
Plea of former recovery. Schriver v. Eckenrode, 161.
A demand for an issue of fact under the Act of April 20, 1846, in a distribution by an auditor is properly refused if the disputed facts are immaterial. Amanda Martin's Appeal, 484.
Upon the refusal of a witness to appear before an examiner, the Court will issue an attachment. (C. P.) Bowen v. Thornton, 575.
Trial and its incidents. What evidence is admissible to rebut the effect of plaintiff's book of original entries. (C. P.) Wanamaker v. Price, 112.
Matters not in the bill of particulars may be admissible on collateral questions arising during the trial. (C. P.) Wilson v. Deacon, 47.
A point duly certified as part of the record showing that it was affirmed and bill sealed, although afterwards withdrawn, may be reviewed by the Supreme Court. Pass. R. W. Co. v. Gibson, 533.
Province of Court and jury in negligence case. P. & R. R. R. Co. v. Boyer, 497. Germantown Pass. R. W. Co. v. Walling, 467. Penna. R. R. Co. v. Bock, 281.
Province of Court and jury in life insurance case. (U. S. S. C.) Moulor v. Ins. Co., 81.
It is not error to permit counsel, after the charge of the Court, to state to the jury the specific items for which he claims damages. Drew v. Peer, 33.
Inadequacy of damages, when not ground for setting verdict aside. (U. S. C. C.) Reading v. Texas R. R. Co., 175.
Form of verdict in replevin. See REPLEVIN. Wright v. Funck, 249.
Other matters. When execution against personalty may issue upon transcript from magistrate. (C. P.) Weir v. Lawrence, 207.
The Court of Common Pleas cannot entertain any question in a cause after the record has been removed to the Supreme Court by writ of error. (C. P.) Martzinger v. Smith, 274.
To enter a judgment containing a reference to an Act of Assembly, and to a case in the Reports, is not a fatal error, but it may be amended by striking out such references. Hartley v. White, 286.
See AFFIDAVIT OF DEFENCE LAW. AMENDMENT. ATTACHMENT. EQUITY. DIVORCE. ERRORS AND APPEAL. EXECUTION. EVIDENCE. JUDGMENT. JUSTICE OF THE PEACE. ORPHANS' COURT. PLEADING.

PRINCIPAL AND AGENT. Principal, how far bound by the acts and declarations of agent. See BANKS AND BANKING. EVIDENCE. Steckel v. Bank, 17. Ziegler v. Bank, 19. Resh v. Bank, 21. James v. Building Association, 325. Gass v. Citizens' Loan Assoc., 326. Comp. v. Bank, 453. Coller v. Passenger Railway Co., 477. Knight v. Ins. Co., 501. Balt. & Ohio R. R. Co. v. School District, 568.

PURCHASER FOR VALUE. Subsequent judgment-creditors are not purchasers for value. Shrewsbury Savings Institution's Appeal, 166.
Holder of check, when not a holder for value. See BILLS AND NOTES. Dougherty v. Bank, 1.

QUO WARRANTO. The Supreme Court and the Judges thereof have exclusive original jurisdiction to issue writs of quo warranto to Associate Judges of the Common Pleas. Commonwealth v. Dumbauld, 369, 417, and 529.

RAILROADS. Rights of passenger railways on Broad Street in Philadelphia. (C. P.) Commonwealth v. Baldwin, 233.
Lease of railroad, when invalid. See CORPORATION. (U. S. C. C.) Thomas v. West Jersey Railroad Co., 65.
Injunction to prevent interruption of free use of track of junction railroad company. (U. S. C. C.) Lathrop v. Junction R. R. Co., 277.
Limitation of damages against railroad company for negligent killing. Phila. & Reading R. R. Co. v. Boyer, 497.
Action by passenger against passenger railway for negligence. See COMMON CARRIER. P. & R. R. R. Co. v. Boyer, 497. Pass. R. W. Co. v. Gibson, 533. See NEGLIGENCE. (C. P.) Coller v. P. R. W. Co., 477. Germantown Pass. R. W. Co. v. Walling, 467.
Obligations of passenger railway company to keep streets in repair. (C. P.) Mayberry v. Pass. R. W. Co., 404.
Liability of railroad company for maintenance of nuisance in construction of track. See NUISANCE. Northern Central R. W. Co. v. Commonwealth, 129.
Action against railroad for construction of defective drain. See NEGLIGENCE. B. and O. R. R. Co. v. School District, 568.
Action against railroad for defective spark-arrester. See NEGLIGENCE. P. & R. R. R. Co. v. Schultz, 146.
Action against railroad by trespasser on cars. See NEGLIGENCE. Duff v. R. R. Co., 504.
Action against railroad by trespasser on track. See NEGLIGENCE. Cauley v. R. R. Co., 505.
RATIFICATION. In order to render a ratification effective, the assent of the ratifying party must be given with a knowledge of the precise provisions of the contract. Roberts's Appeal, 118.
Long acquiescence by a bank corporation in acts of its president otherwise beyond the scope of his authority will operate as a ratification of these acts. Winton v. Little, 37.
What acts of ratification or adoption will estop one whose name is written to an instrument from setting up the forgery. (C. P.) Brooke v. Harman, 462.
The mere recognition by the Legislature of the fact that a lease has been made is not sufficient to amount to a ratification of the power to lease. (U. S. S. C.) Thomas v. West Jersey R. R. Co., 65.
RECEIVER OF OIL WELL. When appointed. See EQUITY. Enterprise Transportation Company's Appeal, 225. Emerson and Wall's Appeal, 227.
RECORDER, OF PHILADELPHIA, right of, to collect taxes on pool tables. See TAXES. Albrecht v. Lane, 377.
RECORDER OF DEEDS. Limitation of liability for false search. See LIMITATIONS, STATUTE OF. Owen v. Savings Fund, 465.
REFEREE, report of, reviewable by Common Pleas. (C. P.) Monaghan v. Ferry Co., 368.
RELIGIOUS SOCIETY. Control of election. See CORPORATION.
REPLEVIN. A pledgee of goods on storage who has never made himself known to the bailee nor obtained possession of the goods, cannot maintain replevin against the bailee who has parted with the goods by order of the pledgor to a *bona fide* purchaser

REPLEVIN—*Continued.*
for value before the writ of replevin issued. People's Bank v. Gayley, 49.
In an action of replevin it is proper for the jury to find some of the goods for the plaintiff and the rest for the defendant. Judgment may be entered upon such a verdict. Wright v. Funck, 249.

REPRESENTATIVES. Construction of word. See WILL. Appeal of the Trustees of the University, 520.

RES ADJUDICATA. When proceedings in the Federal Courts conclude parties from subsequent proceedings concerning the same subject matter in the State Court. Hidel's Appeal, 212.

An injunction granted by a Court of Common Pleas restraining the State treasurer from collecting certain fees from a county treasurer, does not bar a claim for the same in the settlement of the county treasurer's account by the auditor general and State treasurer. Kilgore v. Commonwealth, 184.

The affirmance by the Supreme Court of a judgment of the Common Pleas in a feigned issue where no exception had been taken nor error assigned to the jurisdiction of the Court to try the issue, is not necessarily an implied affirmance of such jurisdiction, and does not prevent a subsequent impeachment of the jurisdiction under further proceedings in the same controversy. Gordon's Appeal, 55.

RESIDENCE. See DOMICILE.

ROADS, HIGHWAYS, AND BRIDGES. A turnpike road constructed by a turnpike corporation on which tolls are collected is a public highway in so far that an indictment will lie against one obstructing it as for a public nuisance. Northern Central Railway Co. v. Commonwealth, 129.

No appeal lies to the Court of Quarter Sessions from the action of the Board of Surveyors confirming a plan. *In re* Plan No. 166, 43.

Petitions for opening streets under the Act of March 22, 1813, are to be heard before a Judge of the Court of Quarter Sessions sitting in Common Pleas. (Q. S.) *In re* Volkmar Street, 169, 201.

Right of coaches to license to run on Broad Street. (C. P.) Commonwealth v. Baldwin, 233.

Action against township for defect in highway. See NEGLIGENCE. Scott Township v. Montgomery, 389.

Railroad crossing highway. See NUISANCE.

RULES OF COURT. Additional rules of Orphans' Court, 420.

SALE. A delivery of chattels made on condition that the title shall pass on the payment of the purchase-money at a future day does not effect a bailment but vests on the transferee a conditional title, which is absolute so far as the rights of creditors or innocent purchasers are concerned. Krause v. Commonwealth, 61.

No recovery can be had for liquors sold which were impure, vitiated, or adulterated. (C. P.) Glenn v. Keenan, 170.

Under what circumstances a defect in the quality of an article sold for a particular purpose is no defence to an action for the price. (C. P.) Roebling v. Brown, 170.

Where, upon an action for the price of goods sold, an affidavit of defence is filed averring that the goods were warranted to be of a certain quality which in fact they were not, necessitates the submission of the question to a jury. (C. P.) Badger v. McKay, 528.

SATISFACTION. See JUDGMENT. MORTGAGE. MUNICIPAL CLAIMS.

SCHOOL DISTRICT. A school district is not strictly a municipal corporation. Colvin v. Beaver, 396.

SET-OFF. Even in actions *ex delicto* an equitable defence in the nature of set-off as to matters growing out of the same transaction may be admissible. Lehr v. Taylor, 401.

Usurious interest actually received by a national bank in the renewals of a series of notes cannot be set off in a suit brought by the bank on the last renewal note in the series. The forfeiture of the interest only occurs where illegal interest has been stipulated for but not paid. Bank v. Dushane, 472.

Right of bank to set off notes of insolvent decedent against his deposit. See BANKS AND BANKING.

SHERIFF. Liability of for false return. (C. P.) Curran v. Elliott, 367.

SHIPS AND SHIPPING. See ADMIRALTY.

SPECIFIC PERFORMANCE. See EJECTMENT, EQUITY, FRAUDS, STATUTE OF.

STATUTES. Local statutes, when not repealed by implication. Kilgore v. Commonwealth, 184.

Statutes are to be construed so as to best effectuate the intention of the makers, which sometimes may be collected from the cause or occasion of passing the statute, and when discovered, it ought to be followed with judgment and discretion in the construction, though that construction may seem contrary to the letter of the statute. Big Black Creek Improvement Co. v. Commonwealth, 74.

STOCK EXCHANGE. See UNINCORPORATED SOCIETY.

STOPPAGE IN TRANSITU. Liability of carrier to assignee of bill of lading for refusing to deliver goods stopped by vendor in transitu. See DAMAGES, MEASURE OF. (U. S. C. C.) Schmidt v. Pennsylvania, 351.

Doctrine of stoppage in transitu applied to relation of bank and depositor. See BANKS AND BANKING. Dougherty v. Bank, 1.

SUBROGATION. See EQUITY. Brice's Appeal, 227. (O. C.) Burnell's Estate, 334.

SUNDAY LAW. See CONSTITUTIONAL LAW. Waldo v. Commonwealth, 200.

SURETY. Where an agreement of suretyship for a consignee provided "such consignments not to exceed in amount the sum of five thousand dollars at any one time, and to be continued from time to time as sales were made," and several consignments were made exceeding the stipulated amount, this was such a variance of the terms of the contract that the surety was absolutely discharged from any liability upon his contract. Brex v. Warner, 45.

Mere forbearance, however prejudicial to a surety, will not discharge him; the failure of a creditor to revive a judgment does not discharge a surety unless there was an express agreement at the time of giving the judgment that it should be kept revived for the benefit of the surety. Winton v. Little, 87.

The failure of a landlord promptly to use his right of distress does not discharge the surety of the tenant. Loftus v. Corles, 333.

A principal, when released from all liability growing out of an action against a surety, is a competent witness for the surety. Evans v. Jenks, 139.

SURVEYORS, BOARD OF, in Philadelphia, powers of. See ROADS, HIGHWAYS, AND BRIDGES. *In re* Plan 166, 43.

TAXES AND TAXATION. Where a corporation declares less than six per cent. dividends for the purpose of assessing the stock for taxation, under the Act of June 7, 1879, the actual value in cash of the stock is to be ascertained by the prices at which it sold between the first and fifteenth days of November,

TAXES AND TAXATION—*Continued.*

and not by the average sales during the year ending on the first Monday of November. Pennsylvania R. R. Co. *v.* Commonwealth, 179.

The Act of April 24, 1874, providing for the taxation of coal mining corporations, applies to corporations authorized to hold and lease coal lands, to be worked by others, although the corporation itself is expressly prohibited by its charter from mining. Big Black Creek Imp. Co. *v.* Commonwealth, 74.

Taxation of national banks. See BANKS AND BANKING. Lackawanna County *v.* First Nat. Bank, 549. Truby's Appeal, 550.

The Recorder of Philadelphia has no jurisdiction of a suit to collect the license fees upon billiard tables. (C. P.) Albrecht *v.* Lane, 377.

Irregular tax levy, effect of. See MUNICIPAL CORPORATIONS. Matthews *v.* Scranton, 507.

Municipal claim for water tax, when defective. See MUNICIPAL CLAIM. Allentown *v.* Hower, 198.

What municipal claims are covered by exemption from taxation. See MUNICIPAL CLAIMS. Olive Cemetery Co. *v.* Philadelphia, 85.

Service of scire facias upon municipal claim for taxes, when sufficient. See MUNICIPAL CLAIMS. O'Byrne *v.* Philadelphia, 41.

Special tax for maintenance of meadow banks, how far constitutional. See CONSTITUTIONAL LAW. Rutherford *v.* Maynes, 221, 561.

TENDER of judgment for amount admitted to be due before a justice of the peace, how to be evidenced. See JUSTICE OF THE PEACE. Driesbach *v.* Morris, 57.

TERRE-TENANT. Right of, to intervene. See PRACTICE. (C. P.) Hobson *v.* Webster, 206.

THEATRE. A ticket to a reserved seat in a theatre confers more than a revocable license, and partakes more of the nature of a lease, entitling the holder to peaceable ingress and egress, and exclusive possession of the seat during the designated performance. Drew *v.* Peer, 33.

TICKET SCALPING, Act punishing, not unconstitutional. See CONSTITUTIONAL LAW. (Q. S.) Commonwealth *v.* Wilson, 291.

TOWNSHIP. The corporate status of counties and townships, their powers and duties, and powers of road supervisors considered. Union Township *v.* Gibboney, 390.

One of several township supervisors may bind the township in merely ministerial matters, within the scope of his duty; but the consent of a majority given at a regularly convened meeting of the board is necessary in all matters requiring deliberation, consultation, and judgment. Ib.

The ordinary repairs of roads and bridges are classed with ministerial duties, but the law contemplates that this work shall be paid for by the road tax which the taxpayers may work out. Ib.

Whether a debt should be contracted for such ordinary repairs is a matter for deliberation and judgment, and the joint action of the supervisors acting within their very limited power to contract debts is necessary to bind the township. Ib.

Even if a township is not a corporation proper, such as a city or a borough, nor invested with power to tax for road purposes beyond one percentum on the county valuation, it is nevertheless bound to erect walls or barriers along the sides of its roads, if that is necessary to the safety of travellers. Scott Township *v.* Montgomery, 389.

See NEGLIGENCE.

TRADE-MARK. A trade-mark, adopted by a manufacturer or merchant for his goods, to be clothed with the attributes of property, entitling the appropriator to protection in its exclusive use, must designate the true ownership and origin of the goods. (C. P.) White *v.* Schlect, 77.

TRESPASS. Action for excessive distress. See LANDLORD AND TENANT. Royse *v.* May, 104.

See ACTION ON THE CASE.

TRESPASSER, action against railroad company by. See NEGLIGENCE.

TROVER. Trover is not maintainable where the right of possession is in the defendant. Lehr *v.* Taylor, 401. See HUSBAND AND WIFE. Commonwealth *v.* Keeper, 314.

TRUSTS AND TRUSTEES. A receipt signed by one who has taken the title of real estate in his own name, setting forth that one-fourth of the purchase-money has been furnished by another, and duly witnessed, is a sufficient declaration of trust, and may be recorded as such. Roberts's Appeal, 118.

Money received by one joint tenant for the sale of his co-tenant's interest in their joint estate is trust money; the rules, therefore, which forbid the charging of interest upon interest as between debtor and creditor have no application. Ib.

When there is a dry trust for the sole and separate use of a woman, neither married nor in contemplation of marriage, the mere fact that, on a certain contingency which might never happen, the trustee was directed to execute a conveyance after the death of the cestui que trust, will not change the dry character of the trust and make it active. Philadelphia Trust Co.'s Appeal, 289.

The Orphans' Court will remove a trustee where his continuance in office, though not jeoparding the trust, might probably work disadvantage or inconvenience to the cestuis que trustent. (O. C.) Hilles's Estate, 421.

TURNPIKE. See ROADS, HIGHWAYS, AND BRIDGES.

ULTRA VIRES. Lease of railroad. See CORPORATIONS. (U. S. S. C.) Thomas *v.* West Jersey Railroad Company, 65.

Loans by national banks on real estate. See BANKS AND BANKING. Winton *v.* Little, 37.

See CORPORATIONS. Steckel *v.* Bank, 17.

UNINCORPORATED SOCIETY. Where there is a provision in the constitution of an unincorporated association for the suspension of members upon their insolvency, if the insolvent member admits to the association his insolvency it is not necessary that he should have a formal hearing and trial; he, in effect, pleads guilty. Moxey's Appeal, 441.

A regulation that if a suspended member fails to comply with all his contracts within a year, his seat shall be sold, and the proceeds of the sale be distributed among such of his creditors as are members of the association is valid. Moxey's Appeal, 441.

Such a regulation may give the members an advantage over other creditors, but they have a right to stipulate for it, and all members are parties assenting to the law. Ib.

A court of equity will restrain by injunction the unlawful suspension of a member of an unincorporated association. (C. P.) Powell *v.* Abbott, 231.

A by-law, if inconsistent with the constitution, is invalid. Ib.

The quasi-judicial powers of unincorporated beneficial societies must be exercised in exact conformity to law. The power to expel does not include a power to suspend, for the latter might work great injustice by depriving a member of the right to benefits while leav-

INDEX. 603

UNINCORPORATED SOCIETY—*Continued.*
ing him subject to the payment of dues. (C. P.) Schassberger v. Staendel, 379.

A member of an unincorporated beneficial association cannot maintain a suit at law against its officers. (C. P.) Kurz v. Eggert, 126.

See PARTNERSHIP. Roberts's Appeal, 118.

USE AND OCCUPATION. See LANDLORD AND TENANT.

USURY. By national bank. See BANKS AND BANKING. National Bank of Fayette v. Dushane, 472.

VENDOR AND VENDEE. While strictly any interval of time, however short, between the delivery of a deed and the entry of judgment for the purchase-money will suffice to let liens upon the vendee's equitable title in upon the legal estate, yet where the circumstances plainly reveal an intention on the part of both vendor and vendee to preserve the vendor's lien, a judgment is entered within a reasonable time (*e. g.*, early the following morning), the priority of the lien for the purchase-money is preserved. Snyder's Appeal, 177.

Vendor's right of entry for default in payment of purchase-money. See EJECTMENT. Welch v. Emerson, 372.

Where one gives a due-bill for the purchase-money of real estate, he cannot defend against its payment on the ground of his inability to obtain an unincumbered title. Roberts's Appeal, 118.

Eviction. Breach of covenant for quiet enjoyment. See DAMAGES, MEASURE OF. Lanigan v. Kille, 481.

Contract for sale of land, breach of, measure of damages. See DAMAGES, MEASURE OF. (C. P.) Sharp v. Robb, 475. See EQUITY. EJECTMENT. FRAUDS, STATUTE OF.

VOLUNTARY SETTLEMENT, by husband on wife. See DEBTOR AND CREDITOR.

WAGES. When a preferred claim upon the proceeds of an execution. See EXECUTION. Stechter v. Malley, 28.

WAREHOUSE RECEIPTS. In order that a receipt for goods on storage may be a warehouse receipt with the quality of negotiability, as contemplated by the Act of September 24, 1866, the person issuing such receipt must be in possession of the goods in his own right, and not merely as agent for a principal. People's Bank v. Gayley, 49.

WATER-COURSE. The special Act of April 14, 1853, providing that compensation shall be made for damages sustained by the owners of land upon which a spring or stream of water is situated, or through which it flows, by permanent appropriation therein described, applies not only for the benefit of owners of natural channels, but applies equally to artificial water-courses so ancient that the memory of man runneth not to the contrary. Reading v. Althouse, 22.

WILL. Under what circumstances the subsequent marriage of a woman will not operate as a revocation of a will previously made by her. See HUSBAND AND WIFE. Lant's Appeal, 209.

An executor named in a will is a person sufficiently interested in its probate, to appeal from an order of the register of wills refusing its probate and to demand an issue. (O. C.) King's Estate, 207.

Practice in the Orphans' Court upon an appeal from such an order on a demand for an issue. Ib.

Under what circumstances a deed of trust containing a power of revocation, will be revoked by a will containing no reference to the power. (C. P.) Taylor v. Smiley, 30.

WILL—*Continued.*
A bequest to a widow of personalty for life coupled with a condition subsequent in restraint of marriage is *in terrorem* and void, and the widow takes an absolute estate. But the condition is validated by a limitation over in the event of remarriage, for such limitation shows that the condition was not intended as a menace, but as the basis of a distinct gift. Bondbright's Appeal, 475.

An absolute direction by a testator to his executors to sell real estate and divide the proceeds among the heirs, works an equitable conversion, and the addition of a provision that the heirs may agree to a division among themselves and that the executors need not then sell, does not operate to prevent a conversion. Jones v. Caldwell, 459.

Such provision is mere surplusage and may be stricken from the will without altering its legal effect. It merely gives the heirs a right which the law secures to them independently of the will. Ib.

A. bequeathed a fund in trust for B. for life, and after his death to such person or persons as he, by last will and testament should appoint, and in default of such appointment to the heirs of B., who should be entitled under the intestate laws. B. bequeathed the fund to his wife, "to be appropriated to clearing off so far as it may, any encumbrance on any of my real estate, the remainder, if any, to be used in keeping up the repairs of the farm or other property." The appointee died in the lifetime of her husband, who himself afterwards died insolvent, all his property both real and personal being sold to pay his debts; *held* that the appointment failed by reason of the death of the appointee and the absence of any property upon which it might be applied, and that the fund should be paid to B.'s heirs under the intestate laws in accordance with the provisions of A.'s will. Schiveley's Appeal, 566, reversing (O. C.) Schiveley's Estate, 223.

A testator provided as follows: "I give and bequeath $7500 unto A. B., but it is my will that whatsoever amount her son C. D. shall owe me, principal and interest, shall be taken to have been so much paid on account of said legacy, and his notes shall be handed over to her or her representatives:" *held*, in the absence of any other evidence as to the testator's intent, that this clause did not contain sufficient to prevent a lapse of the legacy to A. B. by reason of her death during the testator's lifetime. Appeal of the Trustees of the University, 520.

Legacies. In what order payable and when abatable. See LEGACIES. Appeal of the Trustees of the University, 520.

Legacies, when lapsed. See LEGACIES. Appeal of the Trustees of the University, 520.

A testator after directing his real estate to be sold, gave and bequeathed his estate upon the death of his wife to his seven children (naming them), and to his grandson A., share and share alike, "and in case my said grandson A. shall at any time die without issue, I then give and bequeath the bequest of him the said A. so dying, unto all my children, viz. (naming them as before), to share and share alike." A., the grandson, survived the testator and died without leaving issue: *held* that it was evident the testator intended a definite failure of issue at the time of the grandson's death, and that therefore the bequest over to the testator's children took effect. Snyder's Appeal, 213.

The words "heirs of the body lawfully begotten," are the proper and technical words to create an estate tail, and where nothing in the will qualifies or changes their import, they must have their legal

WILL—*Continued.*
effect, whatever the testator may have intended. Philadelphia Trust Company's Appeal, 289.

In the absence of a clear intent to the contrary, technical words in a will are presumed to have been used by the testator in their technical sense. This presumption will be less easily overcome in an artistically drawn will, than in one bearing on its face the evidence that it was drawn by an ignorant testator. Porter's Appeal, 457.

The legal meaning of a technical word will not be affected by a direction in the will which is capable of a construction consistent with that meaning. Ib.

What is sufficient evidence of a testamentary intent to turn a debt into an advancement. Ib.

WILL—*Continued.*
An obscure will interpreted, especially in relation to a bequest to a widow of "so much of the *proceeds* of said property as she may deem necessary for her support." Roberts's Appeal, *in re* estate of J. Edgar Thomson, 118.

There is a presumption that the provisions of a will were contemplated, conceived, and framed in knowledge of and conformably with, the law of the land (O. C.) Wolf's Estate, 260.

Where a bequest is immediate to children as a class, children in existence at the death of a testator alone are entitled. (O. C.) Wunder's Estate, 384.

WITNESS. See EVIDENCE. PRACTICE.

END OF VOLUME IX.

Lightning Source UK Ltd.
Milton Keynes UK
UKHW011139180119
335792UK00010B/604/P